Quick Tax and Benefits Facts

RETIREMENT PLAN COLAS

	2012	2011	2010
Maximum annual benefit for DB plan	200,000	195,000	195,000
Maximum contribution for DC plan	50,000	49,000	49,000
Annual compensation limit	250,000	245,000	245,000
401(k) elective deferrals	17,000	16,500	16,500
Maximum annual tax sheltered annuity deferral	17,000	16,500	16,500
Catch-up contributions (non-SIMPLE)	5,500	5,500	5,500
Tax credit ESOP maximum balance	1,015,000	985,000	985,000
Amount for lengthening of 5-year ESOP period	200,000	195,000	195,000
Highly compensated employee limit	115,000	110,000	110,000
SIMPLE plan employee deferral limit	11,500	11,500	11,500
Catch-up contributions (SIMPLE)	2,500	2,500	2,500
Minimum compensation for SEP coverage	550	550	550
Compensation limit for SEPs	250,000	245,000	245,000
Deferral limits for plans of state and local governments and tax-exempt organizations	17,000	16,500	16,500
Grandfathered compensation rule for government plans	375,000	360,000	360,000

PBGC MAXIMUM MONTHLY BENEFIT

Maximum monthly guarantee	4,653.41	4,500.00	4,500.00
Maximum annual guarantee	55,840.92	54,000.00	54,000.00

SOCIAL SECURITY

	2012	2011	2010
Employer/Employee	7.65%/5.65%*	7.65%/5.65%	7.65% (6.2% OASDI, 1.45% HI)
Self-employed	13.30%** (10.4% OASDI, 2.9% HI)	13.30% (10.4% OASDI, 2.9% HI)	15.30% (12.4% OASDI, 2.9% HI)
Taxable wage base			
OASDI maximum taxable earnings	110,100	106,800	106,800
Taxable wage base: HI maximum taxable earnings	unlimited	unlimited	unlimited
Quarter of coverage	1,130	1,120	1,120
Retirement earnings test exempt amounts			
Upon attaining full retirement age (FRA)	unlimited	unlimited	unlimited
Year of attainment of FRA	3,240 per month	3,140 per month	3,140 per month
	38,880 per year	37,680 per year	37,680 per year
Under FRA	14,640 per year	14,160 per year	14,160 per year
Maximum benefits if benefits begin at FRA (66)	2,513 per month	2,366 per month	2,346 per month

* Through February 29, 2012 (P.L. 112-78), employers and employees pay separate rates. *Employer* rate: 7.65% (6.2% OASDI, 1.45% HI); *Employee* rate: 5.65% (4.2% OASDI, 1.45% HI). (A 2% recapture tax, to be collected in 2013, applies to wages received in excess of $18,350, up to $110,100, through February 29, 2012.) Unless extended for the remainder of 2012, the employee rate would return to 7.65% (6.2% OASDI, 1.45% HI) on March 1, 2012.

** Applies only to self-employment income, for tax years beginning in 2012, up to the difference between $18,350 and any wages subject to a reduced tax rate for OASDI of 4.2% during the period January 1, 2012, and February 29, 2012.

CCH

KEY EXCISE TAXES AND PENALTIES

Failure to meet funding standards	10% of initial tax (5% for multiemployer plans); 100% additional tax if not corrected
Excess contribution to qualified plans	10% nondeductible excise tax on contribution exceeding deduction limit
Excess contribution to 401(k) plan	10% excise tax on excess contribution or excess aggregate contribution
Excess contribution to IRA	Lesser of 6% of excess contribution or 6% of value of account
Early distribution from qualified plans and IRAs	10% of early distribution
Excess accumulation in qualified plans and IRAs	50% of required minimum distribution
Prohibited transactions	15% of amount involved in prohibited transaction; 100% if correction not made within 90 days after notice of deficiency mailed
Reversion of excess amounts from terminating plan	20% of reversion amount; 50% of reversion amount if employer does not establish a successor plan

PENALTIES FOR REPORTING, NOTICE AND DISCLOSURE VIOLATIONS

Failure to file Form 5500	IRS: $25 per day, up to $15,000 DOL: up to $1,100 per day PBGC: up to $1,100 per day
Failure to file Schedule B of Form 5500	IRS: $1,000 for each failure
Failure to provide notice of rollover information	$100 for each failure, up to $50,000 for all failures in a calendar year
Breach of ERISA fiduciary duties	20% of applicable recovery amount
Failure to pay PBGC premiums	Up to 100% of premium (plus interest)
Failure to provide notice or material information regarding PBGC plan termination insurance	Up to $1,100 per day

To contact a Wolters Kluwer, Law & Business Sales Representative, please call 1-888-224-7377

CCH®

CCH®

U.S. Master
Pension Guide

March 2012

Wolters Kluwer
Law & Business

CCH Editorial Staff

Coordinating Editor

Nicholas Kaster, J.D.

Contributing Authors

Nicholas Kaster, J.D.

Kathleen Kennedy-Luzcak, J.D.

Kerry McInerney, J.D.

Linda Panszczyk, J.D.

Elizabeth Pope, J.D.

John Strzelecki, J.D.

Glenn Sulzer, J.D.

Production Editor

Karen Pavletich

ISBN 978-0-8080-2874-1

4025 W. Peterson Ave., Chicago, IL 60646-6085

1-800-248-3248

hr.cch.com

A WoltersKluwer Company

Printed in the United States of America

SUSTAINABLE FORESTRY INITIATIVE   Certified Sourcing
www.sfiprogram.org
SFI-00453

GUIDANCE ON RETIREMENT PLANS

The assets of all tax-favored retirement plans, including qualified employer plans, governmental plans, and IRAs, constitute the largest single source of private investment capital in the U.S. economy.

Qualified plans are one of the most valued elements in an employee's total compensation package and are the major form of investment and savings for most American workers. From the employer's standpoint, qualified plans offer many tax advantages and can help attract and retain the best employees. However, the rules for establishing, maintaining, and terminating qualified plans are complex and constantly changing. The U.S. MASTER™ PENSION GUIDE provides a comprehensive overview of qualified retirement plans. The book begins with a survey of the different types of plans from which an employer may choose, then describes the procedures for obtaining plan qualification.

Plans must meet numerous requirements established by both the IRS and the Department of Labor, including minimum participation, coverage and vesting rules, nondiscrimination requirements, and rules relating to distributions, reporting and disclosure, funding, and fiduciary standards. These topics are covered in separate chapters and set out in an easy-to-understand format in this publication. Examples and pointers are used throughout to illustrate the rules. The final five chapters of the book cover the special rules applicable to 401(k) plans, employee stock ownership plans, tax- sheltered annuities, IRAs, and nonqualified arrangements.

The book incorporates key regulations, rulings, and court decisions issued in 2011. In addition, the book contains numerous cross references to the CCH PENSION PLAN GUIDE where more detailed information may be obtained on a given topic.

The PENSION PLAN GUIDE is a fourteen-volume full text looseleaf reporter that contains explanations, full text of law, regulations and rulings, leading court cases, expert commentary, and sample plans. The GUIDE also is available on the Internet.

March 2012

TABLE of CONTENTS

2012 U.S. Master™ Pension Guide

6   Table of Contents

Calendars and Tables

¶ 50

Plan Reporting Calendar

Employee benefit plans are subject to numerous reporting and disclosure requirements. In addition, various information returns must be filed for employee benefit plans. See ¶ 2200 for a discussion of the reporting and disclosure requirements applicable to employee benefit plans.

A comprehensive calendar summarizing various reporting requirements appears on the following pages. The calendar indicates the date by which reports must be filed or documents must be provided to participants and other parties. All types of reports, whether or not there is an official form, are listed. The calendar shows who is required to file and who must be given copies, and provides a concise description of the subject matter.

☐ See ¶ 2859 for a detailed reporting calendar that indicates deadlines for plan termination-related reports and disclosures.

2012 Filing Due Dates for 2011 Calendar Year Plans

(1) Due Date	(2) Document	(3) Form	(4) Who Files	(5) Furnished To
See Col. (5)	Summary plan description (SPD) and statement of ERISA rights	None prescribed	Administrator of following plans: defined benefit, money purchase, profit-sharing, stock bonus, annuity, multiemployer, collectively-bargained, employer- or union-sponsored IRA, welfare, nonqualified (other than unfunded excess benefit plans) and electing church plans	Each participant or beneficiary within 90 days after he or she becomes a participant or beneficiary, or if later, within 120 days after the plan becomes subject to the reporting and disclosure requirements, and to the Dept. of Labor only upon request

(1) Due Date	(2) Document	(3) Form	(4) Who Files	(5) Furnished To
See Col. (5)	Updated summary plan description	None prescribed	Administrator of following plans: defined benefit, money purchase, profit-sharing, stock bonus, annuity, multiemployer, collectively-bargained, employer- or union-sponsored IRA, welfare, nonqualified (other than unfunded excess benefit plans) and electing church plans	Participants and beneficiaries within 210 days after the end of the appropriate plan year—generally, every 5 years if there are plan amendments but, if no plan amendments, every 10 years, and to the Dept. of Labor only upon request
See Col. (5)	Summary of material modifications (SMMs) or changes in information made during 2011 and not included in a timely summary plan description	None prescribed	Administrator of following plans: defined benefit, money purchase, profit-sharing, stock bonus, annuity, multiemployer, collectively-bargained, employer- or union-sponsored IRA, welfare, nonqualified, and electing church plans	Participants and beneficiaries not later than 210 days after the end of the plan year in which the change is adopted, and to the Dept. of Labor only upon request
See Col. (5)	First-time notice of election not to have withholding apply to periodic payments (*Note:* There is a mandatory 20% withholding on periodic payments that are (1) payable over less than 10 years or the participant's life or life expectancy (or the joint lives or life expectancies of the participant and designated beneficiary) and (2) are not directly transferred to another qualified plan or IRA. Participants may not elect out of this withholding. Mandatory withholding does not apply to nonqualified plans or IRAs.)	None prescribed	Payer of periodic annuity, pension, retirement pay, or IRA payments under the following plans: defined benefit, money purchase, profit-sharing, stock bonus, annuity, multiemployer, collectively-bargained, IRA, government (including Code Sec. 457 plans) and church plans	Recipient of periodic annuity, pension, or retirement pay no earlier than 6 months before and no later than the first payment

(1) Due Date	(2) Document	(3) Form	(4) Who Files	(5) Furnished To
See Col. (5)	Short notice of election for periodic payments (*Note:* There is a mandatory 20% withholding on periodic payments that are (1) payable over less than 10 years or the participant's life or life expectancy (or the joint lives or life expectancies of the participant and designated beneficiary) and (2) are not directly transferred to another qualified plan or IRA. Participants may not elect out of this withholding. Mandatory withholding does not apply to nonqualified plans or IRAs.)	None prescribed	Payer of periodic annuity, pension, retirement pay, or IRA payments who furnished full withholding notice prior to making first payment	Recipient of periodic annuity, pension, retirement pay, or IRA payments when first payment is made
See Col. (5)	Annual notice of election not to have withholding apply to periodic payments or revocation of such election (*Note:* There is a mandatory 20% withholding on periodic payments that are (1) payable over less than 10 years or the participant's life or life expectancy (or the joint lives or life expectancies of the participant and designated beneficiary) and (2) are not directly transferred to another qualified plan or IRA. Participants may not elect out of this withholding. Mandatory withholding does not apply to nonqualified plans or IRAs.)	None prescribed	Payer of periodic annuity, pension, retirement pay, or IRA payments under the following plans: defined benefit, money purchase, profit-sharing, stock bonus, annuity, multiemployer, collectively-bargained, IRA, government (including Code Sec. 457 plans) and church plans	Recipient of periodic annuity, pension, retirement pay, or IRA payments approximately the same time each calendar year after the notice that is provided with the first payment

(1) Due Date	(2) Document	(3) Form	(4) Who Files	(5) Furnished To
See Col. (5)	Written notice to eligible rollover distribution recipients explaining the rollover rules, tax treatment of distributions, direct rollover option and mandatory 20% income tax withholding rules. (*Note:* There is a mandatory 20% withholding on eligible rollover distributions that are not directly transferred to another qualified plan or IRA. An eligible rollover distribution is, in general, a distribution of all or any portion of a participant's benefit under a qualified plan excluding: (1) periodic payments payable over a period of 10 or more years or the participant's life or life expectancy (or joint lives of the participant and participant's designated beneficiary), (2) minimum required distributions, and (3) certain other specified payments. Recipients may not elect out of this withholding.)	None prescribed	Payer of eligible rollover distribution from the following plans: defined benefit, money purchase, profit-sharing, stock bonus, annuity, multiemployer, collectively-bargained, government and church plans	Recipient of eligible rollover distribution no less than 30 days and no more than 180 days before the date of the distribution
See Col. (5)	Written notice of participant's right to defer an immediate cash-out distribution and of the consequences of failing to defer the distribution when the participant's nonforfeitable accrued benefit is over $5,000	None prescribed	Administrators of retirement, 403(b), governmental, 457, or nonelecting church plans	Plan participant no less than 30 days and no more than 180 days before date of distribution

(1) Due Date	(2) Document	(3) Form	(4) Who Files	(5) Furnished To
See Col. (5)	Written notice that mandatory distributions between $1,001 and $5,000 may be rolled over automatically, without cost, to IRAs when participants do not elect to take distributions in cash or have the amounts transferred to qualified plans or different IRAs	None prescribed	Administrator of retirement, 403(b), governmental 457, or nonelecting church plans that provide that nonforfeitable accrued benefits whose present value does not exceed $5,000 will be immediately distributed to participants	Recipient of eligible rollover distribution: rollover notices (that include the plan's automatic rollover provisions) must be furnished no less than 30 days and no more than 180 days before the date of distribution; under DOL safe harbor final regulations, for participant or beneficiary, SPDs (that include the plan's automatic rollover provisions) within 90 days after her or she becomes a participant or beneficiary, or if later, within 120 days after the plan becomes subject to reporting and disclosure requirements, updated SPDs (that include the plan's automatic rollover provisions) within 210 days after the end of the appropriate plan year—generally, every 5 years if there are plan amendments and every 10 years if there are no plan amendments, and SMMs (that include the plan's automatic rollover provisions) not later than 210 days after the end of the plan year in which a change is adopted

¶50

(1) Due Date	(2) Document	(3) Form	(4) Who Files	(5) Furnished To
See Col. (5)	Disclosure statement pertaining to establishment of IRA and automatic rollover of benefits between $1,001 and $5,000 by plan administrator after participant fails to elect to receive a cash distribution or to have the benefits directly rolled over to an eligible retirement plan, such statement providing revocation period	None prescribed	Trustee or issuer of IRA	Participant not later than the earlier of the date of establishment or purchase of the account or annuity
See Col. (5)	Notice of election not to have withholding apply to nonperiodic payments (*Note:* This only applies to distributions that are not eligible rollover distributions. As described above, there is a mandatory 20% withholding on eligible rollover distributions that are not directly transferred to another qualified plan or IRA. Recipients may not elect out of this withholding.)	None prescribed	Payer of distribution (other than an eligible rollover distribution) from the following plans: defined benefit, money purchase, profit-sharing, stock bonus, annuity, multiemployer, collectively-bargained, IRA, nonqualified, government (including Code Sec. 457 plans) and church plans	Recipient of total distribution or withdrawal no earlier than 6 months before distribution but recipient must be given reasonable time between notice and payment. The "reasonable time" requirement is satisfied if the notice is included in the basic claim for benefits application
At any time	Election of nonwithholding on periodic or nonperiodic pension or annuity payments (*Note:* Recipients of eligible rollover distributions do not have the option of claiming exemption from withholding. Tax will be withheld from an eligible rollover distribution at a flat 20% rate, unless the recipient of such distribution elects to have more than 20% withheld on Form W-4P). However, no tax will be withheld if the eligible rollover distribution is directly rolled over to an IRA or another qualified plan.)	W-4P (line 1)	Recipient of periodic or nonperiodic payments from the following plans: defined benefit, money purchase, profit-sharing, stock bonus, annuity, multiemployer, collectively-bargained, IRA, certain nonqualified plans (unless distributions are Form W-2 wages), government (including Code Sec. 457 plans) and church plans	Payer of periodic or nonperiodic pension or annuity payments

(1) Due Date	(2) Document	(3) Form	(4) Who Files	(5) Furnished To
At any time	Withholding certificate for claiming specified number of withholding allowances (and any extra amount) to change amount of tax withheld on periodic pension or annuity payments (*Note:* Recipients of eligible rollover distributions do not have this option. The rate is a flat 20% rate, unless the recipient elects to have more than 20% withheld on Form W-4P. However, no tax will be withheld if the eligible rollover distribution is directly rolled over to an IRA or another qualified plan.)	W-4P (lines 2 and 3)	Recipient not electing exemption from withholding on periodic payments from the following plans: defined benefit, money purchase, profit-sharing, stock bonus, annuity, multiemployer, collectively-bargained, IRA, certain nonqualified plans (unless distributions are Form W-2 wages), government (including Code Sec. 457 plans) and church plans	Payer of periodic pension or annuity payments
At any time	Revocation of previously filed exemption from withholding on periodic or nonperiodic pension or annuity payments (*Note:* Recipients of eligible rollover distributions do not have the option of claiming an exemption from withholding; the rate is a 20% flat rate unless the recipient elects to have more than 20% withheld on Form W-4P. However, no tax will be withheld if such distribution is directly rolled over to an IRA or another qualified plan.)	W-4P (line 1 or lines 2 and 3, as per instructions to W-4P)	Recipient of periodic or nonperiodic pension or annuity payments from the following plans: defined benefit, money purchase, profit-sharing, stock bonus, annuity, multiemployer, collectively-bargained, IRA, certain nonqualified plans (unless distributions are Form W-2 wages), government (including Code Sec. 457 plans) and church plans	Payer of periodic or nonperiodic pension or annuity payments
1/31/12	Statement of participant's account balance as of 12/31/11 and account activity in SIMPLE during 2011	Any written format	Trustee of SIMPLE or issuer of annuity for SIMPLE IRA	Participant
See Col. (5)	Report of income tax amounts withheld from nonqualified plan payments that are treated as wages and reported on Form W-2	941 (line 2)	Employer	Internal Revenue Service quarterly, the last day of the month that follows the end of the quarter

¶50

(1) Due Date	(2) Document	(3) Form	(4) Who Files	(5) Furnished To
1/31/12	Report of income tax amounts withheld from nonqualified plan payments that are treated as wages and reported on Form W-2	944	Small employers that are notified by the Internal Revenue Service to file Form 944 instead of Form 941 (beginning with tax year 2010, employers can notify the IRS that they want to file Form 941 instead of Form 944)	Internal Revenue Service annually; however, if deposits were made in full payment of the taxes for the year by January 31, 2012, the employers have 10 more calendar days to file the return
1/31/12	Report of 2011 distributions from a nonqualified deferred compensation or nongovernmental 457(b) plan (except for distributions from a commercial annuity or to a deceased employee's beneficiary, which are reported on Form 1099-R) or a prior year deferral under a nonqualified or 457(b) plan that became taxable for Social Security and Medicare taxes this year because there is no longer a substantial risk of forfeiture of the recipient's right to the deferred amount	W-2 (Box 1 and Box 11 or Boxes 3, 5, and 11)	Employer	Recipient of nonqualified plan distributions
1/31/12	Statement of amounts includible in gross income (and treated as wages) that an employee has actually or constructively received during 2011 under a nonqualified deferred compensation plan that does not meet the requirements of Code Sec. 409A	W-2 (Box 1 and Box 12 using Code Z)	Employer	Participant of nonqualified deferred compensation plan subject to Code Sec. 409A
1/31/12	Statement of amounts includible in gross income (and not treated as wages) that a nonemployee has actually or constructively received during 2011 under a nonqualified deferred compensation plan that does not meet the requirements of Code Sec. 409A	1099-MISC (Box 7 and Box 15b)	Payer	Nonemployee recipient

(1) Due Date	(2) Document	(3) Form	(4) Who Files	(5) Furnished To
1/31/12	Report of designated Roth contributions to 401(k), 403(b), and 457(b) deferred compensation plans	W-2 (Boxes 1, 3, and 5, and Box 12 using Codes AA, BB, and EE)	Employer	Participants of 401(k) or 403(b) plans
1/31/12	Report of elective deferrals to 401(k) plans, 403(b) plans, and salary reduction SEPs, elective deferrals and employer contributions to 457(b) deferred compensation plans, and employee salary reduction contributions to SIMPLEs	W-2 (Box 12, using Codes D, E, F, G, and S, respectively)	Employer	Plan participants
1/31/12	Report of taxable cost of group term life insurance over $50,000, 20% excise tax on excess golden parachute payments, and income from exercise of nonstatutory stock options	W-2 (Box 12, using Codes C, K, and V)	Employer	Employees
1/31/12	Statement for recipient of total distribution or periodic or installment payments for calendar year 2011	1099-R (Copy B and C)	Payer of distribution under the following plans: defined benefit, money purchase, profit-sharing, stock bonus, annuity, multiemployer, collectively-bargained, IRA, Roth IRA, SIMPLE, SEP, nonqualified (but only if the distribution is from a commercial annuity or to a deceased employee's beneficiary; otherwise, report nonqualified plan distributions on Form W-2, not Form 1099-R), government (including Code Sec. 457 plans) and church plans	Recipient of distribution

(1) Due Date	(2) Document	(3) Form	(4) Who Files	(5) Furnished To
1/31/12	Report of income tax amounts withheld from plan payments	945	Employer, plan administrator, or other payer under following plans: defined benefit, money purchase, profit-sharing, stock bonus, annuity, multiemployer, collectively-bargained, IRA, nonqualified (but only with respect to a distribution from a commercial annuity or to a deceased employee's beneficiary; otherwise, use Form 941), government (including Code Sec. 457 plans) and church plans	Internal Revenue Service; for 2011, file by 1/31/12; however, if deposits were made on time in full payment of the taxes for the year, the return may be filed by 2/10/12
1/31/12	Report of corporation's transfer of employer stock to employee pursuant to employee's exercise of incentive stock option	3921	Employer/corporation	Employee
1/31/12	Report of transfer of stock by employee acquired through exercise of option granted under employee stock purchase plan	3922	Employer/corporation	Employee
1/31/12	Statement of fair market value of IRA, Roth IRA, SEP, or SIMPLE participant's account balance as of 12/31/11	Any written format	Custodian, trustee, or issuer of IRA, Roth IRA, SEP, or SIMPLE	Participant

(1) Due Date	(2) Document	(3) Form	(4) Who Files	(5) Furnished To
1/31/12	If a minimum distribution from an IRA is required for 2012 and the IRA owner is alive at the beginning of 2012, a statement must be provided of either the amount of the required distribution and the date it must be distributed or a statement that a minimum distribution is required and the date by which it must be distributed and an offer to furnish upon request a calculation of the required amount. The statement must also inform the IRA owner that the trustee will be reporting to the IRS that the IRA owner must receive a required minimum distribution for the calendar year	None prescribed	Trustee, custodian, or issuer of IRA as of December 31, 2011	IRA owner, surviving spouse of deceased IRA owner if spouse is sole beneficiary and elects to treat the IRA as the spouse's own IRA
See Col. (5)	Request for extension of time to file Forms W-2, 1099-R, 3921, 3922, and 5498 (paper forms or electronically)	8809	Payer of total distributions or periodic or installment payments under the following plans: defined benefit, money purchase, profit-sharing, annuity, multiemployer, collectively-bargained, IRA, Roth IRA, nonqualified (but only if the distribution is from a commercial annuity or to a deceased employee's beneficiary; otherwise, report nonqualified plan distributions on Form W-2 not Form 1099-R), government and church plans, SEPs and SIMPLEs	Internal Revenue Service, no later than the due date of the return
2/28/12	Copy A of statement of amounts includible in gross income (and not treated as wages) that a nonemployee has actually or constructively received during 2011 under a nonqualified deferred compensation plan that does not meet the requirements of Code Sec. 409A	1099-MISC (Box 7 and Box 15b)	Payer	Internal Revenue Service along with transmittal Form 1096 (for paper forms only); if filed electronically, the due date is 4/2/12

(1) Due Date	(2) Document	(3) Form	(4) Who Files	(5) Furnished To
2/28/12	Copy A of statement for recipient of total distribution or periodic or installment payments from profit-sharing, retirement plan, or individual retirement arrangement (IRA) for calendar year 2011	1099-R	Payer of total distribution under the following plans: defined benefit, money purchase, profit-sharing, stock bonus, annuity, multiemployer, collectively-bargained, IRA, Roth IRA, nonqualified (but only if the distribution is from a commercial annuity or to a deceased employee's beneficiary, otherwise, report nonqualified plan distributions on Form W-2 not Form 1099-R), government (including Code Sec. 457 plans) and church plans, SEPs and SIMPLEs	Internal Revenue Service along with transmittal Form 1096 (for paper forms only); if filed electronically, the due date is 4/2/12
2/28/12	Copy A of report of corporation's transfer of employer stock to employee pursuant to employee's exercise of incentive stock option	3921	Employer/corporation	Internal Revenue Service; if filed electronically, the due date is 4/2/12
2/28/12	Copy A of report of transfer of stock by employee acquired through exercise of option granted under employee stock purchase plan	3922	Employer/corporation	Internal Revenue Service; if filed electronically, the due date is 4/2/12
2/29/12	Copy A of statement of amounts includible in gross income that an employee has actually or constructively received during 2011 under a nonqualified deferred compensation plan that does not meet the requirements of Code Sec. 409A (Box 1 and Box 12, using Code Z)	W-2	Employer	Social Security Administration along with transmittal Form W-3; if filed electronically, the due date is 4/2/12
2/29/12	Copy A of report of designated Roth contributions to 401(k), 403(b), and 457(b) deferred compensation plans	W-2	Employer	Social Security Administration along with transmittal Form W-3; if filed electronically, the due date is 4/2/12

(1) Due Date	(2) Document	(3) Form	(4) Who Files	(5) Furnished To
2/29/12	Copy A of report of elective deferrals to 401(k) plans, 403(b) plans, and salary reduction SEPs, elective deferrals and employer contributions to 457(b) deferred compensation plans, and employee salary reduction contributions to SIMPLEs	W-2	Employer	Social Security Administration along with transmittal Form W-3; if filed electronically, the due date is 4/2/12
2/29/12	Copy A of report of taxable cost of group term life insurance over $50,000, 20% excise tax on excess golden parachute payments, and income from exercise of nonstatutory stock options	W-2	Employer	Social Security Administration along with transmittal Form W-3; if filed electronically, the due date is 4/2/12
2/29/12	Estimated flat-rate premium payment for plan year beginning 1/1/12 (2012 plan year)	PBGC Comprehensive Premium Filing (formerly, Form 1-ES)	Administrator of defined benefit or annuity plan, or other plan subject to ERISA Title IV, which has 500 or more participants for the plan year preceding the premium payment year	Pension Benefit Guaranty Corporation (PBGC) online at PBGC's website

(1) Due Date	(2) Document	(3) Form	(4) Who Files	(5) Furnished To
See Col. (5)	Personal benefit statement of accrued and vested benefits	None prescribed	Administrator of individual account plan (except one-participant retirement plan)	Each participant and beneficiary (1) at least once each calendar quarter when the participant or beneficiary has the right to direct the investment of assets in his or her account (see Employee Benefits Security Administration (EBSA) Field Assistance Bulletin 2006-03 for guidance on good faith compliance with disclosure deadline); (2) at least once each calendar year when the participant or beneficiary has an account but does not have the right to direct the investment of his or her account assets (see EBSA Field Assistance Bulletin 2006-03 for guidance on good faith compliance with disclosure deadline and EBSA Field Assistance Bulletin 2007-03 for further deadline relief); (alternatively, a statement may be provided that enables the participants or beneficiaries to determine their nonforfeitable vested benefits); and (3) on written request to a plan beneficiary not described in (1) or (2) above (but not more than once during any twelve-month period); automatically to terminated and break-in-service employees

(1) Due Date	(2) Document	(3) Form	(4) Who Files	(5) Furnished To
See Col. (5)	Personal benefit statement of accrued and vested benefits	None prescribed	Administrator of defined benefit plan (except one-participant retirement plan)	Each participant with nonforfeitable accrued benefits who is employed by an employer maintaining the plan at the time the statement is to be furnished at least once every three years; and to each participant or beneficiary upon written request (but not more than once during any twelve-month period); alternatively, the notice requirements for the employed participants with nonforfeitable accrued benefits are met if at least once each year they are provided a notice of the availability of the pension benefit statements and the ways to obtain the statements (not later than December 31, 2007, per Employee Benefits Security Administration Field Assistance Bulletin 2006-03); automatically to terminated and break-in-service employees
See Col. (5)	Notice of benefit determination	None prescribed	Plan administrator of employee benefit plans generally	Claimants (participants and beneficiaries) within a reasonable time, but no later than 90 days after receipt of a claim; a claimant must be given at least 60 days to appeal a claim denial; if denial is appealed, the named fiduciary must furnish decision on review

(1) Due Date	(2) Document	(3) Form	(4) Who Files	(5) Furnished To
3/15/12	Withholding statement for nonresident alien recipient of pension or lump-sum distribution for calendar year 2011 (paper or electronically)	1042-S	Payer of annuity or pension payments under the following plans: defined benefit, money purchase, profit-sharing, stock bonus, annuity, multiemployer, collectively-bargained, nonqualified, government and church plans	Internal Revenue Service with Form 1042; copy to recipient of distribution
4/2/12 (for 2010 excesses)	Return for payment of excise tax for excess contributions and excess aggregate contributions	5330	Employer who made excess contributions to plan maintaining cash or deferred arrangement; employer who made excess aggregate contributions under employee and matching employer contribution rules	Internal Revenue Service
See Col. (5)	Return for IRA (including Roth IRAs), and qualified retirement plan (including SIMPLEs) penalty taxes	5329	Participants who owe taxes for IRA excess contributions, IRA or qualified plan excess accumulations (i.e., participants who did not receive their minimum required distributions), IRA or qualified retirement plan early distributions (under certain conditions), or Roth IRA early distributions (under certain conditions)	Internal Revenue Service as an attachment to Form 1040 tax return by the due date (including extensions) of Form 1040
4/17/12	Return for nondeductible IRA contributions, distributions from IRA, SEP, or SIMPLE IRA, distributions from Roth IRA, conversions from IRA, SEP, or SIMPLE IRA to Roth IRA, certain distributions from designated Roth accounts allocable to in-plan Roth rollovers, for calendar year 2011	8606	Participants	Internal Revenue Service as an attachment to Form 1040 series tax return

(1) Due Date	(2) Document	(3) Form	(4) Who Files	(5) Furnished To
4/17/12	Return to directly deposit tax refund to more than one account, including an IRA, Roth IRA, or SEP-IRA	8888	Participant in IRA, Roth IRA, or SEP-IRA	Internal Revenue Service as an attachment to Form 1040 series tax return (Caution: participants who want the refund/contribution to relate back to the prior tax year should file sufficiently before the filing deadline for Form 1040 to ensure that the refund is deposited by that filing deadline) (Note: participants who want their whole refund deposited directly into one account may use the appropriate line in the Form 1040 series)
4/17/12	Return for retirement savings contributions credit for contributions to a traditional or Roth IRA, elective deferrals to a 401(k), 403(b), governmental 457, SEP, or SIMPLE plan, or voluntary employee contributions to a qualified retirement plan for calendar year 2011	8880	Participant who makes contributions or elective deferrals	Internal Revenue Service as an attachment to Form 1040 series tax return
4/17/12	Return for qualified disaster recovery assistance retirement plan distributions and repayments	8930	Participant adversely affected by the Midwestern severe storms, tornadoes, or flooding and who received a qualified disaster recovery assistance distribution from a qualified pension, profit-sharing, or stock bonus (including a 401(k) plan), a qualified annuity plan, a tax-sheltered annuity contract, a governmental 457 deferred compensation plan, or a traditional IRA, SEP, SIMPLE, or Roth IRA	Internal Revenue Service as an attachment to Form 1040 series tax return

(1) Due Date	(2) Document	(3) Form	(4) Who Files	(5) Furnished To
4/17/12	Exempt organization unrelated business income tax return	990-T	Plan fiduciary reporting and paying the tax for the following plans: defined benefit, money purchase, profit-sharing, stock bonus, annuity, multiemployer, collectively-bargained, government and church plans, IRAs, Roth IRAs, SEPs, SIMPLEs, and MSAs; signed by fiduciary or authorized officer of trust and paid preparer	Internal Revenue Service; not required if unrelated business income is less than $1,000
4/30/12	Copy of annual statement of assets and liabilities of common or collective trust or pooled fund and other information necessary for 2011 annual return/report	None prescribed	Bank, insurance company, or plan sponsor maintaining the information on defined benefit, money purchase, profit-sharing, stock bonus, annuity, multiemployer, collectively-bargained, employer- or union-sponsored IRA, welfare, nonqualified, and electing church plans	Plan administrator
4/30/12	Flat-rate premium payment for 2011 plan year and, if single-employer plan with unfunded vested benefits, additional variable-rate premium payment for 2011 plan year	PBGC Comprehensive Premium Filing (formerly Form 1, 1-EZ, and Schedule A)	Administrator of defined benefit or annuity plan subject to ERISA Title IV, which has less than 100 participants for whom flat-rate premiums were payable for the plan year preceding the premium payment year	Pension Benefit Guaranty Corporation (PBGC) online at PBGC's website
5/31/12	Individual retirement arrangement information reporting regular IRA and Roth IRA contributions made in 2011 and through 4/17/12 for 2011, SEP and SIMPLE contributions made in 2011, any rollover contributions made in 2011, fair market value of participant's account as of 12/31/11, for endowment contracts only, the amount allocable to life insurance cost	Form 5498 (Copy A)	Custodian, trustee, or issuer of IRA, Roth IRA, SEP, or SIMPLE	Internal Revenue Service (along with transmittal Form 1096 for paper forms only)

¶50

(1) Due Date	(2) Document	(3) Form	(4) Who Files	(5) Furnished To
5/31/12	Contribution information for IRA, Roth IRA, SEP, or SIMPLE participants for calendar year 2011	Sponsor-designed form or Copy B of Form 5498 with required information	Custodian, trustee, or issuer of IRA, Roth IRA, SEP, or SIMPLE	Participant
6/30/12	Notice of substantial employer status	None prescribed	Administrator of defined benefit or annuity plan, or other plan subject to ERISA Title IV, to which more than one employer contributes (other than a multiemployer plan) and which has at least two contributing sponsors not under common control	Each contributing employer who was a substantial employer for plan year
See Col. (5)	Application to change plan and/or trust year (for plans that do not qualify for automatic approval)	5308	Employer (administrator, if a multiple employer plan) sponsoring the following plans: defined benefit, money purchase, annuity, multiemployer, collectively-bargained; employers sponsoring profit-sharing, stock bonus, government and non-electing church plans need only file Form 5308 to change trust year (not plan year)	Internal Revenue Service, on or before the last day of the end of the short period required to make the change
See Col. (5)	Application for extension of time to file Form 5500, 5500-EZ, 5500-SF, 8955-SSA, or 5330	5558	Administrator, employer or agent; filed for defined benefit, money purchase, profit-sharing, stock bonus, annuity, multiemployer, collectively-bargained, employer- or union-sponsored IRA, welfare, nonqualified, and electing church plans	Internal Revenue Service before the normal due date of the annual return/report and Form 8955-SSA; sufficiently before the normal due date for Form 5330 for the Internal Revenue Service to consider and act on it
7/31/12	Statement of deferred vested benefits	None prescribed	Plan administrator who is required to file annual registration statement	Separated participant on or before the date in Col. (1)

(1) Due Date	(2) Document	(3) Form	(4) Who Files	(5) Furnished To
7/31/12	Annual return/report for 2011 plan year	5500 for all large and small (less than 100 participants), except for one-participant plans (See Form 5500-EZ and Form 5500-SF below).	Plan administrator of or employer maintaining defined benefit, money purchase, profit-sharing, stock bonus, annuity, multiemployer, collectively-bargained, employer- or union-sponsored IRA, welfare, nonqualified, or electing church plan	Employee Benefits Security Administration, electronically either online through EFAST2's web-based filing system or through an EFAST2-approved vendor; copy to any participant and beneficiary within 30 days of written request
7/31/12	Annual return/report for 2011 plan year	5500-EZ, generally for one-participant plans not subject to ERISA Sec. 104(a) and not filing Form 5500-SF, and certain foreign pension plans	Plan administrator or employer maintaining the plan	Internal Revenue Service
7/31/12	Short form annual return/report for 2011 plan year	5500-SF	Plan administrator or employer maintaining certain small (i.e., generally fewer than 100 participants at the beginning of 2011 plan year) pension and welfare benefit plan, and certain one-participant plans (ESOPs, DFEs, and multiemployer plans are not eligible plans)	Employee Benefits Security Administration electronically either online through EFAST2's web-based filing system, or through an EFAST2-approved vendor
7/31/12	Insurance information	5500, Schedule A	Administrator of the following large and small (fewer than 100 participants) plans if any benefits are provided by an insurance company, insurance service or other similar organization: defined benefit, money purchase, profit-sharing, stock bonus, annuity, multiemployer, collectively-bargained, welfare, nonqualified, and electing church plans	Employee Benefits Security Administration, electronically either online through EFAST2's web-based filing system or through an EFAST2-approved vendor with Form 5500

(1) Due Date	(2) Document	(3) Form	(4) Who Files	(5) Furnished To
7/31/12	Service provider information	5500, Schedule C	Administrator of following large plans if service provider was paid $5,000 or more in direct or indirect compensation and/or accountant or an actuary was terminated: defined benefit, money purchase, profit-sharing, stock bonus, multiemployer, collectively-bargained, (with only one employer-contributor), welfare, nonqualified, and electing church plans	Employee Benefits Security Administration, electronically either online through EFAST2's web-based filing system or through an EFAST2-approved vendor with Form 5500
7/31/12	Direct filing information/ participating plan information	5500, Schedule D	Administrators of large and small pension and welfare plans that participated or invested in one or more common/collective trusts (CCTs), pooled separate accounts (PSAs), master trust investment accounts (MTIAs), and 103-12 Investment Entities (103-12 IEs) at any time during the plan year and a CCT, PSA, MTIA, 103-12, or group insurance arrangement (GIA) as a direct filing entity	Employee Benefits Security Administration, electronically either online through EFAST2's web-based filing system or through an EFAST2-approved vendor with Form 5500
7/31/12	Financial transaction schedules	5500, Schedule G (The actual use of Schedule G now is mandatory, when applicable)	Plan administrator of large pension and welfare plans and Direct Filing Entities (DFE) if, on Schedule H, lines 4b, 4c, or 4d are answered "yes"	Employee Benefits Security Administration, electronically either online through EFAST2's web-based filing system or through an EFAST2-approved vendor with Form 5500
7/31/12	Financial information for large plans and DFEs	5500, Schedule H	Plan administrator for large pension and welfare plans (100 or more participants) and Direct Filing Entities (DFEs), except insured, unfunded, or combination unfunded/insured welfare plans and certain fully insured pension plans. If Schedule I was filed for the 2010 plan year and the plan covered fewer than 121 participants as of the beginning of the 2011 plan year, Schedule I may be completed instead of Schedule H	Employee Benefits Security Administration, electronically either online through EFAST2's web-based filing system or through an EFAST2-approved vendor with Form 5500

28

(1) Due Date	(2) Document	(3) Form	(4) Who Files	(5) Furnished To
7/31/12	Financial information for small plans	5500, Schedule I	Plan administrator of small pension and welfare plans (fewer than 100 participants), except for insured, unfunded or combination unfunded/ insured welfare plans and certain fully insured pension plans. If Schedule I was filed for the 2010 plan year and the plan covered fewer than 121 participants as of the beginning of the 2011 plan year, Schedule I may be completed instead of Schedule H	Employee Benefits Security Administration, electronically either online through EFAST2's web-based filing system or through an EFAST2-approved vendor with Form 5500
7/31/12	Multiemployer defined benefit plan and certain money purchase plan actuarial information	5500, Schedule MB	Employer or plan administrator of multiemployer defined benefit plan subject to minimum funding standards and money purchase plans (including target benefit plans) that are currently amortizing a funding waiver; may include annuity, collectively bargained, and electing church plans; also certain money purchase plans filing Form 5500-SF, completing entire schedule, if applicable (however, for Form 5500-EZ (and for one-participant plans that can file Form 5500-EZ, but instead file Form 5500-SF), the schedule is not filed, but instead is retained with plan records)	Employee Benefits Security Administration, electronically either online through EFAST2's web-based filing system or through an EFAST2-approved vendor with Form 5500 or Form 5500-SF

¶50

(1) Due Date	(2) Document	(3) Form	(4) Who Files	(5) Furnished To
7/31/12	Retirement plan information	5500, Schedule R	Administrator of large and small pension plans, both qualified and nonqualified, unless (1) the sole funding vehicle for providing benefits is a tax-deferred annuity arrangement under Code Sec. 403(b)(1), a custodial account for regulated investment company stock under Code Sec. 403(b)(7), and/or individual retirement accounts for annuities under Code Sec. 408, or (2) the plan is not a defined benefit plan or otherwise subject to the minimum funding standards of Code Sec. 412 or ERISA Sec. 302; no plan benefits in a form other than cash, annuity contracts issued by an insurance company, life insurance contracts, marketable securities, or plan loan offset amounts were distributed during the plan year; no benefits reportable on Form 1099-R were distributed during the plan year by payors other than the plan sponsor or plan administrator; and, unless the plan is a profit-sharing, ESOP, or stock bonus plan, no plan benefits of living or deceased participants were distributed during the plan year in the form of a single-sum distribution	Employee Benefits Security Administration, electronically either online through EFAST2's web-based filing system or through an EFAST2-approved vendor with Form 5500

(1) Due Date	(2) Document	(3) Form	(4) Who Files	(5) Furnished To
7/31/12	Actuarial information	5500, Schedule SB	Plan sponsor or administrator of single-employer defined benefit plan (including multiple employer defined benefit plan) subject to minimum funding standards; may include annuity, collectively bargained, nonqualified, and electing church plans; also plans filing Form 5500-SF, completing entire schedule, if applicable (however, for Form 5500-EZ (and for one-participant plans that can file Form 5500-EZ, but instead file Form 5500-SF), the schedule is not filed, but instead is retained with plan records)	Employee Benefits Security Administration, electronically either online through EFAST2's web-based filing system or through an EFAST2-approved vendor with Form 5500 or Form 5500-SF
7/31/12	Annual registration statement identifying separated participants with deferred vested benefits	8955-SSA	Administrators of plans subject to ERISA Sec. 203 vesting standards including: defined benefit, money purchase, profit-sharing, stock bonus, annuity, collectively-bargained, multiple employer, multiemployer, nonqualified, and electing church plans	IRS (paper or electronically)
7/31/12	Opinion of independent qualified public accountant	None prescribed, but an opinion as required by ERISA Sec. 103 and the regulations thereunder	Administrator of large pension and welfare plans including the following plans: defined benefit, money purchase, profit-sharing, stock bonus, annuity, multiemployer, collectively-bargained, welfare (other than a plan that is unfunded, fully insured, or both), nonqualified, and electing church plans; and group insurance arrangements (GIAs) and investment entities filing under ERISA Reg. Sec. 2520.103-12 (103-12 IEs)	Employee Benefits Security Administration, electronically either online through EFAST2's web-based filing system or through an EFAST2-approved vendor with Form 5500
7/31/12	Notice of change in name of plan	5500 or 5500-SF at specified line item	Plan administrator	Employee Benefits Security Administration

(1) Due Date	(2) Document	(3) Form	(4) Who Files	(5) Furnished To
7/31/12	Notice of change in name, employee identification number, or plan number of plan sponsor	5500 or 5500-SF at specified line item	Plan administrator	Employee Benefits Security Administration
7/31/12	Notice of plan termination	5500, Schedule H (for large plans) and Schedule I (for small plans), at specified line item	Plan administrator	Employee Benefits Security Administration
See Col (5)	Return for payment of initial excise taxes for prohibited transaction	5330	Disqualified person who participated in prohibited transaction in regard to following plans: defined benefit, money purchase, profit-sharing, stock bonus, annuity, multiemployer, collectively-bargained, employer-or union-sponsored IRA, and electing church plans	Internal Revenue Service by the last day of the 7th month after the end of the disqualified person's tax year
See Col (5)	Return for payment of excise taxes for prohibited tax shelter transactions	5330	Any plan entity manager of tax-exempt entity who approves entity as party to, or otherwise causes entity to be party to, prohibited tax shelter transaction and knows or has reason to know transaction is prohibited tax shelter transaction	Internal Revenue Service by the 15th day of the 5th month following the close of the entity manager's tax year in which the tax-exempt entity becomes a party to the transaction
See Col. (5)	Return for payment of excise taxes for underfunding or for failure to meet liquidity requirement	5330	Employer who failed to meet minimum funding standards or liquidity requirement of a defined benefit or defined contribution (money purchase) plan	Internal Revenue Service by the later of: (1) the last day of the 7th month after the end of the employer's tax year, of (2) 8½ months after the last day of the plan year that ends with or within the filer's tax year
See Col. (5)	Return for payment of excise taxes for nondeductible employer contributions	5330	Employer who made nondeductible contributions to the following plans: defined benefit, money purchase, profit-sharing, stock bonus, annuity, multiemployer, collectively-bargained, and church (if employer has always been tax-exempt) plans and SEPs	Internal Revenue Service no later than the last day of the 7th month after the end of the employer's tax year

(1) Due Date	(2) Document	(3) Form	(4) Who Files	(5) Furnished To
See Col. (5)	Return for payment of 20% or 50% excise tax on employer plan assets reversion	5330	Employer maintaining defined benefit, money purchase, profit-sharing, stock bonus, annuity, multiemployer, or collectively-bargained plan	Internal Revenue Service no later than the last day of the month following the month in which the reversion occurs
See Col. (5)	Summary annual report (SAR) for 2011	For Form 5500 filers, fill-in-the-blank format prescribed by ERISA Reg. Sec. 2520.104b-10(d)(3)	Administrator of the following plans: money purchase, profit-sharing, stock bonus, annuity, multiemployer, collectively-bargained, employer-or union-sponsored IRA, welfare, nonqualified and electing church plans	Participants and beneficiaries receiving benefits under the plan (other than beneficiaries under a welfare plan) within 9 months after the end of the plan year or 2 months after the due date for filing Form 5500 or Form 5500-SF with an extension
10/15/12	Flat-rate premium payment for 2012 plan year and, if single-employer plan with unfunded vested benefits, additional variable-rate premium payment for 2012 plan year	PBGC Comprehensive Premium Filing (formerly Form 1, 1-EZ, and Schedule A)	Administrator of defined benefit or annuity plan subject to ERISA Title IV, which has 100 or more but less than 500 participants for whom flat-rate premiums are payable in the premium payment year	Pension Benefit Guaranty Corporation (PBGC) online (an amended filing to reconcile the final variable-rate premium with the estimated variable-rate premium payment is due April 30, 2013)
10/15/12	Variable-rate premium payment for 2012 plan year, if single-employer plan with unfunded vested benefits	PBGC Comprehensive Premium Filing (formerly Form 1, 1-EZ, and ScheduleA)	Administrator of defined benefit or annuity plan subject to ERISA Title IV, with 500 or more participants for whom flat-rate premiums are payable in the premium payment year	Pension Benefit Guaranty Corporation (PBGC) online at PBGC's website (an amended filing to reconcile the final flat-rate premium with the estimated flat-rate premium payment is due October 15, 2012 and/or an amended filing to reconcile the final variable-rate premium with the estimated variable-rate premium payment is due April 30, 2013)
12/31/12	Plan number, name of EIN of plan sponsor	None prescribed	Administrator of following plans: defined benefit, money purchase, profit-sharing, stock bonus, annuity, multiemployer, collectively-bargained, welfare, nonqualified and electing church plans	Bank or insurance company maintaining common or collective trust or pooled fund

(1) Due Date	(2) Document	(3) Form	(4) Who Files	(5) Furnished To
See Col. **(5)**	Annual financial and actuarial reports	None prescribed	Generally, contributing sponsor and each member of contributing sponsor's controlled group that maintains single-employer and multiple-employer defined benefit plans if: funding target attainment percentage at the end of preceding plan year is less than 80%; conditions for imposition of lien for plan have been met; or minimum funding waivers in excess of $1,000,000 have been granted for plan and any portion is still outstanding	Pension Benefit Guaranty Corporation (PBGC) online at PBGC's website on or before the 105th day after the close of the filer's fiscal (or calendar year if controlled group members have different fiscal years); if required plan actuarial information is unavailable at the above deadline, filer must submit the actuarial information within 15 days after the deadline for filing Form 5500 for plan year ending within filer's fiscal (or calendar) year, provided certain requirements are met
4/1/13 **(for 2011** **excesses)**	Return for payment of excise tax for excess contributions and excess aggregate contributions	5330	Employer who made excess contributions to plan maintaining cash or deferred arrangement; employer who made excess aggregate contributions under employee and matching employer contribution rules	Internal Revenue Service
See Col. **(5)**	Notice of merger or consolidation, or spin-off or transfer of assets or liabilities to another plan	5310-A; also reported on 5500, Schedule H (for large plans) and Schedule I (for small plans) at specified line item	Sponsor or administrator of following plans: defined benefit, money purchase, profit-sharing, stock bonus, 401(k), annuity, collectively-bargained, (but see below for multiemployer plan subject to ERISA, Title IV), nonqualified, government and electing church plans	Internal Revenue Service no less than 30 days before the transaction
See Col. **(5)**	Notice of merger or transfer between multiemployer plans	None prescribed	Plan sponsor of multiemployer plan subject to ERISA, Title IV	Pension Benefit Guaranty Corporation at least 120 days before effective date of merger or transfer

(1) Due Date	(2) Document	(3) Form	(4) Who Files	(5) Furnished To
See Col. (5)	Notice of qualified separate lines of business (QSLOBs)	5310-A	Employer maintaining single-employer defined benefit, defined contribution, or annuity plan(s)	Internal Revenue Service on or before notification date for the testing year (i.e., the later of: (a) October 15 of the year following the testing year, or (b) the 15th day of the 10th month after the close of the plan year of the plan of the employer that begins earliest in the testing year)
See Col. (5)	Notice of failure to make required contributions	PBGC Form 200	Contributing sponsor and/or parent of controlled group of single-employer defined benefit plan	Pension Benefit Guaranty Corporation no later than 10 days after the due date for the required payment
See Col. (5)	Post-event notice of reportable events	PBGC Form 10	Generally, administrator and each contributing sponsor of single-employer defined benefit plan	Pension Benefit Guaranty Corporation generally within 30 days after a plan administrator or contributing sponsor know or has reason to know that a reportable event has occurred
See Col. (5)	Advance notice of reportable events	PBGC Form 10-Advance	Each contributing sponsor of single-employer defined benefit plan	Pension Benefit Guaranty Corporation generally no later than 30 days before the effective date of the reportable event

¶50

(1) Due Date	(2) Document	(3) Form	(4) Who Files	(5) Furnished To
See Col. (5)	Missing participant information	Schedule MP	Administrator of single-employer defined benefit plan terminating in a standard or distress termination (will apply to terminating multiemployer defined benefit plans, and may be utilized by terminating qualified pension plans not subject to the Pension Benefit Guaranty Corporation's (PBGC's) termination insurance program (i.e., defined contribution plans, defined benefit plans with no more than 25 active participants that are maintained by professional service employers, the portion of defined benefit plans that provide benefits based on participants' separate accounts, and plans that at no time after the enactment of ERISA provided for employer contributions), for distributions made after the PBGC issues final regulations)	Pension Benefit Guaranty Corporation generally no later than 30 days after final distribution of plan assets is completed
See Col. (5)	Notice of insolvency	None prescribed	Sponsor of multiemployer defined benefit plan in reorganization	Pension Benefit Guaranty Corporation, employers required to contribute to plan, employee organizations representing plan participants, and participants and beneficiaries no later than 30 days after the sponsor determines that the plan is or may become insolvent (notice to participants and beneficiaries in pay status can be delivered concurrently with the first benefit payment made more than 30 days after the determination of insolvency)

(1) Due Date	(2) Document	(3) Form	(4) Who Files	(5) Furnished To
See Col. (5)	Notice of insolvency benefit level	None prescribed	Sponsor of multiemployer defined benefit plan in reorganization	Pension Benefit Guaranty Corporation, participants and beneficiaries who are in pay status or are reasonably expected to enter pay status during the insolvency year no later than 60 days before the beginning of the insolvency year, except that if the insolvency determination is made fewer than 120 days before the beginning of the insolvency year, the notices should be furnished within 60 days after the date of the determination (the notice does not have to be delivered to contributing employers, employee organizations representing plan participants, and participants and beneficiaries not in pay status for an insolvency year immediately following the plan year in which a notice of insolvency was required to be delivered if the notice was in fact delivered)
See Col. (5)	Notice of significant reduction in the rate of future benefit accruals, including reductions in certain early retirement benefits or retirement-type subsidies	None prescribed	Administrator of defined benefit or money purchase plans	Participants, alternate payees under QDROs, employee organizations representing participants, and contributing employers (for multiemployer plans) at least 45 days before the effective date of the plan amendment (for multiemployer plans, small plans, and amendments in connection with an acquisition or disposition at least 15 days before the effective date of the plan amendment)

(1) Due Date	(2) Document	(3) Form	(4) Who Files	(5) Furnished To
See Col. (5)	Explanation of participant's right to choose between a qualified joint and survivor annuity and other forms of distributions, and generally for plan years beginning after December 31, 2007, terms and conditions of qualified optional survivor annuity	None prescribed	Administrator of defined benefit and money purchase plans	Participants no less than 30 days and no more than 180 days before the annuity starting date
See Col. (5)	Explanation for participant concerning a qualified pre-retirement survivor annuity	None prescribed	Administrator of defined benefit and money purchase plans	Participants before the latest of the following periods: (1) the period beginning with the first day of the plan year preceding the plan year in which the participant reaches age 32 and ending with the end of the plan year preceding the plan year in which the participant reaches age 35; (2) a reasonable period of time after the end of the subsidization of a survivor benefit for a participant by the plan; (3) a reasonable period of time after an individual becomes a plan participant; (4) a reasonable period of time after the survivor benefit provisions of the Code become applicable to a participant; or (5) in the case of a participant who separates from service before age 35, a reasonable period of time after the separation

(1) Due Date	(2) Document	(3) Form	(4) Who Files	(5) Furnished To
See Col. (5)	Statement attached to income tax returns for taxable year in which taxpayer participated, directly or indirectly, in reportable transactions that have characteristics common to tax shelters, such as transactions in which taxpayers claim deductions for contributions to a qualified CODA or matching contributions made to a defined contribution plan where contributions are attributable to compensation earned by plan participants after the end of the taxable year	8886	Taxpayers that are corporations, individuals, trusts, partnerships, and S corporations	Internal Revenue Service by due date for income tax return or information return
See Col. (5)	Disclosure of information concerning each prohibited tax shelter transaction to which a tax-exempt entity is party	8886-T	Entity manager of plan entity (i.e., qualified plan, annuity plan, 403(b) plan, 457(b) deferred compensation plan, IRA, custodial account treated as annuity contract under Code Sec. 403(b)(7)(A), Archer medical savings account, and health savings account); if plan entity is fully self-directed qualified plan, IRA, or other savings arrangement, entity manager is plan participant, beneficiary, or owner who approved or caused entity to be party to prohibited tax shelter transaction	Internal Revenue Service (a) for a tax-exempt entity that is a party to a prohibited tax shelter transaction because it facilitates the transaction due to its tax-exempt, tax-indifferent, or tax-favored status, on or before May 15 of the year following the close of the calendar year during which the tax-exempt entity entered the transaction, (b) for a tax-exempt entity that became a party to a prohibited tax shelter transaction that is determined to be a listed transaction by the IRS after the entity became a party to the transaction, on or before May 15 of the calendar year following the close of the calendar year during which the transaction was identified as a listed transaction

(1) Due Date	(2) Document	(3) Form	(4) Who Files	(5) Furnished To
See Col. (5)	Notice to interested parties of application for determination of qualified status of plan	None prescribed	Employer or administrator of pension, profit-sharing, or stock bonus plan, annuity plan, nonelecting church plan	Generally, current employees who are eligible to participate in the plan and all other current employees whose principal place of employment is the same as that of the eligible employees, not less than 10 days nor more than 24 days before the date the application is made
See Col. (5)	Notice of blackout period during which participants' and beneficiaries' rights to direct or diversify investments in their accounts or to obtain a loan or receive a distribution under the plan would be temporarily suspended, limited, or restricted for more than 3 consecutive business days	None prescribed	Administrators of individual account plans, except one-participant retirement plans	All affected participants and beneficiaries at least 30 days, but not more than 60 days, in advance of the last date on which the participants and beneficiaries could exercise their affected rights immediately before the commencement of any blackout period
See Col. (5)	Notice of blackout period during which participants' and beneficiaries' rights to direct or diversify investments in their accounts or to obtain a loan or receive a distribution under the plan would be temporarily suspended, limited, or restricted for more than 3 consecutive business days	None prescribed	Administrators of individual account plans, except for one-participant retirement plans	Issuer of any employer securities held by the plan that is subject to the blackout period at least 30 days, but not more than 60 days, in advance of the last date on which the participants and beneficiaries could exercise their affected rights immediately before the commencement of any blackout period
See Col. (5)	Blackout notice concerning a "qualified change in investment options" containing comparison of existing and new investment options and description of default investments that will be made absent contrary instructions from participants or beneficiaries	None prescribed	Administrators of individual account plans, except for one-participant retirement plans	All affected participants and beneficiaries at least 30 days, but not more than 60 days prior to effective date of change

(1) Due Date	(2) Document	(3) Form	(4) Who Files	(5) Furnished To
See Col. (5)	Annual funding notice disclosing identifying information about plan, number of participants, plan's funding policy and asset allocation of investments, any plan amendments, Pension Benefit Guaranty Corporation's guarantee of benefits, where to obtain a copy of plan's annual report, and other information about plan funding and assets, among other things	None prescribed	Administrators of single-employer and multiemployer defined benefit plans to which Title IV of ERISA applies	Participants, beneficiaries, labor organizations representing participants and beneficiaries, contributing employers (for multiemployer plans), and Pension Benefit Guaranty Corporation generally no later than 120 days after end of plan year relating to annual funding notice; small plans should provide notice upon filing of annual Form 5500
See Col. (5)	Certification that a restricted amendment provides for an increase in annual contributions that will exceed the increase in annual charges to the funding standard account attributable to the amendment	None prescribed	Enrolled actuary for under-funded single-employer defined benefit plan maintained by commercial passenger airlines, which meet specified requirements	Internal Revenue Service on or before the due date for filing Form 5500 for the plan year
See Col. (5)	Notice of election to contest certain withdrawal liability findings by plan sponsor through arbitration proceeding or court action without having to pay the withdrawal liability	None prescribed	Electing employer	Sponsor of multiemployer defined benefit plan within 90 days after sponsor notifies electing employer of its withdrawal liability
See Col. (5)	Notice of right to divest investments in employer securities and of the importance of investment diversification	None prescribed	Administrators of 401(k) plans and other participant-directed defined contribution plans and individual account plans that hold publicly traded employer securities (except certain ESOP plans and one-participant retirement plans)	Participants (for employer contributions other than elective deferrals, participants must have completed 3 years of service), alternate payees, or beneficiaries of participants no later than 30 days before the first date on which the participants or beneficiaries become eligible to divest employer securities

¶50

(1) Due Date	(2) Document	(3) Form	(4) Who Files	(5) Furnished To
See Col. (5)	Notice of information relating to the provision of investment advice about securities or other property offered as an investment option	None prescribed	Fiduciary adviser	Participants and beneficiaries of 401(k) plans and other defined contribution plans who direct the investments in their plan accounts, and beneficiaries of IRAs before the initial provision of investment advice, and during the provision of advisory services, at least annually, at a time reasonably contemporaneous to any material change to provided information, or upon request
See Col. (5)	Notice of participants' rights and obligations concerning how contributions and earnings will be invested and information about default investment procedures	None prescribed	Fiduciary of individual account plan that permits participants to exercise control over the investment of the assets in their accounts	Participants or beneficiaries within a reasonable time before each plan year (under Employee Benefits Security Administration final regulations), (1) at least 30 days before the date of plan eligibility, or at least 30 days before the first investment in a qualified default investment alternative, or (2) on or before the date of plan eligibility, provided the participant has the opportunity to make withdrawals authorized under Code Sec. 414(w); at least 30 days before each subsequent plan year; and initial advance or annual notice may be distributed with SPDs or other materials provided to participants and beneficiaries

(1) Due Date	(2) Document	(3) Form	(4) Who Files	(5) Furnished To
See Col. (5)	Notice of employee's rights and obligations under a design-based safe harbor for satisfying the ADP and ACP tests	None prescribed	Sponsor of 401(k) plan that has a contribution safe harbor	Eligible employees within a reasonable time before each plan year (i.e., at least 30 days and no more than 90 days before the beginning of each plan year, or in the case of an employee who becomes eligible after the 90th day before the beginning of the plan year, no more than 90 days before the employee becomes eligible and no later than the date the employee becomes eligible)
See Col. (5)	Notice of employee's rights and obligations under a qualified automatic contribution arrangement (alternative safe harbor for satisfying the ADP and ACP tests) or under an eligible automatic contribution arrangement	None prescribed	Sponsor and administrator of 401(k) plans that have qualified automatic enrollment arrangements, or of 401(k), 403(b), or 457(b) plans, SARSEPs, or SIMPLE plans that have eligible automatic contribution arrangements	Eligible employees within a reasonable time before each plan year (i.e., at least 30 days and no more than 90 days before the beginning of each plan year, or in the case of an employee who becomes eligible after the 90th day before the beginning of the plan year, generally no more than 90 days before the employee becomes eligible and no later than the date the employee becomes eligible)
See Col. (5)	Notice of employee's rights and obligations concerning an automatic contribution arrangement	None prescribed	Small employer maintaining SIMPLE IRA that has automatic contribution arrangement	Eligible employees immediately before eligible employees' annual or initial 60-day election period (i.e., 60-day period immediately preceding the beginning of the calendar year, or 60-day period that includes either the date an employee becomes eligible or the day before that date)

(1) Due Date	(2) Document	(3) Form	(4) Who Files	(5) Furnished To
See Col. (5)	Notice of employee's rights and obligations concerning an automatic contribution arrangement	None prescribed	Administrator of DB/K plan of which the 401(k) portion has an automatic enrollment and contribution arrangement	Eligible employees within a reasonable time before each plan year (applicable to plan years beginning after December 31, 2009)
See Col. (5)	Notice designating a transfer of excess pension assets to a retiree health benefits account as a collectively bargained transfer	None prescribed	Employer maintaining defined benefit plans (other than multiemployer plans)	Each employee organization that is a party to the collective bargaining agreement before the transfer (the rules regarding collectively bargained transfers will not apply to transfers made after 12/31/13)
See Col. (5)	Notice of failure to make installment or other payment required to meet the minimum funding standard	None prescribed	Employer of single-employer defined benefit plan that fails to make the required payment before the 60th day following the due date for the payment	Each participant, beneficiary, or alternate payee following the 60-day grace period after the due date
See Col. (5)	Notice of receipt of domestic relations order (DRO) and procedures for determination of qualified status of order; also notice of determination	None prescribed	Administrators of qualified defined benefit and defined contribution plans in which employees participate (also 403(b) plans)	Participant and each alternate payee promptly of receipt of the order; and within a reasonable period after receipt of the order, the determination of the status of the DRO
See Col. (5)	Summary plan information about contributing employers, participants, funding status of plan, plan assets and liabilities (when there has been plan merger), plan's contribution schedules and benefit formulas, and entitlement to additional plan documents	None prescribed	Administrators of multiemployer plans	Employee organizations and contributing employers within 30 days after due date of Form 5500
See Col. (5)	Actuarial and financial information upon written request	None prescribed	Administrator of multiemployer plans	Participants, beneficiaries, employee representatives, and contributing employers requesting such information not later than 30 days after written request is received

(1) Due Date	(2) Document	(3) Form	(4) Who Files	(5) Furnished To
See Col. (5)	Notice of potential withdrawal liability	None prescribed	Sponsor or administrator of multiemployer plans	Contributing employers requesting such information within 180 days after request is made
See Col. (5)	Special terminal report for abandoned individual account plan	Most recent Form 5500 available as of the date qualified termination administrator winds up affairs of plan and distributes benefits	Qualified termination administrator	Employee Benefits Security Administration within 2 months after end of month that administrator winds up affairs of plan and distributes benefits
See Col. (5)	Final notice for abandoned individual account plan	None prescribed	Qualified termination administrator	Office of Enforcement, Employee Benefits Security Administration no later than 2 months after end of month that administrator winds up affairs of plan and distributes benefits
See Col. (5)	Notice of plan becoming subject to limits on benefits and distributions	None prescribed	Administrator of single-employer defined benefit plan	Participants and beneficiaries (except those in pay status who would not be eligible for lump-sum payments regardless of imposition of funding-based restriction) within 30 days of plan becoming subject to limits on unpredictable contingent event benefits and accelerated benefit distributions

(1) Due Date	(2) Document	(3) Form	(4) Who Files	(5) Furnished To
See Col. (5)	Notice of plan experiencing a severe funding shortfall and becoming subject to limits on shutdown benefits and other unpredictable contingent event benefits, accelerated benefit distributions, and/or benefit accruals	None prescribed	Administrator of single-employer defined benefit plan	Participants and beneficiaries (except those in pay status who would not be eligible for lump-sum payments regardless of imposition of funding-based restriction) within 30 days after the plan becomes subject to a restriction of unpredictable contingent event benefits and accelerated benefits; for plans with limits on benefit accruals, the valuation date for the plan year in which the adjusted funding target attainment percentage for the plan is less than 60% (or if earlier, the date the percentage is deemed to be less than 60% under ERISA Sec. 206(g)(7)); and other times as may be determined by the Treasury Secretary
See Col. (5)	Certification of whether plan is in endangered, or is or will be in critical status for plan year (also, whether plan is making scheduled progress if plan was previously certified as endangered or critical and is in funding improvement or rehabilitation period)	None prescribed	Actuary for multiemployer defined benefit plan in effect July 16, 2006	Internal Revenue Service and plan sponsor no later than 90th day of each plan year (sunsets for plan years beginning after 2014 for new certifications, but continues to apply to plans already in endangered or critical status at end of 2014)
See Col. (5)	Notice of plan's status and explanation of possibility that adjustable benefits may be reduced	None prescribed	Sponsor of multiemployer defined benefit plan in effect July 16, 2006	Participants, beneficiaries, contributing employers, employee representatives, Pension Benefit Guaranty Corporation, and Department of Labor within 30 days after date that plan actuary certifies that plan is or will in endangered or critical status for plan year

(1) Due Date	(2) Document	(3) Form	(4) Who Files	(5) Furnished To
See Col. (5)	Schedule or schedules showing revised benefit and/or contribution structures which, if adopted, might reasonably be expected to allow endangered plan to achieve applicable funding benchmarks	None prescribed	Sponsor of endangered multiemployer defined benefit plan in effect July 16, 2006	Contributing employers and employee representatives within 30 days of adoption of funding improvement plan
See Col. (5)	Schedule or schedules showing revised benefit and/or contribution structures which, if adopted, might reasonably be expected to allow critical plan to emerge from critical status	None prescribed	Sponsor of multiemployer defined benefit plan in critical status and in effect July 16, 2006	Contributing employers and employee representatives within 30 days of adoption of rehabilitation plan
See Col. (5)	Notice of reduction of adjustable benefits	None prescribed	Sponsor of multiemployer defined benefit plan in critical status and in effect July 16, 2006	Participants, beneficiaries, contributing employers, and employee representatives 30 days before reduction of adjustable benefits
See Col. (5)	Notice of application for an extension of the amortization period for unfunded liability	None prescribed	Sponsor of a multiemployer pension plan or authorized representative	Each employee organization representing participants, participant, beneficiary, alternate payee, and Pension Benefit Guaranty Corporation within 14 days prior to the date of submission of the application of extension

(1) Due Date	(2) Document	(3) Form	(4) Who Files	(5) Furnished To
See Col. (5)	Starting April 1, 2012, disclosure of direct and indirect compensation and fees paid to service providers	None prescribed	Covered service providers that enter into contracts or arrangements with plans and reasonably expect $1,000 or more in compensation, direct or indirect, to be received from providing fiduciary or registered investment adviser services, certain recordkeeping or brokerage services, and other services (including accounting, auditing, actuarial, banking, consulting, investment advising, and third-party administration)	Plan fiduciaries of defined contribution and defined benefit plans, except SEPs, SIMPLEs, and IRAs, in general reasonably in advance of the date the contract is entered into, extended, or renewed for initial disclosures, and in general for changes to initial arrangements as soon as practicable, but not later than 60 days from the date the service providers are informed of the changes; upon request by plan fiduciary or plan administrator for reporting and disclosure purposes in general not later than 30 days following receipt of a written request
See Col. (5)	Starting April 1, 2012, failure of covered service provider to disclose required compensation and fee information upon written request	None prescribed	Plan fiduciary	DOL—if the service provider fails to comply with the written request within 90 days of the request—not later than 30 days following the earlier of the service provider's refusal to furnish information or 90 days after the written request is made

(1) Due Date	(2) Document	(3) Form	(4) Who Files	(5) Furnished To
See Col. (5)	Disclosure of investment-related information, administrative plan fees and expenses, and fees and expenses that may be charged against a participant's or beneficiary's individual account (starting with the later of 60 days after the first day of the first plan year beginning on or after November 1, 2011, or 60 days after the effective date of the fiduciary-level disclosure regulations)	None prescribed	Administrator of participant-directed individual account retirement plans, except SEPs or SIMPLE IRAs	Participants or beneficiaries on or before the date they can first direct investments and at least annually thereafter, may be provided as part of the plan's SPD or pension benefit statement if these documents are furnished at the above frequencies; if there are changes to administrative plan information, at least 30 days, but not more than 90 days, before the effective date of the changes
See Col. (5)	Statement of administrative or individual plan fees and expenses that are actually charged against a participant's or beneficiary's individual account during the preceding quarter and a description of the services for which the charges were made (starting with the later of 60 days after the first day of the first plan year beginning on or after November 1, 2011, or 60 days after the effective date of the fiduciary-level disclosure regulations)	None prescribed	Administrator of participant-directed individual account retirement plans, except SEPs or SIMPLE IRAs	Participants or beneficiaries at least quarterly, may be included in quarterly benefit statements

(1) Due Date	(2) Document	(3) Form	(4) Who Files	(5) Furnished To
See Col. (5)	Disclosure of information in a chart or similar format of each designated investment alternative offered under the plan, including performance data, benchmark information, fee and expense information, plus an internet website address for access to specific additional investment information and a glossary of terms (or internet website address that provides access to a glossary of terms) (starting with the later of 60 days after the first day of the first plan year beginning on or after November 1, 2011, or 60 days after the effective date of the fiduciary-level disclosure regulations)	None prescribed	Administrator of participant-directed individual account retirement plans, except SEPs or SIMPLE IRAs	Participants or beneficiaries on or before the date they can first direct investments and at least annually thereafter, may be provided as part of the plan's SPD or pension benefit statement if these documents are furnished at the above frequencies; if there are changes to administrative plan information, at least 30 days, but not more than 90 days, before the effective date of the changes; either on or before the date participants or beneficiaries can first direct investments and at least annually thereafter or upon request, prospectuses, financial reports, and statements of valuation and of assets held by an investment option
See Col. (5)	Notice to interested parties of letter ruling request on whether a plan is a church plan	Model notice	Letter ruling applicant for (i.e., plan sponsor of) nonelecting church plan	Plan participant, beneficiary, alternate payee, employee organizations representing employees who are participants, and, for plans covering more than one employer, contributing employers other than the applicant within 30 days before the letter ruling request is submitted to the IRS (the notice must also be submitted to the IRS with the letter ruling request)

¶ 55
Mortality Table

The adjustment of benefits paid before or after a participant has reached the social security retirement age must generally be made using a mortality table prescribed by the IRS and stipulated interest rates.[1] Code Sec. 417(e)(3) provides rules for the determination of the present value of plan benefits. Code Sec. 417(e)(3)(A) generally provides that for purposes of Code Sec. 417(e)(1) and (e)(2), the present value is not permitted to be less than the present value calculated by using the applicable mortality table and the applicable interest rate as defined in Code Sec. 417(e)(3)(B) and (C) respectively. For plan years beginning on or after January 1, 2008, Code Sec. 417(e)(3)(B) defines the term "applicable mortality table" as the mortality table specified for the plan year under Code Sec. 430(h)(3)(A) (without regard to Code Sec. 430(h)(3)(C) or (D)). In addition, Code Sec. 411(a)(11)(B) provides that the determination of present value for purposes of Code Sec. 411(a)(11)(A) is calculated in accordance with Code Sec. 417(e)(3).

The static mortality tables that apply under Code Sec. 430(h)(3)(A) for valuation dates occurring in years 2011 and 2012 are set forth below.[2] The mortality rates in these tables have been developed from the base rates, projection factors, and weighting factors set forth in IRS Reg. § 1.430(h)(3)-1, using the blending techniques described in the preamble to those regulations.[3]

The static mortality tables that apply under Code Sec. 417(e)(3) for distributions with annuity starting dates occurring during stability periods beginning in years 2011 and 2012 are set forth below in the column labeled "Unisex." The rates in these tables were derived from the tables used for Code Sec. 430(h)(3)(A) following the procedures set forth in IRS Rev. Rul. 2007-67.[4]

Age	MALE 2012 Non-Annuitant Table	MALE 2012 Annuitant Table	MALE 2012 Optional Combined Table for Small Plans	FEMALE 2012 Non-Annuitant Table	FEMALE 2012 Annuitant Table	FEMALE 2012 Optional Combined Table for Small Plans	UNISEX 2012 Table for Distributions Subject to § 417(e)(3)
1	0.000369	0.000369	0.000369	0.000331	0.000331	0.000331	0.000350
2	0.000249	0.000249	0.000249	0.000216	0.000216	0.000216	0.000233
3	0.000207	0.000207	0.000207	0.000161	0.000161	0.000161	0.000184
4	0.000161	0.000161	0.000161	0.000121	0.000121	0.000121	0.000141
5	0.000148	0.000148	0.000148	0.000109	0.000109	0.000109	0.000129
6	0.000141	0.000141	0.000141	0.000102	0.000102	0.000102	0.000122
7	0.000136	0.000136	0.000136	0.000096	0.000096	0.000096	0.000116
8	0.000125	0.000125	0.000125	0.000085	0.000085	0.000085	0.000105
9	0.000121	0.000121	0.000121	0.000081	0.000081	0.000081	0.000101
10	0.000123	0.000123	0.000123	0.000082	0.000082	0.000082	0.000103
11	0.000127	0.000127	0.000127	0.000083	0.000083	0.000083	0.000105
12	0.000132	0.000132	0.000132	0.000086	0.000086	0.000086	0.000109
13	0.000139	0.000139	0.000139	0.000090	0.000090	0.000090	0.000115
14	0.000151	0.000151	0.000151	0.000099	0.000099	0.000099	0.000125
15	0.000160	0.000160	0.000160	0.000110	0.000110	0.000110	0.000135
16	0.000169	0.000169	0.000169	0.000118	0.000118	0.000118	0.000144
17	0.000179	0.000179	0.000179	0.000126	0.000126	0.000126	0.000153
18	0.000188	0.000188	0.000188	0.000128	0.000128	0.000128	0.000158
19	0.000197	0.000197	0.000197	0.000126	0.000126	0.000126	0.000162
20	0.000206	0.000206	0.000206	0.000124	0.000124	0.000124	0.000165
21	0.000219	0.000219	0.000219	0.000121	0.000121	0.000121	0.000170
22	0.000230	0.000230	0.000230	0.000122	0.000122	0.000122	0.000176
23	0.000248	0.000248	0.000248	0.000127	0.000127	0.000127	0.000188
24	0.000264	0.000264	0.000264	0.000134	0.000134	0.000134	0.000199
25	0.000287	0.000287	0.000287	0.000141	0.000141	0.000141	0.000214
26	0.000321	0.000321	0.000321	0.000154	0.000154	0.000154	0.000238
27	0.000334	0.000334	0.000334	0.000161	0.000161	0.000161	0.000248
28	0.000343	0.000343	0.000343	0.000170	0.000170	0.000170	0.000257
29	0.000360	0.000360	0.000360	0.000179	0.000179	0.000179	0.000270
30	0.000388	0.000388	0.000388	0.000201	0.000201	0.000201	0.000295
31	0.000436	0.000436	0.000436	0.000247	0.000247	0.000247	0.000342
32	0.000491	0.000491	0.000491	0.000282	0.000282	0.000282	0.000387

Age	MALE 2012 Non-Annuitant Table	MALE 2012 Annuitant Table	MALE 2012 Optional Combined Table for Small Plans	FEMALE 2012 Non-Annuitant Table	FEMALE 2012 Annuitant Table	FEMALE 2012 Optional Combined Table for Small Plans	UNISEX 2012 Table for Distributions Subject to § 417(e)(3)
33	0.000551	0.000551	0.000551	0.000309	0.000309	0.000309	0.000430
34	0.000613	0.000613	0.000613	0.000332	0.000332	0.000332	0.000473
35	0.000675	0.000675	0.000675	0.000352	0.000352	0.000352	0.000514
36	0.000735	0.000735	0.000735	0.000371	0.000371	0.000371	0.000553
37	0.000790	0.000790	0.000790	0.000389	0.000389	0.000389	0.000590
38	0.000819	0.000819	0.000819	0.000409	0.000409	0.000409	0.000614
39	0.000845	0.000845	0.000845	0.000431	0.000431	0.000431	0.000638
40	0.000869	0.000869	0.000869	0.000469	0.000469	0.000469	0.000669
41	0.000895	0.000922	0.000895	0.000515	0.000515	0.000515	0.000705
42	0.000926	0.001028	0.000927	0.000567	0.000567	0.000567	0.000747
43	0.000964	0.001187	0.000967	0.000623	0.000623	0.000623	0.000795
44	0.001008	0.001399	0.001015	0.000684	0.000684	0.000684	0.000850
45	0.001059	0.001664	0.001073	0.000727	0.000732	0.000727	0.000900
46	0.001104	0.001982	0.001128	0.000770	0.000828	0.000771	0.000950
47	0.001153	0.002353	0.001191	0.000812	0.000972	0.000816	0.001004
48	0.001203	0.002777	0.001260	0.000878	0.001164	0.000888	0.001074
49	0.001256	0.003254	0.001337	0.000949	0.001404	0.000968	0.001153
50	0.001309	0.003786	0.001421	0.001055	0.001692	0.001087	0.001254
51	0.001363	0.003840	0.001486	0.001174	0.001810	0.001211	0.001349
52	0.001419	0.003845	0.001585	0.001344	0.002025	0.001395	0.001490
53	0.001519	0.003898	0.001746	0.001541	0.002302	0.001613	0.001680
54	0.001630	0.003949	0.001929	0.001769	0.002635	0.001872	0.001901
55	0.001805	0.004101	0.002279	0.002034	0.003031	0.002223	0.002251
56	0.002024	0.004337	0.002758	0.002343	0.003501	0.002674	0.002716
57	0.002284	0.004652	0.003179	0.002629	0.003987	0.003091	0.003135
58	0.002586	0.005075	0.003681	0.002874	0.004474	0.003494	0.003588
59	0.002856	0.005509	0.004179	0.003143	0.005029	0.003965	0.004072
60	0.003156	0.006033	0.004777	0.003433	0.005637	0.004525	0.004651
61	0.003579	0.006754	0.005591	0.003743	0.006290	0.005222	0.005407
62	0.003935	0.007440	0.006425	0.004067	0.006991	0.005996	0.006211
63	0.004423	0.008378	0.007548	0.004401	0.007736	0.006909	0.007229
64	0.004803	0.009270	0.008535	0.004742	0.008542	0.007798	0.008167

	MALE	MALE	MALE	FEMALE	FEMALE	FEMALE	UNISEX
Age	2012 Non-Annuitant Table	2012 Annuitant Table	2012 Optional Combined Table for Small Plans	2012 Non-Annuitant Table	2012 Annuitant Table	2012 Optional Combined Table for Small Plans	2012 Table for Distributions Subject to § 417(e)(3)
65	0.005175	0.010266	0.009671	0.005084	0.009422	0.008794	0.009233
66	0.005688	0.011595	0.011194	0.005421	0.010376	0.009939	0.010567
67	0.006039	0.012837	0.012504	0.005750	0.011401	0.011043	0.011774
68	0.006198	0.013923	0.013644	0.006066	0.012520	0.012212	0.012928
69	0.006499	0.015380	0.015126	0.006366	0.013776	0.013500	0.014313
70	0.006597	0.016663	0.016401	0.006649	0.015221	0.014930	0.015666
71	0.007444	0.018437	0.018180	0.007258	0.016572	0.016288	0.017234
72	0.009138	0.020471	0.020235	0.008476	0.018432	0.018162	0.019199
73	0.011679	0.022802	0.022600	0.010303	0.020100	0.019868	0.021234
74	0.015067	0.025438	0.025276	0.012739	0.022277	0.022083	0.023680
75	0.019302	0.028943	0.028818	0.015784	0.024128	0.023986	0.026402
76	0.024384	0.032259	0.032177	0.019438	0.026583	0.026486	0.029332
77	0.030313	0.036581	0.036532	0.023701	0.029844	0.029781	0.033157
78	0.037089	0.041439	0.041416	0.028573	0.032898	0.032869	0.037143
79	0.044712	0.046947	0.046941	0.034054	0.036320	0.036312	0.041627
80	0.053179	0.053179	0.053179	0.040147	0.040147	0.040147	0.046663
81	0.060671	0.060671	0.060671	0.044435	0.044435	0.044435	0.052553
82	0.069094	0.069094	0.069094	0.049260	0.049260	0.049260	0.059177
83	0.077020	0.077020	0.077020	0.054696	0.054696	0.054696	0.065858
84	0.087312	0.087312	0.087312	0.060831	0.060831	0.060831	0.074072
85	0.096919	0.096919	0.096919	0.069078	0.069078	0.069078	0.082999
86	0.107454	0.107454	0.107454	0.078529	0.078529	0.078529	0.092992
87	0.121344	0.121344	0.121344	0.089273	0.089273	0.089273	0.105309
88	0.136910	0.136910	0.136910	0.099435	0.099435	0.099435	0.118173
89	0.151302	0.151302	0.151302	0.112543	0.112543	0.112543	0.131923
90	0.169960	0.169960	0.169960	0.124375	0.124375	0.124375	0.147168
91	0.185121	0.185121	0.185121	0.136580	0.136580	0.136580	0.160851
92	0.204586	0.204586	0.204586	0.148872	0.148872	0.148872	0.176729
93	0.220697	0.220697	0.220697	0.164072	0.164072	0.164072	0.192385
94	0.236783	0.236783	0.236783	0.175976	0.175976	0.175976	0.206380
95	0.257507	0.257507	0.257507	0.187249	0.187249	0.187249	0.222378
96	0.273309	0.273309	0.273309	0.197713	0.197713	0.197713	0.235511

¶55

Age	MALE 2012 Non-Annuitant Table	MALE 2012 Annuitant Table	MALE 2012 Optional Combined Table for Small Plans	FEMALE 2012 Non-Annuitant Table	FEMALE 2012 Annuitant Table	FEMALE 2012 Optional Combined Table for Small Plans	UNISEX 2012 Table for Distributions Subject to § 417(e)(3)
97	0.288660	0.288660	0.288660	0.211187	0.211187	0.211187	0.249924
98	0.309359	0.309359	0.309359	0.219730	0.219730	0.219730	0.264545
99	0.323989	0.323989	0.323989	0.227030	0.227030	0.227030	0.275510
100	0.338068	0.338068	0.338068	0.232996	0.232996	0.232996	0.285532
101	0.358628	0.358628	0.358628	0.244834	0.244834	0.244834	0.301731
102	0.371685	0.371685	0.371685	0.254498	0.254498	0.254498	0.313092
103	0.383040	0.383040	0.383040	0.266044	0.266044	0.266044	0.324542
104	0.392003	0.392003	0.392003	0.279055	0.279055	0.279055	0.335529
105	0.397886	0.397886	0.397886	0.293116	0.293116	0.293116	0.345501
106	0.400000	0.400000	0.400000	0.307811	0.307811	0.307811	0.353906
107	0.400000	0.400000	0.400000	0.322725	0.322725	0.322725	0.361363
108	0.400000	0.400000	0.400000	0.337441	0.337441	0.337441	0.368721
109	0.400000	0.400000	0.400000	0.351544	0.351544	0.351544	0.375772
110	0.400000	0.400000	0.400000	0.364617	0.364617	0.364617	0.382309
111	0.400000	0.400000	0.400000	0.376246	0.376246	0.376246	0.388123
112	0.400000	0.400000	0.400000	0.386015	0.386015	0.386015	0.393008
113	0.400000	0.400000	0.400000	0.393507	0.393507	0.393507	0.396754
114	0.400000	0.400000	0.400000	0.398308	0.398308	0.398308	0.399154
115	0.400000	0.400000	0.400000	0.400000	0.400000	0.400000	0.400000
116	0.400000	0.400000	0.400000	0.400000	0.400000	0.400000	0.400000
117	0.400000	0.400000	0.400000	0.400000	0.400000	0.400000	0.400000
118	0.400000	0.400000	0.400000	0.400000	0.400000	0.400000	0.400000
119	0.400000	0.400000	0.400000	0.400000	0.400000	0.400000	0.400000
120	1.000000	1.000000	1.000000	1.000000	1.000000	1.000000	1.000000

Age	MALE 2011 Non- Annuitant Table	MALE 2011 Annuitant Table	MALE 2011 Optional Combined Table for Small Plans	FEMALE 2011 Non- Annuitant Table	FEMALE 2011 Annuitant Table	FEMALE 2011 Optional Combined Table for Small Plans	UNISEX 2011 Table for Distributions Subject to § 417(e)(3)
1	0.000377	0.000377	0.000377	0.000338	0.000338	0.000338	0.000358
2	0.000254	0.000254	0.000254	0.000220	0.000220	0.000220	0.000237
3	0.000211	0.000211	0.000211	0.000164	0.000164	0.000164	0.000188
4	0.000164	0.000164	0.000164	0.000123	0.000123	0.000123	0.000144
5	0.000151	0.000151	0.000151	0.000111	0.000111	0.000111	0.000131
6	0.000144	0.000144	0.000144	0.000104	0.000104	0.000104	0.000124
7	0.000138	0.000138	0.000138	0.000098	0.000098	0.000098	0.000118
8	0.000128	0.000128	0.000128	0.000087	0.000087	0.000087	0.000108
9	0.000124	0.000124	0.000124	0.000083	0.000083	0.000083	0.000104
10	0.000125	0.000125	0.000125	0.000083	0.000083	0.000083	0.000104
11	0.000130	0.000130	0.000130	0.000085	0.000085	0.000085	0.000108
12	0.000135	0.000135	0.000135	0.000088	0.000088	0.000088	0.000112
13	0.000142	0.000142	0.000142	0.000092	0.000092	0.000092	0.000117
14	0.000154	0.000154	0.000154	0.000101	0.000101	0.000101	0.000128
15	0.000163	0.000163	0.000163	0.000112	0.000112	0.000112	0.000138
16	0.000172	0.000172	0.000172	0.000119	0.000119	0.000119	0.000146
17	0.000183	0.000183	0.000183	0.000128	0.000128	0.000128	0.000156
18	0.000192	0.000192	0.000192	0.000130	0.000130	0.000130	0.000161
19	0.000201	0.000201	0.000201	0.000128	0.000128	0.000128	0.000165
20	0.000210	0.000210	0.000210	0.000126	0.000126	0.000126	0.000168
21	0.000223	0.000223	0.000223	0.000123	0.000123	0.000123	0.000173
22	0.000234	0.000234	0.000234	0.000124	0.000124	0.000124	0.000179
23	0.000252	0.000252	0.000252	0.000130	0.000130	0.000130	0.000191
24	0.000268	0.000268	0.000268	0.000136	0.000136	0.000136	0.000202
25	0.000290	0.000290	0.000290	0.000143	0.000143	0.000143	0.000217
26	0.000323	0.000323	0.000323	0.000156	0.000156	0.000156	0.000240
27	0.000335	0.000335	0.000335	0.000163	0.000163	0.000163	0.000249
28	0.000345	0.000345	0.000345	0.000172	0.000172	0.000172	0.000259
29	0.000362	0.000362	0.000362	0.000181	0.000181	0.000181	0.000272
30	0.000390	0.000390	0.000390	0.000203	0.000203	0.000203	0.000297
31	0.000438	0.000438	0.000438	0.000249	0.000249	0.000249	0.000344
32	0.000493	0.000493	0.000493	0.000284	0.000284	0.000284	0.000389

Age	MALE 2011 Non-Annuitant Table	MALE 2011 Annuitant Table	MALE 2011 Optional Combined Table for Small Plans	FEMALE 2011 Non-Annuitant Table	FEMALE 2011 Annuitant Table	FEMALE 2011 Optional Combined Table for Small Plans	UNISEX 2011 Table for Distributions Subject to § 417(e)(3)
33	0.000554	0.000554	0.000554	0.000311	0.000311	0.000311	0.000433
34	0.000616	0.000616	0.000616	0.000335	0.000335	0.000335	0.000476
35	0.000679	0.000679	0.000679	0.000356	0.000356	0.000356	0.000518
36	0.000738	0.000738	0.000738	0.000376	0.000376	0.000376	0.000557
37	0.000794	0.000794	0.000794	0.000394	0.000394	0.000394	0.000594
38	0.000824	0.000824	0.000824	0.000414	0.000414	0.000414	0.000619
39	0.000851	0.000851	0.000851	0.000437	0.000437	0.000437	0.000644
40	0.000876	0.000876	0.000876	0.000477	0.000477	0.000477	0.000677
41	0.000903	0.000930	0.000903	0.000522	0.000522	0.000522	0.000713
42	0.000936	0.001038	0.000937	0.000575	0.000575	0.000575	0.000756
43	0.000974	0.001201	0.000977	0.000633	0.000633	0.000633	0.000805
44	0.001021	0.001418	0.001028	0.000695	0.000695	0.000695	0.000862
45	0.001073	0.001689	0.001087	0.000739	0.000744	0.000739	0.000913
46	0.001120	0.002014	0.001144	0.000783	0.000842	0.000784	0.000964
47	0.001171	0.002393	0.001210	0.000827	0.000989	0.000831	0.001021
48	0.001223	0.002826	0.001281	0.000894	0.001185	0.000904	0.001093
49	0.001277	0.003314	0.001360	0.000967	0.001430	0.000986	0.001173
50	0.001333	0.003856	0.001447	0.001073	0.001722	0.001106	0.001277
51	0.001389	0.003914	0.001515	0.001193	0.001839	0.001231	0.001373
52	0.001448	0.003923	0.001618	0.001363	0.002054	0.001414	0.001516
53	0.001550	0.003978	0.001781	0.001560	0.002330	0.001633	0.001707
54	0.001663	0.004030	0.001968	0.001787	0.002662	0.001891	0.001930
55	0.001839	0.004181	0.002323	0.002050	0.003056	0.002241	0.002282
56	0.002062	0.004416	0.002809	0.002357	0.003522	0.002690	0.002750
57	0.002323	0.004733	0.003234	0.002642	0.004007	0.003107	0.003171
58	0.002628	0.005158	0.003741	0.002889	0.004496	0.003512	0.003627
59	0.002902	0.005599	0.004247	0.003159	0.005054	0.003985	0.004116
60	0.003207	0.006131	0.004854	0.003451	0.005665	0.004548	0.004701
61	0.003633	0.006857	0.005676	0.003761	0.006322	0.005248	0.005462
62	0.003995	0.007553	0.006522	0.004087	0.007026	0.006026	0.006274
63	0.004486	0.008496	0.007655	0.004423	0.007775	0.006944	0.007300
64	0.004871	0.009401	0.008656	0.004766	0.008584	0.007837	0.008247

Age	MALE 2011 Non-Annuitant Table	MALE 2011 Annuitant Table	MALE 2011 Optional Combined Table for Small Plans	FEMALE 2011 Non-Annuitant Table	FEMALE 2011 Annuitant Table	FEMALE 2011 Optional Combined Table for Small Plans	UNISEX 2011 Table for Distributions Subject to § 417(e)(3)
65	0.005249	0.010411	0.009808	0.005110	0.009470	0.008839	0.009324
66	0.005763	0.011748	0.011342	0.005449	0.010428	0.009989	0.010666
67	0.006118	0.013006	0.012668	0.005779	0.011458	0.011099	0.011884
68	0.006286	0.014121	0.013838	0.006096	0.012583	0.012274	0.013056
69	0.006591	0.015599	0.015341	0.006398	0.013846	0.013568	0.014455
70	0.006698	0.016917	0.016651	0.006683	0.015298	0.015006	0.015829
71	0.007553	0.018718	0.018457	0.007297	0.016672	0.016386	0.017422
72	0.009263	0.020783	0.020543	0.008524	0.018543	0.018271	0.019407
73	0.011828	0.023149	0.022943	0.010365	0.020242	0.020008	0.021476
74	0.015247	0.025826	0.025661	0.012819	0.022434	0.022239	0.023950
75	0.019521	0.029354	0.029226	0.015887	0.024323	0.024180	0.026703
76	0.024650	0.032717	0.032633	0.019568	0.026798	0.026700	0.029667
77	0.030634	0.037063	0.037013	0.023863	0.030054	0.029991	0.033502
78	0.037473	0.041943	0.041920	0.028772	0.033130	0.033100	0.037510
79	0.045167	0.047469	0.047463	0.034294	0.036576	0.036568	0.042016
80	0.053716	0.053716	0.053716	0.040430	0.040430	0.040430	0.047073
81	0.061222	0.061222	0.061222	0.044749	0.044749	0.044749	0.052986
82	0.069651	0.069651	0.069651	0.049608	0.049608	0.049608	0.059630
83	0.077641	0.077641	0.077641	0.055082	0.055082	0.055082	0.066362
84	0.087928	0.087928	0.087928	0.061260	0.061260	0.061260	0.074594
85	0.097602	0.097602	0.097602	0.069495	0.069495	0.069495	0.083549
86	0.108212	0.108212	0.108212	0.078924	0.078924	0.078924	0.093568
87	0.122076	0.122076	0.122076	0.089632	0.089632	0.089632	0.105854
88	0.137598	0.137598	0.137598	0.099834	0.099834	0.099834	0.118716
89	0.152062	0.152062	0.152062	0.112881	0.112881	0.112881	0.132472
90	0.170642	0.170642	0.170642	0.124750	0.124750	0.124750	0.147696
91	0.185864	0.185864	0.185864	0.136991	0.136991	0.136991	0.161428
92	0.205202	0.205202	0.205202	0.149320	0.149320	0.149320	0.177261
93	0.221361	0.221361	0.221361	0.164401	0.164401	0.164401	0.192881
94	0.237495	0.237495	0.237495	0.176329	0.176329	0.176329	0.206912
95	0.258023	0.258023	0.258023	0.187624	0.187624	0.187624	0.222824
96	0.273856	0.273856	0.273856	0.198110	0.198110	0.198110	0.235983

¶55

Age	MALE 2011 Non- Annuitant Table	MALE 2011 Annuitant Table	MALE 2011 Optional Combined Table for Small Plans	FEMALE 2011 Non- Annuitant Table	FEMALE 2011 Annuitant Table	FEMALE 2011 Optional Combined Table for Small Plans	UNISEX 2011 Table for Distributions Subject to § 417(e)(3)
97	0.289239	0.289239	0.289239	0.211398	0.211398	0.211398	0.250319
98	0.309669	0.309669	0.309669	0.219950	0.219950	0.219950	0.264810
99	0.324314	0.324314	0.324314	0.227257	0.227257	0.227257	0.275786
100	0.338406	0.338406	0.338406	0.233229	0.233229	0.233229	0.285818
101	0.358628	0.358628	0.358628	0.244834	0.244834	0.244834	0.301731
102	0.371685	0.371685	0.371685	0.254498	0.254498	0.254498	0.313092
103	0.383040	0.383040	0.383040	0.266044	0.266044	0.266044	0.324542
104	0.392003	0.392003	0.392003	0.279055	0.279055	0.279055	0.335529
105	0.397886	0.397886	0.397886	0.293116	0.293116	0.293116	0.345501
106	0.400000	0.400000	0.400000	0.307811	0.307811	0.307811	0.353906
107	0.400000	0.400000	0.400000	0.322725	0.322725	0.322725	0.361363
108	0.400000	0.400000	0.400000	0.337441	0.337441	0.337441	0.368721
109	0.400000	0.400000	0.400000	0.351544	0.351544	0.351544	0.375772
110	0.400000	0.400000	0.400000	0.364617	0.364617	0.364617	0.382309
111	0.400000	0.400000	0.400000	0.376246	0.376246	0.376246	0.388123
112	0.400000	0.400000	0.400000	0.386015	0.386015	0.386015	0.393008
113	0.400000	0.400000	0.400000	0.393507	0.393507	0.393507	0.396754
114	0.400000	0.400000	0.400000	0.398308	0.398308	0.398308	0.399154
115	0.400000	0.400000	0.400000	0.400000	0.400000	0.400000	0.400000
116	0.400000	0.400000	0.400000	0.400000	0.400000	0.400000	0.400000
117	0.400000	0.400000	0.400000	0.400000	0.400000	0.400000	0.400000
118	0.400000	0.400000	0.400000	0.400000	0.400000	0.400000	0.400000
119	0.400000	0.400000	0.400000	0.400000	0.400000	0.400000	0.400000
120	1.000000	1.000000	1.000000	1.000000	1.000000	1.000000	1.000000

[1] Code Sec. 415(b)(2)(E).

[2] IRS Notice 2008-85, I.R.B. 2008-42, 10-20-2008, CCH Pension Plan Guide ¶ 17,140M.

[3] Preamble to IRS final regulations, CCH PENSION PLAN GUIDE ¶ 24,508Z.

[4] IRS Rev. Rul. 2007-67, I.R.B. 2007-48, 11-26-2007, Appendix, CCH PENSION PLAN GUIDE ¶ 19,948Z-207.

¶ 60

Cost-of-Living Adjustments (COLAs)

The following cost of living adjustment (COLA) charts are for figuring statutory inflationary increases in compensation and benefit amounts for retirement plans and Social Security.

Retirement Plans and IRAs[1]

Subject to COLA	Code Sec.	2012	2011	2010
Maximum benefit for defined benefit plan	415(b)(1)(A)	$200,000	$195,000	$195,000
Maximum contribution for defined contribution plan	415(c)(1)(A)	$50,000	$49,000	$49,000
Exclusion for elective deferrals limit	402(g)(1)	$17,000	$16,500	$16,500
Maximum annual tax sheltered annuity deferral limit		$17,000	$16,500	$16,500
Catch-up contributions (non-SIMPLE)[5] . .	414(v)(2)(B)(i)	$5,500	$5,500	$5,500
Lengthening benefit limit for tax credit ESOPs	409(o)(1)(C)(ii)	$200,000 and $1,015,000	$195,000 and $985,000	$195,000 and $985,000
Highly compensated employee limit[2] . . .	414(q)	$115,000	$110,000	$110,000
Annual compensation limit	401(a)(17) and 404(l)	$250,000	$245,000	$245,000
Grandfather rule for government plans[3] .	401(a)(17)	$375,000	$360,000	$360,000
Deferral limits for deferred compensation plans of state and local governments and tax-exempt organizations	457(b)(2), 457(c)(1), and 457(e)(15)	$17,000	$16,500	$16,500
Minimum compensation for SEPs	408(k)(2)(C)	$550	$550	$550
Compensation limit for SEPs	408(k)(3)(C)	$250,000	$245,000	$245,000
SIMPLE plan deferral limit[4]	408(p)(2)(A) and 408(p)(2)(E)	$11,500	$11,500	$11,500
Catch-up contributions (SIMPLE)[5]	414(v)(2)(B)(ii)	$2,500	$2,500	$2,500
Definition of key employee in top-heavy plan	416(i)(1)(A)(i)	$165,000	$160,000	$160,000
Maximum contribution for IRAs	219(b)	$5,000	$5,000	$5,000
Fringe benefit valuation compensation amount for "control employee" who is officer of employer and earning at least $50,000	61(a)(1)	$100,000	$95,000	$95,000
Fringe benefit valuation compensation amount for "control employee" whose compensation is at least $100,000	61(a)(1)	$205,000	$195,000	$195,000

[1] Sources: IR-2011-103, 10-20-11 (CCH PENSION PLAN GUIDE ¶ 17,037Q); IR-2010-108, 10-28-10 (CCH PENSION PLAN GUIDE ¶ 17,037O); IR-2009-94, 10-15-09 (CCH PENSION PLAN GUIDE ¶ 17,037N). General Agreement on Tariffs and Trade (GATT) requires rounding down when annually adjusting limits for inflation. The figures are rounded down to the next lowest multiple of $5,000 except for the minimum coverage for SEPs, which is rounded down to the next lowest multiple of $50, the elective deferral and catch-up contributions limits, which are rounded down to the next lowest multiple of $500, and the maximum compensation limit, which is rounded down to the next lowest multiple of $10,000.

[2] The Small Business Job Protection Act (P.L. 104-188) simplified and combined with definitions of highly compensated employees for plan years beginning in 1997.

[3] The annual compensation limitation under Code Sec. 401(a)(17) for eligible participants in certain governmental plans that, under the plan in effect on July 1, 1993, allowed cost-of-living adjustments under the plan under Code Sec 401(a)(17) to be taken into account.

[4] SIMPLE plans were added by the Small Business Job Protection Act (P.L. 104-188) effective for plan years beginning in 1997.

[5] Catch-up contributions were added by the Economic Growth and Tax Relief Reconciliation Act of 2001 (P.L. 107-16) effective for contributions in tax years beginning in 2002.

Social Security[6]

Subject to COLA	2012	2011	2010
Tax rate—FICA-Medicare[7]			
Employee	5.65%	5.65%	7.65%
	(4.20% OASDI, 1.45% HI)	(4.20% OASDI, 1.45% HI)	(6.20% OASDI, 1.45% HI)
Self-employed[8]	13.30%	13.30%	15.30%
	(10.40% OASDI, 2.90% HI)	(10.40% OASDI, 2.90% HI)	(12.40% OASDI, 2.90% HI)
Taxable wage base—OASDI maximum earnings taxable	$110,100	$106,800	$106,800
Taxable wage base—HI maximum earnings taxable[9]	unlimited	unlimited	unlimited
Quarter of coverage	$1,130	$1,120	$1,090
Retirement earnings test exempt amounts			
Month worker attains full retirement age[10]	Earnings test eliminated	Earnings test eliminated	Earnings test eliminated
Year worker reaches full retirement age[11]	$38,880 per yr.	$37,680 per yr.	$37,680 per yr.
Under full retirement age	$14,640 per yr.	$14,160 per yr.	$14,160 per yr.
Maximum Social Security benefit (workers retiring at full retirement age)[12]	$2,513 per mo.	$2,346 per mo.	$2,323 per mo.
Supplemental Security Income federal payment standard			
Individual	$698 per mo.	$674 per mo.	$674 per mo.
Couple	$1,048 per mo.	$1,011 per mo.	$1,011 per mo.
Supplemental Security Income resource limits			
Individual	$2,000	$2,000	$2,000
Couple	$3,000	$3,000	$3,000

[6] Sources: Social Security Administration news releases—10/19/11 (CCH PENSION PLAN GUIDE ¶ 24,009Z); 10/15/10 (CCH PENSION PLAN GUIDE ¶ 24,007Y); 10/15/09 (CCH PENSION PLAN GUIDE ¶ 24,006). Based on the decrease in the Consumer Price Index for Urban Wage Earners and Clerical Workers (CPI-W) from the third quarter of 2008 through the third quarter of 2010, Social Security beneficiaries and Supplemental Security Income recipients did not receive a COLA increase for benefit payments received beginning in January 2010 and January 2011. The 3.6% COLA for 2012 reflects an increase in the CPI-W from the third quarter of 2008 through the third quarter of 2011.

[7] Through February 29, 2012 (P.L. 112-78), employers and employees pay separate rates. *Employer* rate: 7.65% (6.20% OASDI, 1.45% HI); *Employee* rate: 5.65% (4.20% OASDI, 1.45% HI). (A 2% recapture tax applies to wages received in excess of $18,350, up to $110,100, through February 29, 2012.) Unless extended for the remainder of 2012, the employee rate will return to 7.65% (6.20% OASDI, 1.45% HI) on March 1, 2012. The 7.65% represents the combined Social Security and Medicare tax rate. The Social Security portion (OASDI) is 6.20% on wages up to the applicable maximum taxable amount. The Medicare portion (HI) is 1.45% on all wages.

[8] Applies only to self-employment income, for tax years beginning in 2012, up to the difference between $18,350 and any wages subject to a reduced tax rate for OASDI of 4.2% during the period January 1, 2012 and February 29, 2012.

[9] The maximum was eliminated be the Omnibus Budget Reconciliation Act of 1993 (P.L. 103-66).

[10] There is no limit on earnings beginning the month an individual attains full retirement age (66 years for those born in 1943-1954).

[11] Applies only to earnings for months prior to attaining full retirement age.

[12] The age at which a retiree is entitled to his or her full benefit amount—i.e., the age at which benefits are no longer reduced on account of early retirement—is gradually increasing to age 67.

Average Monthly Social Security Benefits

(Payable in January 2012)

	Before 3.6% COLA	*After 3.6% COLA*
All retired workers	$1,186	$1,229
Aged couple, both receiving benefits	$1,925	$1,994
Widowed mother and two children	$2,455	$2,543
Aged widow(er) alone	$1,143	$1,184
Disabled worker, spouse, and one or more children	$1,826	$1,892
All disabled workers	$1,072	$1,111

¶ 65
PBGC Maximum Monthly Benefit

The Pension Benefit Guaranty Corporation guarantees benefits for participants retiring at age 65 in underfunded single-employer defined benefit pension plans that are terminating. The maximum monthly guaranteed amounts for plans terminating each year for the past 25 years are set forth below.

Year of Plan Termination	Maximum Monthly Guarantee	Maximum Annual Guarantee
2012	$4,653.41	$55,840.92
2011	$4,500.00	$54,000.00
2010	$4,500.00	$54,000.00
2009	$4,500.00	$54,000.00
2008	$4,312.50	$51,750.00
2007	$4,125.00	$49,500.00
2006	$3,971.59	$47,659.08
2005	$3,801.14	$45,613.68
2004	$3,698.86	$44,386.32
2003	$3,664.77	$43,977.24
2002	$3,579.55	$42,954.60
2001	$3,392.05	$40,704.60
2000	$3,221.59	$38,659.08
1999	$3,051.14	$36,613.68
1998	$2,880.68	$34,568.16
1997	$2,761.36	$33,136.32
1996	$2,642.05	$31,704.60
1995	$2,573.86	$30,886.32
1994	$2,556.82	$30,681.84
1993	$2,437.50	$29,250.00
1992	$2,352.27	$28,227.24
1991	$2,250.00	$27,000.00
1990	$2,164.77	$25,977.24
1989	$2,028.41	$24,340.92
1988	$1,909.09	$22,309.08
1987	$1,857.95	$22,295.40

¶ 70
For More Information

See the CCH PENSION PLAN GUIDE beginning at ¶ 36 for other tables of information pertinent to the administration of retirement plans, including tax rate tables, withholding tax tables, and interest rate tables.

Types of Pension and Savings Plans

¶ 101

Overview of Types of Pension and Savings Plans

Employers may provide retirement income for their employees through a wide variety of mechanisms depending on the financial circumstances of the employer and the retirement needs of their employees. This chapter introduces the various retirement plan options available to employers and employees.

Qualified plans

Certain retirement arrangements, such as pension plans, profit-sharing plans, and stock bonus plans, "qualify" for favorable tax treatment. If strict requirements are satisfied, an employer may deduct contributions to a plan and an employee's tax liability is deferred until plan distributions are received.

Nonqualified plans

Nonqualified plans are used by employers to provide supplemental deferred compensation to executives and key employees. An employer maintaining a non-qualified plan does not receive a deduction until benefits are actually paid to the employee. However, nonqualified plans are not subject to many of the requirements applicable to qualified plans.

Small business plans

Certain types of plans, such as Simplified Employee Pensions (SEPs) or Savings Incentive Match Plans for Employees (SIMPLEs) are targeted to small businesses. (Small businesses can sponsor regular defined benefit and defined contribution plans as well.) Small employers with no more than 100 employees are eligible to receive a tax credit for some of the costs of establishing new retirement plans, effective for costs paid or incurred in tax years after 2001. The credit equals 50% of the start up costs incurred to create or maintain a new employee retirement plan. The credit is limited to $500 in any tax year and may be claimed for qualified costs incurred in each of the three years beginning with the tax year in which the plan becomes effective. An eligible employer plan includes a new qualified defined benefit plan, defined contribution plan, SIMPLE plan, or SEP.[1]

Other types of plans

In addition to the general types of plans discussed above, employers may wish to consider 401(k) plans, cafeteria plans, and tax-sheltered annuities. Individual retirement arrangements, simplified employee pensions, and Keogh plans are popular among small employers.

---

[1] Code Sec. 45E.

¶ 103
PENSION PLANS: Defined Benefit and Defined Contribution Plans

Pension plans can be broadly classified as defined benefit plans and defined contribution plans. "Hybrid plans" have features of both defined benefit and defined contribution plans.

Defined contribution plans

A defined contribution plan provides for an individual account for each participant and for benefits based solely on (1) the amount contributed to the participant's account and (2) any income, expenses, gains and losses, and forfeitures of accounts of other participants which may be allocated to the participant's account.[1]

A defined contribution plan does not guarantee an employee a fixed level of benefits when the employee retires. Instead, the employer contributes a fixed amount to the individual accounts of the participants and the accounts rise or fall based on the trust fund's investment performance, along with, in some plans, the amounts generated from forfeitures from the accounts of terminated participants who have not vested.[2] Thus, under a defined contribution plan, an employee will not know in advance what the amount of assets in his or her account will be at retirement.

Common defined contribution arrangements are profit-sharing plans (¶ 117) (including 401(k) plans (¶ 177)), money purchase pension plans (¶ 109), and stock bonus plans (¶ 140) (including employee stock ownership plans (ESOPs) (¶ 143)).

Defined benefit plans

A defined benefit plan is any retirement plan which is not a defined contribution plan.[3] Specifically, a defined benefit plan measures an employee's benefits under a definite formula, such as 1% of compensation for each year of service, or 30% of average annual compensation or $200 a month.

Defined benefit plans allow an employee to anticipate a fixed or determinable pension upon retirement. Employer contributions necessary to provide such benefits are then determined on an actuarial basis.

Hybrid plans

A "hybrid plan" is a plan that has the features of both a defined contribution and a defined benefit plan. Types of hybrid plans include floor offset plans, cash balance plans, and target benefit plans.[4]

Floor offset plans. Essentially, a floor offset plan is a defined contribution plan with a defined benefit floor. Benefits provided under the defined benefit plan are reduced, or offset, by the value of the individual's account in the defined contribution plan. The appeal of the floor offset arrangement, however, is that it shields employees from investment losses incurred by the defined contribution plan while allowing them to take advantage of investment gains that may produce a greater benefit than that provided under the defined benefit plan.

Under the floor offset plan, an employee who leaves employment before retirement age would receive the amount in the individual account. An employee who stays on until retirement, however, would receive the greater of the defined contribution accumulation or the promised defined benefit pension.

Cash balance plans. A cash balance plan is considered to be a defined benefit hybrid, under which a separate account is maintained for each participant. The employer credits a certain percentage of compensation to each account and credits each account with interest earned. The amounts to be contributed are actuarially determined to insure sufficient funds to provide for the benefits promised. If, at retirement, the balance in a participant's individual account is less than the amount promised by the employer, the participant will receive the promised amount. Participants may elect to receive their benefits in a lump sum or as an annuity.

Because benefits are not based solely on actual contributions and forfeitures allocated to an employee's account and the actual investment experience and expenses of the plan allocated to the account, the arrangement is treated as a defined benefit plan, rather than as a defined contribution plan. Accordingly, the plan is required to provide definitely determinable benefits, use a fixed interest rate, and adhere to the minimum funding standards (see ¶ 1400—¶ 1494).

CCH Pointer: Amounts accrued in a cash balance plan are not frozen in value when an employee changes jobs. Employees may roll over amounts in the plan of their former employer into the plan of their new employer, or into an IRA, because a hypothetical account balance is required to be maintained by the former employer.

CCH Pointer: Employers bear the risk of investment losses under a cash balance plan, unlike a defined contribution plan where employees assume investment risks. (See ¶ 2375 for a discussion of participant-directed accounts and investment risk.) The cash balance plan, however, helps employers reduce future benefit accruals, and employer contributions to the plan may be deducted.[5]

CCH Pointer: The Pension Protection Act of 2006 (P.L. 109-280) provided greater legal certainty to cash balance/hybrid plan arrangements, which have been the subject of much recent litigation. The Act provided rules for testing hybrid plans for age discrimination under the Code, ERISA, and the Age Discrimination in Employment Act. In the case of a conversion from a defined benefit to a cash balance plan, the "wearaway" of benefits that a participant has earned at the time of conversion is prohibited. Hybrid plans may treat the hypothetical account balance as the lump-sum value.

¶103

☐ See ¶ 867 for a discussion on conversions from defined benefit plans to cash balance plans.

Target benefit plan. Under a target benefit plan, an employer contributes an amount necessary to pay a *target* benefit for employees at retirement age. Each employee's *actual* benefit is based on the amount in his or her individual account.[6]

Employer contributions are determined actuarially, as though the plan was a defined benefit plan. Assumptions underlying the initial contribution formula, however, are not required to be adjusted for investment experience or other developments, and the employer does not guarantee the targeted amount. Its only obligation is to pay whatever benefit can be provided by the amount in the participant's account.

☐ Target benefit plans are subject to the minimum funding standards (see ¶ 1402).

Combined defined benefit/401(k) (DB/K) plan. Pursuant to the Pension Protection Act of 2006 (P.L. 109-280), employers with 500 or fewer employees are authorized, effective for plan years beginning *after 2009*, to establish a combined plan, consisting of a defined benefit (DB) plan and an automatic enrollment 401(k) plan. The arrangement would provide employees the guaranteed employer-provided retirement benefit offered by a DB plan supplemented by tax deferred elective employee contributions under a 401(k) plan.

The DB/K plan will only be required to file a single Form 5500 annual report. However, the assets of the plan must be held in a single trust and must be clearly identified and allocated to the DB plan and the 401(k) plan, to the extent necessary for the separate application of the rules of the Internal Revenue Code and ERISA.[7]

The plan must meet specified benefit, contribution, vesting, and nondiscrimination requirements. A plan that satisfies the applicable requirements will be deemed not to be top-heavy and to satisfy the ADP/ ACP tests.

CCH Pointer: Generally, the provisions of the IRC and ERISA will apply to a DB plan and 401(k) plan that are part of the DB/K plan as if each were not part of the DB/K plan.[8] Thus, the Code Sec. 415 limitations will apply separately to contributions under the 401(k) and the DB plan. Similarly, the spousal protection rules will apply to the DB plan, but not to the 401(k) plan.

---

[1] ERISA Sec. 3(34).

[2] Code Sec. 414(i); ERISA Sec. 3(34).

[3] ERISA Sec. 3(35).

[4] ERISA Sec. 3(35).

[5] IRS Notice 96-8, 1996-1 CB 359, 2-5-96, CCH PENSION PLAN GUIDE ¶ 17,109X.

[6] House Report No. 93-1280, 93rd Cong., 2d Sess., p. 344.

[7] Code Sec. 414(x)(2)(A), as added by P.L. 109-280 (Pension Protection Act of 2006), Act Sec. 903(a); ERISA Sec. 210(e)(2)(A), as added by P.L. 109-280 (Pension Protection Act of 2006), Act Sec. 903(b).

[8] Code Sec. 414(x)(1), as added by P.L. 109-280 (Pension Protection Act of 2006), Act Sec. 903(a); ERISA Sec. 210(e)(1), as added by P.L. 109-280 (Pension Protection Act of 2006), Act Sec. 903(b).

¶ 106

PENSION PLANS: Requirements for Pension Plans

A pension plan is established and maintained by an employer primarily to provide systematically for the payment of definitely determinable benefits to its employees over a period of years, usually for life, after retirement. In addition, benefits and contributions under a pension plan are not based on profits.

Definitely determinable benefits

The requirement that benefits be "definitely determinable" does not mean that the amount of the pension which will be received must be predicted with certainty.

Under a defined benefit plan, an employee's benefits are measured under a definite formula. The formula may calculate benefits as a particular percentage of the employee's average compensation over the entire period of service or over a particular number of years. It may provide for a flat monthly payment, or it may provide a definite amount for each year of service, expressed either as a percentage of the employee's compensation for each year of service or as a flat dollar amount for each year of service. Variations are practically endless, but, in any event, there is a *known formula* by which benefits may be determined, given such factors as level of compensation and length of service.

Employer contributions are determined actuarially. That is, an actuary using certain assumptions concerning mortality, interest, turnover, etc., determines how much the employer must contribute in order to ensure sufficient funds to provide for the benefits promised by the plan. [1]

Forfeitures may not increase benefit level. Benefits under a pension plan generally are not definitely determinable if funds arising from forfeitures upon termination of service, or other reason, may be used to provide increased benefits for the remaining participants instead of being used to reduce the amount of contributions by the employer.[2]

Withdrawal of benefits prior to retirement

Because the purpose of a pension plan is primarily to provide for retirement benefits, a plan may not permit participants, prior to the severance of employment or termination of the plan, to withdraw all or part of the funds accumulated on their behalf consisting of employer contributions or the earnings thereon.[3] Under certain circumstances, however, the employee may withdraw his or her own contributions to the plan prior to retirement or separation from service.[4]

Loans. A plan may make loans to participants if the loans are made in a uniform and nondiscriminatory manner. Loans may constitute "distributions," however, if there is a tacit understanding that repayment is not intended or if, for some other reason, the transaction does not create a debtor-creditor relationship.[5] A loan from a qualified plan to an employee is to be treated as a distribution to the extent that it exceeds prescribed limits (see ¶ 2000).[6]

Payment of incidental nonretirement benefits

The primary purpose of a pension plan must be to provide retirement benefits.[7] Generally, a pension plan may not provide nonretirement benefits such as layoff benefits or benefits for sickness, accident, hospitalization, or medical expenses. However, certain nonretirement benefits, such as death benefits, may be provided in a pension plan as long as they are "incidental" to the primary purpose of providing retirement benefits.[8]

Disability benefits. A pension plan may provide for the payment of a pension due to disability. Such a benefit is treated as a "retirement" benefit since the disability contemplated is a permanent disability.[9]

Retirement benefits usually for life

A pension plan pays retirement benefits over a period of years, usually for life.[10] The fact that retirement benefits usually are paid for life, however, does not mean that benefits paid for a fixed number of years will disqualify a pension plan. A pension plan may properly provide for systematic payments after retirement over a period certain.[11] A plan which pays benefits only as a lump sum, however, will not qualify as a pension plan, according to the IRS, since such a plan is not established primarily to provide payments over a period of years, usually for life, after the retirement of employees.[12]

Contributions and benefits not determined by profits

An employer may neither limit contributions to a pension plan to years in which it makes a profit, nor may an employer modify its contributions in response to the level of profits.[13] Contributions to a defined benefit plan are based on what is actuarially necessary to provide the benefits promised by the plan. Similarly, contributions to most defined contribution plans are fixed without reference to profits. If contributions are based on profits, the plan is a profit-sharing plan (see ¶ 120).

---

[1] IRS Reg. § 1.401-1(b)(1)(i).

[2] IRS Reg. §§ 1.401-1(a)(3); 1.401-1(b)(1); 1.401-7(a); and 1.401-7(b).

[3] Rev. Rul. 56-693, 1956-2 CB 282, CCH Pension Plan Guide ¶ 18,102; Rev. Rul. 74-254, 1974-1 CB 91, CCH Pension Plan Guide ¶ 19,327; Rev. Rul. 74-417, 1974-2 CB 131, CCH Pension Plan Guide ¶ 19,351; Rev. Rul. 73-533, 1973-2 CB 129, CCH Pension Plan Guide ¶ 19,284.

[4] Rev. Rul. 69-277, 1969-1 CB 116, CCH Pension Plan Guide ¶ 18,732.

[5] See, e.g., Rev. Rul. 67-288, 1967-2 CB 157, CCH Pension Plan Guide ¶ 18,580; Rev. Rul. 71-437, 1971-2 CB 185, CCH Pension Plan Guide ¶ 19,091;

Rev. Rul. 81-126, 1981-1 CB 206, CCH Pension Plan Guide ¶ 19,580; IRS Letter Ruling 8008059, 11-28-79, CCH Pension Plan Guide ¶ 17,371K.

[6] Code Sec. 72(p).

[7] IRS Reg. § 1.401-1(b)(1).

[8] *Ibid.*

[9] IRS Reg. § 1.401-1(b)(1)(i).

[10] IRS Reg. § 1.401-1(b)(1).

[11] Rev. Rul. 57-312, 1957-2 CB 255, CCH Pension Plan Guide ¶ 18,122.

[12] Rev. Rul. 62-195, 1962-2 CB 125, CCH Pension Plan Guide ¶ 18,430.

[13] IRS Reg. § 1.401-1(b)(1)(i).

¶106

¶ 109

PENSION PLANS: Money Purchase Plans

A money purchase pension plan is an arrangement, other than a profit-sharing or stock bonus plan, under which an individual account is maintained for each participant to which the employer makes fixed or determinable contributions. Contributions to a money purchase plan are not related to profits. Typically, they are a fixed percentage of an employee's compensation. Given a fixed rate of contributions, an actuary can determine the amount of eventual benefits as accurately as he or she can calculate the contributions necessary to provide a fixed benefit. Accordingly, the IRS regards a money purchase plan as providing "definitely determinable benefits," and, thus, classifies it as a pension plan.[1]

Structuring a money purchase plan

A typical money purchase plan formula requires an employer to make an annual contribution of 10% of the base pay of each shareholder or other employee eligible to participate in the plan. If the plan is contributory, usually the employer and employee contribute at the same rate. For example, the corporation contributes 5% of the base pay of each plan participant, and each participant contributes the same amount. The employee's contribution and the employer's contributions (on the employee's behalf) will be allocated to the employee's account. These sums may increase through accretion of interest or investment earnings. The employee's benefits at retirement will be equal to the balance in the account at that time.

Because of its similarities to a profit-sharing plan, a money purchase plan is subject to some of the same rules that apply to profit-sharing and stock bonus plans. For example, a money purchase plan is required to have a definite formula for allocating contributions and is required to provide for an annual valuation of plan assets. A money purchase plan also is subject to rules that apply to defined benefit pension plans such as the minimum funding requirements (see ¶ 1402).

---

[1] IRS Reg. § 1.401-1(b)(1)(i).

¶ 115

PENSION PLANS: Trusteed and Annuity Plans Distinguished

The Internal Revenue Code draws a distinction between "trusteed plans" and "annuity plans." A plan is "trusteed" if it is funded through a trust. A plan that is funded through the purchase of annuity contracts, without intervention of a trust, is an annuity plan.[1]

Domestic trust necessary

In order for a trust forming part of a pension, profit-sharing, or stock bonus plan to qualify for tax exemption, it must be a domestic trust (one "created or organized in the United States") and maintained at all times as a domestic trust.[2] It is possible, however, for a plan to utilize a foreign trust and still realize most of the tax benefits incident to qualified status.

Custodial accounts

Qualified plans may be funded through custodial accounts.[3] This is done by treating a custodial account as a trust. The use of a custodial account or annuity contract as part of a plan does not preclude the use of a trust as part of the same plan. A plan under which a custodial account or an annuity contract is used may be considered in connection with other plans of the employer in determining whether the qualification requirements of the Code are met.

Insured plans

If plan funds are held and invested by a trust and no insurance company is involved, the plan is referred to as "trusteed" (sometimes also called "self- insured"). If the funds ultimately are held by an insurance company, even though they may have passed through a trust on the way, the plan is "insured."

> **CCH Pointer:** Insured plans and custodial accounts are good at shielding the employer from fiduciary liability for fund losses, but trust accounts give the trustee optimum control over the direction of the plan's investment policy.

Annuity plans

An annuity plan is generally an annuity contract provided by an insurance company. Annuity plans usually are funded by individual contracts, issued in the name of the plan participant. Contributions are made directly by the employer to the insurance company in the form of premiums. The insurance company has responsibility for making distributions under the plan.

An important restriction applicable to individual or group annuity contracts is that, if the contract is not held by a trust, it may not be transferred by the employee.[4] Thus, if the contract is not held by a trust, it may not be sold, assigned, discounted, or pledged as collateral for a loan or as security for the performance of an obligation. An annuity contract, however, is not considered transferable if the contract allows an employee to designate a beneficiary to receive the proceeds of the annuity contract in the event of death or to elect a joint and survivor annuity.

---

[1] IRS Reg. § 1.404(a)-3(a).

[2] Code Sec. 401(a); IRS Reg. § 1.401-1(a)(3)(i).

[3] Code Sec. 401(f); IRS Reg. § 1.401(f)-1.

[4] IRS Reg. § 1.401-9.

¶ 117

PROFIT-SHARING PLANS: Profit-Sharing Plans In General

A profit-sharing plan is established and maintained by an employer to provide for the participation in its profits by its employees or their beneficiaries. The plan must provide a definite predetermined formula for allocating the contributions made to the plan among the participants and for distributing the funds accumulated under the plan after a fixed number of years, the attainment of a stated age, or upon the prior occurrence of some event such as layoff, illness, disability, retirement, death, or severance of employment. In addition, a profit- sharing plan must provide for "recurring and substantial contributions." [1]

A profit-sharing plan is *primarily* a plan of deferred compensation. Amounts allocated to the account of a participant may be used to provide *incidental* life or accident or health insurance for the participant or his or her family, however.

---

[1] IRS Reg. § 1.401-1(b)(1)(ii) and 1.401-1(b)(2).

¶ 120

PROFIT-SHARING PLANS: The Role of Profits

An employer's contributions to a profit-sharing plan need *not* be made out of current or accumulated profits.[1] This fact has increased the difficulty of distinguishing a profit-sharing plan from a money purchase plan (see ¶ 109). Thus, a plan that is intended to be a money purchase plan or a profit-sharing plan cannot be qualified unless that intention is expressed at such time and in such manner as is prescribed by the IRS.

What is a profit?

A profit-sharing plan should include a definition of a profit. The IRS is not generally concerned with how profits are defined, however. Because contributions need not be made out of profits, a plan may define profit to permit contributions in years during which, under any sound accounting definition, the employer sustained a loss or did not accumulate profits.

Provision of deferred compensation

Plans which provide for current distribution of profits ("cash" or "immediate" profit-sharing plans) are not true profit-sharing plans. In order for an arrangement to be a profit-sharing plan, it must primarily be a plan of *deferred compensation.* An exception to this rule has been made for 401(k) plans (see below).

Generally, a profit-sharing plan may not permit distributions of employer contributions to plan participants until the contributions have been held by the profit-sharing trust for at least two years, unless the distribution is made after a fixed number of years, upon the attainment of a stated age, or upon the prior occurrence of some event, such as layoff, illness, disability, retirement, death, or severance of employment.[2]

Exception for 401(k) plans. The rule disqualifying plans that permit current distribution of profits does not apply to qualified cash or deferred arrangements (401(k) plans). A profit-sharing plan or a stock bonus plan is not disqualified merely because the plan permits an employee to elect to have the employer make contributions to the trust or to the employee directly in cash.

---

[1] Code Sec. 401(a)(27).

[2] IRS Reg. § 1.401-1(b)(1)(ii); Rev. Rul. 71-295, 1971-2 CB 184, CCH PENSION PLAN GUIDE ¶ 19,061.

¶ 123

PROFIT-SHARING PLANS: Definite Allocation Formula

All funds in a profit-sharing plan must be allocated to participants in accordance with a *definite predetermined formula* that is not subject to the discretion of the employer.[1] That is, an employer may not simply make contributions to a general fund and later determine how the fund will be divided among the employees. A formula is considered definite if, for example, it provides for an allocation in proportion to the basic compensation of each participant.[2] A profit-sharing plan may not, at infrequent or irregular intervals, allocate trust earnings to participants or value trust investments, and it may not use different valuation methods for different participants.[3]

Withdrawal of employee contributions is limited

Employee contributions may not be withdrawn from a profit-sharing plan if that would result in the "manipulation" of the formula allocating employer contributions. Thus, the IRS rejected a provision in a profit-sharing plan that permitted participants to withdraw at any time, and without forfeiture of employer contributions and earnings, their required and optional contributions to which the employer contributions were geared.[4]

---

[1] IRS Reg. § 1.401-1(b)(1)(ii).

[2] IRS Publication 778 (discontinued), Sec. 2(t).

[3] Rev. Rul. 80-155, 1980-1 CB 84, CCH PENSION PLAN GUIDE ¶ 19,530.

[4] Rev. Rul. 74-55, 1974-1 CB 89, CCH PENSION PLAN GUIDE ¶ 19,299, modifying Rev. Rul. 72-275, 1972-1 CB 109, CCH PENSION PLAN GUIDE ¶ 19,154.

¶ 126

PROFIT-SHARING PLANS: Substantial and Recurring Contributions

An employer is not required to contribute to a profit-sharing plan every year or to contribute the same amount every year. An employer does not establish a profit-sharing plan, however, by merely making a single or occasional contribution out of profits for employees. According to the IRS, a profit-sharing plan requires "recurring and substantial" contributions.[1]

---

[1] IRS Reg. § 1.401-1(b)(2). But see *Lincoln Electric Co. Employees' Profit-Sharing Trust v. Commissioner*, CA-6 (1951), rev'g and rem'g TC, 51-2 USTC ¶ 9731, 190 F2d 326, and *Sherwood Swan and Co., Ltd., Employees' Benefit Fund v. Commissioner*, CA-9 (1965), 65-2 USTC 9742, 352 F2d 306, aff'g TC (1964), 42 TC 299, CCH Dec. 26,773. The IRS has announced that it will not follow the *Swan* decision. Rev. Rul. 66-251, 1966-2 CB 121, CCH PENSION PLAN GUIDE ¶ 18,525.

¶ 130

PROFIT-SHARING PLANS: Provision of Insurance

Profit-sharing plans may furnish life insurance protection to their participants.

Distribution from the trust

In the event that a profit-sharing trust purchases life insurance protection payable on the death of employee participants, a distribution occurs if the proceeds are payable to a beneficiary (other than the trust). If the proceeds are payable to the trust, a distribution occurs if the plan requires the trustee to pay over *all* such proceeds to a beneficiary of the employee.[1] If the trustee has the right to retain any part of the proceeds, however, there is no distribution and the purchase is treated as an investment of the trust.

Purchase of insurance will not disqualify plan

Because a profit-sharing trust may make distributions after a "fixed number of years" (at least two years), the purchase of life insurance with funds that have been accumulated for at least two years does not disqualify the trust.[2] In addition, current funds (those not held for at least two years) may be used to provide life insurance that is *incidental* to the main purpose of the plan, which is the deferral of compensation.

The purchase of life insurance contracts is considered incidental if:

1. the premiums for life insurance in the case of each participant are *less than one-half* of the contributions and forfeitures allocated to the participant at any particular time, and

2. the plan requires the trustee either to (a) convert the entire value of the contract at or before retirement into cash or an annuity so that no portion of such value may be used to continue life insurance protection after retirement, or (b) distribute the contract to the participant.[3]

Health and accident insurance

A profit-sharing plan may also provide health and accident insurance.[4] If accident and health insurance may be purchased only with funds that have been accumulated for the period required by the plan for deferral of distributions (at least two years), there is no limit on the amount of insurance that may be purchased.[5] If the plan permits the use of funds that have not been accumulated to purchase insurance, however, the amount of the premiums must be no more than incidental. The purchase of health or accident insurance will be considered incidental if the amount expended for premiums does not exceed 25% of the funds allocated to an employee's account that have not been accumulated for the period prescribed by the plan for deferral of distributions.

---

[1] IRS Reg. § 1.401-1(b)(1)(ii).

[2] Rev. Rul. 60-83, 1960-1 CB 157, CCH Pension Plan Guide ¶ 18,211.

[3] Rev. Rul. 54-51, 1954-1 CB 147, CCH Pension Plan Guide ¶ 18,016 as modified by Rev. Rul. 57-213, 1957-1 CB 157, CCH Pension Plan Guide ¶ 18,119 and Rev. Rul. 60-84, 1960-1 CB 159, CCH Pension Plan Guide ¶ 18,212; Rev. Rul. 61-164, 1961-2 CB 58, CCH Pension Plan Guide ¶ 18,413;

Rev. Rul. 66-143, 1966-1 CB 79, CCH Pension Plan Guide ¶ 18,509; Rev. Rul. 68-31, 1968-1 CB 151, CCH Pension Plan Guide ¶ 18,606; Rev. Rul. 73-501, 1973-2 CB 127, CCH Pension Plan Guide ¶ 19,276; Rev. Rul. 74-307, 1974-2 CB 126, CCH Pension Plan Guide ¶ 19,334.

[4] IRS Reg. § 1.401-1(b)(1)(ii).

[5] Rev. Rul. 61-164, 1961-2 CB 58, CCH Pension Plan Guide ¶ 18,413.

¶130

¶ 133

PROFIT-SHARING PLANS: Comparison of Profit-Sharing Plans and Pension Plans

The chart below summarizes some of the major distinctions between pension and profit-sharing plans.

Subject	Pension Plans	Profit-Sharing Plans
PRIMARY PURPOSE	Provide definitely determinable retirement benefits.	Provide for the deferred sharing of employer profits with employees.
LIFE INSURANCE BENEFITS	May provide only incidental life insurance benefits to employees.	May provide unlimited life insurance coverage if purchased out of accumulated contributions. If purchased out of current contributions, life insurance protection must only be incidental.
HEALTH AND ACCIDENT BENEFITS	May provide post-retirement health and accident benefits if such benefits are incidental.	May provide unlimited health and accident benefits if purchased out of accumulated contributions. If purchased out of current contributions, health and accidental benefits must only be incidental.
DISABILITY BENEFITS	May provide disability benefits.	May provide disability benefits.
LAYOFF BENEFITS	May not provide layoff benefits.	May provide layoff benefits.
WITHDRAWAL OF FUNDS	Employer contributions may not be withdrawn by employee. Employee contributions may be withdrawn under certain circumstances.	Both employer and employee contributions may be withdrawn. Employer contributions may be withdrawn only after a fixed number of years, attainment of stated age, or upon the occurrence of certain events.
CONTRIBUTIONS AND PROFITS	Employer contributions must not be dependent upon profits.	Employer contributions need not be dependent upon profits.
ALLOCATION OF CONTRIBUTIONS	No requirement for a definite predetermined formula for allocating employer contributions among participants.	A definite predetermined allocation formula is required.
FUNDING	Minimum funding requirements apply.	Minimum funding requirements do not apply.

Subject	Pension Plans	Profit-Sharing Plans
VESTING	Minimum vesting requirements apply.	Minimum vesting requirements apply.
FORFEITURES	Forfeitures may not be used to provide increased benefits for the remaining participants.	Forfeitures may be used to provide increased benefits for the remaining participants.

¶ 140

STOCK OWNERSHIP PLANS: Stock Bonus Plans

A stock bonus plan is established and maintained by an employer to provide benefits similar to those of a profit-sharing plan, except that the contributions by the employer are not necessarily dependent upon profits and the benefits are distributable in stock of the employer company.[1] Under certain circumstances, however, a stock bonus plan may pay benefits in cash in lieu of employer stock.

A stock bonus plan is always a defined contribution plan. As with profit-sharing plans, stock bonus plans must have a definite predetermined formula for allocating contributions among participants.

---

[1]　Code　Sec.　401(a)(23);　IRS　Reg. § 1.401-1(b)(1)(iii).

¶ 143

STOCK OWNERSHIP PLANS: Employee Stock Ownership Plans (ESOPs)

An employee stock ownership plan (ESOP) is a tax-qualified defined contribution plan that is designed to be invested primarily or exclusively in the stock of the employer maintaining the plan. [1]

ESOPs are used as financing vehicles for the employer corporation. Typically, the plan borrows money (usually from a commercial lender) to purchase the employer's stock. This loan is secured by the stock and is typically guaranteed by the employer corporation. The borrowed money is then paid to the employer for its stock. The plan repays its loan to the lender with cash contributions made each year to the plan by the employer.

Under an ESOP, contributions ordinarily are not based on profits, but rather are fixed. This insures that the loan can be repaid with tax-deductible dollars even though the employer may not realize profits in a particular year.

Contribution limits for ESOPs

The general limitation on annual contributions to a defined contribution plan applies to ESOPs (see ¶ 525). [2]

☐ ESOPs are discussed in detail beginning at ¶ 3000.

---

[1] Code Sec. 4975(e)(7); ERISA Sec. 407(d)(6).

[2] Code Sec. 415(c)(6).

¶ 146
STOCK OWNERSHIP PLANS: Statutory Stock Options

A stock option is an agreement on the part of a company to sell a given number of shares of stock at a given price to an employee within a specified period of time. The decision to exercise the option is left entirely to the employee in most cases. A company, however, may reserve the right to withdraw the option.

Special tax treatment was provided to qualified stock options and restricted stock options prior to implementation of the Tax Reform Act of 1976. [1] Employee stock purchase plans (¶ 150) and incentive stock options (¶ 153) are the only statutory stock options that remain valid.

[1] Code Secs. 422 and 424, prior to repeal by P.L. 101-508.

¶ 150
STOCK OWNERSHIP PLANS: Employee Stock Purchase Plans

An employee stock purchase plan provides employees with the option to buy company stock out of earnings. The employee authorizes the employer to deduct a given percentage of salary and accumulate the funds in an account from which stock purchases may be made.

Generally, the stock must not be disposed of within two years of the date of the granting of the option or within one year after the transfer of the stock to the individual.[1] In addition, options may be granted only to employees of the granting corporation, its parent, or its subsidiary.

☐ Employee stock purchase plans are discussed in detail at ¶ 3310.

[1] Code Sec. 423; IRS Reg. § 1.423-2.

¶ 153
STOCK OWNERSHIP PLANS: Incentive Stock Options

An incentive stock option gives an employee (typically an executive) the right to pay a fixed price for the employer's stock at a future date. *No tax consequences result from the grant or exercise of an incentive stock option.* Upon sale of the stock, the employee treats any gain as a capital gain if the stock has been held for at least two years from the date the option was granted and at least one year after the stock was transferred to the employee.

The terms of the incentive stock option must be approved by the stockholders within 12 months before or after the plan is adopted. [1] In addition, the term of the option may not exceed ten years and the option price must equal or exceed the value of the stock.

☐ Incentive stock options are discussed in detail at ¶ 3315.

¹ Code Sec. 422(b) and (d); IRS Temp. Reg.
§ 14a.422A-1.

¶ 155

SURVEY OF RETIREMENT AND SAVINGS PLANS:
Thrift or Savings Plans

A thrift or savings plan is a hybrid retirement plan to which employees make contributions. Employer contributions are usually geared to the amounts that are contributed by the employees. The plan may take the form of a pension, profit-sharing, or stock bonus plan. Typically, thrift or savings plans are profit-sharing or money purchase plans.

Employee contributions

Contributions by employees are the building blocks for a thrift or savings plan. The plan is based on funds, or units, that accumulate in an employee's account through his or her own contributions (and those of the employer), plus earnings that may accrue to the fund.

The amount that employees may be required to contribute is subject to a limit (generally, 6% of compensation) in order to prevent discrimination in favor of more highly paid employees. In addition, even in cases where employee contributions are voluntary and in no way connected with benefits from employer contributions, there is a limit to the amount that employees may contribute. According to the IRS, an employee's voluntary contributions, which are unrelated to benefits from employer contributions, may not exceed 10% of the employee's compensation.[1]

Employer contributions

The employer's contributions to a thrift or savings plan are normally made on a "matching" basis. Typically, an employer's contributions are set by the plan as a fixed percentage of the employees' contributions. The rate of the employer's contributions may be tied in to an employee's length of service.

¹ Rev. Rul. 80-350, 1980-2 CB 133, superseding Rev. Rul. 59-185, 1959-1 CB 86 and Rev. Rul. 69-217, 1969-1 CB 115; Rev. Rul. 74-385, 1974-2 CB 130, CCH Pension Plan Guide ¶ 19,346.

¶ 157

SURVEY OF RETIREMENT AND SAVINGS PLANS:
Cafeteria Plans and Flexible Spending Arrangements (FSAs)

A "cafeteria plan" is a written plan under which all participants are permitted to choose between cash and certain qualified benefits. Most benefits that are excludable from income tax under the Internal Revenue Code may be offered under a cafeteria plan.

A cafeteria plan may not provide deferred compensation. As part of its benefits package, however, a cafeteria plan may offer certain tax-deferred retirement plan contributions, such as those contained in a 401(k) plan. Thus, employer contributions made to a 401(k) plan will be treated as eligible nontaxable benefits under a cafeteria plan.[1]

☐ Cafeteria plans are discussed in detail in the CCH U.S. MASTER EMPLOYEE BENEFITS GUIDE.

Flexible spending arrangements

A flexible spending arrangement (FSA) is an employer-sponsored benefit program that is offered as part of a cafeteria plan and designed to provide covered employees with a method of paying for certain covered expenses (e.g., medical or dependent care) with pre-tax dollars.[2] Generally, a covered employee makes contributions through payroll deductions to a health or a dependent care FSA. Because contributions to an FSA reduce an employee's gross income, these amounts, though compensatory in nature, are not subject to federal income tax, Social Security tax, or, in many areas of the country, state and local income taxes. However, amounts selected, but unused by the employee at the end of the plan year, are forfeited under the "use it or lose it" rule.

An FSA will not reduce an employee's pension benefits that are based on pay. Pension, life insurance, and profit-sharing contributions are based on an employee's pay before any spending account deduction.

☐ Flexible spending arrangements are discussed in detail in the CCH U.S. MASTER EMPLOYEE BENEFITS GUIDE.

---

[1] Code Sec. 125(d).

[2] IRS Proposed Reg. § 1.125-2, Q&A-7.

¶ 160

SURVEY OF RETIREMENT AND SAVINGS PLANS: Church Plans

A church plan is an arrangement that is established and maintained by a tax-exempt church or a convention or association of churches. [1] A church plan's principal purpose is to administer or fund a program providing retirement benefits, welfare benefits, or both, for the employees of a church, a church convention, or a religious order or religious organization.

Church plans are exempt from federal income tax. In addition, church plans that do not elect to be covered by ERISA are exempt from its requirements.

☐ Church plans are discussed in greater detail in the CCH PENSION PLAN GUIDE, beginning at ¶ 8049.

---

[1] Code Sec. 414(e)(1)-(3); ERISA Sec. 3(33)(A)-(C); IRS Reg. § 1.414(e)-1(c) and (f).

¶ 163

SURVEY OF RETIREMENT AND SAVINGS PLANS:
Keogh Plans

A Keogh plan is a retirement plan that covers one or more self-employed individuals (sole proprietors and partners). [1] It may be a profit-sharing plan, a money purchase pension plan, a defined benefit plan, or a thrift plan.

☐ Keogh plans are discussed further at ¶ 3242 and following.

[1] Code Sec. 401(c) and (d).

¶ 165

SURVEY OF RETIREMENT AND SAVINGS PLANS:
Individual Retirement Accounts (IRAs)

Individual retirement accounts (IRAs) are domestic trusts or custodial accounts that are established by an employee or self-employed person and to which contributions are made and deducted subject to certain restrictions. [1] The three general types of IRAs that are available to an individual are: deductible IRAs, nondeductible IRAs, and backloaded Roth IRAs.

An individual's contribution to an IRA may not exceed $5,000 per year (in 2012), or, if less, 100% of compensation. Although contributions to Roth IRAs are never deductible, individuals who participate in other IRAs and who are not active participants in employer-sponsored plans may fully deduct IRA contributions. The deduction available to active participants in an employer-sponsored plan is limited, but such individuals may still make nondeductible contributions to an IRA.

Generally, amounts in an IRA are taxed upon distribution. Qualified distributions from Roth IRAs, however, are not included in the individual's gross income upon distribution. To be a qualified distribution from a Roth IRA, the distribution must satisfy a five-year holding period and must meet one of four requirements (see ¶ 3225).

☐ IRAs are discussed in detail beginning at ¶ 3202.

[1] Code Sec. 408.

¶ 170

SURVEY OF RETIREMENT AND SAVINGS PLANS:
SIMPLE Plans

Employers with 100 or fewer employees receiving at least $5,000 in compensation from the employer in the preceding year may adopt a simplified retirement plan, the Savings Incentive Match Plan for Employees (SIMPLE plan), if they do not currently maintain another qualified plan. [1] The plan allows employees to make elective contributions of up to $11,500 per year (in 2012) and requires employers to make matching contributions. Assets in the account are not taxed until they are distributed to an employee, and an employer may generally deduct contributions to the employees' accounts.

A primary advantage of the SIMPLE plan is that it is not subject to the nondiscrimination rules (including top-heavy provisions) or other complex requirements applicable to qualified plans. In addition, the reporting requirements that normally apply to plans under ERISA are significantly relaxed for SIMPLE plans.

SIMPLE plan may be IRA or 401(k)

SIMPLE plans may be structured as an IRA or as a 401(k) qualified cash or deferred arrangement.

☐ SIMPLE IRA plans are discussed further at ¶ 3224.

☐ The rules governing SIMPLE 401(k) plans are explained at ¶ 2994 and ¶ 2995.

---

[1] Code Secs. 401(k)(11) and 408(p).

¶ 172

SURVEY OF RETIREMENT AND SAVINGS PLANS: Simplified Employee Pensions (SEPs)

A simplified employee pension (SEP) is an individual retirement account or annuity that is allowed to receive an increased rate of contributions from the IRA holder's employer. SEPs are subject to special requirements regarding participation, discrimination, withdrawals, and an employer allocation formula. [1] However, SEPs may be excluded from filing annual return/reports (Form 5500 series) and from furnishing summary annual reports or summary plan descriptions to participants and beneficiaries.

Contributions to a SEP on behalf of an employee are limited to the lesser of $50,000 (in 2012) or 25% of the employee's compensation. The amounts contributed to a SEP by an employer on behalf of an employee are excludable from the employee's gross income.

☐ SEPs are discussed further beginning at ¶ 3226.

---

[1] Code Sec. 408(j), (k), and (l).

¶ 174

SURVEY OF RETIREMENT AND SAVINGS PLANS: Top-Heavy Plans

Under a "top-heavy" plan, more than 60% of benefits or contributions are designated for key employees. Top-heavy plans are subject to additional qualification requirements governing vesting and minimum non-integrated contributions or benefits for non-key employees. [1] The rules are designed to ensure that the plan does not discriminate in favor of officers, large shareholders, or highly compensated employees.

☐ Top-heavy plans are discussed beginning at ¶ 900.

¹ Code Sec. 416; IRS Reg. § 1.416-1.

¶ 177
SURVEY OF RETIREMENT AND SAVINGS PLANS:
401(k) Plans

Under a 401(k) plan (also known as a "cash or deferred arrangement" or a "salary reduction plan"), an employee may elect to defer current taxation on a portion of salary contributed by the employer to a qualified plan on behalf of the employee.[1] Such an arrangement must be part of a profit-sharing or stock bonus plan, a pre-ERISA money purchase plan, or a rural electric or telephone cooperative plan.

Code Sec. 401(k) plans are subject to special, additional qualification requirements. Special discrimination rules also apply to these plans.

☐ 401(k) plans are discussed in detail beginning at ¶ 2940.

¹ Code Sec. 401(k).

¶ 179
SURVEY OF RETIREMENT AND SAVINGS PLANS:
Government Plans

A government plan is an arrangement established and maintained by the federal government, or by the government of any state or political subdivision, or by an agency or instrumentality thereof, for its employees.[1] A plan that is administered by an employee organization, such as a union, may be a government plan if the arrangement is maintained exclusively for the benefit of government employees, the organization's membership is limited to government employees, and the plan is funded exclusively by the government or by the government and employees of the government belonging to the sponsoring organization.

Government plans are exempt from ERISA's participation, minimum coverage, vesting, and funding standards.[2] However, a government plan will lose its exemption from ERISA Title I once the governmental entity relinquishes responsibility for the plan to a private entity.

☐ Additional information on government plans is provided at CCH PENSION PLAN GUIDE ¶ 250.

¹ ERISA Sec. 3(32).   ² ERISA Sec. 4(b)(1).

¶ 180
SURVEY OF RETIREMENT AND SAVINGS PLANS:
Code Sec. 457 Plans

Code Sec. 457 plans are nonqualified deferred compensation arrangements that are available to employees of state and local governments and employees of nongovernmental tax-exempt organizations. [1] Under a Code Sec. 457 plan, an employee is not taxed on contributions made by the governmental employer or earnings on those contributions until the amounts are distributed. The amount of compensation that an individual may elect to defer is limited to the lesser of $17,000 (in 2012) or 100% of the participant's includible compensation.[2] In addition, an agreement governing the deferral must be in effect prior to the month that the deferral is made. An additional $5,500 (in 2012) catch-up deferral limit is permitted for a participant age 50 or older in a governmental 457 plan.[3]

Trust requirement

Generally effective for plan assets held on or after August 20, 1996, amounts deferred under a Code Sec. 457 plan maintained by a state or local government must be held in a trust (or a custodial account or annuity contract) for the exclusive benefit of plan participants and their beneficiaries. [4]

☐ Further information on Code Sec. 457 plans is provided beginning at CCH PENSION PLAN GUIDE ¶ 8003.

---

[1] Code Sec. 457. See also IRS Proposed Reg. Secs. 1.457-1—1.457-12 at CCH PENSION PLAN GUIDE ¶ 20,260K.

[2] Code Sec. 457(b)(2) and (e)(15).
[3] Code Sec. 414(v)(2).
[4] Code Sec. 457(g).

¶ 183

SURVEY OF RETIREMENT AND SAVINGS PLANS: Tax-Sheltered Annuities (TSAs)

A tax-sheltered annuity (TSA), or a "403(b) plan," is a deferred compensation retirement arrangement that may be entered into only by employees of public education systems or other specific tax-exempt organizations, such as hospitals and non-profit groups. [1] TSAs are funded primarily through salary reduction agreements under which employees reduce their salary by a fixed amount or forego a future increase in salary.

☐ TSAs are discussed in detail beginning at ¶ 3100.

---

[1] Code Sec. 403(b); ERISA Reg. § 2510.3-2(f).

¶ 185

SURVEY OF RETIREMENT AND SAVINGS PLANS: Multiemployer (Union Management Trust Fund) Plans

A multiemployer plan is an employee benefit plan to which more than one employer contributes and that is established and maintained through the collective bargaining process.[1] In addition, multiemployer plans must be established for a "substantial business purpose" as defined in Labor Department regulations.[2] In contrast to a single-employer plan, which is established by one employer on behalf of its employees, a multiemployer plan generally covers union employees working for several employers within a given industry. All trades or businesses operating under "common control" are considered to be a single employer for purposes of these rules.

There are generally two types of multiemployer plans: multiemployer welfare plans and multiemployer pension plans. The multiemployer welfare plan may provide group life insurance, disability insurance, coverage for hospitalization, and other medical coverage. The multiemployer pension plan provides retirement income.

☐ The termination rules applicable to multiemployer plans are discussed in detail beginning at ¶ 2868.

[1] Code Sec. 414(f)(1), (2), and (5); ERISA Secs. 3(37)(A), (B), and (E).

[2] ERISA Reg. § 2510.3-37.

¶ 187

SURVEY OF RETIREMENT AND SAVINGS PLANS:
Voluntary Employees' Beneficiary Associations (VEBAs)

A voluntary employees' beneficiary association (VEBA), or 501(c)(9) trust, is a tax-exempt trust designed to provide for the payment of life, sick, accident, or other welfare benefits to employees or their dependents or designated beneficiaries. [1] No part of the net earnings of the association may inure (other than through such payments) to the benefit of any private shareholder or individual. [2]

Generally, a VEBA must be an association of employees. [3] Membership in the organization must be voluntary,[4] and the eligibility of employees must be determined by objective standards that reflect an employment-related bond among employees.[5] In addition, no class of benefits under the VEBA may be provided to a classification of employees that discriminates in favor of highly compensated employees.[6]

☐ VEBAs are discussed in detail in the CCH U.S. MASTER EMPLOYEE BENEFITS GUIDE.

[1] Code Sec. 501(c)(9); IRS Reg. § 1.501(c)(9).
[2] *Ibid.*
[3] IRS Reg. § 1.509(c)(9)-1(a).

[4] IRS Reg. § 1.501(c)(9)-1(b).
[5] IRS Reg. § 1.509(c)(9)-2(a)(1).
[6] Code Sec. 505(b).

¶ 190

SURVEY OF RETIREMENT AND SAVINGS PLANS:
Employee Welfare Benefit Plans

An employee welfare benefit plan is any plan, fund, or program, which is established or maintained by an employer, an employee organization, or both, to provide the following benefits for its participants or their beneficiaries: [1]

1. medical, surgical, or hospital care or benefits;

2. benefits in the event of sickness, accident, disability, death, or unemployment;

3. vacation benefits;

4. apprenticeship or other training programs;

5. day care centers;

6. scholarship funds; or

7. prepaid legal services.

Practices excluded from treatment as welfare plans

The Department of Labor and courts have identified benefits practices and arrangements that will not be treated as employee welfare benefit plans and, thus, will not be subject to ERISA's reporting and disclosure requirements. [2] These practices include group insurance programs, strike funds, and compensation payments made by an employer to an employee for services, including overtime pay, shift premiums, holiday premiums, or weekend premiums.

☐ Employee welfare benefit plans are discussed in detail in the CCH U.S. MASTER EMPLOYEE BENEFITS GUIDE.

---

[1] ERISA Sec. 3(1).

[2] ERISA Reg. § 2510.3-1(b)-(k).

¶ 195
SURVEY OF RETIREMENT AND SAVINGS PLANS:
Nonqualified Plans

Qualified pension, profit-sharing, and annuity plans effectively provide retirement income for employees in general, but they cannot be used to provide supplementary compensation for executives or key employees. [1] This is because qualified plans must benefit all eligible employees, and the benefits under such plans must be uniform and nondiscriminatory. Deferred compensation that is limited solely to executives or other key employees, however, may be provided under a nonqualified plan. Simply stated, a nonqualified plan is an arrangement that does not meet the requirements of Code Sec. 401.

Nonqualified arrangements include excess benefit plans, "top-hat" plans, nonqualified stock options, phantom or shadow stock plans, stock appreciation rights (SARs), stock repurchase plans, golden parachutes, rabbi and secular trusts, and nonqualified annuities.

CCH Pointer: Code Sec. 409A provides specific rules for elections and distributions under nonqualified deferred compensation plans. Individual participants who defer compensation under plans that fail to comply with the rules are subject to current taxation on all deferrals and enhanced penalties.

☐ Nonqualified plans are discussed in detail beginning at ¶ 3300.

---

[1] ERISA Secs. 201(2), 301(a)(3), 401(a)(1), and 4021(b)(6).

¶ 198
For More Information

☐ For more detailed information on the various types of pension and savings plans, see CCH PENSION PLAN GUIDE ¶ 100—¶ 365.

Advantages of Plan Qualification—Obtaining Qualified Status

¶ 200

Overview

Although a large number of rules must be met in order to qualify a retirement plan, plan qualification offers a number of tax advantages. The major advantages of plan qualification include:

1. plan earnings are not taxed;

2. employer contributions are deductible when made;

3. employees are not currently taxed on amounts contributed on their behalf by the employer; and

4. favorable tax treatment may be available for some kinds of distributions.

These benefits are available only if the plan is qualified and retains qualified status. Meeting and continuing to comply with the myriad of qualification rules can be burdensome. These rules are discussed at ¶ 300 and following.

Obtaining determination from IRS

The IRS has established procedures allowing an employer to obtain, in advance of an IRS examination of its tax returns, a determination as to whether the employer's pension or profit-sharing plan or trust qualifies for favorable tax treatment. In response to an employer's inquiry, a "determination letter" normally is issued. These procedures are outlined beginning at ¶ 225.

¶ 205

ADVANTAGES OF PLAN QUALIFICATION: Plan Earnings Not Taxed

Internal Revenue Code qualification provisions are primarily directed at those plans that are funded. "Funded" plans are those plans in which contributions by employers, employees, or both, are set aside in a separate fund held by a third party and invested.[1] When a plan is qualified, the earnings on these invested funds are not currently taxed.[2] This is an important advantage of achieving qualified status.

In general, there are several types of third-party fundholders:

1. a trust;[3]

2. an insurance company;[4]

3. a bank acting as a custodian; and

4. an investment company issuing face-amount certificates.[5]

Trust as fundholder

For income tax purposes, a trust is a separate tax entity whose earnings are subject to income tax. For trusts that are part of a qualified plan, however, trust earnings are exempt from tax.[6] Note that there may be a special tax on "unrelated business income," even for exempt trusts.

Insurance company as fundholder

When the fundholder is an insurance company, a trust need not always be involved. In such a case, the contributions are in the form of premiums paid to the insurance company for annuity contracts. The insurance company, which invests the money represented by the premiums, is itself a taxable entity and its investment earnings are subject to tax.[7] A qualified plan may use a segregated asset account maintained by a life insurance company as an investment medium.[8]

Custodian as fundholder

Banks, savings and loan associations, and others are permitted to hold plan funds in custodial accounts. If the plan is qualified, the custodial account is treated as a trust, and its earnings are exempt from tax.

Investment company as fundholder

A plan can be funded through annuity contracts. Included in the definition of "annuity contracts" are "face amount certificates" issued by an investment company operating under the Investment Company Act of 1940. [9] Thus, a plan can be funded in whole or in part through the direct purchase of face amount certificates. No tax is due until these certificates begin to pay out.

---

[1] Rev. Rul. 71-91, 1971-1 CB 116, CCH Pension Plan Guide ¶ 19,020.

[2] Code Sec. 501(a).

[3] Code Sec. 401(a).

[4] Code Sec. 401(f)

[5] Code Sec. 401(g).

[6] Code Sec. 501(a).

[7] Code Sec. 801; Code Sec. 803(a)(3).

[8] Rev. Rul. 72-610, 1972-2 CB 400, CCH Pension Plan Guide ¶ 19,202; Rev. Rul. 73-67, 1973-1 CB 330, CCH Pension Plan Guide ¶ 19,213; Rev. Rul. 74-189, I.R.B. 1974-17, 10, CCH Pension Plan Guide ¶ 19,320.

[9] Code Sec. 401(g).

¶ 210

ADVANTAGES OF PLAN QUALIFICATION: Employer's Contributions Deductible When Made

An employer may deduct contributions made in order to fund a qualified plan. [1] The employer deduction is available even though employees do not receive current plan distributions, the employees are not vested in plan benefits, and the trust earnings on the contributions are not taxed.

The amount of an employer's deduction is subject to statutory limitations, which, as a practical matter, typically govern the amount that the employer contributes to a plan. [2] These limitations vary in the case of pension and annuity plans[3] on the one hand and profit-sharing and stock bonus plans on the other. [4]

It is not absolutely necessary for a plan to be qualified in order for contributions to be deductible by the employer. If the plan is not qualified, however, the employer is allowed a deduction only if the rights of the employees to the fund are vested (i.e., not subject to forfeiture). [5]

☐ For a complete analysis of the deduction of contributions, see the discussion beginning at ¶ 600.

---

[1] Code Sec. 404.

[2] Code Sec. 404(a).

[3] Code Sec. 404(a)(1); Code Sec. 404(a)(2).

[4] Code Sec. 404(a)(3).

[5] Code Sec. 404(a)(5).

¶ 215

ADVANTAGES OF PLAN QUALIFICATION:
Employees Not Currently Taxed on Plan Contributions

Employer contributions to an employees' pension, profit-sharing, or other retirement plans are in the nature of compensation to the employees. Ordinarily, compensation is taxable to an employee when paid to him or her. However, employees participating in qualified plans, whether or not their rights to benefits are vested, are not treated as receiving compensation until they actually receive distributions from the plan. [1] As a result, in many cases, the amounts which the employee has a right to receive at a later date are not taxed until that date.

> **CCH Pointer:** The employee ordinarily does not receive distributions from the plan until he or she retires. The advantage of tax-deferred retirement vehicles is that, at retirement, the employee's overall earnings likely will be less than they were during his or her working years and, therefore, the tax bracket may be lower. An additional benefit will be realized if tax rates are lower in such later years. Also, certain types of plan distributions receive special tax treatment (see ¶ 220).

[1] Code Sec. 402(a); Code Sec. 403(a)(1).

¶ 220

ADVANTAGES OF PLAN QUALIFICATION: Special Treatment of Certain Types of Plan Distributions

Recipients of distributions from qualified plans may be able to receive favorable tax treatment for certain types of plan distributions. Tax advantages are available, for instance, for rollovers from qualified plans, lump-sum distributions, and distributions of employer securities.

Rollovers

Certain distributions of money or property in a qualified plan may be rolled over tax-free, within 60 days after the participant receives the distribution, to another qualified plan or to an IRA (see ¶ 1954). [1] An employee's surviving spouse may also roll over a QDRO distribution attributable to the employee (see ¶ 1966).

Lump-sum distributions

A lump-sum distribution may be eligible for special tax treatment, such as 10-year averaging. In general, a lump-sum distribution is the distribution or payment, within one tax year, of an employee's entire interest in a qualified plan. To be a lump-sum distribution, the distribution must be made because of the employee's death, disability, separation from service, or the attainment of age 59½.[2]

Formerly, five-year averaging for lump-sum distributions was available for distributions made in tax years prior to 2000 (see ¶ 1944). Ten-year averaging will still be available for people who reached age 50 before January 1, 1986 (see ¶ 1946).

Distributions of employer's securities

In some cases, an employee or beneficiary may receive a distribution from a trust that includes securities of the employer. If the distribution is a total distribution that would qualify for the special rates mentioned above, any unrealized appreciation in the value of the securities of the employer is not included in the employee's income.[3]

If the distribution is not a total distribution, the rule is slightly different. In this case, only that part of the unrealized appreciation attributable to the employee's contributions (other than deductible employee contributions) toward the purchase of the securities is excluded from the employee's income. Unrealized appreciation is the excess of the aggregate market value of all the securities distributed over their aggregate cost to the trust.

☐ The rules for taxing plan distributions are discussed at ¶ 1900 and following.

[1] Code Sec. 402(c).

[2] Code Sec. 402(e)(4)(D).
[3] Code Sec. 402(e)(4)(A).

¶ 225
OBTAINING QUALIFIED STATUS: General Rules

Although the tax advantages involved in plan qualification are many, the qualification rules that must be followed are even more numerous.

An employer may obtain an IRS determination that its plan is "qualified" under the Internal Revenue Code and meets certain ERISA requirements as well. Consistent with this policy, the IRS has established procedures allowing an employer to obtain, in advance of an IRS examination of its tax returns, a determination as to whether the employer's pension or profit-sharing plan or trust qualifies for favorable tax treatment. In response to an employer's inquiry, a favorable "determination letter" normally is issued.

If an employer seeks tax qualification of a plan, it should file all appropriate forms and statements with the IRS, including information required by the Labor Department.[1] Employers must notify any employee who is an interested party to the plan (see ¶ 270) that a determination letter has been requested. [2]

When a request for a tax determination of qualification is received by the IRS (or withdrawn by the employer-applicant), the IRS must notify the Labor Department and the PBGC. In addition, employees, the Labor Department, and the PBGC must be given an opportunity to comment on an advance determination application at any time within 45 days after receipt of the application. [3]

Note that the above rules not only relate to requests for a determination of tax qualification for new plans but also to plan amendments and plan terminations. Participants are entitled to inspect the employer's application for plan qualification, including supporting papers and IRS responses, except for information relating to the compensation of any participant. [4]

[1] ERISA Sec. 3001(a).
[2] ERISA Sec. 3001(a).

[3] ERISA Sec. 3001(b)(1).
[4] ERISA Sec. 3001(b)(4).

¶ 230

OBTAINING QUALIFIED STATUS: Roles of IRS, DOL, and the Courts

The IRS has jurisdiction over the question of whether a plan is qualified to receive tax benefits. Taxpayers may—but are not required to—request advance determinations from the IRS as to whether a plan is qualified.

Labor Department

Technically, the Labor Department has no role in the determination of whether a plan is qualified under the Internal Revenue Code. However, many qualification requirements have become substantive requirements of law under Title I of ERISA, which is enforced mainly by the Labor Department.

ERISA Reorganization Plan. The ERISA Reorganization Plan splits enforcement responsibility between the IRS and the Labor Department. [1] The Plan gives the IRS authority over minimum standards of funding, participation, and vesting of benefit rights. The Labor Department has been given responsibility for fiduciary standards and prohibited transactions. As a result, requests under Code or ERISA provisions pertaining to the minimum funding standards, participation, and vesting should be submitted only to the IRS.[2] Requests for opinions, and rulings under the fiduciary responsibility and prohibited transaction provisions of the Code or ERISA should be submitted to the Labor Department. [3]

Role of the courts

The U.S. Tax Court may judicially review an IRS determination—or a failure to make a determination—involving plan qualification. [4] A declaratory judgment by the Tax Court may be obtained by the employer, by the plan administrator, by an employee who qualifies as an "interested party" under IRS regulations, or by the PBGC. An IRS determination may be reviewed as to both initial qualification and continuing qualification.

In the case of the failure by the IRS to make a determination, review is available in the case of initial qualification without restriction, but, in the case of continuing qualification, review is available only if the controversy arises out of a plan amendment or a plan termination.

[2] IRS Announcement 79-6, I.R.B. 1979-4.

[1] Reorganization Plan of 1978 (ERISA Reorganization Plan).

[3] ERISA Secs. 3001—3004; IRS Reg. § 1.401-1(e).

[4] Code Sec. 7476.

¶ 235

OBTAINING QUALIFIED STATUS: Requesting Determination Letters from the IRS

In order to request a determination letter, an applicant must file required material with IRS Employee Plans (EP) Determinations (see ¶ 240). The filing of the application, when accompanied by all information and documents required, generally provides the IRS with the information required to make the requested determination.

In making the determination, however, the IRS may require the submission of additional information. Information submitted to the IRS in connection with an application for determination may be subject to public inspection. [1]

Important changes to determination letter procedures for 2012. The IRS has issued revised procedures for issuing determination letters on the qualified status of pension, profit-sharing, stock bonus, annuity, and employee stock owner-ship plans (ESOPs), and the status for exemption of any related trusts or custodial accounts. The revised procedures are effective February 1, 2012, for plans under the five-year remedial amendment cycle (other than terminating plans), and May 1, 2012, for terminating plans and for plans under the six-year remedial amendment cycle. The 2012 procedures include the following changes:

- ☐ elimination of elective demonstrations concerning minimum participation, coverage, and nondiscrimination requirements;

- ☐ plans will no longer be reviewed for, and a determination letter does not constitute a ruling or determination as to, whether the plan is a governmental plan under Code Sec. 414(d) or a church plan under Code Sec. 414(e); and

- ☐ an applicant must include Employee Plans Compliance Resolution System (EPCRS) documentation, if any, with an application.

File Form 5300

A determination letter request is made by filing the appropriate form and following the instructions contained on the form. For individually-designed plans and collectively bargained plans, Form 5300 (Application for Determination for Employee Benefit Plan) should be filed to request a determination letter.

Schedule Q. Under revised procedures announced in 2012, the filing of Schedule Q (Elective Determination Requests) and accompanying demonstrations regarding the coverage and nondiscrimination requirements should not be submitted with any determination letter application for the plan because such demonstrations will no longer be considered in the review.

Include complete copy of plan

With the exception of applications involving master and prototype plans (see ¶ 250) or minor amendments (see ¶ 255), a complete copy of the plan and trust instrument must be included with the determination letter application. [2]

The application should also include a copy of interim and other plan amendments adopted since the most recent determination letter application to show that the conditions for eligibility for the applicable remedial amendment period are satisfied.

Provide copy of previous determination letter

Plans that have received a favorable determination letter in the past must include a copy of the latest determination letter, if available, with the application. [3]

If the submitted plan is the result of a merger of two or more plans, applicants should include a copy of the prior determination letter for all the plans that combined to result in the merged plan. If a prior determination letter is not available, an explanation must be included with the application. For each plan involved in a merger, the applicant must provide all of the amendments adopted after the date of the most recent determination, opinion or advisory letter for each of the merged plans, as well as the prior plan document.

Interested party notification

The applicant must notify interested parties that an application for an advance determination regarding plan qualification has been filed (see ¶ 270).

Contrary authority must be distinguished

If the determination letter application involves an issue where contrary authorities exist, failure to disclose or distinguish these significant contrary authorities may result in requests for additional information. This will delay action on the application. [4]

Code Sec. 414(l) plans

A separate application must be filed for each single plan within the meaning of Code Sec. 414(l), pertaining to the merger and consolidation of plans. [5] The requirement does not apply to applications regarding the qualified status of group trusts.

Determination of employer/employee relationship

The IRS will make a determination regarding the existence of an employer-employee relationship if requested to do so by the applicant. In such cases, the application (Form 5300) should contain required information and documents and be accompanied by a completed Form SS-8 (Determination of Employee Work Status for Purposes of Federal Employment Taxes and Income Tax Withholding). Other information and copies of documents the applicant·deems appropriate to establish its status also should be submitted. In addition, the IRS may require further information that it considers necessary to determine the employment status of the individuals involved or the qualification of the plan. [6]

Incomplete applications

If an applicant does not comply with all the requirements for applying for a determination letter, EP Determinations may return the application, pointing out those requirements that have not been met. The request will also be returned if the correct user fee (see ¶ 287) is not attached.

If a determination letter request is returned to the applicant, the 270-day remedial amendment period under Code Sec. 7476(b)(3) (for purposes of the

¶235

exhaustion of administrative remedies rule) does not begin to run until the time the application is deemed complete. [7]

Failure to disclose material facts

A failure to disclose a material fact or a misrepresentation of a material fact on the application may adversely affect the reliance that a plan would otherwise obtain through a favorable determination letter. Similarly, failure to accurately provide any of the information called for on any form required may jeopardize effective reliance on the determination letter. [8]

> **CCH Pointer:** *Staggered remedial amendment periods.* The IRS has created a system of staggered remedial amendment period cycles for both pre-approved and individually-designed plans. The new system is intended to limit the number of determination letter applications any one plan would need to submit.
>
> Individually-designed plans have a regular five-year amendment cycle, while pre-approved plans have a regular six-year remedial amendment cycle. (The applicable cycle is generally determined by the tax identification number of the plan sponsor.)[9]
>
> ☐ For further information on staggered remedial amendment periods, see CCH PENSION PLAN GUIDE ¶ 1833.

[1] Rev. Proc. 2012-6, I.R.B. 2012-1, Sec. 6.04, CCH PENSION PLAN GUIDE ¶ 17,299T-86; IRS Announcement 2011-82, I.R.B. 2011-52, CCH PENSION PLAN GUIDE ¶ 17,097T-61.

[2] Rev. Proc. 2012-6, I.R.B. 2012-1, Sec. 6.05.

[3] Rev. Proc. 2012-6, I.R.B. 2012-1, Sec. 6.08.

[4] Rev. Proc. 2012-6, I.R.B. 2012-1, Sec. 6.11.

[5] Rev. Proc. 2012-6, I.R.B. 2012-1, Sec. 6.07.

[6] Rev. Proc. 2012-6, I.R.B. 2012-1, Sec. 6.12.

[7] Rev. Proc. 2012-6, I.R.B. 2012-1, Sec. 6.13.

[8] Rev. Proc. 2012-6, I.R.B. 2012-1, Sec. 6.14.

[9] Rev. Proc. 2007-44, I.R.B. 2007-28, CCH PENSION PLAN GUIDE ¶ 17,299S-25; as modified by Rev. Proc. 2008-56, I.R.B. 2008-40, CCH PENSION PLAN GUIDE ¶ 17,299S-70; Rev. Proc. 2009-36, I.R.B. 2009-35, CCH PENSION PLAN GUIDE ¶ 17,299T-13; IRS Notice 2009-97, I.R.B. 2009-52, CCH PENSION PLAN GUIDE ¶ 17,144D; IRS Notice 2010-77, I.R.B. 2010-51, CCH PENSION PLAN GUIDE ¶ 17,146A; and IRS Announcement 2012-3, I.R.B. 2012-4, CCH PENSION PLAN GUIDE ¶ 17,097T-65.

¶ 240

OBTAINING QUALIFIED STATUS: Where to File Determination Letter Requests

Requests for determination letters should be addressed to EP Determinations at the following address:

Internal Revenue Service
P.O. Box 12192
Covington, KY 41012-0192.

Applications shipped by Express Mail or a delivery service, should be sent to:

Internal Revenue Service
201 West Rivercenter Blvd.
Attn: Extracting Stop 312
Covington, KY 41011.[1]

Determination letter applications will not be accepted via fax.

[1] Rev. Proc. 2012-6, I.R.B. 2012-1, Sec. 6.15, CCH
PENSION PLAN GUIDE ¶ 17,299T-86.

¶ 245

OBTAINING QUALIFIED STATUS: Withdrawal of a Determination Letter Request

The applicant's request for a determination letter may be withdrawn by written request at any time prior to the issuance of a final adverse determination letter. If an appeal to a proposed adverse determination letter is filed, a request for a determination letter may be withdrawn at any time prior to the forwarding of the proposed adverse action to the Chief, Appeals Office. [1]

If a determination letter request application is withdrawn, the IRS will not issue a determination of any type. A failure to issue a determination letter as a result of a withdrawal is not considered a failure by the IRS to make a determination. The IRS, however, may consider the information submitted in connection with the withdrawn request in a subsequent plan examination. Generally, the IRS will not refund user fees if the application is withdrawn.

[1] Rev. Proc. 2012-6, I.R.B. 2012-1, Sec. 6.17, CCH
PENSION PLAN GUIDE ¶ 17,299T-86.

¶ 250

OBTAINING QUALIFIED STATUS: Pre-Approved Plans

The IRS maintains two programs that offer employers and plan sponsors the opportunity to adopt or market plans that are "pre-approved" under Code Sec. 401(a) and Code Sec. 403(a).

Master and prototype program. Master and prototype (M&P) plans are plans (including plans covering self-employed individuals) made available by a sponsor for adoption by employers. M&P plans consist of a basic plan document, an adoption agreement and, if not included in the plan document, a trust or custodial account document. These documents may not be amended by adopting employers, except by choosing among permitted options under the adoption agreement. (A "master" plan utilizes a single funding medium for the joint use of all adopting employers; under a "prototype" plan, a separate funding medium is established for each adopting employer.)[1]

Volume Submitter Plan. A volume submitter plan is a profit-sharing plan, a 401(k) plan, a money purchase pension plan, or a defined benefit plan which meets certain criteria established by the IRS and which is submitted according to procedures for volume submitter advisory letters (for a specimen plan) and determination letters (for an employer's adoption of a plan that is substantially similar to an approved specimen plan). The IRS will not accept volume submitter requests with respect to ESOPs, cash balance plans, or plans that include "fail safe" provisions for the nondiscrimination or average benefits test.[2]

CCH Pointer: The M&P and VS programs originated to serve different purposes and to some extent operate under different rules. Prior to 2005, the IRS published those rules in different revenue procedures. Given the narrowing of the differences between the two programs, the IRS elected in 2005 to set forth the rules for both programs in a single procedure.

Important changes to the M&P and VS programs for 2012

Opinion and advisory letters. The IRS updated the procedures for requesting opinion and advisory letters on the acceptability of the form of M&P and VS plans. The IRS has made many changes to the procedures, including minor revisions and clarifying language. Changes were made to both the M&P pre-approved plan program and the VS pre-approved plan program, including several definitions and descriptions, the list of areas not covered by opinion or advisory letters, the qualifications of plan sponsors, the proper format of adoption agreements, the rules regarding plan amendments, the procedures for requesting advisory letters, the procedures for transferring advisory letters, the rules for submitting identical plans and off-cycle filings, and reasons for revocation or clarification of an advisory letter.[3]

Form 5307 determination letter applications limited. Effective May 1, 2012, determination letter applications filed on Form 5307 will be accepted **only** from adopters of VS plans that modify the terms of the pre-approved VS specimen plan (and only if the modifications are not so extensive as to cause the plan to be treated as an individually designed plan). The IRS will not accept determination letter applications that are filed on Form 5307 on or after May 1, 2012, by adopters of VS plans that have not made any changes to the terms of the pre-approved VS specimen plan (except to select among options under the plan) or by adopters of M&P plans.[4]

Form 5300. An application for a determination letter for an M&P or VS plan that is filed on Form 5300 is treated as an application for an individually designed plan. Thus, the plan must be restated to take into account the Cumulative List in effect when the application is filed.[5]

Reliance on M&P and VS plans

Recent guidance, effective for 2012, describes the procedures for requesting opinion letters and advisory letters on M&P and VS plans and the extent to which adopting employers of such plans may rely on favorable opinion or advisory letters without having to request individual determination letters.[6]

Required information. Generally, letter requests for pre-approved plans must include the following:

1. an adoption agreement showing which elections the employer is making with respect to the elective provisions contained in the plan;

2. a copy of the plan's most recent opinion letter; and

3. in the case of a determination letter request for an M&P plan that uses a separate trust or custodial account, a copy of the employer's trust or custodial account agreement.[7]

Where to file

Opinion and advisory letters. Applications for opinion and advisory letters, for M&P and VS mass submitters, must be sent to the following address:

Internal Revenue Service
P.O. Box 2508
Cincinnati, OH 45201
Attn: Pre-Approved Plans Coordinator
Room 5106.[8]

Remedial amendment period

The IRS has issued extensive guidance for employers adopting remedial amendments to plans in the wake of legislative changes. See ¶ 235 and ¶ 316.

☐ For more information on the rules pertaining to master and prototype plans and regional prototype plans determination letter requests (including special rules for standardized plans), see CCH PENSION PLAN GUIDE ¶ 485. Detailed information on determination letter requests for volume submitter plans is located at ¶ 490 of the PENSION PLAN GUIDE. Information on multiple employer plans is at PENSION PLAN GUIDE ¶ 495.

---

[1] Rev. Proc. 2011-49, I.R.B. 2011-44, Sec. 4.01 and 4.02, CCH PENSION PLAN GUIDE ¶ 17,299T-69; as modified by Announcement 2012-3, I.R.B. 2012-4, CCH PENSION PLAN GUIDE ¶ 17,097T-65 and Rev. Proc. 2012-6, I.R.B. 2012-1, CCH PENSION PLAN GUIDE ¶ 17,299T-86.

[2] Rev. Proc. 2011-49, I.R.B. 2011-44, Sec. 16.03, CCH PENSION PLAN GUIDE ¶ 17,299T-69; as modified by Announcement 2012-3, I.R.B. 2012-4, CCH PENSION PLAN GUIDE ¶ 17,097T-65 and Rev. Proc. 2012-6, I.R.B. 2012-1, CCH PENSION PLAN GUIDE ¶ 17,299T-86.

[3] Rev. Proc. 2011-49, I.R.B. 2011-44, Sec. 16.03, CCH PENSION PLAN GUIDE ¶ 17,299T-69; as modified by Announcement 2012-3, I.R.B. 2012-4, CCH PENSION PLAN GUIDE ¶ 17,097T-65 and Rev. Proc. 2012-6, I.R.B. 2012-1, CCH PENSION PLAN GUIDE ¶ 17,299T-86.

[4] Rev. Proc. 2012-6, I.R.B. 2012-1, Sec. 8.02, at CCH Pension Plan Guide ¶ 17,299T-86.

[5] Rev. Proc. 2012-6, I.R.B. 2012-1, Sec. 8.02, at CCH Pension Plan Guide ¶ 17,299T-86.

[6] Rev. Proc. 2011-49, I.R.B. 2011-44, Sec. 19.04, CCH PENSION PLAN GUIDE ¶ 17,299T-69; as modified by Announcement 2012-3, I.R.B. 2012-4, CCH PENSION PLAN GUIDE ¶ 17,097T-65 and Rev. Proc. 2012-6, I.R.B. 2012-1, Sec. 8.03.

[7] Rev. Proc. 2012-6, I.R.B. 2012-1, Sec. 8.02 and 9.02.

[8] Rev. Proc. 2011-49, I.R.B. 2011-44, Sec. 20.01 and 20.02, CCH PENSION PLAN GUIDE ¶ 17,299T-69; as modified by Announcement 2012-3, I.R.B. 2012-4, CCH PENSION PLAN GUIDE ¶ 17,097T-65 and Rev. Proc. 2012-6, I.R.B. 2012-1, Sec. 8.01.

¶ 255

OBTAINING QUALIFIED STATUS: Minor Amendments of Previously Approved Plans

Form 6406 has been eliminated. Effective July 9, 2007, Form 6406, Short Form Application for Determination for Minor Amendment of Employee Benefit Plan, may not be used to apply for a determination letter. An application submitted with this form will no longer be accepted by the IRS.[1]

---

[1] Rev. Proc. 2007-44, I.R.B. 2007-28, Sec. 12.04, CCH PENSION PLAN GUIDE ¶ 17,299S-25.

¶ 260

OBTAINING QUALIFIED STATUS: Requests for Minimum Funding Waivers

If a defined contribution plan wishes to obtain a waiver of the minimum funding requirements, one of three alternatives may be used. The plan may request (1) a waiver ruling only (without submitting a plan amendment); (2) a waiver ruling only, with submission of a plan amendment; or (3) a waiver ruling and a determination letter request. The first two alternatives are submitted to EP. Only the combined request for a waiver ruling and a determination letter on the effect of any funding amendment on the qualified status of the plan must be submitted by the taxpayer to Employee Plans Technical (EP Technical). Such a request is treated as a mandatory request for technical advice.[1]

Deadline for filing waiver request

In the case of a single-employer plan, no funding waiver may be granted for any plan year unless an application is submitted to the IRS no later than the 15th day of the third month beginning after the close of that plan year. The IRS may not extend this deadline. A request for waiver with respect to a multiemployer plan generally must be submitted no later than the close of the plan year following the plan year for which the waiver is requested.[2]

---

[1] Rev. Proc. 2012-6, I.R.B. 2012-1, Sec. 15.03 and 15.04, CCH PENSION PLAN GUIDE ¶ 17,299T-86. Note that procedures set forth in Rev. Proc.

2004-15 (I.R.B. 2004-7, at CCH PENSION PLAN GUIDE ¶ 17,299R-15) may also apply. See ¶ 1482. See CCH PENSION PLAN GUIDE ¶ 3120.

[2] Rev. Proc. 2012-6, I.R.B. 2012-1, Sec. 15.06.

¶ 265

OBTAINING QUALIFIED STATUS: Interested Parties' Rights to Notice and Comments

People who qualify as interested parties have the following rights: [1]

1. to receive notice that an application for an advance determination will be filed regarding qualification;

2. to submit written comments with respect to the qualification of these plans to the IRS;

3. to request the Labor Department to submit a comment to the IRS on behalf of the interested parties; and

4. to submit written comments to the IRS on matters with respect to which the Department of Labor was requested to comment but declined.

Comments by interested parties

Interested parties must submit their comments so that they are received by EP Determinations by the 45th day after the day EP Determinations has received the application for determination.[2] Where the Labor Department has been asked to comment, the request must be received by the DOL by the 25th day after the day the application for determination is received by EP Determinations. If the parties requesting the DOL to submit a comment wish to preserve the right to comment to EP Determinations in the event the DOL declines to comment, the request must be received by the DOL by the 15th day after the day the application for determination is received by EP Determinations. [3]

Right to comment if DOL declines to comment

If the Labor Department declines to comment on a plan qualification matter, the parties submitting the request may still submit a comment to EP Determinations. The parties' comments must be received by the later of (1) the 45th day after the day the application for determination is received by EP Determinations or (2) the 15th day after the day on which Labor Department notified the parties that it declines to submit a comment. In no event may the comment be received later than the 60th day after the day the application for determination is received.[4]

---

[1] Rev. Proc. 2012-6, I.R.B. 2012-1, Sec. 17.01, CCH PENSION PLAN GUIDE ¶ 17,299T-86.

[2] Rev. Proc. 2012-6, I.R.B. 2012-1, Sec. 17.02.
[3] Rev. Proc. 2012-6, I.R.B. 2012-1, Sec. 17.03.
[4] Rev. Proc. 2012-6, I.R.B. 2012-1, Sec. 17.04.

¶ 270

OBTAINING QUALIFIED STATUS: Notice Provided to Interested Parties

Notice that an application will be submitted to the IRS for an advance determination regarding plan qualification must be given to all interested parties.[1] Interested parties include (1) all present employees of the employer who are eligible to participate in the plan and (2) all other present employees of the employer who share the same principal place of employment as the present employees of the employer who are eligible to participate in the plan.[2]

Time when notice must be given

Notice must be given not less than 10 days or more than 24 days before the day the application for an advance determination is made.[3]

If an application is returned to the applicant for failure to adequately satisfy the notification rules for a particular group or class of interested parties, the applicant does not need to issue another notice to those groups or classes of interested parties who were properly notified.[4]

Content of notice

Information that must be provided in the notice includes: a brief description of the class or classes of interested parties to whom the notice is addressed; the name of the plan, the plan identification number, and the name of the plan administrator; the name and taxpayer identification number of the applicant; a description of the class of employees eligible to participate in the plan; and a statement informing the person to whom the notice is addressed of the right to submit comments to the IRS on the qualification issue.[5]

The notice must also indicate whether or not the IRS has issued a previous determination as to the qualified status of the plan; inform the party that an application for qualified status is being made to the IRS; and reveal whether the application relates to an initial qualification, plan amendment, termination or partial termination.

Additional information available

Unless provided in the notice, the following information must be made available to interested parties:[6]

1. an updated copy of the plan and the related trust agreement (if any); and

2. the application for determination.

Special rules apply if there are less than 26 participants.

☐ A Sample Notice is provided at CCH PENSION PLAN GUIDE ¶ 540.

Electronic notification permitted

Notice may be provided electronically or by any other method that is reasonably calculated to ensure that each interested party is notified of the application for determination.[7]

---

[1] Rev. Proc. 2012-6, I.R.B. 2012-1, Sec. 18.01, CCH PENSION PLAN GUIDE ¶ 17,299T-86.

[2] IRS Reg. § 1.7476-1(b)(1).

[3] Rev. Proc. 2012-6, I.R.B. 2012-1, Sec. 18.02.

[4] *Ibid.*

[5] Rev. Proc. 2012-6, I.R.B. 2012-1, Sec. 18.03.

[6] Rev. Proc. 2012-6, I.R.B. 2012-1, Sec. 18.05.

[7] IRS Reg. § 1.7476-2(c)(1).

¶ 275

OBTAINING QUALIFIED STATUS: Processing Determination Letter Requests

How does the IRS process determination letter requests?

Oral advice

The IRS does not issue determination letters on oral requests. However, personnel in EP Determinations ordinarily will discuss with taxpayers or their representatives inquiries regarding: substantive tax issues, whether the IRS will issue a determination letter on particular issues, and questions relating to procedural matters about submitting determination letter requests. [1]

Any discussion of substantive issues is done at the IRS's discretion and on a time-available basis, is not binding on the IRS, and cannot be relied upon as a basis for obtaining retroactive relief.

Conferences

EP Determinations may grant a conference upon written request from a taxpayer or his or her representative, if the request shows that a substantive plan, amendment, etc., has been developed for submission to the IRS, and that special problems or issues are involved.[2]

Determination based solely on administrative record

In the case of a request for a determination letter, the determination of EP Determinations or the Appeals Office on the qualification or nonqualification of a retirement plan is based solely upon the facts contained in the administrative record.[3] The administrative record consists of such items as the determination request, the retirement plan and any related trust instruments, and any written modifications or amendments made by the applicant during the proceedings with the IRS, all other documents submitted to the IRS by the applicant with regard to the determination request, and written comments and correspondence between the IRS and the applicant.

Any oral representation or modification of the facts as represented or alleged in the determination application or in a comment filed by an interested party, which is *not* reduced to writing will *not* become a part of the administrative record and will *not* be taken into account in the determination of the qualified status of the retirement plan by EP Determinations or the Appeals Office. [4]

Notice of final determination

A notice of final determination is the letter issued by EP Determinations or the Appeals Office stating that the applicant's plan does or does not satisfy the Code's qualification requirements. [5]

EP Determinations or the Appeals office will send the notice of final determination to the applicant, to the interested parties who have previously submitted comments on the application to the IRS (or to the persons designated by them to receive the notice), to the Department of Labor in the case of a comment submitted by the Department, and to the PBGC if it has filed a comment. [6]

---

[1] Rev. Proc. 2012-6, I.R.B. 2012-1, Sec. 19.01, CCH PENSION PLAN GUIDE ¶ 17,299T-86.

[2] Rev. Proc. 2012-6, I.R.B. 2012-1, Sec. 19.02.

[3] Rev. Proc. 2012-6, I.R.B. 2012-1, Sec. 19.03.
[4] *Ibid.*
[5] Rev. Proc. 2012-6, I.R.B. 2012-1, Sec. 19.04.
[6] Rev. Proc. 2012-6, I.R.B. 2012-1, Sec. 19.05.

¶ 280

OBTAINING QUALIFIED STATUS: Exhaustion of Administrative Remedies

Applicants, interested parties, and the PBGC need to exhaust their administrative remedies before seeking a declaratory judgment from the Tax Court as to the initial or continuing qualified status of a plan. [1] Administrative remedies are considered to have been exhausted if the steps outlined below are completed.

Applicants

For applicants, the steps for exhausting administrative remedies include: [2]

1. filing a completed application with EP Determinations;

2. complying with the requirements pertaining to notice to interested parties; and,

3. appealing to the Appeals Office, in the event a notice of proposed adverse determination is issued by EP Determinations.

Interested parties and PBGC

For interested parties or the PBGC, the steps needed to exhaust required administrative remedies with respect to a matter relating to qualification include:[3]

1. submitting to EP Determinations a comment raising the matter, or

2. requesting the Labor Department to submit to EP Determinations a comment with respect to the matter and, if the Labor Department declines to comment, submitting the comment, so that it may be considered by the IRS through the administrative process.

In any event, an applicant, an interested party, or the PBGC will not be deemed to have exhausted administrative remedies prior to the earlier of: (1) the completion of the steps described above, or (2) the expiration of the 270-day period described in Code Sec. 7476(b)(3), which can be extended in certain circumstances.

IRS must act on appeal

The exhaustion of administrative remedies will not be considered complete until the IRS has had a reasonable time to act on the appeal.[4]

---

[1] Rev. Proc. 2012-6, I.R.B. 2012-1, Sec. 20.01, CCH PENSION PLAN GUIDE ¶ 17,299T-86.

[2] Rev. Proc. 2012-6, I.R.B. 2012-1, Sec. 20.02.

[3] Rev. Proc. 2012-6, I.R.B. 2012-1, Sec. 20.04.

[4] Rev. Proc. 2012-6, I.R.B. 2012-1, Sec. 20.06.

¶ 285

OBTAINING QUALIFIED STATUS: Effect of Determination Letters

A determination letter contains only the IRS's opinion as to a plan's qualification under Code Secs. 401 and 403(a) and the status of a related trust, if any, under Code Sec. 501(a). A determination letter is based on the facts presented to the IRS in connection with the application for the determination letter and may not be relied upon after a change in material fact or the effective date of a change in law, except as provided by the IRS.

An applicant's failure to disclose a material fact or misrepresentation of a material fact may adversely affect the reliance which would otherwise be obtained through the issuance by the IRS of a favorable determination letter. Similarly, a failure to accurately provide any of the information called for on any required form may result in no reliance.[1]

---

[1] Rev. Proc. 2012-6, I.R.B. 2012-1, Sec. 21.01, CCH PENSION PLAN GUIDE ¶ 17,299T-86.

¶ 287

OBTAINING QUALIFIED STATUS: User Fees

The IRS has authority to require the payment of user fees for requests for rulings, opinion letters, determination letters, and other similar requests.[1]

The fees charged under the program vary according to categories (or subcategories) established by the IRS. They are to be determined after taking into account the average time for, and difficulty of, complying with requests in each category and subcategory.[2] Fees must be paid in advance.

Scope of user fees

With certain exceptions, user fees apply to all requests for letter rulings, opinion letters, notification letters, determination letters, and advisory letters submitted by or on behalf of taxpayers, sponsoring organizations, or other entities.[3]

Nonpayment or payment of incorrect amount

IRS offices responsible for issuing a ruling or letter may exercise discretion in deciding whether to immediately return submissions that are not accompanied by a properly completed check or money order or that are accompanied by a check or money order for less than the correct amount.[4] The return of a submission to the requester may adversely affect substantive rights if the submission is not perfected and resubmitted to the IRS within 30 days of the date of the cover letter returning the submission.

Overpayment

If a check or money order is for more than the correct amount, the submission will be accepted, and the amount of the excess payment will be returned to the requester.[5]

Refunds

In general, a user fee will not be refunded unless the IRS declines to rule on all issues for which a ruling is requested. [6]

☐ A complete user fee schedule is at CCH PENSION PLAN GUIDE ¶ 570.

☐ A list of applicable IRS mailing addresses is at CCH PENSION PLAN GUIDE ¶ 575.

Relief for small employer plans

IRS user fees have been eliminated for determination letter requests by eligible small employer plans.[7] An eligible small employer is not required to pay a user fee for any determination letter request with respect to the qualified status of a pension benefit plan that the employer maintains if the request is made before the later of (1) the fifth year that the plan is in existence, or (2) the end of any remedial amendment period beginning within the first five years of the plan. User fees are not eliminated for any opinion or advisory letter request made by a sponsor of a master, prototype, or volume submitter plan that the plan sponsor intends to market to participating employers.[8]

For purposes of this provision, an eligible employer is defined as an employer which had no more than 100 employees who received at least $5,000 in compensation from the employer for the preceding year. In addition, the employer must have at least one employee who is not a highly compensated employee (as defined in Code Sec. 414(q) and is participating in the plan. The determination of eligible employer status is made as of the date of the determination letter request.

Recent guidance simplifies process for establishing exemption. To simplify this user fee exemption analysis, the IRS states that it will treat a plan's application as having been filed by the last day of the plan's remedial amendment period beginning within the five plan years if both of the following conditions are met:[9]

☐ the application is filed with the IRS by the last day of the submission period for the plan's current remedial amendment cycle, and

☐ the plan first came into existence no earlier than January 1 of the tenth calendar year immediately preceding the year in which the submission period for the plan's current remedial amendment cycle begins.

The IRS notes that there may be situations where an application that is filed by the last day of a plan's remedial amendment period beginning within the first five plan years would not be treated as such under the above conditions because the remedial amendment period ends on the last day of a submission period that begins more than ten years after the year in which the plan first came into existence. The IRS states that, in these cases, where the other requirements for the user fee

¶287

exemption are met, the applicant should not include a user fee payment with the application, but should explain in a cover letter how the application meets the exemption requirements. If the IRS determines that the application is not exempt, the applicant will be asked to pay the user fee.

[1] Code Sec. 7528, as added by P.L. 108-89 (which extended the Temporary Assistance for Needy Families Block Grant Program) and was made permanent by P.L. 110-28 (U.S. Troop Readiness, Veterans' Care, Katrina Recovery, and Iraq Accountability Appropriations Act of 2007), Act Sec. 8244.

[2] Rev. Proc. 2012-8, I.R.B. 2012-1, Sec. 3, CCH PENSION PLAN GUIDE ¶ 17,299T-88.

[3] Rev. Proc. 2012-8, I.R.B. 2012-1, Sec. 4.01.

[4] Rev. Proc. 2012-8, I.R.B. 2012-1, Sec. 9.03.

[5] *Ibid.*

[6] Rev. Proc. 2012-8, I.R.B. 2012-1, Sec. 10.01.

[7]P.L. 107-16 (Economic Growth and Tax Relief Reconciliation Act of 2001), Sec. 620. NOTE: This provision was subject to sunset after 2010. P.L. 108-89 repealed EGTRRA Sec. 620, but retained the user fee exception applicable to eligible small employers. The fact that P.L. 108-89 repealed Act Sec. 620, but retained the small employer exception, effectively negated the impact of EGTRRA's sunset provision on the small employer exception. Thus, under Code Sec. 7528, the small employer exception will not expire after 2010. See also IRS Notice 2002-1, I.R.B. 2001-53, CCH PENSION PLAN GUIDE ¶ 17,122W and IRS Notice 2003-49, I.R.B. 2003-32, CCH PENSION PLAN GUIDE ¶ 17,126V.

[8]Under P.L. 108-89, after 2004, user fee relief will be provided for sponsors of prototype plans that are not covered by the small employer user fee exemption.

[9] IRS Notice 2011-86, I.R.B. 2011-45, CCH PENSION PLAN GUIDE ¶ 17,148G.

¶ 290

OBTAINING QUALIFIED STATUS: Defect Resolution Programs

As a general matter, a failure to meet the qualification rules results in plan disqualification. The economic impact of noncompliance can be very harsh. The IRS, however, has several programs, which can be termed "defect resolution programs" or "administrative enforcement programs," to resolve plan defects without resorting to plan disqualification. These programs are embodied in the IRS's Employee Plans Compliance Resolution System (EPCRS).

Although plans are not disqualified under the programs, defects must be corrected retroactively and prospectively. Each program has its own eligibility criteria and imposes different requirements on the plan sponsor as a condition of maintaining qualification.

☐ The various defect resolution programs are described in greater detail beginning at ¶ 360.

¶ 295

OBTAINING QUALIFIED STATUS: Maintaining Participant Accounts

Once developed, most pension and profit-sharing plans require that the company or employer-union group sponsoring a plan set up and maintain detailed basic records for each plan member. Careful recordkeeping is necessary to comply with the many requirements imposed by federal law. These records serve to establish participants' service, contributions, vesting, etc., so that payments in the right amount may be made to plan members when they become eligible for benefits. The records also serve as the basic information source for periodic actuarial valuations of a pension plan, as a means of controlling disbursements from pension and profit-sharing funds, as factual materials relevant to estimating the effects of plan changes, and as the source from which summary reports to plan members may be made from time to time on an individual basis.

Reporting and disclosure calendar

An adequate system for filing reports with the government or making required disclosures to participants should incorporate a comprehensive reporting and disclosure calendar. Such a calendar is provided at ¶ 50.

¶ 299
For More Information

☐ For more information on the advantages of plan qualification, see ¶ 801— ¶ 827 of the CCH PENSION PLAN GUIDE. For more information on obtaining qualified status, see ¶ 458—¶ 615 and ¶ 841—¶ 854 of the CCH PENSION PLAN GUIDE.

Basic Plan Qualification Rules

¶ 300

Overview of Qualification Rules

Pension, profit-sharing, stock bonus, and annuity plans that attain qualified status can provide major tax advantages to employers and employees. Employer contributions to a qualified plan are deductible; employees are not currently taxed on amounts contributed on their behalf; and plan earnings are not taxed (see ¶ 205—¶ 220). Before these tax benefits can be realized, however, plans must comply with a myriad of complex and detailed rules. Basically, a plan must be a definite written program that is designed to be permanent and that is maintained for the exclusive benefit of employees and their beneficiaries.

IRS administrative enforcement

The IRS operates a series of administrative enforcement and voluntary compliance programs that allow a plan sponsor to maintain qualified status for a year in which form or operational plan defects occurred. Sanctions may be imposed and each program requires retroactive correction of the plan defects. In all cases where it is necessary, prospective plan amendments curing plan failures should be adopted.

¶ 303

QUALIFICATION RULES: General Qualification Requirements

Pension, profit-sharing, stock bonus, and annuity plans must meet a formidable array of requirements stipulated by the Internal Revenue Code in order to attain qualified status.[1] The qualification requirements highlighted in the following checklist generally apply to all types of plans.

☐ The plan must be a definite written program setting forth all provisions essential for qualification (see ¶ 306). If the plan utilizes a trust, there must be a written trust instrument (see ¶ 309).

☐ The plan must be communicated to employees (¶ 306).

☐ The plan must be established by an employer (see ¶ 315).

☐ Contributions must be made by the employer, the employees, or both (see ¶ 318).

☐ The plan must be permanent (see ¶ 348).

☐ The plan must be for the exclusive benefit of employees or their beneficiaries (see ¶ 321 and ¶ 324).

☐ Prior to the satisfaction of all liabilities with regard to employees and beneficiaries, it must be impossible under the plan, for any part of the plan's assets to be used for, or diverted to, purposes other than for the exclusive benefit of the employees or their beneficiaries (see ¶ 327).

☐ Contributions or benefits provided under the plan must not discriminate in favor of highly compensated employees (see ¶ 1100 and following).

☐ The plan must satisfy minimum vesting standards (see ¶ 800 and following).

☐ The plan must satisfy minimum participation (¶ 700 and following) and coverage requirements (see ¶ 1000 and following).

☐ A defined benefit plan, money purchase plan, and, in some cases, a profit-sharing plan, must provide automatic survivor benefits in the form of a qualified joint and survivor annuity and a qualified preretirement survivor annuity (see ¶ 1700 and following).

☐ The plan must not provide contributions and benefits for individual employees that exceed certain limitations (see ¶ 500 and following).

☐ The plan may not require employees to forfeit any part of an accrued benefit derived from employer contributions (that is at least 50% vested) solely because of their withdrawal of any part of the benefits derived from their own contributions (see ¶ 896).

☐ The plan must provide that, unless the participant elects otherwise, payment of benefits must begin no later than 60 days after the close of the plan year in which the latest occurs: (a) the participant attains the earlier of age 65 or normal retirement age under the plan, (b) the tenth anniversary of the time when the participant began participation in the plan, or (c) the participant terminates his service with the employer (see ¶ 1800).

☐ The plan must provide that a participant's benefits will not be reduced because of changes in the Social Security benefit level or wage base that occur after the earlier of receipt of benefits or separation from service with vested benefits (see ¶ 866).

☐ The plan must provide before- and after-death required distribution rules (see ¶ 1800 and following).

☐ The plan must provide that, in the event of termination or partial termination of the plan, the rights of all participants to benefits accrued to the date of termination or partial termination, to the extent funded, will vest (see ¶ 2804).

☐ The plan must provide that immediately following any merger or consolidation of plans, or any transfer of assets or liabilities from one plan to another, each participant is entitled to receive a benefit that is not less than the value of the benefit he or she would have been entitled to receive immediately before the transaction (see ¶ 2861).

☐ The plan must provide that benefits under the plan may not be assigned or alienated (see ¶ 1500 and following).

☐ Qualified plans and tax-sheltered annuities must provide recipients with the option of having eligible rollover distributions paid in a direct rollover to an eligible retirement plan (see ¶ 1970).

☐ A defined benefit plan that determines the amount of any benefit on the basis of actuarial assumptions must specify the assumptions in the plan in a way that precludes employer discretion (see ¶ 1400).

☐ A qualified pension plan must provide for the payment of definitely determinable benefits to employees over a period of years, usually for life, after retirement. Benefits and contributions under the plan are not based on profits (see ¶ 106).

☐ A defined benefit plan may not allocate forfeitures among remaining participants to increase their benefits (see ¶ 106).

☐ A plan must provide that only the includible amount of an employee's compensation may be taken into account in determining contributions or benefits under the plan (see ¶ 545).

¶303

☐ A defined benefit plan must benefit no fewer than the lesser of (1) 50 employees, or (2) the greater of (a) 40% or all of the employer's employees, or (b) two employees (or one employee, if the employer has only one employee) (see ¶ 1182).

☐ An employee stock ownership plan (ESOP) must provide an annual diversification election period for qualified participants for the 90-day period following the close of the ESOP plan year (see ¶ 3086). In addition, any valuation of employer securities contributed to or purchased by an ESOP must be determined by an independent appraiser.

☐ A stock bonus plan must meet requirements regarding the right to demand employer securities under Code Sec. 409(h) and distribution and payment rules under Code Sec. 409(o) (see ¶ 3065 and ¶ 3075).

☐ A plan which is intended to be a money purchase pension plan or a profit-sharing plan must designate its intention at such time and in such manner as is prescribed by the IRS (see ¶ 109 and ¶ 117).

☐ A 401(k) plan, under which elective deferrals may be made for any individual during a calendar year, must restrict deferrals under the plan and all other plans, contracts, or arrangements of the employer maintaining the plan to the limitation on elective deferrals for taxable years beginning in such calendar year (see ¶ 2981).

---

[1] Code Sec. 401(a) and (d); ERISA Sec. 503; ERISA Reg. § 2560.503-1.

¶ 306

QUALIFICATION RULES: Plan Must Be Written

A qualified plan must be a definite written program setting forth all provisions essential for qualification.[1]

A written plan does not exist where only tentative and abstract agreements concerning eligibility, participation, vesting standards, percentage contribution formula, and benefit-triggering event rules are contained in a group of written memoranda and notes. Accordingly, a plan that provides eligibility for some employees upon satisfaction of alternate eligibility requirements "approved by the trustees" will fail to qualify as a definite written program.[2]

Plan assets must also be held pursuant to a written trust instrument (see ¶ 309). However, the plan is not necessarily coexistent with the trust instrument. Although it is possible for the trust instrument to embody all the provisions of the plan, in practice, the plan and the trust instrument are usually separate documents. Similarly, all the terms of an annuity plan may be embodied in the terms of a group annuity contract, but the plan may also be a document separate from the contract.

CCH Pointer: An employer must follow the written terms of the plan document, even if its actions (which may not be provided for in the plan) are in compliance with the Code. Thus, violations of the governing plan document or adoption agreement will raise a qualification issue, even if the requirements of the Code are not breached. If an employer's procedures are proper, however, it may be able to amend the plan to reflect its practices. See ¶ 360 and following.

Communication of plan to employees

Employees must be notified of the establishment of the plan and informed of its salient features.[3] A plan will not be qualified until it is communicated to employees, even if it has been reduced to writing and approved by the employer in an earlier year.[4]

For purposes of qualification, the plan need be communicated only to those employees who are or could become participants in the plan. Thus, a plan restricted to "salaried only" employees does not fail to qualify merely because hourly paid employees are not notified of the plan's adoption and its salient provisions.[5]

ERISA requirements. ERISA further requires plan administrators to furnish each plan participant with a summary description of the plan and a summary of the annual report filed with the Secretary of Labor (see ¶ 2220).[6]

Other ERISA requirements

ERISA requires as a matter of substantive law, and not only as a condition to qualification for favorable tax treatment, that every plan must meet the following requirements:[7]

1. Provide a procedure for establishing and carrying out a funding policy and method that are consistent with the objectives of the plan and the requirements of Title I of ERISA (relating to protection of employee benefit rights).

2. Describe any plan procedure for the allocation of responsibilities for the operation and administration of the plan, including delegation of responsibility for asset management to an investment manager.

3. Provide a procedure for amending the plan and identify the persons who have authority to amend the plan.

4. Specify the basis on which payments are to be made to and from the plan.

---

[1] IRS Reg. § 1.401-1(a)(2); ERISA Sec. 402.

[2] Rev. Rul. 74-466, 1974-2 CB 131, CCH Pension Plan Guide ¶ 19,357.

[3] IRS Reg. § 1.401-1(a)(2).

[4] Rev. Rul. 72-509, 1972-2 CB 221, CCH Pension Plan Guide ¶ 19,187.

[5] Rev. Rul. 73-78, 1973-1 CB 190, CCH Pension Plan Guide ¶ 19,214.

[6] ERISA Secs. 102 and 104(b).

[7] ERISA Sec. 402(b).

¶ 309

QUALIFICATION RULES: Trust Qualification Requirements

The assets of qualified pension, profit-sharing, and stock bonus plans generally must be held in a written trust. Among other things, the trust must be:

1. created and organized in the United States (i.e., a domestic trust) and maintained at all times as a domestic trust;[1]

2. valid under local law; and

3. formed or used only for the purpose of distributing to the employees or their beneficiaries the corpus and income of the fund accumulated by it in accordance with the plan.

CCH Pointer: Trusts that are part of qualified plans, IRAs (including Roth IRAs and deemed IRAs), and governmental 457(b) plans may pool their assets in a group trust without affecting the exempt status of separate trusts, provided the group trust is organized and maintained at all times as a domestic trust.[2]

Exclusive benefit rule

A qualified plan must be maintained for the exclusive benefit of participating employees or their beneficiaries (see ¶ 321). Thus, it must be impossible under the trust instrument, at any time prior to the satisfaction of all liabilities, with respect to employees and their beneficiaries under the trust, for any part of the principal or income of the trust to be used for, or diverted to, purposes other than for the exclusive benefit of the employees or their beneficiaries. The instrument evidencing the trust agreement must be in writing and contain sufficient words to make the prohibited diversion impossible.[3]

Custodial accounts and annuity contracts

Custodial accounts, annuity contracts, and insurance contracts may be treated as trusts.[4] Funds in the custodial account must be held by a bank or by another entity that can demonstrate to the IRS that the manner in which the funds will be held will be consistent with qualification requirements of the Code. The custodian of the custodial account of a qualified plan may be an entity other than a bank. The nonbank custodian must meet net worth requirements and satisfy rules regarding the proper exercise of fiduciary powers.[5]

A qualified annuity plan need not maintain a trust because contributions are made directly to an insurance company in the form of premiums. The annuity contract or insurance contract must be issued by an insurance company qualified to do business in a state and must not provide life, health or accident, property, casualty, or liability insurance.[6]

---

[1] Code Sec. 401(a)(1), (2), and (24); IRS Reg. §§ 1.401-1, 1.401-2, 1.401(a)-2, 1.401(f)-1.

[2] Rev. Rul. 2004-67, I.R.B. 2004-28, 7-12-04, CCH PENSION PLAN GUIDE ¶ 19,948Z-77.

[3] Rev. Rul. 69-231, 1969-1 CB 118, CCH PENSION PLAN GUIDE ¶ 18,723.

[4] Code Sec. 401(f).

[5] IRS Reg. § 1.408-2(e)(2)- 1.408-2(e)(6).

[6] Code Sec. 401(f).

¶ 312

QUALIFICATION RULES: Tax Advantages Require Plan to Be in Effect

In order for the various tax advantages stemming from qualified status to apply in a tax year, the plan must be in effect in that year. Generally, a plan is in effect when all requirements for qualification have been met. A newly established plan, however, will be considered to have met all qualification requirements in the taxable year in which the plan otherwise took effect if the requirements are met within the period for the filing of the employer's tax return for that year (including extensions).[1]

Existence of trust

The issue of whether or not a plan was in effect during a tax year often revolves around whether the trust that was intended to be part of the plan was in effect. The IRS has long taken the position that for a trust to be in effect it must be a valid and existing trust under local law. Accordingly, the arrangement must have a grantor, a trustee, beneficiaries, a trust corpus, and must satisfy other conditions required in a particular jurisdiction.

CCH Pointer: Because an annuity plan is funded by contracts issued by an insurance company, these arrangements need not have a trustee.

Employer contributions to trust

A valid and existing trust generally requires a trust corpus. Therefore, a trust does not exist until contributions are made. However, an employer is not required to make a contribution for any tax year until the time prescribed for filing its return, including extensions. Thus, despite the lack of a trust corpus, the trust will be deemed to have been in existence if it is valid in all other respects under local law and if a contribution is made by the employer within the time prescribed by law for filing the employer's income tax return.[2]

Trust may not be established by oral agreement

Although an oral agreement is sufficient for the establishment of a trust in most jurisdictions, the IRS requires a written trust instrument. The IRS will not consider the trust to be in effect for any taxable year in which an instrument is lacking.[3]

---

[1] Code Sec. 401(b); IRS Reg. § 1.401(b)-1.

[2] Rev. Rul. 81-114, 1981-1 CB 207, CCH Pension Plan Guide ¶ 19,576.

[3] Rev. Rul. 69-231, 1969-1 CB 118, CCH Pension Plan Guide ¶ 18,723.

¶ 315

QUALIFICATION RULES: Establishment of Plan by Employer

A qualified plan must be established by an "employer." [1] A plan established by a person other than an employer will not be qualified, and, therefore, contributions made to the arrangement will not be deductible as contributions to a qualified plan.[2]

The term "employer" encompasses self-employed individuals and partnerships.

Employee-only contributing plans

A plan may require contributions by employees only. The plan must be *established* by the employer, however.[3]

Multiple-employer plans

A plan need not be sponsored by a single employer. Industry-wide or area-wide plans in which a number of employers participate may be qualified.[4] However, the failure by a single employer to satisfy an applicable qualification requirement may disqualify all of the employers participating in a collectively bargained plan or a plan maintained by more than one employer.[5]

[1] Code Sec. 401(a).

[2] Rev. Rul. 66-59, 1966-1 CB 142, CCH PENSION PLAN GUIDE ¶ 18501; Rev. Rul. 68-422, 1968-2 CB 207, CCH PENSION PLAN GUIDE ¶ 18661.

[3] Code Sec. 401(a); IRS Reg. § 1.401-1(a)(2).

[4] IRS Reg. § 1.401-1(d).

[5] IRS Reg. §§ 1.413-1(a)(3)(ii) and 1.413-2(a)(3)(ii).

¶ 316

QUALIFICATION RULES: Plan Amendments

Generally, ERISA requires a plan to contain a specific procedure for describing how the plan and trust, if any, can be amended after its initial establishment.[1] The Supreme Court has ruled that ERISA permits the use of a standard reservation of rights clause, such as "the Company reserves the right at any time to amend the plan." [2] The plan also must identify who has authority to make amendments.[3]

Amendment procedures must be followed

Only a formal written amendment will amend the plan. An employer cannot amend a plan merely by providing notice to beneficiaries that coverage under the plan has changed. Such notice is not an adequate substitute for use of the plan's amendment procedure.[4]

Plan amendments or provisions causing disqualification

If a plan amendment causes a plan to become disqualified, the plan will be able to maintain its qualified status if the disqualifying features are removed from the plan within the "remedial amendment period."

A remedial amendment period begins, in the case of a new plan, as of the date the plan is put into effect. For an existing plan, the remedial amendment period begins on the date the provision is adopted or put into effect, whichever is earlier.[5] The remedial amendment period ends on the due date of the employer's income tax return, including extensions, for the tax year in which the plan or amendment was adopted. An employer, however, may extend the deadline by filing a request with the IRS for approval of the amendment in a determination letter (see below).

Thus, a curative amendment must be made within the remedial amendment period, and, in all cases, it must be made retroactive to the time when the plan was put into effect (in the case of a new plan) or to the earlier of the time when the amendment was adopted or put into effect (in the case of an amended plan).[6]

Determination letter request extends remedial amendment period

The IRS is empowered to give employers additional time in which to adopt curative amendments in appropriate cases. For example, in situations where the employer files a request for a determination letter as to the initial qualification of the plan or as to the effect of a disqualifying provision of the plan before the time to cure the plan by amendment has expired (without regard to extensions), then the period during which the plan may be cured is automatically extended up to 91 days *after* either: (1) the IRS issues a favorable determination letter, (2) the determination letter application is withdrawn, (3) the IRS otherwise disposes of the case (*e.g.,* an adverse determination), or (4) the U.S. Tax Court issues a final determination based on a timely filed declaratory judgment petition.[7]

> **CCH Pointer:** By extending the close of the remedial amendment period, the determination letter application provides the IRS and the plan sponsor with an opportunity to resolve disputes over plan language and provides the plan sponsor with time to adopt amendments in final form based on discussions with the IRS.

"Disqualifying" defects arising from changes in qualification requirements

The remedial amendment period rules also apply to "disqualifying" defects that typically arise when a plan has not been amended to comply with changes in the qualification requirements. Thus, a plan that fails to satisfy the qualification requirements of the Code solely as a result of a "disqualifying" defect may retain qualified status by being amended to comply with the qualification amendment by the last day of the applicable remedial amendment period. The amendment must be made retroactively effective to the beginning of the remedial amendment period.[8]

The remedial amendment period applicable to a disqualifying provision generally begins with the date on which the change becomes effective, or, if the provision is integral to a qualification requirement that has been changed, the first day on which the plan was operated in accord with the provision as amended.[9]

The remedial amendment period ends with the later of (1) the date, including extensions, by which the employer must file its income tax return for the tax year that includes the date on which the remedial amendment period begins, or (2) the last day of the plan year that includes the date on which the remedial amendment period begins.

Discretionary extensions of remedial amendment period

At its discretion, the IRS may extend the remedial amendment period, allow a particular plan to be amended after the remedial amendment period, and extend an extension of the remedial amendment period.[10]

Staggered remedial amendment periods

In order to provide a more even workflow for both IRS and practitioners, the IRS developed a new approach for applications for favorable determination, advisory, and opinion letters to comply with the submission dates for remedial amendment periods. Overall, the submission dates for pre-approved plans generally follow a six-year cycle. The submission dates for individually-designed plans (IDPs) generally follow a five-year cycle. The new system, which began February 1, 2006 and was later updated, is intended to limit the number of determination letter applications any one plan would need to submit.[11]

Individually-designed plans. Individually-designed plans have a regular five-year amendment cycle, beginning February 1, 2006. The cycles are staggered, so that the cycles of different plans commence in different years. The applicable cycle is generally determined by the tax identification number of the plan sponsor. The system is designed to allow plan sponsors of individually-designed plans to adopt remedial amendments of disqualifying provisions, and apply for new determination letters, only once every five years.

Pre-approved plans. Similarly, pre-approved plans (master and prototype and volume submitter plans) have a regular six-year remedial amendment cycle. The intended effect is that plan sponsors and adopters of pre-approved plans will generally need to apply for a new opinion letter, advisory letter or determination letter only once every six years.

There are two separate six-year cycles for pre-approved plans: one for defined benefit plans and one for defined contribution plans.

The rules have been clarified on when an employer is entitled to remain in the six-year remedial amendment cycle (six-year cycle) after adopting an individually designed plan and making certain types of amendments.[12]

Cumulative list. The IRS intends to publish each November an annual Cumulative List of Changes in Plan Qualification Requirements, in order to identify all changes in qualification requirements that are required to be reflected in the written plan document, due to changes in laws, regulations and IRS guidance. Except as otherwise provided on the applicable cumulative list, the IRS will not consider guidance or statutes issued or enacted after the October 1st preceding the date the applicable cumulative list is issued, qualification requirements that become effective in a calendar year following the calendar year in which the submission period begins with respect to the applicable cumulative list, or statutes that are first effective in the year in which the submission period begins with respect to the applicable cumulative list, for which there is no guidance specified on the cumulative list.[13]

¶316

Retroactive effect of amendments under Pension Protection Act of 2006

A plan amendment made pursuant to the changes made by the Pension Protection Act of 2006 (or regulations issued under the PPA) may be retroactively effective without violating the anti-cutback rule, if, in addition to meeting the other applicable requirements, the amendment is made on or before the last day of the first plan year beginning on or after January 1, 2009 (or, in the case of a governmental plan, on or before the last day of the first plan year beginning on or after January 1, 2011).[14]

☐ The remedial amendment periods applicable to qualified plans are detailed at CCH PENSION PLAN GUIDE ¶ 869 and ¶ 1833.

---

[1] ERISA Sec. 402(b)(3).

[2] *Curtiss-Wright Corporation v. Schoonejongen*, US Sup Ct (1995), 514 U.S. 73.

[3] ERISA Sec. 402(b)(3).

[4] *Kuehnen v. International Brotherhood of Electrical Workers, Local Union 400 Welfare Fund*, CA-3 (1994), No. 94-5084 (not designated for publication).

[5] IRS Reg. § 1.401(b)-1(d).

[6] IRS Reg. § 1.401(b)-1(a).

[7] IRS Reg. § 1.401(b)-1(e)(3).

[8] IRS Reg. § 1.401(b)-1(b).

[9] IRS Reg. § 1.401(b)-1(d).

[10] IRS Reg. § 1.401(b)-1(f).

[11]Rev. Proc. 2009-36 , I.R.B. 2009-36, CCH PENSION PLAN GUIDE ¶ 17,299T-13, which amended Rev. Proc. 2008-56, I.R.B. 2008-40, CCH PENSION PLAN GUIDE ¶ 17,299S-70 and Rev. Proc. 2007-44, I.R.B. 2007-28, CCH PENSION PLAN GUIDE ¶ 17,299S-25, which modified and superseded Rev. Proc. 2005-66, I.R.B. 2005-37, CCH PENSION PLAN GUIDE ¶ 17,299R-69.

[12]Rev. Proc. 2009-36, I.R.B. 2009-36, CCH PENSION PLAN GUIDE ¶ 17,299T-13, which amended Rev. Proc. 2008-56, I.R.B. 2008-40, CCH PENSION PLAN GUIDE ¶ 17,299S-70 and Rev. Proc. 2007-44, I.R.B. 2007-28, CCH PENSION PLAN GUIDE ¶ 17,299S-25Rev. Proc. 2007-44.

[13]Rev. Proc. 2009-36, I.R.B. 2009-36, CCH PENSION PLAN GUIDE ¶ 17,299T-13, which amended Rev. Proc. 2008-56, I.R.B. 2008-40, CCH PENSION PLAN GUIDE ¶ 17,299S-70 and Rev. Proc. 2007-44, I.R.B. 2007-28, CCH PENSION PLAN GUIDE ¶ 17,299S-25Rev. Proc. 2007-44.

[14]Pension Protection Act of 2006 (P.L. 109-280), Act Sec. 1107. The "anti-cutback" rule bars the reduction of a participant's accrued benefit by a plan amendment. See Code Sec. 411(d)(6)(A)and ERISA Sec. 204(g)(1).

¶ 318

QUALIFICATION RULES: Employer or Employee Contributions

In order for a plan or trust to qualify, contributions must be made by (1) the employer, (2) the employees, or (3) both.[1] It is not necessary that both employers and employees contribute to the plan. Many plans do not require employee contributions. In addition, the IRS has ruled that it is not necessary for an employer to contribute currently to a plan.[2]

---

[1] Code Sec. 401(a)(1).

[2] Rev. Rul. 80-306, 1980-2 CB 131, CCH PENSION PLAN GUIDE ¶ 19,545, superseding Rev. Rul. 66-205, 1966-2 CB 119 and Rev. Rul. 54-152, 1954-1 CB 149.

¶ 321

QUALIFICATION RULES: Plan for Exclusive Benefit of Employees

A qualified plan must be maintained for the *exclusive* benefit of *employees* and their beneficiaries.[1] The exclusive benefit rule, however, does not require a qualified plan to cover all employees.[2] Certain employees or groups of employees may be excluded so long as the result is not to favor officers, shareholders, or the highly compensated.

Plan must benefit employees. A corporation cannot maintain a qualified trust or plan at a time when it does not have any employees, active or retired, who are covered by the plan. In addition, the plan of a corporation, once qualified, will not continue to qualify once the corporation ceases to have any employees, active or retired, who are participants under the plan.[3]

A plan covering a single employee may qualify.[4] Plans covering non-employees, however, do not qualify.[5]

CCH Pointer: *Exclusive benefit rule does not bar participation in plan by working owner.* The exclusive benefit rule does not bar participation in a tax-qualified plan by working owners (e.g. sole shareholders). Sole proprietors, for example, may establish tax-favored Keogh plans or one-participant 401(k) plans. Similarly, ERISA's anti-inurement rule does not prevent a working owner from participating in a qualified employee benefit plan. A working owner may participate in a qualified ERISA plan, as long as the plan covers one or more employee other than the business owner and his or her spouse.[6]

U. S. citizens employed by foreign subsidiaries

United States citizens who are employed by foreign subsidiaries of domestic corporations are considered employees of the domestic parent companies for retirement plan purposes and are permitted to participate in qualified pension, profit-sharing, annuity, stock bonus, and bond purchase plans maintained by the parent companies.[7]

Former or absent employees

A qualified plan may cover former employees, as well as present employees and employees who are temporarily on leave (e.g. military service). A qualified plan may benefit only former employees, as long as it does so in a nondiscriminatory manner.[8]

A plan may not provide benefits for periods after an employee has been terminated, however.[9] Although a qualified plan may cover former employees, such coverage is allowed only for the purpose of providing pension benefits for the period during which the individuals were the employees of the employer and does not contemplate additional credit for periods after the termination of the employee's service. Therefore, a pension plan that permits former employees to earn additional pension credits for the period between the termination of their service and the time they reach retirement age does not qualify.

☐ More information on the "exclusive benefit" rule, including the treatment of leased employees, independent contractors, and self-employed persons are discussed in the CCH PENSION PLAN GUIDE beginning at ¶ 985.

[1] Code Sec. 401(a); IRS Reg. §§ 1.401-1(a)(3)(ii); 1.401-2(a)(1); 1.401-2(a)(3).

[2] IRS Reg. § 1.401-1(b)(3).

[3] Rev. Rul. 70-316, 1970-1 CB 91, CCH PENSION PLAN GUIDE ¶ 18,836.

[4] Rev. Rul. 55-81, 1955-1 CB 392, CCH PENSION PLAN GUIDE ¶ 18,033.

[5] Rev. Rul. 69-493, 1969-2 CB 88, CCH PENSION PLAN GUIDE ¶ 18,759.

[6] *Yates v. Hendon*, US Sup Ct (2004), No. 02-458.

[7] Code Sec. 406(a); IRS Reg. § 1.406-1(b)(1).

[8] Rev. Rul. 81-106, 1981-1 CB 169, CCH PENSION PLAN GUIDE ¶ 19,573; Rev. Rul. 66-175, 1966-1 CB, CCH PENSION PLAN GUIDE ¶ 18,514.

[9] Rev. Rul. 73-238, 1973-1 CB 193, CCH PENSION PLAN GUIDE ¶ 19,229.

¶ 324

QUALIFICATION RULES: Rights of Beneficiaries

A plan must be maintained for the exclusive benefit of employees *or* their beneficiaries.[1] The plan, however, must primarily benefit employees. Benefits offered to beneficiaries must be merely incidental. Accordingly, a plan does not qualify if the benefits it provides are not payable to an employee, but only to the beneficiary upon the death of the employee.[2]

Benefits payable to an employee's beneficiary will be considered incidental if the plan contains provisions which assure that the present value of the payments to be made to the participant is more than 50% of the present value of the total payments to be made to the participant and his or her beneficiaries.[3] Even if the present value of the participant's benefits is less than 50%, however, a plan may distribute a participant's interest over the lives of the employee and his or her spouse, provided that each payment to the beneficiary is not greater than each payment to the participant during the participant's lifetime.[4]

Restrictions on designation of beneficiaries

A qualified plan may restrict beneficiaries to specified persons, or a group of persons, who are the natural objects of the employee's bounty, the employee's estate, or the employee's dependents.[5]

[1] Code Sec. 401(a).

[2] Rev. Rul. 56-656, 1956-2 CB 280, CCH PENSION PLAN GUIDE ¶ 18,097; Rev. Rul. 73-445, 1973-2 CB 127, CCH PENSION PLAN GUIDE ¶ 19,270; Rev. Rul. 74-360, 1974-2 CB 130, CCH PENSION PLAN GUIDE ¶ 19,345.

[3] Rev. Rul. 72-241, 1972-1 CB 108, CCH PENSION PLAN GUIDE ¶ 19,150.

[4] Rev. Rul. 72-240, 1972-1 CB 108, CCH PENSION PLAN GUIDE ¶ 19,149. Similarly, Rev. Rul. 74-325, 1974-2 CB 127, CCH PENSION PLAN GUIDE ¶ 19,336, and Rev. Rul. 60-59, 1960-1 CB 154, CCH PENSION PLAN GUIDE ¶ 18,209.

[5] Rev. Rul. 70-173, 1970-1 CB 87, CCH PENSION PLAN GUIDE ¶ 18,813.

¶ 327

QUALIFICATION RULES: Prohibited Diversion of Funds

The trust instrument underlying a qualified pension, profit-sharing, or stock bonus plan must prohibit any part of the principal or income of the trust, prior to the satisfaction of all benefit obligations to employees and their beneficiaries, from being used for, or diverted to, purposes other than the exclusive benefit of the employees or their beneficiaries.[1] Although an employer is not required to relinquish all power to modify or terminate the rights of certain employees covered by the trust, it must be impossible for the trust funds to be used for or diverted for purposes other than for the exclusive benefit of employees.

ERISA's anti-diversion rule

ERISA also prohibits plan assets from inuring to the benefit of any employer. Plan assets must be held for the exclusive purpose of providing benefits to participants and their beneficiaries and defraying reasonable expenses of administering the plan.[2] The rule applies even where the plan does not sustain a loss as a result of the inurement of plan assets to the employer.[3]

Exceptions. Exceptions to the anti-inurement rule are provided for the return of contributions made in error by an employer to a plan (see ¶ 345), refunds of overpayments of withdrawal liability (see ¶ 2908), return of payments conditioned on initial qualification or on deductibility (see ¶ 342), transfers to retiree health plans under Code Sec. 420, and the recovery of excess assets following the termination of a single-employer plan (see ¶ 2839).

---

[1] Code Sec. 401(a)(2); IRS Reg. §1.401-2; IRS Reg. §1.401(a)-2(a); Rev. Rul. 69-231, 1969-1 CB 118, CCH PENSION PLAN GUIDE ¶ 18,723.

[2] ERISA Sec. 403(c)(1).

[3] *Sandoval v. Simmons,* DC Ill (1985), 622 FSupp 1174.

¶ 330

QUALIFICATION RULES: Reversion of Trusteed Funds to Employer

The rule prohibiting the diversion of trust funds prior to the satisfaction of benefit liabilities would seem to allow the employer to recover the balance remaining in the trust upon termination of the plan, if all liabilities to employees have been met. The employer may recover such a balance, however, only if it is due to an "erroneous actuarial computation." [1] Employers are not allowed to shelter funds far in excess of those necessary to provide benefits for employees and then recover those funds after termination of the trust and after satisfaction of liabilities to the employees. Therefore, the IRS holds, in effect, that the employer can recover the balance left in a terminated trust only if the balance resulted from an "honest" error.

Erroneous actuarial computation

A balance due to an "erroneous actuarial computation" is the surplus that arises when actual requirements differ from the expected requirements even though the latter were based upon previous actuarial valuations of liabilities or determinations of costs of providing pension benefits under the plan and were made by a competent person using reasonable assumptions and proper procedures as to the method of funding.[2] Contributions to a fixed benefit pension plan are based on the amounts that an actuary determines will be necessary to provide the benefits called for in the plan.

Excise tax on reversions

If a reversion does occur, the employer is subject to a 20% excise tax on the amount.[3] If the employer does not establish a successor plan or provide for pro rata benefit increases, however, the tax increases to 50% (see ¶ 2841).[4]

ERISA authorizes reversions

ERISA also permits an employer to recover residual assets upon the termination of a single employer plan once all benefit liabilities of the plan have been satisfied (see ¶ 2839). However, plan assets attributable to employee contributions remaining after the satisfaction of all liabilities must be distributed to the contributing participants and other beneficiaries.[5] In addition, the employer reversion can occur only if specifically authorized by the plan and if the distribution does not contravene any provision of law.[6]

Amendment authorizing reversion not effective for 5 years. Any plan provision that provides for either a reversion of excess assets to an employer or an increase in the amount that may revert is not effective before the end of the fifth calendar year following the date the provision was adopted.[7] If a plan has been in effect for less than five years and the plan has provided for the distribution of residual assets to the employer since the effective date of the plan, however, such a distribution will be allowed.[8]

No reversion from multiemployer plan. ERISA does not authorize the distribution of excess plan assets to contributing employers upon the termination of a multiemployer plan.[9]

[1] IRS Reg. § 1.401-2(b)(1); Rev. Rul. 60-33, 1960-1 CB 152, CCH Pension Plan Guide ¶ 18,208; Rev. Rul. 70-421, 1970-2 CB 85, CCH Pension Plan Guide ¶ 18,851.

[2] IRS Reg. § 1.401-2(b)(1).

[3] Code Sec. 4980(a).

[4] Code Sec. 4980(d)(1).

[5] ERISA Sec. 4044(d)(3).

[6] ERISA Secs. 403(c)(1) and 4044(d)(1); PBGC Opinion Letter 78-2.

[7] ERISA Sec. 4044(d)(2)(A).

[8] ERISA Sec. 4044(d)(2)(B).

[9] ERISA Opinion Letter 94-39A, 11-28-94.

¶ 333
QUALIFICATION RULES: Refund of Annuity Plan Premiums

In a nontrusteed annuity plan, contributions are made directly to an insurance company without the intervention of a trust. In order for an employer to deduct such premiums and for an employee to escape tax on premiums paid by the employer, any refund of premiums must be used to reduce the employer's future premium payments.[1] The refunds may not be made to the employer in cash.

Refund of premiums

Premiums may be refunded in the form of various credits that may become payable to the employer from time to time. Credits may arise when an employee severs employment and forfeits the right to benefits under the plan, when an employee continues employment after normal retirement age, or when experience justifies a dividend or rate credit.

Written arrangement required

A written arrangement between the employer and the insurer must be adopted in order to assure that premium refunds are applied against future premiums. The arrangement may be either part of the annuity contract or a separate written direction from the employer to the insurer, stipulating that refunds of premiums be applied within the tax year of the employer in which received or within the next succeeding tax year toward the purchase of retirement annuities under the plan.[2]

---

[1] Code Sec. 404(a)(2), incorporated by reference in Code Sec. 403(a)(1).

[2] IRS Reg. § 1.404(a)-8(a)(3).

¶ 336
QUALIFICATION RULES: Reversion When Trust Invests in Insurance Contracts

In many small plans, the employer will contribute to a trust and the trust in turn will invest in an individual retirement income, retirement annuity, or other types of insurance contract. In such a case, credits and dividends on the contracts may be paid to the trustee.

The trustee may not pass the credits and dividends on to the employer. There is no reversion to the *employer*. However, if the employer continues to base its contributions on the full premiums charged by the insurance company and the trust continues to take all credits and dividends in cash, the trust will soon accumulate a reserve. This reserve will never be liquidated unless the employer reduces its contributions to the trust.

The IRS has ruled that, if such a reserve is large, the qualification of the plan could be adversely affected.[1] The concern of the IRS is presumably that upon termination of the plan, the reserve would either (1) revert to the employer or (2) be distributed to employees. In the former event, the reversion would *not* be due to an actuarial error since the employer would be aware that continuing to contribute amounts based on full premiums while the trust received cash credits would result in an overfunded condition. In the latter event, the distribution of the balance to employees would seem to violate the rule that benefits under a pension plan must be definitely determinable.

If the reserve is small, however, the qualification of the plan would not be adversely affected.[2]

[1] Rev. Rul. 60-33, 1960-1 CB 152, CCH PENSION PLAN GUIDE ¶ 18,208.

[2] *Ibid.*

¶ 339

QUALIFICATION RULES: Profit-Sharing and Stock Bonus Plans

An employer may not recover contributions to a profit-sharing or stock bonus plan after the termination of the plan, or at any other time. Employer contributions to profit-sharing or stock bonus plans are not based on the amounts necessary to provide stipulated retirement benefits, as is the case with a fixed formula pension plan. Because contributions are not determined actuarially, there is no possibility of an actuarial error. Furthermore, every dollar contributed is allocated to the respective accounts of participants according to a definite predetermined formula. Accordingly, forfeitures by participants must be reallocated to other plan participants and may not revert to the employer.[1]

Money purchase plans

The same reasoning preventing the recovery of contributions to profit- sharing or stock bonus plans applies to money purchase plans, even though these arrangements are pension plans, because contributions are fixed and there is no benefit stipulation.

[1] Rev. Rul. 71-149, 1971-1 CB 118, CCH PENSION PLAN GUIDE ¶ 19033.

¶ 342

QUALIFICATION RULES: Contributions Conditioned on Qualification or Deductibility

An employer may make contributions to a trust even though it is not certain that the plan will qualify. To protect itself, the employer may include a provision in the trust instrument allowing the trust to be revoked and contributions returned to the employer if the IRS subsequently determines that the plan is not qualified.

Such provisions do not violate the anti-diversion rule.[1] However, the provision may apply only to contributions made to a plan *prior to the initial determination by the IRS Commissioner as to qualification.*[2] A provision permitting the recovery of contributions after a plan has been disqualified for discriminatory practices subsequent to initial qualification is not acceptable.

ERISA authorizes return of contributions within one year

Under ERISA, the anti-diversion rule is not violated if contributions conditioned on qualification are recoverable by the employer *within one year after the date of denial of qualification*.[3] Contributions may be returned within one year if they are conditioned on the initial qualification of the plan, the plan does not qualify initially, and the application for the determination relating to initial qualification is filed by the due date of the employer's return for the taxable year in which the plan was adopted.

Return of contributions conditioned on deductibility

ERISA also permits the recovery of contributions conditioned on *deductibility* within one year after the date of disallowance.[4]

The Internal Revenue Code does not address the issue. The IRS, however, has also ruled that a provision permitting a return of contributions that are not deductible does not disqualify a plan.[5]

De minimis excess contributions do not require IRS ruling. An employer's excess contributions to a defined benefit plan that are conditioned on deductibility may be recovered without a ruling from the IRS if the amount of the nondeductible contributions is less than $25,000 and if the terms of the plan specifically permit the return of nondeductible contributions. The contributions must be explicitly conditioned on deductibility in writing, either in the plan or in the plan in combination with a certified corporate board resolution, *before* or *at the same time* that the nondeductible contributions are made to the plan.[6]

---

[1] See, e.g. *Meldrum & Fewsmith, Inc. v. Commissioner*, CA-6 (1956), 56-1 USTC ¶ 9269, 230 F2d 283; Rev. Rul. 91-4, 1991-1 CB 57, CCH PENSION PLAN GUIDE ¶ 19,740.

[2] Rev. Rul. 91-4, 1991-1 CB 57, CCH PENSION PLAN GUIDE ¶ 19740.

[3] ERISA Sec. 403(c)(2)(B).

[4] ERISA Sec. 403(c)(2)(C).

[5] Rev. Rul. 91-4, 1991-CB 57, CCH PENSION PLAN GUIDE ¶ 19740.

[6] Rev. Proc. 90-49, 1990-2 CB 620, CCH PENSION PLAN GUIDE ¶ 17299L-82.

¶ 345

QUALIFICATION RULES: Return of Contributions Made in Error

The anti-diversion rule is not violated if a contribution made by an employer to a plan (other than a multiemployer plan) through a mistake in fact is returned to the employer within one year after it is made.[1]

Under IRS rules, the amount which may be returned to the employer is the excess of (1) the amount contributed over (2) the amount that would have been contributed had there not occurred a mistake of fact (or a mistake in determining the deduction).[2]

Contributions made by an employer under a mistake of law may not be recovered by the employer.[3]

Multiemployer plans

A broader rule applies in the case of a multiemployer plan. A plan contribution or withdrawal liability payment made by an employer to a multiemployer plan because of a mistake of fact or law may be returned within six months after the plan administrator determines that the contribution or liability payment was made by a mistake (see ¶ 2908).[4] The exception, however, does not apply to contributions or payments made under a mistake relating to whether the plan was qualified.

Employer has no right of action to recover mistaken contributions

Employers may not bring an action under ERISA Sec. 403 to recover contributions made due to a mistake of fact.[5] However, employers have been allowed to bring suit under theories of equitable restitution[6] and unjust enrichment.[7]

[1] ERISA Sec. 403(c)(2)(A)(i).

[2] Rev. Rul. 91-4, 1991-CB 57, CCH PENSION PLAN GUIDE ¶ 19740.

[3] See, e.g., *Martin v. Hamil,* CA-7 (1979), 608 F2d 725.

[4] ERISA Sec. 403(c)(2)(A)(ii); Code Sec. 401(a)(2).

[5] See, e.g., *I.A.M. National Pension Fund Benefit Plan v. Towner Manufacturing Co.,* DC Dof C (1987), No. 85-0777; *Dime Coal Co., Inc. v. Combs,* CA-5 (1986), 796 F2d 394.

[6] See, e.g., *Soft Drink Industry Local Union No. 744 Pension Fund v. Coca Cola Bottling Co. of Chicago,* DC Ill (1988), 679 FSupp 207.

[7] See, e.g., *Peckham and Woolum v. Board of Trustees of the International Brotherhood of Painters and Allied Trades Union and Industry National Pension Fund,* CA-10 (1983), 719 F2d 1063.

¶ 348
QUALIFICATION RULES: Plan Permanency

In order for a plan to qualify, it must be "permanent." The Internal Revenue Code does not mention permanence, but, according to the IRS, the term "plan" implies a permanent as distinguished from a temporary program.[1] Thus, although the employer may reserve the right to change or terminate the plan, and to discontinue contributions, the abandonment of the plan for any reason other than business necessity within a few years after it has taken effect will be *evidence* that the plan, from its inception, was not a bona fide program for the exclusive benefit of employees.

Early termination is not determinative

The permanency of the plan will be indicated by all of the surrounding facts and circumstances, including the likelihood of the employer's ability to continue contributions as provided under the plan. Early termination is merely evidence, and not determinative, of whether a plan was a sham from its inception. The presumption that the plan was not intended to be permanent from the beginning may be rebutted by showing that abandonment of the plan was due to business necessity (e.g., bankruptcy, insolvency, discontinuance of business, sale of business in arm's length transaction, or financial inability to continue a plan that were not reasonably foreseeable at the time that the plan was adopted).[2] However, if a plan has already been discontinued at the time of its submission for a ruling as to qualification, and such discontinuance was not disclosed at the time, this will be prima facie evidence that the plan was not a bona fide program.[3]

Curtailment of plan risks disqualification. A plan is disqualified when it is *curtailed* for reasons other than business necessity.[4] A curtailment includes modifications that reduce benefits or employer contributions or tighten eligibility or vesting requirements. An amendment requiring employee contributions to provide the same benefits that previously were provided exclusively by employer contributions results in a curtailment.

Retroactive plan disqualification

If the IRS finds that the plan was not a bona fide program for the exclusive benefit of employees from its inception, it will attempt to disqualify the plan retroactively for all years open under the statute of limitations. This could result in retroactive disallowance of employer contribution deductions, assessment of back taxes on plan earnings, and assessment of back taxes against employees for amounts that would have been includible in gross income for each employer contribution.

Negotiated plans

Pension, annuity, profit-sharing, or stock bonus plans that are negotiated pursuant to a union contract that runs for a specified number of years, typically may not be terminated or changed prior to the expiration of the bargaining agreement. The fact that the contract allows the employer to terminate or amend the plan after the expiration of the agreement does not mean that the plan is not permanent.[5]

[1] IRS Reg. § 1.401-1(b)(2).

[2] Rev. Rul. 69-24, 1969-1 CB 110, CCH PENSION PLAN GUIDE ¶ 18,691.

[3] Rev. Rul. 69-25 (Sec. 3.06), 1969-1 CB 113, CCH PENSION PLAN GUIDE ¶ 18,692.

[4] Rev. Rul. 69-24, 1969-1 CB 110, CCH PENSION PLAN GUIDE ¶ 18,691.

[5] Rev. Rul. 83-83, 1983-1 CB 86, CCH PENSION PLAN GUIDE ¶ 19,639.

¶ 360

IRS ADMINISTRATIVE ENFORCEMENT PROGRAMS: Types of IRS Administrative Enforcement Programs

The IRS operates a comprehensive system of correction programs that allow a plan sponsor to maintain the qualified status of a plan for any plan year in which a form or operational failure has occurred.[1] The programs are consolidated in a large coordinated program, known as the Employee Plans Compliance Resolution System (EPCRS). The IRS enforcement programs are the:

1. Self-Correction Program (SCP) (see ¶ 363),
2. Audit Closing Agreement Program (Audit CAP) (see ¶ 366), and
3. Voluntary Correction Program (VCP) (see ¶ 369).

The IRS administrative enforcement programs included within the EPCRS allow a plan sponsor to maintain the qualified status of a plan without the sanction of disqualification for any plan year in which qualification failures occurred. Each program has its own eligibility criteria and imposes different requirements on the plan sponsor as a condition to maintaining qualification. The program that is available to a plan sponsor is determined by whether the plan defects are discovered internally or by IRS audit, and whether the defects are of a form or operational nature.

> **CCH Pointer:** *Congress officially authorizes EPCRS program.* In 2006 Congress belatedly provided formal legislative authorization for the Treasury Secretary to establish and implement EPCRS and any successor program.[2] Accordingly, the Secretary is authorized to waive income, excise or other taxes to ensure that any tax, penalty or sanction associated with EPCRS is not excessive. A reasonable relationship must exist between the tax, penalty or sanction with the nature, extent and severity of the failure. Congress also specifically directed the Treasury Secretary to continue to update the EPCRS program as events warrant.

Retroactive correction required. All of the programs require retroactive correction of plan defects. As necessary, prospective plan amendments will be required to bring a plan into compliance with the requirements for qualified status.

DOL's VFCP. In order to encourage the full correction of breaches of fiduciary duty and the restoration to participants and beneficiaries of losses resulting from such breaches, the Employee Benefits Security Administration (EBSA) maintains the Voluntary Fiduciary Correction Program (VFCP) (see ¶ 2737). Similar to the Employee Plans Compliance Resolution System (EPCRS) maintained by the IRS for redressing qualification defects, the VFCP is a remedial mechanism that allows fiduciaries (e.g., plan sponsors, plan administrators, and parties in interest) to avoid civil actions and civil penalties for specified breaches of fiduciary duty by voluntarily undertaking specified corrective actions prior to an EBSA audit or investigation.

☐ Operational, demographic, and eligibility failures under a 403(b) plan are addressed under the Voluntary Correction of Tax-Sheltered Annuity Failure (VCT) Program. See ¶ 3194.

---

[1]Rev. Proc. 2008-50, I.R.B. 2008-35, 9-2-08, at CCH PENSION PLAN GUIDE ¶ 17,299S-66, modifying and superseding Rev. Proc 2006-27, I.R.B. 2006-22, 5-30-2006, at CCH PENSION PLAN GUIDE ¶ 17,299R-86, modifying and superseding Rev.

Proc. 2003-44, I.R.B. 2003-25, 6-23-2003 at CCH PENSION PLAN GUIDE ¶ 17,299Q-78.

[2]P.L. 109-280 (Pension Protection Act of 2006), Act Sec. 1101, effective August 17, 2006 (date of enactment).

¶ 362

IRS ADMINISTRATIVE ENFORCEMENT PROGRAMS: EPCRS Correction Principles

EPCRS is based on the following general principles:[1]

1. Sponsors of eligible plans should be encouraged to establish administrative practices and procedures that ensure that plans are operated properly in accordance with the applicable requirements.

2. Sponsors of tax-qualified retirement plans should maintain plan documents satisfying the tax qualification requirements.

3. Plan sponsors should make voluntary and timely correction of any plan failures, whether involving discrimination in favor of highly compensated employees, plan operations, or the terms of the plan document. Timely and efficient correction protects participating employees by providing them with their expected retirement benefits, including favorable tax treatment.

4. Voluntary compliance is promoted by providing for limited fees for voluntary corrections approved by the IRS, thereby reducing employers' uncertainty regarding their potential tax liability and participants' potential income tax liability.

5. Fees and sanctions should be graduated in a series of steps so that there is always an incentive to correct promptly.

6. Sanctions for plan failures identified on audit should be reasonable in light of the nature, extent, and severity of the violation.

7. Administration of EPCRS should be consistent and uniform.

8. Sponsors should be able to rely on the availability of EPCRS in taking corrective actions to maintain the tax-favored status of their plans.

---

[1]Rev. Proc.2008-50, I.R.B. 2008-35, 9-2-08, at CCH PENSION PLAN GUIDE ¶ 17,299S-66, modifying and superseding Rev. Proc. 2006-27, I.R.B. 2006-22, Sec. 1.02, 5-30-2006 at CCH PENSION PLAN GUIDE ¶ 17,299R-86, modifying and superseding Rev. Proc. 2003-44, I.R.B. 2003-25, 6-23-2003 at CCH PENSION PLAN GUIDE ¶ 17,299Q-78.

¶ 363

IRS ADMINISTRATIVE ENFORCEMENT PROGRAMS: Self-Correction Program

The Self-Correction Program (SCP) is available to plan sponsors only for the correction of operational failures. Qualified plans and 403(b) plans are eligible for SCP with respect to "significant" and "insignificant" operational failures. SEPs and SIMPLE IRA plans are eligible for SCP with respect to insignificant operational failures only.[1] The SCP does not require disclosure or payment of fees to the IRS.

Revised SCP in 2009. Beginning in 2009, the IRS updated and expanded the EPCRS, including changes to the SCP. The updated procedure expands the SCP in situations where employers discover failures in their plans and have begun the correction process.

Established practices and procedures

In order to qualify for SCP, the plan sponsor or administrator must have established formal or informal practices and procedures (in addition to the plan document) that are reasonably designed to promote and facilitate compliance with applicable Code requirements.[2] For example, a plan administrator may use a check sheet for tracking allocations and for noting whether or not an employee was a key employee for purposes of the top-heavy rules.

Full retroactive correction required

The plan sponsor must make a full correction of all operational failures for all years for which the failures exist.[3] The correction must restore to current and former participants, and their beneficiaries, the benefits and rights they would have had if the violations had not occurred.

De minimis exception to corrective distribution. A plan sponsor is not required to make a corrective distribution if the reasonable direct costs of processing and delivering the distribution to the participant or beneficiary would exceed $50.[4]

Determination of significant failures

Factors that determine whether an operational failure is significant or insignificant include: the number of violations during the examination period; the percentage of plan assets and contributions involved in the failure; the number of years that the failure occurred; the number of participants affected relative to the total number of participants in the plan; whether the failures were corrected within a reasonable time after discovery; and the reason for the failures (e.g., data errors).[5]

Time to self-correct expanded for 2009

Under the revised SCP, beginning in 2009, the time by which a plan sponsor substantially corrects a significant operational failure and is therefore entitled to use the SCP has been liberalized.[6] Sample correction methods for improperly excluded employees for both employer and employee contributions have been added to Appendix A. In addition, sample correction methods for the failure to implement an employee's elective deferral election and to provide matching contributions have been added to Appendix B.

Correction of significant operational failures

A significant operational failure must generally be corrected by the last day of the second plan year following the plan year for which the failures occurred.[7] However, the failure to comply with the ADP or ACP nondiscrimination tests (see ¶ 2951 and ¶ 2952, respectively) may be corrected by the last day of the second plan year following the plan year that includes the last day of the additional period for correction permitted under Code Secs. 401(k)(8) and 401(m)(6) (see ¶ 2977 and ¶ 2978, respectively).

In addition, an operational failure that relates only to transferred assets, or to a plan assumed in connection with a corporate merger, acquisition, or other similar employer transaction may be corrected by the last day of the first plan year that begins after the merger, acquisition, or other similar transaction.[8]

Substantial completion of correction. A significant operational failure will be considered to have been corrected if the correction is "substantially completed" by the last day of the correction period.[9] The correction of an operational failure will be substantially completed if, during the correction period, the sponsor initiates correction procedures and completes the correction within 90 days after the last day of the correction period.

Alternatively, the correction of a significant operational failure will be substantially completed if, during the correction period, (a) correction is completed with respect to 85 percent of all participants affected by the failure and (b) thereafter, correction of the failure is completed with respect to the remaining participants in a "diligent" manner.[10]

Audit prevents use of SCP for significant failures. A plan sponsor may not self-correct a significant operational failure for a plan year if the failure is first discovered during a plan audit for that year. In addition, the correction period ends on the first date the plan comes under examination for the plan year.[11]

Correction of insignificant operational failures

Insignificant operational failures may be corrected under SCP, even if the plan or plan sponsor is under examination and even if the operational failure is discovered by an IRS agent on examination.[12]

Multiple operational failures. Plans that have more than one operational failure in a year, or that experience operational failures in more than one year, may self-correct under SCP if all of the operational failures are insignificant in the aggregate.[13]

CCH Pointer: Operational failures will not be considered significant merely because they occur in more than one year.

[1]Rev. Proc. 2008-50, I.R.B. 2008-35, 9-2-08, at CCH PENSION PLAN GUIDE ¶ 17,299S-66, modifying and superseding Rev. Proc. 2006-27, Sec. 4.01, I.R.B. 2006-22, 5-30-2006 at CCH PENSION PLAN GUIDE ¶ 17,299R-86. The Self-Correction Program replaced the Administrative Policy Regarding Self-Correction (APRSC) in 2001.

[2]Rev. Proc. 2008-50, I.R.B. 2008-35, 9-2-08, at CCH PENSION PLAN GUIDE ¶ 17,299S-66, modifying and superseding Rev. Proc. 2006-27, Sec. 4.04, I.R.B. 2006-22, 5-30-2006 at CCH PENSION PLAN GUIDE ¶ 17,299R-86, modifying and superseding Rev. Proc. 2003-44, I.R.B. 2003-25, 6-23-2003, at CCH PENSION PLAN GUIDE ¶ 17,299Q-78.

[3] Rev. Proc. 2008-50, I.R.B. 2008-35, 9-2-08, at CCH PENSION PLAN GUIDE ¶ 17,299S-66, modifying and superseding Rev. Proc. 2006-27, Sec. 6.02, I.R.B. 2006-22, 5-30-2006 at CCH PENSION PLAN GUIDE ¶ 17,299R-86, modifying and superseding Rev. Proc. 2003-44, I.R.B. 2003-25, 6-23-2003, at CCH PENSION PLAN GUIDE ¶ 17,299Q-78.

[4]Rev. Proc. 2008-50, I.R.B. 2008-35, 9-2-08, at CCH PENSION PLAN GUIDE ¶ 17,299S-66, modifying and superseding Rev. Proc. 2006-27, Sec. 6.02(5)(b), I.R.B. 2006-22, 5-30-2006 at CCH PEN-SION PLAN GUIDE ¶ 17,299R-86, modifying and su-

perseding Rev. Proc. 2003-44, I.R.B. 2003-25, 6-23-2003, at CCH PENSION PLAN GUIDE ¶ 17,299Q-78.

[5]Rev. Proc. 2008-50, I.R.B. 2008-35, 9-2-08, at CCH PENSION PLAN GUIDE ¶ 17,299S-66, modifying and superseding Rev. Proc. 2006-27, Sec. 8.02, I.R.B. 2006-22, 5-30-2006 at CCH PENSION PLAN GUIDE ¶ 17,299R-86, modifying and superseding Rev. Proc. 2003-44, I.R.B. 2003-25, 6-23-2003, at CCH PENSION PLAN GUIDE ¶ 17,299Q-78.

[6]Rev. Proc. 2008-50, I.R.B. 2008-35, 9-2-08, at CCH PENSION PLAN GUIDE ¶ 17,299S-66, modifying and superseding Rev. Proc. 2006-27, Sec. 9.02, I.R.B. 2006-22, 5-30-2006 at CCH PENSION PLAN GUIDE ¶ 17,299R-86, modifying and superseding Rev. Proc. 2003-44, I.R.B. 2003-25, 6-23-2003, at CCH PENSION PLAN GUIDE ¶ 17,299Q-78.

[7] Rev. Proc. 2008-50, I.R.B. 2008-35, 9-2-08, at CCH PENSION PLAN GUIDE ¶ 17,299S-66, modifying and superseding Rev. Proc. 2006-27, Sec. 9.02, I.R.B. 2006-22, 5-30-2006 at CCH PENSION PLAN GUIDE ¶ 17,299R-86, modifying and superseding Rev. Proc. 2003-44, I.R.B. 2003-25, 6-23-2003, at CCH PENSION PLAN GUIDE ¶ 17,299Q-78.

[8]Rev. Proc. 2008-50, I.R.B. 2008-35, 9-2-08, at CCH PENSION PLAN GUIDE ¶ 17,299S-66, modifying

and superseding Rev. Proc. 2006-27, Sec. 9.02, I.R.B. 2006-22, 5-30-2006 at CCH Pension Plan Guide ¶ 17,299R-86, modifying and superseding Rev. Proc. 2003-44, I.R.B. 2003-25, 6-23-2003, at CCH Pension Plan Guide ¶ 17,299Q-78.

[9] Rev. Proc. 2008-50, I.R.B. 2008-35, 9-2-08, at CCH Pension Plan Guide ¶ 17,299S-66, modifying and superseding Rev. Proc. 2006-27, Sec. 9.04, I.R.B. 2006-22, 5-30-2006 at CCH Pension Plan Guide ¶ 17,299R-86, modifying and superseding Rev. Proc. 2003-44, I.R.B. 2003-25, 6-23-2003, at CCH Pension Plan Guide ¶ 17,299Q-78.

[10] *Ibid.*

[11] Rev. Proc. 2008-50, I.R.B. 2008-35, 9-2-08, at CCH Pension Plan Guide ¶ 17,299S-66, modifying and superseding Rev. Proc. 2006-27, Sec. 9.02(3), I.R.B. 2006-22, 5-30-2006 at CCH Pension Plan

Guide ¶ 17,299R-86, modifying and superseding Rev. Proc. 2003-44, I.R.B. 2003-25, 6-23-2003, at CCH Pension Plan Guide ¶ 17,299Q-78.

[12] Rev. Proc. 2008-50, I.R.B. 2008-35, 9-2-08, at CCH Pension Plan Guide ¶ 17,299S-66, modifying and superseding Rev. Proc. 2006-27, Sec. 8.01, I.R.B. 2006-22, 5-30-2006 at CCH Pension Plan Guide ¶ 17,299R-86, modifying and superseding Rev. Proc. 2003-44, I.R.B. 2003-25, 6-23-2003, at CCH Pension Plan Guide ¶ 17,299Q-78.

[13] Rev. Proc. 2008-50, I.R.B. 2008-35, 9-2-08, at CCH Pension Plan Guide ¶ 17,299S-66, modifying and superseding Rev. Proc. 2006-27, Sec. 8.03, I.R.B. 2006-22, 5-30-2006 at CCH Pension Plan Guide ¶ 17,299R-86, modifying and superseding Rev. Proc. 2003-44, I.R.B. 2003-25, 6-23-2003, at CCH Pension Plan Guide ¶ 17,299Q-78.

¶ 366

IRS ADMINISTRATIVE ENFORCEMENT PROGRAMS: Audit Closing Agreement Program

The Audit Closing Agreement Program (Audit CAP) is available for qualified plans, 403(b) plans, SEPs and SIMPLE IRAs for correction of all failures found on examination that have not been corrected under SCP (see ¶ 363) or VCP (see ¶ 369).[1]

Restrictions on Audit CAP eligibility

Audit CAP encompasses nearly every operational failure, except (similar to SCP and VCP) cases involving the diversion of assets in violation of the exclusive benefit rule.[2] Audit CAP kicks in once a plan sponsor has received notice of an audit or of an impending employee plans or exempt organizations audit.

Correction of failures and dollar sanction

If a plan is eligible for Audit CAP, a plan sponsor will be required to (1) correct all plan failures; (2) pay a negotiated dollar sanction; (3) implement procedures that may be required by the IRS; and (4) enter into a closing agreement with the IRS.[3]

Correction of plan defects. Correction of all plan failures must be retroactive.[4] If necessary, prospective plan amendments should be adopted to bring a plan into compliance with the rules for qualification. As with the SCP, retroactive correction requires that the plan and affected plan participants be made whole as if the qualification failures never occurred. Prospective correction involves making plan amendments and implementing the procedures necessary to bring the plan into compliance with Code Sec. 401(a).

Dollar sanction. Unlike the SCP, Audit CAP requires a plan sponsor (and the trust and plan participants) to pay a dollar sanction roughly equivalent to the tax that would have to be paid if the plan was disqualified.[5] The amount of the sanction will be the result of negotiations between the IRS and the plan sponsor. For an ongoing plan that has been in existence for a number of years with significant trust assets, the dollar sanction under Audit CAP can be substantial.

Sanctions cannot be "excessive" and must bear a "reasonable relationship to the nature, extent, and severity of the failures." [6] Also, the extent to which correction has occurred prior to the IRS audit must be weighed as a factor in determining the sanction.[7] Therefore, if the plan sponsor had taken immediate and correct steps to correct the failures—albeit not in time or not of the type to fall within SCP—those efforts must be considered in determining the ultimate sanction.

Mitigating factors. The IRS must consider various mitigating factors favorable to the taxpayer in determining the amount of the sanction. Factors include the steps taken by the plan sponsor to ensure that the plan had no failures and the extent to which correction had progressed before the examination began.[8]

Limited trust liability for Audit CAP sanctions. In the event that the trust has a tax liability as the result of disqualification and therefore, as a matter of law, is required to pay a portion of the dollar sanction, the employees' retirement fund will be adversely affected because those funds generally are never recouped by the trust. Accordingly, the IRS generally requires Audit CAP sanctions to be paid by parties other than the trust, such as the employer or the fiduciary responsible for the disqualifying defect.[9] However, trust assets may be used to pay the sanction if the employer establishes financial distress.

---

[1] Rev. Proc. 2008-50, I.R.B. 2008-35, 9-2-08, at CCH Pension Plan Guide ¶ 17,299S-66, modifying and superseding Rev. Proc. 2006-27, Sec. 13-14, I.R.B. 2006-22, 5-30-2006 at CCH Pension Plan Guide ¶ 17,299R-86, modifying and superseding Rev. Proc. 2003-44, I.R.B. 2003-25, 6-23-2003, at CCH Pension Plan Guide ¶ 17,299Q-78.

[2] Rev. Proc. 2008-50, I.R.B. 2008-35, 9-2-08, at CCH Pension Plan Guide ¶ 17,299S-66, modifying and superseding Rev. Proc. 2006-27, Sec. 4.12, I.R.B. 2006-22, 5-30-2006 at CCH Pension Plan Guide ¶ 17,299R-86, modifying and superseding Rev. Proc. 2003-44, I.R.B. 2003-25, 6-23-2003, at CCH Pension Plan Guide ¶ 17,299Q-78.

[3] Rev. Proc. 2008-50, I.R.B. 2008-35, 9-2-08, at CCH Pension Plan Guide ¶ 17,299S-66, modifying and superseding Rev. Proc. 2006-27, Sec. 13.01, I.R.B. 2006-22, 5-30-2006 at CCH Pension Plan Guide ¶ 17,299R-86, modifying and superseding Rev. Proc. 2003-44, I.R.B. 2003-25, 6-23-2003, at CCH Pension Plan Guide ¶ 17,299Q-78.

[4] Rev. Proc. 2008-50, I.R.B. 2008-35, 9-2-08, at CCH Pension Plan Guide ¶ 17,299S-66, modifying

and superseding Rev. Proc. 2006-27, Sec. 6, I.R.B. 2006-22, 5-30-2006 at CCH Pension Plan Guide ¶ 17,299R-86, modifying and superseding Rev. Proc. 2003-44, I.R.B. 2003-25, 6-23-2003, at CCH Pension Plan Guide ¶ 17,299Q-78.

[5] Rev. Proc. 2008-50, I.R.B. 2008-35, 9-2-08, at CCH Pension Plan Guide ¶ 17,299S-66, modifying and superseding Rev. Proc. 2006-27, Sec. 14.01, I.R.B. 2006-22, 5-30-2006 at CCH Pension Plan Guide ¶ 17,299R-86, modifying and superseding Rev. Proc. 2003-44, I.R.B. 2003-25, 6-23-2003, at CCH Pension Plan Guide ¶ 17,299Q-78.

[6] *Ibid.*

[7] Rev. Proc. 2008-50, I.R.B. 2008-35, 9-2-08, at CCH Pension Plan Guide ¶ 17,299S-66, modifying and superseding Rev. Proc. 2006-27, Sec. 14.02, I.R.B. 2006-22, 5-30-2006 at CCH Pension Plan Guide ¶ 17,299R-86, modifying and superseding Rev. Proc. 2003-44, I.R.B. 2003-25, 6-23-2003, at CCH Pension Plan Guide ¶ 17,299Q-78.

[8] *Ibid.*

[9] IRS Field Directive, 2-21-95.

¶ 369

IRS ADMINISTRATIVE ENFORCEMENT PROGRAMS: Voluntary Correction Program

Under the Voluntary Correction Program (VCP), eligible plan sponsors may correct all qualification failures.[1] Qualified plans, 403(b) plans, SEPs and SIMPLE IRAs are eligible for VCP. At any time before an audit, plan sponsors may use the VCP to pay a set fee and receive the IRS's approval for correction.[2]

Streamlined VCP procedures beginning in 2009

Beginning in 2009, the updated EPCRS procedure added streamlined application procedures under VCP for numerous categories of plan failures.[3] A standardized application form is included in the revised Appendix F, which should be used for all streamlined applications. Appendix F has been expanded to permit corrections for the following failures:

- ☐ interim and certain discretionary nonamender failures;

- ☐ nonamender failures (besides those in Schedule 1, Section 11.02);

- ☐ SEP and SARSEP failures;

- ☐ SIMPLE IRA plan failures;

- ☐ plan loan failures (including Code Sec. 72(p) violations, even when the plan does not provide for loans);

- ☐ employer eligibility failures;

- ☐ failure to distribute elective deferrals in excess of the Code Sec. 402(g) limit; and

- ☐ failure to pay required minimum distributions timely under Code Sec. 401(a)(9).

For all other VCP applications, a sample application form is provided in Appendix D. Providing sample application forms and expanding the streamlined application procedures to include several common failures should help ensure that applications are complete and will provide a significant time savings in case processing.

In addition, beginning in 2009, relief from taxes such as the additional tax on early distributions under Code Sec. 72(t) and excise tax under Code Sec. 4973 may be provided under VCP. Also, the VCP compliance fee is reduced in certain instances if a plan's sole failure is that loans do not meet the requirements of Code Sec. 72(p)(2).

2003 procedure consolidation

With the issuance of Rev. Proc. 2003-44, which was generally effective October 1, 2003, the IRS consolidated all voluntary correction procedures into a single VCP. Prior to that time, the VCP had set forth separate procedures for the following types of submissions:

1. submissions involving only operational failures, entitled Voluntary Correction of Operational Failures (VCO);

2. submissions in which limited operational failures are being corrected using standardized corrections, entitled Voluntary Correction of Operational Failures Standardized (VCS);

3. anonymous submissions, entitled Anonymous (John Doe) Submission Procedure; and

4. group submissions, entitled Voluntary Correction of Group Failures (VCGroup).

In addition, the VCP included special procedures for failures associated with TSAs, and with SEPs.[4]

Under Rev. Proc. 2003-44, this structure was largely eliminated, so that plan sponsors seeking voluntary correction may follow one set of procedures, regardless of the type of plan or the type of defect being corrected. Special rules continue to apply, however, for anonymous submissions and for group submissions.[5]

VCP general procedures

In general, VCP is a voluntary compliance program that is satisfied if the plan sponsor pays a compliance fee and implements the corrective action specified in a compliance statement.[6] The VCP accepts plan document, operational, demographic, and employer eligibility failures.[7]

A plan sponsor requesting relief under VCP will identify the self-discovered failures in its submission. Generally, it is those failures that will be covered by the formal compliance statement.[8] In exchange for signing a compliance statement and complying with its terms, the plan will maintain its tax-favored status.[9]

Compliance fee

The IRS provides a fixed fee schedule for all VCP submissions.[10] The fee is determined with reference to the number of plan participants (employees, in the case of 403(b) plans) and, for qualified plans and 403(b) plans, can range from $750 dollars to $25,000 dollars. For a SEP or SIMPLE IRA plan submission, the fee is generally $250. (Special compliance fee procedures apply in the case of egregious errors.)

Anonymous submissions

Plan sponsors of qualified plans, 403(b) plans, SEPs and SIMPLE IRAs may use submit plans under VCP without first identifying either the applicable plans, the plan sponsors or the eligible organization. Regular VCP application procedures should be followed, except that information identifying the plan or the plan sponsor may be deleted, and the power of attorney and the penalty of perjury statement need not be included with the initial submission. (For processing purposes the State of the plan sponsor must be identified in the initial submission.)

¶369

Once a compliance agreement has been agreed upon, the plan sponsor will have 21 calendar days from the date of the agreement to identify the plan and the plan sponsor.[11]

Note that anonymous submitters do not enjoy the protection from plan audit that normal VCP submitters do. Thus, if an anonymously submitted plan comes under examination before being identified to the IRS, it will no longer be eligible under VCP.[12]

Group submissions

An "eligible organization" may correct operational and plan document failures with respect to a qualified plan, a 403(b) plan, a SEP or a SIMPLE IRA.[13] An eligible organization is (1) a sponsor of a master or prototype plan, (2) insurance company or other entity that has issued annuity contracts and provides services with respect to 403(b) plan assets, or (3) an entity that provides plan administrative services (i.e., third party administrators).[14]

Systemic error affecting 20 or more plans. An eligible organization may not correct a failure using a group submission unless the failure results from a "systemic error" that affects at least 20 plans and that results in at least 20 plans implementing a correction.[15]

[1] Rev. Proc. 2008-50, I.R.B. 2008-35, 9-2-08, at CCH PENSION PLAN GUIDE ¶ 17,299S-66, modifying and superseding Rev. Proc. 2006-27, Sec. 4.02, I.R.B. 2006-22, 5-30-2006, at CCH PENSION PLAN GUIDE ¶ 17,299R-86, modifying and superseding Rev. Proc. 2003-44, I.R.B. 2003-25, 6-23-2003 at CCH PENSION PLAN GUIDE ¶ 17,299Q-78.

[2] Rev. Proc. 2008-50, I.R.B. 2008-35, 9-2-08, at CCH PENSION PLAN GUIDE ¶ 17,299S-66, modifying and superseding Rev. Proc. 2006-27, Sec. 10.01, I.R.B. 2006-22, 5-30-2006, at CCH PENSION PLAN GUIDE ¶ 17,299R-86, modifying and superseding Rev. Proc. 2003-44, I.R.B. 2003-25, 6-23-2003 at CCH PENSION PLAN GUIDE ¶ 17,299Q-78.

[3] Rev. Proc. 2008-50, I.R.B. 2008-35, 9-2-08, at CCH PENSION PLAN GUIDE ¶ 17,299S-66, modifying and superseding Rev. Proc. 2006-27, Sec. 4.02, I.R.B. 2006-22, 5-30-2006, at CCH PENSION PLAN GUIDE ¶ 17,299R-86, modifying and superseding Rev. Proc. 2003-44, I.R.B. 2003-25, 6-23-2003 at CCH PENSION PLAN GUIDE ¶ 17,299Q-78.

[4] Rev. Proc. 2008-50, I.R.B. 2008-35, 9-2-08, at CCH PENSION PLAN GUIDE ¶ 17,299S-66, modifying and superseding Rev. Proc. 2002-47, Secs. 10-11, I.R.B. 2002-29, 7-22-2002, at CCH PENSION PLAN GUIDE ¶ 17,299Q-24.

[5] Rev. Proc. 2003-44, Sec. 4.02, I.R.B. 2003-25, 6-23-2003 at CCH PENSION PLAN GUIDE ¶ 17,299Q-78.

[6] Rev. Proc. 2008-50, I.R.B. 2008-35, 9-2-08, at CCH PENSION PLAN GUIDE ¶ 17,299S-66, modifying

and superseding Rev. Proc. 2006-27, Sec. 10.01, I.R.B. 2006-22, 5-30-2006, at CCH PENSION PLAN GUIDE ¶ 17,299R-86, modifying and superseding Rev. Proc. 2003-44, I.R.B. 2003-25, 6-23-2003 at CCH PENSION PLAN GUIDE ¶ 17,299Q-78.

[7] Rev. Proc. 2008-50, I.R.B. 2008-35, 9-2-08, at CCH PENSION PLAN GUIDE ¶ 17,299S-66, modifying and superseding Rev. Proc. 2006-27, Sec. 4.02, I.R.B. 2006-22, 5-30-2006, at CCH PENSION PLAN GUIDE ¶ 17,299R-86, modifying and superseding Rev. Proc. 2003-44, I.R.B. 2003-25, 6-23-2003 at CCH PENSION PLAN GUIDE ¶ 17,299Q-78.

[8] Rev. Proc. 2008-50, I.R.B. 2008-35, 9-2-08, at CCH PENSION PLAN GUIDE ¶ 17,299S-66, modifying and superseding Rev. Proc. 2006-27, Sec. 10.02, I.R.B. 2006-22, 5-30-2006, at CCH PENSION PLAN GUIDE ¶ 17,299R-86, modifying and superseding Rev. Proc. 2003-44, I.R.B. 2003-25, 6-23-2003 at CCH PENSION PLAN GUIDE ¶ 17,299Q-78.

[9] Rev. Proc. 2008-50, I.R.B. 2008-35, 9-2-08, at CCH PENSION PLAN GUIDE ¶ 17,299S-66, modifying and superseding Rev. Proc. 2006-27, Sec. 10.08, I.R.B. 2006-22, 5-30-2006, at CCH PENSION PLAN GUIDE ¶ 17,299R-86, modifying and superseding Rev. Proc. 2003-44, I.R.B. 2003-25, 6-23-2003 at CCH PENSION PLAN GUIDE¶ 17,299Q-78.

[10] Rev. Proc. 2008-50, I.R.B. 2008-35, 9-2-08, at CCH PENSION PLAN GUIDE ¶ 17,299S-66, modifying and superseding Rev. Proc. 2006-27, Sec. 12, I.R.B. 2006-22, 5-30-2006, at CCH PENSION PLAN GUIDE ¶ 17,299R-86, modifying and superseding Rev.

Proc. 2003-44, I.R.B. 2003-25, 6-23-2003 at CCH Pension Plan Guide ¶ 17,299Q-78.

[11] Rev. Proc. 2008-50, I.R.B. 2008-35, 9-2-08, at CCH Pension Plan Guide ¶ 17,299S-66, modifying and supersedingRev. Proc. 2006-27, Sec. 10.10(1), I.R.B. 2006-22, 5-30-2006, at CCH Pension Plan Guide ¶ 17,299R-86, modifying and superseding Rev. Proc. 2003-44, I.R.B. 2003-25, 6-23-2003 at CCH Pension Plan Guide ¶ 17,299Q-78.

[12]Rev. Proc. 2008-50, I.R.B. 2008-35, 9-2-08, at CCH Pension Plan Guide ¶ 17,299S-66, modifying and superseding Rev. Proc. 2006-27, Sec. 10.10(2), I.R.B. 2006-22, 5-30-2006, at CCH Pension Plan

Guide ¶ 17,299R-86, modifying and superseding Rev. Proc. 2003-44, I.R.B. 2003-25, 6-23-2003 at CCH Pension Plan Guide ¶ 17,299Q-78.

[13]Rev. Proc. 2008-50, I.R.B. 2008-35, 9-2-08, at CCH Pension Plan Guide ¶ 17,299S-66, modifying and superseding Rev. Proc. 2006-27, Sec. 10.11, I.R.B. 2006-22, 5-30-2006, at CCH Pension Plan Guide ¶ 17,299R-86, modifying and superseding Rev. Proc. 2003-44, I.R.B. 2003-25, 6-23-2003 at CCH Pension Plan Guide ¶ 17,299Q-78.

[14] *Ibid.*

[15] *Ibid.*

¶ 378

IRS ADMINISTRATIVE ENFORCEMENT PROGRAMS: Discrepancy Adjustment Program

The Discrepancy Adjustment Program (DAP)[1] allows the IRS to adjust the income tax returns of employers and plan participants when there is a discrepancy between the returns and the records of employee plans. The DAP (which is not a voluntary compliance program under EPCRS) allows the IRS to extend the statute of limitations for Forms 1120 and 1040 and to make adjustments to the forms in the event of plan disqualification, the disallowance of deductions for contributions, and distribution reporting errors.

A discrepancy adjustment is not a full audit of a taxpayer's individual or corporate tax return. A discrepancy adjustment is based solely on the books and records of the employee plan or exempt organization. If there is a discrepancy between those records and one or more entries on a related filed income tax return, an adjustment will be proposed by the EP or EO Specialist.

☐ The DAP is discussed further at CCH Pension Plan Guide ¶ 6250.

---

[1]IRM 7.6.4 (4/15/99).

¶ 380

For More Information

☐ For a thorough review of plan qualification rules, see ¶ 801-1759 of the CCH Pension Plan Guide. A complete discussion of the IRS enforcement programs is at CCH Pension Plan Guide ¶ 6200-6250.

Limits on Benefits and Contributions

¶ 500
General Rules

A qualified plan is subject to stipulated benefit and contribution limits. Employer contributions to a defined benefit plan may not exceed the amount necessary to fund an employee's maximum annual benefit. For 2012, the highest annual benefit payable under a defined benefit plan is the *lesser* of $200,000 or 100% of the employee's compensation. Annual additions to a participant's account under a defined contribution plan may not exceed the *lesser* of $50,000 or 100% of the participant's compensation.

The amount of annual compensation to be considered in determining contributions or benefits is capped at $250,000 for 2012. A plan may not base contributions or benefits on compensation in excess of the limit.

Plan limits are reduced actuarially for early retirement benefits. Similarly, plan limits are increased actuarially for benefits that begin after retirement age. The adjustment of benefits is made under a mortality table prescribed by the IRS and in accord with stipulated interest rates.

Contributions or benefits provided by an employer in excess of the applicable limits may not be deducted. In addition, an employer may not deduct contributions to a plan to fund anticipated cost-of-living adjustments.

¶ 505

Plans Subject to Benefit and Contribution Limits

The benefit and contribution limits apply to a trust which is part of a pension, profit-sharing, or stock bonus plan, an annuity contract purchased by an exempt organization or public school, an employee annuity under Code Sec. 403(a), and a simplified employee pension plan under Code Sec. 408(k). Plans of self-employed persons and S corporations also are subject to the overall limitations.

Cash balance plans are defined benefit plans for purposes of Code Sec. 415. In addition, 403(b) plans (other than those that provide for individual accounts under Code Sec. 414(i)) are also treated as defined benefit plan sponsors for purposes of the Code Sec. 415 rules.[1]

The plans must meet the benefit and contribution limits in order to qualify under Code Sec. 401(a).[2]

---

[1] Reg. § 1.415(b)-1(a)(2).

[2] Code Secs. 401(a)(16) and 415(a)(1).

¶ 507

Multiple Plans Treated as Single Plan—Aggregation

For purposes of the limitations on benefits and contributions, all defined benefit plans of an employer and all defined contribution plans of an employer, whether or not terminated, must be treated as one plan.[1] Similarly, all of the defined benefit plans and defined contribution plans of corporations, partnerships, and proprietorships which are under common control are aggregated.[2] Thus, the limitations cannot be avoided merely by creating multiple plans.

Multiemployer plans

A multiemployer plan is not aggregated with non-multiemployer plans for purposes of applying the 100%-of-compensation benefit limit to non-multiemployer plans under Code Sec. 415(b)(1)(B). In addition, a multiemployer plan is not aggregated with any other multiemployer plan for purposes of determining any Code Sec. 415 limitation.[3]

Plan disqualification

If the limitations are exceeded for a particular limitation year because of the application of the aggregation rules, one or more of the plans (and the underlying trusts) will be disqualified.[4] The disqualification of the plan (and the underlying trust) would be effective as of the first day of the first plan year containing any portion of the particular limitation year.[5] However, no plan that has been terminated may be disqualified until all other plans and trusts have been disqualified.[6]

If the Code Sec. 415(b) limits are exceeded in a limitation year solely because of the application of the Code Sec. 415(f) aggregation requirement, one or more of the plans will be disqualified pursuant to specified ordering rules, until (without regard to annual benefits under the disqualified plan or plans) the remaining plans satisfy the applicable 415 limits.[7]

Under the ordering rules, if there are two or more plans that have not been terminated during the limitation year, and if one of those plans is a multiemployer plan, one or more of the plans that has not been terminated and is not a multiemployer plan will be disqualified in that limitation year.[8]

Employer may elect plan to be disqualified. An employer may elect which of its plans are to be disqualified. Affiliated employers may make the election. However, the election must be made by all of those affected employers.[9]

---

[1] Code Sec. 415(f); IRS Reg. § 1.415(f)-1(a)(1).

[2] Code Sec. 415(g); IRS Reg. § 1.415(a)-1(f)(1).

[3] Code Sec.415(f)(3) , as added by P.L. 107-16 (Economic Growth and Tax Relief Reconciliation Act of 2001) and redesignated as Code Sec. 415(f)(2) by P.L. 110-458 (Worker, Retiree, and Employer Recovery Act), effective for years beginning after December 31, 2005.

[4] IRS Reg. § § 1.415(g)-1(a) and (b)(3).

[5] IRS Reg. § 1.415(g)-1(b)(1).

[6] Code Sec.415(g).

[7] IRS Reg. § 1.415(g)-1(b)(3).

[8] IRS Reg. § 1.415(g)-1(b)(3)(ii).

[9] IRS Reg. § 1.415(g)-1(b)(3)(iii)(A).

¶ 510
Special Aggregation Rules

Any defined benefit or defined contribution plan maintained by any member of an affiliated service group is deemed to be maintained by all members of the affiliated service group.[1] Formerly affiliated plans of an employer are taken into account in applying the aggregation rules. However, limits apply to the extent to which a plan maintained by an employer must aggregate benefits accrued under a plan that was formerly maintained by the employer or that was maintained by an entity that was formerly affiliated with the employer under the affiliated employer rules of IRS Reg. § 1.415(a)-1(f). Specifically, a formerly affiliated plan of an employer is treated as if it were a plan that terminated immediately prior to the "cessation of affiliation" with sufficient assets to pay benefit liabilities under the plan, and had purchased assets to provide plan benefits.[2]

Formerly affiliated plan. A formerly affiliated plan of an employer is a plan that, immediately prior to the cessation of affiliation, was actually maintained by one or more of the entities that constitute the employer (as determined under the employer affiliation rules) and that immediately after the cessation of affiliation, is not actually maintained by any of the entities that constitute the employer (as determined under the employer affiliation rules).[3]

Cessation of affiliation. A cessation of affiliation is defined as an event that causes an entity to no longer be aggregated with one or more entities as a single employer under the employer affiliation rules (e.g., sale of subsidiary outside of a controlled group), or that causes a plan to not actually be maintained by any of the entities that constitute the employer under the employer affiliation rules (e.g., transfer of plan sponsorship outside of a controlled group).[4]

---

[1] IRS Reg. § 1.415(a)-1(f)(2).

[2] IRS Reg. § 1.415(f)-1(b)(2).

[3] IRS Reg. § 1.415(f)-1(b)(2)(ii).

[4] *Ibid.*

¶ 515

Annual Defined Benefit Plan Limit

Employer contributions to a defined benefit plan may not exceed the amount necessary to fund a participant's maximum annual benefit. The highest annual benefit that may be paid is the lesser of:

1. $160,000 ($200,000, as indexed for 2012—see below), or

2. 100% of the average compensation for the participant's "high three years" (the period of not more than three consecutive calendar years during which the participant had the greatest aggregate compensation from the employer).[1]

A plan may use compensation of only $250,000 in 2012 ($245,000 in 2011) for the purpose of benefit accruals or allocations.[2] See ¶ 545.

Example: Ray started working for ABC Corp. when he was age 43 and immediately became a participant in ABC's defined benefit plan. The annual benefit accrual under the plan is 1.5% of the average of Ray's highest three consecutive calendar years during which he was an active participant in the plan. Ray's average compensation for his highest three years is $160,000. Accordingly, Ray's annual benefit at age 63 would be $48,000 (30% (1.5% × 20 years) of $160,000). Because the annual benefit does not exceed the maximum allowable annual benefit, the plan qualifies with regard to the annual benefit payable to Ray.

Aggregation rules. For purposes of the limitations, all defined benefit plans maintained by an employer (including terminated plans) are treated as a single defined benefit plan.[3] The percentage-of-compensation limitation, above, is computed separately for each defined benefit plan of an employer.

Limit indexed for inflation

The annual defined benefit plan limit is subject to cost-of-living adjustments in $5,000 increments.[5] For 2012, the maximum limitation for the annual benefit for defined benefit plans is $200,000 ($195,000 in 2011).

Annual benefit

A participant's annual benefit, for purposes of the Code Sec. 415 limits, is a benefit that is payable in the form of a straight life annuity.[6] A straight life annuity is payable in equal installments for the life of a participant, and terminates upon the participant's death.

Employee contributions. The annual benefit under a DB plan does not include the annual benefit attributable to mandatory employee contributions. However, while these benefits are not subject to the 415(b) limit, they are subject to the 415(c) annual additions limit.

A mandatory employee contribution encompasses amounts contributed to the plan by the employer that are required as condition of employment, as a condition of participation in the plan, or as a condition of obtaining benefits (or additional benefits) under the plan that are attributable to employer contributions.[7]

Employee contributions to a DB plan that are not maintained in separate accounts, as defined in Code Sec. 414(k), also constitute mandatory employee contributions, even if an employee can elect whether to make contributions or Code Sec. 411 does not apply to the plan. The reason for this rule, the IRS explains, is that, depending on the investment performance of plan assets, employee contributions may be needed to pay a portion of the participant's benefit that is conditioned on those employee contributions.[8] Note, any other employee contributions (plus earnings) are treated as a separate DC plan, rather than as part of the DB plan.[9]

The annual benefit attributable to mandatory employee contributions does not include: (1) contributions that are picked up by a governmental employer (pursuant to Code Sec. 414(h)(2)); (2) repayment of any loan made to a participant from the plan; and (3) repayment of any amount that was previously distributed.[10] Such benefits are subject to the 415(b) limit. In addition, note that while the repayment of an employee contribution is not treated as an employee contribution for purposes of the 415 limits, the original contribution is considered an employee contribution.

Benefits attributable to rollover contributions. The annual benefit under a DB plan does not include the annual benefit attributable to rollover contributions made from an eligible retirement plan (including IRAs and 403(b) plans) to a DB plan (i.e., rollover contributions that are not maintained in a separate account treated as a separate DC plan under Code Sec. 414(k)).[11]

Benefits under terminated plan

The rules governing the treatment of benefits under a terminated DB plan vary depending on whether the plan has sufficient assets to pay accrued benefits.

In the event a DB plan is terminated with sufficient assets to pay accrued benefits and a participant in the plan has not yet begun receiving benefits under the plan, all other DB plans maintained by the employer that maintained the terminated plan must, for purposes of applying the 415(b) limit to the participant, take into account the benefits provided pursuant to the annuities purchased to provide benefits under the terminated plan at each possible annuity starting date.[12]

¶515

By contrast, if a DB plan terminates without sufficient assets to pay the accrued benefits of all plan participants, all other DB plans maintained by the employer that maintained the terminated plan must, for purposes of applying the 415(b) limit to a participant, take into account the benefits that are actually provided to the participant under the terminated plan.[13]

Conversion of benefit to straight life annuity

Benefits paid in a form other than a straight life annuity must be adjusted (i.e., converted) to an actuarially equivalent straight life annuity beginning at the same time, in order to determine the annual benefit with respect to that distribution.[14] Generally, the annual benefit is determined as the greater of the actuarially equivalent straight life annuity determined under the plan's actuarial assumptions or the actuarially equivalent straight life annuity determined under statutorily prescribed actuarial assumptions. In the event the equivalent annuity exceeds the 415(b) limit, the benefit will need to be reduced.

Application of minimum present value rules affects actuarial assumptions. The final regulations reflect statutory changes that specify the actuarial assumptions (i.e., interest rate and mortality assumptions) to be used for the equivalency calculation.[15] The applicable rules vary depending on whether benefits are paid in a form (e.g., lump-sum and installment payment) to which the minimum present value rules of Code Sec. 417(e)(3) apply.

Benefits not subject to Code Sec. 417(e)(3). The interest rate assumption for benefits not subject to Code Sec. 417(e)(3) may not be less than the rate of 5 percent or the interest rate specified in the plan.[16] However, the interest rate assumption for benefits that are subject to Code Sec.417(e)(3) may not be less than the greater of: (1) 5.5 percent, (2) the rate that provides a benefit of not more than 105 percent of the benefit that would be provided if the applicable interest rate for determining minimum lump-sums were the interest rate assumption; or (3) the interest rate specified in the plan.[17]

Church plans

Benefits accrued for church plan participants who are not highly compensated will not be reduced if the benefit exceeds 100 percent of their average compensation for their highest paid three years.[18] Accordingly, benefits under a church plan for such participants will be limited only to the annually adjusted dollar limit of Code Sec. 415(b)(1)(A).

---

[1] Code Sec. 415(b)(1), as amended by P.L. 109-280 (Pension Protection Act of 2006), Act Sec. 832(a). See also IR-2011-103, 10-20-2011 at CCH PENSION PLAN GUIDE ¶ 17,037Q.

[2] Code Sec. 401(a)(17); IRS Reg. § 1.401(a)(17)-1(b)(3).

[3] Code Sec. 415(f)(1).

[5] Code Sec. 415(d). See also IR-2011-103, 10-20-2011 at CCH PENSION PLAN GUIDE ¶ 17,037Q.

[6] IRS Reg. § 415(b)-1(b)(i)(A).

[7] Code Sec.411(c)(2)(C); IRS Reg. § 1.411(c)-1(c)(4).

[8] Preamble to IRS Reg. § 1.415-1(b).

[9] IRS Reg. § 1.415(b)-1(b)(2)(iv).

[10] IRS Reg. § 1.415(b)-1(b)(2)(ii).

[11] Reg. § 1.415(b)-1(b)(2)(v).

[12] IRS Reg. § 1.415(b)-1(b)(5)(i).

[13] IRS Reg. § 1.415(b)-1(b)(5)(ii).

[14] Code Sec.415(b)(2)(B).

[15]IRS Reg. § 1.415(b)-1(c). The final regulations became effective April 5, 2007.

[16]Code Sec.415(b)(2)(E)(i).

[17]Code Sec. 415(b)(2)(E)(ii), as amended by P.L. 109-280 (Pension Protection Act of 2006), Act Sec. 303(a), effective for distributions made in years beginning after December 31, 2005. Special rules

apply to small employers, effective for tax years beginning after December 31, 2008. See Code Sec. 415(b)(2)(E)(vi), as added by P.L. 110-458 (Worker, Retiree, and Employer Recovery Act of 2008).

[18]Code Sec.415(b)(11), as amended by P.L. 109-280 (Pension Protection Act of 2006), Act Sec. 867(a).

¶ 525
Defined Contribution Plan Limits

Annual additions to a participant's account under a defined contribution plan (including target benefit and hybrid plans (see ¶ 103)) may not exceed the lesser of $40,000 or 100% of the participant's compensation.[1] The $40,000 figure is adjusted for inflation in $1,000 increments.[2] The figure for 2012 is $50,000 ($49,000 in 2011).[3]

Application of Code Sec. 401(a)(17) compensation limit

A plan may not base allocations under a defined contribution plan on compensation in excess of the annual limitation under Code Sec. 401 (a)(17) ($250,000 for 2012, $245,000 in 2011).[4] Accordingly, compensation used by a plan in applying the 415 limits may not exceed the applicable Code Sec. 401(a)(17) limit for the year.

Limitation year

The limitation year, for purposes of determining whether annual additions comply with the 415 limits, is generally the calendar year. Alternatively, the plan may specify the use of any other consecutive 12 month period as the limitation period.[5]

Annual additions

Annual additions for purposes of the Code Sec. 415 limits include:

1. elective deferrals (other than catch-up contributions);
2. employer matching contributions;
3. employer nonelective contributions;
4. employee after-tax contributions (mandatory and voluntary);
5. forfeitures allocated to a participant's individual account following the termination of nonvested or partially vested participants; and
6. employer contributions to other defined contribution plans, such as profit-sharing plans, money purchase plans, and ESOPs.[6]

Limit on elective contributions to a 401(k) plan

A maximum annual deferral limit ($17,000 for 2012; $16,500 for 2011) is imposed on elective contributions to 401(k) plans for each employee.[7] These contributions are included in the annual addition for purposes of the limits on contributions under defined contribution plans.

☐ Contributions or benefits in excess of the applicable limits may not be deducted. See ¶ 580.

[1] Code Sec. 415(c)(1).

[2] Code Sec. 415(d).

[3] IR-2011-103, 10-20-2011, CCH Pension Plan Guide ¶ 17,037Q.

[4] IRS Reg. § 1.415(c)-2(f).

[5] IRS Reg. § 1.415(j)-1(a) and (b).

[6] Code Sec.415(c)(2).

[7] Code Sec. 402(g). Note that 401(k) plans may permit or require certain contributions of the dol-

lar equivalent of participants' unused paid time off (PTO) in accordance with the governing nondiscrimination requirements and contribution limits. Rev. Rul. 2009-31, I.R.B. 2009-39, 9-28-2009 at CCH Pension Plan Guide ¶ 19,948Z-267; Rev. Rul. 2009-32, I.R.B. 2009-39, 9-28-2009 at CCH Pension Plan Guide ¶ 19,948Z-268. See ¶ 2981 for more information.

¶ 527
Exceptions to Annual Addition Rule

For purposes of the limits on defined contribution plans (see ¶ 525), annual additions include mandatory and voluntary employee contributions.[1] However, annual additions do not include: rollover contributions, repayment by the participant of loans made by the plan to the participant, repayments of cash-out benefits under Code Sec. 411(a)(7), or the direct transfer of employee contributions from one qualified plan to another.[2] In addition, the repayment to the plan of distributions of mandatory employee contributions[3] and employee contributions to simplified employee pension plans[4] are not treated as annual additions.

Restorative payments. Restorative payments that are allocated to participants' accounts do not give rise to an annual addition for any limitation year. Restorative payments are generally payments made to restore losses to a plan resulting from actions by a fiduciary for which there is a reasonable risk of liability for breach of fiduciary duty, where similarly situated plan participants are treated similarly with respect to the payments. Payments made in order to restore some or all of the plan's losses due to an action (or a failure to act) that creates a reasonable risk of liability for such breach of fiduciary duty under ERISA or under other applicable federal or state law (e.g., payments made pursuant to a DOL order or court-approved settlement or under the DOL's Voluntary Fiduciary Correction Program) also may be treated as restorative payments.[5]

[1] IRS Reg. § 1.415(c)-1(b)(3).

[2] *Ibid.*

[3] IRS Reg. § 1.411(a)-7(d)(6)(iii).

[4] Code Sec. 415(c)(2).

[5] Reg. § 1.415(c)-1(b)(2)(ii)(C).

¶ 530
Time for Crediting Annual Additions

An annual addition is credited to a participant's account for a particular limitation year if it is *allocated* to the participant's account during the limitation year.[1] The contribution must be made within 30 days after the end of the period during which plan contributions for the year can be made. Contributions made by tax-exempt employers can be made by the 15th day of the tenth calendar month following the close of the taxable year, or fiscal year, if there is no taxable year.[2]

Voluntary or mandatory employee contributions are not credited to a participant's account unless the contributions are actually made to the plan no later than 30 days after the limitation year.

[1] IRS Reg. § 1.415(c)-1(b)(6)(i)(A).   [2]Reg. § 1.415(c)-1(b)(6)(i)(B).

¶ 535
Forfeitures

Forfeitures are treated as annual additions for the limitation year that contains the date as of which the amounts are allocated to a participant's account as a forfeiture.[1] Any income attributable to the forfeiture is also considered an annual addition.

Erroneous contributions

Contributions that are made to a participant's account because of an erroneous forfeiture in a prior limitation year or because of an erroneous failure to allocate amounts in a prior limitation year, are considered annual additions for the prior limitation year.[2]

[1] Code Sec. 415 (c)(2); IRS Reg. § 1.415(c)-1(b)(6)(i)(D).   [2] IRS Reg. § 1.415(c)-1(b)(6)(ii)(A).

¶ 537
Correcting Excess Annual Additions

In the event that the limit on annual additions for a participant is exceeded because of the allocation of forfeitures, reasonable errors in the estimation of a participant's annual compensation or the determination of the amount of elective deferrals, or other limited circumstances, the excess amounts are not considered annual additions for a limitation year, provided they are corrected under methods and procedures specified by the IRS in the Employee Plans Compliance Resolution System (EPCRS).[1]

[1]Reg. § 1.415(c)-1; Reg. § 1.401(a)-2(b); Reg. § 1.401(a)(9)-5, A-9(b)(1), and Reg. § 1.402(c)-2, A-4(a). Under prior IRS Reg. § 1.415-6(b)(6), in order to correct excess annual additions, plans could reallocate the excess to participants; reduce employer contributions; hold excess in suspense account; distribute deferrals or return employee contributions. The use of EPCRS to correct excess annual additions is effective for limitation years beginning on or after July 1, 2007.

¶ 540
Compensation for Purposes of the Limitations

Generally, a participant's compensation for purposes of the limitations on contributions and benefits includes the participant's wages, salaries, fees for professional service, and other amounts received (in cash or kind) for personal services actually rendered in the course of employment with the employer maintaining the plan, to the extent includible in the participant's gross income.[1] Compensation also includes: commissions paid to salespersons; amounts based on a percentage of profits; commissions on insurance premiums; tips; bonuses; fringe benefits; reimbursements; expense allowances under nonaccountable plans;[2] employer contributions to a Code Sec. 403(b) tax sheltered annuity, whether or not the amounts are excludable from an employee's gross income; employer contributions to a simplified employee pension plan (SEP) that are excludable from an employee's gross income; elective deferrals to a 401(k) plan (including contributions to a SIMPLE 401(k) plan) that are not includible in the employee's income in the year of contribution; elective or salary reduction contributions to a SIMPLE IRA; elective contributions to a Code Sec. 457(b) eligible deferred compensation plan; elective or salary reduction contributions made to a cafeteria plan; qualified transportation benefits provided pursuant to salary reduction arrangements under Code Sec. 132(f); amounts received through employer-provided accident and health insurance under Code Secs. 104(a)(3) and 105(a) (or through a self-insured medical reimbursement plan under Code Sec. 105(h)), to the extent included in gross income; reimbursed moving expenses to the extent that it is reasonable to believe that they are not deductible under Code Sec. 217; the value of a nonstatutory stock option includible in the employee's gross income for the tax year in which granted; the amount includible in an employee's gross income following an election under Code Sec. 83(b) to be taxed on the value of property transferred in connection with the performance of services; and the earned income of a self-employed individual. Compensation further encompasses foreign earned income, whether or not excludable from the participant's income. In addition, effective for limitation years beginning on or after July 1, 2007, compensation includes amounts includible in the gross income of an employee under Code Sec. 409A or Code Sec. 457(f)(1)(A), or because the amounts were constructively received.

What compensation does not include

Compensation for purposes of the limits on contributions and benefits does not include the following.[3]

1. Distributions from a deferred compensation plan (other than an unfunded nonqualified plan), even if the amounts are includible in the gross income of the employee when distributed;

2. Amounts realized from the exercise of a nonqualified stock option, or when restricted stock (or property) held by an employee becomes freely transferable or is no longer subject to a substantial risk of forfeiture; and

3. Amounts realized from the sale, exchange, or other disposition of stock acquired under a qualified stock option; and premiums for group-term life insurance, to the extent the premiums are not includible in an employee's gross income.

Alternative definition of compensation

In lieu of using the basic definition of compensation described above, a plan may define compensation as either:

1. wages as defined for purposes of income tax withholding under Code Sec. 3401(a), determined without regard to any rules that

limit remuneration included in wages on the basis of the nature or location of the employment or the services performed; or

2. wages as defined under Code Sec. 3401(a), plus all other payments of compensation to an employee by his or her employer (in the course of the employer's business) for which the employer is required to furnish the employee Form W-2.[4]

---

[1] Code Sec. 415(c)(3); IRS Reg. § 1.415(c)-2(g)(6).

[2] IRS Reg. § 1.62-2(c).
[3] IRS Reg. § 1.415(c)-2(c).
[4] IRS Reg. § 1.415-2(c)-2(d)(4).

¶ 545
Includible Compensation

In computing qualified plan contributions or benefits for each participant, the amount of annual compensation that must be taken into account by a plan for any plan year is subject to an inflation-adjusted $250,000 limit in 2012 ($245,000 in 2011).[1]

Application of limitation

The dollar limit applies in two ways. First, a plan may not base contributions or benefits on compensation in excess of the annual limit. Second, the amount of a participant's annual compensation taken into account in applying the nondiscrimination rules is subject to the annual limitation.[2]

---

[1] Code Sec. 401(a)(17), as amended by P.L. 107-16 (Economic Growth and Tax Relief Reconciliation Act of 2001). In pre-2002 years, the limit

was a statutory $150,000, adjusted to reflect cost of living increases. See also IR-2011-103, 10-20-2011, CCH PENSION PLAN GUIDE ¶ 17,037Q.
[2] IRS Reg. § 1.401(a)(17)-1(a)(1).

¶ 550
Qualified Cost-of-Living Arrangements

Defined benefit pension plans may maintain a qualified cost-of-living arrangement under which employer and employee contributions are used to fund cost-of-living increases to the primary benefit under the plan.[1] Cost-of-living adjustments are based on increases in the cost of living after the annuity starting date, as generally determined by one or more indexes prescribed by the IRS.

Nondiscrimination requirements

A qualified cost-of-living arrangement is subject to limitations on the amount of the benefit and nondiscrimination requirements. Basically, the right to participate in a qualified cost-of-living arrangement must be open to all plan participants, except key employees.[2]

Arrangement is not mandatory

A qualified cost-of-living arrangement is elective, not mandatory. Accordingly, the arrangement is also subject to rules governing its election by a participant.

☐ Qualified cost-of-living arrangements are discussed in detail at CCH Pension Plan Guide ¶ 1600.

---

[1] Code Sec. 415(k)(2)(B).

[2] Code Sec. 415(k)(2)(D).

¶ 555

Adjustment of Defined Benefit Limit for Retirement Before Age 62 and After Age 65

An adjustment to the Code Sec. 415(b) dollar limit must be made for benefits in the form of a straight life annuity that begin before the participant attains age 62.[1] The dollar limit is also adjusted for benefits that begin after the participant attains age 65.[2] Generally, the applicable benefit limit is reduced to an actuarially equivalent benefit for a participant who elects pre-age 62 retirement, and increased to an actuarially equivalent benefit for participants who elect post-age 65 retirement. The adjustments are calculated using statutory factors or plan factors (whichever results in a lower limit).

Statutory factors. In determining the adjustment using statutory factors, for a distribution with an annuity starting date that occurs before a participant attains age 62 (or after the participant attains age 65), the age-adjusted Code Sec. 415(b)(1)(A) dollar limit is determined as the actuarial equivalent of the annual amount of a straight life annuity commencing at the annuity starting date that has the same actuarial present value as a deferred straight life annuity beginning at age 62 (or age 65) where: (1) annual payments under the straight life annuity beginning at age 62 or age 65 are equal to the dollar limitation of Code Sec. 415(b)(1)(A) (as adjusted under Code Sec. 415(d)), and (2) the actuarially equivalent straight life annuity is computed using a 5 percent interest rate and the applicable mortality table under IRS Reg. § 1.417(e)-1(d)(2) that is effective for the annuity starting date (and expressing the participant's age based on completed calendar months as of the annuity starting date).[3]

Plan factors. In the event a plan provides for an immediately commencing straight life annuity, an alternative method using plan factors can be used to determine the applicable adjustment.[4] The amount of the pre-age 62 adjustments determined using plan factors is the Code Sec. 415(b)(1)(A) dollar limit (as adjusted) multiplied by the ratio of the annual amount of the immediately commencing straight life annuity under the plan to the annual amount of the straight life annuity under the plan commencing at age 62. For purposes of this calculation, both annual amounts are determined without applying the rules of Code Sec. 415.[5]

Similarly, the amount of the post-age 65 adjustment using plan factors is determined by multiplying the adjusted 415(b) dollar limit by an adjustment ratio, which is equal to the annual amount of the adjusted immediately commencing straight life annuity to the adjusted age 65 straight life annuity.[6]

Mortality adjustments

In determining the actuarially equivalent amount for distributions beginning before age 62 or after age 65, a mortality adjustment will not be required, to the extent a forfeiture does not occur upon a participant's death before the annuity starting date. Under such a condition, no adjustment is required in order to reflect the probability of the participant's death between the annuity starting date and the participant's attainment of age 62 or between the participant's attainment of age 65 and the annuity starting date (i.e., the relevant time period), unless the plan provides for such adjustment. In the event a forfeiture does occur upon the participant's death before the annuity starting date, an adjustment is required to reflect the probability of the participant's death between the annuity starting date and the participant's attainment of age 62 or the participant's attainment of age 65.[7] A specified method is provided for applying the mortality adjustment rules.

[1] Code Sec. 415(b)(2)(D); IRS Reg. § 1.415(b)-1(e)(1)(i). Note, prior to 2002, if retirement benefits under a defined benefit plan began before the participant's attainment of social security retirement age, the $90,000 indexed limit ($140,000 for 2001) was reduced to equal the actuarial equivalent of an annual benefit of $90,000 beginning at the social security retirement age.

[2] Code Sec. 415(b)(2)(D).

[3] IRS Reg. § 1.415(b)-1(d)(1)(i) and IRS Reg. § 1.415(b)-1(e)(1)(i).

[4] IRS Reg. § 1.415(b)-1(d)(1)(i).

[5] IRS Reg. § 1.415(b)-1(d)(1)(i)-(ii).

[6] IRS Reg. § 1.415(b)-1(e)(1); IRS Reg. § 1.415(b)-1(e)(2)(i).

[7] IRS Reg. § 1.415(b)-1(d)(2); IRS Reg. § 1.415(b)-1(e)(3).

¶ 565

Reduction of Dollar Limit for Less Than 10 Years of Participation

The dollar limit on defined benefit plan benefits is reduced by 10% for each year that the retiree's participation is less than 10 years.[1] However, benefits will never be reduced below 10% of the applicable limit.[2] The dollar limit is $200,000 in 2012 ($195,000 in 2011).

Example: Ben participated in the defined benefit pension plan of LAN Corp. until he retired in 2012, at normal retirement age, after 6 years of service. At retirement, Ben's compensation was $150,000. Because Ben completed less than 10 years of participation in the plan, his benefit would be limited to the lesser of 100% of compensation reduced by 10% per year for years of participation below 10 ($150,000 × 6/10 = $90,000) or the defined benefit plan limit in 2011 reduced in a similar manner ($195,000 × 6/10 = $117,000).

Disregard service prior to plan participation

An employee's service with the employer prior to becoming a plan participant is disregarded in determining the dollar limit on benefits payable under the plan. However, for purposes of the 100% compensation limitation, years of service rather than years of participation are used in determining the reduction.[3]

[1] Code Sec. 415(b)(5)(A).

[2] Code Sec. 415(b)(5)(C).

[3] Code Sec. 415(b)(5)(B).

¶ 567
Aggregate Limit for Combined Plans—Repealed

The overall limit on contributions made on behalf of an employee who participates in both a defined contribution plan and a defined benefit plan maintained by the same employer is repealed, effective for limitation years beginning after December 31, 1999.[1] Accordingly, with respect to limitation years beginning on or after January 1, 2000, a 401(k) plan, or other defined contribution plan, will not fail to satisfy the requirements of Code Sec. 415 merely because the annual additions for any participant exceed the combined plan limit of Code Sec. 415(e).[2] Similarly, a defined benefit plan will not fail to meet Code Sec. 415 merely because the plan, effective for limitation years beginning after 1999, allows a participant who has not begun to receive benefits as of January 1, 2000, to receive benefits in excess of the combined limit.

[1] P.L. 104-188 (Small Business Job Protection Act), Sec. 1452(a), repealing Code Sec. 415(e).

[2] IRS Notice 99-44, I.R.B. 1999-16, Q&A-1, CCH PENSION PLAN GUIDE ¶ 17,116Z.

¶ 570
$10,000 *De Minimis* Exception

An annual defined benefit plan may pay a benefit of $10,000 or less that is derived from employer contributions, regardless of the limitations on benefit payments.[1]

Example: Teri's average compensation for her highest three years was $8,500. Assuming that all other conditions are satisfied, Teri's employer's plan could pay her an annual benefit of $9,000 (or any other amount that does not exceed $10,000), even though this is more than the average of her highest three years of compensation.

Consider payments from all plans

The benefit paid to the participant from all defined benefit plans of the employer must not exceed $10,000 for the plan year or any prior plan year.

Mandatory employee contributions not a separate DC plan

In the event a defined benefit plan provides for mandatory employee contributions, these contributions are not considered to be a separate defined contribution plan maintained by the employer. Thus, a contributory defined benefit plan may utilize the de minimis dollar limitation.[2] Under any other circumstances, however, such voluntary or mandatory employee contributions are considered a separate defined contribution plan maintained by the employer.

Multiemployer plans

The $10,000 *de minimis* exception is applicable to a participant in a multiemployer plan without regard to whether the participant ever participated in one or more other plans maintained by an employer who also maintains the multiemployer plan. However, none of the other plans could be maintained as a result of collective bargaining involving the same employee representative as the multiemployer plan.[3]

---

[1] Code Sec. 415(b)(4); IRS Reg. § 1.415(b)-1(a)(7) and IRS Reg. § 1.415(b)-1(f).

[2] IRS Reg. § 1.415(b)-1(f)(4).

[3] IRS Reg. § 1.415(b)-(f)(3).

¶ 575
Rules for Tax-Sheltered Annuities

The contribution limitation for tax-sheltered annuities under Code Sec. 403(b) is the same as that for qualified plans. 403(b) plans are treated as defined contribution plans and any contributions made by the employer are to be treated as employer contributions to a defined contribution plan.[1]

☐ The rules for tax-sheltered annuities are covered at ¶ 3100 and following.

---

[1] Prior to 2002, an exclusion allowance permitted certain employers to in effect exceed a 20% limitation on excluding employer contributions if a shortfall in contributions had occurred in earlier years. See P.L. 107-16 (Economic Growth and Tax Relief Reconciliation Act of 2001), Act Sec. 611(a)(5)(A), striking Code Sec. 415(c)(4).

¶ 577
Exception to Limits for Reemployed Veterans

Qualified retirement plans may allow veterans returning to employment from military service to make up employee contributions and elective deferrals that were not made during the employee's period of military service without risking disqualification for violating the applicable limits on contributions and benefits.[1] Qualified plans may also allow employers to make matching contributions at the rate that would have applied had the employee's employment not been interrupted by military service.[2]

Survivor and disability payments

Qualified plans (as well as 403(b) and 457(b) plans) are required to provide, with respect to a participant who dies while performing qualified military service, that the survivors of the participant are entitled to any additional benefits (other than benefit accruals relating to the period of qualified military service) that would have been provided under the plan had the participant resumed employment with the employer maintaining the plan and then terminated employment on account of death.[3] Thus, if a plan provides for accelerated vesting, ancillary life insurance benefits, or other survivor benefits that are contingent upon a participant's termination of employment on account of death, the plan must provide such benefits to the beneficiary of a participant who dies during qualified military service.[4]

Limit on make-up contributions

Make-up contributions (including elective deferrals) may not exceed the amount of contributions that would have been permitted under the applicable limits for the year for which the contributions are made if the individual had continued to be employed by the employer during the period of service.[5]

[1] Code Sec. 414(u)(1).

[2] Code Sec. 414(u)(2).

[3] Code Sec.401(a)(37), as added by P.L. 110-245 (Heroes Earnings Assistance and Tax Relief Act of 2008), Act Sec. 104(G), generally effective with

respect to deaths and disabilities occurring on or after January 1, 2007.

[4] IRS Notice 2010-15, Q&A-1, I.R.B. 2010-6, 2-8-2010, at CCH Pension Plan Guide ¶ 17,144L.

[5] Code Sec. 414(u)(2)(B).

¶ 580
No Deduction for Amounts in Excess of Limits

Contributions or benefits provided on behalf of an employee that exceed the Code Sec. 415 limits for defined contribution plans or for defined benefit plans may not be deducted.[1] The IRS has also disqualified a plan for making excess contributions.[2]

No advance funding for COLAs

An employer may not deduct contributions to a qualified defined benefit pension plan that are designed to fund anticipated cost-of-living adjustments to the dollar limit.

[1] Code Sec. 404(j).

[2] *Buzzetta Construction Corp. v. Commissioner,* TC (1989), 92 TC 641, CCH Dec. 45,555.

¶ 585
For More Information

☐ For more information on benefit and contribution limits, see ¶ 1554-1645 and ¶ 2111-2117 of the CCH Pension Plan Guide.

Contributions and Deductions

¶ 600

Overview of Limits on Deductible Contributions

An employer's deduction for contributions to pension and profit-sharing plans, as well as other types of arrangements, is subject to restrictions governing the type and amount of the contribution.

Ordinary and necessary business expenses

Generally, contributions to qualified plans must be ordinary and necessary business expenses. In addition, contributions may not exceed a reasonable amount of compensation.

Limits on amount of contributions

Specific limitations also apply to the deduction of contributions to qualified plans. Contributions to a pension and annuity plan may not exceed the actuarial cost of the benefits promised by the plan. Contributions to a profit-sharing or stock bonus plan may not exceed a percentage of the compensation otherwise paid to covered employees.

Timing of contribution deduction

Contributions to qualified plans are generally deductible in the year in which the contribution is made. Contributions made to nonqualified plans may be deducted only in the year in which the contribution is includable in the employee's income.

Excise taxes

A 10% excise tax is assessed on nondeductible contributions that exceed the deductible limits. A 10% excise tax is also imposed on excess contributions and excess aggregate contributions under the plan.

SAVER's credit

A nonrefundable tax credit is available for contributions or deferrals to certain retirement plans and IRAs. The credit, known as the "saver's credit," is described in detail at ¶ 2983.

¶600

¶ 605

REQUIREMENTS FOR DEDUCTIBLE CONTRIBUTIONS: Business Expense Requirement

In order to be deductible, a contribution to a pension, annuity, profit-sharing, or stock bonus plan must be an "ordinary and necessary" expense incurred during the year:[1]

1. while carrying on a trade or business, or

2. for the production of income.

In addition, the contributions must be compensation for services actually rendered by the employee.

Deduction for "reasonable" compensation

Compensation for personal services is an ordinary and necessary business expense only if it is reasonable. If an employee receives more compensation than is determined to be reasonable, the excess amount is not deductible as a trade or business expense or as an income production expense.[2]

Adjusting deduction for contributions. Contributions based on an unreasonable amount of compensation must be adjusted to reflect the lower, reasonable amount of compensation. Any reasonable method may be used for adjusting deductions for contributions made by an employer to a profit-sharing or stock bonus trust.[3]

Standard of reasonableness. Whether compensation is reasonable is determined on a case-by-case basis. Factors that are examined include the employee's qualifications, the nature, extent, and scope of the work performed, the prevailing economic conditions, the prevailing rates of compensation for comparable work, and the size and complexity of the business.

Type of plan determines limit

The amount that an employer may deduct each year as a contribution to a qualified plan will depend on the type of plan involved. Separate limitations apply to contributions under a pension or annuity plan (see ¶ 647) and contributions under a profit-sharing or stock bonus plan (see ¶ 670).

---

[1] Code Sec. 404; IRS Reg. § 1.404(a)-1(b).

[2] IRS Reg. § 1.404(a)-1(b).

[3] Rev. Rul. 67-341, 1967-2 CB 156, CCH PENSION PLAN GUIDE ¶ 18,856.

¶ 610

REQUIREMENTS FOR DEDUCTIBLE CONTRIBUTIONS: Timing of Contributions

Deductions for contributions to a qualified plan are generally deductible in the year in which the contribution or compensation is paid, and not just accrued.[1] A contribution is deemed to have been made on the last day of the preceding tax year if it is made on account of that tax year and is made no later than the time for filing the return for that tax year, including extensions.[2] For example, if a calendar-year employer makes a contribution to the company retirement plan by March 15, the contribution may be deducted from its taxes for the previous year.

> **CCH Pointer:** In order to be deductible, contributions must be an ordinary and necessary expense incurred by the employer *during* the tax year in carrying on a trade or business or for the production of income. Thus, employer matching contributions are not deductible if they are attributable to compensation earned *after* the close of the plan year, if the plan year is different from the calendar year, and the contributions are all made within the same calendar year.[3]

Independent contractors

Contributions made on behalf of non-employee participants, such as independent contractors, also may not be deducted until the year in which the contribution is includable in the employee's income.[4]

Contributions must be made before deduction is claimed

Employers must actually make the contribution to a deferred compensation plan before they may claim a deduction for the payment.[5] A payment by check within prescribed time limits constitutes payment.[6]

Payment after close of tax year

A payment that is made after the close of the employer's tax year may still be deducted as if contributed for that tax year if it is made on account of that tax year and is made no later than the time for filing the return for that tax year, including extensions.[7] In addition, the plan must treat the post year-end payment as it would treat a payment actually received on the last day of the preceding year and the employer must designate in writing to the plan administrator that the contribution is for the prior year, or deduct the payment on its prior year tax return. Any designation of a payment as being on account of a preceding tax year is irrevocable.[8]

Extended deadline for disasters

The deadline for contributions to pension plans and IRAs may be extended by reason of a Presidentially declared disaster.[9]

Treatment of contributions to a multiemployer plan

An employer's determination of whether a contribution to a multiemployer plan is on account of a prior tax year is not treated as a method of accounting.[10] Therefore, an employer's decision to begin deducting contributions as allowed under Code Sec. 404(a)(6) is not a change in accounting method under Code Sec. 446, and is not subject to an adjustment under Code Sec. 481.

---

[1] Code Sec. 404(a).

[2] Code Sec. 404(a)(6).

[3] Internal Revenue Service Industry Specialization Program (ISP), coordinated issue paper, 9-5-95.

¶610

[4] Code Sec. 404(d); IRS Temporary Reg. § 1.404(d)-1T; Rev. Rul. 88-68, 1988-2 CB 117, CCH PENSION PLAN GUIDE ¶ 19,713A.

[5] Code Sec. 404(a).

[6] *Sachs v. Commissioner*, CA-3 (1953), 208 F2d 313; *Time Oil Co. v. Commissioner*, CA-9 (1958), 258 F2d 237; *Wasatch Chemical Co. v. Commissioner*, CA-10 (1963), 313 F2d 843. See also, *Don E. Williams Co. v. Commissioner*, US Sup Ct (1977), 429 U.S. 569 (employer's promissory note, even though payable on demand and fully secured, was not a payment of assets).

[7] Code Sec. 404(a)(6).

[8] Code Sec. 404(a)(6); Rev. Rul. 76-28, 1976-1 CB 106, CCH PENSION PLAN GUIDE ¶ 19,402.

[9] See IRS Reg. § 301.7508A-1(c)(1). The Victims of Terrorism Tax Relief Act (P.L. 107-134), signed into law on January 23, 2002, authorizes the Treasury, Labor Department, and PBGC to postpone filing and other deadlines for up to one year for reason of disasters, terrorism, or military actions.

[10] P.L. 107-16 (Economic Growth and Tax Relief Reconciliation Act of 2001), Sec. 658(a), effective for years ending after June 7, 2001, the date of enactment.

¶ 612

REQUIREMENTS FOR DEDUCTIBLE CONTRIBUTIONS: Plan Requirement

A contribution to a plan may not be deducted until the plan actually exists. A mere oral agreement to create a plan is not sufficient to establish a valid trust. Thus, a deduction may not be claimed for a contribution unless, before the end of the employer's tax year, there exists a valid trust, evidenced under a written executed instrument that prevents the diversion of funds other than for the exclusive benefit of employees or their beneficiaries.[1]

[1] Rev. Rul. 69-231, 1969-1 CB 118, CCH PENSION PLAN GUIDE ¶ 18,723.

¶ 615

REQUIREMENTS FOR DEDUCTIBLE CONTRIBUTIONS: Cash or Noncash Contributions

Contributions may be made in cash or other property, such as land or securities. The deduction for non-cash contributions is based on the fair market value of the property at the time the contribution is made.[1] A taxable gain may result if the property's value is greater than its basis at the time of contribution.

Contributions of company stock

If a corporation contributes its own stock, the amount deductible is the stock's fair market value at the time of the contribution but no gain or loss can be recognized by the employer under Code Sec. 1032.[2]

Prohibited transactions

An employer's contribution of property to a plan in satisfaction of its funding obligation may constitute a prohibited transaction.[3] See ¶ 2416.

[1] Rev. Rul. 62-217, 1962-2 CB 59, CCH PENSION PLAN GUIDE ¶ 18,433.

[2] *Ibid.*

[3] *Commissioner v. Keystone Consolidated Industries, Inc.*, US Sup Ct (1993), 113 SCt 2006; PWBA Interpretive Bulletin 94-3, 12-28-94, CCH PENSION PLAN GUIDE ¶ 19,972.

¶ 620

REQUIREMENTS FOR DEDUCTIBLE CONTRIBUTIONS: Return of Contributions Made by Mistake

The anti-diversion rule of ERISA (see ¶ 327) is not violated if a contribution made by an employer to a plan (other than a multiemployer plan) through a mistake of fact is returned to the employer within one year after it is made.[1]

The amount that may be returned to the employer is the excess of:[2]

1. the amount contributed over

2. the amount that would have been contributed if a mistake of fact (or an error in determining the deduction) had not occurred.

De minimis contributions

An employer may recover excess contributions to a defined benefit plan that are conditioned on deductibility if: (1) the amount of the nondeductible contributions is less than $25,000, and (2) the plan allows for the return of contributions to the employer in the event that the IRS finds them to be nondeductible.[3] The plan administrator or sponsor must also obtain an actuarial certificate indicating that a return of the nondeductible contribution is appropriate.

Multiemployer plans

Multiemployer plans are not required under ERISA to refund overpayments. However, a multiemployer plan may return employer contributions made under a mistake of law or fact.[4]

---

[1] ERISA Sec. 403(c)(2)(A)(i).

[2] *Martin v. Hamil*, CA-7 (1979), 608 F2d 725.

[3] Rev. Proc. 90-49, 1990-2 CB 620, CCH PENSION PLAN GUIDE ¶ 17299L-82.

[4] ERISA Sec. 403(c)(2)(A)(ii).

¶ 625

REQUIREMENTS FOR DEDUCTIBLE CONTRIBUTIONS: Incidental Benefits

Contributions to plans that provide only unemployment benefits, sickness, accident, hospitalization, medical benefits, recreation, welfare, severance, or similar benefits, or a combination of such benefits, are not deductible under Code Sec. 404(a).[1] However, if the contributions to a pension, profit-sharing, stock bonus, or other plan of deferred compensation can be used to provide any of the aforementioned benefits, the contributions are deductible under Code Sec. 404(a).[2]

---

[1] IRS Reg. § 1.404(a)-1(a)(2).

[2] IRS Reg. § 1.404(a)-1(a)(3).

¶ 630

REQUIREMENTS FOR DEDUCTIBLE CONTRIBUTIONS: Plans Covering U.S. Citizens Employed by Foreign Subsidiaries

The American parent corporation of a foreign subsidiary is not allowed to deduct contributions to a qualified retirement plan on behalf of U.S. citizens employed by the subsidiary.[1] However, the subsidiary may take a deduction equal to the amount that would have been deductible by the American parent corporation if the individual had been employed by the American employer.[2] Because the subsidiary's U.S. employees are considered employees of the parent company for retirement plan purposes, contributions made to the plan are not currently taxed to those employees.[3]

[1] Code Sec. 406(d)(1).

[2] Code Sec. 406(d)(2)

[3] Code Sec. 406(e).

¶ 640

REQUIREMENTS FOR DEDUCTIBLE CONTRIBUTIONS: Plan Management Fees

Expenses incurred by an employer in connection with a plan, such as trustee and actuary fees, that are not provided for by plan contributions, may be deducted, to the extent they are ordinary and necessary.[1] Payments made by an employer *directly* to a plan's investment manager or brokerage firm may be deducted and are not deemed to be plan contributions.[2] However, payments by an employer *reimbursing* plan trustees for fees paid to investment managers or brokerage firms are not deductible by the employer.[3]

[1] IRS Reg. § 1.404(a)-3(d).

[2] IRS Letter Ruling 8940013, Ruling Request (2), 6-30-89, CCH PENSION PLAN GUIDE ¶ 17,379C; IRS Letter Ruling 8940014, Ruling Request (2), 6-30-89, CCH PENSION PLAN GUIDE ¶ 17,379D.

[3] Rev. Rul. 86-142, 1986-2 CB 60, CCH PENSION PLAN GUIDE ¶ 19,696; IRS Letter Ruling 9124036, 3-19-91, CCH PENSION PLAN GUIDE ¶ 17,381G, revoking IRS Letter Ruling 8940013, Ruling Request (1), 6-30-89, CCH PENSION PLAN GUIDE ¶ 17,379C; IRS Letter Ruling 9124037, 3-19-91, CCH PENSION PLAN GUIDE ¶ 17,381H, revoking IRS Letter Ruling

8940014, Ruling Request (1), 6-30-89, CCH PENSION PLAN GUIDE ¶ 17,379D. **Note:** The IRS, in Letter Rulings 8940013 and 8940014, held that payments by an employer reimbursing plan trustees for fees incurred in connection with the investment of plan assets were deductible and were not deemed to be plan contributions. In revoking the rulings on the deductibility of such employer payments, however, the IRS did not clearly state whether or not payments reimbursing plan trustees for such investment fees would be treated as plan contributions.

¶ 645

REQUIREMENTS FOR DEDUCTIBLE CONTRIBUTIONS: Cost Capitalization of Pension Contributions and Other Employee Benefit Expenses

Amounts contributed by certain employers to pension, profit-sharing, or stock bonus plans that are otherwise deductible in the year paid may be subject to uniform capitalization rules and, thus, not currently deductible.[1] These rules require, in general, that manufacturers, wholesalers, and retailers capitalize direct costs and indirect costs, such as pension contributions and certain employee benefit expenses, allocable to real or intangible personal property produced by the taxpayer (regardless of whether the property is sold or used in the taxpayer's trade or business) and real property or tangible and intangible personal property acquired by the taxpayer for resale.[2]

---

[1] Code Sec. 263A; IRS Reg. § 1.263A-1(e)(3)(ii)(C).

[2] Code Sec. 263A; IRS Reg. § 1.263A-1(a)(3).

¶ 647

LIMITS ON DEDUCTIBLE CONTRIBUTIONS TO PENSION AND ANNUITY PLANS: Allowable Deduction Limits

Employers may claim a tax deduction for amounts contributed to fund a pension plan, even where the employer makes greater contributions than are required.[1] However, the amount that may be deducted is limited.

Employer deduction limits

The deduction limitation is based either on:

1. the amount necessary to fund, in a level manner, the current and past service costs over the remaining future service of each employee, or

2. the normal costs of the plan, plus the amount necessary to amortize unfunded past service costs (and interest thereon) in equal annual payments over a 10-year period.[2]

Thus, the annual deduction limitation for contributions to a single-employer defined benefit plan will be the greater of (1) the minimum contribution required under Code Sec. 430, or (2) an alternative amount computed under Code Sec. 404(o)(1)(A).[3]

See ¶ 1404 for more information.

---

[1] Code Sec. 404(a)(1)(A).

[2] Code Sec. 404(a)(1)(A)(ii) and (iii).

[3] Code Sec. 404(a)(1) and Code Sec. 404(o)(1)(A) as amended by P.L. 109-280 (Pension Protection Act of 2006) and effective for years beginning after December 31, 2007. Transition rules applied to years beginning in 2006 and 2007. See Notice 2007-28, I.R.B. 2007-14, 4/2/2007, CCH Pension Plan Guide ¶ 17,136F.

¶ 650

LIMITS ON DEDUCTIBLE CONTRIBUTIONS TO PENSION AND ANNUITY PLANS: Valuing Assets and Determining Costs

Generally, any method of valuing assets, including fair market value or cost, is acceptable for estimating the cost of a trusteed employee pension plan for purposes of determining the limitations on the deduction for employer contributions to the plan. However, the method must be followed consistently and otherwise result in costs which are reasonable. Asset valuation bases, such as the lower of cost or market for individual securities or classes of securities, or cost less a reserve for market fluctuations, are not acceptable.[1]

Costs for purposes of the deduction limitations cannot exceed costs based on assumptions and methods which are reasonable in view of the provisions and coverage of the plan, the funding medium, reasonable expectations as to the effect of mortality and interest, factors such as withdrawal and deferred retirement (whether or not discounted) which can be expected to reduce costs materially, reasonable expenses of operation, and all other relevant conditions and factors.

Allocated and unallocated funding methods

Defined benefit plans generally use an allocated or unallocated funding method.

1. ***Allocated funding.*** Under the allocated funding method, contributions are currently allocated to purchase insurance or annuities for individual participants. In an allocated insurance contract, contributions are immediately applied as premiums to purchase benefits for individual participants. Examples include annual premium retirement annuities and retirement income contracts and unit credit group annuity contracts.

2. ***Unallocated funding.*** Under an unallocated funding method, some or all of the contributions are accumulated in an unallocated fund to be used to pay benefits as they come due or to purchase annuities for employees as they retire or separate from service. Unallocated funding is associated with trust funds and deposit administration group annuity contracts issued by life insurance companies.

Presumption of actuarial reasonableness. Contributions under an allocated funding method will be considered reasonable (i.e., the premiums charged by the insurance company are deemed to be based on reasonable actuarial assumptions) if:[2]

1. all benefits provided by the plan are provided by allocated contracts with a rigid premium structure issued by an unrelated insurance company;

2. premiums paid to the insurance company are paid by the employer either directly to the insurance company or through a trust; and

3. the benefit purchased for each participant does not anticipate future increases in compensation.

Plans using unallocated funding methods are not entitled to the benefit of any similar presumption of actuarial reasonableness.

Methods and assumptions generally may not be changed

The amount that is deductible for one tax year may affect the amount that is deductible for other tax years. Accordingly, the methods, factors, and assumptions used in determining costs and the method of determining the limitations under which the deduction for the tax year has been determined generally may not be changed for that tax year. However, changes may be authorized where the IRS determines that the methods, factors, assumptions, or limitations were not proper, or when a change is necessitated by reason of the use of different methods, etc., for another tax year.[3]

See ¶ 1452—1493L for more on actuarial requirements.

[1] Rev. Rul. 63-11, 1963-1 CB 194, CCH PENSION PLAN GUIDE ¶ 18,435.

[2] Rev. Rul. 72-557, 1972-2 CB 227, CCH PENSION PLAN GUIDE ¶ 19,194.

[3] IRS Reg. § 1.404(a)-3(c); Rev. Rul. 67-365, 1967-2 C.B. 154, CCH PENSION PLAN GUIDE ¶ 18,590.

¶ 655

LIMITS ON DEDUCTIBLE CONTRIBUTIONS TO PENSION AND ANNUITY PLANS: Adjustment for Decreased Liability

In determining costs for the purpose of the deduction limitations under Code Sec. 404(a)(1), the effects of expected mortality and interest must be discounted and the effects of expected withdrawals, changes in compensation, retirement at various ages, and other pertinent factors may be discounted or otherwise reasonably recognized. A properly weighted retirement age based on adequate analyses of representative experience may be used as an assumed retirement age. Different basic assumptions or rates may be used for different classes of risks or different groups where justified by conditions or required by contract. In no event shall costs for the purpose of Code Sec. 404(a)(1) exceed costs based on assumptions and methods which are reasonable in view of the provisions and coverage of the plan, the funding medium, reasonable expectations as to the effects of mortality and interest, reasonable and adequate regard for other factors, such as withdrawal and deferred retirement (whether or not discounted) which can be expected to reduce costs materially, reasonable expenses of operation, and all other relevant conditions and circumstances.[1]

When determining costs and limitations, an adjustment must be made on account of any experience more favorable than that assumed in the basis of limitations for prior years. Unless such adjustments are consistently made every year by reducing the limitations otherwise determined by any decrease in liability or cost arising from experience in the next preceding taxable year which was more favorable than the assumptions on which the costs and limitations were based, the adjustment must be made by some other method approved by the IRS.

---

[1] IRS Reg. § 1.404(a)-(3)(b).

¶ 660

LIMITS ON DEDUCTIBLE CONTRIBUTIONS TO PENSION AND ANNUITY PLANS: Money Purchase Pension Plans

Money purchase plans and other defined contribution plans that are subject to the funding rules are treated in the same manner as a profit-sharing plan or stock bonus plan for purposes of the deduction rules under Code Sec. 404 (a)(3).[1] See ¶ 670-673 for the general deduction rules for profit-sharing plans.

Combined deductible limit

If an employer contributes to both a defined contribution plan and a defined benefit plan, the total amount deductible for contributions to both plans is the greater of: (1) 25% of the compensation otherwise paid or accrued during the tax year to beneficiaries, or (2) the amount of contributions made to or under the defined benefit plans to the extent they do not exceed the employer contributions necessary to meet the plans' minimum funding obligation for the year.[2] The overall deduction limitation for contributions to combination plans does not apply to defined benefit plans when contributions to defined contribution plans do not exceed six percent of compensation.[3]

The combined limit will not reduce any amount otherwise deductible under a defined benefit plan or money purchase plan if no employee is a beneficiary under more than one plan. Note that the deduction limit that generally applies when an employer maintains a combination of plans will not be imposed when the only contributions made to the defined contribution plan during the tax year are elective deferrals.[4]

> **CCH Pointer:** If a single-employer plan is insured by the Pension Benefit Guaranty Corporation (PBGC), then the plan is not taken into account in applying the overall limitation on deductions.[5]

---

[1] Code Sec. 404(a)(3)(A).

[2] Code Sec. 404(a)(7).

[3] Code Sec. 404(a)(7)(C)(iii), as added by P.L. 109-280 (Pension Protection Act of 2006), Act Sec. 803(a), and amended by P.L. 110-458 (Worker, Retiree, and Employer Recovery Act of 2008), Act Sec. 108(c), effective for tax years beginning after December 31, 2005.

[4] Code Sec. 404(a)(7)(C), as amended by P.L. 107-147 (Job Creation and Worker Assistance Act of 2002).

[5] Code Sec. 404(a)(7)(C)(iv), as added by P.L. 109-280 (Pension Protection Act of 2006), Act Sec. 801(b), effective for plan years beginning after December 31, 2007.

¶ 663

LIMITS ON DEDUCTIBLE CONTRIBUTIONS TO PENSION AND ANNUITY PLANS: Annuity Plans

Annuity plans are retirement plans that provide benefits under annuity or insurance contracts without a trust. In addition to the limitations on deductions applicable to pension plans (see ¶ 647), contributions to annuity plans must:

1. be paid toward the purchase of retirement annuities under an annuity plan for the exclusive benefit of the employees or their beneficiaries; and

2. be paid in a taxable year of the employer which ends with or within a year of the plan for which it meets the applicable requirements of Code Sec. 401.

In addition, a definite written arrangement between the employer and the insurer must provide that refunds of premiums, if any, will be applied, within the taxable year of the employer in which they are received or within the next succeeding taxable year, toward the purchase of retirement annuities under the plan.[1]

---

[1] Code Sec. 404(a)(2); IRS Reg. § 1.404(a)-8(a).

¶ 667

LIMITS ON DEDUCTIBLE CONTRIBUTIONS TO PENSION AND ANNUITY PLANS: Carryover of Excess Contributions to Pension Plan

Contributions paid by an employer to or under a qualified pension plan or annuity plan that exceed the limitations on deductible contributions for any year, but otherwise satisfy the conditions for deduction, may be carried over and deducted in succeeding taxable years in which employer contributions do not reach the prescribed limits.[1] The amount deductible in each succeeding year is the difference between the amount paid and deductible in such year and the maximum amount which could have been deducted in such year.

Example:

TAXABLE YEAR ENDING DEC. 31, 2011:

Amount of contribution paid in year		$100,000
Limitation applicable to year	$50,000	
Amount deductible in year		50,000
Excess carried over to succeeding years		$50,000

TAXABLE YEAR ENDING DEC. 31, 2012:

Amount of contribution paid in year	$30,000

Carried over from previous years		$50,000
Total subject to limitation		$80,000
Limitation applicable to year	$50,000	
Amount deductible in year		50,000
Excess carried over to succeeding years		$30,000

---

[1] Code Sec. 404(a)(1)(E); IRS Reg. § 1.404(a)-7.

¶ 670

LIMITS ON DEDUCTIBLE CONTRIBUTIONS TO PROFIT-SHARING PLANS: Deductible Contributions Limited to 25% of Compensation

Contributions by an employer to a profit-sharing plan may be deducted only up to 25% of the compensation otherwise paid or accrued during the taxable year to employees or their beneficiaries under the plan. This includes all compensation except that for which a deduction is allowable under a qualified plan. In determining the deduction limit, no more than $250,000 (for 2012; $245,000 in 2011) of any one employee's annual compensation may be taken into account.[1]

Exception for retirement benefits

The percentage limitation does not apply to plans that are designed to provide benefits upon retirement and covering a period of years, assuming the amounts to be contributed by the employer can be actuarially determined.

☐ The amount that an employer may deduct is also subject to the overall limitations on contributions contained in Code Sec. 415.[2] These limitations are discussed beginning at ¶ 500.

Disabled employees

Deductible contributions made on behalf of a disabled employee are subject to the percentage of compensation limit. Compensation is based on the amount of compensation the employee had earned immediately before becoming disabled.

Definition of compensation

The definition of compensation for purposes of the deductible contribution limits is generally the definition used for other qualified plan purposes.[3]

---

[1] Code Sec. 404(a)(3)(A)(i)(I); Code Sec. 401(a)(17); IR-2011-103, 10-20-2011, CCH PENSION PLAN GUIDE ¶ 17,037Q.

[2] Code Secs. 404(a)(3)(A)(i), 404(a)(3)(A)(iii), 404(j), 404(l); IRS Reg. § 1.404(a)-9(b)(2).

[3] Code Sec. 404(a)(12).

¶ 673

LIMITS ON DEDUCTIBLE CONTRIBUTIONS TO PROFIT-SHARING PLANS: Carryover of Excess Contributions to Profit-Sharing Plans

Profit-sharing plans are not required to adopt a fixed contribution formula. However, if a profit-sharing plan does contain such a formula, an employer may be required to contribute to the plan an amount in excess of 25% of compensation otherwise paid or accrued. The employer's deduction is still limited to 25% of compensation, but the excess contributions may be carried forward and deducted in succeeding taxable years when contributions fall below the allowable deduction for such years.

> **Example:** A corporation maintains a profit-sharing plan that provides for contributions of 10% of company profits. In a given year, the corporation had profits of $1,100,000. During the year, company employees received total compensation of $400,000. Thus, the corporation's contribution to the plan would be limited to $100,000 and it would have to carry the $10,000 excess contribution forward to the next year.

Deduct carryover in succeeding year

In the event that contributions exceed the allowable limit, the contribution carryover is deductible in succeeding taxable years, in order of time, with the following limitations.[1]

1. If the succeeding taxable year ends with or within a taxable year of the plan when the plan is exempt, the excess is deductible in any succeeding taxable year in which contributions are less than the 25% limitation for that year. The total amount deductible cannot exceed 25% of compensation or the sum of the contributions for the succeeding year plus the carryover, whichever amount is smaller.

2. If the succeeding taxable year ends with or within a taxable year of the plan in which the plan is not exempt, or if the succeeding taxable year ends after the trust has terminated, the amount deductible cannot exceed 25% of compensation or the unclaimed contributions from prior years, whichever is less.

---

[1] Code Sec. 404(a)(3)(A); IRS Reg. § 1.404(a)-9(e)(1).

¶ 675

CONTRIBUTIONS TO MULTIEMPLOYER PLANS: Deductibility of Contributions to Multiemployer Plans

The applicable deduction limitations under Code Sec. 404(a) for contributions to a plan maintained by more than one employer and established after 1988 are determined as if each employer maintained a separate plan.[1] The deduction limitations applicable to plans established before 1989 are determined as if all plan participants were employed by a single employer.[2]

In the event that each employer is treated as maintaining a separate plan, the amounts contributed by each employer, for the portion of the employer's taxable year that is included within the applicable plan year, are considered not to exceed the applicable limitation if the anticipated employer contributions for such plan year do not exceed the limitation.[3]

Controlled group plans

The applicable deduction limits for plans adopted by more than one member of a controlled group of corporations are determined as if all of the employers were a single employer.[4]

Collectively bargained plans

The deduction limits applicable to collectively bargained plans are determined as if all participants in the plan were employed by a single employer.[5] The amount contributed by each employer who is party to the agreement, for the portion of the tax year that is included within the plan year, will not exceed the applicable limitation if anticipated employer contributions for the plan year do not exceed the limitation.

Deduction limitation

The maximum amount of the deduction limitation for contributions to multiemployer plans cannot be less than 140 percent of the current liability of the plan minus the value of the plan's assets.[6]

[1] Code Sec. 413(c)(6)(A).

[2] Code Sec. 413(c)(6)(B).

[3] Code Sec. 413(c)(6)(B)(ii).

[4] Code Sec. 414(b).

[5] Code Sec. 413(b)(7).

[6] Code Sec. 404(a)(1)(D), as amended by P.L. 109-280 (Pension Protection Act of 2006), Act Sec. 802(a), and applicable for years beginning after December 31, 2007. A transition rule was provided for years beginning in 2006 and 2007. In those years, the maximum amount of the deduction limitation for contributions to multiemployer plans cannot be less than 140 percent of the current liability of the plan minus the value of the plan's assets. See Code Sec. 404(a)(1)(D)(i), as amended by P.L. 109-280 (Pension Protection Act of 2006), Act Sec. 802(a).

¶ 677

CONTRIBUTIONS TO OVERLAPPING PENSION AND PROFIT-SHARING PLANS: Limits on Deductions

Employers may provide employees with a pension or annuity plan plus a profit-sharing or stock bonus plan. If any employee of an employer providing both a pension and a profit-sharing plan is a beneficiary of both plans, the total allowable deduction is limited to 25% of compensation otherwise paid or accrued to the employees or the amount of contributions necessary to satisfy the minimum funding standards.[1]

Combined deductible limit

The combined deduction limit of 25% of compensation does not apply if the only amounts contributed to the defined contribution plan are elective deferrals. If employer contributions to defined contribution plans are less than six percent of compensation, the defined benefit plan is not subject to the overall deduction limit. If such contributions exceed six percent of compensation, only the contributions in excess of six percent are counted toward the overall deduction limit.[2]

---

[1] Code Sec. 404(a)(7)(C)(ii).

[2] Code Sec. 404(a)(7)(C)(iii), as added by P.L. 109-280 (Pension Protection Act of 2006), Act Sec.

803(a) and (d) and amended by P.L. 110-458 (Worker, Retiree, and Employer Recovery Act of 2008), Act Sec. 112, and effective for tax years beginning after December 31, 2005.

¶ 679

CONTRIBUTIONS TO OVERLAPPING PENSION AND PROFIT-SHARING PLANS: Carryover Contributions

If an employer maintains a pension or annuity plan and a profit-sharing or stock bonus plan with employees participating in both, excess contributions may be carried over to future years. However, in no event may the deductions for contributions to overlapping plans and the carryovers of excess contributions to overlapping plans exceed 25% of the compensation otherwise paid or accrued to employees.[1]

---

[1] Code Sec. 404(a)(7)(B).

¶ 681

EXCISE TAXES: Excise Tax on Nondeductible Contributions

A 10% excise tax is imposed on nondeductible contributions exceeding deductible limits.[1] The tax applies to all tax-qualified plans, including tax-exempt trusts, 403(a) annuity plans, and simplified employee plans.[2]

Nondeductible contributions are determined as of the close of the employer's tax year[3] and equal the total contribution for the year less the amount allowable as a deduction for the year.[4] If an excess contribution is made during the tax year, the excise tax applies for that year and each succeeding year that the excess is not eliminated.

---

[1] Code Sec. 4972(b).

[2] Code Sec. 4972(d).

[3] Code Sec. 4972(a).

[4] Code Sec. 4972(c). Note that the Working Families Tax Relief Act of 2004 (P.L. 108-311) clarified Code Sec. 4972(c)(6), effective after De-

cember 31, 2001, by removing references to elective deferrals. This change is intended to conform Code Sec. 4972 with Code Sec. 404(n), as added by EGTRRA (P.L. 107-16), pursuant to which elective deferrals are not taken into account in determining the limit on an employer's deductible contributions. See ¶ 2987.

¶ 683

EXCISE TAXES: Excise Tax on Excess Contributions

A 10% excise tax is assessed on excess contributions and excess aggregate contributions under the plan for the plan year ending in the tax year.[1] The excise tax is assessed on the employer maintaining the plan[2] and applies to qualified pension, profit-sharing, or stock bonus plans, 403(a) annuity plans, 403(b) tax-sheltered annuities, simplified employee pensions (SEPs), and certain trusts created before June 25, 1959.[3]

Excess contributions to 401(k) plan

With respect to 401(k) plans, excess contributions are the excess of the aggregate amount of elective deferrals paid to the 401(k) plan and allocated to the accounts of highly compensated employees over the maximum amount of elective deferrals that could be allocated to the accounts of highly compensated employees without violating the nondiscrimination requirements applicable to the 401(k) plan.[4]

Excess aggregate contributions

Excess aggregate contributions are the excess of the aggregate amount of employer matching contributions and employee contributions (and any qualified nonelective contribution or elective contribution taken into account in computing the compensation percentage) actually paid on behalf of highly compensated employees over the maximum amount of such contributions permitted under the contribution percentage requirement.[5]

Carry over excess contributions to avoid excise tax

A company whose plan contributions exceed the deductible contribution limits may avoid the excise tax by carrying over the excess to the following tax year (see ¶ 667 and 673).[6]

Exception for amounts distributed 2½ months after plan year

The excise tax is not assessed if the excess contributions or the excess aggregate contributions, together with income earned on the excess, are distributed to employees no later than 2½ months after the close of the plan year in which the excess contributions were made.[7]

> **CCH Pointer:** *Expansion of corrective distribution period for excess contributions to automatic enrollment arrangements.* Effective for plan years beginning after December 31, 2007, with respect to an eligible automatic enrollment arrangement, the excise tax on excess contributions does not apply if the distribution (or forfeiture) of the excess contributions or aggregate excess contributions together with related earnings occurs within six months after the end of the plan year.[8] See ¶ 2940B for more on the automatic enrollment provisions.

Exception for SEPs

An employer that maintains a SEP that accepts elective contributions may avoid the excise tax by notifying employees of the excess contributions within 2½ months following the plan year for which the excess contributions are made.[9] The notice must inform employees of the amount of the excess contribution and the applicable tax consequences, including the penalties for failure to withdraw the contributions.

---

[1] Code Sec. 4979(a).

[2] Code Sec. 4979(b).

[3] Code Sec. 4979(e).

[4] Code Sec. 4979(c).

[5] Code Sec. 401(m)(6)(B).

[6] IRS Letter Ruling 9107033, 11-21-90, CCH PENSION PLAN GUIDE ¶ 17,380R.

[7] Code Sec. 4979(f)(1); IRS Reg. § 54.4979-1(c).

[8] Code Sec. 4979(f), as amended by P.L. 109-280, Pension Protection Act of 2006, Act Sec. 902(e)(1)(A)-(B).

[9] IRS Reg. § 54.4979-1(a)(4)(i).

¶ 685

NONQUALIFIED PLANS: Deductible Contributions to Nonqualified Plans

Code Sec. 404 governs the deductibility of any compensation paid or accrued on account of any employee under a plan deferring the receipt of compensation.[1] Accordingly, an employer may deduct contributions to a nonqualified plan only if they are ordinary and necessary and reasonable (see ¶ 605).[2] In addition, deductions may be taken for contributions to nonqualified plans only in the year in which the contribution is includible in the income of employees participating in the plan.[3] Similarly, no deduction may be taken for contributions to a nonqualified plan on behalf of independent contractors until the compensation is includable in the gross income of participants.[4]

Vesting of employee's interest

An employee must include in income a contribution to a nonqualified trust or premium for a nonqualified annuity when the interest in the contribution or premium becomes vested. If an employee's interest is vested at the time the contribution is made or the premium is paid, the employer is entitled to a deduction at the same time. The employee may elect, within 30 days following the employer's nonvested contribution, to include the contribution in income. If the employee makes this election, the employer is entitled to a deduction for the same year.[5] If the employee's interest is not vested when the contribution is made, and the election noted above is not made, no part of the contribution need be included in the employee's income at that time and the employer is not entitled to a deduction.

Deduction requires separate accounting

A nonqualified plan that benefits more than one employee must maintain a separate account for each participant in order for vested contributions to be deducted when made.[6] A contribution that is made to a plan under which separate accounts are not maintained, may not be deducted by the employer in the year in which benefits are paid to the employee or in any other year.[7]

Contributions to funded and unfunded plans

Contributions to a funded plan are deductible only to the extent of the original contribution and no deduction is allowed for investment earnings and gains.[8]

Unfunded deferred compensation is deductible when paid and in the amount paid. Under an unfunded plan, an employer may accumulate funds in a segregated account but still retain the right to use the funds in the ordinary course of its business.

Foreign deferred compensation plans

A deduction is permitted for amounts paid by an employer on behalf of participants under a foreign deferred compensation plan.[9]

☐ Nonqualified plans are discussed in greater detail, beginning at ¶ 3300.

---

[1] Code Sec. 404(a).

[2] IRS Reg. § 1.401(a)(1)(b).

[3] IRS Letter Ruling 9051014, 9-21-90, CCH PENSION PLAN GUIDE ¶ 17,380P.

[4] Code Sec. 404(d).

[5] Code Secs. 83(b), 402(b), 403(c); IRS Reg. §§ 1.402(b)-1, 1.403(c)-1 and 1.404(a)-12. Limits

exist on a taxpayer's ability to revoke an election under Code Sec. 83. See Rev. Proc. 2006-31, I.R.B. 2006-27, 7-3-06, CCH PENSION PLAN GUIDE ¶ 17,299R-89.

[6] Code Sec. 404(a)(5).

[7] IRS Reg. § 1.404(a)-12(b)(3).

[8] IRS Reg. § 1.404(a)-12(a).

[9] Code Sec. 404A.

¶ 690

EMPLOYEE CONTRIBUTIONS TO QUALIFIED PLANS: Limits on Employee Contributions

Employee contributions to pension or annuity plans are generally not deductible for federal income tax purposes. In addition, if the amount of a contribution is withheld from an employee's pay, he or she must still report the amount withheld as income in the year of the withholding. Amounts withheld from the salary of an employee and deposited to his credit in a retirement fund are also includible in the employee's gross income.[1] Such contributions are nondeductible personal expenses.[2]

Deductible losses

If an employee's entire interest is distributed in cash upon separation from service, and if the amount received is less than the employee's contributions, the employee has experienced a deductible loss (provided that deductions are itemized).[3] If the distribution is in stock or other property other than cash, there is no deductible loss at the time of the distribution, even if the property is worth less than the employee's contributions. Any loss would have to await the sale of the property.[4]

A cash distribution of an employee's entire interest may also result in a deductible loss, even if the employee does not separate from the employer's service. However, if an employee merely withdraws that portion of his interest in the plan attributable to his own contributions, with the distribution being less than those contributions, the employee may not have a deductible loss, if he continues to have an interest in the plan attributable to employer contributions. In such a case there would not be the "closed transaction" required for a deductible loss.

¹See, e.g. *I. Megibow v. Commissioner,* CA-3 (1955), 218 F2d 687, aff'g TC; *J. Davidson v. Commissioner,* TC (1964), 42 TC 766, CCH Dec. 26,894.

²I. T. 1265, I-1 CB 193; *J. Anderson v. Commissioner,* TC (1980), 40 TCM 530, CCH Dec. 37,029(M); IRS Letter Ruling 8037101, 6-20-80.

³ Rev. Rul. 72-328, 1972-2 CB 224, CCH PENSION PLAN GUIDE ¶ 19,166.

⁴ Rev. Rul. 71-251, 1971-1 CB 129, CCH PENSION PLAN GUIDE ¶ 19,052; Rev. Rul. 72-15, 1972-1 CB 114, CCH PENSION PLAN GUIDE ¶ 19,121.

¶ 695
For More Information

☐ For more information on deductible contributions, see ¶ 2835, ¶ 3200—¶ 3355 and ¶ 9560—¶ 9570 of the CCH PENSION PLAN GUIDE.

Minimum Participation Standards

¶ 700

General Rules

Employee retirement plans are subject to minimum participation standards that govern employee eligibility under the plan. Generally, a retirement plan may not require an employee, as a condition of participation, to complete a period of service extending beyond the date on which the employee attains age 21, or the date on which the employee has completed one year of service. Years of service are determined in accord with an initial eligibility computation period and an eligibility computation period following the initial eligibility computation period.

Employees who incur breaks in service may be required to perform additional service before regaining their eligibility to participate in the plan upon reemployment. However, the rules are modified for individuals who incur a break of service because of parental leave or military service.

The minimum participation standards apply to most retirement plans. However, welfare plans and other arrangements, such as governmental plans and plans maintained by exempt organizations, are not subject to the rules.

¶ 705
Plans Subject to Minimum Participation Requirements

ERISA's minimum participation standards must be met by pension, profit-sharing, stock bonus, and annuity plans that hope to qualify for federal tax benefits under the Internal Revenue Code. In addition, under the provisions of Title I of ERISA, the standards must also be met as a matter of substantive law by the vast majority of retirement plans, whether qualified for tax benefits or not.[1]

---

[1] Code Secs. 410(c); ERISA Secs. 4(a), 4(b), and 202.

¶ 710
Plans Exempt from Minimum Participation Rules

ERISA's participation standards do not apply to welfare plans.[1] In addition, the rules do not apply to the following arrangements:

1. Governmental plans established and maintained for employees of the federal government, state governments and political subdivisions, and agencies or instrumentalities of the foregoing.[2]

2. Church plans established and maintained by a church or tax exempt association of churches for their employees.[3] Church plans, however, may irrevocably elect coverage under the participation standards.[4]

3. Plans maintained solely for the purpose of complying with worker's compensation, unemployment, or disability laws.[5]

CCH Pointer: A plan that provides benefits that are not required for compliance with a state's disability insurance law is not maintained solely for the purpose of complying with such a law.[6] Thus, disability plans subscribed to by a state's schools and universities were not exempt from ERISA because the plans provided additional benefits from the first through the seventh day of disability, while the state only required benefits to begin on the eighth day of disability.[7]

4. Plans maintained outside of the United States primarily for the benefit of persons substantially all of whom are nonresident aliens.[8]

5. Excess benefit plans maintained by an employer solely for the purpose of providing benefits for certain employees in excess of the limitations on contributions and benefits under Code Sec. 415.[9]

6. Plans established and maintained by a fraternal beneficiary society, order or association described in Code Sec. 501(c)(8) or by a voluntary employee beneficiary association (VEBA) described in Code Sec. 501(c)(9), provided that no contributions have been made by employers.[10]

7. Unfunded plans maintained primarily to provide deferred compensation to a select group of management or highly compensated employees.[11]

8. Union plans that do not provide for employer contributions after September 2, 1974.[12]

9. Individual retirement accounts or annuities under Code Sec. 408.[13]

10. Pension trusts funded only through contributions by employees, as described in Code Sec. 501(c)(18).[14]

11. Agreements providing payments to a retired partner or to a deceased partner's successor in interest under Code Sec. 736.[15]

12. Any plan, fund, or program under which an employer, all of whose stock is directly or indirectly owned by employees, former employees, or their beneficiaries, proposes through an unfunded arrangement to compensate retired employees for benefits that were forfeited by such employees under a pension plan maintained by a former employer prior to the date such pension plan became subject to ERISA.[16]

Exemption from qualification requirement

Generally, the minimum participation standards must be met by any qualified plan. However, the following plans may qualify without meeting the minimum participation standards so long as they meet the coverage requirements of Code Sec. 401(a)(3), as it read before amendment by ERISA:[17]

1. A church plan that has not elected to be covered by the participation requirements.

2. A plan that has not provided for employer contributions since September 2, 1974.

3. A plan established and maintained by a society, order, or association described in Code Sec. 501(c)(8) or (9) if no part of the contributions to or under the plan are made by employers of participants in the plan.

---

[1] ERISA Secs. 201(1) and 3(1).

[2] ERISA Secs. 3(32), 4(b)(1) and 201.

[3] ERISA Sec. 4(b)(2).

[4] Code Sec. 410(d); ERISA Sec. 4(b)(2); IRS Reg. § 1.410(d)-1(a).

[5] ERISA Sec. 4(b)(3).

[6] *Shaw v. Delta Airlines, Inc.*, US Sup Ct (1983), 463 U.S. 85.

[7] ERISA Opinion Letter 97-21A, 9-10-97.

[8] ERISA Sec. 4(b)(4).

[9] ERISA Secs. 201(7) and 3(36).

[10] ERISA Sec. 201(3)(A).

[11] ERISA Sec. 201(2).

[12] ERISA Sec. 201(4).

[13] ERISA Sec. 201(6).

[14] ERISA Sec. 201(3)(B).

[15] ERISA Sec. 201(5).

[16] ERISA Sec. 201(8).

[17] Code Sec. 410(c); IRS Reg. § 1.410(a)-1.

¶ 715

Minimum Age and Service Conditions

A retirement plan generally may not require an employee, as a condition of participation, to complete a period of service extending beyond the later of:

1. the date on which the employee attains age 21, or

2. the date on which the employee has completed one year of service (see ¶ 735).[1]

Thus, an employee who otherwise qualifies must become eligible for participation when he or she attains age 21 *and* has completed one year of service. The employee's actual admission to participation must occur no later than the earlier of:

1. the first day of the first plan year beginning after the date on which the employee satisfies the age and service requirements, or

2. the date six months after the date on which the employee satisfies such requirements.[2]

Example 1: David Hogan is hired by his employer on January 1, 2011, when he is 19 years old. His birthday is August 15. The pension plan maintained by his employer uses a calendar year. Assuming that Hogan is employed full time, he will satisfy the age and service requirements on August 15, 2012, the date on which he will have attained 21 years of age and completed at least one year of service. His actual participation in the plan must begin no later than January 1, 2013 (the beginning of the first plan year following satisfaction of the age and service requirement, as this is less than six months after the satisfaction of that requirement).

Example 2: Jennifer Green is hired by her employer on April 1, 2011. At that time she is 30 years old. Her employer's profit-sharing plan is maintained on a calendar year basis. Assuming that Green is employed full time, she will satisfy the age and service requirements at the end of the day on March 31, 2012. Her actual participation must begin no later than October 1, 2012 (the date six months after satisfaction of the age and service requirements, since this occurs before the first day of the first plan year beginning after satisfaction of those requirements).

Example 3: A plan provides that an employee is eligible to participate in the plan on the first day of the first plan year beginning after the employee's employment commencement date. The plan has no other requirements for participation. The plan meets the participation requirements since it ensures that an employee always will be able to participate in the plan within a 12-month period after he or she begins employment.

As a matter of administrative convenience, many plans may prefer to establish two plan entry dates—one at the beginning of each plan year and one on a date six months after the beginning of the plan year. Employees satisfying the age and service requirements during the first six months of the plan's year could be enrolled at the mid-year entry point. This option would satisfy the participation requirements without requiring the plan to enroll each such employee on the date six months after the age and service requirements were met. Also, a single entry date can be maintained by lowering the age requirement to age 20½.[3]

> **CCH Pointer:** The IRS offers a set of "Alert Guidelines" and related worksheets relating to plan qualification requirements, including minimum participation standards.[4] These are used by IRS employee plans specialists during their review of retirement plans. The guidelines may also be used by employers and sponsors in drafting their plans, and completed copies of the worksheets may be submitted with plan applications to facilitate plan review.

Conditions other than age and service may apply

Note that an employee does not automatically become eligible for participation in a plan merely because he or she satisfies the plan's age and service requirements. For example, if a plan permissibly excludes a certain classification of employees and in so doing does not violate the nondiscrimination rules of the Code, those employees can be denied participation regardless of age and periods of service.

Indirect age and service restrictions. The IRS will treat plan provisions as imposing an impermissible age or service requirement even though the provisions do not specifically refer to age or service if the plan provisions have the *effect* of imposing an impermissible requirement. Take the example of a corporation that is divided into two Divisions, A and B. In order to work in Division B, an employee had to be employed in Division A for five years. A plan provision that required Division B employment for participation would disqualify the plan. The requirement would be treated as a service requirement because it has the effect of requiring five years of service.[5]

---

[1] Code Sec. 410(a); ERISA Sec. 202; IRS Reg. § 1.410(a)-4(b).

[2] Code Sec, 410(a)(4); IRS Reg. § 1.410(a)-4(b).

[3] T.I.R. No. 1334, P-2, 1-8-75.

[4] IRS Alert Guidelines, Worksheet and Explanation 1, CCH Pension Plan Guide ¶ 41,003B.

[5] IRS Reg. 1.401(a)-3(e).

¶ 720

Participation Computation Periods

In determining eligibility to participate, service is measured in terms of years of service. Years of service in turn are determined according to computation periods. A computation period is generally a consecutive 12-month period used to measure completion of a year of service. To constitute a year of service, an employee must have at least 1,000 hours of service during the 12-month period (see ¶ 735).

Eligibility computation periods

Two computation periods have been approved for measuring eligibility to participate: an initial eligibility computation period and an eligibility computation period following the initial eligibility computation period.

Initial eligibility computation period. The initial eligibility computation period is generally a consecutive 12-month period that begins on the employee's employment commencement date.[1] This date is the first day on which an employee is entitled to be credited with an hour of service for the performance of duties. A plan may provide that no allocation will be made to the account of an employee who terminates before the allocation date.[2]

Eligibility computation period following the initial period. Eligibility computation periods following the initial period are distinguished from the initial period in order to allow a plan to shift to the plan year as its computation period. As a result, after the initial eligibility computation period, a plan may:[3]

1. continue to use a computation period based on the anniversary of the employee's employment commencement date, or

2. use the plan year.

If the plan elects to use the plan year, the plan must begin with the plan year that includes the first anniversary of the employee's employment commencement date as the eligibility computation period after the initial eligibility computation period (without regard to whether the employee is entitled to credit for 1,000 hours of service during this period).

Overlapping computation periods. The shift from the initial eligibility computation period based on the employment commencement date to a computation period based on the plan year necessarily involves some overlapping of computation periods. In order to ensure that this circumstance does not lead to an evasion of the participation requirements, an employee who is credited with 1,000 hours of service in the initial eligibility computation period and 1,000 hours of service in the following eligibility computation period based on the plan year must be given credit for two years of service.

Alternative eligibility computation period

A plan's recordkeeping system may not allow it to identify the date on which an employee began employment. However, a plan may be able to identify the payroll period during which an employee's first day of employment occurred.

Accordingly, a plan may calculate eligibility computation periods on the basis of the period used for recordkeeping rather than on the basis of the employee's employment date.[4] Under this method, a plan must begin the initial eligibility computation period on the first day of a period of no more than 31 days during which an employee's employment commencement date occurred—that is, on the first day of the recordkeeping period within which the employee started work. This computation period will end on the first anniversary of the last day of the record-keeping period during which the employee started work.

[1] ERISA Reg. § 2530.202-2(a).

[2] Rev. Rul. 76-250, 1976-2 CB 124.

[3] ERISA Reg. § 2530.202-2(b).

[4] ERISA Reg. § 2530.202-2(e).

¶ 725

Plans with Full Vesting

A qualified plan that offers full and immediate vesting may condition eligibility to participate in the plan on up to two years of service.[1] A 401(k) plan, however, must allow participation after the completion of one year of service.

[1] Code Sec. 410(a)(1)(B); ERISA Sec. 202(a)(1)(B)(i).

¶ 730

Exempt Educational Organizations

Plans maintained for employees of an educational organization by an employer that is tax-exempt under Code Sec. 501(a) are provided with an exception from the general age and service rule.[1] Plans that provide for 100% vesting for each participant with at least one year of service may set the maximum age at 26. Such a plan would have to cover each employee who is 26 years of age and who had completed at least one year of service.

[1] Code Sec. 410(a)(1)(B)(ii); ERISA Sec. 202(a)(1)(B)(ii).

¶ 735

Year of Service

A "year of service" is a consecutive 12-month period in which the employee has at least 1,000 hours of service. Usually, the 12-month period begins on the first day of employment.[1] However, where the employee doesn't complete 1,000 hours of service by the anniversary of the first employment date, the 1,000 hours may be counted from the first day of the plan year.

Hour of service

An "hour of service" is each hour for which an employee is directly or indirectly paid or entitled to payment by the employer for the performance of duties, including each hour for which back pay has been either awarded or agreed to by the employer. An hour of service for participation purposes also includes each hour during which no duties are performed and for which an employee is paid or entitled to payment for vacation, holiday, illness, incapacity (including disability), layoff, jury duty, military duty, or leave of absence.[2]

Year of service for the maritime industry

Service may be measured in the maritime industry by days of service rather than hours of service. In this industry, 125 days of service rather than 1000 hours of service are required for a year of service.

---

[1] Code Sec. 410(a)(3); ERISA Sec. 202(a)(3).   [2] ERISA Reg. § 2530.200b-2(a).

¶ 740

Break-in-Service Rules

In general, all of an employee's years of service with an employer maintaining a plan must be counted for minimum participation purposes.[1] However, a plan may treat an employee as incurring a one-year break in service if the employee fails to complete more than 500 hours of service during an applicable computation period.[2] A plan may not, however, apply a break-in-service rule retroactively.[3]

Employees who incur at least a one-year break in service with the employer maintaining the plan need not be readmitted to the plan until they have completed at least one year of service following reemployment.[4] On the other hand, an employee who has a break in service of less than one year, and has completed at least one year of service prior to the break, is eligible to participate immediately upon reemployment.

> **Example:** A calendar year defined benefit plan provides that an employee may enter the plan on the first semi-annual entry date following attainment of age 21 and completion of one year of service. Rae, after working ten years, separates from service in 2006 with a vested benefit. On March 3, 2011, Rae returns to employment that is covered by the plan and is allowed to resume plan participation on July 1 of that year. Under these circumstances, Rae's prior service may not be disregarded because she had a vested benefit upon separation from service. Thus, the plan may not postpone Rae's participation until July 1 as it did here, but, rather, must allow Rae to participate as of her return on March 3, 2011 (subject to Rae's completion of a year of service after returning to work for her employer). Consequently, in addition to the two semi-annual entry dates described above, the plan must also provide for the reentry of vested employees who return after a break in service (and who complete a year of service after returning) and of employees who separate from service and later return without incurring a one-year break in service.[5]

Eligibility computation period. A one-year break in service occurs when an employee fails to complete more than 500 hours of service during (a) a calendar year, (b) a plan year, or (c) any other 12-month period, so long as the period used applies equally to all participants.

For purposes of the participation rules, in determining whether an employee incurs a one-year break in service, a plan must use the eligibility computation period used to measure years of service after the initial eligibility computation period.

Exception for military service. Under the Uniformed Services Employment and Reemployment Rights Act, time away from work due to military service will not be treated as a break in service for purposes of the plan participation rules. In addition, in certain situations, service members may extend an absence from work that is related to military service without incurring a break in service. For example, depending upon the length of military service, a service member returning to employment is entitled to take from one to ninety days to report to work. The employer is required to treat this period as a period of continuous service.[6]

---

[1] Code Sec. 410(a)(5) and 411(a)(6); ERISA Sec. 202(b) and 203(b); Reg. § 2530.200b-4(a).

[2] IRS Reg. § 1.410(a)-5(c).

[3] *Swackard v. Commission House Drivers Union Local No. 400,* CA-6 (1981), 647 F2d 712, *cert. denied* 11/9/81.

[4] Code Secs. 410(a)(5) and 411(a)(6); ERISA Secs. 202(b) and 203(b); IRS Reg. § 1.410(a)-5(c)(3); ERISA Reg. § 2530.200b-4(a)(1) and (2).

[5] Rev. Rul. 80-360, 1980-2 CB 142, CCH PENSION PLAN GUIDE ¶ 19,550A.

[6] 38 U.S.C. 4318(a)(2), enacted October 13, 1994, P.L. 103-353. See also 20 CFR § 1002.259 (December 19, 2005, 70 FR 75246).

¶ 745
Break-in-Service Rules for Nonvested Participants

A special break-in-service rule applies to nonvested participants (i.e., those who do not have a nonforfeitable right under a plan to an accrued benefit derived from employer contributions).

Under the "rule of parity," pre-break years of service for a nonvested participant must be taken into account for participation purposes after a break in service unless the number of one-year breaks in service equals or exceeds the greater of (a) five consecutive one-year breaks in service or (b) the aggregate number of years of service earned before the break in service.[1] The rule effectively allows a participant who returns to work within five years (before five full consecutive one-year breaks) to receive credit for any years of service before the break, as the break in service period will always be less than the *greater* of five consecutive one-year breaks or aggregate pre-break service years.

> **Example 1:** Liv, age 23, a nonvested participant with two years of service under a plan, terminates her employment. The plan requires one year of service and the attainment of age 21 before an employee can participate in the plan. Liv fails to work for a period equal to four consecutive one-year breaks in service.
>
> Because the number of one-year breaks (four) does not equal or exceed the greater of (1) five years or (2) the aggregate number of years of service before the break (one year), the plan may not disregard Liv's one year of service for participation purposes upon her resumption of employment. Thus, if Liv resumes work with her employer after the four one-year breaks in service, she can participate in the plan without having to once again meet the one year of service and age 21 participation requirements.
>
> **Example 2:** Tony, age 23, is a nonvested participant with two years of plan service. He fails to work for a period of seven consecutive one-year breaks in

service. The plan conditions participation on one year of service and the attainment of age 21. Because the period of the break exceeds the greater of (1) five consecutive one-year breaks or (2) two years prior aggregate service, the plan is not required to credit Tony with the years of service he worked before the break. Accordingly, if Tony resumes employment with the employer after the seven one-year breaks in service, he may be kept from participating in the plan until he has completed one year of post-break service.

Under the rule of parity, years of service that need not be taken into account because of breaks in service are not required to be taken into account for participation purposes if there is a subsequent break in service.[2]

☐ The "rule of parity" also applies to the minimum vesting rules. See ¶ 888.

---

[1] Code Sec. 410(a)(5)(D)(i); ERISA Sec. 202(b)(4)(A).

[2] Code Sec. 410(a)(5)(D)(ii); ERISA Sec. 202(b)(4)(B).

¶ 750

Service Following a Break in Service

In determining whether an employee has completed one year of service after returning to employment following a one-year break in service, a plan must use a 12-consecutive month period beginning on the employee's date of reemployment. The reemployment commencement date, which is analogous to the employment commencement date, is defined as the first day on which the employee is entitled to be credited with an hour of service for the performance of duties after the first eligibility computation period in which the employee incurs a one-year break in service following an eligibility computation period in which the employee is credited with more than 500 hours of service.[1]

---

[1] IRS Reg. § 2530.200b-4(b).

¶ 755

Plans With Two-Year Vesting

A modified break-in-service rule applies to plans that provide 100% vesting after two years of service (see ¶ 725).[1] In the event that a participant incurs a one-year break in service before reaching two years of service, the pre-break service may be ignored on reemployment. The participant will have to start over in completing the two-year service requirement. However, the plan may not require, as a condition of participation, that the employee complete two *consecutive* years of service with the employer.[2]

---

[2] T.I.R. 1334, P-4, 1-8-75.

[1] Code Sec. 410(a)(5)(B); ERISA Sec. 202(b)(2); IRS Reg. §§ 1.410(a)-5(c) and 1.410(a)-8T.

¶ 760

Break-in-Service Rules for Parental Leave

In determining whether a break in service has occurred for participation purposes, an individual taking parental leave is treated as having completed hours of service. The rule applies to an individual who is absent from work:

1. by reason of the pregnancy of the individual,

2. by reason of the birth of a child of the individual,

3. by reason of the placement of a child in connection with the adoption of the child by the individual, or

4. for purposes of caring for the child during the period immediately following the birth or placement for adoption.[1]

Credit hours of service during leave period

During the period of absence, the individual is treated as having completed:

1. the number of hours that normally would have been credited but for the absence, or

2. if the normal work hours are unknown, eight hours of service for each normal workday during the leave.[2]

The total number of hours of service required to be treated as completed for any period shall not exceed 501 hours. The hours of service required to be credited must be credited only:

1. in the year in which the absence begins for one of the permitted reasons, if the crediting is necessary to prevent a break in service in that year, i.e., if the participant fails to complete more than 500 hours that year, or

2. in the following year.[3]

CCH Pointer: When coupled with the break-in-service rules for nonvested participants (see ¶ 745), the parental leave provision would allow a parent to take parental leave in one year, then incur up to five consecutive one-year breaks in service, and, upon returning to work, receive participation credit for her earlier work with the employer.

Employee certification

An employer may require an individual to certify that the leave was taken for the permitted reasons.[4] This certification could include, for example, a statement from a doctor that the leave was taken because of the birth of the individual's child. In addition, the employer may require that the individual supply information relating to the number of normal workdays for which there was an absence.

☐ The break-in-service rules applicable to parental leave for participation purposes also apply for vesting purposes. See ¶ 890.

[1] Code Sec. 410(a)(5)(E)(i); ERISA Sec. 202(b)(5)(A); P.L. 98-397 (Retirement Equity Act of 1984), Sec. 302(a).

[2] Code Sec. 410(a)(5)(E)(ii); ERISA Sec. 202(b)(5)(B).

[3] Code Sec. 410(a)(5)(E)(iii); ERISA Sec. 202(b)(5)(C).

[4] Code Sec. 410(a)(5)(E)(v); ERISA Sec. 202(b)(5)(E).

¶ 765

Controlled Groups Treated as Single Employer

All employees of all corporations that are members of a controlled group of corporations (as defined in Code Sec. 1563(a)) are to be treated as employed by a single employer for purposes of the minimum participation standards.[1] The same rule applies to partnerships, sole proprietorships, and other unincorporated businesses under common control.

[1] Code Secs. 414(b) and (c); ERISA Sec. 210(c).

¶ 770

Affiliated Service Groups

All employees of corporations or partnerships that are members of an affiliated service group are generally treated as employed by a single employer for purposes of the minimum participation rules.[1]

Two or more related service/management organizations. An affiliated service group typically is comprised of two or more related service or management organizations. Employees of affiliated service group members are treated as employed by a single employer for purposes of the plan qualification rules.

[1] Code Sec. 414(m)(1).

¶ 775

Plans Maintained by More Than One Employer

The participation requirements are generally to be applied, in the case of a plan maintained by more than one employer, as if all employees of each of the employers who maintain the plan were employed by a single employer.[1] Thus, service with any member employer is to be counted for purposes of the plan. In determining eligibility to participate, all covered service and all "contiguous noncovered service" with an employer or employers maintaining the plan must be taken into account.

Contiguous noncovered service

Noncovered service is "contiguous" if: (1) the noncovered service precedes or follows covered service, and (2) no quit, discharge, or retirement occurs between such covered and noncovered service.

Collectively bargained plans

A slightly different rule applies to plans maintained under a collective bargaining agreement and to all trusts that are part of the plan. In the case of such a plan, the participation requirements are to be applied as if all employees of each of the employers who are parties to the agreement and *who are subject to the same benefit computation under the plan* were employed by a single employer.[2]

[1] Code Sec. 413(c)(1); ERISA Sec. 210(a)(1); IRS Reg. § 1.413-2(b).

[2] Code Sec. 413(b)(1); IRS Reg. § 1.413-1(b).

¶ 780
Counting Service for Predecessor Employer

Service provided for a predecessor employer must be counted as service for the successor employer if the successor employer maintains the plan of the predecessor.[1] This requirement cannot be evaded by the nominal discontinuation of the plan.[2]

In addition, an employer that maintains a plan which is not the same plan maintained by a predecessor employer may still be required to credit service for the predecessor under certain circumstances.[3]

[1] Code Sec. 414(a); ERISA Sec. 210(b)(1).

[2] P.L. 93-406 (ERISA), House Rep't 93-1280, 93rd Cong., 2d Sess., p. 263.

[3] Code Sec. 414(a)(2); ERISA Sec. 210(b)(1).

¶ 785
Maximum Age Conditions

A qualified plan may generally not impose maximum age conditions that effectively exclude employees from participation.[1] Specifically, a qualified plan may not exclude an employee from participating in the plan if his or her age is less than five years from the normal retirement age in the plan.[2]

Example: BIGCO maintains a plan that calls for normal retirement at age 65. Under the plan, an employee who is age 21 and has completed one year of service may participate in the plan. Barney, age 61, is hired by BIGCO. Barney must be eligible to participate in the plan no later than the date when he completes one year of service with the employer. The plan may not impose a maximum age requirement for participation in the plan.

[1] Code Sec. 410(a)(2); ERISA Sec. 202(a)(2).

[2] IRS Reg. § 1.410(a)-4(a).

¶ 790
Additional Minimum Participation Requirements

In order to prevent qualified plans from discriminating in favor of highly compensated individuals, an additional set of minimum participation rules are applied. Generally, a qualified defined benefit plan must benefit no fewer than the lesser of:

1. 50 employees of the employer, or
2. the greater of (a) 40% of all employees of the employer or (b) two employees (or one employee if the employer has only one employee).[1]

The 50 employee-40% rule does not apply to defined contribution plans.

☐ The additional minimum participation requirements are discussed in detail at ¶ 1178 and following.

[1] Code Sec. 401(a)(26)(A).

¶ 795

For More Information

☐ For more information on the minimum participation standards, see ¶ 1089—¶ 1119 and ¶ 1942—¶ 1954 of the CCH PENSION PLAN GUIDE.

Vesting and Accrual of Benefits

¶ 800

Overview of Vesting and Accrual of Benefits

Vesting rules under the Internal Revenue Code and ERISA govern when and to what extent an employee has a nonforfeitable right to contributions and benefits from a qualified retirement plan. Generally, all qualified plans are subject to the vesting rules.

A qualified plan must provide that an employee's right to normal retirement benefits is nonforfeitable upon the attainment of normal retirement age. The extent to which benefits are vested prior to normal retirement age varies depending upon whether benefits stem from employee or employer contributions. Employee contributions vest immediately when made. In contrast, employer contributions generally vest according to a vesting schedule set forth in the employer's plan.

¶ 805

GENERAL VESTING RULES: Nonforfeitable Right to Benefits

A plan participant has a nonforfeitable right to plan contributions and benefits if the contributions and benefits cannot be taken away once they are paid into the plan.[1] An employee becomes vested in plan benefits when he or she is entitled to claim immediate payment. The employee's failure to actually claim payment does not render the right to payment forfeitable as long as the employee retains the exclusive power to claim payment.

Accrued benefit

Under a defined contribution plan, an employee's accrued benefit is generally the balance in the employee's account. Under a defined benefit plan, the employee's accrued benefit is determined according to a formula contained in the plan.[2]

□ The accrual of benefits is discussed further, beginning at ¶ 845.

¹ IRS Reg. § 1.411(a)-4.   ² Code Sec. 411(a)(7).

¶ 810

GENERAL VESTING RULES: Plans Subject to Vesting Rules

In general, all qualified plans must satisfy the minimum vesting rules.[1] In addition, the vesting rules contained in Title I of ERISA (but not those contained in the Internal Revenue Code) apply generally to any employee benefit plan established or maintained by (1) an employer engaged in interstate commerce or in any industry or activity affecting interstate commerce, (2) an employee organization or organizations representing employees engaged in interstate commerce or any industry affecting interstate commerce, and (3) both an employer and an employee organization.[2]

CCH Pointer: As a practical matter, most pension plans seek qualified status under the Code and are accordingly subject to the Code's vesting rules.

¹ Code Secs. 401(a)(7) and 411.   ² ERISA Sec. 4(a).

¶ 815

GENERAL VESTING RULES: Plans Exempt from Vesting Rules

The following types of plans are exempt from the vesting rules.

Governmental plans

Governmental plans are plans established and maintained by the government of the United States, any state, or political subdivision. Plans established by any government agency or instrumentality are also exempt.[1]

Church plans

A church plan is a plan established and maintained by a church or convention or association of churches which is tax-exempt under Code Sec. 501 for its employees. Church plans are exempt from the vesting rules unless they elect to be covered (see ¶ 160).[2]

Fraternal organization plans

Plans maintained by fraternal beneficiary societies and voluntary employees' beneficiary associations that are tax-exempt under Code Sec. 501(c)(8) or (9) are exempt from the vesting rules if no contributions to the plan are made by the employers of its participants.[3] In addition, a pension trust that is established before June 25, 1959 and that is tax-exempt under Code Sec. 501(c)(18) is exempt from the vesting rules.[4]

Union-sponsored plans

The Internal Revenue Code provides an exemption for a plan that has not, at any time after September 2, 1974 (the effective date of ERISA), provided for employer contributions.[5] ERISA exempts a plan that is established and maintained by a labor organization described under Code Sec. 501(c)(5) and that does not provide for employer contributions.[6]

Workers' compensation plans

A plan maintained solely to comply with workers' compensation, unemployment compensation, or disability insurance laws is exempt from the vesting rules.[7]

Foreign plans

A plan maintained outside the United States primarily for persons substantially all of whom are nonresident aliens is exempt from the vesting rules.[8]

Welfare plans

A welfare plan may provide medical, surgical, unemployment, and disability benefits, as well as prepaid legal services, scholarships, and day care.[9] Courts generally have refused to apply ERISA's vesting rules to welfare plans offering medical benefits,[10] retiree health benefits,[11] and disability benefits.[12] Severance pay plans have also been excluded.[13] Parties to a welfare plan, however, may agree to allow welfare benefits to vest.[14]

"Top Hat" plans

An unfunded plan that is maintained primarily to provide deferred compensation for a select group of management or highly compensated employees (top hat plan) is exempt from the vesting rules.[15]

Excess benefit plans

An excess benefit plan is maintained solely for the purpose of providing benefits for certain employees in excess of the limits on benefits imposed by Code Sec. 415. An excess benefit plan is exempt from the vesting standards, whether or not it is funded.[16]

Partnership buy-out

Payments to a retired partner or to a deceased partner's successor in interest that are described in Code Sec. 736 are exempt from the vesting standards.[17]

Individual retirement accounts

An individual retirement account or annuity under Code Sec. 408 is exempt from the vesting rules.[18]

Self-employed persons

For purposes of ERISA Title I, a Keogh plan that covers only self-employed persons and does not cover any common-law employees is not an employee benefit

¶815

pension plan.[19] Accordingly, such a plan would be exempt from all of Title I, including the vesting standards.

---

[1] Code Secs. 411(e)(1)(A) and 414(d); ERISA Sec. 3(32); IRS Reg. § 1.411(a)-1(c)(1)(i). (Under P.L. 109-280 (Pension Protection Act of 2006), certain plans maintained by Indian tribal governments are government plans. See Code Sec.414(d), as amended by P.L. 109-280, Act Sec. 906(a)(1).)

[2] Code Secs. 410(d) and 411(e)(1)(B); ERISA Sec. 4(b)(2); IRS Reg. § 1.411(a)-1(c)(1)(ii).

[3] Code Sec. 411(e)(1)(D); ERISA Sec. 201(3)(A); IRS Reg. § 1.411(a)-1(c)(1)(iv).

[4] ERISA Sec. 201(3)(B).

[5] Code Sec. 411(e)(1)(C); IRS Reg. § 1.411(a)-1(c)(1)(iv).

[6] ERISA Sec. 201(4); ERISA Reg. § 2630.201-2.

[7] ERISA Sec. 4(b)(3).

[8] ERISA Sec. 4(b)(4).

[9] ERISA Sec. 3(1). Also viewed as welfare benefits are any benefits, other than pension or death benefits, that are described in Sec. 302(c) of the Labor Management Relations Act of 1947. Benefits described in LMRA Sec. 302(c) generally mirror the list of ERISA welfare benefits, but also include apprenticeship or other training programs.

[10] See, e.g., *Tusting v. Bay View Federal Savings and Loan Association,* DC Cal (1991), 762 FSupp 1381.

[11] See *Wise v. El Paso Natural Gas Company,* CA-5 (1993), 986 F2d 929.

[12] ERISA Opinion Letter 90-03A, 2-13-90.

[13] See, e.g. *Adams v. Avondale Industries,* CA-6 (1990), 905 F2d 943.

[14] *In re White Farm Equipment Co.,* CA-3 (1986), 788 F2d 1186.

[15] ERISA Sec. 201(2).

[16] ERISA Sec. 201(7).

[17] ERISA Sec. 201(5).

[18] ERISA Sec. 201(6).

[19] ERISA Reg. § 2510.3-3(b) and (c).

¶ 817

GENERAL VESTING RULES: Coordination with Nondiscrimination Rules

A plan must coordinate its vesting requirements with the Code's general rule that a qualified plan may not discriminate in favor of highly compensated employees.[1]

A plan that satisfies the vesting rules will not be considered discriminatory with respect to vesting, unless:

1. there has been a pattern of abuse under the plan (such as dismissal of employees before their accrued benefits become nonforfeitable) tending to discriminate in favor of highly compensated employees, or

2. there has been, or there is reason to believe that there will be, an accrual of benefits or forfeitures tending to discriminate in favor of highly compensated employees.[2]

☐ The nondiscrimination rules are discussed in detail beginning at ¶ 1100.

---

[1] Code Sec. 401(a)(4).

[2] Code Sec. 411(d)(1).

¶ 820

VESTING SCHEDULES: Minimum Vesting Schedules for Most Qualified Plans

The vesting schedules applicable for employer contributions to **defined benefit plans** differ from those applicable to **defined contribution** plans.[1]

Defined benefit plans. For most qualified **defined benefit** plans, an employee's employer-provided accrued benefit must vest at least as rapidly as under one of the following two vesting schedules.[2]

1. *Five-year "cliff" vesting.* An employee who has completed at least five years of service must have a nonforfeitable right to 100% of his accrued benefit derived from employer contributions.

2. *Three-to-seven-year "graded" vesting.* An employee must have a nonforfeitable right to a percentage of his accrued benefit derived from employer contributions determined under the following schedule:

Years of Service	Nonforfeitable percentage
3	20
4	40
5	60
6	80
7 or more	100

Defined contribution plans. An accelerated vesting schedule applies to employer contributions made under defined contribution plans.[3] Employer contributions must vest at least as rapidly as under one of the following two minimum vesting schedules:

1. **Three-year cliff vesting,** under which a participant acquires a nonforfeitable right to 100 percent of employer matching contributions upon completion of three years of service; or

2. **Two-to-six-year graded vesting,** under which a participant will have a nonforfeitable right to 20 percent of employer matching contributions upon the completion of two years of service and will fully vest in the employer matching contributions after six years of service, in accord with the following schedule:

Years of Service	Nonforfeitable percentage
2	20
3	40
4	60

Years of Service	Nonforfeitable percentage
5	80
6 or more	100

The vesting schedules apply only to *employer-provided* contributions. The accrued benefit from an employee's own contributions to a plan must be 100% vested *at all times*.[4]

> **CCH Pointer:** *Separate vesting schedules.* A plan may maintain separate vesting schedules for employer contributions subject to the vesting schedules under the Pension Protection Act of 2006 and for those contributions not subject to PPA. The plan must separately account for the contributions made under (1) the vesting schedule in effect prior to the first day of the plan year beginning after December 31, 2006, and (2) the vesting schedule for employer nonelective contributions for plan years beginning after December 31, 2006.[5]

Prior law

For plan years beginning before 2007, the accelerated vesting schedules described above applied only to employer *matching* contributions.[6] For all other plans (including defined benefit plans), the 5-year cliff and 3-7 year graded vesting schedules remained in effect.

More generous vesting is permitted

Satisfaction of one of the minimum vesting schedules is required to maintain a plan's qualified status. However, a plan's vesting schedule may be more generous than the schedules described above.

---

[1] Code Sec. 411(a)(2), as amended by P.L. 109-280 (Pension Protection Act of 2006), Act Sec. 904(a); ERISA Sec. 203(a), as amended by P.L. 109-280 (Pension Protection Act of 2006), Act Sec. 904(b), generally effective for plan years beginning after December 31, 2006. Special effective dates apply to collectively-bargained plans and to ESOPs. See Act Sec. 904(c).

[2] Code Sec. 411(a)(2); ERISA Sec. 203(a)(2); IRS Temp. Reg. § 1.411(a)-3T.

[3] Code Sec. 411(a)(2), as amended by P.L. 109-280 (Pension Protection Act of 2006), Act Sec.

904(a); ERISA Sec. 203(a), as amended by P.L. 109-280 (Pension Protection Act of 2006), Act Sec. 904(b), generally effective for plan years beginning after December 31, 2006. Special effective dates apply to collectively-bargained plans and to ESOPs. See Act Sec. 904(c).

[4] Code Sec. 411(a)(1); ERISA Sec. 203(a)(1).

[5] Notice 2007-7, Sec. VII, I.R.B. 2007-5, January 29, 2007, CCH Pension Plan Guide ¶ 17,135R.

[6] Code Sec. 411(a)(2), prior to amendment by P.L. 109-280, and Code Sec. 411(a)(12), prior to being stricken by P.L. 109-280.

¶ 825

VESTING SCHEDULES: Multiemployer Plans

Multiemployer plans are subject to the same vesting rules that apply to single-employer plans.[1] Thus, multiemployer defined benefit plans have to provide that a participant's accrued benefits are fully vested after five years of service or over a period of three to seven years.[2]

---

[1]P.L. 104-188 (Small Business Job Protection Act), Sec. 1442(a) and (b). For plan years prior to 1997, accrued benefits in multiemployer plans for employees covered under a collective bargaining agreement had to be vested no later than upon the participant's completion of 10 years of service. See Code Sec. 441(a)(2)(C) and ERISA Sec.

203(a)(2)(C), prior to repeal by P.L. 104-188 (Small Business Job Protection Act).

[2]See ¶ 820 for accelerated vesting schedules applicable to defined contribution plans, as enacted under P.L. 109-280 (Pension Protection Act of 2006). Though these changes are generally effective for plan years beginning after December 31, 2006, special effective dates apply to collectively-bargained plans. See Act Sec. 904(c).

¶ 827
VESTING SCHEDULES: Top-Heavy Plans

Employer-provided benefits must vest more rapidly under top-heavy plans than under most qualified plans. For any plan year for which a plan is a top-heavy plan, an employee's *employer-provided* accrued benefit must vest at least as rapidly as under one of the following two vesting schedules.[1]

1. *Three-year vesting.* An employee who has completed at least three years of service must have a nonforfeitable right to 100% of his accrued benefit derived from employer contributions.

2. *Six-year "graded" vesting.* An employee must have a nonforfeitable right to a percentage of his accrued benefit from employer contributions determined under the following schedule:

Years of Service	The nonforfeitable percentage is:
2	20
3	40
4	60
5	80
6 or more	100

A plan that ceases to be top-heavy may change its vesting schedule to conform to the general vesting rules. See ¶ 830.

☐ For additional information on top-heavy plans, see the discussion beginning at ¶ 900.

---

[1] Code Sec. 416(b)(1).

¶ 830
VESTING SCHEDULES: Vesting Schedule Changes

Plans may change their vesting schedule by plan amendment. However, a plan generally may not amend its vesting schedule with respect to employees who participated in the plan as of the later of (1) the date the amendment is adopted or

(2) the date the amendment becomes effective, if the nonforfeitable percentage of the employee's accrued benefit derived from employer contributions (as determined on that date) would be reduced as a result.[1]

Option to remain under prior vesting schedule

A plan that changes a vesting schedule must give an employee with at least three years of service the option of remaining under the pre-amendment schedule.[2] An employee who does not elect to remain under the pre-amendment schedule will be subject to the new vesting schedule. However, the new vesting schedule may not result in a forfeiture of benefits that are already vested.

The period during which a participant may make the election must begin no later than the date the plan amendment is adopted and must end no earlier than the latest of: (a) 60 days after the amendment is adopted; (b) 60 days after the date the amendment becomes effective; or (c) 60 days after the participant is given written notice of the amendment by the employer or the plan administrator.[3]

A plan is not required to provide for the election of a former vesting schedule where an employee's vesting percentage would not be less under the new vesting schedule.[4]

CCH Pointer: An amended vesting schedule must comply with the approved vesting schedules. However, the amended schedule does not have to be the same schedule followed by the plan prior to the amendment. Thus, a plan that provides for 100% vesting only after five years of service may be amended to allow three-to-seven year vesting.[5]

---

[1] Code Sec. 411(a)(10)(A); ERISA Sec. 203(c)(1)(A); IRS Reg. § 1.411(a)-8(a).

[2] Code Sec. 411(a)(10)(B); ERISA Sec. 203(c)(1)(B).

[3] IRS Temp. Reg. § 1.411(a)-8T(b)(2).

[4] IRS Temp. Reg. § 1.411(a)-8T(b)(1).

[5] IRS Alert Guidelines, Explanation VI to Worksheet No. 2 (Minimum Vesting Standards: Defined Contribution Plans) and Explanation VI to Worksheet No. 2A (Minimum Vesting Standards: Defined Benefit Plans).

¶ 840

VESTING SCHEDULES: Full Vesting at Normal Retirement Age

A qualified retirement plan must provide for full vesting of an employee's normal retirement benefit, regardless of years of service, once the employee attains "normal retirement age." [1] Normal retirement age is the *earlier* of:

1. the time when an employee attains normal retirement age as defined in the plan, or

2. the later of (a) age 65, or (b) five years after the time that the participant commences participation in the plan.[2]

---

[1] Code Sec. 411(a); ERISA Sec. 203(a).

[2] Code Sec. 411(a)(8); ERISA Sec. 3(24).

¶ 845

ACCRUAL OF BENEFITS: Accrued Benefits

The "accrued benefit" referenced in the vesting schedules is the amount of benefit an employee has accumulated at a given time.[1] It is not, however, the amount of benefit to which the employee has a nonforfeitable vested right. That amount is calculated under the vesting schedules (see ¶ 820). Once a benefit amount has accrued, strict limitations are placed on the reduction of the benefit (see ¶ 866).

Under a defined contribution plan, an employee's accrued benefit is the balance in the individual's account (see ¶ 850). An employee's accrued benefit under a defined benefit plan generally includes only pension or retirement benefits, and does not include ancillary benefits not directly related to retirement benefits, such as medical benefits (see ¶ 853).

Investment gain is not an accrued benefit

Participants in a defined benefit plan generally have a nonforfeitable right only to their accrued benefits. According to the United States Supreme Court, this statutory entitlement is not affected by the plan's actual investment experience.[2]

---

[1] Code Sec. 411(a)(7).

[2] *Hughes Aircraft Co. v. Jacobson*, US Sup Ct (1999), 525 U.S. 432.

¶ 850

ACCRUAL OF BENEFITS: Defined Contribution Plans

An employee's accrued benefit under a defined contribution plan is the balance in his or her plan account.[1] Separate accounts must be maintained for each employee.[2]

When benefits accrue

Benefits do not accrue under a defined contribution plan until they are formally "allocated" to a participant's account. ERISA does not prohibit an employer from eliminating previously offered benefits that have not vested or accrued.[3]

The plan may authorize the employer to determine when an allocation is actually made. However, the accrued benefit of a participant in a defined contribution plan includes amounts to which the participant is entitled under the terms of the plan, even if the amounts have not actually been credited to the participant's account because of bookkeeping delays.[4]

---

[1] Code Sec. 411(a)(7); ERISA Sec. 3(23); IRS Reg. § 1.411(a)-7(a)(2).

[2] ERISA Sec. 204(b)(2)(B); IRS Reg. § 1.411(b)-1(e)(2).

[3] *Phillips v. Amoco Oil Co.*, CA-11 (1986), 799 F2d 1464, *cert. denied* 481 U.S. 1016.

[4] IRS Letter Ruling 9735001, 2-20-97 [National Office Technical Advice Memorandum], CCH Pension Plan Guide ¶ 17,397.

¶ 853

ACCRUAL OF BENEFITS: Defined Benefit Plans

Under a defined benefit plan, an employee's accrued benefit is the accrued benefit determined under the terms of the plan, and is generally expressed in the form of an annual benefit commencing at normal retirement age (see ¶ 840).[1] The term "accrued benefit" refers to pension or retirement benefits. It does not apply to medical or disability benefits, life insurance benefits payable as a lump sum, or other such ancillary benefits.[2]

Benefit accrual formulas

A qualified defined benefit plan must provide a formula under which each participant's actual accrued benefit under the plan can be determined in each plan year.[3]

The rate at which an employee's benefits may accrue may be determined under three alternative formulas:[4]

1. the 133⅓% rule;

2. the 3% rule, and

3. the fractional rule.

Essentially, these rules are aimed at preventing the excessive "back loading" of a defined benefit plan. Back loading is the practice of providing a faster rate of accrual after an employee has attained a specified age or performed specified years of service. For instance, back loading would occur where a plan provides a benefit of 1.5% of compensation for each year of service before age 55 and 2% thereafter.

133⅓% rule. The basic requirement of the 133⅓% formula is that the benefit accrued for a later year not be more than 133⅓% of the benefit accrued for the current year. As a result, unlimited front loading is permitted while back loading is restricted. The accrual rate can be based on either a dollar amount or a percentage. In order to use this formula, the plan must provide that the accrued benefit payable at normal retirement age be equal to the normal retirement benefit.[5] Benefit accruals, therefore, must continue until the employee is eligible to retire with actuarially unreduced benefits.

Example 1: Plan X provides a monthly pension equal to 1% of the average compensation for the employee's highest five years for each year of participation through age 50. For years of participation beyond age 50, the plan can provide for benefit accrual of no more than 1⅓% without violating the 133⅓% rule.

Amendment may increase accrual rate. The 133⅓% rule will not be violated merely because a plan amendment (or scheduled benefit increase) increases the accrual rate for the current or future years without providing past service credits. Thus, Plan X in the above example could increase its accrual rate to 2% for years of participation through age 50 and 2⅔% for years of participation beyond age 50 without violating the 133⅓% rule.

In addition, changes in a plan's accrual rate will be disregarded for purposes of the 133⅓% rule if the accrual rate change will not apply to plan participants or those who could be plan participants. However, a violation of the 133⅓% rule occurs if, under the plan, the base for the computation of retirement benefits changes solely by reason of an increase in the number of years of participation.[6] By contrast, a plan may change the base because of salary increases or factors other than a participant's length of service.

3% rule. Under the 3% rule, the benefit accrued in any year must be at least 3% of the normal retirement benefit to which the employee would be entitled if he or she commenced participation in the plan at the earliest possible entry age and served continuously until age 65 or an earlier normal retirement age provided under the plan.[7]

> **Example 2:** Plan Y provides for flat-amount pensions payable at a normal retirement age of 65 which are based on the participant's years of service. Ms. Jones became a participant at age 25 (her entry age). Her pension at age 65 (40 years of service) would be $1,500 per month. Ms. Jones' monthly benefit must accrue at least at the rate of $45 (3% of $1,500) per year for 33⅓ years, when her pension will be fully accrued. No accrual is required thereafter.

The 3% rule is applied cumulatively. Therefore, an employee's minimum accrued benefit is computed by multiplying 3% of his normal retirement benefit by the number of years (not in excess of 33⅓) that he has participated in the plan, including years of participation after normal retirement age has been attained.[8]

Benefit based on highest average compensation. If the plan provides benefits based on the individual's compensation during any period, the maximum benefit will be computed on the basis of the individual's average compensation for his most highly compensated consecutive years of service, although this period cannot exceed 10 years.[9] It will be assumed that the employee continued to earn this average amount of compensation until normal retirement age. If, for instance, the plan calls for benefits based upon the employee's average compensation for his highest three-year period, this average (based on facts at the time of the computation) will be assumed to continue until normal retirement age.

Fractional rule. Under the fractional rule, a participant's accrued benefit is a fraction of the annual benefit to which he would have been entitled at normal retirement age if, under the plan as in effect at the time of the determination, he had continued to earn the same rate of compensation until normal retirement age. The fraction, which cannot exceed 1, is as follows:

$$\frac{\text{Participant's total years of participation as of the date of his separation}}{\text{Total years participant would have participated if he had continued until normal retirement age}}$$

If retirement benefits are computed under the plan as a percentage of average compensation over a period of years, no more than the last ten years before the determination can be taken into account.[10] The fractional rule requirements will not be violated simply because no benefits accrue to a participant who continues service with the employer after he or she has attained normal retirement age.[11]

Example 3: At normal retirement age of 65, Plan X provides a benefit equal to 2% of the employee's average compensation for his highest three years, minus 30% of the primary Social Security benefit. Mr. Green terminated his services at age 55 after 20 years of service. His benefits were 100% vested. His highest three years' compensation were $19,000, $20,000, and $21,000. At the time he left the service of the employer, the primary Social Security benefit payable to him at age 65 (under the Social Security law in effect when he terminated) would be $6,000 if he continued to work for the employer at the same annual rate of compensation until normal retirement age. Mr. Green's accrued benefit would be $6,800, figured as follows:

1. Had Green remained in service until age 65, he would have had 30 years' service. Thirty times 2% for each year of service equals 60%. Sixty percent of the average of his highest three years' compensation ($20,000) is $12,000. Twelve thousand dollars minus 30% of his primary Social Security benefits ($6,000) equals $10,200 ($12,000 minus $1,800). Thus, $10,200 is the projected benefit to which the fraction set out above is applied.

2. The fraction used to determine Mr. Green's accrued benefit at the time of his separation is

$$\frac{20 \text{(years of participation when separated)}}{30 \text{(projected years of participation before normal retirement)}}$$

Mr. Green's accrued benefit as of the date of his separation from the employer's service therefore is $6,800 ($^{20}/_{30}$ of $10,200).

More than one formula may be used

A plan can compute benefits under more than one formula provided that the aggregate benefits satisfy the fractional rule, the 3% rule, or the 133⅓% rule. Furthermore, a plan is not precluded from applying different methods in determining accrued benefits for different classifications of employees.[12]

Exception for insurance-funded plans

A defined benefit plan is not required to satisfy one of the minimum accrual formulas if the plan is funded through the purchase of specified individual insurance contracts or through a group insurance arrangement having similar characteristics. The insurance contracts and plan benefits must satisfy the requirements of Code Sec. 412(i) and the employee's accrued benefit on any applicable date must not be less than the cash surrender value of the insurance contracts under Code Sec. 412(i).[13]

CCH Pointer: "Code Sec. 412(i) plans." Fully insured defined benefit plans that are funded solely by the purchase of individual insurance contracts are sometimes referred to as "Code Sec. 412(i) plans." These plans can alleviate administrative burdens faced by small employers. For example, insurance contract plans can relieve small employers of the requirement of making the complex quarterly contribution calculations. In addition, small employers may save the expense of hiring an enrolled actuary to assure the funding of the plan because an insurance contract plan is not required to file Schedule B of Form 5500.[14]

☐ Additional information on the benefit accrual formulas may be found at CCH PENSION PLAN GUIDE ¶ 2555.

---

[1] Code Sec. 411(a)(7).

[2] IRS Reg. § 1.411(a)-7(a)(1).

[3] T.I.R. 1403, 9-17-75, Question V-14.

[4] Code Sec. 411(b)(1)(B).

[5] Code Sec. 411(b)(1)(B); ERISA Sec. 204(b)(1)(B); IRS Reg. § 1.411(b)-1(b)(2).

[6] IRS Reg. § 1.411(b)-1(b)(2)(ii)(F).

[7] Code Sec. 411(b)(1)(A); ERISA Sec. 204(b)(1)(A); IRS Reg. § 1.411(b)-1(b)(1).

[8] Code Sec. 411(b)(1)(A); ERISA Sec. 204(b)(1)(A); IRS Reg. § 1.411(b)-1(b)(1).

[9] IRS Reg. § 1.411(b)-1(b)(1)(ii)(A).

[10] Code Sec. 411(b)(1)(C); ERISA Sec. 204(b)(1)(C); IRS Reg. § 1.411(b)-1(b)(3)(i).

[11] IRS Reg. § 1.411(b)-1(b)(3)(ii)(C).

[12] IRS Reg. § 1.411(b)-1(a)(1). Under a limited exception to this rule proposed in 2008, certain plans (such as cash balance plans) that determine

a participant's benefits as the greatest of the benefits determined under two or more separate formulas would be permitted to demonstrate satisfaction of the 133 ⅓ percent rule by demonstrating that each separate formula satisfies the 133 ⅓ percent rule (see Proposed Reg. § 1.411(b)-1 (73 FR 34665, 6-18-2008) at CCH PENSION PLAN GUIDE ¶ 20,262L).

[13] Code Secs. 411(b)(1)(F) and 412(i); IRS Reg. § 1.411(b)-1(d)(2); IRS Reg. § 1.412(i)-1.)

[14] Note that amendments to Code Sec. 412 made by the Pension Protection Act of 2006, effective for plan years beginning after 2007, changed the Code location of the definition of insurance contract plans from Code Sec. 412(i) to Code Sec. 412(e)(3). The substance of the provision remains unchanged. See Code Sec. 412(e)(3), as amended by P.L. 109-280 (Pension Protection Act of 2006), Act Sec. 111(a).

¶ 855

ACCRUAL OF BENEFITS: Actuarial Adjustments

The accrued benefit under a plan must be provided by an annual benefit beginning at normal retirement that is in the form of a single life annuity with no ancillary benefits. An actuarial adjustment will be needed if the benefit provided by the plan is other than a single life annuity (with no ancillary benefits) commencing at normal retirement age, or if it is other than an annual benefit.[1] No actuarial adjustment is required merely because an employee postpones retirement beyond normal retirement age.

> **Example:** ABC plan stipulates a normal retirement age of 65 and provides a benefit of $500 a month starting at age 65. Ben retires at age 68 and will be paid the same $500 benefit, with no upward adjustment.[2]

Note, however, that benefit accruals may not be discontinued or reduced because of age (see ¶ 867).

---

[1] Code Sec. 411(c)(3); ERISA Sec. 204(c)(3); IRS Reg. § 1.411(c)-1(e).

[2] IRS Reg. § 1.411(c)-1(f)(2).

¶ 857

ACCRUAL OF BENEFITS: Change in Actuarial Basis

A plan may be amended to change the actuarial basis used to determine an accrued benefit. However, such a change may not reduce a participant's accrued benefit (see ¶ 866).

A plan may require that the actuarial equivalent of the accrued benefit on or after the date of the change be determined as the sum of (1) the actuarial equivalent of the accrued benefit as of the date of change computed on the old basis, and (2) the actuarial equivalent, computed on the new basis of the excess of (a) the total accrued benefit over (b) the accrued benefit as of the date of change.

Alternatively, the plan may require that the actuarial equivalent of the accrued benefit on or after the date of the change be determined as the greater of (1) the actuarial equivalent of the accrued benefit as of the date of change computed on the old basis or (2) the actuarial equivalent of the total accrued benefit computed on the new basis.[1]

---

[1] Rev. Rul. 81-12, 1981-1 CB 228, CCH PENSION PLAN GUIDE ¶ 19,556.

¶ 863

ACCRUAL OF BENEFITS: Allocation of Accrued Benefits Between Employer and Employee Contributions

Accrued benefits derived from an employee's own contributions are always 100% vested. However, accrued benefits derived from employer contributions may be partly or entirely forfeitable. Thus, it may be necessary to allocate the total accrued benefit between the portion derived from employee contributions and the portion derived from employer contributions.

Generally, an employee's accrued benefit derived from employer contributions is the excess of the employee's total accrued benefit over that portion derived from his or her own contributions.[1] In other words, the accrued benefit from employer contributions will equal the employee's total accrued benefit *minus* the accrued benefit derived from the employee's own contributions.

Separate accounting requirement

A separate accounting must be made for the portion of an employee's accrued benefit which is derived from voluntary contributions to a defined benefit plan.[2] In addition, a plan other than a defined benefit plan must make a separate accounting for each employee's accrued benefit.

Defined benefit plan allocation

Separate rules apply to voluntary and mandatory employee contributions.

Voluntary employee contributions. The portion of an accrued benefit derived from *voluntary* employee contributions to a defined benefit plan is treated in the same manner as are employee contributions to a *defined contribution* plan for which a separate account is maintained. Thus, the accrued benefit from an employee's voluntary contributions is the amount of those contributions, plus all income, expenses, gains, and losses attributable to the contributions.[3]

Mandatory employee contributions. The accrued benefit from mandatory employee contributions is an amount equal to the employee's accumulated contributions, expressed as an annual benefit commencing at normal retirement age. The conversion of the employee's contributions (plus interest) to an annuity is calculated in accord with the interest rate used under the plan to determine the present value of accrued benefits.[4]

Accumulated contributions. An employee's "accumulated contributions" refers to all mandatory employee contributions, plus interest.[5]

Actuarial adjustments. If a defined benefit plan provides that an employee's accrued benefit may be determined as an amount other than an annual benefit commencing at normal retirement age, or that the accrued benefit derived from employee contributions may be determined with respect to a benefit in a form other than a single life annuity, the accrued benefit must be the actuarial equivalent of the benefit or the amount that would be payable at normal retirement age.[6]

Defined contribution plan allocation

In the case of a defined contribution plan (or any plan except a defined benefit plan), if separate accounts are maintained, the accrued benefit derived from employee contributions is the balance of the employee's account consisting only of his contributions and the income, expenses, gains, and losses attributable to the contributions.[7]

If separate accounts for employee contributions are not maintained, the amount allocated to the accrued benefit from employee contributions is in the same ratio to the total accrued benefits as that of employee contributions (less withdrawals) is to the total of employer contributions (less withdrawals) and employee contributions (less withdrawals).[8]

$$\text{Accrued Benefit from Employee Contributions} = \text{Total Accrued Benefit} \times \frac{\text{Employee Contributions (less withdrawals)}}{\text{Employee Contributions (less withdrawals)} + \text{Employer Contributions (less withdrawals)}}$$

[1] Code Sec. 411(c)(1); ERISA Sec. 204(c)(1); IRS Reg. § 1.411(c)-1(a).

[2] Code Sec. 411(b)(3); ERISA Sec. 204(b)(3).

[3] Code Sec. 411(d)(5); IRS Reg. § 1.411(c)-1(b)(1).

[4] Code Sec. 411(c)(2)(B); ERISA Sec. 204(c). See also IRS Proposed Reg. § 1.411(c)-1(c)(2).

[5] Code Sec. 411(c)(2)(C); ERISA Sec. 204(c)(2)(D).

[6] Code Sec. 411(c)(3); IRS Reg. § 1.411(c)-1(e); ERISA Sec. 204(c)(3); Rev. Rul. 78-202, 1978-1 C.B. 124, CCH Pension Plan Guide ¶ 19,461.

[7] Code Sec. 411(c)(2)(A); ERISA Sec. 204(c)(2)(A); IRS Reg. § 1.411(c)-1(b)(1).

[8] IRS Reg. § 1.411(c)-1(b)(2).

¶ 865

ACCRUAL OF BENEFITS: First Two Years of Service Rule

A plan will continue to satisfy the accrued benefit rules even though the accrual of benefits under a plan does not become effective until the employee has completed two continuous years of service which are not separated by a break in service (see ¶ 882). However, for years of service after the first two years, the accrued benefit must not be less than that to which the employee would be entitled without application of the special rule.[1]

Example: A plan provides for a rate of accrual of 1% of average compensation for the highest three years of compensation beginning with a participant's third year of service. The plan will *not* be treated as satisfying the accrued benefits requirements because, as of the time the employee completes three continuous years of service, there is no accrual during the first two years of service.

[1] IRS Reg. § 1.411(b)-1(d)(1).

¶ 866

ACCRUAL OF BENEFITS: Reductions in Accrued Benefits Generally Prohibited

The accrued benefits of plan participants generally may not be eliminated or decreased by plan amendments (the "anti-cutback rule").[1] A plan amendment that has the effect of eliminating or reducing an early retirement benefit or a retirement-type subsidy, or eliminating an optional form of benefit (see below) with respect to benefits attributable to service before the plan amendment is treated as reducing accrued benefits.

Suspension of benefits violates anti-cutback rules. The Supreme Court has ruled that a plan amendment expanding the categories of post-retirement employment that trigger the suspension of payments of early retirement benefits that have previously accrued violates the anti-cutback rule.[2]

Optional forms of benefit

An optional form of benefit is a distribution alternative that is available under a plan for the payment of a participant's accrued benefits.[3] Different optional forms of benefit may result from variations in plan terms relating to: the payment schedule; timing, commencement, and medium of distribution (e.g., cash or in-kind) for payments; election rights; eligibility requirements; or the portion of the benefit to which the distribution alternative applies. For example, different optional forms of benefit exist if a distribution alternative does not provide payments on substantially the same terms as another distribution alternative.

Pre-retirement age 70½ distributions

Generally, a plan amendment that eliminates an employee's right to commence pre-retirement benefit distributions after age 70½, or that imposes additional conditions on that right, would violate Code Sec. 411(d)(6), if the amendment applied to benefits accrued as of the later of the adoption or the effective date of the amendment.[4] However, the IRS will allow a plan to be amended to eliminate a participant's right to a pre-retirement age 70½ distribution without violating Code Sec. 411(d)(6).[5]

Benefits that may be reduced

A qualified plan may be amended to reduce or eliminate ancillary life insurance protection; accident or health insurance benefits; Code Sec. 411(a)(9) Social Security supplements; the availability of loans (other than the distribution of an employee's accrued benefit upon loan default); the right to make after-tax employee contributions or elective deferrals; the right to direct investments; the right to a form of investment (such as employer stock or securities); the right to allocation dates for contributions, forfeitures, and earnings, the time for making contributions, and the valuation date for account balances; the right to receive hardship distributions; and rights relating to the administration and operation of the plan.[6]

Defined contribution plans

Generally, a defined contribution plan will not be treated as reducing the accrued benefit of a participant if a plan amendment eliminates a form of distribution previously available under the plan. However, a single-sum distribution must be available to the participant at the same time or times as the form of distribution being eliminated and the single-sum distribution must be based on the same or greater portion of the participant's account as the form of distribution being eliminated.[7] In general, a defined contribution plan to which benefits are transferred is not treated as eliminating a protected optional form of benefit if certain requirements are satisfied. The transfer must be a direct transfer from one plan to another, pursuant to the terms of both the transferor and transferee plans, voluntarily elected by the participant after receiving proper notice, and the transferee plan must allow the beneficiary to receive a single sum distribution.[8]

> **CCH Pointer:** *Utilization test.* The IRS provides a utilization test under which a plan amendment with a de minimis impact on participants is permitted to eliminate or reduce early retirement benefits, retirement-type subsidies, or optional forms of benefit. A plan is not permitted to eliminate *core* options. In order to eliminate a *noncore* optional form of benefit under the utilization test, the plan must satisfy two conditions. First, the generalized optional form must have been available to at least a minimum number of participants who are taken into account during the relevant look-back period. Second, no participant must have elected the optional form of benefit that is part of the generalized optional form with an annuity commencement date that is within the look-back period.[9]

Reduction of accrued protected benefits

A plan may be amended to eliminate or reduce protected benefits that have not accrued as of the date the amendment is adopted or made effective.[10] In addition, a plan amendment may eliminate or reduce protected benefits that have already accrued, if: the amendment is adopted to enable the plan to comply with a change in law affecting plan qualification, the reduction or elimination of an accrued benefit is necessary to enable the plan to retain tax qualified status, and the Commissioner of the IRS authorizes relief under Code Sec. 7805(b).[11]

☐ The IRS has identified additional situations in which accrued benefits may be reduced or eliminated by plan amendment.[12] These situations are discussed at CCH PENSION PLAN GUIDE ¶ 2685.

Notice of amendment reducing benefit accruals

A defined benefit plan, a money purchase pension plan, or another individual account plan that is subject to the minimum funding rules may not be amended to provide for a "significant" reduction in the rate of future benefit accruals unless the plan administrator provides sufficient notice (i.e., the "ERISA 204(h) notice") of the amendment to affected participants and alternate payees.[13]

Limiting multiple notices. With respect to an amendment that triggers a 204(h) notice requirement as well as certain other statutory notice requirements, if a plan provides the latter notice in accordance with the applicable standards for such a notice, then the plan is treated as having timely complied with the requirement to provide a 204(h) notice. [14]

Notice of the amendment must be provided within a "reasonable time" before the effective date of the plan amendment.[15] This means that, in most situations, notice must be provided at least 45 days prior to the effective date of the plan amendment.[16] Sponsors of small plans and multiemployer plans may, in most situations, delay notice until up to 15 days prior to the effective date of the amendment.[17] In addition, a similar 15-day requirement applies to notice of amendments relating to mergers and acquisitions.[18] Notice may be provided via an approved electronic medium.[19]

Notice is required for a plan amendment that provides for a "significant reduction" (1) in the rate of future benefit accrual (including the elimination of accruals) or (2) of an early benefit or retirement-type subsidy.[20]

If sufficient notice is not provided, an excise tax of $100 per day in the noncompliance period will apply, for each participant and beneficiary with respect to which a failure to meet the notice requirements occurs.[21] In addition, ERISA Sec. 204(h) specifies special rules for "egregious" failures to provide notice, under which participants are generally entitled to the greater of the benefit provided under the plan prior to amendment or the benefit under the amended plan.[22]

> **CCH Pointer: *Conversion of money purchase plan.*** An amendment that is adopted to convert a money purchase plan to a profit-sharing or other individual account plan that is not subject to the minimum funding rules of Code Sec. 412 (including a merger, consolidation, or transfer of the plan) is in all cases deemed to be an amendment that provides for a significant reduction in the rate of future benefit accrual, for which notice is required.[23]

Social Security benefits of terminated employees

A qualified plan may not reduce the benefits being received by retired employees because of increases in the Social Security benefit level or wage base.[24] This rule also applies to individuals who are receiving disability benefits under Social Security and a private plan.[25] In addition, the nonforfeitable benefits of a participant who has separated from service, but subsequently returns to work and resumes participation in the plan may not be decreased because of any post-separation Social Security increases that would decrease such benefits below the level of benefits to which the participant would have been entitled had he not returned to service.[26]

☐ Age-related reductions are discussed at ¶ 867.

---

[1] Code Sec. 411(d)(6)(A); IRS Reg. §1.411(d)-4, Q&A-1(c); ERISA Sec. 204(g)(1).

[2] *Central Laborers' Pension Fund v. Heinz*, 541 U.S. 739 (2004). See IRS Reg. §1.411(d)-3(a)(3).

[3] IRS Reg. §1.401(a)(4)-4(e)(1).

[4] IRS Reg. §1.411(d)-4, Q&A-10(a).

[5] IRS Reg. §1.411(d)-4, Q&A-10(b).

[6] IRS Reg. §1.411(d)-4, Q&A-1(d) and Q&A-2(b)(2)(x).

[7] Code Sec. 411(d)(6)(E) and ERISA Sec. 204(g)(2).

[8] Code Sec. 411(d)(6)(D) and ERISA Sec. 204(g)(4). See also IRS Reg. §1.411(d)-4.

[9] Reg. §1.411(d)-3 (August 9, 2006, 71 FR 45379).

[10] IRS Reg. §1.411(d)-4, Q&A-2(a).

[11] IRS Reg. §1.411(d)-4, Q&A-2(b)(2)(i).

[12] IRS Reg. §1.411(d)-4, Q&A-2(b).

[13] Code Sec. 4980F(e); ERISA Sec. 204(h). Effective for plan years after 2007, the notice must be furnished to each employer who has an obligation to contribute to a multiemployer plan. See Code Sec. 4980F(e)(1) and ERISA Sec. 204(h)(i), as amended by P.L. 109-280 (Pension Protection Act of 2006), Act Sec. 502(c).

[14] IRS Reg. §54.4980F-1, Q&A-9 (11/24/2009, 74 FR 6120), applicable to 204(h) amendments that are effective on or after January 1, 2008. The relevant other statutory notice requirements are listed at IRS Reg. §54.4980F-1, Q&A-9(g)(3). These regulations are intended to eliminate the need for a plan to furnish multiple notices at different dates and with substantially the same function and information to affected persons. Note, however, that this special treatment for multiple notices does not apply if a plan is amended to implement benefit reductions independent of the

permitted reductions in the list of statutory notice requirements.

[15] Code Sec. 4980F, as added by P.L. 107-16 (Economic Growth and Tax Relief Reconciliation Act of 2001); ERISA Sec. 204(h)(3), as amended by P.L. 107-16 (Economic Growth and Tax Relief Reconciliation Act of 2001).

[16] IRS Reg. §54.4980F-1, Q&A-9(a).

[17] IRS Reg. §54.4980F-1, Q&A-9(b) and (c).

[18] IRS Reg. §54.4980F-1, Q&A-9(d)(1).

[19] Reg. §54.4980F-1, Q&A-13(c)(1), (May 22, 2007, 72 FR 28604).

[20] Code Sec. 4980F(e)(1), as added by P.L. 107-16 (Economic Growth and Tax Relief Reconciliation Act of 2001); Code Sec. 4980F(f)(3), as amended by P.L. 107-147 (Job Creation and Worker Assistance Act of 2002); ERISA Sec.

204(h)(1)), as amended by P.L. 107-16. See also IRS Reg. §54.4980F-1, Q&A-5(a)-(c).

[21] Code Secs. 4980F(a), 4980F(b)(1), and 4980F(b)(2), as added by P.L. 107-16 (Economic Growth and Tax Relief Reconciliation Act of 2001). See also IRS Reg. §54.4980F-1, Q&A-14(c).

[22] ERISA Sec. 204(h)(6), as amended by P.L. 107-16 (Economic Growth and Tax Relief Reconciliation Act of 2001).

[23] IRS Reg. §54.4980F-1, Q&A-8(b); Rev. Rul. 2002-42, I.R.B. 2002-28, at CCH PENSION PLAN GUIDE ¶ 19,946Z.

[24] Code Sec. 401(a)(15); ERISA Sec. 206(b).

[25] Code Sec. 401(a)(15); IRS Reg. §1.401(a)-15(a).

[26] IRS Reg. §1.401(a)-15(a)(2).

¶ 867

ACCRUAL OF BENEFITS: Age-Based Benefit Accrual (Cash Balance Plans)

A defined benefit plan may not discontinue an employee's benefit accrual or reduce the rate of an employee's benefit accrual because of age.[1] Similarly, a defined contribution plan may not discontinue allocations to an employee's account or reduce the rate at which amounts are allocated to an employee's account because of age.[2] However, a plan may impose a limitation on the number of years of service or plan participation taken into account for purposes of determining benefit accrual under the plan. This limitation must be imposed without regard to age.[3]

Continued accrual beyond normal retirement age

Benefit accruals required to be continued after normal retirement age may be reduced or offset either by the value of actuarial adjustments to an employee's normal retirement benefit or by the value of benefit distributions made to an employee.[4]

Cash balance plans

A cash balance plan is a hybrid defined benefit plan that provides guaranteed benefits for employees. Generally, cash balance plans result from the conversion of traditional defined benefit plans. Cash balance plans establish a separate hypothetical account for each employee. They do not provide a benefit based on a combination of the employee's length of service and salary. Since the benefits are not based solely on actual contributions and forfeitures, nor on investment experiences and plan expenses allocated to the account, the arrangement is treated as a defined benefit plan rather than as a defined contribution plan.

The Pension Protection Act of 2006 made several changes related to cash balance plans. These changes include clarification of the age discrimination and minimum present value rules applicable to defined benefit plans, including cash balance plans. [5]

Three-year vesting rule. A cash balance plan must provide that an employee who has completed at least three years of service has a nonforfeitable right to 100 percent of the employee's accrued benefit derived from employer contributions to avoid violation of the age discrimination prohibition.[6]

Nondiscrimination rules. A defined benefit pension plan, including a hybrid cash balance plan, does not violate the age discrimination prohibition in Code Sec. 411(b)(1)(H)(i) if a participant's entire accrued benefit (as determined as of any date under the terms of the plan) is equal to or greater than that of any similarly situated, younger individual who is or could be a participant.[7] This requires a comparison of the accumulated benefit of each individual who is or could be a participant in the plan with the accumulated benefit of each other similarly situated, younger individual who is or could be a participant in the plan. For example, the safe harbor is not satisfied in the case of a plan that contains a suspension of benefits provision that reduces or eliminates interest credits for participants who continue in service after normal retirement age. [8]

CCH Pointer: The IRS has issued final and proposed regulations regarding cash balance plans. The final regulations generally apply to plan years that begin on or after January 1, 2011.[9] Different effective dates apply to certain rules on interest crediting rates.[10] The effective date for the proposed rules will be included in the final regulations but the date will not be earlier than for plan years beginning on or after January 1, 2013.[11]

Conversion of defined benefit plan to cash balance plan. If a defined benefit plan is converted to a cash balance plan after June 29, 2005, each participant's accrued benefit after the conversion cannot be less than the sum of:

1) The participant's accrued benefit for years of service before the effective date of the conversion amendment, determined pursuant to the pre-amendment plan terms, plus

2) The participant's accrued benefit for years of service after the effective date of the conversion amendment, determined pursuant to the post-amendment plan terms. [12]

A conversion amendment must be both adopted and effective on or after June 29, 2005, in order for the conversion protection provisions to apply.[13]

CCH Pointer: The Supreme Court, in *CIGNA Corp. v. Amara*, discussed which enforcement remedies under ERISA Sec. 502 were available to participants who claimed notice violations in connection with a cash balance plan conversion.[14] See ¶ 2702.

Determination letters for cash balance plan conversions. The status of determination letters for cash balance plan conversions has been somewhat clarified since the enactment of the Pension Protection Act of 2006. [15]

¶867

☐ For more on cash balance plans, see ¶ 2577-2577D of the CCH PENSION PLAN GUIDE.

---

[1] Code Sec. 411(b)(1)(H); ERISA Sec. 204(b)(1)(H); ADEA Sec. 4(i)(1).

[2] Code Sec. 411(b)(2); ERISA Sec. 204(b)(2); ADEA Sec. 4(i)(1).

[3] Code Sec. 411(b)(1)(H)(ii); ERISA Sec. 204(b)(1)(H)(ii); ADEA Sec. 4(i)(2).

[4] Code Sec. 411(b)(1)(H)(iii); ERISA Sec. 204(b)(1)(H)(iii).

[5] P.L. 109-280, August 17, 2006. Generally, the PPA rules on cash balance and other hybrid plans apply to periods beginning on or after June 29, 2005. Special effective dates may apply in some cases. See P.L. 109-280, Act Sec. 701(e).

[6] Code Sec.411(a)(13) and ERISA Sec.204(f)(2), as added by P.L. 109-280 (Pension Protection Act of 2006), Act Secs. 701(a)(2) and 701(b)(2). See also Reg. § 1.411(a)(13)-1(c).

[7] Code Sec. 411(b)(5)(A)(i) and ERISA Sec. 204(b)(5)(A)(i), as added by P.L. 109-280 (Pension Protection Act of 2006), Act Sec. 701(a)(1) and 701(b)(1).

[8] Reg. § 1.411(b)(5)-1(b) (T.D. 9505, 75 FR 64123, 10/19/2010).

[9] Reg. §§ 1.411(a)(13)-1 and 1.411(b)(5)-1 (T.D. 9505, 75 FR 64123, 10/19/2010). Additional proposed rules issued in 2011 would conform the rules for termination of a cash balance plan to reflect changes to benefit determination rules made in the Pension Protection Act of 2006 (P.L. 109-280). See ERISA Prop. Reg. § 4022.120 et seq. (10/31/2011, 76 FR 67105) at CCH PENSION PLAN GUIDE ¶ 20,538D.

[10] Originally, these rules were to be effective for plan years beginning on or after January 1, 2012. The IRS now intends to amend the final regulations to delay the effective date to a date no earlier than plan years beginning on or after January 1, 2013. Until the final regulations are amended, plan sponsors may rely on Notice 2011-85 with respect to the postponement of the effective/applicability date. IRS Notice 2011-85, I.R.B. 2011-44, 10/31/2011 at CCH PENSION PLAN GUIDE ¶ 17,148F.

[11] IRS Notice 2011-85, I.R.B. 2011-44, 10/31/2011 at CCH PENSION PLAN GUIDE ¶ 17,148F.

[12] Code Sec. 411(b)(5)(B)(ii), (iii) and (v)(I) and ERISA Sec. 204(b)(5)(B)(ii), (iii), and (v)(I), as added by P.L. 109-280 (Pension Protection Act of 2006), Act Sec. 701(a)(1) and 701(b)(1); IRS Notice 2007-6, I.R.B. 2007-3, 1-16-07, at CCH PENSION PLAN GUIDE ¶ 17,135Q. The conversion amendments apply to plan amendments adopted on or

after, and taking effect on or after, June 29, 2005, except that the plan sponsor may elect to have such amendments apply to plan amendments adopted before, and taking effect on or after, such date. See P.L. 109-280 (Pension Protection Act of 2006), Act Sec. 701(a)(5), as amended by P.L. 110-458 (Worker, Retiree, and Employer Recovery Act of 2008), Sec. 207(c)(2)(C).

[13] Reg. § 1.411(b)(5)-1(c) (T.D. 9505, 75 FR 64123, 10/19/2010).

[14] *CIGNA Corp. v. Amara* (US Sup Ct 2011), No. 09-804, at CCH PENSION PLAN GUIDE ¶ ¶ 24,009E.

[15] Prior to the enactment of the PPA, there was relatively little guidance on cash balance plans. The IRS, in September 1999, in response to possible age discrimination issues under Code Sec. 411(b) raised by cash balance conversions, especially the "wearing away" of participants' benefits during the period after conversion, placed a moratorium on the approval of cash balance conversions, including pending applications (see IRS Memorandum, 9-15-99, at ¶ 17,102A). Proposed rules issued by the IRS in December 2002 would have enabled employers to convert traditional pension plans to cash balance plans without jeopardizing the qualified status of their plans, as long as the conversion was implemented on an age-neutral basis. However, the IRS subsequently withdrew those proposed regulations and announced that it would not lift the moratorium and issue determination letters until guidance was finalized. (See IRS Proposed Reg. § 1.401(a)(4)-3, 1.401(a)(4)-9, and 1.411(b)-2 (67 FR 76123), at CCH PENSION PLAN GUIDE ¶ 20,260S [withdrawn by IRS Announcement 2003-22, 4-28-03, at CCH PENSION PLAN GUIDE ¶ 17,097S-15 and IRS Announcement 2004-57, 7-6-04, at CCH PENSION PLAN GUIDE ¶ 17,097S-40] and IRS Announcement 2003-1, I.R.B. 2003-2, at CCH PENSION PLAN GUIDE ¶ 17,097T.) After the enactment of the Pension Protection Act of 2006, the IRS resumed processing the determination letters and examination cases that were the subject of the earlier moratorium, subject to certain rules (see IRS Notice 2007-6, I.R.B. 2007-3, 1-16-2007, at CCH PENSION PLAN GUIDE ¶ 17,135Q.) Subsequently, in 2008, the IRS permitted a defined benefit plan that had been converted into a cash balance plan prior to the effective date of the PPA to determine benefits as the "greater of" amounts calculated under pre-conversion and post-conversion formulas (see Rev. Rul. 2008-7, I.R.B. 2008-7, 2-19-08, at CCH PENSION PLAN GUIDE ¶ 19,948Z-220). While the ap-

plicability of this relief is limited to plan years beginning before 2009, IRS proposed rules would effectively extend such relief to plan years begin-ning on or after January 1, 2009 (see IRS Proposed Reg. § 1.411(b)-1 (73 FR 34665, 6-18-2008) at CCH PENSION PLAN GUIDE ¶ 20,262L).

¶ 869

ACCRUAL OF BENEFITS: Cash-Out of Benefits

Amounts of $5,000 or less may be involuntarily cashed out and distributed to the participant by the plan.[1] However, if the present value of a participant's nonforfeitable accrued benefit exceeds $5,000, no portion of the benefit may be immediately distributed without the written consent of the participant and, if applicable, the participant's spouse. For purposes of determining whether a participant's benefit exceeds $5,000, the nonvested portion of the participant's accrued benefit is to be disregarded.

> **CCH Pointer:** A plan that provides for a cash-out distribution of a nonforfeitable account balance that does not exceed $5,000 must use a direct rollover as the default option for involuntary distributions that exceed $1,000. Department of Labor regulations provide a safe harbor for fiduciaries involved in the selection of a financial institution to provide an individual retirement plan and the selection of investments.[2]

Consent requires notice of rights

A participant's consent to a distribution is not valid unless he or she has received a general description of the material features of the optional forms of benefit available under the plan and an explanation of the relative values of the optional forms of benefit.[3] Consent to a distribution is also not valid if a "significant detriment" is imposed on any participant who does not consent.[4]

Provide notice within 30-90 days of distribution. A plan must provide participants with notice of their rights regarding consent no less than 30 days and no more than 90 days before the date that the distribution begins.[5]

> **CCH POINTER:** *Proposed regulations double length of notice and consent period.* Proposed regulations double the length of the notice and consent period for mandatory "cash-out" distributions from 90 days to 180 days for years beginning after December 31, 2006.[6] The proposed regulations, issued pursuant to the Pension Protection Act of 2006 (P.L. 109-280), may be relied upon for notices provided, and election periods beginning on the first day of the first plan year beginning on or after January 1, 2007 and ending on the effective date of the regulations.[7]

Participant may waive 30-day minimum period. Participants may affirmatively elect to receive a distribution less than 30 days after receiving the notice, as long as the participant is informed that he or she has at least 30 days in which to consider consent to the distribution.[8]

Exceptions to consent requirement. The consent requirements are deemed satisfied if the present value of a participant's nonforfeitable total accrued benefit does not exceed $5,000.[9] In addition, the consent requirements do not apply: to benefits that are not immediately distributable (i.e., distributable before the participant attains or would have attained the later of normal retirement age or age 62);[10] after the death of the participant;[11] to payments made to an alternate payee under a QDRO (except as specified in the QDRO);[12] or to distributions that are made in order to satisfy the minimum required distribution rules of Code Sec. 401(a)(9).[13]

Determining present value of lump-sum distribution

The present value of a lump-sum distribution, for purposes of the $5,000 cash-out rule, must generally be determined under:

1. the applicable mortality table, as prescribed by the IRS; and

2. the annual interest rate on 30-year Treasury securities for the month prior to the distribution (or an earlier time determined by the IRS).[14]

---

[1] Code Sec. 411(a)(11)(A); ERISA Sec. 203(e)(1).

[2] ERISA Reg. Sec. 2550.404a-2(e); Code Sec. 401(a)(31)(B). The final regulations apply to the rollovers of mandatory distributions made on or after March 28, 2005. When enacted originally under the Economic Growth and Tax Relief Reconciliation Act of 2001 (P.L. 107-16), the effective date of the rules requiring automatic rollover of cash out distributions was delayed, pending the issuance of the DOL rules providing the safe harbor. See Act Sec. 657(c)(2)(A). The automatic rollover requirements apply to any mandatory distribution that exceeds $1,000 and that is an eligible rollover distribution subject to the direct rollover requirements of Code Sec. 401(a)(31). However, the IRS notes that a plan loan offset amount is not subject to the automatic rollover rules. See IRS Notice 2005-5, I.R.B. 2005-3, CCH Pension Plan Guide ¶ 17,130N.

[3] IRS Reg. § 1.411(a)-11(c)(2)(i).

[4] IRS Reg. Sec. 1.411(a)-11(c)(2)(i). Note that an allocation of administrative expenses incurred by a defined contribution plan to the individual accounts of participants who do not consent to a distribution is not a significant detriment, if the allocation is reasonable and otherwise satisfies the requirements of ERISA Title I (such as a pro rata allocation). See Rev. Rul. 2004-10, I.R.B. 2004-7, 2-17-04.

[5] IRS Reg. § 1.411(a)-11(c)(2)(iii). Act Sec. 1102(a)(1)(B) of the Pension Protection Act of 2006 (P.L. 109-280) directs the Treasury Secretary to amend the regulations in order to double the length of the notice and consent period from 90 days to 180 days.

[6] IRS Proposed Reg. § 1.411(a)-11 (73 FR 59575, 10-9-2008), CCH Pension Plan Guide ¶ 20,262R.

[7] Proposed Reg. § 1.411(a)-11 (73 FR 59575, 10-9-2008), CCH Pension Plan Guide ¶ 20,262R. See also P.L. 109-280 (Pension Protection Act of 2006), Act Sec. 1102(a)(1)(B).

[8] Ibid.

[9] Code Sec. 411(a)(11); IRS Reg. § 1.411(a)-11(c)(3). Note that the "lookback rule" has been eliminated. As a result, an accrued benefit that is valued at $5,000 or less on the date that the distribution begins may be distributed without participant or spousal consent, even if the benefit was valued at more than $5,000 at the time of a previous distribution. See IRS Reg. § 1.411(a)-11(c)(3), as amended by T.D. 8891, July 19, 2000 (65 FR 44679).

[10] IRS Reg. § 1.411(a)-11(c)(4).

[11] IRS Reg. § 1.411(a)-11(c)(5).

[12] IRS Reg. § 1.411(a)-11(c)(6).

[13] IRS Reg. § 1.411(a)-11(c)(7).

[14] Code Secs. 411(a)(11)(B) and 417(e)(3); ERISA Secs. 203(e)(2) and 205(g)(3)(A); IRS Reg. § 1.417(e)-1(d). The mortality table to be used for calculating lump-sum distributions is based on the mortality table specified for the plan year under the post-2007 minimum funding standard rules for single-employer defined benefit plans. The applicable interest rate is the adjusted first, second and third segment rates applied under the minimum funding rules of Code Sec. 430(h)(2)(C) and ERISA Sec. 303(h)(2)(C) as in effect after 2007, with certain modifications, for the month before the date of distribution or such other time as prescribed by the IRS. Different rules apply to pre-1995 plan years. See CCH Pension Plan Guide ¶ 2667.

¶ 870

ACCRUAL OF BENEFITS: Excluded Benefit Accrual Service

Generally, for purposes of benefit accrual, all service, beginning on the earliest date an employee is a participant in a plan, must be taken into account. However, the following service may be disregarded for purposes of benefit accrual under a defined benefit plan:

1. service before an employee first becomes a participant;

2. service which is not required to be taken into account because of a one-year break in service;

3. service which is less than 1,000 hours during a 12-consecutive month period; and

4. service before the conclusion of a series of consecutive one-year breaks in service that permit the plan to disregard service which need not be counted for vesting because of the rule of parity (see ¶ 888).[1]

Repayment of cash-out distribution

In determining an employee's accrued benefits, service for which the employee received a cash-out distribution (see ¶ 869) generally may be disregarded.[2] However, a different rule applies to participants who received a cash-out distribution that was less than the present value of their accrued benefit and who resumed employment covered under the plan. Under such circumstances, a plan may not disregard service with respect to which a participant has received a cash-out distribution unless the participant is allowed to repay the full amount of the distribution (with interest (for defined benefit plans)), and the plan, after receiving repayment, recomputes the participant's accrued benefit by taking into account the disregarded service.[3]

☐ An employee's years of participation, for purposes of benefit accrual, are measured by an accrual computation period. See ¶ 876.

---

[1] Code Sec. 411(b)(4); ERISA Sec. 204(b)(4); ERISA Reg.§ 2530.204-1(b).

[2] Code Sec. 411(a)(7)(B); IRS Reg. § 1.411(a)-7(d)(4); ERISA Sec. 204(d).

[3] Code Sec. 411(a)(7)(C); IRS Reg. § 1.411(a)-7(d)(4)(iv).

¶ 875

CREDITING SERVICE: General Rules

In order to apply ERISA's vesting schedules and benefit accrual rules, the amount of includible employee service with an employer must be determined. A plan must first designate a computation period during which a participant may accumulate hours of service. See ¶ 876. Whether an employee is credited with a year of service is determined by the number of hours of service which are credited to the employee during the applicable computation period. See ¶ 878. Employers may select from three alternative methods of counting hours of service. See ¶ 879.

¶ 876

CREDITING SERVICE: Computation Period for Crediting Service

A plan must designate a computation period (generally, a 12-consecutive month period) during which a participant may accumulate hours of service.[1] In order to determine whether an employee has accumulated the required hours of service for purposes of vesting and benefit accrual, a plan must generally designate a vesting computation period. A defined benefit plan may also be required to designate an accrual computation period for measuring years of participation for benefit accrual.

Vesting computation period

A plan may designate any 12-month period as the vesting computation period.[2] The period must apply to all participants.

The actual vesting computation periods need not be the same for all employees, as is the case when the vesting computation period begins on the date each employee begins employment. However, the plan may not use any period that would cause vesting credit to be artificially postponed. Thus, a plan may not use a period measured by the anniversary of the date four months following the employee's date of employment.

Computation period may be changed. A plan may change a vesting computation period to a different 12-consecutive month period. However, such an amendment may be made only if no employee's vested percentage of accrued benefits from employer contributions would be less on any date after the change than it would be if there had been no change.[3]

Some plans are not required to provide vesting computation period. Plans that use the elapsed time method of counting service or that do not use years of service as a factor in determining a participant's vested interest need not designate a vesting computation period.[4]

Accrual computation period

Accrual computation periods are used to measure years of participation for purposes of benefit accrual. The accrual computation period is also used to measure completion of 1,000 hours of service in determining whether an employee is entitled to partial credit for accrual. A defined benefit plan must designate an accrual computation period unless it uses a benefit accrual method that meets one of the benefit accrual rules under all circumstances.

A plan may designate any 12-consecutive month period as an accrual computation period, as long as the designated period applies to all participants.[5] However, the actual accrual computation period need not be the same for all employees.

Accrual computation and vesting computation periods may differ. The accrual computation period need not be the same as the vesting computation period. For example, the computation period used by a plan in applying the vesting schedule may differ from the one used to determine benefit accrual. In addition, the computation period need not correspond with the plan year.[6]

Partial year of participation. A plan is not required, in calculating an employee's period of service, to take into account a 12-consecutive month period during which the employee has performed less than 1,000 hours of service.[7] However, an employee who has performed at least 1,000 hours of service during an accrual computation period must be credited, for purposes of benefit accrual, with a partial year of participation that is equivalent to no less than a ratable portion of a full year of participation, even if the employee's service is less than the service required under the plan for a full year of participation.[8] Alternatively, the plan may credit the employee with a greater portion of a full year of participation than a ratable portion or may credit the employee with a full year of participation.[9]

In determining whether an employee meets the 1,000 hours of minimum service requirement, a plan must take into account all hours of service within the accrual computation period, including service performed prior to the date the employee began participating in the plan.[10]

Accrual computation period may be changed. A plan may change its accrual computation period to a different 12-consecutive month period.[11] However, accrual credit must be given for a partial year of participation.

---

[1] ERISA Reg. § 2530.200b-1(a).

[2] ERISA Sec. 203; ERISA Reg. § § 2530.203-1 and 2530.203-2(a).

[3] ERISA Reg. § 2530.203-2(c).

[4] IRS Alert Guidelines, Explanation 1 to Worksheet No. 2 (Minimum Vesting Standards: Defined Contribution Plans) and Explanation 1 to Worksheet No. 2A (Minimum Vesting Standards: Defined Benefit Plans).

[5] Code Sec. 411(b)(4); ERISA Sec. 204(b)(4); ERISA Reg. § 2530.204-2(a).

[6] ERISA Reg. § 2530.200b-1(a).

[7] Code Sec. 411(b)(3)(C); ERISA Sec. 204(b)(3)(C).

[8] ERISA Reg. § 2530.204-2(c)(1).

[9] ERISA Reg. § 2530.204-3(c)(2).

[10] ERISA Reg. § 2530.204-2(c)(3).

[11] ERISA Reg. § 2530.204-2(e).

¶ 878

CREDITING SERVICE: Year of Service

Whether an employee is credited with a year of service is determined by the number of hours of service which are credited to the employee during the applicable computation period. For example, an employee who is credited with 1,000 hours of service during a vesting computation period must generally be credited with a year of service for purposes of the minimum vesting rules.[1]

---

[1] Code Sec. 411(a)(5); ERISA Sec. 203(b)(2)(A); ERISA Reg. § 2530.200b-1(a).

¶ 879

CREDITING SERVICE: Determining Credited Service

Employers may adopt one of the following three methods to count the number of hours of service to be credited to an employee.[1]

Counting hours of service method

Under the counting hours of service method, an hour of service is each hour for which an employee is paid or entitled to payment for hours worked or for specified reasons other than the performance of duties. Thus, an hour of service includes:

1. each hour for which an employee is paid or entitled to payment for the performance of duties;

2. each hour during which no duties are performed and for which an employee is paid or entitled to payment for vacation, holiday, illness, incapacity (including disability), layoff, jury duty, military duty, or leave of absence; and

3. each hour for which back pay is awarded or agreed to by the employer.[2]

Hours of service not credited. Hours of service need not be credited where, among other circumstances, the employee is neither paid nor entitled to payment; payment is made or due under a plan solely for the purpose of complying with applicable worker's compensation, unemployment compensation, or disability insurance laws; and the payment reimburses an employee for medical or medically-related expenses.[3]

Equivalencies method

Under the equivalencies method, instead of determining hours worked and hours for which payment is due, a plan adopts an equivalency based on (1) working time only, (2) periods of employment, or (3) earnings. These equivalencies enable a plan to determine the amount of service to be credited on the basis of records which do not reflect the actual number of hours of service to be credited.[4] Any equivalency used by the plan must be set forth in the plan document.

A plan may use different methods of crediting service for different classifications of employees, provided that the classifications are reasonable and are consistently applied. However, a classification is not reasonable if it is designed to preclude an employee from satisfying minimum vesting, participation, or benefit accrual standards. In addition, the equivalencies method may be used only to the extent that it does not result in a violation of the nondiscrimination rules under Code Sec. 401(a).[5]

Elapsed time method

Under the elapsed time method, in contrast to the methods previously discussed, satisfaction of the vesting, benefit accrual, and participation rules does not require a specified number of hours of service to be credited during a computation period.[6] Instead, entitlement to benefits is determined by reference to the total period of time which elapses while an employee is employed. This method is usually less costly to administer because the plan is only required to keep records of the appropriate period of time, without regard to hours of service.[7]

The method generally requires a plan to take into account the period of time which elapses while the employee is employed, regardless of the actual number of hours completed during such period. Service must be taken into account from the date the employee commences employment to the date service with the employer is severed.[8]

Treatment of parental leave. When applying the elapsed time method to parental leave, the severance from service date of an employee who is absent from service beyond the first anniversary of the first date of absence by reason of a parental leave absence is the second anniversary of the first date of such absence. The period between the first and second anniversaries of the first date of absence from work is neither a period of service nor a period of severance.[9]

Plans may alternate methods of crediting service

A plan may use different methods of determining service for different classes of employees. The plan, however, must specifically authorize the transfer between methods of crediting service.[10]

---

[1] ERISA Reg. § 2530.200b-2; ERISA Reg. § 2530.200b-3(c); IRS Reg. § 1.410(a)-7.

[2] ERISA Sec. 202(a)(3)(C); ERISA Sec. 203(b)(2)(B); ERISA Reg. § 2530.200b-2(a).

[3] ERISA Reg. § 2530.200b-2(a).

[4] ERISA Reg. § 2530.200b-3(c).

[5] ERISA Reg. § 2530.200b-3(c)(3).

[6] IRS Reg. § 1.410(a)-7.

[7] IRS Reg. § 1.410(a)-7(a)(1).

[8] IRS Reg. § 1.410(a)-7(a)(2).

[9] IRS Reg. § 1.410(a)-9(a). Note that an employer does not necessarily violate the Pregnancy Discrimination Act when it pays pension benefits calculated in part under an accrual rule (which is applied only prior to the enactment of the PDA) that awarded fewer service credits for pregnancy absences than for medical leaves in general. See *AT&T Corporation v. Hulteen,* 129 SCt 1962 (2009), at CCH PENSION PLAN GUIDE ¶ 24,004Z.

[10] IRS Reg. § 1.410(a)-7(f).

¶ 880

CREDITING SERVICE: Recordkeeping Requirements

A plan must determine the hours of service to be credited from records of hours worked and hours for which payment is made or due. A plan may also use an equivalency method (see ¶ 879). Any records may be used, even if they are kept for other purposes, provided that they accurately reflect the actual number of hours of service required to be credited. Payroll records, for example, may be adequate. However, if existing records do not accurately reflect the actual number of hours of service with which an employee must be credited, the plan must either develop and maintain such records or use one of the permitted equivalencies. Plan documents are not required to indicate the records to be used to determine hours of service.[1]

A plan may credit hours of service under any method that results in the crediting of no less than the actual number of hours of service required even though such method may result in crediting hours of service in excess of the number required by ERISA.

---

[1] ERISA Reg. § 2530.200b-3(a).

¶ 881

CREDITING SERVICE: Service for Vesting Purposes

All service of an employee must generally be taken into consideration in determining his or her place on the vesting schedules.[1] Service for vesting purposes includes that performed both before and after the employee was eligible to participate in the plan and service performed before the plan was subject to the vesting standards.[2]

Excluded service

For purposes of the vesting schedules, a plan need not give an employee credit for the following service:

1. Service provided before age 18.

2. Service during a period for which the participant declined to contribute to a plan requiring employee contributions.

3. Service during any period for which the employer did not maintain the plan or a predecessor plan.

4. Service before January 1, 1971, unless the participant has completed at least three years of service (including pre-1971 service) after December 31, 1970.

5. Certain seasonal service.

6. Broken periods of service, under some circumstances (see ¶ 882).

CCH Pointer: *Partially terminated plans.* The period for which a plan is not maintained by an employer includes the period after the plan is terminated. A partial termination resulting from a freezing of accruals or otherwise, however, is not a termination of the plan. Thus, service provided by an employee after a plan has been partially terminated may not be excluded in calculating a participant's vested benefits.[3]

Multiemployer plans. Years of service with an employer may be disregarded if they occur after the employer has withdrawn from the plan or after the multiemployer plan has terminated.

Predecessor employer. Service provided for the predecessor of an employer may not be ignored if the predecessor's plan is continued by the present employer.[4]

---

[1] Code Sec. 411(a)(4); ERISA Sec. 203(b)(1).

[2] Code Sec. 411(a)(5)(A) and (C); ERISA Sec. 203(b)(2)(A) and (C).

[3] IRS Reg. § 1.411(a)-5(b)(3)(iii); Rev. Rul. 2003-65; I.R.B. 2003-65, 6-25-2003, at CCH Pension Plan Guide ¶ 19,948Z-1.

[4] Code Sec. 414(a); ERISA Sec. 210(b).

¶ 882

BREAKS IN SERVICE: One-Year Break in Service

For vesting purposes, an employee who is not credited with at least 501 hours of service in a 12-consecutive month period incurs a one-year break in service.[1] The consequences of a one-year break in service can be severe. For example, if an employee incurs a one-year break in service, years of service before the break are not required to be taken into account until the employee completes a year of service upon his or her return (see ¶ 884).[2] In addition, the following rules apply:

1. Under a defined contribution plan, years of service after five consecutive one-year breaks in service are not required to be taken into account in determining an employee's vested right to the accrued benefit derived from employer contributions which accrued before the break (see ¶ 886).

2. An employee who has no vested percentage in an accrued benefit derived from employer contributions upon incurring a break in service may be subject to the "rule of parity," under which the employee will lose credit for service performed before the break (see ¶ 888).[3]

3. A plan that requires two years of service for eligibility to participate in the plan may provide that an employee who incurs a one-year break in service before meeting the eligibility requirement loses all credit for service before the one-year break in service.

Computation periods

The computation periods used for measuring one-year breaks in service will be the same as the computation periods used for measuring years of service before any breaks in service. Thus, in determining whether an employee has performed a year of service for vesting purposes, the plan must apply the vesting computation period used by the plan (see ¶ 876).

---

[1] Code Sec. 411(a)(6)(A); ERISA Sec. 203(b)(3)(A); IRS Reg. §1.411(a)-6(a); ERISA Reg. §2530.200b-4(a).

[2] Code Sec. 411(a)(6)(B).

[3] Code Sec. 411(a)(6)(D).

¶ 884

BREAKS IN SERVICE: Treatment of Service Following a Break in Service

A plan may require employees who have incurred a one-year break in service to perform a year of service before allowing them credit for years of service completed before the break.[1] However, once the year of service has been completed, the employee must receive credit for vesting and benefit accrual purposes for all pre-break and post-break service (including the waiting period year).[2]

Example: Plan Y is on a calendar year basis. Mr. Short commenced work for the employer on January 1, 2005 and was eligible to participate in the plan on January 1, 2006. His work record was as follows:

Year	Hours of Service
2006	2,000
2007	2,000
2008	2,000
2009	500
2010	2,000
2011	2,000

In 2010, Plan Y would not be required to give Short credit for 2006-2009. In 2011, however, the plan must give Short credit for all years except 2009. Thus, he would have five years' credit for vesting schedule purposes and four years' credit for benefit accrual purposes.

[1] Code Sec. 411(a)(6)(B); ERISA Sec. 203(b)(3)(B); ERISA Reg. § 2530.200b-4.

[2] Conference Report on P.L. 93-406 (ERISA); T.I.R. 1403, 9-17-75, (Question V-15).

¶ 886

BREAKS IN SERVICE: Five Breaks in Service Under Defined Contribution Plans

Years of service completed by a vested participant in a defined contribution plan, or in a defined benefit pension plan funded solely by insurance contracts, after a break in service are generally counted for purposes of determining the vested percentage of the participant's accrued benefit derived from employer contributions before the break in service. However, if the participant incurs at least five consecutive one-year breaks in service, years of service after the five-year period need not be taken into account for purposes of determining the vested percentage of employer-provided benefits accrued before the five-year period.[1]

Vested interest at separation

If a participant has five or more consecutive breaks in service, all service (both pre-break and post-break) must be counted in determining the vesting percentage in the post-break account balances in two circumstances. First, such service must be counted when a participant has any vested interest in the accrued benefit attributable to employer contributions at the time of separation from service. Second, such service must be counted when the number of years of service before the break exceeds the number of consecutive break-in-service years.

Thus, in the case of a participant with a vested interest at the time of separation, the length of the break in service is irrelevant with respect to counting pre-break service for the percent of vesting in post-break account balances upon reemployment. However, the length of the break is relevant with respect to counting post-break service for the percent of vesting in pre-break accrued benefits (where the participant was not 100% vested upon the break) if the break in service is at least five consecutive years.[2]

[1] Code Sec. 411(a)(6)(C); ERISA Sec. 203(b)(3)(C).

[2]IRS Alert Guidelines No. 2 (Minimum Vesting Standards—Defined Contribution Plans), Sec. III.

¶ 888

BREAKS IN SERVICE: Rule of Parity

Under the "rule of parity," years of service before a break in service by a nonvested participant must be taken into account after a break in service unless the number of one-year breaks in service equals or exceeds the greater of (a) five consecutive one-year breaks in service or (b) the aggregate number of years of service earned before the consecutive breaks in service.[1] Effectively, this means that a participant who returns to work within five years (before five full consecutive one-year breaks) must be credited for any years of service before the break since the break in service period will always be less than the *greater* of five consecutive one-year breaks or aggregate pre-break service years.[2]

Example 1: Amy, a nonvested participant with three years of service under a plan, terminates her employment. She fails to work for a period equal to four consecutive one-year breaks in service. The plan may not disregard Amy's three years of service for vesting purposes upon her resumption of employment with the employer because the number of one-year breaks (four) does not equal or exceed the greater of (1) five years or (2) the aggregate number of years of service before the break (three years).

Example 2: Hal, a nonvested participant with four years of plan service, failed to work for a period of seven consecutive one-year breaks in service. Because the period of the break exceeds the greater of (1) five consecutive one-year breaks or (2) four years prior aggregate service, the plan is not required to credit the years of service Hal worked before the break for vesting purposes.

Years of service that are not required to be taken into account because of a period of breaks in service under the "rule of parity," are not required to be taken into account under ERISA for participation or vesting purposes if there is a subsequent break in service.

[1] Code Sec. 411(a)(6)(D); ERISA Sec. 203(b)(3)(D).

[2] Code Sec. 411(a)(6)(D)(iii); ERISA Sec. 203(b)(3)(D)(iii); IRS Reg. § 1.410(a)-7(d)(7).

¶ 889

BREAKS IN SERVICE: Rights of Veterans

Reemployed veterans are entitled under the Uniformed Services Employment and Reemployment Rights Act of 1994 (USERRA) to the seniority, rights, and benefits based on seniority that they would have attained with reasonable certainty had they remained continuously employed. The requirements of USERRA apply to qualified plans. Thus, reemployed veterans may not be treated as incurring a break in service under the employer's plan during a period of military service.[1] In addition, a reemployed veteran's period of military service will constitute service with the employer for purposes of determining the nonforfeitability of the individual's accrued benefits and the accrual of benefits under the plan.

Death benefits under USERRA-qualified service. If a plan provides for benefits that are contingent upon a participant's termination of employment on account of death, such as accelerated vesting or ancillary life insurance benefits, the plan must provide such benefits to the beneficiary of a participant who dies during qualified military service.[2]

---

[1] Code Sec. 414(u)(8). Final rules issued under USERRA in 2005 reiterate that an employee returning from military service is treated as not having incurred a break in service with the employer for purposes of participation, vesting and accrual of benefits. See Department of Labor, Veterans' Employment and Training Service, 20 CFR § 1002.259 (December 19, 2005, 70 FR 75246).

[2] Code Sec. 401(a)(37), as added by P.L. 110-245 (Heroes Earnings Assistance and Tax Relief Act of 2008), Act Sec. 104(b), effective for deaths occurring after January 1, 2007.

¶ 890
BREAKS IN SERVICE: Parental Leave

In determining whether a break in service has occurred for participation (see ¶ 700) and vesting purposes, an individual taking parental leave is considered to have completed hours of service. Specifically, the rule applies to an employee who is absent from work (1) because of the employee's pregnancy, (2) because of the birth of the employee's child, (3) because of the placement of a child in connection with the adoption of the child by the individual, or (4) for purposes of caring for the child during the period immediately following the birth or placement for adoption.[1]

CCH Pointer: Any period of employee leave granted under the Family and Medical Leave Act of 1993 will be treated as continued service (i.e., no break in service) for purposes of vesting and eligibility to participate. If, for example, the plan requires an employee to be working on a specific date in order to be credited with a year of service for vesting or participation purposes, an employee on family leave who subsequently returns to work shall be deemed to have been working on that date.

Credit hours of service during leave period

During the period of absence, the individual is treated as having completed (1) the number of hours that normally would have been credited but for the absence, or (2) if the normal work hours are unknown, eight hours of service for each normal work day during the leave. The total number of hours of service treated as completed for any period may not exceed 501 hours.[2]

The hours of service required to be credited must be credited only (1) in the year in which the absence begins for one of the permitted reasons, if the crediting is necessary to prevent a break in service in that year, or (2) in the following year.[3]

Example: Karen completed 501 hours of service in a year before leaving employment because of pregnancy. She is therefore entitled to a credit of up to 501 hours in the next year, because the credit is not needed in the year in which her absence begins.

CCH Pointer: When coupled with the break in service rules for nonvested participants (see ¶ 888), the parental leave provision would allow a parent to take leave in a year, then incur up to five consecutive one-year breaks in service, and, upon returning to work, receive participation and vesting credit for earlier work with the employer.

Effect on benefit accrual

Hours credited under these rules for maternity and paternity leave are not required to be taken into account for purposes of determining a participant's year of participation under the benefit accrual rules.[4]

---

[1] Code Sec. 411(a)(6)(E); ERISA Sec. 203(b)(3)(E).

[2] Code Sec. 411(a)(6)(E).

[3] Code Sec. 411(a)(6)(E).

[4] Code Sec. 411(b)(4)(A); ERISA Sec. 203(b)(3)(A).

¶ 892

FORFEITURES OF ACCRUED BENEFITS: Vested Benefits Generally Nonforfeitable

A right to an accrued benefit is considered to be nonforfeitable at a particular time if, at that time and thereafter, it is an unconditional right.[1] A right that, at a particular time, is conditioned under the plan upon a subsequent event, performance, or forbearance that will cause the loss of such right is a forfeitable right at that time. Thus, rights that are conditioned upon a sufficiency of plan assets in the event of a termination or partial termination are considered to be forfeitable because of such condition. In addition, certain adjustments to plan benefits, such as adjustments in excess of reasonable actuarial reductions, can result in rights being forfeitable.

"Bad boy" clauses may not be enforceable

One of the main effects of ERISA's nonforfeiture provisions is to prevent the enforcement of so-called "bad boy" clauses. A "bad boy" clause typically prevents employees who have defrauded the employer, have otherwise engaged in an act of dishonesty with respect to employer assets, or have been convicted of a felony which occurred while they were an employee, from receiving pension benefits.

No fraud exception to nonforfeiture rule. Courts have refused to recognize a fraud exception to the nonforfeitability provisions of ERISA, holding that it would be improper to create a fraud exception that would allow companies to deny vested pension benefits to disloyal employees.[2] Thus, an employee who was convicted of defrauding a subsidiary of his employer was nevertheless entitled to pension benefits under ERISA.

Excess benefits may be forfeited. Benefits in excess of ERISA's minimum vesting requirements may be forfeited. However, the plan must be cautious that the reduction of benefits not result in discrimination prohibited by Code Sec. 401(a)(4).[3]

---

[1] Code Secs. 401(a)(19), 411(a)(3) and (d)(6), and 412(c)(8); ERISA Secs. 203(a)(3), 204(g), and 302(c)(8).

[2] *Crausman v. Curtiss-Wright Corporation,* DC NJ (1988), No. 875-3587; *Vink v. SVH North American*

Holding Corporation, DC NY (1982), 549 FSupp 268.

[3] Rev. Rul. 85-31, 1985-1 CB 153, CCH PENSION PLAN GUIDE ¶ 19,672.

¶ 893

FORFEITURES OF ACCRUED BENEFITS: Death of Participant Prior to Retirement

A plan may provide for the forfeiture of a participant's vested benefit from employer contributions in the event of his death before retirement. However, the forfeiture rule does not relieve the plan from paying a survivor annuity to the surviving spouse of a vested participant who dies before retirement.[1]

☐ The joint and survivor annuity rules are discussed beginning at ¶ 1700.

---

[1] Code Secs. 401(a)(11) and 411(a)(3)(A); ERISA Secs. 203(a)(3)(A) and 205; IRS Reg. § 1.401(a)-11; IRS Reg. § 1.411(a)-4(b)(1)(i).

¶ 894

FORFEITURES OF ACCRUED BENEFITS: Resumption of Work by Retiree

A plan may provide for the suspension of benefit payments attributable to employer contributions if a retiree is reemployed by the employer under whose plan he is receiving benefits. Payments attributable to employee contributions, however, may not be suspended. In the case of a multiemployer plan, a suspension of benefit payments is permitted when a retiree resumes work in the same industry, in the same trade or craft, and also in the same geographical area covered by the plan when the benefits were being paid.[1]

Resumption of payments

Benefit payments that have been suspended must resume no later than the first day of the third calendar month after the calendar month in which the employee ceases to be employed in service under ERISA Sec. 203(a)(3)(B).[2] The employee must comply with any reasonable procedure adopted by the plan for notifying the plan that such employment has ceased.

---

[1] Code Sec. 411(a)(3)(B); ERISA Sec. 203(a)(3)(B).

[2] ERISA Reg. § 2530.203-3(b)(2).

¶ 896

FORFEITURES OF ACCRUED BENEFITS:
Withdrawal of Employee Contributions

Whenever a participant whose benefit attributable to employer contributions is less than 50% vested withdraws all or any part of his own contributions, a forfeiture of the benefit attributable to employer contributions is permitted.[1] Evidently, this applies to a withdrawal of voluntary contributions as well as to a withdrawal of mandatory contributions. If the benefit attributable to employer contributions is 50% or more vested, no forfeiture is permitted.

Restoration of benefit

The plan must provide for the restoration of the participant's forfeited accrued benefit if the full amount of the distribution, plus, in the case of a defined benefit plan, interest computed from the date of withdrawal, is repaid.[2]

---

[1] Code Sec. 401(a)(19); IRS Reg. § 1.401(a)-19(b); ERISA Sec. 206(c).

[2] Code Sec. 411(a)(3)(D); ERISA Sec. 203(a)(3)(D); IRS Reg. § 1.411(a)-7(d)(2).

¶ 897

FORFEITURES OF ACCRUED BENEFITS:
Multiemployer Plans

Vested benefits under a multiemployer plan may be forfeited upon an employer's withdrawal from the plan. In addition, a provision in a multiemployer plan that prohibits benefits of a participant that accrued as a result of service with an employer *before* the employer was required to contribute to the plan from being payable if the employer ceases contributions to the plan does not result in a prohibited forfeiture of a participant's vested benefit derived from employer contributions.[1]

Employer withdrawal affects participant's vested percentage

If an employer completely withdraws from a multiemployer plan, a participant's years of service with the employer that are completed after withdrawal need not be taken into account in determining the participant's vested percentage in his or her accrued benefits under the plan. This rule also applies to certain partial withdrawals involving the decertification of the collective bargaining representative. If a multiemployer plan terminates for purposes of termination insurance, an employee's years of service completed after the date of termination do not have to be taken into account in determining a participant's vested percentage in his accrued benefits under the plan.[2]

---

[1] Code Sec. 411(a)(3)(E).

[2] Code Sec. 411(a)(4)(G).

¶ 898
FORFEITURES OF ACCRUED BENEFITS: Matching Contributions

A matching contribution is not forfeitable for purposes of compliance with minimum vesting standards merely because it may be forfeited if the related contribution is treated as an excess contribution under Code Sec. 401(k)(8)(B), Code Sec. 402(g)(2)(A) (relating to limitations on elective deferrals), or Code Sec. 401(m)(6)(B) (relating to distributions of excess aggregate contributions).[1]

CCH Pointer: For plan years beginning after December 31, 2007, erroneous automatic contributions to a 401(k) plan will also be treated as a permitted forfeiture with respect to the treatment of forfeited matching contributions for purposes of compliance with the minimum vesting standards.[2]

[1] Code Sec. 411(a)(3)(G).

[2] Code Sec. 411(a)(3)(G), as amended by P.L. 109-280 (Pension Protection Act of 2006), Act Sec. 902(d).

¶ 899
For More Information

☐ For more information on vesting, see ¶ 1149-1212 and ¶ 2500-2695 of the CCH PENSION PLAN GUIDE.

Top-Heavy Plan Rules

¶ 900

General Rules

A "top-heavy" plan is generally one in which more than 60% of benefits or contributions under the plan are for key employees.[1] Qualified corporate and non-corporate plans that are classified as "top-heavy" plans must meet additional qualification requirements, including accelerated vesting, and providing a minimum benefit or minimum contribution for non-key employees.[2]

Application to different types of plans

Qualified pension, profit-sharing, or stock bonus plans are subject to the top-heavy rules.[3] Qualified annuity plans and simplified employee pensions are also subject to top-heavy rules. Governmental plans and SIMPLE plans are, however, exempted from the top-heavy plan rules.[4]

Post-EGTRRA rules

The top-heavy rules were significantly modified by the Economic Growth and Tax Relief Reconciliation Act of 2001 (EGTRRA), effective for years beginning in 2002, to limit the number of individuals that will be considered key employees and to better allow employers to provide the required minimum benefit or the required minimum contribution to key employees. The amended rules apply for purposes of determining whether a plan is top-heavy for the first plan year beginning after

December 31, 2001, even if the determination date for that plan year is before the effective date of the EGTRRA amendment.[5]

---

[1] IRS Reg. § 1.416-1, G-2.

[2] Code Sec. 401(a)(10)(B)(iii).

[3] Code Sec. 416(a).

[4] Code Secs. 401(k)(11)(D)(ii), 416(g)(1)(A), and 416(g)(4)(G).

[5]IRS Notice 2001-56, 2001-2 CB 277, CCH Pension Plan Guide ¶ 17,122A.

¶ 905
When Is a Plan Top-Heavy?

A defined benefit plan is a top-heavy plan for a plan year if, as of the determination date:

1. the present value of the accumulated accrued benefits for participants who are key employees (see ¶ 925) for the plan year exceeds 60% of the present value of the accumulated accrued benefits for all employees under the plan, or

2. the plan is part of a top-heavy group (see ¶ 910).[1]

A defined contribution plan is a top-heavy plan for a plan year if, as of the determination date:

1. the sum of the account balances of participants who are key employees for the plan year exceeds 60% of the sum of the account balances of all employees (see ¶ 925) under the plan, or

2. the plan is a part of a top-heavy group (see ¶ 910).[2]

What is "the determination date"?

The determination date for any plan year is (1) the last day of the preceding plan year, or (2) in the case of the first plan year of any plan, the last day of such plan year.[3] Also, to the extent provided in regulations, the determination date may be determined on the basis of a year other than a plan year.[4]

Valuation of account balances and accrued benefits

Defined contribution plans. Generally, account balances and accrued benefits are valued as of the determination date. The value of an account balance in a defined contribution plan is the sum of (a) the account balance as of the most recent valuation date occurring within a 12-month period ending on the determination date, and (b) an adjustment for contributions due as of the determination date.[5]

Defined benefit plans. For a defined benefit plan, the present value of an accrued benefit must be determined as of the most recent valuation date which is within a 12-month period ending on the determination date.[6] There are no prescribed actuarial assumptions that must be used for determining the present value of accrued benefits. Although the assumptions used must be reasonable, they need not relate to the actual plan and investment experience.[7]

Distributions during lookback period. In determining whether a plan is top-heavy, a participant's accrued benefit or account balance is increased by distributions made to the participant during the applicable lookback period (see ¶ 915).[8]

Accrual of benefits

If benefits under all plans of an employer accrue at the same rate, that accrual rate is to be used in determining whether the plans are top-heavy.[9] If no single accrual rate is used by all of the plans of an employer, a plan's top-heavy status is determined by treating the benefits of all participants in each plan as accruing no more rapidly than the slowest permitted rate under the fractional rule. Generally, under the fractional rule, each participant's accrued benefit at the end of the year must be at least equal to a fractional portion of the retirement benefit to which the participant would be entitled under the plan's benefit formula if the participant continued to earn annually the same rate of compensation until normal retirement age. However, the plan may use either of two other accrual schedules available (the 3% rule or the 133⅓% rule). See ¶ 853 for a discussion of these accrual schedules.

Application to SEPs

For purposes of the top-heavy plan rules, a simplified employee pension is treated as a defined contribution plan.[10] An alternative rule applies to a SEP for purposes of determining whether a plan is top-heavy.[11] Under this rule, in testing against the 60% limit, the employer may elect to use the aggregate employer contributions made for employees covered by the SEP instead of the sum of their account balances. If a SEP is determined to be top-heavy, an employer must make a minimum contribution on behalf of each participant who is not a key employee (see ¶ 940).[12]

Multiple-employer plans

The top-heavy status of a multiple-employer plan is determined with respect to each individual employer.[13] If the multiple-employer plan fails to satisfy the top-heavy plan rules with respect to the employees of one employer, all of the employers are maintaining a plan that is not a qualified plan.

Safe harbor 401(k) plans are not top-heavy

An exception to the top-heavy requirements is provided by safe harbor 401(k) plans under Code Secs. 401(k)(12) and 401(m)(11). A plan that consists solely of a cash or deferred arrangement that satisfies the design-based safe harbor of Code Sec. 401(k)(12) and matching contributions that satisfy the safe harbor of Code Sec. 401(m)(11) will not be considered to be top-heavy.[14]

CCH Pointer: The Pension Protection Act of 2006 (P.L. 109-280), effective for plan years beginning after 2007, amends Code Sec. 416(g)(4)(H) to provide that a 401(k) plan whose only contributions are made pursuant to an qualified automatic enrollment feature (see ¶ 2940A) is not subject to the top-heavy rules.[15] Further, for plan years beginning after 2009, a 401(k) plan and a defined benefit plan that are part of a DB/K plan (see ¶ 103) are treated as meeting the top-heavy requirements of Code Sec. 416.[16]

¶905

☐ The rules governing safe harbor 401(k) plans are discussed in detail at ¶ 2975.

Terminated or frozen plans

Terminated or frozen plans generally are subject to the same top-heavy rules as plans that have not ceased benefit accruals.[17]

---

[1] Code Sec. 416(g)(1)(A)(i) and (B).

[2] Code Sec. 416(g)(1)(A)(ii) and (B).

[3] Code Sec. 416(g)(4)(C).

[4] Code Sec. 416(g)(4)(D).

[5] IRS Reg. § 1.416-1, T-24.

[6] IRS Reg. § 1.416-1, T-25.

[7] IRS Reg. § 1.416-1, T-26 (a).

[8] Code Sec. 416(g)(3).

[9] Code Sec. 416(g)(4)(F).

[10] Code Sec. 416(i)(6)(A).

[11] Code Sec. 416(i)(6)(B).

[12] Code Sec. 408(k)(1)(B).

[13] IRS Reg. § 1.416-1, G-2.

[14] Code Sec. 416(g)(4)(H), as added by P.L. 107-16 (Economic Growth and Tax Relief Reconciliation Act of 2001).

[15] Code Sec. 416(g)(4)(H), as amended by P.L. 109-280 (Pension Protection Act of 2006).

[16] Code Sec. 414(x)(4), as added by P.L. 109-280 (Pension Protection Act of 2006).

[17] IRS Reg. § 1.416-1, T-4 and T-5.

¶ 910
Top-Heavy Groups

Two or more plans of a single employer may have to be aggregated to determine whether the plans, as a group, are top-heavy. Certain plans are required to be aggregated, while other plans are permitted to be aggregated at an employer's option.

Required aggregation group

The aggregation group must include (1) any plan that covers a key employee, and (2) any other plan that enables a plan covering a key employee to meet the qualification requirements under the coverage or nondiscrimination rules.[1] This is referred to as a "required aggregation group."

Permissive aggregation

In addition, an employer may elect to expand the aggregation group to take into account any other plan maintained by the employer, if such expanded aggregation group continues to satisfy the coverage and nondiscrimination rules.[2] This is referred to as a "permissive aggregation group."

Multiemployer plans, multiple-employer plans, and simplified employee pensions may be permissively aggregated with a plan covering key employees or a required aggregation group so long as the benefits and contributions are comparable.[3]

When is an aggregation group top-heavy?

An aggregation group is a top-heavy group if, as of the determination date, the sum of (1) the present value of the accumulated accrued benefits for key employees under all defined benefit plans included in the group, and (2) the account balances of key employees under all defined contribution plans included in the group, exceeds 60% of the same amount determined for all participants under all plans included in the group.[4]

Controlled group

The top-heavy rules apply to all plans of related employers (controlled groups of corporations, commonly controlled trades or businesses, and affiliated service groups) that are treated as a single employer.[5]

---

[1] Code Sec. 416(g)(2)(A)(i).

[2] Code Sec. 416(g)(2)(A)(ii).

[3] IRS Reg. § 1.416-1, T-8.

[4] Code Sec. 416(g)(2)(B).

[5] Code Sec. 414(b), (c), and (m)(4); IRS Reg. § 1.414(c)-1.

¶ 915

Present Values and Account Balances

For purposes of determining the present value of accumulated accrued benefits under a defined benefit plan and the sum of the account balances under a defined contribution plan (see ¶ 905), benefits derived from both employer contributions and employee contributions are taken into account (but accumulated deductible employee contributions under a plan are disregarded).[1]

Distributions during lookback period

The present value of the accumulated accrued benefit of a participant in a defined benefit plan or the account balance of a participant in a defined contribution plan generally includes any amount distributed to a participant within the one-year period ending on the determination date.[2]

One-year distribution rule after 2001. Effective beginning in 2002, the 5-year distribution rule that had been in effect was reduced to one year. Accordingly, in determining whether a plan is top-heavy, a participant's accrued benefit or account balance is increased by distributions made to the participant during the one year period ending on the determination date.[3]

5-year lookback period for in-service distributions. The 5-year lookback period will continue to apply after 2001 to in-service distributions (i.e., distributions made for purposes other than severance from employment, death or disability).[4] In-service distributions subject to the 5-year lookback period would include corrective distributions of excess contributions, hardship distributions, and distributions from a terminated plan.

Lookback period for former employees. In determining whether a plan is top-heavy, the accrued benefit or account balance of an individual who has not performed services for the employer during the one-year period (5-year period prior to 2002) ending on the determination date is disregarded.[5] However, if an employee resumes service after the layoff, his or her total accrued benefit or account balance will be included in the top-heavy calculation.[6]

Death benefits

Death benefit distributions will be counted only to the extent that they do not exceed the present value of an employee's accumulated accrued benefit existing immediately before death.[7] A distribution from a defined contribution plan (including the cash value of life insurance policies) of a participant's accumulated account balance on account of death is treated as a distribution.

[1] Conference Report No. 97-760, 97th Cong., 2d Sess., p. 625.

[2] Code Sec. 416(g)(3).

[3] Code Sec. 416(g)(3), as amended by P.L. 107-16 (Economic Growth and Tax Relief Reconciliation Act of 2001).

[4] Code Sec. 416(g)(3)(B), as amended by P.L. 107-147 (Job Creation and Worker Assistance Act of 2002), Act Sec. 411(k)(2).

[5] Code Sec. 416(g)(4)(E).

[6] IRS Reg. § 1.416-1, T-1(d).

[7] IRS Reg. § 1.416-1, T-31.

¶ 920

Rollovers and Plan-to-Plan Transfers

Rollovers and transfers between plans raise the issue of which plan must count the rollover or transfer in calculating its top-heavy status. The answer depends on whether the rollover or transfer was initiated by the employee.

Rollovers and transfers not initiated by employees

A rollover of a plan distribution not initiated by an employee or a transfer from one plan of an employer to another plan of the same or related employer is not taken into account by the plan providing such a rollover for purposes of the top-heavy plan computations.[1] However, it is counted by the plan accepting the rollover in calculating top-heavy plan status. These transfers are known as "related rollovers."

Rollovers and transfers initiated by employees

Where the rollover or transfer is initiated by the employee from one plan of an employer to another plan of an unrelated employer, the plan providing the distribution must reflect this as a distribution when making its top-heavy plan computations. These transfers are labeled as "unrelated rollovers" by IRS regulations.

[1] Code Sec. 416(g)(4)(A); IRS Reg. § 1.416-1, T-32.

¶ 925

Key Employees

A key employee is any employee who at any time during the preceding plan year containing the determination date for the preceding plan year is:

1. an officer of the employer, with compensation in excess of $165,000 ($160,000 in 2011).

2. a 5% owner of the employer, or

3. a 1% owner of the employer having an annual compensation of more than $150,000.[1]

Company officers

Company officers are generally administrative executives who are employed in regular and continued service. The authority of the employee and not the employee's title is determinative of whether the employee is an officer.[2]

Limit on number of key employee officers. The number of officers who may be considered key employees is limited to the lesser of (1) 50 employees, or (2) the greater of 3 employees or 10 percent of all employees.[3] Thus, if the employer has less than 30 employees (including part-time employees), no more than 3 officers may be treated as key employees. Similarly, if the employer has over 500 employees, the maximum number of officers who may be key employees is 50.[4]

5% and 1% owners

A 5% owner is an employee who owns more than a 5% interest in the employer. Similarly, a 1% owner is an employee who owns more than a 1% interest in the employer.[5] For purposes of the 1% owner requirement in (3) above, compensation means compensation as defined in Code Sec. 415(c) plus elective deferrals under qualified plans, SEPs, tax-sheltered annuities, and cafeteria plans.[6] Note, the $150,000 compensation limit is not adjusted for changes in the cost of living.

Application of family ownership attribution rules. Under the family ownership attribution rules, an individual is considered to own the stock owned by his or her spouse, children, grandchildren, and parents.[7] The family ownership attribution rules are applied in the determination of 5-percent owner status and one-percent owner status.[8]

Deceased and former employees

A deceased employee also can be considered a key employee. A former key employee is excluded entirely from calculation to determine top-heaviness.[9]

Terminated employee must have completed service during lookback period. Terminated and former employees are generally not included in the top-heavy determination if they have not performed services in the one-year lookback period. Similarly, if a key employee ceases to be a key employee for any plan year, any accrued benefits for such employee (or the account balance of the employee) is not taken into account following the last plan year for which the employee was treated as a key employee.[10]

CCH Pointer: An individual may satisfy more than one of the criteria for being a key employee (e.g., an officer and a 5% owner). However, an employee who qualifies as a key employee for multiple reasons is only considered to be one key employee. In addition, in determining whether the plan is top heavy, the individual's accrued benefit is only counted once.[11]

Self-employed individuals

In determining whether a self-employed individual who is a 1% owner is a key employee, compensation means earned income from the trade or business under which the plan is maintained.[12]

Leased employees

A leased employee who performs services for another person (the recipient) may be treated as the recipient's employee where the services are performed under an agreement between the recipient and the leasing organization.

☐ See CCH PENSION PLAN GUIDE ¶ 1002 for more information on the definition of who is a leased employee.

---

[1] Code Sec. 416(i)(1)(A), as amended by P.L. 107-16 (Economic Growth and Tax Relief Reconciliation Act of 2001). IR-2011-103, 10-20-11, CCH PENSION PLAN GUIDE ¶ 17,037Q.

[2] IRS Reg. § 1.416-1, T-13.

[3] Code Sec. 416(i).

[4] IRS Reg. § 1.416-1, T-14.

[5] IRS Reg. § 1.416-1, T-16.

[6] Code Sec. 416(i)(1)(D).

[7] Code Secs. 318(a) and 416(i)(1)(B)(iii); IRS Reg. § 1.416-1, T-18.

[8] Conference Committee Report to P.L. 107-16 (Economic Growth and Tax Relief Reconciliation Act of 2001).

[9] IRS Reg. § 1.416-1, T-12.

[10] Code Sec. 416(g)(4)(B).

[11] IRS Reg. § 1.416-1, Q&A T-14.

[12] Code Sec. 416(i)(3).

¶ 930
Vesting

For any plan year for which a plan is a top-heavy plan, an employee's right to the accrued benefit derived from employer contributions must become nonforfeitable (vested) under either one of the vesting schedules discussed below.[1]

Three-year vesting

An employee who has completed at least three years of service with the employer or employers maintaining the plan must have a nonforfeitable right to 100% of his or her accrued benefit derived from employer contributions.[2]

Six-year graded vesting

An employee must have a nonforfeitable right to a percentage of his accrued benefit from employer contributions determined under the following schedule:[3]

Years of Service	Nonforfeitable percentage
2	20
3	40
4	60
5	80
6 or more	100

The top-heavy plan requirement that either one of the above minimum vesting schedules be used applies to all accrued benefits under a plan. This includes benefits accrued before years beginning after 1983 (the effective date of the top-heavy rules) and benefits accrued before a plan becomes top-heavy.[4] However, if a plan becomes top-heavy, the accrued benefits of any employee who does not have an hour of service after the plan becomes top-heavy are not required to be subject to a top-heavy minimum vesting schedule. In addition, accrued benefits that have been forfeited before a plan becomes top-heavy need not vest when a plan becomes top-heavy.

Minimum benefits that must be provided under Code Sec. 416(c) to non-key employees (see ¶ 935) may not be forfeited under the suspension-of-benefit rules (Code Sec. 411(a)(3)(B)) or the withdrawal-of-mandatory-contribution rules (Code Sec. 411(a)(3)(D)), to the extent required to be nonforfeitable under the top-heavy vesting requirements.[5] Thus, if benefits are suspended during a period of reemployment, the benefit payable upon the subsequent resumption of payments must be actuarially increased to reflect the nonpayment of benefits during such period of reemployment.

Not top-heavy in subsequent years

For any year or years in which a previously top-heavy plan which has met the special vesting rule is not a top-heavy plan, the vesting schedule could be revised to a less rapid vesting schedule which meets the general vesting rules (that is, 5-year vesting or 3- to 7-year graded vesting—see ¶ 820). However, in such case, the ERISA rules regarding vesting schedule changes must be observed. Thus, if the vesting schedule is changed because a top-heavy plan subsequently ceases to be top-heavy, an employee with at least five years of service must be allowed to elect to remain under the top-heavy vesting schedule.[6] If the participant does not make the election (or make it within a reasonable time), he will be subject to the revised vesting schedule; however, the revised vesting schedule cannot reduce any benefits which are already vested.

Years of service

For purposes of determining service under these vesting schedules, the minimum vesting standards under Code Sec. 411 relating to years of service, breaks in service, and certain permitted forfeitures, etc., apply.[7] The years of service are to include those years when the plan is not a top-heavy plan.

---

[1] Code Sec. 416(b)(1).

[2] Code Sec. 416(b)(1)(A).

[3] Code Sec. 416(b)(1)(B).

[4] IRS Reg. § 1.416-1, V-3.

[5] IRS Reg. § 1.416-1, V-5.

[6] IRS Reg. § 1.416-1, V-7.

[7] Code Sec. 416(b)(2).

¶ 935
Minimum Benefit for Non-Key Employees

A qualified plan that is a top-heavy plan must provide a minimum benefit or contribution for each non-key employee who is a participant in the plan.

For a plan year, a top-heavy defined benefit plan generally must accrue a benefit for each plan participant who is not a key employee for the year. When expressed as an annual retirement benefit, the benefit must not be less than 2% of the employee's average annual compensation from the employer during the employee's testing period, multiplied by the employee's years of service with the employer.[1] However, an employee's minimum benefit is not required to exceed 20% of such average annual compensation.[2]

Example: John Brown, a participant in a defined benefit plan which is a top-heavy plan for all plan years, retires after 15 years of service. John, who is a non-key employee, was paid an average of $36,000 by his employer for his high-five years of employment. The minimum benefit to which he is entitled is $7,200 (20% × $36,000).

Years of service

All years of service otherwise required to be taken into account under the plan for vesting purposes generally are required to be taken into account except a year of service (1) completed in a plan year beginning before January 1, 1984, or (2) within which ends a plan year for which the plan is not a top-heavy plan.[3]

Service in "frozen" plans. For purposes of determining the minimum benefit under a defined benefit plan, an employee's years of service will not include any year in which no key employee or former key employee benefits under the plan.[4] Thus, service in such a "frozen" plan will not be considered in determining the minimum benefit under a defined benefit plan.

All accruals taken into account

All accruals of employer-derived benefits, whether or not attributable to years for which the plan is top-heavy, may be used to satisfy the defined benefit minimum.[5] Thus, if a non-key employee had already accrued a benefit of 20% of final average pay at the time the plan became top-heavy, no additional minimum accruals are required (although the accrued benefit would increase as final average pay increased). Accrued benefits attributable to employee contributions must be ignored in determining minimum benefits.

Testing period

An employee's testing period is the period of the employee's consecutive years of service (not exceeding five) during which the employee had the greatest aggregate compensation from the employer.[6] However, a year of service need not be included in the employee's testing period if it ends in a plan year beginning before January 1, 1984, or if it begins after the close of the last year in which the plan was a top-heavy plan.[7]

Annual retirement benefit

The term annual retirement benefit is defined as a benefit payment annually in the form of a single life annuity (with no ancillary benefits) beginning at the normal retirement age under the plan.[8] Thus, if post-retirement death benefits are also provided, the 2% minimum annuity benefit may be adjusted. The 2% minimum annuity benefit may not be adjusted due to the provision of pre-retirement ancillary benefits.[9] If the form of benefit is other than a single life annuity, the employee must receive an amount that is the actuarial equivalent of the minimum single life annuity benefit.[10]

¶935

Benefits commencing before or after normal retirement age

If the benefit begins at a date other than at normal retirement age, the employee must receive at least an amount that is the actuarial equivalent of the minimum single life annuity benefit beginning at normal retirement age. Consequently, the employee may receive a lower benefit if the benefit begins before the normal retirement age, but the employee must receive a higher benefit if the benefit commences after the normal retirement age. No specific actuarial assumptions are mandated providing different actuarial equivalents but assumptions must be reasonable.

Minimum benefit for plan participants

Each non-key employee who is a participant in a top-heavy defined benefit plan and who has at least 1,000 hours of service for an accrual computation period must accrue a minimum benefit in the plan for that accrual computation period.[11] For a top-heavy plan that does not base accruals on accrual computation periods, minimum benefits must be credited for all periods of service required to be credited for benefit accrual.

Non-key employees must accrue the minimum benefit even if the employees are excluded from participation in the plan because their compensation is less than a stated amount or because of their failure to make mandatory employee contributions.[12]

Minimum benefit not reduced by Social Security. The minimum benefit is a nonintegrated benefit, meaning that an employee's Social Security benefits are disregarded for purposes of the minimum benefit rules.[13] Thus, the required minimum benefit for an employee may not be eliminated or reduced on account of the employee's Social Security benefits attributable to employer contributions.

Right to roll over does not make employee a participant. Employees who have not satisfied the minimum age and service requirements for a plan year will not be treated as participants for purposes of the minimum benefit rule merely by making, or being eligible to make, rollover contributions under the plan from the plan of their former employer.[14] Accordingly, such employees are not required to accrue minimum benefits for years in which the plan is top-heavy.

Employee pay-all plan. The defined benefit minimum in an "employee pay-all" plan is the same as that for a plan which has employer contributions.[15]

Cap on includible compensation

Top-heavy plans are generally subject to the same cap on includible compensation as other qualified plans (i.e., $250,000 for 2012; $245,000 for 2011) (see ¶ 545).[16]

---

[1] Code Sec. 416(c)(1)(A) and (B)(i).

[2] Code Sec. 416(c)(1)(B)(ii).

[3] Code Sec. 416(c)(1)(C); IRS Reg. § 1.416-1, M-2(b).

[4] Code Sec. 416(c)(1)(C)(iii), as amended by P.L. 107-16 (Economic Growth and Tax Relief Reconciliation Act of 2001).

[5] IRS Reg. § 1.416-1, M-2(e).

[6] Code Sec. 416(c)(1)(D)(i)

[7] Code Sec. 416(c)(1)(D)(iii).

[8] Code Sec. 416(c)(1)(E).

[9] IRS Reg. § 1.416-1, M-2(d).

[10] IRS Reg. § 1.416-1, M-3.

[11] IRS Reg. § 1.416-1, M-4.

[12] Ibid.

[13] Code Sec. 416(e).

[14] Rev. Rul. 96-48, 1996-2 CB 31, CCH PENSION PLAN GUIDE ¶ 19,844.

[15] IRS Reg. § 1.416-1, M-6.

[16] Code Sec. 401(a)(17)(A), as amended by P.L. 107-16 (Economic Growth and Tax Relief Reconciliation Act of 2001). This figure is adjusted for inflation, under Code Sec. 417(a)(17)(B), as amended by P.L. 107-16 (Economic Growth and Tax Relief Reconciliation Act of 2001), in $5,000 increments.

¶ 940

Minimum Contribution for Non-Key Employees

An employer that has a defined contribution top-heavy plan generally must contribute on behalf of each plan participant who is a non-key employee for the year an amount that is not less than 3% of the participant's compensation.[1]

Less than 3% contribution rate

If the employer's contribution rate for each participant who is a key employee for the plan year is less than 3%, the required minimum contribution rate for each non-key employee is limited to not more than the highest contribution rate for any key employee.[2]

The special rule providing for a less than 3% contribution rate does not apply, however, to any defined contribution plan required to be included in an aggregation group if such plan enables a defined benefit plan required to be included in such group to meet the coverage or nondiscrimination rules.[3] In such a case, the required minimum contribution rate for a non-key employee is 3% even if the contribution rate on behalf of a key employee is less than 3%. For purposes of the special rule, as well as for purposes of the minimum contribution rules generally, all defined contribution plans required to be included in an aggregation group are to be treated as a single plan.

Employees excluded from participation entitled to contribution

Under the top-heavy plan rules, a non-key employee may not fail to receive a defined contribution minimum (or a defined benefit minimum) because either (1) the employee is excluded from participation (or accrues no benefit) merely because the employee's compensation is less than a stated amount, or (2) the employee is excluded from participation (or accrues no benefit) merely because of a failure to make mandatory employee contributions or, in the case of a cash or deferred arrangement, elective contributions.[4]

Service requirements

Non-key employees who are participants in a top-heavy defined contribution plan who have not separated from service by the end of the plan year must receive the defined contribution minimum. Non-key employees who have become participants but who subsequently fail to complete 1,000 hours of service (or the equivalent) for an accrual computation period must receive the defined contribution minimum. If one of two defined contribution plans of an employer provides the defined contribution minimum for each non-key employee who participates in both plans, the other plan need not provide an additional contribution for such employees.[5] However, the other plan must provide for top-heavy plan vesting and must limit compensation (based on all compensation for all aggregated employers) in providing benefits.

Social Security contribution

Amounts paid by the employer for the year to provide Social Security benefits are disregarded in computing the minimum contribution rate.[6]

SEPs

In the event that a simplified employee pension plan is top-heavy (see ¶ 905), the employer must make a minimum contribution on behalf of each participant who is not a key employee.[7]

401(k) plans

Top-heavy 401(k) plans must specifically provide for minimum contributions and limit the amount of compensation taken into account in providing contributions. In order for an arrangement to be treated as a 401(k) plan, an employer may not condition benefits upon an employee's elective deferrals (see ¶ 2981).[8] Thus, elective deferrals may not be used to satisfy the minimum contribution required on behalf of non-key employees in a top-heavy plan.

Elective contributions made by an employer to a 401(k) plan on behalf of non-key employees may not be treated as employer contributions for the purpose of meeting the top-heavy minimum contribution requirements.[9] However, elective contributions made on behalf of key employees may be taken into account in determining the minimum required contribution.

Matching contributions. Employer matching contributions may be used to satisfy the minimum contribution requirement. Matching contributions allocated to key employees are treated as employer contributions for purposes of determining the required minimum contribution.[10]

In addition, effective for years beginning after 2001, employer matching contributions for non-key employees will be taken into account for purposes of the required minimum contribution.[11] As a result, employer matching contributions may be taken into account for purposes of both the nondiscrimination and the top-heavy rules.

QNECs. Qualified nonelective contributions (QNECs) under Code Sec. 401(m)(4)(C) may be treated as employer contributions for purposes of the top-heavy minimum contribution requirement.[12] In addition, QNECs may be treated as employer contributions, even if they are taken into account under the ADP and ACP tests (see ¶ 2951B and ¶ 2954).

[1] Code Sec. 416(c)(2)(A).

[2] Code Sec. 416(c)(2)(B)(i).

[3] Code Sec. 416(c)(2)(B)(ii)(II).

[4] IRS Reg. § 1.416-1, M-10.

[5] IRS Reg. § 1.416-1, M-8.

[6] Code Sec. 416(e).

[7] Code Sec. 408(k)(1)(B).

[8] Code Sec. 401(k)(4)(A).

¶ 945

Non-Key Employees in Both DB and DC Plans

If a non-key employee participates in both a defined benefit plan and a defined contribution plan maintained by an employer, the employer is not required to provide the non-key employee with both the full, separate minimum benefit and the full, separate minimum contribution.

According to IRS regulations, if employees are covered under both defined benefit and defined contribution plans, and if the contributions and forfeitures under the defined contribution plan equal 5% of compensation each year the plan is top-heavy, such a minimum will be presumed to satisfy the minimum contribution/ benefit limits.[1]

---

[1] Code Sec. 416(f); Conference Report No. 97-760, 97th Cong., 2d Sess., p. 629; IRS Reg. § 1.416-1, M-12.

¶ 950

Employees Covered by Collective Bargaining Agreement

The extra qualification requirements for top-heavy plans relating to rapid vesting and minimum contributions and benefits do not apply to any employee included in a collective bargaining unit. Furthermore, top-heavy provisions do not have to be included in a plan if it:

1. is not top-heavy and
2. covers only employees under a collective-bargaining agreement (as determined by the Secretary of Labor).[1]

---

[1] Code Secs. 416(i)(4) and 7701(a)(46); IRS Reg. § 1.416-1, T-38.

¶ 955

Aggregate Limit on Contributions and Benefits

Prior to limitation years beginning in 2000, special rules relating to the aggregate limit on benefits and contributions applied to a key employee who participated in both a defined benefit plan and a defined contribution plan that were included in a top-heavy group. Generally, unless certain requirements were met, for any year for which the plans were included in a top-heavy group, 1.0 was substituted for 1.25 in the denominators of the defined benefit plan and defined contribution fractions used in computing the aggregate limit (see ¶ 567).[1] In addition,

"$41,500" was substituted for "$51,875" in the numerator of the transition fraction for a defined contribution plan.

The combined plan limit rules have been repealed, effective for limitation years beginning after 1999.[2] The rules governing the aggregate limit on contributions and benefits that applied before 2000 are detailed at CCH PENSION PLAN GUIDE ¶ 1711.

Transitional rule

A transitional rule provides that if, at the time the general top-heavy plan limit (where 1.0 is substituted for 1.25) begins to apply, the aggregate of a key employee's accrued benefits and annual additions exceed 1.0 as applied to the dollar limits, the general rule will be suspended so long as there are no further benefit accruals or annual additions on behalf of the key employee.[3] Benefit accruals and annual additions may not resume until (1) the aggregate of the key employee's accrued benefits and annual additions is less than 1.0 (as applied to the dollar limits), or (2) the aggregate limit for the key employee is increased to 1.25 (as applied to the dollar limits).[4]

---

[1] Code Sec. 416(h)(1), stricken by P.L. 104-188, applicable to limitation years beginning after December 31, 1999.

[2] Small Business Job Protection Act (P.L. 104-188), Sec. 1452.

[3] Code Sec. 416(h)(3), stricken by P.L. 104-188, applicable to limitation years beginning after December 31, 1999.

[4] Conference Report No. 97-760, 97th Cong., 2d Sess.

¶ 960
Top-Heavy Provisions in Plan Documents

Since the additional rules for top-heavy plans (vesting, minimum benefits, and contributions, etc.) are qualification rules, a top-heavy plan is a qualified plan only if these rules are met.[1] Moreover, a plan (whether or not top-heavy in fact) constitutes a qualified plan only if it includes provisions that (1) will automatically take effect if the plan becomes a top-heavy plan and (2) meet the top-heavy requirements.

However, a plan is not required to adopt these provisions if no employee of the employer maintaining the plan is or could be a key employee.

---

[1] Code Sec. 401(a)(10)(B).

¶ 965
Avoidance by Use of Personal Service Corporations

Rules are provided to ensure that an employer cannot avoid the top-heavy plan rules by establishing a one-person corporate shell. These rules cover situations in which all of the services of a personal service corporation are performed for another corporation, partnership, or other entity and where such personal service corporation is formed principally for the purpose of avoiding or evading federal income tax by reducing the income of, or securing the benefit of any expense, deduction, credit, exclusion, or other allowance for, any employee-owner which would not be otherwise available.

Income and deductions to be allocated

In such a case, the Secretary of the Treasury is authorized to allocate any such income, deduction, etc., between the personal service corporation and its employee-owners if the Secretary determines it is necessary to do so in order to prevent tax avoidance or evasion or clearly to reflect the income of the personal service corporation or any of its employee-owners.[1]

---

[1] Code Sec. 269A(a).

¶ 970

For More Information

☐ For more information on top-heavy plans, see CCH PENSION PLAN GUIDE ¶ 1669-1729.

Coverage Requirements

¶ 1000

Overview of Coverage Rules

Under the minimum coverage rules, generally, a qualified plan must benefit a certain percentage of employees.[1] A plan may also qualify if it benefits a certain class of employees, so long as it does not discriminate in favor of highly paid employees.

To meet the coverage requirements, most plans must satisfy one of the two following tests:

1. the ratio percentage test, or

2. the average benefits test.

Excluded employees

A plan will not be disqualified merely because it limits coverage to salaried or clerical employees. Moreover, a plan may exclude employees covered by a collective bargaining agreement if retirement benefits were a subject of good-faith bargaining and may exclude nonresident aliens who receive no U.S. earned income.

Integration with Social Security

A plan may integrate with Social Security only if the plan meets certain disparity limits relating to the integration of contributions or benefits. For further details on integrated plans, see ¶ 1200 and following.[2]

Ratio percentage test

Under the ratio percentage test, the percentage of nonhighly compensated employees benefiting under the plan must be at least 70% of the percentage of highly compensated employees benefiting under the plan.[3]

Average benefits test

A plan meets the average benefits test if:

1. the plan benefits such employees as qualify under a classification set up by the employer and found by the IRS not to be discriminatory in favor of highly compensated employees ("nondiscriminatory classification test"), and

2. the average benefit percentage for nonhighly compensated employees of the employer is at least 70% of the average benefit percentage for highly compensated employees of the employer ("average benefit percentage test").

Average benefit percentage. The term "average benefit percentage" means, with respect to any group of employees, the average of the benefit percentages calculated separately with respect to each employee in such group (whether or not a participant in any plan). The term "benefit percentage" means the employer-provided contributions (including forfeitures) or benefits of an employee under all qualified plans of the employer, expressed as a percentage of such employee's compensation. If benefit percentages are determined on the basis of employer-provided contributions, all employer-provided benefits must be converted into contributions for testing purposes. If benefit percentages are determined on the basis of employer-provided benefits, all employer-provided contributions must be converted into benefits.

For purposes of determining benefit percentages, all pre-tax contributions or benefits provided under a qualified plan are considered employer-provided and must be taken into account.

Satisfying the average benefit percentage test requires that the employer determine an average benefit percentage for each employee and then separately average the percentages of all employees in the highly compensated and rank-and-file groups. In general, benefit percentages must be determined on either a

¶1000

contributions or a benefits basis. However, an optional rule allows an employer to test its defined benefit and defined contribution plans separately by ignoring benefits and contributions under any plans of a different type. See ¶ 1075.

Nondiscriminatory classification test. There is a three-part test for determining whether a group of employees constitutes a "nondiscriminatory classification" (see ¶ 1070):

First, the classification of employees must be reasonable. This means that it must reflect a bona fide business classification of employees, such as salaried employees and hourly employees, rather than a classification designed to increase qualified plan benefit disparities.

Second, the classification must satisfy an "objective test" that has both a safe harbor and an unsafe harbor for determining whether a classification is nondiscriminatory.

Third, there is a facts-and-circumstances test for those cases that fall in between the safe and unsafe harbors.[4]

Plans that need not satisfy coverage requirements

Certain types of plans need not satisfy either the ratio percentage test or the average benefits test. These include:

1. plans offering benefits only to highly compensated employees;
2. plans offering no benefits for highly compensated employees; and
3. church and government plans.

---

[1] Code Sec. 410(b).

[2] Code Secs. 401(a)(5) and 401(l).

[3] Code Sec. 410(b); IRS Reg. §1.410(b).

[4] IRS Reg. §1.410(b)-2(b).

¶ 1005

Process of Testing for Coverage Requirements

To determine whether a plan meets the minimum coverage requirements, an employer has to make the following determinations:

1. Who is the employer?

2. Who are the employees includable in the testing? Which employees are excludable from testing? Which employees are considered to be "benefiting" under a plan for testing purposes? Which employees are highly compensated and nonhighly compensated? How are former employees to be tested?

3. What is the plan to be tested? Do plans of the employer have to be aggregated or disaggregated for purposes of testing coverage?

4. During what period must coverage be satisfied?

5. Does the plan pass either the ratio percentage test or average benefit percentage test, or any of the tests under which a plan is deemed to satisfy coverage?

Once the employer and employees (including former employees) are properly defined for testing purposes, it is determined whether plans need to be aggregated, and the testing period is defined, the employer must run either the ratio percentage test or average benefit percentage test. If either test is satisfied or the plan complies with a rule under which it is deemed to satisfy coverage, then the plan has met the minimum coverage requirements for the testing period. In the following paragraphs each of these requirements will be discussed.

¶ 1008

EMPLOYERS AND EMPLOYEES TESTED: Determining the Employer

An employer, for coverage purposes, is defined as (1) the employer maintaining the plan, and also (2) those other employers that are required to be aggregated with the employer.

Several additional rules apply in determining employers for testing coverage:[1]

1. An individual who owns the entire interest of an unincorporated business is treated as an employer.

2. A partnership is treated as the employer of each partner and of each employee of the partnership.

3. Each separate line of business under Code Sec. 414(r) may be treated as an employer for testing coverage. See ¶ 1300 and following.

4. There is a special rule for certain business acquisitions and dispositions included in a controlled group or affiliated service group.[2] If a person (legal entity) ceases to be a member of a controlled group or affiliated service group, the coverage rules are satisfied by a plan for a limited period of time after an acquisition or disposition if it meets two conditions:[3]

   a. the plan satisfied coverage immediately before the acquisition or disposition; and

   b. there is no immediate change in the plan or coverage of the plan other than the acquisition or disposition.

The transition relief applies to component plans, if each plan separately satisfies the Code Sec. 401(a)(4) and Code Sec. 410(b) requirements immediately before the acquisition or disposition and there is no significant change in the plan or the plan coverage during the transition period.[4]

The *limited transition period* begins with the date of acquisition or disposition and ends with the last day of the first plan year beginning after the acquisition or disposition.[5]

The terms acquisition and disposition mean an asset or stock acquisition, merger, or other similar transaction involving a change in employer of the employees of a trade or business.[6]

[1] IRS Reg. § 1.410(b)-9.

[2] IRS Reg. § 1.410(b)-2(f).

[3] Code Sec. 410(b)(6)(C)(i).

[4] See Rev. Rul. 2004-11, 2004-1 CB 480, February 17, 2004, CCH PENSION PLAN GUIDE ¶ 19,948Z-44.

[5] Code Sec. 410(b)(6)(C)(ii).

[6] IRS Reg. § 1.410(b)-2(f).

¶ 1010

EMPLOYERS AND EMPLOYEES TESTED: Determining Employees Benefiting Under a Plan—In General

A plan will only satisfy coverage if it meets either the ratio percentage test or average benefit percentage test, or is a plan that automatically satisfies coverage[1] *with respect to employees* for a plan year. In addition, a plan must satisfy separate coverage rules with regard to former employees for a plan year (see ¶ 1030).[2] The whole purpose of nondiscriminatory minimum coverage is to ensure that a required percentage of employees are covered under a plan. However, employees are only required to be taken into account for testing purposes if they benefit under the plan being tested and are not excludable from coverage.[3] Thus, testing requires determining which employees benefit under a plan and running either the ratio percentage or average benefit percentage test to determine if coverage satisfies Code Sec. 410(b).

Therefore, an employer must define its total employees (see ¶ 1015), exclude those employees who may be excluded under the regulations (see ¶ 1020), and then determine whether they benefit under the plan for testing purposes (see ¶ 1025). The next step is to determine whether the remaining employees are either highly compensated or nonhighly compensated (see ¶ 1035).

[1] IRS Reg. § § 1.410(b)-2(b)(4) through (7).

[2] IRS Reg. § 1.410(b)-2(c).

[3] IRS Reg. § 1.410(b)-3 and -6.

¶ 1015

EMPLOYERS AND EMPLOYEES TESTED: Defining Employees

An employee is defined as an individual who performs services for the employer either as a:[1]

1. common-law employee,

2. self-employed individual who is treated as an employee under Code Sec. 401(c)(1), or

3. leased employee (not excluded under Code Sec. 414(n)(5)) who is treated as an employee of the employer-recipient under Code Sec. 414(n)(2) or 414(o)(2).

[1] IRS Reg. § 1.410(b)-9.

¶ 1020
EMPLOYERS AND EMPLOYEES TESTED:
Excludable Employees

Certain classes of employees *must* or *may be* excluded in applying the minimum coverage rules. These "excludable employees" are generally not taken into consideration for testing purposes even if they benefit under a plan.[1]

Employees not benefiting

Excludable employees must be distinguished from employees who are not treated as "benefiting" under a plan. The latter class of employees are taken into account for some purposes but not others. The concept of which employees benefit under a plan will also be discussed below.

General rules for excludable employees

For purposes of determining excludable employees, several general rules apply:[2]

1. Excludable employees are determined separately under each plan when testing coverage.

2. In determining whether two or more plans that are permissively aggregated and treated as a single plan (under IRS Reg. § 1.410(b)-7(d)) satisfy the ratio percentage test, the excludable employee rules are applied exclusively to the deemed single plan.

3. For purposes of the average benefit percentage test, all plans in the testing group are treated as one plan.

Groups of excludable employees

The following groups of employees are excludable for coverage purposes:

Minimum age or service. If a plan requires that an employee be 21 years of age or complete one year of service before participation and excludes all employees who do not satisfy such requirements, the employer is to disregard these employees in applying the minimum coverage rules.[3]

Employees who do not satisfy a plan's minimum service requirement are not treated as benefiting under the plan, and remain excludable employees, even though they may elect to make rollover contributions under the plan.[4]

Multiple age or service requirements. Some plans have more than one minimum age or service eligibility requirement. In that situation, only those employees who fail to satisfy *all of the different sets of conditions* are excludable employees under that plan.[5]

Example 1: Atlas Corp. maintains Plan A for hourly employees and Plan B for salaried employees. Plan A has no minimum age or service condition. Plan B has no minimum age condition and requires one year of service. Atlas treats

Plans A and B as a single plan for purposes of the minimum coverage rules. Since Plan A has no minimum age or service conditions, *no employees* are excludable in testing Plans A and B for purposes of the minimum coverage rules.

Example 2: Butler Corp. maintains three plans. Plan F has no minimum age or service conditions. Plan G benefits employees who are age 18 with one year of service. Plan H benefits employees who are 21 with 6 months of service. For purposes of the average benefit percentage test, all three plans are treated as a single plan. Since Plan F has no minimum age and service conditions, no employee is excludable for purposes of the average benefit percentage test.

Separate testing for otherwise excludable employees. If a plan does not bar from participation all employees who could have been barred under the Code Sec. 410(a) minimum participation standards ("otherwise excludable employees"), that plan may be treated as two plans for testing purposes: one for the "otherwise excludable employees" and one for the other employees who benefit under the plan. Therefore the "otherwise excludable employees" are excluded from testing coverage in the plan covering the other employees.[6]

In effect, then, employees who would be excludable but for the fact that the plan does not apply the greatest permissible minimum age and service conditions under Code Sec. 410(a)(1)(A) *may be treated as excludable* with respect to the plan. This rule only applies, however, if the "otherwise excludable employees" separately satisfy the minimum coverage rules after excluding the following employees: (a) those employees who have satisfied the greatest minimum age and service requirements, and (b) if the plan provides minimum age or service conditions that are lower than the maximum permissible age or service conditions, those employees who have not satisfied the lower minimum age and service conditions.[7]

Example 3: Plan A requires attainment of age 18 and three months of service. Employees who are eligible to benefit under the plan but have not reached age 21 or completed one year of service may be excluded in testing the plan if such employees separately satisfy the minimum coverage rules. In testing these otherwise excludable employees, those employees who have not attained age 18 or three months of service are excludable.

Example 4: An employer maintains Plan J, which does not apply any minimum age or service conditions. Plan J benefits all employees in Division 1 but does not benefit employees in Division 2. Although Plan J has no minimum age or service condition, the employer wants to exclude employees who have not attained age 21 or completed one year of service. The employer has 110 employees who either do not have one year of service or are not at least age 21. Of these 110 employees, 10 are highly compensated employees and 100 are nonhighly compensated employees. Five of these highly compensated employees, or 50%, work in Division 1 and thus benefit under Plan J. Thirty-five of these nonhighly compensated employees, or 35%, work in Division 1 and thus benefit under Plan J. Plan J satisfies the ratio percentage test of Code Sec. 410(b) with respect to employees who do not satisfy the greatest permissible minimum age and service requirement because the ratio percentage of that group of employees is 70%. Thus, in determining whether or not Plan J satisfies Code Sec. 410(b), the 110 employees may be treated as excludable employees.

Nonresident aliens. Employees who are nonresident aliens and who receive no U.S. source earned income are excluded even if they are benefiting under the plan.[8] An employer may also exclude nonresident aliens who receive U.S. source income if that income is exempt from U.S. income tax under a treaty and the employer excludes all employees in this category.[9] A nonresident alien is defined under Code Sec. 7701(b)(1)(B) as an individual who is neither a U.S. citizen nor a U.S. resident.

QSLOBs. Employees of a qualified separate line of business under Code Sec. 414(r) are excludable with respect to testing coverage under another QSLOB of the same employer. This exclusion of employees does not apply, however, for purposes of satisfying the nondiscrimination classification prong of the average benefit test under Code Sec. 410(b)(5)(B).[10]

Terminating employees. Employees terminated before the last day of the plan year with no more than 500 hours *may be* excluded if (a) the employee does not benefit under the plan for the plan year, (b) the employee is eligible to participate in the plan, (c) the plan has a minimum period of service requirement or a requirement that an employee be employed on the last day of the plan year (last-day requirement) to receive a benefit, and (d) the employee fails to accrue a benefit or receive an allocation under the plan solely because of the failure to satisfy the minimum period of service or last-day requirement.[11]

This is an optional rule, but if it is used for any employee it must be used for all like employees during the plan year.[12] If a plan uses the elapsed time method of determining years of service, it may use either 91 consecutive calendar days or three consecutive months instead of 500 hours of service provided that the same convention is used for all employees for a plan year.[13]

> **Example 1:** An employer has 35 employees who are eligible to participate under a defined contribution plan. The plan provides that an employee will not receive an allocation of contributions for a plan year unless the employee is employed by the employer on the last day of the plan year. Only 30 employees are employed by the employer on the last day of the plan year. Two of the five employees who terminated employment before the last day of the plan year had 500 or fewer hours of service during the plan year, and the remaining three had more than 500 hours of service during the year. Of the five employees who were no longer employed on the last day of the plan year, the two with 500 hours of service or less during the plan year are treated as excludable employees and the remaining three who had over 500 hours of service during the plan year are taken into account in testing the plan under Code Sec. 410(b) but are treated as not benefiting under the plan.

> **Example 2:** An employer maintains two plans, Plan A for salaried employees and Plan B for hourly employees. Of the 100 salaried employees, two do not receive an allocation under Plan A for the plan year because they terminate employment before completing 500 hours of service. Of the 300 hourly employ-

ees, 50 do not receive an allocation under Plan B for the plan year because they terminate employment before completing 500 hours. In applying Code Sec. 410(b) to Plan A, the two employees who did not receive an allocation under Plan A are excludable employees, but the 50 who did not receive an allocation under Plan B are not excludable employees, because they were not eligible to participate under Plan A.

Employees of governmental and tax-exempt organizations. State and local government employees cannot participate in a qualified 401(k) plan.[14] In testing a 401(k) plan (or a 401(m) plan that is provided under the same general arrangement as a 401(k) plan), an IRS regulation provides that an employer may exclude employees of tax-exempt entities *if more than* 95% of the employees of the employer who are not precluded from being eligible to benefit under the plan for the plan year.[15]

> **CCH Pointer:** Regulations finalized by the IRS in 2006 provide that employees of a tax-exempt 501(c)(3) organization who are eligible to participate in a 403(b) plan of the organization may be excluded in testing whether the employer's 401(k) or 401(m) plan complies with the minimum coverage requirements. Such employees may be disregarded, however, only if: (1) no employees of the tax-exempt organization are eligible to participate in the 401(k) or 401(m) plan and (2) at least 95% of the employees of the employer who are not employees of the tax-exempt organization are eligible to participate in the 401(k) or 401(m) plan.[16] The regulations effectively allow a tax-exempt organization to continue to maintain a 403(b) plan and a 401(k) plan without having to provide coverage for employees under both plans.

Collectively bargained plans treated separately. The mandatory disaggregation rules of IRS Reg. § 1.410(b)-7(b) and (c) require that a plan benefiting both collectively bargained and noncollectively bargained employees be treated as two separate plans covering each group of employees.[17] Thus, a collectively bargained employee is always an excludable employee with respect to the mandatorily disaggregated portion of any plan that benefits noncollectively bargained employees; and vice versa.

A collectively bargained employee is defined as an employee who is included in a unit of employees covered by an agreement that the Secretary of Labor determines to be a good faith collective bargaining agreement (CBA) between employee representatives and one or more employers. An employee can be a collectively bargained employee even if the employee benefits under another plan of the employer. There may be situations where an employee performs hours of service as a collectively bargained employee and as a noncollectively bargained employee. In those cases the employee will be treated as either a collectively or noncollectively bargained employee with regard to the particular hours of service performed.[18]

> **CCH Pointer:** The category of excluded employees was modified by the Pension Protection Act of 2006 (P.L. 109-280) to provide that certain management pilots are treated as covered by a collective bargaining agreement.[19]

Former employees. Former employees are tested separately from employees for each plan year.[20] A plan is tested for nondiscriminatory coverage by taking all former employees into account, except that the following classes of former employees may be excluded from testing:[21]

   a. former employees who terminated their employment prior to January 1, 1984, or prior to the tenth calendar year preceding the calendar year in which the current plan year begins;

   b. former employees who terminated their employment in a calendar year preceding the earliest calendar year in which any former employee who benefits under the plan in the current plan year became a former employee;

   c. former nonhighly compensated employees who are treated as employees of the employer solely because they have increases in accrued benefits under a defined benefit plan that are based on ongoing service or compensation credits after they cease to perform services for the employer (including imputed service or compensation;[22] and

   d. former employees who were excludable employees under a class of employees described above during the plan year in which the former employees terminated employment, even if the former employees are benefiting under the plan.[23]

Reemployed veterans. Qualified retirement plans subject to the requirements of the Uniformed Services Employment and Reemployment Act of 1994 (USERRA) may allow veterans returning to employment from military service to make up employee contributions and elective deferrals that were not made during the employee's period of military service without risking disqualification of the plan for violating the limits on contributions and benefits applicable to qualified plans.[24] In addition, make up contributions, additional elective deferrals, employer matching contributions, and employee contributions made on behalf of reemployed veterans in compliance with USERRA will not cause a plan to violate the coverage rules applicable to qualified plans.

Differential wage payments, effective for remuneration paid after December 31, 2008, will be treated as compensation for purposes of the USERRA requirements.[25] Plan contributions and benefits that are based on differential wage payments will not cause the plan to fail to meet the minimum participation and nondiscrimination requirements applicable to qualified plans. However, all employees of the sponsoring employer who perform military service must be entitled to receive differential wage payments on reasonably equivalent terms. In addition, all employees eligible to participate in a retirement plan maintained by the employer must be entitled to make contributions based on the differential payments on reasonably equivalent terms.

Special rules for multiemployer plans. IRS regulations provide a number of rules that are specifically applicable to employees in multiemployer plans, and that are exceptions to the general rules above.[26] For example, when testing coverage, a noncollectively bargained employee who benefits under the plan may be treated as a collectively bargained employee with regard to all of his hours of service if (i) the employee is or was covered by a CBA, and (ii) that CBA or successor agreement provides for the employee to benefit under the plan in the current year.[27] See CCH PENSION PLAN GUIDE ¶ 1975 for more information on the special rules applicable to multiemployer plans.

---

[1] Code Sec. 410(b)(3) and (4); IRS Reg. §1.410(b)-6(a).

[2] IRS Reg. §1.410(b)-6(a)(2).

[3] IRS Reg. §1.410(b)-6(b)(1).

[4] Rev. Rul. 96-48, 1996-2 CB 31, 9-30-96, CCH PENSION PLAN GUIDE ¶ 19,844.

[5] IRS Reg. §1.410(b)-6(b)(2).

[6] Code Sec. 410(b)(4)(B); IRS Reg. §1.410(b)-6(b)(3).

[7] IRS Reg. §1.410(b)-6(b)(3)(ii).

[8] Code Sec. 410(b)(3)(C); IRS Reg. §1.410(b)-6(c).

[9] IRS Reg. §1.410(b)-6(c)(2).

[10] IRS Reg. §1.410(b)-6(e).

[11] IRS Reg. §1.410(b)-6(f).

[12] IRS Reg. §1.410(b)-6(f)(1)(vi).

[13] IRS Reg. §1.410(b)-6(f)(1)(v).

[14] Code Sec. 401(k)(4)(B).

[15] IRS Reg. §1.410(b)-6(g).

[16] IRS Reg. §1.410(b)-6(g)(2) and (3) as issued under T.D. 9275 (71 FR 41357).

[17] IRS Reg. §1.410(b)-6(d)(1).

[18] IRS Reg. §1.410(b)-6(d)(2)(i).

[19] Code Sec. 410(b)(3), as modified by P.L. 109-280 (Pension Protection Act of 2006), Act Sec. 402(h)(1).

[20] IRS Reg. §1.410(b)-2(c).

[21] IRS Reg. §1.410(b)-6(h)(1)-(3).

[22] IRS Reg. §1.410(b)-6(i).

[23] IRS Reg. §1.410(b)-6(h)(3).

[24] Code Sec. 414(u). See also Department of Labor regulations implementing USERRA, published in the *Federal Register* on March 10, 2005, and December 19, 2005 (70 FR 75246 and 75313), CCH PENSION PLAN GUIDE ¶ 16,453A and following.

[25] Code Sec. 414(u)(12)(C), as added by P.L. 110-245 (Heroes Earnings Assistance and Tax Relief Act of 2008), Act Sec. 105(b)(1).

[26] IRS Reg. §1.410(b)-6(d)(2)(ii).

[27] IRS Reg. §1.410(b)-6(d)(2)(ii)(A).

¶ 1025

EMPLOYERS AND EMPLOYEES TESTED: Employees Benefiting Under a Plan

Once the employer has determined its total employees and has subtracted excludable employees, the next step is to determine which employees are "benefiting" under the plan for testing purposes.[1]

In order to satisfy the minimum coverage rules a plan must satisfy either the ratio percentage test or average benefit percentage test. Both of these tests look to ensure that a specified percentage and classification of employees "benefit" under the plan in a nondiscriminatory manner.[2] The regulations provide separate rules for determining whether employees benefit under a defined contribution or a defined benefit plan.

What tests require determination of benefit to employee?

Tests that require a determination of whether an employee benefits under a plan include:

1. Ratio percentage test. *(IRS Reg. §1.410(b)-2(b)(2)).*

2. Nondiscriminatory classification requirement of the average benefit test. *(IRS Reg. §1.410(b)-4).*

3. Safe and unsafe harbors under the nondiscriminatory classification requirement. *(IRS Reg. § 1.410(b)-4(c))*.

4. Rule that treats the minimum coverage rules as satisfied when a plan does not benefit any highly compensated employees. *(IRS Reg. § 1.410(b)-2(b)(6))*.

5. Testing of former employees. *(IRS Reg. § 1.410(b)-2(b)(2) and 3(b)*.

General rule for "benefiting" under a plan

An employee is considered to benefit for a plan year under a defined contribution plan if the employer receives an allocation that is taken into account under IRS Reg. § 1.401(a)(4)-2(c)(2)(ii).[3] Therefore, if an employee is a plan participant but does not receive an allocation because the employee is not employed by the employer on the last day of the plan year, the employee is not considered to benefit under the plan for that plan year.[4]

Under a defined benefit plan, an employee is considered to benefit if the employee has an increase in a benefit accrued or treated as an accrued benefit under Code Sec. 411(d)(6).[5] Under this general rule, increases in the dollar amount of an employee's accrued benefit attributable to the passage of time or a change in COLAs or other indices affecting the accrued benefit do not cause an employee to be treated as benefiting.[6]

Exceptions to the general rule

The regulations provide rules for determining whether an employee benefits under a plan in specific situations:[7]

401(k) and 401(m) plans. An employee is treated as benefiting under a 401(k) plan only if the employee is eligible to participate for that year even though elective deferrals are not actually made to his account.[8] Similarly, an employee is treated as benefiting under a 401(m) plan only if the employee is eligible to make after-tax contributions (and have matching contributions made for his benefit) in the plan year, even though no contributions are actually made.[9]

An election to make a rollover contribution is not a cash or deferred election. Accordingly, employees who are not eligible to make salary deferral contributions because they have not met the plan's service requirement will not be treated as benefiting under the plan even though they are eligible to make rollover contributions to the plan from the plan of their former employer.[10] Similarly, employees who are not eligible to receive allocations of matching contributions for a plan year because they have not met a minimum service requirement are not treated as benefiting under the plan even though they are allowed to make rollover contributions under the plan.[11] Nor will employees who do not receive allocations of nonelective contributions because they do not meet the applicable service requirements be treated as benefiting under the plan merely because they may make rollover contributions under the plan.[12]

Section 415 limits. Certain plan provisions pertaining to Code Sec. 415 are to be disregarded in determining whether an employee benefits under a defined benefit plan.[13] These are provisions:

a. that implement the Code Sec. 415 limits.[14]

b. that provide for an increase in an employee's accrued benefit under the plan due solely to COLA adjustments to the annual dollar limitation under Code Sec. 415(d)(1);

c. that provide additional years of service or participation under Code Sec. 415(b)(5); or

d. that provide changes in the defined contribution fraction under Code Sec. 415(e).

If it applies the rule on a consistent basis to all employees, a defined contribution plan can determine which employees benefit by disregarding those plan provisions that implement the 415 limits.[15]

Effect of failure to receive an allocation or increase in accrual. An employee will be treated as benefiting under a plan if the employee satisfies all the criteria necessary to receive an allocation or accrue a benefit, *but fails to* have an increase in his accrued benefit or to receive an allocation solely due to any one of the following reasons:[16]

a. the employee's benefit would otherwise exceed a limit that is applicable to all employees on a uniform basis;[17]

b. the benefit previously accrued by the employee is greater than the benefit that would be determined under the plan if the benefit that was accrued previously was disregarded;[18]

c. under an offset arrangement described in IRS Reg. § 1.401(a)(4)-3(f)(9), the plan offsets the employee's current benefit accrual;[19]

d. under a target benefit plan that satisfies the safe harbor (see IRS Reg. § 1.401(a)(4)-8(b)(3)), the employee's theoretical reserve is greater than or equal to the actuarial present value of the fractional rule benefit;[20] or

e. an employee has attained normal retirement age under a defined benefit plan and fails to accrue a benefit because of the provisions of Code Sec. 411(b)(1)(H)(iii) regarding adjustments for delayed retirement.[21]

Insurance contract plans. An employee is treated as benefiting under an insurance contract plan described in Code Sec. 412(i) only if a premium is paid on behalf of an employee for the plan year.[22] Even if a premium is not paid on an employee's behalf, he will be treated as benefiting under an insurance contract plan if: (a) the sole reason the premium is not paid is one of the reasons set forth under "Effect of failure to receive an allocation or increase in accrual" above, or (b) the sole reason the premium is not paid is that the insurance contracts that have been purchased previously on behalf of the employee guarantee to provide the employee's projected normal retirement benefit without regard to future premium payments.[23]

---

[1] Code Sec. 410(b)(1) and (2); IRS Reg. § 1.410(b)-3.

[2] IRS Reg. §§ 1.410(b)-2(b)(2), -4, and -5.O

[3] IRS Reg. § 1.410(b)-3(a)(1).

[4] Preamble to the 1991 final regulations. T.D. 8363 published in the *Federal Register* on September 19, 1991 (56 FR 47638). To the extent that Rev. Rul. 76-250, 1976-2 CB 124, and Rev. Rul. 81-210, 1981-2 CB 89, conflict with this rule, the IRS considers the revenue rulings to be superseded.

[5] IRS Reg. § 1.410(b)-2(c) and -3(b).

[6] Preamble to T.D. 8487, September 3, 1993 (58 FR 46835).

[7] IRS Reg. § 1.410(b)-3(a)(2).

[8] See IRS Reg. § 1.410(b)-3(a)(2)(i) and § 1.401(k)-1(g)(4) for the definition of an eligible employee under a 401(k) plan.

[9] See IRS Reg. § 1.410(b)-3(a)(2)(i) and § 1.401(m)-1(f)(4) for the definition of an eligible employee under a 401(m) plan.

[10] Rev. Rul. 96-48, 1996-2 CB 31, 9-30-96, CCH PENSION PLAN GUIDE ¶ 19,844.

[11] *Ibid.*

[12] *Ibid.*

[13] IRS Reg. § 1.410(b)-3(a)(2)(ii)(A).

[14] See IRS Reg. § 1.410(b)-3(a)(2)(ii)(B) for rules regarding the relationship between Code Secs. 401(a)(4), 410(b), and 415, in determining defined benefit plan accrual rates.

[15] IRS Reg. § 1.410(b)-3(a)(2)(ii)(C).

[16] IRS Reg. § 1.410(b)-3(a)(2)(iii)(A).

[17] IRS Reg. § 1.410(b)-3(a)(2)(iii)(B).

[18] IRS Reg. § 1.410(b)-3(a)(2)(iii)(C).

[19] IRS Reg. § 1.410(b)-3(a)(2)(iii)(D).

[20] IRS Reg. § 1.410(b)-3(a)(2)(iii)(E).

[21] IRS Reg. § 1.410(b)-3(a)(2)(iii)(F).

[22] IRS Reg. § 1.410(b)-3(a)(2)(iv)(A).

[23] IRS Reg. § 1.410(b)-3(a)(2)(iv)(B).

¶ 1030

EMPLOYERS AND EMPLOYEES TESTED: Former Employees Benefiting Under a Plan

A "former employee" is an individual who was, but has ceased to be, an employee of the employer. Former employee status begins on the first day after the day on which an individual no longer performs services as an employee for a particular employer.

Former employees are tested separately from employees for nondiscriminatory coverage purposes.[1] Therefore the employer must identify its former employees and then determine which former employees within this class benefit under the plan for testing purposes.[2]

Testing of former employees

Because former employees are tested separately from employees, they are disregarded in applying the ratio percentage test, nondiscriminatory classification test, and average benefit percentage test for current employees under the plan. Similarly, employees are disregarded when former employees are tested for nondiscriminatory coverage.[3]

The IRS provides a facts-and-circumstances test under which a plan will satisfy coverage only if, in the group of former employees benefiting under the plan, it "does not discriminate significantly" in favor of highly compensated former employees.[4]

Former employees benefiting under a plan

A former employee is considered to benefit for a plan year only if the plan provides an allocation or benefit increase to the former employee for the plan year.[5]

The rules applicable to allocations or benefit increases for former employees are summarized below.[6]

COLA amendment. If a former employee recovers benefits under a defined benefit plan that is amended to provide an ad-hoc cost-of-living adjustment in the former employee's benefits, the former employee benefits under the plan.

Example 1: Employer A amends its defined benefit plan in the 2012 plan year to provide an ad hoc cost-of-living increase of 5% for all retirees. Former employees who receive this increase are treated as benefiting under the plan for the 2012 plan year.

Accrual or allocation due to employee's status. Any accrual or allocation during the plan year that arises from the individual's status as a former employee is treated as an accrual or allocation of a former employee.

Example 2: Employer B maintains a defined benefit plan with a calendar plan year. In the 2012 plan year, Employer B amends the plan to provide that an employee who has reached early retirement age under the plan and who retires before July 31 of the 2012 plan year will receive an unreduced benefit, even though the employee has not yet reached normal retirement age. This early retirement window benefit is provided to employees based on their status as employees. Thus, although individuals who take advantage of the benefit become former employees, the window benefit is treated as provided to employees and is not treated as a benefit for former employees.

Example 3: The facts are the same as Example 2, except that on September 1, 2012, Employer B also amends the defined benefit plan to provide an ad hoc cost-of-living increase effective for all former employees. An individual who ceases performing services for the employer before July 31, 2012, under the early retirement window, and then receives the ad hoc cost-of-living increase, is treated as both an employee and a former employee for 2012 (see below).

CCH Pointer: A plan amendment that applies the increased Code Sec. 401(a)(17) compensation limit under EGTRRA to former employees does not violate the coverage requirements.[7]

Simultaneous status as "employee" and "former employee"

An individual may be both an employee and former employee during the plan year. Because it is possible for an individual to accrue a benefit during a plan year both as an employee and former employee, that plan year is bifurcated based on the individual's status. Accordingly, for the year in which an individual terminates employment with the employer, the individual is treated as both an employee and former employee for testing coverage.[8]

---

[1] IRS Reg. § 1.410(b)-2(c).

[2] IRS Reg. § 1.410(b)-3(b).

[3] IRS Reg. § 1.410(b)-2(c)(1).

[4] IRS Reg. § 1.410(b)-2(c)(2).

[5] IRS Reg. § 1.410(b)-3(b)(1).

[6] *Ibid.*
[7] Rev. Rul. 2003-11, 2003-1 CB 285, CCH Pension Plan Guide ¶ 19,948G.

[8] Reg. § 1.410(b)-3(b)(1).

¶ 1035
EMPLOYERS AND EMPLOYEES TESTED: Highly Compensated and Nonhighly Compensated Employees

Up to this point, the employer has calculated its total number of employees (and total former employees), identified excludable employees, and determined those employees who benefit under the plan for testing whether coverage is nondiscriminatory. Now the employer must determine whether employees are highly compensated (HCE) or nonhighly compensated (nonHCE), and whether former employees are highly compensated or nonhighly compensated.

This determination must be made because the ratio percentage and average benefit percentage test (including the nondiscriminatory classification test) compare coverage of highly and nonhighly compensated employees.[1]

Highly compensated employee

An employee is an HCE if he or she:

1. was a 5% owner at any time during the current year or the preceding year, or

2. had compensation from the employer in excess of a statutory $80,000 during the preceding year ($110,000 in 2011; $115,000 in 2012), and, if the employer so elects, was in the top-paid group (i.e., top 20 percent of employees by compensation) of the employer for the preceding year.[2]

Code Sec. 415 compensation. In determining the compensation of a highly compensated employee, the Code Sec. 415(c)(3) definition of compensation applies.[3] Compensation also includes elective deferrals to a 401(k) plan, SIMPLE plan, TSA or SEP, and salary reduction contributions under a cafeteria plan.

Compensation amount adjusted for inflation. The statutory $80,000 compensation amount is adjusted for inflation at the same time and in the same way as the adjustments to the defined benefit limit under Code Sec. 415(d).[4] However, the base period is the calendar quarter ending September 30, 1996. Thus, the $80,000 limit increases to $110,000 in 2011 and $115,000 in 2012.[5]

CCH Pointer: By electing to treat employees in the top 20% of compensation as highly compensated, an employer may be required to include fewer employees in the highly compensated employee group. As a result, employees who are still relatively highly paid may be categorized as nonhighly compensated, thereby increasing the plan's chances of passing the nondiscrimination tests.

In addition, for employees in the same general salary range, an employer may be able to designate those employees with higher benefit percentages as being in the nonhighly compensated group, which may also enable it to pass the nondiscrimination tests more easily.

Determination of HCE on controlled group basis. The identity of the highly compensated employees is to be determined on a controlled group basis. Also, employees who are treated as highly compensated employees are to be determined on a controlled group basis.[6]

Exclusion of nonresident aliens. Nonresident aliens without U.S. source income from the employer are disregarded for all purposes in determining the identity of the highly compensated employees of the employer.[7]

Top-paid group. An employee is in the top-paid group of employees for any year if he or she is in the top 20% of the employees based on compensation paid during the year.[8] An employer, however, may exclude the following employees in determining the members of the top-paid group: (1) employees who have not completed 6 months of service; (2) employees who normally work less than 17½ hours per week; (3) employees who normally work fewer than six months a year; (4) employees who are included in a unit of employees covered by a collective bargaining agreement, except to the extent provided in regulations (see below); (5) employees who have not attained age 21; and (6) employees who are nonresident aliens and who receive no earned income from the U.S. employer.[9]

Note that an employee who does not meet the plan's eligibility requirements, but who has completed six months of service, or is a foreign national receiving U.S. source income, or is not otherwise excludable under Code Sec. 414(q)(5) or (8), must be included in the determination of the top-paid group.

Applicable period for determination year or look-back year. For purposes of determining the group of highly compensated employees, the determination year calculation is based on the "applicable year" of the plan or other entity for which a determination is being made.[10] The look-back year calculation is based on the 12-month period immediately preceding such determination year. Thus, if a plan has a calendar year plan year, the determination year and look-back year calculations must be made based on a calendar year. If a plan has a fiscal year, for example, a July 1 to June 30 plan year, the determination year and look-back year calculation is based on the July 1 to June 30 plan year.

Applicable year. The "applicable year" is the plan year of the qualified plan or other employee benefit arrangement to which the definition of highly compensated employees is applicable as defined in the written plan document or otherwise in regulations.[11]

The look-back year may never be less than a twelve month period.[12]

CCH Pointer: Because the determination of whether an employee is highly compensated is based on the employee's status in the preceding year, a newly hired employee who is not more than a 5 pecent owner may not be a highly compensated employee in the year of hire.

Calendar year data election for fiscal year plans. An employer that maintains one or more plans on a fiscal year basis may use calendar year data in order to simplify the determination of whether an employee is a highly compensated employee. See CCH PENSION PLAN GUIDE ¶ 1987 for more information on the election to use calendar year data.

Amend qualified plan to reflect elections. A qualified plan that contains the Code Sec. 414(q) definition of highly compensated employees must be amended to reflect a top-paid group or calendar year data election that has been made for a determination year.[13] Thus, an employer may not make the change to a top-paid group election operationally, or rely on general authorization in the plan, but must actually amend the plan.[14] In addition, the plan must be amended to reflect any change made by the employer to the top-paid group or calendar year data election. However, a plan that does not contain a definition of highly compensated employees is not required to add such definition merely to reflect a top-paid group or calendar year data election.

When must the plan be amended? Qualified plans must be amended to reflect the Code Sec. 414(q) definition of highly compensated employees, as amended by the Small Business Job Protection Act of 1996.[15] A plan provision reflecting the definition of highly compensated is a disqualifying provision. Thus, any plan amendments adopted to reflect the Code Sec. 414(q) definition of highly compensated and to reflect top-paid group or calendar year data elections need not be made until the end of the prescribed GUST remedial amendment period (see ¶ 316).

The IRS emphasizes, however, that the plan must operate in accordance with the amended definition of highly compensated under the SBA'96 as of the statutory effective date and that amendments adopted to reflect those changes must be retroactively effective as of the statutory effective date. The retroactive amendments must reflect any top-paid group or calendar year data elections (and changes to the elections) and the first date that the plan operated in accordance with those elections or election changes.

Attribution of ownership interest rules. In determining whether an individual is highly compensated under the more than 5% owner test, an individual is considered to own any stock owned directly or indirectly by his or her spouse (other than a legally separated spouse), children, grandchildren, or parents. See CCH PENSION PLAN GUIDE ¶ 1987 for more information on attribution rules.

Former employees. An employee who has separated from service is treated as a highly compensated employee if the individual was a highly compensated employee when the employee separated from service.[16] In keeping with the rules for employees treated as highly compensated, an employee is treated as highly compensated if the employee was highly compensated at any time during the current or the preceding year. Also, a former employee will be treated as highly compensated if he or she was a highly compensated employee at any time after attaining age 55.[17]

Top-paid group election. Employers may make a top-paid group election for a determination year, under which an employee (other than an employee who has been a more than 5% owner at any time during the determination year or the lookback year) who earned compensation in excess of the statutory limit of $80,000 (adjusted to $110,000 in 2010 and 2011) for the look-back year will be a highly compensated employee only if the employee was in the top-paid group for the look-back year.[18]

---

[1] IRS Reg. § 1.410(b)-2(b), -4, -5, and -9.

[2] Code Sec. 414(q)(1), as amended by P.L. 104-188 (Small Business Job Protection Act of 1996).

[3] Code Sec. 414(q)(4).

[4] Code Sec. 414(q).

[5] IR-2011-103, 10-20-2011, CCH PENSION PLAN GUIDE ¶ 17,037Q.

[6] Code Sec. 414(q)(10), redesignated as (7) by P.L. 104-188 (Small Business Job Protection Act).

[7] Code Sec. 414(q)(11), redesignated as (8) by P.L. 104-188 (Small Business Job Protection Act).

[8] Code Sec. 414(q)(4), redesignated as (3) by P.L. 104-188 (Small Business Job Protection Act).

[9] Code Sec. 414(q)(5) and 414(q)(8).

[10] IRS Temp. Reg. § 1.414(q)-1T, Q/A-14(a)(1).

[11] IRS Temp. Reg. § 1.414(q)-1T, Q/A-14(a)(2).

[12] IRS Temp. Reg. § 1.414(q)-1T, Q/A-14(a)(3).

[13] IRS Notice 97-45, 1997-2 CB 296, 8-18-97, CCH PENSION PLAN GUIDE ¶ 17,112W.

[14] Steven Forbes, Pension Publications of Denver, 1997 ERISA workshop.

[15] *Ibid.*

[16] Code Sec. 414(q)(9)(A), redesignated as Code Sec. 414(q)(6) by P.L. 104-188 (Small Business Job Protection Act).

[17] Code Sec. 414(q)(9)(B), redesignated as Code Sec. 414(q)(6) by P.L. 104-188 (Small Business Job Protection Act).

[18] Code Sec. 414(q)(1)(B)(ii).

¶ 1040

PLANS TESTED: Aggregation Rules—Definition of Plan

For purposes of some minimum coverage rules, several plans *may* be aggregated and, therefore, treated as one plan. However, for purposes of other coverage tests, several plans *must* be aggregated and, therefore, treated as one plan. In addition, in some cases, a plan *may (or must)* be separated into more than one plan.[1]

This aggregation and disaggregation of plans is a two-part process. Before an employer starts pulling its plan apart and gluing it back together so that it can comply with coverage, it first needs to know how to define its plan. Then it must apply certain mandatory disaggregation and permissive aggregation rules to that definition of the plan. This resulting plan definition will be used in complying with both Code Sec. 410(b) coverage rules and 401(a)(4) nondiscrimination rules.[2]

What is a plan for coverage purposes?

A plan means a plan described in Code Sec. 414(l) or an annuity plan described in Code Sec. 403(a). The Code Sec. 414(l) definition refers to a single plan, so that each single plan is a separate plan for purposes of testing coverage.[3] A plan will not fail to be a single plan merely because:[4]

1. it has several distinct benefit structures that apply to the same or different participants;

2. it has several plan documents;

3. employers, whether or not affiliated, contribute to the plan;

4. the assets of the plan are invested in several trusts or annuity contracts; or

5. separate accounting is maintained for purposes of cost allocation but not for purposes of providing benefits under the plan.

However more than one plan will exist if a portion of the plan assets is not available to pay some of the benefits, even if each plan has the same benefit structure or plan document.[5]

Example: After acquiring Corporation B, Corporation A amends Corporation B's defined benefit plan (Plan B) to provide the same benefits as Corporation A's defined benefit plan (Plan A). The assets of Plan B are transferred to the trust containing the assets of Plan A in such a manner that the assets of each plan: (1) are separately accounted for, and (2) are not available to pay benefits of the other plan. Because of condition (2), there are still two plans and, therefore, a merger did not occur. As a result, Code Sec. 414(l) does not apply.

Additional rules

Building on this single plan concept, the coverage regulations provide the following rules and examples regarding the definition of a plan:[6]

1. if only a portion of the assets of a defined benefit plan is available, on an ongoing basis, to provide the benefits of certain employees, and the remaining assets are available only in certain limited cases to provide such benefits (but are available in all cases for the benefit of other employees), there are two separate plans.

2. the defined contribution portion of a Code Sec. 414(k) plan—a DB plan that provides a benefit derived from employer contributions which is based in part on the balance of the separate account of a participant—is a separate plan from the defined benefit portion of that same plan.

3. a single plan under Code Sec. 414(l) is a single plan for purposes of the minimum coverage requirements even though the plan comprises separate written documents and separate trusts, each of which has received a separate determination letter from the IRS.

4. a plan does not comprise separate plans merely because assets are separately invested in individual insurance or annuity contracts for employees.

5. a defined contribution plan will not comprise separate plans merely because it includes more than one trust, or merely because it provides for separate accounts and permits employees to direct the investment of the amounts directed to their accounts.

---

[1] IRS Reg. § 1.410(b)-7.

[2] IRS Reg. § 1.410(b)-7(a).

[3] *Ibid.;* IRS Reg. § 1.414(l)-1(b)(1); and preamble to T.D. 8363, published in the *Federal Register* on September 19, 1991 (54 FR 47638).

[4] IRS Reg. § 1.414(l)-1(b)(1).

[5] *Ibid.*

[6] IRS Reg. § 1.410(b)-7(b).

¶ 1045

PLANS TESTED: Aggregation and Disaggregation

For purposes of applying the ratio percentage and nondiscriminatory classification tests,[1] an employer *may* take two or more of its separate plans and treat them as a single plan.[2] Once this election is made, the employer must carry this over to Code Sec. 401(a)(4) and treat those separate plans as a single plan for testing nondiscrimination in contributions and benefits.[3]

However, an employer may *not* aggregate the following plans for purposes of the ratio percentage and nondiscriminatory classification tests:[4]

1. separate plans that are required to be disaggregated under IRS Reg. § 1.410(b)-7(c),

2. separate plans that would be disaggregated under IRS Reg. § 1.410(b)-7(c) if they were portions of the same plan, and

3. ESOPs, except as permitted under IRS regulations.[5]

Also, plans having different plan years may not be aggregated.[6]

A plan cannot be combined with two or more plans to form more than one single plan.

> **Example:** An employer maintains plans A, B, and C. Neither plans A and B or A and C can be aggregated to form two single plans. However, the permissive aggregation rules may be used to form any one of the following combinations— plan ABC; plans AB and C; plans AC and B; or plans A and BC.[7]

Permissive aggregation regarding separate lines of business

For purposes of applying the ratio percentage and nondiscriminatory classification tests, an employer may aggregate the portions of two or more plans that benefit employees of the same qualified separate line of business. This aggregation may be done regardless of whether the employer aggregates the portions of the same plans that benefit employees of the other qualified separate lines of business of the employer.[8]

Mandatory disaggregation

If a single plan[9] benefits employees of more than one "disaggregation population," the plan must be disaggregated and treated as separate plans, each separate plan consisting of the portion of the plan benefiting the employees of each disaggregation population.[10]

Disaggregation populations of employees. A disaggregation population is determined by the employees benefiting under the plan. The following rules apply:[11]

1. *If the plan benefits employees of more than one qualified separate line of business (QSLOB),* the employees of each QSLOB are separate disaggregation populations.[12] Here the portion of the plan benefiting employees of each QSLOB is treated as a separate plan maintained by that QSLOB. However, if the plan is tested as an employer-wide plan rather as separate QSLOBs, employees of different QSLOBs are *not* separate disaggregation populations.[13]

2. *If a plan covers both collectively bargained and noncollectively bargained employees,* each group of employees is a separate disaggregation population.[14] A separate disaggregation population also exists for each group of employees covered by separate collective bargaining agreements.

3. *If a plan benefits employees of more than one employer,* the employees of each employer are separate disaggregation populations.[15] The portion of the plan benefiting the employees of each employer is treated as a separate plan maintained by each employer. Each such separate plan has to comply with Code Sec. 410(b) by reference only to that employer's employees.

Treatment of benefit accruals and allocations. Generally, when an employer applies the mandatory disaggregation rules, the portion of the plan benefiting disaggregated populations of employees consists of all benefits accrued by (or allocations made to) employees while they were members of the disaggregation population.[16]

However, if employees who benefit under a plan change from one disaggregation population to another, benefits they accrue while in the second disaggregation population that are attributable to years of service credited while they were in the first disaggregation population can be treated as provided to them while in the first disaggregation population.[17]

In addition, if employees change from one disaggregation population to another, benefits they accrued while in the first population may be treated as provided to them in their current status.

---

[1] IRS Reg. § 1.410(b)-2(b)(2) and -4.

[2] IRS Reg. § 1.410(b)-7(d)(1).

[3] *Ibid.*

[4] IRS Reg. § 1.410(b)-7(d)(2) and (3).

[5] IRS Reg. § 54.4975-11(e).

[6] IRS Reg. § 1.410(b)-7(d)(3).

[7] IRS Reg. § 1.410(b)-7(d)(5).

[8] IRS Reg. § 1.410(b)-7(d)(4).

[9] A single plan is defined under Code Sec. 414(l).

[10] IRS Reg. § 1.410(b)-7(c)(4)(i)(A).

[11] IRS Reg. § 1.410(b)-7(c)(4)(ii)(A)-(C).

[12] IRS Reg. § 1.410(b)-7(c)(4)(ii)(A).

[13] IRS Reg. § 1.414(r)-1(c)(2)(ii) provides the rules for employer-wide testing.

[14] IRS Reg. § 1.410(b)-7(c)(4)(ii)(B).

[15] IRS Reg. § 1.410(b)-7(c)(4)(ii)(C).

[16] IRS Reg. § 1.410(b)-7(c)(4)(i)(B).

[17] IRS Reg. § 1.410(b)-7(c)(4)(i)(C)(1).

¶ 1050

NONDISCRIMINATION: Nondiscrimination Tests— In General

A plan's coverage must be nondiscriminatory for each plan year. A plan can establish that its coverage is nondiscriminatory by satisfying either (1) the ratio percentage test, (2) the average benefit percentage test (including the nondiscriminatory classification test), or (3) one of several tests relating to specific situations.[1]

---

[1] IRS Reg. § 1.410(b)-2, -4, and -5.

¶ 1055

NONDISCRIMINATION: Nondiscrimination Tests— Specific Situations

A plan may, in specific situations, satisfy the coverage requirements under Code Sec. 410(b) without having to run either the ratio percentage or average benefit percentage tests.[1]

Tax credit ESOPs

An ESOP will satisfy coverage if:[2]

1. it is a tax credit ESOP described in Code Sec. 409(a),

2. it is the only plan of the employer that the employer intends to be qualified under Code Sec. 401(a),

3. it benefits 50% or more of all the employees who are eligible under a nondiscriminatory classification, and

4. the total amount allocated to each participant's account for the year does not exceed 2% of the compensation of that participant during that year.

The second criteria is not met if the mandatory disaggregation rules require that the single plan of the employer must be treated as two or more separate plans.[3]

No nonhighly compensated employees

A plan will satisfy coverage for a plan year if the employer does not have any nonhighly compensated employees for that period.[4]

No highly compensated employees

A plan will satisfy coverage for a plan year if the plan benefits no highly compensated employees for the plan year.[5]

Collectively bargained employees

If a plan benefits only collectively bargained employees, it satisfies coverage. In those cases where a plan is mandatorily disaggregated because it benefits both collectively bargained employees and noncollectively bargained employees, the portion of the plan that benefits only collectively bargained employees satisfies coverage.[6]

Tax-sheltered annuities

A tax-sheltered annuity plan that provides only for nonelective contributions (i.e., contributions other than salary reduction elective contributions) must satisfy the coverage requirements of Code Sec. 410(b). This includes tax-sheltered annuity plans maintained by church employers.[7]

Government and church plans

The nondiscrimination rules generally applicable to tax-sheltered annuities do not apply to governmental plans.[8]

CCH Pointer: Not all governmental TSAs are exempt from the nondiscrimination rules. The Tax Relief Act of 1997 did not exempt all TSAs maintained by government employers from complying with the nondiscrimination rules. Governmental TSAs must still comply with the nondiscrimination requirements applicable to elective deferrals under Code Sec. 403(b)(12)(A)(ii).[9] The exemption provided by the Act is limited to nonelective contributions made to governmental TSAs.

The coverage requirements of Code Sec. 410(b) do not apply to state and local government plans.[10] However, the compensation limit of Code Sec. 401(a)(17) continues to apply to governmental plans. Governmental plans will be treated as meeting the nondiscrimination rules for all tax years beginning before August 5, 1997.[11]

The coverage requirements of Code Sec. 410(b), as amended by TRA '86, do not apply to church plans (as defined in Code Sec. 414(e)) unless the employer has made an election under Code Sec. 410(d) to have Code Sec. 410(b) coverage apply. Qualified church plans, however, must satisfy the coverage requirements of Code Sec. 410, as in effect prior to ERISA.

---

[1] IRS Reg. § 1.410(b)-2(b)(4) -(7).

[2] IRS Reg. § 1.410(b)-2(b)(4).

[3] *Ibid.*; IRS Reg. § 1.410(b)-7(c).

[4] IRS Reg. § 1.410(b)-2(b)(5).

[5] IRS Reg. § 1.410(b)-2(b)(6).

[6] IRS Reg. § 1.410(b)-2(b)(7) and § 1.410(b)-7(c)(5), the latter of which discusses disaggregation.

[7] IRS Reg. § 1.410(b)-2(d). See also Code Sec. 403(b)(12)(A)(i).

[8] Code Sec. 403(b)(12)(C).

[9] Comments of Theresa Lensander, President of American Pension Co., Santa Barbara, CA, speaking at the Western Region IRS/Practitioners Benefits Conference on September 18, 1997.

[10] Code Sec. 401(a)(5)(G).

[11] P.L. 105-34 (Taxpayer Relief Act of 1997), Sec. 1505(d)(2).

¶ 1060

NONDISCRIMINATION: Ratio Percentage Test

One of the two tests by which a plan may satisfy the minimum coverage requirements is referred to in regulations as the "ratio percentage test."

The ratio percentage test is satisfied for a plan year if the percentage obtained by dividing the percentage of the nonhighly compensated employees who benefit under the plan by the percentage of highly compensated employees who benefit under the plan is at least 70 percent. The percentage of employees in each category who benefit under the plan is determined by dividing the number of employees in each category who benefit under the plan by the total number of employees in that category. Percentages are rounded off to the nearest 100th of a percentage point.[1]

Example: For a plan year, the retirement plan of Apex Corporation benefits 98% of Apex's highly compensated employees and 69% of its nonhighly compensated employees. The ratio percentage of the plan for that plan year is 70.41% (69% divided by 98%). Accordingly, the plan satisfies the ratio percentage test. If the plan benefited only 68% of the nonhighly compensated employees, the test would not be satisfied because the ratio percentage would be only 69.39%.

---

[1] IRS Reg. § 1.410(b)-9.

¶ 1065

NONDISCRIMINATION: Average Benefit Test—An Overview

The alternative test by which a plan may satisfy the minimum coverage requirements is the "average benefit test." It consists of two subtests, both of which must be satisfied. These are (1) the nondiscriminatory classification test (see ¶ 1070) and (2) the average benefit percentage test (see ¶ 1075).[1]

---

[1] Code Sec. 410(b)(2); IRS Reg. §§ 1.410(b)-2(b)(3), -4, and -5.

¶ 1070

NONDISCRIMINATION: Nondiscriminatory Classification Test

A plan will meet this prong of the average benefit test if: (1) the plan benefits those employees who qualify under a classification established by the employer and (2) that classification of employees does not discriminate in favor of highly compensated employees.[1]

Reasonable classification of employees

A plan must establish a reasonable classification (based on objective business criteria) that identifies the employees who benefit under the plan (see ¶ 1025). A reasonable classification may be based on specified job categories, type of compensation (e. g., salaried or hourly), or a similar objective business criterion. An itemization of employees by name or by other specific criteria having the same effect as an itemization by name is not considered a reasonable classification.[2]

Nondiscriminatory classification

The reasonable classification must be also be nondiscriminatory. A plan can establish that the classification is nondiscriminatory by satisfying either a safe harbor test or a facts and circumstances test.[3] However, the facts-and-circumstances method is only available if the plan first avoids an *un* safe harbor that is built into the safe harbor test.[4]

Safe harbor nondiscrimination test. A classification is conclusively established to be nondiscriminatory only if the plan's "ratio percentage" for the plan year equals or exceeds its "safe harbor percentage" for that year.[5]

Ratio percentage. A plan's ratio percentage is determined as follows:[6]

Step #1   Divide the number of nonhighly compensated employees who benefit under the plan by the employer's total number of nonhighly compensated employees.

Step #2   Divide the number of highly compensated employees who benefit under the plan by the employer's total number of highly compensated employees.

Step #3   Divide (1) by (2).

The percentage determined under (3) is rounded to the nearest hundredth of a percentage point.

Safe harbor percentage. As indicated below, an employer's safe harbor percentage starts at 50%, and is then reduced by ¾ of a percentage point for each whole percentage point by which the "nonhighly compensated employee concentration percentage" (CP) exceeds 60%.[7] For example, if 64% of an employer's employees are nonhighly compensated employees, the safe harbor ratio percentage for the employer's plans is 47%. If 96% of an employer's employees are nonhighly compensated employees, the safe harbor ratio percentage for the employer's plans is 23%.

Alternative facts-and-circumstances nondiscrimination test. Even if a classification does not come within the described safe harbor, a plan may still satisfy the nondiscriminatory classification test if:[8]

1. the classification of employees must satisfy a relevant-facts-and-circumstances test, and

2. the ratio percentage equals or exceeds the "unsafe harbor percentage".

Safe and unsafe harbor percentages. A safe harbor and an unsafe harbor percentage are set forth for each "nonhighly compensated employee concentration percentage" (CP) that exceeds 60 percent.[9] The CP is the percentage of all employees of the employer who are not highly compensated employees. In determining the CP, excludable employees are not taken into account.[10]

An incremental scale *un* safe harbor begins at a ratio percentage of 40% and decreases to 20% as the concentration of nonhighly compensated employees in the employer's workforce increases. Therefore, any plan with a ratio percentage below 20% necessarily falls within an *un* safe harbor and does not satisfy coverage. A plan with a ratio percentage between the safe and *un* safe harbor ratio percentages may satisfy the nondiscrimination requirement on the basis of the facts-and-circumstances test.

The safe and *un* safe harbor percentages are shown in the following table:[11]

Nonhighly Compensated Employee Concentration Percentage	Safe Harbor Percentage	Unsafe Harbor Percentage
0—60%	50%	40%
61%	49.25%	39.25%
62%	48.50%	38.50%
63%	47.75%	37.75%
64%	47%	37%
65%	46.25%	36.25%
66%	45.50%	35.50%
67%	47.75%	34.75%
68%	44%	34%
69%	43.25%	33.25%
70%	42.50%	32.50%
71%	41.75%	31.75%
72%	41%	31%
73%	40.25%	30.25%
74%	39.50%	29.50%
75%	38.75%	28.75%
76%	38%	28%
77%	37.25%	27.25%
78%	36.50%	26.50%
79%	35.75%	25.75%
80%	35%	25%
81%	34.25%	24.25%
82%	33.50%	23.50%
83%	32.75%	22.75%
84%	32%	22%
85%	31.25%	21.25%
86%	30.50%	20.50%
87%	29.75%	20%
88%	29%	20%
89%	28.25%	20%
90%	27.50%	20%
91%	26.75%	20%
92%	26%	20%

Nonhighly Compensated Employee Concentration Percentage	Safe Harbor Percentage	Unsafe Harbor Percentage
93%	25.25%	20%
94%	24.50%	20%
95%	23.75%	20%
96%	23%	20%
97%	22.25%	20%
98%	21.50%	20%
99%	20.75%	20%

Example 1: Reliable Corporation has 240 employees (after an adjustment for excludable employees). Of these, 190 are nonhighly compensated employees and 50 are highly compensated employees. Reliable maintains a plan that benefits 80 nonhighly compensated employees and 40 highly compensated employees. Thus, the plan's ratio percentage is 52.63%—i.e., [$^{80}/_{190}$] divided by [$^{40}/_{50}$] = 42.1053% divided by 80% = 52.63%, which is below the percentage to satisfy the ratio percentage test. Reliable's CP is 79.17% ($^{190}/_{240}$); thus, Reliable's safe harbor percentage is 35.75% and its unsafe harbor percentage is 25.75%. Because the plan's ratio percentage is greater than the safe harbor percentage, the plan's classification satisfies the safe harbor test.

Example 2: The facts are the same as in Example (1), except that the plan benefits only 36 nonhighly compensated employees. The plan's ratio percentage is 26.32% ([$^{36}/_{190}$] divided by [$^{40}/_{50}$] = 18.9474% divided by 80% = 23.68%). Because this is less than the *un* safe harbor percentage (25.75%), the classification must be considered to be discriminatory.

Example 3: The facts are the same as in Example (1), except that the plan benefits 50 nonhighly compensated employees. The plan's ratio percentage is 32.89% ([$^{50}/_{190}$] divided by [$^{40}/_{50}$] = 26.3158% divided by 80% = 32.89%). This is above the *un* safe harbor percentage (25.75%) and below the safe harbor percentage (35.75%). Accordingly, the IRS may or may not determine that the classification is nondiscriminatory after considering all relevant facts and circumstances.

Relevant facts and circumstances. As noted above, a plan with a ratio percentage between the safe and *un* safe harbor ratio percentages may satisfy the nondiscrimination requirement on the basis of the facts-and-circumstances test. In determining whether a classification is discriminatory under the facts-and-circumstances test, the following (but not necessarily only the following) are considered to be relevant by the IRS:[12]

> 1. *The underlying business reason* for the classification. The more compelling the business reason underlying the classification, the more likely is that classification to be found nondiscriminatory. Reduction of the employer's cost of providing pension benefits is not a relevant business reason.

2. *The percentage of the employees benefiting.* The higher the percentage of an employer's employees who benefit under the plan, the more likely is the classification to be found nondiscriminatory.

3. *Whether the number of employees benefiting under the plan in each salary range is representative of the number of employees in each such range in the employer's work force.* In general, the more representative the percentages of employees benefiting under the plan in each salary range, the more likely is the classification to be nondiscriminatory.

4. The difference between the plan's ratio percentage and its safe harbor percentage. The smaller the difference, the more likely is the classification to be found nondiscriminatory.

5. The extent to which the plan's average benefit percentage exceeds 70 percent. (The average benefit percentage is discussed at ¶ 1075.)

¹ IRS Reg. § 1.410(b)-4(a).

² IRS Reg. § 1.410(b)-4(b).

³ IRS Reg. § 1.410(b)-4(c)(1).

⁴ IRS Reg. § 1.410(b)-4(c)(3).

⁵ IRS Reg. § 1.410(b)-4(c)(2).

⁶ IRS Reg. § 1.410(b)-9.

⁷ IRS Reg. § 1.410(b)-4(c)(4)(i).

⁸ IRS Reg. § 1.410(b)-4(c)(3).

⁹ IRS Reg. § 1.410(b)-4(c)(4).

¹⁰ IRS Reg. § 1.410(b)-4(c)(4)(iii).

¹¹ IRS Reg. § 1.410(b)-4(c)(4)(iv).

¹² IRS Reg. § 1.410(b)-4(c)(3)(ii).

¶ 1075

NONDISCRIMINATION: Average Benefit Percentage Test

The second part of the average benefit test—the average benefit percentage test—requires that the average benefit percentage (AB%) be at least 70%.[1]

The AB% is determined by dividing the actual benefit percentage for the nonhighly compensated employees in plans in the testing group for the testing period by the actual benefit percentage for the highly compensated employees in plans in the testing group for the testing period.[2] The resulting percentage is the AB%.

The actual benefit percentage for the nonhighly compensated employees (and the highly compensated respectively) is the average of the employee benefit percentages (EB%) of each employee in the group. The EB% is determined separately for each employee in the group for the testing period. In applying this aspect of the test, all employees of the employer who are not excludable under IRS Reg. § 1.410(b)-6 are taken into account, even if they are not benefiting under any plan that is taken into account.[3] (See ¶ 1020 for excludable employees.)

The determination of employee benefit percentages (EB%) under IRS regulations is quite complex. There is a general rule for determining EB%[4] and alternative methods for doing the same.[5] These rules are discussed below.

Plans benefiting both union and non-union employees

The general coverage rules relating to collectively bargained plans provide that a plan covering only employees covered under a collective bargaining agreement (CBA employees) is automatically considered to satisfy the minimum coverage requirements of the Code. Also, if a plan covers both CBA employees and non-CBA employees, the portions covering each are considered to be separate plans (with the CBA portion automatically satisfying the coverage requirements).[6]

Apparently, for the benefit of the non-CBA portion (because the CBA portion need not be concerned with the AB% test), the regulations provide that the AB% test may be satisfied on an aggregated basis (i.e., considering both CBA and non-CBA employees). In other words, even if the non-CBA portion cannot satisfy the test when considered as a separate plan, it will be considered to satisfy it if, when the two portions are aggregated, the test is satisfied. Under the regulations, the AB% test is satisfied by the aggregated plan if:[7]

1. the provisions of the plan applicable to each participant are identical to the provisions of the plan applicable to every other participant, including the plan benefit or allocation formula, any optional forms of benefit, any ancillary benefits, and any other right or feature under the plan; and

2. the plan, as aggregated, would satisfy the ratio percentage test (see ¶ 1060) if the excludable employee and mandatory disaggregation rules for CBA and non-CBA employees did not apply.[8]

Calculation of individual employee benefit percentages

In order to apply the AB% test, it is necessary to determine the benefit percentage for each individual employee (the "employee benefit percentage" or "EB%"). The following general principles must be applied in making this determination.

Contributions taken into account. Only employer-provided contributions and benefits are taken into account in determining EB%. Employee contributions (whether or not allocated to separate accounts) and benefits derived from them are not considered.[9] EB% may be determined either on a contributions or a benefits basis, as long as the same basis applies to all plans in the testing group.[10]

Testing group. The determination of the average benefit percentage and employee benefit percentages requires determining testing groups and testing periods. The "testing group" refers to the plan(s) being tested rather than the employees being tested. All plans included in the testing group, and only those plans, are taken into account in determining an employee's employee benefit percentage.[11]

Testing period. An employee's EB% is determined on the basis of plan years ending with or within the same calendar year.[12]

¶1075

Basic methods of determining employee benefit percentages. The determination of the employee benefit percentages (EB%) is coordinated with the determination of accrual rates under the nondiscrimination regulations.[13]

In general, the EB% is equal to the applicable accrual or allocation rates determined under the Code Sec. 401(a)(4) nondiscrimination regulations if all plans in the testing group for purposes of the average benefit percentage test are one aggregated plan for minimum participation and nondiscrimination testing.[14] Thus, the methods and options available for determining EB% are generally the same methods and options that an aggregated plan has under the nondiscrimination provisions (which are dependent on the types of plans being tested and on whether the aggregated plan is tested on a contributions, benefits or cross-tested basis). Additional options for determining employee benefit percentages are also provided.

Plans with differing plan years. When plans in the same testing group do not share the same plan year or accrual computation period, the EB% is determined for each group of plans that do share the same plan year or accrual computation period. The results of the separate determinations for the separate plan year groups are then aggregated for all plans in the testing group so that an employee's EB% is determined as the sum of the separate EB%.[15] Note that this rule is really an exception to the general rule that would ordinarily prohibit these plans from being aggregated if they do not share the same plan year.[16]

Plans providing early retirement benefits. If a defined benefit plan provides early retirement benefits in addition to normal retirement benefits to any highly compensated employee and the average actuarial reduction for any of these benefits beginning in the five years preceding the plan's normal retirement age is less than 4% per year, then the aggregate most valuable allocation rate, equivalent most valuable allocation rate, aggregate most valuable accrual rate, or most valuable accrual rate must be substituted for the related normal rates in determining EB%.[17]

The above modification does not apply if early retirement benefits with average actuarial reductions of less than 4% are currently available under plans in the testing group to a percentage of nonexcludable highly compensated employees that is at least 70% of the percentage of nonexcludable highly compensated employees to whom these benefits are currently available.[18]

Optional rules for determining employee benefit percentages

There are various optional rules that may be used—alone or in combination—in determining EB% for a testing period. For example, the EB% may be determined as the sum of separately determined rates or it may be determined with regard to plans of one type, such as plans that are defined contribution plans, while treating plans of another type as if they were not part of the test group.[19]

[1] IRS Reg. § 1.410(b)-5(a).

[2] IRS Reg. § 1.410(b)-5(b).

[3] IRS Reg. § 1.410(b)-5(c).

[4] IRS Reg. § 1.410(b)-5(d).

[5] IRS Reg. § 1.410(b)-5(e).

[6] IRS Reg. § 1.410(b)-2(b)(7).

[7] IRS Reg. § 1.410(b)-5(f).

[8] See IRS Reg. §§ 1.410(b)-6(d) and -7(c)(5).

[9] IRS Reg. § 1.410(b)-5(d)(2).

[10] IRS Reg. § 1.410(b)-5(d)(4).

[11] IRS Reg. § 1.410(b)-5(d)(3)(i).

[12] IRS Reg. § 1.410(b)-5(d)(3)(ii).

[13] IRS Reg. § 1.410(b)-5(d)(5).

[14] *Ibid.*

[15] IRS Reg. § 1.410(b)-5(d)(5)(ii).

[16] IRS Reg. § 1.410(b)-7(d)(5) and -5(d)(5)(ii).

[17] IRS Reg. § 1.410(b)-5(d)(7)(i).

[18] IRS Reg. § 1.410(b)-5(d)(7)(ii).

[19] IRS Reg. § 1.410(b)-5(e)(1).

¶ 1080

NONDISCRIMINATION: Testing Period

A plan must be tested for nondiscriminatory coverage over one of three optional time periods.[1]

1. ***Daily testing.*** Coverage must be satisfied on each day of the plan year.

2. ***Quarterly testing.*** Here a plan is deemed to satisfy coverage if it meets any one of the coverage tests on at least one day in each quarter of the plan year.

3. ***Annual testing.*** Coverage must be satisfied as of the last day of the plan year, taking into account all employees (or former employees) who were such on any day of the plan year. The annual testing option must be used for 401(k) and 401(m) plans, and when applying the average benefit percentage test.

Additional rules

Whichever option is used for coverage testing must be used when applying Code Sec. 401(a)(4) testing to a plan for a plan year. In the event that an employer permissibly retroactively amends a plan to correct coverage defects, these amendments are considered to be in effect as of the last day of the plan year.[2]

☐ See CCH PENSION PLAN GUIDE ¶ 1938 and ¶ 2039 for a discussion of retroactive correction of plan defects.

[1] IRS Reg. § 1.410(b)-8(a).

[2] *Ibid.*

¶ 1098

For More Information

☐ For more information on minimum coverage requirements, see CCH PENSION PLAN GUIDE ¶ 1125-1146 and ¶ 1957-2043.

Nondiscrimination Rules

¶ 1100

Overview of Nondiscrimination Rules

Ensuring that a plan complies with the form and operational requirements of the Internal Revenue Code's various nondiscrimination rules is a difficult task facing plan sponsors. Nondiscrimination simply means that contributions and benefits under a qualified plan cannot favor highly compensated employees of the employer, and that employees of the employer must participate in the plan on the same basis. While that statement of the nondiscrimination requirements is fairly uncomplicated, the rules that enforce it are formidable.

A brief review of the following nondiscrimination rules that must be satisfied bears witness to this burden:

1. Code Sec. 401(a)(4)—nondiscrimination in the amount of contributions and benefits (¶ 1110 and following).

2. Code Sec. 410(b)—nondiscriminatory coverage of employees. In general a plan can meet the minimum coverage test by satisfying either a ratio percentage test or average benefit test (¶ 1000 and following).

3. Code Sec. 401(a)(17)—determination of whether a plan observes the limitation on annual compensation of each employee ($245,000 for 2011; $250,000 for 2012) that may be taken into account under the plan (¶ 545 and following).

4. Code Sec. 414(s)—permissible definitions of compensation that do not result in highly compensated employees receiving nondiscriminatory contributions or benefits (¶ 1170 and following).

5. Code Secs. 401(l) and 401(a)(5)—integration of plan benefits with Social Security—"permitted disparity" (¶ 1135 and following).

6. Code Sec. 414(r)—whether an employer may test the minimum coverage and minimum participation requirements under the separate line of business (SLOB) regulations (¶ 1300 and following).

7. Code Sec. 410(a) minimum participation requirements (¶ 700 and following).

8. Code Sec. 401(a)(26) additional minimum participation requirements that impact on the employer's establishment of its plan and benefit structures (¶ 1178 and following).

Each of these rules is explained either in this chapter or other chapters so that plan sponsors can be familiar with how the nondiscrimination requirements affect plan drafting and plan operation.

¶ 1102

NONDISCRIMINATION IN CONTRIBUTIONS AND BENEFITS: General Rules

A plan will not qualify unless the contributions or benefits provided under the plan do not discriminate in favor of highly compensated employees.[1] A highly compensated employee is any employee who:[2]

1. was a 5% owner at any time during the year or preceding year, or

2. for the preceding year

    a. had compensation from the employer in excess of $115,000 for 2012 ($110,000 for 2011),[3] and

    b. if the employer elects, was in the top-paid group of employees (i.e., top 20% of employees by compensation) for that preceding year.

---

[1] Code Sec. 401(a)(4).

[2] Code Sec. 414(q)(1).

[3] This amount is indexed for inflation under Code Sec. 415(d). See IR-2011-103, 10-20-2011, CCH Pension Plan Guide ¶ 17,037Q.

¶ 1105

NONDISCRIMINATION IN CONTRIBUTIONS AND BENEFITS: Relation to Other Nondiscrimination Rules

The Internal Revenue Code provides a multitude of rules that a plan must satisfy to comply with the requirements for plan qualification, all of which are geared generally to preventing plans from favoring HCEs over nonHCEs and to ensuring that promised benefits are paid at retirement or when required under the terms of the plan. Code Sec. 401(a)(4), which requires that contributions and benefits be provided in a nondiscriminatory manner, interacts with all these other provisions. In this regard, an employer has to be concerned with the following qualification requirements:

1. Whether its plan provides nondiscriminatory coverage of employees.[1]

2. Whether the plan provides for the limitation on annual compensation ($250,000 for 2012; $245,000 for 2011) for each employee that may be taken into account under the plan.[2]

3. Whether the plan sets forth permissible definitions of compensation.[3]

4. Whether, and to what extent, there is "permitted disparity," i.e., the level to which a plan may integrate its benefits with Social Security.[4]

5. Whether an employer may test the minimum coverage and minimum participation requirements under the separate line of business (SLOB) regulations.[5] Those regulations provide an employer with a certain amount of flexibility in splitting its employee workforce into separate testing groups generally depending on the organizational and structural separateness of its lines of business.

6. Whether there are additional minimum participation requirements that impact on the employer's establishment of its plan and benefit structures. This provision requires all qualified retirement plans to cover the lesser of (a) 50 employees or (b) the greater of (i) 40% of the employee workforce or (ii) two employees (or one employee, if that is the only employee).[6]

Medical benefits for retired employees

If a pension or annuity plan provides medical benefits for retired employees under a separate account as described in Code Sec. 401(h), that account and the portion of the plan that provides retirement benefits are tested separately. Therefore, the 401(h) medical account is not required to satisfy the nondiscriminatory amount requirement.[7]

Collectively bargained plans

A collectively bargained plan (including one maintained by a government entity) will automatically satisfy Code Sec. 401(a)(4) if it satisfies certain minimum coverage rules.[8] A collectively bargained plan automatically satisfies the minimum coverage requirements if it benefits only collectively bargained employees.

If a plan covers both collectively bargained and noncollectively bargained employees, the portion of the plan that benefits solely collectively bargained employees automatically satisfies this requirement.

Rollovers

If there has been a tax-free rollover of a portion of a plan participant's accrued benefit[9] or an elective transfer,[10] those transferred assets are not subject to testing under the discriminatory amount requirement (relating to benefits and contributions) in the transferee plan.[11]

CCH Pointer: In the case of rollovers to qualified plans, it is not necessary for the distributing plan to have a determination letter from the IRS.[12]

Allocation of earnings

A defined contribution plan will not satisfy the nondiscriminatory amount requirement for contributions or benefits if the manner in which income, expenses, gains, or losses are allocated to employees' accounts causes discrimination in favor of HCEs.[13]

¶1105

Reemployed veterans

Qualified retirement plans subject to the requirements of the Uniformed Services Employment and Reemployment Act of 1994 (USERRA) may allow veterans returning to employment from military service to make up employee contributions and elective deferrals that were not made during the employee's period of military service. USERRA allows this without risking disqualification of the plan for violating the limits on contributions and benefits applicable to qualified plans.[14] In addition, make up contributions, additional elective deferrals, employer matching contributions, and employee contributions made on behalf of reemployed veterans in compliance with USERRA will not cause a plan to violate the nondiscrimination rules.

Defining the plan

IRS regulations provide special rules for defining the "plan" that is to be used for testing purposes. Because of the close relationship between the testing of coverage under Code Sec. 410(b) and contribution or benefits under Code Sec. 401(a)(4), the definition of a plan must be the same for both purposes. Therefore, if the mandatory disaggregation rules or permissive aggregation rules are applied under Code Sec. 410(b), the resulting plan or plans must also be used for testing under Code Sec. 401(a)(4).[15]

Restructuring

Under certain circumstances, a plan may be restructured into two or more plans on the basis of employee groups. If restructuring is permitted, each resulting plan must separately satisfy Code Secs. 401(a)(4) for benefits and contributions and 410(b) for coverage. The benefit of restructuring is that it provides an opportunity to comply with Code Sec. 401(a)(4) by using component plans where the single plan does not comply. It does not necessarily follow, however, that a restructured plan will satisfy both Code provisions so care in testing is essential.[16] Restructuring is not allowed for 401(k) and 401(m) plans to comply with ADP/ACP testing.[17]

Plan year

As a general rule, it is the plan year that is used for testing of discrimination in contributions and benefits. Therefore, compensation, benefit accruals, timing of contributions, and other events that relate to the application of the nondiscrimination regulations are based on the plan year. The plan year is the plan year that is defined in the written document or, in the absence of a plan definition, as the calendar year.[18]

Vesting

In addition to a general rule which provides that a plan's vesting schedule must not discriminate in the manner in which benefits are accrued, there is a special rule relating to the "deemed equivalence of statutory vesting schedules." [19]

"Deemed equivalence" works pursuant to the following rule. The manner in which employees vest in their accrued benefits under the vesting schedules in

Code Secs. 411(a)(2)(A) and (B) are treated as equivalent to each other; and the ways in which employees vest in their accrued benefits under Code Sec. 416(b)(1)(A) and (B) for top-heavy plans are treated as equivalent to each other.[20]

There is also a safe harbor. It provides that the manner in which employees vest in their accrued benefits under a plan is deemed nondiscriminatory if each combination of plan provisions that affects the nonforfeitability of any employee's accrued benefit would satisfy the nondiscriminatory availability requirements (IRS Reg. § 1.401(a)(4)-4) if that combination was another right or feature.[21]

Crediting service

There are extensive rules regarding the manner in which an employee's service is credited under a plan. Unless these rules are complied with, a plan will not satisfy the nondiscriminatory amount or availability requirements under IRS Reg. § 1.401(a)(4)-1(b)(2) and (3). In applying these rules, only actual service with the employer may be taken into account.[22]

Government plans

Government plans are exempt from the rule barring discrimination in contributions and benefits in favor of highly compensated employees.[23]

CCH Pointer: The exemption from the nondiscrimination rules for all government plans was enacted by the Pension Protection Act of 2006 (P.L. 109-280), effective for years beginning after August 17, 2006. Prior to amendment by PPA, the exemption technically applied only to plans maintained by state and local governments, although non-state and local government plans had been deemed to satisfy the nondiscrimination rules pending issuance of final regulations.[24]

---

[1] Code Sec. 410(b).

[2] Code Sec. 401(a)(17); IR-2011-103, 10-20-2011, CCH Pension Plan Guide ¶ 17,037Q.

[3] Code Sec. 414(s).

[4] Code Sec. 401(l).

[5] Code Sec. 414(r).

[6] Code Sec. 401(a)(26). See the Small Business Job Protection Act of 1996 (P.L. 104-188), Act Sec. 1432(a).

[7] IRS Reg. § 1.401(a)(4)-1(c)(14).

[8] See IRS Reg. § 1.410(b)-2(b)(7) and IRS Reg. § 1.401(a)(4)-1(c)(5).

[9] Code Secs. 402(c), 402(e)(6), 403(a)(4) or (5), or 408(d)(3).

[10] IRS Reg. § 1.411(d)-4, Q&A-3(b).

[11] IRS Reg. § 1.401(a)(4)-1(c)(9).

[12] P.L. 105-34 (Taxpayer Relief Act of 1997), Sec. 1509.

[13] IRS Reg. § 1.401(a)(4)-1(c)(8).

[14] Code Sec. 414(u).

[15] IRS Reg. § 1.401(a)(4)-9(a). In general, the aggregation/disaggregation rules refer to the combining of more than one plan into a single plan for testing purposes, or the separating of a single plan into two or more plans. IRS Reg. § 1.401(a)(4)-9(b) sets forth these rules as they pertain to nondiscrimination in contributions or benefits.

[16] IRS Reg. § 1.401(a)(4)-9(c).

[17] IRS Reg. § 1.401(a)(4)-9(c)(3)(ii).

[18] IRS Reg. § 1.401(a)(4)-1(c)(3) and § 1.401(a)(4)-12.

[19] IRS Reg. § 1.401(a)(4)-11(c).

[20] IRS Reg. § 1.401(a)(4)-11(c)(2).

[21] IRS Reg. § 1.401(a)(4)-11(c)(3).

[22] IRS Reg. § 1.401(a)(4)-1(c)(11) and -11(d).

[23] Code Sec. 401(a)(5)(G), as amended by P.L. 109-280 (Pension Protection Act of 2006), Act Sec. 861(a)(1).

[24] See IRS Notice 2003-6, 2003-1 CB 298, January 21, 2003, CCH Pension Plan Guide ¶ 17,125P, modifying Notice 2001-46, 2001-2 CB 122, August 6, 2001, CCH Pension Plan Guide ¶ 17,121R.

¶ 1110

NONDISCRIMINATION IN CONTRIBUTIONS AND BENEFITS: Discrimination in Amount—An Overview

The IRS has developed comprehensive rules for testing whether contributions and benefits are nondiscriminatory "in amount" under defined contribution and defined benefit plans. These rules are summarized as follows:

In the case of DC and DB plans, the nondiscriminatory amount requirement can be met in the following ways:

1. by safe harbor testing;

2. by a much more burdensome general nondiscrimination test where discrimination is tested on a participant-by-participant basis;

3. on a cross-testing basis where, in the case of a DC plan, allocations are converted into equivalent accruals as under a DB plan; and in the case of a DB plan, where accruals are converted to equivalent allocations as under a DC plan, including a special safe harbor for the DB portion of a floor-offset arrangement; or

4. on a restructured basis.

Data collection requirements

The IRS provides detailed rules relating to data substantiation guidelines that must be followed by employers demonstrating compliance with the nondiscrimination requirements for benefits and contributions.[1]

---

[1] Rev. Proc. 93-42, 1993-2 CB 540, superseded in part by Rev. Proc. 95-34, 1995-2 CB 385.

¶ 1115

NONDISCRIMINATION IN CONTRIBUTIONS AND BENEFITS: Discrimination in Contributions and Benefits

The fact that highly compensated employees may receive a greater absolute portion of the benefits provided by a plan does not mean that the plan is discriminatory within the meaning of the Internal Revenue Code. There are two situations that will not be considered discriminatory in and of themselves:

1. The first is where the contributions or benefits under the plan bear a uniform relationship to compensation. Thus, if a plan provides for contributions equal to 10% of an employee's salary, the fact that an employee earning $120,000 will have a contribution of $12,000 made on his or her behalf, while a $20,000 a year

employee will have only a $2,000 contribution made on his or her behalf, does not make the plan discriminatory.[1]

2. Plans may take into account Social Security benefits in addition to compensation in determining whether contributions or benefits bear a uniform relationship to compensation. However, a plan must meet disparity limits relating to contributions or benefits under such an integrated plan.[2] See ¶ 1200 and following.

In the case of contributions and benefits, a plan may not be discriminatory on paper, but may prove to be discriminatory in practical operation. The law is concerned not only with the wording of the plan, but also with how the plan operates in practice.[3]

Basic requirements

IRS regulations provide the structure for determining whether a plan is discriminatory in contributions or benefits, and set forth three basic requirements.[4]

1. *Either* contributions or benefits provided under a plan must be nondiscriminatory in amount. A plan is not required to prove nondiscrimination in amount for both contributions and benefits.

2. Benefits, rights, and features provided under the plan must be made available to participants in a nondiscriminatory manner.

3. The timing of plan amendments must not have the effect of discriminating significantly in favor of highly compensated employees, and plan terminations must be nondiscriminatory.

The manner in which employees vest in their accrued plan benefits also must not discriminate in favor of highly compensated employees.[5]

Testing mechanisms. The IRS provides two basic testing alternatives for determining nondiscrimination in the amounts of contributions and benefits. These are safe-harbor testing and general testing.

Safe-harbor testing focuses primarily on the provisions of the plan and provides design-based or simplified testing methods for plans with essentially uniform benefits. The uniformity requirements of the safe harbors sufficiently reduce the risk of discrimination in the amount of contributions or benefits so that no further testing of actual results is considered necessary.[6]

In contrast, general testing focuses on actual results under the plan and permits plans providing for diversity in contributions or benefits to demonstrate that, despite this diversity, the plan satisfies the nondiscrimination requirements.

---

[1] Code Sec. 401(a)(5)(B).

[2] Code Sec. 401(a)(5)(C).

[3] IRS Reg. § 1.401(a)(4)-1(a).

[4] IRS Reg. § 1.401(a)(4)-1.

[5] IRS Reg. § 1.401(a)(4)-11(c).

[6] Preamble to T.D. 8485, published in the *Federal Register* on September 3, 1993 (58 FR 46773).

¶ 1120

NONDISCRIMINATION IN CONTRIBUTIONS AND BENEFITS: Contributions and Benefits Under Multiple Plans

A pension and profit-sharing plan may be combined and treated as a single plan for purposes of the coverage requirements. The fact that the plans meet the coverage requirements when considered as a single plan does not mean that the single plan is necessarily qualified. It still must not discriminate in favor of highly paid employees in contributions and benefits. When a defined benefit pension plan and a profit-sharing plan are treated as a single plan, the two plans will be considered comparable and the combined plan as qualified, if it can be shown that *either* the benefits or the contributions are nondiscriminatory.[1] This comparison ordinarily involves actuarial computations converting the profit-sharing contributions into projected benefits.

Special rules apply where an employer maintains two or more plans considered as a single plan where contributions or benefits vest at different rates. The following rules apply to contributions or benefits for purposes of determining whether two or more plans of an employer satisfy the general nondiscrimination rules when considered as a single plan.

Contributions

If two or more plans of an employer are considered as a single plan, the plans will not be discriminatory simply because the rights of employees to, or derived from, the employer contributions under the separate plans do not become nonforfeitable at the same rate. This rule applies if the amount of contributions on behalf of the employees allowed as a plan deduction for the taxable year, taken together, bears a uniform relationship to the compensation of the employees.[2]

Benefits

If the employees' rights to benefits under the separate plans do not become nonforfeitable at the same rate, but the level of benefits provided by the separate plans satisfy IRS requirements that take into account such differences in rates, the plan will not be considered discriminatory simply because of the difference in rates.[3]

---

[1] Code Sec. 401(a)(5)(E).

[2] Code Sec. 401(a)(5)(E)(i).
[3] Code Sec. 401(a)(5)(E)(ii).

¶ 1125

NONDISCRIMINATION IN CONTRIBUTIONS AND BENEFITS: Benefits Test for Pension Plans

Employer-provided benefits under a defined benefit plan must be nondiscriminatory in amount. There are design-based safe harbors that enable unit credit and flat benefit plans that furnish uniform benefits to meet the nondiscriminatory amount test without making a determination and comparison of actual benefits under the plan.[1] Plans that do not offer uniform benefits must meet a general test that requires a determination of individual benefit accrual rates.

Uniformity requirements

The safe harbors generally require that:[2]

1. A uniform benefit formula provide all plan participants with an annual benefit payable in the same form and beginning at the same uniform normal retirement age.

2. Benefits beginning after normal retirement age must be provided at the same percentage of average annual compensation or the same dollar amount as benefits payable at normal retirement age to employees with the same years of service at normal retirement age.

3. Each subsidized optional benefit (such as early retirement or joint and survivor benefits) must be available to substantially all employees in the plan.

4. The same vesting schedule and definition of years of service apply to all employees for all purposes under the plan.

5. The plan may not be a contributory defined benefit plan.

Example: Plan A provides a normal retirement benefit equal to 2% of average annual compensation times each year of service commencing at age 65 for all employees. Plan A provides that employees of Division S receive their benefit in the form of a straight life annuity and that employees of Division T receive their benefit in the form of a life annuity with an automatic cost-of-living increase. Plan A does not provide a uniform normal retirement benefit because the annual benefit is not payable in the same form to all employees.

CCH Pointer: A defined benefit plan that utilizes a safe harbor may take into account the increased Code Sec. 415 limits implemented by EGTRRA (see ¶ 515) as of the first day of the first limitation year for which the increased limits are effective for the plan without violating the uniformity requirements of IRS Reg. § 1.401(a)(4)-3(b)(2).[3]

Safe harbor for unit credit plans

The first safe harbor applies to unit credit plans. A unit credit plan is an arrangement that contains a benefit formula under which all employees accrue a fixed benefit (either as a percentage of compensation or a fixed dollar amount) for each year of service, and all employees with the same number of years accrue the same benefit.

133⅓% rule safe harbor. A unit credit plan will meet the safe harbor if:

1. The benefit accrued for a later year is not more than 133⅓% of the benefit accrued for the current year.

2. Accrued plan benefits for any plan year are calculated by application of the plan's benefit formula to an employee's years of service and (if applicable) average annual compensation, as of that plan year.[4] The rule ensures that employees with the same years of service have an accrued benefit that is the same percentage of compensation or the same dollar amount.

Safe harbor for fractional accrual plans

This safe harbor allows plans that calculate retirement benefits under a unit credit formula, but that accrue benefits under the fractional accrual rules of Code Sec. 411(b)(1)(C) to qualify as nondiscriminatory on the basis of plan design even if all employees with the same number of years of service do not accrue the same benefit.[5] No employee under the rule may accrue in a plan year a portion of the normal retirement or post-normal retirement benefit (expressed as a percentage of average annual compensation or as a dollar amount) that is more than $\frac{1}{3}$ larger than the portion of the same benefits accrued by any other employee in the plan (disregarding employees with more than 33 years of projected service).[6]

Safe harbor for flat benefit plans. The safe harbor for fractional accrual plans has special provisions that apply to flat benefit plans that satisfy the fractional accrual rule (i.e., a plan providing a benefit of 50% of average annual compensation, accrued ratably over all years of service). A flat benefit is a benefit provided at the same percentage of average annual compensation, or the same dollar amount, for all plan participants with a minimum number of years of service at normal retirement age (reduced pro rata for employees with less than minimum service at retirement age). The maximum flat benefit must be accrued over a period of at least 25 years.

Alternative safe harbor for flat benefit plans. An alternative flat benefit safe harbor does not condition the benefit on 25 years of service. Here the average accrual rate of nonhighly compensated employees as a group must be at least 70% of the average accrual rate of highly compensated employees as a group. The safe harbor is applied by taking into consideration all nonexcludable employees of the employer, whether or not they are covered by the plan, and disregarding contributions and benefits under other plans of the employer.

Safe harbor for insurance contract plans

A final safe harbor is provided for insurance contract plans,[7] an arrangement that is funded exclusively through the purchase of individual insurance contracts (or similarly structured group contracts).[8] The plan's benefit formula must also satisfy either the unit credit fractional accrual safe harbor or the flat benefit accrual safe harbor if the normal retirement benefit were accrued ratably over each employee's period of participation through normal retirement age. Accordingly, an employee's years of service prior to participation in the plan may not be recognized in the benefit formula because the definition of years of service for determining the normal retirement benefit would differ from the definition of years of service for determining the accrued benefit.

¶1125

Benefits offset

A defined benefit plan may still qualify for a safe harbor even if, subject to certain conditions, it offsets benefits under the plan by benefits received by an employee under another plan maintained by the same or another employer.[9]

☐ See ¶ 1854-1858 of the CCH PENSION PLAN GUIDE for a detailed discussion of the defined benefit safe harbors, including certain plan provisions that do not affect the safe harbors and the unavailability of the safe harbors.

General test

Defined benefit plans that do not qualify for any of the safe harbors must satisfy a general test under which discrimination is tested on a participant-by-participant basis.

Rate groups. Under the general test, a rate group is established for each highly compensated employee (or lower paid employee with an equally high accrual rate) benefiting under the plan. Employees with accrual rates in the same group are treated as having the same rates. Each group must meet the minimum coverage requirements of Code Sec. 410(b) as though it were a separate plan. If each of the rate groups meets the minimum coverage test, the plan in total will be nondiscriminatory in amount.[10]

> **Example:** Y Company has only six nonexcludable employees, all of whom benefit under its retirement plan. The HCEs are H1 and H2, and the nonHCEs are N1 through N4. For the plan year, H1 and N1 through N4 have an allocation rate of 5% of plan year compensation. For the same plan year, H2 has an allocation rate of 7.5% of plan year compensation. There are two rate groups under the plan. Rate group 1 consists of H1 and all those employees who have an allocation rate greater than or equal to H1's allocation rate (5%). Thus, rate group 1 consists of H1, H2, and N1 through N4. Rate group 2 consists only of H2 because no other employee has an allocation rate greater than or equal to H2's allocation rate (7.5%).
>
> The ratio percentage for rate group 2 is zero percent—i.e., zero percent (the percentage of all nonhighly compensated nonexcludable employees who are in the rate group) divided by 50% (the percentage of all highly compensated nonexcludable employees who are in the rate group). Therefore, rate group 2 does not satisfy the ratio percentage test. Rate group 2 also does not satisfy the nondiscriminatory classification test. Therefore, rate group 2 does not satisfy Code Sec. 410(b) and, as a result, does not satisfy the general nondiscrimination test.

☐ See ¶ 1858 and 1866-1878 of the CCH PENSION PLAN GUIDE for a detailed discussion of the defined benefit plan general nondiscrimination test, including testing by automatic compliance, determination of accrual rates, compensation rules, and special testing rules.

¶1125

Restructuring

Employers may restructure or divide a single defined benefit plan into component plans and test each of the components separately in order to meet the safe harbors or the general test. If each component satisfies the nondiscrimination rules as a separate plan, the plan will be treated as nondiscriminatory.[11] An employer may utilize any criteria in allocating employees to a component plan. However, each employee may be included in only one component plan for a plan year. In addition, each plan must consist of the allocations, accruals, and other benefits, rights, and features provided to a selected group of employees in the plan.[12]

Testing on basis of equivalent contributions

A defined benefit plan may alternatively satisfy the nondiscrimination requirement on the basis of equivalent contribution allocation rates ("cross- testing").[13] IRS rules contain methods for converting benefits to equivalent normal and most valuable allocation rates.

Compensation rules for defined benefit plans

A definition of compensation is required in a qualified plan where compensation is used as the basis for determining plan contributions or benefits. Generally, Code Sec. 414(s) provides the definition of compensation for this purpose, and must be relied upon where it is referred to specifically by other Code provisions.[14]

Early retirement window benefits

Early retirement window benefits are taken into account for defined benefit testing, even if these benefits are not offered under permanent plan provisions and even if they are only offered to employees whose employment terminates within a specified period of time.[15]

An early retirement window benefit is defined as an "early retirement benefit, retirement-type subsidy, QSUPP, or other optional form of benefit under a plan that is available, or a change in the plan's benefit formula that is applicable only to employees who terminate employment within a limited period of time specified by the plan (not to exceed one year) under circumstances specified by the plan." An amendment that only extends the limited window period is not treated as a separate early retirement window benefit provided that the extended period satisfies the foregoing rules. Any other amendment to an early retirement window benefit creates a separate benefit.[16]

Social Security retirement age

For plan years beginning on and after January 1, 1997, the Social Security retirement age (SSRA) is to be treated as a uniform retirement age.[17] This expands the definition of testing age under the regulations.[18] The regulations provide that, if a plan does not provide a uniform normal retirement age, the employees' testing age is 65. Now, whatever the SSRA is at a given time, it is treated as uniform.

---

[1] IRS Reg. § 1.401(a)(4)-3(b).

[2] IRS Reg. § 1.401(a)(4)-3(b)(2).

[3] Rev. Rul. 2001-51, Q&A-11, 2001-2 CB 427, CCH Pension Plan Guide ¶ 19,945N.

[4] IRS Reg. § 1.401(a)(4)-3(b)(3).

[5] IRS Reg. § 1.401(a)(4)-3(b)(4).

[6] IRS Reg. § 1.401(a)(4)-3(b)(4)(i)(C).

[7] As defined in Code Sec. 412(i) and that satisfies the accrual rule of Code Sec. 411(b)(1)(F) and stipulated funding requirements.

[8] IRS Reg. § 1.401(a)(4)-3(b)(5).

[9] IRS Reg. § 1.401(a)(4)-11(d)(3)(i)(D).

[10] IRS Reg. § 1.401(a)(4)-3(c).

[11] IRS Reg. § 1.401(a)(4)-9(c).

[12] IRS Reg. § 1.401(a)(4)-9(c)(2).

[13] IRS Reg. § 1.401(a)(4)-8(c)(2).

[14] IRS Reg. § 1.401(a)(4)-3(e).

[15] IRS Reg. § 1.401(a)(4)-3(f)(4).

[16] IRS Reg. § 1.401(a)(4)-3(f)(4)(iii).

[17] Code Sec. 401(a)(5)(F)(i).

[18] IRS Reg. § 1.401(a)(4)-12.

¶ 1130

NONDISCRIMINATION IN CONTRIBUTIONS AND BENEFITS: Contributions Test for Defined Contribution Plans

The amount of contributions under a defined contribution plan may not discriminate in favor of highly compensated employees. Plans that provide uniform allocations may utilize one of two safe harbors to establish nondiscrimination in amount.[1] Defined contribution plans that do not satisfy the safe harbors must meet a general test that requires employers to demonstrate nondiscrimination in allocation rates.[2]

☐ For nondiscrimination testing for 401(k) plans, including utilization of the safe harbor for 401(k) plans, see ¶ 2975.

Uniform allocation formula safe harbor

This design-based safe harbor provides the most traditional DC plan formula under which contributions and forfeitures are allocated to participants' accounts based on the same percentage of compensation, the same dollar amount for every participant, or the same dollar amount for each uniform unit of service (not to exceed one week) performed by the employee during the plan year.[3] Permitted disparity may be used in conjunction with this safe harbor.[4] See ¶ 1135.

The classic example of this safe harbor is the plan that allocates contributions and forfeitures to each participants account under the following formula:

$$\text{Contribution} = 15\% \text{ of profits} \times \frac{\text{Each participant's compensation}}{\text{Total compensation}}$$

CCH Pointer: A defined contribution plan that utilizes a safe harbor may take into account the increased Code Sec. 415 limits implemented by EGTRRA (see ¶ 525) as of the first day of the first limitation year for which the increased limits are effective for the plan without violating the uniformity requirements of IRS Reg. § 1.401(a)(4)-2(b).[5]

Uniform allocation formula weighted for age or service

This safe harbor pertains to "uniform points plans" and should not be confused with age-weighted DC plans under which discrimination is tested under the more strict, general nondiscrimination test. Generally, a uniform points plan will satisfy the safe harbor if the average rate of allocation for HCEs does not exceed the average rate of allocation for nonHCEs. There is a two-prong requirement for this safe harbor:[6]

1. The safe harbor is only applicable to plans in which points are provided to participants on a uniform basis taking into account compensation, age, and service.

2. An employee's allocation for a plan year is determined by multiplying the total amount to be allocated to all employees by a fraction, the numerator of which is the employee's points for the plan year and the denominator of which is the sum of the points for all employees in the plan for the plan year.

The dollar amount of allocations *may vary solely on account of* compensation, age, years of service, or years of plan participation. However, each participant in the plan must receive the same number of points for each year of age, year of service, and the same number of points for each unit of plan year compensation. Points need not be given for both age and service, but must be given for at least one of them.[7] A uniform points plan may not be an ESOP,[8] nor may the permitted disparity rules be used for this safe harbor.[9]

Example: Plan A has a single allocation formula that applies to all employees, under which each employee's allocation for the plan year equals the product of the total of all amounts taken into account for all employees for the plan year and a fraction, the numerator of which is the employee's points for the plan year and the denominator of which is the sum of the points of all employees for the plan year. Plan A grants each employee 10 points for each year of service (including pre-participation service and imputed service credited under Plan A) and one point for each $100 of plan year compensation. For the plan year, the total allocations are $71,200, and the total points for all employees are 7,120. Each employee's allocation for the plan year is set forth in the table below.

Employee	Years of Service	Plan Year Compensation	Points	Amount of Allocation	Allocation Rate
H1	20	$150,000	1,700	$17,000	11.3%
H2	10	$150,000	1,600	$16,000	10.7%
H3	30	$100,000	1,300	$13,000	13.0%
H4	3	$100,000	1,030	$10,300	10.3%
N1	10	$40,000	500	$5,000	12.5%
N2	5	$35,000	400	$4,000	11.4%
N3	3	$30,000	330	$3,300	11.0%
N4	1	$25,000	260	$2,600	10.4%

¶1130

Employee	Years of Service	Plan Year Compensation	Points	Amount of Allocation	Allocation Rate
Total	—	—	7,120	$71,120	—

For the plan year, Plan A allocates amounts under a uniform points allocation formula.

For the plan year, the average allocation rate for the HCEs (HI through H4) is 11.3% and the average allocation rate for nonHCEs (N1 through N4) is 11.3%. Because the average of the allocation rates for the HCEs does not exceed the average of the allocation rates for the nonHCEs, Plan A satisfies the safe harbor rule for the plan year.

General test

Defined contribution plans that do not satisfy any of the safe harbors must meet a general test under which no highly compensated plan participant may have an allocation rate greater than that of any rank-and-file participant.[10]

Rate groups. Under the general test, a rate group is established for each highly compensated employee (or lower paid employees with equally high allocation rates) benefiting under the plan. Each group must meet the minimum coverage requirement of Code Sec. 410(b) as though it were a separate plan. If each of the rate groups meet the minimum coverage test, the plan in total will be nondiscriminatory in amount.[11] A rate group exists for each HCE in the plan and consists of that HCE and all other HCEs and nonHCEs in the plan who have an allocation rate greater than or equal to that HCE's allocation rate.[12]

Allocation rate defined. An employee's allocation rate is the sum of employer contributions and forfeitures for the plan year, expressed either as a percentage of compensation or as a dollar amount.[13] These rates must be determined in a consistent manner for all employees.[14]

Allocation taken into account. In determining allocation rates, amounts taken into account include all employer contributions and forfeitures for the plan year, but not earnings, expenses, gains, or losses.[15] Employer contributions include annual additions,[16] and allocations are subject to the Code Sec. 415 annual benefit limitations.[17]

Grouping of allocation rates. Grouping allows a plan to take all allocation rates that fall within 5% of a mid-point and treat them as being equal to that mid-point rate. For example, 8.49% and 7.51 may be treated as 8%. Allocation rates within a given range may not be grouped if the allocation rates of the HCEs within the range generally are significantly higher than the allocation rates of nonHCEs in that range.[18] Similarly, if allocation rates are determined as a percentage of plan year compensation, the lowest and highest allocation rates need not be within 5% of the midpoint rate if they are no more than ¼ of a percentage point above or below the mid-point rate.[19] For example, 2.24% and 1.76 can each treated as a 2% allocation rate.

Example 1: Employer X maintains two defined contribution plans, Plan A and Plan B, that are aggregated and treated as a single plan. Employee M has plan year compensation of $10,000 and receives an allocation of $200 under Plan A and an allocation of $800 under Plan B. Employee M's allocation rate under the aggregated plan for the plan year is 10% (i.e., $1,000 divided by $10,000).

Example 2: The employees in Plan C have the following allocation rates (expressed as a percentage of plan year compensation): 2.75%, 2.80%, 2.85%, 3.25%, 6.65%, 7.33%, 7.34%, and 7.35%. Because the first four rates are within a range of no more than one quarter of a percentage point above and below 3% (a midpoint rate chosen by the employer), the employer may treat the employees who have those rates as having an allocation rate of 3% (provided that the allocation rates of HCEs within the range generally are not significantly higher than the allocation rates of NHCEs within the range). Because the last four rates are within a range of no more than five percent above and below 7% (a midpoint rate chosen by the employer), the employer may treat the employees who have those rates as having an allocation rate of 7% (provided that the allocation rates of HCEs within the range generally are not significantly higher than the allocation rates of NHCEs within the range).

Overlapping of allocation rates

Grouping of allocation rates is only permissible if the specified ranges, within which all employees are treated as having the same allocation rate, do not overlap.[20]

Restructuring

Employers may restructure or divide a single defined contribution plan (other than a 401(k) or 401(m) plan) into component plans and test each of the components separately in order to meet the safe harbors or the general test.[21] If each component satisfies the nondiscrimination rules as a separate plan, the plan will be treated as nondiscriminatory.[22]

If a DC plan has different contribution formulas for different employees and the plan can be restructured into component parts, taking these differences into account, the restructured plans can satisfy the nondiscrimination in contributions requirement.[23]

Testing on basis of equivalent benefits

A defined contribution plan (other than an ESOP, 401(k), or 401(m) plan) may alternatively meet the nondiscriminatory amount requirement on the basis of equivalent benefits ("cross-testing").[24] See ¶ 1155.

---

[1] IRS Reg. § 1.401(a)(4)-2(b).

[2] IRS Reg. § 1.401(a)(4)-2(c).

[3] IRS Reg. § 1.401(a)(4)-2(b)(2).

[4] IRS Reg. § 1.401(a)(4)-2(b)(2)(ii).

[5] Rev. Rul. 2001-51, Q&A-11, 2001-2 CB 427, CCH PENSION PLAN GUIDE ¶ 19,945N.

[6] IRS Reg. § 1.401(a)(4)-2(b)(3).

[7] IRS Reg. § 1.401(a)(4)-2(b)(3)(i)(A).

[8] IRS Reg. § 1.401(a)(4)-2(b)(3)(i).

[9] IRS Reg. § 1.401(a)(4)-2(b)(2)(ii) allows disparity for the uniform allocation safe harbor, but there is not a similar provision under (b)(3) for the uniform points plan safe harbor.

[10] IRS Reg. § 1.401(a)(4)-2(c).

[11] IRS Reg. § 1.401(a)(4)-2(c)(3).

[12] IRS Reg. § 1.401(a)(4)-2(c)(2).

[13] IRS Reg. § 1.401(a)(4)-2(c)(2)(i).

[14] IRS Reg. § 1.401(a)(4)-2(c)(2)(iv).

[15] IRS Reg. § 1.401(a)(4)-2(c)(2)(ii) and (iii).

[16] As described in IRS Reg. § 1.415-6(b)(2)(i).

[17] IRS Reg. § 1.401(a)(4)-2(c)(2)(ii).

[18] IRS Reg. § 1.401(a)(4)-2(c)(2)(iv).

[19] IRS Reg. § 1.401(a)(4)-2(c)(2)(v)(A).

[20] *Ibid.*

[21] IRS Reg. § 1.401(a)(4)-2(a)(2).

[22] IRS Reg. § 1.401(a)(4)-2(a)(2).

[23] IRS Reg. § 1.401(a)(4)-9(c)(1).

[24] IRS Reg. § 1.401(a)(4)-9(c)(3)(ii). Each new plan must also satisfy the Code Sec. 410(b) coverage requirements.

¶ 1135

NONDISCRIMINATION IN CONTRIBUTIONS AND BENEFITS: Imputation of Permitted Disparity

Permitted disparity relates to the integration of Social Security retirement benefits into the overall benefits/contributions formula of a qualified retirement plan.[1] It recognizes Congressional intent that certain plans not be considered discriminatory merely because they provide greater contributions or benefits for HCEs because the employer-provided benefit only comes into play for compensation in excess of the contribution or benefit level of Social Security.

Code Sec. 401(a)(5)(C) provides that "a plan shall not be considered discriminatory within the meaning of [Code Sec. 401(a)(4)] merely because the contributions or benefits of, or on behalf of, the employees under the plan favor HCEs . . . in a manner permitted under [Code Sec. 401(l)]." It is Code Sec. 401(l) which sets forth the rules under which integration with Social Security benefits in a qualified defined contribution and defined benefit plan is acceptable.

While Code Sec. 401(l) explains the limits on permitted disparity, the Code Sec. 401(a)(4) regulations demonstrate how permitted disparity is taken into account in testing whether the amount of contributions or benefits under an integrated plan is discriminatory.

Use of safe harbors

The determination of whether a plan satisfies Code Sec. 401(a)(4) may take into account permitted disparity. For purposes of satisfying the DB or DC safe harbors to establish that a plan is not discriminatory in amount, the plan must demonstrate that it satisfies the permitted disparity rules of Code Sec. 401(l) as to form.[2]

General test for nondiscrimination in amount

If a plan does not use the safe harbor rules, permitted disparity is taken into account by using specified formulas that adjust allocation or accrual rates to reflect the amount of permitted disparity that may be taken into account.[3] The adjusted rates effectively transform the allocations or accruals under the plan for each employee to determine the excess rate each employee would receive if the same dollar value of allocation or accrual had been received under a plan formula containing the maximum permitted disparity under Code Sec. 401(l). The resulting excess rates are the allocation or accrual rates that are compared to determine whether the plan is nondiscriminatory in amount.

[1] Code Secs. 401(a)(5)(C) and 401(l); and IRS Reg. § 1.401(a)(4)-7.

[2] IRS Reg. §§ 1.401(a)(4)-7(a), 1.401(l)-2, and 1.401(l)-3.

[3] IRS Reg. § 1.401(a)(4)-7(a), (b) and (c).

¶ 1140

NONDISCRIMINATION IN CONTRIBUTIONS AND BENEFITS: Availability of Benefits, Rights, and Features

The second overall test that must be complied with for a plan to satisfy Code Sec. 401(a)(4) concerns the availability of benefits, rights, and features (BR&F).[1] BR&F includes all optional forms of benefit, ancillary benefits, and other rights and features available to any employee under the plan. It is the *availability* of these BR&F that must be nondiscriminatory. On its face and in operation, a plan must provide BR&F in a nondiscriminatory manner by satisfying a dual "current availability" and "effective availability" requirement. Moreover, *each of the BR&F under the plan must separately satisfy* this dual regulatory requirement.[2]

Optional forms of benefit

This refers to a distribution alternative (including the normal form of benefit under the plan) that is available with respect to plan participants' (1) protected accrued benefits and (2) early retirement benefits and retirement-type subsidies, including qualified Social Security supplements. Generally distribution options are in the form of single sum distributions, periodic payments, or life annuities.[3] Different optional forms of benefit will exist under a plan "if the distribution alternative is not payable on substantially the same terms as another distribution alternative." Different optional forms of benefit may result from differences in payment schedules, timing, commencement, mode of distribution, election rights, differences in eligibility requirements, or the portion of the benefit to which the distribution alternative applies.[4]

If different optional forms of benefit exist, the employer must make certain that each separately satisfies the nondiscriminatory availability requirement.

Example: Plan A is a defined benefit plan that benefits all employees of Divisions S and T. The plan offers a qualified joint and 50% survivor annuity at normal retirement age, calculated by multiplying an employee's single life annuity payment by a factor. For an employee of Division S whose benefit commences at age 65, the plan provides a factor of 0.90, but for a similarly situated employee of Division T the plan provides a factor of 0.85. The qualified joint and survivor annuity is not available to employees of Divisions S and T on substantially the same terms, and thus it constitutes two separate optional forms of benefit.

Defined contribution plans may eliminate some optional forms of benefit. See ¶ 866.

Ancillary benefits

Ancillary plan benefits include Social Security supplements (other than qualified Social Security supplements),[5] disability benefits not in excess of a qualified disability benefit,[6] ancillary life insurance and health insurance benefits, death benefits under a defined contribution plan, preretirement death benefits under a defined benefit plan, plant shut-down benefits not protected from reduction under Code Sec. 411(d)(6), and other similar benefits. Different ancillary benefits exist "if an ancillary benefit is not available on substantially the same terms as another ancillary benefit." [7]

Other rights or features

This refers to any right or feature under the plan, *other than:* [8]

1. optional forms of benefit or ancillary benefits;
2. rights or features that can not reasonably be expected to be of a meaningful value to an employee; and
3. plan terms that are taken into account in determining whether separate optional forms of benefit or ancillary benefits exist.

Different rights or features will exist under a plan "if a right or feature is not available on substantially the same terms as another right or feature." [9]

Examples of "other rights and features" include:[10]

1. plan loans;
2. the right to direct investments;
3. the right to a particular form of investment;
4. the right to a particular class or type of employer security;
5. the right to determine each type of elective contribution under a cash or deferred arrangement;
6. the right to make after-tax contributions to a DB plan that are not allocated to separate accounts;
7. the right to determine each rate of employee contributions to a plan to which matching contributions can be made;[11]
8. the right to an allocation of matching employer contributions;[12]
9. the right to purchase additional retirement or ancillary benefits; and
10. the right to make and receive rollovers or transfers;

Current availability criteria

A benefit, right, or feature (BRorF) is only made available to participants in a nondiscriminatory manner if it separately satisfies a "current availability" requirement and an "effective availability" requirement.[13]

To satisfy the current availability requirement, the regulations apply the minimum coverage regulations under Code Sec. 410(b) to provide the exclusive testing mechanism. This requirement will be met only if a group of employees in the plan to which the BRorF is currently available satisfies either the ratio percentage test or the nondiscriminatory classification test. The average benefit percentage test need not be satisfied here.[14] See ¶ 1000.

Effective availability criteria

The "effective availability" test requires that, based on all the facts and circumstances, BR&F must be available for all employees without substantially favoring HCEs.[15] There is little IRS guidance on how to determine whether BR&F are effectively available. However, the IRS has provided examples which describe situations in which BR&F fail the effective availability requirement because they substantially favor HCEs.[16]

From the three examples, we know that (1) even if the group of employees to whom the BRorF is currently available satisfies the ratio percentage test of Reg. § 1.410(b)-2(b)(2), the IRS may still decide that the BRorF substantially favors HCEs, and (2) the IRS will look very carefully at the manner in which a BRorF is made available to employees, because while the form of a plan provision or amendment may be nondiscriminatory, its effect in operation may be discriminatory.

Subsidized early retirement benefits

Subsidized early retirement benefits and joint and survivor annuities will not be treated as being unavailable to employees on the same terms merely because such benefits or annuities are based in whole or in part on an employee's Social Security retirement age.[17]

Mergers and acquisitions

Where there is a change in control of a business through a stock or asset acquisition, merger, or similar transaction, a BRorF is deemed to satisfy the nondiscriminatory current and effective availability tests if the following requirements are met:[18]

1. The BRorF must satisfy the current and effective availability tests on a date selected by the employer as the latest date by which an employee must be hired by or transferred to the acquired trade or business for an employee to be included in the acquired group of employees.

2. The BRorF must be available under the plan of the current employer after the transaction on the same terms as it was available under the plan of the prior employer before the transaction. If, for example, the current employer expands the coverage of the BRorF to cover more employees than were previously covered, this criteria is not met.

Example: Sumo Corporation maintains a defined benefit plan (Plan A) with a single sum optional form of benefit for all employees. Sumo acquires Bear Corporation and merges its plan into Plan B, a defined benefit plan maintained by Bear that does not otherwise provide a single sum optional form of benefit.

Bear continues to provide the single sum optional form of benefit under Plan B on the same terms as it was offered under Plan A to all employees who were acquired in the transaction with Sumo (and to no other employees). The optional form of benefit satisfies the nondiscrimination regulations immediately following the transaction (determined without taking into account Code Sec. 410(b)(6)(C)) when tested with reference to Plan B and Bear's nonexcludable employees. Under these facts, Plan B is treated as satisfying the nondiscrimination rules with respect to the single sum optional form of benefit for the plan year of the transaction and all subsequent plan years.

Frozen participants

The nondiscriminatory availability requirements must be satisfied for each BR&F for "frozen participants," i.e., those nonexcludable employees with accrued benefits who are not currently benefiting under the plan.[19] A plan will satisfy the nondiscriminatory availability requirement if it meets any one of the following four criteria:[20]

1. The BRorF would satisfy the current and effective availability requirements if it were not available to any employee currently benefiting under the plan.

2. The BRorF would satisfy the current and effective availability requirements if all the frozen plan participants were treated as currently benefiting employees.

3. The availability of the BRorF for any frozen participant does not change that is first effective for the current year.

4. Any change in the availability of a BRorF that is first effective in the current plan year for a frozen participant is made in a nondiscriminatory manner. For example, any expansion of a BRorF to a frozen HCE or contraction of a BRorF to a nonHCE must be applied consistently for all frozen employees so that HCE and nonHCEs are treated uniformly.

Limited participants

Limited participants are employees who do not benefit under the plan and who are not frozen participants. A plan must separately satisfy the nondiscriminatory availability requirements for each benefit, right, or feature that is made available under the plan to limited participants.

Employees who have not met a plan's service requirements are not considered benefiting employees or frozen participants merely because they make rollover contributions to the plan.[21] However, the right to make a rollover contribution is a right or feature that must be made available to limited participants in a manner that does not discriminate in favor of nonexcludable highly compensated employees. Under a safe harbor issued by the IRS, a benefit, right or feature will not be discriminatory if it is currently available only to limited participants who are excluded from participation in the plan solely because they fail to meet the plan's age and service requirements.[22] The benefit, right, or feature must also satisfy the effective availability requirement of IRS Reg. § 1.401(a)(4)-4(c). A plan would meet the safe harbor if it allows rollovers by all employees who will participate once they satisfy the plan's minimum age and service requirements, but does not extend the rollover option to other employees who are excluded from participation.

Early retirement window benefits

An early retirement benefit that is only available to participants within a specified time period—i.e., a window period—is referred to as an early retirement window benefit. These are also referred to as early-out benefits and often occur when companies are attempting to pare down their workforce. If a BRorF meets the definition of an early retirement window benefit under regulations,[23] it is disregarded when applying the nondiscriminatory availability requirement to an employee, for all plan years other than the first plan year in which the BRorF is currently available to an employee.[24]

Permissive aggregation of certain BRorFs

While the general rule requires each BRorF to be tested separately, more than one BRorF may be aggregated with another BRorF if the following two requirements are met:[25]

1. One BRorF is inherently equal or greater in value than the other.

2. The BRorF that is of inherently equal or greater value separately satisfies the nondiscriminatory availability rules.

The regulations allow a pyramiding with permissive aggregation, so that a BRorF may be aggregated with another BRorF that has already been aggregated and therefore treated as a single BRorF.[26]

Certain spousal benefits

Where two or more plans have been permissively aggregated pursuant to the minimum coverage rules, the resulting plan will satisfy the nondiscriminatory availability test with respect to any nonsubsidized qualified joint and survivor annuity, qualified preretirement survivor annuity, or spousal death benefit, but only if each plan that is part of the aggregated plan satisfies the joint and survivor rules of Code Sec. 401(a)(11).[27]

Unpredictable contingent event benefits

A BRorF that is dependent upon an unpredictable contingent event occurring is tested as if the event actually occurred.[28]

---

[1] IRS Reg. § 1.401(a)(4)-4.

[2] IRS Reg. § 1.401(a)(4)-4(a).

[3] IRS Reg. § 1.401(a)(4)-4(e)(1)(i).

[4] *Ibid.*

[5] IRS Reg. § 1.401(a)(4)-12 refers to IRS Reg. § 1.411(a)-7(c)(4)(ii) for the following definition of Social Security supplement: "A benefit for plan participants which (1) commences before the age

and terminates before the age when participants are entitled to old-age insurance benefits, unreduced on account of age, under Title II of the Social Security Act and (2) does not exceed such old-age insurance benefit."

[6] Code Sec. 411(a)(9) defines a qualified disability benefit as a disability benefit provided by a plan which does not exceed the benefit which would be

provided for the participant if he separated from service at normal retirement age.

[7] IRS Reg. § 1.401(a)(4)-4(e)(2).

[8] IRS Reg. § 1.401(a)(4)-4(e)(3)(i) and (ii).

[9] Ibid.

[10] IRS Reg. § 1.401(a)(4)-4(e)(3)(iii).

[11] See IRS Reg. § 1.401(m)-1(f)(6) for a listing of those types of employee contributions.

[12] IRS Reg. § 1.401(m)-1(f)(12) defines "matching contribution" for this purpose.

[13] IRS Reg. § 1.401(a)(4)-4(a), (b), and (c).

[14] IRS Reg. §§ 1.410(b)-2(b)(2) and 1.410(b)-4.

[15] IRS Reg. § 1.401(a)(4)-4(c)(1).

[16] IRS Reg. § 1.401(a)(4)-4(c)(2) sets forth the three examples.

[17] Code Sec. 401(a)(5)(F)(i).

[18] IRS Reg. § 1.401(a)(4)-4(d)(1)(i).

[19] IRS Reg. § 1.401(a)(4)-4(d)(2).

[20] IRS Reg. § 1.401(a)(4)-3(f)(4)(iii).

[21] Rev. Rul. 96-48, 1996-2 CB 31, 9-30-96, CCH PENSION PLAN GUIDE ¶ 19,844.

[22] Ibid.

[23] IRS Reg. § 1.401(a)(4)-3(f)(4)(iii).

[24] IRS Reg. § 1.401(a)(4)-4(d)(3).

[25] IRS Reg. § 1.401(a)(4)-4(d)(4)(i).

[26] IRS Reg. § 1.401(a)(4)-4(d)(4)(ii).

[27] IRS Reg. § 1.401(a)(4)-4(d)(5).

[28] IRS Reg. § 1.401(a)(4)-4(d)(7).

¶ 1145

NONDISCRIMINATION IN CONTRIBUTIONS AND BENEFITS: Nondiscriminatory Effect of Plan Amendments and Plan Terminations

The third overall nondiscriminatory test that a plan must comply with to satisfy the Code Sec. 401(a)(4) is the requirement that the effect of a plan amendment or plan termination must not discriminate significantly in favor of HCEs.[1]

Plan amendments

IRS regulations consolidate the rules pertaining to plan amendments and grants of past service credit, in part because grants of past service credit are accomplished through plan amendment and both can be tested by a facts-and-circumstances analysis. As a general rule, the IRS looks at whether the timing of a plan amendment or series of plan amendments has the effect of discriminating "significantly" in favor of HCEs or former HCEs. This determination is made at the time the plan amendment first becomes effective, and is based on relevant facts-and-circumstances. A plan amendment or series of plan amendments includes: the establishment or termination of a plan; change in a benefit, right, or feature; change in benefit formulas; and modification of allocation formulas.[2]

Facts-and-circumstances test for significant discrimination. Several of the applicable factors used to determine the existence of significant discrimination include:

1. Relative numbers of current and former HCEs and nonHCEs affected by the plan amendment;

2. The relative accrued benefits of HCEs and nonHCEs before and after the amendment;

3. Any additional benefits provided to current and former HCEs and nonHCEs under other plans;

4. The relative length of service of current and former HCEs and nonHCEs;

5. The length of time the plan or plan provision being amended has been in effect;

6. The turnover of employees prior to the amendment; and

7. In the case of past service credits, the benefits employees and former employees would have received if the plan, as amended, had been in effect throughout the entire period for which the past service credits are granted.

Example 1: Plan A is a defined benefit plan that covered both HCEs and nonHCEs for most of its existence. The employer decides to wind up its business. In the process of ceasing operations, but at a time when the plan covers only HCEs, Plan A is amended to increase benefits and thereafter is terminated. The timing of this plan amendment has the effect of discriminating significantly in favor of HCEs.

Example 2: Plan B is a defined benefit plan that provides a Social Security supplement that is not a qualified Social Security supplement. After substantially all of the HCEs of the employer have benefited from the supplement, but before a substantial number of nonHCEs have become eligible for the supplement, Plan B is amended to reduce significantly the amount of the supplement. The timing of this plan amendment has the effect of discriminating significantly in favor of HCEs.

CCH Pointer: A plan amendment that provides benefit increases resulting from the increased Code Sec. 415 limits implemented by EGTRRA, as of the effective date of the increased limits (i.e., limitation years beginning after 2001) to either: (1) all current and former employees who have accrued benefits under the plan immediately before the effective date of the increased Code Sec. 415 limits, or (2) all employees participating in the plan that have one hour of service after the effective date of the increased Code Sec. 415 limits for the plan, will satisfy the nondiscrimination requirements.[3] Also, a plan amendment that applies EGTRRA's increased compensation limit to former employees does not violate the nondiscrimination rules.[4]

Past service credits

The rules covering past service credit (PSC) set forth both a safe harbor and the facts-and-circumstances criteria noted above, as alternative tests, to determine whether a plan amendment that grants PSC is discriminatory.[5]

Past service credit safe harbor. There are four criteria, each of which must be met to qualify for the safe harbor.[6] The timing of a plan amendment that credits past service (or increases benefits attributable to past service) is deemed not to discriminate significantly in favor of HCEs if:

1. The period for which the credit is granted does not exceed the five years immediately preceding the year in which the amendment is first effective;

2. The PSC (or benefit increase) is granted on a reasonably uniform basis to all employees;

3. Benefits attributable to the period are determined by applying the current plan formula; and

4. The service credited is service with the employer or a previous employer.

The fact that a plan grants PSC for a period longer than five years may not mean that the plan violates this nondiscrimination requirement. All it means is that the safe harbor is not an available method of testing, and that a facts-and-circumstances test will be used.[7]

Example: Widget Manufacturing Co. currently has six nonexcludable employees, two of whom, H1 and H2, are HCEs, and the remaining four of whom, N1 through N4, are nonHCEs. The ratio of present HCEs to former HCEs is significantly higher than the ratio of current nonHCEs to former nonHCEs. Widget Manufacturing establishes a defined benefit plan providing a benefit of 1% of average annual compensation per year of service, including *all* years of service prior to the establishment of the plan. H1 and H2 each have 15 years of prior service, N1 has nine years of past service, N2 has five years, N3 has three years, and N4 has one year. The timing of this plan establishment has the effect of discriminating significantly in favor of HCEs.

Pre-termination restrictions

The pre-termination restriction regulations deal specifically with the restrictions on distributions to HCEs from DB plans to prevent discrimination in favor of the HCEs in the event of early plan termination.[8] The early termination restrictions also apply to a money purchase pension plan, but only if the plan has a Code Sec. 412(a) accumulated funding deficiency or a Code Sec. 412(d) unamortized funding waiver.[9]

---

[1] IRS Reg. §§ 1.401(a)(4)-1(b)(4) and 1.401(a)(4)-5.

[2] IRS Reg. § 1.401(a)(4)-5(a)(1) and (2).

[3] Rev. Rul. 2001-51, Q&A-12, 2001-2 CB 427, CCH PENSION PLAN GUIDE ¶ 19,945N. In addition, the requirements will be met if, as of the effective date of the increased Code Sec. 415 limits for the plan, benefit increases are provided to either of the above two groups through the operation of the plan's existing provisions. However, if the increased benefits are provided only to current or former employees who are not described above through the adoption of a plan amendment, or if the plan is amended to reflect the increased limits effective later than the effective date of the EGT-RRA limits, the timing of the amendment is subject to the facts and circumstances test of IRS Reg. § 1.401(a)(4)-5(2).

[4] Rev. Rul. 2003-11, 2003-1 CB 285, CCH PENSION PLAN GUIDE ¶ 19,948G.

[5] IRS Reg. § 1.401(a)(4)-5(a)(1)-(3).

[6] IRS Reg. § 1.401(a)(4)-5(a)(3).

[7] Preamble to 1991 final regulations, 1991-2 CB 98, 107.

[8] IRS Reg. § 1.401(a)(4)-5(b)(1).

[9] IRS Reg. § 1.401(a)(4)-5(b)(4).

¶ 1150

NONDISCRIMINATION IN CONTRIBUTIONS AND BENEFITS: Contributory Defined Benefit Plans

There are distinct rules for determining whether a contributory DB plan—a plan to which employer and employee contributions are made—satisfies the nondiscriminatory amount requirement under Code Sec. 401(a)(4).[1]

A contributory DB plan must satisfy the nondiscriminatory amount requirement separately for both the benefits derived from employer contributions and benefits derived from employee contributions where the latter are not allocated to separate accounts.[2] Because of the differences in the value of the employee-provided accrual benefit, a contributory DB plan cannot take advantage of the safe-harbor testing method.

Determining the amount of the employer-derived benefit

An employee's employer-derived benefit equals the employee's total plan benefit minus the employee's employee-derived benefit under the plan, both determined as of the plan year.[3]

Employee-derived benefits

A contributory DB plan must be nondiscriminatory in the amount of the employee-derived benefit as well as the employer-derived benefit.

☐ See ¶ 1890 of the CCH PENSION PLAN GUIDE for a detailed discussion of these rules.

---

[1] IRS Reg. § 1.401(a)(4)-6.

[2] IRS Reg. § 1.401(a)(4)-6(a), (b), and (c).

[3] Code Sec. 411(c) provides the primary rules for determining the employer-derived benefit.

¶ 1155

NONDISCRIMINATION IN CONTRIBUTIONS AND BENEFITS: Cross-Testing of Contributions and Benefits

Cross-testing of contributions and benefits provides an alternative methodology for a defined contribution or a defined benefit plan to satisfy the general requirement that a plan must be nondiscriminatory in the amount of benefits and contributions that it provides.

Cross-testing for defined contribution plans

The IRS finalized regulations on cross-testing for defined contribution plans in June 2001.[1] The regulations allow certain defined contribution plans (other than ESOPs) to demonstrate compliance with the nondiscrimination requirements based on plan benefits rather than contributions. In a cross-tested defined contribution plan, contributions are converted to equivalent benefits payable at normal retirement age, using actuarial assumptions. Then these equivalent benefits are tested in a manner similar to the testing of employer-provided benefits under a defined benefit plan.[2]

In its final regulations on cross-testing, the IRS sought to address its concerns with disparate allocations in "new comparability" plans that used cross-testing in such a way that complied with the nondiscrimination requirements, but at the same time, in the IRS's view, may not have been entirely consistent with the basic principles of the nondiscrimination rules. New comparability plans utilize disparate allocation rates for highly compensated employees (or classifications of participants consisting mostly of highly compensated employees), as contrasted with the allocation rates used for other employees. The IRS undertook a review of new comparability plans prior to its finalization of the regulations on cross-testing because of its concern that in many instances highly compensated employees in such plans were receiving allocations that were high (in the 18% or 20% range), while nonhighly compensated employees were receiving allocations that were significantly lower (the IRS cited allocation rates of 3% of compensation for nonhighly compensated employees in such plans, though this rate cited by the IRS as the typical allocation rate for nonhighly compensated employees in such plans was disputed by some practitioners). The nonhighly compensated employees in these plans were receiving the lower allocation rate regardless of age of years of service.

The IRS's concern with new comparability plans extended to various other plan designs that were similar to new comparability plans, such as super-integrated plans. Super-integrated plans utilize an additional allocation rate for compensation that is in excess of a specified threshold.[3]

In the final regulations, the IRS permits the continued use of cross-testing by new comparability and other plans, but requires plans that use cross-testing to meet certain minimum requirements. More specifically, under these rules, a defined contribution plan can test on a benefits basis if it provides broadly available allocation rates, age-based allocations, or passes a gateway requiring allocation rates for nonhighly compensated employees to be at least 5% of pay or at least 1/3 of the highest allocation rate for highly compensated employees.[4]

Transition allocations. In determining whether a plan has "broadly available allocation rates," an employee's allocation can be disregarded if it is a defined benefit replacement allocation (DBRA) or another type of transition allocation (specifically, a pre-existing replacement allocation or a pre-existing merger and acquisition allocation).[5] The DBRAs and other transition allocations must satisfy various conditions in order to be excluded in determining whether a plan had broadly available allocation rates. The conditions for DBRAs are designed to allow employers to provide, in a nondiscriminatory manner, allocations replacing the retirement benefits that would have been provided under a defined benefit plan, without having to satisfy the minimum allocation gateway.[6]

DB/DC plans. Defined benefit and defined contribution plans that are tested together as a single, aggregated plan (and that are not primarily defined benefit or broadly available separate plans) may test on a benefits basis after passing a similar gateway. The DB/DC plan satisfies the minimum aggregate allocation gateway if each nonhighly compensated employee has an aggregate normal allocation rate

¶1155

that is at least one-third of the aggregate normal allocation rate of the highly compensated employee who has the highest rate or, if less, 5% of pay (provided that the highly compensated employee's rate does not exceed 25% of compensation).[7] The minimum aggregate allocation gateway is deemed to be satisfied if the allocation rate for nonhighly compensated employees is at least 7 1/2% of pay.[8]

[1] IRS Reg. § 1.401(a)(4)-8 and 1.401(a)(4)-9.

[2] Preamble to TD 8954, 66 FR 34535, June 29, 2001.

[3] *Ibid.*

[4] IRS Reg. § 1.401(a)(4)-8(b)(1)(vi).

[5] IRS Reg. § 1.401(a)(4)-8(b)(1)(iii).

[6] Rev. Rul. 2001-30, 2001-2 CB 46, July 16, 2001, CCH PENSION PLAN GUIDE ¶ 19,945C.

[7] IRS Reg. § 1.401(a)(4)-9(b)(2)(v)(D)(1).

[8] IRS Reg. § 1.401(a)(4)-9(b)(2)(v)(D)(2).

¶ 1157

NONDISCRIMINATION IN CONTRIBUTIONS AND BENEFITS: Plan Aggregation

It is essential to remember the tie-in between the minimum coverage regulations and the nondiscriminatory contributions/benefits requirements. See ¶ 1105. If two or more plans are permissively aggregated and therefore treated as a single plan under Code Sec. 410(b) for purposes of satisfying either the ratio percentage test or nondiscriminatory classification test,[1] they must also be treated as a single plan for Code Sec. 401(a)(4) nondiscrimination testing.[2]

An example would be where an employee participates in more than one defined benefit (DB) plan of an employer, and those plans have been aggregated and therefore treated as a single plan for purposes of the ratio percentage coverage test.[3] In that case the employee's benefits under both plans must be taken into account in determining the employee's accrual rates under the DB general nondiscrimination test.

DB/DC plans

There are situations where an employer will maintain a DB and a DC plan, and aggregate them for purposes of satisfying the minimum coverage rules. These aggregated plans are referred to as *DB/DC plans*. A separate set of rules are provided for testing discrimination in amount and discrimination in the availability of BR&F.[4] The general rule for DB/DC plans is that they are to be treated as a single plan for testing purposes. Because of the hybrid nature of a DB/DC plan, however, the designed-based safe harbors are not available.[5]

Nondiscrimination in availability of BR&F under a DB/DC plan. There are separate rules for satisfying the current and effective availability requirements for BR&F.[6] A DB/DC plan can automatically satisfy the *current availability* requirement[7] if:

1. the BRorF that is provided under the DC or DB plan is also provided in the DB/DC plan, and

2. the BRorF is currently available to all nonHCEs in all plans of the same type (DC or DB).

The *effective availability* requirement is met if, based on all the facts and circumstances, the group of employees to whom a BRorF is "effectively available" does not substantially favor HCEs.[8] IRS regulations provide little guidance with regard to DB/DC plans. They state that it might be difficult or impossible to provide a BRorF under a plan of a different type than the plan under which it is provided. This, in itself, is a factor that can be taken into account in determining whether the effective availability requirement is met.[9]

Example: XYZ Company amends its plan on June 30, 2011, to provide for a single sum optional form of benefit for employees who terminate from employment with XYZ after June 30, 2011, and before January 1, 2012. The availability of this single sum optional form of benefit is conditioned on the employee's having a particular disability at the time of termination of employment. The only employee of the employer who meets this disability requirement at the time of the amendment and thereafter through December 31, 2011, is a HCE. The IRS takes the position that the disability condition is disregarded in determining the current availability of the single sum optional form of benefit. Nevertheless, under these facts, the group of employees to whom the single sum optional form of benefit is effectively available substantially favors HCEs.

---

[1] IRS Reg. §§ 1.410(b)-7(d)(1), 1.410(b)-2(b)(2), and 1.410(b)-4.

[2] IRS Reg. § 1.401(a)(4)-9(a).

[3] IRS Reg. § 1.410(b)-2(b)(2).

[4] IRS Reg. § 1.401(a)(4)-9(b).

[5] IRS Reg. §§ 1.401(a)(4)-2 and 1.401(a)(4)-3.

[6] IRS Reg. § 1.401(a)(4)-4(b)(1).

[7] IRS Reg. § 1.401(a)(4)-9(b)(2)(i).

[8] IRS Reg. § 1.401(a)(4)-4(c).

[9] IRS Reg. § 1.401(a)(4)-9(b)(3)(ii).

¶ 1160

NONDISCRIMINATION IN CONTRIBUTIONS AND BENEFITS: Restructuring

Restructuring is a concept that allows a single plan (or a number of plans that are treated as one plan under the aggregation rules) to be treated as one consisting of two or more "component plans." Each component plan must separately satisfy the nondiscrimination in benefits/contribution requirements of Code Sec. 401(a)(4) and coverage requirements of Code Sec. 410(b). If each component plan satisfies these requirements, as if it was a separate plan, then the primary plan is treated as satisfying Code Sec. 401(a)(4).[1] Restructuring only helps a plan pass Code Sec. 401(a)(4), even though as a condition precedent it must satisfy Code Sec. 410(b) to do so.

Determining component plans on a restructured basis

IRS rules provide a great deal of flexibility in determining how to restructure a single plan into component plans. The bottom line is that each component plan must satisfy the nondiscrimination requirements under Code Secs. 401(a)(4) and 410(b). Each component plan must consist of all the allocations, accruals, and other benefits, rights, and features, provided to a select group of employees in the plan. An employer may devise any criteria to select the group of employees in the component plan, and these criteria may change from year to year. However, every employee must be covered under one and only one component plan for each year.[2]

Grouping related to employment can be based on a number of factors: the same worksite; employment in the same job category; employment with the same division or subsidiary, or for a unit acquired in a merger or acquisition; employment for the same number of years; employment as salaried or hourly paid employees; or coverage under the same allocation or benefit formula, or on any other basis regardless of whether it would be considered reasonable under the nondiscriminatory classification test.[3]

How a component plan satisfies the nondiscrimination requirement

A component plan must satisfy Code Sec. 401(a)(4) as if it were a single plan. For example, if there is a reference to the plan being tested, the reference should be to the component plan. If component plans are used to satisfy the defined contribution or defined benefit safe harbors, each component plan must be tested on a design basis. Moreover, if an employer attempts to satisfy the nondiscriminatory amount requirement on a cross-tested basis, equivalences are determined only after restructuring.[4]

Example: Employer X maintains a defined benefit plan. The plan provides a normal retirement benefit equal to 1% percent of average annual compensation times years of service to employees at Plant S, and 1.5% of average annual compensation times years of service to employees at Plant T. The plan may be treated as consisting of two component defined benefit plans: one providing retirement benefits equal to 1% of average annual compensation times years of service to the employees at Plant S, and another providing benefits equal to 1.5% of average annual compensation times years of service to employees at Plant T. If each component plan satisfies Code Secs. 401(a)(4) and 410(b) as if it were a separate plan, then the entire plan satisfies the nondiscrimination rules of Code Sec. 401(a)(4).

Inapplicability of restructuring

A component plan *may not use* either the safe harbor for DC plans with uniform points allocation formulas,[5] or the special nondiscrimination tests in Code Secs. 401(k)(3) and 401(m)(2) for elective, employee, and matching contributions.[6]

---

[1] IRS Reg. § 1.401(a)(4)-9(c)(1).

[2] IRS Reg. § 1.401(a)(4)-9(c)(2).

[3] IRS Reg. § 1.410(b)-4. These examples were in the 1991 final regulations (IRS Reg. § 1.401(a)(4)-9(c)(2)) but were not carried over to the 1993 final regulations. It does not seem here that the fact that they were deleted should make

them any less valid. They should provide guidance as possible methods of grouping employees.

[4] IRS Reg. § 1.401(a)(4)-9(c)(3).

[5] IRS Reg. § 1.401(a)(4)-2(b)(3).

[6] IRS Reg. § 1.401(a)(4)-9(c)(4). See IRS Reg. §§ 1.401(k)-1(b)(3)(iii) and 1.401(m)-1(b)(3)(iii) for rules regarding the inapplicability of restructuring to these situations.

¶ 1162

NONDISCRIMINATION IN CONTRIBUTIONS AND BENEFITS: Service-Crediting Rules

In general, for purposes of determining whether either a DB or DC plan satisfies the requirements that a plan be nondiscriminatory in the amount of contributions or benefits and in the availability of benefits, rights, and features (BR&F), a plan does not credit service for periods during which the employee did not perform services for the employer, or in which the employee was not a participant in that plan.

However, the IRS has issued service-crediting rules that allow plans to recognize service with another employer by applying (1) past service credit, (2) pre-participation service, and (3) imputed service. Each of these types of service credit periods has its own requirements.[1] When applying these service-crediting rules, it is essential to note that these rules apply separately to service credited under a plan for each different purpose under the plan. These different purposes might include: application of a benefit formula, accrual method, or vesting schedule; entitlement to BR&F; or application of the requirements for eligibility to participate in the plan.[2]

[1] IRS Reg. § 1.401(a)(4)-11(d).   [2] IRS Reg. § 1.401(a)(4)-11(d)(1)(i).

¶ 1164

NONDISCRIMINATION IN CONTRIBUTIONS AND BENEFITS: Testing of Former Employees

A facts-and-circumstances test is applied for determining whether the amount of contributions or benefits under a plan discriminates significantly in favor of former HCEs. If it does, the plan fails Code Sec. 401(a)(4).[1]

If there are not any former employees who currently benefit under a plan,[2] the plan automatically satisfies this test. Contributions and benefits under a plan generally include all contributions and benefits provided to former employees. However, at the employer's option, they may include only those contributions or benefits arising out of a plan amendment providing contributions or benefits.[3] The permitted disparity rules generally apply to former employees and current employees in the same manner.[4] A significant difference is that the permitted disparity rate that applies to a former employee is determined as of the age the former employee began receiving benefits.[5]

Defining employees and former employees

An "employee" is defined as an employee who benefits as an employee under the plan for the plan year.[6] Under the coverage regulations an employee is an individual who performs services for the employer and who is either a common-law employee, a self-employed person, or a leased employee. A "former employee" is defined as a person who has ceased performing services for the employer.[7]

Nondiscrimination in availability of benefits, rights, or features

This requirement is met with regard to former employees so long as any change in the availability of a benefit, right, or feature to any former employee is applied in a manner that, under all the relevant facts and circumstances, does not discriminate significantly in favor of former HCEs. IRS regulations do not provide any guidance as to what factors influence significant discrimination.[8]

---

[1] IRS Reg. § 1.401(a)(4)-10(b)(1).

[2] As defined in IRS Reg. § 1.410(b)-3(b).

[3] IRS Reg. § 1.401(a)(4)-10(a).

[4] Code Sec. 401(l) and IRS Reg. § 1.401(a)(4)-7.

[5] See IRS Reg. § 1.401(a)(4)-10(b)(2) and IRS Reg. § 1.401(a)(4)-3(e).

[6] IRS Reg. § 1.401(a)(4)-12.

[7] IRS Reg. § 1.410(b)-9.

[8] IRS Reg. § 1.401(a)(4)-10(c).

¶ 1166

NONDISCRIMINATION IN CONTRIBUTIONS AND BENEFITS: Correction and Sanctions

If a plan fails to comply with the nondiscrimination requirements—either in form or operation as a technical matter—it loses its qualified and tax-exempt status. There is, however, a mechanism which allows a plan that is out of operational compliance with the nondiscrimination rules to correct retroactively certain—but not all types of—disqualifying defects. In general, a permitted corrective amendment will cure the operational defect for a plan year by treating the amendment as if it were adopted and effective on the first day of the plan year in which the defect occurred.[1]

Scope of retroactive amendments

The retroactive correction mechanism only applies to the following situations:[2]

1. If a plan does not satisfy the minimum coverage rules of Code Sec. 410(b), the nondiscriminatory amount requirement under IRS Reg. § 1.401(a)(4)-1(b)(2), or the nondiscriminatory plan amendment requirement under IRS Reg. § 1.401(a)(4)-1(b)(4), an employer may amend the plan retroactively to either increase accruals or allocations for employees who benefited under the plan for the previous year, or to grant accruals or allocations for those employees who did not benefit under the plan for the preceding year.

2. If a plan does not satisfy the nondiscriminatory *current availability* requirement, the employer can correct the defect by making the benefit, right, or feature available to employees to whom it should have been made available.

The regulations provide an overriding caveat. A corrective amendment will not be taken into account to the extent the amendment affects nonvested employees whose employment terminated on or before the close of the preceding year, and who would not have received any economic benefit from the amendment if it had been made in the prior year.[3]

Example: Employer Y maintains a plan that discriminates in benefits. Employer Y amends the plan to increase the benefits of certain employees retroactively. In designing the amendment, Employer Y identifies those employees who have terminated without vested benefits during the period after the end of the prior plan year and before the adoption date of the amendment. The amendment provides increases in benefits primarily to those employees. The IRS takes the position that it would be inconsistent with the purpose of preventing discrimination in favor of HCEs for the IRS to treat the amendment as retroactively effective.

Conditions required for retroactive correction

The regulations provide a number of conditions, each of which must be satisfied for retroactive correction to be available:[4]

1. There cannot be any reduction to an employee's benefits (including a benefit, right, or feature) based on the plan's terms immediately before the amendment, as the result of a retroactive amendment.

2. The retroactive amendment must be effective as if the amendment had been made on the first day of the preceding plan year.

3. Any retroactive amendment must be adopted and implemented no later than the 15th day of the tenth month after the close of the preceding plan year.

4. Additional allocations or accruals for the preceding plan year must separately satisfy Code Sec. 401(a)(4) for the preceding plan year and must benefit a group of employees that separately satisfies all coverage requirements.

5. The requirements of (4) above do not have to be met if any failure to comply arises out of a defined contribution or defined benefit safe harbor, or if correction is made to ensure that the plan continues to meet an applicable safe harbor.

6. Code Sec. 401(k) cash and deferred arrangements and plans to which employee and employer matching contributions may be made[5] have their own correction procedures where there is a violation of the actual deferral or actual contribution percentages. However, the retroactive correction mechanism under the Code Sec. 401(a)(4) regulations provide separate additional rules.

7. A corrective amendment of a benefit, right, or feature (BRorF), can be made only if (a) correction is not part of a pattern of amendments to correct repeated failures pertaining to a particular BRorF, (b) the relevant plan provisions in effect immediately after the corrective amendment is adopted remains in effect until the end of the first plan year beginning after the date of the amendment, and (c) the corrective amendment either (i) expands the group of employees to whom the BRorF is cur-

rently available or (ii) eliminates the BRorF to extent permitted under Code Sec. 411(d)(6).[6]

☐ See ¶ 1938 and ¶ 7520 of the CCH PENSION PLAN GUIDE for the rules on correcting operational plan defects.

[1] IRS Reg. § 1.401(a)(4)-11(g).
[2] IRS Reg. § 1.401(a)(4)-11(g)(2).
[3] IRS Reg. § 1.401(a)(4)-11(g)(4).
[4] IRS Reg. § 1.401(a)(4)-11(g)(3).
[5] Code Sec. 401(m).
[6] IRS Reg. § 1.401(a)(4)-11(g)(3)(vi).

¶ 1170

DEFINING COMPENSATION UNDER NONDISCRIMINATION RULES: General Rules

Code Sec. 414(s) provides the rules for defining compensation under qualified retirement plans.[1] Whenever any other Code provision specifically refers to Code Sec. 414(s), the rules under Code Sec. 414(s) for defining compensation must be applied. The other Code provisions that specifically refer to Code Sec. 414(s) are called "applicable provisions." [2] For example, the amount of plan contributions or benefits, expressed as a percentage of compensation within the meaning of Code Sec. 414(s), is generally one of the key factors in determining whether these nondiscrimination requirements are satisfied.

Determination period

Compensation is calculated during a "determination period." This is the "period during which the amount of compensation is measured for use in determining whether the requirements of an applicable provision are satisfied." In situations where an applicable provision does not provide a period for measuring compensation, the determination period will always be the period during which the applicable provision must be satisfied.[3]

How can compensation be defined?

IRS regulations provide a number of ways for defining compensation. The structure of the regulations breaks these definitions down as follows:

Specific definitions. There are four specific definitions, one of which includes the basic definition of Code Sec. 414(s) compensation, which is compensation as defined in Code Sec. 415(c)(3). (See discussion at ¶ 1172.) There is also a safe harbor definition, one that includes elective deferrals and deferred compensation, and a definition that is modified to exclude any portion of the compensation of some or all highly compensated employees.[4]

Alternative definitions. Any definition of compensation may be used so long as it (a) does not by design discriminate in favor of highly compensated employees, (b) is reasonable, and (c) satisfies a separate nondiscrimination requirement.[5]

Rate of compensation. This definition of compensation looks at *the rate of* each employee's pay rather than actual compensation. A rate of compensation definition must also satisfy the three criteria required of the alternative definitions of compensation set forth above.[6]

Prior-employer and imputed compensation. A defined benefit plan may credit compensation with another employer (both for periods before and after employment with the employer maintaining the plan) or during a leave of absence.[7]

Consistency requirement

Whatever definition of compensation that an employer uses to satisfy Code Sec. 414(s) must be used on a consistent basis to define the compensation of all employees under the plan. Therefore, for example, if an employer defines compensation for purposes of Code Sec. 401(a)(4) as "Code Sec. 415(c)(3) compensation," [8] that definition must be used consistently for all employees in determining whether contributions or benefits are provided in a nondiscriminatory manner. However, an employer may change its definition for a subsequent determination period.[9]

If all employees do not receive all the types of compensation included in the definition of compensation, that does not necessarily result in a violation of the consistency requirement. For example, a definition of compensation may include salary, regular or scheduled pay, bonuses, and overtime. The fact that only salaried employees receive salary and bonuses, and hourly employees receive regular or scheduled pay and overtime, does not violate the consistency requirement.[10] Depending on the facts, however, the definition may result in operational plan discrimination in contributions or benefits in favor of highly compensated employees.

Special rule for self-employed individuals

The general rule is that any definition of compensation that complies with Code Sec. 414(s) can be used if the related applicable Code provision specifically refers to Code Sec. 414(s).[11] This general rule does not apply to self-employed individuals. The compensation of a self-employed individual can be determined according to either of the following methods:[12]

1. *Compensation within the meaning of Code Sec. 415(c)(3).*

2. *An equivalent alternative definition of compensation determined under IRS Reg. § 1.414(s)-1(g)(1).*

This special rule does not require that either of these two definitions be used for common-law employees who are also covered under the plan. Any definition of compensation can be used for the common-law employees so long as it satisfies Code Sec. 414(s).[13]

---

[1] See also IRS Reg. § 1.414(s)-1.

[2] Code Sec. 414(s)(4) and IRS Reg. § 1.414(s)-1(h)(1). "Applicable provisions" include Code Secs. 401(a)(5)(B), 401(a)(5)(E)(i), 401(k)(9), 401(l)(5)(B), 401(m)(3)(B), 402(h)(2)(A), 408(k)(7)(B), 410(b)(2)(C)(i), and 505(b)(6).

[3] IRS Reg. § 1.414(s)-1(h)(2).

[4] IRS Reg. § 1.414(s)-1(c).

[5] IRS Reg. § 1.414(s)-1(d).

[6] IRS Reg. § 1.414(s)-1(e).

[7] IRS Reg. § 1.414(s)-1(f).

[8] IRS Reg. § 1.414(s)-1(c)(2).

[9] IRS Reg. § 1.414(s)-1(b)(2)(i).

[10] IRS Reg. § 1.414(s)-1(b)(2)(ii).

[11] IRS Reg. § 1.414(s)-1(b)(1).

[12] IRS Reg. § 1.414(s)-1(b)(3).

[13] IRS Reg. § 1.414(s)-1(b)(3).

¶ 1172

DEFINING COMPENSATION UNDER NONDISCRIMINATION RULES: Definitions of Compensation

IRS regulations provide four specific definitions of compensation that can be used in a plan. Those definitions are as follows:[1]

Compensation under Code Sec. 415(c)(3)

Using the definition of compensation that is provided in Code Sec. 415(c)(3) allows a plan to follow the limits on benefits and contributions. A plan that defines compensation as "415(c)(3) compensation" has three optional methods to define compensation:[2]

1. "415(c)(3) compensation" can be defined by including certain compensation and excluding all other types of compensation.[3] This includes wages for purposes of income tax withholding, salaries, fees, tips, bonuses, and all other amounts received for professional or personal services to the extent the amounts are includable in gross income, and earned income if the employee is a self-employed individual.[4] Once it is determined what compensation must be included, all other forms of remuneration must be excluded. Examples are deferred compensation, distributions from a plan of deferred compensation, employer contributions to a simplified employee pension plan (SEP), amounts realized from the sale of stock acquired under a qualified stock option, and certain fringe benefits.

2. IRS rules provide a "safe harbor" definition of "415(c)(3) compensation" which can also be used.[5] Under the safe harbor, an employer may define compensation as including only certain types of compensation, i.e., regular or base salary or wages, plus commissions, tips, overtime and other premium pay, and bonuses.[6] This definition of compensation automatically satisfies Code Sec. 415(c)(3).

3. "415(c)(3) compensation" can also be defined under an alternative definition.[7] This definition relies on modified versions of the wage reporting rules. It may not be used in the case of a self-employed individual described in Code Sec. 401(c)(1). Under this alternative, compensation is defined either as (i) wages within the meaning of Code Sec. 3401 plus all other payments to an employee that an employer must report on the Form W-2 (i.e., those payments required to be reported by Code Secs. 6041, 6051, and 6052), or as (ii) wages within the meaning of Code Sec. 3401(a). However, compensation here is determined without regard to any rules that limit the amount of

remuneration included in wages that is based on the nature or location of employment or the services performed.

Safe harbor alternative definition

Here compensation is any of the alternative definitions for "415(c)(3) compensation" as defined in the immediately preceding paragraphs *reduced by* the following specific items: reimbursements or other expense allowances, cash and noncash fringe benefits, moving expenses, deferred compensation, and welfare benefits. These specific items must be subtracted for this definitional purpose even if they are includible in gross income.[8]

Inclusion of elective contributions and deferred compensation

Elective contributions, such as contributions to 401(k) plans, tax-sheltered annuities, simplified employee pensions (SEPs), or cafeteria plans under salary reduction agreements, will be included in the definition of compensation unless the employer elects not to include them as compensation.[9]

Compensation where exclusions pertain solely to HCEs

A plan can define compensation by using either the 415(c)(3) definition or safe harbor alternative definition (see (1) and (2) above), and modifying it to exclude any portion of the compensation earned by one or more of the highly compensated employees under the plan.[10]

CCH Pointer: Adjustments can be made to this definition of compensation by changing the amount of pre-tax deferrals under cafeteria plans, 401(k) plans, Code Sec. 457, and 403(b) tax-sheltered annuities. An advantage of making this type of adjustment to include additional income as compensation under Code Sec. 414(s) to increase qualified plan benefits.

Alternative definitions of compensation

In addition to the specific definitions of compensation set forth above, the regulations provide that any other alternative definition of compensation may be used if (1) it is reasonable, (2) does not by design favor highly compensated employees, and (3) satisfies a nondiscrimination requirement. This alternative rule does not apply to self-employed individuals.[11] See ¶ 2101 of the CCH PENSION PLAN GUIDE for a detailed discussion, including determining reasonableness and satisfying the nondiscrimination requirement.

Rate of compensation

Also known as "rate-of-pay," the rate of compensation rule permissibly defines the amount of each employee's basic or regular compensation using the employee's basic or regular rate of compensation rather than using the employee's actual basic or regular compensation. As a condition to using rate-of-pay as a method of compensation, the definition must satisfy two rules:[12]

¶1172

1. The definition of compensation must actually be used to calculate the benefits, contributions, and amounts that are subject to the particular Code provision, e.g., Code Sec. 401(a)(4).

2. The requirements for the alternative definitions of compensation must all be satisfied. If "rate of pay" is used, the previously discussed definitions of compensation do not apply. Often employers will use rate-of-pay in the benefit formula because it reduces data collection, and is more predictable and easily administered.

HCEs accruing duplicate benefits

The IRS has ruled that an empoyer's amendment of its defined benefit pension plan violated the nondiscrimination requirements of Code Sec. 401(a)(4) because the amendment created a second, spin-off plan that allowed highly compensated employees to accrue duplicate benefits without any type of offset from the first plan.[13]

---

[1] IRS Reg. § 1.414(s)-1(c).

[2] IRS Reg. § 1.414(s)-1(c)(2).

[3] IRS Reg. § 1.415-2(d)(1), (2), and (3).

[4] Code Sec. 401(c)(1).

[5] IRS Reg. § 1.415-2(d)(10).

[6]Described in IRS Reg. § 1.415-2(d)(2)(i).

[7]This is set forth in IRS Reg. § 1.415-2(d)(11).

[8] IRS Reg. § 1.414(s)-1(c)(3).

[9] Code Sec. 414(s)(2), as amended by P.L. 104-188 (Small Business Job Protection Act of 1996), Act Sec. 1434(b)(2).

[10] IRS Reg. § 1.414(s)-1(c)(5).

[11] IRS Reg. § 1.414(s)-1(d).

[12] IRS Reg. § 1.414(s)-1(e)(1).

[13] Rev. Rul. 99-51, 1999-2 CB 652, CCH PENSION PLAN GUIDE ¶ 19,942V.

¶ 1174

DEFINING COMPENSATION UNDER NONDISCRIMINATION RULES: Compensation with a Prior Employer and Imputed Compensation

A defined benefit plan can credit compensation with another employer (both for periods before and after employment with the employer maintaining the plan) or during a leave of absence, provided certain facts-and-circumstances standards are met.[1] Specifically, for purposes of determining whether a defined benefit plan satisfies the nondiscrimination requirements of Code Secs. 401(a)(4) and 410(b), an alternative definition of compensation that includes prior-employer compensation or imputed compensation can satisfy Code Sec. 414(s) as a reasonable definition of compensation.[2]

Prior-employer compensation

This is compensation from an employer other than the employer (determined at the time that the compensation is paid) maintaining the plan. It must be credited for periods prior to the employee's employment with the employer maintaining the plan and for periods during which the employee performed services for the other employer.[3]

Imputed compensation

This is compensation credited for periods after an employee has commenced or recommenced participation in a plan for time while the employee (1) is not compensated by the employer maintaining the plan, or (2) is compensated at a reduced rate by that employer because the employee is not performing services as an employee for the employer. This would include a period in which the employee performs services for another employer, such as a joint venture, or because the employee has a reduced work schedule.[4]

☐ See ¶ 2107 of the CCH PENSION PLAN GUIDE for the detailed tests that must be met to comply with the prior-employer compensation/imputed compensation requirement.

---

[1] IRS Reg. § 1.414(s)-1(f).

[2] IRS Reg. § 1.414(s)-1(f)(1).

[3] *Ibid.*

[4] *Ibid.*

¶ 1178

ADDITIONAL MINIMUM PARTICIPATION REQUIREMENTS: Background

Code Sec. 401(a)(26) has the specific purpose of preventing employers from providing higher benefits to HCEs under one plan and lower benefits for its nonHCEs under another plan. Prior to the Tax Reform Act of 1986, in determining whether several different plans that were designated as a single plan provided nondiscriminatory contributions or benefits, the IRS required that the employer demonstrate that the different plans making up the single plan provided "comparable" contributions or benefits. Rev. Rul. 81-202 provided the rules for determining whether the amount of employer-derived benefits or contributions provided under more than one plan discriminated in favor of HCEs.[1]

Rather than continue to rely on Rev. Rul. 81-202 as the method for curbing discrimination in this situation, Code Sec. 401(a)(26) was enacted as a more effective way of preventing discrimination through the implementation of a "minimum number of participants" rule. This provision eliminated much of the favorable treatment for HCEs that was provided under Rev. Rul. 81-202 by requiring a plan to benefit no fewer than a specified number of employees.

The effect of this provision limits one of the practical shortcomings of Rev. Rul. 81-202 from Congress's view. It limits the extent to which a defined benefit plan consisting of small professional or other corporations can operate as an individual account for a small group of employees; and restricts the ability of an employer to design different benefit formulas for different employees to maximize benefit differences in favor of HCEs.[2]

Significant elements to minimum participation rule

A number of general rules apply to understanding this requirement:

1. A plan must satisfy the minimum participation requirements of Code Sec. 401(a)(26) for the plan year.[3]

2. The rules apply separately to each plan of the employer. Therefore, plans of the employer can not be aggregated to satisfy this provision even if the plans are identical in all respects or where the plans are aggregated and treated as a single plan for purposes of Code Secs. 401(a)(4) and 410(b).[4]

3. There are a number of exceptions from these requirements, and if any one of the exceptions is met, Code Sec. 401(a)(26) is automatically satisfied.[5]

4. A plan must also meet certain requirements with respect to its prior benefit structure.[6]

5. Former employees who benefit under a plan are tested separately during a plan year.[7]

6. Certain employees can be excluded from testing.[8]

7. These requirements must be met either on each day of the plan year *or* on any single day of the plan year if it is reasonably representative of coverage and the employee workforce.[9]

8. The retroactive correction mechanism that applies to Code Sec. 401(a)(4) also applies to the additional minimum participation requirements.[10] See ¶ 1166.

9. This requirement *only applies to defined benefit plans.* [11]

---

[1] Rev. Rul. 81-202, 1981-2 CB 93. In view of the finalization of the various nondiscrimination regulations, this revenue ruling was obsoleted by Rev. Rul. 93-87, 1993-2 CB 124.

[2] Preamble to the T.D. 8375, published in the *Federal Register* on December 4, 1991 (56 FR 63410).

[3] IRS Reg. § 1.401(a)(26)-1(a).

[4] Preamble to T.D. 8375, published in the *Federal Register* on December 4, 1991 (56 FR 63410).

[5] IRS Reg. § 1.401(a)(26)-1(a).

[6] IRS Reg. §§ 1.401(a)(26)-1(a) and 1.401(a)(26)-3.

[7] IRS Reg. § 1.401(a)(26)-4.

[8] IRS Reg. § 1.401(a)(26)-6.

[9] IRS Reg. § 1.401(a)(26)-7.

[10] This mechanism is set forth in IRS Reg. § 1.401(a)(4)-11(g). IRS Reg. § 1.401(a)(26)-7.

[11] P.L. 104-188 (Small Business Job Protection Act), Act Sec. 1432(a).

¶ 1180

ADDITIONAL MINIMUM PARTICIPATION REQUIREMENTS: Plans Excepted from the "Minimum Number of Participants" Rule

In some situations, there can be automatic compliance with the minimum participation requirements. Therefore, if the criteria of a respective exception is met, there is automatic compliance without the need for any further testing. The exceptions are as follows:[1]

1. plans that benefit only nonHCEs;[2]

2. plans that benefit only employees covered by a collective bargaining agreement. This includes that portion of a multiemployer plan that benefits only employees covered by a collective bargaining agreement and that can be treated as a separate

plan. The portion of the plan not covering collectively bargained employees must separately satisfy these rules (see example below);[3]

3. certain underfunded defined benefit plans;[4]

4. certain government and tax-exempt employer 401(k) or 401(m) plans;[5] and

5. employers involved in a merger or acquisition.[6]

Example: A multiemployer plan covers 7,000 total employees—6,970 collectively bargained and 30 noncollectively bargained. That portion of the plan covering the collectively bargained employees automatically satisfies Code Sec. 401(a)(26).

CCH Pointer: For tax years beginning on or after August 5, 1997, governmental plans (including tax-sheltered annuities) do not have to comply with these additional minimum participation requirements. For years prior to that date, governmental plans are treated as satisfying these requirements for all tax years.[7] The exception from the minimum participation rules applies to *all* government plans, for years after August 17, 2006.[8] This provision was added by the Pension Protection Act of 2006 (P.L. 109-280). Prior to amendment by the PPA, the exception applied only to state and local government plans.

---

[1] IRS Reg. § 1.401(a)(26)-1(a) and (b).

[2] IRS Reg. § 1.401(a)(26)-1(b)(1).

[3] IRS Reg. § 1.401(a)(26)-1(b)(2)(i), (b)(2)(ii)(A), and (b)(2)(ii)(B).

[4] IRS Reg. § 1.401(a)(26)-1(b)(3).

[5] IRS Reg. § 1.401(a)(26)-1(b)(4).

[6] IRS Reg. § 1.401(a)(26)-1(b)(5)(i) and (ii).

[7] Code Secs. 401(a)(26)(G), as amended by P.L. 105-34 (Taxpayer Relief Act of 1997) and P.L. 108-311 (Working Families Tax Relief Act of 2004), and 403(b)(12)(C), as amended by P.L. 105-34 (Taxpayer Relief Act of 1997).

[8] Code Sec. 401(a)(26)(G), as amended by P.L. 109-280 (Pension Protection Act of 2006), Act Sec. 861(a)(1).

¶ 1182

ADDITIONAL MINIMUM PARTICIPATION REQUIREMENTS: "Minimum Number of Participants" Rule

A defined benefit plan must benefit no fewer than the lesser of:[1]

1. 50 employees, or

2. the greater of (i) 40% of all employees of the employer or (ii) two employees (or if there is only one employee, that employee).

This "50-40" rule does not apply to *defined contribution plans* for plan years after 1996.

What is a plan for testing purposes?

Code Sec. 401(a)(26) applies separately to each plan of the employer. Therefore, plans of the employer *cannot* be aggregated to satisfy this provision even if the plans are identical in all respects or where the plans are aggregated and treated as a single plan for other testing purposes.[2]

A plan is a single plan if, on an ongoing basis, all of its assets are available to pay benefits to covered employees and their beneficiaries. For example, if only a portion of the plan assets under a defined benefit plan is available, on an ongoing basis, to provide the benefits of certain employees, and the remaining assets are available only in certain limited circumstances to provide those benefits (but are available, in all cases, for the benefit of other employees), there are two separate plans.[3]

☐ See ¶ 2056 of the CCH PENSION PLAN GUIDE for a detailed discussion of plan testing, including mandatory disaggregation of plans, permissive disaggregation of plans, separate lines of business, collectively bargained employees, excludable employees, and frozen plans.

---

[1] Code Sec. 401(a)(26)(A).
[2] See Code Secs. 401(a)(4) and 410(b). IRS Reg. § 1.401(a)(26)-2(c).

[3] The IRS adopted the definition of a single plan that is contained in IRS Reg. §§ 1.414(l)-1(b)(1) and 1.410(b)-7(b).

¶ 1184

ADDITIONAL MINIMUM PARTICIPATION REQUIREMENTS: Prior Benefit Structure

A defined benefit plan that is not excepted from the minimum participation requirements must satisfy certain rules with regard to its prior benefit structure.[1] This requirement is in addition to complying with the "50-40" minimum number of participants requirement. The purpose of the prior benefit structure rule is to ensure that a plan does not exist primarily to preserve benefits for a small group of employees and thereby function more as an individual plan for that particular group or for the employer.

Complying with the prior benefit structure requirement

Each defined benefit plan has only one prior benefit structure, which is made up of all accrued plan benefits *as of the beginning of a plan year*. This includes benefits that have been rolled over or transferred to the plan.[2] A plan will only satisfy the prior benefit structure rule if it "provides *meaningful* benefits to a group of employees that includes the lesser of 50 employees or 40% of the employer's employees." [3] Therefore, if the lesser of 50 employees or 40% of the employer's employees currently accrue *meaningful* benefits under the plan, this requirement is met. See below for the definition of "meaningful benefits."

Defining "meaningful benefits"

This is determined by a facts-and-circumstances test involving the following factors:[4]

1. level of current benefit accruals;
2. comparative rate of accruals under the current benefit formula compared to the prior rates of accrual;

3. the projected accrued benefits under the current benefit formula compared to accrued benefits as of the close of the immediately preceding year;

4. the length of time the current benefit formula has been in effect;

5. the number of employees with accrued benefits under the plan; and

6. the length of time the plan has been in effect.

---

[1] IRS Reg. § 1.401(a)(26)-3.

[2] IRS Reg. § 1.401(a)(26)-3(b).

[3] IRS Reg. § 1.401(a)(26)-3(c)(1).

[4] IRS Reg. § 1.401(a)(26)-3(c)(2).

¶ 1186

ADDITIONAL MINIMUM PARTICIPATION REQUIREMENTS: Excludable Employees

There are specified classes of employees who are not taken into account when applying the "50-40" rule. As a general rule, these exclusions must be applied uniformly and consistently, and only with regard to the particular plan of the employer.[1]

Employees excludable for failure to meet minimum age and service conditions

Code Sec. 410(a)(1) sets forth age and service conditions that can be included in a plan as a condition for plan participation. If a plan contains those conditions so that all employees are excluded from benefiting under the plan until they satisfy the conditions, then those employees may be treated as excludable employees.[2] If a plan adopts age and service conditions that are less restrictive than allowed under Code Sec. 410(a)(1), all employees who are ineligible to participate under those more liberal age and service conditions are also excludable employees.[3]

Example: Employer X maintains a defined benefit plan under which employees who have not completed one year of service are not eligible to participate. Employer X has six employees. Two of the employees participate in the plan. The other four employees have not completed one year of service and are therefore not eligible to participate in the plan. The four employees who have not completed one year of service are excludable employees and may be disregarded for purposes of applying the minimum participation test. Therefore, the plan satisfies Code Sec. 401(a)(26) because both of the two employees who must be considered are participants in the plan.

Air pilots

Air pilots who are excludable employees for purposes of satisfying the minimum coverage rules under Code Sec. 410(b)(3)(B) are also excludable employees for purposes of the "50-40" rule.[4]

Nonresident aliens

A nonresident alien employee who is an excludable employee for purposes of satisfying the minimum coverage rules under Code Sec. 410(b)(3)(C) is also an excludable employee for purposes of the "50-40" rule.[5]

Collectively bargained employees

This rule may be applied separately to each collective bargaining agreement (CBA).[6]

> **Example 1:** WXY Company has 70 collectively bargained employees and 30 non-collectively bargained employees. WXY maintains a plan that benefits only the 30 non-collectively bargained employees. The 70 collectively bargained employees may be treated as excludable employees and thus may be disregarded in applying Code Sec. 401(a)(26) to WXY's plan.

> **Example 2:** XYZ Industries has 100 collectively bargained employees. Thirty of its employees are represented by Collective Bargaining Unit 1 and covered under Plan 1. Seventy of its employees are represented by Collective Bargaining Unit 2 and covered under Plan 2. For purposes of testing Plan 1, the employees of Collective Bargaining Unit 2 may be treated as excludable employees. Similarly, for purposes of testing Plan 2, the employees of Collective Bargaining Unit 1 may be treated as excludable employees.

When testing the "50-40" rule in a plan that benefits only collectively bargained employees, an employee who is not covered by the CBA may be excluded.[7]

> **Example 3:** Ferris Company has 30 collectively bargained employees and 70 non-collectively bargained employees. Ferris maintains a plan that benefits only the 30 collectively bargained employees. Ferris may treat the non-collectively bargained employees as excludable employees and disregard them in applying Code Sec. 401(a)(26) to the collectively bargained plan.

Terminating employees

The clear advantage here is that by excluding these terminating employees, the employer lowers the number of employees that must be counted for testing purposes. Here, an employee may be excluded from testing for a plan year if:[8]

1. the employee did not benefit under the plan for the plan year;
2. the employee is eligible to participate in the plan;
3. the plan has a minimum period of service requirement or a requirement that an employee be employed on the last day of the plan year for the employee to accrue a benefit or receive an allocation for the plan year;
4. the employee terminates employment during the plan year with no more than 500 hours of service;
5. the employee is not an employee on the last day of the plan year; and

6. the plan applies this terminating employee rule to all employees if it applies the rule to one employee.

Qualified separate lines of business

There are a number of rules that are applicable to the "50-40" rule where an employer is treated as operating qualified separate lines of business (QSLOB). The QSLOB rules under Code Sec. 414(r) are definitional only; they do not provide any operational rules. If an employer is treated as operating QSLOBs by complying with Code Sec. 414(r), then an employer can test Code Secs. 401(a)(26) and 410(b) on a "QSLOB basis." [9] The following rules summarize the interplay of Code Secs. 401(a)(26) and 414(r):

1. As a general rule an employer must test the "50-40" rule on an employer-wide basis. This means that all nonexcludable employees of the employer must be taken into account.[10]

2. If an employer operates QSLOBs, the "50-40" rule must be applied separately to the employees of each QSLOB for purposes of testing all plans of the employer that begin in the testing year.[11] In testing a plan that benefits employees of one QSLOB, the employees of the other QSLOBs are treated as excludable employees.[12]

3. In applying the "50-40" rule on a QSLOB basis, the portion of a plan that benefits employees of one QSLOB is treated as a separate plan from the portions of the same plan that benefit employees of other QSLOBs of that same employer.[13]

CCH Pointer: The requirement that a line of business have at least 50 employees does not apply in determining whether a plan satisfies the minimum participation rule on a separate line of business basis.[14] Thus, the additional minimum participation rule can be applied separately to an employer's line of business that has less than 50 employees, so long as it otherwise qualifies as a separate line of business.

Excludable former employees

The general rule is that all former employees of the employer must be taken into account for testing the 50-40 rule with respect to former employees. However, the following classes of former employees may be treated as excludable employees by the employer.[15]

1. Former employees who left (a) either before January 1, 1984, or before the 10th calendar year before the calendar year in which the current plan year begins, and (b) in a calendar year that precedes the earliest calendar year in which any former employee who benefits under the plan in the current plan year became a former employee.

2. Former employees who were excludable employees (under any of the foregoing rules regarding which employees an employer

may treat as excludable employees) during the plan year in which they became former employees.

3. Former employees whose vested accrued benefits do not exceed $5,000. See Code Secs. 411(a)(11) and 417(e) for the rules to be applied in making this determination.

Police and firefighters

An employer may apply the "50-40" rule separately with respect to any classification of any qualified public safety employees for whom a separate plan is maintained. Therefore, all employees not in that classification are excludable employees when testing a separate plan that includes those employees included within the classification.[16]

A "qualified public safety employee" means any employee of any police or fire department of a state or political subdivision if the employee provides police protection, fire fighting services, or emergency medical services.[17]

Independent contractors

Independent contractors are not employees eligible to participate in a qualified plan. The distinction between an independent contractor and an employee can be ambiguous, but the ambiguity will not excuse violation of the participation requirements. Thus, individuals who were under a sole shareholder's control, received company health insurance, provided an integral service to the company, and were engaged in a permanent working relationship with the company, were not independent contractors.[18] The exclusion of the employees from the plan subjected the plan to disqualification and the sole shareholder to the assessment of a tax deficiency.

Similarly, individuals who signed agreements declaring them to be independent contractors and denying their eligibility for benefits were entitled to benefits because they performed services for the company under conditions that made them common law employees.[19] The agreements did not negate the fact that the workers were employees who did not waive their rights to be treated as employees under the company's plans.

---

[1] IRS Reg. § 1.401(a)(26)-6(a).

[2] IRS Reg. § 1.401(a)(26)-6(b)(1)(i).

[3] IRS Reg. § 1.401(a)(26)-6(b)(1)(ii).

[4] Code Sec. 401(a)(26)(B)(i) and IRS Reg. § 1.401(a)(26)-6(b)(2).

[5] Code Sec. 401(a)(26)(B)(i) and IRS Reg. § 1.401(a)(26)-6(b)(3)(i). See Code Sec. 7701(b)(1)(B) for the definition of nonresident alien.

[6] IRS Reg. § 1.401(a)(26)-6(b)(4).

[7] IRS Reg. § 1.401(a)(26)-6(b)(5).

[8] IRS Reg. § 1.401(a)(26)-6(b)(7).

[9] Code Sec. 401(a)(26)(F); IRS Reg. § 1.410(a)(26)-6(b)(8).

[10] IRS Reg. § 1.401(a)(26)-9(a).

[11] *Ibid.*

[12] IRS Reg. § 1.410(a)(26)-6(b)(8) and § 1.414(r)-9(b).

[13] IRS Reg. § 1.414(r)-9(c)(2).

[14] Code Secs. 401(a)(26)(H), as amended by P.L. 104-188 (Small Business Job Protection Act of 1996), and P.L. 108-311 (Working Families Tax Relief Act of 2004).

[15] IRS Reg. § 1.401(a)(26)-6(c).

[16] IRS Reg. § 1.401(a)(26)-6(d).

[17] *Ibid.*

[18] *Kenney v. Commissioner,* TC (1995), 70 TCM 614; CCH Dec. 50,879M.

[19] *Vizcaino v. Microsoft Corp.,* CA-9 (1997), 120 F3d 1006 (en banc); aff'g CA-9 (1996), 97 F3d 1187.

¶ 1190
For More Information

☐ For more information on nondiscrimination in contributions and benefits, see ¶ 1050-1068, 1800-1940, and 2048-2109 of the CCH PENSION PLAN GUIDE.

Permitted Disparity

¶ 1200
General Rules

Employers are allowed to adjust contributions to and benefits under qualified retirement plans to reflect the employer-paid portion of Social Security. Such "integrated plans" are qualified provided that they do not discriminate in favor of highly compensated employees.[1] Three Code sections have primary importance here—Code Secs. 401(a)(4), 401(a)(5), and 401(l).

Code Sec. 401(a)(4) provides that a plan cannot discriminate in favor of the highly compensated employees with regard to the amount of contributions or benefits. Code Sec. 401(a)(5) provides that a plan does not discriminate merely because the contributions or benefits under the plan bear a uniform relationship to compensation, taking into account the permitted disparity rules set forth in Code Sec. 401(l).

---

[1] Code Secs. 401(a)(5)(C) and 401(l); IRS Reg. § 1.401(a)(4)-1(b)(2).

¶ 1205
Explanation of Permitted Disparity

Permitted disparity relates to the integration of Social Security retirement benefits into the overall benefits/contributions formula of a qualified retirement plan.[1] The concept of "integration with Social Security" or "permitted disparity" is a long-established principle that predates ERISA. It recognizes a Congressional acceptance that certain plans will not be considered as discriminatory in favor of highly compensated employees if those contributions or benefits only result from compensation in excess of the contribution or benefit level of Social Security.

Code Sec. 401(a)(5)(C) provides that "a plan shall not be considered discriminatory merely because the contributions or benefits of, or on behalf of, the employees under the plan favor highly compensated employees . . . in a manner permitted under Code Sec. 401(l)."[2] It is Code Sec. 401(l) which sets forth the rules under which integration with Social Security benefits in a qualified defined benefit and defined contribution plan is acceptable.

---

[1] Code Secs. 401(a)(5)(C) and 401(l). IRS Reg. §§ 1.401(l)-1(a)(1) and 1.401(a)(4)-7.

[2] This refers to discrimination under Code Sec. 401(a)(4).

¶ 1210
Relationship to Other Requirements

While it is the regulations under Code Sec. 401(l) that explain the limits on permitted disparity, it is Code Sec. 401(a)(4) and its regulations that demonstrate how permitted disparity is taken into account in testing whether the amount of contributions or benefits under an integrated plan are discriminatory. The regulations under Code Secs. 401(a)(4) and 401(l) were developed with the intended goal of maximizing the coordination between the two provisions.

Even if disparities in employer contributions or employer-derived benefits are permitted under Code Sec. 401(l), and thus may be disregarded in testing for discrimination under Code Sec. 401(a)(4), the plan may still fail to satisfy Code Sec. 401(a)(4) for other reasons. Similarly, even if disparities in employer contributions or employer-derived benefits are not permitted under Code Sec. 401(l), and thus may not be disregarded in testing for discrimination under Code Sec. 401(a)(4), the plan may still be found to be nondiscriminatory under Code Sec. 401(a)(4).[1]

Unless provided otherwise, Code Sec. 401(l) does not provide an exception to any other requirement of Code Sec. 401(a). For example, if a plan complies with the permitted disparity rules, it cannot as a result provide a benefit lower than the minimum benefit requirements under the top-heavy rules of Code Sec. 416. In addition, a plan cannot adjust benefits in a way that results in a decrease in an employee's accrued benefit in violation of Code Secs. 411(d)(6) and 411(b)(1)(G).[2]

Plans not subject to permitted disparity

There are a number of situations where plans or portions of a plan cannot benefit from the permitted disparity rules:[3]

1. Plans of employers that are not subject to the employer FICA tax (Code Sec. 3111) or employer Railroad Retirement Tax (Code Sec. 3221) may not avail themselves of the permitted disparity rules.

2. A plan, or portion of a plan, that is an employee stock ownership plan (ESOP) under Code Sec. 4975(e)(7) or a tax credit ESOP under Code Sec. 409(a).

3. Elective contributions under a 401(k) plan (IRS Reg. § 1.401(k)-1(g)(3)), or employee or matching contributions under a 401(m) plan (IRS Reg. § 1.401(m)-1(f)(6) or (f)(12).

4. SEP contributions under a salary reduction arrangement.

5. SIMPLE Retirement Accounts.[4]

6. Roth IRAs.[5]

---

[1] IRS Reg. § 1.401 (l)-1 (a) (1).

[2] IRS Reg. § 1.401 (l)-1 (b). Other examples are provided in the regulation.

[3] IRS Reg. § 1.401 (l)-1 (a) (4).

[4] Code Sec. 408(p).

[5] Code Sec. 408A.

1215

Permitted Disparity Rules for Defined Contribution Plans

In determining whether a defined contribution plan discriminates in contributions in violation of Code Sec. 401(a)(4), a disparity in the rates of employer contributions and forfeitures allocated to the accounts of participants is disregarded if the requirements discussed below are met.[1]

Plan must be an excess plan

The plan must be a defined contribution excess plan.[2] This means that the rate at which employer contributions are allocated to the account of an employee with respect to plan year compensation above the integration level is greater than the rate at which employer contributions are allocated to the account of an employee with respect to plan year compensation at or below the integration level. (Compensation here is expressed as a percentage of plan year compensation.)

Disparity must not be greater than maximum excess allowance

A defined contribution plan meets the disparity limits for integrated plans only if the "excess contribution percentage" [3] under the plan does not exceed the "base contribution percentage" [4] by a specified amount.

The "maximum excess allowance," i.e., the excess contribution percentage, is not to exceed the base contribution percentage by more than the lesser of:[5]

1. the base contribution percentage, or

2. the greater of (a) 5.7 percentage points, or (b) the percentage rate of tax under Code Sec. 3111(a) (imposing the employer FICA tax) that is attributable to the old age insurance portion of the Old Age, Survivors and Disability Insurance (OASDI) provisions of the Social Security Act.

See ¶ 2131 of the CCH PENSION PLAN GUIDE for situations in which the integration level must be reduced.

Disparity must be uniform

The disparity under the plan is uniform only if the plan uses the same base contribution percentage and the same excess contribution percentage for all employees in the plan.[6]

Definitions

Excess contribution percentage. This is the percentage of compensation that is contributed by the employer under the plan with respect to that portion of each participant's compensation in excess of the integration level specified under the plan for the year.[7]

Base contribution percentage. This is the percentage of compensation contributed by the employer under the plan with respect to that portion of each participant's compensation not in excess of the integration level specified under the plan for the year.[8]

Compensation. For purposes of the above rules, "compensation" is the definition used in the plan, provided that the definition is reasonable and is nondiscriminatory under Code Sec. 414(s).[9] See ¶ 2085 and following of the CCH PENSION PLAN GUIDE.

The following examples illustrate the operation of the permitted disparity rules for defined contribution plans. In each example, assume that 5.7% exceeds the percentage rate of the employer FICA tax attributable to the old-age insurance portion of OASDI.

Example 1: For its plan year beginning in 2012, a profit-sharing plan provides contributions of 5% of compensation up to and including the taxable wage base for 2012 ($110,100)[10] and 10.5% of compensation in excess of the taxable wage base for 2012. The plan fails to meet the disparity limits because the excess contribution percentage (10.5%) exceeds the base contribution percentage (5%) by 5.5%, which is more than the lesser of the base contribution percentage (5%) or 5.7%.

Example 2: For its plan year beginning in 2012, a money purchase pension plan provides contributions of 6% of compensation up to and including the taxable wage base for 2012 ($110,100), and 11.5% of compensation in excess of the taxable wage base for 2012. The plan meets the disparity limits because the excess contribution percentage (11.5%) exceeds the base contribution percentage (6%) by 5.5%, which is less than the lesser of the base contribution percentage (6%) or 5.7%.

---

[1] IRS Reg. 1.401(l)-2.

[2] IRS Reg. 1.401(l)-1(c)(16)(ii).

[3] IRS Reg. 1.401(l)-1(c)(15).

[4] IRS Reg. 1.401(l)-1(c)(4).

[5] IRS Reg. 1.401(l)-2(b)(2)(ii).

[6] IRS Reg. 1.401(l)-2(c)(1).

[7] IRS Reg. 1.401(l)-1(c)(15).

[8] IRS Reg. 1.401(l)-1(c)(4).

[9] Code Sec. 401(l)(5)(B).

[10] Social Security Administration News Release (October 19, 2011).

¶ 1220

Permitted Disparity Rules for Defined Benefit Excess Plans

Permitted disparity under a defined benefit plan is only allowable if the plan is a defined benefit excess plan.[1] A defined benefit excess plan is a defined benefit plan under which the rate of benefits from employer contributions ("employer-derived benefits") with respect to compensation above a level specified in the plan (expressed as a percentage of compensation)—the "integration level"—is greater than the rate of employer-derived benefits with respect to compensation below that level.[2]

Permitted disparity requirements

In determining whether a defined benefit excess plan discriminates in benefits in violation of Code Sec. 401(a)(4), a disparity in the rates of employer benefits is disregarded if the requirements listed below are met:

1. The disparity provided for the plan year does not exceed the maximum excess allowance.[3]

2. The disparity provided is uniform so that the plan uses the same base benefit percentage and the same excess benefit percentage for all employees with the same number of years of service.[4]

3. The integration level satisfies the integration level requirements.[5]

4. Each benefit, right, or feature provided under the plan with respect to employer-provided benefits attributable to average annual compensation above the integration level must also be provided on the same terms with respect to employer-provided benefits attributable to average annual compensation up to the integration level.[6]

☐ See ¶ 2144-2164 of the CCH PENSION PLAN GUIDE for a detailed explanation of these requirements.

[1] IRS Reg. § 1.401(l)-3(a)(1).
[2] IRS Reg. § 1.401(l)-1(c)(16)(i).
[3] IRS Reg. § 1.401(l)-3(a)(3).
[4] IRS Reg. § 1.401(l)-3(a)(4).
[5] IRS Reg. § 1.401(l)-3(a)(5).
[6] IRS Reg. § 1.401(l)-3(a)(6).

¶ 1225

Permitted Disparity Rules for Defined Benefit Offset Plans

A defined benefit offset plan is a defined benefit plan that is not an excess plan and that provides that each employee's employer-provided benefit is reduced or offset by a specified percentage of the employee's final average annual compensation up to the offset level under the plan.[1]

Final average compensation

Final average compensation for an employee means the average compensation for the 3-consecutive-year period ending with or within the plan year.[2] The year in which an employee terminates employment may be disregarded in determining final average compensation. If, as of a plan year, an employee's entire period of employment with the employer is less than three consecutive years, the employee's final average compensation must be determined by averaging the annual compensation received by the employee from the employer during the employee's entire period of employment with the employer. The definition of final average compensation used in the plan must be applied consistently with respect to all employees.[3]

In determining an employee's final average compensation, compensation in excess of the Social Security taxable wage base in effect at the beginning of the plan year must not be taken into account. A plan may provide that each employee's final average annual compensation for a plan year is limited to the employee's average annual compensation for the plan year.[4] A plan must use the same definition of compensation to determine final average compensation as the plan uses to determine average annual compensation.[5]

Permitted offset requirements—in general

In determining whether a defined benefit offset plan discriminates in violation of Code Sec. 401(a)(4), a disparity in the rate of employer-provided benefits under an offset plan is permitted if the plan meets the following requirements:

1. The disparity provided for the plan year does not exceed the maximum offset allowance.[6] This is the maximum disparity for defined benefit offset plans.

2. The disparity provided is uniform in that the plan uses the same gross benefit percentage and the same offset percentage for all employees with the same number of years of service.[7]

3. The offset level satisfies certain offset level requirements.[8]

4. Each benefit, right, or feature provided under the plan with respect to employer-provided benefits before application of the offset (the "gross benefit, right, or feature") must be provided on the same terms as those used to determine the offset applied to the gross benefit, right or feature.[9]

Safe harbor for PIA offset plans

A PIA offset plan is one where benefits provided under the plan are offset by a portion of the employee's primary insurance amount (PIA) under the Social Security Act. IRS regulations on permitted disparity contain a PIA offset safe harbor.

Under the deemed uniformity rules set forth in the permitted disparity regulation, a plan will not fail to provide uniform disparity merely because it contains certain provisions. One of those provisions is the PIA offset.[10] A PIA offset plan can satisfy the Code Sec. 401(l) permitted disparity requirements (and thus satisfy the nondiscriminatory amount requirement under Code Sec. 401(a)(4) on a safe harbor basis) if the plan limits the offset to the maximum offset permitted under Code Sec. 401(l) (the section 401(l) overlay), which is determined as a percentage of covered compensation rather than PIA.[11]

The percentage of PIA must be the same for all employees with the same number of years of service. Rev. Rul. 84-85 applies in determining the compensation history on which an employee's PIA can be based.[12]

¶1225

☐ See ¶ 2177-2197 of the CCH PENSION PLAN GUIDE for a detailed discussion of these requirements, including the safe harbor for PIA offset plans.

☐ See ¶ 2206-2210 of the CCH PENSION PLAN GUIDE for a discussion of the requirements for adjusting the maximum allowances when the integration or offset levels exceed covered compensation.

☐ See ¶ 2215-2219 of the CCH PENSION PLAN GUIDE for a discussion of the requirements for adjusting the maximum allowances when the plan pays benefits before the Social Security retirement age.

Employee contributions

In determining whether the maximum permitted disparity is exceeded in the case of either a defined benefit excess plan or defined benefit offset plan, benefits attributable to contributions by employees are not taken into account.[13]

☐ See ¶ 1890 of the CCH PENSION PLAN GUIDE for a detailed discussion of employer/employee contributions under the nondiscrimination rules of Code Sec. 401(a)(4).

---

[1] IRS Reg. § 1.401(l)-1(c)(25).

[2] IRS Reg. § 1.401(l)-1(c)(17)(i). This is determined under Code Sec. 414(s).

[3] Averaging annual compensation is determined under Code Sec. 414(s).

[4] IRS Reg. § 1.401(l)-1(c)(17)(ii).

[5] IRS Reg. § 1.401(l)-1(c)(17)(iii).

[6] IRS Reg. § 1.401(l)-3(a)(3).

[7] IRS Reg. § 1.401(l)-3(a)(4).

[8] IRS Reg. § 1.401(l)-3(a)(5).

[9] IRS Reg. § 1.401(l)-3(a)(6).

[10] IRS Reg. § 1.401(l)-3(c)(2) generally and -3(c)(2)(ix) specifically.

[11] Preamble to T.D. 8486, published in the *Federal Register* on September 3, 1993 (58 FR 46828).

[12] 1984-1 CB 115.

[13] IRS Reg. § 1.401(l)-3(h) and § 1.401(a)(4)-6.

¶ 1230
Overall and Cumulative Permitted Disparity

There is a requirement for an "annual overall permitted disparity limit" if an employee benefits under more than one plan for the plan year. Additionally, there is a "cumulative overall permitted disparity limit" that may be provided for an employee's total years of service under one or all plans of the employer.[1]

A plan must, by its terms, provide that the overall permitted disparity limits may not be exceeded and must also specify how employer-provided contributions or benefits under the plan are adjusted. Any adjustment must be uniformly applied to all employees.[2] All plans of the employer are taken into account; and all plans of any other employer must be taken into account for all periods of service with the other employer for which the employee receives credit for benefit accrual purposes.[3] The reason for taking the other employer's plan into account is to ensure that the current employer does not duplicate the disparity provided for years of service with the other employer, thus exceeding the disparity limits.[4]

☐ See ¶ 2224-¶ 2236 of the CCH PENSION PLAN GUIDE.

---

[1] IRS Reg. § 1.401(l)-5(a)(1).

[2] IRS Reg. § 1.401(l)-5(a)(2).

[3] IRS Reg. § 1.401(l)-5(a)(3).

¶ 1235

Alternative Method of Integrating Defined Benefit Plans—Final Pay Plans

In general, a final pay plan is one that limits an employee's benefit to the total of the employee's final pay and the employee's employer-provided primary insurance amount (PIA). Because Code Sec. 401(a)(5) is written in terms of whether certain plan provisions are discriminatory, a plan is not considered to discriminate in benefits in favor of highly compensated employees merely because the plan provides that each participant's employer-derived accrued benefit is limited to the excess (if any) of:[1]

1. final pay, over

2. the employer-derived Social Security retirement benefit that is attributable to the participant's service for the employer.

Exceptions to the final pay plan rules

This limitation on the employer-derived accrued benefit does not apply in the following cases:

1. **Reduction in accrued benefit.** [2] It does not apply to the extent that its application results in a decrease in a participant's accrued benefit on account of any increase in his age or service,[3] or because of any plan amendment.[4]

2. **Employer not subject to FICA tax.** If the employer maintaining the plan is not subject to FICA or Railroad Retirement taxes imposed by Code Secs. 3111 and 3221, the limitation does not apply.[5]

Employer-derived accrued benefit

The participant's employer-derived accrued retirement benefit as of any plan year is the accrued retirement benefit under the plan attributable to employer contributions. The accrued benefit is determined on an actual, rather than a projected, basis.[6] See ¶ 2552-¶ 2575 of the CCH PENSION PLAN GUIDE for determining the allocation of the accrued benefit between the portion provided by employer contributions and the portion provided by employee contributions.

Final pay defined

As of any plan year, a participant's final pay is the compensation[7] during the "year" (ending within the five-plan-year period and with the plan year in which employment is terminated) in which compensation is the highest. For this purpose, a "year" is any 12-month period specified by the plan, provided it is uniformly and consistently applied to all participants. Compensation in excess of the limitation under Code Sec. 401(a)(17) ($250,000 for 2012; $245,000 for 2011) is not taken into account.[8]

Example: Acme Corporation maintains a defined benefit plan. The plan year is the fiscal year ending June 30. For purposes of determining a participant's final pay, the plan provides that the relevant "year" is the calendar year. Jones, a participant, retires on June 30, 2012. Accordingly, the five-plan-year period ending with the plan year in which employment terminates is the period July 1, 2007, through June 30, 2012. Jones's compensation during the five calendar years ending with or within that 5-plan-year period is as follows:

2011	$29,000
2010	25,000
2009	26,000
2008	30,000
2007	28,000

Under these circumstances, Jones's final pay is $30,000.

Employer-derived Social Security retirement benefit attributable to service for employer

A participant's employer-derived Social Security retirement benefit that is attributable to the participant's service for the employer is:[9]

1. fifty percent (50%) of the participant's projected primary insurance amount payable under Section 215 of the Social Security Act

multiplied by

2. a fraction (not exceeding the whole number one) whose numerator is the participant's number of complete years of covered service for the employer under the Social Security Act and whose denominator is 35.

Projected primary insurance amount. A participant's projected primary insurance amount (PIA) as of any plan year is determined as of the end of that plan year (the "determination date"). It is the PIA payable to the participant upon attainment of Social Security retirement age, assuming that the participant's annual compensation from the employer that is treated as wages under the Social Security Act remains the same from the determination date until the participant's attainment of Social Security retirement age.[10]

In the case of service for the employer before the determination date, actual compensation is taken into account. Actual compensation for years preceding service for the employer is also taken into account if the employee provides the employer with satisfactory evidence of the amounts. Otherwise, it is assumed that the participant received compensation in an amount "computed by using a six percent salary scale projected backwards from the termination date to the participant's 21st birthday." [11]

Each participant must be given notice of the right to provide the actual history of compensation from prior employment. This notice must be given each time a participant receives a summary plan description and also upon termination of employment. It must advise the participant that it is possible to obtain an actual compensation history from the Social Security Administration.[12]

If a participant has two or more employers, an employer maintaining a plan may not take into account any compensation from the others while it employs the participant.[13]

Example: The following examples illustrate the application of the final pay plan rules. The Genesis Corporation maintains a defined benefit pension plan on a calendar year basis. The plan provides a normal retirement benefit at age 65 of $500 a year, times the employee's years of service for Genesis, limited to the excess of the amount of the employee's final pay from Genesis over the employee's employer-provided primary insurance amount attributable to the employee's service for Genesis. Rickman retires at age 65 with 35 years of service with final pay of $20,000. His annual primary insurance amount (PIA) is $9,000, of which $4,500 is the employer-provided portion attributable to his service for Genesis. Under the plan's benefit formula, Rickman would be entitled to receive a normal retirement benefit of $17,500 ($500 times 35 years). However, under the plan, his benefit is limited to the excess of the amount of his final pay from Genesis over his employer-provided primary insurance amount attributable to service for Genesis. Accordingly, Rickman's normal retirement benefit is $15,500 ($20,000 final pay less the $4,500 that is the employer-provided portion of the PIA). This plan meets the final pay limitations and therefore does not discriminate in favor of highly compensated employees on this basis.

Other benefits not taken into account. In determining whether a plan meets the nondiscrimination requirements of Code Secs. 401(a)(4) and 401(a)(5), other benefits created under state or federal law may not be taken into account. Examples of these state or federal laws include benefits provided by worker's compensation or black lung benefits.[14]

---

[1] Code Sec. 401(a)(5)(D); IRS Reg. §§ 1.401(a)(5)-1(e)(1) and 1.401(l)-3(e)(l).

[2] IRS Reg. § 1.401(a)(5)-1(e)(6)(i).

[3] Code Sec. 411(b)(1)(G).

[4] Code Sec. 411(d)(6).

[5] IRS Reg. § 1.401(a)(5)-1(e)(6)(ii).

[6] IRS Reg. § 1.401(a)(5)-1(e)(5).

[7] Code Sec. 414(q)(4).

[8] IRS Reg. § 1.401(a)(5)-1(e)(2); See IR-2011-103, 10-20-11, CCH PENSION PLAN GUIDE ¶ 17,037Q.

[9] IRS Reg. § 1.401(a)(5)-1(e)(3).

[10] IRS Reg. § 1.401(a)(5)-1(e)(4).

[11] *Ibid.*

[12] *Ibid.*

[13] *Ibid.*

[14] IRS Reg. § 1.401(a)(5)-1(e)(6)(iv).

¶ 1240

Railroad Retirement Benefits

In determining the qualification of a plan which includes employees of a railroad employer who are entitled to benefits under the Railroad Retirement Act of 1974, rules similar to those governing integration with Social Security benefits apply.[1] These rules take into account the employer-derived portion of the employees' tier 2 railroad retirement benefits and any supplemental annuity under the Railroad Retirement Act of 1974.[2]

---

[1] Code Sec. 401(l)(6).

[2] The rules referred to are found in IRS Reg. § 1.401(l)-(4) and should be consulted for details.

¶ 1245

For More Information

☐ For more information on permitted disparity, see ¶ 2118-2278 of the CCH Pension Plan Guide.

Separate Lines of Business

¶ 1300

General Rules

All employees of a single employer must generally be taken into account in applying minimum coverage rules of Code Sec. 410(b) and the minimum participation requirements of Code Sec. 401(a)(26). Employees of corporations that are members of a controlled group, employees of trades or businesses that are under common control, and employees of members of an affiliated service group are treated as being employed by a single employer. However, there is an exception to this "single employer" requirement that applies to employers that operate "qualified separate lines of business" (QSLOBs).[1] An employer that meets this exception may apply the minimum coverage and minimum participation requirements separately to the employees of each separate line of business.

The exception will not apply to all employers. In order to qualify for the exception, an employer must have at least 100 employees and operate more than one line of business. Accordingly, the separate line of business rules will be of particular significance to large diversified employers. However, employers that qualify for the exception will effectively be able to satisfy the minimum coverage and minimum participation requirements on a basis that more accurately reflects their business operations.

Qualified Separate Lines of Business (QSLOBs)

The rules for determining whether an employer is eligible to apply the SLOB rules to its plan are complex. Under the SLOB rules, every plan of the employer must satisfy, on an employer-wide basis, either a percentage test,[2] a ratio test,[3] or an average benefit percentage test.[4] In addition, to satisfy the average benefit percentage test, an employer must pass a nondiscriminatory classification test[5] and an average benefit percentage test in which the average benefit percentage for nonhighly compensated employees is at least 70% of that of highly compensated employees.[6]

¹Code Sec. 414(r).
²Code Sec. 410(b)(1)(A).
³Code Sec. 410(b)(1)(B).

⁴Code Sec. 410(b)(2).
⁵Code Sec. 410(b)(2)(A)(i).
⁶Code Sec. 410(b)(2)(A)(ii).

¶ 1305

Determining Whether an Employer Operates a Qualified Separate Line of Business

There is a four-step process for determining whether an employer operates a qualified separate line of business (QSLOB).

STEP 1—The employer must employ at least 100 nonexcludable employees, because each QSLOB must have at least 50 employees.[1] If it does not, these rules are not applicable to the employer.

STEP 2—If an employer employs 100 employees, then the *second step* is for the employer to define its lines of business (LOBs). See ¶ 1325.

STEP 3—Once the employer defines what constitutes its LOBs, then the *third step* is to determine whether the LOBs are separate lines of business (SLOBs). See ¶ 1315 below.

STEP 4—If the LOBs are separate under the regulations, then the *fourth and final step* consists of a three-part test to determine whether the SLOB is a qualified separate line of business (QSLOB). This three-part test requires the following:

1. Each SLOB must satisfy a fifty-employee rule (¶ 1320).[2]
2. The employer must provide notice to the IRS of its application of the SLOB rules.[3]
3. Each SLOB must satisfy the requirements of "administrative scrutiny." [4]

The governing regulations set forth a flowchart that illustrates the steps an employer must follow in order to utilize the QSLOB rules.[5] The flowchart is reproduced at CCH PENSION PLAN GUIDE ¶ 2291.

¹Whether an employee is nonexcludable for this purpose is determined under Code Sec. 414(q)(5), relating to the definition of highly compensated employees. All references to the "fifty-employee rule" or to "fifty employees" takes into account that they must be nonexcludable.
²Code Sec. 414(r)(2)(A) and IRS Reg. §1.414(r)-4(b).

³Code Sec. 414(r)(2)(B), IRS Reg. §1.414(r)-4(c), and Rev. Proc. 93-40, 1993-2 CB 535, CCH PENSION PLAN GUIDE ¶ 17,299M-76.

⁴Code Sec. 414(r)(2)(C), IRS Reg. §1.414(r)-5, and Rev. Proc. 93-41, 1993-2 CB 536, CCH PENSION PLAN GUIDE ¶ 17,299M-77.

⁵IRS Reg. §1.414(r)-0(c).

¶ 1310

Basic Testing Rule

The employer is given the discretion of determining its own LOB[1] so long as the determination is *reasonable* and *consistent with its existing bona fide business operations.*[2] The essence of this aspect of the regulations is to place the emphasis on the degree to which the LOBs are organized and operated separately from one another in a self-sustaining manner. Thus, an employer may combine dissimilar types of property or services within one LOB.[3] Similarly, an employer is not required to combine all related types of property or services within one LOB. However, an employer's discretion must be exercised in accord with governing IRS regulations.

The basic rule requires an employer to determine its LOBs for a "testing year" [4] by (1) identifying all the property and services it provides to its customers for the "testing year" and (2) then by designating which portion of the property and services is provided by each of its LOBs.[5]

> **Example 1:** Company X is in the business of manufacturing and selling food and beverages and providing data processing services. Company X can designate three LOBs—one providing food products, one providing beverage products, and one providing data processing services. Alternatively, Company X can combine the food and beverage products into one LOB.

> **Example 2:** In a testing year, XYZ Company, a shipbuilder, enters into a contract with a customer to construct a new cargo ship for delivery two years later. XYZ incurs significant costs designing and planning for the production of the new ship during the testing year, but receives no payments from the customer during that year. Even though XYZ has not received consideration during the testing year, it is treated as providing the cargo ship to the customer during the testing year.

---

[1]IRS Reg. § 1.414(r)-2.
[2]IRS Reg. § 1.414(r)-1(d)(2).
[3]IRS Reg. § 1.414(r)-2(b)(3).

[4]IRS Reg. § 1.414(r)-11(b)(5) defines "testing year" as the calendar year.

[5]IRS Reg. § 1.414(r)-2(b)(1).

¶ 1315
Requirement of Separateness

Once the employer designates its LOBs, it must show that these LOBs are organized and operated separately from one another.[1] There are four objective criteria (together with supplementary rules), each of which must be met for the testing year, for determining legitimate separation of LOBs.[2]

1. **Separate organizational unit**—The LOB must be a formal organizational unit, such as a corporation, partnership, division, or other similar unit, which must be present on every day of the testing year.

2. **Separate financial accountability**—The LOB must be a separate profit center or group of profit centers within the employer, on each day of the testing year.

3. **Separate employee workforce**—The LOB must have its own workforce. In order to satisfy the requirement, 90 percent of the employees who provide services to the LOB may not be "substantial service employees" and may not be substantial service

employees with respect to any other LOB.[3] A substantial-service employee is an employee who provides at least 75% of his services to a particular LOB for the testing year. Additionally, if an employee provides at least 50% and less than 75% of his services to a LOB for a testing year, the employer may treat that employee as a substantial-service employee of that LOB so long as the employee is treated that way for all purposes.[4]

Example: Company T operates five LOBs, one of which manufactures sneakers, shoes, and boots. Employee P makes soles for all the footwear, and Employee M manages the production. Here the services of Employees P and M contribute to the sale of sneakers, shoes, and boots to customers of Company T's footwear LOB. Further, the only services that Employees P and M provide are to the footwear customers of Employer T. This makes both P and M substantial-service employees of Company T's footwear LOB because at least 75% of their services are for that LOB.

4. **Separate management**—A LOB must have its own separate management. A LOB has its own separate management if at least 80 percent of the LOB's top-paid employees (i.e., employees who are in the top 10 percent of compensation and provide at least 25 percent of their services to the LOB) are substantial service employees.[5]

□ See ¶ 2303 and 2307 of the CCH PENSION PLAN GUIDE for the rules for those employees and services that must be taken into account in determining separateness of LOBs; and the optional rule for vertically integrated LOBs.

---

[1]IRS Reg. § 1.414(r)-3.

[2]IRS Reg. § 1.414(r)-11(b)(5) defines "testing year" as the calendar year.

[3]IRS Reg. § 1.414(r)-3(b)(4).

[4]IRS Reg. § 1.414(r)-11(b)(2).

[5]IRS Reg. § 1.414(r)-3(b)(5) and § 1.414(r)-11(b)(3).

¶ 1320
Qualified Separate Lines of Business

If an employer can jump over the first two hurdles by (1) designating its own line of business (LOB) within IRS guidelines and (2) having the LOB treated as a separate line of business (SLOB), the last hurdle is a demonstration that it maintains *qualified* separate lines of business (QSLOBs). To do so this, each of three statutory requirements set forth in Code Sec. 414(r)(2) must be satisfied:

1. Each SLOB must have at least 50 employees.

2. The employer must provide notice to the IRS on Form 5310-A that it treats itself as operating QSLOB.

3. Each QSLOB must satisfy additional administrative guidelines by meeting the requirements for administrative scrutiny.

Fifty-employee rule

A SLOB must have 50 employees on each day of the "testing year" who provide their services to the SLOB and do not provide services to any other SLOB of the employer for the testing year. All employees of the employer are taken into account (including collectively bargained employees), except employees who do not meet certain age and minimum service requirements and certain nonresident aliens.[1]

Notice requirements

The employer must provide notice to the IRS that it is applying the SLOB rules.[2] Rev. Proc. 93-40 provides the following rules for satisfying this notice requirement:[3]

1. Notice that the employer wishes to be treated as operating QSLOBs must be given to the IRS by filing Form 5310-A, *Notice of Plan Merger or Consolidation, Spinoff, or Transfer of Plan Assets or Liabilities; Notice of Qualified Separate Lines of Business.*

2. Form 5310-A must be filed with the Internal Revenue Service, P.O. Box 12192, Covington, KY 41012-0192.

3. A schedule must be attached to Form 5310-A, and it must contain the following information:

    (i) the identification of each QSLOB of the employer;

    (ii) the identification of each plan maintained by the employer;

    (iii) the QSLOBs that have employees benefiting under each such plan; and

    (iv) the Code section(s) for which the employer is testing on a QSLOB basis (e.g., Code Secs. 401(a)(26) or 410(b)).

4. Form 5310-A notice for a testing year must be given on or before the "Notification Date" of the testing year. This is the later of:

    (i) October 15th of the year following the testing year, or

    (ii) the 15th day of the 10th month after the close of the plan year of the plan of the employer that begins earliest in the testing year.

Administrative scrutiny—statutory and administrative safe harbors

The administrative scrutiny requirement[4] is the third requirement for qualified separate line of business status. It is satisfied if the SLOB meets either (1) the safe harbor set forth in the IRC[5] or (2) any one of the five administrative safe harbors that are solely created by IRS regulations.[6] If a SLOB does not satisfy any of these safe harbors, it can still satisfy the administrative scrutiny requirement if the employer applies for and receives a determination from the IRS that the SLOB complies with the standards for administrative scrutiny.[7]

Statutory safe harbor

The statutory safe harbor is a straight mathematical test. A SLOB will satisfy this safe harbor if the highly compensated employee percentage ratio (HCE%) of the SLOB is both (1) at least 50% and (2) no more than 200%. The HCE% is determined by the following fraction:[8]

% of the Employees of the SLOB who are HCEs

over

% of all Employees of the Employer who are HCEs

In addition, the 50% test has its own safe harbor. If at least 10% of all HCEs of the employer provide services solely for that LOB and do not provide services to any other LOB for the testing year, a SLOB is deemed to satisfy the 50% test.[9] The SLOB must still satisfy the 200% test.

Example: Smith Industries operates three separate lines of business, consisting of an ironworks, a telecommunications company, and a plastics processing plant. Smith Industries employs a total of 400 employees, 100 of whom are highly compensated employees. Thus, the percentage of all employees of Smith who are highly compensated employees is 25%. The distribution of highly and nonhighly compensated employees among Smith's separate lines of business is as follows:

	Employer-Wide	Ironworks	Telecommunications	Plastics
Number of Employees ..	400	100	150	150
Number of HCEs	100	20	50	30
Number of Non-HECs ..	300	80	100	120
HCE Percentage ..	25% (100/400)	20% (20/100)	33% (50/150)	20% (30/150)
HCE Percentage Ratio	N/A	80% (20%/25%)	133% (33%/25%)	80% (20%/25%)

Because the highly compensated employee percentage ratio of each SLOB is at least 50% and no more than 200%, each of Smith Industries's SLOBs satisfies the requirements of the safe harbor.

¶1320

Lookback rule

Under the "preceding year look-back rule," a SLOB that satisfied the statutory safe harbor for the "immediately preceding testing year" is deemed to satisfy it for the "current testing year." [10]

Administrative safe harbors

There are five administrative safe harbors, which, if met, result in an automatic determination that SLOBs meet the requirements of administrative scrutiny. These encompass instances where:[11]

1. SLOBs are in different industries;

2. SLOBs are reported as industry segments;

3. SLOBs provide the same average benefits as other SLOBs;

4. SLOBs are acquired through certain mergers and acquisitions; or

5. SLOBs provide minimum or maximum benefits.

Consequences of failure to comply

An employer is not obligated to apply the QSLOB rules. In addition, the failure to comply with those rules does not create a disqualification problem. It is only when an employer operates as a QSLOB and then attempts to use those rules to satisfy Code Sec. 410(b) or 401(a)(26) that qualification becomes an issue.

If a plan fails to satisfy the requirements of the SLOB regulations pertaining to the (1) satisfaction of the Code Sec. 410(b)(5)(B) on an employer-wide basis, (2) satisfaction of Code Sec. 410(b)(5) on a QSLOB basis, (3) coordination of Code Sec. 401(a)(4) with 410(b), or (4) the requirements of Code Sec. 401(a)(26) that are applicable to a plan of the employer, that plan *(and any plan of which it is a portion)* will fail to satisfy the qualification requirements of Code Sec. 401(a).[12]

---

[1] Code Sec. 414(r)(2)(A) and IRS Reg. §1.414(r)-4(b). See IRS Reg. §1.414(q)-1, Q&A-9(g) for the excluded employees.

[2] Code Sec. 414(r)(2)(B); IRS Reg. §1.414(r)-4(c) and -1(b)(2)(iv)(C).

[3] Sec. 3 at 1993-2 CB 535. Notice is required for plan years beginning on or after January 1, 1994.

[4] Code Sec. 414(r)(2)(C).

[5] Code Sec. 414(r)(3)(A).

[6] IRS Reg. §1.414(r)-5(c)—5(g).

[7] Code Sec. 414(r)(2)(C), IRS Reg. §1.414(r)-6, and Rev. Proc. 93-41, 1993-2 CB 536, CCH PENSION PLAN GUIDE ¶ 17,299M-77.

[8] Code Sec. 414(r)(4); IRS Reg. §1.414(r)-5(b)(1) and (2).

[9] IRS Reg. §1.414(r)-5(b)(4).

[10] Code Sec. 414(r)(3)(B); IRS Reg. §1.414(r)-5(b)(5); P.L. 100-647 (Technical and Miscellaneous Revenue Act of 1988), Sec. 3021(b)(2)(A).

[11] IRS Reg. §1.414(r)-5(c)-(g).

[12] IRS Reg. §§1.414(r)-8(d)(4) and -9(c)(4).

¶ 1325

Individual IRS Determination of Lines of Business

If the SLOB does not satisfy either the statutory safe harbor or any one of the five administrative safe harbors, it can still satisfy the statutory requirement of administrative scrutiny if "the employer receives a determination from the Secretary that such line of business may be treated as separate."[1]

IRS Rev. Proc. 93-41: sets forth the exclusive procedures relating to the issuance of an administrative scrutiny determination for a testing year; prescribes the conditions under which an employer is permitted to request a determination that a SLOB meets administrative scrutiny; and describes the factors that will be taken into account in determining whether to grant a determination that a SLOB satisfies the requirements for administrative scrutiny.[2]

A request for a ruling on compliance with the administrative scrutiny conditions requires payment of a user fee.

---

[1]Code Sec. 414(r)(2)(C); IRS Reg. § 1.414(r)-6.   [2]1993-2 CB 536.

¶ 1330

Determining the Employees of the Employer's QSLOB

In applying the rules under Code Sec. 414(r), it is necessary for an employer to determine which of its employees work for which QSLOB. There are special rules for determining the employees of a QSLOB.[1] However, these rules are limited to determining whether a SLOB satisfies:[2]

1. the statutory safe harbor under Code Sec. 414(r)(3)(A) and IRS Reg. § 1.414(r)-5(b);

2. the merger and acquisition safe harbor under IRS Reg. § 1.414(r)-5(d) for a testing year;

3. the average benefits safe harbor under IRS Reg. § 1.414(r)-5(f) for a testing year;

4. the minimum and maximum benefits safe harbors under IRS Reg. § 1.414(r)-5(g) for a testing year; and

5. Code Secs. 401(a)(4), 410(b), and 401(a)(26) for a plan year.[3]

IRS regulations address the allocation of headquarters personnel among the employer's LOB and the treatment of other employees providing services for more than one LOB or employees not in the LOB.[4] These rules provide the procedures for assigning employees among the employer's QSLOBs and the methods for allocating "residual shared employees." As a general rule, the employees of a QSLOB consist of all employees who provide substantial services to the QSLOB, and all other employees who are allocated to the QSLOB under the regulations.

☐ See ¶ 2333-2341 of the CCH PENSION PLAN GUIDE for a discussion of the "assignment procedures for substantial-service employees" and "allocation of residual shared employees."

---

[1]IRS Reg. § 1.414(r)-7.

[2]IRS Reg. § 1.414(r)-7(a)(2)(i)-(iv).

[3]IRS Reg. § 1.414(r)-7(a)(2)(v)-(vi).

[4]Code Sec. 414(r)(6). See also H.R. Conf. Rep. 99-841 at II-524-525.

¶ 1335
Relationship of SLOB Rules to Other Code Provisions

The SLOB rules may also be applied to plans of government and tax-exempt employers and to health and welfare plans.

Governmental and tax-exempt employers

Non-governmental tax-exempt employers may apply the QSLOB rules to comply with the requirements of Code Secs. 410(b) and 401(a)(26). However, IRS regulations do not address specific QSLOB rules for plans of tax-exempt employers. Pending the issuance of guidance by the IRS, tax-exempt employers will be considered to be in compliance with the QSLOB rules if they make a "reasonable good faith effort . . . to satisfy the requirements of section 414(r) consistent with the statutory and regulatory requirements." [1]

Health and welfare plans

While there are many other Code provisions that set forth nondiscriminatory coverage tests for retirement, health, and welfare plans, the QSLOB rules may not be applied to employees covered under such arrangements. Included in this prohibition are Code Secs. 79(d)(3) (group-term life insurance), 105(h) (accident and health plans), 117(d)(3) (qualified tuition reductions), 120(c)(2) (qualified group legal services plans), 125(g)(3) (cafeteria plans), 127(b)(2) (educational assistance plans), 132 (certain fringe benefit arrangements), 401(a)(3) (as in effect on September 1, 1974, prior to ERISA) (coverage), 414(q)(3) (top-paid group definition), 501(c)(17)(A)(ii) or 501(c)(17)(B)(iii) (supplemental unemployment compensation benefits), 501(c)(18)(B) (pre-June 25, 1959, employer-funded pension plans), and 505(b)(1)(A) (Voluntary Employees' Beneficiaries Associations).[2]

Cash or deferred arrangements

Where an employer satisfies the rules for QSLOBs for purposes of applying the minimum coverage rules under Code Sec. 410(b), and applies the special rule for employer-wide plans to the portion of the plan that consists of the CODA, then the requirements of Code Sec. 401(k) also must be applied on an employer-wide basis (rather than a QSLOB basis) to all plans or portions of plans taken into account in determining whether the CODA is a qualified CODA.[3]

[1] IRS Reg. § 1.414(r)-1(d)(5). Also, see the preamble to T.D. 8376, published in the *Federal Register* on December 4, 1991 (56 FR 63420). The revised 1994 final QSLOB regulation did not provide any further guidance. T.D. 8548, published in the *Federal Register* on June 27, 1994 (59 FR 32911).

[2] IRS Reg. § 1.414(r)-1(c)(5).

[3] IRS Reg. § 1.401(k)-1(e)(9). This provision was issued with the 1991 final QSLOB regulations, and amends the final Code Sec. 401(k) regulations that were previously issued on August 8, 1991. Generally, the same rule applies to employee and employer matching contributions under Code Sec. 401(m). See IRS Reg. § 1.401(m)-1(c)(3), as issued on December 2, 1991, and as amending the final regulations previously issued on August 8, 1991. It was not changed by the 1994 final regulations under Code Sec. 414(r).

¶ 1340
For More Information

☐ For more information on separate lines of business, see ¶ 2283-2383 of the CCH PENSION PLAN GUIDE.

Funding and Actuarial Requirements

¶ 1400

Overview of Funding and Actuarial Requirements

Inadequately financed pension plans create the risk that the funds needed to provide employees with promised benefits upon retirement will not be available. Accordingly, employers that maintain defined benefit plans, as well as certain defined contribution plans, such as money purchase plans and target benefit plans, must adhere to funding standards stipulated in ERISA and the Internal Revenue Code. However, arrangements such as profit-sharing plans, welfare benefit plans, stock bonus plans, ESOPs, plans funded exclusively by insurance contracts, church plans, municipal plans, and state plans are exempt from the funding rules.

The minimum funding rules were substantially modified, generally effective beginning after 2007, by the Pension Protection Act of 2006. The following is a brief synopsis of the minimum funding requirements applicable before 2008 and subsequent to amendment.

Minimum funding requirements for single-employer defined benefit plans: Pre-2008

An employer maintaining a single-employer defined benefit pension plan must make an annual minimum funding contribution to ensure that the plan has sufficient assets with which to pay promised retirement benefits. The funding standards generally require an employer to contribute an amount to the plan that is sufficient to: (1) pay the normal cost of funding the plan; and (2) amortize unfunded past service liability and changes in past service liability due to plan amendments, assumption changes, and experience gains and losses over a period that can exceed 30 years.

Full funding limit. Employers are not required to make contributions to a defined benefit plan in excess of the full funding limitation. The full funding limit is the excess, if any, of: (1) the accrued liability under the plan (including normal cost); over (2) the lesser of (a) the market value of plan assets, or (b) the actuarial value of plan assets. However, the full funding limit may not be less than the excess of 90 percent of the plan's current liability over the actuarial value of plan assets. In

¶1400

determining whether a plan is at the 90 percent limit, plan assets are not reduced by credit balances.

Employers may also generally not take a deduction for contributions in a tax year that exceed the full funding limitation. The effect of the full funding limit is to prevent employers from making additional contributions to a fully funded plan even if the accrued liability of the plan is greater than plan assets.

Funding standard account. The administrative mechanism used to implement the funding requirements is the funding standard account. Every plan subject to the minimum funding rules must maintain a funding standard account that is: (1) charged with amounts that must be paid to satisfy the plan's funding obligations; and (2) credited with contributions to the plan, decreases in plan liabilities due to plan or assumption changes, and experience gains.

A plan satisfies the minimum funding requirements if an accumulated funding deficiency does not exist at the end of the plan year. The accumulated funding deficiency is the excess of total charges to the funding standard account over total credits to the account. Generally, the minimum contribution for a plan year is the amount by which the charges to funding standard account would exceed credits to the account if no contributions were made to the plan.

Charges to funding standard account. Charges to the funding standard account include: (1) normal costs for the plan year; (2) amortization of: unfunded past service liability (generally over a 30-40 year period), the net increase in unfunded past service liability for plan amendments (over a 30-year period), net experience loss (over a five-year period for single-employer plans) and net loss from changes in actuarial assumptions (over a 10-year period for single-employer plans); (3) amounts necessary to amortize each waived funding deficiency (over five plan years for single-employer plans); (4) and the amount necessary to amortize over five plan years the amount credited to the account from an alternative funding standard account that may be adopted in addition the regular funding standard account under a plan sponsor's funding method.

Extension of amortization periods. The IRS may, at the request of the plan administrator or plan sponsor, extend the amortization periods described above for up to 10 years if necessary to adequately protect the interests of participants and beneficiaries. The amortization period may be extended only if the failure to authorize the extension would: (1) be adverse to the interests of plan participants in the aggregate; and (2) cause a substantial risk to the plan's continued operation or substantially curtail retirement benefits or employee compensation.

Special relief for airline plans. Generally effective for plan years ending after August 17, 2006, special funding relief is available for single-employer defined benefit plans sponsored by commercial passenger airlines and catering businesses that primarily serve commercial airlines. The relief allows eligible sponsors of plans that restrict benefit accruals and benefit increases to elect to amortize the plan's unfunded liability over a 17-year period. Alternatively, plans that do not satisfy the specified restrictions on benefit accruals and benefit increases may elect to amortize the plan's shortfall amortization base over a 10-year period.

¶1400

Credits to funding standard account. Credits to the funding standard account include: (1) employer contributions for the plan year; (2) amortization in equal annual installments of the net decrease in unfunded past service liability from plan amendments (over a 30-year period), net experience gain (over a five-year period for single-employer plans), and any net gain resulting from changes in actuarial assumptions (over 10 years for single-employer plans); (3) amount of the waived funding deficiency for the plan year; and (4) the excess of the debit balance in the funding standard account over the debit balance in the alternative funding standard account, if the funding deficiency was determined under the alternative funding standard account for the plan year.

Deficit reduction required of underfunded plans. Single-employer defined benefit plans (covering more than 100 participants on each day in the preceding plan year) with unfunded current liability must be funded more rapidly than single-employer plans without unfunded liabilities. Plans having a funded current liability percentage of less than 90 percent may be required to make an additional "deficit reduction contribution" (of 18-30 percent of unfunded current liability) over a specified amortization period. The minimum contribution required of such underfunded plans is the greater of: (1) the amount determined under the normal funding rules (discussed above); or (2) the deficit reduction contribution and the amount required to be contributed on account of unpredictable contingent events.

The deficit reduction contribution, for purposes of the additional funding contribution, is the total of the unfunded old liability amount and the unfunded new liability amount. The deficit reduction contribution must also include: (1) the expected increase in current liability that is attributable to benefits accruing during the plan year; and (2) the amount needed to amortize increased current liability that is attributable to future changes in required mortality tables (i.e., the unfunded mortality increase amount).

Calculation of the amounts underlying the deficit reduction contribution is based upon the plan's current liability, which generally encompasses all plan obligations to employees and their beneficiaries. Current liability is calculated through the use of prescribed mortality tables and specified interest rates.

Interest rates used in calculating current liability. Determining the present value of an underfunded plan's liabilities requires the discounting of future payments at a designated interest rate. Thus, the discount rate is not based on the interest the plan is actually earning on its investments. Under the law applicable in 2004 and 2005, the interest rate to be used in determining a plan's current liability could not be above and could not be more than 10 percent below (i.e., between 90 percent to 100 percent) the weighted average of the rate of interest on amounts conservatively invested in long-term corporate bonds for the four-year period ending on the last day before the plan year begins.

Prior to 2002, the permissible range for purposes of determining current liability was based on the weighted average of the rate of interest on 30-year Treasury securities during the four-year period ending on the last day before the beginning of the plan year. The Job Creation and Worker Assistance Act of 2002 authorized an increase in the maximum interest rate to be used in determining

¶1400

current liability from 105 percent to 120 percent of the weighted average interest rate of 30-year Treasury securities for 2002 and 2003 plan years. The higher interest rate, by effectively decreasing the value of plan liabilities, reduced the plan sponsor's funding obligation.

The Pension Funding Equity Act of 2004 (PFEA) replaced the previously applicable 30-year Treasury rate used in funding calculations with the four-year weighted average of the long-term corporate bond rate, referenced above. However, the interest rates authorized under the PFEA applied only through 2005. Accordingly, in 2006, current liability is determined pursuant to an interest rate that is 90-105 percent of the average of interest rates on 30-year Treasury securities for the four-year period ending on the last day before the plan year begins. The Pension Protection Act of 2006, effective August 17, 2006, authorized the use of the replacement interest rate through 2007.

Mortality table for calculating current liability. The prescribed mortality table for calculating current liability is the 1983 Group Annuity Mortality Table (GAM 83). An employer must use the GAM 83 table and may not adopt a plan-specific mortality table or a table that reflects the increase in average life expectancy since 1983.

90-percent funding exemption from additional contribution requirement. The additional funding contribution required of underfunded single-employer defined benefit plans (other than plans with 100 or fewer participants) does not apply to an underfunded plan in a plan year in which the funded current liability percentage is at least 90 percent. Thus, an employer is required, under current law, to fund only 90 percent of the plan's current liabilities to preclude the deficit reduction contribution requirement from applying. Moreover, the additional funding contribution will not apply to an underfunded plan in a plan year in which: (1) the funded current liability percentage is at least 80 percent; and (2) the funded current liability percentage for each of the two immediately preceding years (or each of the second and third immediately preceding years) is at least 90 percent (i.e., the "volatility" rule).

Alternative deficit reduction contribution for airlines and steel industry. The PFEA authorized specified employers maintaining underfunded single-employer defined benefit plans to elect a reduction in the amount of required contributions. The alternative deficit reduction contribution relief was available in 2004 and 2005 and was limited to plans maintained by commercial passenger airlines; companies primarily engaged in the production or manufacture of steel mill products or the processing of iron ore pellets; and the Transportation Communications Union. The amount of the alternative deficit reduction contribution that could be elected by an eligible employer was limited to the greater of: (1) 20 percent of the additional contribution that would otherwise be required; or (2) the additional contribution that would be required if the deficit reduction contribution for the plan year was based solely on the expected increase in current liability due to benefits accruing during the plan year. The Pension Protection Act of 2006, effective for plan years ending after August 17, 2006 extended the alternative deficit reduction election to plan years beginning after December 27, 2003 and before December 28, 2007. However, the relief is limited to commercial passenger airlines.

Plan asset valuation. In determining whether a plan's assets are sufficient to cover liabilities, assets may be valued under any reasonable actuarial method that takes fair market value into account. Fair market value is defined as the price at which the property would change hands between a willing buyer and a willing seller.

Alternatively, a plan's valuation method may be based on the average value of plan assets over a period not in excess of the five most recent plan years, including the current year. Average asset valuation (i.e., smoothing) is permitted to the extent actuarial value is between 80 and 120 percent of current fair market value. Note, plan liabilities may be amortized over a four-year period.

Employers are generally required to use a current year valuation date. The valuation date must be within the plan year relating to the valuation, or within one month prior to the start of the plan year. Alternatively, employers may elect to value plan assets as of any date within the plan year prior to the plan year to which the valuation refers.

Credit balances. In the event a plan's accumulated funding deficiency at the end of a plan year is larger than the full funding limitation, the excess is credited to the funding standard account as a credit balance. A credit balance may result from contributions in excess of minimum required contributions or from large net experience gains. The credit balance may be further enhanced by interest at the rate used by the plan to determine costs. However, the credit balance is also reduced by charges to the funding standard account unless the charge is offset by contributions. The value of a credit balance is that it is automatically applied against charges to the funding standard account and, thus, will reduce required contributions, regardless of the plan's funded status.

In determining whether the plan is required to make a deficit reduction contribution because it has a funded current liability that is under 90 percent, plan assets are not reduced by credit balances in the funding standard account. However, the value of plan assets will be reduced by the credit balance in determining the amount of the deficit reduction contribution.

Benefit limits. A single-employer defined benefit plan may entitle participants to an unpredictable contingent event benefit that is payable upon the occurrence during the plan year of specified events, such as the shutdown of an employer's operations. In the event a plan is required to pay a benefit arising from an unpredictable contingent event while its assets are less than its current liabilities, an additional funding contribution must be made. However, unpredictable contingent event benefits are generally not taken into account for purposes of determining a plan's funding liabilities until the event has occurred.

Plan amendments that increase a plan's current liability (e.g., accelerated lump-sum payments) may not be adopted if the plan's funded current liability percentage is less than 60 percent, unless the employer provides security to the plan. In addition, plan amendments that increase a plan's benefit liabilities because of an increase in benefits, change in the rate of accrual of benefits, or change in the rate at which benefits vest under the plan may not be adopted while the employer is in bankruptcy or during the period of an IRS-approved funding waiver or amortization extension.

Finally, lump-sum distributions may not be made under a plan that has a liquidity shortfall (i.e., fund assets are less than three times the plan disbursements for the year). However, current law does not restrict future benefit accruals in underfunded plans, and employers are allowed under current law to use credit balances to reduce required contributions.

□ The minimum funding rules applicable before 2008 are detailed at ¶ 2800 — ¶ 3135 of the CCH PENSION PLAN GUIDE.

Minimum funding standards applicable after 2007

Effective for plan years beginning after 2007, the funding standard account mechanism and the current two-tiered funding system will be replaced with a single funding method. An employer maintaining a single-employer defined benefit plan that is not 100-percent funded will not be required to make a deficit reduction contribution, but will be required to make a minimum contribution based on the plan's assets (reduced by credit balances), funding target, and target normal cost and that is sufficient to amortize unfunded plan liabilities over a period of seven years. Unlike current law, under which employers are required to fund up to 90 percent of a plan's total liabilities, the Pension Protection Act increases the funding target to 100 percent of target or current liabilities.

In addition, the Pension Protection Act radically changes the actuarial assumptions and methods used to determine present value, authorizing a new interest rate and a new mortality table. Specifically, the Pension Act, while retaining the blended rate of corporate bonds, introduces a segmented "yield curve" that would consist of three different interest rates (based on the unweighted average of interest rates on investment grade corporate bonds) applicable to benefits payable in different time periods.

"At-risk" plans, as determined by the plan's funded status and not by the credit rating of the employer sponsoring the plan, will be further subject to an at-risk liability assumption that all plan participants eligible for benefits within a 10-year period will elect benefits at the highest present value. The at-risk rules, which are limited to plans with over 500 participants, will increase a plan's target liability.

Employer liability for contributions. Employer sponsors of the plan are responsible for managing the minimum required contribution. In addition, each member of a controlled group is jointly and severally liable for the contribution.

Benefit limits applicable to underfunded plans. Single-employer defined benefit plans that fall below specified funding levels will be subject to new limits on: the payment of unpredictable contingent event benefits (e.g. shutdown benefits), plan amendments, lump-sum distributions, and benefit accruals. The restrictions, which are based on the ratio of the plan assets to target liability and triggered at varying thresholds, will generally be effective beginning in 2008. The limits require benefit accruals to be frozen and prevent underfunded plans that have been in effect for over five years from implementing amendments adding benefits or otherwise increasing plan liabilities or paying the full amount of a lump-sum distribution, without additional contributions by the plan sponsor. Employees must receive written notice of any benefit limitation within 30 days.

☐ The minimum funding rules applicable to single-employer plans after 2007 are discussed at ¶ 1493—1493J.

Multiemployer Plan Funding Rules

Multiemployer plans are also subject to minimum funding requirements. A multiemployer plan is a plan to which more than one unrelated employer contributes, that is established pursuant to one or more collective bargaining agreements, and that satisfies such other requirements as the Secretary of Labor may prescribe by regulation. In general, the required level of contributions to a multiemployer plan is specified in the applicable collective bargaining agreements, and the level of plan benefits is established by the plan trustees.

Minimum funding standard. A multiemployer plan satisfies the minimum funding standard for a plan year if, as of the end of that plan year, the plan does not have an accumulated funding deficiency. An accumulated funding deficiency exists for any plan year if the total charges to the plan's funding standard account for all plan years (see below) exceed the total credits to the account for all plan years.

Funding standard account. A multiemployer plan must have a funding standard account. For each plan year, the funding standard account is charged with the normal cost of the plan and credited with employer contributions. The normal cost is the cost of future benefits allocated to the year by the funding method used by the plan for current employees and (under some funding methods) for separated employees.

Amortization of supplemental costs. Changes in supplemental costs are also either charged or credited to the funding standard account. A supplemental cost for a plan year is the cost of future benefits that would not be met by future contributions or plan assets. For example, an unfunded past service liability existing on the date that the plan is first effective or an increase or decrease in unfunded past service liabilities caused by plan amendments is amortized in equal payments generally over 30 years and charged or credited to the funding standard account. Any gain or loss resulting from changes in actuarial assumptions is amortized in equal payments generally over 30 years and charged or credited to the funding standard account. Any increase or decrease resulting from changes in the plan's net experience gain or loss are amortized in equal payments over 15 years and charged or credited to the funding standard account.

Plans in reorganization status. Special rules apply to any multiemployer plan that is in "reorganization status." Typically this situation will arise if the plan's funding level is low and current accruals are small relative to the vested accrued liabilities. A plan is in reorganization status for a year if the required funding contribution exceeds the plan's vested benefits charge. The vested benefits charge is generally the amount needed to amortize, in equal annual installments, unfunded vested benefits under the plan over: (1) 10 years, in the case of vested benefits payable to individuals who are already receiving benefit payments; and (2) 25 years, in the case of benefits payable to other individuals.

When a plan is in reorganization status: (1) benefits derived from employer contributions that exceed a de minimis amount must be paid in the form of a life annuity; (2) the plan is eligible for a special funding credit; (3) year-to-year increases in contributions are capped; and (4) the plan may be amended to reduce or eliminate accrued benefits in excess of those guaranteed by the PBGC.

Multiemployer minimum funding rules applicable after 2007

The funding rules for multiemployer plans have been set out separately from the single-employer plan funding rules. The same general framework remains, but changes have been made for plan years beginning after 2007 that will: (1) reduce the amortization periods for certain supplemental costs to 15 years, (2) change the amortization extension and funding waiver interest rate to the plan rate, (3) tighten the reasonableness requirement for actuarial assumptions, (4) eliminate the alternative minimum funding standard, (5) make available an automatic five-year amortization extension with an additional five-year extension, and (6) provide a route for deemed approval of changes in the use of the shortfall funding method.

Additional funding rules for significantly underfunded multiemployer plans. All multiemployer plans are now required to obtain an annual actuarial certification regarding their funding status. Special funding and operational requirements apply for plans that are certified to be in "endangered" or "critical" status. The new requirements generally apply to plan years beginning after 2007 for multiemployer plans in effect on July 16, 2006. The requirements are subject to a sunset provision, so that for plan years beginning after 2014 there will be no new certifications of endangered or critical status. The requirements will continue to apply to plans that are already in endangered or critical status at the end of 2014.

☐ The minimum funding rules applicable to multiemployer plans after 2007 are discussed at ¶ 1493K and ¶ 1493L.

¶ 1402

COVERED PLANS: Plans Covered by Funding Standards

Defined benefit plans and certain defined contribution plans, such as money purchase plans or target benefit arrangements, are subject to funding standards. Funding standards are found in both ERISA and the Internal Revenue Code (IRC). The funding requirements of the IRC, however, apply only to qualified pension plans.[1] The funding standards of ERISA, on the other hand, apply, in general, to both qualified and nonqualified pension plans.[2] Thus, certain plans that are not qualified under the IRC must still comply with the minimum funding standards.

Plan maintained by entity engaged in interstate commerce

A plan is subject to ERISA's funding requirements if it is maintained by:

1. an employer that is engaged in interstate commerce or any activity that affects interstate commerce;

2. an employee organization (union) representing employees engaged in interstate commerce or in an activity affecting interstate commerce; or

3. both such an employer and employee organization.[3]

Money purchase plans subject to funding rules

Employer contributions under a money purchase plan are typically fixed as a set percentage of each employee's compensation. However, for purposes of the funding requirements, a plan will be treated as a money purchase plan (and, thus, subject to the minimum funding requirements) even though its obligation to contribute may be contingent on the amount of contributions made by participating employees.[4] Thus, a plan under which the employer is required to contribute 6% of an employee's salary, but no more than the amount contributed by the employee, is subject to the minimum funding standards.

☐ Money purchase plans are discussed at ¶ 109.

☐ Plans exempt from the funding requirements are discussed at ¶ 1403.

---

[1] Code Sec. 412(e) (post-2007).

[2] ERISA Secs. 4(a) and 301(a).

[3] ERISA Sec. 4(a).

[4] P. L. 93-406 (ERISA), Conference Report.

¶ 1403

COVERED PLANS: Plans Exempt from Funding Standards

The following plans are exempt from the funding standards for both tax and regulatory purposes:

1. Profit-sharing, stock bonus, or employee stock ownership plans.[1] Plans that do not provide for employer contributions after September 2, 1974.[2]

2. Plans that are funded exclusively through the purchase of specified insurance contracts (see below).[3]

3. Governmental plans, including Railroad Retirement Plans, established and maintained for employees by the government of the United States, any state or political subdivision thereof, or any of their agencies or instrumentalities.[4]

4. Church plans that do not elect coverage.[5]

5. Plans of fraternal organizations and employee beneficiary associations that are tax-exempt under Code Sec. 501(c)(8) and (9). However, no part of the contributions under the plan may be made by employers of plan participants.[6] In addition, in order to maintain its tax-qualified status, the plan must comply with the applicable funding requirements of pre-ERISA law.[7]

The following plans are exempt from the funding standards for regulatory purposes. These are plans that normally would not seek qualified status under the Internal Revenue Code:

1. Employee welfare benefit plans.[8] These are plans that provide medical, surgical, or hospital care or benefits, or benefits in the event of sickness, accident, disability, death or unemployment, or vacation, training, severance, and other benefits. Benefits described in Sec. 302 of the Labor Management Relations Act of 1947, other than pensions on retirement or death benefits and associated insurance, are also encompassed by this exemption.[9]

2. Unfunded nonqualified plans maintained by employers primarily to provide deferred compensation to a select group of management or highly compensated employees.

   CCH POINTER: *Restrictions on funding of nonqualified plans by employers maintaining underfunded pension plans.* Nonqualified deferred compensation plans are not subject to the minimum funding rules. However, an employer's failure to comply with the funding standards will compromise its ability to fund a nonqualified plan. Specifically, effective for transfers or other reservations of assets occurring after August 17, 2006, assets set aside for the payment of deferred compensation under a nonqualified plan to a covered employee (e.g., insider employee under SEC rules) by an employer maintaining an at-risk pension plan (see ¶ 1493E) will be subject to tax under (Code Sec. 83 as property transferred in connection with the performance of services.[11] Such assets would also be subject to interest and penalty tax under Code Sec. 409A (see ¶ 3302).

3. Excess benefit plans.[12] These supplemental plans are designed solely for the purpose of providing benefits to certain employees in excess of the limitations on contributions and benefits contained in Code Sec. 415.[13]

4. Individual retirement accounts or annuities under Code Sec. 408.[14]

5. Individual account plans, other than money purchase plans. This exemption includes defined benefit plans that are treated as individual account plans, other than money purchase plans.[15]

6. Payments to a retired partner or to a deceased partner's successor in interest under Code Sec. 736.[16]

7. Plans maintained to comply with workers' compensation or unemployment compensation laws or disability insurance laws.[17]

8. Plans maintained outside the United States primarily for the benefit of persons substantially all of whom are nonresident aliens.[18]

9. Plans designed by an employer, whose stock is owned by employees, former employees, or beneficiaries, under an unfunded arrangement, to compensate retired employees for benefits that were forfeited under a plan

maintained by a former employer prior to the date that such plan became subject to ERISA.[19]

Insurance contract plans

Fully insured defined benefit plans that are funded solely by the purchase of individual insurance contracts (insurance contract plans) are exempt from the minimum funding standards.[20]

> **CCH POINTER:** Insurance contract plans, prior to 2008, were defined under Code Sec. 412(i). Accordingly, such arrangements were known as "412(i) plans." The Pension Protection Act of 2006, incident to an overhaul of the minimum funding rules (see discussion beginning at ¶ 1493), effective for plan years beginning after December 31, 2007, eliminated Code Sec. 412(i). [21] However, the substantive provisions of Code Sec. 412(i) were retained in new Code Sec. 412(e)(3).

Insurance contract plans are typically used by small employers with a steady cash flow to alleviate administrative burdens. For example, insurance contract plans can relieve small employers of the requirement of making the complex quarterly contribution calculations. In addition, small employers may save the expense of hiring an enrolled actuary to assure the funding of the plan because an insurance contract plan is not required to file Schedule B of Form 5500.

Funding exemption conditions. An insurance contract plan is exempt from the applicable minimum funding requirements:

(1) it is funded exclusively through the purchase of individual insurance contracts;

(2) the contracts provide for level annual premiums to be paid, extending no later than the retirement age for each individual participating in the plan, and commencing with the date the individual becomes a participant in the plan (or in the case of an increase in benefits, commencing at the time the increase in benefits becomes effective);

(3) benefits provided by the plan are equal to the benefits provided under each contract at normal retirement age under the plan and are guaranteed by a license insurance carrier;

(4) premiums payable for the plan year, and all prior plan years, under the contract have been paid before lapse, or there is reinstatement of the policy;

(5) no rights under the contracts have been subject to a security interest at any time during the plan year; and

(6) no policy loans are outstanding at any time during the plan year.[22]

☐ The rules governing insurance contract plans, including the conversion of pension plans to insurance contract plans, are discussed in detail at CCH PENSION PLAN GUIDE ¶ 2815—¶ 2825.

---

[1] Code Sec. 412(e)(2)(A). Note, prior to 2008, the governing rules were provided under Code Sec. 412(h).

[2] Code Sec. 412(e)(2)(E); ERISA Sec. 301(a)(5).

[3] Code Sec. 412(e)(2)(B); ERISA Sec. 301(a)(2).

[4] Code Sec. 412(e)(2)(C); ERISA Sec. 4(b)(1).

[5] Code Sec. 412(e)(2)(D); ERISA Sec. 4(b)(2).

[6] Code Sec. 412(e)(2)(F); ERISA Sec. 301(a)(4)(A).

[7] Code Sec. 412(e)(2).

[8] ERISA Sec. 301(a)(1); *Adams v. Avondale Industries*, CA-6 (1990), 905 F2d 943.

[9] ERISA Sec. 3(1).

[11] Code Sec. 409A(b)(3).

[12] ERISA Sec. 4(b)(5) and 301(a)(9).

[13] ERISA Sec. 3.

[14] ERISA Sec. 301(a)(7).

[15] ERISA Sec. 301(a)(8).

[16] ERISA Sec. 301(a)(6); ERISA Opinion Letter 90-03A, 2-13-90.

[17] ERISA Sec. 4(b)(3).

[18] ERISA Sec. 4(b)(4).

[19] ERISA Sec. 301(a)(10).

[20] Code Sec. 412(e)(2); ERISA Sec. 301(a)(2).

[21] P.L. 109-280 (Pension Protection Act of 2006), Act Sec. 111(a).

[22] Code Sec. 412(e)(3); ERISA Sec. 301(b).

¶ 1404

EMPLOYER DEDUCTION: Deduction for Funding Contributions

Employers may claim a tax deduction for amounts contributed to fund a pension plan, even where the employer makes greater contributions than are required.[1] However, the amount that may be deducted is limited.

Employer deduction limits

The annual deduction limitation for contributions to a single-employer defined benefit plan is the greater of (1) the minimum contribution required under Code Sec. 430 (see ¶ 1493B) or (2) an alternative amount computed under Code Sec. 404(o)(1)(A) (applicable to at-risk plans).

At-risk plans. The alternative amount for plans that are "at-risk" under Code Sec. 430(i) will be the excess of the sum of (1) the funding target for the plan year, (2) the target normal cost for the plan year, and (3) the "cushion amount" for the plan year, over the value of the assets held by the plan as of the valuation date for the plan year, under Code Sec. 430(g)(2), or the sum of the minimum required contribution under Code Sec. 430. [2]

Limit may not be less than minimum required contribution. In the event the plan is not "at-risk," the alternative amount may not be less than the sum of the funding target and the target normal cost for the plan year (both determined as if it were an at-risk plan) less the value of the plan assets, over the Code Sec. 430(g)(3) definition of the actuarial value of assets.[3]

Cushion amount is 50% of funding target. The "cushion amount" is generally the sum of 50 percent of the funding target for the plan year and the amount by which the funding target would increase for the year if the plan took into account expected future increases in compensation or, if the plan does not base benefits for past services on compensation, expected increases in benefits in succeeding plan years. [4] The determination of expected increases in benefits must be based on the average annual increase in benefits over of the previous six plan years.

In computing the cushion amount, the plan's actuary must assume that the annual compensation limitation under Code Sec. 404(l) and the annual benefit limitation under Code Sec. 415(b) apply. In the case of a plan covered by the PBGC, the plan's actuary may take into account cost-of-living compensation limitation increases expected to occur in succeeding plan years under Code Sec. 401(a)(17), notwithstanding Code Sec. 404(l).[5]

Cushion amount for plans with 100 or fewer participants. In determining the cushion amount, the funding target of a plan with 100 or fewer participants for the plan year does not include benefit increases for highly compensated individuals, as defined in Code Sec. 414(q), resulting from a plan amendment made or effective (whichever is later) within the previous two years.[6]

The application of the cushion amount and the determination of the deductible limit is illustrated at CCH PENSION PLAN GUIDE ¶ 2835.

Adoption of new plan treated as plan amendment. The IRS has clarified that the adoption of a new plan will not be treated as a plan amendment only if the employer did not maintain a defined benefit plan covering only HCEs covered by the new plan during the past two years.[7] For example, assume a highly compensated employee is covered by the defined benefit plan of an employer (with a tax year that is the calendar year) at any time during 2008 or 2009. In the event a new plan is established during the 2010 tax year that covers that HCE, the new plan would be considered a plan amendment for purposes of Code Sec. 404(a)(1)(D)(ii).

Aggregation rules. For purposes of determining the number of plan participants, all defined benefit plans maintained by the same employer (or any member of the employer's controlled group) are treated as one plan. However, only participants of the employer (or controlled group member) are taken into account.[8]

Deduction limits for multiemployer plans. The maximum amount of the deduction limitation for contributions to multiemployer plans cannot be less than 140 percent of the current liability of the plan (determined under Code Sec. 431(c)(6)(D)) minus the value of the plan's assets (determined under Code Sec. 431(c)(2)).[9]

Excess may be carried over

Contributions in excess of the full funding limitation may be carried over and deducted in succeeding years.[10] In each succeeding year, the amount deductible would be the difference between the amount paid and deductible in the year and the maximum which could have been deducted in the year. In cases where the full funding limit exceeds the deductible limit, the full funding limit will not reduce the employer's deduction. Even where no contributions are made during a tax year, a taxpayer may take a deduction for carryover amounts that do not exceed the full funding limits.[11]

Excise tax on nondeductible contributions continues to apply. Although employers may carry over and deduct excess contributions, the 10 percent excise tax assessed on nondeductible contributions for a year (see ¶ 1492) continues to apply.

¶1404

Types of deductible contributions

Not all types of employer contributions qualify for the tax deduction under Code Sec. 404(a). The United States Supreme Court has ruled that the delivery of a promissory note of the employer was not a deductible contribution, even though the note was payable on demand and further secured.[12] Subsequently, in *Commissioner v. Keystone Consolidated Industries*, the Supreme Court further held that a transfer of property that was executed in order to satisfy a plan's minimum funding obligation constituted a prohibited transaction.[13] Thus, plan sponsors who make a contribution of property in satisfaction of the minimum funding requirement will commit a prohibited transaction. However, the Labor Department has granted an individual prohibited transaction exemption to a company that has, under tightly defined conditions, contributed nonpublicly traded stock of a subsidiary to pension plans in satisfaction of the minimum funding obligation.[14]

Penalty for overstatement of pension liabilities

An employer is subject to a penalty, assessed as an addition to tax, on a substantial overstatement of pension liability.[15] Pension liabilities are substantially overstated if the employer's actuarial determination is 200% or more of the actual amount of the liabilities.[16] However, the penalty is not imposed unless the tax underpayment caused by the overstatement of liability is over $1,000.[17]

Plans with 100 participants or less

For years prior to 2002, a special rule applied to defined benefit plans (other than multiemployer plans) with more than 100 participants.[18] Generally, the maximum deduction for contributions to such a plan could not be less than the unfunded current liability for the plan, as determined under the additional funding requirements of repealed ERISA Sec. 302(d).

In determining if a plan had more than 100 participants, all defined benefit plans maintained by the same employer (or any member of the employer's controlled group) were treated as one plan. However, only employees of the member of the controlled group or the employer were taken into account in making this determination.

Special rules governing deductibility extended to multiemployer plans. The special rule allowing employers to deduct contributions up to 100 percent of a plan's unfunded current liability was extended, effective for plan years beginning after 2001, to all defined benefit plans, including multiemployer plans and plans with 100 or fewer participants.[19] However, if a plan has 100 or fewer participants for the plan year, unfunded current liability will not include the liability attributable to benefit increases for highly compensated employees that result from plan amendments that are made or become effective, whichever is later, within the last two years.[20]

Money purchase pension plans treated as profit-sharing plans

Money purchase pension plans and other defined contribution plans that are subject to the Code Sec. 412 minimum funding rules are treated in the same manner as a profit-sharing or stock bonus plan for purposes of the deduction rules under Code Sec. 404(a)(3) (see ¶ 670 and ¶ 2987). Thus, an employer may deduct contributions to a money purchase plan in an amount not to exceed the greater of (1) 25% of compensation paid or accrued during the tax year to beneficiaries of the plan, or (2) the amount that the employer is required to contribute to the trust under Code Sec. 401(k)(11) for the year.[21]

Special deduction election for collectively bargained plans

Collectively bargained plans that become fully funded as the result of a plan amendment may make a special deduction election. Under the election, the maximum deduction will equal the lesser of the full funding limitation (under Code Sec. 431(c)(6) (see ¶ 1493K), accounting for the decrease in the present value of unamortized liability resulting from the amendment, or normal plan costs minus the amount needed to amortize the benefit reduction (principal and interest) over a period of 10 years.[22] If the election is made, the amounts deductible in future years will be reduced by the amount required to amortize the benefit reduction.

Deduction influenced by contribution and benefit limits

The amount of annual benefits that may be provided by a qualified pension plan is also limited (see ¶ 500 and following).[23] This limitation influences the funding of a plan and the employer's deduction for plan contributions. Accordingly, deductions may not be based upon amounts contributed to a defined benefit plan to reflect anticipated cost-of-living increases to the Code Sec. 415 limitations on contributions and benefits.[24]

Detailed discussion of the rules governing the deduction of funding contributions is at CCH PENSION PLAN GUIDE ¶ 2835.

[1] Code Sec. 404(a)(1)(A).

[2] Code Sec. 404(o)(2)(A), as added by P.L. 109-280 (Pension Protection Act of 2006), Act Sec. 801(a)(2).

[3] Code Sec. 404(o)(2)(B), as added by P.L. 109-280 (Pension Protection Act of 2006), Act Sec. 801(a)(2).

[4] Code Sec. 404(o)(3), as added by P.L. 109-280 (Pension Protection Act of 2006), Act Sec. 801(a)(2).

[5] Code Sec.404(o)(3)(B)(ii), as added by P.L. 109-280 (Pension Protection Act of 2006), Act Sec. 801(a)(2).

[6] Code Sec. 404(o)(4)(A), as added by P.L. 109-280 (Pension Protection Act of 2006), Act Sec. 801(a)(2).

[7] IRS Notice 2007-28, Q/A-5, I.R.B. 2007-14, 4-2-07, at CCH PENSION PLAN GUIDE ¶ 17,136F.

[8] Code Sec. 404(o)(4)(B), as added by P.L. 109-280, (Pension Protection Act of 2006), Act Sec. 801(a)(2).

[9] Code Sec. 404(a)(1)(D)(i), as amended by P.L. 109-280 (Pension Protection Act of 2006), Act Sec. 802(a).

[10] Code Sec. 404(a)(1)(E).

[11] Rev. Rul. 82-125, 1982-1 CB 64, CCH PENSION PLAN GUIDE ¶ 19,620A.

[12] *Don E. Williams Co. v. Commissioner*, U.S. Sup Ct (1977), 492 U.S. 569..

[13] *Commissioner of Internal Revenue v. Keystone Consolidated Industries, Inc.*, U.S. Sup Ct (1993), 508 U.S. 152 at CCH PENSION PLAN GUIDE ¶ 23,876E; Prohibited Transaction Exemption 2003-6 (Northwest Airlines Pension Plan for Salaried Employees, the Northwest Airlines Pension Plan for Pilot Employees, and the Northwest Airlines Pension Plan for Contract Employees, Located in Eegan, MN), 8-19-2003 (68 FR 49792), at CCH PENSION PLAN GUIDE ¶ 19,980.

[14] Prohibited Transaction Exemption 2003-6 (Northwest Airlines Pension Plan for Salaried Employees, the Northwest Airlines Pension Plan for Pilot Employees, and the Northwest Airlines Pension Plan for Contract Employees, Located in

Eegan, MN), 8-19-2003 (68 FR 49792), at CCH PENSION PLAN GUIDE¶ 19,980.

[15] Code Sec. 6662(f).

[16] Code Sec. 6662(f)(1).

[17] Code Sec. 6662(f)(2).

[18] Code Sec. 404(a)(1)(D) prior to amendment by P.L. 107-16 (Economic Growth and Tax Relief Reconciliation Act of 2001).

[19] Code Sec. 404(a)(1)(D)(i), as amended by P.L.107-16 (Economic Growth and Tax Relief Reconciliation Act of 2001).

[20] Code Sec. 404(a)(1)(D)(ii), as amended by P.L.107-16 (Economic Growth and Tax Relief Reconciliation Act of 2001).

[21] Code Sec. 404(a)(3)(A)(v), as amended by P.L. 107-16 (Economic Growth and Tax Relief Reconciliation Act of 2001).

[22] Code Sec. 404(a)(1)(B).

[23] Code Sec. 415(b); ERISA Sec. 2004(d).

[24] Code Sec. 404(j)(2).

¶ 1405

SPECIAL RULES FOR PLANS OF MORE THAN ONE EMPLOYER: Plans of More Than One Employer

The minimum funding rules apply to multiple employer plans as if each employer were maintaining a separate plan.[1] Specifically, employers will be treated as maintaining separate plans unless the method for determining required contributions under a plan established after 1988 assures that each employee will contribute no less than the amount that would be required if each employer were operating a separate plan. [2] If this requirement is satisfied, the multiple employer plan will be required to file only a single Form 5500 and only a single Schedule B for the entire plan.[3] With respect to other plans (i.e., those established before 1989) the funding requirements will be applied as if all the participants in the plan were employed by a single employer, unless the plan administrator elects to have the condition under Code Sec. 413(c)(4)(A) apply.[4]

Determination of deduction limitation

In the case of a plan established after 1988, each applicable deduction limitation under Code Sec. 404(a) is determined as if each employer were maintaining a separate plan.[5] For plans established before 1989, the deduction limitations are determined, absent a contrary election by the plan administrator, as if all participants are employed by a single employer. [6]

☐ The rules governing plans established prior to 1989 are fully discussed in the CCH PENSION PLAN GUIDE at ¶ 2840.

Assets and liabilities

The assets and liabilities of each plan that is treated as a separate plan are the assets and liabilities that would be allocated to a plan maintained by the employer if the employer withdrew from the multiple employer plan.[7]

[1] Code Sec. 413(c)(1).

[2] Code Sec. 413(c)(4)(A).

[3] Conference Report to P.L. 100-47 (Technical and Miscellaneous Revenue Act of 1988).

[4] Code Sec. 413(c)(4)(B).

[5] Code Sec. 413(c)(6)(A).

[6] Code Sec. 413(c)(6)(B).

[7] Code Sec. 413(c)(7).

¶ 1406

SPECIAL RULES FOR PLANS OF MORE THAN ONE EMPLOYER: Collectively Bargained and Multiemployer Plans

The minimum funding standards for collectively bargained plans and multiemployer plans are determined as if all participants are employed by a single employer.[1] Similarly, the limitation on deductible contributions is determined as if all plan participants are employed by a single employer.[2]

Deductible contributions under collectively bargained plans

Deductible amounts may be allocated among employers in a collectively bargained plan.[3] However, a participating employer may not deduct its entire contribution if total employer contributions would exceed the Code Sec. 404(a) deduction limits.[4] The contributions would be restricted to the amount of the deduction limit for the year. However, amounts contributed in excess of the limits could be deducted in subsequent years.[5]

---

[1] Code Sec. 413(b)(5); ERISA Sec. 210(a)(3).

[2] Code Sec. 413(b)(7).

[3] *Ibid.*

[4] IRS General Counsel's Memorandum 39677 [no date given], CCH PENSION PLAN GUIDE ¶ 17,516.

[5] Code Sec. 404(a)(1)(E).

¶ 1407

AMORTIZATION OF PENSION COSTS: General Amortization Rules: Pre-2008

A major cause of financial instability among pension plans has been that employers often underfund the cost of providing an employee with retirement benefits for the employee's years of service before the plan was adopted. Accordingly, ERISA requires that an employer's annual contribution to the plan be sufficient to pay the normal costs of funding the plan *and* to amortize unfunded past service liability and changes in past service liability due to plan amendments, assumption changes, and experience gains and losses.[1] The amortization payments must be calculated on a level payment basis, and the payments must include interest and principal.

> **CCH POINTER:** *New funding rules to apply in plan years beginning after 2007.* Effective for plan years beginning after 2007, the funding standard account mechanism and the current two-tiered funding system will be replaced with a single funding method. An employer maintaining a single-employer defined benefit plan that is not 100-percent funded will not be required to make a deficit reduction contribution, but will be required to make a minimum contribution that is (a) based on the plan's assets (reduced by credit balances), funding target, and target normal cost and (b) sufficient to amortize unfunded plan liabilities over a period of seven years. Unlike current law, under which employers are required to fund up to 90 percent of a plan's total liabilities, the

Pension Act increases the funding target to 100 percent of target or current liabilities.[2]

In addition, the Pension Act radically changes the actuarial assumptions and methods used to determine present value, authorizing a new interest rate and a new mortality table. Specifically, the Pension Act, while retaining the blended rate of corporate bonds, introduces a segmented "yield curve" that would consist of three different interest rates (based on the unweighted average of interest rates on investment grade corporate bonds) applicable to benefits payable in different time periods.

☐ The governing rules are discussed in detail beginning at ¶ 1493.

☐ The amortization rules applicable prior to 2008 are discussed at CCH PENSION PLAN GUIDE ¶ 2850—¶ 2890.

---

[1] Code Sec. 412(a)-(b); ERISA Sec. 302(a)-(b).

[2] ERISA Sec. 303, as added by P.L. 109-280 (Pension Protection Act of 2006), Act Sec. 102(a);

Code Sec. 430, as added by P.L. 109-280 (Pension Protection Act of 2006), Act Sec. 112(a).

¶ 1413

AMORTIZATION OF PENSION COSTS: Special Funding Rules for Plans Maintained by Commercial Airlines

Generally effective for plan years ending after August 17, 2006, special funding relief is available for single-employer defined benefit plans sponsored by commercial passenger airlines and catering businesses that primarily serve commercial airlines. The relief allows eligible sponsors of plans that restrict benefit accruals and benefit increases to elect to amortize the plan's unfunded liability over a 17-year period. Alternatively, sponsors of plans that do not satisfy the specified restrictions on benefit accruals and benefit increases may elect to amortize the plan's shortfall amortization base over a 10-year period.[1]

Election of alternative funding schedule

An eligible employer that satisfies the benefit accrual and benefit increase restrictions must make an election in order to use the alternative funding schedule.[2] The plan sponsor may select the plan year to which the election applies. However, the employer must select a plan year beginning in 2006 or 2007 as the first plan year to which the election applies.[3] The election for a plan year beginning in 2006 was required to have been made by December 31, 2006. Similarly, the election for a plan year beginning in 2007 must be made no later than December 31, 2007.

The IRS has clarified that an election applies beginning in the "first applicable year," which must be a plan year that begins in 2006 or 2007. In the event an eligible employer makes the election, the minimum funding contribution rules under PPA Sec. 402(e) will apply for purposes of determining the minimum funding requirements for plan years that begin on or after January 1, 2008.[4]

The IRS has issued guidance detailing the procedural requirements applicable to the election.[5] In addition, the IRS has specified the information that must be provided with the election (including the EIN of the employer and the first plan year for which the alternative funding schedule provisions are to apply).[6]

Election must be signed by officer of employer. The election must be signed by an officer of the employer maintaining the plan. An authorized representative of the employer, a plan administrator, or an enrolled actuary may not sign the election on behalf of the employer.

Election may specify new plan year. An employer may specify a new plan year in the election. The change in plan year will not require IRS approval.[7] However, note the election to use the alternative funding schedule may only be revoked with IRS consent.[8]

Election to amortize shortfall amortization base

Plans that do not satisfy the benefit accrual and benefit increase restriction requirements must make the election to amortize the shortfall amortization no later than December 31, 2007.[9]

Benefit accrual restrictions

In order to elect the alternative funding schedule, a plan maintained by an eligible employer must, as of the first day of the applicable plan year, and at all times thereafter while the election is in effect, restrict the accrual of benefits. Specifically, the plan must require that any pension, death or disability benefits, and any Social Security supplemental benefits (under Code Sec. 411(a)(9)) be frozen at the level existing immediately before the first day of the plan year of the election.[10] In addition, all other benefits under the plan must be eliminated.[11]

Freeze must be permitted under anti-cutback rules. The freezing or elimination of benefits is required, however, only to the extent that it would be permitted under the anti-cutback rules, if implemented by a plan amendment adopted immediately before the first day of the plan year of the election.[12]

Notice of reduction in benefit accruals. Plan administrators must provide timely notice of a plan amendment that provides for a significant reduction in the rate of future benefit accrual. [13] In the event a plan amendment is adopted in order to comply with the relief under PPA Sec. 402, the ERISA Sec. 204(h) notice must be provided within 15 days of the effective date of the plan amendment. [14] The IRS has further clarified that the ERISA Sec. 204(h) notice must be furnished at least 15 days before the effective date of the amendment. [15]

Restrictions on benefit increases

The availability of the alternative funding schedule further requires that no benefit increase have taken effect at any time during the period beginning on July 26, 2005 and ending on the day before the first day of the applicable plan year.[16] A benefit increase subject to restriction is an increase in plan liabilities implemented by a plan amendment (or otherwise) which would occur during the plan year by reason of: (1) any increase in benefits, (2) any change in the accrual of benefits, or (3) any change in the rate at which benefits become nonforfeitable under the plan.[17]

Exception for imputed disability service

The restrictions on benefit accruals and benefit increases do not apply to any accrual or increase with respect to imputed service provided to a participant during a period of disability occurring on or after the effective date of the plan amendment implementing the benefit accrual restrictions (or after July 26, 2005, with respect to benefit increase restrictions).[18]

Minimum required contribution

The minimum required contribution for any plan year during the amortization period that the election is in effect is the amount necessary to amortize the plan's unfunded liability (i.e., unfunded accrued liability calculated under the unit credit funding method), determined as of the first day of the plan year, in equal annual installments over the remainder of the amortization period.[19] The amortization period is the 17-plan year period beginning with the plan year of the election.[20] Thus, the annual amortization amount must be redetermined each year, based on the plan's unfunded liability at that time and the remainder of the amortization period.[21]

Smoothing of asset values

The value of plan assets, for purposes of the special airline funding rules, is the fair market value of assets. Accordingly, the special rules did not allow for the "smoothing" of plan asset values. [22]

However, effective for plan years beginning after December 31, 2007, the Worker, Retiree, and Employer Recovery Act of 2008 (P.L. 110-458) also allows airlines to use average asset valuation (i.e., "smoothing"), which provides for the determination of the value of plan assets by averaging fair market values.[23] For the purposes of smoothing plan asset values under Code Sec. 430(g)(3) and ERISA Sec. 303(g)(3), the average asset method must: (1) be permitted under regulations to be promulgated by the Secretary of the Treasury, and (2) may not provide for the averaging of fair market value over more than the period beginning on the last day of the 25th month preceding the month in which the valuation date occurs and ending on the valuation date (or a similar period if the valuation date is not the first day of the month). In addition, the smoothing method must result in a plan asset valuation of between 90 and 110 percent of the fair market value of the assets. Any such averaging shall be adjusted for contributions and distributions (as provided by the Secretary of the Treasury).

> **CCH POINTER:** *Minimum funding standards apply after end of amortization period.* Effective for plan years beginning after the end of the amortization period, the plan will be subject to the new minimum funding rules enacted by the Pension Protection Act (generally applicable beginning in 2008) including the benefit limitations applicable to underfunded plans (see ¶ 1493H).[24] However, the prefunding balance and the funding standard carryover balance

as of the first day of the first year beginning after the end of the amortization period will be zero.[25]

Effect of election on funding standard account and credit balance. Following an election, any charge or credit in the funding standard account and any prefunding balance or funding standard carryover balance, as of the day before the first day of the first plan year of election, will be reduced to zero.[26]

Plan terminations during the election period

Special rules apply to plans for which an amortization election has been made that are terminated within the 10-year period beginning on the first day of the first plan year of the election. Specifically: (1) the plan will be treated as terminated on the first day of the first plan year of the election, and (2) the PBGC guaranteed benefit (see ¶ 2811) will be computed on the basis of plan assets and liabilities as of that assumed termination date.[27]

Difference in benefits to be paid from plan assets. The difference between the amount of guaranteed benefits, determined as of the assumed termination date, and the amount of guaranteed benefits, determined as of the actual termination date, is to be paid from plan assets before other benefits.[28]

Termination premium. In the event a plan for which an amortization election has been made terminates within the 5-year period beginning on the first day of the first plan year of the election, the generally applicable termination premium of $1,250 per participant will increase to $2,500 per participant.[29] The additional termination premium may be waived if the Labor Department determines that the plan termination resulted from extraordinary circumstances, such as a terrorist attack or similar event.[30] Extraordinary circumstances would be limited to a "substantial, system-wide adverse effect on the airline industry, such as the terrorist attack which occurred on September 11, 2001," (but not economic events, such as increased oil prices).[31]

Alternative election to amortize shortfall amortization base

Employers maintaining plans that do not satisfy the benefit accrual and benefit increase restrictions may elect for the first tax year beginning in 2008, to amortize the shortfall amortization base for the tax year over a period of 10 plan years (rather than 7 plan years), beginning with such plan year.[32]

Applicable interest rate. In determining the funding target for each of the plan years during the 10-year period, an interest rate of 8.25 percent (rather than the segment rates calculated on the basis of the corporate bond yield curve (see ¶ 1493D)) may be used. [33]

In the event an employer makes the alternative election, the restrictions on benefit accruals and benefit increases, as well as other conditions applicable under the amortization election, will not apply.[34] However, note that the special interest rate applies only for purposes of determining a plan's funding target. The interest rate may not be applied in determining a plan's target normal cost (see ¶ 1493D).[35]

¶1413

Prescribed election procedures. The IRS has established procedures for electing the alternative funding schedule under PPA Sec. 402(a)(2). [36] The Appendix to IRS Announcement 2008-2 (set forth at CCH PENSION PLAN GUIDE ¶ 17,097T-20) specifies the information that must be disclosed in the election (e.g., EIN of the employer and plan number of plan) and the address to which the election must be sent. Note, the election requires a signature by an officer of the employer maintaining the plan.

[1] P.L. 110-28 (U.S Troop Readiness, Veterans' Care, Katrina Recovery, and Iraq Accountability Appropriations Act of 2007, Act Sec. 6615, amending P.L. 109-280 (Pension Protection Act of 2006), Act Sec. 402(a)(2).

[2] P.L. 109-280 (Pension Protection Act of 2006), Act Sec. 402(d).

[3] P.L. 109-280 (Pension Protection Act of 2006), Act Sec. 402(d)(1).

[4] IRS Announcement 2008-2, I.R.B. 2008-3, 1-22-08, at CCH PENSION PLAN GUIDE ¶ 17,097T-20.

[5] IRS Announcement 2006-70, I.R.B. 2006-40, 10-2-06, at CCH PENSION PLAN GUIDE ¶ 17,097S-90.

[6] IRS Announcement 2008-2, I.R.B. 2008-3, 1-22-08, at CCH PENSION PLAN GUIDE ¶ 17,097T-20.

[7] P.L. 109-280 (Pension Protection Act of 2006), Act Sec. 402(d)(1)(C).

[8] P.L. 109-280 (Pension Protection Act of 2006), Act Sec. 402(d)(2).

[9] P.L. 109-280 (Pension Protection Act of 2006), Act Sec. 402(d)(1)(B).

[10] P.L. 109-280 (Pension Protection Act of 2006), Act Sec. 402(b)(2)(A)(i).

[11] P.L. 109-280 (Pension Protection Act of 2006), Act Sec. 402(b)(2)(A)(ii).

[12] P.L. 109-280 (Pension Protection Act of 2006), Act Sec. 402(b)(2)(B).

[13] Code Sec. 4980F; ERISA Sec. 204(h).

[14] P.L. 109-280 (Pension Protection Act of 2006), Act Sec. 402(h)(4).

[15] IRS Reg. § 54.4980F-1, A-9(f).

[16] P.L. 109-280 (Pension Protection Act of 2006), Act Sec. 402(b)(3)(A).

[17] P.L. 109-280 (Pension Protection Act of 2006), Act Sec. 402(b)(3)(B).

[18] P.L. 109-280 (Pension Protection Act of 2006), Act Sec. 402(b)(4).

[19] P.L. 109-280 (Pension Protection Act of 2006), Act Sec. 402(e)(1).

[20] P.L. 109-280 (Pension Protection Act of 2006), Act Sec. 402(e)(3)(B).

[21] Joint Committee on Taxation, Technical Explanation of the Pension Protection Act of 2006 (JCX-38-06).

[22] P.L. 109-280 (Pension Protection Act of 2006), Act Sec. 402(e).

[23] P.L. 110-458 (Worker, Retiree, and Employer Recovery Act of 2008), Act Sec. 126(a), amending P.L. 109-280 (Pension Protection Act of 2006), Act Sec. 402(e)(4)(C).

[24] P.L. 109-280 (Pension Protection Act of 2006), Act Sec. 402(e)(2).

[25] *Ibid.*

[26] P.L. 109-280 (Pension Protection Act of 2006), Act Sec. 402(f)(1).

[27] ERISA Sec. 4022(h)(1), as added by P.L. 109-280 (Pension Protection Act of 2006), Act Sec. 402(g)(2)(A).

[28] ERISA Sec. 4022(h)(2), as added by P.L. 109-280 (Pension Protection Act of 2006), Act Sec. 402(g)(2)(A).

[29] P.L. 109-280 (Pension Protection Act of 2006), Act Sec. 402(g)(2)(B)(i).

[30] P.L. 109-280 (Pension Protection Act of 2006), Act Sec. 402(g)(2)(B).

[31] Joint Committee on Taxation, Technical Explanation of the Pension Protection Act of 2006 (JCX-38-06).

[32] P.L. 109-280 (Pension Protection Act of 2006), Act Sec. 402(a)(2).

[33] P.L. 109-280 (Pension Protection Act of 2006), Act Sec. 402(a)(2), as amended by P.L. 110-28 (U.S. Troop Readiness, Veterans' Care, Katrina Recovery, and Iraq Accountability Appropriations Act), Act Sec. 6615(a); IRS Reg. § 1.430(h)(2)-1(b)(6)(i).

[34] Joint Committee on Taxation, Technical Explanation of the Pension Protection Act of 2006 (JCX-38-06).

[35] IRS Proposed Reg. § 1.430(h)(2)-1(b)(6)(ii).

[36] IRS Announcement 2008-2, I.R.B. 2008-3, 1-22-08, at CCH PENSION PLAN GUIDE ¶ 17,097T-20.

¶ 1415

FUNDING STANDARD ACCOUNT: Funding Standard Account: Pre-2008 Rules

Under the funding rules applicable before 2008, each plan that was subject to the minimum funding standards of ERISA was required to maintain a funding standard account to ensure that the funding requirements were met.[1] The funding standard account was basically an administrative mechanism that was charged with amounts necessary to meet the minimum funding requirement and credited with employer contributions to the plan, experience gains, and decreases in plan liabilities.

CCH POINTER: *New funding rules apply in plan years beginning after 2007.* Effective for plan years beginning after 2007, the funding standard account mechanism and the current two-tiered funding system will be replaced with a single funding method. An employer maintaining a single-employer defined benefit plan that is not 100-percent funded will not be required to make a deficit reduction contribution, but will be required to make a minimum contribution that is (a) based on the plan's assets (reduced by credit balances), funding target, and target normal cost and (b) sufficient to amortize unfunded plan liabilities over a period of seven years. Unlike current law, under which employers are required to fund up to 90 percent of a plan's total liabilities, the Pension Act increases the funding target to 100 percent of target or current liabilities.[2]

☐ The governing rules applicable after 2007 are discussed in detail beginning at ¶ 1493.

☐ The funding standard account requirements applicable prior to 2008, including the rules governing the deficit reduction contribution, the calculation of current liability, and the restoration funding method are discussed in detail at CCH PENSION PLAN GUIDE ¶ 2895—¶ 3000

---

[1] Code Secs. 412(a) and (b); ERISA Sec. 302(a) and (b).

[2] ERISA Sec. 303, as added by P.L. 109-280 (Pension Protection Act of 2006), Act Sec. 102(a); Code Sec. 430, as added by P.L. 109-280 (Pension Protection Act of 2006), Act Sec. 112(a).

¶ 1452

ACTUARIAL REQUIREMENTS: Actuarial Requirements: Pre-2008 Rules

An integral component of an employer's funding obligation is the actuarial determination of plan costs and liabilities. Actuarial assumptions must be made for employee mortality, disability, turnover, and retirement, and for interest rates and salary growth. In addition, actuarial assumptions must reflect investment return and plan administrative expenses. The actuarial assumptions selected can effectively reduce plan costs.

CCH POINTER: *New funding rules to apply in plan years beginning after 2007.* Effective for plan years beginning after 2007, the funding standard account mechanism and the current two-tiered funding system will be replaced with a single funding method. An employer maintaining a single-employer defined benefit plan that is not 100-percent funded will not be required to make a deficit reduction contribution, but will be required to make a minimum contribution that is (a) based on the plan's assets (reduced by credit balances), funding target, and target normal cost and (b) sufficient to amortize unfunded plan liabilities over a period of seven years. Unlike prior law, under which employers were required to fund up to 90 percent of a plan's total liabilities, the Pension Act increases the funding target to 100 percent of target or current liabilities.[1]

In addition, the Pension Act radically changes the actuarial assumptions and methods used to determine present value, authorizing a new interest rate and a new mortality table. Specifically, the Pension Act, while retaining the blended rate of corporate bonds, introduces a segmented "yield curve" that would consist of three different interest rates (based on the unweighted average of interest rates on investment grade corporate bonds) applicable to benefits payable in different time periods.

☐ The governing rules are discussed in detail beginning at ¶ 1493B.

☐ The rules governing actuarial assumptions under prior law, including those applicable to the valuation of assets, the valuation of liabilities and experience gains and losses, and changes in assumptions, are detailed at CCH PENSION PLAN GUIDE ¶ 3003—¶ 3085.

Qualification standards for enrolled actuaries

An enrolled actuary must satisfy the standards and qualifications set forth by the Joint Board for the Enrollment of Actuaries and must be approved by the Board (or its designees) to perform actuarial services. [2] A previously unenrolled actuary must file an application for enrollment (Form 5434) with the Executive Director of the Joint Board. The applicant will be required to remit a reasonable fee and submit to a written or oral examination.

In order to continue to perform actuarial services under ERISA, each enrolled actuary must further file an application for renewal of enrollment every three years. [3] A reasonable nonforfeitable fee may be charged for each application for renewal that is filed. The renewal of enrolled status is conditioned on satisfaction of the completion of 36 hours of continuing professional education during each full enrollment cycle.[4]

The Joint Board has prescribed standards of performance to which an enrolled actuary must adhere. [5] Among the requirements is that an enrolled actuary may not perform actuarial services in any situation in which he has a conflict of interest as to the performance of services.[6] However, the enrolled actuary may continue to represent a client, despite a conflict of interest, if: the actuary reasonably believes that he or she will able to provide competent and diligent representation to each affected client; the representation is not prohibited by law; each affected client waives the conflict of interest and provides informed consent at the time the existence of the conflict is known by the actuary.

The governing requirements, which continue to apply under the new minimum funding rules, are detailed at CCH PENSION PLAN GUIDE ¶ 3055—¶ 3075.

---

[1] ERISA Sec. 303, as added by P.L. 109-280 (Pension Protection Act of 2006), Act Sec. 102(a); Code Sec. 430, as added by P.L. 109-280 (Pension Protection Act of 2006), Act Sec. 112(a).

[2] JBEA Reg. § 901.10(a).

[3] JBEA Reg. § 901.10(d).

[4] JBEA Reg. § 901.11(e).

[5] JBEA Reg. § 901.20.

[6] JBEA Reg. § 901.20(d).

¶ 1480

RELIEF FROM FUNDING REQUIREMENTS: Waiver of Minimum Funding Standards: Pre-2008 Rules

An employer that was unable to make the required funding contributions without incurring "temporary substantial business hardship" was authorized, under pre-2008 law, to seek a waiver of the funding standards if meeting the requirements would harm the interests of plan participants.[1] The IRS would not authorize a waiver of the funding standards, however, unless stringent requirements regarding notice, security, and amortization of the waived amount were met. In addition, single employer plans were limited to 3 waivers within a period of 15 consecutive plan years. Multiemployer plans were allowed 5 waivers within the 15-year period.

> **CCH POINTER:** *Liability for required minimum contributions under post-2007 minimum funding rules.* Effective for plan years beginning after 2007, employers maintaining single-employer defined benefit plans are subject to new funding rules that will require them to make a minimum contribution to the plan based on the plan's assets (reduced by credit balances), funding target, and target normal cost.[2] A temporary waiver of the minimum funding requirements may be provided to an employer that is unable to satisfy the minimum funding standard for a plan year without "substantial business hardship." An employer maintaining a single-employer defined benefit plan may be required to provide security to the plan as a condition for a waiver of the minimum funding standards. In addition, no plan amendment that has the effect of increasing plan liabilities may generally be adopted during the waiver period.[3]

☐ The governing rules are discussed beginning at ¶ 1493.

☐ The rules governing the waiver of minimum funding standards applicable prior to 2008, including those controlling: the determination of business hardship, notice of waiver requests, interest rates on waived contributions, wavier application procedures, and plan amendments during the waiver period, are detailed at CCH PENSION PLAN GUIDE ¶ 3090—¶ 3120.

---

[1] Code Sec. 412(d)(1); ERISA 303(a).

[2] ERISA Sec. 302(a)(2), as added by P.L. 109-280 (Pension Protection Act of 2006), Act Sec. 101;

Code Sec. 412(a)(2), as amended by P.L. 109-280 (Pension Protection Act of 2006), Act Sec. 111(a).

[3] Code Sec. 412(d)(1); ERISA Sec. 303(a).

¶ 1492

ENFORCEMENT OF FUNDING STANDARDS: Penalties for Failure to Meet Funding Standards: Pre-2008 Rules

Employers are subject to excise tax penalties for underfunding a plan and for overstating pension liabilities.

Under pre-2008 law, if a plan failed to meet the funding requirements, employers, and all members of the controlled group of which the employer is a member, were subject to two successive nondeductible excise taxes. First, a 10% initial tax was imposed on the plan's accumulated funding deficiency. [1] Multiemployer plans were subject to a 5% tax. If the funding deficiency was not corrected within a specified time, an additional 100% tax was assessed.[2] However, the 100 percent additional tax could be waived by the Secretary of the Treasury if the employer was able to establish substantial business hardship.

Under the rules applicable after 2007, employers that fail to make minimum required contributions and that do not obtain a waiver will remain subject to excise tax.

□ The penalties applicable after 2007 for the failure to make required contributions are discussed at ¶ 1493F.

□ The penalties imposed prior to 2008 for the failure to meet the minimum funding standards are discussed at CCH PENSION PLAN GUIDE ¶ 3135.

---

[1] Code Sec. 4971(a).

[2] Code Sec. 4971(b).

¶ 1493

MINIMUM FUNDING RULES APPLICABLE AFTER 2007: Minimum Funding Rules Applicable After 2007: Overview

The Pension Protection Act of 2006, enacted on August 17, 2006, radically changed the minimum funding rules applicable to single employer defined benefit plans. Final regulations issued in October 2009, applicable to plan years beginning on or after January 1, 2010, implement the new rules.

New funding requirements

Under the new rules, the funding standard account mechanism and two-tiered funding system have been replaced with a single funding method (see ¶ 1493A). Employers are generally required to fully fund the present value of all benefits earned or accrued under the plan as of the beginning of the year (see ¶ 1493B). Liabilities are to be calculated using interest rates derived from a three-segment yield curve based on yields of high grade corporate bonds averaged over two years (see ¶ 1493D). The minimum contribution is based on plan assets and accrued liabilities and must be sufficient to amortize a funding shortfall over seven years.

At-risk plans with over 500 participants that are funded below a specified threshold level that reflects the ratio of assets to liabilities are subject to an increased funding target that will require plan sponsors to make larger minimum funding contributions (see ¶ 1493E). At-risk liabilities are to be determined pursuant to the assumption that plan participants within 10 years of retirement will retire at the earliest date and with the most valuable form of benefit allowed under the plan.

Existing credit balances may be retained and future credit balances may be used for funding purposes. Pre-2008 funding standard carryover credit balances are distinguished from prefunding credit balances accumulated after 2008. Plan sponsors are provided the option of using a credit balance to reduce the required minimum contribution or waiving the balance. However, an employer's ability to use a credit balance to pay any required minimum contribution is subject to restrictions, based on the plan's funded status (see ¶ 1493C).

Benefit limits applicable to underfunded plans

Single-employer defined benefit plans that fall below specified funding levels (based on the ratio of plan assets to target liability) are subject to limits on: the payment of unpredictable contingent event benefits (e.g., shutdown benefits), plan amendments, lump-sum distributions, and benefit accruals. The limits further require benefit accruals to be frozen and prevent underfunded plans that have been in effect for over five years from implementing amendments adding benefits or otherwise increasing plan liabilities or paying the full amount of a lump-sum distribution, without additional contributions by the plan sponsor. Employees must receive written notice of any benefit limitations within 30 days.

☐ The governing rules are detailed at ¶ 1493H.

Waiver of minimum funding requirements

A temporary waiver of the minimum funding requirements may be provided to an employer that is unable to satisfy the minimum funding standard for a plan year without "substantial business hardship." An employer maintaining a single-employer defined benefit plan may be required to provide security to the plan as a condition for a waiver of the minimum funding standards. In addition, no plan amendment may that has the effect of increasing plan liabilities may generally be adopted during the waiver period.

☐ The governing rules are discussed at ¶ 1493I.

Temporary relief from funding rules for certain defined benefit plans

The new single-employer defined benefit plan funding rules do not apply to certain multiple employer plans maintained by rural cooperatives for plan years beginning before January 1, 2017. In addition, the new rules do not apply to certain Pension Benefit Guaranty Corporation (PBGC) settlement plans for plan years beginning before January 1, 2014. Finally, the new rules generally do not apply to plans maintained by certain government defense contractors before plan years beginning before the earlier of (1) the date certain new rules regarding pension

¶1493

costs to be issued by the Cost Accounting Standards Board become effective or (2) January 1, 2011. For plan years beginning after December 31, 2007, and before the first plan year for which the new funding rules apply, all such plans must use a specific interest rate to determine the plan's funding status.

☐ The applicable rules are explained at ¶ 1493J.

Minimum funding rules for multiemployer plans

The Pension Protection Act also modified the funding rules governing multiemployer plans. Under the Act, the funding rules for multiemployer plans have been set out separately from the single-employer plan funding rules. The same general framework remains, but changes have been made for plan years beginning after 2007 that: (1) reduce the amortization periods for certain supplemental costs to 15 years, (2) change the amortization extension and funding waiver interest rate to the plan rate, (3) tighten the reasonableness requirement for actuarial assumptions, (4) eliminate the alternative minimum funding standard, (5) make available an automatic five-year amortization extension with an additional five-year extension, and (6) provide a route for deemed approval of changes in the use of the shortfall funding method.

☐ The governing rules are set forth at ¶ 1493K.

Additional funding rules for significantly underfunded multiemployer plans

All multiemployer plans are required to obtain an annual actuarial certification regarding their funding status. Multiemployer plans that are so underfunded as to be in "endangered" or "critical" status are required adopt funding improvement and rehabilitation plans and to comply with specified funding and operational requirements in order to improve their funding status over a multiyear period. Excise taxes and civil penalties may be imposed if a plan does not adopt or comply with a required funding improvement or rehabilitation plan.

The new requirements generally apply to plan years beginning after 2007 for multiemployer plans in effect on July 16, 2006. However, under a sunset provision applies, pursuant to which no new certifications of endangered or critical status will be required for plan years beginning after 2014. Note, the requirements will continue to apply to plans that are already in endangered or critical status at the end of 2014.

☐ The applicable rules are detailed at ¶ 1493L.

Annual funding notice

Single-employer defined benefit plans (and multiemployer plans) are required under ERISA Sec.101(f) to provide annual funding notices to participants, beneficiaries, unions, and contributing employers of multiemployer plans. Each annual funding notice must be provided within 120 days of the end of the plan year and must contain identifying information (i.e., name of plan and plan number), as well as information concerning he plan's funding policy and asset allocations. See ¶ 2220.

¶1493

¶ 1493A

MINIMUM FUNDING RULES APPLICABLE AFTER 2007: Minimum Funding Standards for Single-Employer Defined Benefit Plans

Effective for plan years beginning after 2007, the funding standard account mechanism and the current two-tiered funding system will be replaced with a single funding method.[1] An employer maintaining a single-employer defined benefit plan that is not 100-percent funded will not be required to make a deficit reduction contribution (see ¶ 1400), but will be required to make a minimum contribution based on the plan's assets (reduced by credit balances), funding target, and target normal cost and that is sufficient to amortize unfunded plan liabilities over a period of seven years. Unlike current law, under which employers are required to fund up to 90 percent of a plan's total liabilities, the Pension Act increases the funding target to 100 percent of target or current liabilities (see ¶ 1493B).

In addition, the Pension Act radically changes the actuarial assumptions and methods used to determine present value, authorizing a new interest rate and a new mortality table. Specifically, the Pension Act, while retaining the blended rate of corporate bonds, introduces a segmented "yield curve" that would consist of three different interest rates (based on the unweighted average of interest rates on investment grade corporate bonds) applicable to benefits payable in different time periods (see ¶ 1493C).

Finally, the Pension Act subjects "at-risk" plans, as determined by the plan's funded status and not by the credit rating of the employer sponsoring the plan, to an at-risk liability assumption that all plan participants eligible for benefits within a 10-year period will elect benefits at the highest present value. The at-risk rules, which are limited to plans with over 500 participants, will increase a plan's target liability (see ¶ 1493E).

Effective date of new rules

The new funding rules generally apply to plan years beginning on or after January 1, 2008. Final regulations issued by the IRS in October 2009, implementing the funding requirements under Code Secs. 430 and 436, apply to plan years beginning on or after January 1, 2010. However, for plan years before January 1, 2010, plans may rely on the regulations in order to comply with the governing requirements.[2]

---

[1] ERISA Sec. 303, as added by P.L. 109-280 (Pension Protection Act of 2006), Act Sec. 102(a); Code Sec. 430, as added by P.L. 109-280 (Pension Protection Act of 2006), Act Sec. 112(a).

[2] IRS Reg. § 1.430(d)-1(g) and IRS Reg. § 1.436-1(k).

¶ 1493B

MINIMUM FUNDING RULES APPLICABLE AFTER 2007: Minimum Required Contribution

An employer's contribution to a single-employer defined benefit plan for a plan year may not, under the new rules, in the aggregate be less than the "minimum required contribution." [1]

The rules governing the determination of the minimum required contribution apply to plan years beginning on or after January 1, 2008. Final regulations issued by the IRS in 2009 apply to plan years beginning on or after January 1, 2010. [2] However, plans with plan years beginning before January 1, 2010 may rely on the final regulations in complying with the minimum required contribution requirements.

Determining the minimum required contribution

The minimum required contribution applicable to plans in which plan assets (reduced by credit balances) are less than the "funding target" of the plan for the year will be the sum of the following factors:[3]

1. **Target normal cost**: (for plans that are not at risk for any plan year) the excess of: (1) the sum of (a) the present value (as of the valuation date) of all benefits that are expected to accrue or to be earned under the plan during the plan year, plus (b) the amount of plan-related expenses expected to be paid from plan assets during the plan year, over (2) the amount of mandatory employee contributions expected to be made during the plan year. [4]

   Benefits that accrue, are earned, or otherwise allocated to service for the plan year are based, under the final regulations, on the actual benefits accrued, earned or otherwise allocated to service for the plan year through the valuation date and benefits expected to accrue, be earned or otherwise be allocated to service for the plan year from the period from the valuation date through the end of the plan year. [5] For example, with respect to a plan with a valuation date other than the first day of the plan year, the actual benefits earned during the part of the year before the valuation date must be included in target normal cost. [6]

   Benefits attributable to increase in compensation. As under prior law, if any benefit attributable to services performed in a preceding year is increased because of an increase in compensation during the current plan year, the increase in the benefit will be treated as having accrued during the current plan year. [7]

   Target normal cost for plans in at-risk status is discussed at ¶ 1493E.

   CCH POINTER: The final regulations clarify that the target normal cost of the plan for the plan year must be adjusted (not below zero) by adding the amount of plan-related expenses expected to be paid from plan assets during the plan year.[8]

2. **Shortfall amortization charge for the plan year**: the total (not less than zero) of the amounts (i.e., the shortfall amortization installments) required to amortize shortfall amortization bases for the plan year and six preceding years.[9]

   Note, sponsors of single-employer plans have the option of temporarily extending the period by which to amortize funding shortfalls pursuant to a "2 plus 7" amortization schedule or a 15-year amortization schedule. The extended amortization schedules are discussed below.

3. **Waiver amortization charge for the plan year**: the aggregate total of the amounts (i.e., the waiver amortization installments) required to amortize the "waiver amortization base" for the plan year over a five-year period.[10] The rules governing the waiver of the minimum funding standards are discussed in detail at ¶ 1493I.

If the value of a plan's assets (reduced by any credit balance) equals or exceeds the funding target (i.e., 100 percent of the target liability), the minimum required contribution will be the target normal cost of the plan for the plan year reduced (but not below zero) by the amount by which the plan's assets (reduced by a credit balance) exceed the funding target.[11]

Funding target

The funding target of a plan is the present value (determined as of the valuation date) of all benefits accrued, earned, or otherwise allocated to year of service prior to the first day of the plan year.[12]

Funding target attainment percentage. The funding target attainment percentage (FTAP) (discussed in detail with respect to the limits imposed on underfunded plans at ¶ 1493H) is the ratio (expressed as a percentage) of the value of plan assets (determined under IRS Reg. § 1.430(g)-1) for the year (as reduced by prefunding and funding standard carryover credit balances) to the funding target of the plan for the plan year (determined without regard to at-risk status). [13]

Plans with zero funding target. The FTAP for a plan with a funding target of zero for a plan year is 100 percent for the year. [14] The application of this rule is not limited to plans that have no predecessor plan.

Present value determination. The present value of a participant's benefit is determined as of the valuation date by multiplying the amount of that benefit by the probability that the benefit will be paid at a future date and then discounting the resulting product, using the applicable interest rate.[15] The probability that the benefit will be paid to a participant at such future date is determined pursuant to actuarial assumptions regarding the probability of future service, advancement in age, and other benefits (e.g., death, disability, termination of employment, and selection of optional forms of benefit) that affect whether the participant or beneficiary will be eligible for the benefit and whether the benefit will be paid at that future date.

Benefits taken into account. Benefits taken into account in determining the target normal cost and the funding target include all benefits earned or accrued

¶1493B

under the plan that have not been paid as of the valuation date (including retirement–type and ancillary benefits). [16] The benefits taken into account are based on the status of the participant or beneficiary (e.g., active employee, vested or partially vested terminated employee, or disable participant) as of the valuation date.

Allocation of benefits. The benefits taken into account are allocated to the funding target or target normal cost. Specifically, the determination of the plan's funding target and target normal cost require that the future benefits to be paid from the plan be allocated among: prior plan years (where they will taken into account in determining the funding target for the current plan year); the current plan year (where they will be taken into account in determining the target norm cost for the current plan year); and future plan years (where they will be taken into account in determining either the funding target or the target normal cost for the current plan year).

The final regulations specify the rules for the allocation of benefits where: benefits are a function of the accrued benefits; benefits are a function of participant years of service; benefits are determined as the excess of a function of the participant's service over a function of the participant's accrued benefit; and under other circumstances (i.e., where the amount of a benefit that is expected to be paid is neither a function of the accrued benefit at the time the benefit is expected to be paid nor a function of the participant's service at the time). [17]

Recognition of Code Sec. 436 benefit limitation. Under the final regulations, benefits that were not paid or accrued prior to the valuation date because of the imposition of the benefit limits under Code Sec. 436 (see ¶ 1493H) are generally not included in the determination of the funding target and the target normal cost. [18] However, the determination of the funding target and the target normal cost may not anticipate any future application of the Code Sec. 436 benefit restrictions (e.g., funding based limits on unpredictable contingent event benefits).

Account for limits on benefit accruals. The determination of the funding target for a plan must take into account any limitation on benefit accruals under Code Sec. 436(e) that applied before the valuation date. [19] The nonrecognition of the benefit accrual limitations effectively requires an employer sponsoring a plan that provides for ongoing benefit accruals to include the present value of those accruals in the target normal cost, even if the plan is temporarily prohibited from allowing for accruals.

Effect of frozen plan. A plan freeze implemented by the plan sponsor must be reflected in target normal cost. In addition, the final regulations state that, if the plan requires missed benefit accruals to be automatically restored once the plan's AFTAP is above 60 percent (taking into account the missed benefit accruals) any missed benefit accruals from the prior plan year must be taken into account in determining the funding target, if (as of the valuation date) the period of the missed benefit accruals is 12 months or less.[20]

Benefits funded by insurance contracts. A plan's funding target and target normal cost generally must reflect the liability for benefits that are funded by insurance contracts held by the plan. The corresponding insurance contracts must, further, be included in plan assets. [21] However, the liability for benefits provided under insurance contracts may be excluded from the plan's funding target and target normal cost (and the insurance contracts excluded from plan assets) if: (1) the contract is purchased from a state licensed insurance company, and (2) the participant's or beneficiary's right to receive the benefits is an irrevocable contractual right (i.e., plan trustee may not surrender contract to insurer for cash value) under the insurance contracts, based on premiums paid to the insurance company prior to the valuation date. [22]

Reflect plan terms by valuation date. The determination of a plan's funding target and target normal cost for a plan year are generally based on plan provisions that are adopted no later than the valuation date for the plan year and that take effect on or before the last day of the plan year. [23] However, an amendment would not be taken into account in determining the funding target and target normal cost if it did not take effect until a future year.

Note, the final regulations provide guidance on determining when an amendment that increases or decreases benefits takes effect. [24]

Plan amendment adopted on first day of plan year. In determining whether a plan amendment is treated as having been adopted on the first day of the plan year (including an amendment adopted 2½ months after the close of the plan year) the rules of Code Sec. 412(d) apply. Accordingly, if an amendment is adopted after the valuation date for a plan year (and no later than 2½ months after the close of the plan year) but takes effect by the last day of the plan year, the amendment will be taken into account in determining the plan's funding target and target normal cost for the plan year, if the plan administrator makes the Code Sec. 412(d)(2) election (i.e., to treat the amendment as having been made on the first day of the plan year). [25]

Amendments after valuation date that increase liabilities. The final regulations require that an amendment adopted after the valuation date for the plan year be taken into account in determining a plan's funding target and target normal cost for the plan year, if the amendment increases the target normal cost for the plan year. [26] Specifically, if such an amendment would have caused the benefit limits of Code Sec. 436(c) to apply if the increase in the target normal cost were included in the plan's funding target (after taking into account all unpredictable contingent event benefits permitted to be paid for unpredictable contingent events that occurred during the current plan year, and plan amendments that went into effect in the current plan year), the amendment must be taken into account in determining the plan's funding target and target normal cost for the plan year.

CCH POINTER: The rule is designed to prevent the avoidance of the Code Sec. 436(c) benefit restrictions through the adoption of a mid-year plan amendment that purports not to increase benefits earned prior to the beginning of the plan year. [27]

Include all individuals entitled to benefits in valuation. The plan population for purposes of determining the funding target or target normal cost, must be determined as of the valuation date. The final regulations require currently em-

¶1493B

ployed plan participants, formerly employed participants (including retirees and terminated vested participants) and other individuals currently entitled to benefits under the plan to be included in the valuation. [28] The effect of this rule is that plan participants who could have been excluded from participation in the plan under Code Sec. 410(a) may not be excluded from the valuation.

Valuation may not anticipate future participation. For purposes of making any determination of the funding target or target normal cost, the actuarial assumptions and funding method used for the plan may not anticipate the affiliation with the plan of future participants not employed in the service of the employer on the plan valuation date. However, the affiliation with the plan of current employees who have not satisfied the applicable age and service requirements as of the valuation date may be anticipated.[29]

Actuarial assumptions of funding method. The determination of present value must be made on the basis of actuarial assumptions and a funding method. Note, generally, the same actuarial assumptions and funding methods are to be use for computations under Code Secs. 430 and 436. [30]

The actuarial assumptions used to determine present value would (in compliance with Code Sec. 430(h)(1)) need to be individually reasonable (taking into account the experience of the plan and reasonable expectation) and, in combination offer the plan's enrolled actuary's best estimate of anticipated experience under the plan. [31]

The interest rate and mortality table specified under Code Sec. 430(h) must be used in determining present value. [32] However, the actuarial assumptions for a plan that has less than 100 participants and beneficiaries who are not in pay status, may assume no pre-retirement mortality, if that assumption would be reasonable.

Changes in assumptions and funding method. The actuarial assumptions established for a plan year may not be changed for that year, absent a determination by the IRS that the assumptions were unreasonable. Similarly, the funding method may not be changed for a plan year absent an IRS determination that the method for that year is not permissible. [33]

CCH POINTER: ***Change in funding method.*** Under Code Sec. 412(d)and ERISA Sec. 302(d)(2), as enacted by the Pension Protection Act of 2006, any change in a plan's funding method must be approved by the IRS. This rule follows the requirement under Code Sec. 412(c)(5) and ERISA Sec. 302(c)(5), prior to amendment by PPA.

Automatic approval of change in funding method. Rev Proc. 2000-40 (see CCH PENSION PLAN GUIDE ¶ 17,299P-40) authorized automatic approval for certain changes in the funding method resulting from a change in valuation software and for changes in a funding method that occurred with respect to "takeover" plans (i.e., plan for which both the enrolled actuary and business organization providing actuarial services are changed) (see CCH PENSION PLAN GUIDE ¶ 3040). Rev. Proc. 2000-40, however, has not been updated to reflect the funding changes enacted by PPA and relies on calculations that are not used under the new rules.

The final regulations issued in October 2009 and effective for plan years beginning after January 1, 2010 explain that a plan's funding method includes not only the overall funding method used by the plan, but also each specific method of computation used in applying the overall method. [34]Thus, a change in valuation software may result in a change in funding method that requires approval by the IRS.

The final regulations provide that any changes in the funding method that are not inconsistent with the requirements of Code Sec. 430 are treated as having been approved by the IRS and thus, do not require specific approval. [35] In addition, any change in a plan's funding method for the first year that begins on or after January 1, 2010 will not require specific approval. [36]

Similar to the relief under Rev Proc. 2000-40, the final rules authorize general approval for a change in funding method, which includes a change resulting from a change in valuation software, for the first year beginning on or after January 1, 2010. [37] However, the IRS explains that, if the rules under IRS Reg. § 1.430(f)-1, IRS Reg. § 1.430(g)-1 IRS Reg. § 1.430(i)-1, and IRS Reg. § 1.436-1 were applied to a plan for a plan year beginning on or after January 1, 2009, but before, January 1, 2010, approval is provided with respect to such a plan for a change in funding method for that plan year, in lieu of general approval for changes for the first plan year beginning on or after January 1, 2010.

Subsequent to the release of the final regulations, the IRS, in December 2009, issued guidance, effective for plan years beginning on or after January 1, 2009, that provides automatic approval for change in the funding method of single employer plans that result from either a change in the valuation software used to determine the plan's or from a change in the enrolled actuary and business organization providing actuarial services to the plan. [38]

With respect to takeover plans, approval requires (among other conditions) that the funding target and target normal cost (without regard to any adjustments for employee contributions and plan-related expenses) as determined for the prior plan year by the new enrolled actuary (using the actuarial assumptions of the prior enrolled actuary) both be within 5 percent of those values, as determined by the prior enrolled actuary.

Automatic approval for a change in funding method resulting from a change in valuation software requires (among other conditions) that the funding target and target normal cost (without regard to any adjustments for employee contributions and plan related expenses) under the new valuation software (for either the current plan or the prior plan year) each be within 2 percent of the respective values under the prior valuation software (all other factors being held constant).

Establish assumptions and funding method by Form 5500 filing date. The actuarial assumptions and funding method used by a plan for a plan year are established by the date of the timely filing (with extensions) of the actuarial report (Schedule SB) of the plan's Form 5500 annual report for that plan year. If the plan is not required to file an actuarial report, the assumptions and funding method are established by the delivery of the completed report to the employer, no later than the due date (with extensions) for filing the actual report, if such a filing were required. [39]

Scope of funding method. The final regulations clarify that a plan's funding method includes each specific method of computation used in applying the overall funding method. However, the choice of actuarial assumptions to be used under the overall funding method or in a specific method of computation is not part of the funding method. [40]

Actuarial valuation must reflect probability of lump-sum distribution. The determination of present value must, under the final regulations, take into account the probability that future benefits will be paid in a lump-sum distribution or other optional form of benefit, determined on the basis of the plan's experience and other relevant assumptions. [41] Thus, the IRS cautions that the present value of future distribution is not necessarily the current amount of a participant's hypothetical account balance. [42]

The plan's enrolled actuary is further required to take into account any difference in the present value of those future benefit payments that results from the use of actuarial assumptions in determining benefit payments that differ from those prescribed under Code Sec. 430. [43]

Distributions based on assumptions under Code Sec. 417(e)(3). The final regulations provide rules that apply when a distribution is determined using the interest rate and mortality table under Code Sec. 417(e)(3), rather than the actuarial assumptions under Code Sec. 430(h). Under the rules, if a distribution is subject to Code Sec. 417(e)(3), and is determined using the applicable interest rate and mortality table under Code Sec. 417(e)(3), the computation of the present value of the distribution is treated as having taken into account any difference in present value resulting from the use of actuarial assumptions that differ from those under Code Sec. 430(h) only if the present value of the distribution is determined by valuing the annuity that corresponds to the distribution using prescribed actuarial assumptions. [44]

Unpredictable contingent event benefits. The determination of present value or other required computations must take into account the probability (based on information as of the valuation date) that future benefits (or increased benefits) will become payable because of the occurrence of an unpredictable contingent event benefit. [45] However, the probability of the unpredictable contingent event may be assumed to be zero, if (as of the valuation date) there is no more than a de minimis likelihood that the event will occur.

Reasonable valuation techniques. Any reasonable technique may be use to determine the present value of benefits expected to be paid during a plan year, based on the applicable interest rate and mortality assumptions of the plan year. [46]

IRS approval of significant changes in actuarial assumptions. The final regulations specify that the actuarial assumptions used to determine a plan's funding target for a plan year may not be changed from the assumptions used for the preceding year without IRS approval if: (1) the plan is sponsored by a member of controlled group which maintains plans with over $50 million in unfunded vested benefits and (2) the change in assumptions results in a decrease in the plan's funding shortfall for the current plan year that exceeds $50 million, or that exceeds $5 million and is 5 percent or more of the funding target of the plan before the change.[47] However, the final rules also authorize a plan that is not in at-risk status for the current plan year, but was at-risk for the prior plan year (not to exceed a period of 5 consecutive plan years) to use the assumptions that applied before the plan entered at-risk status and that were used in combination with the required at-risk assumptions during the period the plan was in at-risk status without prior IRS approval.[48]

Shortfall amortization charge

For purposes of determining the shortfall amortization charge, a plan's "funding shortfall" for a year is the excess of the plan's funding target for the plan year over the value of plan assets (reduced by any credit balance) for the plan year which are held by the plan on the valuation date.[49] In the event of a funding shortfall, the plan's minimum required contribution will be increased by the shortfall amortization charge.

Shortfall amortization installments. The amount necessary to amortize the shortfall amortization base in level installments over the seven-year period beginning with the plan year is the shortfall amortization installment.[50] The shortfall amortization installment for any plan year in the seven-year period (i.e., the current plan year and the six preceding plan years) with respect to any shortfall amortization base is the annual installment determined for the year for the shortfall amortization base.[51]

CCH POINTER: Special amortization rules allow commercial airlines (and catering firms serving airlines) to amortize funding shortfall over 10 years. In addition, commercial airlines that have frozen their plans may elect, prior to 2008, to amortize funding target liability over 17 years at a specified interest rate. The governing rules are discussed at ¶ 1413.

Shortfall amortization base. The shortfall amortization base for a plan year is the funding shortfall for the plan year reduced by the present value (determined using the segment rates of ERISA Sec. 303(h)(2)(C) and Code Sec. 430(h)(2)(C)) (discussed below) of the aggregate total of the shortfall amortization installments and waiver amortization installments that have been determined for the plan year and any succeeding plan year with respect to any shortfall amortization bases and waiver amortization bases for preceding plan years.[52] Thus, if the value of plan assets (as reduced by credit balances) is equal to or greater than the funding target of the plan, then the shortfall amortization base for the plan year will be zero.[53] By contrast, if the value of plan assets is less than the funding target for the plan year, a shortfall amortization base is established for the plan year. [54]

Timing rules applicable to interest rates used for determining shortfall amortization installments. The interest rate used to determine the amount of the shortfall amortization installments (and waiver amortization installments (see be-

¶1493B

low)) are determined based on the date those installments are assumed to be paid, using the same timing rules that apply in determining target normal cost. [55]

Funding shortfall. IRS Proposed Regulations define a funding shortfall as the excess of the funding target of the plan for the plan year, over the value of plan assets for the year (as reduced to reflect the subtraction of the funding standard carryover balance and prefunding balance). [56]

Note: The proposed regulations implementing the rules under Code Sec. 430(a) were released in April 2008. The rules have not yet been issued in final form.

Example: ABC maintains a calendar year plan with a valuation date of January 1. The plan has a funding target of $2,500,000 and assets totaling $1,800,000, as of January 1, 2008. The 2008 actuarial valuation is performed using the 24-month average segment rates applicable to September 2007. A $700,000 shortfall amortization base is established for 2008, which is equal to the $2,500,000 funding target less $1,800,000 of assets.

With respect to the $700,000 shortfall amortization base, there is a shortfall amortization installment of $116,852 ($700,000 shortfall amortization base amortized over 7 years) for each year from 2008 through 2014. The amount of the shortfall amortization installment is determined by discounting the first 5 installments, using the first segment rate of 5.26 percent and by discounting the sixth and seventh installments, using the second segment rate of 5.82 percent. [57]

Shortfall amortization charge may not be less than zero. The shortfall amortization charge may not be less than zero. The amortization schedule will reflect shortfall increases as well as decreases in the funding shortfall, such as those that may be caused by favorable investment experience or an increase in interest rates. Thus, depending on whether the present value of remaining installments with respect to prior year amortization bases is more or less than the plan's funding shortfall, a shortfall amortization base may be positive or negative. However, the shortfall amortization must still be amortized over seven years. In addition, although shortfall amortization installments for a plan year with respect to positive and negative amortization bases are netted in determining the shortfall amortization charge for the plan year, the resulting shortfall amortization charge may not be less than zero.[58] Accordingly, negative amortization installments may not offset the waiver amortization installment or normal cost.

CCH POINTER: Under the current rules, employers do not have the option that was available prior to 2008 of amortizing past service liabilities over 30 years or losses over 10 years. In addition, the deficit reduction contribution rules, which require amortization of the underfunded amounts over a four to seven year period, will not apply. Furthermore, the IRS is no longer empowered to grant an extension of the amortization period.

Exception to shortfall amortization base for well-funded plans. A plan will not be required to establish a shortfall amortization base for a plan year if the value of plan assets (reduced by a prefunding balance that the employer elects to use to reduce contributions for the year (see below) is equal to or greater than the funding target for the plan year. Under such circumstances, the shortfall amortization base for the plan year will be zero.[59]

Transition rules. A transition (or phase-in) rule applies for plan years beginning after 2007 and before 2011. Under the transition rule, a shortfall amortization base does not have to be established for a plan year during the transition period if the value of plan assets for the plan year is at least equal to a specified applicable percentage of the plan's funding target for the year (92% for 2008, 94% for 2009, and 96% for 2010).[60] The transition relief, as enacted by the Pension Protection Act did not apply to a plan for any plan year beginning after 2008, unless for each preceding plan year beginning after 2007, the plan's shortfall amortization base was zero.[61] Accordingly, if a plan's funding target for any year in the transition period was below the applicable percentage (necessitating a shortfall amortization base), the funding target for the current year and subsequent year would be 100 percent.[62] Under such circumstances, the plan would need to establish a shortfall amortization base. Note, IRS Proposed Regulations would not provide for any adjustment to the applicable percentage prescribed by the transition rule for plans for which the effective date of Code Sec. 430 is delayed under PPA Sec. 104-106. [63]

The Worker, Retiree, and Employer Recovery Act of 2008, effective for plan years beginning after 2008, modified the governing rule so that the plan's shortfall amortization base is no longer required to be zero for each of the preceding years beginning after 2007. [64] Thus, the relief may be available to a plan in 2009 and 2010, even if it fell below the 92 percent funding target for 2008. Note, however, consistent with prior law, the relief is not available for plans that were subject to the deficit reduction contribution rules in 2007.

Deemed amortization upon attainment of funding percentage. In the event that the value of a plan's assets (reduced by any credit balance) is equal to or greater than the plan's funding target for the year (thereby, resulting in a funding shortfall of zero), any shortfall amortization bases for preceding plan years will be eliminated. Specifically, in determining the shortfall amortization charge for the plan year and succeeding plan years, the shortfall amortization bases for all preceding plan years (and all shortfall amortization installments for such bases) will be reduced to zero.[65]

Shortfall amortization charge included in termination liability to PBGC trustee. Under pre-PPA rules, in the event a plan terminated in a distress termination or in a termination instituted by the Pension Benefit Guaranty Corporation (PBGC), and the plan was subject to PBGC trusteeship proceedings, each contributing sponsor and each member of its controlled group were liable to the trustee appointed by the PBGC for: (1) the outstanding balance of the accumulated funding deficiencies; (2) the outstanding balance of the amount of funding deficiencies that was waived before the termination date; and (3) the outstanding balance of the amount of decreases in the minimum funding standard allowed before the termination date, plus interest from the termination date.[66] The liability was due and payable to the trustee, as of the termination date, in cash or securities acceptable to the trustee.

Under current law, liability to the PBGC trustee consists of: (1) the sum of the shortfall amortization charge for the plan year in which the termination date occurs, plus the aggregate total of shortfall amortization installments determined for succeeding plan years (including any increases resulting from the denial of all pending waiver applications); and (2) the sum of the waiver amortization charge under ERISA Sec. 303(e) for the plan year in which the termination date occurs, plus the aggregate total of waiver amortization installments determined for succeeding plan years.[67]

Election of temporary extension of amortization schedules

The plan sponsor of a single-employer defined benefit pension plan may elect to determine shortfall amortization installments with respect to the shortfall amortization base under two alternative extended amortization schedules: (1) the two plus seven amortization schedule, or (2) the 15-year amortization schedule. [68] Plan sponsors eligible to elect the relief include any member of the plan sponsor's controlled group (as defined in Code Sec. 412(d)(3) or ERISA Sec. 302(d)(3). [69]

2 plus 7 amortization schedule. Under the two plus seven amortization schedule, the plan sponsor may elect to amortize the shortfall amortization base for the applicable plan year over a nine-year period beginning with that election year. The installment for each of the first two years is determined by multiplying the amount of the shortfall amortization base established for the election year by the effective interest rate for the plan for the election year. The installment for each of the remaining 7 years is the level amount calculated so that the present value of the 9 installments as of the valuation date for the election year equals the amount of the shortfall amortization base established for the election year. [70] The present value of the 9 installments is determined using the segment rates or rates from the full yield curve used to determine the target normal cost (or the funding target, if the target normal cost is zero) for the election year.

> **Example:** Assume ABC, the sponsor of a plan with a calendar year plan year and a January 1 valuation date, elects to amortize the shortfall amortization base of $1,000,000 established for the 2010 plan year using the 2 plus 7-year amortization schedule. The first and second segment rates used to determine the target normal cost for the 2010 plan year are 4.81% and 6.69%, respectively, and the effective interest rate for the plan for the 2010 plan year is 6.00%.
>
> Each of the shortfall amortization installments for the 2010 and 2011 plan years is $60,000, determined by multiplying the amount of the shortfall amortization base by the effective interest rate for the plan for the 2010 plan year ($1,000,000 × 6% = $60,000). After taking into account these installments, the remaining shortfall amortization base is equal to the amount of the shortfall amortization base, minus the first two installments adjusted to the January 1, 2010 valuation date using the first segment rate of 4.81%, or $882,754 ($1,000,000 –$60,000 – ($60,000 divided by 1.0481)). The shortfall amortization installment for each of the next 7 plan years (2012 through 2018) is $168,458, determined as the level amount necessary to amortize the remaining balance of $882,754 using the first segment rate of 4.81% for the shortfall amortization installments for 2012 through 2014, and the second segment rate of 6.69% for

the shortfall amortization installments for 2015 through 2018. The total present value of all 9 payments is $1,000,000, calculated using the first segment rate of 4.81% for installments due for plan years 2010 through 2014 and the second segment rate of 6.69% for plan years 2015 through 2018. [71]

15-year amortization schedule. Pursuant to the 15-year amortization schedule, the plan sponsor may elect to amortize the shortfall amortization base for an applicable plan year in level annual installments over a 15-year period beginning with the election year using the segment rates or rates from the full yield curve used to determine the target normal cost (or funding target if the target normal cost is zero) for the election year. [72]

Example: Assume ABC in the above example elects to use the 15-year amortization schedule. The shortfall amortization installment due for each of the 15 plan years from 2010 through 2024 is $99,394. The shortfall amortization installment is determined using the first segment rate of 4.81% for the installments due for plan years 2010 through 2014 and the second segment rate of 6.69% for the installments due for plan years 2015 through 2024. [73]

Eligible plan year. For purposes of the provision, an eligible plan year is a plan year beginning in 2008, 2009, 2010, or 2011, but only if the due date for the payment of the minimum required contribution for the plan year occurs on or after June 25, 2010 (the date of enactment of the provision under the Preservation of Access to Care for Medicare Beneficiaries and Pension Relief Act of 2010 (P.L. 111-192)).[74] Thus, a plan sponsor may not elect an alternative amortization schedule for a plan year beginning on October 1, 2008 and ending September 30, 2009, because the due date for contributions for that plan year was June 25, 2010. [75]

Note, while generally plan years ending on or after October 10, 2009 and beginning before January 1, 2012 are eligible for the relief, plans described in PPA Sec. 206 (see ¶ 1493J) may elect the alternative amortization schedule only for a plan year beginning in 2011. [76]

Limits on election of extended amortization schedule. An election to use an extended amortization schedule may not be used for more than two eligible plan years with respect to a plan.

A plan sponsor is not required to make an extended amortization schedule election for more than one eligible plan year or for consecutive eligible plan years. However, a plan sponsor who does make an election for two eligible plan years must elect the same extended schedule for each year.[77]

Example: Plan sponsor ABC elects to use 15-year amortization for the plan year beginning in 2010. ABC may elect to use the same schedule for 2011, but cannot elect to use a two plus seven amortization schedule for 2011.

Notice requirements. Plan sponsors must provide notice to participants, beneficiaries and the PBGC of the elected relief. [78]

Due date for notice. The pension funding relief notice must be provided to participants and beneficiaries of the plan by 120 days after the end of the plan year for which an alternative amortization schedule is elected, or by May 2, 2011, if later.

¶1493B

[79] For example, if an alternative amortization schedule is elected for a plan year beginning June 1, 2010, then the notice must be provided to participants and beneficiaries by September 28, 2011. If the election for a plan is made simultaneously for two plan years, the notices for both elections can be combined as long as the notice identifies both years for which the election is made.

Required information. The notice must (in addition to other information) provide a general description of the effect of the election (highlighting the fact that the election will delay pension funding) and indicating which of the two schedules has been elected. [80]

The IRS has provided examples that illustrate the information that must be contained in the pension funding relief notice. [81].

Notifying PBGC of election. A copy of an election made for a plan that is covered by the PBGC must be e-mailed to the PBGC at single-employer.funding.relief.election@pbgc.gov. The subject line of the e-mail must contain the plan sponsor's employer identification number, the plan number, and the name of the plan. Note, additional information may be required for elections made before January 1, 2011. [82]

The PBGC notification must be made by the later of: (i) 30 days after the date the election is made or (ii) January 31, 2011. [83]

Procedures for electing alternative amortization schedule. A plan sponsor may elect the relief, on or after January 2, 2011, by providing written notification of the election to the plan's enrolled actuary and the plan administrator. The election must be signed and dated by the plan sponsor and must disclose specified information, including: which of the two alternative amortization schedules is being elected; the plan year for which the election is being made; and whether an alternative amortization schedule has been elected for another year, and, if so, a statement that the same alternative amortization schedule is being elected. [84]

Election deadline. The election must be made by the latest of: (i) the last day of the plan year for which the election is made, (ii) 30 days after the valuation date for the plan year for which the election is made, or (iii) January 31, 2011. Thus, if the valuation date for a plan is the first day of the plan year, an election for the plan year that begins on January 1, 2009, or January 1, 2010, must be made by January 31, 2011; for the plan year that begins on January 1, 2011, the election must be made by December 31, 2011. [85]

Increase in required installments for certain plans. Increases in alternate required shortfall amortization installments must be made in cases involving the payment of excess compensation or extraordinary dividends or stock redemptions. The shortfall amortization installment otherwise determined and payable is increased by any installment acceleration amount with respect to a plan for any plan year in the restriction period with respect to an election year.[86] The increase may not result in the amount of the installment exceeding the present value of that installment and all succeeding installments with respect to the shortfall amortization base (determined without regard to the increase). Thus, the installment adjustment accelerates, but does not increase the amount of the otherwise required installment. [87]

Subsequent shortfall amortization installments with respect to the shortfall amortization base will, in reverse order of the otherwise required installments, be reduced to the extent necessary to limit the present value of the subsequent shortfall amortization installments to the present value of the remaining unamortized shortfall amortization base. The present value of the remaining payment is determined using the segment rates on the full yield curve use to determine the target normal cost (or the funding target, if the target normal cost is zero) for the year for which the acceleration adjustment is added to the shortfall amortization installment. [88]

CCH POINTER: *Restriction period.* The term "restriction period" with respect to an election year for a plan sponsor that elects to use the two plus seven amortization schedule means the three-year period beginning with the election year (or, if later, the first plan year beginning after December 31, 2009). If the plan sponsor elects 15-year amortization for the shortfall amortization base for the election year, the restriction period is the five-year period beginning with the election year (or, if later, the first plan year beginning after December 31, 2009). [89]

Installment acceleration amount. The "installment acceleration amount" with respect to any plan year in a restriction period is the aggregate amount of excess employee compensation with respect to all employees for the plan year and the aggregate amount of extraordinary dividends and redemptions for the plan year (excess shareholder payment amount). [90]

Annual limit on installment acceleration amount. The installment acceleration amount is limited annually to the aggregate amount of funding relief received by the plan sponsor in prior years as a result of an election to use an extended amortization period for an eligible plan year. [91] Accordingly, the installment acceleration amount for a plan year may not be greater than the excess of: (i) the sum (without interest) of the shortfall amortization installments for the plan year and all preceding plan years, determined as if the sponsor had not elected the alternative amortization schedule, over (ii) the sum (without interest) of the actual shortfall amortization installments for the plan year and all preceding plan years, reflecting the alternative amortization schedule elected by the plan sponsor. [92] Accordingly, as of the end of the plan year for which a shortfall amortization installment for a shortfall amortization base is increased, the cumulative amount of the shortfall amortization installments for that base, including any increase on account of an installment acceleration amount, will not be greater than the cumulative amount of the shortfall amortization installments for that base determined as if the alternative amortization schedule had not been elected.

Carryover of excess installment. In the event the annual limitation applies to any installment acceleration amount, the excess is generally carried over and added to the increase in the shortfall amortization installment for that base for the following year, if that plan year is within the carryover period. [93] Note, any carryover of an

¶1493B

excess installment amortization amount is added only to the installments for the shortfall amortization base for which it was originally attributed.

Ordering rules. In applying the annual limit for a plan year, the following ordering rules apply: (1) the installment acceleration amount for the plan year, determined prior to the addition of any carryover amount from a preceding year, is applied first against the annual limit, and (2) then any installment acceleration amounts carried over to the plan year are applied against the annual limit on a first-in, first-out basis. [94]

Excess employee compensation: $1 million threshold. Excess employee compensation is compensation with respect to any employee (including former employees and self-employed individuals treated as employees under Code Sec. 401(c)) in excess of $1 million for any plan year. [95] Beginning in 2011, the $1 million threshold is indexed to the Consumer Price Index for Urban Consumers, rounded to the next lowest $1,000.

Includible compensation. The compensation amount for an employee for a plan year is equal to the amount that is includible in the employee's income for the calendar year in which the plan year begins and that constitutes remuneration for services performed by the employee for the plan sponsor (including remuneration for services performed by the employee for the plan sponsor in earlier years that is includible in the employee's income for the calendar year in which the plan year begins. [96] Compensation for any employee during a calendar year also encompasses any amount that the plan sponsor directly or indirectly sets aside or reserves in, or transfers to, a trust (or other arrangement specified by the Secretary of the Treasury) during the calendar year for purposes of paying deferred compensation to the employee under a nonqualified deferred compensation plan (as defined in Code Sec. 409A) of the plan sponsor, unless such amount is otherwise includible in income as remuneration by the employee in that calendar year. No amount taken into account when set aside, reserved or transferred to a trust or other arrangement will be taken into account more than once. [97].

Grant of service recipient stock. Remuneration does not include any amount includible in income with respect to the granting, after February 28, 2010, of service recipient stock (within the meaning of Code Sec. 409A) that, upon such grant, is subject to a substantial risk of forfeiture for at least 5 years from the date of that grant. [98].

Excludable compensation. Compensation, for purposes of the increase in re-quired shortfall amortization installments, does not include any amount otherwise includible in the employee's income with respect to the granting of service recipient stock (within the meaning of Code Sec. 409A) after February 28, 2010, that is, at the time of grant, subject to a substantial risk of forfeiture (as defined under Code Sec.83(c)(1)) for at least five years from the date of grant. Under the provision, the Secretary of the Treasury may provide for the application of this exception for restricted service recipient stock to persons other than corporations. [99]

In addition, compensation does not include any remuneration payable to an employee on a commission basis solely on account of income directly generated by that employee's individual performance. IRS stresses that remuneration is not payable on a commission basis if the remuneration is paid on account of standards other than individual performance, such as the income produced by a business unit of the employer or the disposition of a business unit that is not in the ordinary course of business of the employer. [100]

Finally, compensation does not include any remuneration consisting of non-qualified deferred compensation, restricted stock, stock options, or stock appreciation rights payable or granted under a binding written contract in effect on March 1, 2010, and not modified in any material respect before the remuneration is paid.[101] IRS cautions that nonqualified deferred compensation does not include remuneration that is not deferred for more than a brief period of time after the end of the employer's taxable year. Accordingly, compensation is not considered to consist of nonqualified deferred compensation for purposes of the exception to the extent that such compensation is received on or before the 15th day of the 3rd calendar month after the end of the employer's taxable year in which the related services are rendered.

Extraordinary dividends and redemptions. The aggregate amount of extraordinary dividends and redemptions (i.e., excess shareholder amount payments) for a plan year is equal to the amount by which the sum of the dividends declared during the plan year by the plan sponsor for the year in which the installment amount is calculated and the aggregate amount paid for the redemption of stock of the plan sponsor redeemed during the plan year exceeds the greater of: (1) the plan sponsor's adjusted net income (within the meaning of ERISA Sec. 4043) for the preceding plan year, determined without regard to any reduction by reason of interest, taxes, depreciation, or amortization, or (2) in the case of a plan sponsor that determined and declared dividends in the same manner for at least five consecutive years immediately preceding the plan year, the aggregate amount of dividends determined and declared for the plan year in that manner. [102]

Exemptions from excess shareholder payment amounts. The following amounts are disregarded in calculating the dividends declared and amounts paid for the redemption of stock during the plan year:

(1) Dividends paid by one member of the plan sponsor's controlled group (as defined in Code Sec. 412(d)(3)) and ERISA Sec. 302(d)(3)) to another member of the controlled group. [103]

(2) Redemptions made pursuant to an employee benefit plan or that are made on account of the death, disability or termination of employment of an employee or shareholder. [104]

Note, a redemption is made on account of death, disability, or termination of employment only if, as a result of the death, disability, or termination of employment of the employee or shareholder, either (i) the plan sponsor or any member of the plan sponsor's controlled group is required to redeem the stock held by the shareholder (even if the shareholder is not required to tender the stock) or (ii) the shareholder is required to tender the stock for redemption (even if the plan

¶1493B

sponsor or a member of the plan sponsor's controlled group is not required to redeem the stock tendered). [105]

(3) Dividends and redemptions with respect to applicable preferred stock on which dividends accrue at a specified rate in all events and without regard to the plan sponsor's income and with respect to which interest accrues on any unpaid dividends. Applicable preferred stock is preferred stock originally issued before March 1, 2010, and preferred stock issued after March 1, 2010 that is held by an employee benefit plan subject to Title I of ERISA. [106]

Waiver amortization charge

In the event that a plan has a waived funding deficiency for any of the five preceding plan years (pursuant to the rules discussed at ¶ 1493I), the minimum required contribution for the plan year will be increased by a waiver amortization charge for the plan year. The waiver amortization charge for a plan year is the aggregate total of waiver amortization installments for the plan year with respect to the waiver amortization base for each of the five preceding plan years.[107]

Waiver amortization installment. The waiver amortization installment is the amount necessary to amortize the waived amortization base (i.e., the amount of the waived funding deficiency for the plan year) in level annual installments over the five- year period beginning with the succeeding plan year.[108] The waiver amortization installment for any plan year in the five-year period with respect to a waiver amortization base is the annual installment determined for the shortfall amortization base.[109]

Application of segment rate in determination of installment. The IRS Proposed Regulations would further provide that the installments are determined assuming that the installments are paid on the valuation date for each plan year and using the interest rate applicable under Code Sec. 430(h)(2). [110] Accordingly, in the event the plan is using segment rates, the installments are determined by applying the first segment rate to the first four installments and the second segment rate to the fifth (and final) installment. The waiver amortization installments established with respect to a waiver amortization base are determined using the interest rates that apply for the plan year for which the waiver is granted (even though the first installment with respect to the waiver amortization base is not due until the subsequent plan year) and are not redetermined in subsequent plan years to reflect changes in interest rates under Code Sec. 430(h)(2) for those subsequent plan years.

> **CCH POINTER:** *Preexisting funding waiver.* In the case of a plan that received a funding waiver under Code Sec. 412 for a plan year for which Code Sec. 430 was not yet effective with respect to the plan, the IRS Proposed Regulations provide that the waiver is treated as giving rise to a waiver amortization base, and the amortization charges with respect to that funding waiver are treated as waiver amortization installments.[111] With respect to such a preexisting funding waiver, the amount of the annual waiver amortization installment is equal to the amortization charge with respect to that waiver determined using the interest rate or rates that applied for the pre-effective

plan year. Thus, for a plan that received a waiver in the past, the plan sponsor would have to contribute the amounts needed to amortize that waiver over the original schedule as previously established.

Plan assets in excess of funding target. In the event that the value of a plan's assets (reduced by any credit balance) is equal to or greater than the plan's funding target for the year (resulting in a funding shortfall for the plan year of zero), the waiver amortization bases for preceding plan years will be eliminated. Specifically, in determining the waiver amortization charge for the plan year and succeeding plan years, the waiver amortization base for all preceding plan years and all the waiver amortization installments for such bases, will be reduced to zero.[112]

Short plan year

IRS Proposed Regulations provide rules for determining the amount of a minimum required contribution for a short plan year, under which amortization installments would be prorated for the short plan year. [113] The IRS Proposed Regulations do not authorize the proration of the target normal cost, but the determination of target normal cost would reflect actual accruals that accrue or are expected to accrue during the plan year. Specifically, the shortfall amortization installments and waiver amortization installments would be determined by multiplying the amount of the installment that would be taken into account for a 12 month plan year by the following fraction: duration of short plan year/1 year. [114]

---

[1] ERISA Sec. 303(a)(2), as added by P.L. 109-280 (Pension Protection Act of 2006), Act Sec. 102(a); Code Sec. 430(a)(2), as added by P.L. 109-280 (Pension Protection Act of 2006), Act Sec. 112(a).

[2] IRS Reg. § 1.430(d)-1(g).

[3] ERISA Sec. 303(a)(1), as added by P.L. 109-280 (Pension Protection Act of 2006), Act Sec. 102(a); Code Sec. 430(a)(1), as added by P.L. 109-280 (Pension Protection Act of 2006), Act Sec. 112(a).

[4] ERISA Sec. 303(b)(1) and Code Sec.430(b)(1), as amended by P.L. 110-458 (Worker, Retiree, and Employer Recovery Act of 2008), Act Sec. 101(b). Prior to amendment, target normal cost was defined as the present value of all benefits expected to accrue or be earned under the plan during the plan year, including benefits attributable to service in a preceding year that are increased because of an increase in compensation during the current plan year (i.e., funding target).

[5] IRS Reg. § 1.430(d)-1(b)(1)(ii).

[6] Preamble to IRS Reg. § 1.430(d)-1, at CCH PENSION PLAN GUIDE ¶ 24,509G.

[7] ERISA Sec. 303(b)(2) and Code Sec.430(b)(2), as amended by P.L. 110-458 (Worker, Retiree, and Employer Recovery Act of 2008), Act Sec. 101(b);IRS Reg. § 1.430(d)-1(b)(1)(ii).

[8] IRS Reg. § 1.430(d)-1(b)(iii).

[9] ERISA Sec. 303(c), as added by P.L. 109-280 (Pension Protection Act of 2006), Act Sec. 102(a); Code Sec. 430(c), as added by P.L. 109-280 (Pension Protection Act of 2006), Act Sec. 112(a).

[10] ERISA Sec. 303(e), as added by P.L. 109-280 (Pension Protection Act of 2006), Act Sec. 102(a); Code Sec. 430(e), as added by P.L. 109-280 (Pension Protection Act of 2006), Act Sec. 112(a).

[11] ERISA Sec. 303(a)(2), as added by P.L. 109-280 (Pension Protection Act of 2006), Act Sec. 102(a); Code Sec. 430(a)(2), as added by P.L. 109-280 (Pension Protection Act of 2006), Act Sec. 112(a).

[12] ERISA Sec. 303(d), as added by P.L. 109-280 (Pension Protection Act of 2006), Act Sec. 102(a); Code Sec. 430(d), as added by P.L. 109-280 (Pension Protection Act of 2006), Act Sec. 112(a); Joint Committee on Taxation, Technical Explanation of the Pension Protection Act of 2006 (JCX-380-06); IRS Reg. § 1.430(d)-1(b)(2).

[13] ERISA Sec. 303(d)(2), as added by P.L. 109-280 (Pension Protection Act of 2006), Act Sec. 102(a); Code Sec. 430(d)(2), as added by P.L. 109-280 (Pension Protection Act of 2006), Act Sec. 112(a); Joint Committee on Taxation, Technical Explanation of the Pension Protection Act of 2006 (JCX-380-06); IRS Reg. § 1.430(d)-1(b)(3).

[14] IRS Reg. § 1.430(d)-1(b)(3)(iii).

[15] IRS Reg. § 1.430(d)-1(b)(4).

[16] IRS Reg. § 1.430(d)-1(c)(1).

[17] IRS Reg. § 1.430(d)-1(c)(1)(ii).

[18] IRS Reg. § 1.430(d)-1(c)(1)(iii).

[19] IRS Reg. § 1.430(d)-1(c)(1)(iii)(D).

[20] IRS Reg. § 1.430(d)-1(c)(1)(iii)(D).

[21] IRS Reg. § 1.430(d)-1(c)(2).

[22] IRS Reg. § 1.430(d)-1(c)(2)(ii).

[23] IRS Reg. § 1.430(d)-1(d)(1)(ii).

[24] IRS Reg. § 1.430(d)-1(d)(1)(iii).

[25] IRS Reg. § 1.430(d)-1(d)(1)(ii).

[26] IRS Reg. § 1.430(d)-1(d)(1)(ii).

[27] Preamble to IRS Reg. § 1.430(d)-1(d)(1), at CCH PENSION PLAN GUIDE ¶ 24,509G.

[28] IRS Reg. § 1.430(d)-1(e)(1).

[29] IRS Reg. § 1.430(d)-1(e)(3).

[30] IRS Reg. § 1.430(d)-1(f).

[31] IRS Reg. § 1.430(d)-1(f)(3).

[32] IRS Reg. § 1.430(d)-1(f)(2).

[33] IRS Reg. § 1.430(d)-1(f)(1).

[34] IRS Reg. § 1.430(d)-1(f)(1)(iv).

[35] IRS Reg. § 1.430(d)-1(g)(3)(i).

[36] IRS Reg. § 1.430(d)-1(g)(3)(ii)(A).

[37] IRS Reg. § 1.430(d)-1(g)(3)(ii)(B).

[38] IRS Announcement 2010-3, I.R.B. 2010-4, 1-25-2010, at CCH PENSION PLAN GUIDE 17,099T-48.

[39] IRS Reg. § 1.430(d)-1(f)(1)(iii).

[40] IRS Reg. § 1.430(d)-1(f)(1)(iv).

[41] IRS Reg. § 1.430(d)-1(f)(4)(ii)(A).

[42] Preamble to IRS Reg. § 1.430(d)-1, at CCH PENSION PLAN GUIDE ¶ 24,509G.

[43] IRS Reg. § 1.430(d)-1(f)(4)(ii)(B).

[44] IRS Reg. § 1.430(d)-1(f)(4)(iii)(A).

[45] IRS Reg. § 1.430(d)-1(f)(6).

[46] IRS Reg. § 1.430(d)-1(f)(7).

[47] IRS Reg. § 1.430(d)-1(f)(8).

[48] IRS Reg. § 1.430(d)-1(f)(3)(iii).

[49] ERISA Sec. 303(c)(4), as added by P.L. 109-280 (Pension Protection Act of 2006), Act Sec. 102(a); Code Sec. 430(c)(4), as added by P.L. 109-280 (Pension Protection Act of 2006), Act Sec. 112(a).

[50] ERISA Sec. 303(c)(2)(A), as added by P.L. 109-280 (Pension Protection Act of 2006), Act Sec. 102(a); Code Sec. 430(c)(2)(A), as added by P.L. 109-280 (Pension Protection Act of 2006), Act Sec. 112(a).

[51] ERISA Sec. 303(c)(2)(B), as added by P.L. 109-280 (Pension Protection Act of 2006), Act Sec. 102(a); Code Sec. 430(c)(2)(B), as added by P.L. 109-280 (Pension Protection Act of 2006), Act Sec. 112(a).

[52] ERISA Sec. 303(c)(3), as added by P.L. 109-280 (Pension Protection Act of 2006), Act Sec. 102(a); Code Sec. 430(c)(3), as added by P.L. 109-280 (Pension Protection Act of 2006), Act Sec. 112(a).

[53] ERISA Sec. 303(c)(5)(A), as added by P.L. 109-280 (Pension Protection Act of 2006), Act Sec. 102(a); Code Sec. 430(c)(5)(A), as added by P.L. 109-280 (Pension Protection Act of 2006), Act Sec. 112(a).

[54] IRS Prop. Reg. § 1.430(a)-1.

[55] IRS Reg. § 1.430(h)(2)-1(f)(2).

[56] IRS Prop. Reg. § 1.430(a)-1(f)(2).

[57] IRS Prop. Reg. § 1.430(a)-1(g), Example 1.

[58] Joint Committee on Taxation, Technical Explanation of the Pension Protection Act of 2006 (JCX-380-06).

[59] ERISA Sec. 303(c)(5)(A), as added by P.L. 109-280 (Pension Protection Act of 2006), Act Sec. 102(a); Code Sec. 430(c)(5)(A), as added by P.L. 109-280 (Pension Protection Act of 2006), Act Sec. 112(a).

[60] ERISA Sec. 303(c)(5)(B)(i), as added by P.L. 109-280 (Pension Protection Act of 2006), Act Sec. 102(a); Code Sec. 430(c)(5)(B)(i), as added by P.L. 109-280 (Pension Protection Act of 2006), Act Sec. 112(a).

[61] ERISA Sec. 303(c)(5)(B)(iii), as added by P.L. 109-280 (Pension Protection Act of 2006), Act Sec. 102(a); Code Sec. 430(c)(5)(B)(iii), as added by P.L. 109-280 (Pension Protection Act of 2006), Act Sec. 112(a).

[62] IRS Prop. Reg. § 1.430(a)-1(h)(4).

[63] Preamble to IRS Prop. Reg. § 1.430(a)-1, at CCH PENSION PLAN GUIDE ¶ 20,262K.

[64] ERISA Sec. 303(c)(5)(B) and Code Sec. 430(c)(5)(B), as amended by P.L. 110-458 (Worker, Retiree, and Employer Recovery Act of 2008), Act Sec. 101(b).

[65] ERISA Sec. 303(c)(6), as added by P.L. 109-280 (Pension Protection Act of 2006), Act Sec. 102(a); Code Sec. 430(c)(6), as added by P.L. 109-280 (Pension Protection Act of 2006), Act Sec. 112(a).

[66] ERISA Sec. 4062(c), as amended by P.L. 109-280 (Pension Protection Act of 2006), Act Sec. 112(a).

[67] Ibid.

[68] ERISA Sec. 303(c)(2)(D)(iv) and Code Sec. 430(c)(2)(D)(iv) as added by P.L. 111-192 (Preservation of Access to Care for Medicare Beneficiaries and Pension Relief Act of 2010).

[69] ERISA Sec. 303(c)(7)(F)(i) and Code Sec. 430(c)(7)(F)(v) as added by P.L. 111-192 (Preser-

vation of Access to Care for Medicare Beneficiaries and Pension Relief Act of 2010).

[70] ERISA Sec. 303(c)(2)(D)(ii) and Code Sec. 430(c)(2)(D)(ii) as added by P.L. 111-192 (Preservation of Access to Care for Medicare Beneficiaries and Pension Relief Act of 2010); IRS Notice 2011-3, Q G-3, I.R.B. 2011-2, 1-10-11, at ¶ 17,146M.

[71] IRS Notice 2011-3, Q G-3, I.R.B. 2011-2, 1-10-11, at ¶ 17,146M.

[72] ERISA Sec. 303(c)(2)(D)(iii) and Code Sec. 430(c)(2)(D)(iii), as added by P.L. 111-192 (Preservation of Access to Care for Medicare Beneficiaries and Pension Relief Act of 2010); IRS Notice 2011-3, Q G-3, I.R.B. 2011-2, 1-10-11, at ¶ 17,146M

[73] IRS Notice 2011-3, Q G-4, I.R.B. 2011-2, 1-10-11, at ¶ 17,146M.

[74] ERISA Sec. 303(c)(2)(D)(v) and Code Sec. 430(c)(2)(D)(v), as added by P.L. 111-192 (Preservation of Access to Care for Medicare Beneficiaries and Pension Relief Act of 2010).

[75] IRS Notice 2010-55 , I.R.B. 2010-33, 8-16-10, at ¶ 17,145N.

[76] IRS Notice 2011-3, Q G-1(b), I.R.B. 2011-2, 1-10-11, at ¶ 17,146M.

[77] ERISA Sec. 303(c)(2)(D)(iv) and Code Sec. 430(c)(2)(D)(iv), as added by P.L. 111-192 (Preservation of Access to Care for Medicare Beneficiaries and Pension Relief Act of 2010); IRS Notice 2011-3, Q G-2(a), I.R.B. 2011-2, 1-10-11, at ¶ 17,146M.

[78] ERISA Sec. 303(c)(2)(D)(vi) and Code Sec. 430(c)(2)(D)(vi), as added by P.L. 111-192 (Preservation of Access to Care for Medicare Beneficiaries and Pension Relief Act of 2010).

[79] IRS Notice 2011-3, Q N-1, I.R.B. 2011-2, 1-10-11, at ¶ 17,146M.

[80] IRS Notice 2011-3, Q N-4, I.R.B. 2011-2, 1-10-11, at ¶ 17,146M.

[81] IRS Notice 2011-3, Q N-4(c), I.R.B. 2011-2, 1-10-11, at ¶ 17,146M.

[82] IRS Notice 2011-3, Q N-6 and Q T-1, I.R.B. 2011-2, 1-10-11, at ¶ 17,146M.

[83] IRS Notice 2011-3, Q N-7, I.R.B. 2011-2, 1-10-11, at ¶ 17,146M.

[84] IRS Notice 2011-3, Q N-7, I.R.B. 2011-2, 1-10-11, at ¶ 17,146M.

[85] IRS Notice 2011-3, Q E-2, I.R.B. 2011-2, 1-10-11, at ¶ 17,146M.

[86] ERISA Sec. 303(c)(7)(A) and Code Sec. 430(c)(7)(A), as added by P.L. 111-192 (Preservation of Access to Care for Medicare Beneficiaries and Pension Relief Act of 2010).

[87] IRS Notice 2011-3, Q I-3, I.R.B. 2011-2, 1-10-11, at ¶ 17,146M.

[88] IRS Notice 2011-3, Q I-3, I.R.B. 2011-2, 1-10-11, at ¶ 17,146M.

[89] ERISA Sec. 303(c)(7)(F)(ii) and Code Sec. 430(c)(7)(F)(ii), as added by P.L. 111-192 (Preservation of Access to Care for Medicare Beneficiaries and Pension Relief Act of 2010).

[90] ERISA Sec. 303(c)(7)(C)(i) and Code Sec. 430(c)(7)(C)(i), as added by P.L. 111-192 (Preservation of Access to Care for Medicare Beneficiaries and Pension Relief Act of 2010).

[91] ERISA Sec. 303(c)(7)(C)(ii) and Code Sec. 430(c)(7)(C)(ii), as added by P.L. 111-192 (Preservation of Access to Care for Medicare Beneficiaries and Pension Relief Act of 2010).

[92] IRS Notice 2011-3, Q I-4, I.R.B. 2011-2, 1-10-11, at ¶ 17,146M.

[93] IRS Notice 2011-3, Q I-5, I.R.B. 2011-2, 1-10-11, at ¶ 17,146M.

[94] ERISA Sec. 303(c)(7)(C)(iii) and Code Sec. 430(c)(7)(C)(iii), as added by P.L. 111-192 (Preservation of Access to Care for Medicare Beneficiaries and Pension Relief Act of 2010); IRS Notice 2011-3, Example I-3, I.R.B. 2011-12, 1-10-11, at ¶ 17,146M.

[95] ERISA Sec. 303(c)(7)(D) and Code Sec. 430(c)(7)(D), as added by P.L. 111-192 (Preservation of Access to Care for Medicare Beneficiaries and Pension Relief Act of 2010).

[96] ERISA Sec. 303(c)(7)(D) and Code Sec. 430(c)(7)(D), as added by P.L. 111-192 (Preservation of Access to Care for Medicare Beneficiaries and Pension Relief Act of 2010); IRS Notice 2011-3, Q C-3(a), I.R.B. 2011-2, 1-10-11, at ¶ 17,146M.

[97] ERISA Sec. 303(c)(7)(D)(ii) and Code Sec. 430(c)(7)(D)(ii), as added by P.L. 111-192 (Preservation of Access to Care for Medicare Beneficiaries and Pension Relief Act of 2010).

[98] ERISA Sec. 303(c)(7)(D)(iv) and Code Sec. 430(c)(7)(D)(iv), as added by P.L. 111-192 (Preservation of Access to Care for Medicare Beneficiaries and Pension Relief Act of 2010); IRS Notice 2011-3, Q C-5, I.R.B. 2011-2, 1-10-11, at ¶ 17,146M.

[99] ERISA Sec. 303(c)(7)(D)(iv) and Code Sec. 430(c)(7)(D)(iv), as added by P.L. 111-192 (Preservation of Access to Care for Medicare Beneficiaries and Pension Relief Act of 2010); IRS Notice 2011-3, Q C-5, I.R.B. 2011-2, 1-10-11, at ¶ 17,146M.

[100] IRS Notice 2011-3, Q C-6, I.R.B. 2011-2, 1-10-11, at ¶ 17,146M.

[101] ERISA Sec. 303(c)(7)(D)(v) and Code Sec. 430(c)(7)(D)(v), as added by P.L. 111-192 (Preservation of Access to Care for Medicare Beneficiaries and Pension Relief Act of 2010); IRS Notice 2011-3, Q C-7, I.R.B. 2011-2, 1-10-11, at ¶ 17,146M.

[102] ERISA Sec. 303(c)(7)(E)(i) and Code Sec. 430(c)(7)(E)(i), as added by P.L. 111-192 (Preservation of Access to Care for Medicare Beneficiaries and Pension Relief Act of 2010); IRS Notice 2011-3, Q S-1, I.R.B. 2011-2, 1-10-11, at ¶ 17,146M.

[103] ERISA Sec. 303(c)(7)(E)(iii) and Code Sec. 430(c)(7)(E)(iii), as added by P.L. 111-192 (Preservation of Access to Care for Medicare Beneficiaries and Pension Relief Act of 2010); IRS Notice 2011-3, Q S-8, I.R.B. 2011-2, 1-10-11, at ¶ 17,146M.

[104] ERISA Sec. 303(c)(7)(E)(iv) and Code Sec. 430(c)(7)(E)(iv), as added by P.L. 111-192 (Preservation of Access to Care for Medicare Beneficiaries and Pension Relief Act of 2010).

[105] IRS Notice 2011-3, Q S-7, I.R.B. 2011-2, 1-10-11, at ¶ 17,146M.

[106] ERISA Sec. 303(c)(7)(E)(v) and Code Sec. 430(c)(7)(E)(v), as added by P.L. 111-192 (Preservation of Access to Care for Medicare Beneficiaries and Pension Relief Act of 2010); IRS Notice 2011-3, Q S-8, I.R.B 2011-2, 1-10-11, at ¶ 17,146M.

[107] ERISA Sec. 303(e)(1), as added by P.L. 109-280 (Pension Protection Act of 2006), Act Sec. 102(a); Code Sec. 430(e)(1), as added by P.L. 109-280 (Pension Protection Act of 2006), Act Sec. 112(a).

[108] ERISA Sec. 303(e)(2)(A), as added by P.L. 109-280 (Pension Protection Act of 2006), Act Sec. 102(a); Code Sec. 430(e)(2)(A), as added by P.L. 109-280 (Pension Protection Act of 2006), Act Sec. 112(a).

[109] ERISA Sec. 303(e)(2)(B), as added by P.L. 109-280 (Pension Protection Act of 2006), Act Sec. 102(a); Code Sec. 430(e)(2)(B), as added by P.L. 109-280 (Pension Protection Act of 2006), Act Sec. 112(a).

[110] IRS Prop. Reg. § 1.430(a)-1(d)

[111] IRS Prop. Reg. § 1.430(a)-1(h)(3))

[112] ERISA Sec. 303(e)(5), as added by P.L. 109-280 (Pension Protection Act of 2006), Act Sec. 102(a); Code Sec. 430(e)(5), as added by P.L. 109-280 (Pension Protection Act of 2006), Act Sec. 112(a).

[113] IRS Prop. Reg. § 1.430(a)-1(b)(2)(ii)(A)

[114] IRS Prop. Reg. § 1.430(a)-1(g)(7, Example 7.

¶ 1493C

MINIMUM FUNDING RULES APPLICABLE AFTER 2007: Credit Balances

Under pre-2008 law, a credit balance automatically reduced any required contribution, regardless of the plan's funded status. The current rules do not eliminate existing credit balances or prevent excess contributions from being maintained as a credit balance after the new rules goes into effect for plan years beginning after 2007. However, existing credit balances will be separated from credit balances that may be accumulated and maintained after the funding rules go into effect. Specifically, the rules divide credit balances into: (1) a funding standard carryover balance, which reflects a balance in the funding standard account at the end of the 2007 plan year; and (2) a prefunding balance, which may be elected by a plan to accumulate excess contributions after application of the new rules for plan years beginning after 2007.[1]

The funding standard carryover balance and the prefunding balance may be credited against the minimum required contribution (if the plan is sufficiently funded), reducing the amount that must be paid for the year. However, credit balances used to offset the required minimum contribution will also reduce the value of plan assets. Accordingly, plan sponsors are allowed the alternative option of electing to reduce or waive the funding standard carryover and the prefunding credit balance so as to prevent the reduction of plan assets.

Final rules apply in 2010

The new funding rules generally apply to plan years beginning on or after January 1, 2008. Final regulations issued by the IRS in October 2009, implementing the funding requirements under Code Sec. 430(f), apply to plan years beginning on or after January 1, 2010. However, for plan years before January 1, 2010, plans may rely on the regulations in order to comply with the requirements of Code Sec. 430(f). [2]

Application of rules to multiple employer plans

The funding rules under Code Sec. 430(f) apply to multiple employer plans as single-employer defined benefit plans subject to Code Sec. 412. [3] If the plan complies with Code Sec. 413(c)(4)(A) (i.e., no employer contributes less than the amount that would be required if the employer maintained a separate plan) the rules apply to each employer under the plan as if each employer maintained a separate plan. Accordingly, each employer under a multiple employer plan may have a separate funding standard carryover balance and prefunding balance for the plan. [4]

Funding standard carryover balance

The employer sponsor of a single-employer defined benefit plan that has a positive credit balance in the funding standard account at the end of such plan year was authorized under the PPA to *elect* to maintain a funding standard carryover balance until the balance is reduced to zero.[5] The balance would be adjusted to reflect the plan's investment experience.

Election not required to maintain funding standard carryover balance. The final rules provide that a funding standard carryover balance is automatically established for a plan that had a positive balance in the funding standard account under Code Sec. 412(b) (prior to amendment by the Pension Protection Act of 2006) as of the end of the pre-effective plan year for the plan. [6] An employer that does not wish to have a funding standard carryover balance established may elect to reduce it to zero. [7]

Decrease in funding standard carryover balance. The funding standard carryover balance will be reduced (but not below zero), as of the first day of each plan year by the amount of the funding standard carryover balance used to offset the minimum required contribution of the plan for the preceding year and by any reduction in the carryover balance elected by the sponsor in order to reduce the amount by which plan assets are reduced in determining the minimum required contribution.[8]

Prefunding balance

A plan sponsor may elect to maintain a prefunding balance for a plan. The prefunding balance will consist of a beginning balance of zero. The balance will be: (1) increased by an amount (elected by the employer) of contributions that exceed the required minimum funding contribution, and (2) decreased (but not below zero) by the amount of the prefunding balance used to offset the minimum required contribution of the plan for the preceding plan year.[9] The prefunding balance will be further adjusted to reflect actual investment return for the plan year and interest.

CCH POINTER: *Special election not required to establish prefunding balance.* The plan sponsor's initial election to add to the prefunding balance

¶1493C

constitutes an election to maintain a prefunding balance. [10] Accordingly, no special election is needed in order to establish a prefunding balance.

Determination of increase in prefunding balance. In the event the plan sponsor elects to increase the prefunding balance, as of the first day of a plan year, the prefunding balance will be increased by the amount elected for the plan year. The amount added to the prefunding balance, however, may not exceed the present value of the excess contribution for the preceding year, increased for interest. [11]

Present value of excess contributions. The present value of the excess contribution for the preceding plan year is the excess of the present value (determined as of the preceding plan year using the plan's effective interest rate) of employer contributions (other than contributions made to avoid or terminate the Code Sec. 436 benefit limits (see ¶ 1493H)) to the plan for such preceding plan year, over the minimum required contribution for the preceding year.[12] However, the present value of excess contributions may not include a contribution made during the plan year to correct an unpaid minimum required contribution for a prior plan year. [13]

The present value of the excess contribution is adjusted for interest (at the plan's effective interest rate) accruing between the valuation date for the preceding plan year to the first day of the current plan year. [14] Interest, for purposes of the adjustment, is generally the plan's effective interest rate (under Code Sec.430(h)(2)(A)) of the preceding plan year.

Decrease in prefunding balance. The prefunding balance of a plan, as of the first day of each plan year, must be reduced (but not below zero) by: (a) any amount of the prefunding balance that was used to offset the minimum required contribution of the plan for the preceding plan year, and (2) any reduction in the prefunding balance for the plan year. [15]

Excess contribution added to prefunded balance. Excess contributions may be added to the prefunding balance even if the excess results solely from an election to use the funding standard carryover balance or prefunding balance to offset required minimum contributions. However, the interest adjustment with respect to the contribution must be based on the plan's actual investment experience for the plan year, and not the effective interest rate under Code Sec. 430(h)(2)(A). Under this rule, the funding standard carryover balance and prefunding balance will be adjusted by the plan's actual investment return, when the balances are not used to satisfy the minimum required contribution for the plan year, regardless of whether an election has been made to use the balance to offset the contribution and the prefunding balance is subsequently replenished. [16]

Credit balance adjusted for investment experience

The plan sponsor will be required to adjust the prefunding balance and the funding standard carryover balance of the plan, as of the first day of the plan year (after subtracting amounts used to offset the minimum required contribution for the preceding plan year and after any reduction of balances for that preceding year), to reflect the actual rate of return (gain or loss) on plan assets from the preceding plan year.[17] The actual rate of investment return will be determined on the basis of fair market value, taking into account the amount and timing of all

¶1493C

contributions, distributions, and other plan payments made during the period.[18] Thus, a plan's credit balance will no longer be determined under the plan's assumed interest rate, irrespective of the plan's investment performance.

Ordering rules for adjustment of actual return. The adjustment for actual rate of return on plan assets, under the final regulations, is applied to the balance, after any reduction of prefunding and funding standard carryover balances for that preceding plan year and after subtracting amounts used to offset the minimum required contribution for the preceding plan year (see below).[19]

Subtract credit balances from plan assets. The amount of a plan's prefunding balance or funding standard carryover balance must generally be subtracted from the value of plan assets for purposes of the rules under Code Secs. 430 and 436. [20] The final regulations clarify that, in determining whether a plan is exempt from the requirement under Code Sec. 430(c)(5) to establish a new shortfall amortization base (see ¶ 1493B), the amount of the prefunding balance is subtracted from the value of plan assets only in an election to use a portion of the prefunding balance to offset the minimum required contribution is made for the plan year. [21] However, the funding standard carryover balance is not subtracted from the value of plan assets in determining the exemption from the shortfall amortization base, regardless of whether any portion of the funding standard carryover balance or the prefunding balance is used to offset the minimum required contribution for the plan year.[22]

Agreement with PBGC may prevent use of credit balance to reduce plan assets. The plan sponsor and the PBGC may negotiate a binding written agreement (executed prior to the valuation date for the plan year) preventing the use of a credit balance to reduce the minimum required contribution for the plan year.[23]

CCH POINTER: *Annual funding notice.* Administrators of single-employer and multiemployer defined benefit plans are required to provide an annual funding notice (to the PBGC, participants and beneficiaries, labor organizations, and contributing employers) for each plan year. With respect to single-employer plans, the notice must provide a statement of total assets (separately stating the prefunding balance and the funding standard carryover balances) and liabilities of the plan (determined in the same manner as under ERISA Sec. 303) for the plan year to which the notice relates (rather than the plan year for which the latest annual report was field) and for the two preceding plan years, as reported in the annual report for each plan year. [24]

The funding notice requirements are detailed at ¶ 2220.

Election to apply credit balance against minimum required contribution

Under pre-2008 law, a credit balance automatically reduces a required contribution in a future year. Employers, under current law, are not precluded from continuing to use credit balances to pay required contributions. Thus, employers are not prohibited or discouraged from pre-funding their plans. Rather, the sponsor of a plan that is not below a threshold funding level may "elect" to credit all or a portion of the prefunding balance or the funding standard carryover balance plan year against the minimum required contribution for the current plan year. The minimum required contribution for the plan year will be reduced, as of the first day of the plan year (i.e., valuation date), by the credited amount. [25] However, the amount credited may not exceed the minimum required contribution.

CCH POINTER: Employers sponsoring underfunded plans are prohibited from using credit balances to reduce the required minimum contribution. Thus, an underfunded plan may not use a prefunding balance to offset the portion of a required contribution that exceeds the amount exceeding target normal cost or 25 percent of the minimum required contribution.

This rule is in contrast to pre-2008 law under which the value of plan assets was not reduced by any credit balance in determining whether the plan's funded current liability percentage is under 90 percent and, thus, whether a deficit reduction contribution is required. The new rules do not require the value of plan assets to be reduced by the full amount of the prefunding balance in determining the minimum required contribution.[26]

Ordering rule for applying credit balance against required contribution. Under the final regulations, the amount of the prefunding and funding standard carryover balance that may be used to offset the minimum required contribution for a plan year must take into account any decrease in those balances that results from a prior election either to use the balance for offset purposes or to reduce the balances. [27]

The election to reduce the funding standard carryover balance or prefunding balance is deemed to occur on the valuation date for the plan before any election to use the balance to offset the minimum required contribution for the current year. [28] Thus, the IRS cautions, if an election to apply a credit balance to offset the minimum required contribution for the plan year has been made prior to the election to reduce the prefunding or funding standard carryover balance, the amount available to offset the required contribution for the plan year will be retroactively reduced, resulting in a missed quarterly contribution. [29] By contrast, the election to reduce a credit balance for a plan year will not offset a prior election to use a prefunding balance of funding standard carryover balance to offset a minimum required contribution for a prior plan year.

Reflect investment experience. The prior plan year's prefunding and funding standard carryover balances must be adjusted to reflect investment experience for that prior plan year before the amount of the balances available for the election can be determined. [30]

Exhaust funding standard carryover balance before using prefunding balance. A plan with a funding standard carryover balance greater than zero may use no amount of the prefunding balance to offset the minimum required contribution. [31] Accordingly, a plan's funding standard carryover balance must be exhausted before the plan's prefunding balance may be use to offset the required contribution.

Election may not be made by underfunded plans. A plan may not elect to use the prefunding or funding standard carryover balance to offset the required contribution for a plan year if the plan's funding ratio for the prior plan year was less than 80 percent. [32] The plan's prior year funding ratio generally is equal to the following fraction (expressed as a percentage): value of plan assets on the valuation date for the preceding plan year, reduced by the prefunding balance (and not the funding standard carryover balance)/ funding target of the plan for the preceding plan year.

Special rule for new plans. A special rule is provided for new plans that did not result from a merger and were not involved in a spinoff. Under the rule, if the prior plan year was the first year of the plan and the funding target for the prior plan year was zero, the plan's prior year funding ratio will be deemed 80 percent, for purposes of the limitation on the use of credit balances. [33] This rule effectively allows the sponsor of a new plan that has no funding target in its first year to use a prefunding balance that resulted from first year contributions in excess of the target normal cost in order to offset the minimum required contribution in the second year of the plan. [34]

Election to reduce credit balance

Because plan assets are generally reduced by the amount of a credit balance in determining the minimum required contribution, a plan sponsor may alternatively elect to permanently reduce (or waive) a prefunding balance and the funding standard carryover balance for any plan by any amount (but not below zero).[35] The reduction will take effect before the valuation of plan assets for the year and before the application of an election to use the balance to offset the required minimum contribution. Pursuant to the election, the amount of the credit balance that must be subtracted from the value of plan assets will be smaller and, accordingly, the value of plan assets for purposes of Code Sec. 430 or 436 will be larger.[36] Accordingly, by making the election, a plan sponsor may protect plan assets from being reduced by the credit balance in determining the minimum required contribution.

Funding standard carryover balance must be exhausted. The funding standard carryover balance must be exhausted before the prefunding balance may be reduced.[37]

Election procedures

The final regulations specify requirements that govern the manner in which an election to apply credit balances to offset required contributions or to reduce credit balances are to be executed. [38]

Written notice of election to plan actuary and plan administrator. The final regulations require the plan sponsor to provide written notification of the election to the plan's enrolled actuary and to the plan administrator. [39] The notice would need to disclose the specific dollar amount involved in the election. Accordingly, a conditional or formula-based election will generally not satisfy the notice requirements. [40]

Standing election to increase or use credit balance. A plan sponsor is authorized, under the final rules, to provide a standing election, in writing, to the plan's enrolled actuary to use a credit balance to offset the required contribution for the plan year, or to add the maximum amount possible each year to the prefunding balance. [41]

¶1493C

Timing rules. An election to add to the prefunding balance or to use the prefunding balance or funding standard carryover balance to offset the minimum required contribution for the plan year must be made no later than the last date for making the minimum required contribution for the plan year. [42]Generally, the election may not be made before the first day of the plan year to which the election relates. However, an exception is provided where a change in the enrolled actuary results in a revocation of a standing election. [43]

An election to reduce a credit balance for a plan year (e.g., in order to avoid or terminate a benefit restriction under Code Sec. 436) must be made by the end of the plan year to which the election relates. [44]

CCH POINTER: The timing deadlines specified in the final regulations do not preclude a plan sponsor from making an earlier election. [45] The IRS notes that circumstances may require an earlier election in order to allow the plan sponsor to make a required quarterly contribution.

Election is irrevocable. A plan sponsor's election with respect to the plan's prefunding balance or funding standard carryover balance is irrevocable and unconditional. [46]

However, an election to use the prefunding balance or funding standard carryover balance to offset the minimum required contribution for a plan year (including an election to satisfy the quarterly contribution requirements for a plan year) may be revoked to the extent that the amount the plan sponsor elected to use to offset the required contribution exceeded the minimum required contribution for a plan year (determined without regard to offset). The election may be revoked, the IRS cautions, only by providing written notification of the revocation to the plan's enrolled actuary and plan administrator. [47]

The election must, further, generally be revoked by the end of the plan year. [48] However, for plans with a valuation date other that the first day of the plan year, the election must be revoked by the deadline for plan contributions for the year (under Code Sec. 430(j)(1) (see ¶ 1493F). [49]

Note, for the first plan year beginning in 2008, the deadlines for the revocation for all plans is deferred to the due date (including extension) of Form 5500, Schedule SB (Single Employer Defined Benefit Actuarial Information).[50]

The final regulations provide numerous examples illustrating the governing rules (see CCH PENSION PLAN GUIDE ¶ 13,151L-12).

---

[1] ERISA Sec. 303(f), as added by P.L. 109-280 (Pension Protection Act of 2006), Act Sec. 102(a); Code Sec. 430(f), as added by P.L. 109-280 (Pension Protection Act of 2006), Act Sec. 112(a).

[2] IRS Reg. § 1.430(f)-1(h).

[3] IRS Reg. § 1.430(f)-1(a).

[4] IRS Reg. § 1.430(f)-1(a)(2).

[5] ERISA Sec. 303(f), as added by P.L. 109-280 (Pension Protection Act of 2006), Act Sec. 102(a); Code Sec. 430(f), as added by P.L. 109-280 (Pension Protection Act of 2006), Act Sec. 112(a).

[6] IRS Reg. § 1.430(f)-1(b)(2).

[7] Preamble to IRS Reg. § 1.430(f)-1, at CCH PENSION PLAN GUIDE ¶ 24,509G.

[8] ERISA Sec. 303(f)(7)(C), as added by P.L. 109-280 (Pension Protection Act of 2006), Act Sec. 102(a); Code Sec. 430(f)(7)(C), as added by P.L. 109-280 (Pension Protection Act of 2006), Act Sec. 112(a); IRS Reg. § 1.430(f)-1(b)(2)(ii).

[9] ERISA Sec. 303(f)(6), as added by P.L. 109-280 (Pension Protection Act of 2006), Act Sec. 102(a); Code Sec. 430(f)(6), as added by P.L. 109-280 (Pension Protection Act of 2006), Act Sec. 112(a).

¶1493C

[10] IRS Reg. § 1.430(f)-1(b)(1).

[11] ERISA Sec. 303(f)(6)(B), as added by P.L. 109-280 (Pension Protection Act of 2006), Act Sec. 102(a); Code Sec. 430(f)(6)(B), as added by P.L. 109-280 (Pension Protection Act of 2006), Act Sec. 112(a); IRS Reg. § 1.430(f)-1(b)(1)(ii)(A)

[12] IRS Reg. § 1.430(f)-1(b)(1)(ii)(B) and (iv).

[13] IRS Reg. § 1.430(f)-1(b)(1)(ii)(C).

[14] ERISA Sec. 303(f)(6)(B)(ii), as added by P.L. 109-280 (Pension Protection Act of 2006), Act Sec. 102(a); Code Sec. 430(f)(6)(B)(ii), as added by P.L. 109-280 (Pension Protection Act of 2006), Act Sec. 112(a); IRS Reg. § 1.430(f)-1(b)(1)(iv).

[15] IRS Reg. § 1.430(f)-1(b)(1)(iii).

[16] Preamble to IRS Reg. § 1.430(f)-1, at CCH PENSION PLAN GUIDE ¶ 24,509G.

[17] ERISA Sec. 303(f)(8), as added by P.L. 109-280 (Pension Protection Act of 2006), Act Sec. 102(a); Code Sec. 430(f)(8), as added by P.L. 109-280 (Pension Protection Act of 2006), Act Sec. 112(a); IRS Reg. § 1.430(f)-1(b)(3).

[18] *Ibid.*

[19] IRS Reg. § 1.430(f)-1(b)(3).

[20] IRS Reg. § 1.430(f)-1(c).

[21] IRS Reg. § 1.430(f)-1(c)(2)(i).

[22] IRS Reg. § 1.430(f)-1(c)(2)(ii).

[23] ERISA Sec. 303(f)(4)(B)(ii), as added by P.L. 109-280 (Pension Protection Act of 2006), Act Sec. 102(a); Code Sec. 430(f)(4)(B)(ii), as added by P.L. 109-280 (Pension Protection Act of 2006), Act Sec. 112(a); IRS Reg. § 1.430(f)-1(c)(3).

[24] ERISA Sec.101(f)(2)(B)(II), as amended by P.L. 110-458 (Worker, Retiree, and Employer Recovery Act of 2008), Act Sec. 105(a)(2).

[25] ERISA Sec. 303(f)(3)(A), as added by P.L. 109-280 (Pension Protection Act of 2006), Act Sec. 102(a); Code Sec. 430(f)(3)(A), as added by P.L. 109-280 (Pension Protection Act of 2006), Act Sec. 112(a); IRS Reg. § 1.430(f)-1(d).

[26] ERISA Sec. 303(f)(4)(B), as added by P.L. 109-280 (Pension Protection Act of 2006), Act Sec. 102(a); Code Sec. 430(f)(4)(B), as added by P.L. 109-280 (Pension Protection Act of 2006), Act Sec. 112(a).

[27] IRS Reg. § 1.430(f)-1(d)(1)(ii)(A).

[28] IRS Reg. § 1.430(f)-1(d)(1)(ii)(B).

[29] Preamble to IRS Reg. § 1.430(f)-1, at CCH PENSION PLAN GUIDE ¶ 24,509G.

[30] IRS Reg. § 1.430(f)-1(d)(1)(ii)(C).

[31] IRS Reg. § 1.430(f)-1(d)(2).

[32] IRS Reg. § 1.430(f)-1(d)(3).

[33] IRS Reg. § 1.430(f)-1(d)(3)(ii).

[34] Preamble to IRS Reg. § 1.430(f)-1, at CCH PENSION PLAN GUIDE ¶ 24,509G.

[35] ERISA Sec. 303(f)(5), as added by P.L. 109-280 (Pension Protection Act of 2006), Act Sec. 102(a); Code Sec. 430(f)(5), as added by P.L. 109-280 (Pension Protection Act of 2006), Act Sec. 112(a); IRS Reg. § 1.430(f)-1(e).

[36] IRS Reg. § 1.430(f)-1(e)(1).

[37] ERISA Sec. 303(f)(5)(B), as added by P.L. 109-280 (Pension Protection Act of 2006), Act Sec. 102(a); Code Sec. 430(f)(5)(B), as added by P.L. 109-280 (Pension Protection Act of 2006), Act Sec. 112(a) IRS Reg. § 1.430(f)-1(e)(2).

[38] IRS Reg. § 1.430(f)-1(f).

[39] IRS Reg. § 1.430(f)-1(f)(1).

[40] Preamble to IRS Reg. § 1.430(f)-1, at CCH PENSION PLAN GUIDE ¶ 24,509G.

[41] IRS Reg. § 1.430(f)-1(f)(1)(ii).

[42] IRS Reg. § 1.430(f)-1(f)(2)(i).

[43] IRS Reg. § 1.430(f)-1(f)(2)(ii).

[44] IRS Reg. § 1.430(f)-1(f)(2)(iii).

[45] IRS Reg. § 1.430(f)-1(f)(2)(iv).

[46] IRS Reg. § 1.430(f)-1(f)(3).

[47] IRS Reg. § 1.430(f)-1(f)(3)(ii).

[48] IRS Reg. § 1.430(f)-1(f)(3)(iii).

[49] *Ibid.*

[50] *Ibid.*

¶ 1493D

MINIMUM FUNDING RULES APPLICABLE AFTER 2007: Valuation Rules

Under prior law, plan sponsors were empowered with the discretion to select any day during the plan year as the valuation date. In addition, the value of plan assets was determined on the basis of any reasonable actuarial method. The Pension Protection Act of 2006 modified the prior rules, designated the valuation date for a plan as the first day of the plan year and required the value of plan assets to be fair market value. [1]

The valuation rules enacted by the PPA generally apply to plan years beginning on or after January 1, 2008. Final regulations issued by IRS in 2009, implementing the new requirements, apply to plan years beginning on or after 2010. [2]

Valuation date

A plan's valuation date would (with the exception of plans with 100 or fewer participants) be the first day of the plan year. [3] Thus, the determination of the plan's funding target, target normal cost, and the value of plan assets will be made as of the first day of the plan year.

Small plan exemption. Small plans are allowed to designate any day during the plan year as the valuation date for that plan year and succeeding years. [4] A small plan is defined, generally, as a plan that, on each day during the preceding plan year, had 100 or fewer participants, including active and inactive participants and all other individuals entitled to future benefits.

For purposes of the small plan exemption, all defined benefit plans (other than multiemployer plans) maintained by an employer (including all members of the employer's controlled group and certain predecessor employers) are treated as one plan. However, only participants with respect to the employer are taken into account.

New plans. With respect to the first plan year of any plan, the small plan exemption is applied by taking into account the number of participants that the plan is reasonably expected to have on each day during the first plan year.

CCH POINTER: *Valuation date is part of funding method.* The selection of the plan's valuation date is part of the plan's funding method and, accordingly may only be changed with IRS consent. [5] However, if a plan ceases to be eligible for the small plan exemption for a plan year because the number of participants exceeds 100 in the prior plan year, the change in the valuation date to the first day of the plan year (as required by Code Sec. 430) will be automatically approved by the IRS and does not need to be pre-approved.

Valuation of assets

The value of plan assets was determined, under prior law on the basis of any reasonable actuarial method that accounted for fair market value. Under current law, the value of plan assets may be determined as: (1) the fair market value of plan assets on the valuation date, [6] or (2) as the average of the fair market value of assets on the valuation date and the adjusted fair market value of assets, subject to a 90-100 percent corridor. [7]

Note, the method by which the value of plan assets is determined is part of the plan's funding method and may only be changed with IRS consent. However, any change in a plan's asset valuation method or valuation date that is made for the first plan year beginning in 2008, the first plan year beginning in 2009, or the first plan year beginning in 2010 will be automatically approved and will not require prior IRS approval. [8]

Fair market value of assets. Under the final regulations, assets must be valued at their fair market value on the valuation date or at the average value of assets on the valuation date. [9] The fair market value of an asset would be the price at which an asset would change hands between a willing buyer and a willing seller, neither being under a compulsion to buy or sell and both having reasonable knowledge of relevant facts. [10]

"Smoothing" of plan asset values. A plan may, alternatively, determine the value of plan assets by averaging fair market values.[11] The Pension Protection Act, did not eliminate such "smoothing" of asset values. However, the averaging method must: (1) be permitted under regulations promulgated by the Secretary of the Treasury; and (2) may not provide for the averaging of fair market value over more than the period beginning on the last day of the 25th month preceding the month in which the valuation date occurs and ending on the valuation date (or a similar period if the valuation date is not the first day of the month).[12] Thus, assets may only be averaged or smoothed over the 24-month period immediately preceding the valuation date. Note, prior law allowed plan assets to be smoothed over 5 years and liabilities over 4 years.

Smoothing method must result in asset valuation of 90-110 percent of fair market value. Prior law allowed for smoothing techniques that could produce actuarial values of between 80-120 percent of current fair market value. Under the rules applicable after 2007, the smoothing method must result in a plan asset valuation of between 90-110 percent of the fair market value of the assets on the valuation date.[13]

Averaging of fair market value under final regulations. Under the final rules, the value of plan assets may be determined as the value of the average of the fair market value of assets on the valuation date and the adjusted fair market value of assets determined for one or more earlier determination dates. [14]

Determination dates. The valuation date would be treated as the determination date. The period of time between the valuation date and each of the earlier determination dates must be equal and may not exceed 12 months. [15] In addition, the earliest of the determination dates may not be earlier than the last day of the 25th month before the valuation date of the plan year (or a similar period in the case of a valuation date that is not the first day of the month).

Note, typically, the earliest determination date will be the two immediately preceding valuation dates. However, more frequent determination dates (e.g., monthly or quarterly) are authorized.

Adjusting fair market value for contributions and distributions. The adjusted fair market value of plan assets for a prior determination date is the fair market value of plan assets on that date: (1) increased for contributions included in the plan's asset balance on the earlier determination date, and (2) reduced for benefits and all other amounts paid from plan assets during the period beginning with the prior determination date and ending immediately before the valuation; and (3) adjusted for expected earnings. [16]

The fair market value of assets as of the determination date includes any contribution for a plan year that ends with or prior to the determination date that is receivable as of the determination date (if the contribution is actually made within

8½ months after the end of the applicable plan year). [17] The present value of a contribution that is receivable for the applicable plan year is determined using the effective interest rate (under Code Sec. 430(h)(2)) for the applicable plan year.

Application of the 90-110 percent corridor. As noted, the averaging of fair market value must, under Code Sec. 430(g)(3)(B)(iii), result in a plan asset valuation of between 90—110 percent of the fair market value of the assets on the valuation date. The final regulations provide that, if the value of plan assets determined under the averaging method would otherwise be less than 90 percent of the fair market value of plan assets, the value of the plan assets will be equal to 90 percent of the fair market value of plan assets. [18] Similarly, if the value of plan assets under the averaging method would otherwise be greater than 110 percent of the fair market value of the plan assets, the value of plan assets will be equal to 110 percent of the fair market value of plan assets. [19]

Accounting for prior year contributions. In the event contributions attributable to a prior plan year are made after the valuation date for a plan year, only the present value of the contribution (discounted using the effective interest rate for the prior plan year) is included in the valuation of plan assets. [20] However, the contribution for the prior year may be considered only if it is made by the deadline for contributions for the immediately preceding plan year.

Current year contributions before valuation date. If a contribution is made before the valuation date of a plan year to which it is attributable, the contribution (including interest accrued for the period between the contribution date and the valuation date) must be subtracted from plan assets in determining the value of plan assets as of the valuation date. [21] In the event the calculation results in a number less than zero, the value of plan assets as of the valuation date will be zero.

CCH POINTER: *Smoothing relief allows adjustment for earnings.* Responding to the severe decline in the stock market in 2008, the Worker, Retiree, and Employer Recovery Act of 2008, effective for plan years beginning on or after January 1, 2008, allows for the adjustment of plan asset values (over the 24 month period preceding the valuation date) by contributions, distributions, and expected earnings. [22] The earnings are to be determined by the plan's actuary on the basis of an assumed earnings rate that is specified by the actuary, but may not exceed the third segment rate applicable under Code Sec. 430(h)(2)(C) and ERISA Sec. 303(h)(2)(C), discussed below. Note, however that, consistent with the rules enacted under the Pension Protection Act, the smoothing method may not result in a valuation over 110 percent of the fair market value of the plan's assets on the valuation date.

The final regulations issued in 2009 do not address the adjustment for expected earnings. The IRS is to issue proposed rules on the subject. Interim guidance released by IRS in 2009 and the final regulations, however, authorize the use of an assumed earnings rate of zero for purposes of determining the actuarial value of plan assets for a plan year beginning during 2008, using the averaging rules. This option applies even if zero does not represent the actuary's best estimate of the anticipated annual rate of return on plan assets. [23]

The governing rules are detailed at CCH Pension Plan Guide ¶ 3137C.

Interest rate assumptions: Segmented yield curve

The determination of present value and other funding computations will be made on the basis of reasonable actuarial assumptions and methods that take into account the experience of the plan and offer an actuary's best estimate of anticipated experience under the plan.[24]

The interest rates used in determining the present value of benefits that are included in the target normal cost and the funding target for the plan for the plan year are based on the performance of corporate bonds as reflected in a segmented yield curve that reflects the age of an employer's work force.[25]

The yield curve will essentially consist of different interest rates applicable to benefits payable in three different time periods (i.e., segments). The applicable interest rate will be determined by the segment in which the expected payment due date falls, ranging from 0-5 years, 5-20 years, or over 20 years. Generally, employers with an older work force will be required to use a short-term corporate bond rate, resulting in higher contributions.

Note, the final rules implementing the interest rate assumption apply to plan years beginning on January 1, 2010. For plan years beginning before January 1, 2010, plans may rely on the final regulations in complying with Code Sec. 430. [26]

CCH POINTER: The yield curve is an acknowledgment that an employer's funding liabilities are, to a large degree, a function of the demographic profile of the plan's population. Accordingly, an employer with an older plan population nearing retirement age will have a larger funding obligation based on its applicable interest rates, as compared to a new company with a younger plan population, because its liabilities would be discounted at short-term interest rates.

Segment rates. The interest rates are based on the 24-month moving averages of 3 separate segment rates for the month that includes the valuation date, which are determined based on the monthly corporate bond yield curve for the preceding 24 months.

First segment rate. The first segment rate applies to benefits that can be reasonably determined to be payable during the five-year period beginning on the first day of the plan year. Thus, the first segment rate will be used to discount benefits that are expected to be paid during the 5-year period beginning on the valuation date for a plan year. [27] The applicable interest rate will be the single rate of interest determined on the basis of the average of the monthly corporate bond yield curves for the 24-month period ending with the month preceding that month, taking into account only the first 5 years of those yield curves. [28]

Second segment rate. The second segment rate applies to benefits that can be reasonably determined to be payable after five years, but within 20 years.[29] The applicable interest rate will be based on the monthly corporate bond yield curve for the 24-month period ending with the month preceding that month, taking into account only the portion of the yield curve that is based on bonds maturing during the 5-20 year period.

Third segment rate. The third segment is based on the portion of the corporate bond yield curve over the period between 20 and 60 years, and applies to benefits that can be reasonably determined to be payable in over 20 years.[30] For example, the IRS explains, if a series of monthly payments is assumed to be made beginning on the valuation date, the second segment rate will apply to the 61st such payment and the third segment rate will apply beginning with the 241st such payment. [31]

Corporate bond yield curve. The yield curve applicable in a month will be prescribed by the Secretary of the Treasury and will reflect the unweighted average, for the 24-month period ending with the month preceding such month, of yields on investment grade corporate bonds with varying maturities that are in the top three quality levels available.[32] The interest rate for each segment is based on the average of all rates in the segment.

Calculating the yield curve. The Treasury is required to publish, on a monthly basis, the corporate bond yield curve and the interest rate used for the determination of minimum present value (i.e., segment rates).[33] The IRS has issued guidance detailing the methodology applied in determining the corporate bond yield curve and the segment rates.[34] The yield curve is calculated for each business day of the month based on investment grade corporate bonds in the top three quality levels.

Note, the special interest rate that applies in determining the funding target for plans maintained by commercial airlines that make the 10-year amortization election is discussed at ¶ 1413.

Month to which segment rate applies. The month to which the segment rate applies will generally be the month that includes the valuation date of the plan for the plan year.[35] However, at the election of the plan sponsor, the applicable month may be any of the four months preceding the month including the plan's valuation date. The sponsor must provide written notification to the plan's enrolled actuary of the election. [36]

Pursuant to this election, the segment rate could be used in any of the four months preceding the month in which the plan year begins. This election will apply in all succeeding plan years, unless revoked with the consent of the Secretary of the Treasury.

Election of alternative to segment rates: Corporate bond yield curve without 24-month averaging. A plan sponsor, in determining the minimum required contribution may elect to use alternative interest rates. [37] The elections must be made by providing written notice to the plan's enrolled actuary.

The election may be made without IRS consent or approval. However, once adopted, the election will apply for all plan years and may be revoked only with IRS consent.[38]

A plan sponsor that is using the segment rate may, as an alternative to using the month that includes the valuation date for the plan year as the applicable month, use one of the 4 months preceding that month as the applicable month.[39]

¶1493D

Pursuant to such an election, the segment rates for an applicable month would be based on data through the end of the applicable month.

In determining the funding target, target normal cost, shortfall amortization installment, wavier amortization installment, and present value of these installments, the plan sponsor may elect to use interest rates under the monthly corporate bond yield curve (i.e., a set of spot rates for the month preceding the valuation date) in lieu of the segment rates. [40]

Interest rates for shortfall amortization installments and waiver amortization installments. The interest rate used to determine the amount of the shortfall amortization installments and waiver amortization installments (and the present value of those installments) are determined based on the date those installments are assumed to be paid, using the same timing rules that apply in determining target normal cost. [41]

Mortality tables

The Secretary of the Treasury is required to prescribe mortality tables to be used in determining present value or making any required funding computation. The tables are to be based on the actual experience of pension plans and projected trends in experience.[42] In addition, the Treasury is required to revise the tables at least every 10 years to reflect the actual experience of pension plans and projected trends in experience.[43]

> **CCH POINTER:** *Generally applicable mortality tables*. Final regulations issued by the IRS in 2008, applicable for plan years beginning on or after January 1, 2009, under Code Sec. 430, specifically base the mortality table to be used in determining present value and making computations under Code Sec. 430 (as well as determining current liability for multiemployer plans under Code Sec. 431(c)(6)(D)(iv)(II)) on the RP-2000 Mortality Tables. [44] Thus, the tables are based on expected mortality as of 2000 and reflect the impact of expected improvements in mortality.
>
> Similar to the mortality tables contained in the final regulations under Code Sec. 412, the mortality tables in the final regulations under Code Sec. 430 are gender distinct. Note, gender distinct tables are necessary, according to the IRS, because of significant differences between male mortality and expected female mortality.
>
> *Separate tables for annuitants and nonannuitants*. The final regulations provide separate mortality tables for annuitants (i.e., plan participants who are receiving benefits) and nonannuitants (i.e., plan participants, such as active employees, who have not yet begun receiving benefits).
>
> The nonannuitant mortality table is applied by determining the probability of survival for a nonannuitant for the period before the nonannuitant is projected to begin receiving benefits. The annuitant mortality table is applied to determine the present value of benefits for each annuitant, and for each nonannuitant for the period beginning when the nonannuitant is projected to begin receiving benefits. [45]

¶1493D

Static or generational tables for projecting mortality improvement. The final regulations allow plan sponsors to apply the projection of mortality improvement through the use of: (1) static tables that are updated annually to reflect expected improvements in mortality, or (2) generational tables.[46] Under the generational mortality tables, the probability of an individual's death at a particular age is determined as of the individual's base mortality rate (pursuant to the applicable mortality rates from tables under IRS Reg. § 1.430(h)(3)-1(d) (set forth at CCH PENSION PLAN GUIDE ¶ 13,151L-20) for the age at which the probability of death is being determined, multiplied by a specified mortality improvement factor.[47]

The static mortality tables are projected from the base tables for the year 2000 through the year of valuation with further projections to reflect the approximate expected duration of liabilities. The static mortality table for annuitants reflects plan population through the year of valuation with a further projection of 7 years. The static mortality table for nonannuitants reflects projection through the year of valuation and a further projection of 15 years.[48]

Valuation dates occurring during 2009-2013. The final regulations set forth the static mortality tables that are to be used with respect to valuation dates occurring during 2008. [49] However, the tables are updated annually to reflect expected improvements in mortality experience.

The IRS subsequently, in IRS Notice 2008-35, released static mortality tables that are to be used in calculating the funding target and other items for valuation dates occurring during calendar years 2009 through 2013. [50] The static mortality tables (which are reproduced at CCH PENSION PLAN GUIDE ¶ 17,140M) contain mortality rates that have been developed from the base rates, projection factors, and weighting factors set forth in IRS Reg. § 1.430(h)(3)-1, using prescribed blending techniques.

Small plan tables. The final rules provide an option for small plans (i.e., plans with 500 or fewer total active and nonactive participants on the valuation date) that elect to use static mortality tables as an alternative to the separate static tables for annuitants and nonannuitants.[51] The option will enable small plans to simplify actuarial valuation by using a combined static table that applies the same mortality rates to both annuitants and nonannuitants

Substitute plan specific tables

A plan sponsor will be allowed to apply a substitute plan-specific mortality table, but only with approval of the Secretary of the Treasury and under strictly defined conditions.[52] The Secretary, however, will not approve a plan-specific table absent credible information, based on the number of participants and the period of time the plan has been maintained, that is sufficient to allow a determination that the proposed table reflects actual plan experience and projected trends in general mortality experience.[53]

The plan-specific table may only be used in determining present value or making other computations for a period of consecutive plan years specified in the request, but not to exceed 10 years.[54] In addition, a plan-specific mortality table may no longer be used (even if the specified period has not elapsed) in the event of significant change in plan participation, caused by a plan spinoff, merger, or other circumstance. The table will also cease to apply at an earlier date if the table no longer reflects the actual experience of the plan maintained by the sponsor and projected trends in general mortality experience.

Final rules effective beginning in 2009 govern use of substitute tables. The IRS has issued final regulations governing the use of substitute mortality tables that apply for plan years beginning on or after January 1, 2009. [55]

Plan-specific table must be applied over consecutive years. The period of years over which the plan-specific mortality table may be used must be consecutive. Thus, a plan sponsor may not apply a plan-specific table to only selected years within a specified period.

Base table and base year. The development of a substitute mortality table requires the creation of a base table and the identification of a base year. [56] The base year is the calendar year that contains the day before the midpoint of the experience study period.[57]

The base table for the plan population must be developed from a study of the mortality experience of the plan using amounts-weighted data. [58] Amounts-weighted mortality rates may be derived from amount-weighted mortality rates for age groups. The final regulations provide for the grouping of ages and alternative methods of graduation in order to simplify the construction of substitute mortality tables.

Gender-specific tables: Credible mortality experience. The final rules require separate mortality tables to be established for each gender under the plan. In addition, a substitute mortality table may be used only if the plan has credible mortality experience with respect to the gender. Credible mortality experience for a gender within a plan requires at least 1000 deaths within that gender over the period covered by the experience study. [59]

CCH POINTER: *Disregard mortality experience of disabled individuals.* A plan may use separate mortality tables for disabled individuals (see below).[60] However, in the event separate mortality tables are used for disabled individuals, those parties will be disregarded for all purposes with respect to substitute mortality tables under Code Sec. 430(h)(3)(C). [61] Under this rule, the mortality experience of disabled individuals under a plan that uses the separate Code Sec. 430(h)(3)(D) tables will be excluded from the determination of mortality rate for substitute mortality tables.

Generational mortality table. A substitute mortality table must be a generational mortality table, under which the probability of an individual's death at a particular age is determined as the individual's base mortality rate (i.e., applicable mortality rate from the base mortality table) multiplied by a specified mortality improvement factor. [62]

Separate table for specified population within a gender. Plans are permitted (but not required) to establish substitute mortality tables for separate populations within a gender (e.g., annuitants and nonannuitants, or hourly and salaried individuals). [63]

¶1493D

However, individuals of that gender would need to be divided into separate populations, each separate population would need to have credible mortality experience and the separate substitute mortality table for each separate population would need to be developed using mortality experience data for that population. Thus, if a plan has credible mortality experience for both its male hourly and male salaried populations, separate substitute mortality tables may be used for those two separate populations. However, if a plan lacks credible mortality experience for its male salaried population, it may not use substitute mortality tables for its male hourly population and the standard mortality table for its male salaried population. [64]

Substitute mortality table for each plan sponsored by employer. Substitute mortality tables may be used for a plan for a plan year only if, for that plan year (or any portion of that plan year), substitute mortality tables are also approved and used for every other pension plan subject to funding requirements of Code Sec. 430 that is maintained by the sponsor and by each member of the plan sponsor's controlled group.[65] Note, the requirement that employers sponsoring more than one plan apply different plan specific mortality tables to each plan will effectively prevent the situation in which a plan that covers rank and file employees and a plan that covers executive employees use the same mortality table, even where the mortality experience of the plans is substantially different.

Plan within controlled group with different plan year. Plans within a controlled group may have different plan years. Under such circumstances, a plan that uses substitute mortality tables for a plan year may satisfy the requirement that all plans within the group use substitute mortality tables if all plans within the controlled group use substitute mortality tables for some portion of the plan year.

Plans without credible mortality experience not precluded from using substitute tables. For the first year for which a plan uses substitute mortality tables, the plan will not be prevented from using the substitute table for a plan merely because another plan subject to Code Sec. 430 that is maintained by the sponsor (or a member of the sponsor's controlled group) may not use substitute tables because neither the males nor the females under the plan have credible mortality experience for a plan year. [66] Accordingly, the IRS explains, if a sponsor's controlled group contains two pension plans that are subject to Code Sec. 430, each of which has credible mortality experience for at least one gender, both plans must obtain approval from the IRS (pursuant to the procedures detailed below) to use substitute mortality tables or neither plan may use substitute tables. By contrast, if for one of the plans, neither males nor females have credible mortality experience, the plan with credible mortality experience may use the substitute tables. [67]

CCH POINTER: *Limited time period during which newly affiliated plans may prevent plans from using substitute mortality tables.* An issue invited by the proposed regulations had been whether a newly acquired plan that used substitute mortality tables could prevent the use of the substitute tables by the acquiring sponsor that maintained other plans for which the substitute tables were not used. The final regulations state that the use of substitute mortality table is not prohibited merely because a "newly affiliated" plan (i.e., a plan maintained by a plan sponsor (or established in connection with a transfer of assets and liabilities from another plan) incident to a merger, acquisition, or similar transaction) does not use substitute mortality tables. However, the relief applies only through the last day of the plan year of the plan using the substitute mortality tables that contain the last day of the transition period (under Code Sec. 410(b)(6)(C)(ii)) for either the newly affiliated plan or the plan using substitute tables, whichever is later. [68] The mortality tables prescribed under IRS Reg. § 1.430(h)(3)-1 would generally apply with respect to the plan (and all other plans within the sponsor's controlled group). Exceptions are authorized where approval to use substitute mortality tables has been obtained with respect to the newly affiliated plan, or the newly affiliated plan cannot use substitute mortality tables because neither the males nor the females have credible mortality experience.

Length of period during which substitute tables may be used. Substitute mortality tables may be used with respect to a plan for the term of consecutive plan years specified in the plan sponsor's written request to use the tables (see below) and approved by the IRS, or such shorter period prescribed by the IRS in the approval to use the substitute tables. Upon the end of the term of use (or the early termination of use (see below)), the mortality tables set forth in IRS Reg. § 1.430(h)(3)-1 will apply, unless the plan sponsor has obtained approval to use substitute mortality tables for a further term. [69]

Aggregation requirements. In order for a plan sponsor to use a set of substitute mortality tables for two or more plans, the governing rules are applied by treating the plans as a single plan. Under this rule, the substitute mortality tables must be used for the aggregated plans and the tables must be based on data collected with respect to the aggregated plans. [70]

Early termination of the use of tables. A plan's substitute mortality tables may not be used as of the earliest of: (1) the plan year in which the plan fails to satisfy the requirements regarding credible mortality experience requirements and demonstrations; (2) the plan year in which the plan fails to satisfy the requirements for the use of substitute mortality tables by controlled group members; (3) the second plan year following the plan year in which there is a "significant'" change in individuals covered by the plan (i.e., an increase or decrease of at least 20 percent from the average number of individuals included in the experience study); (4) the plan year following the plan year in which a substitute mortality table used for a plan population is no longer accurately predictive of future mortality, as determined by the IRS or as certified by the plan's actuary; or (5) a date specified in guidance related to the replacement of mortality tables under Code Sec. 430(h)(3)(A) and IRS Reg. § 1.430(h)(3)-1 (other than annual updates to the static mortality tables issued under IRS Reg. § 1.430(h)(3)-1(a)(3)). [71]

Submission of request to use substitute mortality tables. A plan sponsor must obtain approval from the IRS in order to use substitute mortality tables. [72] The procedures, including applicable information requirements, are detailed at CCH PENSION PLAN GUIDE ¶ 3137C. The following highlights some of the applicable conditions.

¶1493D

CCH POINTER: The procedures for submitting a request for the use of substitute mortality tables, effective for requests submitted on or after December 1, 2008, are specified in Rev. Proc. 2008-62 (which reflects the final regulations issued in July 2008). [73] The IRS has further provided a checklist in the Appendix to Rev. Proc. 2008-62 that will enable plan sponsors to ensure that a submission is completed. Note, the checklist must be completed, signed, dated, and placed on top of the request.

User fee requirement. A potentially significant factor that should be considered prior to filing a request to use substitute mortality table is the $14,500 user fee that must be sent with all requests. [74] The user fee may be an even greater consideration in light of the fact that a separate request must be made with respect to each plan, or group of plans that are permissively aggregated, for which the use of a substitute mortality table (or tables) is requested.

Disclosure of experience study period. The request must identify the period of time covered by the mortality experience study (i.e., Experience Study Period) used to develop the base table(s) and must identify the base year. Note, a plan sponsor may not use different experience study periods for different populations within the plan. Similarly, a plan sponsor may generally not use different experience study periods for different plans within the permissive group. Accordingly, the IRS explains, a plan that does not have mortality experience for the entire experience study period may not be included in the permissive group.[75]

Demonstrating credible mortality experience. In demonstrating credible mortality experience, the number of deaths during each year of the experience study period (and the total deaths during the experience study period) within each population for which the substitute mortality table is requested must be provided. The information must be set forth in tabular form. [76]

Demonstration of stability. The request must disclose: (1) the average number (or reasonable estimate) of individuals within the population during the experience study period; and (2) the number of individuals within the population as of last day of the plan year immediately preceding the plan year during which the use of the substitute mortality table is requested.[77] The information must be provided in tabular form for each population within the plan (or plans within the permissive group) for which the substitute mortality table is requested, aggregating all plans that have the same year.

In the event of a 20 percent or more discrepancy between the information required in (1) and (2) above, the plan sponsor must submit an analysis indicating that the mortality experience study during the experience study period remains accurately predictive of the future mortality of the population.

Lack of Credible Mortality Experience Demonstration Period. The period of time used to demonstrate the lack of credible mortality experience must generally be identified in the request for all plans maintained by the applicant. [78] As noted above, the Lack of Credible Mortality Experience Demonstration Period must consist of at least 4 consecutive years, with the last year ending less than 3 years before the first day of the plan year for which the lack of credible mortality experience is being demonstrated.

A general exception relieves certain plans (e.g., plan for which substitute tables are requested for all plan populations) of the need to identify a Lack of Credible Mortality Demonstration Period. [79]

Unadjusted mortality experience. The request must include, in tabular form, specified information regarding the mortality experience of the plan population and accrued benefits for all individuals within each population for whom the use of separate mortality tables is requested. The information must cover each year of the experience study period (and for the entire experience study period) for all ages between 18 and 100 (or within 5-year age groups). [80]

Deadline for submitting request. Generally, the plan sponsor must submit the written request to use substitute tables at least 7 months before the first day of the first plan year for which the substitute tables are to apply. [81] Thus, if the first plan year to which substitute mortality tables are to apply is the plan year that begins January 1, 2011, the written request must be submitted by June 1, 2010. [82]

IRS review of request. The IRS has 180 days, beginning on the date the written request is submitted, to review and make a determination with respect to the request to use substitute mortality tables.[83] In the event the IRS does not issue a denial within the specified 180-day period, the request will be deemed to have been approved.

The IRS will deny a request if it determines that a substitute mortality table does not sufficiently reflect the mortality experience of the plan population. The IRS will also reject a request that fails to satisfy the requirements set forth in the governing regulations or Rev. Proc 2008-62.

Request for additional information. The IRS may request additional information with respect to a submission. Failure to provide the requested information on a timely basis is grounds for a denial of a request.

Separate mortality tables for disabled individuals

The Secretary of the Treasury is required to establish alternative mortality tables for individuals who are entitled to plan benefits because of disability. The separate tables will need to be provided for individuals whose disabilities occurred in plan years beginning before January 1, 1995, and for individuals whose disabilities occurred or occur in plan years beginning on or after that date.[84]

Note, the IRS, set forth mortality tables under Rev. Rul. 96-7 that were to be used under Code Sec.412(l)(7)(C)(iii) for disabilities occurring in plan years beginning before January 1, 1995, and for disabilities occurring in plan years beginning after December 31, 1994. [85] The IRS, in March 2008, further stated that until additional guidance is issued, the rules of Rev. Rul. 96-7 (including the disability mortality table and the rules governing the determination of when a benefit is payable on account of disability) will continue to apply for purposes of the new requirements applicable to single employer plans under Code Sec. 430(h)(3)(D) (and multiemployer plans under Code Sec .431(c)(6)(D)(v)). [86]

¶1493D

The alternative mortality tables set forth in Rev. Rul. 96-7, the IRS further explained may be applied where employer-specific mortality tables are used for nondisabled participants.[87] However, the tables may be used only if mortality experience with respect to disabled individuals for which the tables have been used has been excluded in developing mortality rates for the employer-specific mortality tables.

Accounting for probability of lump-sum benefit payments

In determining present value or in making other required funding computations, the plan sponsor must account for the probability that future benefit payments will be made in a lump-sum or in another optional form of benefit authorized under the plan. The assumptions used in determining optional forms of benefit under the plan may differ from the assumptions prescribed by the Pension Protection Act for determining present value. However, the plan sponsor must account for any difference in the present value of such future benefit payments resulting from the use of actuarial assumptions in determining benefit payments in the optional form, which are different from those required under PPA.[88]

Changes in actuarial assumptions require IRS approval

Actuarial assumptions used in determining the funding target for a single-employer plan with large unfunded vested benefits may not be changed without approval of the IRS.[89] The restriction applies to plans with aggregate unfunded vested benefits, as of the close of preceding plan year of the plan and all other plans maintained by contributing sponsors and members of the sponsors' controlled group (other than plans with no unfunded vested benefits) that exceed $50 million.[90]

---

[1] ERISA Sec. 303(g)(2)(A) and (B), as added by P.L. 109-280 (Pension Protection Act of 2006), Act Sec. 102(a); Code Sec. 430(g)(2)(A) and (B), as added by P.L. 109-280 (Pension Protection Act of 2006), Act Sec. 112(a).

[2] IRS Reg. § 1.430(g)-1.

[3] IRS Reg. § 1.430(g)-1(b).

[4] IRS Reg. § 1.430(g)-1(b)(2).

[5] IRS Reg. § 1.430(g)-1(b)(2)(iv).

[6] ERISA Sec. 303(g)(3)(A), as added by P.L. 109-280 (Pension Protection Act of 2006), Act Sec. 102(a); Code Sec. 430(g)(3)(A), as added by P.L. 109-280 (Pension Protection Act of 2006), Act Sec. 112(a).

[7] ERISA Sec. 303(g)(3)(B), as added by P.L. 109-280 (Pension Protection Act of 2006), Act Sec. 102(a); Code Sec. 430(g)(3)(B), as added by P.L. 109-280 (Pension Protection Act of 2006), Act Sec. 112(a).

[8] IRS Reg. § 1.430(g)-1(f)(3).

[9] IRS Reg. § 1.430(g)-1(c)(1)(i).

[10] IRS Reg. § 1.430(g)-1(c)(1)(ii).

[11] ERISA Sec. 303(g)(3)(B), as added by P.L. 109-280 (Pension Protection Act of 2006), Act Sec. 102(a); Code Sec. 430(g)(3)(B), as added by P.L. 109-280 (Pension Protection Act of 2006), Act Sec. 112(a).

[12] ERISA Sec. 303(g)(3)(B)(iii), as added by P.L. 109-280 (Pension Protection Act of 2006), Act Sec. 102(a); Code Sec. 430(g)(3)(B)(iii), as added by P.L. 109-280 (Pension Protection Act of 2006), Act Sec. 112(a).

[13] ERISA Sec. 303(g)(3)(B)(iii), as added by P.L. 109-280 (Pension Protection Act of 2006), Act Sec. 102(a); Code Sec. 430(g)(3)(B)(iii), as added by P.L. 109-280 (Pension Protection Act of 2006), Act Sec. 112(a).

[14] IRS Reg. § 1.430(g)-1(c)(2).

[15] IRS Reg. § 1.430(g)-1(c)(2)(ii).

[16] IRS Reg. § 1.430(g)-1(c)(2)(ii)(B).

[17] *Ibid.*

[18] IRS Reg. § 1.430(g)-1(c)(2)(iii)(B).

[19] IRS Reg. § 1.430(g)-1(c)(2)(iii)(C).

[20] IRS Reg. § 1.430(g)-1(d)(1).

[21] IRS Reg. § 1.430(g)-1(d)(2).

[22] ERISA Sec. 303(g)(3)(B) and Code Sec. 430-(g)(3)(B) as amended by P.L. 110-458 (Worker, Retiree, and Employer Recovery Act of 2008), Act Sec. 121(a) and (b).

[23]IRS Notice 2009-22, I.R.B. 2009-14, 4-6-09, at CCH PENSION PLAN GUIDE ¶ 17,142G; IRS Reg. § 1.430(g)-1(f)(2)(ii).

[24] ERISA Sec. 303(h), as added by P.L. 109-280 (Pension Protection Act of 2006), Act Sec. 102(a); Code Sec. 430(h), as added by P.L. 109-280 (Pension Protection Act of 2006), Act Sec. 112(a).

[25] ERISA Sec. 303(h)(2)(B), as added by P.L. 109-280 (Pension Protection Act of 2006), Act Sec. 102(a); Code Sec. 430(h)(2)(B), as added by P.L. 109-280 (Pension Protection Act of 2006), Act Sec. 112(a).

[26]IRS Reg. § 1.430(h)(2)-1.

[27] IRS Reg. § 1.430(h)(2)-1(b)(2) and (c)(2).

[28] ERISA Sec. 303(h)(2)(B)(i) and (h)(2)(C)(i), as added by P.L. 109-280 (Pension Protection Act of 2006), Act Sec. 102(a); Code Sec. 430(h)(2)(B)(i) and (h)(2)(C)(i), as added by P.L. 109-280 (Pension Protection Act of 2006), Act Sec. 112(a); IRS Reg. § 1.430(h)(2)-1(c)(2)(i).

[29] ERISA Sec. 303(h)(2)(C)(ii), as added by P.L. 109-280 (Pension Protection Act of 2006), Act Sec. 102(a); Code Sec. 430(h)(2)(C)(ii), as added by P.L. 109-280 (Pension Protection Act of 2006), Act Sec. 112(a).

[30] ERISA Sec. 303(h)(2)(C)(iii), as added by P.L. 109-280 (Pension Protection Act of 2006), Act Sec. 102(a); Code Sec. 430(h)(2)(C)(iii), as added by P.L. 109-280 (Pension Protection Act of 2006), Act Sec. 112(a).

[31] Preamble to IRS Reg. § 1.430(h)(2)-1, at ¶ 24,509G.

[32] ERISA Sec. 303(h)(2)(D), as added by P.L. 109-280 (Pension Protection Act of 2006), Act Sec. 102(a); Code Sec. 430(h)(2)(D), as added by P.L. 109-280 (Pension Protection Act of 2006), Act Sec. 112(a). IRS Reg. § 1.430(h)(2)-1(d)

[33]P.L. 109-280 (Pension Protection Act of 2006), Act Sec. 430(h)(2)(F); IRS Reg. § 1.430(h)(2)-1(d)(2).

[34]IRS Notice 2007-81, I.R.B. 2007-44, 10-29-07, at CCH PENSION PLAN GUIDE ¶ 17,137C.

[35] ERISA Sec. 303(h)(2)(E), as added by P.L. 109-280 (Pension Protection Act of 2006), Act Sec. 102(a); Code Sec. 430(h)(2)(E), as added by P.L. 109-280 (Pension Protection Act of 2006), Act Sec. 112(a).

[36]IRS Reg. § 1.430(h)(2)-1(e)(2).

[37] ERISA Sec. 303(h)(2)(D)(ii), as added by P.L. 109-280 (Pension Protection Act of 2006), Act Sec.

102(a); Code Sec. 430(h)(2)(D)(ii), as added by P.L. 109-280 (Pension Protection Act of 2006), Act Sec. 112(a); IRS Reg. § 1.430(h)(2)-1(e).

[38]IRS Reg. § 1.430(h)(2)-1(e)(1).

[39]IRS Reg. § 1.430(h)(2)-1(e)(2).

[40]IRS Reg. § 1.430(h)(2)-1(e)(4).

[41]IRS Reg. § 1.430(h)(2)-1(f)(2).

[42] ERISA Sec. 303(h)(3), as added by P.L. 109-280 (Pension Protection Act of 2006), Act Sec. 102(a); Code Sec. 430(h)(3), as added by P.L. 109-280 (Pension Protection Act of 2006), Act Sec. 112(a).

[43] ERISA Sec. 303(g)(3)(B), as added by P.L. 109-280 (Pension Protection Act of 2006), Act Sec. 102(a); Code Sec. 430(h)(3)(B), as added by P.L. 109-280 (Pension Protection Act of 2006), Act Sec. 112(a).

[44]IRS Reg. § 1.430(h)(3)-1

[45]IRS Reg. § 1.430(h)(3)-1(b)(1).

[46]IRS Reg. § 1.430(h)(3)-1(a)(2).

[47]IRS Reg. § 1.430(h)(3)-1(a)(4)(i).

[48]IRS Reg. § 1.430(h)(3)-1(c)(2).

[49]IRS Reg. § 1.430(h)(3)-1(a)(3).

[50]IRS Notice 2008-35, I.R.B. 2008-42, 10-20-08, at CCH PENSION PLAN GUIDE ¶ 17,140M

[51]IRS Reg. § 1.430(h)(3)-1(b)(2).

[52] ERISA Sec. 303(h)(3)(C), as added by P.L. 109-280 (Pension Protection Act of 2006); ERISA Sec. 303(h)(3)(C)(i), as added by P.L. 109-280 (Pension Protection Act of 2006), Act Sec. 102(a); Code Sec. 430(h)(3)(C)(i), as added by P.L. 109-280 (Pension Protection Act of 2006), Act Sec. 112(a).

[53] ERISA Sec. 303(h)(3)(C)(iii), as added by P.L. 109-280 (Pension Protection Act of 2006), Act Sec. 102(a); Code Sec. 430(h)(3)(C)(iii), as added by P.L. 109-280 (Pension Protection Act of 2006), Act Sec. 112(a).

[54] ERISA Sec. 303(h)(3)(C)(i) and (ii), as added by P.L. 109-280 (Pension Protection Act of 2006), Act Sec. 102(a); Code Sec. 430(h)(3)(C)(i) and (ii), as added by P.L. 109-280 (Pension Protection Act of 2006), Act Sec. 112(a).

[55]IRS Reg. § 1.430(h)(3)-2.

[56]IRS Reg. § 1.430(h)(3)-2(c)(2).

[57]IRS Reg. § 1.430(h)(3)-2(c)(2)(iii).

[58]IRS Reg. § 1.430(h)(3)-2(c)(2)(ii).

[59]IRS Reg. § 1.430(h)(3)-2(c)(1)(ii).

[60]Code Sec.430(h)(3)(D).

[61]IRS Reg. § 1.430(h)(3)-2(c)(1)(iv).

[62]IRS Reg. § 1.430(h)(3)-2(c)(3).

[63]IRS Reg. § 1.430(h)(3)-2(c)(4).

[64]IRS Reg. § 1.430(h)(3)-2(c)(4)(iii).

[65]IRS Reg. § 1.430(h)(3)-2(d)(1).

[66]IRS Reg. § 1.430(h)(3)-2(d)(1)(ii)(A).

[67] Preamble to IRS Reg. § 1.430(h)(3)-2, at CCH PENSION PLAN GUIDE ¶ 24,508Z.

[68]IRS Reg. § 1.430(h)(3)-2(d)(1)(iii).

[69]IRS Reg. § 1.430(h)(3)-2(d).

[70]IRS Reg. § 1.430(h)(3)-2(d)(3)(i).

[71]IRS Reg. § 1.430(h)(3)-2(d)(4).

[72]ERISA Sec.303(h)(3)(C); Code Sec.430(h)(3)(C)(v)(I); and IRS Reg. § 1.430(h)(3)-2(d)(4).

[73]Rev. Proc. 2008-62, I.R.B. 2008-42, 10-20-08, at CCH PENSION PLAN GUIDE ¶ 17,299S-76. Note, requests submitted before December 1, 2008, would need to comply with Rev. Proc. 2008-62 or IRS Proposed Reg. 1.430(h)(3)-2 and Rev. Proc. 2007-37.

[74]Rev. Proc. 2011-8, I.R.B. 2011-1, 1-3-11, at CCH PENSION PLAN GUIDE ¶ 17,299T-58.

[75]Rev. Proc. 2008-62, Sec. 7, I.R.B. 2008-42, at CCH PENSION PLAN GUIDE ¶ 17,299S-76.

[76]Rev. Proc. 2008-62, Sec. 7.04, I.R.B. 2008-42, at CCH PENSION PLAN GUIDE ¶ 17,299S-76.

[77]Rev. Proc. 2008-62, Sec. 8, I.R.B. 200-42, at CCH PENSION PLAN GUIDE ¶ 17,299S-76.

[78]Rev. Proc. 2008-62, Sec. 9, I.R.B. 2008-42, at CCH PENSION PLAN GUIDE ¶ 17,299S-76.

[79]Rev. Proc. 2008-62, Sec. 9.02, I.R.B 2008-42, at CCH PENSION PLAN GUIDE ¶ 17,299S-76.

[80]Rev. Proc. 2008-62, Sec. 10, I.R.B. 2008-42, at CCH PENSION PLAN GUIDE ¶ 17,299S-76.

[81]IRS Reg. § 1.430(h)(3)-2(b)(1)(ii)(A).

[82]Rev. Proc. 2008-62, Sec. 4, I.R.B. 2008-62, at CCH PENSION PLAN GUIDE ¶ 17,299S-76.

[83]IRS Reg. § 1.430(h)(3)-2(b)(2)

[84] ERISA Sec. 303(h)(3)(D)(i), as added by P.L. 109-280 (Pension Protection Act of 2006), Act Sec. 102(a); Code Sec. 430(h)(3)(D)(i), as added by P.L. 109-280 (Pension Protection Act of 2006), Act Sec. 112(a).

[85] Rev. Rul. 96-7, 1996-1 C.B. 59, at CCH PENSION PLAN GUIDE, ¶ 19,827.

[86]IRS Notice 2008-29, I.R.B. 2008-12, at CCH PENSION PLAN GUIDE, ¶ 17,138W.

[87]IRS Notice 2008-29, I.R.B. 2008-12, at CCH PENSION PLAN GUIDE, ¶ 17,138W; IRS Reg. § 1.430(h)(3)-2(c)(1)(iv).

[88] ERISA Sec. 303(h)(4), as added by P.L. 109-280 (Pension Protection Act of 2006), Act Sec. 102(a); Code Sec. 430(h)(4), as added by P.L. 109-280 (Pension Protection Act of 2006), Act Sec. 112(a).

[89] ERISA Sec. 303(h)(5), as added by P.L. 109-280 (Pension Protection Act of 2006), Act Sec. 102(a); Code Sec. 430(h)(5), as added by P.L. 109-280 (Pension Protection Act of 2006), Act Sec. 112(a).

[90] ERISA Sec. 303(h)(5)(B), as added by P.L. 109-280 (Pension Protection Act of 2006), Act Sec. 102(a); Code Sec. 430(h)(5)(B), as added by P.L. 109-280 (Pension Protection Act of 2006), Act Sec. 112(a).

¶ 1493E
MINIMUM FUNDING RULES APPLICABLE AFTER 2007: At-Risk Plans

Plans with more than 500 participants that have a funded target attainment percentage in the preceding year below designated thresholds will be deemed "at-risk" and subject to increased target liability for plan years beginning after 2007. The funding percentage will be determined by subtracting credit balances from plan assets. The increased at-risk liability payment will be phased in over a five consecutive year period beginning in 2008.[1]

It is important to clarify that a plan's at-risk funding target and a plan sponsor's attendant funding obligation are not determined by the financial condition of the plan sponsor, as reflected in credit ratings. At-risk status is strictly a function of the plan's funded status and specified participant demographics.

CCH POINTER: *Final regulations clarify funding requirements applicable to at-risk plans.* Final regulations issued in October 2009 and generally applicable to plan years beginning on or after January 1, 2010, govern the determination of whether a plan is in at-risk status and the calculation of the plan's funding target attainment percentage (FTAP) and at-risk funding target attainment percentage (AFTAP). The rules also describe the funding target and target normal cost of an at-risk plan, including plans that have been in at-risk status for less than 5 consecutive plan years. [2]

The final regulations apply to plan years beginning on or after January 1, 2010. However, plans with plan years beginning prior to January 1, 2010 may rely on the final regulations in complying with the requirements under Code Sec. 430. [3]

Multiple employer plans

The rules applicable to plans in at-risk status also apply to multiple employer plans (but not to multiemployer plans).[4] With respect to plans that have made an election under Code Sec. 413(c)(4), the rules (e.g., determination of at-risk status) are applied separately for each employer under the plan, as if each employer maintained a separate plan.

"70-80 percent" threshold test for at-risk status

Plans with more than 500 participants during each day of the preceding plan year (aggregating all single-employer defined benefit plans maintained by the employer, predecessor employer or a member of the employer's controlled group) are subject to a two-tiered determination of at-risk status.[5]

CCH POINTER: *Small plan exemption.* In clarifying the scope of the small plan exception, the IRS final regulations explain that active and inactive participants and all other individuals entitled to future benefits are included in the determination of whether the plan had 500 or former participants on each day during the preceding plan year. [6] Note, however, although all defined benefit plans maintained by an employer or any member of the employer's controlled group are treated as one plan, only participants with respect to that employer or controlled group member are to be taken into account. [7] In addition, with respect to the first plan year of any plan, the small plan exception is applied by taking into account the number of participants that the plan is reasonably expected to have on each day during the first plan year. [8]

Two part at-risk test. Specifically, a plan is at-risk if:

1. the funding target attainment percentage (i.e., ratio of plan assets (reduced by credit balances) to the funding target for the preceding plan year, determined without regard to at-risk liability) for the preceding plan year is less than 80 percent; and

2. the at-risk funding target attainment percentage for the preceding plan year, determined by applying the specified at-risk actuarial assumptions, is less than 70 percent.[9]

CCH POINTER: Both components of the test must apply in order for a plan to be treated as at-risk. Thus, if a plan fails the 70-percent at-risk test, but satisfies the 80-percent ongoing liability test, it will not be subject to at-risk liability.

¶1493E

At-risk funding target attainment percentage. The at-risk funding target attainment percentage of a plan for a plan year is: the value of plan assets for the year after the subtraction of the prefunding balance and funding standard carryover balance/ the at-risk funding target of the plan for the plan year (without regard to the loading factor). [10]

Special rule for new plans. The FTAP and AFTAP for new plans that were neither the result of a merger nor involved in a spinoff will equal 100 percent for years before the plan exists. [11] Thus, such plans will not be in at-risk status in the first year.

Special rules for plans with zero funding target. The FTAP and AFTAP for a plan with a funding target for a plan year of zero will be 100 percent for that plan year. [12] Thus, a plan that is established without benefits accruing for periods prior to establishment will not be in at-risk status in its second year. [13]

Phase-in of 80 percent at-risk test. The 80-percent funding target component of the at-risk test is phased in over a four-year period, beginning in 2008. The applicable percentages will be: 65 percent in 2008, 70 percent in 2009, 75 percent in 2010, and 80 percent in 2011 and thereafter.[14]

Estimation of funded status. The 80 percent and 70 percent components of the definition of at-risk status are based on the plan's funded status for the preceding plan year. The Pension Protection Act suggested that only the definition of the 70 percent component for 2008 could be determined using methods of estimation provided by the Treasury. The Worker, Retiree, and Employer Recovery Act clarifies that such methods of estimation may also be applied to the 80 percent component. [15]

CCH POINTER: In applying the 80-percent ongoing liability test and the 70-percent at-risk liability test, funding standard carryover and prefunding credit balances are deducted from plan assets. Thus, the actual value of plan assets will be reduced by credit balances in applying the 80-percent funding target and the 70-percent at-risk funding target.

At-risk actuarial assumptions

The determination of at-risk liability is made by assuming that all employees who will be eligible to elect benefits during the current plan year and in the 10 succeeding plan years will retire at the earliest date authorized under the plan (but not before the end of the plan year for which the at-risk determination is being made).[16] In addition, all employees will be assumed to elect the retirement benefit available under the plan at the assumed retirement age (i.e., earliest retirement date authorized under the plan) that would result in the highest present value of benefits.[17] A loading factor also applies to certain plans (see below).

CCH POINTER: *Exemption for employees of automobile manufacturers who accepted early retirement offers.* An exemption from the at-risk liability assumptions applies to employees of specified automobile and automobile parts manufacturers who rejected early retirement incentive offers made in

2006 that were conditioned on acceptance before 2007 and retirement before 2011.[18]

At-risk plans subject to higher funding target and target normal cost

At-risk plans are subject to a higher funding target and to a higher target normal cost that will effectively require plan sponsors to make larger minimum funding contributions.

Funding target. The funding target for a plan that has been in at-risk status for 5 consecutive years (including the current plan year) will be the present value of all benefits accrued or earned under the plan as of the beginning of the plan year, as determined by application of the at-risk actuarial assumptions.[19]

Loading factor increases funding target. Plans that are at risk for at least two of the four preceding plan years are subject to a "loading factor." The loading factor is designed to reflect the cost of purchasing group annuity contracts in the event that the plan terminates. The funding target will be increased by the sum of $700 per plan participant, plus four percent of the funding target for the plan year determined as if the plan was not in at-risk status.[20] The number of participants considered for purposes of the assessment include active participants, inactive participants, and beneficiaries. [21] Note, the IRS cautions that the at-risk funding target of a plan for a plan year may not be less than the plan's funding target for the plan year. [22]

Retirement age assumptions. In addressing the retirement age assumptions applicable to participants eligible to retire and collect benefits within 11 years (i.e., the end of the 10th plan year after the current plan year), the participant is assumed, under the final regulations, to commence an immediate distribution at the earliest retirement date under the plan (i.e., the earliest date on which a participant may receive an immediate distribution of a fully vested benefit), or if later, at the end of the current plan year.[23]

Note, the special early retirement assumption is not limited to employees, but applies to all participants (e.g., terminated vested participants and beneficiaries) who have not commenced payment. However, the retirement age assumption will not apply to a participant to the extent that the participant is otherwise assumed (under the plan's actuarial assumptions) to commence benefits during the current plan year.

All participants and beneficiaries (and not just those subject to the early retirement presumption) who are assumed to retire on a particular date are assumed to elect the optional form of benefit available under the plan that would result in the highest present value of benefits commencing at that date. [24] The plan's actuary may use reasonable assumptions in determining the optional form of benefits that would result in the highest present value of benefits.[25]

Target normal cost of at-risk plans. The target normal cost of plan in at-risk for 5 consecutive plan years , including the current plan year is equal to the present value (as of the valuation date) of all benefits that accrue during, are earned during,

¶1493E

or are otherwise allocated to service in the plan year, determined using special at-risk assumptions (discussed above). [26]

Special adjustments. The target normal cost of the plan for the plan year is adjusted (not below zero) by adding the amount of plan-related expenses (determined under IRS Reg. 1.430(d)-1(b)(1)(iii)(B)) expected to be paid from plan assets during the plan year and subtracting the amount of any mandatory employee contribution expected to be made during the plan year.[27]

Loading factor. In the case of a plan that also has been in at-risk status for at least two of the four preceding plan years, the target normal cost must be increased by a loading factor equal to four percent of the amount of the target normal cost determined under Code Sec. 430(b)(1)(A) or ERISA Sec. 303(b)(1)(A)(i) (i.e., present value of all benefits expected to accrue or be earned under the plan during the plan year) with respect to the plan year. [28]

The final regulations clarify that the target normal cost is increased by a loading factor equal to 4 percent of the present value (as of the valuation date) of all benefits under the plan that accrue, are earned, or are otherwise allocated to service for the plan year (determined as if the plan were not in at-risk status). [29]

Note: IRS cautions that the at-risk target normal cost of a plan for a plan year may not be less than the target normal cost of a plan that is not in at-risk status.[30]

The target normal cost of a plan not in at-risk status is discussed at ¶ 1493B.

Phase-in rules for at-risk liability

At-risk liability will be phased in at 20 percent per year over a period of five consecutive years effective for plan years beginning after 2007. Specifically, if a plan is in at-risk status for a consecutive period of less than five plan years, the amount of the funding target and target normal cost will be: (1) the funding target and normal target cost determined without reference to the at-risk rules; plus (2) an applicable transition percentage for the plan year of the increased funding target or normal cost attributable to the at-risk rules.[31]

Phase in percentage. The applicable transition percentage is 20 percent multiplied by the number of consecutive plan years (including the current plan year) that the plan has been at-risk status. [32] The transition percentages are 20, 40, 60, and 80 percent for the first, second, third and fourth years, respectively, that the plan is in at-risk status, beginning in 2008.[33]

Plan years beginning before 2008 are not considered for purposes of the transition rules.[34] Similarly, years before the first effective plan year are not considered. [35]

Determining funding target/target normal cost under phase-in rules. In implementing the phase-in rules for at-risk liability, the final regulations clarify that the funding target/target normal cost of a plan that is in at-risk status for the plan year, and that has been in at-risk status for a consecutive period of less than 5 years, is determined as a blend of the funding target/ target normal cost, determined as if the plan were not in at-risk status, and the funding target/ target normal cost,

¶1493E

determined as if the plan had been in at-risk status for each of the previous 5 plan years. [36]

Determination of transition funding target and target normal cost without load. In the event a plan has not been in at-risk status for 2 or more of the preceding 4 plan years (excluding years before the first effective plan year for a plan), the plan at-risk funding target (used in calculating the funding target when the plan has been at-risk for less than 5 plan years) is determined without applying the loading factor.[37] Similarly, if a plan has not been in at-risk status for 2 or more of the preceding 4 plan years (excluding years before the first effective plan year) the plan's at-risk target normal cost (used in calculating the target normal cost of a plan that has been at-risk for less than 5 plan years) is determined without applying the load factor. [38]

[1] ERISA Sec. 303(i), as added by P.L. 109-280 (Pension Protection Act of 2006), Act Sec. 102(a); Code Sec. 430(i), as added by P.L. 109-280 (Pension Protection Act of 2006), Act Sec. 112(a).

[2] IRS Reg. § 1.430(i)-1.

[3] IRS Reg. § 1.430(i)-1(f).

[4] IRS Reg. § 1.430(i)-1(a).

[5] ERISA Sec. 303(i)(4), as added by P.L. 109-280 (Pension Protection Act of 2006), Act Sec. 102(a); Code Sec. 430(i), as added by P.L. 109-280 (Pension Protection Act of 2006), Act Sec. 112(a).

[6] IRS Reg. § 1.430(i)-1(b)(2).

[7] Preamble to IRS Reg. § 1.430(i)-1, at CCH PENSION PLAN GUIDE ¶ 24,509G.

[8] *Ibid.*

[9] ERISA Sec. 303(i)(4)(A), as added by P.L. 109-280 (Pension Protection Act of 2006), Act Sec. 102(a); Code Sec. 430(i)(4)(A), as added by P.L. 109-280 (Pension Protection Act of 2006), Act Sec. 112(a). IRS Reg. § 1.430(i)-1(b)(1).

[10] IRS Reg. § 1.430(i)-1(b)(4).

[11] IRS Reg. § 1.430(i)-1(b)(5)(i).

[12] IRS Reg. § 1.430(i)-1(b)(5)(ii).

[13] Preamble to IRS Reg. § 1.430(i)-1, at CCH PENSION PLAN GUIDE ¶ 24,509G.

[14] ERISA Sec. 303(i)(4)(B), as added by P.L. 109-280 (Pension Protection Act of 2006), Act Sec. 102(a); Code Sec. 430(i)(4)(B), as added by P.L. 109-280 (Pension Protection Act of 2006), Act Sec. 112(a); IRS Reg. § 1.430(i)-1(f)(4).

[15] ERISA Sec. 303(i)(4)(B) and Code Sec.430(i)(4)(B), as amended by P.L. 110-458 (Worker, Retiree, and Employer Recovery Act of 2008), Act Sec. 101(b)(1) and (2).

[16] ERISA Sec. 303(i)(1)(B)(i), as added by P.L. 109-280 (Pension Protection Act of 2006), Act Sec. 102(a); Code Sec. 430(i)(1)(B)(i), as added by P.L. 109-280 (Pension Protection Act of 2006), Act Sec. 112(a).

[17] ERISA Sec. 303(i)(1)(B)(ii), as added by P.L. 109-280 (Pension Protection Act of 2006), Act Sec. 102(a); Code Sec. 430(i)(1)(B)(ii), as added by P.L. 109-280 (Pension Protection Act of 2006), Act Sec. 112(a).

[18] ERISA Sec. 303(i)(4)(C), as added by P.L. 109-280 (Pension Protection Act of 2006), Act Sec. 102(a); Code Sec. 430(i)(1)(B)(ii), as added by P.L. 109-280 (Pension Protection Act of 2006), Act Sec. 112(a).

[19] ERISA Sec. 303(i)(1)(A) and 303(i)(2)(A), as added by P.L. 109-280 (Pension Protection Act of 2006), Act Sec. 102(a); Code Sec. 430(i)(1)(A) and 430(i)(2)(A), as added by P.L. 109-280 (Pension Protection Act of 2006), Act Sec. 112(a); IRS Reg. § 1.430(i)-1(c).

[20] ERISA Sec. 303(i)(1)(C) and 303(i)(2)(B), as added by P.L. 109-280 (Pension Protection Act of 2006), Act Sec. 102(a); Code Sec. 430(i)(1)(C) and 430(i)(2)(B), as added by P.L. 109-280 (Pension Protection Act of 2006), Act Sec. 112(a).

[21] IRS Reg. § 1.430(i)-1(c)(2)(ii)(A).

[22] IRS Reg. § 1.430(i)-1(c)(2)(iii).

[23] IRS Reg. § 1.430(i)-1(c)(3)(ii)(A) and (C).

[24] IRS Reg. § 1.430(i)-1(c)(3)(iii).

[25] IRS Reg. § 1.430(i)-1(c)(3)(iv).

[26] IRS Reg. § 1.430(i)-1(d).

[27] IRS Reg. § 1.430(i)-1(d)(2)(i)(B).

[28] ERISA Sec. 303(i)(2) and Code Sec.430(j)(2), as amended by P.L. 110-458 (Worker, Retiree, and Employer Recovery Act of 2008), Act Sec. 101(b)(1) and (2).

[29] IRS Reg. § 1.430(i)-1(d)(2)(ii).

[30] IRS Reg. § 1.430(i)-1(d)(2)(iii).

[31] ERISA Sec. 303(i)(5), as added by P.L. 109-280 (Pension Protection Act of 2006), Act Sec. 102(a); Code Sec. 430(i)(5), as added by P.L. 109-280 (Pension Protection Act of 2006), Act Sec. 112(a).

[32] IRS Reg. § 1.430(i)-1(e)(3).

[33] ERISA Sec. 303(i)(5)(B), as added by P.L. 109-280 (Pension Protection Act of 2006), Act Sec. 102(a); Code Sec. 430(i)(5)(B), as added by P.L. 109-280 Pension Protection Act of 2006), Act Sec. 112(a).

[34] ERISA Sec. 303(i)(5)(C), as added by P.L. 109-280 (Pension Protection Act of 2006), Act Sec.

102(a); Code Sec. 430(i)(5)(C), as added by P.L. 109-280 (Pension Protection Act of 2006), Act Sec. 112(a).

[35] IRS Reg. § 1.430(i)-1(e)(3).

[36] IRS Reg. § 1.430(i)-1(e)(1) and (2).

[37] IRS Reg. § 1.430(i)-1(e)(4).

[38] *Ibid.*

¶ 1493F
MINIMUM FUNDING RULES APPLICABLE AFTER 2007: Annual Payment of Minimum Required Contribution

The minimum required contribution for a plan year must be paid within 8½ months after the close of the plan year.[1] The payment of the minimum required contribution, however, may not be made before the first day of the plan year. [2]

Payments made on a date other than the valuation date for the plan year must be adjusted for interest accruing for the period from the valuation date to the payment date, at the effective rate of interest for the plan for the year.[3]

CCH POINTER: The requirements under Code Sec. 430(j) generally apply to plan years beginning on or after January 1, 2008. The IRS has issued proposed regulations governing the annual payment of the minimum required contribution that are proposed to apply generally to plan years beginning on or after January 1, 2009. [4] However, when the regulations are finalized, plans will be permitted to apply them to plan years beginning in 2008. In addition, the IRS explains, plans may rely on the proposed regulations in complying with the requirements under Code Sec.430(j) for plan years beginning in 2008. [5]

Adjustment of minimum required contribution. The adjustment of the minimum required contribution, under the proposed rules, depends on whether the contribution is paid before or after valuation date for the plan year. Contributions that are paid after the valuation date for the plan year are discounted to the valuation date using the plan's effective interest rate. By contrast, contributions that are paid before the valuation date for the plan year will be increased for interest at the plan's effective interest rate. [6]

Excise tax for failure to make required contributions

Under pre-2008 law, in the event a plan failed to meet the meet the minimum funding requirements, the employer sponsor and all members of a controlled group of which the employer was a member, were subject to two successive nondeductible excise taxes (see ¶ 1492). Employers that fail to make minimum required contributions under the rules applicable after 2007 (see ¶ 1493B) and that do not obtain a waiver based on substantial hardship (see ¶ 1493I) will remain subject to an excise tax. The sponsor of a single-employer plan will be subject to a 10 percent excise tax on the aggregate unpaid minimum required contribution for all plans that remain unpaid as of the end of any plan year ending with or within the tax year.[7] An initial tax will be assessed on five percent of the accumulated funding deficiency under a multiemployer plan. As under prior law, sponsors may be subject to an additional 100 percent tax on the amount of an unpaid minimum contribution for a single-employer plan (or accumulated funding deficiency for a multiemployer plan) remaining unpaid as of the close of the taxable period.[8]

> **CCH POINTER:** The proposed regulations define an unpaid minimum contribution as any minimum required contribution that is not paid on or before the due date for the plan year.[9] A plan's accumulated funding deficiency under Code Sec. 412 for the pre-effective plan year would be treated as an unpaid minimum required contribution for that plan year until correction is made. [10] In addition, the IRS explains, the total unpaid minimum required contributions are not adjusted with interest.[11]

The proposed regulations contain examples illustrating application of the excise tax that is assessed following the failure to meet the minimum funding standards (see CCH PENSION PLAN GUIDE ¶ 20,262K). [12]

Ordering rule for payment of outstanding contributions. An ordering rule governs the payment of outstanding minimum required contributions. Specifically, any payment to a plan for any plan year will be allocated first to the unpaid minimum required contribution for all preceding plan years on a "first-in, first-out" basis, before being directed to the minimum required contribution for the current plan year.[13]

Accelerated quarterly contribution for underfunded plans

Employers maintaining plans that had a funding shortfall for the preceding plan year (i.e., the value of plan assets (reduced by credit balances) was less than the funding target for the preceding year) must make quarterly contributions to the plan.[14]

> **CCH POINTER:** *Determining funding shortfall pursuant to methods of estimation.* The Worker, Retiree, and Employer Recovery Act of 2008, effective for plan years beginning in 2008, authorized the funding shortfall for the preceding plan year to be determined under methods of estimation to be prescribed by the Treasury. [15]

In the event the employer fails to pay the full amount of a required quarterly installment, interest will be assessed at the plan's specified rate of interest plus five percentage points. Interest will be assessed on the amount of the underpayment for the due date of the installment until the date on which the remaining portion is contributed to the plan.[16]

Ordering rule. In determining the amount of an underpayment, an ordering rule requires contributions to credited against unpaid required installments in the order in which the installment must be paid.[17]

Amount of quarterly installment. The quarterly contribution will be 25 percent of the required annual payment. The required annual payment is defined as the lesser of: (1) 90 percent of the minimum required contribution (determined without regard to the accelerated contribution requirement) for the plan year; or (2) 100 percent of the minimum required contribution (determined without regard to the accelerated contribution requirement or to any waiver under ERISA Sec. 302(c) or Code Sec. 412(c)) for the preceding plan year. [18] If the preceding plan year was not a year of 12 months, the required annual payment will be 90 percent of the minimum required contribution (determined without regard to the accelerated contribution requirement).

Disregard funding balances in determination of quarterly installment. The Proposed IRS Regulations clarify that the minimum required contributions are to be determined as of the valuation date for each year and are not adjusted for interest. [19] In addition, the proposed rules note that the minimum required contribution for a plan year is determined without regard to use of the prefunding balance or funding standard carryover balance in the current year or prior year. [20]

Due date of quarterly installments. The quarterly installments will be due on April 15, July 15, October 15, and January 15 of the following year.[21] Note, the proposed rules specify the following installment schedule: 1st quarter: 15th day of the 4th plan month; 2nd quarter: 15th day of 7th plan month; 3rd quarter: 15th day of the 10th plan month; and 4th quarter: 15th day after close of plan year. [22]

Short plan years

IRS Proposed Regulations would specify rules for determining the amount of the required annual payment, the number and due date of the installments, and the amount of the installment with respect to a short plan year.[23] A short plan year is a plan year that is shorter than 12 months (and is not a 52 week plan year of a plan that uses a 52-53 week plan year). [24]

Calculating annual payment for short plan year. In determining the required annual payment for a short plan year, the amount otherwise determined would be multiplied by the following fraction: duration of short plan year/1 year. [25] In the event a plan has a short plan year, the installment payment is due 15 days after the close of the short plan year. An installment is required for each specified due date that falls within the short plan year. Thus, if the short plan year ends before the 15th day of the 4th plan month of the plan year, only one installment will be due for that plan year, The installment would be due on the 15th day after the close of the short plan year.[26]

CCH POINTER: *Alternative valuation date.* Small plans may use a valuation date other the first day of the plan year. [27] The Treasury is required by the Worker, Retiree, and Employer Recovery Act of 2008 to prescribe regulations for the application of the quarterly contribution rule to plans with valuation dates other than the first day of the plan year. [28]

Use of funding balance to make quarterly contributions

A plan sponsor may use a plan's funding balance to make a required quarterly contribution. However, under the proposed regulations, the use of the pre-funding balance and the funding standard carryover balance will satisfy the sponsor's obligation to make an installment payment on the date of the election. The option applies to the extent of the amount elected, as adjusted with interest at the plan's effective interest rate for the plan year from the valuation date through the due date of the installment. [29]

The IRS further explains that a plan sponsor that uses the plan's prefunding balance or funding standard carryover balance to make the plan's quarterly contribution before the plan's effective interest rate for the plan year has been determined, should assume that the effective interest rate is equal to the lowest of the 3 segment rates (i.e. the first segment rate) in order to adjust the elected amount.

In addition, IRS cautions that the amount of the funding balance used as a quarterly contribution may not be subsequently added back to the prefunding balance. [30] Only contributions in excess of the minimum funding requirement are eligible to be added to prefunding balance, the IRS stresses.[31]

Liquidity requirement

An employer maintaining a plan that had over 100 participants on each day during the preceding plan year will be treated as failing to pay the full amount of a required quarterly installment if the value of the liquid assets (e.g., cash or marketable securities (including insurance and annuity contracts)) paid in the installment is less than the "liquidity shortfall." [32] The proposed regulations further clarify that, in order to satisfy the quarterly contribution requirement for a quarter, liquid assets in the amount of the liquidity shortfall must be contributed after the close of that quarter and on or before the due date for the installment. [33] However, the IRS cautions that a liquidity shortfall may not be remedied through the use of funding balance or the contribution of illiquid assets.

Liquidity shortfall. A "liquidity shortfall" is defined as the excess (as of the last day of the quarter for which the installment is made) of the "base amount" for the quarter over the value (as of the last day of quarter) of the plan's liquid assets.[34] The base amount for any quarter is three times the sum of the adjusted disbursements from the plan for the 12-month period ending on the last day of the quarter.[35] Adjusted disbursements are disbursements from the plan (e.g., purchases of annuities, payment of lump sums and other benefits, and administrative expenses) reduced by the product of the plan's funding target attainment percentage for the plan year and the sum of the annuity purchases, payments of single sums, and other disbursements as specified in Treasury regulations.[36]

Excise tax for failure to pay liquidity shortfall. Failure to pay the liquidity shortfall subjects the employer to an excise tax under Code Sec. 4971(f). The tax is 10 percent of the amount of the excess of the amount of the liquidity shortfall for any quarter, over the amount of such shortfall which is paid by the required installment date under Code Sec. 430(j) for such quarter.

Period of underpayment

For purposes of the 5 percentage point interest adjustment assessed following the failure to make a quarterly contribution, the liquidity increment (i.e., portion of the required quarterly installment that is treated as not paid solely because of the additional contribution required under the liquidity rules) for a quarter will continue to be treated as unpaid until the close of the quarter in which the due date for that installment occurred, without regard to when that portion is paid. [37]

¶1493F

Ordering rule. In the event that a contribution is not sufficient to satisfy the quarterly contribution under Code Sec. 430(j)(3)(E) (and IRS Prop. Reg. § 1.430(j)-1(c)), the amount will be allocated towards satisfying the quarterly contribution and then towards the liquidity increment. [38]

The proposed regulations include examples illustrating the applicable rules (see CCH PENSION PLAN GUIDE ¶ 20, 262K).[39]

[1] ERISA Sec. 303(j)(1), as added by P.L. 109-280 (Pension Protection Act of 2006), Act Sec. 102(a); Code Sec. 430(j)(1), as added by P.L. 109-280 (Pension Protection Act of 2006), Act Sec. 112(a).

[2] IRS Prop. Reg. § 1.430(j)-1(b).

[3] ERISA Sec. 303(j)(2), as added by P.L. 109-280 (Pension Protection Act of 2006), Act Sec. 102(a); Code Sec. 430(j)(2), as added by P.L. 109-280 (Pension Protection Act of 2006), Act Sec. 112(a).

[4] IRS Prop. Reg. § 1.430(j)-1.

[5] Preamble to IRS Prop. Reg. § 1.430(j)-1, at CCH PENSION PLAN GUIDE ¶ 20,262K.

[6] IRS Prop. Reg. § 1.430(j)-1(b)(3).

[7] Code Sec. 4971(a)(2), as amended by P.L. 109-280 (Pension Protection Act of 2006), Act Sec. 114(e).

[8] Code Sec. 4971(b), as amended by P.L. 109-280 (Pension Protection Act of 2006), Act Sec. 114(e).

[9] IRS Prop. Reg. § 54.4971(c)-1(c)(2).

[10] *Ibid.*

[11] IRS Prop. Reg. § 54.4971(c)-1(c)(2).

[12] IRS Prop. Reg. § 54.4971(c)-1(c)(2).

[13] Code Sec. 4971(c)(4), as amended by P.L. 109-280 (Pension Protection Act of 2006), Act Sec. 114(e).

[14] ERISA Sec. 303(j)(3)(A), as added by P.L. 109-280 (Pension Protection Act of 2006), Act Sec. 102(a); Code Sec. 430(j)(3)(A), as added by P.L. 109-280 (Pension Protection Act of 2006), Act Sec. 112(a).

[15] ERISA Sec. 303(j)(3)(A), as amended by P.L. 110-458 (Worker, Retiree, and Employer Recovery Act of 2008), Act Sec. 101(b)(1)(G)(i); Code Sec. 430(j)(3)(A), as amended by P.L. 110-458 (Worker, Retiree, and Employer Recovery Act of 2008), Act Sec. 102(b)(1)(G).

[16] ERISA Sec. 303(j)(3)(B), as added by P.L. 109-280 (Pension Protection Act of 2006), Act Sec. 102(a); Code Sec. 430(j)(3)(B), as added by P.L. 109-280 (Pension Protection Act of 2006), Act Sec. 112(a).

[17] ERISA Sec. 303(j)(3)(B)(iii), as amended by P.L. 109-280 (Pension Protection Act of 2006), Act Sec. 102(a); Code Sec. 430(j)(3)(B)(iii), as added by P.L. 109-280 (Pension Protection Act of 2006), Act Sec. 112(a).

[18] ERISA Sec. 303(j)(3)(D), as amended by P.L. 109-280 (Pension Protection Act of 2006), Act Sec. 102(a); Code Sec. 430(j)(3)(D), as added by P.L. 109-280 (Pension Protection Act of 2006), Act Sec. 112(a).

[19] IRS Prop. Reg. § 1.430(j)-1(c)(3).

[20] IRS Prop. Reg. § 1.430(j)-1(c)(3)(iii).

[21] ERISA Sec. 303(j)(3)(C)(ii), as added by P.L. 109-280 (Pension Protection Act of 2006), Act Sec. 102(a); Code Sec. 430(j)(3)(C)(ii), as added by P.L. 109-280 (Pension Protection Act of 2006), Act Sec. 112(a).

[22] IRS Prop. Reg. § 1.430(j)-1(c)(4).

[23] IRS Prop. Reg. § 1.430(j)-1(c)(5).

[24] IRS Prop. Reg. § 1.430(j)-1(e)(9).

[25] IRS Prop. Reg. § 1.430(j)-1(c)(5)(iii)(A).

[26] IRS Prop. Reg. § 1.430(j)-1(c)(5)(ii)(B).

[27] ERISA Sec. 303(j)(3)(E), as added by P.L. 109-280 (Pension Protection Act of 2006), Act Sec. 102(a); Code Sec. 430(j)(3)(E), as added by P.L. 109-280 (Pension Protection Act of 2006), Act Sec. 112(a).

[28] ERISA Sec. 303(j)(3)(E), as amended by P.L. 110-458 (Worker, Retiree, and Employer Recovery Act of 2008), Act Sec. 101(b)(1)(g)(ii); Code Sec. 430(j)(3)(E), amended by P.L. 110-458 (Worker, Retiree, and Employer Recovery Act of 2008), Act Sec. 101(b)(2)(g)(iii).

[29] IRS Prop. Reg. § 1.430(j)-1(c)(1)(ii).

[30] IRS Prop. Reg. § 1.430(j)-1(b)(1)(ii)(B)..

[31] Preamble to IRS Prop. Reg. § 1.430(j)-1, at CCH PENSION PLAN GUIDE ¶ 20,262K.

[32] ERISA Sec. 303(j)(4)(A), as added by P.L. 109-280 (Pension Protection Act of 2006), Act Sec. 102(a); Code Sec. 430(j)(4)(A), as added by P.L. 109-280 (Pension Protection Act of 2006), Act Sec. 112(a); IRS Proposed Reg. § 1.430(j)-1(e)(5).

[33] IRS Prop. Reg. § 1.430(j)-1(d).

[34] ERISA Sec. 303(j)(4)(E), as added by P.L. 109-280 (Pension Protection Act of 2006), Act Sec. 102(a); Code Sec. 430(j)(4)(E), as added by P.L. 109-280 (Pension Protection Act of 2006), Act Sec. 112(a).

[35] ERISA Sec. 303(j)(4)(E)(ii), as added by P.L. 109-280 (Pension Protection Act of 2006), Act Sec. 102(a); Code Sec. 430(j)(4)(E)(ii), as added by

P.L. 109-280 (Pension Protection Act of 2006), Act Sec. 112(a).

[36] ERISA Sec. 303(j)(4)(E)(iv), as added by P.L. 109-280 (Pension Protection Act of 2006), Act Sec. 102(a); Code Sec. 430(j)(4)(E)(iv), as added by

P.L. 109-280 (Pension Protection Act of 2006), Act Sec. 112(a).

[37] IRS Prop. Reg. § 1.430(j)-1(d)(2).
[38] IRS Prop. Reg. § 1.430(j)-1(d)(2)(iii).
[39] IRS Prop. Reg. § 1.430(j)-1(d)(2)(iii).

¶ 1493G

MINIMUM FUNDING RULES APPLICABLE AFTER 2007: Plan Lien Following Employer Failure to Make Required Funding Contribution

In the event an employer fails to make a required contribution to a single-employer defined benefit plan before the scheduled date for payment (see ¶ 1493F, a lien will be imposed in favor of the plan on the aggregate unpaid balance of the required contribution payments.[1] The lien will not be imposed, however, unless: (1) the funding target attainment percentage for the plan is under 100 percent; and (2) the unpaid balance of the missed payment (including interest) when added to the aggregate balance of a preceding payment for which payment was not made before the due date (including interest), exceeds $1 million.[2] The lien will extend to all property and rights to property (real and personal) belonging to the person required to make the payment and other members of the person's controlled group.[3]

Notice to PBGC

An employer that fails to make a required funding contribution must notify the PBGC of the failure within 10 days of the contribution due date.[4]

Period of lien

The period of the lien will extend from the due date of the required contribution to the last day of the first plan year in which the aggregate unpaid balance of required contributions is under $1 million. The lien will continue to apply even if the plan's funding target attainment percentage is no longer below 100 percent during the prescribed period of the lien.[5]

> **CCH POINTER:** *Enforcement of lien by PBGC or plan sponsor.* A plan lien may generally only be perfected and enforced by the PBGC. [6] However, the PBGC may allow for the enforcement of the lien by the contributing sponsor or any member of the sponsor's controlled group.

[1] ERISA Sec. 303(k)(1) and (2), added by P.L. 109-280 (Pension Protection Act of 2006), Act Sec. 102(a); Code Sec. 430(k)(1) and (2), added by P.L. 109-280 (Pension Protection Act of 2006), Act Sec. 112(a).

[2] ERISA Sec. 303(k)(1)(B), added by P.L. 109-280 (Pension Protection Act of 2006), Act Sec. 102(a); Code Sec. 430(k)(1)(B), added by P.L. 109-280 (Pension Protection Act of 2006), Act Sec. 112(a).

[3] ERISA Sec. 303(k)(1), added by P.L. 109-280 (Pension Protection Act of 2006), Act Sec. 102(a); Code Sec. 430(k)(1), added by P.L. 109-280 (Pension Protection Act of 2006), Act Sec. 112(a).

[4] ERISA Sec. 303(k)(4), added by P.L. 109-280 (Pension Protection Act of 2006), Act Sec. 102(a); Code Sec. 430(k)(4), added by P.L. 109-280 (Pension Protection Act of 2006), Act Sec. 112(a).

[5] ERISA Sec. 303(k)(4)(B), added by P.L. 109-280 (Pension Protection Act of 2006), Act Sec.

102(a); Code Sec. 430(k)(4)(B), added by P.L. 109-280 (Pension Protection Act of 2006), Act Sec. 112(a).

[6] ERISA Sec. 303(k)(5), added by P.L. 109-280 (Pension Protection Act of 2006), Act Sec. 102(a); Code Sec. 430(k)(5), added by P.L. 109-280 (Pension Protection Act of 2006), Act Sec. 112(a).

¶ 1493H

MINIMUM FUNDING RULES APPLICABLE AFTER 2007: Benefit Limitations Under Single-Employer Pension Plans

Single-employer defined benefit plans that fall below specified funding levels are subject to limits on unpredictable contingent event benefits, plan amendments, lump-sum distributions, and benefit accruals.[1] Note, for purposes of the limits on benefits and benefit accruals, single-employer plans are defined as any plan that is not a multiemployer plan.[2]

Plans may continue to provide unpredictable contingent event benefits. However, an unpredictable contingent event benefit may not be paid if the plan's adjusted funding target attainment percentage for the plan year is less than 60 percent or would be less than 60 percent as a consequence of the occurrence of the event.

An employer also may not adopt an amendment to a single-employer defined benefit plan that is less than 80 percent funded that will have the effect of increasing plan liabilities, unless it makes additional contributions to the plan. Plans may continue to authorize accelerated distributions, such as lump-sum payments. However, "prohibited payments" under plans that are below specified funding levels are subject to restrictions.

Single-employer defined benefit plans must further provide for the cessation of all benefit accruals under the plan in the event that the plan's adjusted funding target attainment percentage is less than 60 percent. The limitations will not, however apply during the first five years that a plan (or a predecessor plan) is in effect.

Finally, the plan administrator of a single-employer defined benefit plan must provide "written" notice to plan participants and beneficiaries within 30 days of the plan becoming subject to the limits on unpredictable contingent event benefits, and prohibited payments.

Note, a plan sponsor may take measures to avoid or terminate the benefit limits. The authorized methods include an election to reduce the prefunding balance or the funding standard carryover balance, making a current year contribution, and providing security to the plan.

CCH POINTER: *Final regulations implement benefit limits.* The IRS issued final regulations in October 2009 implementing the benefit limits enacted by the Pension Protection Act of 2006. [3] The final rules apply to plan years beginning on or after January 1, 2010. For plan years beginning before 2010, plans may rely on the final rules or on proposed regulations issued in August 2007. [4]

Amend plan to reflect benefit restrictions. Plan terms must expressly incorporate the limits on unpredictable contingent event benefits, lump-sum payments, plan amendments increasing plan liabilities, and benefit accruals. Thus, an employer must not only operationally comply with or enforce the benefit restriction, but must amend it plan to reflect the limits. The plan should also include the procedures the plan will follow in administering benefit elections that are subsequently subject to restriction.

2010 extension of remedial amendment period. The Pension Protection Act specified that required plan amendments need to be adopted prior to the close of the 2009 plan year (2011 for governmental plans). [5] Subsequently, the IRS, in order to enable plan sponsors to account for the final regulations issued in October 2009, extended the deadline for adopting an interim or discretionary plan amendment under Code Sec. 436, to the last day of the first plan year that begins on or after January 1, 2011. [6]

2011 extension of remedial amendment period. In December 2011 the IRS again extended the deadline for adopting required interim amendments to the latest of: (a) the last day of the first plan year that begins on or after January 1, 2012, (b) the last day of the plan year for which Code Sec. 436 is first effective for the plan, or (c) the due date, including extensions, of the employer's tax return for the tax year that contains the first day of the plan year for which Code Sec. 436 is first effective for the plan. The extension is conditioned on the amendment being effective as of the effective date of Code Sec. 436 with respect to the plan and operation of the plan in accordance with the amendment from and after the effective date of the amendment. [7]

Anti-cutback relief. An interim plan amendment that eliminates or reduces a protected benefit will not cause a plan to violate the anti-cutback requirements of Code Sec. 411(d)(6), if the amendment is adopted by the last day of the first plan year that begins on or after January 1, 2012, and the elimination or reduction is made only to the extent necessary to satisfy the requirements of Code Sec. 436. [8]

Sample plan amendment. The IRS has also provided a sample amendment that satisfies the requirements of Code Sec. 436 and the final regulations. If a plan is amended by adoption of the sample amendment, the terms of the plan will satisfy those statutory and regulatory requirements. [9] The sample amendment is reproduced at CCH PENSION PLAN GUIDE ¶ 17,148Q.

Operational compliance. A plan must continue to operationally comply with all of the applicable requirements as a condition of the extension of the deadline for adopting required amendments.

Adjusted funding target attainment percentage

The benefit limits are based on the plan's adjusted funding target attainment percentage (AFTAP).[10] A plan's "funding target attainment percentage" is the ratio of assets (minus funding standard carryover and pre-funding credit balances) to target liability (i.e., funding target) (disregarding the plan's at-risk status (see

¶1493H

¶ 1493E).[11] The "adjusted funding target attainment percentage" is generally determined in the same way, but reflects plan assets and funding target liabilities as increased by the aggregate amount of annuity purchases made for nonhighly compensated employees by the plan during the preceding two plan years.[12]

Determination of AFTAP. The adjusted funding target attainment percentage (AFTAP) for any plan year, as defined by the final regulations issued in 2009, is the following fraction (expressed as a percentage): adjusted plan assets/ adjusted funding target. [13]

The adjusted plan assets equal the value of plan assets decreased by the plan's funding standard carryover balance and prefunding balance and increased by the aggregate amount of purchases and annuities for participants and beneficiaries (other than participants who were highly compensated employees at the time of the purchase) which were made by the plan during the preceding two plan years, to the extent not included in plan assets under Code Sec. 430. [14]

The final regulations also provide rules for determining the AFTAP for the prior plan year when the first plan year begins in 2008.

See CCH PENSION PLAN GUIDE ¶ 3138 for detailed discussion of the determination of FTAP.

AFTAP determined on valuation date. The AFTAP is determined as of the plan's valuation date. The valuation date is generally the first day of the plan year. However, small plans with less than 100 participants may select any day of the year as the valuation date.[15] Accordingly, the valuation date of a small plan may differ from the date on which AFTAP is determined.

The IRS prescribed transition rules that could be applied for purposes of determining FTAP and AFTAP under small plans with end of the year valuation dates. [16] Note, further, the Worker, Retiree, and Employer Recovery Act of 2008 authorized the Treasury to prescribe rules for applying the benefit restrictions to accommodate a small plan's use of an alternative valuation date. [17]

Limits on unpredictable contingent event benefits

A single-employer defined benefit plan may entitle participants to benefits or an increase in benefits that are payable only upon the occurrence during the plan year of specified unpredictable uncontingent event benefits, such as the full or partial shutdown of an employer's operations. The plan terms must provide that such an unpredictable contingent event benefits may not be paid if the plan's adjusted funding target attainment percentage for the plan is (a) less than 60 percent or (b) is 60 percent or more but would be less than 60 percent if the AFTAP were determined applying an actuarial assumption that the likelihood of an occurrence of the event during the year is 100 percent. [18]

Unpredictable contingent event benefits. The restriction on unpredictable contingent event benefits applies to benefits (e.g., unreduced early retirement annuity) that are payable as a result of a plant shutdown, or a similar event (including the absence of an event) as determined by the Treasury.[19] In addition, the restriction will apply to benefits that are payable solely by reason of an event (or absence of an event) other than the attainment of any age, performance of any service, receipt or derivation of any compensation, or the occurrence of death or disability.[20]

The IRS final regulations clarify that, in the event a plan provides for an unreduced early retirement benefit upon the occurrence of an event other than the attainment of any age, performance of any service, receipt or derivation of any compensation, or the occurrence of death or disability, the unreduced early retirement benefit is to be treated as an unpredictable contingent event benefit to the extent of any portion of the benefit that would not be payable but for the occurrence of the event. This rules applies even if the remainder of the benefit is payable without regard to the occurrence of the event.[21]

Application of limits on participant-by-participant basis. The benefit restrictions apply on a participant-by-participant basis. [22] Accordingly, the application of a benefit restriction to a participant is based on whether the participant satisfies the plan's eligibility requirements (other than the attainment of any age, performance of any service, receipt or derivation of any compensation, or death or disability) for the benefit in the plan year in which the Code Sec. 436 benefits limits apply.

Limit applies upon occurrence of event, not payment. The determination of whether the limitation on unpredictable contingent event benefits applies is made in the year the event occurs, and not when the benefit payments are actually made.[23] Thus, for example, if a plant shutdown occurs in a year in which the plan's funding target attainment percentage is 50 percent, shutdown benefits may not be paid (absent additional contributions by the employer), even if the benefits will not actually be paid until a later year.

Prior unpredictable contingent event benefits. The final regulations clarify that the benefit restrictions do not apply to unpredictable contingent event benefits that are attributable to an event that occurred within a period during which no limits applied. For example, if a plant shutdown or other event occurs during a plan year in which unpredictable contingent event benefits are not subject to limit (e.g., 2010), benefits paid pursuant to the shutdown may be paid in a later plan year (e.g., 2012) even if the plan's adjusted funding target attainment percentage for the subsequent year is less than 60 percent. [24] However, conversely, the shutdown benefits could not be paid in a subsequent year in which the plan's AFTAP was above 60 percent, if the plan was subject to the Code Sec. 436(b) limit in the year of the shutdown.

Multiple contingent event benefits. A plan may condition an unpredictable contingent event benefit upon the occurrence of more than one event. Under such circumstances, the benefit reduction would not apply until the last of the unpredictable contingent events occur. [25]

Cessation of benefits. A plan may provide for the cessation, suspension, or reduction of any benefits upon the occurrence of any event. The final regulations clarify that the cessation of a benefit upon the occurrence of a specified event is not an unpredictable contingent event subject to the limits of Code Sec. 436. [26]

¶1493H

Avoid restriction by making contribution equal to increased funding target caused by occurrence of event. An employer may avoid the restrictions applicable to a plan with a funding target attainment percentage under 60 percent by making a contribution (in addition to the minimum required funding contribution for the plan year) equal to the amount of the increase in the funding target of the plan attributable to the occurrence of the unpredictable contingent event.[27]

The final regulations issued in 2009 clarify that, in the event the AFTAP for the plan year (determined without taking into account the liability attributable to the unpredictable contingent event benefits) is less than 60 percent, the employer contribution must equal the amount of the increase in the funding target of the plan for the plan year that would apply if the benefit attributable to the unpredictable contingent event benefit was included in the determination of the funding target.[28]

By contrast, if the AFTAP for the plan year (determined without taking into account the liability attributable to unpredictable contingent event benefits) is 60 percent or more, the employer contribution would need to be sufficient to result in an AFTAP for the plan year of 60 percent, if the contribution (and any prior contribution under Code Sec. 436 for the plan year) were included as part of the plan assets and the funding target took into account adjustments specified under IRS Reg. § 1.436-1(g).[29]

Limits on amendments increasing benefit liabilities

An employer may not adopt an amendment to a single-employer defined benefit plan that is less than 80 percent funded that will have the effect of increasing plan liabilities, unless it makes additional contributions to the plan. Specifically, if the "adjusted" funding target attainment percentage as of the evaluation date of the plan for the plan year is less than 80 percent (or would be less than 80 percent as a result of the amendment) the plan may generally not be amended during the year to increase benefits, establish new benefits, change the rate of benefit accrual, or change the rate at which benefits become nonforfeitable (i.e., accelerated vesting schedule).[30]

Additional employer contribution may fund benefit increase under amendment. A plan that has an adjusted funding target attainment percentage under 80 percent may be amended to increase benefit liabilities if the employer makes a contribution (in addition to the minimum required contribution for the plan year under ERISA Sec. 303 and Code Sec. 430) equal to the amount of the increase in the funding target of the plan that is attributable to the amendment.[31] Similarly, an employer may adopt an amendment that will have the effect of reducing the plan's adjusted funding target attainment percentage below 80 percent, if the employer contributes an additional amount that is sufficient to restore the plan's adjusted funded target attainment percentage to 80 percent.[32]

Pre-existing plan provisions authorizing restoration of benefit accruals. A plan may include a provision that authorizes the automatic restoration of benefit accruals that were not permitted to accrue because of the limit on benefit accruals under Code Sec. 436(e). The restoration of the benefit is generally treated as a plan amendment subject to restriction under Code Sec. 436(c).[33] However, the automatic restoration of benefit accruals pursuant to the plan provision will not be treated as a plan amendment if: (a) the continuous period of the limitation is 12 months or less, and (b) the AFTAP for the plan (as certified by the plan's enrolled actuary) would not be less than 60 percent, taking into account the restored benefit accruals for the plan year.

Exemption for compensation-based benefit formulas. A plan amendment that provides for an increase in benefits that is based on a participant's compensation is not subject to the restrictions. A plan amendment may also provide for an increase in benefits that is not based on a participant's compensation. However, the rate of the benefit increase may not exceed the contemporaneous rate of increase in average wages of participants covered by the amendment.[34]

The determination of the rate of increase in average wages is made, under the IRS final regulations, by reference to the net increase in average wages during the period beginning with the effective date of the most recent benefit increase applicable to all participants covered by the current agreement and ending on the effective date of the current amendment.[35] The regulations authorize currently employed and terminated participants to be included in the determination of the increase in average wages.[36]

Exemption for amendments implementing mandatory increase in vesting of benefits. An exemption from treatment as an amendment changing the rate at which benefits become nonforfeitable is provided for amendments (or pre-existing plan provisions) that authorize a mandatory increase in the vesting for benefits under the Internal Revenue Code or ERISA (e.g., vesting rate increase pursuant to statute, plan termination amendments, or partial terminations under Code Sec. 411(d)(3) and vesting increase required under the Code Sec. 416 top-heavy rules). [37] However, the exemption only applies if the increase in vesting is necessary to enable the plan to maintain its tax qualified status.

Determining effective date of amendment. Amendments that increase benefits take effect for purposes of Code Sec. 436(c), on the first date on which any individual who is or could be a participant or beneficiary under the plan would obtain a legal right to the increased benefit, if the individual were, on that date, to satisfy the applicable requirements for entitlement to the benefit (i.e., attainment of applicable age or satisfaction of service requirement).[38]

Restrictions on lump-sum distributions and accelerated payments

Under pre-2008 law, plans with a liquidity shortfall were prohibited from making lump-sum benefit payments. The current rules do not prohibit accelerated distributions, such as lump-sum payments. However, "prohibited payments" under plans that are below specified funding levels (i.e., AFTAP under 60 percent) are subject to restrictions.[39]

Exemption for frozen plans. The restrictions under Code Sec. 436(d) do not apply for any plan year if the terms of the plan (as in effect for the period beginning September 1, 2005) provide for no benefit accruals with respect to any participants. [40] However, the exemption would no longer apply if the plan subsequently provides for benefit accruals. [41]

¶1493H

Prohibited payments. Prohibited payments subject to restriction include: monthly payments in excess of the monthly amount paid under a single life annuity (plus Social Security supplements) to a participant or beneficiary whose annuity starting date occurs during a limitation period; any payment for the purchase of an irrevocable commitment from an insurer to pay benefits; any transfer of assets and liabilities to another plan maintained by the same employer (or by any member of the employer's controlled group) that is made in order to avoid or terminate the application of the Code Sec. 436 benefit limits; and other payments identified in IRS guidance as prohibited payments. [42]

Annuity starting date. The annuity starting date is the first day of the first period for which an amount is payable as an annuity, if the amount is being paid as an annuity. [43] If an amount is not being paid as an annuity, the annuity starting date is the annuity starting date for the qualified joint and survivor annuity that is payable at the same time as the benefit that is not payable as an annuity. If the amount is payable under a retroactive annuity starting date, the annuity starting date is the commencement date.

The annuity starting date also includes the date of the purchase of an irrevocable commitment from an insurer to pay benefits under the plan, and the date of any transfer of assets and liabilities to another plan maintained by the same employer that is made in order to avoid or terminate the application of the benefit limits.

Cash-out distributions are not prohibited payments. Prohibited payments do not include the payment of benefits that may be immediately distributed without the consent of the participant (see ¶ 869 and ¶ 2989). [44] Accordingly, the payment of a nonforfeitable accrued benefit would not be a prohibited payment if the present value of the participant's vested benefit did not exceed $5,000.

Suspension of prohibited payments when funding percentage under 60 percent. In the event a plan has an AFTAP under 60 percent, a participant or beneficiary may not elect an optional form of benefit that includes a prohibited payment, and the plan may not make any prohibited payment, with an annuity starting date on or after the Code Sec. 436 measurement date. [45]

Effect of employer bankruptcy. A defined benefit plan may not make a lump-sum distribution or other prohibited payment during any period in which the plan sponsor is in federal or state bankruptcy proceedings.[46] However, payments may be made if the annuity starting date is on or after the date on which the plan's enrolled actuary has certified that the plan's AFTAP is not less than 100 percent.[47]

Additional restrictions on prohibited payments under plans with funding percentage of 60 percent or more. The restrictions on prohibited payments are not limited to benefits paid under a plan that has an adjusted funding target attainment percentage of less than 60 percent. Plans with an adjusted funding target attainment percentage of 60 percent or more, but not greater than 80 percent, are also subject to restriction.

A participant or beneficiary may not elect the payment of an optional form of benefit that includes a prohibited payment, and the plan may not make any prohibited payment with an annuity starting date on or after the Code Sec. 436

measurement date unless the present value (under Code Sec. 417(e)(3)) of the portion of the benefit being paid in a prohibited payment does not exceed the lesser of: (1) 50 percent of the present value of the benefit payable in the optional form of benefit that includes the prohibited payment; or (2) the present value of the applicable maximum PBGC guaranteed benefit (based on the participant's or beneficiary's age at the annuity starting date) under ERISA for the year in which the annuity starting date occurs (see ¶ 2811).[48]

> **CCH POINTER:** *Table of Present Value of Maximum PBGC Guaranteed Benefit.* The PBGC has issued a table that reflects the present value of the PBGC maximum guarantee for purposes of the above restriction. [49] The table reflects, for the calendar year, the applicable present value amount based on the age of the participant. The value in the table for a calendar year applies to distributions with annuity starting dates in that calendar year, regardless of when the plan year begins.

The table is reproduced at CCH PENSION PLAN GUIDE ¶ 19,981S.

Bifurcation of benefit. In the event an optional form of benefit is not available to a participant because the plan's AFTAP is within the 60–80 percent range, the plan must: allow a participant or beneficiary to bifurcate the benefit into unrestricted and restricted portions; offer the participant or beneficiary any other optional form of benefit otherwise available under the plan at the annuity starting date that would satisfy the 50 percent /PBGC maximum benefit guarantee amount limitation; and authorize the right to defer the payment of benefits to a later date. [50]

Unrestricted portion of benefit. The unrestricted portion of the benefit with respect to any option for of benefit is 50 percent of the amount payable under the optional form of benefit. [51] However, if the optional form of benefit is a prohibited payment because of a Social Security leveling feature or a refund of employee contributions, the unrestricted portion of the benefit would be the optional form of benefit applied to only 50 percent of the total benefit. [52]

The unrestricted portion of the benefit must (under the general rule and special rules) be further reduced to the extent necessary to ensure that the present value of the unrestricted portion of the optional form of benefit does not exceed the PBGC maximum benefit guarantee. [53]

Treat unrestricted portion of benefit as participant's entire benefit. If a participant or beneficiary elects to bifurcate the benefit, the plan must provide (with respect to the unrestricted portion) the optional form of benefit elected by the participant, treating the unrestricted benefit as if it were the participant's entire benefit under the plan. The participant or beneficiary may elect to receive the remainder of the benefit in any optional form of benefit available under the plan that does not include a prohibited payment. [54]

Participant's right to delay benefits. A participant who receives a distribution of an optional form of benefit that includes a prohibited payment that may not be made has the right to delay the commencement of benefits. However, the delay in benefits must comply with the terms of the plan and the applicable qualification requirements (i.e., Code Sec. 401(a)(9) distribution rules). [55]

¶1493H

Participant right to elect alternative form of benefit. A plan may offer optional forms of benefit that are available only during the period in which prohibited payments may not be made. The final rules authorize participants and beneficiaries who request a prohibited payment to elect another form of benefit available under the plan. [56] Accordingly, if a participant elects a lump-sum payment which may not be made under a Code Sec. 436 restriction, he or she may elect the annuity form offered under the plan which does not contain prohibited payments. [57] In addition, a plan may prevent participants and beneficiaries who commence benefits during the period in which prohibited payments are subject to the Code Sec. 436 limit, to elect, within a specified period after the date on which the limitation no longer applies, to receive the remaining benefits in the form of a single sum payment equal to the present value of the remaining benefit. However, the optional form of benefit must comply with Code Sec. 436(d) and the governing qualification requirements.

Limit on number of prohibited payments. In addition to the limit on the amount of the payment, the plan may not make more than one prohibited payment to a participant during any period of consecutive plan years to which the limits apply.[58] For purposes of the restriction, a participant and his or her beneficiary (including an alternate payee) are treated as one participant.[59] If, under the terms of a qualified domestic relations order (QDRO), a participant's accrued benefit is to be allocated to an alternate payee and to one or more person, the amount to be distributed will be allocated in the same manner, unless the QDRO provides for different treatment.

Accruals frozen if plan less than 60 percent funded

Single-employer defined benefit plans must provide for the cessation of all future benefit accruals under the plan in the event the plan's adjusted funding target attainment percentage is less than 60 percent.[60] The benefit accruals will cease as of the valuation date for the plan year. The IRS final rules further provide that a plan that is required to cease benefit accruals may not be amended in a manner that would increase plan liabilities because of an increase in benefits or the establishment of new benefits. [61] This restriction applies even if the amendment would otherwise be permissible under Code Sec. 436(c)(3) (governing amendments to increase benefits under a formula based on employee compensation).

See CCH Pension Plan Guide ¶ 3138 for discussion of the temporary modification of the limitation on benefit accruals authorized under the Worker, Retiree, and Employer Recovery Act of 2008 and the Preservation of Access to Care for Medicare Beneficiaries and Pension Relief Act of 2010.

Current year contributions avoid or terminate benefit limits

An employer may make a current year contribution to avoid or terminate the application of the Code Sec. 436 benefit limitations for a plan year that apply to unpredictable contingent event benefits, plan amendments that increase liabilities for benefits, and benefit accruals. [62] The contributions must be paid during the plan year and before the unpredictable contingent event benefits may be paid, the plan amendment is permitted to take effect, or the benefit accruals are permitted to resume. [63]

Interest rate adjustment. A Code Sec. 436 contribution made on a date other than the valuation date for the plan year must be adjusted with interest at the plan's effective interest rate (under Code Sec. 430(h)(2)) for the plan year, or if that rate has not been determined, using the highest rate of the three segment rates applicable to the plan under Code Sec.430(h)(2)(C). [64]

Use of prefunding balance or funding standard carryover balance. An employer may not use a prefunding balance or a funding standard carryover balance in satisfaction of the additional contribution that is required in order to avoid or terminate the application of the limit on unpredictable contingent event benefits, the adoption of amendments increasing benefit liabilities, or benefit accruals to underfunded plans. [65] However, under the final regulations, issued in 2009, a plan sponsor may elect to reduce the funding standard carryover balance or the prefunding balance in order to increase the AFTAP for a plan year. The reduction of the funding standard carryover balance or the prefunding balance by an amount sufficient to avoid the limits, will effectively increase adjusted plan assets and thereby increase the AFTAP. [66]

Note: The final regulations provide general rules that apply to all Code Sec. 436 contributions and then separate rules that are based on the amount of contributions needed to avoid each type of benefit limitation. [67]

Separate contribution from minimum required contributions. The contribution authorized under Code Sec. 436 must be separate from any minimum required contribution under Code Sec. 430. [68] The Code Sec. 436 contribution must be so designated at the time the contribution is used to avoid or terminate the applicable benefit limitation and, generally, may not be recharacterized with respect to any plan year as a contribution to satisfy a minimum required contribution or otherwise.[69] The IRS stresses that a plan will not satisfy the minimum funding requirements for a plan year if it does not make the minimum required contribution, even if the Code Sec. 436 contribution is made.

Security as alternative to additional contributions

An employer required to make an additional contribution in order to prevent application of a benefit limitation may, alternatively, provide security to the plan. Security that is provided by the valuation date for the plan year satisfies specified requirements will be treated as a plan asset for purposes of determining the adjusted funding target attainment percentage.[70] The security must be: a corporate surety bond; cash or United States obligation that matures in three years or less, held in escrow by a bank or similar financial institution; or some other form of security that is approved by the parties involved and the Treasury Department.[71]

Payment of security. The security must be paid to the plan upon the earliest of: (1) the plan termination date; (2) the due date for the payment of a minimum required contribution that is not made for a plan year after the security has been provided; or (3) if the plan's AFTAP is less than 60 percent (without regard to any security provided) for a consecutive 7-year period, the valuation date for the last plan years in the 7-year period. [72] The plan administrator must also notify the surety, bank, or insurance company that issues or holds the security of any event described in (3) above, within 10 days of its occurrence.

Release of security. The security may be returned (and any amounts thereunder returned with interest accrued thereon) as provided in the agreement governing the security. However, the security may not be released until the plan's enrolled actuary certifies that the plan's AFTAP for a plan year is at least 90 percent or until replacement security has been provided. [73]

Contribution of security to plan. Security that is released to the plan is treated as a contribution by the plan sponsor. However, a security that is turned over to the plan, pursuant to the enforcement mechanism, may not be treated as a contribution to avoid or terminate the application of the 436 benefit limits.[74]

Replacement security. The final regulations released in 2009 authorize the replacement of a security. [75] However, the amount of the new security may not be less than the amount of the original security (determined at the time of release of the original security).

Participant notice of limits on distributions and benefit accruals

The plan administrator of a single-employer defined benefit plan must provide "written" notice to plan participants and beneficiaries within 30 days of the plan becoming subject to the limits on unpredictable contingent event benefits, and accelerated benefit distributions under ERISA Sec. 206(g)(1) and (3).[76]

In addition, notice must be provided for a plan that is experiencing a severe funding shortfall and subject to the limits on benefit accruals under ERISA Sec. 206(g)(4). The notice must be provided within 30 days after the valuation date for the plan year in which the adjusted funding target attainment percentage for the plan year is less than 60 percent, or, if earlier, the date the percentage is deemed to be less than 60 percent under ERISA Sec. 206(g)(7) (see below).[77]

Notice satisfies ERISA 204(h) notice requirement. Final regulations issued by IRS in 2009 clarify that, if a plan is required to provide notice of a limit or cessation of benefit accruals under ERISA Sec.101(j) and ERISA Sec. 204(h) (relating to a reduction in future benefit accruals), providing the 101(j) notice would constitute a safe harbor for purposes of the requirement to provide an ERISA 204(h) notice. [78]

Notice of funding based restriction on lump-sum payments not required for participants in pay status. The notice that must be provided to participants and beneficiaries in underfunded plans subject to funding-based restrictions on lump-sum payments need not be furnished to parties in pay status who would not be eligible for lump-sum payments whether or not the plan was subject to the benefit reduction.[79]

$1000 civil penalty. The DOL may impose a civil penalty of up to $1000 per day for each failure by an person to provide the required notice. [80]

Procedural framework for assessment of penalties. Final regulations issued by EBSA, effective March 3, 2009, set forth rules for the computation of the maximum penalty amount, identify circumstances under which a penalty may be assessed, establish procedural rules for service and filing, and provide plan administrators with a mechanism by which to challenge a penalty assessment and request an administrative hearing. [81] The final regulations stress that the penalty is a personal liability of the plan administrator that may not be transferred to the plan as a reasonable expense of plan administration. However, the rules also authorize the DOL to waive or reduce the penalty assessment upon a showing by the plan administrator, in a written reasonable cause statement, of compliance or mitigating circumstances regarding the degree of willfulness of noncompliance.

The governing rules are detailed at CCH PENSION PLAN GUIDE ¶ 3138.

Five-year exception for new plans

The limits on unpredictable contingent event benefits, increased benefits, and benefit accruals under ERISA Sec. 206(g)(1), (2), and (4) and Code Sec. 436(b), (c), and (e) will not apply to a new plan (including a predecessor plan) for the first five plan years.[82]

However, the limit on plan amendments that increase benefit liabilities will apply if the employer is in bankruptcy proceedings during the five-year period. In addition, the limit on prohibited payments under ERISA Sec. 206(g)(3) and Code Sec. 436(d) applies to new plans.[83]

CCH POINTER: IRS final regulations require plan years under a plan to be aggregated with plan years under a predecessor plan.[84] Thus, a plan year would include plan years where the plan was maintained by a predecessor employer and the plan year of another DB plan maintained by the employer or predecessor employer within the preceding 5 years, if plan participants participated in the DB plan. [85] Pursuant to this rule, the only benefit limit that would apply under a plan that is not a successor plan during the first 5 years of its existence would be the limits applicable to accelerated benefit payments (e.g., lump-sum distributions) discussed above.[86]

Application of benefit restrictions after plan termination

The benefit limitations in effect immediately before the termination of a plan continue to apply. However, the limits on accelerated benefit distributions under Code Sec. 436(d) will not apply to prohibited payments that are made in order to terminate the plan in accordance with applicable law (e.g., the plan sponsor's purchase of an irrevocable commitment from an insurer to pay benefit liabilities to participants as required under ERISA Sec. 4041(b)(3)).[87]

Presumption of continued underfunding

Plans subject to a benefit limitation under ERISA Sec. 206(g)(1)-(4) and Code Sec. 436(b)-(e) for the preceding plan year will be presumed to be subject to the limit in the current year until the plan actuary certifies the actual adjusted funding target attainment percentage for the current year. Specifically, the adjusted funding target attainment percentage of the plan as of the valuation date of the plan for the current plan year will be presumed to be equal to the adjusted funding target

¶1493H

attainment percentage of the plan as of the valuation date for the preceding plan year.[88]

The final regulations issued in 2009 set forth rules for the application of the 436 benefit limits prior to and during the period the presumption of continued underfunding applies. The rules describe the interaction of the presumption with plan operations after the plan's enrolled actuary has issued a certification of the plan's AFTAP for the year. [89] The rules further address: the period during which no presumptions apply; modification of the plan's presumed adjusted funding target attainment percentage; and unpredictable contingent event benefits and amendments that increase liability during the period prior to certification.

The rules require a plan that, for any period during which a presumption applies, to apply the 436 limits as if the AFTAP were the presumed AFTAP, in accordance with rules of operation set forth in the final regulations. [90]

Reduction of funding balances. A plan's prefunding balance and funding standard carryover balance must be reduced under Code Sec. 436(f)(3) if the reduction would be sufficient to avoid the applicable limits on the presumed AFTAP. The final regulations compare a presumed adjusted funding target to the interim value of adjusted plan assets to determine the amount of any deemed reduction if the funding standard carryover balance and the prefunding balance. [91]

The presumed adjusted funding target attainment percentage is equal to the interim value of adjusted plan assets for the plan year, divided by the presumed AFTAP. In the event the presumed AFTAP for the plan year changes during the year, the rules regarding the deemed election to reduce funding balances must be reapplied, based on the new presumed AFTAP.

Presumption of underfunding following delayed actuarial certification. In the event the plan's enrolled actuary fails to certify the plan's actual adjusted funding target attainment percentage before the first day of the 10th month of the current year, the plan's adjusted funding target percentage will be conclusively presumed to be less than 60 percent as of the first day of such 10th month.[92] The first day of the 10th month will be deemed to be the valuation date of the plan for the current plan year, for purposes of applying the benefit limits.

The final rules clarify that, if the presumed AFTAP is presumed under Code Sec. 436(h)(2), to be less than 60 percent, no reduction in the funding standard carryover balance and prefunding balance is required. [93] Because a reduction in the balances may not be used to increase the presumed AFTAP to 60 percent, no prohibited payment may be made, no benefit accruals are permitted, and no plan amendments increasing benefits may take effect during the period the plan is deemed to have an AFTAP under 60 percent. However, unpredictable contingent event benefits may be paid if the plan sponsor makes a contribution equal to the increase in the funding target attributable to the unpredictable contingent event benefits.

Presumption of underfunding for "nearly underfunded" plans. A presumption of underfunding also applies to plans that were not subject to benefit limits under ERISA Sec. 206(g) or Code Sec. 436 in the preceding year, but that had an adjusted funding target attainment percentage for the prior plan year that was not more than 10 percentage points greater than the benefit limit threshold (e.g., 60 percent for lump-sum distributions or shut-down benefits). Under the rule, unless the plan's enrolled actuary certifies the actual adjusted funding target attainment percentage of the plan for the current plan year by the first day of the fourth month of the current plan year, the plan's adjusted funding target attainment percentage will be presumed, as of that day, to be 10 percentage points less than the adjusted funding target attainment percentage for the preceding plan year.[94] The first day of the fourth month of the current plan year will be deemed to be the valuation date of the plan for the current plan year for purposes of applying the benefit limitation. Thus, the benefit limitation will apply beginning on that date until the plan's actuary certifies the plan's adjusted funding target attainment percentage.

Certification of AFTAP. The enrolled actuary's certification of the AFTAP for a plan year must be made in writing, must be provided to the plan administrator, and must certify the plan's AFTAP for the plan year.[95] The certification must set forth the value of plan assets, the prefunding balance, the funding standard carryover balance, the value of the funding target used in the determination and other specified information. [96]

As an alternative to certifying a specific number for the plan AFTAP for the plan year, the IRS final regulations allow the enrolled actuary to certify during a plan year that the plan's AFTAP for that year is within a percentage "range" that is either: (1) less than 60 percent; (2) 60 percent or higher, but less than 80 percent; (3) 80 percent or higher; or (4) 100 percent or higher.[97] The range certification would end the application of the presumption, if: (a) the enrolled actuary follows up with a certification of the specific AFTAP (at any time prior to end of the plan year) before the first day of the 10th month of that year, and (b) the certified specific AFTAP is within the range of the earlier certification. Note, if the plan's enrolled actuary does not issue a certification of the specific AFTAP for the plan by the last day of that plan year, the AFTAP for the plan is retroactively deemed to be less than 60 percent as of the first day of the 10 month of the plan year. [98]

Change in certified AFTAP. In the event the certified percentage is superseded by a subsequent determination of the adjusted funding target attainment percentage (e.g., correction of prior error in certification), the later percentage must be applied for the portion of the plan year beginning on the date of the earlier certification. [99] The effect of the change varies depending on whether the change is material (i.e., impacts plan operation) or immaterial.

Benefits resume without plan amendment after end of limitation period

Following the expiration of the period during which a plan is subject to limits on lump-sum payments and other prohibited payments and the restrictions on benefit accruals under ERISA Sec. 206(g)(3) and (4) and Code Sec. 436(d) and (e), the forms of distribution and benefit accrual authorized under the plan will automatically resume, absent a contrary provision in the plan.[100]

---

[1] ERISA Sec. 206(g), as added by P.L. 109-280 (Pension Protection Act of 2006), Act Sec. 103(a);

Code Sec. 436, as added by P.L. 109-280 (Pension Protection Act of 2006), Act Sec. 113(a).

¶1493H

² Code Sec. 436(l), as added by P.L. 110-458 (Worker, Retiree, and Employer Recovery Act of 2008) Act Sec. 101(c)(2)(F).

³ IRS Reg. § 1.436-1.

⁴ IRS Reg. § 1.436-1(k)(3).

⁵ P.L. 109-280 (Pension Protection Act of 2006), Act Sec. 1107.

⁶ IRS Notice 2010-77, I.R.B. 2010-51, 12-20-10, at ¶ 17,146A, *modifying* IRS Notice 2009-97, I.R.B. 2009-52, at CCH PENSION PLAN GUIDE¶ 17,144D.

⁷ IRS Notice 2011-96, I.R.B. 2011-52, 12-27-11, at CCH PENSION PLAN GUIDE¶ 17,148Q.

⁸ *Ibid.*

⁹ *Ibid.*

¹⁰ERISA Sec. 206(g), as added by P.L. 109-280 (Pension Protection Act of 2006), Act Sec. 103(a); Code Sec. 436(b), as added by P.L. 109-280 (Pension Protection Act of 2006), Act Sec. 113(a).

¹¹ERISA Sec.206(g)(9)(A), as added by P.L. 109-280 (Pension Protection Act of 2006), Act Sec. 103(a); Code Sec.436(b), as added by P.L. 109-280 (Pension Protection Act of 2006), Act Sec. 113(a).

¹² ERISA Sec. 206(g)(9)(B), as added by P.L. 109-280 (Pension Protection Act of 2006), Act Sec. 103(a); Code Sec. 436(j)(2), as added by P.L. 109-280 (Pension Protection Act of 2006), Act Sec. 113(a).

¹³ IRS Reg. § 1.436-1(j)(1).

¹⁴ IRS Reg. § 1.436-1(j)(1)(ii)(B).

¹⁵ ERISA Sec. 303(g)(2)(B); Code Sec. 430(g)(2)(B).

¹⁶ IRS Notice 2008-21, I.R.B. 2008-7, Sec. III, at CCH PENSION PLAN GUIDE ¶ 17,138P; IRS Notice 2008-73, I.R.B. 2008-38, at CCH PENSION PLAN GUIDE ¶ 17,140H.

¹⁷ ERISA Sec.206(g)(10) as added by P.L. 110-458 (Worker, Retiree, and Employer Recovery Act of 2008), Act Sec. 101(c)(1)(G); Code Sec. 436(k), as added by P.L. 110-458 (Worker, Retiree, and Employer Recovery Act of 2008), Act Sec. 101(c)(2)(F).

¹⁸ ERISA Sec. 206(g)(1)(A), as added by P.L. 109-280 (Pension Protection Act of 2006), Act Sec. 103(a); Code Sec. 436(b)(1), as added by P.L. 109-280 (Pension Protection Act of 2006), Act Sec. 113(a); IRS Reg. § 1.436-1(b)(1).

¹⁹ ERISA Sec. 206(g)(1)(C)(i), as added by P.L. 109-280 (Pension Protection Act of 2006), Act Sec. 103(a); Code Sec. 436(b)(3)(A), as added by P.L. 109-280 (Pension Protection Act of 2006), Act Sec. 113(a).

²⁰ ERISA Sec. 206(g)(1)(C)(ii), as added by P.L. 109-280 (Pension Protection Act of 2006), Act Sec. 103(a); Code Sec. 436(b)(3)(B), as added by P.L.

109-280 (Pension Protection Act of 2006), Act Sec. 113(a); IRS Reg. § 1.436-1(j)(9).

²¹IRS Reg. § 1.436-1(b).

²²IRS Reg. § 1.436-1(b)(3)(i).

²³ ERISA Sec. 206(g)(1)(A), as added by P.L. 109-280 (Pension Protection Act of 2006), Act Sec. 103(a); Code Sec. 436(b)(1), as added by P.L. 109-280 (Pension Protection Act of 2006), Act Sec. 113(a).

²⁴IRS Reg. § 1.436-1(b)(4).

²⁵IRS Reg. § 1.436-1(b)(3)(ii).

²⁶IRS Reg. § 1.436-1(b)(3)(iii).

²⁷ ERISA Sec. 206(g)(1)(B)(i), as added by P.L. 109-280 (Pension Protection Act of 2006), Act Sec. 103(a); Code Sec. 436(b)(2)(A), as added by P.L. 109-280 (Pension Protection Act of 2006), Act Sec. 113(a); IRS Reg. § 1.436-1(b)(2) and (f)(2)(iii).

²⁸IRS Reg. § 1.436-1(f)(2)(iii)(A).

²⁹IRS Reg. § 1.436-1(f)(2)(iii)(B).

³⁰ ERISA Sec. 206(g)(2)(A), as added by P.L. 109-280 (Pension Protection Act of 2006), Act Sec. 103(a); Code Sec. 436(c)(1), as added by P.L. 109-280 (Pension Protection Act of 2006), Act Sec. 113(a); IRS Reg. § 1.436-1(c)(1).

³¹ ERISA Sec. 206(g)(2)(B)(i), as added by P.L. 109-280 (Pension Protection Act of 2006), Act Sec. 103(a); Code Sec. 436(c)(2)(i), as added by P.L. 109-280 (Pension Protection Act of 2006), Act Sec. 113(a); IRS Reg. § § 1.436-1(c)(2).

³² ERISA Sec. 206(g)(2)(B)(ii), as added by P.L. 109-280 (Pension Protection Act of 2006), Act Sec. 103(a); Code Sec. 436(c)(2)(ii), as added by P.L. 109-280 (Pension Protection Act of 2006), Act Sec. 113(a).

³³IRS Reg. § 1.436-1(f)(2)(iii)(B).

³⁴ ERISA Sec. 206(g)(2)(C), as added by P.L. 109-280 (Pension Protection Act of 2006), Act Sec. 103(a); Code Sec. 436(c)(3), as added by P.L. 109-280 (Pension Protection Act of 2006), Act Sec. 113(a).

³⁵IRS Reg. § 1.436-1(c)(4)(i)(A).

³⁶IRS Reg. § 1.436-1(c)(4)(i)(B) and (C).

³⁷IRS Reg. § 1.436-1(c)(4)(ii).

³⁸IRS Reg. § 1.436-1(c)(5).

³⁹ ERISA Sec. 206(g)(3)(C), as added by P.L. 109-280 (Pension Protection Act of 2006), Act Sec. 103(a); Code Sec. 436(d)(1), as added by P.L. 109-280 (Pension Protection Act of 2006), Act Sec. 113(a).

⁴⁰ERISA Sec. 206(g)(4), as added by P.L. 109-280 (Pension Protection Act of 2006), Act Sec. 103(a) Code Sec. 436(d)(4), as added by P.L. 109-280 (Pension Protection Act of 2006), Act Sec. 103(a).

[41] Preamble to IRS Reg. §1.436-1, at CCH PENSION PLAN GUIDE ¶24,509G.

[42] ERISA Sec. 206(g)(3)(E), as added by P.L. 109-280 (Pension Protection Act of 2006), Act Sec. 103(a); Code Sec. 436(d)(5), as added by P.L. 109-280 (Pension Protection Act of 2006), Act Sec. 113(a).IRS Reg. §1.436-1(j)(6).

[43] IRS Reg. §1.436-1(j)(2).

[44] ERISA Sec. 206(g)(3)(E), as amended by P.L. 110-458 (Worker, Retiree, and Employer Recovery Act of 2008), Act Sec. 101(c)(1)(D); Code Sec. 436(d)(5), as amended by P.L. 110-458 (Worker, Retiree, and Employer Recovery Act of 2008), Act Sec. 101(c)(2)(C).

[45] IRS Reg. §1.436-1(d)(1).

[46] ERISA Sec. 206(g)(3)(B), as added by P.L. 109-280 (Pension Protection Act of 2006), Act Sec. 103(a); Code Sec. 436(d)(2), as added by P.L. 109-280 (Pension Protection Act of 2006), Act Sec. 113(a).

[47] IRS Reg. §1.436-1(d)(2).

[48] ERISA Sec. 206(g)(3)(C), as added by P.L. 109-280 (Pension Protection Act of 2006), Act Sec. 103(a); Code Sec. 436(d)(3)(A), as added by P.L. 109-280 (Pension Protection Act of 2006), Act Sec. 113(a); IRS Reg. §1.436-1(d)(3)(i).

[49] PBGC Technical Update 07-4, 12-7-07, at CCH PENSION PLAN GUIDE ¶19,975Z-17.

[50] IRS Reg. §1.436-1(d)(3)(ii).

[51] IRS Reg. §1.436-1(d)(3)(iii)(D)(1).

[52] IRS Reg. §1.436-1(d)(3)(iii)(D)(2).

[53] IRS Reg. §1.436-1(d)(3)(iii)(D)(3).

[54] IRS Reg. §1.436-1(d)(3)(ii)(B).

[55] IRS Reg. §1.436-1(d)(5).

[56] IRS Reg. §1.436-1(d)(6).

[57] Preamble to IRS Reg. §1.436-1, at CCH PENSION PLAN GUIDE ¶24,509G.

[58] ERISA Sec. 206(g)(3)(C)(ii)(I), as added by P.L. 109-280 (Pension Protection Act of 2006), Act Sec. 103(a); Code Sec. 436(d)(3)(B)(i), as added by P.L. 109-280 (Pension Protection Act of 2006), Act Sec. 113(a); IRS Reg. §1.436-1(d)(3)(iv)(A).

[59] ERISA Sec. 206(g)(3)(C)(ii)(II), as added by P.L. 109-280 (Pension Protection Act of 2006), Act Sec. 103(a); Code Sec. 436(d)(3)(B)(ii), as added by P.L. 109-280 (Pension Protection Act of 2006), Act Sec. 113(a); IRS Reg. §1.436-1(d)(3)(iv)(B).

[60] ERISA Sec. 206(g)(4)(A), as added by P.L. 109-280 (Pension Protection Act of 2006), Act Sec. 103(a); Code Sec. 436(e)(1), as added by P.L. 109-280 (Pension Protection Act of 2006), Act Sec. 113(a).

[61] IRS Reg. §1.436-1(e)(1).

[62] IRS Reg. §1.436-1(f)(2).

[63] IRS Reg. §1.436-1(f)(2)(i)(B).

[64] Code Sec. 430(h)(2)(C).

[65] IRS Reg. §1.436-1(f)(2)(i)(C).

[66] Preamble to IRS Reg. §1.436-1, at CCH PENSION PLAN GUIDE ¶24,509G.

[67] IRS Reg. §1.436-1(f)(2)(iii)—(v).

[68] IRS Reg. §1.436-1(f)(2)(ii).

[69] Preamble to IRS Reg. §1.436-1, at CCH PENSION PLAN GUIDE ¶24,509G.

[70] ERISA Sec. 206(g)(5)(A)(i), as added by P.L. 109-280 (Pension Protection Act of 2006), Act Sec. 103(a); Code Sec. 436(f)(1)(A), as added by P.L. 109-280 (Pension Protection Act of 2006), Act Sec. 113(a); IRS Reg. §1.436-1(f)(3).

[71] ERISA Sec. 206(g)(5)(A)(ii), as added by P.L. 109-280 (Pension Protection Act of 2006), Act Sec. 103(a); Code Sec. 436(f)(1)(B), as added by P.L. 109-280 (Pension Protection Act of 2006), Act Sec. 113(a); IRS Reg. §1.436-1(f)(3)(ii).

[72] IRS Reg. §1.436-1(f)(3)(iii).

[73] IRS Reg. §1.436-1(f)(3)(iv).

[74] IRS Reg. §1.436-1(f)(3)(v).

[75] IRS Reg. §1.436-1(f)(3)(vi).

[76] ERISA Sec. 101(j)(1), as added by P.L. 109-280 (Pension Protection Act of 2006), Act Sec. 103(b).

[77] ERISA Sec. 101(j)(2), as added by P.L. 109-280 (Pension Protection Act of 2006), Act Sec. 103(b).

[78] IRS Reg. §54.4980F-1, A-9(g)(3)(ii)(B).

[79] IRS Employee Plan News, October 2009.

[80] ERISA Sec. 502(c)(4), as added by P.L. 109-280 (Pension Protection Act of 2006), Act Sec. 103(b)(2); ERISA Reg. §2560.502c-4.

[81] ERISA Reg. §2560.502c-4.

[82] ERISA Sec. 206(g)(6), as added by P.L. 109-280 (Pension Protection Act of 2006), Act Sec. 103(a); Code Sec. 436(g), as added by P.L. 109-280 (Pension Protection Act of 2006), Act Sec. 113(a).

[83] *Ibid.*

[84] IRS Reg. §1.436-1(a)(3).

[85] IRS Reg. §1.436-1(a)(3)(i).

[86] IRS Reg. §1.436-1(a)(3).

[87] IRS Reg. §1.436-1(a)(3)(ii).

[88] ERISA Sec. 206(g)(7), as added by P.L. 109-280 (Pension Protection Act of 2006), Act Sec. 103(a); Code Sec. 436(h)(1), as added by P.L. 109-280 (Pension Protection Act of 2006), Act Sec. 113(a).

[89] IRS Reg. §1.436-1(g).

[90] IRS Reg. §1.436-1(g)(2).

[91] IRS Reg. §1.436-1(g)(4).

[92] ERISA Sec. 206(g)(7)(B), as added by P.L. 109-280 (Pension Protection Act of 2006), Act Sec. 103(a); Code Sec. 436(h)(2), as added by P.L.

109-280 (Pension Protection Act of 2006), Act Sec. 113(a). IRS Reg. § 1.436-(h)(2).

[93]IRS Reg. § 1.436-1(g)(2)(ii)(B)(2).

[94] ERISA Sec. 206(g)(7)(C), as added by P.L. 109-280 (Pension Protection Act of 2006), Act Sec. 103(a); Code Sec. 436(h)(3), as added by P.L. 109-280 (Pension Protection Act of 2006), Act Sec. 113(a).

[95]IRS Reg. § 1.436-1(h)(3).

[96]IRS Reg. § 1.436-1(h)(4)(i)(A).

[97]IRS Reg. § 1.436-1(h)(4)(ii).

[98]Preamble to IRS Reg. § 1.436-1(h), at CCH PENSION PLAN GUIDE¶ 24,509G.

[99]IRS Reg. § 1.436-1(h)(4)(iii).

[100] ERISA Sec. 206(g)(8)(A), as added by P.L. 109-280 (Pension Protection Act of 2006), Act Sec. 103(a); Code Sec. 436(i)(1), as added by P.L. 109-280 (Pension Protection Act of 2006), Act Sec. 113(a).

¶ 1493I

MINIMUM FUNDING RULES APPLICABLE AFTER 2007: Waiver of Minimum Funding Requirements

Employer sponsors and members of a controlled group are jointly and severally liable for the required minimum funding contribution.[1] However, a temporary waiver of the minimum funding requirements may be provided to an employer that is unable to satisfy the minimum funding standard for a plan year without "substantial business hardship." An employer maintaining a single-employer defined benefit plan may be required to provide security to the plan as a condition for a waiver of the minimum funding standards. In addition, no plan amendment may that has the effect of increasing plan liabilities may generally be adopted during the waiver period.[2]

Joint and several liability for contributions

The minimum required funding contribution must be paid by the employer sponsor responsible for making contributions to the plan.[3] In the event the employer is a member of a controlled group (as defined under Code Sec. 414(b), (c), (m), or (o)), each member of the group is jointly and severally liable for the payment.[4] Note, joint and several liability also applies with respect to the funding contribution due under a multiemployer plan.

Waiver of minimum funding requirements: Business hardship

As under pre-2008 law, the Secretary of the Treasury is authorized to waive the minimum funding requirements applicable to all or any portion of the minimum funding standard for an employer that is unable to satisfy the minimum funding standard for a plan year without "temporary substantial business hardship." [5] The Secretary of the Treasury is similarly empowered to waive all or any portion of the minimum funding requirements applicable to a multiemployer plan in which 10 percent or more of the participating employers to the participating employer are unable to meet the minimum funding standards for a plan year without substantial business hardship.

Application of funding standard must be adverse to interests of plan participants. An employer under a single-employer plan or a multiemployer plan will not be able to justify a waiver of the minimum funding standard solely on the basis of business hardship. As under pre-2008 law, application of the minimum funding standard must also be adverse to the interests of plan participants in the aggregate.[6]

Relief of limited duration

The available funding relief is of a limited duration. As under pre-2008 law, the Treasury may not waive the minimum funding standards applicable to plan years beginning after 2007 for more than three of any 15 consecutive plan years for a single-employer plan or for more than five of any 15 consecutive plan years for a multiemployer plan.[7]

Waiver reduces minimum required contribution

In the event a waiver is granted for a single-employer plan, the minimum required contribution for the plan year will be reduced by the amount of the waived funding deficiency and amortized under ERISA Sec. 303(e) and Code Sec. 430(e) (see the discussion at ¶ 1493B).[8]

Waiver of funding deficiency. A "waived funding deficiency" refers to the portion of the minimum funding standard (determined without regard to the waiver) for a plan year that has been waived by the Secretary of the Treasury and not satisfied by employer contributions.[9] However, no portion of the minimum funding standard for a plan year that is attributable to any waived funding deficiency for any preceding plan year may be waiver.[10]

CCH POINTER: *Amortization of waived amount.* Under pre-2008 law, the amount waived for a single-employer plan could amortized in no more than five equal annual payments. With respect to a multiemployer plan, the amount waived could be amortized in no more than 15 equal annual payments. For plan years beginning after 2007, the waiver amortization charge is the aggregate total of the waiver amortization installments for the plan year with respect to the waiver amortization base for each of the five preceding plan years. [11] The waiver amortization installment is the amount necessary to amortize the waiver amortization base (i.e., the amount of the waived funding deficiency for the plan year).[12]

Note, the waiver amortization charge will be included in the determination of the minimum required contribution, under the rules discussed at ¶ 1493B.

Security for waiver of minimum funding standard

As under pre-2008 law, an employer maintaining a single-employer defined benefit plan may be required to provide security to the plan as a condition for a waiver of the minimum funding standards.[13] Any security provided as a condition for a waiver may be perfected and enforced only by the Pension Benefit Guaranty Corporation (PBGC) or, at the direction of the PBGC, by a contributing sponsor or member of the sponsor's controlled group).[14]

Treasury must provide notice to PBGC of waiver. The Secretary of the Treasury may not grant or modify a waiver without providing the PBGC with notice of the application for a waiver, and opportunity to comment on the application within 30 days after receipt of the notice.[15] The Treasury must consider comments

¶ 1493I

from the PBGC and from employee organizations representing plan participants that are submitted in writing to the Treasury.

Exception to security requirement

An exception to the security requirement is authorized for a waiver involving a plan with respect to which the sum of: (1) the aggregate unpaid minimum required contributions for the plan year (including any increase that would result from a denial of a pending waiver request) and all preceding plan years; and (2) the present value of all waiver amortization installments determined for the plan year and all succeeding plan years, is less than $1 million.[16]

Application and notice of waiver

Single-employer plans must file an application for a waiver of the minimum funding standard for a plan year no later than the 15th day of the 3rd month beginning after the close of the plan year.[17] A waiver will not be granted absent satisfactory evidence that the applicant has provided advance notice of the filing of the waiver application to each affected party (as defined under Code Sec. 4001(a)(21)). The notice must describe the extent to which the plan is funded for guaranteed benefits and for benefit liabilities.[18]

Plan amendments during waiver period

An employer may amend the pension plan during the period that a waiver of the minimum funding requirements is in effect. As under pre-2008 law, however, no plan amendment may be adopted during the waiver period that increases plan liabilities because of an increase in benefits, change in the accrual of benefits, or change in the rate at which benefits become nonforfeitable.[19] In addition, the amendment may not be adopted if a retroactive amendment that reduces the accrued benefits of a participant has been made in the preceding 12 months (24 months for multiemployer plans). [20]

Plan amendments that provide de minimis increase in benefits authorized. The restriction on plan amendments during the waiver period will not apply to plan amendments that the Secretary of the Treasury determines to be reasonable and which provides for only a de minimis increase in benefits.[21]

CCH POINTER: *IRS approval of change in funding method and valuation date.* As under Code Sec. 412(c)(8) in effect prior to 2008, a change in the plan's funding method or plan year may not take effect without approval by the Treasury.[22]

Retroactive plan amendments

A plan may retroactively adopt an amendment up to 2 ½ months after the close of the plan year (2 years after the close of the plan year for multiemployer plans). In the event the amendment does not reduce the accrued benefit of a participant, determined as of the beginning of the first plan year to which the amendment applies and as of the time the amendment is adopted, the plan administrator may elect to treat the amendment as having been made on the first day of the plan year. [23] However, no retroactive amendment reducing a participant's accrued benefit may be adopted unless the Treasury either approves the amendment or fails to disapprove the amendment within 90 days after being notified of the amendment.

Plans exempt from new rules

The new rules regarding liability for required contributions for plan years beginning after 2007 are limited to tax qualified plans under Code Sec. 401(a) and annuity plans under Code Sec. 403(a).[24] The rules do not apply to: profit-sharing or stock bonus plans; insurance contract plans; governmental plans; church plans; plans which have not provided for employer contributions after September 2, 1974; or plans established by fraternal orders under Code Sec. 501(c)(8) or Voluntary Employees's Beneficiary Associations (VEBAs) under Code Sec. 501(c)(9) if no contributions to the plan are made by employers of plan participants.[25]

---

[1] ERISA Sec. 302(b), as added by P.L. 109-280 (Pension Protection Act of 2006), Act Sec. 101(b); Code Sec. 412(b), as amended by P.L. 109-280 (Pension Protection Act of 2006), Act Sec. 111(a).

[2] ERISA Sec. 302(c)(1), as added by P.L. 109-280 (Pension Protection Act of 2006), Act Sec. 101(b); Code Sec. 412(c)(1)(A)(i), as amended by P.L. 109-280 (Pension Protection Act of 2006), Act Sec. 111(a).

[3] ERISA Sec. 302(b)(1), as added by P.L. 109-280 (Pension Protection Act of 2006), Act Sec. 101(b); Code Sec. 412(b)(1), as amended by P.L. 109-280 (Pension Protection Act of 2006), Act Sec. 111(a).

[4] ERISA Secs. 302(b)(2) and 302(d), as added by P.L. 109-280 (Pension Protection Act of 2006), Act Sec. 101(b); Code Sec. 412(c)(5)(B), as amended by P.L. 109-280 (Pension Protection Act of 2006), Act Sec. 111(a).

[5] ERISA Sec. 302(c)(1)(A)(i), as added by P.L. 109-280 (Pension Protection Act of 2006), Act Sec. 101(b); Code Sec. 412(b)(2) and 412(d)(3) as amended by P.L. 109-280 (Pension Protection Act of 2006), Act Sec. 111(a).

Factors indicating substantial business hardship include whether: (1) the employer is operating at an economic loss; (2) there is substantial unemployment or underemployment in the employer's industry; (3) sales and profits in the industry are depressed or declining; and (4) it is reasonable to expect that the plan will continue only if the waiver is granted (ERISA Sec.302(c)(2), as added by P.L. 109-280 (Pension Protection Act of 2006), Act Sec. 101(b); Code Sec.412(c)(2), as added by P.L. 109-280 (Pension Protection Act of 2006) Act Sec. 111(a)).

[6] ERISA Sec. 302(c)(1)(A)(ii), as added by P.L. 109-280 (Pension Protection Act of 2006), Act Sec. 101(b); Code Sec. 412(c)(1)(A)(ii), as amended by

P.L. 109-280 (Pension Protection Act of 2006), Act Sec. 111(a).

[7] ERISA Sec. 302(c)(1)(A), as added by P.L. 109-280 (Pension Protection Act of 2006), Act Sec. 101(b); Code Sec. 412(c)(1)(A), as amended by P.L. 109-280 (Pension Protection Act of 2006), Act Sec. 111(a).

[8] ERISA Sec. 302(c)(1)(B)(i), as added by P.L. 109-280 (Pension Protection Act of 2006), Act Sec. 101(b); Code Sec. 412(c)(1)(B)(i), as amended by P.L. 109.

[9] ERISA Sec. 302(c)(3), as added by P.L. 109-280 (Pension Protection Act of 2006), Act Sec. 101(b); Code Sec. 412(c)(3), as amended by P.L. 109-280 (Pension Protection Act of 2006), Act Sec. 111(a).

[10] ERISA Sec. 302(c)(1)(C), as added by P.L. 109-280 (Pension Protection Act of 2006), Act Sec. 101(b); Code Sec. 412(c)(1)(C), as amended by P.L. 109-280 (Pension Protection Act of 2006), Act Sec. 111(a).

[11] ERISA Sec.303(e)(1), as added by P.L. 109-280 (Pension Protection Act of 2006), Act Sec. 101(b); Code Sec.430(e)(1), as added by P.L. 109-280 (Pension Protection Act of 2006), Act Sec. 111(a).

[12] ERISA Sec.303(e)(2), as added by P.L. 109-280 (Pension Protection Act of 2006), Act Sec. 102(a); Code Sec.430(e)(2), as added by P.L. 109-280 (Pension Protection Act of 2006), Act Sec. 112(a).

[13] ERISA Sec. 302(c)(4)(A), as added by P.L. 109-280 (Pension Protection Act of 2006), Act Sec. 101(b); Code Sec. 412(c)(4)(A), as amended by P.L. 109-280 (Pension Protection Act of 2006), Act Sec. 111(a).

[14] ERISA Sec. 302(c)(4)(A)(ii), as added by P.L. 109-280 (Pension Protection Act of 2006), Act Sec. 101(b); Code Sec. 412(c)(4)(A)(ii), as amended by P.L. 109-280 (Pension Protection Act of 2006), Act Sec. 111(a).

¶1493I

[15] ERISA Sec. 302(c)(4)(B), as added by P.L. 109-280 (Pension Protection Act of 2006), Act Sec. 101(b); Code Sec. 412(c)(4)(B), as amended by P.L. 109-280 (Pension Protection Act of 2006), Act Sec. 111(a).

[16] ERISA Sec. 302(c)(4)(C)(i), as added by P.L. 109-280 (Pension Protection Act of 2006), Act Sec. 101(b); Code Sec. 412(c)(4)(C)(i), as amended by P.L. 109-280 (Pension Protection Act of 2006), Act Sec. 111(a).

[17] ERISA Sec. 302(c)(5)(A), as added by P.L. 109-280 (Pension Protection Act of 2006), Act Sec. 101(b); Code Sec. 412(c)(5)(A), as amended by P.L. 109-280 (Pension Protection Act of 2006), Act Sec. 111(a).

[18] ERISA Sec. 302(c)(6)(A), as added by P.L. 109-280 (Pension Protection Act of 2006), Act Sec. 101(b); Code Sec. 412(c)(6)(A), as amended by P.L. 109-280 (Pension Protection Act of 2006), Act Sec. 111(a).

[19] ERISA Sec. 302(c)(7)(A), as added by P.L. 109-280 (Pension Protection Act of 2006), Act Sec. 101(b); Code Sec. 412(c)(7)(A), as amended by P.L. 109-280 (Pension Protection Act of 2006), Act Sec. 111(a).

[20] ERISA Sec.302(c)(7), as amended by P.L. 110-458 (Worker, Retiree, and Employer Recovery Act of 2008), Act Sec. 101(a)(1)(B); Code Sec.412(c)(7), as amended by P.L. 110-458 (Worker, Retiree, and Employer Recovery Act of 2008), Act Sec. 101(a)(2)(B).

[21] ERISA Sec. 302(c)(7)(B)(i), as added by P.L. 109-280 (Pension Protection Act of 2006), Act Sec. 101(b); Code Sec. 412(c)(7), as amended by P.L. 109-280 (Pension Protection Act of 2006), Act Sec. 111(a).

[22] ERISA Sec. 302(d)(1), as added by P.L. 109-280 (Pension Protection Act of 2006), Act Sec. 101(b); Code Sec. 412(d)(1), as amended by P.L. 109-280 (Pension Protection Act of 2006), Act Sec. 111(a). Note, the reference in Code Sec.412(d)(1), as enacted by the Pension Protection Act, to the plan's "valuation date" was removed , in the interest of clarity, by P.L. 110-458 (Worker, Retiree, and Employer Recovery Act of 2008) Act Sec. 112, because a change in the valuation date is the equivalent of a change in the plan's funding method.

[23] ERISA Sec. 302(d)(2), as added by P.L. 109-280 (Pension Protection Act of 2006), Act Sec. 101(b); Code Sec. 412(d)(2), as added by P.L. 109-280 (Pension Protection Act of 2006), Act Sec. 111(a).

[24] Code Sec. 412(e)(1), as amended by P.L. 109-280 (Pension Protection Act of 2006), Act Sec. 111(a).

[25] Code Sec. 412(e)(2), as amended by P.L. 109-280 (Pension Protection Act of 2006), Act Sec. 111(a).

¶ 1493J

MINIMUM FUNDING RULES APPLICABLE AFTER 2007: Temporary Relief from Funding Rules for Certain Defined Benefit Plans

Certain defined benefit plans are provided a temporary exemption from the application of the new minimum funding rules. Specifically, the new single-employer defined benefit plan funding rules will not apply to certain multiple employer plans maintained by rural cooperatives for plan years beginning before January 1, 2017.[1] In addition, the new rules will not apply to certain Pension Benefit Guaranty Corporation (PBGC) settlement plans for plan years beginning before January 1, 2014.[2] Finally, the new rules will generally not apply to plans maintained by certain government defense contractors before plan years beginning before the earlier of (1) the date certain new rules regarding pension costs to be issued by the Cost Accounting Standards Board become effective or (2) January 1, 2011.[3] For plan years beginning after December 31, 2007, and before the first plan year for which the new funding rules apply, all such plans must use a specific interest rate to determine the plan's funding status.

Note, the Preservation of Access to Care for Medicare Beneficiaries and Pension Relief Act of 2010 (P.L. 111-192) authorized funding relief for underfunded plans with delayed effective dates, pursuant to which the plan's deficit reduction contribution may be calculated under a two-year look back rule and the plan's unfunded new liability may be determined under a 15-year amortization schedule (see CCH PENSION PLAN GUIDE ¶ 2970).[4]

Third segment rate

In applying the funding rules to multiple employer plans maintained by rural cooperatives, PBGC settlement plans, and plans of government defense contractors, for plan years beginning after December 31, 2007, and before the first plan year for which the new funding rules apply, a specific interest rate must be used.[5] The plans must use the third segment rate of the segmented yield curve adopted under the Pension Act (see ¶ 1493D). The yield curve consists of different interest rates applicable to benefits payable in three different time periods. The third segment normally applies to benefits that can be reasonably determined to be payable in 20 years.[6] The applicable interest rate, which will be determined by the Treasury, will be based on the corporate bond yield curve for the month, taking into account only that portion of the yield curve which is based on bonds maturing during periods beginning after the 20-year period beginning on the first day of the plan year.[7]

> **CCH POINTER:** Using the third segment rate to determine funding liabilities, rather than the entire segmented yield curve, will allow affected employers to apply a higher discount rate assumption when calculating the present value of plan liabilities. As a consequence, the present value of plan liabilities may be smaller than it would be if the entire yield curve approach required by the new law were used. A decrease in plan liabilities under a higher discount rate reduces the plan sponsor's funding obligation.

Funding relief extended to eligible charity plans

The delayed effective date and special interest rate rules for multiple employer plans of certain cooperatives have been expanded (generally effective for plan years beginning after 2007) to include eligible charity plans. A plan is an eligible charity plan for the year if the plan is maintained by more than one employer (determined without regard to Code Sec. 414(c)) and 100 percent of the employers are described in Code Sec. 501(c)(3) (i.e., tax-exempt organizations). [8]

The amendments relating to eligible charity plans apply to plan years beginning after December 31, 2007. However, a plan sponsor may elect to apply the provision to plan years beginning after December 31, 2008, pursuant to elections made at the time and in the manner prescribed by the Secretary of the Treasury and revocable only with the Secretary's consent.[9]

---

[1]P.L. 109-280 (Pension Protection Act of 2006), Act Sec. 104.

[2]P.L. 109-280 (Pension Protection Act of 2006), Act Sec. 105.

[3]P.L. 109-280 (Pension Protection Act of 2006), Act Sec. 106.

[4]Act Sec. 107(a) of P.L. 109-280 (Pension Protection Act of 2006), as added by P.L. 111-192 (Preservation of Access to Care for Medicare Beneficiaries and Pension Relief Act of 2010).

[5]P.L. 109-280 (Pension Protection Act of 2006), Act Secs. 104(b), 105(b), and 106(b).

[6] ERISA Sec. 303(h)(2)(B)(iii), as added by P.L. 109-280 (Pension Protection Act of 2006), Act Sec. 102(a).

[7] ERISA Sec. 303(h)(2)(C)(iii), as added by P.L. 109-280 (Pension Protection Act of 2006), Act Sec. 102(a).

[8] Act Sec. 104(d) of P.L. 109-280 (Pension Protection Act of 2006) , as added by P.L. 111-192 (Preservation of Access to Care for Medicare Beneficiaries and Pension Relief Act of 2010).

[9] Act Sec. 202(c) of P.L. 109-280 (Pension Protection Act of 2006) , as added by P.L. 111-192 (Preservation of Access to Care for Medicare Beneficiaries and Pension Relief Act of 2010).

¶ 1493K

MINIMUM FUNDING RULES APPLICABLE AFTER 2007: Minimum Funding Rules for Multiemployer Plans After 2007

The funding rules for multiemployer plans that were primarily found in Code Sec. 412 have been set out separately in new Code Sec. 431 and ERISA Sec. 304. The rules have been left largely intact, except for changes that will: (1) reduce the amortization periods for certain supplemental costs to 15 years, (2) change the amortization extension period and funding waiver interest rate to the plan rate, (3) tighten the reasonableness requirement for actuarial assumptions, (4) eliminate the alternative minimum funding standard, (5) make available an automatic five-year amortization extension with an additional five-year extension, and (6) provide a route for deemed approval of changes in the use of the shortfall funding method.

Note, a funding standard account must still be maintained for a multiemployer plan (unlike a single-employer plan).

Uniform 15-year amortization period

The 30-year amortization periods for various supplemental costs charged or credited to a multiemployer plan's standard funding account, effective after 2007, will be reduced to a uniform 15 year period. These changes apply to certain supplemental costs charged or credited to the standard funding account for amounts first amortized in plan years beginning in 2008 and thereafter. The amortization periods may be extended for up to 10 years (see below).

Charges to the funding standard account. Under the new law, the amortization period will be 15 years rather than 30 years for the following charges to the standard funding account:

1. unfunded past service liabilities under the plan on the first day of the first plan year for plans that come into existence on or after January 1, 2008,

2. net increases in unfunded past service liabilities arising from plan amendments, and

3. net losses resulting from changes in actuarial assumptions.[1]

Credits to standard funding account

Under the new law, the amortization period is 15 years rather than 30 years for the following credits to the standard funding account:

1. net decreases in unfunded past service liabilities arising from plan amendments, and

2. net gains resulting from changes in actuarial assumptions.[2]

Experience gains and losses

The amortization period for experience gains and losses remains the same at 15 years.[3] To the extent that a plan amendment increases the unfunded past service liability by reason of a short-term increase in benefits payable under the plan for a period that does not exceed 14 years from the effective date of the amendment, the 15-year amortization period is changed to the number of years of the period of increased benefits.[4]

> **CCH POINTER:** The change brings the multiemployer plan amortization periods in line with the single-employer plan amortization periods. Shortening the amortization periods results in quicker reflection of funding liability changes to the standard funding account. It also increases the volatility of pension funding obligations. Plan sponsors will have to fund increased costs by making larger yearly outlays because the payments will be spread over fewer years.

> ***Funding relief provided for multiemployer plans that suffered investment losses.*** A plan sponsor of a multiemployer plan that meets a solvency test may use either one or both of two special funding relief rules for either or both of the first two plan years that end after August 31, 2008. One method allows separate amortization of net investment losses. The other method (discussed below under "Expanded asset valuation smoothing period") allows an extended smoothing period for asset valuation. Note, use of both the amortization period relief and the smoothing relief for a plan year is subject to specified restrictions.

> ***Solvency test.*** The solvency test is met only if the plan actuary certifies that the plan is projected to have sufficient assets to pay expected benefits and anticipated expenditures over the amortization period in a timely manner, taking into account the changes in the funding standard account caused by the relief elected by the plan. [5]

> *Applicable period for solvency determination.* The applicable period for purposes of a solvency certification under Code Sec. 431(b)(8)(C) is the period beginning with the plan year for which the solvency certification is made. If the special amortization rule (but not the special asset valuation rule) applies, the period will end with the last plan year in the 30-plan year period beginning with the eligible loss year. If the special asset valuation rule (but not the special amortization rule) applies, the period will end with the last plan year in the 10-year period over which the change in unfunded accrued liability attributable to the change in asset valuation method is amortized.[6] If both the special amortization rule and the special asset valuation rule apply, the period ends with the last plan year in the 30-plan year period over which the change in unfunded accrued liability attributable to the change in asset valuation methods is amortized.

¶1493K

Effect of solvency certification. The solvency certification must be made before a formal decision is made to apply either or both of the special funding rules. In the event the plan passes the solvency test as of the plan year in which a formal decision is made to apply the special funding rules, the plan will be deemed to pass the test as of any preceding plan year.[7]

Actuarial basis for solvency certification. The plan actuary must use the same actuarial basis (e.g., actuarial assumptions, data, and terms of an existing funding improvement or rehabilitation plan) in making the solvency certification that is used in certifying the plan funded status under Code Sec. 432(b)(3) for the plan year in which the solvency certification is made. [8]

Deadline for electing funding relief. The deadline for making a formal decision to apply either or both of the special funding rules is the earliest of: (1) the deadline for certification of the plan's status under Code Sec. 432(b)(3) for the first plan year beginning on or after January 1, 2011; (2) the date of certification of the plan's status under Code Sec. 432(b)(3) for the first plan year beginning on or after January 1, 2011, or (3) June 30, 2011.[9]

Election to stop applying amortization relief. Plan sponsors may make the formal decision to discontinue applying the special amortization rule as of any future plan year. [10] As a consequence, any portion of an eligible net investment loss recognized in a subsequent year will be taken into account under the generally applicable rules of Code Sec. 431(b)(2) or (3).

Notice requirements. Once a formal decision to elect the special funding rules is made, the plan sponsor has 30 days (from the deadline for the decision to apply for the relief) in which to give participants and beneficiaries a notice of the election. Note, the notice need only be provided once, even if the funding relief under Code Sec. 431(b)(8) applies for more than one year. [11]

Notice to PBGC. The Pension Benefit Guaranty Corporation must also be sent a copy of the notice provided to participants and beneficiaries by the later of: (1) 30 days after the plan sponsor makes a formal election to use the special funding rules, or (2) January 18, 2011.[12].

Note, if the plan sponsor makes separate decisions on different dates regarding which of the special funding rules to apply, or the plan years for which the relief will apply, separate notices must be provided to the PBGC with respect to each application of the special funding rules.

Contents of Notice. The notice must disclose: (1) the name of the plan, taxpayer identification number, and plan number for the plan, (2) an explanation of which of the special funding rules apply and the plan year or years for which they apply, (3) the effect of the application of the special funding rules (i.e., the amortization of losses beyond the otherwise applicable 15-plan-year period and/or the recognition of losses in the value of plan assets over a period as long as 10 years), (4) a general description of the effect of applying the special funding rules, including the fact that applying the special rules will decrease the amount of required minimum contributions that are taken into account in determining the appropriate contribution rates under collective bargaining agreements and may also affect the plan's status under

Code Sec. 432(b) for the current and future plan years, (5) a statement that the plan is not permitted to increase benefits during the two plan years immediately following any plan year in which either or both of the special funding rules apply, unless certain conditions are met, and (6) the name, address, and telephone number of the plan administrator or other contact person from whom more information may be obtained. [13]

Certification of status. Once a formal decision to apply either or both of the special funding rules under Code Sec. 431(b)(8) has been made, the application of the special rules must be taken into account in any contemporaneous or subsequent certification of status required under Code Sec. 432(b)(3) and in any contemporaneous or subsequent required adoption or update of a funding improvement plan or rehabilitation plan. [14]

Recertification of plan status. In the event a formal decision to apply the special funding rules is made after the certification of a plan's status for a plan year, the application of the special funding rules will not be reflected in the certification of the plan's status until the following plan year. However, the plan sponsor is permitted to request that the plan actuary redetermine the plan's status under Code Sec. 432(b)(3) for a plan year, taking into account the application of the special funding rules. [15]

Amortization of net investment losses. Under the relief, a multiemployer plan that passes a solvency test may treat the portion of any experience loss or gain attributable to net investment losses incurred in either or both of the first two plan years ending after August 31, 2008, as an item separate from other experience losses. The amount would be amortized in equal annual installments (until fully amortized) over the period: (1) beginning with the plan year in which such portion is first recognized in the actuarial value of assets, and (2) ending with the last plan year in the 30-plan year period beginning with the plan year in which such net investment loss was incurred.[16]

Duration of relief. The IRS has clarified that the special amortization rule under Code Sec. 431(b)(8)(A) applies beginning with the first recognition year with respect to an eligible net investment loss and ending with the earliest of: (a) the plan year in which the entire unrecognized balance of the eligible net investment loss as of the preceding plan year is recognized in the actuarial value of assets, (b) the plan year for which, if the special amortization rule were to apply to establish a new special amortization base, the amortization period applicable to that base would be 15 plan years, or (c) the plan year for which the plan sponsor chooses to end the application of the special amortization rule. [17]

Separate application of relief to losses in two loss years. If the special amortization rule in Code Sec. 431(b)(8)(A) applies with respect to net investment losses incurred in two eligible loss years, the relief will apply separately to each portion of a net experience gain or loss that is attributable to an eligible net investment loss incurred in a different eligible loss year. [18]

Note, if a plan takes advantage of this special amortization relief for any plan year, no extension of the amortization period will be allowed under Code Sec.

431(d). If an extension was granted for any plan year prior to the election, such election may not result in the amortization period exceeding 30 years.[19]

Net investment losses. Net investment losses are to be determined in the manner prescribed by the Secretary of the Treasury on the basis of the difference between actual and expected returns. [20]

Calculating eligible net investment loss. The IRS has clarified that for plans with valuation dates on either the first day of the plan year or the last day of the plan year, the net investment loss incurred in an eligible loss year (an "eligible net investment loss") is equal to the excess of the expected market value of plan assets as of the end of the eligible loss year over the market value of the assets as of that date, including any difference attributable to a criminally fraudulent investment arrangement. [21] The expected market value of plan assets as of the end of the eligible loss year is defined as equal to (1) the market value of plan assets at the beginning of the eligible loss year, plus (2) contributions made during the eligible loss year, minus (3) disbursements made during the eligible loss year, with all such amounts adjusted to the end of the eligible loss year with interest at the plan's valuation rate for the plan year.

The actuarial value of assets under the plan's asset valuation method may, alternatively, be determined using the difference between the actual return of the plan year and the expected return on the actuarial value of assets for the plan year. Under this calculation, the eligible net investment loss for the plan year is equal to that actual return minus the expected return. [22]

If the valuation date for a plan year is neither the first day of the plan year nor the last day of the plan year, eligible net investment loss for the plan year is calculated as of the valuation date, based on the difference between the actual return (determined on a market value basis as of the valuation date) and the expected return (based on either market or actuarial value, as the case may be, as of the valuation date for the prior year). [23]

Bifurcation of next experience loss. In the event a plan has a net experience loss for a year in which a portion of an eligible net investment loss is recognized in the value of assets (i.e., recognition year), the net experience loss is bifurcated into: (a) the portion attributable to the eligible net investment loss and (b) the portion not attributable to the eligible net investment loss (i.e., the portion attributable to other gains or losses).[24]

A separate amortization base applies to the portion attributable to the eligible net investment loss. That portion is amortized over the period beginning with the recognition year and ending with the last plan year in the 30-plan-year period beginning with the eligible loss year. Accordingly, if a plan uses a valuation date of the first day of the plan year, so that a portion of an eligible net investment loss is first recognized in the actuarial value of assets for the plan year after the eligible loss year, the amortization period for that portion is the 29-plan-year period beginning with that recognition year. [25]

Alternative bifurcation rule. An alternative bifurcation applies if the net experience loss for the plan year is less than the amount attributable to the eligible net

¶1493K

investment loss, if the amount attributable to the eligible net investment loss is an actuarial gain, or if there is an overall experience gain for the plan year. Under such circumstances, two amortization bases are established. [26]

The initial balance of the first base (gain base or loss base) is the amount attributable to the eligible net investment loss and amortized over the extended period described above.

The initial balance of the second base (gain base or a loss base) is the amount that, when combined with the initial balance of the first base, equals the plan's net experience gain or loss for that plan year. The second base is amortized over 15 plan years.

Net investment loss in two eligible loss years. If the special amortization rule applies with respect to net investment losses incurred in two eligible loss years, the governing rules will apply separately to each portion of a net experience gain or loss that is attributable to an eligible net investment loss incurred in a different eligible loss year. [27]

Criminally fraudulent investment arrangement. Net investment loss includes any difference attributable to any criminally fraudulent investment arrangement. Whether an arrangement is criminally fraudulent is determined under rules substantially similar to the Code Sec. 165 rules used by the IRS for determining whether a loss from a Ponzi scheme can be taken as a theft loss rather than a capital loss. [28]

Full funding limit

Multiemployer plans are subject to a full funding limit. The full funding limit is the excess (if any) of: (1) the accrued liability (including normal cost) under the plan (determined under the entry age normal funding method if such accrued liability cannot be directly calculated under the funding method used for the plan), over (2) the lesser of: (a) the fair market value of the plan's assets, or (b) the value of such assets. [29]

Current liability under prescribed mortality tables

The IRS has prescribed rules under Code Sec. 431(c)(6)(D) applicable to the mortality tables that are generally to be used in determining current liability. The standards governing the mortality tables are to be the same as the standards for mortality tables prescribed under Code Sec. 430(h)(3)(A) for single employer defined benefit plans (see ¶ 1493D).

In addition, the IRS is required under PPA '06 to establish mortality tables that are to be used, in lieu of the generally applicable tables, for individuals who are entitled to benefits under the plan on account of disability. [30] Separate tables are to be established for individuals whose disabilities occurred in plan years beginning before January 1, 1995, and for individuals whose disabilities occurred or occur in plan years beginning after December 31, 1994. However, the mortality table for individuals whose disabilities occur in plan years beginning after December 31, 1994 will apply only to individuals who are considered disabled under Title II of the Social Security Act. [31]

¶1493K

The IRS, in Rev. Rul. 96-87, set forth mortality tables that were to be used under Code Sec. 412(l)(7) for disabilities occurring in plan years beginning before January 1, 1995, and for disabilities occurring in plan years beginning after December 31, 1994. The IRS, in March 2008, indicated that until further guidance is issued, the rules of Rev. Rul. 96-7 (including the disability mortality table and the rules governing the determination of when a benefit is payable on account of disability) will continue to apply for purposes of the new requirements under Code Sec. 431(c)(6)(D)(v). [32]

In July 2008, the IRS issued final regulations, effective for plan years beginning on or after January 1, 2008, that apply the mortality assumptions specified for single employer plans under IRS Reg. § 1.430(h)(3)-1(a)(2) to the determination of a multiemployer plan's current liability under Code Sec. 431(c)(6). A multiemployer plan is permitted to apply either the static mortality tables or the generational mortality tables provided under IRS Reg. § 1.430(h)(3)-1(a)(3) and (4). However, a multiemployer plan may not use substitute mortality tables that are authorized under IRS Reg. § 1.430(h)(2)-2. [33]

The mortality tables specified under IRS Reg. § 1.430(h)(3)-1 are detailed at ¶ 1493D.

Extension of amortization period

The sponsor of a multiemployer plan may apply to the IRS for an automatic extension of the period required to amortize any unfunded past service liability, investment loss, or experience loss. The IRS must extend the amortization period for a period of up to five years. However, the plan's actuary must certify that: (1) absent the extension, the plan would have an accumulated funding deficiency in the current plan year or any of the nine succeeding plan years, (2) the plan sponsor has adopted a plan to improve the plan's funding status, (3) taking into account the extension, the plan is projected to have sufficient assets to pay its expected benefit liabilities and other anticipated expenditures in a timely manner, and (4) required advance notice has been provided to affected parties. Note, the automatic extension will not apply with respect to applications submitted after December 31, 2014. [34]

Additional five-year amortization period. The plan sponsor can apply for an additional extension of the amortization period of up to five years over and above the automatic five-year extension (i.e., "alternative extension"). The plan must show that the additional extension would provide adequate protection for participants and their beneficiaries, and denial of the extension would (1) substantially risk the continuation of the pension plan or might cause a substantial curtailment of retirement benefits or employee compensation, and (2) be adverse to the interests of the participants. The IRS must act on the application within 180 days after submission. If the IRS rejects the application, it must notify the plan of the specific reason for the rejection. [35]

Procedures for applying for extension of amortization period. The IRS has provided procedures for submitting an application for a ruling on an amortization extension under Code Sec. 431(d). [36]

Parties authorized to submit applications. An application for approval to extend the period of years required to amortize an unfunded liability must be submitted by the plan sponsor (i.e., board of trustees of the plan) or by an authorized representative of the applicant. The application must be signed by an authorized trustee who is a current member of the board or by an authorized representative of the applicant. [37] Note, IRS cautions that an individual will not qualify as an authorized representative of the applicant merely on account of being an administrator or trustee of the plan.

Advance notice requirement for amortization period requests. Within 14 days prior to the date of the application, the applicant must provide a copy of a written notice to all affected parties. [38]

Affected parties. Affected parties include participants, beneficiaries of deceased participants, alternate payees under an applicable qualified domestic relations order (QDRO), employee organizations representing participants, and the Pension Benefit Guaranty Corporation (PBGC). [39] The notice must include a description of the extent to which the plan is funded for guaranteed benefits and for benefit limitations. Note, the IRS must take into consideration any comments by an affected party in response to the notice. [40]

Consolidation of extension applications. An applicant may request the automatic extension and the alternative extension in a single application. [41] The combined application will be considered in a single ruling request. However, the IRS may approve the automatic extension without approving the alternative extension.

Application for automatic extension. An applicant for an automatic extension must furnish the following information: (1) a list of the charge bases for which an extension of the amortization periods is requested; (2) the length of the extension of the amortization period being requested for each of the charge bases listed (note, no extension will be granted with respect to an amortization period for net investment losses under Code Sec. 431(b)(8)(A)(i)); and (3) a certification by the plan's actuary that (based on reasonable assumptions): (a) absent the extension the plan would have accumulated a funding deficiency in the current plan year or any of the succeeding plan years, (b) the plan sponsor has adopted a plan to improve the plan's funding status, (c) the plan is projected to have sufficient assets to timely pay expected benefits and anticipated expenditures over the extended amortization period, and (d) the required notice to affected parties has been provided. [42] In addition, the notice must disclose whether a prior application for an automatic or alternative amortization extension under Code Sec. 431(d) or Code Sec. 412(e), as in effect before the effective date of PPA, was or was not approved, including, the length of any approved extension, and, alternatively the reason for the denial of an extension and an explanation of why the reason for the denial no longer applies.

Note, these procedures will remain in effect until December 31, 2014.

Alternative extension applications. An applicant for an alternative extension must furnish appropriate evidence that the extension of the amortization period would carry out the purposes of ERISA and the PPA and would provide adequate protection for participants and their beneficiaries. In addition, the applicant must provide evidence that the failure to permit the extension would (1) result in a substantial risk to the voluntary continuation of the plan, or a substantial curtailment of pension benefit levels or employee compensation and (2) be adverse to the interests of plan participants in the aggregate. [43]

Information about participating employers. Applicants are required to furnish general facts about the participating employers; the financial condition of the principal employers (e.g., latest available annual financial report of the employer and other members of the controlled group (including balance sheets, profit and loss statements, and cash flow statements)); information concerning the extension of the amortization period (including: a list of the charge bases for which the extension is requested; the amount of each base, and the years remaining in the amortization period; the reasons why the extension is needed; the requested length of the amortization period extension; and projections of the funding standard account credit balance/accumulated funding deficiencies, actuarial value of assets, market value of assets, current liabilities, and funding ratios); and facts concerning the pension plan (including the most recent actuarial period, plus any available actuarial reports for the preceding two plan years; a description of how the plan is funded; a list of the contributions actually paid to the plan in each month (from the 24th month prior to the beginning of the fist year for which the extension would apply through the date of the application); and the appropriate contribution required to meet the minimum funding standard for the first plan year for which the extension would apply. [44]

Checklist. The IRS has provided a checklist that may be used by a plan sponsor (or authorized representative) submitting an application for an alternative extension. The checklist must be signed and dated by the applicant or authorized representative and placed on top of the application (see CCH Pension Plan Guide ¶ 17,299T-42).

Update information in event of bankruptcy. In the event that a significant number of contributing employers or any of the principal employers file a bankruptcy petition after the application for an extension of an amortization period is submitted, the applicant must provide the IRS with updates to required information. The IRS is especially interested in updates to financial information regarding the principal employer and information related to the extension of the amortization period. [45]

Deadline for submitting extension applications. All extension applications must be submitted by the 15th day of the third calendar month following the last day of the first plan year for which the extension is intended to take effect. [46] The IRS will consider applications for extensions submitted after this date only upon a showing of good cause. It is generally advised that an application for alternative extension not be submitted earlier than 90 days prior to the end of the plan year for which the extension is requested. This 90-day period, however, does not apply to applications for an automatic extension.

The IRS will notify the applicant of the date on which it has received all of the required information. However, the IRS will close the file, without issuing a ruling, on a submission for which all of the required documentation is not provided in a timely manner.

Model Notice. The IRS has provided a Model Notice of Action for Amortization Extension (see CCH PENSION PLAN GUIDE ¶ 17,299T-42).

Interest rates for funding waivers and amortization extension periods

The new rules eliminate the special rate of interest based on the short-term federal rate for funding waivers and amortization period extensions that apply in plan years beginning before 2008. A plan, beginning in the 2008 plan year, must charge or credit the funding standard account with interest consistent with the rate or rates that the plan uses to determine costs.[47]

Extensions of amortization periods that are granted pursuant to applications filed on or before June 30, 2005 can continue to be applied by using the old special rate, which was based on the federal short-term rate.[48] As under pre-2008 law, the plan's general funding interest rate, which is used to calculate costs for purposes of determining its current liabilities, has to be within a permissible range. The permissible range is not more than 5 percent above, and not more than 10 percent below, the weighted average of the rates of interest on 30-year Treasury securities during the 4-year period ending on the last day before the beginning of the plan year.[49] Previously, the permissible range was not more than 10 percent above and 10 percent below the weighted average of the 30-year Treasury bond rates.

Reasonableness of each actuarial assumption and method

The reasonableness requirement is changed for actuarial assumptions and methods used to determine costs, liabilities, interest rates and other factors with respect to multiemployer plans is modified for plan years beginning after 2007. Rather than requiring reasonable actuarial assumptions and methods in the aggregate, each actuarial assumption and method used must be reasonable, taking into account the plan's experience and reasonable expectations. Also, as under pre-2008 law, the actuarial assumptions and methods must, in combination, offer the actuary's best estimate of anticipated experience under the plan.[50]

Valuation of plan assets. In determining the charges and credits to be made to the plan's funding standard account maintained for a multiemployer plan, the value of a plan's assets may be calculated pursuant to any reasonable actual method of valuation that takes into account fair market value and which is permitted under regulations to be prescribed by the Treasury Secretary.[51] Accordingly, the actuarial value of a plan's assets under a reasonable actuarial valuation method may be used instead of fair market value. A reasonable actuarial valuation method generally may include a smoothing methodology that takes into account reasonable expected investment returns and the average value of the plan assets, to the extent the smoothing or averaging period does not exceed the five most recent plan years, including the current plan year.

In addition, any reasonable actuarial valuation method used by the plan must result in a value of plan assets that is not less than 80 percent of the current fair

¶1493K

market value of the asset and not more than 120 percent of the current fair market value. [52]

Note, the actual valuation method is considered to be part of the plan's funding method. The same method must be used each plan year. A change in the valuation method must be approved by the Treasury Secretary. [53]

Expanded asset valuation smoothing period. The 2010 Pension Relief Act allows a multiemployer plan that meets a solvency test (i.e., plan projected to have sufficient assets to pay expected benefits and anticipated expenditures over the amortization period in a timely manner) to change its asset valuation method in order to spread (i.e., recognize) the difference between expected and actual returns for either or both of the first two plan years ending after August 31, 2008, over a period of not more than 10 years.

The change in the asset valuation method to extend the period (up to 10 years) over which an eligible net investment loss is recognized in the value of an asset will be automatically approved, even if the difference between expected and annual returns for other plan years is spread over a different number of years. [54] Note, a plan that does not use market value as the asset valuation method will need to obtain approval from the IRS before implementing the change.

Asset valuation corridor. The relief may not result in a value of assets (when compared to the current fair market value of the plan assets) that is outside the asset valuation corridor. The 2010 Pension Relief Act, however, expanded the asset valuation corridor by providing that for either or both of the first two plan years beginning after August 31, 2008, the value of plan assets at any time shall not be less than 80 percent of the current fair market value of assets and not greater than 130 percent (up from 120 percent) of the current fair market value. [55]

Note, the expanded valuation corridor is available whether or not the plan sponsor increases the period for spreading the difference between expected and actual returns under its asset valuation method. In the event a plan elects to take advantage of this smoothing relief, the plan's asset valuation method is not to be treated as unreasonable solely because of the changes in such method, and such changes shall be deemed approved by the Secretary of the Treasury[56]

Amortization of reduction in unfunded accrued liability. In the event a plan elects to use both amortization period relief (see above) and smoothing relief for any plan year, the plan must treat any reduction in unfunded accrued liability resulting from the application of this section as a separate experience amortization base that would be amortized in equal annual installments (until fully amortized) over a period of 30 plan years, rather than the period such liability would otherwise be amortized. [57]

Restrictions on benefit increases. If a multiemployer plan elects amortization or smoothing relief for any plan year, a plan amendment increasing benefits may not go into effect during either of the two plan years immediately following such plan year unless either: (1) the plan actuary certifies that (a) any such increase is paid for out of additional contributions that are not allocated to the plan as of the end of the immediately preceding plan year, and (b) the plan's funded percentage and projected credit balances for such plan years are reasonably expected to be at least as high as such percentage and balances would have been if the benefit increase had not been adopted, or (2) the amendment is required as a condition of plan qualification or to comply with other applicable law. [58]

Note, the relief afforded under Code Sec. 431(b)(8) generally took effect on the first day of the first plan year ending after August 31, 2008. However, the restriction on plan amendments under Code Sec. 431(b)(8)(D) is effective on June 25, 2010. [59] Accordingly, benefit increases that were effective on or after June 25, 2010 are subject to the restriction, even if adopted before that date. [60]

Notice requirements. A plan sponsor of a plan using either of these forms of relief must notify participants and beneficiaries of the plan, and inform the Pension Benefit Guaranty Corporation (PBGC) of the relief used. [61]

Deemed approval of shortfall funding method

Multiemployer plans may elect to determine charges to the funding standard account pursuant to a shortfall funding method. Under the shortfall method, the net shortfall charge to the funding standard account is computed on the basis of estimated units of service or production for which a certain amount per unit is charged. For example, charges can be computed based on hours worked under a collective bargaining agreement. Except for the first plan year, for which the plan can elect to use the shortfall method without IRS approval, a plan has to obtain IRS approval to adopt or discontinue use of the shortfall method.[62] Under the rules effective after 2007, a multiemployer plan will be deemed to have the IRS's approval to adopt, use, or cease to use the shortfall funding method for plan years beginning after 2007, and beginning before 2015, if: (1) the plan has not used the shortfall funding method during the preceding five-year period and, (2) no extension of an amortization period with respect to the plan is in effect or has been in effect for such five-year period. [63]

Limit on plan amendments during use of shortfall funding method . Plan amendments increasing benefits generally cannot be adopted while the shortfall funding method is in use [64] The provision should not be construed as affecting a plan's ability to adopt the shortfall funding method with IRS approval or its right to change funding methods as otherwise permitted.[65] Deemed approval of the shortfall method will not apply to plan years beginning after December 31, 2014. [66]

Sunset provision. The provisions of, and amendments relating to, the use of the shortfall funding method by multiemployer plans that are collectively bargained plans will not apply to plan years beginning after December 31, 2014.[67]

[1] ERISA Sec. 304(b)(2), as added by P.L. 109-280 (Pension Protection Act of 2006), Act Sec. 201(a); Code Sec. 431(b)(2), as added by P.L. 109-280 Pension Protection Act of 2006, Act Sec. 211(a).

[2] ERISA Sec. 304(b)(3), as added by P.L. 109-280 (Pension Protection Act of 2006), Act Sec. 201(a); Code Sec. 431(b)(3), as added by P.L. 109-280 Pension Protection Act of 2006, Act Sec. 211(a).

[3] ERISA Sec. 304(b)(2) and (3), as added by P.L. 109-280 (Pension Protection Act of 2006), Act Sec. 201(a); Code Sec. 431(b)(2) and (3), as added by P.L. 109-280 Pension Protection Act of 2006, Act Sec. 211(a).

[4] ERISA Sec. 304(b)(7)(G), as added by P.L. 109-280 (Pension Protection Act of 2006), Act Sec. 201(a); Code Sec. 431(b)(7)(G), as added by P.L.

109-280 Pension Protection Act of 2006), Act Sec. 211(a).

5 ERISA Sec. 304(b)(8)(C) and Code Sec. 431(b)(8)(C), as added by P.L. 111-192 (Preservation of Access to Care for Medicare Beneficiaries and Pension Relief Act of 2010).

6IRS Notice 2010-83, Q S-1, I.R.B. 2010-51, 12-20-10, at CCH PENSION PLAN GUIDE ¶ 17,146C.

7IRS Notice 2010-83, Q S-2, I.R.B. 2010-51, 12-20-10, at CCH PENSION PLAN GUIDE ¶ 17,146C.

8IRS Notice 2010-83, Q S-3, I.R.B. 2010-51, 12-20-10, at CCH PENSION PLAN GUIDE ¶ 17,146C.

9IRS Notice 2010-83, Q D-2, I.R.B. 2010-51, 12-20-10, at CCH PENSION PLAN GUIDE ¶ 17,146C.

10IRS Notice 2010-83, Q D-3, I.R.B. 2010-51, 12-20-10, at CCH PENSION PLAN GUIDE ¶ 17,146C.

11IRS Notice 2010-83, Q N-1, I.R.B. 2010-51, 12-20-10, at CCH PENSION PLAN GUIDE ¶ 17,146C.

12IRS Notice 2010-83, Q N-5 and N-6, I.R.B. 2010-51, 12-20-10, at CCH PENSION PLAN GUIDE ¶ 17,146C.

13IRS Notice 2010-83, Q N-3, I.R.B. 2010-51, 12-20-10, at CCH PENSION PLAN GUIDE ¶ 17,146C.

14IRS Notice 2010-83, Q C-1, I.R.B. 2010-51, 12-20-10, at CCH PENSION PLAN GUIDE ¶ 17,146C.

15IRS Notice 2010-83, Q C-3, I.R.B. 2010-51, 12-20-10, at CCH PENSION PLAN GUIDE ¶ 17,146C.

16 ERISA Sec. 304(b)(8)(A)(i) and Code Sec. 431(b)(8)(C)(A)(i), as added by P.L. 111-192 (Preservation of Access to Care for Medicare Beneficiaries and Pension Relief Act of 2010).

17IRS Notice 2010-83, Q A-8, I.R.B. 2010-51, 12-20-10, at CCH PENSION PLAN GUIDE ¶ 17,146C.

18IRS Notice 2010-83, Q A-9, I.R.B. 2010-51, 12-20-10, at CCH PENSION PLAN GUIDE ¶ 17,146C.

19 ERISA Sec. 304(b)(8)(A)(ii) and Code Sec. 431(b)(8)(C)(A)(ii), as added by P.L. 111-192 (Preservation of Access to Care for Medicare Beneficiaries and Pension Relief Act of 2010).

20IRS Notice 2010-83, Q A-1, I.R.B. 2010-51, 12-20-10, at CCH PENSION PLAN GUIDE ¶ 17,146C.

21IRS Notice 2010-83, Q A-1, I.R.B. 2010-51, 12-20-10, at CCH PENSION PLAN GUIDE ¶ 17,146C.

22IRS Notice 2010-83, Q A-1, I.R.B. 2010-51, 12-20-10, at CCH PENSION PLAN GUIDE ¶ 17,146C.

23IRS Notice 2010-83, Q A-1, I.R.B. 2010-51, 12-20-10, at CCH PENSION PLAN GUIDE ¶ 17,146C.

24IRS Notice 2010-83, Q A-3, I.R.B. 2010-51, 12-20-10, at CCH PENSION PLAN GUIDE ¶ 17,146C.

25IRS Notice 2010-83, Q A-3, I.R.B. 2010-51, 12-20-10, at CCH PENSION PLAN GUIDE ¶ 17,146C.

26IRS Notice 2010-83, Q A-4, I.R.B. 2010-51, 12-20-10, at CCH PENSION PLAN GUIDE ¶ 17,146C.

27IRS Notice 2010-83, Q A-4, I.R.B. 2010-51, 12-20-10, at CCH PENSION PLAN GUIDE ¶ 17,146C.

28 ERISA Sec. 304(b)(8)(A)(iii) and Code Sec. 431(b)(8)(C)(A)(iii), as added by P.L. 111-192 (Preservation of Access to Care for Medicare Beneficiaries and Pension Relief Act of 2010); IRS Notice 2010-83, Q A-2, I.R.B. 2010-51, 12-20-10, at CCH PENSION PLAN GUIDE ¶ 17,146C.

29Code Sec. 431(c)(6), as added by P.L. 109-280 (Pension Protection Act of 2006), Act Sec. 211(a).

30Code Sec. 431(c)(6)(D)(v)(I)(, as added by P.L. 109-280 (Pension Protection Act of 2006), Act Sec. 211(a).

31Code Sec. 431(c)(6)(D)(v)(II)(, as added by P.L. 109-280 (Pension Protection Act of 2006), Act Sec. 211(a).

32IRS Notice 2008-29, I.R.B. 2008-12, 3-5-08, at CCH PENSION PLAN GUIDE ¶ 17,138W.

33IRS Reg. § 1.431(c)(6)-1.

34 ERISA Sec. 304(d)(1), as added by P.L. 109-280 (Pension Protection Act of 2006), Act Sec. 201(a); Code Sec. 431(d)(1), as added by P.L. 109-280 (Pension Protection Act of 2006).

35 ERISA Sec. 304(d)(1), as added by P.L. 109-280 (Pension Protection Act of 2006), Act Sec. 201(a); Code Sec. 431(d)(1), as added by P.L. 109-280 (Pension Protection Act of 2006).

36 Rev. Proc. 2008-67, 2008-48, I.R.B. 1211, at CCH PENSION PLAN GUIDE ¶ 17,299S-80 (applicable to plan years starting after 2007); Rev. Proc. 2010-52, I.R.B. 2010-52, 12-27-10, at CCH PENSION PLAN GUIDE ¶ 17,299T-42 (applicable to ruling requests submitted on or after January 1, 2011). For ruling requests submitted prior to January 1, 2011, plan sponsor may follow the new rules or continue to follow Rev. Proc. 2008-67.

37Rev. Proc. 2010-52, Sec. 3.01, I.R.B. 2010-52, 12-27-10, at CCH PENSION PLAN GUIDE ¶ 17,299T-42.

38Rev. Proc. 2010-52, Sec. 3.05, I.R.B. 2010-52, 12-27-10, at CCH PENSION PLAN GUIDE ¶ 17,299T-42.

39 ERISA Sec. 4001(a)(21).

40 ERISA Sec. 304(d)(3), as added by P.L. 109-280 (Pension Protection Act of 2006), Act Sec. 201(a); Code Sec. 431(d)(3), as added by P.L. 109-280 (Pension Protection Act of 2006).

41Rev. Proc. 2010-52, Sec. 3.07, I.R.B. 2010-52, 12-27-10, at CCH PENSION PLAN GUIDE ¶ 17,299T-42.

42Rev. Proc. 2010-52, Sec. 4.01, I.R.B. 2010-52, 12-27-10, at CCH PENSION PLAN GUIDE ¶ 17,299T-42.

[43]Rev. Proc. 2010-52, Sec. 5.01, I.R.B. 2010-52, 12-27-10, at CCH Pension Plan Guide ¶ 17,299T-42.

[44]Rev. Proc. 2010-52, Sec. 5.01(3), I.R.B. 2010-52, 12-27-10, at CCH Pension Plan Guide ¶ 17,299T-42.

[45]Rev. Proc. 2010-52, Sec. 7, I.R.B. 2010-52, 12-27-10, at CCH Pension Plan Guide ¶ 17,299T-42.

[46]Rev. Proc. 2010-52, Sec. 6, I.R.B. 2010-52, 12-27-10, at CCH Pension Plan Guide ¶ 17,299T-42.

[47] ERISA Sec. 304(b)(6), as added by P.L. 109-280 (Pension Protection Act of 2006), Act Sec. 201(a); Code Sec. 431(b)(6), as added by P.L. 109-280 Pension Protection Act of 2006, Act Sec. 211(a).

[48]P.L. 109-280 (Pension Protection Act of 2006), Act Secs. 201(d) and 211(b).

[49] ERISA Sec. 304(c)(6)(E)(ii), as added by P.L. 109-280 (Pension Protection Act of 2006), Act Sec. 201(a); Code Sec. 431(c)(6)(E)(ii), as added by P.L. 109-280 Pension Protection Act of 2006, Act Sec. 211(a).

[50] ERISA Sec. 304(c)(3), as added by P.L. 109-280 (Pension Protection Act of 2006), Act Sec. 201(a); Code Sec. 431(c)(3), as added by P.L. 109-280 Pension Protection Act of 2006, Act Sec. 211(a).

[51] ERISA Sec. 304(c)(2), as added by P.L. 109-280 (Pension Protection Act of 2006), Act Sec. 201(a); Code Sec. 431(c)(2), as added by P.L. 109-280 Pension Protection Act of 2006, Act Sec. 211(a).

[52]IRS Reg. § 1.412(c)(2)-1(b).

[53]Code Sec. 412(d)(2).

[54]IRS Notice 2010-83, Q V-2, I.R.B. 2010-51, at CCH Pension Plan Guide ¶ 17,146C.

[55] ERISA Sec. 304(b)(8)(B)(i) and Code Sec. 431(b)(8)(B)(i), as added by P.L. 111-192 (Preservation of Access to Care for Medicare Beneficiaries and Pension Relief Act of 2010).

[56] ERISA Sec. 304(b)(8)(B)(ii) and Code Sec. 431(b)(8)(B)(ii), as added by P.L. 111-192 (Preservation of Access to Care for Medicare Beneficiaries and Pension Relief Act of 2010).

[57] ERISA Sec. 304(b)(8)(B)(iii) and Code Sec. 431(b)(8)(B)(iii), as added by P.L. 111-192 (Preservation of Access to Care for Medicare Beneficiaries and Pension Relief Act of 2010).

[58] ERISA Sec. 304(b)(8)(D) and Code Sec. 431(b)(8)(D), as added by P.L. 111-192 (Preservation of Access to Care for Medicare Beneficiaries and Pension Relief Act of 2010).

[59] P.L. 111-192 (Preservation of Access to Care for Medicare Beneficiaries and Pension Relief Act of 2010), Act Sec. 211(b)(2).

[60]IRS Notice 2010-83, Q R-2, I.R.B. 2010-51, at CCH Pension Plan Guide ¶ 17,146C.

[61] ERISA Sec. 304(b)(8)(E) and Code Sec. 431(b)(8)(E), as added by P.L. 111-192 (Preservation of Access to Care for Medicare Beneficiaries and Pension Relief Act of 2010).

[62] IRS Reg. § 1.412(c)(1)-2(i).

[63]P.L. 109-280 (Pension Protection Act of 2006), Act Sec. 201(b)(2).

[64]P.L. 109-280 (Pension Protection Act of 2006), Act Sec. 201(b)(4).

[65]P.L. 109-280 (Pension Protection Act of 2006), Act Sec. 201(b)(5).

[66]P.L. 109-280 (Pension Protection Act of 2006), Act Sec. 221(c).

[67]P.L. 109-280 (Pension Protection Act of 2006), Act Secs. 221(c)(1) and 221(c).

¶ 1493L

MINIMUM FUNDING RULES APPLICABLE AFTER 2007: Additional Funding Rules for Significantly Underfunded Multiemployer Plans

Multiemployer plans that are so underfunded as to be in "endangered" or "critical" status will be required, generally effective after 2007, to adopt funding improvement and rehabilitation plans and take certain actions to improve their funding status over a multi-year period.[1] Excise taxes and civil penalties may apply if a plan does not adopt or comply with a required funding improvement or rehabilitation plan.

¶1493L

All multiemployer plans will be further required to obtain an annual actuarial certification regarding their funding status. Special funding and operational requirements apply for plans that are certified to be in "endangered" or "critical" status.[2]

The new requirements will generally apply to plan years beginning after 2007 for multiemployer plans in effect on July 16, 2006.[3] However, the requirements are subject to a sunset provision, under which no new certifications of endangered or critical status will be required for plan years beginning after 2014. The requirements will continue to apply to plans that are already in endangered or critical status at the end of 2014.

Actuarial certification of funded status

Not later than the 90th day of each plan year, the actuary for every multiemployer plan must certify to the IRS and to the plan sponsor whether or not the plan is in endangered status and whether or not it is or will be in critical status for the year. If a plan has previously been certified as endangered or critical and is currently in a funding improvement or rehabilitation period, the actuary must certify whether or not the plan is making the scheduled progress in meeting the requirements of its funding improvement or rehabilitation plan.[4] If the actuary fails to provide the required certification in time, the Secretary may assess a penalty of up to $1,100 per day against the plan administrator.[5]

Projections of present value of plan liabilities. In determining a plan's status or its progress, the actuary must use reasonable actuarial estimates, assumptions and methods that offer the actuary's best estimate of anticipated experience under the plan in making projections of the current value of the plan's assets and the present value of the plan's liabilities. [6] Those projections are made for each plan year as of the beginning of the year.

Notice of certification. If the plan actuary certifies that a plan is in or will be in endangered or critical status for a plan year, the plan sponsor must, within 30 days after the date of the certification, provide notification of the plan's status to the participants and beneficiaries, the bargaining parties, the Pension Benefit Guaranty Corporation (PBGC), and the Secretary of Labor. [7] The bargaining parties include any employer who has an obligation to contribute under the plan and any union that represents the employees of such an employer.

Notice must explain reduction in benefits. If the plan actuary certifies that the plan is or will be in critical status, the notice must include an explanation of the possibility that adjustable benefits may be reduced for participants and beneficiaries who begin receiving benefits after the notice is provided.[8] The Department of Labor is to develop a model notice for this purpose.[9]

Proposed Model Notice of Critical Status. The Employee Benefits Security Administration has issued a proposed regulation that provides a Model Notice of Critical Status that may be used by multiemployer defined benefit pension plans to notify plan participants and others that the plan is in critical funding status and of the possibility that adjustable benefits may be reduced or eliminated (see CCH PENSION PLAN GUIDE ¶ 20,537L). [10] The IRS has also advised that the sponsor of a plan in critical status may use the model notice to notify participants and others of the status of the plan in satisfaction of its content obligations under Code Sec. 432(b)(3)(D).

The proposed regulation will become effective 60 days after the date of publication of the final regulation in the Federal Register. However, because ERISA Sec. 305(b)(3)(D) and Code Sec. 432(b)(3)(D) are effective with respect to plan years beginning after 2007, for purposes of notices required to be furnished before the effective date of the final regulation, EBSA, the Treasury Department and the IRS will view utilization of the model notice as satisfying the notice requirements of ERISA Sec. 305(b)(3)(D) and Code Sec. 432(b)(3)(D).

Provide notice to DOL and PBGC. Plans are required to furnish a copy of the notice to EBSA and may mail notices to the U.S. Department of Labor, Employee Benefits Security Administration, Public Disclosure Room, N-1513, 200 Constitution Ave., NW, Washington, DC 20210. Alternatively, notices may be e-mailed to criticalstatusnotice@dol.gov.

Plans must also furnish a copy of the notice to the Pension Benefit Guaranty Corporation, at Multiemployer Program Division, Pension Benefit Guaranty Corporation, 1200 K Street, NW, Suite 930, Washington, DC 20005. Alternatively, notices may be e-mailed to multiemployerprogram@pbgc.gov.

Note, although the model notice relates to plans in critical status, EBSA has suggested that the model may be useful in preparing notices required to be furnished by plans in endangered status as well. However, EBSA also cautions that plans may not use the model notice to satisfy the notice requirements under ERISA Sec. 305(e)(8)(C). [11]

Election to delay designation of multiemployer plans as in endangered or critical status. The Worker, Retiree, and Employer Recovery Act of 2008 authorizes the sponsor of a multiemployer plan to make an election, pursuant to which the funding status of the plan for its first plan year beginning during the period starting on October 1, 2008, and ending on September 30, 2009, will be the same as the status of the plan as determined under Code Sec. 432(b)(3) and ERISA Sec. 305(b)(3) for the plan year preceding such plan year. [12] Thus, a calendar year plan that is not in critical or endangered status for 2008 may elect to retain its non-critical and non-endangered status for 2009 and a plan that was in either critical or endangered status for 2008 may elect to retain such status for 2009. [13]

In addition, if the plan was in endangered or critical status for the plan year preceding the plan year beginning during the October 1, 2008 to October 1, 2009 period, the plan would not be required to update the funding improvement plan or schedules (in accordance with the requirements of Code Sec. 432(c)(6) and ERISA Sec. 305(c)(6)(applicable to endangered plans) or Code Sec. 432(e)(3)(B) and ERISA Sec. 305(e)(3)(B) (applicable to critical plans)), until the plan year following the first plan year beginning during the relief period. [14]

Note, however, in order to avoid the requirement, the plan must update its funding improvement plan or rehabilitation plan unless it makes a 204 election, even if its Code Sec. 432 funding status for the election year would be the same, whether or not an election was made. [15]

¶1493L

CCH POINTER: *Effect of 204 election.* The 204 election enabled a multiemployer plan to be operated in accord with its funding status as determined pursuant to the election, rather than the Code Sec. 432 status to which the actuary certified for the election year. Accordingly, the sponsor of a multiemployer plan that would have been in critical status for the election year, but for the election to freeze funding status, could not assess employer surcharges under Code Sec. 432(e)(7), reduce adjustable benefits, or restrict lump-sum distributions under Code Sec. 432(f)(2).[16]

The applicable rules are detailed at CCH PENSION PLAN GUIDE ¶ 3139A.

Critical status

A multiemployer plan is in critical status for a plan year if the plan actuary determines that it meets any one of four specified tests as of the beginning of the plan year (see CCH PENSION PLAN GUIDE ¶ 3139A).[17] Generally, a plan that is less than 65% funded will be in critical status if it is projected that the plan: it will have an accumulated funding deficiency within five years; or (2) will not have sufficient assets to pay the promised benefits within seven years.

Any plan, regardless of its funded percentage, will be in critical status if it is projected that:

1. it will have an accumulated funding deficiency within four years;
2. it will not have sufficient assets to pay promised benefits within five years; or
3. all of the following are true:

    (a) the present value of benefits for inactive participants is greater than the present value of benefits for active participants;

    (b) expected contributions are less than the sum of the plan's normal cost and the interest on its unfunded liabilities; and

    (c) the plan will have an accumulated funding deficiency within five years.

Endangered status

A multiemployer plan is in endangered status if the plan actuary determines that it is not in critical status for the plan year but that it meets either of two tests at the beginning of the plan year.[18]

Under the first test, a plan is in endangered status if its funded percentage is less than 80 percent.[19] Under the second test, a plan is in endangered status if it has an accumulated funding deficiency for the current plan year or is projected to have an accumulated funding deficiency for any of the next six plan years, taking into account any extension of amortization periods (under Code Sec. 431(d) and ERISA Sec. 304(d) (see ¶ 1493K)).[20]

Seriously endangered plans. A plan that satisfies both of the tests discussed above is in "seriously endangered" status.[21]

CCH POINTER: Under Accounting Standards Update No. 2011-09 (Compensation–Retirement Benefits–Multiemployer Plans (Subtopic 715-80): Disclosures about an Employer's Participation in a Multiemployer Plan) the Financial Accounting Standards Board will require employers to disclose the following information regarding their financial obligations to multiemployer pension plans: the amount of employer contributions made to each significant plan and to all plans in the aggregate; an indication of whether the employer's contributions represent more than 5% of total contributions to the plan; an indication of which plans, if any, are subject to a funding improvement plan; the expiration date(s) of the collective bargaining agreement(s) and any minimum funding arrangements; the most recent certified funded status of the plan, as determined by the plan's "zone status" (if the zone status is not available, an employer will be required to disclose whether the plan is less than 65% funded, between 65% and 80% funded, and at least 80% funded); and a description of the nature and effect of any changes affecting comparability for each period in which a statement of income is presented. Note, however, employers are not required to disclose estimated withdrawal liability.

For public entities, the enhanced disclosures will be required for fiscal years ending after December 15, 2011. For nonpublic entities, the enhanced disclosures will be required for fiscal years ending after December 15, 2012. However, early application will be permitted.

Requirements for endangered plans: Funding improvement plans

An endangered plan must adopt and implement a funding improvement plan (FIP) designed to allow the plan to meet applicable funding improvement benchmarks during a funding improvement period. In addition, the plan must satisfy special operational requirements after the date of the certification and throughout the funding improvement period.[22]

Funding improvement plan. The sponsor of an endangered plan must adopt a FIP not later than the 330th day (i.e., 240 days after the required 90 day period for actuarial certification of endangered status) of the plan year for which the plan is first certified as endangered (the initial determination year).[23] A FIP is a plan that specifies the actions, including options or a range of options to be proposed to the bargaining parties, which based on reasonably anticipated experience and under reasonable actuarial assumptions will result in the plan meeting certain funding improvement benchmarks.[24] Specifically, the FIP will provide contribution and benefit schedules, including a default schedule setting out the reductions in future benefit accruals necessary for the endangered plan to improve its status.

Two benchmarks measure success of FIP. The FIP must be designed to allow an endangered plan to achieve two benchmarks. If the plan is not in seriously endangered status, the adoption of the measures contained in the FIP must be projected to result in the plan (1) reducing its unfunded percentage, by the end of a ten-year funding improvement period, by at least 33 percent; and (2) not having an accumulated funding deficiency for any plan year during the funding improvement period. [25] The applicable rules are illustrated at see CCH PENSION PLAN GUIDE ¶ 3139A.

Funding improvement period. The funding improvement period is generally the 10-year period beginning on the first day of the first plan year beginning after the second anniversary of the adoption of the funding improvement plan.[26]

For "seriously endangered" plans, the time frame for the period for the funding improvement plan is extended to 15 years. [27]

Election of temporary extension of funding improvement period. The Worker, Retiree, and Employer Recovery Act of 2008 (effective for plan years beginning after December 31, 2007) authorized a temporary extension of the funding period for endangered plans from 10 to 13 years (18 years for seriously endangered plans).

A plan must specifically elect the extension.[28] However, the temporary extension is not available unless the plan has elected to freeze its funding status in order to avoid certification as endangered or critical.

Time frame for election. The election must be made by the earlier of: (1) the last day of the plan year as of which the election is being made, or (2) the date a funding improvement plan, rehabilitation plan, or update is adopted that takes the election into account. Initially, the election was not required to have been made before April 30, 2009.[29] However, subsequently, the IRS extended the date before which no election may be required to June 30, 2009. [30]

Contents of election. The content requirements of the election under Worker Act Sec. 204, detailed above, also apply to election under Worker Act Sec. 205 to extend the funding improvement period.

Interaction of election to freeze funding status with election of extension of funding improvement period. As noted, a plan may elect for plan years beginning in 2009, to freeze its funding status as neither endangered nor critical, rather than operate in accord with an actuarial certification of endangered or critical status for that year.

However, the IRS cautions that, if the plan is subsequently certified as being in endangered or critical status, for the plan year beginning in 2010, the election to extend the funding improvement period or rehabilitation period to 13 years (or 18 years) would not be available, because the initial endangered year or initial critical year of the plan (the year when the plan first enters endangered or critical status) would not be until 2010 (when the election to extend the funding improvement period is no longer available). [31]

By contrast, if the 204 election is not made, the plan may make the election to extend the funding improvement period to 13 (or 18 years) for as long as the funding improvement plan or rehabilitation plan remains in effect. [32]

A plan sponsor may elect for the 2009 plan year to freeze the plan's funding status and to extend the funding improvement period to 13 years. However, the IRS explains that, if the plan is subsequently certified as being in critical status for the 2010 plan year, the election to extend the funding improvement period would no longer be applicable, as the funding improvement plan would need to be replaced by a rehabilitation plan. In addition, IRS advises that the sponsor would not then be able to extend the rehabilitation period to 13 years, because the initial critical year for the plan would not be until 2010 (at which time the 204 election would not be available).[33]

Requirements for endangered plans: Operational requirements

Special operational requirements apply to endangered plans. At no time during the funding plan adoption period or the funding improvement period may the plan sponsor adopt any collective bargaining agreement or participation agreement that provides for (1) lower contributions for any participants, (2) a suspension of contributions with respect to any period of service, or (3) any new direct or indirect exclusion of younger or newly hired employees from plan participation.[34]

Excise taxes may be imposed on noncompliant endangered plans

Several excise tax liabilities may arise with respect to an endangered plan. An employer that fails to timely make a contribution required under an endangered plan's FIP is subject to an excise tax in the amount of 100 percent of the contribution. [35] If a seriously endangered plan fails to satisfy the applicable benchmarks by the end of the funding improvement period, the plan is treated as having an accumulated funding deficiency (subject to the excise tax under Code Sec. 4971) for the last year of the funding improvement period (and each succeeding year until the applicable benchmarks are met) equal to the greater of the amount of contributions necessary to meet the applicable benchmarks or the amount of the plan's accumulated funding deficiency as calculated under the general rules. [36] For endangered plans, these excise taxes are imposed in addition to the usual excise tax on accumulated funding deficiencies under Code Sec. 4971. [37]

Penalties. The Secretary of Labor may assess a penalty of up to $1,100 per day against a plan sponsor for each violation of the requirement to: (1) timely adopt a required funding improvement (or rehabilitation) plan; or (2) in the case of a plan that is not seriously endangered, meet the applicable benchmarks by the end of the funding improvement period for the plan. [38]

Final rules specify procedures for assessment of civil penalties. EBSA final regulations provide rules and procedures: governing the computation of the maximum penalty; detailing the circumstances under which the penalty may be assessed or waived; and specifying the means by which a plan sponsor may contest a liability assessment. [39] Note, the final rules also apply to penalties applicable to the failure of a critical plan to adopt a rehabilitation plan (see below).

Partial violations subject to penalty. The final regulations clarify that a failure or refusal, in whole or in part, to adopt a funding improvement plan (or rehabilitation plan) or to meet the applicable benchmarks will subject the plan sponsor to penalty. [40]

Amount of penalty. The amount of the penalty assessed for each separate violation (computed from the date of the violation) is determined by the DOL, taking into consideration the degree or willfulness of the violation. [41] The final rules further indicate that, although the statutorily prescribed penalty is $1,100 per day, the penalty may be adjusted under the Federal Civil Penalties Inflation Adjustment Act.

¶1493L

Notice requirements. Prior to assessing a penalty, the DOL is required to provide the plan sponsor with written notice of its intent to assess a penalty, the amount of the penalty, the period to which the penalty applies, and the reasons the penalty is being assessed (e.g., violation of ERISA Sec. 305(c)(1) or ERISA Sec. 305(e)(1)). [42]

Waiver of penalty. The DOL is empowered to reduce or waive all or part of the authorized penalty, in the event the plan sponsor can show evidence of compliance with the statutory requirements or circumstances mitigating the noncompliance. [43] Under such circumstances, the plan sponsor is required to file a written statement of reasonable cause (including a perjury declaration) within 30 days from the date of service of the notice from the DOL of the intent to assess a penalty. [44] The failure to file a timely statement would be deemed to be a waiver of the right to appear and contest the facts alleged in the DOL notice, and an admission of the facts alleged for purposes of any proceeding involving the assessment of the penalty. [45] The notice would then become a final order 45 days from the date of service of the notice.

Joint and several liability. All persons responsible as the plan sponsor for the failure or refusal (in whole or in part) to adopt a funding improvement plan or a rehabilitation plan, or to meet the applicable benchmarks, are jointly and severally liable for the failure. [46] Thus, the EBSA explains, the entire joint board of trustees would be jointly and severally liable for any failure. [47]

In addition, the final regulations do not account for the allocation of fault. Each member of the board of trustees would be jointly and severally liable for an assessed penalty, whether or not, for example, a trustee voted for or against a rehabilitation or improvement plan. [48]

Personal liability may not be paid by plan. Any penalty assessed under ERISA Sec. 502(c)(8) is a personal liability. [49] Accordingly, the liability assessment may not be paid by the plan. The payment of the penalty from plan assets, EBSA cautions would not constitute a reasonable expense of plan administration under ERISA Sec. 403 and ERISA Sec. 404. [50]

Requirements for critical plans: Rehabilitation plan

A plan in critical status must adopt and implement a rehabilitation plan designed to enable the plan to emerge from critical status (and must satisfy certain special operational requirements, discussed below) throughout the rehabilitation plan adoption and rehabilitation periods.[51] A plan in critical status is not subject to the general funding requirements if it has adopted and is in compliance with the requirements of a rehabilitation plan. [52]

The sponsor of a critical plan must adopt a rehabilitation plan not later than the 330th day of the plan year (i.e., 240 days after the 90 day period for actual certification of critical status) for which the plan is first certified as critical (the initial critical year). [53] The rehabilitation plan must provide contribution and benefit schedules, including a default schedule, that set out reductions in future benefit accruals necessary for the plan to emerge from critical status by the end of the rehabilitation period. Note, a plan in critical status is not subject to the general funding requirements if it has adopted and is in compliance with the requirements of a rehabilitation plan.[54]

Schedule of revised benefit/contribution structures. A rehabilitation plan must include one or more schedules showing revised benefit and/or contribution structures which, if adopted, may reasonably be expected to allow the plan to emerge from critical status. The schedules must reflect reductions in future benefit accruals and adjustable benefits and increases in contributions that the sponsor determines are reasonably necessary to emerge from critical status. One such schedule, the default schedule, must assume that there are no increases in contributions under the plan other than those necessary to emerge from critical status after future benefit accruals and other benefits have been reduced as much as the law allows [55] The schedules must include an allowance for funding the benefits of participants for whom contributions are not currently required. [56]

CCH POINTER: *Imposition of default schedules.* The FIP and the rehabilitation plan are subject to collective bargaining. However, if, upon the expiration of a collective bargaining agreement, an employer and its employees' union are unable to reach a new agreement that includes appropriate contribution or benefit schedules, the plan sponsor must impose the default schedule.

The date by which the default schedule will be imposed is 180 days after the expiration of the old collective bargaining agreement. The date may not be accelerated by a certification that the parties are at an impasse.[57]

In addition, note that the failure to make contributions as required by an imposed default schedule is a delinquent contribution, just like a failure to make a contribution required by a collective bargaining agreement, and is redressable in the same way. Thus, plan fiduciaries can sue to enforce the contribution schedule. [58]

Emergence from critical status. A plan has emerged from critical status when the plan actuary certifies, in its annual certification, that the plan is not projected to have an accumulated funding deficiency for the current year or any of the next nine plan years, without use of the shortfall method or any extension of amortization periods (under Code Sec. 431(d) and ERISA Sec. 304(d) (see ¶ 1493K). [59]

Rehabilitation period. The rehabilitation period for a critical plan is generally the 10-year period beginning on the first day of the first plan year beginning after the second anniversary of the adoption of the rehabilitation plan.[60]

Temporary extension of rehabilitation period. The Worker, Retiree, and Employer Recovery Act of 2008 (effective for plan years beginning after December 31, 2007) authorized a temporary extension of the rehabilitation period for critical plans from 10 to 13 years [61] As with the extension of the funding improvement period for endangered plans, the critical plan must elect the relief and must have elected to freeze its funding status, pursuant to the relief provided by the Worker Act discussed above.

Cutbacks of adjusted benefits in critical plans

¶1493L

Although the anti-cutback rule of ERISA Sec. 204(g) generally prohibits reductions in benefits that have already been earned, certain cutbacks are allowed when a plan is in critical status. The sponsor of a critical plan must make cutbacks in "adjustable benefits" that it decides are appropriate. Generally, no cutback may be made in the benefits of any participant or beneficiary who has already begun receiving benefits. However, an increase in benefits that was adopted or took effect within 60 months of the first day of the initial critical year may be reduced or eliminated. [62]

Adjustable benefits. Adjustable benefits generally include nearly every aspect of a plan apart from normal retirement benefits in the form of a joint-and-survivor annuity.[63] Such benefits include: (1) other benefits, rights and features under the plan, including post-retirement death benefits, 60-month guarantees, disability benefits not yet in pay status, and similar benefits; (2) any early retirement benefits or retirement-type subsidies; (3) any benefit payment option other than the qualified joint-and-survivor annuity; and (4) benefit increases that were adopted or took effect less than 60 months before the first day of the initial critical year.

Notice of reduction in adjustable benefits. Before implementing a reduction in adjustable benefits the sponsor must give 30 days notice of the change to all participants and beneficiaries, each employer who contributes to the plan, and each union representing participants employed by any employer. The notice must contain information sufficient to enable the participants and beneficiaries to understand the effect of the reductions on their benefits, including an estimate of any affected benefit for which the individual would otherwise have been eligible as of the effective date of the change, and information as to the individual's rights and remedies and how to contact the Department of Labor for more information and assistance. [64]

The notice must be written so as to be understandable by the average plan participant. It may be provided on paper, electronically or in any other form, so long as it is reasonably accessible to the recipients.

Model Notice. The Department of Labor is required to promulgate regulations including a model notice and prescribing the form and manner in which the notice is to be given.[65] Note, final regulations issued by IRS in 2009 do not allow the notice provided by a multiemployer plan in critical status, in compliance with Code Sec. 432(e)(8), to also satisfy the timing and content requirements of an ERISA Sec. 204(h) notice. The IRS and Treasury are developing guidance (presumably for release in 2010) that will establish requirements for the Code Sec. 432(e)(8)(C) notice and address the interaction of the notice with the 204(h) notice rules.

CCH POINTER: *Benefit reductions disregarded.* Reductions in benefits under a rehabilitation plan are disregarded in determining a plan's unfunded vested benefits (i.e., amount by which the value of nonforfeitable benefits under the plan exceeds the value of plan assets) for purposes of determining an employer's withdrawal liability. [66]

A Technical Update released by the PBGC in July 2010 furnished a simplified method for applying the requirement to disregard benefit reductions in determining withdrawal liability. [67] Under this method:

(1) the value of the affected benefits (i.e., benefit reductions which are to be disregarded under Code Sec. 432(e)(9)(A)in determining a plan's unfunded vested benefits for purposes of determining an employer's withdrawal liability) will be determined pursuant to the same assumptions that are used by the plan to determine unfunded vested benefits for purposes of ERISA Sec. 4211, and

(2) the unamortized balance of the affected benefits as of a plan year will be the value of that amount as of the end of the year in which the reductions took effect (base year), reduced as if that amount were being fully amortized in level annual installments over 15 years, at the plan's valuation interest rate, beginning with the first plan year after the base year.

An employer's proportional share of the unamortized balance of the affected benefits will be the product of:

(i) the unamortized balance as of the end of the plan year preceding the withdrawal, and

(ii) the following fraction: the sum of all contributions required to be made by the employer under the plan for the last 5 plan years ending before withdrawal/ the total amount contributed under the plan by all employers for the last 5 plan years ending before the withdrawal, increased by any employer contributions owed with respect to earlier periods which were collected in those plan years, and decreased by any amount contributed to the plan during those plan years by employers who ceased to be obligated to contribute or ceased covered operations.

Requirements for critical plans: Operational requirements

Special operational requirements apply to critical plans.[68] Generally, plans will be restricted from paying out lump-sum benefits and may not be amended to contain terms inconsistent with the rehabilitation plan.

Restrictions on lump-sum benefits. After notice of the plan's critical status has been sent to the bargaining parties and participants, the plan generally is not allowed to pay out large lump-sum benefits. Specifically, the plan may not pay:

1. any amount greater than the monthly amount paid under a single life annuity;

2. any payment for an irrevocable commitment from an insurer to pay benefits; or

3. any other payments prohibited by regulations.[69]

Exception for involuntary cashouts. The restrictions discussed above do not apply to involuntary cash-outs of benefits up to $5,000 or to any retroactive payment with respect to a prior period. [70]

Restriction on reduced contributions. During the rehabilitation plan adoption period, the plan sponsor may not accept any collective bargaining agreement or participation agreement that provides for reduced contributions by reason of: (1) lower contributions for any participants, (2) a suspension of contributions with respect to any period of service, or (3) any new direct or indirect exclusion of younger or newly hired employees from plan participation. [71] A critical plan cannot be amended during the adoption period in any way that increases plan liabilities by reason of an increase in benefits, change in accruals or change in the vesting rate, unless the amendment is necessary to maintain the plan's qualified status or required by law [72]

Plan amendment may not be inconsistent with rehabilitation plan. Once a rehabilitation plan has been adopted, the multiemployer plan may not be amended in a way inconsistent with the rehabilitation plan, and amendments increasing benefits, including future benefit accruals, are restricted. A critical plan can be amended to increase benefits only if the plan actuary certifies that the increase is paid for out of increased contributions not contemplated by the rehabilitation plan, and that after taking into account the increased benefits the plan is still reasonably projected to emerge from critical status by the end of the rehabilitation period on the schedule contemplated in the rehabilitation period. [73]

Employer surcharges. Employers contributing to critical plans are encouraged to renegotiate their collective bargaining agreements to adopt a schedule of contributions and benefits consistent with the rehabilitation plan by the imposition of a surcharge on contributions. [74]. A temporary surcharge in the amount of five percent of the required contribution is imposed on all contributing employers for the first year a plan is in critical status. In later years, for as long as the plan remains in critical status, the surcharge is ten percent of the required contribution. The surcharge amounts themselves cannot be the basis for any benefit accruals under the plan. The surcharge takes effect 30 days after the employer has been notified by the sponsor that the plan is in critical status and that the surcharge is in effect. The surcharges are due and payable on the same schedule as the contributions on which they are based, and any failure to make the required payment is treated as a delinquent contribution under ERISA. [75] However, the surcharge does not apply with respect to employees who are covered by a collective bargaining agreement that includes terms consistent with a schedule provided by the sponsor under the rehabilitation plan. [76]

Excise tax imposed for failure to adopt rehabilitation plan. In the event a critical plan does not adopt the rehabilitation plan within the required 240-day period, the plan sponsor (e.g., association, committee, joint board of trustee or similar group of representatives of the parties who established or maintain the plan) is subject to an excise tax of $1,100 multiplied by the number of days during the tax year which are included in the period beginning on the day following the close of the 240-day period and ending on the day on which the rehabilitation plan is adopted. [77] Note, the excise tax does not begin to accrue at the beginning of the 240-day period.

Joint and several liability. Similar to single-employer plans, all members of a controlled group under a multiemployer plan will be jointly and severally liable for the excise tax.[78]

¶1493L

Effective dates

The provisions imposing additional funding rules on multiemployer plans in endangered or critical status apply with respect to plan years beginning after 2007.

Sunset provision. The provisions of, and amendments relating to, the additional funding rules for multiemployer plans in endangered or critical status contained in Pension Protection Act Secs. 202 and 212 will not apply to plan years beginning after December 31, 2014.[79]

☐ The additional funding requirements applicable to underfunded multiemployer plans are discussed in detail at CCH PENSION PLAN GUIDE ¶ 3139A.

---

[1] ERISA Sec.305, as added by P.L. 109-280 (Pension Protection Act of 2006), Act Sec. 202(a); Code Sec. 432, as added by P.L. 109-280 (Pension Protection Act of 2006), Act Sec. 212(a).

[2] *Ibid.*

[3] P.L. 109-280 (Pension Protection Act of 2006), Act Secs. 202(f) and 212(e).

[4] ERISA Sec. 305(b)(3)(A), as added by P.L. 109-280 (Pension Protection Act of 2006), Act Sec. 202(a); Code Sec. 432(b)(3)(A), as added by P.L. 109-280 (Pension Protection Act of 2006), Act Sec. 212(a).

[5] ERISA Sec. 305(b)(3)(C), as added by P.L. 109-280 Pension Protection Act of 2006), Act Sec. 202(a); Code Sec. 432(b)(3)(C), as added by P.L. 109-280 (Pension Protection Act of 2006), Act Sec. 212(a).

[6] ERISA Sec. 305(b)(3)(A), as added by P.L. 109-280 Pension Protection Act of 2006), Act Sec. 202(a); Code Sec. 432(b)(3)(A), as added by P.L. 109-280 (Pension Protection Act of 2006), Act Sec. 212(a).

[7] ERISA Sec. 305(b)(3)(D)(i), as added by P.L. 109-280 Pension Protection Act of 2006), Act Sec. 202(a); Code Sec. 432(b)(3)(D)(i), as added by P.L. 109-280 (Pension Protection Act of 2006), Act Sec. 212(a).

[8] ERISA Sec. 305(b)(3)(D)(ii), as added by P.L. 109-280 Pension Protection Act of 2006), Act Sec. 202(a); Code Sec. 432(b)(3)(D)(ii), as added by P.L. 109-280 (Pension Protection Act of 2006), Act Sec. 212(a).

[9] ERISA Sec. 305(b)(3)(D)(iii), as added by P.L. 109-280 Pension Protection Act of 2006), Act Sec. 202(a); Code Sec. 432(b)(3)(D)(iii), as added by P.L. 109-280 (Pension Protection Act of 2006), Act Sec. 212(a).

[10] ERISA Proposed Reg. § 2540.305-1

[11] Preamble to ERISA Proposed Reg. § 2540.305-1, Footnote 3, at CCH PENSION PLAN GUIDE ¶ 20,537L.

[12] P.L. 110-458 (Worker, Retiree, and Employer Recovery Act of 2008), Act Sec. 204(a).

[13] Technical Explanation of P.L. 110-458 (Worker, Retiree, and Employer Recovery Act of 2008), JCX 85-08.

[14] P.L. 110-458 (Worker, Retiree, and Employer Recovery Act of 2008), Act Sec. 204(a).

[15] IRS Notice 2009-31, Sec. III, I.R.B. 2009-16, at CCH PENSION PLAN GUIDE ¶ 17,142K.

[16] *Ibid.*

[17] ERISA Sec. 305(b)(2), as added by P.L. 109-280 (Pension Protection Act of 2006), Act Sec. 202(a); Code Sec. 432(b)(2), as added by P.L. 109-280 (Pension Protection Act of 2006), Act Sec. 212(a).

[18] ERISA Sec. 305(b)(1), as added by P.L. 109-280 (Pension Protection Act of 2006), Act Sec. 202(a); Code Sec. 432(b)(1), as added by P.L. 109-280 (Pension Protection Act of 2006), Act Sec. 212(a).

[19] ERISA Sec. 305(b)(1)(A), as added by P.L. 109-280 (Pension Protection Act of 2006), Act Sec. 202(a); Code Sec. 432(b)(1)(A), as added by P.L. 109-280 (Pension Protection Act of 2006), Act Sec. 212(a).

[20] ERISA Sec. 305(b)(1)(B), as added by P.L. 109-280 (Pension Protection Act of 2006), Act Sec. 202(a); Code Sec. 432(b)(1)(B), as added by P.L. 109-280 (Pension Protection Act of 2006), Act Sec. 212(a).

[21] ERISA Sec. 305(b)(1), as added by P.L. 109-280 (Pension Protection Act of 2006), Act Sec. 202(a); Code Sec. 432(b)(1), as added by P.L. 109-280 (Pension Protection Act of 2006), Act Sec. 212(a).

[22] ERISA Sec. 305(a)(1), as added by P.L. 109-280 (Pension Protection Act of 2006), Act Sec. 202(a); Code Sec. 432(a)(1), as added by P.L. 109-280 (Pension Protection Act of 2006), Act Sec. 212(a).

[23] ERISA Sec. 305(c)(1)(A), as added by P.L. 109-280 (Pension Protection Act of 2006), Act Sec.

202(a); Code Sec. 432(c)(1)(A), as added by P.L. 109-280 (Pension Protection Act of 2006), Act Sec. 212(a).

24 ERISA Sec. 305(c)(3)(A), as added by P.L. 109-280 (Pension Protection Act of 2006), Act Sec. 202(a); Code Sec. 432(c)(3)(A), as added by P.L. 109-280 (Pension Protection Act of 2006), Act Sec. 212(a).

25 ERISA Sec. 305(c)(3)(A) and (4)(A), as added by P.L. 109-280 (Pension Protection Act of 2006), Act Sec. 202(a); Code Sec. 432(c)(3)(A) and (4)(A), as added by P.L. 109-280 (Pension Protection Act of 2006), Act Sec. 212(a).

26 ERISA Sec. 305(c)(4)(A), as added by P.L. 109-280 (Pension Protection Act of 2006), Act Sec. 202(a); Code Sec. 432(c)(4)(A), as added by P.L. 109-280 (Pension Protection Act of 2006), Act Sec. 212(a).

27 ERISA Sec. 305(c)(4)(B), as added by P.L. 109-280 (Pension Protection Act of 2006), Act Sec. 202(a); Code Sec. 432(c)(4)(B), as added by P.L. 109-280 (Pension Protection Act of 2006), Act Sec. 212(a).

28 P.L. 110-458 (Worker, Retiree, and Employer Recovery Act of 2008), Act Sec. 205(a).

29 IRS Notice 2009-31, Sec. IV.1, I.R.B. 2009-16, at CCH PENSION PLAN GUIDE ¶ 17,142K.

30 IRS Notice 2009-42, Sec. I, I.R.B. 2009-20, at CCH PENSION PLAN GUIDE ¶ 17,142P.

31 IRS Notice 2009-31, Sec. III, I.R.B. 2009-16, at CCH PENSION PLAN GUIDE ¶ 17,142K.

32 *Ibid.*

33 *Ibid.*

34 ERISA Sec. 305(d)(1)(A) and (2)(B), as added by P.L. 109-280 (Pension Protection Act of 2006), Act Sec. 202(a); Code Sec. 432(d)(1)(A) and (2)(B), as added by P.L. 109-280 (Pension Protection Act of 2006), Act Sec. 212(a).

35 Code Sec. 4971(g)(2), as added by P.L. 109-280 (Pension Protection Act of 2006), Act Sec. 202(b).

36 Code Sec. 4971(g)(3), as added by P.L. 109-280 (Pension Protection Act of 2006), Act Sec. 202(b).

37 Code Sec. 4971(g)(1)(B), as added by P.L. 109-280 (Pension Protection Act of 2006), Act Sec. 202(b).

38 ERISA Sec. 502(c)(8) as added by P.L. 109-280 (Pension Protection Act of 2006), Act Sec. 202(b).

39 ERISA Reg. § 2560.502c-8.

40 ERISA Reg. § 2560.502c-8(a)(2).

41 ERISA Reg. § 2560.502c-8(b).

42 ERISA Reg. § 2560.502c-8(c).

43 ERISA Reg. § 2560.502c-8(d).

44 ERISA Reg. § 2560.502c-8(e).

45 ERISA Reg. § 2560.502c-8(e); ERISA Reg. § 2570.164.

46 ERISA Reg. § 2560.502c-8(j).

47 Preamble to ERISA Reg. § 2560.502c-8), at CCH PENSION PLAN GUIDE ¶ 24,808N.

48 *Ibid.*

49 ERISA Reg. § 2560.502c-8(j)(2).

50 Preamble to ERISA Reg. § 2560.502c-8), at CCH PENSION PLAN GUIDE ¶ 24,808N.

51 ERISA Sec. 305(a)(2), as added by P.L. 109-280 (Pension Protection Act of 2006), Act Sec. 202(a); Code Sec. 432(a)(2) as added by P.L. 109-280 (Pension Protection Act of 2006), Act Sec. 212(a).

52 ERISA Sec. 302(b)(3), as added by P.L. 109-280 (Pension Protection Act of 2006), Act Sec. 202(d); Code Sec. 412(b)(3) as added by P.L. 109-280 (Pension Protection Act of 2006), Act Sec. 212(c).

53 ERISA Sec. 305(e)(1)(A), as added by P.L. 109-280 (Pension Protection Act of 2006), Act Sec. 202(a); Code Sec. 432(e)(1)(A) as added by P.L. 109-280 (Pension Protection Act of 2006), Act Sec. 212(a).

54 ERISA Sec. 302(b)(3), as added by P.L. 109-280 (Pension Protection Act of 2006), Act Sec. 202(d); Code Sec. 412(b)(3) as added by P.L. 109-280 (Pension Protection Act of 2006), Act Sec. 212(c).

55 ERISA Sec. 305(e)(3)(A), as added by P.L. 109-280 (Pension Protection Act of 2006), Act Sec. 202(a); Code Sec. 432(e)(3)(A) as added by P.L. 109-280 (Pension Protection Act of 2006), Act Sec. 212(a).

56 ERISA Sec. 305(e)(8)(A)(ii), as added by P.L. 109-280 (Pension Protection Act of 2006), Act Sec. 202(a); Code Sec. 432(e)(8)(A)(ii) as added by P.L. 109-280 (Pension Protection Act of 2006), Act Sec. 212(a).

57 ERISA Sec. 305(c)(7)(B), as amended by P.L. 110-458 (Worker, Retiree, and Employer Recovery Act of 2008), Act Sec. 102(b); Code Sec. 432(c)(7)(B) and (e)(3)(C) as amended by P.L. 110-458 (Worker, Retiree, and Employer Recovery Act of 2008), Act Sec. 102(b).

58 ERISA Sec. 305(c)(7) and (e)(3)(C)(iii), as amended by P.L. 110-458 (Worker, Retiree, and Employer Recovery Act of 2008), Act Sec. 102(b).

59 ERISA Sec. 305(e)(4)(B), as amended by P.L. 110-458 (Worker, Retiree, and Employer Recovery Act of 2008), Act Sec. 202(a); Code Sec. 432(e)(4)(B) as amended by P.L. 110-458 (Worker, Retiree, and Employer Recovery Act of 2008), Act Sec. 212(a).

[60] ERISA Sec. 305(e)(4)(A), as added by P.L. 109-280 (Pension Protection Act of 2006), Act Sec. 202(a); Code Sec. 432(e)(4)(B) as added by P.L. 109-280 (Pension Protection Act of 2006), Act Sec. 212(a).

[61] P.L. 110-458 (Worker, Retiree, and Employer Recovery Act of 2008), Act Sec. 205(a).

[62] ERISA Sec. 305(e)(8)(A), as added by P.L. 109-280 (Pension Protection Act of 2006), Act Sec. 202(a); Code Sec. 432(e)(8)(A) as added by P.L. 109-280 (Pension Protection Act of 2006), Act Sec. 212(a).

[63] ERISA Sec. 305(e)(8)(C)(iv), as added by P.L. 109-280 (Pension Protection Act of 2006), Act Sec. 202(a); Code Sec. 432(e)(8)(C)(iv) as added by P.L. 109-280 (Pension Protection Act of 2006), Act Sec. 212(a).

[64] ERISA Sec. 305(e)(8)(C)(ii), as added by P.L. 109-280 (Pension Protection Act of 2006), Act Sec. 202(a); Code Sec. 432(e)(8)(C)(ii) as added by P.L. 109-280 (Pension Protection Act of 2006), Act Sec. 212(a).

[65] ERISA Sec. 305(e)(8)(C), as added by P.L. 109-280 (Pension Protection Act of 2006), Act Sec. 202(a); Code Sec. 432(e)(8)(C) as added by P.L. 109-280 (Pension Protection Act of 2006), Act Sec. 212(a).

[66] ERISA Sec. 305(e)(9)(A), as added by P.L. 109-280 (Pension Protection Act of 2006), Act Sec. 202(a); Code Sec. 432(e)(9)(A) as added by P.L. 109-280 (Pension Protection Act of 2006), Act Sec. 212.

[67] PBGC Technical Update 10-3, July 15, 2010, at CCH PENSION PLAN GUIDE ¶ 19,975Z-28.

[68] ERISA Sec. 305(f), as added by P.L. 109-280 (Pension Protection Act of 2006), Act Sec. 202(a); Code Sec. 432(f), as added by P.L. 109-280 (Pension Protection Act of 2006), Act Sec. 212.

[69] ERISA Sec. 305(f)(2)(A), as added by P.L. 109-280 (Pension Protection Act of 2006), Act Sec. 202(a); Code Sec. 432(f)(2)(A), as added by P.L. 109-280 (Pension Protection Act of 2006), Act Sec. 212.

[70] ERISA Sec. 305(f)(2)(B), as added by P.L. 109-280 (Pension Protection Act of 2006), Act Sec.

202(a); Code Sec. 432(f)(2)(B), as added by P.L. 109-280 (Pension Protection Act of 2006), Act Sec. 212.

[71] ERISA Sec. 305(f)(4)(A), as added by P.L. 109-280 (Pension Protection Act of 2006), Act Sec. 202(a); Code Sec. 432(f)(4)(A), as added by P.L. 109-280 (Pension Protection Act of 2006), Act Sec. 212.

[72] ERISA Sec. 305(f)(4)(B), as added by P.L. 109-280 (Pension Protection Act of 2006), Act Sec. 202(a); Code Sec. 432(f)(4)(B), as added by P.L. 109-280 (Pension Protection Act of 2006), Act Sec. 212.

[73] ERISA Sec. 305(f)(1), as added by P.L. 109-280 (Pension Protection Act of 2006), Act Sec. 202(a); Code Sec. 432(f)(1), as added by P.L. 109-280 (Pension Protection Act of 2006), Act Sec. 212.

[74] ERISA Sec. 305(e)(7)(A), as added by P.L. 109-280 (Pension Protection Act of 2006), Act Sec. 202(a); Code Sec. 432(e)(7)(A), as added by P.L. 109-280 (Pension Protection Act of 2006), Act Sec. 212.

[75] ERISA Sec. 305(e)(7)(B), as added by P.L. 109-280 (Pension Protection Act of 2006), Act Sec. 202(a); Code Sec. 432(e)(7)(B), as added by P.L. 109-280 (Pension Protection Act of 2006), Act Sec. 212.

[76] ERISA Sec. 305(e)(7)(C), as added by P.L. 109-280 (Pension Protection Act of 2006), Act Sec. 202(a); Code Sec. 432(e)(7)(C), as added by P.L. 109-280 (Pension Protection Act of 2006), Act Sec. 212.

[77] Code Sec. 432(i)(9), as added by P.L. 110-458 (Worker, Retiree, and Employer Recovery Act of 2008), Act Sec. 102(b)(2)(G); Code Sec. 4971(g)(4), as amended by P.L. 110-458 (Worker, Retiree, and Employer Recovery Act of 2008), Act Sec. 102(b).

[78] Code Sec. 4971(e)(2)(A) , as amended by P.L. 109-280 (Pension Protection Act of 2006), Act Sec. 212(b)(2), as amended by P.L. 110-458 (Worker, Retiree, and Employer Recovery Act of 2008), Act Sec. 102(b)(3)(B).

[79] P.L. 109-280 (Pension Protection Act of 2006), Act Sec. 221(c)(1).

¶ 1494

For More Information

☐ For more information on funding and actuarial requirements, see ¶ 2800-3150 of the CCH PENSION PLAN GUIDE.

Assignment and Alienation of Benefits

¶ 1500
General Rules

A qualified retirement plan must provide that benefits under the plan cannot be assigned or alienated.[1] Generally, this means that benefits under the plan cannot be anticipated, assigned, or alienated, and are not subject to attachment, garnishment, levy, execution, or other legal process.[2]

IRS levy exempt

The anti-alienation provisions of a plan (commonly called "spendthrift" provisions) do not preclude the enforcement of the federal tax levy or the collection by the United States of a judgment resulting from unpaid tax assessment. The IRS may levy upon all property and rights to property of a taxpayer, including pension benefits, in order to collect tax liabilities.[3]

Additional exceptions

Additional exceptions to the general anti-alienation rule include:

1. limited assignments of benefit payments (see ¶ 1510),
2. loans secured by the participant's nonforfeitable benefits (see ¶ 1515), and
3. benefits with respect to a participant under a qualified domestic relations order (see ¶ 1600).[4]

In addition, note that welfare benefits, unlike pension benefits, may be freely assigned or encumbered.[5]

Offset of fiduciary's plan benefits

A limited exception to the anti-alienation rule allows a participant's pension benefits to be reduced where the participant has breached a fiduciary duty to the plan or committed a criminal act against the plan. A participant's benefits in a qualified pension plan may be offset against an amount that the participant is ordered or required to pay to the plan pursuant to:

1. a judgment or conviction for a crime involving the plan;

2. a civil judgment (or consent order or decree) entered by a court in an action brought in connection with a breach or alleged breach of fiduciary duty under ERISA; or

3. a settlement agreement entered into by the participant and either the Secretary of Labor or the PBGC in connection with a breach of fiduciary duty under ERISA by a fiduciary or any other person.[6]

In addition, the judgment, order, decree, or settlement agreement must expressly provide for the offset of the amount to be paid to the plan against the participant's plan benefits.[7]

Spousal consent generally required. If the participant is married at the time his or her plan benefits are offset and if the survivor annuity requirements of ERISA Sec. 205 (or Code Sec. 401(a)(11)) apply to distributions under the plan, the participant's spouse must generally either consent in writing to the offset or waive his or her rights to a qualified joint and survivor annuity or a qualified preretirement survivor annuity.[8] In order to be valid, the spousal consent must be witnessed by a notary public or representative of the plan. In the event that spousal consent may not be obtained, the plan representative must be satisfied that there is no spouse, the spouse cannot be located, or other circumstances that may be prescribed in Treasury regulations apply.[9] For more information, see ¶ 1715.

Exceptions to spousal consent rule. Spousal consent need not be obtained if:

1. the spouse is required under the judgment, order, decree, or settlement to make a payment to the plan in connection with a breach of fiduciary duty;[10] or

2. the spouse retains the right under the judgment, order, decree, or settlement to receive a survivor annuity under a qualified joint and survivor annuity and under a qualified preretirement survivor annuity.[11]

Survivor annuity. The survivor annuity must be determined as if:

1. the participant terminated employment on the offset date;

2. there was no offset;

3. the plan allowed benefits to begin only on or after the normal retirement age;

4. the plan provided only the minimum required qualified joint and survivor annuity (see below); and

5. the amount of the qualified preretirement survivor annuity is equal to the amount of the survivor annuity payable under the minimum required qualified joint and survivor annuity.[12]

Minimum required qualified joint and survivor annuity. The minimum required qualified joint and survivor annuity is a qualified joint and survivor annuity that is the actuarial equivalent of the participant's accrued benefit and under which the survivor annuity is 50 percent of the amount of the annuity that is payable during the joint lives of the participant and the spouse.[13]

Bankruptcy

Prior to the enactment of The Bankruptcy Abuse Prevention and Consumer Protection Act of 2005 (BAPCPA) (P.L. 109-8), on April 20, 2005, the determinative factors in the protection of a debtor's retirement assets were: (1) whether the assets were held in "ERISA-qualified" plans or (2) whether the assets were held in similar plans and were reasonably necessary for the support of the debtor and dependents. BAPCPA, effective for bankruptcy cases commencing on or after October 17, 2005, significantly expands the bankruptcy protection afforded retirement assets held in plans that are not covered by ERISA (e.g., IRAs). Specifically, the Act amends the Bankruptcy Code to authorize an exemption from the bankruptcy estate for retirement assets held in funds or accounts that are exempt from taxation under Code Secs. 401, 403, 408, 408A, 414, 457, or 501, irrespective of whether the funds are held in ERISA-qualified plans. Thus, the Act shields funds in traditional and Roth IRAs (including rollover amounts) from a debtor's creditors, regardless of whether the funds are reasonably necessary for the support of the debtor.[14]

In addition, the Act creates a new exclusion from the bankruptcy estate for employee contributions to: ERISA Title I plans, Code Sec. 414(d) governmental plans, 457 plans, 403 tax-deferred annuities, and state regulated health insurance plans.[15]

Prior to the effective date of BAPCPA, the following discussion applies.

A debtor's interest in an ERISA-qualified plan sponsored by his employer is excludable from his bankruptcy estate under the Bankruptcy Code's "applicable nonbankruptcy law" exception, the U.S. Supreme Court has ruled.[16] The Bankruptcy Code excludes property from the bankruptcy estate that is subject to a restriction on transfer enforceable under nonbankruptcy law. The Court held that the anti-alienation provision in a qualified plan was a restriction on transfer enforceable under applicable nonbankruptcy law.

☐ The ability of creditors to reach a participant's plan assets is discussed at ¶ 2560.

Employees must participate in plan. In order for the exemption from assignment and alienation to apply, the plan must be a pension plan under ERISA.[17] An employee benefit plan under ERISA does not include arrangements in which no employees participate.[18] The Department of Labor has clarified, however, that plans covering sole owners and their spouses are excluded from Title I coverage as ERISA plans only if the plans include no other non-owner employees as participants. Thus, according to the DOL, a plan that covers one or more common law employees as participants, in addition to the self-employed individual, will qualify as an ERISA plan.[19] The United States Supreme Court relying heavily on ERISA Opinion Letter 99-04A has further ruled, resolving a dispute among the Federal

¶1500

Appeals Courts, that the working owner of a business may qualify as a participant in an ERISA plan and thereby benefit from the plan's anti-alienation provision, as long as the plan covers one or more employees other than the business owner and his or her spouse.[20] Accordingly, the sole shareholder in a profit-sharing plan that covered the shareholder, his spouse, and non-owner employees could shield loan repayments made to the plan from personal bankruptcy creditors.

IRAs. The U. S. Supreme Court in 2005 resolved a split among the Circuits on whether IRAs qualify for the bankruptcy exception for payments from a stock bonus, pension, profit-sharing, annuity, or similar plan under Bankruptcy Code Sec. 522(d)(10)(E).[21] Specifically, the Court held that IRA assets were exempt from the bankruptcy estate because: (1) they conferred a right to receive payment "on account of age" and (2) were "similar plans or contracts" to those enumerated under Bankruptcy Code Sec. 522(d)(10)(E).

It is important to note that the Court did not address the third prong of the exemption authorized under Bankruptcy Code Sec. 522(d)(10)(E): that the assets be reasonably necessary for the support of the debtor and/or his dependents. Thus, IRA assets could be excluded under Federal bankruptcy law from the bankruptcy estate only to the extent that the funds were reasonably necessary for the support of the debtor and/or the debtor's dependents.

Paid benefits not protected

The anti-alienation rules of ERISA Sec. 206(d)(1) only provide protection for pension benefits prior to distribution.[22] Benefits that have already been paid are not protected by the spendthrift provisions. For instance, pension benefits deposited in a bank account were not protected.[23] The bank account, and not the benefits, was subject to garnishment.[24]

---

[1] Code Sec. 401(a)(13); ERISA Sec. 206(d); IRS Reg. § 1.401(a)-13(b).

[2] IRS Reg. § 1.401(a)-13(b).

[3] Code Secs. 6331 and 6334(a)(6); *United States v. National Bank of Commerce*, US Sup Ct (1985), 472 U.S. 713.

[4] Code Sec. 401(a)(13); ERISA Sec. 206(d).

[5] *Mackey v. Lanier Collection Agency & Service, Inc.*, US Sup Ct (1988), 486 U.S. 825.

[6] Code Sec. 401(a)(13)(C)(i); ERISA Sec. 206(d)(4).

[7] Code Sec. 401(a)(13)(C)(ii); ERISA Sec. 206(d)(4)(B).

[8] Code Sec. 401(a)(13)(C)(iii); ERISA Sec. 206(d)(4)(C).

[9] Code Sec. 401(a)(13)(C)(iii)(I); ERISA Sec. 206(d)(4)(C)(i)(I).

[10] Code Sec. 401(a)(13)(C)(iii)(II); ERISA Sec. 206(d)(4)(C)(ii).

[11] Code Sec. 401(a)(13)(C)(iii)(III); ERISA Sec. 206(d)(4)(C)(iii).

[12] Code Sec. 401(a)(13)(D)(i); ERISA Sec. 206(d)(5)(A).

[13] Code Sec. 401(a)(13)(D)(ii); ERISA Sec. 206(d)(5)(B).

[14] 11 U.S.C. §§ 522(b)(3)(C) and 522(d)(12), as added by P.L. 109-8 (Bankruptcy Abuse Prevention and Consumer Protection Act of 2005), Act Sec. 224(a).

[15] 11 U.S.C. § 541(b)(7), as added by P.L. 109-8 (Bankruptcy Abuse Prevention and Consumer Protection Act of 2005), Act Sec. 323.

[16] *Patterson v. Shumate*, US Sup Ct (1992), 504 U.S. 753, aff'g CA-4 (1992), 943 F2d 362.

[17] ERISA Sec. 206(d).

[18] ERISA Reg. § 2510.3-3(b).

[19] ERISA Opinion Letter 99-04A, 2-4-99, CCH PENSION PLAN GUIDE ¶ 19,987K.

[20] *Raymond B. Yates, M.D., P.C. Profit-Sharing Plan v. Hendon*, US Sup Ct (2004), 541 U.S. 1, CCH PENSION PLAN GUIDE ¶ 23,987K.

[21] *Rousey v. Jacoway*, US Sup Ct (2005), 544 U.S. 320, CCH PENSION PLAN GUIDE ¶ 23,991C.

[22] *Hawxhurst v. Hawxhurst,* NJ Super Ct (1998), 723 A2d 58.

[23] *Guidry v. Sheet Metal Workers National Pension Fund,* CA-10 (1994), 39 F3d 1078.

[24] *Trucking Employees of North Jersey Welfare Fund, Inc. v. Colville,* CA-3 (1994), 16 F3d 52.

¶ 1505

What Is an Assignment or Alienation of Benefits?

The term "assignment" or "alienation" includes any arrangement providing for the payment to the employer of plan benefits that would otherwise be due the participant.[1] It also includes any direct or indirect arrangement under which a party acquires from a participant or beneficiary an enforceable right or interest against the plan in, or to, all or any part of a benefit plan payment, which is, or may become, payable to the participant or beneficiary.

The following are not considered to be assignments or alienations:

1. an arrangement under ERISA Sec. 4045(b) for the recovery of certain benefits paid by a terminated plan;

2. an arrangement for withholding federal, state, or local taxes from benefit payments;

3. an arrangement for the recovery of overpayments of benefits previously paid to a participant;

4. an arrangement for the transfer of benefit rights from one plan to another; and

5. an arrangement for direct deposit of benefit payments to a participant's account in a bank, savings and loan association, or credit union.[2]

---

[1] IRS Reg. § 1.401(a)-13(c)(1).

[2] IRS Reg. § 1.401(a)-13(c)(2).

¶ 1510

Limited Assignment of Benefit Payments

A plan may provide that, once a participant or beneficiary begins to receive plan benefits, assignments totaling not more than 10% of any benefit payment may be made.[1] However, the assignments or alienations must be voluntary and revocable. They must not have the purpose or effect of defraying any plan administration costs. An attachment, garnishment, levy, execution or other legal or equitable process is not a voluntary assignment or alienation.

---

[1] IRS Reg. § 1.401(a)-13(d)(1).

¶ 1515

Participant Loans

Loans from a plan to a participant or beneficiary may be secured by the participant's accrued, nonforfeitable benefit.[1] However, loans from a party other than the plan may not be secured by benefits that accrued (or are to be accrued), whether or not vested.

If the loan is made to a participant or beneficiary who is a disqualified person under the prohibited transaction rules of Code Sec. 4975(e)(2), it must be exempt from the prohibited transaction excise tax by reason of meeting the requirements of Code Sec. 4975(d)(1). Code Sec. 4975(d)(1) requires that loans be available to all participants or beneficiaries on a reasonable basis and that they bear a reasonable rate of interest. The loan must meet the requirements of Code Sec. 4975(d)(1) even if the participant or beneficiary is not a disqualified person.

Low interest rates

A loan to a qualified plan participant that is secured by the participant's accrued nonforfeitable benefit is an impermissible assignment or alienation if the loan is made at an unreasonably low interest rate.[2]

☐ See ¶ 2000 for more information on plan loans, including plan qualification issues and repayment requirements.

---

[1] Code Sec. 401(a)(13)(A); ERISA Sec. 206(d)(2); IRS Reg. § 1.401(a)-13(d)(2).

[2] Rev. Rul. 89-14, 1989-1 CB 111, CCH Pension Plan Guide ¶ 19,718.

¶ 1520

Third-Party Payments

A plan may permit a participant or beneficiary to direct the plan to pay part or all of a benefit payment to a third party (including the employer of a participant).[1] However, the arrangement must be revocable by the participant or beneficiary.

Acknowledgment filed with plan administrator

The third party must file an acknowledgment with the plan administrator, stating that he or she has no enforceable right in or to any benefit payment or portion thereof, except to the extent of payments actually received. The acknowledgment must be filed with the plan administrator no later than 90 days after the arrangement is entered into. A blanket acknowledgment for all participants covered under the arrangement may be filed by the third party.

---

[1] IRS Reg. § 1.401(a)-13(e).

¶ 1525

Excluded Plans

Only plans subject to the vesting standards of Code Sec. 411 must contain anti-alienation provisions.[1] Thus, an anti-alienation provision is not necessary for a welfare plan, government plan, a nonelecting church plan, or a plan that provides for employer contributions.

---

[1] IRS Reg. § 1.401(a)-13(a).

¶ 1530
For More Information

☐ See the PENSION PLAN GUIDE ¶ 1329-1345 for more information on the assignment and alienation of benefits.

Qualified Domestic Relations Orders (QDROs)

¶ 1600

General Rules

Qualified domestic relations orders require plan benefits to be paid to alternate payees other than the plan participant, such as a spouse, former spouse, or child. They are specifically exempted from the anti-alienation rule (see ¶ 1500), which requires plans to provide that benefits cannot be assigned or alienated.[1]

What is a QDRO?

A domestic relations order, under Code Sec. 414(p), is a judgment, decree, or order (including approval of a property settlement agreement) made pursuant to a state's domestic relations or community property law. A domestic relations order relates to the provision of child support, alimony, or marital property rights to a spouse, former spouse, child, or other dependent of a plan participant.[2]

Not all domestic relations orders are "qualified" domestic relations orders. For the order to be a *qualified* order, it must clearly specify:[3]

1. the name and the last known mailing address (if any) of the participant and the name and mailing address of each "alternate payee" (e.g., the spouse, former spouse, child, or dependent who is recognized by the order as having a right to benefits);

2. the amount or percentage of the participant's benefits to be paid to each alternate payee or the manner in which the amount or percentage is to be determined;

3. the number of payments or the period to which the order applies; and

4. each plan to which the order applies.

CCH Pointer: The order must be presented to the employer or plan administrator for a determination as to its status as a QDRO (see ¶ 1625).

Rights of alternate payees. An alternate payee under a QDRO is generally considered a beneficiary under the plan. Accordingly, the alternate payee must be furnished, upon request, with copies of the SPD and other documents under which the plan is established or operated. In addition, in the event of plan termination, the rights of an alternate payee must be taken into account as if the terms of the QDRO were part of the plan.

Impermissible QDRO terms. A domestic relations order is generally *not* a qualified order if:[4]

1. it requires a plan to provide any type or form of benefit, or any option, not otherwise provided by the plan;

2. it requires the plan to provide increased benefits (determined on the basis of actuarial value); or

3. it requires the payment of benefits to an alternate payee that are required to be paid to another alternate payee under a previous qualified order.

Example: A plan provides for the payment of benefits only in the form of a total distribution. An order providing for the payment of benefits to the alternate payee of a lifetime annuity would not be a qualified domestic relations order since it specifies a form of benefit other than a total distribution.

CCH Pointer: The Employee Benefits Security Administration (EBSA) has issued final regulations, pursuant to requirements of the Pension Protection Act of 2006, clarifying that a QDRO otherwise meeting ERISA's QDRO requirements will not fail to be treated as a QDRO solely because of when it is issued or because it is issued after, or revises, another domestic relations order or QDRO.[5] In addition, the regulations clarify that domestic relations orders are subject to the requirements and protections that apply to all QDROs under ERISA Sec. 206(d)(3). The regulations, which are effective on August 9, 2010, include examples to address various circumstances involving domestic relations orders.

Types of plans subject to QDROs

Generally, the qualified domestic relations provisions under the Internal Revenue Code and ERISA do not apply to any plan that is exempt from the assignment or alienation restrictions under the Internal Revenue Code or ERISA.[6] However, distributions from governmental plans and church plans are treated as made pursuant to a qualified domestic relations order if made under a domestic relations order that creates or recognizes an alternate payee's right to receive part or all of the benefits payable to a plan participant.[7] Also, a distribution of an annuity contract from a tax-sheltered annuity is treated as a plan to which the assignment or alienation restrictions apply. Thus, the QDRO rules apply to Code Sec. 403(b) tax-sheltered annuities.[8]

Taxation of distributions

Distributions from a qualified plan to a spouse or former spouse under a QDRO are taxable to the spouse in the year of distribution.[9] Absent a QDRO, plan distributions paid to a spouse or former spouse are taxed to the participant.

[1] Code Secs. 401(a)(13)(B) and 414(p); ERISA Sec. 206(d)(3)(A); IRS Reg. § 1.401(a)-13(g).

[2] Code Sec. 414(p)(1)(B); ERISA Sec. 206(d)(3)(B)(ii).

[3] Code Sec. 414(p)(2); ERISA Sec. 206(d)(3)(C).

[4] Code Sec. 414(p)(3); ERISA Sec. 206(d)(3)(D).

[5] ERISA Reg. § 2530.206, 75 FR 32846, June 10, 2010.

[6] Code Sec. 414(p)(9); ERISA Sec. 206(d)(3)(L).

[7] Code Sec. 414(p)(11).

[8] Code Sec. 414(p)(9).

[9] Code Sec. 402(e)(1)(A).

¶ 1605
Earliest Retirement Age Rule

Generally, a QDRO may not allow an alternate payee to receive a benefit before the date on which the participant attains the "earliest retirement age" under the plan. However, a participant may not delay an alternate payee's receipt of benefits by passing up an early retirement option that is available under the plan, if the order is drafted to provide that payments to the alternate payee may begin on or after the date on which the participant attains the "earliest retirement age" under the plan, whether or not the participant actually retires on that date.[1]

What is "the earliest retirement age" under a plan?

In the case of a defined benefit or a defined contribution plan, the "earliest retirement age" is defined as the earlier of:

1. the earliest date benefits are payable under the plan to the participant; and

2. the later of (a) the date on which the participant attains age 50 and (b) the date on which the participant could obtain a distribution from the plan if the participant separated from service.[2]

For example, in the case of a plan that provides for payment of benefits upon separation from service, but not before, the earliest date on which a QDRO can require payments to an alternative payee to begin is the date on which the participant separates from service. In the case of a profit-sharing plan that allows a participant to withdraw some, but not all, of his account balance before separation from service, the QDRO may provide for payment to the former spouse of up to the amount that the participant may withdraw.

Amount of benefits

If an order requires payments to begin on the earliest retirement age under the plan, benefits will be calculated as if the participant had retired on the date when benefit payments are to commence under the order. Only benefits actually accrued on that date are to be taken into account, and any employer subsidy for early retirement is not taken into account. An employer subsidizes an early retirement benefit to the extent that the benefit provided is greater than the actuarial equivalent of a retirement benefit—based on the accrued benefit at the date of early retirement—commencing at normal retirement age.

Actuarial equivalency is to be computed using the interest rate specified in the plan. If the plan does not specify an interest rate for determining actuarial equivalency (as would be the case if the employer were subsidizing the benefit), a 5% interest rate is to be employed.[3]

> **Example:** A domestic relations order permits a former wife to begin receiving court-awarded benefits at any time after her husband reaches early retirement age of 55 under his employer's pension plan. She elects to begin receiving her court-awarded benefits when her husband reaches age 55 although he does not retire then. She would be entitled to payments based on the present value of the benefit actually accrued by her former husband when he reached age 55, without taking into account any employer subsidy for early retirement. Since she chose to begin receiving payments before her former husband actually retired, she would not be entitled to any subsequent increase in his accrued benefits attributable to his working past age 55.

Future recalculation of benefits

If the employee should take early retirement at some date after the earliest possible date and after unsubsidized payments to the alternate payee have commenced, it is permissible for an order to require the recalculation of the share of the alternate payee so that he or she may share in the subsidy then actually being paid.[4]

Form of benefit

A QDRO may allow the alternate payee to elect to receive an early retirement benefit in any form available under the plan, except for a joint and survivor annuity with a subsequent spouse.

Preretirement survivor annuity

If a participant dies before the earliest retirement age, no retirement benefits will be paid to him or her. However, a qualified plan is required to provide the surviving spouse with a "preretirement survivor annuity" to the extent of the participant's vested interest at date of death. The non-employee spouse may be treated as a surviving spouse with respect to all or any part of the employee's benefits.[5] See ¶ 1610.

---

[1] Code Sec. 414(p)(4)(A); ERISA Sec. 206(d)(3)(E)(i).

[2] Code Sec. 414(p)(4)(B); ERISA Sec. 206(d)(3)(E)(ii).

[3] Code Sec. 414(p)(4)(A); ERISA Sec. 206(d)(3)(E)(i).

[4] Senate Finance Committee Report to P.L. 98-397 (Retirement Equity Act of 1984).

[5] Code Sec. 414(p)(5); ERISA Sec. 206(d)(3)(F); IRS Reg. § 1.401(a)-13(g)(4)(i).

¶ 1610

Former Spouse Treated as Surviving Spouse

The requirements of Code Secs. 401(a)(11) and 417 involving the payment of benefits in the form of a qualified joint and survivor annuity (QJSA) or a qualified pre-retirement survivor annuity (QPSA) are to be construed to include an employee's former spouse as a "surviving spouse" to the extent that a qualified domestic relations order so provides.[1] However, the employee and former spouse must have been married for at least one year. This requirement applies if the plan does not provide a joint and survivor annuity or preretirement survivor annuity for a surviving spouse who was not married to the employee for at least one year preceding the earlier of the annuity starting date or the date of death of the employee. If married for at least one year, the surviving former spouse is treated as meeting the one-year marriage requirement.

The former spouse does not automatically become a surviving spouse. Rather, the divorce court has the power to order that he or she be treated as the surviving spouse for purposes of the QJSA or QPSA.

Spousal consent

As a corollary to the treatment of a former spouse as a spouse, for purposes of the survivor annuity spousal consent rules, a QDRO may provide that the current spouse of a participant is not to be treated as a spouse.[2] For example, a QDRO could provide for the division of a participant's accrued benefits under a pension plan as part of a separation agreement. It could further provide that the participant's current spouse is not entitled to receive any survivor benefits with respect to such accrued benefits. Thus, the plan administrator would not be required to secure spousal consent to the participant's election to waive a survivor benefit.

More than one person treated as surviving spouse

If, because of a QDRO, more than one person is to be treated as the surviving spouse, a plan may provide that the total amount to be paid in the form of a QPSA or survivor portion of a QJSA may not exceed the amount that would be paid if there were only one surviving spouse.[3] The QPSA or survivor portion of the QJSA payable to each surviving spouse must be paid as an annuity based on the life of each spouse.

If the QDRO divides the participant's accrued benefit between the participant and a former spouse, the surviving spouse of the participant is entitled to a QPSA or QJSA based on the participant's accrued benefit as of the date of death, or the annuity starting date, *less* the separate account or percentage that is payable to the former spouse.[4]

Death of former spouse

If a former spouse who is treated as a current spouse dies before the participant's annuity date, the actual current spouse of the participant is treated as the current spouse, except as otherwise provided in a QDRO.[5]

---

[1]Code Sec. 414(p)(5); ERISA Sec. 206(d)(3)(F); IRS Reg. § 1.401(a)-13(g)(4)(i)(A).

[2]IRS Reg. § 1.401(a)-13(g)(4)(i)(B).

[3]IRS Reg. § 1.401(a)-13(g)(4)(i)(C)(1).

[4]IRS Reg. § 1.401(a)-13(g)(4)(i)(C)(2).

[5]IRS Reg. § 1.401(a)-13(g)(4)(iii)(C).

¶ 1612
Distributions to Alternate Payees

A QDRO may provide an alternate payee (and only the alternate payee) with all or any portion of the benefits payable to a plan participant. In dividing the participant's benefits, a QDRO may adopt a "separate interest" or a "shared interest" approach, or a combination of these methods.[1]

Separate interest method

Under the separate interest method, the participant's benefit (rather than just the payments) is divided into two separate portions so as to allow the alternate payee to receive a portion of the benefit at a time and in a form different from that chosen by the participant. Typically, under the separate interest approach, the alternate payee is assigned a percentage or a dollar amount of the participant's account balance as of a certain date. The separate interest will be held in a separate account under the plan and the alternate payee will be allowed to exercise the rights of a participant with respect to the account.

Shared payment method

Under the shared payment method, an alternate payee is provided with a portion of the benefit payments made to a participant. The QDRO may require that any or all payments made to a participant be shared with the alternate payee. QDROs that provide for shared payments from a 401(k) plan should clearly specify the amount or percentage of the participant's payments that will be allocated to the alternate payee and the number of payments or period of time during which the allocation to the alternate payee is to be made.

CCH Pointer: QDROs that divide benefits under a 401(k) plan should address the possibility of contingencies that may affect a participant's account balance (and, therefore, the alternate payees's share) during the determination period.[2] Accordingly, parties drafting the QDRO should specify the source of the alternate payee's share of the participant's account that is to be invested in multiple investments because the different possible methods for determining the alternate payee's share could affect the value of that share. In addition, the QDRO should address the allocation of any income or losses attributable to the participant's account that may accrue during the determination period. If the QDRO allocates a specific dollar amount, rather than a percentage, to an alternate payee as a shared payment, the order should account for the possibility that the participant's account balance or the additional individual payment may be less than the dollar amount specified in the order.

Time frame for distributing benefits

A QDRO that requires shared payments must specify the date on which the alternate payee will begin to share the participant's payments. A QDRO that adopts the separate interest method may specify either the time at which the alternate payee will receive the separate interest, or assign to the alternate payee the same right that the participant would have had under the plan to control the timing of the payment.

Payments may not begin until plan has received the QDRO. Under either the shared payment or the separate interest method, the QDRO may not require payments to be made to the alternate payee before the plan has received the order.

Taxation of distributions

The spouse or former spouse of a participant is subject to income tax on distributions received under a QDRO as an alternate payee.[3] However, the spouse may roll over the distribution.

Premature distribution penalty tax does not apply. Distributions to an alternate payee pursuant to a QDRO do not subject the participant to the 10 percent penalty tax that generally applies to distributions made before a participant separates from service, attains age 59½, or is otherwise entitled to a distribution.[4]

---

[1] "QDROs: The Division of Pensions Through Qualified Domestic Relations Orders," Department of Labor, 1997. See also IRS Notice 97-11, 1997-1 CB 379, CCH PENSION PLAN GUIDE ¶ 17,112E.

[2] *Ibid.*

[3] Code Sec. 402(e)(1)(A) and (B).

[4] Code Sec. 72(t)(2)(C).

¶ 1615

Interaction of QDROs with Survivor Annuity Rules

The following example illustrates how qualified domestic relations orders operate and how they interact with the minimum survivor annuity rules.[1]

The example involves a defined benefit plan, referred to as Plan X, under which the normal retirement age is 65, the earliest retirement age is 55, and the normal retirement benefit is a single annuity for the participant's life. The plan also offers a lump-sum settlement option, a qualified joint and survivor annuity option (and a qualified preretirement survivor annuity option) with respect to a participant and the participant's spouse, and a 60-month certain and life annuity. P, a participant in Plan X, is divorced from his spouse S1 at age 45. The state court, applying the domestic relations law of State A, enters a domestic relations order awarding S1 a one-half interest in P's accrued benefits to the extent they are attributable to the period of their marriage.

Example: P retires at age 65 with a total accrued benefit of $1,000 per month. At that time S1 is age 62. Under the laws of State A, $400 per month of P's accrued benefit is considered attributable to P's marriage to S1. The order provides that S1 is to receive her one-half interest in that portion of P's total benefit when P actually retires. P has since remarried S2. P and S2 choose not to waive the qualified joint and survivor annuity. Under the terms of the order, S1 may elect to receive her court-awarded interest in any form available to P—other than a qualified joint and survivor annuity. S1 elects an immediate single-life annuity. The plan is required to convert her one-half interest in that portion of P's accrued benefits attributable to their marriage from a $200 per month annuity for P's life—50 percent of $400—beginning at P's age 65 to an actuarially equivalent monthly annuity for S1's life beginning at her age 62. Only the $800 per month balance of P's accrued benefit remaining would be taken into account in determining P's qualified joint and survivor annuity.

☐ Additional examples, illustrating the interaction between the rules governing QDROs and the survivor annuity requirements are set forth in the CCH PENSION PLAN GUIDE at ¶ 1381.

---

[1]*Congressional Record*, August 9, 1984, p. H8761 (discussing the Retirement Equity Act of 1984).

¶ 1620

Waiver of Distribution Requirements

A plan does not fail to meet the requirements of Code Sec. 409(d) (which relates to the ESOP provision that requires deferral of distributions for 84 months), the qualification requirements under Code Secs. 401(a) and 401(k), and the tax-sheltered annuity requirements under Code Sec. 403(b), solely because of payments to an alternative payee pursuant to a qualified domestic relations order.[1] Such payments may, therefore, be made with respect to a participant who has not separated from service and may commence even before the participant attains the earliest retirement age under the plan.

---

[1]Code Sec. 414(p)(10).

¶ 1625

Procedures for Plan Administrator

The plan administrator must determine the qualified status of a domestic relations order, and administer distributions under the qualified order, pursuant to reasonable written plan procedures (see ¶ 1640).[1] In addition, the plan administrator must promptly notify the participant and each alternate payee named in the order of its receipt by the plan and of the plan's procedures for determining the order's qualified status.

A qualified domestic relations order must contain the elements described at ¶ 1600. In making the determination that a judgment or decree is a QDRO, the plan administrator also looks to whether it relates to the provision of child support, alimony payments, or marital property rights to a spouse, former spouse, child, or other dependent of the participants, and that it is made pursuant to a state domestic relations law by a state authority with jurisdiction.

---

[1]Code Sec. 414(p)(6)(A); ERISA Sec. 206(d)(3)(G).

¶ 1630

Deferral of Payment Pending QDRO Determination

While the qualified status of the order is being determined, the plan administrator may not distribute benefits to the plan participant, but must separately account for the benefits that would otherwise be payable to the alternate payee under the QDRO during that period. However, the administrator need not set up an escrow account for such amounts.[1] If an order is determined to be qualified within 18 months after the date on which the first payment would be required to be made under the order, the plan administrator must pay the separated amounts (including any interest on those amounts) to the person or persons entitled to them.[2]

Nonqualified order

If, within that period, it is determined that the order is not qualified or if the matter remains unresolved, the administrator must pay the separated amounts (and any interest thereon) to the person or persons who would have received them if the order had not been issued.[3]

Prospective effect only

Any determination that an order is qualified after expiration of the 18-month period will have prospective effect only.[4]

---

[1]Code Sec. 414(p)(7)(A); ERISA Sec. 206(d)(3)(H)(i).

[2]Code Sec. 414(p)(7)(B); ERISA Sec. 206(d)(3)(H)(ii).

[3]Code Sec. 414(p)(7)(C); ERISA Sec. 206(d)(3)(H)(iii).

[4]Code Sec. 414(p)(7)(D); ERISA Sec. 206(d)(3)(H)(iv).

¶ 1635

Fiduciary Liability

Any determination regarding an order's qualified status is subject to judicial review in federal or state court on the initiative of either the participant or alternate payee. However, if the plan administrator acts in accordance with the fiduciary standards of ERISA (see ¶ 2300) in making any determination or payment under the above rules, he or she will be discharged from any liability to a participant or alternate payee with respect to the payment.[1]

The fiduciary standards would be construed to require the administrator to provide the parties with an adequate period of time in which to seek judicial review of the administrator's determination as to the qualified status of the order before a distribution is made.

Participants remain liable for payments

The fact that the plan administrator may make payment of all separated amounts to the participant if the administrator determines that an order is not qualified, or if a determination is not made within the 18-month period (see ¶ 1630), does not mean that the participant is necessarily relieved of liability to pay over those amounts to the alternate payee. It is only the administrator who is relieved of liability to the alternate payee.

---

[1] ERISA Sec. 206(d)(3)(I).

¶ 1640

Written Procedures

Every plan is required to have written procedures for determining the qualified status of domestic relations orders and for administering the payment of benefits under such orders. These procedures must provide for notification of the interested parties promptly following receipt of the order and must permit an alternate payee to designate a representative for receipt of copies of notices sent to the alternate payee.[1]

The procedures need not be set forth in the qualified plan document, but must be contained in the plan's SPD.[2] The IRS has provided sample language that may be used in drafting a QDRO.[3]

CCH Pointer: Reasonable expenses incurred in determining whether an order is a QDRO constitute administrative plan expenses that are payable from plan assets. In addition, reasonable expenses incurred by the plan administrator in making a QDRO determination may be imposed on the account of the participant or beneficiary seeking the determination.[4]

---

[1] Code Sec. 414(p)(6)(B); ERISA Sec. 206(d)(3)(G)(ii).

[2] Code Sec. 414(p)(6)(B); ERISA Sec. 206(d)(3)(G)(ii); ERISA Reg. Sec. 2520.102-3(l).

[3] IRS Notice 97-11, 1997-1 CB 379, CCH Pension Plan Guide ¶ 17,112E.

[4] EBSA Field Assistance Bulletin 2003-3, May 19, 2003, CCH Pension Plan Guide ¶ 19,980E; ERISA Opinion Letter 94-32A, 8-4-94, CCH Pension Plan Guide ¶ 23,898D, is superseded.

¶ 1645

For More Information

☐ For more information on QDROs, see CCH Pension Plan Guide ¶ 1347-1387.

Joint and Survivor Annuities

¶ 1700

General Rules

A retirement plan must provide automatic survivor benefits to the surviving spouse of a retiree under a "joint and survivor annuity" or to the surviving spouse of a vested participant who dies before retirement under a "preretirement survivor annuity." [1] Plans that are required to provide benefits in the form of a qualified joint and survivor annuity must also offer a "qualified optional survivor annuity." See below.

What is a qualified joint and survivor annuity?

A qualified joint and survivor annuity (QJSA) is an annuity for the life of the participant with a survivor annuity for the life of the spouse. The annuity for the life of the spouse must not be less than 50% (and not greater than 100%) of the amount that is payable during the joint lives of the participant and spouse. [2] The QJSA must be the actuarial equivalent of a single life annuity for the life of the participant.

In the case of a married participant, the qualified joint and survivor annuity must be at least as valuable as any other optional form of benefit payable under the plan at the same time. [3] In the case of an unmarried participant, the QJSA may be less valuable than other optional forms of benefit payable under the plan.

Earliest retirement age. A plan must permit a participant to receive a distribution of a QJSA when the participant attains the earliest retirement age. [4] The earliest retirement age generally is defined as the earliest date on which, under the plan, the participant could elect to receive retirement benefits. [5] In the case of a plan that provides for voluntary distributions that begin on the participant's separation from service, the earliest retirement age is the earliest age at which a participant could separate from service (including death of the participant) and receive distributions. [6] In the case of a plan that provides for in-service distributions, the earliest retirement age is the earliest age at which such distributions may be made. [7]

What is a qualified preretirement survivor annuity?

A qualified preretirement survivor annuity (QPSA) is an annuity for the life of the surviving spouse of the participant where the participant dies before receiving retirement benefits. Under a qualified preretirement survivor annuity, the amount of payments to the surviving spouse is to be the same as (or the actuarial equivalent of) the amount of the payments that would have been made under the qualified joint and survivor annuity under the following circumstances:[8]

1. In the case of a participant who dies after attaining the earliest retirement age under the plan, the amount of the payments under the QPSA may not be less than the payments that would have been made if the participant had retired with an immediate qualified joint and survivor annuity on the day before his or her death.

2. In the case of a participant who dies on or before the earliest retirement age under the plan, the amount of the payments under the QPSA may not be less than the payments that would have been made under the QJSA if the participant had separated from service on the date of death, survived to the earliest retirement age, retired with an immediate qualified joint and survivor annuity at the earliest retirement age, and died on the day after the day on which he or she would have attained the earliest retirement age. However, in the case of a participant who separated from service prior to his or her death, the amount of a qualified preretirement survivor annuity is to be calculated by reference to the actual date of separation and not from the date of the participant's death.

In the case of a defined contribution plan, the payments under a qualified preretirement survivor annuity are not to be less than the payments under a single life annuity, the present value of which is at least equal to 50% of the participant's account balance to which the participant had a nonforfeitable right on the date of death.[9]

The plan is not to prohibit the commencement of the qualified preretirement survivor annuity to the surviving spouse later than the month in which the participant would have reached the earliest retirement age under the plan.[10]

What is a qualified optional survivor annuity?

Generally effective for plan years beginning after December 31, 2007, a participant may elect to have benefits paid in the form of a "qualified optional survivor annuity."[11] A qualified optional survivor annuity is:

1. an annuity for the life of the participant with a survivor annuity for the life of the spouse that is equal to the applicable percentage of the amount of the annuity that is payable during the joint lives of the participant and the spouse; and

2. the actuarial equivalent to a single annuity for the live of the participant.

If the survivor annuity under the plan's qualified joint and survivor annuity is less than 75% of the annuity payable during the joint lives of the participant and spouse, the applicable percentage is 75%. If the survivor annuity under the plan's qualified joint and survivor annuity is greater than or equal to 75% of the annuity payable during the joint lives of the participant and spouse, the applicable percentage is 50%.

While spousal consent is required for a participant to waive a plan's QJSA form of distribution and elect an alternative distribution form, a participant may elect out of the QJSA, in favor of an actuarially equivalent alternative joint and survivor annuity that satisfies the conditions to be a QJSA, without spousal consent. If the QOSA is not actuarially equivalent to the QJSA, spousal consent is required for the participant to waive the QJSA and elect the QOSA.[12]

[1] Code Secs. 401(a)(11) and 417; ERISA Sec. 205.

[2] Code Sec. 417(b); ERISA Sec. 205(d).

[3] IRS Reg. § 1.401(a)-20, Q&A-16.

[4] IRS Reg. § 1.401(a)-20, Q&A-17(a).

[5] Code Sec. 417(f)(3); ERISA Sec. 205(h)(3); IRS Reg. § 1.401(a)-20, Q&A-17(b)(4).

[6] IRS Reg. § 1.401(a)-20, Q&A-17(b)(2).

[7] IRS Reg. § 1.401(a)-20, Q&A-17(b)(3).

[8] Code Sec. 417(c)(1)(A); ERISA Sec. 205(e)(1)(A); IRS Reg. § 1.401(a)-20, Q&A-18.

[9] Code Sec. 417(c)(2); ERISA Sec. 205(e)(2); IRS Reg. § 1.401(a)-20, Q&A-20.

[10] Code Sec. 417(c)(1)(B); ERISA Sec. 205(e)(1)(B); IRS Reg. § 1.401(a)-20, Q&A-22.

[11] Code Sec. 417(a)(1)(A), as amended, and Code Sec. 417(g), as added, by P.L. 109-280 (Pension Protection Act of 2006).

[12] IRS Notice 2008-30, I.R.B. 2008-12, 3-24-08, CCH PENSION PLAN GUIDE ¶ 17,138X.

¶ 1705

Application to Different Types of Plans

The joint and survivor annuity rules apply to defined benefit plans and certain types of defined contribution plans.

Defined benefit plans

A defined benefit plan is required to provide automatic survivor benefits:[1]

1. in the case of a vested participant who does not die before the annuity starting date, in the form of a qualified joint and survivor annuity, and

2. in the case of a vested participant who dies before the annuity starting date and who has a surviving spouse, in the form of a qualified preretirement survivor annuity.

Defined contribution plans

The survivor annuity requirements apply to defined contribution plans that are subject to the minimum funding standards of Code Sec. 412.[2] The only defined contribution plans that are subject to those standards are money purchase pension plans. Therefore, the survivor annuity rules apply to money purchase pension plans that are not exempt from the minimum funding standards.

Profit-sharing and stock bonus plans. The automatic survivor coverage rules also apply to profit-sharing plans and stock bonus plans unless the following conditions are satisfied:[3]

First, the plan must provide that, on the death of the participant, the vested accrued benefit will be paid in full to the surviving spouse or, if there is no surviving spouse or if the surviving spouse consents, to a designated beneficiary.

Second, the participant must not elect that benefits be paid in the form of a life annuity.[4]

Third, as to the participant, the plan must not be a direct or indirect transferee of a plan required to provide automatic survival benefits.

ESOPs. Under Code Sec. 409(h), a participant in an ESOP is entitled to demand that his benefits be paid in the form of the employer's stock. The portion of the participant's accrued benefit that is subject to Code Sec. 409(h) is regarded as being provided by a plan that is not subject to the minimum funding standards. Accordingly, that portion is not subject to the survivor annuity requirements if the above three conditions are satisfied.[5]

Government and church plans. As discussed above, the survivor annuity requirements do not apply to individual account plans that are not subject to the funding standards under Code Sec. 412.[6] Government plans and church plans are exempt from the funding standards and are, therefore, exempt from the survivor annuity requirements.[7]

Frozen or terminated plans

A plan that is otherwise subject to the survivor annuity rules is not generally excused from compliance with those rules just because it is frozen or terminated.[8]

PBGC-administered plan

If the Pension Benefit Guaranty Corporation is administering a plan, it will pay benefits in the form required by the survivor annuity rules (i.e., a QPSA or a QJSA).[9]

Nonqualified plans

Both ERISA and the Internal Revenue Code contain provisions requiring plans to provide survivor annuities. ERISA Sec. 205, which prescribes survivor annuity rules that are essentially the same as those set forth in the Internal Revenue Code, applies to many plans that are not—and do not seek to be—qualified under Code Sec. 401.

IRAs

Individual retirement accounts and annuities are not subject to the survivor annuity requirements of ERISA.[10]

---

[1] Code Sec. 401(a)(11)(A) and (B)(i) and (ii); ERISA Sec. 205(a) and (b)(1)(A) and (B).

[2] Code Sec. 401(a)(11)(B)(ii).

[3] Code Sec. 401(a)(11)(B)(iii); IRS Reg. § 1.401(a)-20, Q&A-3.

[4] IRS Reg. § 1.401(a)-20, Q&A-4.

⁵ Code Sec. 401(a)(11)(C); IRS Reg. § 1.401(a)-20, Q&A-3(c).

⁶ Code Sec. 401(a)(11)(A) and (B)(i) and (ii); ERISA Sec. 205(a) and (b)(1)(A) and (B).

⁷ Code Sec. 412(h)(3) and (4); ERISA Sec. 4(b)(1) and (2).

⁸ IRS Reg. § 1.401(a)-20, Q&A-6. An exception was provided for plans with a termination date preceding September 17, 1985, if assets were promptly distributed.

⁹ IRS Reg. § 1.401(a)-20, Q&A-7.

¹⁰ ERISA Sec. 201(6).

¶ 1710

Application to Married and Unmarried Participants

Plans subject to the survivor annuity requirements must satisfy those requirements even for unmarried participants. A qualified joint and survivor annuity for an unmarried participant is a life annuity.[1] Thus, an unmarried participant must be provided with a life annuity unless he or she elects another form of benefit. An unmarried participant is deemed to have waived the qualified preretirement survivor requirements. This deemed waiver is null and void if the participant later marries.

---

[1] IRS Reg. § 1.401(a)-20, Q&A-25(a).

¶ 1715

Election Against Survivor Annuity

A plan must provide each participant with an opportunity to elect not to receive the qualified joint and survivor annuity or the qualified preretirement survivor annuity (QPSA) (or both) during an applicable election period.[1] Spousal consent is necessary in most cases (see "**When consent is not required**," below). In addition, the participant is permitted to revoke any waiver during the applicable election period. There is no limit on the number of times a participant may waive a survivor benefit or revoke a waiver.

Election period

In the case of a qualified joint and survivor annuity, the applicable election period is the 180-day period ending on the annuity starting date. In the case of a qualified preretirement survivor annuity, the applicable election period is a period beginning on the first day of the plan year in which the participant attains age 35 and ending on the date of the participant's death.[2]

> **Example 1:** In 2005, John White, who is married, becomes a participant in his employer's pension plan when he is age 28. The plan uses the calendar year for its plan year. His election period with respect to the qualified preretirement survivor annuity will begin on January 1, 2012, the first day of the plan year in which he reaches age 35, if he is still an active participant in the plan.

If the participant separates from service, the applicable election period begins on that date with respect to benefits accrued before the separation from service.[3]

> **Example 2:** Assume the same facts as in Example (1), except that at age 30, White separates from his employer's service with vested, accrued benefits of

$4,000. White will be able to waive the qualified preretirement survivor annuity with respect to the benefits of $4,000 at the time of his separation from service, if he so wishes. Suppose, however, that White returns to his employer's service at age 32. The applicable election period with respect to benefits accrued after he returns does not begin until January 1, 2012, the first day of the plan year in which he becomes age 35.

White will have automatic survivor coverage during the period from age 32 to 35 with respect to the vested benefits accrued during that period, even if he waived the coverage with respect to the pre-separation accrued benefits. Of course, at age 35, the participant may waive any preretirement survivor annuity coverage. However, any waiver election by White during either of the election periods described in this example will have to be consented to by his wife.

Waivers before age 35. A plan may provide for a waiver (with spousal consent) of a QPSA benefit before age 35 if a written explanation of the QPSA is given to the participant and the waiver becomes invalid upon the beginning of the plan year in which the participant reaches age 35.[4] If there is no new waiver after that date, the participant's spouse must receive the QPSA benefit upon the participant's death.

Spousal consent requirement

A spouse's consent to an election to waive a qualified joint and survivor annuity or a qualified preretirement survivor annuity is not valid unless, in writing:[5]

1. the election designates a beneficiary (or a form of benefit) which may not be changed without spousal consent, or the consent of the spouse permits designations of beneficiaries by the participant without any requirement of further consent by the spouse, and

2. the spouse's consent acknowledges the effect of such election and it is witnessed by a plan representative or a notary.

Sample language for spousal consent to waiver

The IRS has issued sample language that plan administrators may incorporate into forms designed to enable a spouse to consent to:

1. a participant's waiver of a QJSA or a QPSA under a defined benefit or a defined contribution plan;

2. a participant's choice of a nonspouse beneficiary for a survivor's benefit under a defined benefit or a defined contribution plan; and

3. a participant's selection of a nonspouse beneficiary for the participant's account balance in a defined contribution plan that is not subject to the QJSA or QPSA rules.[6]

The sample language is limited to spousal consent and does not apply to the waiver of a QJSA or QPSA by a participant.

¶1715

When consent is not required

Spousal consent to a waiver is not necessary if there is no spouse or if the spouse cannot be located.[7] In addition, spousal consent is not required (unless a qualified domestic relations order provides otherwise) if the participant is legally separated or if the participant has been abandoned (within the meaning of local law) and there is a court order to that effect. See ¶ 1600.

---

[1] Code Sec. 417(a)(1); ERISA Sec. 205(c)(1).

[2] Code Sec. 417(a)(6); ERISA Sec. 205(c)(7). NOTE: The Pension Protection Act of 2006 (P.L. 109-280) expanded the applicable election period for a participant to waive the QJSA form of benefit from 90 to 180 days, effective for years beginning after December 31, 2006. This is reflected in proposed IRS regulations published on October 9, 2008 (73 FR 59575), CCH Pension Plan Guide ¶ 20,262R.

[3] Code Sec. 417(a)(6), last sentence; ERISA Sec. 205(c)(7), last sentence.

[4] IRS Reg. § 1.401(a)-20, Q&A-33(b).

[5] Code Sec. 417(a)(2)(A); ERISA Sec. 205(c)(2)(A).

[6] IRS Notice 97-10, 1997-1 CB 370; CCH PENSION PLAN GUIDE ¶ 17,112D.

[7] IRS Reg. § 1.401(a)-20, Q&A-27.

¶ 1720

Plan Assets Pledged as Security for Loan

If a participant could use his or her accrued benefit as security for a loan made by the plan, the spouse's right to a qualified joint and survivor annuity or qualified preretirement survivor annuity could be defeated. To prevent this, the law requires spousal consent if any portion of the accrued benefit is to be used as security for a loan.[1]

Consent must be in writing and must be made during the 90-day period ending with the date on which the loan is to be secured. Spousal consent is required even if the accrued benefit is not the primary security for the loan.

If use of a participant's accrued benefit as security for a loan meets the consent requirements, nothing in the survivor benefit requirements will prevent any distribution required by reason of a failure to comply with the terms of such loan.[2]

When consent is not necessary

As in the case of spousal consent to waivers of QJSAs and QPSAs (see ¶ 1715), no spousal consent is necessary where there is no spouse or the spouse cannot be located.[3] In addition, no consent is required if the plan is not subject to the survivor annuity rules. The same is true if the accrued benefit subject to the security does not exceed $5,000.[4]

---

[1] Code Sec. 417(a)(4); ERISA Sec. 205(c)(4); IRS Reg. § 1.401(a)-20, Q&A-24.

[2] Code Sec. 417(f)(5); ERISA Sec. 205(j).

[3] Code Sec. 417(a)(4); ERISA Sec. 205(c)(4).

[4] IRS Reg. § 1.401(a)-20, Q&A-24; IRS Reg. § 1.411(a)-11(c)(3).

¶ 1725

Written Explanation

A plan that is required to provide a qualified joint and survivor annuity or a qualified preretirement survivor annuity form of benefit also must provide to each participant a written explanation of:[1]

1. the terms and conditions of the qualified joint and survivor annuity or qualified preretirement survivor annuity,

2. the participant's right to make, and the effect of, an election to waive the joint and survivor annuity or preretirement survivor annuity form of benefit,

3. the rights of the participant's spouse, and

4. the right to make, and the effect of, a revocation of an election.

The explanation must be furnished to vested participants and to those nonvested participants who are currently employed by the employer who maintains the plan.[2]

CCH Pointer: The written explanation must also include the terms and conditions of the "qualified optional survivor annuity." See ¶ 1700.

Explanation of optional forms of benefits

The IRS has issued final regulations that effectively consolidate the content requirements applicable to written explanations of QJSAs and QPSAs. [3]

Content of QPSA explanation. The written QPSA explanation must contain a description of the QPSA, the circumstances under which the QPSA will be paid if elected, the availability of the election of the QPSA, and the financial effect of the election of the QPSA on the participant's benefits. The financial effect of the election of a QPSA on a participant's benefits can be described by estimating the extent to which a participant's estimated normal retirement benefit would be reduced by the QPSA election.[4] In lieu of providing a specific description of the financial effect of the QPSA election, plans may provide a general description of the financial effect of the election.[5]

Content of QJSA explanation. A QJSA explanation must, with respect to each optional form of benefit available to a participant, describe:[6]

1. the optional form of benefit;

2. the eligibility conditions for the optional form of benefit;

3. the financial effect of electing the optional form of benefit;

4. (for defined benefit plans) the relative value of the optional form of benefit compared to the value of the QJSA; and

5. any other material features of the optional form of benefit.

Relative value of optional benefit form. The required description of the relative value of an optional form of benefit compared to the value of the QJSA must be expressed to a participant in a manner that provides a "meaningful comparison" of the relative economic value of the forms of benefit and that does not require the participant to make calculations using interest or mortality assumptions.[7] The IRS explains that, in order to provide the meaningful comparison, the benefits under one or both optional forms of benefit must be converted, taking into account the time value of money and life expectancies, so that the value of both optional forms of benefit are expressed in the same form.

Approximately equal rule. The relative value of all optional forms of benefit that have an actuarial present value that is at least 95% of the actuarial present value of the QJSA and no greater than 105% of the actuarial present value of the QJSA is permitted to be described by stating that these optional forms of benefit are approximately equal in value to the QJSA, or that all of these forms of benefit and the QJSA are approximately equal in value.[8] Thus, optional forms of benefit that have greater differences in present value may not be described as having approximately the same value. Moreover, this rule applies regardless of whether the comparison is made to the QJSA for married participants or the QJSA for unmarried participants. To give employers sufficient time to perform the additional calculations that may be required to implement this rule, a special effective date applies so that this change to the regulations need not be applied for disclosures made before January 1, 2007.[9]

Estimates of financial effect and relative value. In describing the financial effect of electing an optional form of benefit available to a participant and in describing the relative value of an optional form of benefit compared to the value of the QJSA, a plan may provide "reasonable estimates" (e.g., reasonable assumptions for the age of a participant's spouse) including reasonable estimates of the applicable interest rate under Code Sec. 417(e)(3).[10]

Simplified presentations of financial effect and relative value. The 2006 final regulations permit simplified presentations of financial effect and relative value for a plan that offers a significant number of substantially similar optional forms of benefit. The 2006 rules also permit simplified presentations of relative value and financial effect for a plan that permits the participant to make separate benefit elections with respect to parts of a benefit.[11]

General information alternative to participant-specific information. As an alternative to providing participant-specific information regarding each presently available optional form of benefit, the written QJSA explanation may provide generally applicable information. Specifically, the QJSA explanation, in lieu of providing a statement of the financial effect of electing an optional form of benefit or a comparison of relative values, based on the actual age and benefit of a participant, may include a chart (or other comparable device) indicating the financial effect and relative value of optional forms of benefit in a series of examples specifying the amount of the optional form of benefit payable to a hypothetical participant at a representative range of ages and the comparison of relative values at the same representative ages.[12]

When to provide QJSA explanation

The explanation for a qualified joint and survivor annuity must be furnished to participants no less than 30 days and no more than 180 days before the annuity starting date.[13]

QJSA explanation provided after annuity starting date

Plans may provide the QJSA election explanation after the annuity starting date as long as the election period lasts for 30 days after the explanation is provided.[14] In addition, a participant may elect, with any required spousal consent, to waive the requirement that the written explanation be provided at least 30 days before the annuity starting date, if the distribution begins more than seven days after the explanation is provided.[15] The participant may also waive the requirement that, in the event the explanation is provided after the annuity starting date, the applicable election period not end until 30 days after the explanation is provided.

Retroactive payment of benefits. Code Sec. 417(a)(7)(A), by authorizing a plan to provide the QJSA explanation after the annuity starting date (as long as the applicable election period does not end less than 30 days after the date on which the election is provided) allows for the retroactive payment of benefits attributable to the period before the QJSA explanation is provided.

IRS final regulations, applicable to plan years beginning on or after January 1, 2004, allow benefits to be based on a retroactive annuity starting date if authorized by the plan and affirmatively elected by plan participants.[16]

Authorization of the retroactive annuity is limited to defined benefit plans.[17] However, defined benefit plans are not required to allow for retroactive annuity starting dates and may continue to require that the QJSA explanation be provided before the annuity starting date.

Election of retroactive annuity starting date. A participant must affirmatively elect to use an annuity starting date that occurs on or before the Code Sec. 417(a)(3) written explanation is provided to the participant.

Benefit subject to Code Sec. 415 limits. The benefit determined as of the retroactive annuity starting date must comply with the benefit limits of Code Sec. 415 (and Code Sec. 417(e)(3), if applicable), with the applicable interest rate and the applicable mortality table determined as of that date.[18]

Spousal consent requirement. A participant's spouse (including an alternate payee who is treated as a spouse under a QDRO), determined as of the time distributions actually begin, must consent to the retroactive annuity starting date election.[19]

When to provide QPSA explanation

A plan must provide a written explanation of a qualified preretirement survivor annuity and the right to decline such an annuity within the later of:[20]

1. the period beginning with the first day of the plan year in which a participant reaches age 32 and ending with the end of the plan year preceding the plan year in which he reaches age 35,

2. a reasonable period after the individual becomes a plan participant,

3. a reasonable period of time after the end of the subsidization of a survivor benefit with respect to a participant by a plan, or

4. a reasonable period of time after the survivor benefit provisions of Code Sec. 401(a)(11) become applicable to a participant.

Separation from service before age 35. If a participant separates from service before reaching age 35, the applicable period means the period beginning one year before the separation from service and ending one year after the separation.[21] If such a participant returns to service, the plan also must comply with the general rule. A reasonable period after the enumerated events described in (2), (3), and (4) above is the end of the one-year period beginning with the date the applicable event occurs.[22] The applicable period for such events begins one year prior to the occurrence of the enumerated events.

Delivery of explanation

The written explanation may be provided by first class mail to the last known address of the participant or by hand delivery.[23]

Notice exemption where plan subsidizes costs

A plan is not required to provide a written explanation of the qualified joint and survivor annuity or the qualified preretirement survivor annuity if:[24]

1. the plan fully subsidizes the cost of the benefit, and

2. the plan does not permit a participant to waive the benefit or designate another beneficiary.

Electronic transmission of notices

The IRS has issued regulations providing for the use of electronic methods for complying with QJSA notices and elections.[25] The regulations authorize the use of an electronic acknowledgment or notarization to comply with the Code Sec. 417 requirement that any spousal consent to a waiver of a QJSA be witnessed by a plan representative or a notary public.

---

[1] Code Sec. 417(a)(3); ERISA Sec. 205(c)(3).

[2] IRS Reg. § 1.401(a)-20, Q&A-34.

[3] T.D. 9099 (2003) and T.D. 9256 (2006). Initially, the final regulations were effective for QJSA explanations provided with respect to annuity starting dates on or after October 1, 2004 and to QPSA explanations provided after July 1, 2004. IRS Reg. § 1.417(a)(3)-1(f), as issued under T.D. 9099 (2003).

Subsequently, the IRS, in June 2004, postponed the effective date of the regulations for specified QJSA explanations. Under the relief, the final rules will apply to QJSA explanations provided with respect to distributions with annuity starting dates beginning on or after February 1, 2006, rather than October 1, 2004. IRS Announcement 2004-58, I.R.B. 2004-29, CCH Pension Plan Guide ¶ 17,097S-46.

The extended effective date was adopted in final regulations issued by the IRS in March 2006. Thus, under the 2006 regulations, the 2003 regulations are generally effective for QJSA explanations provided with respect to annuity starting dates beginning on or after February 1, 2006. IRS Reg. § 1.417(a)(3)-1(f), as issued under T.D. 9256 (2006). However, the 2006 regulations retain the effective date under the 2003 regulations for explanations with respect to any optional form of benefit subject to Code Sec. 417(e)(3) that has a lower actuarial present value than the QJSA. For example, a QJSA explanation provided with respect to an annuity starting date beginning on or after October 1, 2004, must comply with the final rules under IRS Reg. § 1.417(a)(3)-1 to the extent that the plan provides for payment to the participant in the form of a single-sum distribution that does not reflect an early retirement subsidy available under the QJSA. However the change to IRS Reg. § 1.417(a)(3)-1(c)(2)(iii)(C), relating to disclosures of optional forms of benefit that are approximately equal in value to the QJSA (see below), does not apply to a QJSA explanation provided before January 1, 2007. A reasonable good faith effort to comply with the 2006 regulations (including substantial compliance with the 2003 regulations) will be deemed to satisfy the QJSA explanations provided before January 1, 2007, except for any portion of a QJSA explanation that is subject to the earlier effective dates of IRS Reg. § 1.417(a)(3)-1(f)(2) discussed above.

[4] IRS Reg. § 1.417(a)(3)-1(b)(3).

[5] IRS Reg. § 1.417(a)(3)-1(d)(3).

[6] IRS Reg. § 1.417(a)(3)-1(c)(1).

[7] IRS Reg. § 1.417(a)(3)-1(c)(2).

[8] IRS Reg. § 1.417(a)(3)-1(c)(2)(iii)(C), as issued under T.D. 9256 (2006); Preamble to T.D. 9256, at CCH PENSION PLAN GUIDE ¶ 24,508C.

[9] IRS Reg. § 1.417(a)(3)-1(f)(2)(iii), as issued under T.D. 9256 (2006); Preamble to T.D. 9256, at CCH PENSION PLAN GUIDE ¶ 24,508C.

[10] IRS Reg. § 1.417(a)(3)-1(c)(3)(i).

[11] IRS Reg. § 1.417(a)(3)-1(c)(5), as issued under T.D. 9256 (2006).

[12] IRS Reg. § 1.417(a)(3)-1(d)(2)(i).

[13] IRS Reg. § 1.417(e)-1(b)(3)(ii). NOTE: The Pension Protection Act of 2006 (P.L. 109-280) expanded the applicable election period for a participant to waive the QJSA form of benefit from 90 days to 180 days, effective for years beginning after December 31, 2006. This is reflected in Prop. IRS Reg. § 1.417(e)(1)(b)(3)(ii). The Act also directed the Secretary of the Treasury to make a conforming modification to the regulations under the Code and ERISA that apply to distributions of survivor annuities in order to double the length of the notice and consent period.

[14] Code Sec. 417(a)(7)(A); ERISA Sec. 205(c)(8)(A).

[15] Code Sec. 417(a)(7)(B); ERISA Sec. 205(c)(8)(B).

[16] IRS Reg. § 1.417(e)-1(b)(3)(iv).

[17] IRS Reg. § 1.417(e)-1(b)(3)(iv)(A).

[18] IRS Reg. § 1.417(e)-1(b)(3)(iv)(B).

[19] IRS Reg. § 1.417(e)-1(b)(3)(v)(A).

[20] Code Sec. 417(a)(3)(B); ERISA Sec. 205(c)(3)(B); IRS Reg. § 1.401(a)-20, Q&A-35(a).

[21] IRS Reg. § 1.401(a)-20, Q&A-35(b).

[22] IRS Reg. § 1.401(a)-20, Q&A-35(c).

[23] IRS Reg. § 1.417(a)(3)-1(a)(3).

[24] Code Sec. 417(a)(5)(A); ERISA Sec. 205(c)(5)(A); IRS Reg. § 1.401(a)-20, Q&A-37.

[25] IRS Reg. § 1.401(a)-21; Preamble to T.D. 9294, CCH PENSION PLAN GUIDE ¶ 24,508I.

¶ 1730

One-Year Marriage Requirement

A qualified joint and survivor annuity or a qualified preretirement survivor annuity need not be provided by a plan unless the participant and the spouse have been married throughout the one-year period ending on the earlier of:[1]

1. the participant's annuity starting date (the first day of the first period for which an amount is received as an annuity whether by reason of retirement or disability), or

2. the date of the participant's death.

Under this rule, if a participant dies after the annuity starting date, the spouse to whom the participant was married during the one-year period ending on the annuity starting date is entitled to the survivor annuity under the plan whether or not the participant and spouse are married on the date of the participant's death.

Exception to one-year rule

An exception to the one-year marriage requirement provides that a participant and his or her spouse will be treated as having been married throughout the one-year period ending on the participant's annuity starting date if:[2]

1. the participant marries *within* one year before the annuity starting date and

2. the participant has been married to that spouse for at least one year ending on the date of the participant's death.

---

[1] Code Sec. 417(d)(1); ERISA Sec. 205(f)(1); Reg. § 1.401(a)-20, Q&A-25(b).　　[2] Code Sec. 417(d)(2); ERISA Sec. 205(f)(2).

¶ 1735
Restrictions on "Cash-Outs" and Distributions

Code Secs. 411(a)(11) and 417(e) restrict the ability of a qualified plan to distribute benefits without the consent of the participant or, if the participant is not alive, the surviving spouse of the participant.

Consent before benefit is no longer immediately distributable

A plan may not distribute a QJSA or QPSA without the consent of the participant, or the participant's spouse, if the benefit is "immediately distributable." Thus, consent is required before the participant attains, or would have attained (in the case of a deceased participant), the later of normal retirement age (as defined in Code Sec. 411(a)(8)), or age 62, and the benefit is no longer immediately distributable.[1] However, spousal consent is not required for a distribution of a QJSA at any time. In addition, benefits may be paid to a nonspouse beneficiary after a participant's death without the beneficiary's consent.[2]

Distributions in a form other than a QJSA

A plan may not make a distribution of a participant's accrued benefits in a form other than a QJSA unless the QJSA has been waived by the participant and the participant's spouse has consented to the waiver.[3] However, written consent of the participant and, if the participant is married on the annuity starting date, the participant's spouse, is not required for the distribution of a benefit in form other than a QJSA if the present value of the nonforfeitable benefit is not greater than $5,000.[4]

Where benefit is not greater than $5,000

The present value of a QJSA or QPSA may be immediately distributed, or "cashed-out," before the annuity starting date, if the present value of the nonforfeitable benefit does not exceed $5,000.[5]

CCH Pointer: Under the "lookback" rule, the present value of a vested accrued benefit was deemed to exceed the cash-out limit if the value of the benefit exceeded the cash-out limit at the time of any previous distribution.[6] Accordingly, once payments had begun, a plan could not cash out a QJSA or

QPSA in the event that the present value of the benefit declined below $5,000. IRS regulations, effective for distributions made on or after October 17, 2000, eliminated the lookback rule. As a result, an accrued benefit that is valued at $5,000 or less on the date that the distribution begins may be distributed without participant or spousal consent, even if the benefit was valued at more than $5,000 at the time of a previous distribution.[7] However, the final regulations strengthen the spousal consent rules by requiring consent after the annuity starting date for the immediate distribution of the present value of an accrued benefit that is being distributed in any form, including a QJSA or QPSA, regardless of the present value of the benefit.[8] Thus, a cash-out may not be made after the annuity starting date, even if the value of the benefit at the annuity starting date is under $5,000 and the benefit is distributed in a nonannuity form.

A cash-out distribution of a QJSA or a QPSA with a present value over $5,000 may only be made with the consent of the participant and the participant's spouse.[9]

CCH Pointer: The present value of a plan benefit may be calculated without including amounts received by the distributing plan that are attributable to rollover contributions and earnings allocable to rollover contributions.[10] A QJSA or QPSA may also exclude a participant's rollover contributions (and earnings thereon) from the present value of the participant's benefit for purposes of determining whether the participant or participant's spouse must consent to the cash-out of the benefit.[11]

Consent in writing

The consent to commencement of benefits must be in writing.[12] Written consent of the participant and the participant's spouse to the distribution must be made not more than 180 days before the annuity starting date.[13] However, no consent is valid unless the participant has received a general explanation of the material features and relative values of the optional forms of benefit available under the plan in a manner that would satisfy the notice requirements for QJSAs and QPSAs.[14]

QJSA may be waived less than 30 days after notice. Plan participants must be provided with the written explanation of their rights to a QJSA and their corollary rights to waive the QJSA no less than 30 days and no more than 180 days before the annuity starting date.[15] See ¶ 1725. However, after receiving the written explanation, a participant may affirmatively elect (with spousal consent, if applicable) to waive the QJSA and elect a benefit other than a QJSA (i.e., a single life annuity) with an annuity starting date that is less than 30 days after the written explanation was provided to the participant, if the following conditions are met:

1. The plan administrator provides information to the participant clearly indicating that the participant has at least 30 days to decide whether to waive the QJSA and take a distribution in a form other than a QJSA.

2. The participant is allowed a period of time in which to revoke the distribution election that lasts at least until the later of the

annuity starting date or any date prior to the expiration of the seven-day period beginning with the day after the explanation of the QJSA is given to the participant.

3. The annuity starting date is after the date that the QJSA explanation is provided to the participant. However, the annuity starting date may precede the date that the participant elects a distribution and be before the date that the distribution is permitted to begin.

4. Distributions in accord with the participant's election do not beg0in before the end of the seven-day period that begins after the explanation of the QJSA is provided.

Determining present value

The present value of a qualified joint and survivor annuity or a preretirement survivor annuity, must be determined by using an applicable mortality table and an applicable interest rate.[16]

CCH Pointer: The Pension Protection Act of 2006 (P.L. 109-280) changed the applicable mortality table and interest rate used to calculate the minimum value of a lump-sum distribution paid from a defined benefit plan.[17] Generally, the post-PPA rules will reduce the lump sum that would have otherwise been payable by increasing the applicable interest rate. The mortality table to be used for calculating lump-sum distributions is based on the mortality table specified for the plan year under the post-2007 minimum funding rules for single-employer defined benefit plans (see ¶ 869). [18] The IRS has prescribed tables for use in determining minimum lump sums.[19]

Pre-2008 rules. For pre-2008 plan years, the applicable mortality table to be used is a gender neutral mortality table issued by the IRS that is based on the prevailing commissioner's standard table used to determine reserves for group annuity contracts issued on the date as of which present value is being determined.[20] The applicable interest rate is the annual interest rate on 30-year Treasury securities for the month prior to the distribution (or an earlier time that the IRS may determine).[21]

---

[1] IRS Reg. § 1.417(e)-1(b)(1).

[2] *Ibid.*

[3] *Ibid.*

[4] IRS Reg. § 1.417(e)-1(b)(2).

[5] Code Sec. 417(e)(1); ERISA Sec. 205(g)(1); IRS Reg. § 1.417(e)-1(b)(2).

[6] IRS Reg. § 1.417(e)-1(b)(2), prior to amendment by T.D. 8891 (65 FR 44679).

[7] IRS Reg. § 1.411(a)-11(c)(3) and IRS Reg. § 1.417(e)-1(b)(2)(i).

[8] Code Sec. 417(e)(1); IRS Reg. § 1.417(e)-1(b)(2)(i).

[9] Code Sec. 417(e)(2).

[10] Code Sec. 411(a)(11)(D); ERISA Sec. 203(e)(4).

[11] Code Sec. 417(e)(1) and (2); ERISA Sec. 205(g)(1).

[12] IRS Reg. § 1.417(e)-1(b)(2).

[13] IRS Reg. § 1.417(e)-1(b)(3)(i). NOTE: The Pension Protection Act of 2006 (P.L. 109-280), Act Sec. 1102(a)(1)(B), directs the Secretary of the Treasury to modify the regulations under the Internal Revenue Code that apply to distributions of survivor annuities (IRS Reg. § 1.417(e)-1(b)) in order to double the length of the notice and consent period from 90 to 180 days. The required modifications apply to years beginning after De-

cember 31, 2006. This is reflected in Prop. IRS Reg. § 1.417(e)(1)(b)(3)(i).

[14] IRS Reg. § 1.417(e)-1(b)(2).

[15] IRS Reg. § 1.417(e)-1(b)(3)(ii). NOTE: The Pension Protection Act of 2006 (P.L. 109-280), Act Sec. 1102(a)(1)(B), directs the Secretary of the Treasury to modify the regulations under the Internal Revenue Code that apply to distributions of survivor annuities (IRS Reg. § 1.417(e)-1(b)) in order to double the length of the notice and consent period from 90 to 180 days. The required modifications apply to years beginning after December 31, 2006. This is reflected in Prop. IRS Reg. § 1.417(e)(1)(b)(3)(ii).

[16] Code Sec. 417(e)(3)(A) and ERISA Sec. 205(g)(3)(A), as amended by P.L 109-280 (Pension Protection Act of 2006), Act Sec. 302.

[17] Code Sec. 417(e)(3) and ERISA § 205(g), as amended by P.L. 109-280 (Pension Protection Act of 2006), Act Sec. 302.

[18] Code Sec. 417(e)(3)(B) and ERISA § 205(g)(3)(B)(i), as amended by P.L. 109-280 (Pension Protection Act of 2006), Act Sec. 302.

[19] Rev. Rul. 2007-67, I.R.B. 2007-48, November 26, 2007, CCH PENSION PLAN GUIDE ¶ 19,948Z-207 generally provides that the applicable mortality table under Code Sec. 417(e)(3) for 2008 is based on a fixed blend of 50% of the static male combined mortality rates and 50% of the static female combined mortality rates promulgated under final regulations. Notice 2008-85, I.R.B. 2008-42, 10-20-08, CCH PENSION PLAN GUIDE ¶ 17,140M, sets forth the Code Sec. 417(e)(3) applicable mortality table for distributions with annuity starting dates that occur during stability periods that begin during calendar years 2009-2013.

[20] Code Sec. 417(e)(3)(A)(ii)(I), prior to amendment by P.L. 109-280 (Pension Protection Act of 2006). IRS Reg. § 1.417(e)-1(d)(2). Note, the prevailing commissioner's standard table is defined under Code Sec. 807(d)(5)(A).

[21] IRS Reg. § 1.417(e)-1(d)(3).

¶ 1740
For More Information

☐ For more information on joint and survivor and preretirement survivor annuities, consult the CCH PENSION PLAN GUIDE, ¶ 1477-¶ 1549.

Required Distributions From Qualified Plans

¶ 1800

When Distributions Can and Must Be Made

A retirement plan cannot qualify for favorable tax treatment under Code Sec. 401 unless it provides that the payment of benefits must begin (unless the employee elects otherwise) not later than the 60th day after the *latest* of:[1]

1. the end of the plan year in which the employee attains the earlier of age 65 or normal retirement age under the plan,

2. the end of the plan year in which there occurs the tenth anniversary of the year in which the participant commenced participation in the plan, or

3. the end of the plan year in which the employee terminates service with the employer.

In addition, the IRS provides rules under which qualified plan participants *must* begin receiving minimum distribution amounts once they reach age 70½.[2] These required distribution rules are covered in detail at the paragraphs that follow.

¶1800

Postponing the receipt of benefits

A plan may permit an employee to postpone the receipt of benefits beyond the latest of the three dates mentioned above.[3] To do so, the employee must make an election in the form of a written statement, signed by the employee and submitted to the plan administrator, which describes the benefit and the date when payments will begin.[4] However, an election to postpone payment of benefits under a plan cannot be made if it would cause the payment of benefits to violate the "incidental death benefit" rules described at ¶ 1855.[5]

Early retirement

If the plan provides for early retirement, a participant who has completed the service requirements for early retirement benefits, but has separated from service before reaching the required early retirement age, must be entitled to an actuarially reduced normal retirement age benefit upon reaching early retirement age.[6]

Normal retirement age

Normal retirement age is defined as the earlier of:

1. the time specified in the plan as the normal retirement age, or

2. the later of the time an employee attains age 65 or the fifth anniversary of the time the employee commenced participation in the plan.[7]

Governmental plans. The IRS has extended the effective date by which governmental plans must comply with final regulations defining normal retirement age to plan years beginning on or after January 1, 2013.[8] Previously, the prior compliance deadline for governmental plans, announced was for plan years beginning on or after January 1, 2009. Governmental plans, which are not subject to Code Sec. 411, may define normal retirement age based on years of service, rather than attainment of normal retirement age.

---

[1] Code Sec. 401(a)(14); ERISA Sec. 206(a); IRS Reg. § 1.401(a)-14(a).

[2] Code Sec. 401(a)(9).

[3] IRS Reg. § 1.401(a)-14(b)(1).

[4] IRS Reg. § 1.401(a)-14(b)(2).

[5] IRS Reg. § 1.401(a)-14(b)(3).

[6] Code Sec. 401(a)(14).

[7] Code Sec. 411(a)(8).

[8] IRS Notice 2009-86, I.R.B. 2009-46, November 16, 2009, at CCH PENSION PLAN GUIDE ¶ ¶ 17,143U.

¶ 1805

Required Beginning Date for Distributions Beginning Before Death

Participants in qualified plans, with the exception of 5% owners and IRA holders, must begin to receive distributions no later than April 1 of the calendar year following the later of either:[1]

1. the calendar year in which the employee reaches age 70½, or

2. the calendar year in which the employee retires.

If the employee's entire interest is not distributed by the required beginning date, distributions must begin not later than that date and must be made over one of the following periods (or a combination of them):[2]

1. the employee's life;

2. the lives of the employee and his or her designated beneficiary (see ¶ 1820);

3. a period that does not extend beyond the employee's life expectancy; or

4. a period that does not extend beyond the joint life and last survivor expectancy of the employee and his or her designated beneficiary.

Moratorium for 2009 RMDs

A one-year moratorium was imposed on required minimum distributions (RMDs) for 2009. Thus, any required minimum distributions (RMDs) were waived for 2009 for individual account plans, such as 401(k) plans and 403(b) plans, and for IRAs. This means that most participants and beneficiaries otherwise required to take minimum distributions from these types of plans were not required to withdraw any amount in 2009.

Optional forms of benefits

An employee's right to commence benefit distributions in any form at a particular time is an optional form of benefit under Code Sec. 411(d)(6) (see ¶ 866). Plan amendments that eliminate an optional form of benefit are treated as reducing accrued benefits to the extent that the amendment applies to benefits accrued as of the later of the adoption date or the effective date of the amendment. Thus, a plan amendment that eliminates an employee's right to commence pre-retirement benefit distributions after age 70½, or that restricts that right by imposing additional conditions, would generally violate Code Sec. 411(d)(6), if the amendment applies to benefits accrued as of the later of the adoption or the effective date of the amendment.

However, the IRS will allow a plan to be amended to eliminate an age 70½ distribution option to the extent that it provides for distributions to an employee prior to retirement with the employer maintaining the plan. Generally, the amendment must be limited to future accruals and participants who attain age 70½ before 1999 must be allowed to retain the right to receive pre-retirement distributions after age 70½ with respect to a portion of their benefits. Specifically, the following conditions apply:[3]

1. The amendment eliminating the optional form of benefit applies only to benefits with respect to employees who attain age 70½ in or after a calendar year beginning after the later of December 31, 1998, or the adoption date of the amendment;

2. The plan does not (except to the extent required by Code Sec. 401(a)(9)) preclude an employee who retires after the calendar

year in which the employee attains age 70½ from receiving benefits in any of the same optional forms of benefit that would have been available if the employee had retired in the calendar year in which the employee attained age 70½; and

3. The amendment is adopted no later than the last day of any remedial amendment period that applies to the plan for changes under the Small Business Job Protection Act (see ¶ 316).

Actuarial adjustments required

If an employee, who is a participant in a defined benefit plan, retires in a calendar year after the year in which he attains age 70½, the employee's accrued benefit must be actuarially increased in order to reflect the value of benefits that the employee would have received if he or she had retired at age 70½ and had begun receiving benefits at that time.[4] Accordingly, if an employee retires after the calendar year in which he attains age 70½, the employee's accrued benefit must be actuarially increased starting on April 1 following the calendar year in which the employee attains age 70½. For employees who attained age 70½ prior to 1996, however, the starting date for the period of actuarial increase is January 1, 1997.[5] The ending date of the actuarial increase is the date on which benefits commence after retirement. The actuarial increase rules do not apply to defined contribution plans or to certain defined benefit plans that use an optional distribution rule outlined by the IRS.

Government and church plans

The required beginning date for distributions from a governmental plan or a church plan is the later of:

1. April 1 of the calendar year following the calendar year in which the employee reaches age 70½, or

2. April 1 of the calendar year following the calendar year in which the employee retires.

In addition, the actuarial adjustment rule and the requirement that 5-percent owners and IRA holders take distributions at age 70½ do not apply to governmental or church plans.[6]

The IRS has issued final regulations permitting a governmental plan to comply with the required minimum distribution rules by using a reasonable and good faith interpretation of the statute. This compliance rule applies to an eligible 457 plan maintained by a government and to a 403(b) contract that is part of a governmental plan.

5% owners and IRA holders

Five-percent owners must begin receiving distributions no later than April 1 of the calendar year following the calendar year in which they attain age 70½.[7] Similarly, distributions from an IRA or Individual Retirement Annuity must begin no later than April 1 of the calendar year following the calendar year in which the IRA holder attains age 70½.

¶1805

A 5% owner, if the employer is a corporation, is any person who owns more than 5% of the outstanding stock of the corporation or stock possessing more than 5% of the total combined voting power of all stock of the corporation. If the employer is not a corporation, a 5% owner is any person who owns more than 5% of the capital or profit interest in the employer.[8]

Initial and subsequent distribution years

The "distribution calendar year" is the calendar year in which the minimum distribution is required.[9] However, this *first* distribution need not be made until the *following* calendar year (though not later than April 1). The annual distribution for each *subsequent* calendar year must be made not later than December 31 of that year.[10]

If an employee does not receive a distribution during the calendar year in which age 70½ is attained, he or she must receive distributions for two calendar years in the following year. For a discussion of minimum distribution amounts, see ¶ 1835.

An employee reaches age 70½ as of the date six months after the 70th anniversary of his or her birth.[11]

Distributions before the required beginning date

Distributions made before the calendar year the employee attains age 70½ need not be for any specified amount. However, if the individual selects a certain type of distribution option before the calendar year he or she attains age 70½, the distribution option must satisfy the minimum distribution rules beginning in the year the individual attains age 70½.[12]

---

[1] Code Sec. 401(a)(9)(A) and (C).

[2] Code Sec. 401(a)(9)(A)(ii).

[3] IRS Reg. § 1.411(d)-4, Q&A-10.

[4] Code Sec. 401(a)(9)(C)(iii).

[5] IRS Notice 97-75, I.R.B. 1997-51, 12-22-97, CCH Pension Plan Guide ¶ 17,113N.

[6] Code Sec. 401(a)(9)(C)(iv).

[7] Code Sec. 401(a)(9)(C)(ii).

[8] Code Sec. 416(i).

[9] IRS Reg. § 1.401(a)(9)-5, A-1(b).

[10] IRS Reg. § 1.401(a)(9)-5, A-1(c).

[11] IRS Reg. § 1.401(a)(9)-1, A-3.

[12] IRS Reg. § 1.401(a)(9)-2, A-4.

¶ 1810

Death of Employee After Distribution Has Begun

If an employee dies after distribution of his or her interest has begun, the remaining portion of that interest must be distributed "at least as rapidly" as under the method of distribution being used as of his or her date of death.[1]

In applying this rule (except in the case of certain annuity distributions), the distribution of an employee's interest is considered to begin on the required beginning date, even though payments have actually begun before that date. This is so even though the plan or arrangement has made the minimum distribution for the first calendar year preceding the employee's death in which a minimum distribution is required.[2]

Determining the applicable distribution period

The "at least as rapidly" requirement is satisfied if each annual distribution is at least equal to an amount determined by dividing the account balance by the number of years in the applicable distribution period. If the employee dies on or after the date the distribution has begun, and has a designated beneficiary, the applicable distribution period is the longer of the life expectancy of the designated beneficiary or of the employee. Where there is no beneficiary, it is the remaining life expectancy of the employee.[3]

> **CCH Pointer:** According to final regulations, the distribution period will be the longer of the life expectancy of the designated beneficiary or the deceased employee. Thus, if the designated beneficiary is older than the employee, the distribution period will be longer.

Remaining life expectancy of designated beneficiary

The single life table is used to compute the remaining life expectancy of the designated beneficiary. See ¶ 1835.

One non-spouse designated beneficiary. If the designated beneficiary is not the employee's surviving spouse, annual distributions are based on the beneficiary's life expectancy using the beneficiary's age in the year following the year of the employee's death. For subsequent years, the distribution period is reduced by one for each year that has elapsed since the year of the employee's death.[4]

Spouse as sole beneficiary. If the employee's spouse is the sole beneficiary, the applicable distribution period is measured by the surviving spouse's life expectancy using the spouse's birthday for each distribution calendar year after the calendar year of the employee's death up through the calendar year of the spouse's death. Upon the spouse's death, payouts are made under the method described above (reduce by one method) using the spouse's age on his or her birthday in the year of his or her death.[5]

Multiple beneficiaries. If there are multiple individual designated beneficiaries, distributions are determined based on the life expectancy of the beneficiary with the shortest life expectancy (in other words, the oldest beneficiary).[6] However, if the account is a defined contribution plan, separate accounts may be created. See ¶ 1835.

No designated beneficiary. Where there is no designated beneficiary, distributions are based on employee's life expectancy at the date of death. For subsequent years, the distribution period is reduced by one for each year that has elapsed since the year of the employee's death.[7]

---

[1] Code Sec. 401(a)(9)(B)(i).

[2] IRS Reg. § 1.401(a)(9)-2, A-6(a).

[3] IRS Reg. § 1.401(a)(9)-5, A-5(a).

[4] IRS Reg. § 1.401(a)(9)-5, A-5(c)(1).

[5] IRS Reg. § 1.401(a)(9)-5, A-5(c)(2).

[6] IRS Reg. § 1.401(a)(9)-5, A-7(a).

[7] IRS Reg. § 1.401(a)(9)-5, A-5(c)(3).

¶ 1815

Distributions Beginning After Death

If an employee dies before distributions have begun, there are two methods for distributing the employee's interest.

Under the first method, known as the *five-year rule,* the entire interest of the employee must be distributed within five years of the employee's death regardless of who or what entity receives the distribution.

The second method, referred to as the *life expectancy method,* requires that any portion of an employee's interest which is payable to or for the benefit of a designated beneficiary be distributed, beginning within one year of the employee's death, over the life of the beneficiary or over a period not extending beyond the life expectancy of the beneficiary.

Five-year rule

Under the five-year rule, an employee's entire interest must be distributed as of December 31 of the calendar year containing the fifth anniversary of the date of the employee's death.[1]

Life expectancy rule

Under the life expectancy rule, if the designated beneficiary is not the employee's surviving spouse, distributions must begin on or before December 31 of the calendar year immediately following the calendar year in which the employee died.[2]

Surviving spouse. If the designated beneficiary is the employee's surviving spouse, distributions must begin on or before the later of:[3]

1. December 31 of the calendar year immediately following the calendar year in which the employee died, or

2. December 31 of the calendar year in which the employee would have reached age 70½.

Absence of plan provision

Absent a plan provision or election of the five-year rule, the life expectancy rule would apply in all cases in which the employee has a designated beneficiary.[4]

Death of spouse-beneficiary before distributions begin

If a surviving spouse dies after the employee, but before distributions have begun under the life expectancy rule, the five-year rule and the life expectancy rule are to be applied as if the surviving spouse were the employee. The date of death of the surviving spouse will be substituted for the date of death of the employee. Distributions are considered to have begun to the surviving spouse on the date required for commencement of distributions under the life expectancy rule—even though payments have actually been made before that date.[5]

Employee elections

A plan may also adopt provisions that permit employees or their beneficiaries to elect either the five-year rule or the exception to the five-year rule. Such an election must be made no later than the earlier of:

1. December 31 of the calendar year in which the distribution would be required to commence in order to satisfy requirements for the life expectancy rule, or

2. December 31 of the calendar year which contains the fifth anniversary of the date of death of the employee.

The election must be irrevocable as it applies to the beneficiary as of these dates and must apply to all subsequent years.[6]

---

[1] Code Sec. 401(a)(9)(B)(ii).

[2] Code Sec. 401(a)(9)(B)(iii).

[3] Code Sec. 401(a)(9)(B)(iv)(I).

[4] IRS Reg. § 1.401(a)(9)-3, A-4.

[5] Code Sec. 401(a)(9)(B)(iv).

[6] IRS Reg. § 1.401(a)(9)-3, A-4(c).

¶ 1820

Determination of Designated Beneficiary

An employee does not have to make an affirmative election specifying a beneficiary for a person to be considered a designated beneficiary under a plan.[1] If the terms of the plan specify the beneficiary, then whoever is so specified is the designated beneficiary and will be treated as if designated by the employee.

A designated beneficiary does not have to be specified by name in the plan or by the employee participating in the plan so long as the person who will be the beneficiary is identifiable under the plan on the employee's required distribution beginning date or on the date of the employee's death and at all later times.

The beneficiary may be a class as long as it is identifiable. It will be considered identifiable if it is possible at the appropriate time to identify the class member with the shortest life expectancy.

Example: Larry McDonald designates his spouse and children as beneficiaries under his company's plan, although he never gives the plan their names. Since the spouse and children are identifiable through their relationship with Larry on the required beginning date, they are designated beneficiaries. The class of children who are beneficiaries is capable of expanding in the event that other children are born.

Period for determining designated beneficiary

The determination of the designated beneficiary does not become final until September 30 of the calendar year following the calendar year of the employee's death.[2]

If by September 30, the beneficiary validly disclaims entitlement to the employee's account, thereby allowing other beneficiaries to receive the benefit, the disclaiming person is not taken into account in determining the designated beneficiary.[3]

Surviving spouse. If the employee's spouse is the sole designated beneficiary as of September 30 of the calendar year following the calendar year of the employee's death, and the surviving spouse dies after the employee and before the date on which distributions have begun to the surviving spouse, the rule allowing the surviving spouse to be treated as the employee will apply. Thus, the beneficiary for determining the distribution period after the death of the surviving spouse is the spouse's designated beneficiary.[4]

Death of beneficiary. If the designated beneficiary dies between the date of the employee and September 30 of the calendar year following the calendar year of the employee's death, without disclaiming, he or she will still be treated as the beneficiary for purposes of figuring the minimum distribution period.[5]

Beneficiaries limited to individuals

Generally, only individuals may be designated as beneficiaries. If an entity other than an individual is designated as the beneficiary of an employee's benefit, the employee will be treated as having no designated beneficiary for required distribution purposes.[6]

Trust beneficiaries

A trust may not be the designated beneficiary for minimum distribution purposes. If a trust is named as an employee's beneficiary, all beneficiaries of the trust are treated as if they were designated as beneficiaries of the employee under the plan for purposes of determining the distribution period, provided the following requirements are met:[7]

1. The trust must be a valid trust under state law or be a trust that would be valid except for the fact that it has no corpus;

2. The trust must be irrevocable, or must, by its terms, become irrevocable upon the death of the employee;

3. The beneficiaries of the trust who are beneficiaries of an employee's interest must be identifiable from the trust instrument; and

4. Certain documentation must be furnished to the plan administrator.[8]

Trustees are required to provide the documentation by October 31 of the calendar year immediately following the calendar year in which the employee died.[9]

---

[1] IRS Reg. § 1.401(a)(9)-4, A-1 and A-2.

[2] IRS Reg. § 1.401(a)(9)-4, A-4.

[3] IRS Reg. § 1.401(a)(9)-4, A-4(a).

[4] IRS Reg. § 1.401(a)(9)-4, A-4(b).

[5] IRS Reg. § 1.401(a)(9)-4, A-4(c).

[6] IRS Reg. § 1.401(a)(9)-4, A-3(a).

[7] IRS Reg. § 1.401(a)(9)-4, A-5.

[8] IRS Reg. § 1.401(a)(9)-4, A-6.

[9] IRS Reg. § 1.401(a)(9)-1, D-6(b). Note that if the date for providing this documentation was before October 31, 2003, and the trust satisfied all of the other requirements, then the documentation could be provided by October 31, 2003. See IRS Reg. § 1.401(a)(9)-1, A-2(c).

¶ 1835

Determining the Minimum Distribution Amount for Lifetime Distributions

If the employee's benefits are in an individual account in a qualified plan or IRA, the required minimum distribution is determined by dividing the account balance by the distribution period.

For lifetime required minimum distributions, IRS regulations provide a simple, uniform table that all employees can use to determine the minimum distribution required during their lifetime.[1]

Uniform lifetime distribution table

By using the uniform distribution table below, most employees will be able to determine their required minimum distribution for each year based on nothing more than their current age and their account balance as of the end of the prior year.

Age of employee	Distribution period	Age of employee	Distribution period
70	27.4	92	10.2
71	26.5	93	9.6
72	25.6	94	9.1
73	24.7	95	8.6
74	23.8	96	8.1
75	22.9	97	7.6
76	22.0	98	7.1
77	21.2	99	6.7
78	20.3	100	6.3
79	19.5	101	5.9
80	18.7	102	5.5
81	17.9	103	5.2
82	17.1	104	4.9
83	16.3	105	4.5
84	15.5	106	4.2
85	14.8	107	3.9
86	14.1	108	3.7
87	13.4	109	3.4
88	12.7	110	3.1
89	12.0	111	2.9
90	11.4	112	2.6
91	10.8	113	2.4

| 92 . . . . | 10.2 | 114 . . . . | 2.1 |
| 93 . . . . | 9.6 | 115+ . . . . | 1.9 |

CCH Pointer: The 2002 final regulations modified the uniform table from the table contained in the 2001 proposed regulations. This modification was mandated under the Economic Growth and Tax Relief Reconciliation Act of 2001 (EGTRRA) in order to reflect increased longevity. However, the new table, by extending the period over which minimum distributions must be taken, allows employees to spread out payments and effectively lessen their tax. The uniform table relieves employees of the need to modify the amount of the required minimum distribution during their lifetimes based on a beneficiary designated on the required beginning date and eliminates the need to elect to recalculate or not to recalculate life expectancies at the required beginning date, since recalculation is factored into the uniform table. In addition, by using the uniform table, taxpayers will no longer be required to satisfy the separate incidental death benefit requirement.

Longer distribution period for surviving spouse beneficiary

In the event that an employee' sole beneficiary is his or her spouse, and the spouse is more than 10 years younger than the employee, the employee is authorized to use the longer of (1) the distribution period determined under the uniform table or (2) the joint life and last survivor life expectancy of the employee and the spouse using the employee's and spouse's attained age as of their birthdays in the distribution calendar year.[2]

Multiple beneficiaries

Generally, if more than one individual is designated as a beneficiary, the designated beneficiary with the shortest life expectancy is treated as the designated beneficiary for purposes of determining the distribution period.[3]

However, if an employee's benefit in a defined contribution plan is divided into separate accounts under the plan, then each beneficiary can use his or her own life expectancy to compute the required distributions.[4] In order to determine the distribution period for the separate accounts, the separate accounts must be established by the last day of the year following the calendar year of the employee's death.

Requirements for annuity distributions

An employee may satisfy the minimum distribution requirements by taking payments in the form of an annuity. If so, it is unnecessary to calculate a dollar amount that must be distributed in each year (as is required for nonannuity payments), provided that the annuity satisfies certain requirements. If a plan or arrangement transfers an annuity contract to an employee, this is not treated as a distribution for purposes of the minimum distribution rules; it is the annuity payments that are considered in determining compliance with those rules.

¶1835

CCH Pointer: The IRS has issued final regulations governing the minimum distribution requirements applicable to defined benefit plans and annuity contracts purchased with an employee's account balance under a defined contribution plan, 403(b) plan, 457 plan, or traditional IRA and Roth IRA.[5] The regulations incorporate, with modifications, provisions of earlier temporary regulations that expanded the situations in which annuity payments under annuity contracts purchased with an employee's account balance under a defined contribution plan may provide for increased payments. The final rules retain the basic structure of the temporary regulations, but also: allow for greater flexibility in the payment of annuities, including increased benefit payments; modify the incidental benefit rule for employees receiving distributions before age 70; permit employees and beneficiaries to change the form of future distributions in response to changed circumstances, such as retirement or death; and provide expanded distribution options for governmental plans. In addition, the final rules amend an existing final rule governing separate accounts under defined contribution plans that will enable employers to more easily establish separate accounts for beneficiaries where a plan participant or IRA holder dies late in a calendar year.[6]

To satisfy the minimum distribution requirements, annuity distributions under a defined benefit plan must be made in periodic payments at not less than one-year intervals. The payments must be for the applicable life or lives or over a "period certain" not longer than the applicable life expectancy or joint life and last survivor expectancy.[7]

A further requirement is that payments be nonincreasing. However, there are exceptions for the following cases:

1. Percentage increases under a specified and generally recognized cost-of-living index;

2. An increase to the extent of the reduction in the amount of the employee's benefits to provide for a survivor benefit on death, but only if the beneficiary whose life was used to determine the joint life and last survivor expectancy over which payments were being made dies or is no longer the employee's beneficiary pursuant to a qualified domestic relations order;

3. Increases to provide cash refunds of employee contributions upon the employee's death; and

4. An increase in benefits under the plan.

☐ The annuity distribution rules are discussed beginning at ¶ 1922.

---

[1] IRS Reg. § 1.401(a)(9)-5, A-4(a).

[2] IRS Reg. §§ 1.401(a)(9)-5, A-4(b)(1).

[3] IRS Reg. § 1.401(a)(9)-5, A-7.

[4] IRS Reg. § 1.401(a)(9)-8, A-2(a)(2).

[5] IRS Reg. § 1.401(a)(9)-6.

[6] IRS Reg. § 1.401(a)(9)-8.

[7] IRS Reg. § 1.401(a)(9)-6, A-1(a).

¶ 1840
Special Rules for Rollovers

If an amount is distributed by one plan and is rolled over to another plan, the amount distributed is still treated as a distribution by the distributing plan, notwithstanding the rollover.[1] However, any amount which is required to be distributed is not eligible for rollover treatment (see ¶ 1954).[2]

[1] 2001 IRS Prop. Reg. § 1.401(a)(9)-7, A-1.

[2] Code Secs. 402(c)(4)(B) and 408(d)(3)(E).

¶ 1845
Minimum Distribution Incidental Benefit Requirement

The minimum distribution incidental benefit (MDIB) rules require that death and other nonretirement benefits payable under a pension, stock bonus, or profit-sharing plan must be incidental to the primary purpose of the plan, which is to provide retirement benefits or deferred compensation for the employee.[1] IRS temporary regulations specify how distributions in the form of a joint and survivor annuity must be made in order to satisfy the MDIB requirements.

Annuity distributions for life

If the employee's benefit is payable for the life of an employee in the form of a life annuity, the MDIB requirements are automatically satisfied.[2]

Joint and survivor annuity, nonspouse beneficiary

If distributions take the form of a joint and survivor annuity for the joint lives of the employee and a beneficiary *other than the employee's spouse,* the amount payable to the survivor may not exceed the "applicable percentage" of the annuity payment that would have been paid to the employee had the employee survived. The applicable percentage is based on the excess of the age of the employee over the age of the beneficiary as of their attained ages as of their birthdays in the employee's first distribution calendar year and is derived from a table set out by the IRS.[3]

Joint and survivor annuity, spousal beneficiary

In the event that an employee's sole beneficiary, as of the employee's required beginning date (annuity starting date under 2001 rules), is the employee's spouse and the distribution satisfies the required distribution rules, without regard to the MDIB rules, the distribution to the employee will satisfy the MDIB requirement.[4] A former spouse to whom all or a portion of an employee's benefit is payable pursuant to a qualified domestic relations order as defined in Code Sec. 414(p) will be treated as a spouse of the employee for purposes of the MDIB requirement.[5]

[1] IRS Reg. § 1.401-1(b)(1)(i).

[2] IRS Temporary Reg. § 1.401(a)(9)-6T, A-2(a).

[3] IRS Temporary Reg. § 1.401(a)(9)-6T, A-2(b).

[4] *Ibid.*

[5] IRS Reg. § 1.401(a)(9)-8, A-6.

¶ 1850
Payments to Children

Any amount paid to a child is treated as if it had been paid to the surviving spouse of an employee if the amount becomes payable to the surviving spouse when the child reaches the age of majority.[1]

---

[1] Code Sec. 401(a)(9)(F).

¶ 1855
Incidental Death Benefits

Any distribution required under the incidental death benefit requirements is treated as a required distribution under the required distribution rules.[1] Generally, the incidental death benefit rule specifies that death benefits do not prevent the qualification of a plan if they are incidental (see ¶ 324).

---

[1] Code Sec. 401(a)(9)(G).

¶ 1860
Plan Provisions Needed to Comply With Required Distribution Rules

All qualified stock bonus plans, pension plans, and profit-sharing plans are subject to the distribution rules found in Code Sec. 401(a)(9).[1] The minimum distribution rules also apply to IRAs, SEPs, and tax-sheltered annuities.[2]

Plan provisions on distributions

In order to satisfy Code Sec. 401(a)(9), the plan must contain written provisions explaining the statutory rules of that Code section, including the incidental death benefit requirement.[3] The plan must also provide that distributions will be made in accordance with regulations issued under Code Sec. 401(a)(9) and that the distribution rules of Code Sec. 401(a)(9) will override any inconsistent distribution options in the plan.[4]

---

[1] Code Sec. 401(a)(9).

[2] Code Secs. 403(b)(10) and 408(a)(6).

[3] IRS Reg. § 1.401(a)(9)-1, A-3;

[4] IRS Reg. § 1.401(a)(9)-1, A-4.

¶ 1865
Violation of the Minimum Distribution Rules

Although a plan or arrangement generally cannot enjoy the benefits that attach to status as a qualified retirement plan, a tax-sheltered annuity, an IRA, or an eligible deferred compensation plan unless it satisfies the minimum distribution rules (including the MDIB requirement (see ¶ 1845)), isolated instances in which the rules are not satisfied will not cause disqualification. However, a pattern or regular practice of noncompliance will result in disqualification, even if each failure—standing alone—is minor.[1]

Aside from disqualification, the law provides an additional sanction in the form of an excise tax imposed on the distributee. The tax is 50 percent of the amount by which the required minimum distribution exceeds the actual distribution. The tax must be paid by the recipient.[2]

The IRS is authorized to waive the 50% excise tax for any year for which the taxpayer is able to establish that any shortfall in minimum required distributions is attributable to "reasonable error" and that steps are being taken to remedy the shortfall.[3]

---

[1] Code Secs. 401(a)(9), 403(a)(1), 403(b)(10), 408(a)(6), 408(b)(3), and 457(d)(2)(A).

[2] Code Sec. 4974(a) and (b); IRS Reg. §54.4974-2, Q&A-2.

[3] Code Sec. 4974(d).

¶ 1870
Special Rules for Plans that Invested in Failed Insurers

The impact of insurance company failures may affect the ability of qualified plans to satisfy the minimum distribution requirements. The IRS has set out procedures to be followed when a qualified plan or other qualified arrangement is affected by investments in an insurance company that is undergoing state delinquency proceedings.[1] These "affected investments" may cause a plan to fail to make required distributions or to decrease participants' accrued benefits.

A plan or arrangement that has "affected investments" in a delinquent insurer will not be treated as violating the minimum distribution requirements if the following conditions are met:

1. The plan utilizes all assets other than the unavailable portion of the "affected investment" to make required distributions;

2. All similarly situated individuals receive comparable treatment with respect to distributions; and

3. Any shortfall in payments is made up in the year following receipt of payments from an "affected investment."

Restorative payments to plans investing in GICs

The IRS has also established a closing agreement program that allows employers to make restorative payments to plans whose assets are invested in guaranteed investment contracts issued by life insurance companies that have been placed in state delinquency proceedings.[2] The program, which was initially intended to be of a temporary duration, has been indefinitely extended.

---

[1] Rev. Proc. 92-10, 1992-1 CB 661, CCH Pension Plan Guide ¶ 17,299M-1.

[2] Rev. Proc. 95-52, 1995-2 CB 439 (effective for closing agreement requests made on or after 2-2-95), CCH Pension Plan Guide ¶ 17,299N-53, superseding Rev. Procs. 92-16, 1992-1 CB 673 and 94-19, 1994-1 CB 605.

¶ 1875
For More Information

☐ For more information on required distributions from qualified plans, see ¶ 3601-3629 of the CCH Pension Plan Guide.

Taxation of Distributions

¶ 1900

Overview of Tax Rules for Distributions

Distributions from qualified plans can take many different forms. There are early retirement distributions, involuntary cash-outs, trustee-to-trustee transfers, distributions in the form of a qualified joint and survivor annuity or a qualified preretirement survivor annuity, lump-sum distributions, or distributions in the form of in-service withdrawals or loans from the plan. The tax consequences of a particular distribution will depend partly on the form of the distribution chosen.

Qualified plan distributions are includible in the recipient's gross income when received. Typically, defined benefit plans pay benefits in the form of an annuity, whereas defined contribution plans normally pay benefits in a single sum. Amounts received from qualified plans are generally taxed under the annuity rules of Code Sec. 72. Rollovers of eligible distributions will enable recipients to defer taxation on plan distributions.

☐ The annuity rules are discussed beginning at ¶ 1922.

☐ The lump-sum distribution rules are discussed beginning at ¶ 1940.

☐ Rollovers of lump-sum distributions are discussed beginning at ¶ 1950.

¶ 1902

GENERAL TAX RULES FOR DISTRIBUTIONS: Tax Treatment of Employer Contributions

Employer contributions to a qualified retirement plan on behalf of an employee are not taxable to the employee when made, irrespective of whether the employee's right to the contributions is forfeitable or nonforfeitable at that time.[1]

In the case of a nonqualified plan that is funded, a participant may be taxed when the employer makes contributions to the trust or other funding vehicle employed by the plan. In addition, a participant may be taxed when his or her interest in the plan becomes substantially vested. In the case of an unfunded plan, a participant may be taxed at or before the time compensation is deferred.

☐ The taxation of distributions from nonqualified plans is discussed beginning at ¶ 3300.

---

[1] Code Secs. 402(a) and 403(a)(1); IRS Reg. §§ 1.402(a)-1(a)(1)(i) and 1.403(a)-1(a).

¶ 1904

GENERAL TAX RULES FOR DISTRIBUTIONS: Tax Treatment of Employee Contributions

Distributions by retirement plans are generally taxed under the same rules that apply to payments received under annuity contracts.[1] Under these rules, employees may recover their own contributions ("investment in the contract"), tax-free when a distribution is made by a retirement plan.

The investment in the contract includes, among other things, "the aggregate amount of premiums or other consideration paid for the contract." [2] Where distributions from a qualified plan are taxable under Code Sec. 72, the "investment in the contract" is determined by reference to the amount contributed by the employee.[3]

Contributory plans

A contributory pension plan will not fail to qualify solely because it permits the trustee to transfer funds from a participant's voluntary contributions account to make up a deficiency in the participant's required contributions for any year. However, an amount transferred in excess of the total of the voluntary contributions is a transfer of earnings on the account and constitutes a distribution to be included in the participant's gross income for the transfer year.[4]

---

[1] Code Sec. 402(a).

[2] Code Sec. 72(c)(1)(A).

[3] IRS Reg. § 1.402(a)-1(a)(5).

[4] Rev. Rul. 73-581, 1973-2 CB 131, CCH PENSION PLAN GUIDE ¶ 19,287.

¶ 1906

GENERAL TAX RULES FOR DISTRIBUTIONS: Designation of Contribution

From the tax standpoint, it makes a vast difference whether a particular contribution to a retirement plan is that of the employer or of the employee. If it is the employee's, it generally is not excludable or deductible from gross income. If it is the employer's and the plan is a qualified plan, tax-sheltered annuity, SEP, or SIMPLE plan, the contribution is excluded from the employee's gross income. If the plan is not qualified and funded, an employer's contribution is includible in the employee's gross income only when it becomes substantially vested.[1]

Except for government "pick up" plans,[2] the Code makes it clear that if a contribution to a qualified plan is designated as an employee contribution, it will not be treated as made by the employer.[3]

---

[1] Code Secs. 402(b) and 403(c).

[2] Code Sec. 414(h)(2).

[3] Code Sec. 414(h)(1).

¶ 1908

GENERAL TAX RULES FOR DISTRIBUTIONS: Elective Contributions

If a qualified plan has a qualified cash or deferred arrangement (CODA or 401(k) plan), employees may choose between receiving compensation in cash or having it contributed to the plan.[1] If the contribution is elected, it is treated as a contribution of the employer, provided that it was not available to the employee when the election was made.[2] It is not included in the employee's gross income even if the employee is fully vested in the contribution.

If a CODA used by a qualified plan is not a qualified CODA, contributions thereunder are treated as contributions of the employees—not excludable or deductible from gross income.[3]

One-time irrevocable elections

Contributions made under one-time, irrevocable elections are not treated as elective contributions under a CODA, including 401(k) plans.[4] Thus, the plan under which they are made need not meet the requirements that ordinarily must be satisfied for an arrangement to be a qualified CODA. Nevertheless, the contributions are treated as those of the employer, and are not included in the gross income of the employee.[5]

☐ Cash or deferred arrangements (401(k) plans) are discussed in detail beginning at ¶ 2940.

---

[1] Code Sec. 401(k); IRS Reg. § 1.401(k)-1.

[2] Code Sec. 402(e)(3); IRS Reg. § 1.402(a)-1(d)(2); IRS Reg. § 1.401(k)-1(a)(4)(ii) and (iii).

[3] IRS Reg. § 1.401(k)-1(a)(5)(iii); IRS Reg. § 1.402(a)-1(d)(1). See also IRS General Counsel's Memorandum 39351, 4-3-85, CCH PENSION PLAN GUIDE ¶ 17,506.

[4] IRS Reg. § 1.401(k)-1(a)(3)(iv).

[5] IRS Reg. § 1.401(k)-1(a)(3)(iv); IRS Reg. § 1.402(a)-1(d)(2)(iii).

¶ 1910

GENERAL TAX RULES FOR DISTRIBUTIONS: When Distributions Become Taxable

Benefits under a qualified plan (including deductible employer contributions and earnings thereon) are taxed only when "actually distributed" to the employee or beneficiary and are not taxed if merely "made available" or "constructively received." [1] A deferral of the receipt of benefits results in the deferral of the taxation of the benefits.[2]

Constructive receipt rules, however, apply to nonqualified plans and to governmental plans.

Under proposed IRS regulations, an accident or health insurance premium payment made by a qualified plan constitutes a taxable distribution for the tax year in which the premium is paid. If the premium is paid by a defined contribution plan out of monies not yet allocated to an individual's account, it would be treated as having been allocated to that individual's account and then charged against that individual's benefits.[3]

---

[1] Code Sec. 402(a).

[2] Qualified plan distributions may not be treated as tax-free salary reductions. Thus, amounts distributed from a qualified plan that the distributee elects to have applied to pay health insurance premiums under a cafeteria plan are includible in the distributee's gross income. Rev. Rul. 2003-62, I.R.B. 2003-25, 6-23-2003, CCH PENSION PLAN GUIDE ¶ 19,948X.

[3] Proposed Reg. § 1.402(a)-1(a)(1)(ii).

¶ 1912

GENERAL TAX RULES FOR DISTRIBUTIONS:
Periodic vs. Nonperiodic Distributions

The taxation of distributions from qualified plans depends on the form and timing of the distribution. Typically, defined benefit plans pay benefits in the form of an annuity. Defined contribution plans normally pay benefits in a single sum. All qualified plan distributions are includible in the recipient's gross income when received (see ¶ 1910).

Periodic payments

Periodic payments (amounts received as an annuity) from qualified plans are includible in the recipient's income in the year received.[1] If the recipient has an investment in the contract (also referred to as "basis"), part of each payment may be excluded from taxable income. This is arrived at by applying the following formula:

$$\frac{\text{Investment in the contract}}{\text{expected return under the annuity}} \times \text{Annual annuity payment}$$

☐ For a detailed discussion of the taxation of annuity payments, see ¶ 1922 and following.

Nonperiodic payments

Nonperiodic or single-sum distributions received on or after the annuity starting date (¶ 1930) are fully includible in the recipient's gross income under the annuity rules.[2] However, if the payment satisfies the definition of a lump-sum distribution (¶ 1942), it may be entitled to special tax treatment or it may be transferred tax-free to an eligible retirement plan (see ¶ 1950).

Option to receive annuity in lieu of lump sum

Where an employee exercises an option permitted under his employer's plan to elect, within 60 days after termination of employment, to receive an annuity contract instead of a lump-sum distribution of the balance credited to his account in the plan, no part of the lump-sum payment is includible in the employee's gross income at the time the sum first becomes payable.[3]

☐ Amounts received as loans from qualified plans are considered in-service distributions to the extent they exceed prescribed limits. See ¶ 2000 and following.

---

[1] IRS Reg. § 1.402(a)-1(a)(5).

[2] Code Sec. 72(e).

[3] Code Sec. 72(h); Rev. Rul. 59-94, 1959-1 CB 25, CCH PENSION PLAN GUIDE ¶ 18,186.

¶ 1914

GENERAL TAX RULES FOR DISTRIBUTIONS: Distributions of Noncash Property

Distributions from a retirement plan or arrangement are not always in cash. Generally, noncash distributions are treated in the same manner as cash distributions, with the fair market value of the property substituted for the amount of cash in the relevant calculations.[1] Fair market value becomes the basis of the property distributed to the extent that it is included in determining the distributee's gross income.

---

[1] IRS Reg. § 1.402(a)-1(a)(1)(iii).

¶ 1916

GENERAL TAX RULES FOR DISTRIBUTIONS: Distributions of Employer Securities

In the case of a lump-sum distribution by a qualified plan maintained by a corporation, if a part of the distribution consists of securities of that corporation, the net unrealized appreciation (NUA) in those securities is not taxed at the time of the distribution.[1] Instead, tax is deferred until the securities are disposed of in a taxable transaction. If securities of the employer corporation are distributed other than as part of a lump-sum distribution, tax deferral is also available, but it is limited to that portion of the NUA in the securities that is attributable to contributions of the employee.[2]

The portion of the value of the employer securities that does not represent NUA is treated in the same manner as any other noncash distribution from a qualified plan.[3] Thus, if the security is not rolled over, that value is combined with the value of all other taxable amounts distributed by the plan.

Example: Thirty shares of stock of the employer corporation were included in a total distribution from an exempt employees' trust, within one taxable year, to an employee upon his retirement from service. At the time of distribution, the 30 shares had a fair market value of $3600. Ten of these shares had been acquired by the trust with employee contributions totaling $1000, and the other

20 shares were acquired with employer contributions in the amount of $2000, making a total cost of $3000 for the 30 shares. The appreciation in the amount of $600 is not includible in the employee's income, and his basis in the stock if he subsequently sells it is $3000 for the 30 shares, or $100 per share.

Net unrealized appreciation defined

Net unrealized appreciation is defined as the excess of the market value of such securities, at the time of distribution, over the cost or other basis of such securities to the trust.[4] If the distributions during the year include both appreciated and depreciated securities, unrealized appreciation and unrealized depreciation must be combined to determine the net unrealized appreciation (or depreciation) with respect to the distributed securities as a whole.[5]

Employer securities defined

The term "securities of the employer corporation" includes securities of a parent or subsidiary corporation.[6]

Election to recognize gain

In the case of a lump-sum distribution that includes securities of the employer corporation, the distributee has the option of taking NUA into account in calculating gain or loss.[7] In other words, the distributee may forego the exclusion that would otherwise apply. In such a case, the distributed securities will have a fair market value basis in the hands of the distributee. This option is only available for a distribution that qualifies as a lump-sum distribution.

Cost to the plan

Several methods are available to determine the cost or other basis to the plan of employer securities distributed to a plan participant or beneficiary.[8]

Earmarked securities. If a security is earmarked for the account of a particular participant at the time it is purchased by or contributed to the plan so that its cost or other basis to the plan is reflected in the account of the participant, that cost or other basis must be used in calculating NUA.[9]

Periodic allocations. If, at the end of each plan year or other specified period not exceeding 12 consecutive calendar months, the plan allocates among the accounts of participants all employer securities acquired during that period, the cost or other basis to the plan of the allocated securities is the average cost or other basis to the trust of all securities of the same type that were purchased or otherwise acquired during that period.[10]

Subsequent disposition of stock

The excludable NUA in a distributed employer security is not included in the distributee's basis for that security.[11] The distributee's basis for the security is determined as follows:

(A) If NUA is *less* than the excess of the value of all cash and property received in the distribution over the employee's basis in the plan, the basis of the securities in the hands of the distributee will be the fair market value of those securities at date of distribution less the NUA at date of distribution. (Stated another way, the distributee's basis for the securities is the same as the plan's basis for the securities.)

(B) If NUA is *greater* than the excess of the value of all cash and property received in the distribution over the employee's basis in the plan, the basis of the securities in the hands of the distributee will be the employee's basis in the plan less the amount of cash and fair market value of property (other than employer securities) received in the distribution.

Tax on gain

When an employer security is sold or exchanged by a distributee who received it as part of a lump-sum distribution, the gain, insofar as it does not exceed the amount of the NUA as of the date of distribution, is taxable as a long-term capital gain, regardless of how long the security was held by the distributee.[12] If the gain exceeds the NUA, the character of the excess (long-term or short-term) depends on the holding period of the distributee, which begins with the date of distribution.

In the case of securities received in a distribution that is not a lump-sum distribution, any gain realized on a subsequent taxable disposition (including that not exceeding NUA attributable to employee contributions) is long-term or short-term capital gain depending upon the holding period.

---

[1] Code Sec. 402(e)(4)(B).

[2] Code Sec. 402(e)(4)(A).

[3] Code Sec. 402(a); IRS Reg. § 1.402(a)-1(a)(1)(iii).

[4] IRS Reg. § 1.402(a)-1(b)(1).

[5] IRS Reg. § 1.402(a)-1(b)(2).

[6] Code Sec. 402(e)(4)(E)(ii).

[7] Code Sec. 402(e)(4)(B).

[8] IRS Reg. § 1.402(a)-1(b)(2)(ii).

[9] IRS Reg. § 1.402(a)-1(b)(2)(ii)(a).

[10] IRS Reg. § 1.402(a)-1(b)(2)(ii)(b).

[11] IRS Reg. § 1.402(a)-1(b)(1)(i).

[12] IRS Reg. § 1.402(a)-1(b)(1)(i).

¶ 1917

GENERAL TAX RULES FOR DISTRIBUTIONS:
Distributions During Phased Retirement

Under the Pension Protection Act of 2006, for purposes of the ERISA definition of a pension plan, a distribution from a plan, fund, or program is not treated as made in a form other than retirement income or as a distribution prior to termination of covered employment solely because the distribution is made to an employee who has attained age 62 and who is not separated from employment at the time of the distribution but instead is in a phased retirement program.[1]

Similarly, a pension plan will not fail to meet the Code Sec. 401qualification requirements solely because it provides for a distribution to an employee who has attained age 62 and who is not separated from employment at the time of the distribution but instead is in a phased retirement program.[2]

Normal retirement age

The IRS has issued final regulations permitting distributions to be made from a pension plan upon the attainment of normal retirement age prior to a participant's severance from employment with the employer maintaining the plan. Under the final regulations, a defined benefit or money purchase plan is permitted to pay benefits upon an employee's attainment of normal retirement age, even if the employee has not yet had a severance from employment with the employer maintaining the plan. Included in the rules is a requirement that the normal retirement age under a plan be an "age that is not earlier than the earliest age that is reasonably representative of the typical retirement age for the industry in which the covered workforce is employed." [3]

A "safe harbor age" is established under which a normal retirement age of at least age 62 is deemed to be not earlier than the typical retirement age for the industry in which the covered workforce is employed.

If a plan's normal retirement age is earlier than age 62, the determination of whether the age is not earlier than the earliest age that is reasonably representative of the typical retirement age for the industry in which the covered workforce is employed will be based on relevant facts and circumstances.

If the normal retirement age is between ages 55 and 62, then it is generally expected that a good faith determination of the typical retirement age for the industry in which the covered workforce is employed that is made by the employer (or, in the case of a multiemployer plan, made by the trustees) will be given deference, assuming that the determination is reasonable under the facts and circumstances.

However, a normal retirement age that is lower than age 55 will be presumed to be earlier than the earliest age that is reasonably representative of the typical retirement age for the industry of the relevant covered workforce absent facts and circumstances that demonstrate otherwise.

---

[1] ERISA Sec. 3(2)(A), as amended by the Pension Protection Act of 2006 (P.L. 109-280).

[2] Code Sec. 401(a)(36), as added by P.L. 109-280.

[3] Reg. § 1.401(a)-1(b)(2).

¶ 1918

GENERAL TAX RULES FOR DISTRIBUTIONS: Tax on Premature Distributions

A 10% excise tax is imposed on the distribution from any qualified plan, qualified annuity, or tax-sheltered annuity made before the participant's death, disability, or attainment of age 59½.[1]

The law exempts the following distributions from the additional income tax on early withdrawals:

1. distributions that are part of a series of substantially equal periodic payments (made not less frequently than annually) made for the life of the employee or the joint lives of the employee and his beneficiary;

2. distributions made to employees after attainment of age 55 and after separation from service;

3. distributions made for medical expenses to the extent such expenses are deductible under Code Sec. 213;

4. certain distributions to an ESOP made before January 1, 1990;

5. distributions to an alternate payee under a qualified domestic relations order; and

6. dividend distributions under Code Sec. 404(k).

CCH Pointer: Note that only amounts that would normally be included in gross income are subject to the 10% additional tax on early distributions. Therefore, distributions that do not meet any of the above exceptions, but which are rolled over (¶ 1950 and following), are not subject to the tax.

Substantially equal periodic payments

The exception for substantially equal periodic payments applies to distributions from qualified plans, qualified annuity plans, and tax-sheltered annuities only if the distribution is made after separation from service.[2] A distribution in the form of an annuity typically satisfies the substantially equal payment exception.

Payments will be considered to be substantially equal periodic payments if they are made according to one of the three methods set forth below.[3] The life expectancy tables used to determine distribution periods are: (1) the uniform lifetime table (reproduced in Revenue Ruling 2002-62); (2) the single life expectancy table in IRS Reg. § 1.401(a)(9)-9, A-1, or (3) the joint and last survivor table in IRS Reg. § 1.401(a)(9)-9, A-3.

Minimum distribution method. If the annual payment is determined using a method that would be acceptable for purposes of calculating the required minimum distribution, the payments are considered to be substantially equal periodic payments. For this purpose, the payment may be determined on the life expectancy of the employee or the joint life expectancy of the employee and beneficiary.

Amortization method. Payments will also be treated as substantially equal periodic payments if the amount to be distributed annually is determined by amortizing the taxpayer's account balance over a number of years. The number of years equals the life expectancy of the employee or the joint life expectancy and last survivor expectancy of the taxpayer and beneficiary. The interest rate used may not exceed a reasonable interest rate on the date payments commence.

Annuity factor method. Finally, if the amount to be distributed annually or monthly is determined by dividing the taxpayer's account balance by an annuity factor, the payments will be considered substantially equal periodic payments. The annuity factor is the present value of an annuity of $1 per year beginning at the employee's age attained in the first distribution year and continuing for the life of the employer. The annuity factor must be derived by using a reasonable mortality table and a reasonable interest rate.

¶1918

CCH Pointer: *Early retirees permitted to change distribution methods.* Generally, once chosen, the distribution method may not be changed without penalty.[4] As a result, distribution schedules that may be appropriate in an expanding stock market may not be appropriate in a time of declining stock values. The IRS has attempted to address the rigidities of the substantially equal periodic payment rules by providing the following two methods of relief.[5] First, if as a result of following an acceptable method of determining substantially equal periodic payments, an individual's assets in a plan are exhausted, the individual will not be subject to additional income tax as a result of not receiving substantially equal periodic payments and the resulting cessation of payments will not be treated as a modification of the series of payments. Second, individuals are allowed a one-time opportunity to change to the required minimum distribution method. An individual who begins distributions in a year using either the fixed amortization method or the fixed annuitization method may in any subsequent year switch to the required minimum distribution method to determine the payment for the year of the switch and all subsequent years and the change in method will not be treated as a modification. Once a change is made the required minimum distribution method must be followed in all subsequent years. Any subsequent change will be considered a modification.

☐ There are special rules on premature distributions from IRAs. See ¶ 3222.

Special rule for military reservists

Under the Pension Protection Act of 2006, a qualified reservist distribution from an IRA or attributable to elective deferrals under a 401(k) plan, 403(b) annuity, or certain similar arrangements are not subject to the 10-percent early withdrawal tax if the qualified reservist was ordered or called to active duty for a period in excess of 179 days or for an indefinite period.[6]

The Heroes Earnings Assistance and Relief Tax (HEART) Act of 2008 (P.L. 110-245) makes permanent the rules allowing active duty reservists to make penalty-free withdrawals from retirement plans and IRAs.

[1] Code Sec. 72(t).

[2] Code Sec. 72(t)(3)(B).

[3] IRS Notice 89-25, 1989-1 CB 662, CCH Pension Plan Guide ¶ 17,102A-1.

[4] Code Sec. 72(t)(4)(A).

[5] Revenue Ruling 2002-62, I.R.B. 2002-42, CCH Pension Plan Guide ¶ 19,974L.

[6] Code Sec. 72(t)(2)(G)(iii), as added by the Pension Protection Act of 2006 (P.L. 109-280).

¶ 1920

GENERAL TAX RULES FOR DISTRIBUTIONS: Disaster Relief

In recent years, in several instances, laws were signed to provide relief to victims of natural disasters. In general, this relief took the form of temporarily modifying existing rules governing retirement plan distributions and loans, in order to free up additional funds for disaster victims. For example, in 2005, there was relief for Hurricane Katrina, Rita, and Wilma victims. Later, similar relief was offered to Midwestern storm victims.

¶ 1922

TAXATION OF ANNUITY DISTRIBUTIONS: Taxation of Qualified Plans Under Annuity Rules

The annuity rules under Code Sec. 72 apply to distributions from qualified plans.[1] Thus, if an annuity is purchased for an employee under a qualified plan, the contributions or premiums paid by the employer for the purchase of the annuity are not includible in the employee's income. Generally, distribution of an annuity contract to an employee by a qualified plan is not considered income to the employee unless and until the contract is surrendered, even if the contract has a cash surrender value.[2] If, however, the contract distributed is a retirement income, endowment, or other life insurance contract, the entire cash value of such contract at the time of distribution must be included in the recipient's income under Code Sec. 402(a), unless the contract is irrevocably converted to an annuity contract within 60 days after distribution. An annuity contract issued after 1962 must be nontransferable to qualify for tax-deferred treatment.[3]

If an employee has no *investment in the annuity contract* (also referred to as "basis"), the full amount of each annuity payment is taxable to him as ordinary income.[4] If the employee has an investment in the contract, a portion of each annuity payment is treated as a recovery of employee contributions. The portion which is not taxable (that is, the amount that is excluded from gross income) is determined by multiplying each payment by a fraction, the numerator of which is the individual's investment in the contract and the denominator of which is equal to the total *expected return* under the annuity.[5] This can be expressed as a formula:

$$\frac{\text{Investment in the contract}}{\text{expected return under the annuity}} \times \text{Annual annuity payment}$$

This *exclusion ratio* is applied to each annuity payment received under the contract until the investment in the contract has been recovered tax-free.[6]

The *investment in the contract* is generally the total amount of premiums or other consideration the taxpayer paid, less any amounts the taxpayer received before the annuity starting date and did not include in gross income (see ¶ 1932).

The taxpayer's *expected return* is the amount he expects to receive (see ¶ 1934). If his life expectancy is involved, actuarial tables are used to provide a figure to be multiplied by the amount of the annual payments. If no life expectancy is involved (for example, installment payments for a fixed number of years), the taxpayer merely totals the amounts to be received.

The *annuity starting date* is, in general, the first day of the first period (monthly, quarterly, annually, and so on) for which an amount is received as an annuity under the contract (see ¶ 1930).

If the annuity starting date of an individual is after December 31, 1986, and the last annuitant (that is, the individual and his or her beneficiary under the annuity) dies before receiving the full amount the individual contributed, the amount that was not recovered is deductible on the annuitant's final tax return.[7] An individual whose annuity starting date is earlier than December 31, 1986, is not eligible for this deduction.[8]

As explained at ¶ 1936, if an employee has paid premiums (or made contributions) to acquire a pension or annuity both before July 1, 1986, and after June 30, 1986, and if the duration of the pension or annuity is dependent on life expectancy, the employee is entitled to calculate the exclusion by employing a two-step calculation that uses different life expectancy tables.

There are two ways of computing the annuity exclusion: the general rule (¶ 1936) and the simplified method (¶ 1938).

However, different tax treatment applies where the distribution is nonperiodic ("amounts not received as an annuity"). See ¶ 1928.

Special rules apply to certain qualified plan distributions

Note that the annuity rules of Code Sec. 72 are disregarded to the extent they are inconsistent with Code Sec. 402 (relating to the taxation of qualified plans) or 403 (relating to the taxation of employee annuities).[9] These sections set out special tax rules for lump-sum distributions (¶ 1940 and following), rollovers (¶ 1950 and following), and distributions of employer securities (¶ 1916).

---

[1] Code Sec. 402(a) provides that any amount distributed by a qualified employees' trust is taxable to the distributee under the annuity rules of Code Sec. 72. See "Special rules apply to certain qualified plan distributions," below.

[2] IRS Reg. § 1.402(a)-1(a)(2).

[3] Code Sec. 401(g); IRS Reg. § 1.402(a)-1(a)(2).

[4] Code Secs. 72(a), 402(a), and 403(a)(1); IRS Reg. §§ 1.61-11(a) and 1.72-4(d)(1).

[5] Code Sec. 72(b)(1).

[6] Code Sec. 72(b)(2).

[7] Code Sec. 72(b)(3).

[8] IRS Announcement 87-2, I.R.B. 1987-2, CCH PENSION PLAN GUIDE ¶ 17,097L-25.

[9] IRS Reg. § 1.72-14(d).

¶ 1924

TAXATION OF ANNUITY DISTRIBUTIONS: Requirements for Annuities

To be classified as an annuity, a distribution must satisfy each of the following requirements:[1]

1. It must be received on or after the annuity starting date (see ¶ 1930);

2. It must be payable in periodic installments at regular intervals (whether annually, semiannually, quarterly, monthly, weekly,

or otherwise) over a period of more than one full year from the annuity starting date; and

3. Except in the case of a variable annuity, the total of the amounts payable must be determinable at the annuity starting date either directly from the terms of the contract or indirectly by the use of mortality tables, compound interest calculations, or both, in conjunction with those terms and in accordance with sound actuarial theory.

Common types of annuities

Annuities may be purchased from insurance companies by employers to fund qualified pension plans. Such a policy represents a viable alternative to placing plan assets in a separate trust. Under such contracts there is usually little pure insurance protection, but instead a mechanism for providing for periodic retirement payments for a stated time. There are many types of annuity contracts available from insurance companies. The following are the most common types of annuities sold by insurance companies:

Single premium immediate life annuity. This is a policy which is purchased all at one time by the payment of a lump sum of money. This payment represents an investment of capital. If an annuity policy so purchased provides the annuitant with a monthly or annual income for life, beginning at once, it is called a single premium immediate life annuity.

Single premium deferred life annuity. If a single premium annuity provides for annuity income after a specified future date, it is called a single premium deferred life annuity. These policies are also available on a refund basis or a nonrefund basis.

Annual premium deferred life annuity. If the annuitant takes out a policy, pays an annual premium beginning at once, and receives a life annuity beginning at a specified age—usually between 60 and 65—the policy is an annual premium deferred life annuity. These policies are available on a refund basis or a nonrefund basis. In some policies the annuitant may elect to stop payment of annual premiums and have payments of the annuity begin at any desired time.

Joint and survivorship annuity of nonrefund type. Annuity policies which provide for a specified annuity to be paid to the annuitant for life, and after the purchaser dies, to a specified person for the balance of the second person's life, are called joint and survivorship annuities. These policies are usually purchased for a lump sum and are available on a nonrefund basis.

Joint and survivorship annuity with term certain. An annuity policy which includes a guarantee of the return of part, if not all, of the premiums (capital) to the annuitant during his life, with a balance to a beneficiary if the premiums have not all been returned during the annuitant's life, is called a joint and survivorship annuity with term certain. These are always refund policies. In any annuity contract there is no pure insurance protection at any time. The fact that the contract may provide for return of total premiums paid for the annuity benefits in case of death, and such

¶1924

total premiums may exceed the reserve in the early years, will not be considered as providing insurance protection.

Endowment contract. A retirement income endowment contract is a policy purchased on a level premium basis providing for retirement benefits and for conversion to paid-up endowment insurance upon premium default, with death benefits never to exceed 100 times the monthly annuity.[2]

Variable annuities. A pension or profit-sharing plan may provide variable benefits through the purchase of variable annuities from a life insurance company or through a trusteed self-administered securities investment fund. The usual objective of a variable pension benefit is to produce an amount of retirement income which, when combined with Social Security benefits, will enable the employee to maintain his purchasing power from year to year.

[1] IRS Reg. § § 1.72-1 and 1.72-2(b)(2).

[2] Rev. Rul. 70-581, 1970-2 CB 94, CCH PENSION PLAN GUIDE ¶ 18,876.

¶ 1926

TAXATION OF ANNUITY DISTRIBUTIONS: Separate Programs Maintained by Employer

In applying the annuity rules to distributions from an employer's qualified plan, each separate program of the employer consisting of interrelated contributions and benefits is considered as a single contract.[1] Therefore, all distributions or payments received under each separate program are received under a single contract.

A separate program of interrelated contributions and benefits may be financed partly or completely by either group or individual insurance contracts or through an investment fund. There may be several trusts under one separate program or several separate programs may make use of a single trust.

The following types of benefits are considered as separate programs:[2]

1. Definitely determinable retirement benefits.

2. Definitely determinable benefits payable prior to retirement in case of disability.

3. Life insurance.

4. Accident and health insurance.

Retirement benefits and life insurance will be considered part of the same separate program, however, if provided under retirement income, endowment, or other contracts giving life insurance protection. Annuity distributions which began before October 20, 1960, however, will be taxed as if each trust or plan were a single contract.[3]

[1] IRS Reg. § 1.72-2(a)(3)(i).

[2] IRS Reg. § 1.72-2(a)(3)(ii).

[3] IRS Reg. § 1.72-2(a)(3)(iii).

¶ 1928

TAXATION OF ANNUITY DISTRIBUTIONS: Taxation of Amounts Not Received As an Annuity

The tax treatment of "amounts not received as an annuity" (nonperiodic payments) will depend on whether the amount is received before or after the "annuity starting date" (see ¶ 1930).

Amounts not received as an annuity include amounts received under a life insurance, endowment, or annuity contract that:[1]

1. do not meet the definition of an annuity (see ¶ 1924),

2. meet the requirements for an annuity, but the annuity payments received differ either in amount, duration, or both, from those originally provided under the contract, or

3. meet the requirements for an annuity, but the annuity payments are received by a beneficiary after the death of an annuitant (or annuitants) in full discharge of the obligation under the contract and solely because of a guarantee.

Nonannuity payments also include:

1. dividends or a return of premiums or other consideration,[2]

2. refunds of consideration paid,[3]

3. amounts received on the surrender, redemption, or maturity of a contract,[4]

4. periodic payments received for a different term than originally provided under the contract (as a result of a modification of the contract or an exchange of annuity obligations),[5] and

5. periodic payments received for the same term after a lump-sum withdrawal.[6]

Amounts received on or after annuity starting date

Nonperiodic payments received on or after the annuity starting date are *fully* includible in the recipient's gross income.[7] For example, a cost-of-living increase in a pension after the annuity starting date is an amount not received as an annuity and, as such, is fully taxable.

Amounts received prior to annuity starting date (in-service distributions)

Nonperiodic payments received before the annuity starting date from a qualified plan are not included in gross income to the extent they are allocable to the recipient's investment in the contract (i.e., the recipient's cost). The remainder is includible in the recipient's gross income.[8] The amount of a nonperiodic distribution which is allocated to the employee's cost and, thus, is recoverable tax-free, is that portion which bears the same ratio to the total distribution that the employee's investment in the contract bears to the account balance (or accrued benefit, in the case of defined benefit plans). This can be expressed by the following formula:

$$\text{Amount received} \quad \times \quad \frac{\text{Investment in the contract}}{\text{Account balance}} \quad = \quad \text{Excludable amount}$$

Example: Before she had a right to an annuity, Phyllis Jones received $50,000 from her retirement plan. She had $10,000 invested (cost) in the plan, and her account balance was $100,000. She can exclude $5,000 of the $50,000 received, figured as follows:

$$\$50,000 \quad \times \quad \frac{\$10,000}{\$100,000} \quad = \quad \$5,000$$

Situations where allocation is not required

Distributions for which allocation between income and investment is not required include the following:[9]

1. Distributions in full discharge of a contract received as a refund of what was paid for the contract or for the complete surrender, redemption, or maturity of the contract,

2. Distributions from life insurance or endowment contracts (other than modified endowment contracts) that are not received as an annuity under the contracts, and

3. Distributions under contracts entered into before August 14, 1982, to the extent that they are allocable to cost before August 14, 1982.

---

[1] Code Sec. 72(e)(1)(A); IRS Reg. § 1.72-11(a)(1)(i) and (ii).

[2] Code Sec. 72(e)(1)(B); IRS Reg. § 1.72-11(b).

[3] IRS Reg. § 1.72-11(c).

[4] IRS Reg. § 1.72-11(d).

[5] IRS Reg. § 1.72-11(e).

[6] IRS Reg. § 1.72-11(f).

[7] Code Sec. 72(e)(2)(A).

[8] Code Sec. 72(e)(2)(B), (e)(8)(A) and (B).

[9] Code Sec. 72(e)(5)(B), (C), and (E).

¶ 1930

TAXATION OF ANNUITY DISTRIBUTIONS: Annuity Starting Date

The "annuity starting date" is the first day of the first period for which an amount is received under the contract. The first day of the first period for which an amount is received as an annuity is the later of:[1]

1. the date upon which the obligations under the contract become fixed, or

2. the first day of the period (year, half-year, month, or otherwise, depending on whether payments are to be made annually, semiannually, quarterly, monthly, or otherwise) which ends on the date of the first annuity payment.

Example: Mary Smith retires on January 31, 2012. Under the terms of her employer's pension plan she will receive an annuity of $2,000 a month. The first payment will be received on February 29, 2012, covering the month of February. Her annuity starting date is February 1, 2012.

---

[1] IRS Reg. § 1.72-4(b)(1).

¶ 1932

TAXATION OF ANNUITY DISTRIBUTIONS:
Investment in the Contract

The "investment in the contract" (also referred to as "basis") is, generally speaking, the aggregate amount of premiums or other consideration paid for the contract, less amounts, if any, received prior to the annuity starting date and not included in gross income.[1] Although the law is not absolutely specific on the point, it appears that the reductions in cost for amounts received before the annuity starting date, which were *excludable* from gross income, are to be made even though the taxpayer received no tax benefit from the exclusion. The use of the word "excludable" in the Code,[2] rather than the word "excluded," gives that impression.

Consideration paid

The consideration paid includes the employee's own contributions plus the following contributions made by the employer:[3]

1. Those which were includible in the employee's income, and

2. Those which, if they had been paid directly to the employee at the time of contribution, would not have been includible in the employee's gross income.

Transfer for value

If an annuity contract is transferred from one taxpayer to another for a valuable consideration, the consideration paid by the transferee becomes a part of his or her investment in the contract.[4] This rule does not apply in the case of qualified retirement plans, however, because an interest in such a plan is nonassignable.

Qualified domestic relations orders

In the case of a distribution or payment made to an alternate payee pursuant to a qualified domestic relations order (see ¶ 1600 and following), the "investment in the contract" is allocated on a pro rata basis between the present value of the distribution or payment and the present value of all other benefits payable with respect to the participant.[5]

---

[1] Code Sec. 72(c)(1).

[2] Code Sec. 72(c)(1)(B).

[3] Code Sec. 72(f).

[4] Code Sec. 72(g).

[5] Code Sec. 72(m)(10).

¶ 1934
TAXATION OF ANNUITY DISTRIBUTIONS: Expected Return

The expected return is the total amount that an annuitant can expect to receive under the annuity contract. In the case of an annuity payable over a fixed period of time (for instance, 120 months), the expected return is simply the amount of each payment multiplied by the number of payments to be made.[1] In the case of annuities whose duration is measured in whole or in part by one or more lives, it is necessary to refer to the IRS actuarial tables to determine the life expectancy (or expectancies) of the annuitant(s).[2]

Single life annuities

If the annuity is paid to one annuitant for life, the expected return is determined by multiplying the annual payment by the multiple found in Table I or Table V of IRS Reg. § 1.72-9, whichever is applicable, for the age and, if relevant, sex of the annuitant's life.[3] Table I is the gender-based table used for computations involving pre-July 1986 investment in the contract. Table V is the unisex table used for computations involving post-June 1986 investment in the contract.

> **Example:** George and Gracie each retire from XYZ Corporation at age 66. Each receives a retirement annuity of $1,000 a month. If the investment in the contract of each is entirely pre-July 1986, George will have an expected return of $172,800 (14.4 × $12,000); Gracie will have an expected return of $210,000 (17.5 × $12,000). On the other hand, if the basis of each is entirely post-June 1986, each will have an expected return of $230,400 (19.2 × $12,000).

The multiple from Table I or Table V will have to be adjusted if the annuity payments are made quarterly, semiannually, or annually.[4]

Temporary life annuities

In the case of a settlement under which fixed payments are made to the annuitant until death or until the expiration of a specified limited period, whichever occurs earlier (a "temporary life annuity"), the expected return is determined by multiplying the annuity payments for a year by the multiple found in gender-based Table IV or unisex Table VIII, whichever is applicable, for the age (nearest birthday as of the annuity starting date) and sex (if applicable) of the annuitant and the nearest whole number of years in the specified period. This multiple is not adjusted for payments made quarterly, semiannually, or annually, as it is for single life annuities.[5]

> **Example:** Sally Rogers, age 65 at her nearest birthday, is to receive $200 each month for five years or until she dies, whichever period is shorter. The expected return is figured as follows:
>
> | | |
> |---|---:|
> | Monthly payments of $200 × 12 months .... | $2,400 |
> | Multiple shown in Table VIII for age 65, 5-year term .... | 4.9 |
> | Expected return (4.9 × $2,400) .... | $11,760 |

Decreased payments after specified period

If an annuity is payable for life, but there is a decrease in the amount of each payment after a specified period of time, the expected return is calculated by treating the contract as a combination of (1) a whole life annuity for the smaller amount plus (2) a temporary life annuity for an amount equal to the difference between the larger and the smaller amounts. If payments are made quarterly, semiannually, or annually, the multiple for the whole life annuity must be adjusted in the same way as for a single life annuity (see above).[6]

Increased payments after specified period

If an annuity is payable for life, but there is an increase in the amount of each payment after a specified period of time, the expected return is calculated by treating the contract as a combination of (1) a whole life annuity for the larger amount less (2) a temporary life annuity for an amount equal to the difference between the larger and the smaller amounts. If payments are made quarterly, semiannually, or annually, the multiple for the whole life annuity must be adjusted in the same way as for a single life annuity (see above).[7]

Joint and survivor annuities

If the benefit settlement under a retirement plan calls for a fixed monthly payment to the employee for life and an identical monthly payment for life to a named beneficiary who survives the employee, the expected return is determined by multiplying the annual payment by the multiple obtained from gender-based Table II or unisex Table VI, whichever is applicable, for the ages (nearest birthday as of the annuity starting date) and, if relevant, the sexes of the living annuitants. If payments are to be made quarterly, semiannually, or annually, the multiple must be adjusted in the same way as for a single life annuity (see above).[8]

---

[1] IRS Reg. § 1.72-5(c).

[2] IRS Reg. § 1.72-5(a) and (b).

[3] IRS Reg. § 1.72-5(a)(1). The annuity tables are reproduced at CCH PENSION PLAN GUIDE ¶ 11,199.

[4] The adjustment is determined under the table reproduced in IRS Reg. § 1.72-5(a)(2)(i).

[5] IRS Reg. § 1.72-5(a)(3).

[6] IRS Reg. § 1.72-5(a)(4).

[7] IRS Reg. § 1.72-5(a)(5).

[8] IRS Reg. § 1.72-5(b)(1).

¶ 1936

TAXATION OF ANNUITY DISTRIBUTIONS: Computing the Annuity Exclusion Under the General Rule

If the annuitant is not eligible for, or does not choose to employ, the simplified method discussed at ¶ 1938, the following is the basic procedure for determining the taxable and nontaxable portions of annuity payments received in any tax year.[1] An annuitant who does not wish to calculate the taxable and nontaxable portions of his or her annuity may, for a fee, have this done by the Internal Revenue Service.

STEP 1: Determine the employee's investment in the contract (basis) in the retirement plan.

STEP 2: Determine the expected return from the annuity. The expected return is the anticipated number of annual payments multiplied by the amount of the annual payment.

STEP 3: Divide the amount determined in Step 1 by the amount determined in Step 2. Round the dividend to three (3) decimal places. This is the "exclusion percentage."

STEP 4: Multiply the first regular annuity payment by the exclusion percentage. The result is the excluded (tax-free) portion of that annuity payment. If the annuity starting date is after June 1986, the annuitant may not exclude more than his or her entire basis.

STEP 5: Multiply the tax-free portion of each payment by the number of full payments received during the year and add the taxable portion of any payment for a fractional period. (In the first year of the annuity, the first payment (or part thereof) may be for a fraction of the payment period. This fractional amount is multiplied by the exclusion percentage to get the tax free portion.) These computations will produce the tax-free portion of the total payments received in the tax year.

STEP 6: Subtract the tax-free portion from the total payments received in the tax year. The balance is the taxable portion of the annuity.

Life expectancy tables

In calculating the amount excludable from an annuity payment, different life expectancy tables may be used, depending upon whether the employee had an investment in the contract as of June 30, 1986, and upon elections that the employee may be entitled to make.

The general rule is that the amount of a post-June 30, 1986 annuity payment that is excludable from income is determined by reference to gender-neutral (sometimes called "unisex") life expectancy tables set forth in the IRS regulations. However, if there was no investment in the contract as of June 30, 1986, the employee can determine the amount excludable either by reference to the old gender-based tables contained in the same regulations or by reference to the gender-neutral tables.[2]

Where there was an investment in the contract as of June 30, 1986, and there has been a further investment in the contract after that date, the employee may elect to calculate the exclusion under a special rule. Under this rule, the exclusion is calculated using the gender based tables as if the investment in the contract as of June 30, 1986, was the only investment in the contract. Then a second exclusion is calculated using the gender-neutral tables as if the post-June 30, 1986 investment was the only investment. The two exclusions are added together to produce the final exclusion used in preparing the tax return.[3]

[1]IRS Publication No. 939, General Rule for Pensions and Annuities, CCH PENSION PLAN GUIDE ¶ 17,007, pp. 6-8.

[2] IRS Reg. § 1.72-6(d) and 1.72-9.

[3]IRS Publication No. 939, General Rule for Pensions and Annuities, CCH PENSION PLAN GUIDE ¶ 17,007, pp. 8-10.

¶ 1938

TAXATION OF ANNUITY DISTRIBUTIONS:
Simplified Method for Determining Annuity Exclusion

A simplified method is provided for determining the portion of annuity distribution from a qualified retirement plan, qualified annuity, or tax-sheltered annuity that represents nontaxable return of basis.[1] This simplified method must be used by recipients to comply with the requirements of Code Sec. 72(d) and by payors to report the taxable portion of annuity distributions on Form 1099-R.[2]

For annuity starting dates beginning after November 18, 1996, but before January 1, 1998, the total number of monthly annuity payments expected to be received is based on the primary annuitant's age at the annuity starting date.[3] The applicable expected number of payments remains the same whether the annuitant is receiving a single life or a joint and survivor annuity. The expected number of payments is set forth in the table below.

Age of primary annuitant on the annuity starting date	Number of Anticipated Payments
55 and under	360
56-60	310
61-65	260
66-70	210
71 and over	160

Beginning with annuities with annuity starting dates after 1997, the expected number of payments will be affected by whether payments are based on the life of more than one individual. If an annuity is payable based on the life of one individual, the total number of monthly annuity payments is based on the annuitant's age at the annuity starting date. The expected number of payments for an annuity based on the life on one individual is set forth in the table above.

Example: Max Holden, age 50, receives a $200 per month annuity from his pension plan. His contributions to the plan totaled $36,000. Under the simplified method, the nontaxable part of the annuity payment is $100. This is derived by dividing $36,000 (the investment in the contract) by the number of anticipated payments (360).

Separate table for benefits based on life of multiple annuitants

Prior to 1998, the table for determining anticipated payments discussed above did not vary depending on whether the payment was payable in the form of a single life annuity or a joint and survivor annuity. Applying the table for single life annuities to joint and survivor annuities had a tendency to understate the expected payments under a joint and survivor annuity. Accordingly, effective for annuities

¶1938

with starting dates after 1997, in determining the number of anticipated payments to be used in determining nontaxable return of basis, the following table applies to benefits based on the life of more than one annuitant for amounts received as an annuity:[4]

Combined age of annuitants	Number of Payments
110 and under	410
111-120	360
121-130	310
131-140	260
141 and over	210

This table governs benefits based on the life of multiple annuitants, even if the amount of the annuity varies by annuitant.[5] Thus, the table applies to a 50% joint and survivor annuity. However, the table does not apply to an annuity paid on a single life merely because it has additional features, e.g. a term certain.

Primary annuitant must not have attained age 75

The simplified method does not apply if the primary annuitant has attained age 75 on the annuity starting date unless there are fewer than five years of guaranteed payments under the annuity.[6]

Payments not part of annuity stream

If, in connection with commencement of annuity payments, the recipient receives a lump-sum payment that is not part of the annuity stream, the payment is taxed as "amounts not received as an annuity" (¶ 1928) as if received before the annuity starting date and the investment in the contract used to calculate the simplified exclusion ratio for the annuity payments is reduced by the amount of the payment.

---

[1] Code Sec. 72(d).

[2] IRS Notice 98-2, 1998-1 CB 266, 1-12-98, CCH PENSION PLAN GUIDE ¶ 17,1130.

[3] IRS Notice 98-2, Sec. III, 1998-1 CB 266, 1-12-98, CCH PENSION PLAN GUIDE ¶ 17,1130.

[4] Code Sec. 72(d)(1)(B)(iv).

[5] P.L. 105-34 (Taxpayer Relief Act of 1997), Conference Committee Report.

[6] Code Sec. 72(d)(1)(E).

¶ 1940

TAXATION OF LUMP-SUM DISTRIBUTIONS: Special Tax Treatment Accorded to Lump-Sum Distributions

If the recipient of a lump-sum distribution from a qualified retirement plan does not opt for a nontaxable rollover to an IRA or to another qualified plan (see ¶ 1950), the distribution is taxable. For many years, lump-sum distributions were subject to special, favorable tax treatment. Generally, this treatment will no longer be available for lump-sum distributions made in tax years beginning after 1999.[1] However, favorable tax treatment will still be available for employees who had attained age 50 before January 1, 1986 (see ¶ 1946 and ¶ 1948).

Employees born after 1935

In pre-2000 tax years, for employees born after 1935, the full taxable amount of a lump-sum distribution of the benefits of an employee who was at least age 59½ on the date of distribution is eligible for five-year averaging (see ¶ 1944). For tax years beginning after 1999, five-year averaging is unavailable.

Employees born before 1936

For tax years beginning before the year 2000, there are three types of special tax treatment for a taxpayer who receives a lump-sum distribution of the benefits of an employee who was born before 1936.

1. *The five-year averaging method.* This may be applied either to the full taxable amount of the distribution or to the post-1973 portion.

2. *The 10-year averaging method.* This too may be applied either to the full taxable amount or to the post-1973 portion.

3. *The flat 20% tax.* This may be applied only to the pre-1974 portion of the taxable amount. As to the post-1973 portion, the taxpayer may treat it as ordinary income or may elect to calculate a separate tax by employing either the five-year or ten-year averaging method.

For tax years beginning after 1999, five-year averaging is unavailable. However, the other two varieties of special tax treatment (10-year averaging and 20% capital gain treatment) will continue to be available to employees born before 1936. See ¶ 1946 and ¶ 1948).

Eligible plans

Lump-sum tax treatment is available only for distributions from pension, profit-sharing, and stock bonus plans that are qualified under Code Sec. 401(a).[2]

[1]P.L. 104-188 (Small Business Job Protection Act), Sec. 1401.

[2] Code Sec. 402(e)(4)(D).

¶ 1942

TAXATION OF LUMP-SUM DISTRIBUTIONS: Lump-Sum Distribution Defined

A lump-sum distribution is a distribution made by an employer's qualified plan to a plan participant or beneficiary representing the "balance to the credit" of an employee (that is, an employee's entire balance in the plan excluding certain amounts forfeited or subject to forfeiture).

All of the distribution (or all of the participant's portion of it) must be received by the participant within a single taxable year (the participant's taxable year). The distribution must be made:[1]

1. as a result of the employee's death,

2. after the employee reaches age 59½,

3. on account of the employee's separation from service (not applicable to the self-employed), or

4. after a self-employed person or owner-employee becomes disabled (a regular employee who is disabled must also be age 59½ or separated from service in order for a distribution to be treated as a lump-sum distribution).

In tax years beginning before 2000, a five-year minimum period of service was required in order for a distribution to be considered a "lump-sum distribution." [2]

Balance to the credit of an employee

The entire amount remaining in an employee's account must be paid to the recipient upon the occurrence of one of the specified events in order to qualify the distribution for lump-sum treatment.[3] This amount is referred to as "balance to the credit" of an employee.

If an employer maintains two or more qualified plans, they may have to be treated as a single plan for purposes of determining whether a participant's entire interest has been distributed within one tax year. Specifically, all pension plans must be treated as a single plan; all profit-sharing plans must be treated as a single plan; and all stock bonus plans must be treated as a single plan.[4]

☐ The balance to the credit of an employee does not include amounts payable to an alternate payee under a qualified domestic relations order (QDRO).[5] QDROs are discussed at ¶ 1600 and following.

Distribution made on account of self-employed person's disability

A distribution made on account of the disability of a self-employed person or an owner-employee qualifies for special tax treatment.[6] This requirement probably does not apply to regular employees because total and permanent disability is usually accompanied by separation from service. An individual is considered to be disabled if unable to engage in any substantial gainful activity because of any medically determinable physical or mental impairment that can be expected to result in death or to be of long-continued and indefinite duration.[7]

Separation from service

A distribution to a regular employee who has not yet attained age 59½ must be made on account of "separation of service" in order to qualify for lump-sum treatment. This requirement has been the subject of considerable litigation. Most of the cases and rulings involve the effect of a change in the employer's status due to a merger, sale, or reorganization. In such a circumstance, the individual employees may continue to perform the same jobs as before, but are now arguably performing them for a different "employer." This is known as the "same desk rule." Another problem area involves persons who, although supposedly retired or separated, nonetheless continue to perform services for the employer in some other capacity (as independent contractors, for instance).

---

[1] Code Sec. 402(e)(4)(D)(i).

[2] Code Sec. 402(d)(4)(F), prior to repeal by P.L. 104-188 (Small Business Job Protection Act).

³ Code Sec. 402(e)(4)(D)(i).

⁴ Code Sec. 402(e)(4)(D)(ii).

⁵ Code Sec. 402(e)(4)(D)(v) and (vii).

⁶ Code Sec. 402(e)(4)(D)(i)(IV).

⁷ Code Secs. 402(e)(4)(D)(i)(IV) and 72(m)(7).

¶ 1944

TAXATION OF LUMP-SUM DISTRIBUTIONS: Five-Year Averaging Treatment—Pre-2000 Tax Years

For pre-2000 tax years, if a distribution satisfies the requirements for a lump-sum distribution and if the employee is at least age 59½ at the time of the distribution, then the portion of the distribution attributable to post-1973 participation in the plan qualifies for special five-year averaging treatment. As for the pre-1974 portion, see ¶ 1948.

For tax years beginning after December 31, 1999, five-year averaging for lump-sum distributions is repealed.[1] However, prior law transition rules that permit certain individuals to use 10-year averaging at 1986 rates (¶ 1946) still apply.

The special five-year averaging rule may be used only once.[2] The five-year averaging election can be made by a trust or an estate as well as by an individual.[3]

If a participant makes an election to roll over any portion of a lump-sum distribution into an IRA or a qualified plan, five-year averaging (pre-2000) or 10-year averaging is not available for that distribution.[4]

¹P.L. 104-188 (Small Business Job Protection Act), Sec. 1401.

² Code Sec. 402(d)(1)(B) and 402(d)(4)(B), prior to repeal by P.L. 104-188 (Small Business Job Protection Act).

³ Code Sec. 402(d)(4)(B), prior to repeal by P.L. 104-188 (Small Business Job Protection Act).

⁴ Code Sec. 402(d)(4)(K), prior to repeal by P.L. 104-188 (Small Business Job Protection Act).

¶ 1946

TAXATION OF LUMP-SUM DISTRIBUTIONS: Ten-Year Averaging Treatment for Certain Individuals

Individuals who reached age 50 before January 1, 1986, may elect to use 10-year averaging (using the 1986 tax rates).

Only one election is available with respect to an employee and, if made, it eliminates the ability to elect five-year averaging (for pre-2000 distributions) and capital gains treatment after age 59½.[1] This provision also applies to individuals, estates, or trusts for distributions made with respect to employees who reached age 50 before 1986.

Computing the ten-year averaging tax

The ten-year averaging method is explained in IRS Publication 575 (Pension and Annuity Income).[2] It is essentially the same as the old five-year averaging method, except (1) the tentative tax is based on one-tenth of the taxable amount of the distribution (which is then multiplied by 10), and (2) the tentative tax calculation employs a special rate schedule appearing in the instructions for Form 4972,

Tax on Lump-Sum Distributions From Qualified Plans.[3] This schedule is the 1986 schedule for single persons, adjusted to reflect the $2,480 "zero bracket amount" that was in effect in 1986.

---

[1]P.L. 99-514 (Tax Reform Act of 1986), Sec. 1122(h)(3)(C) and (h)(5).

[2]CCH PENSION PLAN GUIDE ¶ 17,005A.

[3]See CCH PENSION PLAN GUIDE ¶ 10,762.

¶ 1948

TAXATION OF LUMP-SUM DISTRIBUTIONS: Capital Gains Treatment for Pre-1974 Portion

Individuals who reached age 50 before January 1, 1986, may elect "capital gains treatment" with respect to a lump-sum distribution. If such an individual elects to retain the capital gains character of a pre-1974 portion of a lump-sum distribution, the capital gains portion will be taxed at a rate of 20%.[1] This provision also applies to individuals, estates, or trusts for distributions made with respect to employees who reached age 50 before 1986.

Individuals who did not attain age 50 prior to January 1, 1986, may not elect capital gains treatment for the portion of the distribution attributable to pre-1974 participation in the plan.[2]

---

[1]P.L. 99-514 (Tax Reform Act of 1986), Sec. 1122(h)(3) and (h)(6).

[2]P.L. 99-514 (Tax Reform Act of 1986), Sec. 1122(b), repealing Code Secs. 402(a)(2) and

403(a)(2). P.L. 99-514, Sec. 1122(h)(4). Capital gains treatment was phased out between 1987 and 1992, for individuals who had not attained age 50 prior to 1986.

¶ 1950

ROLLOVERS OF DISTRIBUTIONS: Ordinary Rollovers From Qualified Plans

A tax-free rollover from a qualified plan is the transfer of all or part of the balance to the employee's credit in a qualified trust that has been paid to the employee in an "eligible rollover distribution" to an "eligible retirement plan" within sixty days of the receipt of the distribution. In the case of a distribution of property other than cash, the amount transferred to an eligible retirement plan must consist of the property distributed.[1]

Rollover by surviving spouse

If a distribution attributable to an employee is paid to the employee's surviving spouse, the distribution may be rolled over in the same manner as if the spouse were the employee.[2] This includes distributions from qualified annuity plans.[3]

---

[1] Code Sec. 402(c)(1) and (3).

[2] Code Sec. 402(c)(9).

[3] Code Sec.403(a)(4)(B), as amended by P.L. 108-311.

¶ 1952

ROLLOVERS OF DISTRIBUTIONS: When Rollovers Must Be Made

To qualify as a tax-free rollover, a distribution must be rolled over within 60 days of receipt.[1] The IRS is permitted to waive the 60-day rollover period where taxpayers qualify for a hardship exception.[2]

[1] Code Sec. 402(c)(3)(A).

[2] Code Sec. 402(c)(3)(B). Guidance in applying for a waiver of the 60-day rule is supplied in Rev.

Proc. 2003-16, I.R.B. 2003-4, CCH PENSION PLAN GUIDE ¶ 17,299Q-63.

¶ 1954

ROLLOVERS OF DISTRIBUTIONS: Eligible Rollover Distributions

An eligible rollover distribution is generally a distribution of all or any portion of the balance to the credit of an employee in a qualified plan.[1] Basically any amount distributed to an employee from a qualified plan (excluding the exceptions noted below) is an eligible rollover distribution, including qualified disability benefits, hardship distributions, and distributions that are includible in gross income but that are provided to a distributee who is not expected to have income tax liability.[2]

Distributions not eligible for rollover

Eligible rollover distributions do not include:

1. any distribution that is one of a series of substantially equal periodic payments made at least annually over (a) the life of the employee (or joint lives of the employee and his or her designated beneficiary), (b) the life expectancy of the employee (or the joint life and last survivor expectancy of the employee and his or her designated beneficiary), or (c) a specified period of at least 10 years.[3]

2. required minimum distributions (see ¶ 1800 and following).[4]

3. portions of distributions not included in gross income, excluding net unrealized appreciation of employer securities received in certain distributions (for example, a return of the employee's after-tax contributions).[5]

4. returns of Code Sec. 401(k) elective deferrals in excess of the maximum allowed under Code Sec. 415.[6]

5. corrective distributions of 401(k) plan excess deferrals, including income allocable to the corrections.[7]

6. corrective distributions of excess 401(k) contributions and aggregate contributions, including income allocable to the corrections.[8]

7. dividends paid on employer securities held by an ESOP.[9]

8. the costs of life insurance coverage ("PS 58 costs").[10]

9. loans that are treated as distributions because they do not meet IRS requirements or because they are in default—so-called "deemed distributions." [11]

10. any hardship distributions[12]

CCH Pointer: Generally effective for distributions made after 2001, no hardship distribution made under the plan may be an eligible rollover distribution.[13] Accordingly, after 2001, hardship distributions attributable to employer matching and nonelective contributions, as well as those attributable to elective deferrals, may not be rolled over.

Plan loan offset may be an eligible rollover distribution

A distribution made, under the terms of the plan, to reduce, or offset, a participant's accrued benefit in order to repay the loan, may be an eligible rollover distribution.[14] A plan may allow or deny a plan loan offset amount to be directly rolled over.[15] For more on plan loans, see ¶ 2000.

Periodic payments

A payment is not treated as being one of a series of periodic payments, and, thus, may be an eligible rollover distribution, if it is substantially larger or smaller than the other payments in the series. This is the case regardless of whether the payment is made before, with, or after payments in the series.[16]

2009 RMDs

The IRS has offered rollover relief arising out of the 2009 moratorium on required minimum distributions (RMDs) (see ¶ 1805). Under the relief, payments to a plan participant in 2009 will not be treated as ineligible for rollover if the payments equal the 2009 RMDs or are one or more payments in a series of substantially equal periodic payments.[17] Accordingly, such payments can be rolled over, provided the other rules are satisfied. To assist plan participants who already have received distributions in 2009 but might have been unsure of which amounts could be rolled over, the IRS extended the 60-day rollover period, for any 2009 RMDs and for any additional payments that are part of a series of substantially equal periodic payments, so that it ended no earlier than November 30, 2009.

---

[1] Code Sec. 402(c)(4); IRS Reg. §1.402(c)-2, Q&A-3(a).

[2] IRS Reg. §1.402(c)-2, Q&A-3(a); T.D. 8619, 60 FR 49199.

[3] Code Sec. 402(c)(4)(A); IRS Reg. §1.402(c)-2, Q&A-3(b)(1).

[4] Code Sec. 402(c)(4)(B); IRS Reg. §1.402(c)-2, Q&A-3(b)(2).

[5] IRS Reg. §1.402(c)-2, Q&A-3(b)(3).

[6] IRS Reg. §1.402(c)-2, Q&A-4(a).

[7] IRS Reg. §1.402(c)-2, Q&A-4(b).

[8] IRS Reg. §1.402(c)-2, Q&A-4(c).

[9] IRS Reg. §1.402(c)-2, Q&A-4(e).

[10] IRS Reg. §1.402(c)-2, Q&A-4(f).

[11] IRS Reg. §1.402(c)-2, Q&A-4(d); IRS Notice 93-3, 1993-1 CB 293, CCH PENSION PLAN GUIDE ¶ 17,105F.

[12] Code Secs. 402(c)(4)(C).

[13] Code Sec. 402(c)(4)(C), as amended by P.L. 107-16 (Economic Growth and Tax Relief Reconciliation Act), Sec. 636(b)(2).

[14] IRS Reg. §1.402(c)-2, Q&A-9; IRS Notice 93-3, 1993-1 CB 293, CCH PENSION PLAN GUIDE ¶ 17,105F.

[15] IRS Reg. §1.401(a)(31)-1, Q&A-15.

[16] IRS Reg. § 1.402(c)-2, Q&A-6(a).   [17] IRS Notice 2009-82, I.R.B. 2009-41, October 13, 2009, CCH PENSION PLAN GUIDE ¶ 17,143Q.

¶ 1956

ROLLOVERS OF DISTRIBUTIONS: Eligible Retirement Plans

In order for a rollover to be tax-free, the eligible rollover distribution must be transferred into an eligible retirement plan. An eligible retirement plan is:[1]

1. an individual retirement account,

2. an individual retirement annuity,

3. a qualified trust,

4. a qualified annuity,

5. a Code Sec. 457 eligible deferred compensation plan maintained by a state, a political subdivision of a state, or instrumentality of a state or political subdivision of a state, or

6. a Code Sec. 403(b) tax-sheltered annuity plan.

Qualified plans, 457 plans, and 403(b) plans are authorized, but not required to accept rollovers. In order to accept rollovers from a qualified plan, IRA, or 403(b) plan, the recipient 457 plan must agree to account for such rollovers separately.[2] The reason for this separate accounting requirement is that amounts distributed from 457 plans will generally be subject to the 10% additional tax on early withdrawals to the extent that the distributions consist of amounts attributable to rollovers from another type of plan.[3]

According to the IRS, if an eligible retirement plan separately accounts for amounts attributable to rollover contributions to the plan, distributions of those amounts are not subject to the restrictions on permissible timing that apply, under the applicable requirements of the Code, to other plan distributions. Therefore, pursuant to a participant's request, the plan may distribute amounts attributable to rollover contributions at any time.[4]

---

[1] Code Sec. 402(c)(8)(B); IRS Reg. § 1.402(c)-2, Q&A-2.

[2] Code Sec. 402(c)(10).
[3] Code Sec. 72(t)(9).
[4] Rev. Rul. 2004-12, I.R.B. 2004-7, 2/17/04.

¶ 1958

ROLLOVERS OF DISTRIBUTIONS: After-Tax Contributions

Employees may roll over the entire amount of any qualified distribution received from a qualified plan, including the portion of the distribution representing after-tax contributions, to a qualified defined contribution plan or traditional IRA, effective for distributions made after December 31, 2001.[1] The transfer to a qualified defined contribution plan must be made by means of a direct trustee-to-trustee transfer. The recipient plan may not receive this transfer of after-tax contributions unless it agrees to maintain separate accounting records for the after-tax contributions.

Post-2006 contributions

Under the Pension Protection Act, after-tax contributions from qualified retirement plans can be rolled over not only to a defined contribution plan or an IRA, but also to a defined benefit plan or a 403(b) tax-sheltered annuity.[2] A rollover to a defined benefit plan or tax-sheltered annuity must be a direct trustee-to-trustee rollover, and the transferee plan must separately account for after-tax contributions and earnings thereon.

The provision applies to tax years beginning after December 31, 2006.

[1] Code Sec. 401(a)(31)(B)(i) and (ii). Code Sec. 402(c)(2)(A) and (B).

[2] Code Sec. 402(c)(2)(A), as amended by the Pension Protection Act of 2006 (P.L. 109-280).

¶ 1960

ROLLOVERS OF DISTRIBUTIONS: Tax Consequences of Rollover

If the balance to the credit of an employee in a qualified trust is paid to the employee in an eligible rollover distribution and the employee rolls the amount over to an eligible retirement plan within 60 days of receipt, then the distribution, to the extent transferred, is not included in the employee's gross income for tax year in which it is paid.[1] However, unless the distribution is a direct rollover (¶ 1970), it is subject to 20% withholding even though it is not ultimately taxed.

[1] Code Sec. 402(c)(1); IRS Reg. §1.402(c)-2, Q&A-11.

¶ 1961

ROLLOVERS OF DISTRIBUTIONS: Rollovers to Nonspouse Beneficiaries

Under the Pension Protection Act of 2006 (PPA), distributions from a deceased person's eligible retirement plan (as defined under Code Sec. 402(c)(8)(B)) to a nonspouse beneficiary may be rolled over tax-free into an IRA via trustee-to-trustee transfer. Payouts from the transferee IRA must follow the minimum distribution rules that apply to nonspouse beneficiaries. This rule applies to distributions made after 2006.

If a direct trustee-to-trustee transfer is made to an IRA that has been established to receive the distribution on behalf of a beneficiary who is not the participant/owner's surviving spouse, the following treatment applies:[1]

- the transfer is treated as an eligible rollover distribution;
- the transferee IRA is treated as an inherited account; and

- the required minimum distribution rules applicable where the participant/ owner dies before the entire interest is distributed apply to the transferee IRA; the special rules for surviving spouse beneficiaries do not apply.

The rollover rules for distributions from 403(a) employee annuity plans, 403(b) plans and 457 plans specifically provide that the nonspouse beneficiary rollover rule applies.[2]

Post-2009 changes

The Worker, Retiree, and Employer Recovery Act of 2008 (P.L. 110-458) makes several adjustments to the nonspouse beneficiary rollover provisions. Significantly, qualified retirement plans must allow direct rollovers for nonspouse beneficiary distributees, because such rollovers are no longer treated as eligible rollover distributions only for Code Sec. 402(c) rollover purposes. [3] Thus, the mandatory rollover rules in Code Sec. 401(a)(31) apply. Additionally, 403(a) plans, 403(b) plans and 457 plans also must allow direct nonspouse beneficiary rollovers because these plans incorporate the Code Sec. 402(c)(11) rules for nonspouse beneficiary rollovers.

The elimination of the restriction on eligible rollover distribution treatment of a direct nonspouse beneficiary rollover only "for purposes of" Code Sec. 402 also means that the Code Sec. 402(f) notice and Code Sec. 3405(c) mandatory withholding requirements apply.[4] Again, the rules also apply to 403 and 457 plans, by reference. Additionally, plan administrators now are specifically required to provide written notice of distribution options and other related provisions to nonspouse beneficiaries for whom eligible rollover distributions are available. This includes eligible rollover distributions for nonspouse beneficiaries from 403(a) plans, 403(b) plans and 457 plans.[5]

The amendments described above –removing the limitation on eligible rollover distribution treatment to only Code Sec. 402(c) rollovers, and revising the rollover-eligible distribution notice requirements under Code Sec. 402(f) to include non-spouse beneficiary distributees–apply to plan years beginning after December 31, 2009, rather than after the effective date of the Pension Protection Act (December 31, 2006).

Other amendments. The definition of "eligible retirement plan" from which a nonspouse beneficiary rollover can be made has been narrowed in the Code Sec. 402(c)(11)nonspouse beneficiary rollover rules to apply to a "qualified trust." The rules, however, continue to apply to distributions from 403 and 457 plans, because these plans incorporate the nonspouse beneficiary rollover requirements of Code Sec. 402(c)(11). The amendments appear to confirm that, as under existing law, there is no nonspouse rollover available from IRAs. An IRA acquired by an nonspouse beneficiary due to the IRA owner's death is an "inherited" account which may not be rolled over.[6]

Missing nonspouse beneficiaries

A safe harbor is available (see ¶ 2378) for plan fiduciaries of terminated plans and qualified termination administrators (QTAs) of abandoned plans with a fiduciary safe harbor for making distributions on behalf of missing participants or beneficiaries. Under the safe harbor, a deceased participant's benefit be directly rolled over to an inherited IRA established to receive the distribution on behalf of a missing, designated nonspouse beneficiary. [7]

EBSA final regs on distributions to missing nonspousal beneficiaries. EBSA final regulations clarify existing distribution requirements for terminated defined contribution plans, including abandoned plans, to allow rollovers into inherited IRAs for missing nonspouse beneficiaries. These final rules clarify the Pension Protection Act of 2006 provisions regarding missing participants, effective on November 6, 2008.

The final rule amends EBSA's regulatory safe harbor for distributions from terminated (including abandoned) individual account plans to require that a deceased participant's benefit be directly rolled over to an inherited IRA established to receive the distribution on behalf of a missing, designated nonspouse beneficiary. These amendments eliminate the prior safe harbor condition that required a distribution on behalf of a missing nonspouse beneficiary to be made only to an account other than an individual retirement plan. The final rule also makes conforming changes to the content requirements of the mandated participant and beneficiary termination notice.

In light of PPA changes, EBSA has amended PTE 2006-06 to require that, as a condition of relief under the exemption, benefits for a missing, designated nonspouse beneficiary be directly rolled over into an inherited IRA that fully complies with Code requirements. EBSA also clarifies that the exemption provides relief to a QTA that designates itself or an affiliate as the provider of an inherited IRA for a missing, designated nonspouse beneficiary pursuant to the exemption's conditions.

---

[1] Code Sec. 402(c)(11)(A), as added by the Pension Protection Act of 2006 (P.L. 109-280) and as amended by the Worker, Retiree, and Employer Recovery Act of 2008 (P.L. 110-458).

[2] Code Secs. 403(a)(4)(B), 403(b)(8)(B) and 457(e)(16)(B), as amended by P.L. 109-280.

[3] Code Secs. 402(c)(11)(A)(i), as amended by P.L. 110-458.

[4] Code Sec. 402(c)(11)(A)(i), as amended by P.L. 110-458.

[5] Code Sec. 402(f)(2)(A), as amended by P.L. 110-458.

[6] Code Sec. 408(d)(3)(C).

[7] ERISA Reg. § 2550.404a-3(d)(1)(ii).

¶ 1962

ROLLOVERS OF DISTRIBUTIONS: Rollover of Proceeds from Sale of Property

If a rollover distribution from a qualified plan includes property, an individual can roll over tax-free the proceeds from a bona fide sale of the property to an IRA within the usual 60-day period after the distribution.[1] If the rollover consists of the full distribution (including the sales proceeds), gain or loss on sale of the property will not be recognized.

---

[1] Code Sec. 402(c)(6).

¶ 1964

ROLLOVERS OF DISTRIBUTIONS: Frozen Plans

The 60-day period during which a tax-free rollover must be made (see ¶ 1952) does not include any period during which the amount transferred to an employee is a "frozen deposit." A frozen deposit is defined as any deposit which may not be withdrawn because of:

1. the bankruptcy or insolvency of the financial institution or

2. any requirement imposed by the state in which the institution is located by reason of the bankruptcy (or threat of bankruptcy or insolvency) of one or more financial institutions in the state.

In addition, an individual has at least 10 days after the release of the funds to complete the rollover. A deposit is treated as a frozen deposit only if amounts are frozen on at least one day during the 60-day period following the date when the amounts are distributed from the plan.[1]

---

[1] Code Sec. 402(c)(7).

¶ 1966

ROLLOVERS OF DISTRIBUTIONS: Rollover of Benefits Distributed Under Qualified Domestic Relations Orders

Distributions attributable to an employee that are paid to the employee's spouse or former spouse as an alternate payee under a qualified domestic relations order (QDRO), are treated, for rollover purposes, as if the alternate payee was the employee.[1] Thus, a distribution to a spouse or former spouse under a QDRO, including the distribution of ancillary death benefits attributable to the employee, is eligible for rollover if the requirements detailed at ¶ 1954 are met. However, nonspouse alternate payees may not roll over distributions from a qualified plan.[2] Accordingly, distributions to a nonspouse alternate payee are not eligible rollover distributions and are not subject to 20% income tax withholding.

□ QDROs are discussed beginning at ¶ 1600.

---

[1] Code Sec. 402(e)(1)(B); IRS Reg. § 1.402(c)-2, Q&A-12(a); IRS Letter Ruling 9109052, 12-5-90, CCH Pension Plan Guide ¶ 17,380S-3.

[2] IRS Reg. § 1.402(c)-2, Q&A-12(b); IRS Notice 89-25, 1989-1 CB 662, CCH Pension Plan Guide ¶ 17,102A-1.

¶ 1968

ROLLOVERS OF DISTRIBUTIONS: Rollover Treatment Where Employee Returns to Service

For pre-2000 tax years, in determining whether a distribution made to an employee on account of separation from service was eligible to be rolled over to another plan or to an IRA, the balance in the employee's account is determined without consideration of any increased vesting that might occur if the employee returns to work with the same employer.[1]

However, if an employee excluded the distribution from his income on account of the rollover, returns to work with the employer before incurring five consecutive one-year breaks in service, and the vested percentage of benefits accrued before separation increases, any later distributions made to the employee from the plan will not be eligible for the special tax treatment accorded to lump-sum distributions (see ¶ 1940).

---

[1] Code Sec. 402(d)(6); prior to repeal by P.L. 104-188 (Small Business Job Protection Act).

¶ 1970
ROLLOVERS OF DISTRIBUTIONS: Direct Rollover Option

Qualified plans and tax-sheltered annuities (TSAs) must provide recipients with the option of having eligible rollover distributions paid in a *direct rollover* to an eligible retirement plan.[1] A direct rollover is distinguished from an ordinary rollover (¶ 1950) in that the funds are paid *directly* from the plan to an IRA or another plan that accepts such rollovers, rather than being paid to the recipient who then transfers the funds to another plan. An eligible rollover distribution paid in a direct rollover to an eligible retirement plan is not included in the recipient's gross income.[2] For direct rollovers from qualified plans, an eligible retirement plan can only be a defined contribution plan that accepts transfers, IRAs, and qualified annuity plans funded through insurance contracts.[3] If a recipient does not elect to have the eligible rollover distribution paid directly to an eligible retirement plan, the eligible rollover distribution is subject to 20% income tax withholding.[4] The 20% withholding is imposed even if the distribution is rolled over and no tax is ultimately payable.

> **CCH Pointer:** The law does not *require* that plans be amended to accept direct rollovers from other plans. That decision is left to the discretion of the employer. Also, the law does not require plans to add payment options (such as lump-sum payouts) that could qualify for ordinary rollover or direct rollover treatment.

Eligible retirement plans

Prior to 2002, an eligible retirement plan that could receive a direct rollover from a qualified plan was limited to a defined contribution plan that accepted such transfers, an IRA, or a qualified annuity plan.[5] However, effective for distributions after 2001, direct rollovers may also be made from qualified plans to 403(b) plans and governmental 457 plans.[6]

A plan administrator may reasonably conclude that a contribution is a valid rollover contribution even if the distributing plan does not have a determination letter from the IRS regarding its qualified status.[7] For example, if an employee provides a statement from the plan administrator of the distributing plan representing (1) that the plan satisfies the qualification requirements or (2) that the plan is intended to satisfy the qualification requirements and the plan administrator is not aware of any disqualifying plan features, the receiving plan administrator may reasonably conclude that the distributing plan is qualified and that the amount paid as a direct rollover was an eligible rollover distribution.[8]

In the event that a plan administrator determines that a contribution was an invalid rollover contribution, the amount of the invalid rollover contribution, plus any earnings attributed to the contribution, must be distributed to the employee within a reasonable period of time after such determination.

Executing direct rollovers

A direct rollover may be accomplished by any reasonable means of direct payment, such as by wiring a transfer directly to the trustee or custodian of the eligible retirement plan or by mailing a check negotiable only by the trustee or custodian of the eligible retirement plan.[9]

Check may be given to distributee. A plan administrator or custodian may distribute a check to the recipient, instructing the recipient to deliver the check to an eligible retirement plan. The check must be payable to the trustee or custodian of the eligible retirement plan. If the name of the recipient is not included in the name of the eligible retirement plan, the check must indicate it is for the benefit of ("FBO") the recipient. If the eligible retirement plan is not an IRA, the check does not have to identify the trustee by name.[10]

Procedure for electing direct rollover

The plan administrator may prescribe any reasonable procedure for a recipient to elect a direct rollover.[11] The procedure may include any reasonable requirement for information, such as a statement from the recipient plan that it is an eligible retirement plan and that it will accept the direct rollover.

Procedures established by the plan administrator are not reasonable if they effectively eliminate or substantially impair the recipient's ability to elect a direct rollover.[12] Thus, it would not be reasonable for the plan administrator or custodian to require the recipient to obtain a legal opinion that the recipient plan is an eligible retirement plan.

Rollover election deemed irrevocable

The election by a distributee to directly roll over a distribution to an individual retirement plan is deemed to be an irrevocable designation of the direct rollover as a rollover contribution.[13]

Default procedure

A plan administrator may establish a default procedure under which a recipient who fails to make an affirmative election is treated as having either made or not made a direct rollover election.[14] However, distributions under a default procedure can only be made if the distributee has received an explanation of the default procedure and the direct rollover option within the stipulated period of time. A plan may be amended to change the default method of payment of an involuntary cash-out distribution from a direct cash payment to a direct rollover to an IRA established by the employer.[15]

Partial direct rollovers are permitted

A plan administrator must permit a recipient of an eligible rollover distribution to have a portion directly rolled over to an eligible retirement plan and to receive the balance. The plan administrator may require that the amount of the direct rollover equal at least $500. If an eligible rollover distribution does not exceed $500, the plan administrator or custodian does not have to allow the recipient to divide the distribution.[16]

Rollover to more than one plan

A plan is not required (but is permitted) to allow a recipient to have a direct rollover paid to more than one recipient plan.[17] Thus, a distributee may be required to select a single plan to which the rollover will be made.

Rollover not required for *de minimis* distributions

A plan does not have to permit a recipient to elect a direct rollover if it is reasonably expected that the recipient's total eligible rollover distributions for the year will be less than $200. The plan administrator may specify a lower amount.[18]

Periodic payments

A plan may treat a recipient's election to make or not make a direct rollover with respect to one payment in a series of periodic payments as applying to all subsequent payments in the series. The recipient must be permitted at any time to change an election with respect to subsequent payments and must be informed that the rollover election will apply to all future payments unless the election is changed.[19]

Spousal consent rules apply to rollover

A direct rollover is treated as a distribution of an eligible rollover distribution followed by an immediate rollover, and not as a transfer of assets and liabilities. Thus, applicable consent requirements, including spousal consent, must be satisfied before the direct rollover is executed. Also, because the direct rollover is not a transfer of benefits, the eligible retirement plan need not provide, with respect to the direct rollover, the same optional forms of benefits that were provided under the transferor plan.[20]

Direct rollover of loan offset not required

The distribution that results when a participant's accrued benefit is reduced, or offset, by the amount of a plan loan *may* be rolled over. However, the plan is not *required* to offer a direct rollover of the offset distribution.[21]

---

[1] Code Sec. 401(a)(31); IRS Reg. § 1.401(a)(31), Q&A-1.

[2] IRS Reg. § 1.401(a)(31)-1, Q&A-5.

[3] Code Secs. 401(a)(31)(D) and 402(c)(8)(B); IRS Reg. § 1.402(c)-2, Q&A-2.

[4] Code Sec. 3405(c)(2).

[5] IRS Reg. § 1.402(c)(2), Q&A-2.

[6] Code Sec. 402(c)(8)(B).

[7] IRS Reg. § 1.401(a)(31)-1, Q&A-14(a).

[8] IRS Reg. § 1.401(a)(31)-1, Q&A-14(c).

[9] IRS Reg. § 1.401(a)(31)-1, Q&A-3.

[10] IRS Reg. § 1.401(a)(31)-1, Q&A-4.

[11] IRS Reg. § 1.401(a)(31)-1, Q&A-6(a).

[12] IRS Reg. § 1.401(a)(31)-1, Q&A-6(b).

[13] IRS Reg. § 1.402(c)-2, Q&A-13(b).

[14] IRS Reg. § 1.401(a)(31)-1, Q&A-7.

[15] Rev. Rul. 2000-36, I.R.B. 2000-31, 7-31-2000, CCH PENSION PLAN GUIDE ¶ 19,944C.

[16] IRS Reg. § 1.401(a)(31)-1, Q&A-9.

[17] IRS Reg. § 1.401(a)(31)-1, Q&A-10.

[18] IRS Reg. § 1.401(a)(31)-1, Q&A-11.

[19] IRS Reg. § 1.401(a)(31)-1, Q&A-12.

[20] IRS Reg. § 1.401(a)(31)-1, Q&A-14.

[21] IRS Reg. § 1.401(a)(31)-1, Q&A-15; IRS Notice 93-3, 1993-1 CB 293, CCH PENSION PLAN GUIDE ¶ 17,105F.

¶ 1970A

ROLLOVERS OF DISTRIBUTIONS: Direct Rollovers from Eligible Retirement Plans to Roth IRAs

Distributions from eligible retirement plans made after December 31, 2007, can be rolled over directly into a Roth IRA.[1] In addition to traditional IRAs, eligible retirement plans include qualified trusts, tax-sheltered annuities and governmental 457 plans.[2] However, the rollover contribution must meet the rollover requirements applicable to the specific type of retirement plan.

For tax years beginning prior to January 1, 2010, the restrictions that previously applied to rollovers from a traditional IRA into a Roth IRA will apply to any rollover from an eligible retirement plan directly into a Roth IRA. Thus, a rollover to a Roth IRA will be allowed only if, for the tax year of the distribution to which the contribution relates, the taxpayer's adjusted gross income does not exceed $100,000 and the taxpayer is not a married individual filing a separate return.[3]

CCH Pointer: A rollover into a Roth IRA is not tax free. Except to the extent it represents a return of after-tax contributions, any amount that is rolled over to a Roth IRA is includible in gross income as a distribution since qualified distributions from a Roth IRA are not taxed. However, the 10 percent tax on early distributions will not apply to the rollover.

IRS guidance. The IRS has issued guidance clarifying the provisions of the Pension Protection Act of 2006 (P.L. 109-280) which relate to distributions involving rollovers from retirement plans to Roth IRAs after December 31, 2007.[4] . The PPA provisions discussed in the guidance include requirements relating to rollovers from qualified retirement plans to Roth IRAs and the qualified optional survivor annuity rules.

The guidance provides that, if an eligible rollover distribution from an eligible employer plan is rolled over to a Roth IRA and the distribution is not made from a designated Roth account (e.g., a Roth 401(k) plan), then the amount that would be includible in gross income were it not part of a qualified rollover contribution is included in the distributee's gross income for the year of the distribution. If an eligible rollover distribution made from a designated Roth account in an eligible employer plan is rolled over to a Roth IRA, the amount rolled over is not includible in the distributee's gross income, whether or not the distribution is a qualified distribution from the designated Roth account.

The IRS further clarifies that, for distributions not made from an eligible Roth account, an eligible rollover distribution from an eligible employer plan made before January 1, 2010, may not be rolled over to a Roth IRA unless, for the year of the distribution, the distributee's modified adjusted gross income does not exceed $100,000 and, in the case of a married distributee, the distributee files a joint federal income tax return with his or her spouse. The $100,000 limit and the joint filing requirement do not apply to distributions made on or after January 1, 2010. No restrictions based on the income limits and joint filing requirements would apply to a rollover made from a designated Roth account under an eligible employer plan to a Roth IRA.

According to the IRS, post-PPA, eligible rollover distributions from qualified plans can be rolled over to Roth IRAs via a direct plan-to-Roth IRA rollover, or via a distribution from the plan followed by a rollover to the Roth IRA within 60 days. The new definition of qualified rollover contribution in Code Sec. 408A(e) includes distributions from tax-sheltered annuity plans (403(b) plans) and governmental plans (457 plans).

For tax years beginning before January 1, 2010, an individual cannot make a qualified rollover contribution from an eligible retirement plan other than a Roth IRA if, for the year the eligible rollover distribution is made, he or she has a modified adjusted gross income (MAGI) above $100,000, or is married and files a separate return. If a taxable amount rolled into a Roth IRA from an eligible retirement plan other than a Roth IRA is distributed within 5 years, the additional tax under Code Sec. 72(t) applies as if the distribution were includible in gross income.

Plan administrators are required to permit the distributee of an eligible rollover distribution to elect a direct rollover to a Roth IRA, the IRS states, but they are not responsible for assuring that the distributee is eligible to make such a rollover. Withholding is required for rollover distributions paid to the employee, but is not required for direct trustee-to-trustee rollovers, including rollovers to Roth IRAs, even if the distribution is includible in gross income.

---

[1] Code Sec. 408A(e), as amended by the Pension Protection Act of 2006 (P.L. 109-280).

[2] Code Sec. 402(c)(8)(B), as amended by the Pension Protection Act of 2006 (P.L. 109-280).

[3] Code Sec. 408A(c)(3)(b), as amended by the Pension Protection Act of 2006 (P.L. 109-280).

[4] IRS Notice2009-75, I.R.B. 2009-39, September 28, 2009; IRS Notice 2008-30, I.R.B. 2008-12, March 24, 2008.

¶ 1971
ROLLOVERS OF DISTRIBUTIONS: Automatic Rollovers

EBSA regulations clarify the rules governing the satisfaction of fiduciary responsibilities with regard to automatic rollovers of certain mandatory distributions to individual retirement plans. The safe harbor set forth in the regulations requires the proper selection of an individual retirement plan provider and provides conditions for the proper investment of funds in connection with the automatic rollover.[1]

The Economic Growth and Tax Relief Reconciliation Act of 2001 created a new section, Code Sec. 401(a)(31)(B)(i), which provides that, to satisfy the fiduciary responsibility provisions of ERISA § 404(a), a trust which is part of an eligible plan will not be qualified unless the plan provides that where mandatory "cash out" distributions of more than $1,000 and less than or equal to $5,000 are to be made, where the participant has neither elected to receive the distribution directly nor opted to have it paid to an individual retirement plan, the administrator must transfer such distribution directly to an individual retirement plan. The plan administrator must give written notice to the participant of the option to transfer the distribution to another individual retirement plan.

Safe harbor conditions

In order for the safe harbor relief to apply, the following conditions need to be satisfied.[2] Note, however, that compliance with the safe harbor conditions is not the exclusive means by which a fiduciary could satisfy the requirements governing the rollover of cash-out distributions.[3]

1. The present value of the nonforfeitable accrued benefit may not exceed the maximum amount permitted under Code Sec.401(a)(31)(B).

2. The mandatory distribution must be directed to an individual retirement plan as described in Code Sec.408(a) and Code Sec.408(b).

3. Mandatory distributions must be invested in products designed to preserve principal and provide a reasonable rate of return. The final regulations state that this requirement must be set forth in a written agreement between the plan fiduciary and the individual retirement plan provider. The product must be offered by a state or federally regulated financial institution, and must seek to maintain a stable dollar value equal to the amount invested in the product by the individual retirement plan.

4. Fees and expenses attendant to an individual retirement plan may not exceed specified limits. This requirement also must now be set forth in a written agreement between the plan fiduciary and the individual retirement plan provider. Such fees and expenses may not exceed those charged by the provider for comparable individual retirement plans established for rollover distributions that are not subject to the automatic rollover provisions of Code Sec.401(a)(31)(B).

5. Participants must be furnished a summary plan description or a summary of material modifications describing the plan's automatic rollover provisions, with information that includes an explanation of how the mandatory distribution will be invested, how fees and expenses attendant to the individual retirement plan will be allocated, and a name, address, and phone number of a plan contact.

6. The selection of an individual retirement plan and the investment of funds may not result in a prohibited transaction, unless the selection falls under a prohibited transaction exemption issued pursuant to ERISA § 408(a).

Class PTE

EBSA has issued a prohibited transaction class exemption (PTE) that would allow a bank or other regulated financial institution to designate itself as the plan provider to receive mandatory rollovers from plans it sponsors, or from an affiliate sponsor.[4] The PTE would also permit the bank or financial institution to select its own funds or investment products for the rollovers and receive fees in connection with that service. Absent the PTE, the rollovers would have to be directed to a competitor of the bank or financial institution.

> **CCH Pointer:** *Safe harbor covers distributions under $1,000.* The safe harbor provisions of the 2004 final rules also apply to rollovers of mandatory distributions of $1,000 or less, provided that the participant has not made an affirmative distribution election and the rollover executed by the fiduciary satisfies the conditions specified in the final regulations.[5]

The safe harbor applies to distributions of $1,000 or less, although such distributions are not addressed in Code Sec. 401(a)(31)(B), because the DOL believes that the safe harbor protection will increase the likelihood that such distributions will be rolled over and, thereby, promote the preservation of retirement assets, without compromising the interests of plan participants.[6]

Safe harbor does not cover distributions over $5,000. The safe harbor does not extend to distributions of amounts over $5,000. The DOL was not prepared to conclude that the framework for the safe harbor relief, specifically the prescribed investment products, was appropriate for such distributions.[7]

Administrative procedures for processing rollovers

According to the IRS, all plans have until the end of 2005 to establish administrative procedures for processing the automatic rollovers. Specifically, as long as mandatory distributions are made by December 31, 2005, a plan is not treated as failing to operate in accordance with its terms regarding mandatory distributions merely because it does not process mandatory distributions for which a participant does not affirmatively elect direct rollover or direct payment due to a lack of adequate administrative procedures for automatic rollovers, including establishing individual retirement plans to accept automatic rollovers.[8]

Sample amendment provided

According to the IRS, plans which already provide for mandatory distributions and which do not already include the automatic rollover provisions must adopt a good faith plan amendment reflecting the automatic rollover requirements by the end of the first plan year ending on or after March 28, 2005. IRS has provided a sample amendment that individual plan sponsors and sponsors (or volume submitter practitioners) of pre-approved plans can use or adopt to amend their plans to comply with the new automatic rollover rules. Use of this sample plan amendment, or one that is materially similar, is considered to be a "good-faith" plan amendment.[9]

Rollover individual retirement plans do not require participant's participation

The IRS has clarified that rollover individual retirement plans can be set up without the participant's participation. Specifically, if a participant who receives a mandatory distribution fails to elect to have the distribution paid to an eligible retirement plan in a direct rollover or to receive the distribution directly, a plan administrator may execute the necessary documents to establish an individual retirement plan on the participant's behalf with a financial institution chosen by the plan administrator.

According to the IRS, when setting up the rollover individual retirement plan, a plan administrator may use the participant's most recent mailing address as shown in the records of the employer and plan administrator. The individual retirement plan's trustee or issuer must provide a disclosure statement to the participant and provide for a revocation period as described in Reg. § 1.408-6. The trustee or issuer does not fail to satisfy the disclosure requirements merely because the disclosure statement is returned by the Postal Service as undeliverable if this most recent mailing address has been used.[10]

☐ For more information on the direct rollover option, see ¶ 3798 of the CCH PENSION PLAN GUIDE.

---

[1] ERISA Reg. § 2550.404a-2(e).

[2] ERISA Reg. § 2550.404a-2(c).

[3] ERISA Reg. § 2550.404a-2(a)(2).

[4] Prohibited Transaction Class Exemption 2004-16.

[5] ERISA Reg. § 2550.404a-2(d)

[6] Preamble to ERISA Reg. § 2550.404a-2.

[7] Preamble to ERISA Reg. § 2550.404a-2.

[8] IRS Notice 2005-5, I.R.B. 2005-3, 1/18/05.

[9] IRS Notice 2005-5, I.R.B. 2005-3, 1/18/05.

[10] IRS Notice 2005-5, I.R.B. 2005-3, 1/18/05.

¶ 1972
ROLLOVERS OF DISTRIBUTIONS: IRS Model Amendment

The IRS has provided a simplified method for sponsors of master and proto-type (M&P), regional prototype, volume submitter specimen, and individually designed plans which have received favorable opinion, notification, advisory, and determination letters to amend their plans to comply with the direct rollover rules by adopting either a model amendment or a non-model amendment for approval by the IRS.[1]

Sponsors who amend their plans may adopt, on a word-for-word basis, model language prescribed by the IRS. No application to the IRS is required. In lieu of the model amendment, plans may adopt non-model language also described by the IRS.

---

[1] Rev. Proc. 93-12, 1993-1 CB 479, CCH PENSION PLAN GUIDE ¶ 17,299M-51.

¶ 1974

ROLLOVERS OF DISTRIBUTIONS: Notice of Rollover Treatment

Before the administrator of a qualified plan may make an eligible rollover distribution, the administrator is to provide a written explanation to the recipient of the rules that:[1]

1. allow the recipient to have the distribution directly transferred to an eligible retirement plan;

2. require tax to be withheld on the distribution if it is not directly transferred to another eligible retirement plan;

3. shield the distribution from tax if transferred to an eligible retirement plan within 60 days after the date on which the recipient received the distribution;

4. govern lump-sum distributions and other distributions under Code Sec. 402(d) and (e), if applicable; and

5. sets out the potential restrictions and tax consequences that may apply to distributions from the new plan to which the distribution is rolled over that are different from those applicable to the distributing plan, effective for distributions after December 31, 2001.

Plan administrators must also provide a written explanation to a distributee of any default procedures under which a distributee who fails to make an affirmative rollover election is treated a having either made or not made an election.[2]

Post-2006 notices

The Pension Protection Act of 2006 directed the Secretary of the Treasury to modify the regulations under the Code that apply to mandatory "cash-out" distributions, distributions of survivor annuities, and eligible rollover distributions in order to double the length of the notice and consent period. The regulations under ERISA that apply to same distributions are also to be modified to double the length of the notice and consent period. This change applies for years beginning after 2006.

Following the modification of the regulations, a plan must provide a participant with notice of his or her rights no less than 30 days and no more than 180 days before the date that the distribution commences. The participant's consent to the distribution may not be made more than 180 days before the date that the distribution commences.

The Secretary of Treasury is also directed to modify the regulations that apply to mandatory "cash-out" distributions to provide that the description of a participant's right (if any) to defer receipt of a distribution must also describe the consequences of failing to defer such receipt. A plan will not be treated as failing to meet the requirements with respect to any description of consequences made within 90 days after the modifications to the regulations are issued if the plan administrator makes a "reasonable attempt" to comply with such requirements.

Special rules for QJSAs. In regard to QJSAs, a plan must generally provide the written explanation mandated by Code Sec. 417(a)(3) to participants no less than 30 days and no more than 180 days before the annuity starting date. The written consent of the participant and the participant's spouse to the QJSA distribution must be made not more than 180 days before the annuity starting date and, in general, no later than the annuity starting date.

The Pension Act also expands the application election period for a participant to waive the QJSA form of benefit. As a result, a participant may elect to waive a QJSA during the 180-day period ending on the annuity starting date.

Model notice

The IRS has issued an updated notice containing safe harbor explanations that plan administrators may provide to recipients of eligible rollover distributions in order to satisfy the requirements of Code Sec. 402(f).[3]

The first safe harbor explanation applies to a distribution that is not from a designated Roth account. The second safe harbor explanation applies to a distribution from a designated Roth account. These safe harbor explanations update the Code Sec. 402(f) safe harbor explanations that were published earlier. Plans were able to use these new safe harbor explanations immediately or continue to use their prior 402(f) notices, as appropriately modified for law changes, through the end of 2009.

The administrator of a retirement plan is required to give a written explanation to recipients of an eligible rollover distribution, that is, a payment that may be rolled over to an eligible retirement plan, as defined in Code Sec. 402(c)(8)(B). The written explanation must describe the direct rollover rules, the mandatory income tax withholding rules for distributions not directly rolled over, the tax treatment of distributions not rolled over, and when distributions may be subject to different restrictions and tax consequences after being rolled over. These requirements reflect changes in the law due to legislation enacted in 2001 and 2006.

Besides simplifying the description and presentation of the participant's options on receiving an eligible rollover distribution, the new explanations also broaden the information to reflect changes in law, such as information on a distribution from a designated Roth account (e.g., a Roth 401(k) plan). The information has also been expanded to cover special situations, such as where a distribution is made to a surviving spouse or beneficiary or to a nonresident alien. Plan administrators may customize the explanations to their terms and administrative procedures, for example, by omitting any information that does not apply to a plan. An alternative explanation may be provided instead of those contained in the notice, provided that it contains the same information and is written an understandable manner.

In using one of the safe harbor explanations, the plan administrator may customize the safe harbor explanation by omitting any portion that does not apply to the plan. Alternatively, a plan administrator can satisfy Code Sec. 402(f) by providing recipients with an explanation that provides additional information or that is otherwise different from one of the safe harbor explanations, as long as it contains the required information and is written in a manner designed to be easily understood.[4]

The Working Families Tax Relief Act of 2004 (P.L. 108-311) specifically requires rollovers from qualified annuity plans under Code Sec. 403(a) to adhere to the Code Sec. 402(f) notice rules.[5]

Notice must be provided within "reasonable time"

The plan administrator must provide the notice within a reasonable period of time before making an eligible rollover distribution.[6] The reasonable period of time requirement is satisfied only if the written explanation is given to the plan participant at least 30 days, but not more than 90 days, prior to the distribution.[7] Under certain circumstances, however, the 30-day period can be waived.

Waiver of 30-day period allowed

If a participant receives the required rollover notice and affirmatively elects to make or not make a direct rollover, a distribution can be made less than 30 days after the notice is given.[8] Thus, participants are permitted to waive the 30-day period in Code Sec. 402(f) and receive their distributions without waiting 30 days. However, two requirements must be met:[9]

1. the participant must be *given the opportunity* to consider the decision of whether or not to elect a direct rollover for at least 30 days after the notice is provided; and

2. the plan administrator must provide information to the participant clearly indicating that the participant has 30 days in which to decide whether or not to elect a direct rollover. This information may be conveyed to the distributee by any method reasonably designed to attract the attention of the distributee.

Separate notice of periodic payments not required

A plan administrator is not required to provide a separate rollover notice for each distribution in a series of periodic payments that constitute eligible rollover distributions.[10] However, notice must be provided prior to the first payment in the series and at least once annually over the period during which the payments are made. In addition, the notice must inform the distributee that the rollover election will apply to all future payments in the series unless the employee subsequently changes the election.[11]

Posting is not sufficient notice

The written rollover notice must be provided to each individual distributee within the required time period.[12] The notice may not be merely posted at the distributee's place of employment.

¶1974

Penalty for failure to provide notice

A plan administrator who fails to provide the rollover notice within the required period of time is subject to a penalty of $100 for each failure, up to $50,000 for each calendar year.[13] The penalty, however, will not apply if the administrator's failure to provide the notice was due to reasonable cause and not to willful neglect.

2008 IRS proposed rules

The IRS has issued proposed regulations clarifying the content of notices to plan participants of the consequences of failing to defer cash-out distributions. The proposed rules would also expand the time period during which an election to waive or revoke a joint and survivor annuity may be made.

Notice of consequences of failing to defer distributions. The proposed regulations provide that the notice, advising the participant of the right to defer receipt of a distribution and the consequences of failing to defer such receipt, must describe the federal tax implications of failing to defer. In the case of a defined benefit plan, a statement is also required which shows the amount payable to the participant under the normal form of benefit both upon immediate commencement and when the benefit is no longer immediately distributable (that is, the later of age 62 or attainment of normal retirement age).

In the case of a defined contribution (DC) plan, the proposed regulations would require the information in the notice to include a statement that some currently available investment options in the plan may not be generally available on similar terms outside the plan. The notice would also be required to include a statement that fees and expenses outside the plan may be different from fees and expenses that apply to the participant's account. The proposed regulations further require the inclusion of other information which could materially affect a participant's decision on whether to defer receipt of the distribution, such as a description of the eligibility requirements for retiree health benefits if such benefits are limited to participants who have an undistributed benefit under the employer's retirement plan.

Expansion of applicable election and notice periods. Generally, qualified plans are required to provide the accrued benefit payable to a vested participant in the form of a QJSA. Any election to waive the QJSA benefit, or revoke the waiver, must be made within the applicable election period. The PPA expanded the applicable election period from 90 days to 180 days. Consequently, the proposed regulations would expand the definition of an applicable election period, and the time period for the issuance of certain notices, to 180 days prior to the annuity starting date or, in certain cases, the date of distribution.

Effective dates. The proposed regulations are effective for notices provided, and election periods beginning, on or after the first day of the first plan year beginning January 1, 2010, but in no event earlier than the first day of the first plan year beginning 90 days after publication of final regulations. With respect to the proposed regulations relating to the expanded applicable election period and the expanded period for notices, plans may rely on these proposed regulations for notices provided, and election periods beginning, during the period beginning on the first day of the first plan year beginning on or after January 1, 2007 and ending on the effective date of final regulations.

---

[1] Code Sec. 402(f)(1); IRS Reg. §1.402(f), Q&A-1(a).

[2] IRS Reg. §1.401(a)(31), Q&A-7.

[3] IRS Notice 2009-68, I.R.B. 2009-39, September 28, 2009, CCH Pension Plan Guide ¶ 17,143H-5.

[4] IRS Reg. § 1.402(f)-1, Q&A-1(a).

[5] Code Sec.403(a)(4)(B), as amended by P.L. 108-311.

[6] IRS Reg. § 1.402(f)-1, Q&A-1.

[7] IRS Reg. § 1.402(f)-1, Q&A-2.

[8] IRS Notice 93-26, 1993-1 CB 308, 11, CCH Pension Plan Guide ¶ 17,105L.

[9] IRS Reg. § 1.402(f)-1, Q&A-2.

[10] IRS Reg. § 1.402(f)-1, Q&A-3.

[11] IRS Reg. § 1.401(a)(31), Q&A-12(b).

[12] IRS Reg. § 1.402(f)-1, Q&A-4.

[13] Code Sec. 6652(i).

¶ 1980

For More Information

☐ For more information on the taxation of distributions from qualified plans, see ¶ 3633, ¶ 3804, and ¶ 5468-5495 of the CCH Pension Plan Guide.

Loans to Employees Under Qualified Plans

¶ 2000
Loans from Qualified Plans

An attractive feature of many tax qualified plans is a provision that allows employees to borrow against their account balances. A loan provision is particularly useful in encouraging low-paid employees to participate in a 401(k) plan. Without such an option, these employees may be reluctant to tie up funds that they may need to purchase a car or to pay for medical expenses or other large or unexpected expenses.

Plan loans, however, are not without cost to employees. In addition to set up costs and other administrative fees, an employee must repay a loan, with interest, even if the employee terminates employment. Employers also need to be aware, before adopting a loan program, of restrictions imposed by the Internal Revenue Code and ERISA that are designed to assure that loans are true loans and not disguised distributions. Generally: loan terms must be set forth in a written and legally enforceable agreement (see ¶ 2002); the amount of the loan may not exceed the lesser of $50,000 (reduced by previous outstanding loans) or one-half of the present value of the participant's nonforfeitable accrued benefit (see ¶ 2003); the terms of the loan (other than principal residence loans), must require repayment within 5 years (see ¶ 2020); and the loan must be amortized on a substantially level basis with payments made no less frequently than quarterly (see ¶ 2025). A loan that does not meet the applicable requirements is treated as a deemed distribution and is subject to income tax, and, under certain circumstances the 10 percent tax on early distributions (see ¶ 2027).

A loan from a qualified plan to a plan participant is not treated as an actual distribution. However, in order for the loan to avoid being treated as a prohibited transaction, and for the plan to remain qualified, loans to participants must: be available to all participants or beneficiaries on a reasonably equivalent basis; not be available to highly compensated employees in an amount greater than the amount made available to other employees; be made in accordance with specific plan provisions; bear a reasonable rate of interest; and be adequately secured (see ¶ 2029). Plan officials may avoid liability under ERISA for fiduciary breaches incident to loans that constitute prohibited transactions, however, by following prescribed correction procedures under the Voluntary Fiduciary Correction Program.

Truth-In-Lending Disclosures

Plans making 25 or more plan loans (or five or more loans secured by a dwelling) in a current or prior calendar year must make truth-in-lending disclosures under the Truth in Lending Act and governing Regulation Z. [1]

Plan Loans exempt from truth-in-lending disclosures. The Board of Governors of the Federal Reserve System, incident to a sweeping revision of Regulation Z, provided an exemption, effective July 1, 2010, from the truth-in-lending disclosures for loans from employer-sponsored retirement plans. [2] Under new Reg. 226.3(g), an extension of credit to a participant in a Code Sec. 401(a) tax qualified plan, 403(b) plan, or 457(b) plan will be exempt from Regulation Z if: (1) the loan is comprised of fully vested funds from the participant's account and (2) complies with Code Sec. 72 and other requirements under the Internal Revenue Code.

Exemption applies to non-ERISA plans. The fact that loans from plans subject to ERISA are required to comply with detailed disclosure requirements is a factor obviating the application of Regulation Z to plan loans. However this point does not mean that non-ERISA plans remain subject to Regulation Z. The Federal Reserve, noting that Reg. 226.3(g) does not explicitly reference ERISA or the DOL disclosure regulations, explains that the exemption from Regulation Z applies to plans that are not subject to ERISA. The fact that ERISA's disclosure rules do not apply to such plans does not change the nature of the loan that allows for the exemption.

[1] 15 U.S.C. 1601, et seq., 12 CFR 226.2(a)(17).   [2] 12 CFR 226.3(g) (74FR 5244), January 20, 2009.

¶ 2002
Legally Enforceable Agreement

A loan must be evidenced by a legally enforceable agreement set forth in writing (or in another form approved by the IRS) that specifies the amount of the loan, the term of the loan, and the repayment schedule.[1] A loan that is not evidenced by a legally enforceable agreement is a taxable deemed distribution (see ¶ 2027).

CCH POINTER: An employer may amend or discontinue a loan program because the anti-cutback rules, which prevent the elimination of optional forms of benefit, do not apply to plan loans. [2]

Paperless loans. A loan may be evidenced by a legally enforceable agreement that is not in writing, but that is set forth in a form approved by the IRS. A loan agreement may be set forth in an electronic medium.[3] However, plans that use an electronic system must allow participants a reasonable opportunity to review, correct or rescind loan terms before the loan is made.

Use of electronic media authorized. Final regulations provide standards for the use of electronic systems by retirement plans, employee benefit arrangements, and individual retirement plans for the delivery of notices to participants or the delivery of elections by participants to plans, including agreements involving loans to plan participants.[4]

Participant need not sign legally enforceable loan agreement. A participant is not required to sign the document containing the terms of the loan, as long as the loan agreement is legally enforceable and the other requirements for the loan are satisfied.[5]

Spousal consent required under plans subject to survivor annuity requirements. In the event a plan is subject to the survivor annuity requirements and a participant's account balance is pledged as security for a loan, spousal consent must be obtained no earlier than 90 days before the participant's account balance is pledged.[6] Spousal consent is not required for a loan if the plan is not subject to the survivor annuity requirements at the time a participant's account balance is used a security for the plan, or if the participant's total account balance subject to the security is not in excess of the applicable cash-out limits. [7]

---

[1] IRS Reg. § 1.72(p)-1, Q&A-3(b).

[2] IRS Reg. § 1.411(d)-4, Q&A-1(d)(4).

[3] IRS Reg. § 1.72(p)-1, Q&A-3(b).

[4] IRS Reg. Reg. § 1.401(a)-21(a), (b) and (c); Preamble to IRS Reg. 1.401(a)-21, at CCH Pension Plan Guide ¶ 24,508I.

[5] *Ibid*; IRS General Information Letter, 6-26-97, at CCH Pension Plan Guide ¶ 17,396L.

[6] IRS Reg. § 1.401(a)-20, Q&A-24(a).

[7] *Ibid.*

¶ 2003

Dollar Limit on Loans

A loan from a qualified plan to a participant is treated as a distribution and taxed to the extent that it exceeds prescribed dollar limits.[1] A loan from a qualified plan that is repaid within five years is treated as a distribution only to the extent that the amount of the loan, when added to the outstanding loan balance of the employee under all other loans from such plan, exceeds the *lesser* of:

1. $50,000, reduced by the excess of: (a) the highest outstanding balance of loans for the plan during the one-year period ending on the day before the date the loan is made, over (b) the outstanding balance of the loans for the plan on the date the loan is made; or

2. the greater of one-half of the *present* value of the employee's nonforfeitable accrued benefit under the plan, or $10,000.[2]

Aggregation rules

For purposes of the dollar limits, all plans of an employer (including controlled group and affiliated service members) are treated as one plan.[3]

Roth contributions. Designated Roth contributions (see ¶ 2941A) may serve as the basis of a participant loan [4] Thus, if any amount from a designated Roth account is included in a loan to an employee, the plan aggregation rules must be applied in determining the amount of the available loan.

Determine value of vested benefit at the time of the loan

The value of a participant's nonforfeitable benefit is determined at the time the time the loan is made. Thus, for example, an authorized 401(k) plan distribution that occurs after a loan equal to 50 percent of a participant's vested account balance has been made will not produce a deemed distribution, even though the participant's account balance is reduced by the distribution and the loan amount may actually exceed 50 percent of the account balance.[5]

CCH POINTER: *Number of loans.* While a dollar limit applies to plan loans, there is no limit, under the governing Code Sec. 72 regulations on the number of loans that a participant can take, other than that imposed by the dollar restrictions. However, plans may impose restrictions on the number of loans available to participants and place a limit on the minimum amount of a loan.[6] For example, a plan may prohibit loans under $1000.

Credit card loans. The IRS acknowledges that, because the final rules do not impose any limit (other than the applicable dollar limits and plan restrictions) on the number of plan loans that can be made in a year, there will be no barrier to credit card loans that otherwise satisfy the conditions of Code Sec. 72(p).[7]

☐ A chart and examples illustrating the maximum loan limits are at CCH PENSION PLAN GUIDE ¶ 7685B.

[1] Code Sec. 72(p)(1).
[2] Code Sec. 72(p)(2)(A).
[3] Code Sec. 72(p)(2)(D).
[4] IRS Reg. § 1.401(k)-1(f).
[5] IRS Reg. § 1.72(p)-1, Q&A-4 ERISA Reg. § 2550.408b-1(f).
[6] ERISA Reg. § 2550.408b-1(b)(2).

[7] Preamble to IRS Reg. § 1.72(p)-1, Q&A-20. See also ERISA Opinion Letter 95-17A, 6-19-95, CCH PENSION PLAN GUIDE ¶ 19,983T, in which the DOL tacitly sanctioned a loan program pursuant to which participants were able to secure loans, up to a specified limit, from their individual 401(k) account through a credit card issued by the administrator of the program.

¶ 2020
Five-Year Repayment Requirement

A loan made to a participant under a qualified plan, government plan, or tax-sheltered annuity (other than loans used to acquire a personal residence) that is not required to be repaid within five years is automatically treated as a distribution.[1] A loan that is treated as a distribution because of a specified repayment period of more than 5 years will be treated as a distribution, even if it is repaid within 5 years.

Date of loan. The period by which the loan must be repaid is determined at the time the loan agreement is executed. The terms of the loan must specify the repayment date. The date of a loan for purposes of the 5-year repayment period is the date on which the loan is funded. Thus, IRS representatives have explained, the date of a loan is the date on which the check is delivered to the participant (and not the date on which the loan application is signed, or the date on which the note is signed).[2]

Participant bankruptcy

Participant loans under a 401(k) plan are not discharged in bankruptcy. Thus, only loan repayments by payroll deduction are permitted in order to avoid loan defaults and resulting taxation.[3] In addition, the Bankruptcy Abuse Prevention and Consumer Protection Act (BAPCPA) provides that amounts required to repay loans from ERISA qualified plans are not disposable income for purposes of determining amounts required to be applied to unsecured debts under a Chapter 13 plan.[4]

Debtors Not Allowed to Exclude 401(k) Loan Repayments From Chapter 7 Means Test as Mandatory Deduction. A debtor may not exclude 401(k) plan repayments from the means test calculation required for purposes of Chapter 7 relief. Loan repayments made through salary reduction were not viewed as mandatory deductions upon which an employee's employment was conditioned.[5]

Loan repayments are not debts or necessary expenses. The Ninth Circuit, in a case of first impression, has adopted the prevailing position, but with an emphasis on the understanding that loan repayments are not debts or necessary expenses under the bankruptcy law.[6]

Loan repayment is not secured debt. Noting that a debtor is permitted under the Chapter 7 means test to deduct average monthly payments made on account of "secured debts," the court held that a debtor's obligation to repay a loan from a retirement account is not a debt under the Bankruptcy Code that may be deducted from income under the means test. An employee's obligation under a 401(k) loan is to himself, the court explained, stressing that the plan administrator has no right to personal recovery against the debtor in the event of default.

> **CCH POINTER:** *Chapter 13 Debtors Prohibited from Contributing Funds Available Following Repayment of 401(k) Loan to Plan.* Debtors may wish to continue to shield money that was used to repay a 401(k) loan after the loans has been paid by contributing those funds to the plan. However, a Bankruptcy Panel in the Sixth Circuit has ruled that debtors in a Chapter 13 bankruptcy case may not use income which becomes available once 401(k) plan loans are repaid to begin making elective deferrals to the plan.[7] The Panel stressed that property of the bankruptcy estate under Bankruptcy Code Sec. 541(a) and exclusions from property of the estate under Bankruptcy Code Sec. 541(b) must be determined on the date of the filing of the case. Pursuant to this understanding, the Panel explained that only 401(k) contributions that are being made at the commencement of the case may be excluded from the property of the estate under Bankruptcy Code Sec. 541(b)(7).

Loan extensions

A loan may be extended beyond the original repayment date if the original loan period was less than five years. However, if a five-year repayment period is later extended past the original five years, the outstanding balance at the time of the extension is treated as distribution at the time of the extension.

Existing loan may be renewed or modified. An existing plan loan may be renewed, modified, or renegotiated. However, the loan agreement must still indicate an intent by the parties that the loan be repaid. Thus, a participant may not continually renegotiate a loan so as to avoid the 5 year repayment requirement.

Exemption for purchase of principal residence

The 5-year repayment rule does not apply to any loan that is used for the acquisition (and not the reconstruction or rehabilitation) of a dwelling that will be used as the principal residence of the participant within a reasonable time.[8] However, plan loans designed to improve an existing principal residence, to purchase a second home, or to finance the purchase of a home or home improvement for other members of the employee's family are subject to the five-year repayment rule. In addition, employees should be cautioned that a plan *may* require a principal residence loan to be repaid within 5 years.

Loan need not be secured by dwelling unit. A principal residence loan need not be secured by the dwelling unit that is to be used as the recipient's principal residence.[9]

Refinancing as principal residence loan. Refinancings (see ¶ 2027) do not generally qualify a principal residence loans.[10] However, the use of a plan loan to repay a loan from a third party (i.e., a bank) will be treated as a principal residence loan if the plan loan qualifies as a principal residence loan irrespective of the loan from the third party.

Suspension of loan during employee's military service

A plan may (but is not required to) suspend an employee's obligation to repay a plan loan during the period of the employee's military service (even if the individual is not entitled to reemployment) without risking disqualification or engaging in a prohibited transaction (see ¶ 2025).[11]

Deduction of interest

Employees may not deduct the interest on a loan from a 401(k) plan if the loan is secured by elective deferrals under the plan.[12] This restriction has the greatest impact on new employees because the bulk of their vested account balance is derived from elective contributions. However, the deduction restriction also applies to loans made to key employees, regardless of how the loan is secured.

[1] Code Sec. 72(p)(2)(B)(i).

[2] ABA Joint Committee on Employee Benefits, IRS Q&A, May 7, 2004.

[3] P.L. 109-8 (Bankruptcy Abuse Prevention and Consumer Protection Act of 2005), 119 Stat. 23.

[4] 11 U.S.C. 1322(f). See also, *In re Lasowski* CA-8 (2009), No. 09-2017, at CCH PENSION PLAN GUIDE ¶ 24,005W, *aff'g* (U.S. Bank App. Pnl, CA-8 (2008), No. 07-6063, at CCH PENSION PLAN GUIDE ¶ 24,002P), in which the court explained that only

the amount required to repay the 401(k) plan loan is excludable from treatment as disposable income. Thus, the debtor could only exclude payments for the 13 months remaining on the term of the loans, not for the entire 5 years of the bankruptcy plan. The court rejected a debtor's contention that the Bankruptcy Form 22C allowed loan repayment amounts to be calculated on a historical basis in the same manner that monthly income was determined. Because the statute, and not the Bankruptcy Form, controlled the determination of disposable income, the debtor was limited to excluding the $1,600 actually required to repay the loan.

[5] *In re Whitaker*, US Bank OH (2007), No. 06-33109, at CCH PENSION PLAN GUIDE ¶ 24,000X.

[6] *Egjebjerg v. Anderson*, CA-9 (2009), No. 08-55301, at CCH PENSION PLAN GUIDE ¶ 24,005E.

[7] *Burden v. Seafort*, U.S. Bank. App. Pnl. CA-6, Nos. 09-8062 and 09-8063, at CCH PENSION PLAN GUIDE ¶ 24,007W.

[8] Code Sec. 72(p)(2)(B)(ii).

[9] IRS Reg. § 1.72(p)-1,Q&A-6.

[10] IRS Reg. § 1.72(p)-1, Q&A-8.

[11] Code Sec. 414(u); IRS Reg. § 1.72p-1, Q&A-9(b).

[12] Code Sec. 72(p)(3).

¶ 2025
Level Amortization of Payments

A loan must be amortized on a substantially level basis and payments (principal and interest) must be made no less frequently than quarterly over the term of the loan.[1] A plan loan that is payable on demand with interest payable per annum is a taxable distribution, even if it is repaid within five years, if payments of principal and interest are not required *by the terms of the plan* to be made in substantially level payments no less frequently than quarterly.[2]

CCH POINTER: The level amortization requirement must be set forth in the legally enforceable agreement pursuant to which the loan is executed.[3] Thus, the loan amortization requirement must be satisfied in form and in operation.

.

Time for transmitting loan repayments to plan

The provisions of ERISA Reg. § 2510.3-102, requiring elective deferrals to be paid to the trust by the earliest date on which the contributions can be reasonably segregated from the employer's general assets, but no later than the 15th business day of the month following the month in which the contributions would have otherwise been payable in cash to the participants, did not, prior to amendment, specifically apply to participant loan repayments. However, the DOL has held that participant loan repayments are sufficiently similar to participant contributions to justify, in the absence of regulatory guidance, the application of principles similar to those underlying the participant contribution rules in determining when loan repayments become plan assets. [4]Accordingly, participant loan repayments paid to or withheld by an employer for transmittal to the plan become plan assets as of the earliest date on which the repayments may reasonably be segregated from the employer's general assets.

Safe harbor allows employees maintaining small plans 7 days in which to deposit loan repayments. The EBSA has amended the governing plan asset regulations to extend the requirements to loan repayments under all plans and to provide employers maintaining plans with less than 100 participants at the beginning of the plan year a 7-day safe harbor in which to deposit loan repayments to the plan. [5]Under the safe harbor, loan repayments that are deposited within 7 business days from the date the funds are received or withheld from the participant would be deemed repaid to the plan on the earliest date on which the loan repayments could reasonably be segregated from the employer's general assets.

Safe harbor is optional. Use of the safe harbor is not mandatory. Nor is the safe harbor the exclusive means by which an employer may comply with the deposit requirements.

The rules are detailed at ¶ 2948.

Calculation of delinquent and unpaid loan repayments

In the event loan repayments are transferred to the plan later than the time authorized under the governing ERISA rules, an employer must pay the plan the greater of: (1) lost earnings, or (2) restoration of profits resulting from the employer's use of the principal amount. [6] Any penalties, late fees or other charges are to be paid by the employer and may not be paid from participant loan repayments.

If the loan repayments were not paid to the plan, the employer would be required to remit to the plan the principal amount, plus the greater of: (1) lost earnings on the principal amount or (2) restoration of profits resulting from the employer's use of the principal amount. [7] Note, the DOL provides an online calculator that is useful in making the required calculation. See www.dol.gov/ebsa/calculator/main.html.

Payments suspended during one year leave of absence

The level amortization requirement does not apply during a period of up to the lesser of one year or the latest permissible term (i.e., maximum term) of the loan that a participant is on a bona fide leave of absence, either without pay from the employer or at a rate of pay (after income and employment tax withholding) that is less than the amount of the installment payment required by the plan. Thus, a loan that is unpaid while a participant is on leave of absence (pursuant to plan terms) will not be treated as a deemed distribution.[8] However, the loan (including interest that accrues during the period of leave) must still be repaid within 5 years (or the latest permissible term of the loan).

Plan may accelerate payments

The level amortization requirement does not preclude pre-payments or the acceleration of loan payments, nor does it bar the use of a variable interest rate. Thus, a plan is not prohibited from requiring the full repayment of a loan upon a participant's termination of employment.

Payments suspended during military service

A plan may authorize the suspension of loan repayments by an employee during a period of service in the uniformed services (whether or not qualified military services). The suspension of loan repayments is not taken into account for purposes of Code Sec. 72(p)(2). [9]

In the event a plan suspends loan repayments for any part of a period during which an employee is performing military service, the suspension will not cause the loan to be a deemed distribution, even if the period during which the loan is suspended exceeds one year and even if the term of the loan is extended.[10] However, the employee must resume repayments upon the completion of military service and the loan, including interest accrued during the period of military service (up to a 6% cap set forth in the Soldiers' and Sailors' Relief Act Amendments of 1942), must be repaid in substantially level installments over a period that ends no later than the latest "permissible term of the loan" (i.e., 5 years from the date of the loan for non principal residence loans) plus any additional period of suspension authorized for participants on military leave.[11] Thus, the loan repayment schedule may be extended at the end of a participant's military leave, in the event that the original loan had a term of less than 5 years.[12]

[1] Code Sec. 72(p)(2)(C).

[2] *Estate of Gray v. Commissioner*, TC (1995), TC Memo. 1995-421, CCH Dec. 50,868(M).

[3] Reg. § 1.72(p)-1, Q&A-3.

[4] DOL Advisory Opinion 2002-2A, May 17, 2002, at CCH PENSION PLAN GUIDE ¶ 19,988X).

[5] ERISA Reg. § 2510.3-102(a)(2).

[6] EBSA Adoption of Voluntary Fiduciary Correction Program, Sec. 7.1(a)(2), April 19, 2006 (71 FR 20261) at CCH PENSION PLAN GUIDE ¶ 19,953D).

[7] *Ibid.*

[8] Reg. § 1.72(p)-1, Q&A-9(a).

[9] Code Sec. 414(u)(4).

[10] IRS Reg. § 1.72(p)-1, Q&A-9(b).

[11] IRS Reg. § 1.72(p)-1, Q&A-9(b) and (c).

[12] Preamble to IRS Reg. § 1.72(p)-1, Q&A-9.

¶ 2027

Taxation of Loans as Deemed Distributions

A loan that does not meet the requirements detailed at ¶ 2000-2025 is treated as a deemed distribution and is subject to income tax in the year of the deemed distribution.[1] In addition, if the participant has not attained age 59½, or is not otherwise entitled to an early distribution, the Code Sec. 72(t) 10% tax on early distributions will be assessed, unless an exception explicitly authorized under Code Sec. 72(t) applies.[2]

Deemed distribution at time loan is made

If a loan is not evidenced by a legally enforceable agreement, or the terms of the loan do not require the loan to be repaid within 5 years (or the extended period authorized for principal residence loans), or satisfy the level amortization requirement, the *entire amount* of the loan is a deemed distribution at the time the loan is made.[3]

Loan in excess of applicable dollar limit

In the event that a loan satisfies the repayment, level amortization, and enforceable agreement requirements, but exceeds the dollar limits (see ¶ 2003), only the amount of the loan in excess of the applicable limit is a deemed distribution at the time the loan is made.[4] Thus, the full amount of the loan is not taxed.

Deemed distribution upon default

If the loan initially satisfies the applicable rules, but the participant fails to make the required payments when due, a deemed distribution of the remaining balance of the loan occurs at the time of the default.[5]

"Cure period" for missed loan payments. The plan may allow the participant a "cure period" in which to make a required installment payment (and, thus, avoid a deemed distribution). The deemed distribution would not occur until the close of the cure period. However, the cure period may not extend beyond the last day of the calendar quarter following the calendar quarter in which the required installment payment was due.[6]

Entire outstanding balance of loan is taxed. In the event that a participant defaults on a payment (taking into account any cure period authorized by the plan), the amount of the deemed distribution will equal the entire outstanding balance of the loan (including accrued interest) at the time of the default (and not in the year the loan was executed).[7] Thus, the participant is subject to tax not only on the amount of the missed installment, but on the entire amount of the loan that is still outstanding.

Example: Linda has a nonforfeitable account balance of $45,000. On August 1, 2009, she borrows $20,000 from the plan to be repaid over 5 years in level monthly installments due at the end of each month. Linda, makes monthly payments through July 31, 2011, but fails to make the installment payment due on August 31, 2011 or any monthly payment due thereafter. The plan provides for a 3-month cure period.

As a result of her default, Linda has a deemed distribution on November 30, 2011, the last day of the 3 month cure period for the August 31, 2011 installment. The amount of the deemed distribution is $17,157, which is the outstanding balance of the loan on November 30, 2011.

CCH POINTER: *Correction under VCP.* A failure to repay a loan in accordance with loan terms that comply with Code Sec.72(p)(2) may be corrected under the Voluntary Correction Program (VCP). Correction requires: (1) lump sum repayment equal to the additional repayments that the participant would have made to the plan if there had been no failure to repay the plan, plus interest accrued on the missed repayments, (2) reamortization of the outstanding balance of the loan, including interest, over the remaining payment schedule of the original term of the loan or the period that would remain had the loan been amortized over the maximum period that complies with Code Sec. 72(p)(2)(B), measured from the original date of the loan, or (3) any combination of the preceding measures.[8]

Treatment of deemed distribution as actual distribution. A deemed distribution may be treated for tax purposes in the same way as an actual distribution. For example, if the employee's account includes after-tax contributions or other investment in the contract, all or a portion of the deemed distribution may not be taxable.[9] However, the 10 percent tax on early distributions and the separate 10 percent tax applicable under Code Sec. 72(m) to amounts received by 5-percent owners will be imposed as if the deemed distribution was an actual distribution.[10]

A deemed distribution is not treated as an actual distribution for purposes of the qualification rules, the in-service distribution restrictions, or the vesting requirements of IRS Reg. § 1.411(a)-7(d)(5).[11] Similarly, the deemed distribution is not an eligible rollover distribution and is not considered to be an impermissible distribution of an amount attributable to elective contributions to a 401(k) plan.[12]

Loan in default must be repaid

The fact that a participant is taxed on the amount of the loan that is treated as a deemed distribution does not excuse the participant from repaying the loan. A loan that is treated as a deemed distribution continues to exist as a loan until it is repaid. In addition, the loan remains a *plan asset* until it is repaid and interest continues to accrue on the loan until it is repaid with principal and interest.[13]

Termination of employment

Plans typically require an employee to repay the remaining unpaid amount of the loan upon the termination of employment or offsets the distribution of the participant's account by the amount of the outstanding loan balance. A plan may also, less frequently, allow a terminated employee to carry an outstanding loan balance.

Distributed loans are eligible rollover distributions

When a participant terminates employment and receives a distribution, the plan may allow the note representing the loan to be rolled over to another qualified plan (not an IRA), thereby avoiding the triggering of a loan offset, which is a taxable event.

Loan offset is a distribution

A qualified plan may require a loan to be offset against the participant's accrued benefits. The amount of the account balance that is offset against the loan is an actual distribution, and not a deemed distribution.[14] However, generally, a plan may not authorize a loan offset before the participant is eligible to take a distribution (i.e., before a participant separates from service, dies, experiences a hardship or disability, or attains age 59½). Thus, even though a plan loan is generally not treated as a distribution, even if it is secured by the employee's accrued benefits that are attributable to elective contributions, because the reduction or foreclosure of a participant's account following default is a distribution, the plan risks losing qualified status if it reduces or forecloses on the account balance before the occurrence of a distributable event.[15]

Loan offset amount is eligible rollover distribution. The loan offset may be avoided under plans that provide for the direct rollover of the loan upon the termination of employment.[16]

Accrued interest after default is not taxable

A loan in default is a plan asset and, thus, interest continues to accrue, even if the loan is treated as a deemed distribution. However, because a loan that is a deemed distribution is not treated as an outstanding loan, interest that accrues under the plan on the amount that is deemed distributed is not included in a participant's income.[17] In addition, even though interest continues to accrue on the outstanding loan, the additional interest is not treated as an additional loan and does not result in an additional distribution.

Interest included in determining amount of subsequent loan. In the event that a loan is deemed distributed and has not been repaid by plan offset, or otherwise, the unpaid amount of the loan, plus interest accrued after the distribution, is considered to be outstanding and will, accordingly, reduce the amount of any subsequent loan to a participant or beneficiary.[18]

Additional security for loans subsequent to default. Plans may provide loans to participants after a default on a prior loan. However, if a loan is deemed distributed to a participant or beneficiary and has not been repaid (e.g., by plan loan offset), no payment subsequently made to the participant or beneficiary may be treated as a loan, unless specified conditions are satisfied. The loan must comply with the dollar limits of Code Sec. 72(p)(2).[19] In addition, there must be an arrangement between the plan, the participant or beneficiary, and the employer, enforceable under applicable law, pursuant to which repayments will be made by payroll withholding or, alternatively, the plan must receive adequate security from the participant or beneficiary that is in addition to the participant's or beneficiary's accrued benefit under the plan.[20]

Refinanced loans

A plan participant or beneficiary may refinance an outstanding loan or borrow additional amounts from the plan. The loans must collectively satisfy the dollar amount limits of Code Sec. 72(p)(2)(A).[21] In addition, the prior loan and the additional loan must satisfy the requirements of Code Sec. 72(p)(2)(B) and Code Sec. 72(p)(2)(C). Therefore, each loan must be repaid in substantially level installments, not less often than quarterly, over five years (or longer for certain home loans).

Refinanced loans as deemed distributions. A refinanced loan is treated a continuation of the prior loan, plus a new loan, to the extent of any increase in the loan balance.[22] Thus, while a refinanced loan may be repaid over a 5 year period from the date of the refinancing, to the extent that the refinanced loan exceeds the amount of the prior loan, the prior outstanding loan must continue to be repaid in substantially level installments over a period that is no longer than the original term remaining on the prior loan in order for the refinancing not to result in a deemed distribution.

Term of replacement loan may not exceed replaced loan. If the term of the replacement loan ends after the latest permissible term of the replaced loan, the replacement loan and the replacement loan are both treated as outstanding on the date of the transaction. Accordingly, if the term of the replacement loan ends after the latest permissible term of the replaced loan (i.e., generally 5 years from the date of the original loan, absent any extension authorized for a principal residence loan or military leave) and the sum of the replacement loan and the outstanding balance of all other loans (including the replaced loan) on the date of transaction exceeds the dollar limits of Code Sec. 72(p)(2)(A), the replacement loan will result in a deemed distribution. However, a replacement loan will not result in a deemed distribution if the replaced loan and the replacement loan (treated as two separate loans) are repaid by the end of the latest permissible term of the prior loan. [23]

Refinancing of loans with terms under 5 years. The final rules allow for the extension of a prior loan with an original term of less than 5 years.[24]

However, the term of the refinanced loan may not be extended beyond 5 years from the date of the prior loan.

☐ Similar rules apply to participants returning from military leave (see ¶ 2025).

Reporting deemed distributions

The amount taxable to a participant as a deemed distribution (including accrued interest) must be reported on Form 1099-R.[25] In addition, an employer must report defaulted loans on Form 5500 (Schedule H or I) as a plan asset, unless the loan is secured by a participant's account balance or otherwise treated as an asset of the participant. The employer would also be required to report the resumption of loan repayments.

Withholding on deemed distributions

If a loan, when made, is a deemed distribution, or an account balance is reduced (offset) to repay a loan, the amount includible in the participant's income is subject to withholding.[26] However, if a deemed distribution of a loan or a loan repayment by benefit offset results in income after the loan is made, withholding is required only if cash or property (excluding employer securities) is transferred to the participant or beneficiary from the plan at the same time.[27]

Eligible rollover distributions. Loans that are treated as deemed distributions are not eligible rollover distributions that are subject to mandatory 20% withholding.[28] However, a distribution of a plan offset amount is an eligible rollover distribution that must be rolled over to an eligible retirement plan within 60 days in order to avoid 20% withholding.[29]

Loan offset subject to withholding. Withholding applies to the amount of the loan offset and to the cash and property received by the distributee. However, although plan loan offsets are included in the amount subject to withholding, the maximum amount to be withheld for a loan offset that is an eligible rollover distribution may not exceed the sum of the cash and the fair market value of property (other than employer securities) received by the distributee, excluding the loan offset amount.[30] Thus, if the only portion of an eligible rollover distribution that is not paid in a direct rollover consists of a plan loan offset (and not cash or property), withholding is not required.

Example: Tony terminates employment with an account balance of $40,000 and an outstanding loan balance of $5,000. Pursuant to the plan's terms, he elects to take a distribution of his entire $40,000 account balance at termination.

The plan offsets the $40,000 account balance by the $5,000 outstanding loan amount and intends to pay Tony the difference, less any required withholding. The amount of the distribution for purposes of calculating the required withholding is $40,000. Accordingly, the amount that must be withheld is $8,000 (20% of $40,000).

Tony will receive a distribution of $27,000 in cash ($40,000 account balance minus $5,000 loan, minus $8,000 withholding.

---

[1] Code Sec. 72(p)(1).

[2] Courts will not expand upon the exceptions specifically authorized under Code Sec. 72(t). Thus, the 10 percent penalty applied to a taxpayer who was precluded from making loan repayments by an individual bankruptcy plan (*White v. Commissioner*, TC (2005), No. 1815-045, at CCH PENSION PLAN GUIDE ¶ 23,991Q).

[3] IRS Reg. § 1.72(p)-1, Q&A-4(a).

[4] IRS Reg. § 1.72(p)-1, Q&A-4(a).

[5] IRS Reg. § 1.72(p)-1, Q&A-4(a) and 10(a).

[6] IRS Reg. § 1.72(p)-1, Q&A-10(a).

[7] IRS Reg. § 1.72(p)-1, Q&A-10(b); *Duncan v. Commissioner*, TC (2005), No. 329-04, at CCH PENSION PLAN GUIDE ¶ 23,992K. See also *Molina v. Commissioner*, TC (2005), No. 4026-03L, TC Memo 2004-258 at CCH PENSION PLAN GUIDE ¶ 23,990F (loan did not result in a taxable deemed distribution until regular substantially equal loan amortization repayments were discontinued); and *Leon and Tilley v. Commissioner* (TC (2008), No. 26450-06S, at CCH PENSION PLAN GUIDE, at ¶ 24,003K) in which the Tax Court ruled (with respect to a loan made before the effective date of the governing final regulations, which required a loan balance to become due and payable upon a participant's termination of employment, did not negate the plan's 90 day cure period. Accordingly, although the participant had terminated employment in October 2003, because the cure period did not expire until 2004, the deemed distribution of the outstanding loan balance occurred in 2004.

[8] Rev. Proc. 2008-50, I.R.B. 2008-35, Sec. 6.07(3), at CCH PENSION PLAN GUIDE, at ¶ 17,299S-66.

[9] IRS Reg. § 1.72(p)-1, Q&A-11(a).

[10] IRS Reg. § 1.72(p)-1, Q&A-11(b).

[11] IRS Reg. § 1.72(p)-1 , Q&A-12.

[12] *Ibid.*

[13] CCH Interview: Martin Heming, Reish & Luftman, at CCH PENSION PLAN GUIDE ¶ 26,598.

[14] IRS Reg. § 1.72(p)-1, Q&A-13(b); IRS Reg. § 1.401(k)-1(d)(6)(ii).

[15] IRS Reg. § 1.401(k)-1(d)(6)(iii).

[16] IRS Reg. § 1.402(c)-2, Q&A-9 IRS Ltr Rul. 200617037, 1-20-06, at CCH PENSION PLAN GUIDE ¶ 17,424Y (plan loan offset following default was an actual distribution that could be rolled over to an eligible retirement plan).

[17] IRS Reg. § 1.72(p)-1, Q&A-19(a).

[18] IRS Reg. § 1.72(p)-1, Q&A-19(a) and (b).

[19] IRS Reg. § 1.72(p)-1, Q&A-19(b).

[20] IRS Reg. § 1.72(p)-1, Q&A-19(b)(2)(i) and (ii).

[21] IRS Reg. § 1.72(p)-1, Q&A-20(a)(1).

[22] Preamble to IRS Reg. § 1.72(p)-1, Q&A-20.

[23] IRS Reg. § 1.72(p)-1, Q&A-20(a)(2). See, *Marquez v. Commissioner* (TC Summary Opinion 2009-80, No. 25885-07S, at CCH PENSION PLAN GUIDE ¶ 24,005I) and *Billups v. Commissioner* of Internal Revenue (TC Summary Opinion 2009-86, No. 17470-07S, at CCH PENSION PLAN GUIDE ¶ 24,005Q) in which employees who refinanced prior plan loans were deemed to have received taxable distributions because the prior loans and the refinanced loans collectively exceeded the Code Sec. 72(p) limit.

[24] *Ibid.*

[25] IRS Reg. § 1.72(p)-1, Q&A-14(a).

[26] IRS Reg. § 1.72(p)-1, Q&A-15.

[27] *Ibid.*

[28] IRS Reg. § 1.402(c)-2, Q&A-4(d).

[29] IRS Reg. § 1.402(c)-2, Q&A-9(a). See also IRS Letter Ruling 8103063, 10-22-80, at CCH PENSION PLAN GUIDE ¶ 17,372R, in which the IRS privately ruled that a participant could roll over a distribution from a terminating profit-sharing plan, even though part of the distribution was offset by the outstanding amount of a plan loan, as long as any amount attributable to the loan offset was rolled over in cash.

[30] IRS Reg. § 31.3405(c)-1, Q&A-11.

¶ 2028
Pledges and Assignments

A plan participant or beneficiary may assign or pledge (or agree to assign or pledge) a portion of his or her interest in a qualified plan as security for a loan. Under such circumstances, the portion of the individual's interest that is assigned or pledged (or subject to an agreement to assign or pledge) is treated as a loan from the plan to the individual and is subject to the deemed distribution rules.[1] Thus, if a participant pledges his entire vested interest as security for a loan of a lesser amount, only the amount borrowed is taxable income.

Pledge of plan interest may not violate anti-alienation rule. Plan loans may be secured by a participant's vested benefits if: (1) the benefits are used to secure loans from the plan and not from third parties; and (2) the loan: is available to all participants or beneficiaries on a reasonably equivalent basis; is not available to highly compensated employees in an amount greater than the amount made available to other employees; is made in accordance with specific plan provisions; bears a reasonable rate of interest; and is adequately secured.[2]

---

[1]Code Sec. 72(p)(1)(B); Reg. §1.72(p)-1, Q&A-1(b).

[2]Reg. §1.401(a)-13(d)(2).

¶ 2029
Loans Exempt from Prohibited Transaction Rules

Generally, any lending of money or other extension of credit between a plan and a disqualified person or party in interest is a prohibited transaction.[1] However, loans by plans to participants or beneficiaries who are parties in interest are permitted (and the plan will retain qualified status) if the loans:[2]

1. are available to all participants or beneficiaries on a reasonably equivalent basis;

2. are not made available to highly compensated employee in an amount greater than the amount made available to other employees;

   CCH Pointer: Maximum loan amounts available under a plan may vary in accord with the size of a participant's vested account balance. However, a plan may not establish a minimum loan threshold (e.g., $25,000) and require all loans to be secured by a participant's account balance, if the effect of the condition is to limit the availability of a loan to highly compensated employees.[3]

   Employer loans, including below market loans designed to benefit corporate officers, are discussed at ¶ 3340.

3. are made in accordance with specific plan provisions;

   CCH Pointer: A loan must be made pursuant to a participant loan program that is set forth in writing and identifies the administrator of the program. In addition, the loan program should disclose: the procedures for applying for loans, the basis on which loans will be approved or denied, any limitations on the type and amount of loans, applicable procedures for determining a reasonable rate of interest, the collateral that may secure a loan, events constituting a default, and the steps that must be taken to preserve plan assets in the event of a default.[4] The absence of a participant loan program that provides the required information will cause all plan loans to parties in interest to be prohibited transactions.

4. bear a reasonable rate of interest (i.e., an interest rate that provides a return commensurate the rate charged by commercial lenders (e.g., prime rate)); and

5. are adequately secured

15 percent excise tax

Participant loans that do not comply with the governing restrictions subject parties to the transaction to an excise tax of 15 percent of the amount involved with respect to the loan (i.e., interest on the loan). In addition, a 100 percent penalty may be assessed if the loan is not paid within a specified period.[5]

CCH POINTER: Note, a loan that constitutes a prohibited transaction is a recurring transaction on which the penalty tax "pyramids." Accordingly, the tax assessed each year will equal the tax imposed for the prior year, plus the tax on the loan for the current year.

Correction of fiduciary breach under VFCP

In the event that a loan is considered a prohibited transaction, the fiduciary executing the loan will have committed a breach of fiduciary duty. A fiduciary, however, may avoid civil liability for a plan loan made to a party in interest that does not comply with ERISA by correcting the transaction under the EBSA's Voluntary Fiduciary Correction Program (VFCP) (see ¶ 2737). The VFCP generally requires applicants to correct loan violations under the Employee Plans Compliance Resolution System (EPCRS) maintained by the IRS and then submit a copy of the resulting EPCRS compliance statement, along with proof of payment of any required amount, to the EBSA.[6]

---

[1] Code Sec. 4975(c)(1); ERISA Sec. 406(a)(1)(B).

[2] Code Sec. 4975(d)(1); ERISA Sec. 408(b)(1); ERISA Reg. § 2550.408b-1(a)(1).

[3] ERISA Reg. § 2550.40-8b-1(c)(1) and (4), Example 2.

[4] ERISA Reg. § 2550.408b-1(d).

[5] Code Sec. 4975(a) and (b).

[6] EBSA Adoption of Voluntary Fiduciary Correction Program, Sec. 7.3(b), April 19, 2006 (71 FR 20261), at CCH PENSION PLAN GUIDE ¶ 19,953D

¶ 2030

For More Information

☐ For more information on loans from qualified plans, see ¶ 3840-3856 and ¶ ¶ 7685—7685L of the CCH PENSION PLAN GUIDE.

Withholding Rules

¶ 2100

General Rules

Federal income tax withholding rules apply to designated distributions, including periodic payments.[1] Designated distributions include the taxable part of pension, profit-sharing, stock bonus, or individual retirement account (IRA) payments. Designated distributions also include the taxable part of distributions from Code Sec. Code Sec. 457 plans sponsored by governmental employers.[2]

Payments from a deferred compensation plan that are not otherwise considered wages and payments under a commercial annuity contract, whether or not purchased under an employer's plan, also will be considered designated distributions.[3] For purposes of the withholding rules, a commercial annuity is defined as an annuity, endowment, or life insurance contract issued by an insurance company licensed to do business under the laws of any state.[4]

Partial surrender of an annuity contract, certain loans from employee plans and IRAs, and Civil Service Retirement System annuity payments and distributions also will give rise to withholding.[5] In addition, the withholding provisions apply to annuities paid from an employer-deferred compensation plan, an IRA, or a commercial annuity to the surviving spouse or other beneficiary of a deceased employee.[6]

Maximum amount to be withheld

The maximum amount withheld from any designated distribution (including any eligible rollover distribution) may not exceed the sum of the cash and the value of other property (excluding employer securities or plan loan offset amounts) received in the distribution. In other words, it is never necessary to liquidate employer securities to satisfy the withholding obligation. If the distribution is limited to employer securities plus cash in lieu of fractional shares, no withholding is required if the cash does not exceed $200 (see ¶ 2115).[7]

A payor or plan administrator also is not required to withhold tax from an eligible rollover distribution that is *not* rolled over if the distribution is under $200.[8]

Avoidance of withholding

Withholding on a distribution from a qualified retirement plan, a tax-sheltered annuity (TSA), IRA, or Code Sec. 457 plan that is eligible for rollover may be avoided only if the employee instructs the plan to make a direct transfer of the distribution to an IRA, a defined contribution plan that accept transfers, or a qualified annuity plan funded through insurance contracts (see ¶ 1970 and ¶ 2115).[9] Direct rollovers may also be made from qualified plans to 403(b) plans and governmental 457 plans.[10] For other distributions, withholding may be avoided if the employee "elects out" (see ¶ 2125).

Social security and medicare tax

Contributions. Elective contributions, including Roth 401(k) contributions and additional voluntary contributions in excess of the deferral limits are subject to a two-part tax under the Federal Insurance Contributions Act (FICA). An Old-Age, Survivor, and Disability Insurance (OASDI) (i.e., "social security") tax assessed on covered wages, up to the applicable taxable wage base. In addition, a 1.45% Hospital Insurance (i.e., "medicare tax") is imposed on all covered wages, irrespective of the applicable wage base.

In December 2010, the President approved a temporary 2% reduction in the social security tax rate for employees and the self-employed for 2011 as part of the Tax Relief, Unemployment Insurance Reauthorization, and Job Creation Act of 2010 (P.L. 111-312). The social security tax rate for 2011 was 4.2% for employees and 10.4% for the self-employed. The law made no changes to the social security tax rate for employers (6.2%) or to the amount of wages (the wage base) and net self-employment income subject to the social security payroll tax ($106,800 in 2011).

On December 23, 2011, the President approved the continuation of the 4.2% rate for the first two months of 2012 as part of the Temporary Payroll Tax Cut Continuation Act of 2011 (P.L. 112-78). The law also included a new "recapture" provision, which applies only to those employees who receive more than $18,350 in wages during the two-month period (the social security wage base for 2012 is $110,100, and $18,350 represents two months of the full-year amount). The provision imposes an additional income tax on these higher-income employees in an amount equal to 2% percent of the amount of wages they receive during the two-month period in excess of $18,350 (and not greater than $110,100).

This additional recapture tax is an add-on to income tax liability that the employee would otherwise pay for 2012 and is not subject to reduction by credits or deductions. The recapture tax would be payable in 2013 when the employee files his or her income tax return for the 2012 tax year. With the possibility of a full-year

¶2100

extension of the payroll tax cut being discussed for 2012, the IRS will closely monitor the situation in case future legislation changes the recapture provision.

As we go to press, the House and Senate have appointed conferees to work on legislation (H.R. 3630) that would extend the 4.2% rate for all of 2012.

Future tax increase will not apply. Although elective contributions are generally subject to FICA tax, the additional 0.9% Medicare tax, effective January 1, 2013, imposed by the Patient Protection and Affordable Care Act will not apply to such contributions, because the additional tax will only affect amounts in excess of the applicable threshold of $250,000 for joint filers and $200,000 for other taxpayers. As the applicable contribution limits under Code Sec. 402(g) and Code Sec. 415 do not allow for contributions of such magnitude, the additional 0.9% Medicare tax will not apply to elective contributions. [11]

Distributions. The Health Care and Education Reconciliation Act of 2010 (enacted together with the Patient Protection and Affordable Care Act, imposes an additional 3.8% Medicare tax, effective January 1, 2013, on investment income.

The American Society of Pension Professionals and Actuaries (ASPPA) has confirmed that the law excludes distributions from qualified retirement plans, such as Code Sec. 401(k) and pension plans, from the increased Medicare tax. Thus, investment income generated on investments within the plan will not be subject to the new 3.8% Medicare tax on income in excess of the $200,000-$250,000 threshold limits. [12]

Nonqualified plans

Generally, contributions to, and benefits paid from, nonqualified plans are subject to wage withholding at the time they are includible in the recipient's gross income (see ¶ 2135). [13] However, W-2 withholding does not apply if the distribution from a nonqualified plan takes the form of an annuity payable on retirement that is taxed under the annuity rules of Code Sec. 72. [14]

Nonstatutory stock options. The transfer by an employee of an interest in a nonstatutory stock option (see ¶ 3320) or a nonqualified deferred compensation plan (see ¶ 3345) to a former spouse incident to divorce does not subject the employee to taxation. [15] The former spouse, rather than the employee, is required to include an amount in gross income when the former spouse exercises the stock option or when the deferred compensation is paid or made available to the former spouse. The IRS has issued a proposed revenue ruling discussing the application of income tax withholding to such transfers. [16] The income recognized upon the former spouse's exercise of the transferred nonqualified stock options would be subject to income tax withholding, as would be the amounts distributed to the former spouse from a nonqualified deferred compensation plan. The former spouse, however, would be entitled to the credit allowable for income tax withheld at the source on wages.

Statutory stock options. See ¶ 3310 for information on the application of FICA and FUTA tax to certain stock options.

[1] P.L. 97-248 (Tax Equity and Fiscal Responsibility Act of 1982), Sec. 334(e)(1).

[2] P.L. 107-16 (Economic Growth and Tax Relief Reconciliation Act of 2001), Sec. 649 sunset provision, as repealed by P.L. 109-280 (Pension Protection Act of 2006), Sec. 811.

[3] Code Secs. 3405(a) and (d).

[4] IRS Temp. Reg. § 35.3405-1T, Q&A A-4.

[5] P.L. 97-248 (Tax Equity and Fiscal Responsibility Act of 1982), Conference Committee Report.

[6] IRS Temp. Reg. § 35.3405-1T, Q&A A-17.

[7] Code Sec. 3405(e)(8); IRS Reg. § 31.3405(c)-1, Q&A-11; IRS Notice 93-3, 1993-1 CB 293.

[8] IRS Reg. § 31.3405(c)-1, Q&A-14.

[9] Code Secs. 402(c)(8)(B) and 3405(c)(2); IRS Reg. § § 31.3405(c)-1, Q&A-2 and 35.3405-1T, Q&A A-17.

[10] Code Sec. 402(c)(8)(B) sunset provision, as repealed by P.L. 109-280 (Pension Protection Act of 2006), Sec. 811.

[11] Code Sec. 3101(b)(2), as added and amended by Act Sec. 9015 of the Patient Protection and Affordable Act (P.L. 111-148), as amended by Act. Sec. 1402(b) of the Health Care and Education Reconciliation Act of 2010 (P.L. 111-152).

[12] Code Sec. 1411(a)(1), as added by Act sec. 1402(a)(1) of the Health Care and Education Reconciliation Act of 2010 (P.L. 111-152).

[13] IRS Reg. § 35.3405-1T, Q&A A-18.

[14] IRS Reg. § 31.3401(a)-1(b)(1).

[15] Rev. Rul. 2002-22, 2002-1 CB 849, 5-13-02, CCH Pension Plan Guide ¶ 19,946K.

[16] IRS Notice 2002-31, 2002-1 CB 908, 5-13-02, CCH Pension Plan Guide ¶ 17,123W. In Rev. Rul. 2004-60, I.R.B. 2004-24, 6-14-04, CCH Pension Plan Gudie ¶ 19,948Z-72, the IRS largely adopted the proposed rules set forth in Notice 2002-31. The revenue ruling is effective January 1, 2005. For periods before this date, employers may rely on a reasonable, good faith interpretation of the proposed revenue ruling in Notice 2002-31.

¶ 2105

Benefits Excludable from Gross Income

Generally, withholding is not required from any portion of a distribution that the payor reasonably believes will not be included in the recipient's gross income.[1]

Deductible employee contributions (DECs)

Between 1981 and 1987, employees could deduct a limited amount of contributions to a qualified retirement plan. These contributions (referred to as deductible employee contributions or DECs) are not part of an employee's investment in the contract and, thus, are taxable when distributed. However, the IRS takes the position that, unless the payor has specific knowledge that employee contributions distributed by a plan are DECs, it is reasonable to assume that they are excludable from gross income.[2]

Cost of life insurance protection

The cost of life insurance protection provided to a participant by a qualified plan or TSA is included in a participant's gross income. The IRS takes the position that, because the costs are not distributed or deemed to be distributed, withholding is not required on the amount included in the participant's income.[3]

Payments subject to wage withholding

Pension and retirement distributions that constitute "wages" are subject to the W-2 withholding provisions not the 1099-R withholding provisions. [4] Under those rules, pensions and retirement distributions are subject to W-2 withholding unless there is an express exemption in the law or regulations.[5] W-2 withholding does not apply to distributions from qualified retirement plans, qualified annuities, simplified employee pensions (SEPs), or to employee or employer contributions under SIM-PLE plans.[6] In addition, W-2 withholding does not generally apply to distributions made from Code Sec. 457 deferred compensation plans sponsored by a state or other state entity.[7] Qualified distributions from a Roth IRA are nontaxable, and, therefore, are not subject to withholding.

[1] Code Sec. 3405(e)(1)(B)(ii).

[2] IRS Temp. Reg. §35.3405-1T, Q&A A-31.

[3] IRS Temp. Reg. §35.3405-1T, Q&A F-9.

[4] Code Sec. 3405(e)(1)(B)(i); IRS Temp. Reg. § 35.3405-1T, Q&A A-18.

[5] IRS Reg. §31.3401(a)-1(b)(1).

[6] Code Secs. 3401(a)(12)(A)—(D).

[7] Code Sec. 3401(a)(12)(E), as added by P.L. 107-16 (Economic Growth and Tax Relief Reconciliation Act of 2001), Sec. 649, sunset provision, as repealed by P.L. 109-280 (Pension Protection Act of 2006), Sec. 811.

¶ 2110
Periodic Payments

Withholding will apply to periodic payments, such as those provided by an annuity, as if such payments are considered wages subject to the recipient's withholding certificate for the appropriate payroll period. If a withholding certificate is not in effect, the recipient will be treated as a married individual claiming three exemptions for withholding purposes.[1] Generally, this means that tax will be withheld if the pension or annuity payment is at least $1,640 per month during 2012.[2]

Although the payor must withhold from any periodic payment the amount that would be withheld as if the payment were a payment of wages by an employer to an employee for a payroll period, the amount to be withheld from a periodic payment is calculated separately from any amounts that are actually wages paid to the recipient for the same period.[3] Either the percentage method (Code Sec. 3402(b)) or the wage-bracket method (Code Sec. 3402(c)) may be used to determine the withholding liability on a periodic payment.[4]

☐ See ¶ 46—46A of the CCH PENSION PLAN GUIDE for the wage-bracket and percentage method withholding tables that are used to calculate the amounts to be withheld from periodic payments.

More than one beneficiary

Where one check is issued to more than one beneficiary, withholding may be computed as if there were only one recipient. However, where each recipient files a withholding certificate and the payor knows the amount of the payment to which each recipient is entitled, the payor may determine the amount to be withheld with respect to each recipient. If notice of an election not to have withholding apply (see ¶ 2125) is supplied to each recipient and only one recipient makes the election or files a certificate, the payor must assume that the election or filing was made by the recipient on behalf of the other recipients.[5]

When withholding certificate takes effect

If a pension withholding certificate is filed by a recipient, it will generally take effect as provided under wage withholding rules for certificates. If a withholding certificate is furnished by a recipient on or before the date on which payments begin, it applies to payments made more than 30 days after the certificate is submitted, unless the payor elects to make it effective sooner.[6]

---

[1] Code Sec. 3405(a)(1) and (4).

[2] Form W-4P Instructions.

[3] IRS Temp. Reg. § 35.3405-1T, Q&A B-1.

[4] IRS Temp. Reg. § 35.3405-1T, Q&A B-2.

[5] IRS Temp. Reg. § 35.3405-1T, Q&A A-36.

[6] Code Sec. 3402(f)(3); Code Sec. 3405(a)(3); IRS Reg. §§ 31.3402(o)-2; IRS Temporary Reg. § 35.3405-1T; IRS Pub 505.

¶ 2115
Nonperiodic Payments

A nonperiodic distribution is any designated distribution which is not a periodic payment.[1] Income tax withholding is imposed at the rate of 20% on any distribution that is eligible for rollover treatment but that is not transferred directly to an eligible transferee plan.[2] Recipients cannot elect out of withholding on nonperiodic payments that are eligible rollover distributions as they can for withholding on periodic distributions (see ¶ 2125).[3] Withholding at the rate of 10% is imposed on the taxable part of a nonperiodic payment that is not an eligible rollover distribution.[4] However, recipients may elect no withholding from nonperiodic distributions that are not eligible rollover distributions. If the recipient provides a Form W-4P with an incorrect taxpayer identification number (TIN), the payor must withhold 10% from the payment.[5]

No withholding on direct rollovers

No withholding is imposed on a *direct rollover* from a qualified trust to an eligible retirement plan listed below:[6]

1. a trust of a qualified defined contribution plan,
2. an individual retirement account,
3. a qualified annuity,
4. an eligible Code Sec. 457 deferred compensation plan maintained by a state or other state entity, or
5. 403(b) plans.

An eligible rollover distribution that is paid in a direct rollover to a qualified defined benefit plan also is exempt from 20% withholding.[7]

"Ordinary rollovers" subject to withholding

If a distribution is made and the recipient makes an *ordinary*, as opposed to a direct, rollover of the distribution within 60 days, 20% withholding is imposed. In order to roll over the entire amount of the distribution, the taxpayer would have to make up the amount and apply for a tax refund. This may seem like a rather harsh result, but, because a plan administrator must provide a written explanation to a recipient of the direct rollover option within a reasonable time before the distribution (see ¶ 2130), the recipient has time in which to decide whether to make the transfer directly to an eligible plan or to receive the distribution and then roll it over.

Partial rollover exempt from withholding

If an employee elects to have only a portion of a distribution directly rolled over into an eligible retirement plan, the 20% withholding requirement applies only to the part of the distribution that the employee receives, and not to the portion that is transferred in the direct rollover.[8]

Plan administrator is responsible for withholding

Generally, the plan administrator has the responsibility of withholding on the amount of an eligible rollover distribution that the recipient does not elect to directly roll over.[9]

Withholding may be transferred to payor

A plan administrator may shift the withholding responsibility to the payor by following certain procedures set out by the IRS, which include a requirement that the administrator direct the payor in writing to withhold the tax.[10]

Withholding not required on distributions under $200

Withholding is not required on an eligible rollover distribution that is not directly transferred if it is less than $200.[11] In determining whether the $200 floor is reached, all eligible rollover distributions made to a recipient by a plan within one tax year must be aggregated. If, at the time of the first distribution under $200, the plan administrator does not know whether other distributions will be made, withholding is not required. If distributions are made within one tax year by more than one plan of the same employer, the plan administrator or payor may (but need not) aggregate those distributions in determining if the $200 floor has been reached. However, once distributions reach $200, the sum of all payments made during the year is used to calculate the amount to be withheld from subsequent payments made during the year.

Distributions of property subject to withholding

Special rules for withholding on property[12] apply with respect to the 20% mandatory withholding requirement.[13] Under these rules, if property (other than employer securities) is distributed and the cash in the distribution will not satisfy the withholding obligation, an employer must either sell the property or receive cash from the employee in amounts sufficient to pay the withholding.[14] If provided in a sufficient amount, the cash in a distribution may satisfy the withholding due on the entire distribution.[15]

---

[1] Code Sec. 3405(e)(3).

[2] Code Sec. 3405(c)(1); IRS Reg. §31.3405(c)-1, Q&A-1(a).

[3] IRS Reg. §31.3405(c)-1, Q&A-2.

[4] Code Sec. 3405(b)(1).

[5] 2011 Form W-4P Instructions.

[6] Code Sec. 402(c)(8)(B) sunset provision, as repealed by P.L. 109-280 (Pension Protection Act of 2006), Sec. 811. Code Sec. 3405(c)(2); IRS Reg.

§§31.3405(c)-1, Q&A-2 and 35.3405-1T, Q&A A-17.

[7] IRS Reg. §31.3405(c)-1, Q&A-8.

[8] IRS Reg. §31.3405(c)-1, Q&A-6.

[9] IRS Reg. §31.3405(c)-1, Q&A-4.

[10] IRS Reg. §31.3405(c)-1, Q&A-5.

[11] IRS Reg. §31.3405(c)-1, Q&A-14.

[12] IRS Temp. Reg. §35.3405-1T, Q&A F-2 and F-3.

[13] IRS Reg. § 31.3405(c)-1, Q&A-9.   [15] IRS Temp. Reg. § 35.3405-1T, Q&A F-3.
[14] IRS Temp. Reg. § 35.3405-1T, Q&A F-2.

¶ 2120
Reporting and Recordkeeping

The IRS may require an employer or the administrator of a plan making distributions on which withholding is required to make returns and reports to the IRS, recipients, and any other persons designated by the IRS.[1]

Form 1099-R

The return and report requirements are satisfied if Form 1099-R (Distributions From Pensions, Annuities, Retirement or Profit-Sharing Plans, IRAs, Insurance Contracts, etc.) is filed for each recipient.[2]

The recordkeeping requirement is satisfied if the plan administrator maintains the information necessary to complete Form 1099-R and additional information, such as the date on which payments began.[3]

☐ See CCH PENSION PLAN GUIDE ¶ 3872 for more information on the record-keeping requirement.

Primary responsibility of administrator

The IRS initially requires the plan administrator to maintain records and make reports. However, if the plan administrator fails in this responsibility, the employer is responsible for the reports and returns.[4]

Reporting eligible rollover distributions on Form 1099-R

All eligible rollover distributions, including direct rollover distributions, must be reported on Form 1099-R.[5] If part of a distribution is a direct rollover and part is distributed to the recipient, two Forms 1099-R must be prepared.[6]

Reporting amounts received as a direct rollover

Generally, if an eligible rollover distribution is paid directly to an eligible retirement plan (see ¶ 2115), the plan need not report receiving the rollover distribution. However, amounts distributed to an individual retirement account in a direct rollover must be reported on Form 5498 (IRA Contribution Information).[7]

Combined information reporting following merger or acquisition

The persons required to withhold or collect taxes under Code Sec. 3405 are also responsible for filing information reports with respect to those transactions. Generally, the predecessor and successor employers involved in a merger or acquisition must file the Form 1099-R, reporting distributions and withheld amounts. However, under an alternative procedure, a successor employer may assume the information reporting obligations of the predecessor employer for reportable transactions occurring in the acquisition year.[8]

Remitting withheld taxes

The deposit rules are generally the same as those that apply to W-2 wage withholding. Beginning January 1, 2011, depositors were no longer allowed to use the Federal Tax Deposit (FTD) Coupon Book, Form 8109. All deposits must be made electronically unless the de minimis rules apply. All of the users of FTD coupons were pre-enrolled in the Electronic Federal Tax Payment System (EFTPS) for 2011 and thereafter. The de minimis deposit rules remain unchanged. Under the de minimis deposit rules, depositors have several options if the tax deposit liability is less than $2,500. Depositors have the choice of either (1) remitting the employment taxes with the quarterly or annual tax returns, (2) voluntarily making deposits using electronic funds transfers, (3) contracting with a third-party provider, e.g., a tax professional or financial institution, to make the deposits on their behalf, or (4) making a same-day wire transfer. [9]

Payroll taxes are reported on Form 941 (Employer's QUARTERLY Federal Tax Return) or Form 944 (Employer's ANNUAL Federal Tax Return). Nonpayroll withheld taxes are reported on Form 945 (Annual Return of Withheld Federal Income Tax). Do not combine deposits for Forms 945 with other deposits. [10] Nonpayroll taxes include taxes withheld on pensions, annuities, IRAs, and certain other deferred income.[11]

☐ Additional information on the required reporting is in CCH PENSION PLAN GUIDE at ¶ 9955.

[1] Code Sec. 6047(d).

[2] IRS Temp. Reg. § 35.3405-1T, Q&A E-9.

[3] IRS Temp. Reg. § 35.3405-1T, Q&A E-6.

[4] IRS Temp. Reg. § 35.3405-1T, Q&A E-1; IRS Reg. § 31.3405(c)-1, Q&A-15, governing the reporting of eligible rollover distributions.

[5] IRS Reg. § 31.3405(c)-1, Q&A-16.

[6] Instructions for Form 1099-R.

[7] IRS Reg. § 31.3405(c)-1, Q&A-17.

[8] Rev. Proc. 99-50, 1999-2 CB 757, CCH PENSION PLAN GUIDE ¶ 17,299P-6.

[9] IRS Reg. § 31.6302-1, IRS Reg. § 31.6302-2, IRS Reg. § 31.6302-3, IRS Reg. §§ 31.6302-4, as amended by TD 9507, 74 FR 75,897, December 7, 2010, IRS Reg. § 40.6302(c)-1, and IRS Pub. 15.

[10] IRS Reg. § 31.6011(a)-4(a) and (b).

[11] IRS Reg. § 31.6011(a)-4(b)(4).

¶ 2125
Election Not to Have Withholding Apply

Recipients of nonperiodic distributions that are eligible for rollover are subject to mandatory withholding of 20% if they are not transferred directly to an eligible transferee plan, as discussed at ¶ 2115. However, recipients of other types of distributions (i.e., periodic or nonperiodic distributions that do not otherwise constitute eligible rollover distributions) may elect, for any reason, not to have tax withheld.[1] Payees of those periodic or nonperiodic payments can elect not to have taxes withheld or increase the amount withheld by submitting Form W-4P (Withholding Certificate for Pension or Annuity Payments).[2]

☐ See CCH PENSION PLAN GUIDE ¶ 3880 and ¶ 3882 for sample election forms for withholding on periodic payments and nonperiodic payments.

[1] Code Sec. 3405(a)(2) and (b)(2).

[2] Instructions to Form W-4P. Temporary regulations have been issued prescribing the time and

manner of making the election. The temporary regulations also provide sample forms for making the election. See IRS Temp. Reg. §35.3405-1T, Q&A D-22 and D-26.

¶ 2130
Notice Requirements

Whether or not a withholding certificate or other means of determining the amount to be withheld indicates that a designated distribution is subject to withholding, a payor must advise every annuity recipient of the application of the withholding rules.[01] This requirement is imposed to prevent instances in which under-withholding may result for a recipient who has other income and to ensure that all recipients are made aware of the taxability of periodic payments.[02] Payors must also notify recipients of their right to make, renew, or revoke an election not to have the withholding provisions apply. Temporary IRS regulations list content requirements for the notice and provide sample notices.[03]

Notice may be sent via written or electronic media. A payor may provide the required notice to a payee either on a written paper document or through an electronic medium reasonably accessible to the payee if certain conditions are met.[04] Electronic media includes e-mail, plan web sites, and automated telephone systems. The IRS has issued final regulations that provide standards for the use of electronic systems by retirement plans, employee benefits arrangements, and individual retirement plans for the delivery of notices to participants or elections and consents made by participants to plans, including notices required under Code Sec. 3405(e)(10)(B). [05]

Periodic payments

For periodic payments, initial notice of the right to make, renew, or revoke the election must be given no earlier than six months before the anticipated first payment and no later than the date of the first payment.[06] See CCH PENSION PLAN GUIDE ¶ 3880 for a sample notice form for periodic payments.

However, even if notice is given before the first payment, notice must be given when making the first payment. In this situation, an abbreviated notice may be provided.[07] See CCH PENSION PLAN GUIDE ¶ 3884 for a sample form for providing this abbreviated notice.

Annual notice. In addition, annual notice of the right to make, renew, or revoke the election must be provided to recipients of periodic payments.[08]

Nonperiodic payments

For lump-sum distributions or other nonperiodic payments, notice of the election must be provided no later than the time of the distribution.[09] Since notice provided at the time of the distribution could result in delay of receipt of the recipient's benefit check if he or she elects out of withholding, notice for nonperiodic distributions should be given no earlier than six months prior to the distribution and no later than the time that will give the recipient reasonable time to elect not to have withholding apply and to reply to the payor with the election information.[10]

¶2130

"Reasonable time" requirement. What constitutes "reasonable time" depends upon the facts and circumstances in each case. However, the "reasonable time" requirement for a nonperiodic distribution will be satisfied if the notice is included in the basic claim for benefits application that is provided to the participant by the plan administrator.[11]

Distributions from IRAs. The "reasonable time" requirement will be satisfied in the case of a distribution from an individual retirement account (IRA) if the payor provides notice of the election not to have withholding apply at the time the beneficiary requests a withdrawal from his IRA.[12]

Sample notices. See CCH PENSION PLAN GUIDE ¶ 3882 for a sample notice for withholding on nonperiodic payments.

---

[01] Code Sec. 3405(e)(10)(B).

[02] P.L. 97-248 (Tax Equity and Fiscal Responsibility Act of 1982), Conference Committee Report.

[03] IRS Temp. Reg. § 35.3405-1T, Q&A D-18 through D-27.

[04] IRS Reg. § 35.3405-1, Q&A D-35 and D-36.

[05] T.D. 9294, 71 FR 61877, October 20, 2006; IRS Reg. Sec. 35.3405-1, d-35, A, as amended by T.D. 9294.

[06] Code Sec. 3405(e)(10)(B)(i)(I).

[07] IRS Temp. Reg. § 35.3405-1T, Q&A D-4 and D-27.

[08] Code Sec. 3405(e)(10)(B)(i)(III).

[09] Code Sec. 3405(e)(10)(B)(ii).

[10] IRS Temp. Reg. § 35.3405-1T, Q&A D-9.

[11] IRS Temp. Reg. § 35.3405-1T, Q&A D-10.

[12] IRS Temp. Reg. § 35.3405-1T, Q&A D-13.

¶ 2135

Withholding on Nonqualified Plans

Contributions to nonqualified plans, to which employees have *nonforfeitable rights*, constitute taxable income of the employees at the time the contributions are made.[1] An interest is nonforfeitable if there is no contingency under the plan which may cause the employee to lose his rights in the contribution. When an employee's interest in a plan is nonforfeitable at the time of the employer's contribution, the employer is required to withhold taxes from the contribution.[2]

Employer contributions to a plan where employees' interests are *forfeitable* are not subject to federal income tax at the time the contributions are made.[3] It follows that no withholding should be required on such employer contributions at the time of the contributions.

CCH Pointer: The American Jobs Creation Act of 2004 (P.L. 108-357) enacted new Code Sec. 409A, which imposed distribution and funding restrictions on nonqualified deferred compensation plans, generally effective beginning in 2005. Participants who defer compensation under plans that fail to comply with the requirements of Code Sec. 409A are subject to current taxation on all deferrals. For withholding purposes, any amount includible in the gross income of an employee under Code Sec. 409A is included in the employee's wages for the year of inclusion.[4]

The Act also excludes from FICA and FUTA tax remuneration received on account of the transfer of stock pursuant to the exercise of an incentive stock option (¶ 3315) or under an employee stock purchase plan (¶ 3310) or any disposition of such stock.[5]

Reporting and withholding. The IRS issued guidance which clarified and extended the requirements for employers' and payers' reporting of deferrals, withholding from wages for employees, and for compensation includible in income for nonemployees under Code Sec. 409A.[6]

Subsequently, the IRS suspended some of the reporting requirements for compensation deferred in 2005, 2006, 2007, 2008, and thereafter, that otherwise would have been reported on Forms W-2, 941, and 1099-MISC.[7] The relief applies until superseded by future guidance. The IRS does not anticipate any further guidance until recently proposed regulations are finalized.[8]

Thus, for calendar year 2012, an employer is not required to report amounts deferred during the year under a nonqualified deferred compensation plan subject to Code Sec. 409A in Box 12 of Form W-2 using Code Y. In addition, a payer is not required to report amounts deferred during the year under a nonqualified deferred compensation plan subject to Code Sec. 409A in Box 15a of Form 1099-MISC.

For 2012, an employer is required to treat amounts includible in gross income under Code Sec. 409A as wages for income tax withholding purposes. In addition, an employer must report such amounts as wages paid on line 2 of Form 941, Employer's Quarterly Federal Tax Return, and in Box 1 of Form W-2. An employer must also report such amounts as income in Box 12 of Form W-2 using Code Z. Regardless of whether the employee has received other regular wages from the employer during the calendar year, amounts includible in gross income under Code Sec. 409A are treated as supplemental wages for purposes of determining the amount of income tax required to be deducted and withheld under Code Sec. 3402(a).

FICA and FUTA tax. Amounts deferred under nonqualified deferred compensation plans are subject to FICA and FUTA tax when the services are performed or, if later, when there is no substantial risk of forfeiture of the employee's right to such amounts. [9] Thus, if an employee has a vested right to benefits in a nonqualified plan, FICA taxes are applicable each year on contributions to the plans. FUTA taxes also apply to nonqualfiied plan contributions if an employee has a vested right to benefits.

Nonemployees. For nonemployees, a payer must report amounts includible in gross income under Code Sec. 409A and not treated as wages under Code Sec. 3401(a) as nonemployee compensation in Box 7 of Form 1099-MISC. A payer must also report such amounts as Code Sec. 409A income in Box 15b of Form 1099-MISC.

☐ See ¶ 3300 and following for more information on nonqualified plans.

---

[1] IRS Reg. §§ 1.402(b)-1 and 1.403(b)-1.

[2] Rev. Rul. 57-37, 1957-1 CB 18, CCH PENSION PLAN GUIDE ¶ 18,104, as modified by Rev. Rul. 57-528, 1957-2 CB 263, CCH PENSION PLAN GUIDE ¶ 18,138.

[3] IRS Reg. §§ 1.402(b)-1 and 1.403(b)-1.

[4] Code Sec. 3401(a), as amended by P.L 108-357 (American Jobs Creation Act of 2004). NOTE:

Interim guidance on withholding obligations under the American Jobs Creation Act was provided by the IRS in Notice 2005-1, I.R.B. 2005-2, 1-10-05, CCH PENSION PLAN GUIDE ¶ 17,130K.

[5] P.L 108-357 (American Jobs Creation Act of 2004), Sec. 251.

[6] IRS Notice 2005-1, I.R.B. 2005-2, 1-10-05, CCH PENSION PLAN GUIDE ¶ 17,130K; Proposed Regs. Secs. 1.409A-1—1.409A-6, 70 FR 57930, 10-4-05, as

corrected in 70 FR 75090, 12-19-05, 70 FR 76502, 12-27-05, 71 FR 2496, 1-17-06, and by IRS Ann. 2006-11, I.R.B. 2006-6, 2-6-06, CCH PENSION PLAN GUIDE ¶ 20,261T; IRS Notice 2006-79, I.R.B. 2006-43, 10-1-06, CCH PENSION PLAN GUIDE ¶ 17,134Q.

[7] IRS Notice 2005-1, I.R.B. 2005-2, 1-10-05, CCH PENSION PLAN GUIDE ¶ 17,130K; IRS Notice 2005-94, I.R.B. 2005-52, 12-27-05, CCH PENSION PLAN GUIDE ¶ 17,132M, superceded by IRS Notice 2006-100, I.R.B. 2006-51, 11-30-06, CCH PENSION PLAN GUIDE ¶ 17,135; Preamble to TD 9321, 72 FR 19,234, 4-17-2007, CCH PENSION PLAN GUIDE

¶ 25,580O; IRS Notice 2007-89, I.R.B. 2007-46, 10-23-2007, CCH PENSION PLAN GUIDE ¶ 17,137K; and IRS Notice 2008-115, I.R.B. 2008-52, 11-29-2008, CCH PENSION PLAN GUIDE ¶ 17,141L, as modified by IRS Notice 2010-6, IRB 2010-3, January 19, 2010.

[8] Proposed Reg. 148326-05, 73 FR 74,380, 12-8-2009, CCH PENSION PLAN GUIDE ¶ 20,262S and IRS Notice 2008-115, I.R.B. 2008-52, 11-29-2008, CCH PENSION PLAN GUIDE ¶ 17,141L, as modified by IRS Notice 2010-6, IRB 2010-3, January 19, 2010.

[9] Code Sec. 3121(v)(2) and §3306(r)(2).

¶ 2140
Distributions to Nonresident Aliens

Distributions from a qualified plan that qualify as "amounts received as an annuity" are excluded from a recipient's income and are not subject to income tax withholding if:[1]

1. all personal services for which contributions to the plan were made were performed outside the United States by nonresident aliens; and

2. more than 90 percent of the participants in the plan are citizens of the United States.

Withholding on distributions that are not annuities

Currently, distributions to nonresident aliens that do not qualify as an annuity generally are subject to tax at a rate of 30 percent.[2] However, an income tax treaty to which the United States is a party may provide for a reduced rate of tax and many treaties provide a complete exemption from withholding.[3] In order to secure a reduced rate of withholding available under a treaty, the recipient must provide the withholding agent or payor a completed Form W-8BEN (Certificate of Foreign Status of Beneficial Owner for United States Tax Withholding).[4]

No graduated withholding

Payers of distributions from qualified pension plans to nonresident aliens are required to withhold from the distributions in accordance with the 30% flat rate of Code Sec. 1441, rather than the graduated withholding rate of Code Sec. 3405, that is applicable to pension distributions to citizens of the United States.[5] The rule applies to payments from any trust under Code Sec. 401(a), annuity plan under 403(a), annuity, custodial account or retirement income account under 403(b), or IRA under Code Sec. 408, that are made to nonresident aliens.

[1] Code Secs. 871(f) and 1441(c)(7).

[2] Code Secs. 871(a) and 1441; IRS Reg. §§ 1.1441-1 and 1.1441-2.

[3] IRS Reg. § 1.1441-6(a).

[4] IRS Reg. § 1.1441-6(c)(1).

[5] IRS Reg. § 1.1441-4, amended 5-22-2000 by T.D. 8881; IRS Notice 99-25, I.R.B. 1999-20, 5-17-99, CCH PENSION PLAN GUIDE ¶ 17,116H. The rule is effective for payments made on or after January 1, 2001.

¶ 2145

Withholding on Pension Payments to U.S. Citizens Outside the U.S.

Pension, annuity, and other similar deferred income payments are subject to mandatory withholding under Code Sec. 3405 if they are delivered to a U.S. citizen outside of the United States.[1] In general, taxpayers receiving such payments may not elect to forego withholding on such payments. The IRS has provided detailed rules for determining the U.S.-source portion of a pension distribution under a defined benefit plan in cases where the retiree has performed services both in the United States and abroad during his or her employment.[2]

Payments to non-U.S. citizens

However, this mandatory withholding rule does not apply if the recipient certifies to the payor that he or she is not a U.S. citizen, resident alien or a tax avoidance expatriate under Code Sec. 877. The mandatory withholding rule also does not apply to the foreign-delivered payments of a resident alien of the United States who certifies that he or she is not a tax avoidance expatriate.

---

[1] Code Sec. 3405(e)(13).

[2] See Rev. Proc. 2004-37, I.R.B. 2004-26, 6-28-04, CCH Pension Plan Guide ¶ 17,299R-29.

¶ 2150

State Income Tax Withholding

Most states impose their own personal income tax. Thus, in addition to federal withholding requirements, there are a myriad of different state withholding rules on pensions and deferred compensation.

☐ See ¶ 3892 of the CCH Pension Plan Guide for information on the withholding rules applicable in each state.

¶ 2155

For More Information

☐ For more information on withholding, see CCH Pension Plan Guide ¶ 3858-3892.

Reporting to Government Agencies and Participants

¶ 2200

Basic Rules

The federal government requires reporting and disclosure in the administration and operation of employee benefit plans to protect the interests of plan participants and beneficiaries. Both the Internal Revenue Code and ERISA require certain reports to be filed with the IRS, the Department of Labor (DOL), and the Pension Benefit Guaranty Corporation (PBGC), or to be disclosed to plan participants and their beneficiaries.

Who must comply with reporting and disclosure requirements?

The plan administrator of an employee benefit plan must satisfy reporting and disclosure requirements. These requirements include filing reports and statements with various government agencies, as well as providing notices to plan participants and beneficiaries.

What types of reports and disclosures are required?

There are four main areas of reporting and disclosure with which the administrator of an employee benefit plan must comply:

1. reports, notices, and other information required by the IRS;

2. filings required by the DOL;

3. information required by the PBGC; and

4. notices and information required to be distributed to plan participants and other parties.

¶2200

Which plans are subject to federal reporting rules?

The reporting and disclosure provisions of ERISA apply to any employee benefit plan that is established or maintained by an employer engaged in commerce or in an industry affecting commerce, by any employee organization(s) representing employees engaged in commerce or in an industry affecting commerce, or by both.[1] An "employee benefit plan" is defined in ERISA as an employee welfare benefit plan or any employee pension benefit plan.[2]

The following plans are specifically excluded from the reporting and disclosure requirements:[3]

1. governmental plans;

2. church plans that have not elected to be covered by the vesting and participation rules of ERISA;

3. plans maintained solely for the purpose of complying with applicable workers' compensation, unemployment compensation, or disability insurance laws;

4. plans maintained outside of the United States primarily for the benefit of persons substantially all of whom are nonresident aliens; and

5. unfunded excess benefit plans.

Also excluded from coverage under the reporting and disclosure provisions, by virtue of their exclusion from the definition of an employee pension benefit plan under ERISA Sec. 3(2), are certain individual retirement accounts (IRAs) and certain self-employed individuals' (Keogh) plans. In most cases, an individual retirement account established by an individual would not constitute an employee pension benefit plan as defined by ERISA.

---

[1] *Baucom v. Pilot Life Insurance Co.*, DC NC (1987), 674 FSupp 1175.

[2] ERISA Sec. 3(3).

[3] ERISA Sec. 4(b).

¶ 2202
Form 5500 Annual Report

ERISA requires a plan administrator to file a comprehensive annual report, disclosing information relating to the plan's qualified status, financial condition, and operation. Annual reports are filed on the Form 5500 series. The Form 5500 series consolidates the annual report forms of the IRS, the DOL, and the PBGC. The Form 5500 (Annual Return/Report of Employee Benefit Plan) is filed with the Employee Benefits Security Administration (EBSA), which forwards relevant information to the IRS and the PBGC. Note, however, that instead of filing Form 5500, certain plans may file Form 5500-SF (with the EBSA) and are permitted or required to file Form 5500-EZ (with the IRS).

The Form 5500 series consists of one form, three pension schedules, and six general schedules.

Required schedules. The schedules in the 2011 Form 5500 include:

1. Schedule A, Insurance Information;

2. Schedule C, Service Provider Information;

3. Schedule D, DFE (Direct Filing Entity)/Participating Plan Information;

4. Schedule G, Financial Transaction Schedules;

5. Schedule H, Financial Information (for large plans and DFEs);

6. Schedule I, Financial Information—Small Plan;

7. Schedule R, Retirement Plan Information; and

8. Schedule SB, Single-Employer Defined Benefit Plan Actuarial Information, or Schedule MB, Multiemployer Defined Benefit Plan and Certain Money Purchase Plan Actuarial Information.

CCH Note: Starting with the 2009 Form 5500 series, Form 5500 no longer includes any form or schedule from the pre-2009 Form 5500 series that had been required only for the IRS, as part of the move to an all-electronic filing system for the Form 5500 series.[1] As a result, Form 5500-EZ (Annual Return of One-Participant (Owners and Their Spouses) Retirement Plan), and Schedules E and SSA were removed. Note, however, that Form 5500-EZ is filed directly with the IRS.

Schedule SSA has been replaced with Form 8955-SSA (Annual Registration Statement Identifying Separated Participants with Deferred Vested Benefits). Form 8955-SSA must be filed with the IRS on paper or electronically and not through the EFAST2 filing system. For more information, see ¶ 2205.

Schedule B was replaced with two separate schedules: Schedule SB and Schedule MB. Schedule C was revised to clarify the reporting requirements and improve the information plan officials receive regarding direct and indirect compensation and fees paid to plan service providers. Schedule C was modified so that service providers required to be listed will separately report direct compensation paid by the plan and indirect compensation received from sources other than the plan or the plan sponsor (for example, compensation charged against investment assets). The EBSA issued guidance to help filers comply with the expanded reporting requirements of Schedule C.[2]

Also, special limited financial reporting rules for 403(b) plans was eliminated.[3] Thus, 403(b) plans that are subject to Title I of ERISA are subject to the same annual reporting rules that apply to other ERISA-covered retirement plans. However, the EBSA provided transition relief for 403(b) plan administrators that made good faith efforts to comply with the 2009 Form 5500 reporting and audit requirements for annuity contracts and custodial accounts issued before January 1, 2009.[4]

Large and small plan reporting requirements. The Form 5500 reporting requirements applicable to large plans, small plans, and Direct Filing Entities (DFEs) vary. Generally, the Form 5500 for a pension or welfare benefit plan that covered less than 100 participants as of the beginning of the plan year should be completed in accordance with the "small plan" rules. The Form 5500 report filed for a pension or welfare plan that covered 100 or more participants as of the beginning of the plan year should comply with the "large plan" rules.

The following schedules (and any additional information required by the instructions to the schedules) must be attached to a Form 5500 for a small pension plan that is neither exempt from filing nor filing Form 5500-SF (Short Form Annual Return/Report of Small Employee Benefit Plan): Schedule A (if funded in whole or in part by insurance contracts), Schedule SB or MB (if it is a single-employer or multiemployer defined benefit plan subject to minimum funding standards or a certain type of money purchase plan), Schedule D, Part 1 (if applicable), Schedule I, and Schedule R (unless the plan is, among other things, not a defined benefit plan, nor subject to the minimum funding rules, and no benefits were distributed during the year).

The following schedules (and any additional information required by the instructions to the schedules) must be attached to a Form 5500 for a large pension plan: Schedule A (if funded in whole or in part by insurance contracts), Schedule SB or MB (if it is a single-employer or multiemployer defined benefit plan subject to minimum funding standards or a certain type of money purchase plan), Schedule C (if a service provider was paid $5,000 or more in direct or indirect compensation and/or an accountant or actuary was terminated), Schedule D, Part 1 (if applicable), Schedule G (if applicable), Schedule H, and Schedule R (unless the plan is, among other things, not a defined benefit plan, nor subject to the minimum funding rules, and no benefits were distributed during the year).

Forms 5500-EZ and 5500-SF. A one-participant plan may not file an annual return on Form 5500 starting with the 2009 plan year. One-participant plans must either file Form 5500-EZ or, if eligible, Form 5500-SF.[5] Form 5500-EZ must be filed by one-participant plans that are required to file annual returns and are not eligible or choose not to file Form 5500-SF, and by certain foreign plans that are required to file an annual return. A paper copy of Form 5500-EZ must be mailed to the IRS. Filers may obtain an official IRS paper Form 5500-EZ from the IRS, or fill in and print Form 5500-EZ available on the IRS website, www.irs.gov. See the IRS filing address below.

A pension plan is eligible to file Form 5500-SF if the plan: (1) covers fewer than 100 participants; (2) is eligible for the small plan audit waiver under ERISA Reg. § 2520.104-46; (3) holds no employer securities; (4) has 100% of its assets in investments that have a readily ascertainable market value; and (5) is not a multiemployer plan.[6] The form must be filed electronically using EFAST2. For more information on electronic filing, see below.

Most Form 5500-SF filers are not required to file any schedules, although defined benefit pension plans continue to be required to file Schedule MB or SB, where applicable. The Agencies use Form 5500-SF to satisfy the simplified reporting that the Pension Protection Act of 2006 requires for plans with fewer than 25 participants.[7]

☐ For details, see the CCH PENSION PLAN GUIDE ¶ 4085 and ¶ 4086 and the Form 5500 instructions.

Supplemental documents. Form 5500 filers also may be required to submit a report of an independent qualified public accountant expressing an opinion as to the financial statements and schedules in the annual report, the accounting principles and practices in the report, and any changes in accounting principles that might have affected the financial statements.

For plans beginning after 2007, the Pension Protection Act of 2006 requires that a statement be included in the annual report of the extent to which the plan is underfunded if the current value of the plan assets is less than 70% of the funding target (in the case of a single-employer plan) or of the current liability (in the case of a multiemployer plan).[8]

In addition, filers may be required to submit additional statements and schedules providing specific information on plan finances, reportable transactions, and assets in common trusts or pooled accounts.

Who must file annual reports. Annual reports must generally be filed by each plan administrator or employer that maintains an employee benefit plan, including defined benefit and defined contribution plans, unless an exemption applies.[9] Annual reports must be filed for plans even if benefits no longer accrue or contributions are no longer made. The IRS and DOL will impose penalties for a failure to file annual reports on a timely basis (see ¶ 2230).

Employee pension benefit plans for which annual reports must be filed include:

1. profit-sharing, stock bonus, money purchase, 401(k) plans, etc.;
2. tax-sheltered annuities under Code Sec. 403(b)(1);
3. custodial accounts for regulated investment company stock under Code Sec. 403(b)(7);
4. individual retirement accounts maintained by employers for employees;
5. church pension plans electing coverage under the participation, vesting, and funding provisions of the Code;
6. pension plans covering residents of Puerto Rico, the U.S. Virgin Islands, Guam, Wake Island, or American Samoa; and
7. plans that satisfy the actual deferral percentage test by adopting a SIMPLE 401(k) plan under Code Sec. 401(k)(11).[10]

Nonqualified deferred compensation plans must file Form 5500, unless they file a Nonqualified Registration Statement with the EBSA.

CCH Pointer: For defined benefit plans, additional information must be provided on Form 5500 annual reports for plan years beginning after 2007 if liabilities to participants or their beneficiaries under the defined benefit plan consist (either in whole or in part) of liabilities under two or more pension plans as of immediately before the plan year.[11] Besides the above required information, annual reports for multiemployer defined benefit plans must also include, as of the end of the plan year relating to the report, several additional pieces of information.[12] For details, see CCH PENSION PLAN GUIDE ¶ 4085 and ¶ 4086.

Due dates for filing annual reports. The annual report form and its accompanying schedules must be filed with the EBSA on or before the last day of the seventh month following the close of the plan year. Generally, this is July 31 for calendar-year plans. See discussion at ¶ 2205 for due date when July 31 falls on a Saturday, Sunday, or legal holiday.

Filing extensions. An employer looking to extend the due date for filing Form 5500, Form 5500-SF, or Form 5500-EZ has the option of utilizing an automatic filing extension, if applicable, or filing Form 5558 (Application for Extension of Time To File Certain Employee Plan Returns) with the IRS.[13]

An automatic extension of the due date for filing the employer's federal income tax return is available if the plan year and the employer's tax year are the same, the employer has been granted an extension to file the federal income tax return, and a copy of the extension is maintained with the filer's records.

An extension of up to two and one-half months may be requested by filing a Form 5558. All applications for an extension of time to file an annual return that are filed with the IRS before the return's normal due date on a properly completed Form 5558 will be automatically approved. Prior to the 2009 plan year, a photocopy of the extension request was required to be attached to the Form 5500. Starting with the 2009 plan year Form 5500 filing, filers are no longer required to attach a copy of Form 5558 to their Form 5500 filing. Filers just check the relevant box on Form 5500. A copy of the Form 5558 that was filed with the IRS must be kept with the plan records.

IRS final regulations. The IRS issued final regulations that allow plan administrators or sponsors to file Form 5558 in order to obtain an automatic two and one-half month filing extension, applicable to the Form 5500 series, without having to sign the application or provide an explanation for seeking the extension.[14]

Filing extension for Form 8955-SSA. Form 5558 may also be filed to extend the due date for filing Form 8955-SSA.[15] The rules are the same for filing an extension of time to file Form 8955-SSA as they are for filing the Form 5500 series, with one exception. A properly completed Form 5558 for an extension to file Form 8955-SSA must be signed by a plan administrator, plan sponsor, or any authorized representative required to sign Form 8955-SSA.

Where to file the annual report. Form 5500-EZ, and any required schedules, statements, and attachments, are required to be filed at the following location:

Mail:

Paper filing:

Department of the Treasury

Internal Revenue Service

Ogden, UT 84201-0020

Electronic filing. Beginning with the 2009 plan year, annual reports (except Form 5500-EZ) and related schedules must be filed electronically using the ERISA Filing Acceptance System (Form EFAST2). Annual reports are filed online using

EFAST2's web-based filing system or an EFAST2-approved vendor. The plan administrator must maintain the original copy of the annual report with all required signatures as part of the plan's records even though the annual report is filed electronically. The EBSA's website address for obtaining electronic filing information is www.efast.dol.gov.

CCH Pointer: Prior year delinquent or amended Form 5500s must be filed electronically through EFAST2.[16]

Pension Protection Act mandates electronic display of certain Form 5500 information. For plan years beginning after December 31, 2007, the Pension Protection Act of 2006 requires that identification, basic plan information and actuarial information included in the annual report for any plan year be filed with the Secretary of Labor in an electronic format that accommodates Internet display.[17] Within 90 days after the annual report filing date, the DOL is required to display the information on an Internet website that the DOL maintains and other appropriate media. The information also is required to be displayed on any intranet website that the plan sponsor (or the plan administrator on behalf of the plan sponsor) maintains for the purpose of communicating with employees.

The EBSA explains that its new EFAST2 system and its electronic filing rule for Form 5500 will satisfy the Pension Protection Act's requirements for electronic filing and display of Form 5500 information.[18] The EBSA has established a website for posting 2008 Form 5500 actuarial information at www.dol.gov/ebsa/actuarial-search.html. To search for 2009 Form 5500 filings, see www.efast.dol.gov/welcome.html.

[1] ERISA Reg. §2520.103-1(c)(1), 72 FR 64710, November 16, 2007. EBSA, IRS, and PBGC Notice of Adoption of Revisions to the Annual Information Returns/Reports, 72 FR 64731, November 16, 2007. ERISA Reg. §2520.103-1(b)(1). 2009 Instructions to Form 5500.

[2] For example, see FAQs About the 2009 Form 5500 Schedule C, July 14, 2008, CCH PENSION PLAN GUIDE ¶ 19,981X; and Supplemental FAQs About the 2009 Schedule C, October 23, 2009, CCH PENSION PLAN GUIDE ¶ 19,981Z-10.

[3] ERISA Reg. §2520.104-44, and Preamble to final regulations, 72 FR 64710, November 16, 2007.

[4] EBSA Field Assistance Bulletin 2009-02, July 20, 2009, CCH PENSION PLAN GUIDE ¶ 19,981Z-8 and EBSA Field Assistance Bulletin 2010-01, February 17, 2010, CCH PENSION PLAN GUIDE ¶ 19,981Z-17.

[5] 2009 Instructions to Form 5500 and Instructions to Form 5500-EZ.

[6] ERISA Reg. §2520.103-1(c)(2), 72 FR 64710, November 16, 2007; Instructions to Form 5500-SF.

[7] Preamble to EBSA final regulations, 72 FR 64710, November 16, 2007; EBSA/IRS/PBGC Notice of Adoption of Revisions to Annual Return/Report Form, 72 FR 64731, November 16, 2007.

Act Sec. 1103(b) of P.L. 109-280 (Pension Protection Act of 2006).

[8] ERISA Sec. 103(d)(11), as amended by P.L. 109-280 (Pension Protection Act of 2006), Act Sec. 107(a)(3).

[9] Instructions to Form 5500.

[10] IRS Announcement 86-20, I.R.B. 1986-7, 34, CCH PENSION PLAN GUIDE ¶ 17,097L-12; Instructions to Form 5500.

[11] ERISA Sec. 103(f)(1)(A), as added by P.L. 109-280 (Pension Protection Act of 2006), Act Sec. 503(a)(1)(B). Act Sec. 503(f) of P.L. 109-280 (Pension Protection Act of 2006).

[12] ERISA Sec. 103(f)(2), as added by P.L. 109-280 (Pension Protection Act of 2006), Act Sec. 503(a)(1)(B).

[13] Instructions to Form 5558.

[14] IRS Reg. §1.6081-11; Preamble to IRS Reg. §1.6081-11, 73 FR 37362, July 1, 2008.

[15] Instructions to Form 5558.

[16] Frequently Asked Questions about EFAST2, Q4.

[17] Act Sec. 504(b) of P.L. 109-280 (Pension Protection Act of 2006). ERISA Sec. 104(b)(5), as added by P.L. 109-280 (Pension Protection Act of 2006), Act Sec. 504(a).

[18] EBSA/IRS/PBGC Notice of Adoption of Revisions to Annual Return/Report Form, 72 FR 64731, November 16, 2007.

¶ 2205

Reports and Disclosures to the IRS

Plan administrators are required to file various reports with the IRS, such as:

1. actuarial statements for defined benefit plans,

2. registration statements, and

3. notices of plan changes.

In addition, reports for unrelated business income, distributions, withholding, stock options, and other transactions may need to be filed with the IRS.

Actuarial statements

Beginning with the 2008 plan year, single-employer defined benefit plans (including multiple employer defined benefit plans), and multiemployer defined benefit plans that are subject to the minimum funding standards of ERISA, and money purchase plans (including target benefit plans) that are currently amortizing a funding waiver must file Schedule SB or MB, as applicable. For more information, see ¶ 2202. Prior to the 2008 plan year, a defined benefit pension plan subject to the minimum funding standards of ERISA was required to file an actuarial report on Schedule B (Actuarial Information) of Form 5500 for the first plan year, and each plan year thereafter, to which the minimum funding standards apply. Schedule SB or MB must be signed by an enrolled actuary and include a statement that the report is complete and accurate and that the actuarial assumptions are reasonable and represent the actuary's best estimate of anticipated experience under the plan. For further details, see CCH PENSION PLAN GUIDE ¶ 4100 and ¶ 5545.

> **CCH Pointer:** *Plan retirement projections.* For certain defined benefit plans, under the Pension Protection Act of 2006, the actuarial statement should explain the actuarial assumptions and methods used in projecting future retirements and forms of the benefit distributions under the plan.[1] This addition applies to plan years beginning after December 31, 2007.[2] For more information, see CCH PENSION PLAN GUIDE ¶ 4170.

Registration statements

The plan administrator of each plan that is subject to ERISA's vesting rules must file a registration statement: (1) identifying plan participants who are entitled to a deferred vested benefit under the plan as of the end of the plan year, and (2) reporting the nature, amount, and form of the deferred vested benefit to which the participants are entitled.[3] The annual registration statement must be filed by both tax qualified and nonqualified plans.[4] However, government plans and church plans that do not elect to be covered by the minimum participation, funding, and vesting requirements are not required to register.

¶2205

Form 8955-SSA (Annual Registration Statement Identifying Separated Participants With Deferred Vested Benefits) is the form to be used to satisfy the reporting requirements of Code Sec. 6057(a) for plan years beginning on or after January 1, 2009, replacing Schedule SSA. Form 8955-SSA must be filed with the IRS and not through the EFAST2 filing system. Like Schedule SSA, Form 8955-SSA is filed by the last day of the seventh month following the close of the plan year (plus extensions). Form 8955-SSA may be filed on paper or electronically.

Prior to the 2009 plan year, Schedule SSA (Annual Registration Statement Identifying Separated Participants With Deferred Vested Benefits) (Form 5500) was used by plan administrators to report all plan participants with deferred vested benefits who separated from service during the plan year. It was filed as an attachment to Form 5500. Schedule SSA was removed from the 2009 Form 5500 series as part of the conversion to an all-electronic filing system and the requirement that the annual report be displayed on the Internet. For more information, see ¶ 2202.

Required information. Form 8955-SSA, like Schedule SSA, requires, among other things: (1) the name and Social Security number of each plan participant who was separated from service during the year and was entitled to a deferred vested benefit as of the end of the plan year; and (2) the nature, amount, and form of the deferred vested benefit to which each separated plan participant was entitled.

☐ See CCH Pension Plan Guide ¶ 4105 for a more expansive discussion of the registration statement.

Notice of plan changes

A plan administrator who is required to file an annual registration statement also is required to notify the IRS of the following changes in the status of the plan. Notice of the following changes must be submitted:[5]

    1. a change in the name of the plan;

    2. a change in the name or address of the plan administrator;

    3. the termination of the plan; and

    4. the merger or consolidation of the plan or its division into two or more plans.

A notification of a status change must be filed on Form 5500 for the plan year in which the change occurs.

Due dates

If the last day for filing a report with the IRS, or for performing any act required by the Internal Revenue Code, falls on a Saturday, Sunday, or legal holiday, the performance of the act will be considered timely if it is performed on the next succeeding day which is not a Saturday, Sunday, or legal holiday.[6] Any authorized extension of time is included in determining the last day on which the act could be performed.[7]

Special relief in cases of federal disasters or terrorist attacks. Under Code Sec. 7508A, the Secretary of the Treasury may prescribe regulations under which a period of up to 120 days may be disregarded for performing various acts under the Internal Revenue Code, such as filing tax returns, paying taxes, or filing a claim for credit or refund of tax, for any taxpayer determined to be affected by a federally declared disaster.

The Victims of Terrorism Tax Relief Act, signed into law on January 23, 2002, authorizes the Treasury and Labor Departments and the PBGC to postpone filing and other deadlines for pension and other employee benefit plans by up to one year for reason of disaster, terrorism, or other military actions.[8]

The provisions of the Act apply to disasters and terrorist or military actions occurring on or after September 11, 2001, with respect to any action of the Secretary of the Treasury, the Secretary of Labor, or the PBGC occurring on or after January 23, 2002. The IRS, the PBGC, and the DOL subsequently issued guidance.[9]

Summary of plan-related disclosures

Following below is a summary of some of the plan-related disclosures required to be made to the IRS:

Request for change in plan/trust year. Form 5308 (Request for Change in Plan/Trust Year) should be filed to obtain IRS approval of a change in an employee benefit plan year or trust year. Note that automatic approval of a change is available if a number of conditions are met, such as a requirement that no plan year be more than 12 months long.[10] Furthermore, certain types of plans do not need approval to change their plan year, and, thus, are not required to file Form 5308. These plans include profit-sharing plans, stock bonus plans, plans funded with insurance contracts, government plans, and church plans.

Reports by issuers and trustees of IRAs. The trustees of IRAs and the issuers of endowment contracts or individual retirement annuities must make reports concerning such accounts, contracts, or annuities to the Secretary of the Treasury at such time and in such manner as may be specified by regulations adopted by the Secretary. Regulations have been issued requiring a disclosure statement be furnished to the "benefited individual" for whom an account, contract, or annuity is established.

☐ See ¶ 3200 and following for more information about IRAs or see CCH PENSION PLAN GUIDE ¶ 4200 and ¶ 8668 for a more detailed description of the required IRA disclosure statements and other IRA-related reports.

Notice of multiemployer plan insolvency. The plan sponsor of a multiemployer plan that is insolvent or may become insolvent within the next three plan years is required to notify the Secretary of the Treasury of the potential insolvency.[11]

Cash transaction reports. Any person engaged in a trade or business who, in the course of such trade or business, receives cash in an amount of more than $10,000 in a transaction or series of related transactions must file a report with the IRS.[12] Organizations exempt from federal income tax under Code Sec. 501(a), including employee plans, are considered "persons" and are subject to the cash transaction reporting requirement.[13]

Return for unrelated business taxable income of trust. A trust of a qualified plan with $1,000 or more of gross income from an unrelated business is required to file Form 990-T (Exempt Organization Business Income Tax Return) with the IRS.[14]

Distributions to employees or beneficiaries. Form 1099-R (Distributions From Pensions, Annuities, Retirement or Profit-Sharing Plans, IRAs, Insurance Contracts, etc.) is used to report to employees and their beneficiaries information regarding periodic employee distributions, as well as lump-sum distributions. As a rule, reports must be furnished to the participant by January 31 following the year of distribution. Paper Form 1099-R (and Form 1096 (Annual Summary and Transmittal of U.S. Information Returns)) generally must be filed with the IRS no later than the end of February of the year following the calendar year of the distribution. If filed electronically, Form 1099-R need not be filed before March 31 of the year following the calendar year of the distribution. (See **Due dates** above concerning what to do when the normal due date falls on a Saturday, Sunday, or legal holiday.)

Very small distributions are exempted from these reporting rules. Distributions to any person of less than $10 in any calendar year do not have to be reported.[15]

Withholding on pensions, annuities, and deferred income. Federal income tax withholding rules apply to distributions. Taxes withheld on pensions, annuities, IRAs, and certain other deferred income are reported on Form 945 (Annual Return of Withheld Federal Income Tax).[16] For more information on withholding, see ¶ 2100 and following.

Nonresident alien beneficiaries. Form 1042 (Annual Withholding Tax Return for U.S. Source Income of Foreign Persons) is an annual information return of tax withheld on payments to nonresident alien beneficiaries. This return is required with respect to payments to beneficiaries who are aliens residing outside the United States. Form 1042 is substituted for annual information returns on Forms 1096 and 1099-R when the payments are made to nonresident alien beneficiaries.[17]

There are a number of reporting issues that involve nonresident aliens, such as taxpayer identifying numbers and withholding on lump-sum distributions. See CCH PENSION PLAN GUIDE ¶ 4110 for more information.

Stock option reporting requirements. Every corporation must provide written information statements for each calendar year in which it (1) transfers a share of stock to any person pursuant to such person's exercise of a qualified or restricted stock option, or (2) records the transfer of the legal title of a share of stock acquired by a transferor under the exercise of an option under a stock purchase plan where the price is between 85% and 100% of the fair market value of the stock.[18] The statements must be furnished to persons who exercise options on or before January 31 of the following calendar year.

¶2205

CCH Pointer: The IRS has issued final regulations that increase the amount of information employers must provide to the IRS and employees about stock option transfers.[19] The IRS has issued two forms for employers to use to provide the information: Form 3921 (Exercise of an Incentive Stock Option Under Section 422(b)) and Form 3922 (Transfer of Stock Acquired Through an Employee Stock Purchase Plan Under Section 423(c)).

Return for prohibited transactions. Form 5330 (Return of Excise Taxes Related to Employee Benefit Plans) must be filed by a disqualified person who participates in a prohibited transaction involving the plan.

Disclosure of reportable transactions/prohibited tax shelter transactions. A tax-exempt entity, such as a qualified plan, that participates in any reportable transaction and is required to file a federal income tax or information return must file Form 8886 (Reportable Transaction Disclosure Statement). The "entity manager" is required to file Form 8886-T (Disclosure by Tax-Exempt Entity Regarding Prohibited Tax Shelter Transaction) to disclose information for each prohibited tax shelter transaction to which the plan entity is a party. In addition, entity managers who are liable for excise taxes in connection with the prohibited tax shelter transaction are required to file Form 5330 (Return of Excise Taxes Related to Employee Benefit Plans).

Application for identification number. Reports and returns submitted to the IRS, as well as the DOL and the PBGC, must include an employer identification number (EIN) of the plan sponsor or plan administrator.[20] A completed Form SS-4 (Application for Employer Identification Number) may be filed with the IRS to obtain an EIN.

Determination upon termination. A plan sponsor or administrator may file Form 5310 (Application for Determination for Terminating Plan) to request a determination of the qualified status of a plan upon termination.

---

[1] ERISA Sec. 103(d)(12), as added by P.L. 109-280 (Pension Protection Act of 2006), Act Sec. 503(b)(2).

[2] Act Sec. 503(f) of P.L. 109-280 (Pension Protection Act of 2006).

[3] Code Sec. 6057(a).

[4] IRS Reg. § 301.6057-1(a)(3).

[5] Code Sec. 6057(b); IRS Reg. § 301.6057-2(a) and (b).

[6] Code Sec. 7503.

[7] IRS Reg. § 301.7503-1(a).

[8] P.L. 107-134; IRS Reg. § 301.7508A-1.

[9] P.L. 107-134; IRS Notice 2002-7, 2002-1 CB 489, February 11, 2002, CCH Pension Plan Guide ¶ 17,123C.

[10] Rev. Proc. 87-27, 1987-1 CB 769, CCH Pension Plan Guide ¶ 17,299L-33A; Instructions to Form 5308.

[11] Code Sec. 418E(e).

[12] Code Sec. 6050I. IRS Reg. § 1.6050I-1 provides implementing rules and requires that Form 8300 (Report of Cash Payments Over $10,000 Received in a Trade or Business) be completed and returned to the IRS for each transaction.

[13] Code Sec. 7701(a); IRS Notice 90-61, 1990-2 CB 347, CCH Pension Plan Guide ¶ 17,103M.

[14] IRS Reg. § 1.6012-3(a)(5).

[15] Code Sec. 6047(d)(1); Instructions for Forms 1099-R and 5498.

[16] IRS Reg. § 31.6011(a)-4(b)(4).

[17] IRS Reg. § 1.1461-2.

[18] Code Sec. 6039(a).

[19] IRS Reg. § 1.6039-1 and IRS Reg. § 1.6039-2.

[20] IRS Publication 1635.

¶ 2210

Reports and Disclosures to the Pension Benefit Guaranty Corporation

In addition to the reports required by the IRS, plan administrators and employers also may be required to provide the Pension Benefit Guaranty Corporation (PBGC) with a number of reports. These reports include a premium payment form, a notice of a reportable event, a notice of intent to terminate a plan, a notice of withdrawal by a substantial employer, an annual report, a report when a plan terminates, financial and actuarial reports from underfunded plans, a notice of election of alternative deficit reduction contribution, and a number of special reports for multiemployer plans.

Premium payment form

Defined benefit plans must pay for plan termination insurance and file directly with the PBGC. Starting with the 2008 plan year premium filings, the PBGC has replaced Form 1, Schedule A, and Form 1-EZ with one new comprehensive filing.[1] A comprehensive premium filing is used to report the flat-rate premium and related data by all plans, the variable-rate premium and related data by single-employer plans, and additional data, such as identifying information and miscellaneous plan-related data by all plans. Starting with the 2010 plan year filings, the estimated flat-rate premium filing (previously, Form 1-ES) by large plans and instructions has been combined with the comprehensive premium filing instructions.[2]

Forms and instructions for prior years. If a filing is for a previous year, the instructions for that year must be followed. If a paper filing is being made, a filer must use the prior year's form. Prior year instructions and forms are available on the PBGC's website, www.pbgc.gov.

New due date structure. For plan years beginning after 2007, the PBGC's due date structure for the new comprehensive premium filing is based on three categories: large plans—plans that owed premiums for 500 or more participants for the plan year preceding the premium payment year; mid-sized plans—plans that owed premiums for 100-499 participants; small plans—all other plans not included in the "large" or "mid-size" categories.[3]

Small plans (less than 100 participants). For small plans, the same due date will apply to both the flat-rate premium and the variable rate premium. All premiums will be due on the last day of the 16th full calendar month that begins on or after the first day of the premium payment year. For example, for calendar-year plans, the due date is generally April 30th after the plan year end.[4]

Mid-size (100-499 participants). For mid-size plans, the same due date will apply to both the flat-rate premium and the variable rate premium. All premiums will be due on the 15th day of the 10th full calendar month that begins on or after the first day of the premium payment year. For example, for calendar-year plans, the due date is generally October 15th during the plan year.[5] The PBGC permits mid-sized plans to make variable rate premium filings based on estimated liabilities, providing a "true-up" or reconciliation period in which corrections may be made without incurring a penalty.

Large plans (500 or more participants). For large plans, different due dates apply to the flat-rate and the variable rate premiums. For the flat-rate premium, single-employer plans with 500 or more participants for whom flat-rate premiums were payable for the plan year preceding the premium payment year are required to pay the flat-rate per participant premium by the last day of the second full calendar month after the close of the prior plan year ("first filing due date"), Thus, for calendar-year plans, the due date is generally February 28 of the premium payment year.[6] If the participant count is not known in time to meet the February 28 filing deadline, a large plan must make a reconciliation filing containing the participant count, along with the flat-rate premium payment by October 15 of the premium payment year. The due dates and penalty structure for large plan variable rate premiums are the same as the structure for mid-size plans.

For more details, see ¶ 2809.

Electronic premium filing. Insured defined benefit plans must file electronically.[7] Filings may be submitted through the PBGC's online e-filing service center, called "My Plan Administration Account (My PAA)." The secure website, available for defined benefit plan sponsors, administrators, and pension practitioners, enables the establishment of an account, and the electronic creation and signing of premium filings, as well as the submission of the filings and payments to the PBGC. Filers may also use compatible private-sector software to prepare filings for electronic submissions. My PAA processes all types of premium filings.

☐ For additional information on PBGC premium payments and filings, see the "Terminations—Single Employer Plans" division beginning at CCH PENSION PLAN GUIDE ¶ 6460.

Notice of reportable event

Within 30 days after (1) a plan administrator or (2) a contributing sponsor of a plan covered by the plan termination insurance provisions of ERISA knows, or has reason to know, that a "reportable event" has occurred, the administrator or employer must notify the PBGC that such event has occurred.[8] The PBGC has authorized the total or conditional waiver of the 30-day post-event notice requirement. In addition, plan administrators and contributing sponsors are not required to provide notice of any reportable event in the plan's annual report.[9]

Under the regulations for nonmultiemployer plans, the 30-day notice requirement is waived for reportable events involving tax disqualification of the plan; plan amendments that decrease benefits; plan terminations or partial terminations, mergers, and consolidations; and certain transfers of plan assets and liabilities.[10] All reportable event requirements are waived for multiemployer plans.[11]

☐ For additional information on the notice of reportable events, see ¶ 2810.

Notice of intent to terminate

Before the effective date of a distress termination (¶ 2820-2830) of a single-employer pension benefit plan that is covered by the termination insurance provisions of ERISA, the plan administrator must file a notice with the PBGC. The notice is to advise that the plan is to be terminated on a proposed date, which may not be earlier than 60 days after the filing of the notice.[12]

☐ For further information relating to plan coverage and requirements under plan termination insurance, see CCH PENSION PLAN GUIDE ¶ 6400 and following.

Withdrawal of substantial employer

The plan administrator of a single-employer plan that has two or more contributing sponsors, at least two of whom are not under common control, is required to notify the PBGC within 60 days of the withdrawal of a "substantial employer" (see CCH PENSION PLAN GUIDE ¶ 6753) from the plan and request that the PBGC determine the liability of all persons with respect to the withdrawal.[13]

The plan administrator also must notify the PBGC within 60 days after an employer shuts down a facility and, as a result, more than 20% of the plan participants are separated from service of the employer.[14]

Annual reports

For each plan year for a plan covered by the termination insurance provisions of ERISA, the plan administrator shall file with the PBGC an annual report which identifies the plan and the plan administrator and includes information about withdrawals and reportable events.

The annual report requirement of the PBGC will be satisfied through the filing of the Form 5500 series.[15] See ¶ 2202 for a description of the annual report requirement.

Terminal reports

The administrator of any employee pension benefit plan which, regardless of the number of participants remaining in the plan, is winding up its affairs, must file terminal reports with the PBGC. For more on plan terminations, see ¶ 2800 and following.

Financial and actuarial information by underfunded plans

Under ERISA Sec. 4010, contributing sponsors and each member of a contributing sponsor's controlled group that maintain substantially underfunded single-employer plans must submit annual financial and actuarial reports to the PBGC (see ¶ 2810).[16] The PBGC requires this information to be filed electronically.

Special reports for multiemployer plans

The Multiemployer Pension Plan Amendments Act of 1980 requires various notices to be filed with the PBGC by multiemployer plans under the special provisions in the Act. These notices include reports of insolvency (¶ 2876) and employer withdrawals (¶ 2883).

☐ For more information about the multiemployer plan funding notice requirements, see ¶ 2220. For a full discussion of the reporting requirements for multiemployer plans, see the "Terminations—Multiemployer Plans—Withdrawal Liability" division beginning at CCH PENSION PLAN GUIDE ¶ 6900.

Reporting and disclosure using electronic media

The PBGC has issued final regulations that are designed to remove regulatory impediments to electronic filings with the Agency, as well as impediments to electronic issuances to others.[17] The rules cover electronic filing, issuances to third parties, computation of time, and electronic means of recordkeeping.

The rules treat most types of submissions as filed or issued on the date sent rather than on the date received. However, specified filings, including the advance notice of certain reportable events, notices of missed contributions over $1 million, and requests for approval of multiemployer plan amendments, will not be treated as filed until actually received by the PBGC. The rules generally provide for the use of any method of issuance, if the measures used are reasonably calculated to ensure actual receipt of the material by the intended recipient. The rules on methods of issuance include a safe harbor method for providing an issuance by electronic media, similar to existing DOL rules on the disclosure of employee benefit plan information through electronic media.

Disaster and terrorism relief

The Victims of Terrorism Tax Relief Act authorizes the Treasury and Labor Departments and the PBGC to postpone filing and other deadlines for employee benefit plans for up to one year for reason of disaster, terrorism, or other military actions. For more information, see ¶ 2205.

---

[1] 2008 PBGC Comprehensive Premium Payment Instructions.

[2] 2010 PBGC Premium Payment Instructions.

[3] PBGC Reg. § 4007.11.

[4] PBGC Reg. § 4007.11(a)(1).

[5] PBGC Reg. § 4007.11(a)(2)(i) and (ii).

[6] PBGC Reg. § 4007.11(a)(3)(i), (ii), and (iii).

[7] Preamble to PBGC Reg. §§ 4000.3(b)(1) and 4007.3 (71 FR 31077), at CCH PENSION PLAN GUIDE ¶ 24,806Z; PBGC Reg. §§ 4000.3(b)(1) and 4007.3, as amended 6-1-06 (71 FR 31077).

[8] ERISA Sec. 4043(a); PBGC Reg. § 4043.20.

[9] PBGC Reg. §§ 4043.4 and 4065.3(a).

[10] PBGC Reg. §§ 4043.21, 4043.22, 4043.24, 4043.28, and 4043.32(c).

[11] PBGC Reg. § 4043.4(b).

[12] ERISA Sec. 4041(a) and (c).

[13] ERISA Sec. 4063(a).

[14] ERISA Sec. 4062(e).

[15] ERISA Sec. 4065; PBGC Reg. § 4065.3(b).

[16] ERISA Sec. 4010; PBGC Reg. §§ 4010.1-4010.12.

[17] PBGC Reg. §§ 4000.1-4000.15, 4000.21-4000.32, 4000.41-4000.43, and 4000.51-4000.54.

¶ 2215

Reports and Disclosures to the Department of Labor

ERISA and regulations under ERISA require plan administrators to provide certain reports to the DOL, as explained below.

Summary plan description

A summary plan description (SPD) must be filed by the administrator of each employee benefit plan with the Secretary of Labor if the administrator is requested to do so by the DOL.[1] The SPD must be written in a manner designed to be understood by the average plan participant and must be accurate and comprehensive enough to reasonably inform the participants and beneficiaries of their rights and obligations under the plan. See ¶ 2220 for more information on SPDs.

Annual reports

Comprehensive annual reporting to the DOL is required by ERISA.[2] The annual return/report (Form 5500 series) consolidates the annual reporting requirements of the IRS, the DOL, and the PBGC. Form 5500 is filed only with the EBSA. See ¶ 2202 for a description of the annual report requirement.

Material modifications

The administrator of an employee benefit plan subject to ERISA's reporting and disclosure requirements must file a description of any material modification or change in information with the DOL if requested to do so by the Secretary of Labor.[3]

Terminal reports

The administrator of any employee pension benefit plan that is winding up its affairs must file terminal reports as required by the Secretary of Labor. This is true regardless of the number of plan participants. Copies of these reports must also be filed with the PBGC.[4]

The EBSA has issued regulations that provide termination procedures for abandoned individual accounts plans.[5] The regulations facilitate the termination of these plans and the distributions of benefits to participants and beneficiaries by financial institutions and other entities holding the assets of the plans. These regulations, which also provide model notices to be sent to the plan sponsor, the EBSA, and participants and beneficiaries, also establish a simplified method for filing a terminal report. For more information, see ¶ 2378.

Disaster and terrorism relief

The Victims of Terrorism Tax Relief Act authorizes the Treasury and Labor Departments and the PBGC to postpone filing and other deadlines for employee benefit plans for up to one year for reason of disaster, terrorism, or other military actions. For more information, see ¶ 2205.

---

[1] ERISA Sec. 104(a)(6); ERISA Reg. § 2520.104a-8.

[2] ERISA Sec. 101(b)(4) [redesignated as ERISA Sec. 101(b)(1) by P.L. 105-34 (Taxpayer Relief Act of 1997)]; ERISA Sec. 103(a)(1)(A); ERISA Reg. § 2520.103-1.

[3] ERISA Sec. 104(a)(6); ERISA Reg. § 2520.104a-8.

[4] ERISA Sec. 101(c).

[5] ERISA Reg. §§ 2520.103-13, 2550.404a-3, and 2578.1, 71 FR 20820, April 21, 2006.

¶ 2220

Reports and Disclosures to Participants and Other Parties

Participants and beneficiaries may be entitled to receive a number of different types of reports and disclosures. Their entitlement to these documents may depend on whether certain events have occurred, such as plan amendments and plan underfunding. Participants and beneficiaries also may be entitled to disclosure documents if they have requested particular information from their employer or plan administrator. In addition, employers and employee representatives may be entitled to plan-related disclosures. The range of required reports and disclosures includes:

1. summary plan descriptions,
2. notices of material plan changes,
3. statements for separated employees and retirees,
4. summary annual reports,
5. funding notices,
6. periodic benefit statements,
7. descriptions of survivor annuities,
8. notices of rollover distributions,
9. blackout notices,
10. veterans' USERRA rights,
11. multiemployer plan notices, and
12. fee disclosures.

Missing participants

Missing participants can pose a problem for employers and administrators attempting to satisfy their reporting and disclosure obligations. The PBGC defines a "missing participant" as a participant or beneficiary under a terminating plan that the plan administrator cannot locate after a diligent search.[1] The DOL states that the steps a fiduciary must take to locate lost participants are inherently facts-and-circumstances determinations. The DOL reasons that each fiduciary must determine whether the steps he or she uses to locate lost participants satisfy the fiduciary obligations under ERISA.[2] The PBGC requires the plan administrator to question beneficiaries of the missing participant whose names and addresses are known to the administrator and to utilize a commercial locator service.[3]

The IRS will assist plan administrators or sponsors of qualified retirement plans in locating missing participants by forwarding letters that contain beneficial information or serve a "humane" purpose, such as notifying plan participants of benefits.[4]

Benefits of missing participants. Under the PBGC Missing Participant Program, plan administrators terminating plans covered by the PBGC must either purchase an annuity from an insurer for missing participants or pay a "designated benefit" to the PBGC, which will then assume responsibility for locating the missing participants and paying benefits to individuals who are located.[5] A "Pension Search Directory" set up by the PBGC lists the names of missing plan participants on the Internet.[6] The Directory contains the names and last-known addresses of people being sought and the names and headquarters location of the companies at which they earned the pensions. The list is updated quarterly. The directory may be viewed at www.pbgc.gov/search.

> **CCH Pointer:** The Pension Protection Act of 2006 has extended the missing participant program to multiemployer plans. The Act directs the PBGC to issue regulations for terminating multiemployer plans similar to the missing participant rules for single-employer defined benefit plans that are currently in place.[7] In addition, plan administrators of certain qualified pension plans not subject to the PBGC missing participant program and not subject to the termination insurance program under present law will be permitted, but not required, to elect to transfer missing participant benefits to the PBGC upon plan termination.[8] For more information, see CCH Pension Plan Guide ¶ 6800.

Summary plan descriptions

Each participant and each beneficiary who is receiving benefits under an employee benefit plan is entitled to receive, automatically, from the plan's administrator a copy of the summary plan description and a statement of ERISA rights.[9] The summary plan description, commonly known as the "SPD," must accurately reflect the contents of the plan as of a date not earlier than 120 days prior to the date such SPD is furnished.[10]

Contents of SPD. ERISA requires the SPD to contain specific information about the plan, including information on how the plan is administered, the name of the person designated as agent for service of legal process, the name, title, and business address of any trustee or trustees of the plan, and the plan's requirements respecting eligibility for participation and benefits. In addition, the SPD must include a statement of employee rights under ERISA.

For employee pension benefit plans, the SPD also must include a statement describing the plan's normal retirement age, a statement describing any other conditions which must be met before a participant will be eligible to receive benefits, and a description or summary of the benefits.

Plan administrators are required to specify in the SPD the type of pension plan that is being administered (e.g., "ERISA section 404(c) plan," "defined contribution plan," "401(k) plan" and "cash balance plan").[11]

Procedures for automatic rollover of cash-out distributions. Absent an affirmative election by a participant, mandatory distributions (i.e., cash-out distributions) from a qualified plan of more than $1,000 and less than or equal to $5,000, must be directly rolled over to an individual retirement plan of a designated trustee or issuer.[12] DOL final regulations provide a safe harbor for fiduciaries involved in the selection of a financial institution to provide the individual retirement plan and the selection of investments.[13] However, in order for the safe harbor to apply,

¶2220

information regarding a plan's automatic rollover procedures must be included in the plan's SPD or SMM.[14]

CCH Pointer: The DOL changed the name of the Pension and Welfare Benefits Administration (PWBA) to the Employee Benefits Security Administration (EBSA) in 2003. According to the EBSA, plans are not required to change the Agency's name in existing SPDs.[15]

Very small plans. Very small plans may qualify for a special exemption from the SPD requirement. If a plan has only two participants, who are also the plan trustees and 60% shareholders of the company, the plan administrator does not have to provide an SPD. In lieu of furnishing an SPD, the administrator need only furnish free of charge:[16]

1. a copy of the instruments under which the plan is established or operated, upon the written request of any participant, and

2. a copy of each amendment or other change to the plan in the event the plan is amended or changed.

Comprehensibility. The SPD must be written in a manner calculated to be understood by the average plan participant and must be sufficiently accurate and comprehensive so as to reasonably apprise such participants and beneficiaries of their rights and obligations under the plan.[17]

Sample SPDs. For sample SPDs, see the "Plans and Clauses" volume of the CCH PENSION PLAN GUIDE.

Distribution of SPDs. The plan administrator of an employee benefit plan subject to the reporting and disclosure requirements of ERISA must furnish a copy of the SPD and a statement of ERISA rights to each participant covered under the plan and each beneficiary receiving benefits under a pension plan on or before the later of the following dates:[18]

1. within 90 days (a) after the employee becomes a participant in the case of a participant covered under the plan, or (b) after the beneficiary first receives benefits in the case of a beneficiary receiving benefits under a pension plan, or

2. within 120 days after the plan becomes subject to the reporting and disclosure requirements of ERISA.

A plan becomes "subject to" the reporting and disclosure requirements of ERISA on the first day on which an employee is credited with an hour of service.

The SPD must be distributed by a method that is reasonably calculated to ensure actual receipt of the material by plan participants and beneficiaries.[19] The SPD may be sent via first class mail to the participant's last known address, or by electronic means, if certain conditions are met.[20]

Request by participants. Upon written request, a participant must be furnished with a copy of plan documents. The administrator must generally mail the documents within 30 days of the request and may make a reasonable charge to cover the cost of furnishing the documents.[21]

¶2220

Updated SPD

Every fifth year after an employee benefit plan becomes subject to ERISA's reporting and disclosure requirements, the plan administrator must furnish to each plan participant, and to each beneficiary receiving benefits under the plan, an updated SPD which integrates all plan amendments made within such five-year period. If no amendments have been made to the plan during the five-year period, this requirement need not be met. Regardless of whether amendments have been made, however, an SPD must be furnished to plan participants, and beneficiaries receiving benefits under the plan, every tenth year after the plan becomes subject to the reporting and disclosure rules.[22]

Due dates for distributing updated SPD. A plan administrator will have 210 days after the end of the plan year in which the five- or ten-year period described in the preceding paragraph ends to distribute the SPD to participants and beneficiaries. In order to avoid situations where a period of time would not be covered by an SPD, the regulations provide that the five-and ten-year periods are measured from the end of the period covered by the last distributed SPD.

☐ For a full discussion of SPD requirements, see CCH PENSION PLAN GUIDE ¶ 4245—4255.

Material plan changes

A summary description of any material modification to the plan or any change in information required to be included in the SPD must be furnished to each participant and beneficiary not later than 210 days after the close of the plan year in which the modification or change was adopted.[23] The summary must be written in a manner calculated to be understood by the average plan participant.

Example: A calendar-year plan adopts a modification in April 2011. A summary description of the material modification must be furnished on or before July 29, 2012.

Very small plans. Very small plans may qualify for a special exemption from the requirement to provide summaries of material modifications (SMMs). The same such exemption that applies to SPDs applies to SMMs. See the discussion of the exemption under "**Summary plan description**" above.

Statements for separated employees and retirees

Retired participants under a pension plan, beneficiaries receiving benefits from a pension plan, and employees separated from employment with vested rights under a pension plan all have their rights fixed and relatively few changes which the plan makes will affect their situations. As a result, it would be expensive and wasteful to routinely provide these people with updated SPDs and material modifications which have no bearing on their benefits. In fact, this is likely to mislead them. Accordingly, an employee benefit pension plan need only furnish such persons with a copy of the SPD which was current at the time their rights were fixed and with SMMs that have information affecting their benefits.

¶2220

Summary annual report

Each participant and each beneficiary who is receiving benefits under an employee benefit plan is entitled to receive, automatically, from the plan's administrator, a copy of the summary annual report (SAR).[24]

CCH Pointer: *Repeal of SAR requirement for defined benefit plans.* Under the Pension Protection Act of 2006, the requirement to provide a summary annual report to participants will not apply to single-employer and multiemployer defined benefit pension plans for plan years beginning after December 31, 2007.[25] Note, detailed information about a defined benefit plan must be provided to participants in a new annual funding notice. See the discussion below about the defined benefit plan funding notice.

An ERISA regulation governs the content, style, and format of the SAR and prescribes sample forms which plan administrators of pension and welfare plans are to use in furnishing the SAR to plan participants and beneficiaries.[26] Plan administrators complete the sample pension or welfare SAR form by inserting information taken from the most recent annual report. Plan administrators may omit any part of the prescribed pension or welfare benefit form which is not applicable to the plan, or which would require information which is not required to be reported in the plan's annual report.[27] Plan administrators are not permitted to vary the format of the SAR, however. If necessary, explanatory material may be added, in which case it must be placed following the SAR form, and must be headed "Additional Explanation." [28]

Times for furnishing the SAR. Although ERISA provides that an SAR must be distributed within 210 days after the close of the plan year (that is, at the same time the annual report must be filed), the DOL has determined that this would impose unreasonable administrative burdens on plan administrators.[29] Accordingly, the DOL has modified the requirements of the statute in this respect. Thus, under the SAR regulation, SARs are to be furnished to plan participants and beneficiaries within nine months after the close of the plan year.[30] If an extension of time in which to file the annual report has been granted by the IRS, the SAR is generally required to be furnished within two months after the close of the period for which the extension is granted.

Funding notices

Participants, beneficiaries, and certain other parties are entitled to receive notices involving a plan's funding.

Defined benefit plan funding notice. The Pension Protection Act of 2006 expands the annual funding notice rules that previously applied only to multiemployer defined benefit plans so that they also apply to single-employer defined benefit plans.[31] The information that must be provided in the notice has been changed and augmented, and the timing of the notice has been accelerated. The expanded notice requirements generally apply to plan years beginning after December 31, 2007.

¶2220

The purpose of these expanded funding notice requirements is to provide greater awareness of, and transparency to, retirement security. The annual funding notice will provide a timely look at the true financial state of the plan for the most recent and two preceding years. Additional notices are required when benefits limitations are triggered or the company files for bankruptcy.

CCH Pointer: *EBSA guidance and Model Notices allow for good faith compliance.* In February 2009, the EBSA issued interim guidance, which included Model Notices.[32] Under the guidance, the EBSA explained that it would treat a plan administrator as satisfying the requirements of ERISA Sec.101(f) if the administrator complied with the guidance and acted in accordance with a good faith, reasonable interpretation of those requirements concerning matters not specifically addressed by the guidance. The EBSA has released proposed regulations that would implement the annual funding notice requirements of ERISA Sec. 101(f), as amended by the Pension Protection Act of 2006 and the Worker, Retiree, and Employer Recovery Act of 2008.[33] The proposed regulations, which incorporate much of the interim guidance, detail the content, style, and format requirements, the timing and delivery requirements for furnishing the notice, and the persons entitled to receive the notice. Two non-mandatory model notices are also provided.

Defined benefit plan administrators, for both single-employer and multiemployer defined benefit plans to which Title IV of ERISA applies, are required to provide an annual funding notice for each plan year. This annual funding notice must be provided to: (1) the PBGC; (2) each plan participant and beneficiary; (3) each labor organization representing plan participants and beneficiaries; and (4) for multiemployer plans, to each contributing employer.[34]

Contents of notice. Each defined benefit plan annual funding notice must contain identifying information, including (1) the name of the plan, (2) the plan administrator's address and phone number, (3) the address and phone number of the plan's principal administrative officer, (4) each plan sponsor's employer identification number (EIN), and (5) the plan number of the plan.[35] Also, information must be provided concerning the number of participants, the plan's funding policy and asset allocation of investments, any plan amendments, the PBGC's guarantee of benefits, and where to obtain a copy of the plan's annual report.[36] In addition, single-employer and multiemployer plans must each provide more information about plan funding and assets, among other things.

Timing of notice. In general, the defined benefit plan annual funding notice must be provided no later than 120 days after the end of the plan year relating to the notice.[37] For small plans, however, the required defined benefit plan annual funding notice should be provided with the annual Form 5500.[38] For more details, see CCH PENSION PLAN GUIDE ¶ 4205.

Notice of failure to fund. An employer must notify all plan participants and beneficiaries, including alternate payees, if the employer fails to make an installment or other payment required to meet the minimum funding standard to a plan within 60 days following the due date for such installment. This requirement does not apply to multiemployer plans. If the employer has filed a waiver request with respect to the plan year that includes the required installment, no notice is required. If the waiver request is denied, the employer must provide notice within 60 days after the date of the denial.

A sanction is imposed on employers who fail to notify participants and beneficiaries that they did not meet the minimum funding standard. A court may require an employer who fails to make the notification to pay the affected participant and beneficiaries up to $110 per day from the date of the failure.[39]

Periodic benefit statements for participants and beneficiaries

For plan years beginning after December 31, 2006 (with delayed effective dates for collectively bargained plans), a plan administrator of a defined contribution plan (other than a one-participant retirement plan) must provide a pension benefit statement to participants and beneficiaries.[40] The statement must be furnished at least once each calendar quarter to participants and beneficiaries who have the right to direct the investment of the assets of their accounts; once each calendar year to participants and beneficiaries who have accounts but do not have the right to direct the investment of the account assets; and upon written request to a plan beneficiary not described above. A plan administrator of a defined benefit plan (other than a one-participant retirement plan) must provide a pension benefit statement at least once every three years to each participant with a nonforfeitable accrued benefit and who is employed by the employer at the time the statement is furnished, and to a participant or beneficiary of the plan upon written request.[41]

Content of pension benefit statement. In general, a pension benefit statement must indicate, on the basis of the latest information available, the total benefits accrued and the nonforfeitable benefits, if any, that have accrued or the earliest date on which benefits will become nonforfeitable.[42] The statement must also include an explanation of any permitted disparity or any floor-offset arrangement that may be applied in determining any accrued benefits. The statement must be written in a manner calculated to be understood by the average plan participant. It may be delivered in written, electronic, or other appropriate form to the extent that the form is reasonably accessible to the participant or beneficiary. For certain participants and beneficiaries of defined contribution plans, additional information must be provided.

The EBSA has issued guidance implementing the periodic pension benefit statement requirements enacted by the Pension Protection Act of 2006.[43] On the issue of when to furnish the statements, pending the issuance of further guidance, it is the EBSA's view that the furnishing of pension benefit statement information to individual account plan participants or beneficiaries not later than 45 days following the end of the calendar-quarter or calendar-year period will constitute good faith compliance. The EBSA also provides guidance on other issues, including electronic access to the statements and the use of multiple documents or sources for benefit statement information. In addition, the EBSA provides model language to assist with requirement that participants receive an explanation of the importance of a well-balanced and diversified investment portfolio.

¶2220

CCH Pointer: The EBSA has provided further relief for profit-sharing and other non-participant directed individual account plans that must furnish periodic benefits statements to participants and beneficiaries of individual account plans that do not permit participants and beneficiaries to direct the investment of assets in their individual accounts.[44] Under the new relief, plan administrators of non-participant directed individual account plans will be treated as acting in good faith compliance with a reasonable interpretation of ERISA Sec. 105(a)(1)(A)(ii) when statements are furnished to these participants and beneficiaries on or before the date on which the Form 5500 Annual Return/Report is filed by the plan (but in no event later than the date, including extensions, on which the Form 5500 is required to be filed by the plan) for the plan year to which the statement relates.

For more information about pension benefit statements, see CCH PENSION PLAN GUIDE ¶ 4243.

Survivor annuities

A plan that must provide a qualified joint and survivor annuity form of benefit also must provide to each participant, no less than 30 days and no more than 180 days before the annuity starting date, a written explanation of:

1. the terms and conditions of the qualified joint and survivor annuity;

2. the participant's right to make, and the effect of, an election to waive the joint and survivor annuity form of benefits;

3. the rights of the participant's spouse; and

4. the right to make, and the effect of, a revocation of an election.

CCH Pointer: Generally effective for plan years after 2007, the written explanation must also include the terms and conditions of the "qualified optional survivor annuity." See ¶ 1700.

Qualified preretirement annuity. Participants must also be provided with a written explanation of a qualified preretirement annuity. The explanation is to be comparable to that required for the joint and survivor annuity. It must be provided before the latest applicable period:

1. the period beginning with the first day of the plan year preceding the plan year in which the participant reaches age 32 and ending with the end of the plan year preceding the plan year in which the participant reaches age 35;

2. a reasonable period of time after the end of the subsidization of a survivor benefit with respect to a participant by the plan;

3. a reasonable period of time after an individual becomes a plan participant;

4. a reasonable period of time after the survivor benefit provisions of the Code become applicable to a participant; or

¶2220

5. a reasonable period of time after separation from service in the case of a participant who separates from service before age 35.

A plan does not have to provide notice of the right to waive the qualified joint and survivor annuity or the qualified preretirement survivor annuity if (1) the plan fully subsidizes the cost of the benefit and (2) the plan does not permit a participant to waive the benefit or designate another beneficiary.[45]

The IRS has provided guidance on the content requirements that apply to explanations given to participants and spouses of participants of qualified joint and survivor annuities and qualified preretirement survivor annuities, and that provide disclosure requirements that will enable participants to compare the relative values of optional forms of benefits without having to do calculations using interest or mortality assumptions.[46] For more information, see ¶ 1725.

The IRS has also released final regulations that define the conditions under which a qualified defined benefit plan may furnish a written explanation of a participant's right to choose between a qualified joint and survivor annuity and other forms of payment *after* the annuity starting date.[47]

☐ See ¶ 1700 and following for a discussion of these annuities.

Rollover distribution notices

Plan administrators must provide a detailed written explanation to plan participants regarding plan distributions that are eligible for rollover treatment. Within a reasonable amount of time prior to the distribution, distributees must be informed in writing of the provisions:[48]

1. under which the recipient may have the distribution transferred directly to another eligible retirement plan;

2. which require the withholding of tax on the distribution if it is not transferred directly to another eligible retirement plan;

3. under which the distribution will not be subject to federal income tax if transferred to an eligible retirement plan within 60 days after the date on which the recipient received the distribution;

4. which govern lump-sum distributions and other distributions under Code Sec. 402(d) and Code Sec. 402(e), if applicable; and

5. under which distributions from the eligible retirement plan that had received the distribution may be subject to restrictions and tax consequences which are different from those applicable to distributions from the distributing plan.[49]

For the definition of eligible retirement plan, see ¶ 1956.

Notice of default rollover of cash-out distributions. Under EGTRRA, a plan that provides for a cash-out distribution of a nonforfeitable account balance that does not exceed $5,000 must use a direct rollover as the default option for involuntary distributions that exceed $1000.[50] The rollover notice must inform a participant that an automatic direct rollover will be made unless the participant makes a different election.[51] Under Code Sec. 401(a)(31)(B), DOL final regulations, and IRS guidance, the plan administrator must notify the participant in writing, as part of the rollover notice or separately, that the distribution may be transferred without cost to another IRA.[52]

☐ See ¶ 1974 for more information on the rollover distribution notice.

Blackout notices

Plans may institute blackout (or "lockdown" or "lockout") periods during which, incident to a change in plan recordkeepers or providers, participants are prohibited from transferring assets among investment options, taking plan loans, or engaging in other financial transactions involving their accounts. The Sarbanes-Oxley Act of 2002, effective January 26, 2003, amends ERISA to require plan administrators to provide at least 30 days advance notice of blackout periods to participants and beneficiaries under individual account plans.[53] A blackout period that triggers the notice requirement is defined by ERISA as "any period for which any ability of a participant or beneficiary under plan, which is otherwise available under the terms of the plan, to direct or diversify assets credited to their accounts, to obtain loans from the plan, or to obtain distributions from the plan" is suspended, limited, or restricted for more than three consecutive business days.

Exceptions to the notice requirements are provided in addition to the general rule that notices are not required for blackout periods that are less than four business days. Specifically, notice is not required for suspensions, limitations, or restrictions that: (1) occur incident to the application of federal securities law, (2) constitute a change to a plan that provides for a regularly scheduled suspension, limitation, or restriction that is disclosed to participants and beneficiaries, (3) arise pursuant to a QDRO or by reason of a pending determination (by a plan administrator, court, or other party) of whether a domestic relations order filed (or reasonably anticipated to be filed) is a qualified order, or (4) occur because of an act or failure to act by an individual participant or because of an action or claim by a party unrelated to the plan involving the account of an individual participant.[54]

CCH Pointer: The Pension Protection Act of 2006 has created a new exception to the relief from fiduciary liability that ERISA Sec. 404(c) grants to fiduciaries for blackout periods that meet ERISA's requirements.[55] If a "qualified change in investment options" is made to a self-directed plan, fiduciary liability will not accrue to plan administrators or other fiduciaries as long as certain conditions are met.[56]

The term "qualified change in investment options" means a change in the investment options, offered to individual account plan participants or beneficiaries, under which account assets are reallocated among new investment options that are reasonably similar in risk and rate of return characteristics to the options offered prior to the change.[57] For more information, see ¶ 2391.

The notice must describe, in a manner calculated to be understood by the average plan participant: (1) the reason for the blackout period, (2) investments and other rights affected by the blackout, (3) the expected beginning date and length of the blackout period, and (4) other notices that the DOL may require by regulation.[58]

Notice to issuers of securities. The plan administrator is also required to provide "timely notice" of any blackout period to the issuer of employer securities held by the plan and subject to the suspension, limitation, or restriction on plan rights.[59]

Penalties for failure to provide notice. Plan administrators that fail to comply with the blackout notice requirements may be assessed a civil penalty, starting from the date of noncompliance.[60] Plan administrators are subject to a separate penalty of up to $100 per day for each individual participant or beneficiary to whom notice has not been provided.

Final regulations. Final regulations implement and clarify the provisions of the Sarbanes-Oxley Act of 2002, which are effective January 26, 2003 and apply to blackout periods commencing on or after that date.[61] Among other things, the regulations require the notice to: (1) disclose the reasons for the blackout period; (2) provide a description of rights that will be temporarily suspended or restricted by the blackout period; (3) disclose the expected beginning date and ending date of the blackout period (alternatively, the notice may specify the length of the blackout period by reference to the calendar week during which the blackout period is expected to begin and end, as long as information as to whether the blackout period has begun or ended is readily available, without charge, to affected participants and the notice describes how to access the information), (4) contain a statement advising participants and beneficiaries to review their investments in light of their inability to direct or diversify account assets during the blackout period, and (5) where applicable, provide an explanation of why a notice may not have been furnished within the specified time period. In addition, a Model Notice has been provided that plan administrators may use in complying with the applicable requirements. However, plan administrators are not required to use the Model Notice. DOL final rules have also been issued establishing procedures for the assessment and administrative review of the civil penalties authorized under ERISA for the failure or refusal by plan administrators to provide the blackout notices as required.[62]

SEC final rules. The SEC has issued final rules implementing provisions of the Sarbanes-Oxley Act of 2002 that prohibit directors and officers from trading in their company's securities acquired in connection with their employment during a blackout period imposed on participants of the company's individual account plan.[63] The employer maintaining the plan under which the blackout period is imposed (i.e., the issuer of the securities) must provide timely notice of the blackout period to the SEC and to the directors or officers who are subject to the insider trading prohibition.

☐ See CCH Pension Plan Guide ¶ 4325 and ¶ 7526B for more details about blackout notice requirements.

¶2220

Veterans' USERRA rights

The DOL has finalized regulations concerning veterans' reemployment rights under the Uniformed Services Employment and Reemployment Rights Act (USERRA).[64] Among other things, the final regulations require employers to provide employees an explanation of pension and health benefits during service and upon return to the workforce. Employers may provide the notice by posting it where employee notices are customarily placed. Employers may also provide the notice to employees in other ways that will minimize costs while ensuring that the full text of the notice is provided (for example, by handing or mailing out the notice, or by distributing the notice via electronic mail). The DOL has provided model notices that private-sector employers and state government employers may use to meet their notice requirements. The regulations are effective January 18, 2006.

Multiemployer plans

Summary plan information for employers and employee representatives. Within 30 days after the due date of the annual report, multiemployer plan administrators are required to provide to each employee organization and to employers that have an obligation to make plan contributions a report that contains several pieces of information, including information about contributing employers, participants, the funding status of the plan, plan assets and liabilities when there has been a plan merger, and entitlement to additional plan documents.[65]

The Pension Protection Act of 2006 makes it clear that no language that has been added waives any other provision requiring plan administrators to provide information, upon request, to contributing employers.[66] This new disclosure requirement applies to plan years beginning after December 31, 2007.[67] For more information, see CCH PENSION PLAN GUIDE ¶ 4330.

Information requests to multiemployer plans. The ability of participants, beneficiaries, unions, and contributing employers to request and receive plan actuarial and financial information from multiemployer plans has been expanded by the Pension Protection Act of 2006. In addition, contributing employers are entitled to receive, upon written request, a notice of the estimated amount of the employer's withdrawal liability. The expanded access to multiemployer plan information is effective for plan years beginning after December 31, 2007.[68]

Multiemployer actuarial and financial plan information must be provided to the participant, beneficiary, or contributing employer requesting it within 30 days after the request.[69] In general, any required notice of potential withdrawal liability must be provided to the requesting employer within 180 days after the request is made and in a form and manner to be prescribed in Labor Department regulations.[70] Anyone entitled to a copy of any actuarial or financial report or to the notice of potential withdrawal liability does not have a right to receive more than one copy of any report or notice during any 12-month period.[71]

CCH Pointer: The EBSA has issued final regulations clarifying the obligations of multiemployer plan administrators to disclose certain actuarial and financial information.[72] For example, the EBSA clarifies that copies of requested documents must be furnished by the plan administrator no later than 30 days after

¶2220

the date the written request is received. In addition, clarification is provided on what information is or is not subject to disclosure.

For more details, see CCH PENSION PLAN GUIDE ¶ 4306.

Fee disclosures

Effective April 1, 2012, certain service providers to employee pension benefit plans must disclose direct and indirect compensation and fees received by the service providers and their affiliates in connection with services provided to the plans.[73] The disclosures are intended to assist plan fiduciaries in assessing the reasonableness of contracts or arrangements. Employee pension benefit plans include defined benefit and defined contribution plans, except SEPs, SIMPLEs, and IRAs.

In addition, administrators of participant-directed individual account plans (except SEPs or SIMPLE IRAs) must provide participants and beneficiaries with investment-related information (including fees and expenses assessed to and deducted from their individual accounts) on an annual and quarterly basis.[74] Initial disclosures must be furnished no later than the later of 60 days after the first day of the first plan year beginning on or after November 1, 2011, or 60 days after April 1, 2012.

For more details about the fee disclosure requirements, see ¶ 2945.

Electronic transmission of disclosures

Group health plans have been allowed since June 1, 1997 to provide SPDs, summaries of material reductions in covered services or benefits, and other summaries of plan modifications and SPD changes through electronic media, under a safe harbor established by DOL regulations.[75] Effective October 9, 2002, DOL final rules expanded the safe harbor to allow all pension and welfare plans covered by ERISA Title I to use electronic media to provide *all* documents required to be furnished or made available under ERISA Title I.[76] Thus, the safe harbor for electronic media disclosures is not limited to SPDs and related disclosures or to SARs. In addition, the expanded safe harbor allows for electronic delivery of plan information beyond the workplace. For more information, see CCH PENSION PLAN GUIDE ¶ 4310.

The IRS has issued final regulations regarding the use of electronic media to provide notices to plan participants and beneficiaries and to transmit elections or consents.[77] The regulations apply whenever there is a requirement that an applicable notice be provided in writing to participants, beneficiaries, or alternate payees. Such notices include Code Sec. 402(f) notices describing rollover rights, Code Sec. 411(a)(11) notices describing participants' benefit commencement rights, and Code Sec. 204(h) notices to participants of significant reductions in rates of future benefit accruals. The regulations clarify existing rules and extend the signature and witness requirements for spousal consent for QJSAs under Code Sec. 417 to electronic transmissions. For more information, see CCH PENSION PLAN GUIDE ¶ 4311.

---

[1] ERISA Sec. 4050(b)(1).

¶2220

[2] ERISA Opinion Letter 11-86, 8-25-86: PWBA Opinion Letter 96-02A, 2-9-96.

[3] PBGC Reg. § 4050.4(b)(2).

[4] Rev. Proc. 94-22, 1994-1 CB 608, 2-28-94, CCH Pension Plan Guide ¶ 17,299N-4.

[5] PBGC Reg. § 4050.3.

[6] See PBGC Fact Sheet on the PBGC's Missing Participants Program at CCH Pension Plan Guide Transfer Binder, April 1996—June 1999, ¶ 23,929H; PBGC News Release No. 99-28, 7-22-99 at CCH Pension Plan Guide Transfer Binder, July 1999—November 2001, ¶ 23,955D.

[7] ERISA Sec. 4050(c), as added by P.L. 109-280 (Pension Protection Act of 2006), Act Sec. 410(a). The provision extending the program to multiemployer plans is effective for distributions made after the final regulations referenced in ERISA Sec. 4050(c) have been issued.

[8] ERISA Sec. 4050(d), as added by by P.L. 109-280 (Pension Protection Act of 2006), Act Sec. 410(a), and ERISA Sec. 4050(d)(4)(A), as amended by P.L. 110-458 (Worker, Retiree, and Employer Recovery Act of 2008). The provision extending the program to plans not covered by the PBGC is effective for distributions made after the final regulations referenced in ERISA Sec. 4050(d) have been issued.

[9] ERISA Sec. 101(a).

[10] ERISA Reg. § 2520.102-3.

[11] ERISA Reg. § 2520.102-3(d).

[12] Code Sec. 401(a)(31)(B).

[13] ERISA Reg. § 2550.404a-2.

[14] ERISA Reg. § 2550.404a-2(c)(4); Preamble to ERISA Reg. § 2550.404a-2, CCH Pension Plan Guide ¶ 24,806P.

[15] 68 FR 5374, February 3, 2003; Employee Plans News, IRS TE/GE Division, Spring 2003.

[16] Alternative Method of Compliance for the November Electric Company Profit-Sharing Trust (46 FR 57196).

[17] ERISA Sec. 102(a).

[18] ERISA Sec. 104(b); ERISA Reg. § 2520.104b-2(a).

[19] ERISA Reg. § 2520.104b-1(b).

[20] ERISA Reg. § 2520.104b-1(b) and (c).

[21] ERISA Secs. 104(b)(4) and 502(c)(1).

[22] ERISA Sec. 104(b)(1).

[23] ERISA Sec. 104(b)(1); ERISA Reg. § 2520.104b-3; *Ershik v. Greg X-Ray Co., Inc.*, DC Kan (1989), No. 87-2362-5.

[24] ERISA Sec. 104(b)(3); ERISA Reg. § 2520.104b-10.

[25] ERISA Secs. 101(a)(2) and 104(b)(3), as amended by P.L. 109-280 (Pension Protection Act of 2006), Act Sec. 503(c).

[26] ERISA Reg. § 2520.104b-10(d)(3) and (4).

[27] ERISA Reg. § 2520.104b-10(d)(1).

[28] ERISA Reg. § 2520.104b-10(d)(2).

[29] ERISA Sec. 104(b)(3).

[30] ERISA Reg. § 2520.104b-10(c).

[31] ERISA Sec. 101(f), as amended by P.L. 109-280 (Pension Protection Act of 2006), Act Sec. 501(a). Act Sec. 501(d)(1) of P.L. 109-280 (Pension Protection Act of 2006).

[32] EBSA Field Assistance Bulletin 2009-01, February 10, 2009, CCH Pension Plan Guide ¶ 19,981Z-5.

[33] ERISA Proposed Regulations, 75 FR 70625, November 18, 2010.

[34] ERISA Sec. 101(f)(1), as amended by P.L. 109-280 (Pension Protection Act of 2006), Act Sec. 501(a).

[35] ERISA Sec. 101(f)(2)(A), as amended by P.L. 109-280 (Pension Protection Act of 2006), Act Sec. 501(a).

[36] ERISA Sec. 101(f)(2)(B)(iii), (iv), (vi), (viii), and (ix), as amended by P.L. 109-280 (Pension Protection Act of 2006), Act Sec. 501(a).

[37] ERISA Sec. 101(f)(3)(A), as amended by P.L. 109-280 (Pension Protection Act of 2006), Act Sec. 501(a).

[38] ERISA Sec. 101(f)(3)(B), as amended by P.L. 109-280 (Pension Protection Act of 2006), Act Sec. 501(a).

[39] ERISA Secs. 101(d) and 502(c); ERISA Reg. § 2575.502c-3.

[40] ERISA Sec. 105(a)(1)(A), as amended by P.L. 109-280 (Pension Protection Act of 2006), Act Sec. 501(a)(1).

[41] ERISA Sec. 105(a)(1)(B), as amended by P.L. 109-280 (Pension Protection Act of 2006), Act Sec. 501(a)(1), Act Sec. 501(a)(1).

[42] ERISA Sec. 105(a)(2)(A)(i)-(iv), as amended by P.L. 109-280 (Pension Protection Act of 2006), Act Sec. 501(a)(1), Act Sec. 501(a)(1).

[43] EBSA Field Assistance Bulletin 2006-03, December 20, 2006, CCH Pension Plan Guide ¶ 19,981H.

[44] EBSA Field Assistance Bulletin 2007-03, October 12, 2007, CCH Pension Plan Guide ¶ 19,981N.

[45] Code Secs. 417(a)(3) and 417(a)(5)(A); ERISA Secs. 205(c)(3) and 205(c)(5)(A).

[46] IRS Reg. § 1.417(a)(3)-1, T.D. 9099, 68 FR 70141, December 17, 2003; T.D. 9256, 71 FR 14798, March 24, 2006.

¶2220

[47] IRS Reg. § 1.417(e)-1, T.D. 9076, 68 FR 41906, July 16, 2003.

[48] Code Sec. 402(f); IRS Reg. § 1.402(f)-1, Q&A-1.

[49] Code Sec. 402(f)(1)(E).

[50] Code Sec. 401(a)(31)(B).

[51] Code Sec. 402(f)(1).

[52] Code Sec. 401(a)(31)(B). ERISA Reg. § 2550.404a-2; IRS Notice 2005-5, Q&A-15, I.R.B. 2005-3, January 18, 2005, CCH PENSION PLAN GUIDE ¶ 17,130N.

[53] ERISA Sec. 101(i), as added by P.L. 107-204 (Sarbanes-Oxley Act of 2002), Act Sec. 306(b)(1).

[54] ERISA Sec. 101(i)(7)(B), as added by P.L. 107-204 (Sarbanes-Oxley Act of 2002), Act Sec. 306(b)(1); ERISA Reg. § 2520.101-3(d)(1)(ii).

[55] ERISA Sec. 404(c)(1), as amended by the Pension Protection Act of 2006 (P.L. 109-280), Act Sec. 621(a)(1)(B).

[56] ERISA Sec. 404(c)(4)(C), as amended by the Pension Protection Act of 2006 (P.L. 109-280, Act Sec. 621(a)(2).

[57] ERISA Sec. 404(c)(4)(B), as amended by the Pension Protection Act of 2006 (P.L. 109-280), Act Sec. 621(a)(2).

[58] ERISA Sec. 101(i)(2)(A), as added by P.L. 107-204 (Sarbanes-Oxley Act of 2002), Act Sec. 306(b)(1).

[59] ERISA Sec. 101(i)(2)(E), as added by P.L. 107-204 (Sarbanes-Oxley Act of 2002), Act Sec. 306(b)(1).

[60] ERISA Sec. 502(c)(7), as added by P.L. 107-204 (Sarbanes-Oxley Act of 2002), Act Sec. 306(b)(3); ERISA Reg. § 2560.502c-7.

[61] ERISA Reg. § 2520.101-3.

[62] ERISA Reg. § 2560.502c-7.

[63] SEC Release No. 34-47225, 68 FR 4337, January 28, 2003.

[64] 70 FR 75246 and 75313, December 19, 2005.

[65] ERISA Sec. 104(d)(1), as added by P.L. 109-280 (Pension Protection Act of 2006), Act Sec. 503(d)(3).

[66] ERISA Sec. 104(d)(2), as added by P.L. 109-280 (Pension Protection Act of 2006), Act Sec. 503(d)(3).

[67] Act Sec. 503(f) of P.L. 109-280 (Pension Protection Act of 2006).

[68] Act Sec. 502(d) of P.L. 109-280 (Pension Protection Act of 2006).

[69] ERISA Sec. 101(k)(2)(A), as added by P.L. 109-280 (Pension Protection Act of 2006), Act Sec. 502(a)(1)(B).

[70] ERISA Sec. 101(l)(2), as added by P.L. 109-280 (Pension Protection Act of 2006), Act Sec. 502(b)(2)(A).

[71] ERISA Secs. 101(k)(3) and 101(l)(3), as added by P.L. 109-280 (Pension Protection Act of 2006), Act Secs. 502(a)(1)(B) and (b)(1)(B).

[72] EBSA Final Regulations, 75 FR 9334, March 2, 2010.

[73] ERISA Reg. § 2550.408b-2; Preamble to ERISA Interim Final Regulations, CCH PENSION PLAN GUIDE ¶ 24,808T; and Preamble to ERISA Final Regulations, CCH PENSION PLAN GUIDE ¶ 24,809B.

[74] ERISA Reg. § 2550.404a-5 and ERISA Reg. § 2550.404c-1; Preamble to ERISA Interim Final Regulations, CCH PENSION PLAN GUIDE ¶ 24,808W; and Preamble to ERISA Final Regulations, CCH PENSION PLAN GUIDE ¶ 24,809B.

[75] ERISA Reg. § 2520.104b-1(c)(1) and (3).

[76] ERISA Reg. § 2520.104b-1(c); Preamble to ERISA Reg. § 2520.104b-1(c), CCH PENSION PLAN GUIDE ¶ 24,805Z.

[77] IRS Reg. § § 1.401(a)-21, 1.402(f)-1, 1.411(a)-11(f), 1.417(a)(3)-1, and 1.7476-2(c), T.D. 9294, 71 FR 61877, October 20, 2006.

¶ 2230

Penalties for Failure to Report or Disclose

Plan administrators, employers, and other parties are liable for penalties for failing to comply with reporting and disclosure rules. The IRS imposes a penalty of $25 per day (up to $15,000) for not filing returns in connection with pension, profit-sharing, and other retirement plans by the required due date.[1]

The DOL may assess a civil penalty of up to $1,100 per day against a plan administrator from the date of the administrator's failure or refusal to file an annual report until the report is filed.[2]

Delinquent Filer Voluntary Compliance Program

A plan administrator may ameliorate possible penalties for failure to timely file Form 5500 prior to receiving a late filing notice from the DOL by participating in the Delinquent Filer Voluntary Compliance Program (DFVC).[3] Under the DFVC, which is available only prior to the issuance of a late filing notice by the DOL, the plan administrator voluntarily files the delinquent return and pays a reduced penalty that is based on the size of the plan and the length of the filing delay. Penalties under the DFVC may not be paid from plan assets. The plan administrator is personally liable for the assessed penalties.

In order to further encourage delinquent plan filers to voluntarily comply with ERISA's annual reporting requirements, the DOL, effective March 28, 2002, reduced the basic penalty and the maximum penalties under the program.[4] In addition, the IRS has provided administrative relief from penalties for failure to timely comply with the annual reporting requirements under the Internal Revenue Code. The relief applies to late filers who both are eligible for and satisfy the requirements of the DFVC.[5]

☐ See CCH PENSION PLAN GUIDE ¶ 5538 and following for more information on the excise taxes imposed for failure to make required reports or notifications. For more information about reporting penalties and the DFVC, see CCH PENSION PLAN GUIDE ¶ 4085.

---

[1] Code Sec. 6652(e).

[2] ERISA Sec. 502(c)(2); ERISA Reg. §§ 2560.502c-2(b) and 2575.502c-2.

[3] PWBA Notice, April 27, 1995 (60 FR 20874), CCH PENSION PLAN GUIDE ¶ 19,976.

[4] PWBA Notice, March 28, 2002 (67 FR 15051), CCH PENSION PLAN GUIDE ¶ 19,976A, superseding PWBA Notice, April 27, 1995 (60 FR 20874).

[5] IRS Notice 2002-23, 2002-1 CB 742, April 15, 2002, CCH PENSION PLAN GUIDE ¶ 17,123O.

¶ 2235
For More Information

☐ For more information on reporting and disclosure, see CCH PENSION PLAN GUIDE ¶ 4000-¶ 4330.

Fiduciary Responsibility

¶ 2300

Overview of Fiduciary Responsibility Rules

Persons who qualify as fiduciaries with respect to employee benefit plans have special responsibilities under the Employee Retirement Income Security Act (ERISA). Failure to meet these responsibilities may result in fiduciary liability.

A fiduciary includes any person who exercises authority over the management of a plan or its assets. The determination of fiduciary status is crucial because once an individual qualifies as a fiduciary, numerous obligations, or duties, apply to that fiduciary.

Fiduciary duties

ERISA imposes various duties on fiduciaries. That is, fiduciaries must manage the plan for the exclusive benefit of participants and beneficiaries, act prudently, diversify plan investments, and abide by plan provisions.

Fiduciary liability

Once an individual who qualifies as a fiduciary breaches his duties, the issue arises as to the scope of liability. Generally, a fiduciary who breaches any fiduciary duty is liable for any losses the plan suffers because of the breach.

Court review of fiduciary's denial of benefits

ERISA does not explicitly define a standard for courts to use when reviewing the benefits decisions of plan administrators and fiduciaries. The standard of review has evolved under case law. For a discussion of the judicial standard of review when benefits are denied, see ¶ 2730.

¶ 2305

WHO IS A FIDUCIARY?: Fiduciary Defined

Persons who are considered fiduciaries with respect to employee benefit plans have special responsibilities under ERISA. Failure to meet these responsibilities could lead to fiduciary liability. Initially, it is necessary to discuss who in fact is a fiduciary before moving on to what standards govern fiduciary conduct.

ERISA definition

Under ERISA, a fiduciary is a person who:[1]

1. exercises discretionary authority or control respecting management of the plan or exercises any authority or control over the management or disposition of its assets;

2. renders investment advice for a fee or other compensation (direct or indirect) as to any monies or other property of the plan, or has any authority or responsibility to do so; or

3. has discretionary authority or discretionary responsibility in the administration of the plan.

The determination of an individual's fiduciary status is an inherently factual inquiry and will require analysis of the specific facts and circumstances of each case.[2]

"Ministerial" functions

In the day-to-day administration of an employee benefit plan, various individuals are responsible for performing functions that do not involve individual discretion or the rendering of investment advice. These functions are often referred to as "ministerial."

Individuals who perform purely "ministerial" functions for an employee benefit plan within a framework of policies, interpretations, rules, practices, and procedures made by other persons are not fiduciaries. These persons are not fiduciaries because they do not have discretionary authority or exercise discretionary control respecting plan management or the disposition of plan assets and do not render investment advice. For example, an accountant who performs only the ministerial functions expected of a professional and does not provide services beyond day-to-day administration is not a fiduciary. Similarly, attorneys and consultants who prepare year-end reports as required by government agencies are performing ministerial functions and do not qualify as fiduciaries.

Examples of routine administrative activities include:[3]

1. applying rules to determine eligibility for participation or benefits;
2. calculating service and compensation credits for benefits;
3. preparing employee communications material;
4. maintaining participants' service and employment records;
5. preparing reports required by government agencies;
6. calculating benefits;
7. conducting the orientation of new participants and advising participants of their rights and options under the plan;
8. collecting contributions and applying them as provided in the plan;
9. preparing reports concerning a participant's benefits;
10. processing claims; and
11. making recommendations to others with respect to plan administration.

Discretion requirement. An individual need not have absolute discretion with respect to a benefit plan in order to be considered a fiduciary. Fiduciary status exists with respect to any activity enumerated in ERISA over which the individual exercises discretion or control.[4] Generally, a person is a fiduciary only with respect to those aspects of the plan over which he exercises authority and control.[5]

Designated fiduciaries. The term fiduciary also includes any person designated by a named fiduciary to carry out fiduciary responsibilities (other than the responsibilities of a trustee) under the plan. However, formal appointment as a fiduciary is not necessary for a person to be considered a fiduciary. For example, a person may be regarded as a fiduciary by giving the impression of being a fiduciary (for example, by signing documents).[6] See ¶ 2335 for a discussion of named fiduciaries.

Corporate title. Generally, the exercise of actual control over the disposition of plan assets, not an individual's title, will determine fiduciary status.[7]

Participant-directed accounts. A participant in a plan that provides for individual accounts and permits participants and beneficiaries to exercise control over the assets of their accounts is not a fiduciary even though he exercises control over his own account. However, if the participant exercises control over the assets of the accounts of others, he is a fiduciary of the plan.[8] In addition, an individual who is otherwise a plan fiduciary is not liable for losses incurred by the individual accounts of participants as long as he does not exercise control over the assets in their accounts.

☐ For more on participant-directed accounts, see ¶ 2375.

Plan administrators

A plan administrator is not necessarily a fiduciary. A plan administrator who does not possess discretionary authority over the plan but who merely performs ministerial functions (see above) is not a fiduciary.[9]

Third-party administrator. Third-party administrators who exercise discretion in adjudicating benefit claims act as plan fiduciaries under ERISA.[10] However, third-party administrators who perform clerical functions and who do not exercise sufficient discretion and control over plan assets will not be held to be functioning as fiduciaries.[11]

Corporate directors and officers

As noted above, a person is a fiduciary only with respect to those aspects of the plan over which he exercises authority and control. Therefore, if an employer and its board of directors have no power with respect to a plan other than the appointment and oversight of the plan administrator and the trustees, their fiduciary status extends only to those functions.[12] Alternatively, company officers, who were not directly responsible for managing a severance plan, were fiduciaries where the company was responsible for administering the plan.[13]

Corporate directors are typically fiduciaries with regard to some aspect of the plan since they usually, at the very least, appoint plan administrators and investment managers. Directors who merely appoint fiduciaries are not necessarily relieved of all oversight responsibilities in connection with those appointments.

Employers

Employers may be considered fiduciaries to the extent that they maintain any authority or control over the management of the plan's assets, or the plan in general, or have any responsibility for the administration of the plan. Thus, an

¶2305

employer acts as a fiduciary when it maintains discretionary authority over who administers the plan.[14] However, an employer that does not have discretionary authority or control over the plan is not a fiduciary.[15]

> **CCH Pointer:** ERISA permits an employer to function as a benefits administrator. However, the common law of trusts, which ERISA supplanted, prohibited fiduciaries from holding positions that created a conflict of interest with trust beneficiaries.

Employer or plan administrator? Determining when an employer, that also serves as a plan administrator, is acting as a fiduciary is a troublesome issue. An employer will not be held liable for statements about its expected future financial condition or for business decisions that adversely affect the plan. In addition, an employer's decision to amend or terminate a plan is not an act of plan administration.[16] However, the U.S. Supreme Court found that an employer that made intentional misrepresentations to employees about the future of plan benefits during a meeting regarding corporate restructuring *was* acting as a fiduciary.[17] The employer was not obligated by ERISA or the plan to make any statements regarding future benefits. Nor did its statements about a new subsidiary's financial future concern the administration of a plan. However, the meeting focused primarily, and in detail, on benefits. In addition, statements regarding the future security of benefits were made by individuals who had the authority to communicate as fiduciaries and who could be perceived by employees as acting in their fiduciary capacity. In that context, making misrepresentations about the future benefits was an act of plan administration, the Court held.

Partnerships

A general partner may become a fiduciary with respect to a plan whose assets have been invested in the partnership.[18]

Unions

A union's status as a fiduciary under ERISA arises from the exercise of discretion in administering a plan. Thus, a union that presents the benefit claims of its members before an employer's health plan, but does not exercise discretion over the management of plan assets or offer investment advice, is not a fiduciary.[19] On the other hand, a union division authorized to appoint plan trustees is a fiduciary.[20]

Insurance companies

An insurance company may be considered a plan fiduciary, depending upon plan provisions and the agreement made by the insurer. Generally, the fiduciary status of an insurer is dependent on the degree to which the insurer exercises control over plan assets.[21]

An insurance company is generally not a fiduciary with respect to assets that are maintained in a guaranteed benefit policy.[22] A guaranteed benefit policy provides a fixed level of guaranteed benefits in the form of an annuity.

Power to amend contract. However, an insurer is an ERISA fiduciary where it has the power to unilaterally amend an annuity. An insurer's power to amend a contract, and thereby alter its value, is not qualitatively different from the ability to choose investments.[23] Similarly, an insurer is considered a fiduciary if it retains the power to amend *certain terms* of an annuity without corporate consent.[24]

Group annuity products. An insurer that holds assets that are in excess of what is needed to pay guaranteed benefits under a group annuity contract may be a fiduciary with respect to those assets. The U.S. Supreme Court has held that an insurer will be considered a fiduciary with respect to amounts that are not immediately used for the purchase of annuities to guarantee benefits and not subject to a guaranteed rate of return provided by the insurer.[25] Under these circumstances, the amounts are not treated as being part of a guaranteed benefit policy. Therefore, they are not excluded from the definition of "plan assets," and the insurer has fiduciary obligations concerning these assets. (See ¶ 2330 for more on the status of insurance company general accounts as plan assets and ¶ 2470 for a relevant Prohibited Transaction Exemption.)

Banks

A bank has been held to be a fiduciary when it retains the power to appoint a plan's trust administrator.[26]

Professional service providers

Professional service providers such as auditors, accountants, and actuaries may perform functions that place them in the role of fiduciary. Professional service providers become liable for damages when they cross the line from advisor to fiduciary.[27]

Under ERISA, an auditor must be independent from the plan.[28] Thus, auditors are not fiduciaries unless, in specific cases, they have authority or control over plan assets. Absent this authority or control, auditors are not liable to a plan under ERISA for alleged overcharges or malpractice.[29] Similarly, actuaries are not necessarily fiduciaries. Their status as fiduciaries depends on the degree of control they exercise over plan assets. For example, an actuary who fails to disclose the reasoning behind his actuarial assumptions does not exercise the requisite control.[30]

Investment managers. An investment manager has the power to manage, acquire, or dispose of plan assets. Therefore, investment managers are fiduciaries.[31]

An investment manager is any fiduciary, other than a trustee or named fiduciary, who:

1. has the power to manage, acquire, or dispose of any asset of a plan;

2. is registered as an investment adviser under the Investment Advisers Act of 1940; is not registered as an investment adviser under the Investment Advisers Act of 1940, but (a) is registered as an investment adviser in the state in which it maintains its principal office and place of business and (b) has filed a copy of its state fiduciary registration form with the Department of

Labor; is either a bank, or is an insurance company qualified to perform services described in (1) above under the laws of more than one state; and

3. has acknowledged in writing that he is a plan fiduciary.

Investment managers may execute cross-trades between a plan and any other account managed by the same investment manager, if certain conditions are satisfied. Cross-trading is a transaction in which an investment manager uses its authority to sell a security on behalf of one client and to buy that same security on behalf of another client (see ¶ 2447).

Arbitrators. The fiduciary status of an arbitrator depends on specific factual circumstances. An arbitrator may be deemed a fiduciary, for example, if, by determining a participant's right to benefits, the arbitrator would be exercising discretionary authority over the management and administration of the plan.[32]

Detailed fee disclosures to plan fiduciaries. The Department of Labor has issued final regulations that require plan administrators, in satisfaction of their fiduciary duties under ERISA, to provide participants and beneficiaries in participant-directed plans with plan and investment-related information (including details of fees and expenses assessed to and deducted from their individual accounts) on an annual and quarterly basis. The final rules require the disclosure of investment-related fee and expense information (e.g., sales loads, deferred sales charges, redemption fees, service charges, exchange fees, account fees, purchase fees, and the expense ratio for the total operating expenses of the investment) to be made in a chart or similar format that would allow for a comparison of the plan's investment options. The effective date of these has been extended several times. Currently, they are scheduled to take effect so that covered service providers are not required to make initial disclosures prior to April 1, 2012.

Absent compliance by the service provider with the disclosure requirements, the plan fiduciary would be subject to liability for engaging in a prohibited transaction (see ¶ 2945).

For more information, see ¶ 2945 and CCH Pension Plan Guide ¶ 7526E.

Reporting service provider fee information. The Employee Benefits Security Administration (EBSA) has released frequently asked questions (FAQs) to provide guidance on the revised Schedule C/Form 5500 reporting requirements regarding direct and indirect compensation and fees paid to plan service providers. Schedule C has been modified so that, effective beginning with the 2009 plan year, service providers required to be listed will separately report direct compensation paid by the plan and indirect compensation received from sources other than the plan or the plan sponsor, such as compensation charged against investment assets.

Use of electronic media to satisfy participant-level fee disclosure regs. EBSA has issued an interim policy on electronic delivery of disclosures that must be supplied to participants of participant-directed individual account retirement plans under the final participant-level fee disclosure regulations. Required disclosures under the regulations that are allowed to be included in a pension benefit statement (such as procedures for giving investment instructions, and information concerning fees and expenses that may be charged to participants' accounts for general plan administrative services and for individual transactions) may be furnished in the same way that other information included in the same pension benefit statement is provided. For required disclosures that may not be included in a pension benefit statement, EBSA explains that a plan administrator may furnish the disclosures through electronic media by using the safe harbor in ERISA Reg. § 2520.104b-1(c), or, alternatively, pending further guidance, satisfying certain conditions provided in the interim policy.[33]

---

[1] ERISA Sec. 3(21).

[2] ERISA Opinion Letter 95-17A, 6-29-95.

[3] ERISA Reg. § 2509.75-8, Q&A D-2 (ERISA Interpretive Bulletin, 75-8).

[4] *Gelardi v. Pertec Computer Corp.,* CA-9 (1985), 761 F2d 1323.

[5] *Sommers Drug Stores Co. Profit-Sharing Trust v. Corrigan Enterprises,* CA-5 (1986), 793 F2d 1456.

[6] *Donovan v. Mercer,* CA-5 (1984), 747 F2d 304.

[7] *Blatt v. Marshall Lassman,* CA-2 (1987), 812 F2d 810.

[8] ERISA Sec. 404(c); ERISA Opinion Letter 75-24, 10-21-75.

[9] *Pohl v. National Benefits Consultants, Inc.,* CA-7 (1992), 956 F2d 126.

[10] ERISA Opinion Letter 92-24A, 11-6-92; *Harold Ives Trucking Co. v. Spradley & Coker, Inc.,* CA-8 (1999), 178 F3d 523.

[11] *Klosterman v. Western General Management, Inc.,* CA-7 (1994), 32 F3d 1119.

[12] *Leigh v. Engle,* CA-7 (1984), 727 F2d 113.

[13] *Alkire v. Fissel,* DC Kan (1994), No. 94-1075-PFK.

[14] *Elmore v. Cone Mills Corp.,* DC SC (1991), C/A No. 6:88-3258-17, aff'd in part and rev'd in part by CA-4 (1994), 23 F3d 855.

[15] *E.g., First National Life Insurance Company v. Sunshine-Jr. Food Stores, Inc.,* CA-11 (1992), 960 F2d 1546, *cert. denied* 1/19/93.

[16] *Spink v. Lockheed Corp.,* US Sup Ct (1996), 517 US 882; *Curtiss-Wright Corp. v. Schoonejongen,* US Sup Ct (1995), 514 US 73; *Corcoran v. Bell Atlantic Corp.,* DC Pa (1997), No. 97-510. See also *Hughes Aircraft Co., et al. v. Jacobson, et al.,* US Sup Ct (1999), 525 US 432.

[17] *Howe v. Varity Corp.,* US Sup Ct (1996), 516 U.S. 489. *Cf. Sprague v. General Motors Corporation,* CA-6 (1998), 133 F3d 388, in which the Sixth Circuit held that an employer did not act in a fiduciary capacity when it did not deliberately mislead retirees into believing that their health benefits were vested.

[18] ERISA Reg. § 2510.3-101(a)(2).

[19] *Forys v. United Foods and Commercial Workers International, AFL-CIO, and CLC,* CA-7 (1987), 829 F2d 603.

[20] *Licensed Division District No. 1 MEBA/NMU v. DeFries,* CA-4 (1991), 943 F2d 474, *cert. denied* 1/27/92.

[21] See, e.g., *Consolidated Beef Industries, Inc. v. New York Life Insurance Co.,* CA-8 (1991), 929 F2d 960, *cert. denied* 4/20/92; *Witt v. Allstate Insurance Company,* CA-8 (1995), 50 F3d 536.

[22] *Mack Boring and Parts v. Meeker Sharkey Moffitt,* CA-3 (1991), 930 F2d 267.

[23] *Chicago Board Options Exchange v. Connecticut General Life Insurance Co.,* CA-7 (1983), 713 F2d 254.

[24] *Associates in Adolescent Psychiatry, SC v. Home Life Insurance Co.,* CA-7 (1991), 941 F2d 561, *cert. denied* 2/24/92.

[25] *John Hancock Mutual Life Insurance Company v. Harris Trust & Savings Bank,* US Sup Ct (1993), 510 US 86. See also, *Harris Trust & Savings Bank v. John Hancock Mutual Life Insurance Co.,* DC NY (1997), No. 83 Civ. 5401 (DC).

[26] *Associates in Adolescent Psychiatry, SC v. Home Life Insurance Co.,* CA-7, (1991), 941 F2d 561, *cert. denied* 2/24/92.

[27] *Mertens v. Hewitt Associates,* US Sup Ct (1993), 508 U.S. 248.

[28] ERISA Sec. 103(a)(3)(A).

[29] *Painters of Philadelphia District Council No. 21 Welfare Fund v. Price Waterhouse,* CA-3 (1989), 879 F2d 1146.

[30] *Pappas v. Buck Consultants,* CA-7 (1991), 923 F2d 531; *Mertens v. Hewitt Associates,* US Sup Ct (1993), 508 US 248.

[31] ERISA Sec. 3(38).

[32] ERISA Opinion Letter 79-66A, 9-14-79.

[33] ERISA Technical Release No. 2011-03, 12-8-11.

¶ 2310

WHO IS A FIDUCIARY?: Persons Who Render Investment Advice

A person who renders investment advice for a fee or other compensation with respect to plan assets or has the authority or responsibility to do so is treated as a fiduciary.[1] (See¶ 2312 for more information on fiduciary advisers under the Pension Protection Act.)

A person renders investment advice if two requirements are met.

First, the person must render advice to the plan on the value of securities or other property or make recommendations as to the advisability of investing in, purchasing, or selling securities or other property.[2]

Second, the individual must, either directly or indirectly:[3]

1. have discretionary authority or control covering the purchase or selling of securities or other property; or

2. render any advice pursuant to an agreement (written or otherwise) which stipulates that such advice will serve as the primary basis for investment decisions and that the person will render individualized advice to the plan based on the particular needs of the plan.

Individualized investment advice may deal with investment policies or strategy, overall portfolio composition, or diversification of plan investment.[4]

Investment in securities issued by investment company

The investment of a plan's money or other property in securities issued by an investment company registered under the Investment Company Act of 1940 (e.g., a mutual fund), will not by itself cause the investment company or its investment adviser or principal underwriter to be deemed a fiduciary or a party in interest. However, any of these three parties that acts in connection with a benefit plan covering its employees will be considered a fiduciary.[5]

Participant-directed account plans

A financial consultant that is hired by a participant in an ERISA Sec. 404(c) plan to provide investment advice as defined above or management of the participant's plan investments, in exchange for a fee, will be a fiduciary, according to the EBSA.[6] Thus, the financial consultant will be liable for imprudent investment decisions because, even though the participant hired the consultant, those decisions will not have been the direct and necessary result of the participant's exercise of control. The EBSA further advised that the other plan fiduciaries would not be liable as fiduciaries for either the selection of the consultant or the results of the consultant's decisions or recommendations.

In addition, a consultant merely advising a plan participant to take an otherwise permissible plan distribution, even when that advice is combined with a recommendation on how to invest the distribution (such as rolling an account balance over to an IRA to take advantage of investment options not available in the plan), is not providing investment advice, according to the EBSA. However, if the consultant is already a fiduciary and provides the above advice, then the consultant is exercising discretionary authority concerning the management of the plan and must act prudently and solely in the interest of the participant. So, if the consultant advices the participant to roll a plan distribution over to an IRA that is managed by the consultant, the consultant may be using plan assets in his or her own interest, in violation of ERISA.

Participant education

See ¶ 2375 for a discussion of the types of investment education employers may provide to employees covered by 401(k) plans and other participant-directed retirement arrangements without incurring fiduciary liability.

[1] ERISA Sec. 3(21)(A)(ii).

[2] ERISA Reg. § 2510.3-21(c)(1)(i) and (ii).

[3] ERISA Reg. § 2510.3-21(c)(1)(ii)(B).

[4] *Ibid.*

[5] ERISA Sec. 3(21)(B).

[6] ERISA Opinion Letter 2005-23A, 12-7-05. The EBSA assumed that the consultant was neither chosen nor promoted by plan fiduciaries and was not otherwise a fiduciary of the plan.

¶ 2312

WHO IS A FIDUCIARY?: Investment Advice Provided by Fiduciary Advisers

Under the Pension Protection Act of 2006, for investment advice provided after 2006, a new prohibited transaction exemption allows qualified "fiduciary advisers" to offer personally tailored professional investment advice to help employees manage their 401(k) and other plans. Fiduciary advisers may provide investment advice pursuant to "eligible investment advice arrangement" under which (1) portfolio recommendations are generated for a participant based on an unbiased computer model that has been certified and audited by an independent third party, or (2) fiduciary advisers provide their investment advice services by charging a flat fee that does not vary depending on the investment option chosen by the participant. The Secretary of Labor has been directed to determine whether investment advice provided through a computer model is feasible for IRAs and other tax-favored savings accounts.

Employers or plan sponsors are not obligated to monitor the specific advice given to any particular participant or beneficiary, though they retain the responsibility to prudently select and monitor advice providers. Fiduciary advisers are personally liable for the investment advice that they provide.

Individualized investment advice may be provided to 401(k) plan participants without running afoul of the prohibited transaction rules, if fiduciary advisers provide investment advice under an "eligible investment advice arrangement." Such an arrangement requires that investment advice is provided (1) through an unbiased computer model that has been certified and audited by an independent third party, or (2) by fiduciary advisers whose investment advice service fees and commissions do not vary depending on the investment option chosen by the participant.

General rules for investment advice exemption

Under the Pension Protection Act, qualified "fiduciary advisers" can provide investment advice to 401(k) and other plan participants without running afoul of the prohibited transaction rules under the Code and ERISA. Thus, if the applicable requirements are satisfied, the following are exempt from prohibited transaction treatment:

- providing investment advice to a participant or beneficiary regarding any security or property available as a plan investment;
- an investment transaction (i.e., a sale, acquisition, or holding of a security or other property) pursuant to the investment advice; and
- the direct or indirect receipt of fees or other compensation by a fiduciary adviser or its affiliates (or any employee, agent, or registered representative of the fiduciary or adviser or its affiliates) in connection with the providing investment advice or an investment transaction pursuant to the investment advice.[1]

A number of stringent safeguards must be met (see below) in order to be eligible for the prohibited transaction exemption for investment advice.

CCH Pointer: The prohibited transaction exemption provided for investment advice does not alter, in any way, any existing individual or class prohibited transaction exemption provided by statute or by administrative action.

Fiduciary rules and investment advice

Subject to certain requirements, an employer or other person who is a plan fiduciary, other than a fiduciary adviser, is not treated as failing to meet the fiduciary requirements of ERISA solely by reason of providing investment advice as permitted under the provision or by contracting for or otherwise arranging for the advice. This rule applies if: (1) the advice is provided under an arrangement between the employer or plan fiduciary and the fiduciary adviser for the fiduciary adviser to provide investment advice as permitted under the provision; (2) the terms of the arrangement require compliance by the fiduciary adviser with the requirements of the provision; and (3) the terms of the arrangement include a written acknowledgement by the fiduciary adviser that the fiduciary adviser is a plan fiduciary with regard to providing the advice.[2]

The provision does not exempt the employer or a plan fiduciary from fiduciary responsibility under ERISA for the prudent selection and periodic review of a fiduciary adviser who provides investment advice pursuant to an arrangement with the employer or plan fiduciary. The employer or plan fiduciary does not have the duty to monitor the specific investment advice given by a fiduciary adviser. The provision also makes it clear that nothing in the fiduciary responsibility provisions of ERISA is to be construed to preclude using plan assets to pay for reasonable expenses in providing investment advice.

¶2312

Eligible investment advice arrangements

The exemptions provided under the investment advice provision apply in connection with a fiduciary adviser providing investment advice under an "eligible investment advice arrangement." An eligible investment advice arrangement is an arrangement that either (1) provides that any fees (including any commission or compensation) received by the fiduciary adviser for investment advice or with respect to an investment transaction with respect to plan assets do not vary depending on the basis of any investment option selected, or (2) uses a computer model under an investment advice program as described below in connection with the provision of investment advice to a participant or beneficiary.[3] To qualify as an eligible investment advice arrangement, certain audit, disclosure, record retention and other rules (see below) must also be met.

In the case of an eligible investment advice arrangement with respect to a defined contribution plan, the arrangement must be expressly authorized by a plan fiduciary other than (1) the person offering the investment advice program, (2) any person providing investment options under the plan, or (3) any affiliate of (1) or (2).

2011 DOL final regs. EBSA has issued final regulations implementing provisions of the Pension Protection Act of 2006 (PPA; P.L. 109-280) that authorize fiduciary advisers to provide individualized investment advice under eligible investment advice arrangements. The final regulations: define the scope of the fee leveling requirements under an eligible investment advice arrangement; specify the requirements for the certification of model investment advice programs; set forth the conditions under which a fiduciary adviser may elect to be the sole plan fiduciary; explain the circumstances under which an auditor will be deemed sufficiently independent to review an investment arrangement; and provide a voluntary Model Fiduciary Adviser Form for the disclosure of fees, compensation and services. The rules are effective December 27, 2011. See CCH PENSION PLAN GUIDE ¶ 4416 for more information.

The PPA (effective for investment advice provided after 2006) authorized a prohibited transaction exemption that allows "fiduciary advisers" to provide individualized investment advice for a fee to plan participants and beneficiaries under an eligible investment advice arrangement, pursuant to which: (1) portfolio recommendations are generated based on an unbiased computer model that has been audited by an independent third party, or (2) a fiduciary adviser provides investment advice services by charging a flat fee that does not vary depending on the investment option selected by participants (i.e., fee level basis).

The statutory exemption applies to investment advice offered by a fiduciary adviser under an eligible investment advice arrangement to participants and beneficiaries in individual account plans (such as 401(k) plans and IRAs) who are authorized to direct the investment of assets in their individual accounts. Note, the relief does not apply to investment advice provided to plan sponsors and other fiduciaries, but is limited to the recommendations of investment managers to participants and beneficiaries. The final regulations clarify that the conditions of the rules apply only to investment advice that would constitute a prohibited transaction. In addition, the final regulations stress that a plan fiduciary is not statutorily obligated to offer, provide, or otherwise make available investment advice to a participant or beneficiary.

Fiduciary advisers

For purposes of the provision, "fiduciary adviser" is defined as a person who is a fiduciary of the plan by reason of the provision of investment advice to a participant or beneficiary and who is also:

1. registered as an investment adviser under the Investment Advisers Act of 1940 or under laws of the state in which the fiduciary maintains its principal office and place of business;

2. a bank, a similar financial institution supervised by the United States or a state, or a savings association (as defined under the Federal Deposit Insurance Act), but only if the advice is provided through a trust department that is subject to periodic examination and review by federal or state banking authorities;

3. an insurance company qualified to do business under state law;

4. registered as a broker or dealer under the Securities Exchange Act of 1934;

5. an affiliate of any of the preceding; or

6. an employee, agent or registered representative of any of the preceding who satisfies the requirements of applicable insurance, banking and securities laws relating to the provision of advice.[4]

CCH Pointer: A person who develops the computer model or markets the investment advice program or computer model is treated as a person who is a plan fiduciary by reason of the provision of investment advice and is treated as a fiduciary adviser. However, the Secretary of Labor may prescribe rules under which only one fiduciary adviser may elect to be treated as a plan fiduciary.[5]

"Affiliate" means an affiliated person as defined under section 2(a)(3) of the Investment Company Act of 1940. "Registered representative" means a person described in section 3(a)(18) of the Securities Exchange Act of 1934 or a person described in section 202(a)(17) of the Investment Advisers Act of 1940.

A fiduciary adviser is a person who is a plan fiduciary because of the provision of investment advice to participants or beneficiaries.

Computer model for investment advice

As mentioned above, an eligible investment advice arrangement can be an arrangement that uses a qualified computer model under an "investment advice program." The computer model must:

1. apply generally accepted investment theories that take into account the historic returns of different asset classes over defined periods of time,

2. use relevant information about the participant, which may include age, life expectancy, retirement age, risk tolerance, other assets or sources of income, and preferences as to certain types of investments,

3. use prescribed objective criteria to provide asset allocation portfolios comprised of investment options available under the plan,

4. operate in a manner that is not biased in favor of investments offered by the fiduciary adviser or a person with a material affiliation or contractual relationship with the fiduciary adviser, and

5. take into account all investment options under the plan in specifying how a participant's account balance should be invested, and not be inappropriately weighted with respect to any investment option.[6]

The computer model must be certified by an "eligible investment expert" before it is used. The expert must certify, in accordance with any regulations issued by the Secretary of Labor, that the computer model meets the requirements of the law. If, under the regulations, there are material changes to the computer model, a new certification must be obtained for the modified model. An eligible investment expert is any person who meets the requirements of the Secretary of Labor, and who does not bear any material affiliation or contractual relationship with any investment adviser or a related person (or any employee, agent, or registered representative of the investment adviser or related person).[7]

The advice provided by any investment advice program must be exclusive. In other words, it must be the only advice generated by the computer model under the program, and it must occur solely at the direction of the participant or beneficiary. A participant or beneficiary may request other investment advice, but only if the request has not been solicited by any person connected with carrying out the eligible investment advice arrangement.[8]

CCH Pointer: The Secretary of Labor, in consultation with the Secretary of the Treasury, must determine if there is any computer model investment advice program that (1) utilizes relevant information about the account beneficiary, which may include age, life expectancy, retirement age, risk tolerance, other assets or sources of income, and preferences as to certain types of investments, (2) takes into account the full range of investments, including equities and bonds, in determining the options for the investment portfolio of the account beneficiary, and (3) allows the account beneficiary, in directing the investment of assets, sufficient flexibility in obtaining advice to evaluate and select investment options.

Annual audits

A qualified independent auditor must conduct an annual audit of the investment advice arrangement to ensure that it meets the requirements of the new law.[9] The specific findings of the audit must be provided in a written report to the fiduciary that authorized use of the arrangement.[10]

An auditor is deemed "independent" if it is not related to (1) the person offering the arrangement to the plan and (2) any person providing investment options under the plan.[11] An independent auditor is qualified to conduct an audit if written assurance is provided that he or she has the proper technical training or experience and proficiency.[12]

¶2312

Notice and disclosure

Before investment advice is given about securities or other property offered as an investment option, the fiduciary adviser is required to provide to a participant or beneficiary written notification (which may be in electronic form), including information related to:

1. the role of any related party (i.e., any party having a material affiliation or contractual relationship to the financial adviser) with respect to the development of the investment advice program and the selection of available investment options under the plan;

2. the past performance and historical rates of return for each available investment option offered under the plan;

3. any fees or other compensation to be received by the financial adviser or its affiliates (including any compensation provided by a third party) (a) with respect to the provision of the advice or (b) in connection with the sale, acquisition or holding of the security or other property (investment transactions);

4. any material affiliation or contractual relationship of the financial adviser or its affiliate in the security or other property involved in the investment transaction;

5. the manner and circumstances under which any participant or beneficiary information will be used or disclosed;

6. the kinds of services provided by the fiduciary adviser with respect to the advice given;

7. the adviser's status as a fiduciary of the plan; and

8. the ability of the recipient of the advice to enter into a separate arrangement with another adviser that has no material affiliation with, and receives no compensation with respect to, the security or other property.[13]

The information described above must be maintained in accurate form by the fiduciary adviser at all times while the advisory services are being provided to the participant or beneficiary. Further, the information must be provided to the advice recipient, without charge, at least annually or upon request, as well as at a time reasonably contemporaneous to any material change to the information provided. The notification must be conspicuous and clearly written, designed so as to be understood by the average plan participant, and sufficiently accurate and comprehensive so as to reasonably inform participants and beneficiaries of the required information.[14]

CCH Pointer: Investment advisers are liable under the Investment Company Act for breach of fiduciary duty if they charge a fee that is "so disproportionately large that it has no reasonable relationship to the services rendered and could not have been the product of arm's length bargaining," according to the U.S. Supreme Court.[15] Thus, mere disclosure of fees is not sufficient to satisfy Investment Company Act, and the fee assessment may be subject to review if the party alleging the breach can prove that the fee is outside the acceptable range.

Maintaining evidence of compliance. A record retention rule applies to fiduciary advisers under both the Code and ERISA. The fiduciary adviser must maintain any records necessary for determining whether the prohibited transaction exemption requirements were met for at least six years after providing the investment advice.[16]

---

[1] Code Sec. 4975(d)(17) and ERISA Sec. 408(b)(14), as added by the Pension Protection Act of 2006 (P.L. 109-280).

[2] ERISA Sec. 408(g)(1), as added by P.L. 109-280; Joint Committee on Taxation, Technical Explanation of the Pension Protection Act of 2006 (JCX-38-06).

[3] Code Sec. 4975(f)(8)(B) and ERISA Sec. 408(g)(3), as added by P.L. 109-280.

[4] Code Sec. 4975(f)(8)(J) and ERISA Sec. 408(g)(11), as added by P.L. 109-280.

[5] Code Sec. 4975(f)(8)(J) and ERISA Sec. 408(g)(11)(A), as added by P.L. 109-280.

[6] Code Sec. 4975(f)(8)(C)(ii) and ERISA Sec. 408(g)(3)(B), as added by P.L. 109-280.

[7] Code Sec. 4975(f)(8)(C)(iii) and ERISA Sec. 408(g)(3)(C), as added by P.L. 109-280.

[8] Code Sec. 4975(f)(8)(C)(iv) and ERISA Sec. 408(g)(3)(D), as added by P.L. 109-280.

[9] Code Sec. 4975(f)(8)(E)(i) and ERISA Sec. 408(g)(5), as added by P.L. 109-280.

[10] Code Sec. 4975(f)(8)(E)(i)(II) and ERISA Sec. 408(g)(5), as added by P.L. 109-280.

[11] Code Sec. 4975(f)(8)(E)(iii) and ERISA Sec. 408(g)(5), as added by P.L. 109-280.

[12] Code Sec. 4975(f)(8)(E)(i) and ERISA Sec. 408(g)(5), as added by P.L. 109-280.

[13] Code Sec. 4975(f)(8)(F)(i) and ERISA Sec. 408(g)(6)(A), as added by P.L. 109-280.

[14] Code Sec. 4975(f)(8)(F)(ii) and (H)(i) and ERISA Sec. 408(g)(6)(B) and (8)(A), as added by P.L. 109-280.

[15] *Jones, et al. v. Harris Associates*, US Sup Ct (2010),

[16] Code Sec. 4975(f)(8)(I) and ERISA Sec. 409(g)(9), as added by P.L. 109-280.

¶ 2315

WHO IS A FIDUCIARY?: Broker-Dealers

Generally, broker-dealers who execute securities transactions on behalf of employee benefit plans are not fiduciaries. However, broker-dealers who exercise discretionary authority over plan assets will be treated as fiduciaries.

Individuals who may qualify for an exemption from fiduciary status include:[1]

1. brokers or dealers registered under the Securities Exchange Act of 1934;

2. reporting dealers that make primary markets in securities of the U.S. or their agents; and

3. banks supervised by the U.S. or a state.

These individuals escape fiduciary status if they are not affiliated with the fiduciary and if the plan fiduciary's instructions specify the security to be purchased or sold, the price range, a time span (not to exceed 5 business days), and the minimum and maximum quantity which may be purchased or sold.[2] In other words, these persons will not be deemed to be fiduciaries solely because they execute transactions for the purchase or sale of securities on behalf of the plan in the ordinary course of their business as brokers, dealers, or banks, pursuant to instructions of a plan fiduciary.

Broker-dealers as fiduciaries

Broker-dealers, reporting dealers, and banks may be plan fiduciaries if they possess or exercise discretionary control in the management of plan assets in connection with the purchase or sale of securities. However, they are fiduciaries only with respect to assets over which they have discretionary authority, control or responsibility.[3]

[2] ERISA Reg. §2510.3-21(d)(1); IRS Reg. §54.4975-9(d)(1).

[1] ERISA Reg. §2510.3-21(d)(1); IRS Reg. §54.4975-9(d)(1).

[3] ERISA Reg. §2510.3-21(d)(2); IRS Reg. §54.4975-9(d)(2).

¶ 2320

WHO IS A FIDUCIARY?: Persons Banned from Service as Fiduciaries

Individuals who have been convicted of certain crimes are prohibited from serving as fiduciaries of employee benefit plans. This prohibition lasts for 13 years after the date of the conviction or, if the individual is imprisoned following the conviction, 13 years after the end of imprisonment.[1]

List of offenses

The offenses that preclude an individual from serving as a fiduciary include:[2]

1. robbery;
2. bribery;
3. extortion;
4. embezzlement;
5. fraud;
6. grand larceny;
7. burglary;
8. arson;
9. murder;
10. rape;
11. kidnapping;
12. perjury;
13. assault with intent to kill;
14. a felony violation of federal or state law involving "controlled substances" as defined in the Comprehensive Drug Abuse Prevention and Control Act of 1970;
15. any crime described in section 9(a)(1) of the Investment Company Act of 1940;
16. mail fraud;
17. acceptance of kickbacks from public works employees;

18. a violation relating to false statements and concealment of facts concerning documents required under the Welfare and Pension Plans Disclosure Act;

19. influencing or injuring an officer, juror, or witness in any federal court or before a federal magistrate;

20. obstruction of proceedings before federal departments, agencies, or committees;

21. a violation relating to the theft or alteration of records and process and false bail in any federal court;

22. obstruction of investigations of violations of any federal criminal statute;

23. interference with commerce by threats and violence;

24. the offer, acceptance, or solicitation to influence operations of employee benefit plans;

25. a violation of section 302 of the Labor-Management Relations Act, 1947, which places restrictions on financial transactions, such as on the payment or lending of money by an employer to employees, employee representatives, or labor organizations;

26. a violation of the Labor-Management Reporting and Disclosure Act of 1959 (which sets forth numerous bonding requirements);

27. a violation of any provision of ERISA; and

28. any felony involving abuse or misuse of such person's position, or employment in a labor organization or employee benefit plan to seek or obtain an illegal gain at the expense of the members of the labor organization or the beneficiaries of the employee benefit plan.

The same prohibition applies to persons convicted of a conspiracy to commit any of the above-listed crimes or any crime in which any of the above-listed crimes is an element. In addition, no person may knowingly permit any other person to serve as a fiduciary or in certain other roles in violation of the prohibition.

Other affected parties

In addition to the ban on service as a fiduciary, a person convicted of one of the enumerated crimes cannot serve an employee benefit plan in the following capacity:[3]

1. administrator;

2. officer;

3. trustee;

4. custodian;

5. counsel;

6. agent;

7. employee;

8. consultant or adviser; and

9. any capacity that involves decision-making authority or custody or control of assets of an employee benefit plan.

Restoration of right to serve as fiduciary

The prohibition against serving as a fiduciary for an employee benefit plan may be lifted before the end of the prescribed 13-year period in two situations.[4]

The first situation is when a person's citizenship rights have been revoked as a result of the conviction and are later fully restored.

Second, the ban does not apply when a court determines that a convicted person could serve as a fiduciary without violating the purposes of ERISA's provisions on the protection of employee benefit rights. If a federal offense is involved, the sentencing judge makes this determination. In the case of a state offense, a United States district court makes the determination.

No corporation or partnership may be precluded from acting as a fiduciary (or in any capacity listed above) without a notice, hearing, and determination by the court that such service could be inconsistent with the prohibition.

Conviction and appeal

ERISA requires the disqualification of a fiduciary immediately upon conviction. The person cannot remain in office pending the outcome of an appeal.[5] The individual's salary will continue to be paid, but it will be placed into an escrow account. If the person's conviction is overturned on appeal, the amounts will be paid to him. If the person's conviction is sustained on appeal, the amounts will be returned to the individual or organization responsible for paying his salary.[6]

Penalty

The penalty for the intentional violation of the ban on service as a fiduciary is a fine of not more than $10,000 or imprisonment for not more than five years, or both.[7]

---

[1] ERISA Sec. 411(a).

[2] *Ibid.*

[3] *Ibid.*

[4] *Ibid.*

[5] ERISA Sec. 411(c)(1).

[6] ERISA Sec. 411(d).

[7] ERISA Sec. 411(b).

¶ 2325

GENERAL FIDUCIARY RULES: Plans Covered by Fiduciary Rules

Generally, the fiduciary rules of ERISA apply to employee benefit plans that are established or maintained by an employer or an employee organization, or both.[1] The employer or employee organization must be engaged in an industry or activity that affects commerce. The fiduciary rules apply to both pension plans and welfare plans.[2]

Courts have ruled that an employee benefit plan is established under ERISA, if from the "surrounding circumstances," a reasonable person can ascertain the intended benefits, a class of beneficiaries, the source of financing, and procedures for receiving benefits.[3] A plan need not be formalized in writing, as long as it is more than a mere decision to extend benefits.[4]

Plans exempted from fiduciary rules

The fiduciary rules do not apply to certain plans. These exempted plans include:[5]

1. governmental plans;
2. church plans for which no election has been made to have the participation, vesting, and funding provisions of ERISA apply;
3. plans maintained solely for complying with applicable workmen's compensation laws or unemployment or disability insurance laws;
4. plans maintained outside of the U.S. primarily for the benefit of persons substantially all of whom are nonresident aliens;
5. excess benefit plans which are unfunded;
6. unfunded plans maintained by employers primarily for the purpose of providing deferred compensation for a select group of management or highly compensated employees; and
7. any agreement described in Code Sec. 736 which provides payments to a retired or deceased partner or a deceased partner's successor in interest.

ERISA Preemption. As discussed at ¶ 2726, ERISA is intended to be the exclusive law in the area of employee benefit plans. Thus, if one of the above plans is exempt under ERISA, it cannot fall under state fiduciary standards because ERISA preempts state laws that relate to an employee benefit plan.[6]

Mutual funds

The mere investment by a plan in the shares of a mutual fund is not sufficient to cause the assets of the fund to be considered the assets of the plan. On the other hand, a plan's assets do include the shares of a mutual fund held by the plan.[7] However, a mutual fund may be a fiduciary if it acts *in connection with* a plan covering the employees of the investment company, the investment adviser, or its principal underwriter.[8]

Insurance companies

The assets of a plan to which a guaranteed benefit policy is issued by an insurer include that policy but do not, solely because of the issuance of such policy, include any assets of the insurer.[9] A "guaranteed benefit policy" is an insurance policy or contract that provides for benefits that are guaranteed by the insurer. The term also includes any surplus in a separate account, but excludes any other portion of a separate account. If the policy guarantees basic payments but other payments may vary with, for instance, investment performance, then the variable part of the policy and the assets attributable thereto are not to be considered as guaranteed. Instead, they are treated as plan assets subject to the fiduciary rules. Such assets, however, need not be held in trust under the fiduciary rules.[10]

Separate accounts. Typically, assets that are placed in a separate account are managed by the insurance company and payments to plan participants are generally based on the investment performance of these particular assets. Consequently, insurance companies are responsible under the general fiduciary rules with respect to assets held under separate account contracts, and the assets of these contracts are considered as plan assets (but need not be held in trust). However, to the extent that insurance companies place some of their own funds in these separate accounts to provide for contingencies, this separate account "surplus" is not subject to the fiduciary rules.[11]

General accounts. "General accounts" are all assets of an insurance company that are not legally segregated and allocated to separate accounts. The assets in such accounts can be commingled with the insurance companies' own funds. The U.S. Supreme Court has held that certain pension assets held in the general accounts of insurance companies constitute plan assets under ERISA.[12] Therefore, such assets are subject to the fiduciary provisions of ERISA, including the rules prohibiting certain transactions involving the assets of an employee benefit plan. See ¶ 2330.

Group insurance. An "employee welfare benefit plan" does not include a group insurance program offered by an insurer to employees under which:[13]

1. no employer contributions are made;

2. employee participation is completely voluntary;

3. the sole functions of the employer are, without endorsing the program, to permit an insurer to publicize a program to employees, to collect premiums through payroll deductions or dues checkoffs, and to remit the premiums to the insurer; and

4. the only compensation an employer receives is reasonable compensation (excluding profit) for administrative services rendered in connection with premium collection.

Individual retirement accounts

An IRA is not an employee benefit plan as long as:[14]

1. no contributions are made by an employer or employee association;

2. participation is completely voluntary;

3. any involvement of the employer does not include endorsing the program but is limited to permitting the sponsor to publicize the program to employees or members of the employee association and to collecting contributions through payroll deductions and remitting them to the sponsor; and

    4. the employer receives no payments other than reasonable payments for services rendered in connection with the payroll deductions.

Tax-sheltered annuities

A tax-sheltered annuity program maintained pursuant to salary reduction agreements is not a plan covered by ERISA's fiduciary rules if the following requirements are met:[15]

    1. participation is completely voluntary;

    2. all rights under the contract are enforceable only by the employee, beneficiary, or authorized representative;

    3. the employer's involvement is generally limited to permitting annuity contractors to publicize their products; requesting information concerning proposed funding media, products, or annuity contractors; limiting funding media or products available; summarizing relevant information for employee review; collecting salary reduction amounts; and holding group annuity contracts covering its employees in its name; and

    4. the only compensation the employer receives is for duties performed pursuant to the salary reduction agreements.

☐ Tax-sheltered annuities are discussed in detail beginning at ¶ 3100.

Mortgage pool certificates

Where an employee benefit plan acquires mortgage pool certificates that are guaranteed by the Government National Mortgage Association, the Federal National Mortgage Association, the Federal Home Loan Mortgage Company, or the Federal Agricultural Mortgage Corporation, the plan's assets include the certificates but do not include the mortgages underlying these governmental mortgage pools.[16] As a result, the sponsors or managers of these mortgage pools will not be subject to ERISA's fiduciary requirements merely because of a plan's investment in the pool.

---

[1] ERISA Secs. 4(a) and 401(a).

[2] ERISA Sec. 3(3).

[3] See, e.g., *Donovan v. Dillingham*, CA-11 (1982), 688 F2d 1367; *Scott v. Gulf Oil Corp.*, CA-9 (1985) 754 F2d 1499; *Harris v. Arkansas Book Co.*, CA-8 (1986), 794 F2d 358; *Brown v. Ampco-Pittsburgh Corp.*, CA-6 (1989), 876 F2d 546; *Elmore v. Cone Mills Corp.*, CA-4 (1994), 23 F3d 855.

[4] *James v. National Business Systems*, CA-7 (1991), 924 F2d 718; *Ed Miniat, Inc. v. Globe Life Ins. Group, Inc.*, CA-7 (1986), 805 F2d 732, *cert. denied* 482 US 915; *Donovan v. Dillingham*, CA-11 (1982), 688 F2d 1367.

[5] ERISA Sec. 401(a).

[6] ERISA Sec. 514.

[7] ERISA Secs. 3(21)(B) and 401(b)(1); ERISA Reg. §2509.75-3 (ERISA Interpretive Bulletin 75-3).

[8] P.L. 93-406 (ERISA), Conference Committee Report.

[9] ERISA Sec. 401(b)(2).

[10] ERISA Sec. 401(b)(2); P.L. 93-406 (ERISA), Conference Committee Report.

[11] P.L. 93-406 (ERISA), Conference Committee Report.

[12] *John Hancock Mutual Life Insurance Company v. Harris Trust & Savings Bank,* US Sup Ct (1993), 510 US 86.

[13] ERISA Reg. §2510.3-1(j).

[14] ERISA Reg. §2510.3-2(d).

[15] ERISA Reg. §2510.3-2(f)(4).

[16] ERISA Reg. § 2510.3-101(i)(2); ERISA Opinion Letter 99-05A, 2-22-99.

¶ 2330

GENERAL FIDUCIARY RULES: Plan Assets Defined

The issue of what constitutes plan assets is important for two reasons. First, an individual who handles plan assets is considered a fiduciary. Second, once an individual becomes a fiduciary, he violates fiduciary duties if plan assets are handled improperly.

Regulations specify when participant contributions and plan investments are considered plan assets.[1] However, ERISA and the regulations are generally silent on the issue of plan assets under other circumstances.

Participant contributions are plan assets

Amounts that a participant or beneficiary pays to an employer, or amounts that a participant has withheld from wages for contributions to a plan, are plan assets.[2] The amounts become plan assets as of the earliest date on which they can reasonably be segregated from the employer's general assets.[3]

Contributions to pension plans. Employee contributions to pension plans become plan assets and must, therefore, be paid to the plan no later than the 15th business day of the month following the month in which the contributions were withheld or received by the employer.[4] Under prior rules, contributions to pension plans became plan assets no later than 90 days after the date on which the amounts were received by the employer (or would otherwise have been payable to the employee in cash).

Employers that sponsor pension plans may obtain an extension of 10 business days before they will be required to deposit participant contributions received or withheld in a single month.[5]

Contributions to SIMPLE IRAs. The maximum time period by which salary reduction contributions must be made to a SIMPLE IRA is no later than 30 calendar days following the month in which amounts would otherwise have been payable to the employee in cash.[6]

Contributions to welfare plans. Participant contributions to a welfare plan become plan assets as of the earliest date on which they can be reasonably segregated from the employer's general assets, but in no event later than 90 days from the date on which the contributions are received or withheld by the employer.[7]

Union dues. Amounts paid as union dues are not to be characterized as participant contributions merely because a portion of such dues might be used to provide benefits under a welfare or pension plan sponsored by an employee organization.[8]

Violations. Employers who fail to transmit contributions promptly and plan fiduciaries who fail to collect those amounts in a timely manner will violate the fiduciary requirement that plan assets be held in trust (see ¶ 2340). In addition, such employers and fiduciaries may be engaging in prohibited transactions (see ¶ 2400 and following).[9]

Discontinued operations. The fact that 401(k) plan participants received their full distribution upon the plan sponsor's discontinuation of operations did not excuse the company's failure to remit elective deferrals to the plan.[10]

Plan investments

Generally, when a plan invests in another entity, the plan's assets include its investment but do not, solely by reason of the investment, include any of the underlying assets of the entity.[11]

"Look-through rule." A special "look-through" rule provides that the underlying assets of an entity can constitute plan assets. This rule applies where a plan invests in an equity interest of an entity that is neither a publicly offered security nor a security issued by a mutual fund.[12] In this case, plan assets include both the equity interest and an undivided interest in each of the underlying assets of the entity. In these situations, a person who exercises authority or control over the underlying assets or who provides investment advice is a fiduciary of the investing plan.

Exceptions. Thus, the "look-through rule" does not apply to investments in debt instruments. Furthermore, it does not apply to publicly offered securities, even where the offering of securities is made primarily to plans.

The "look-through" rule does not apply where:[13]

1. the entity is an operating company; or
2. equity participation in the entity by benefit plan investors is not significant.

Operating company. An "operating company" is a company which is engaged primarily in the production or sale of a product or service other than the investment of capital. The term includes "real estate operating companies" and "venture capital operating companies." An entity does not constitute a venture capital operating company prior to its first venture capital investment.[14] A partnership that is primarily engaged in the production or the sale of a product or service other than the investment of capital may qualify as a venture capital operating company.[15]

Insignificant equity participation. Equity participation is not significant where, immediately after the most recent acquisition of any equity interest in the entity, plans and certain similar investors do not hold more than 25% of the value of any class of equity interests in an entity.[16] The redemption of a partner's equity interest in a partnership would constitute an "acquisition" for purposes of the preceding definition.[17]

Insurance company separate accounts. The underlying assets of an insurance company's separate account that is maintained for a plan are plan assets if the investors bear all of the investment risk.[18]

¶2330

Other amounts considered as plan assets

While ERISA regulations define plan assets in the case of employee contributions and plan investments, they do not provide guidance in other situations. According to the Labor Department, plan assets generally include any property, tangible or intangible, in which the plan has a beneficial ownership interest.[19] For example, a beneficial interest exists when:

1. an employer establishes a trust on behalf of a plan;
2. the employer sets up a separate account with a bank or other third party in the name of the plan; or
3. the plan documents state that separately maintained funds belong to the plans.

However, the segregation of employer funds to facilitate plan administration would not, in and of itself, show an intent to create a beneficial interest in those assets on behalf of the plan.

Insurance company general accounts

In *John Hancock Mutual Life Insurance Co. v. Harris Trust and Savings Bank*, the U.S. Supreme Court held that certain pension assets held in the general accounts of insurance companies constitute plan assets under ERISA.[20] Therefore, such assets are subject to the fiduciary provisions of ERISA, including the rules prohibiting certain transactions involving the assets of an employee benefit plan. "General accounts" are all assets of an insurance company that are not legally segregated and allocated to separate accounts. The assets in such accounts can be commingled with the insurance companies' own funds.

Safe harbor for transition policies issued before 1999. Congress empowered the Department of Labor with authority to issue regulations clarifying the status of plan assets held in insurance company general accounts, in order to provide relief for insurance companies affected by the *Hancock* decision.[21] The DOL subsequently finalized regulations providing that, when a plan acquires a policy or contract of insurance (other than a guaranteed benefit policy) that is issued by an insurer before 1999, and that is supported by assets of the insurer's general account (i.e., a "transition policy"), the plan's assets include the policy, but will not include any of the underlying assets of the insurer's general account if the insurer satisfies stipulated disclosure rules, termination procedures, and certain other requirements.[22]

Seven-day safe harbor for contributions to small plans. Effective on January 14, 2010, the Employee Benefits Security Administration (EBSA) has finalized regulations, applicable primarily to defined contribution plans with fewer than 100 participants at the beginning of the plan year, that provide a seven-business-day safe harbor period for employers to deposit participant contributions. Thus, for small contributory pension and plans, amounts deposited no later than the seventh business day following the day in which the amounts are received by an employer or withheld from a participant's wages will be deemed contributed to the plan on the earliest date on which the contributions could be reasonably be segregated from the employer's general assets. EBSA has also amended the regulations to explicitly subject repayments of participant loans to the same rules as other participant contributions (i.e., for both the general rule and for the safe harbor).

Criminal penalties

Since ERISA regulations define plan assets only for purposes of ERISA Title I (which relates to the protection of employee benefit rights) and the related prohibited transaction provisions of the Internal Revenue Code, they may not be relied upon to bar criminal prosecutions under 18 U.S.C. § 664. This statute makes it a criminal offense to embezzle, convert, or steal assets of an employee plan or related fund.

[1] ERISA Reg. §§ 2510.3-101 and 2509.75-2.

[2] ERISA Reg. § 2510.3-102(a).

[3] ERISA Reg. § 2510.3-102(a).

[4] ERISA Reg. § 2510.3-102(b).

[5] ERISA Reg. § 2510.3-102(d)(1).

[6] ERISA Reg. § 2510.3-102(b)(2).

[7] ERISA Reg. § 2510.3-102(c).

[8] ERISA Reg. § 2510.3-102(a); Preamble to ERISA Reg. § 2510.3-102, 5-17-88 (53 FR 17628).

[9] Preamble to ERISA Reg. § 2510.3-102, 12-20-95 (60 FR 66036).

[10] U.S. v. Eriksen, (CA-9), (2011).

[11] ERISA Reg. § 2510.3-101(a)(2).

[12] Ibid.

[13] Ibid.

[14] ERISA Opinion Letter 89-15A, 8-3-89.

[15] ERISA Opinion Letter 89-04A, 3-30-89.

[16] ERISA Reg. § 2510.3-101(f).

[17] ERISA Opinion Letter 89-05A, 4-5-89.

[18] ERISA Reg. § 2510.3-101(h)(1)(iii).

[19] ERISA Opinion Letter 92-24A, 11-6-92.

[20] *John Hancock Mutual Life Insurance Company v. Harris Trust & Savings Bank,* US Sup Ct (1993), 510 US 86. *Hancock* overturned two decades of insurance industry practice that had been supported by a DOL interpretive bulletin. The interpretive bulletin provided that if an insurance company issues a contract or policy of insurance to an employee benefit plan and places the consideration of such contract or policy in its general asset account, the assets in such account are not considered to be plan assets. See ERISA Reg. § 2509.75-2.

[21] P.L. 104-188, Small Business Job Protection Act of 1996.

[22] ERISA Reg. § 2550.401c-1(a) and ERISA Reg. § 2550.401d-1(h)(6).

¶ 2335

GENERAL FIDUCIARY RULES: Establishment of Plan—Provision for Named Fiduciaries

Generally, every employee benefit plan that is subject to the fiduciary responsibility requirements must be established and maintained pursuant to a written instrument (see ¶ 306).[1] This instrument is required to provide for one or more named fiduciaries who, jointly or severally, are to have authority to control and manage the operation and administration of the plan.

Named fiduciaries must be named in the plan

A "named fiduciary" is a fiduciary who is named in the plan instrument or who, in accordance with a procedure specified in the plan, is identified as a fiduciary either by an employer or employee organization (or both).[2] An employee benefit plan covering employees of a corporation may designate the corporation as a "named fiduciary."[3]

Examples of named fiduciaries. A named fiduciary may be a person whose name actually appears in the plan document, or may be a person who holds an office specified in the document, such as the company president. A named fiduciary also may be a person who is identified by the employer or union, under a procedure set out in the document. For example, the plan may provide that the employer's board of directors is to choose the person who manages or controls the plan. In addition, a named fiduciary may be a person identified by the employer and union, acting jointly. Thus, the members of a joint board of trustees of a Taft- Hartley plan would usually be named fiduciaries.[4]

Fiduciary liability limited to specific responsibilities. If a plan allocates specific duties to named fiduciaries, each fiduciary is responsible only for those assigned responsibilities.[5] Absent an allegation of co-fiduciary liability (see ¶ 2385), personal liability of a fiduciary is limited to the fiduciary role performed for the plan.[6] Named fiduciaries are not liable for acts or omissions properly allocated to other fiduciaries.[7]

Requirements for plans subject to fiduciary responsibility

In addition, every employee benefit plan subject to the fiduciary responsibility requirements is required to:[8]

1. provide a procedure for establishing and carrying out a funding policy and method consistent with the objectives of the plan and the ERISA requirements relating to the protection of employee benefit rights;

2. describe any procedure under the plan for the allocation of responsibilities for the operation and administration of the plan;

3. provide a procedure for amending the plan and for identifying the persons who have authority to amend the plan; and

4. specify the basis on which payments are made to and from the plan.

The procedures relating to funding enable plan fiduciaries to determine the plan's short- and long-term financial needs and communicate these requirements to the appropriate persons. For example, with a retirement plan, it is expected that under this procedure the persons who manage the plan will determine whether the plan has a short-term need for liquidity (e.g., to pay benefits) or whether liquidity is a long-term goal and investment growth is a more current need. This, in turn, should be communicated to the persons responsible for investments, so that investment policy can be appropriately coordinated with plan needs.[9]

As indicated, plan documents are required to set out the basis for contributions to and payments from the plan. Thus, the plan must specify what part (if any) of the contributions are to come from employees and what part from employers. Also, it must specify the basis on which payments are to be made to participants and beneficiaries.[10]

Allocation and delegation of fiduciary responsibilities

A person who is a named fiduciary with respect to the control or management of plan assets may appoint an investment manager to manage the plan assets.[11]

---

[1] ERISA Sec. 402(a)(1).

[2] ERISA Sec. 402(a)(2).

[3] ERISA Reg. § 2509.75-5, FR-3 (ERISA Interpretive Bulletin 75-5).

[4] P.L. 93-406 (ERISA), Conference Committee Report.

[5] ERISA Reg. § 2509.75-8, FR-16.

[6] ERISA Reg. § 2509.75-8, FR-13.

[7] ERISA Reg. § 2509.75-8, D-4.

[8] ERISA Sec. 402(b).

[9] P.L. 93-406 (ERISA), Conference Committee Report.

[10] *Ibid.*

[11] ERISA Sec. 402(c)(3); P.L. 93-406 (ERISA), Conference Committee Report.

¶ 2340

GENERAL FIDUCIARY RULES: Assets Required to Be Held in Trust

All assets of an employee benefit plan generally must be held in trust by one or more trustees pursuant to a written instrument. The trustees are required to be either named in the trust instrument or plan instrument or appointed by a person who is a named fiduciary.[1]

As noted at ¶ 2330, employers who fail to promptly transmit participant contributions and fiduciaries who fail to timely collect such contributions violate the requirement that plan assets be held in trust.[2] The actions of such employers and fiduciaries may also constitute a prohibited transaction (see ¶ 2400 and following).

Trustees' authority

After the individuals accept their appointment as trustees, they have exclusive authority and discretion to manage and control the assets of the plan. However, this authority and discretion is limited to the extent that:[3]

1. the plan expressly provides that the trustees are subject to the direction of a named fiduciary who is not a trustee; or

2. the authority to manage, acquire, or dispose of assets of the plan is delegated to one or more investment managers.

Consequently, a plan may provide for an investment committee to direct plan investments. Since investment decisions are basic to plan operations, members of such an investment committee must be named fiduciaries. For example, the plan could provide that the investment committee consists of the president, vice-president for finance, and comptroller of the employer. If the plan so provides, a trustee must follow the committee's directions unless it is clear that any actions taken under those directions would be prohibited by the fiduciary responsibility rules or would be contrary to the terms of the plan or trust.[4] If a named fiduciary delegates authority to manage plan assets to an investment manager, the trustee is not liable for any act of the manager.

CCH Pointer: The EBSA has released a Field Assistance Bulletin that provides guidance on the responsibilities under ERISA of a directed trustee to carry out transactions involving employer securities according to instructions from a named fiduciary.[5] The EBSA makes clear that the named fiduciary, not the directed trustee, is primarily responsible for ensuring the prudence of plan investment decisions. A directed trustee is required to question the directing fiduciary's instructions regarding transactions involving publicly traded securities only in rare circumstances. For example, a directed trustee may have to question directions involving the purchase or holding of a security where there are "clear and compelling public indicators" that call into question the issuer's viability as a going concern.

When a directed trustee has non-public information regarding a security that is necessary for a prudent decision by the directing plan fiduciary, the directed trustee has a duty to inquire about the named fiduciary's knowledge and consideration of the information.

Exception for certain types of assets

The requirement that the assets of a plan be held in trust does not apply:[6]

1. to any assets of a plan which consist of insurance contracts or policies issued by an insurance company qualified to do business in a state;

2. to any assets of such an insurance company or any assets of a plan which are held by the insurer;

3. to a plan in which some or all of the participants are self-employed individuals or which consist of IRAs, to the extent that such plan's assets are held in one or more qualified custodial accounts;

4. to a plan which the Secretary of Labor has exempted from the requirement that assets be held in trust and which is not subject to any of the participation, vesting, funding, and plan termination insurance provisions of ERISA; or

5. to a tax-sheltered annuity contract (under Code Sec. 403(b)) to the extent that the assets of the contract are held in one or more custodial accounts (under Code Sec. 403(b)(7)).

---

[1] ERISA Sec. 403(a); ERISA Reg. § 2550.403a-1(a).

[2] Preamble to ERISA Proposed Reg. § 2510.3-102, 12-20-95 (60 FR 66036).

[3] ERISA Sec. 403(a); ERISA Reg. § 2550.403a-1(c).

[4] P.L. 93-406 (ERISA), Conference Committee Report.

[5] Field Assistance Bulletin 2004-03, 12-17-04, CCH PENSION PLAN GUIDE ¶ 19,980R.

[6] ERISA Sec. 403(b); ERISA Reg. § 2550.403b-1(a). Note that the requirement that the assets of a plan be held in trust also does not apply to certain unfunded arrangements that compensate retired employees for benefits that were forfeited by employees under a pre-ERISA plan maintained by a former employer.

¶ 2345

FIDUCIARY DUTIES: Exclusive Benefit Rule

The fiduciary rules provide that the assets of a plan may never inure to the benefit of any employer and must be held exclusively for the purposes of providing benefits to plan participants and their beneficiaries and defraying reasonable expenses of administering the plan.[1]

The U.S. Supreme Court has ruled that the anti-inurement rule does not preclude Title I coverage of working owner participants in ERISA plans that also cover one or more non-owner employees.[2]

Violation of the exclusive benefit rule

Fiduciaries may be liable for violating the "exclusive benefit" rule even where there is no loss to the plan or its beneficiaries. The nature of the breach of duty is not the *loss* of plan assets but instead the *risking* of assets.[3] However, there must be a causal connection between the breach of fiduciary duty and losses incurred by the plan.[4] A breaching fiduciary must restore to the plan any profits made through the improper use of plan assets. See ¶ 2380 for more on fiduciary liability.

Economically targeted investments (ETIs). Economically targeted investments that are selected for the economic benefits they create in addition to the investment return provided to the employee benefit plan, are not incompatible with ERISA's fiduciary standards.

ETIs are governed by the same ERISA standards of exclusivity and prudence that apply to other plan investments. According to the Department of Labor, ETIs are consistent with ERISA's exclusive benefit standard if they:[5]

1. generate a rate of return that is commensurate with competing investments of similar risk characteristics, and

2. are an otherwise appropriate investment for the plan, as determined by standards of investment diversification and the investment policy of the plan.

Handling of plan funds

Fiduciaries must take care to clearly differentiate their own money from plan funds. Failure to do so constitutes a violation of ERISA fiduciary responsibility rules.[6]

Disclosure of plan information

A plan administrator may not have a fiduciary duty to disclose plan information unless it relates to the provision of benefits. In determining that an employer violated its fiduciary duty to act exclusively in the interests of plan participants and beneficiaries by making misrepresentations regarding the future security of plan benefits following a corporate restructure, the U.S. Supreme Court refused to address the issue of whether ERISA imposes upon fiduciaries the duty to disclose truthful information on their own initiative or in response to employee inquiries.[7]

The Court, however, did note that there is more to plan administration than simply complying with the specific duties imposed by the plan or ERISA.

☐ A fiduciary's affirmative duty to disclose benefits information under the prudent person rule is discussed at ¶ 2355.

Failure to make contributions

Fiduciaries must notify insured participants of an employer's failure to make premium payments.[8] "At a minimum," the fiduciary obligation of a trustee requires notification of pensioners that an employer has failed to make required contributions.[9]

Plan audits

The plan trustee's obligation to preserve and maintain trust assets requires it to identify eligible plan beneficiaries. Common law vests trustees with all powers necessary or appropriate for carrying out trust purposes. Accordingly, a plan trustee *may* request an audit of an employer's payroll, tax, and other personnel records to determine whether employees are eligible plan participants.[10] ERISA does *not require* plan trustees to conduct such an audit. However, ERISA also does not prohibit an audit that is authorized by the trust instrument and that serves the legitimate purposes of the plan.

Reasonable expenses of plan administration

Plan assets may be used to defray the reasonable expenses of plan administration. Whether the payment of a particular expense is an appropriate expenditure of plan assets is a facts and circumstances decision that is largely determined by whether payment of the expense is authorized by plan documents and consistent with ERISA standards of fiduciary conduct.[11] Reasonable expenses of plan administration include direct expenses properly and actually incurred in the performance of a fiduciary's duties to the plans.

Decision to pay expenses from plan assets. The determination as to whether to pay expenses from plan assets is a fiduciary act. The payment of the expenses must be authorized by the plan and be in the interests of plan participants and beneficiaries. The expenses also may not exceed a reasonable amount.

Generally, the documents and instruments governing the plan will determine whether plan assets may be used to cover administrative expenses. However, if the plan document is silent as to the payment of administrative expenses, the plan must pay reasonable administrative expenses.[12]

CCH Pointer: The EBSA has issued a Field Assistance Bulletin that clarifies and expands the ability of 401(k) and other defined contribution plans to allocate administrative expenses, including those incurred with respect to QDRO determinations and processing hardship withhdrawals, to the individual accounts of participants and beneficiaries.[13] The IRS has further clarified that defined contribution plans do not fail to satisfy the restrictions on mandatory distributions in Code Sec. 411(a)(11) merely because the plans charge former

¶2345

employees' accounts a pro rata share of the plans' reasonable administrative expenses without charging those expenses to current employees' accounts.[14]

Expenses incident to maintaining tax qualification may be paid from plan assets. The EBSA has previously acknowledged in Advisory Opinion 97-03A that the tax qualified status of a plan confers benefits upon both the plan sponsor and the plan. Accordingly, a portion of the expenses attendant tax-qualified activities may be reasonable plan expenses that may be paid from plan assets.

The EBSA continues to maintain that the formation of a plan as a tax qualified entity is a settlor activity which may not be funded by plan assets. However, implementation of the settlor decision to form the plan may require plan fiduciaries to undertake activities for which a plan may pay reasonable expenses. Such "implementation activities" for which plan assets may be used, include drafting plan amendments required to comply with tax law changes, nondiscrimination testing, and requesting IRS determination letters.[15] By contrast, if maintaining the plan's tax qualified status requires analysis of options for amending the plan from which the plan sponsor makes a choice, the expense incurred in analyzing the options would be settlor expenses.

Apportionment of tax-qualification related expenses not required. Fiduciaries must consider whether tax-qualification activities are settlor in nature in determining whether the costs constitute reasonable plan expenses. However, a fiduciary is not required to take into account the benefit that a plan's tax qualified status confers on the employer.[16] Thus, the fiduciary is not required to apportion all tax-qualification related expenses between the plan and plan sponsor.

Plan termination expenses. Actions taken to implement the termination of the plan (as opposed to the decision to terminate the plan), are generally fiduciary in nature, so reasonable expenses incurred in implementing a plan termination are payable by the plan. Accordingly, a plan may pay expenses incurred in auditing the plan, preparing and filing annual reports, preparing benefit statements and calculating accrued benefits, notifying participants and beneficiaries of their plan benefits, and amending the plan in order to effectuate an orderly termination that benefits participants and beneficiaries.[17]

Plan amendment expenses. Expenses incurred in maintaining a plan's tax qualified status or in obtaining a determination from the IRS regarding the status of a plan in termination may be reasonable expenses of the plan where the plan permits the payment of reasonable expenses from plan assets.[18]

Compliance audits. The DOL has advised that the use of plan assets to purchase an insurance product that includes periodic compliance audits designed to assure that the plan is operated in compliance with plan terms and federal law would be consistent with ERISA's standards of fiduciary conduct, if plan trustees determined that the audits would be a helpful and prudent means of assisting them in implementing their responsibilities, including the duty of operating the plan in accordance with its terms.[19] The DOL cautions that the plan's payments for the audits must be reasonable in light of the benefit conferred on the plan. In addition, payments made for the benefit of parties other than plan participants and beneficiaries, or for services, the cost of which could reasonably be expected to be borne by the plan sponsor or other entity in the normal course of business, would not be reasonable expenses of administering the plan.

IRS sanctions are not reasonable plan expenses. Penalties imposed on plan administrators under Code Sec. 6652 for failure to file stipulated information returns are not reasonable administrative expenses of a plan. The DOL has further suggested that sanctions or penalties imposed on a plan in connection with the settlement of a disqualification matter with the IRS would not be a reasonable administrative expense.[20]

Using plan assets to inform participants about fiduciaries' views on broad public policy issues is not permitted. According to the EBSA, plan fiduciaries may not use plan assets to communicate with plan participants to promote a particular result pertaining to, or disseminate their views on, matters of broad public policy.[21] These expenditures are not for paying out benefits or for plan administration, and, thus, they do not come within the scope of ERISA-permitted expenditures, the EBSA stated. In limited circumstances, however, "where a legislative proposal is near enactment and closely tied to plan issues," a fiduciary could choose to spend plan assets "to educate participants about the need to take the legislation into account in making particular decisions about their options under the plan."

Tax Code requirements

Under the Tax Code, qualified retirement plans must be maintained for the exclusive benefit of the employees and their beneficiaries (see ¶ 321).[22] The IRS has developed general rules that govern the investment of plan assets, including a requirement that the cost of an investment must not exceed fair market value at the time of purchase. In addition, a plan must receive a fair return commensurate with the prevailing rate, sufficient liquidity must be maintained to permit distributions, and the safeguards and diversification that a prudent investor would adhere to must be present.[23] To the extent that a fiduciary meets the prudent man rule of the regulatory provisions of ERISA, he is deemed to meet these aspects of the exclusive benefit requirements under the Tax Code.

[1] ERISA Secs. 403(c)(1) and 404(a)(1)(A).

[2] *Raymond B. Yates, M.D., P.C. Profit Sharing Plan v. Hendon*, US Sup Ct (2004), 541 U.S. 1.

[3] *Sandoval v. Simmons*, DC Ill (1985), 622 FSupp 1174; *Leigh v. Engle*, CA-7 (1984), 727 F2d 113.

[4] *Friend v. Sanwa Bank California*, CA-9 (1994), 35 F3d 466.

[5] PWBA Interpretive Bulletin 94-1, 6-22-94, CCH Pension Plan Guide ¶ 19,970.

[6] *Corley v. The Hecht Co.*, DC D of C (1982), 530 FSupp 1155.

[7] *Howe v. Varity Corp*, US Sup Ct (1996), 516 U.S. 489.

[8] *Rodriguez v. MEBA Pension Trust*, CA-4 (1989), 872 F2d 69.

[9] *Rosen v. Hotel and Restaurant Employees & Bartenders Union*, CA-3 (1980), 637 F2d 592, *cert. denied*, 454 U.S. 898.

[10] *Central States, Southeast and Southwest Areas Pension Fund, et al. v. Central Transport, Inc., et al.*, US Sup Ct (1985), 106 S Ct 17.

[11] DOL Information Letter, 7-26-98.

[12] ERISA Opinion Letter 97-03A, 1-23-97.

[13] EBSA Field Assistance Bulletin 2003-3, 5-19-03, CCH Pension Plan Guide ¶ 19,980E.

[14] IRS Rev. Rul. 2004-10, I.R.B. 2004-7, 2-17-04, CCH Pension Plan Guide ¶ 19,948Z-43.

[15] ERISA Opinion Letter 2001-01A, 1-18-01.

[16] *Ibid.*

[17] *Ibid.*

[18] *Ibid.*

[19]DOL Information Letter, 7-26-98.

[20] *Ibid.*

[21]EBSA Information Letter, 5-3-05, CCH PENSION PLAN GUIDE ¶ 19,980U.

[22] Code Sec. 401(a).

[23]Technical Information Release 1346, 2-5-75.

¶ 2350

FIDUCIARY DUTIES: Exceptions to the Exclusive Benefit Rule

Numerous exceptions apply to the rule that plan assets must be held exclusively for the purposes of providing benefits to plan participants and their beneficiaries and defraying reasonable expenses. The exclusive benefit rule does not apply with respect to:[1]

1. certain mistaken contributions;

2. contributions conditioned on initial plan qualification; and

3. contributions conditioned on their deductibility.

In addition, the exclusive benefit rule does not prevent an employer from recovering excess assets upon the termination of a defined benefit plan.

Mistaken contributions

If a contribution is made by an employer to a single-employer plan under a mistake of fact (such as a clerical or arithmetic error), the exclusive benefit rule does not prohibit the return of the contribution to the employer within one year after the payment of the contribution.[2]

Multiemployer plans. A somewhat broader exception applies in the case of a multiemployer plan. This exception permits the return of a plan contribution or withdrawal liability payment (see ¶ 345) made by an employer to a multiemployer plan by a mistake of fact *or law* within six months after the plan administrator determines that the contribution or liability payment was made by a mistake.[3] Similarly, an overpayment of withdrawal liability may be returned within six months after a determination of overpayment (see ¶ 2908).[4] However, the exception does not apply to contributions or payments made under a mistake relating to whether the plan was qualified.[5]

Contributions conditioned on plan qualification

A return of contributions to the employer is permitted if:[6]

1. the contributions are conditioned on the initial qualification of the plan (under Code Sec. 401(a) or 403(a));

2. the plan does not qualify initially;

3. the application for the determination relating to initial qualification is filed by the due date of the employer's return for the taxable year in which the plan was adopted; and

4. the contributions are returned within one year after the adverse determination as to qualification was made.

In addition, the plan must provide for the return of contributions under these circumstances.[7]

Contributions conditioned on deductibility

If a contribution is conditioned upon its deductibility under Code Sec. 404, then, to the extent the deduction is disallowed, the "exclusive benefit" rule does not prohibit the return to the employer of the contribution within one year after the disallowance of the deduction.[8]

The contribution may be returned only if the plan provides for the return under these circumstances. In the event of a disallowance of deductions, contributions can be returned only to the extent of the amount for which a deduction is denied. For example, if $100 is contributed on the condition it is deductible and $20 is later determined not to be deductible, only $20 can be returned, and not $100.[9]

---

[1] ERISA Sec. 403(c)(2).

[2] ERISA Sec. 403(c)(2)(A)(i).

[3] ERISA Sec. 403(c)(2)(A)(ii).

[4] ERISA Sec. 403(c)(3).

[5] ERISA Sec. 403(c)(2)(A)(ii).

[6] ERISA Sec. 403(c)(2)(B).

[7] P.L. 93-406 (ERISA), Conference Committee Report.

[8] ERISA Sec. 403(c)(2)(C).

[9] P.L. 93-406 (ERISA), Conference Committee Report.

¶ 2355

FIDUCIARY DUTIES: "Prudent Man" Test

In addition to the exclusive benefit rule, a fiduciary must also act prudently with respect to an employee benefit plan. A fiduciary acts prudently if he acts with the care, skill, prudence, and diligence that a "prudent man" acting in a similar capacity would act under similar circumstances.[1]

A fiduciary must act prudently from a procedural standpoint (also known as "procedural diligence"), as well as from a substantive standpoint. That is, fiduciary conduct will be evaluated not only according to the result of fiduciary action (i.e., substantively, such as an investment of plan assets) but also on how the fiduciary goes about reaching that result (i.e., procedurally, such as the criteria considered in making an investment decision).

Investments

The relative riskiness of a specific investment does not alone render it prudent or imprudent under ERISA. The prudence of an investment decision should be judged with regard to the role that the proposed investment plays within the overall plan portfolio.[2]

Specifically, a fiduciary must determine that a particular investment decision, as part of the portfolio, is reasonably designed to further the purposes of the plan by taking into account the risk of loss and the opportunity for gain associated with the investment choice. Further, the following criteria are to be considered by the fiduciary in making an investment decision:[3]

   1. the composition of the portfolio with regard to diversification requirements (see ¶ 2360);

2. the liquidity and current return of the portfolio relative to the anticipated cash flow requirement of the plan; and

3. the projected return of the portfolio relative to the funding objectives of the plan.

Diligence

A trustee's failure to discharge his duties with diligence may constitute a breach of the prudent man standard. Also, a trustee's failure to independently evaluate a proposed plan investment may constitute a fiduciary breach.

Duty to investigate investments. A fiduciary's failure to investigate the investments it administers breaches the duty of prudence only if adequate investigation would have revealed to a prudent fiduciary that the investment at issue was improvident.[4]

CCH Pointer: The DOL has issued a statement explaining that when a mutual fund has been identified as being under investigation by Federal or state regulators, plan fiduciaries must consider the nature of the alleged abuses, the potential impact of the abuses on the plan's investments, the steps taken by the fund to limit such abuses in the future, and any remedial action contemplated to make investors whole.[5] For mutual funds not currently under investigation, fiduciaries will need to consider whether they have sufficient information to conclude that the funds have safeguards in place to limit abuses.

Selection of annuity provider. A fiduciary must exercise prudence in selecting an annuity provider. A fiduciary does not, however, breach its fiduciary duty, even if the annuity provider subsequently goes into receivership, if it has diligently investigated the purchase of the annuity. A fiduciary should retain qualified experts to investigate the insurer, review financial statements, and receive a financial analysis of the insurer. However, the fiduciary should not passively accept the consultant's appraisal, but should also assess the data and conduct an independent analysis of the reasoning underlying the consultant's recommendations.[6] See ¶ 2365.

Investigation of creditworthiness of insurance company. An employer sponsoring a plan does not breach its fiduciary duty by purchasing guaranteed investment contracts (GICs) from an insurance company that subsequently is placed in conservatorship, even if the GICs return less interest than was promised. The employer, however, must take adequate and reasonable steps to investigate the insurance company's creditworthiness before purchasing the GICs.[7]

Participant-directed accounts. A fiduciary that has failed to exercise prudence or to diversify plan investments may be absolved of liability for losses sustained as a result of a participant's exercise of control over his or her account. However, the exemption from fiduciary liability afforded by ERISA Sec. 404(c) is strictly applied (see ¶ 2375).

Term of office

The fiduciary responsibility provisions of ERISA do not specifically address the term of office of a plan trustee. However, the Labor Department has taken the position that a lifetime term of appointment for a pension fund trustee is inconsistent with ERISA's fiduciary responsibility provisions.[8]

Misrepresentation and failure to disclose

A plan fiduciary must not "materially mislead" those to whom the duties of loyalty and prudence are owed. Thus, a fiduciary cannot misrepresent a participant's benefits under the terms of the plan. In addition, a number of courts have held that a plan may not make material misrepresentations to participants or beneficiaries concerning anticipated changes in plan benefits.[9] Also, a fiduciary's obligation to provide information to employees and beneficiaries may entail not only an obligation not to misinform or misrepresent, but also the affirmative duty to inform when the fiduciary knows that silence can be harmful.[10]

The issue of the material misrepresentation often arises in communications by fiduciaries to participants concerning anticipated changes in plan benefits. In such a context, the materiality of the misrepresentation often turns on the question of whether an anticipated change in benefits was under "serious consideration" by the employer. A leading case[11] has concluded that serious consideration of a change in plan benefits exists when a specific proposal is being discussed for implementation by senior management with the authority to implement that change.[12]

Proxy voting

The fiduciary act of managing plan assets that are shares of corporate stock includes the voting of proxies attributable to those shares. The responsibility for voting proxies lies with the plan trustee unless:[13]

1. the trustee is subject to the directions of a named fiduciary; or

2. power to manage, acquire, or dispose of assets has been delegated by a named fiduciary to an investment manager.

Where the authority to manage plan assets has been delegated to an investment manager, no other person may vote the proxies unless the named fiduciary has reserved for itself (or for another named fiduciary, if the plan provides) the right to direct a plan trustee as to proxy voting. If the plan document or investment management agreement does not speak to the issue of proxy voting by the investment manager, the investment manager would have exclusive responsibility for voting proxies. Moreover, an investment manager with the authority to vote proxies would not be relieved of its own fiduciary responsibilities by following directions of another person regarding the voting of proxies, or by delegating the responsibility to another person. However, if the plan document or the investment management contract expressly precludes the investment manager from voting proxies, that responsibility would lie exclusively with the trustee.[14]

In voting proxies, the responsible fiduciary must consider factors that may affect the value of the plan's investment and may not subordinate the interests of the participants and beneficiaries in their retirement incomes to unrelated objectives. Accordingly, the named fiduciary must periodically monitor the management of plan assets by the investment manager, including proxy voting decisions. In order to allow the named fiduciary to effectively monitor an investment manager, proper documentation must be maintained. Thus, the investment manager or other named fiduciary must keep accurate records of proxy voting. The records must enable the named fiduciary to review the investment manager's voting procedures with respect to plan-owned stock and the actions taken by the manager in individual proxy voting situations.[15]

SEC rules. SEC rules allow a beneficial owner of stock to designate a registered investment adviser to vote proxies and to receive proxy and related issuer material in place of the beneficial owner. The rules also permit certain investment managers of ERISA plans to vote proxies.[16] Accordingly, any member of the National Association of Securities Dealers, Inc., that is designated as an investment manager of stock held in a plan, may vote proxies held in accordance with ERISA's fiduciary rules.

Such proxy voting will be allowed only if:

1. a named plan fiduciary designates the investment adviser, and

2. the plan expressly grants discretion to the investment manager to manage, acquire, or dispose of any plan assets and does not expressly reserve the proxy voting right to the named fiduciary.

Eligible individual account plan

In the case of an eligible individual account plan, the prudence requirement (but only to the extent that it would include the element of diversification) (see ¶ 2360) is not violated by the acquisition or holding of qualifying employer securities or qualifying employer real property.[17]

An eligible individual account plan is an individual account plan that is a profit-sharing, stock bonus, thrift, savings, or employee stock ownership plan (ESOP), or a pre-ERISA money purchase pension plan.[18]

☐ See ¶ 2424 for definitions of "qualifying employer securities" and "qualifying employer real property."

---

[1] ERISA Sec. 404(a)(1).

[2] ERISA Reg. § 2550.404a-1.

[3] ERISA Reg. § 2550.404a-1(b)(2).

[4] *Roth v. Sawyer-Cleator Lumber Co.*, CA-8 (1994), 16 F3d 915; *Ershick v. United Missouri Bank*, CA-10 (1991), 948 F2d 660; *Fink v. National Sav. & Trust Co.*, CA-DC (1985), 772 F2d 951; *Katsaros v. Cody*, CA-2 (1984), 744 F2d 270, *cert. denied*, 469 US 1072.

[5] Statement of EBSA Assistant Secretary Ann L. Combs, 2-17-04.

[6] *Riley v. Murdock*, CA-4 (1996), 83 F3d 415 (*unpublished opinion*), *cert. denied*, 519 US 964

(1996); *In re Unisys Savings Plan Litigation*, CA-3 (1996), 74 F3d 420.

[7] *In re Unisys Savings Plan Litigation*, CA-3 (1999), 173 F3d 145, aff'g DC Pa (1997), No. 91-3067.

[8] ERISA Opinion Letter 85-41A, 12-5-85.

[9] See, e.g., *Mullins v. Pfizer, Inc.*, CA-2 (1994), 23 F3d 663; *Pocchia v. Nynex Corp.*, CA-2 (1996), 81 F3d 278.

[10] *Bixler v. Central Pennsylvania Teamsters Health and Welfare Fund*, CA-3 (1993), 12 F3d 1292.

[11] *Fischer v. Philadelphia Electric Co.*, CA-3 (1996), 96 F3d 1533, *cert. denied*, US SupCt (1997), 117 SCt 1247.

[12]See also *Vartanian v. Monsanto Co.*, CA-1 (1997), 131 F3d 264; *Bins v. Exxon Co.*, CA-9 (2000), 220 F3d 1042; *Bradney v. E.I. DuPont de Nemours and Co.*, CA-6 (2000), No. 99-3842.

[13]PWBA Interpretive Bulletin 94-2, 7-29-94, CCH PENSION PLAN GUIDE ¶ 19,971.

[14] *Ibid.*

[15] *Ibid.*

[16]SEC Release No. 34-35681, 5-12-95 (60 FR 25749).

[17] ERISA Secs. 404(a)(2) and 407(d)(3).

[18] ERISA Sec. 407(d)(3).

¶ 2360

FIDUCIARY DUTIES: Pre-2007 Plan Investment Diversification

For plan years beginning before 2007, the fiduciary rules required fiduciaries to diversify plan investments to minimize the risk of large losses, unless it is "clearly prudent" not to do so.[1]

Degree of diversification

The degree of investment concentration that would violate the diversification requirement could not be stated as a fixed percentage because a prudent fiduciary must consider the facts and circumstances of each case. The factors to be considered included:[2]

1. the purposes of the plan;

2. the amount of the plan assets;

3. financial and industrial conditions;

4. the type of investment, e.g., mortgages, bonds, shares of stock, etc.;

5. distribution of investments as to geographical location;

6. distribution of investments as to industries; and

7. the dates of investment maturity.

Under the pre-2007 rules,, a fiduciary usually should not invest all or an unreasonably large proportion of the trust property in a single security. In addition, the fiduciary should not invest all or an unduly large proportion of the trust property in one type of security or in various types of securities that are dependent upon the success of one enterprise or upon conditions in one locality, since the effect is to increase the risk of large losses.[3]

---

[1] ERISA Sec. 404(a)(1)(C).

[2]P.L. 93-406 (ERISA), Conference Committee Report.

[3] *Ibid.*

¶ 2362

FIDUCIARY DUTIES: Post-2006 Plan Investment Diversification Rules

For plan years beginning after 2006, defined contribution plans must meet diversification requirements with regard to any portion of employee contributions, elective deferrals and employer contributions invested in employer securities. With regard to employee contributions and elective deferrals invested in employer securities, an individual must be allowed to elect to direct the plan to divest employer securities into other investment options. An individual who is a participant in the plan with at least 3 years of service or is a beneficiary of such a participant must be able to elect to divest the portion of the account invested in employer securities that is attributable to employer contributions in other investment options.

Under the Pension Protection Act of 2006, a trust that is part of an "applicable defined contribution plan" will not be treated as a qualified trust unless the plan meets certain diversification requirements with regard to investments in employer securities.[1] An "applicable individual account plan" must also meet the diversification requirements.[2]

Employee contributions and elective deferrals

A plan will meet its diversification requirements if it allows an "applicable individual" to direct the plan to divest any employer securities in which a portion of employee contributions and elective deferrals are invested.[3] The individual must then be allowed to direct the reinvestment of an equivalent amount in other investment options that meet requirements discussed below.

An "applicable individual" is any participant in the plan and any beneficiary who has an account under the plan with respect to which the beneficiary is entitled to exercise the rights of a participant.[4]

Employer contributions

The plan meets its diversification requirements if an applicable individual who is a participant in the plan and has completed at least 3 years of service or is a beneficiary of a participant or of a deceased participant is allowed to divest that portion of an account that contains employer contributions, other than elective deferrals, that is invested in employer securities or employer property.[5] The applicable individual must be able to reinvest an equivalent amount in other investment options that meet the requirements discussed below.

The rules on divesting that portion of employer contributions invested in employer securities will be phased in over a three year period. For that portion of the account attributable to employer contributions invested in employer securities and that were acquired in a plan year beginning before January 1, 2007, the applicable individual may only divest an applicable percentage. The applicable percentage will be determined as follows:

- 33-percent in the first plan year;
- 66-percent in the second plan year; and
- 100 percent in the third and following plan years.

Each class of securities will be treated separately. The three year phase in rules do not apply to an applicable individual participant who has attained age 55 and who has completed at least 3 years of service before the first plan year beginning after December 31, 2005.

Investment options

Not less than three investment options other than employer securities must be offered in which an applicable individual may direct the proceeds from the divestment of employer securities. Each of the investment options must be diversified and have materially different risk and return characteristics.[6]

A plan may limit the time for divestment and reinvestment of employer securities to periodic, reasonable opportunities occurring no less frequently than quarterly. Such a limit will not cause the plan to fail to meet the diversification requirements. However, the plan will fail to meet the diversification requirements if the plan imposes restrictions or conditions with respect to the investment of employer securities that are not imposed on the investment of other assets. This requirement will not apply to any restrictions or conditions required by securities laws.

Applicable defined contribution or individual account plan

The term "applicable defined contribution plan" means any defined contribution plan that holds any publicly traded employer securities. An "applicable individual account plan" means any individual account plan as defined by ERISA Sec. 3(34) that holds any publicly traded employer securities. Publicly-traded securities are securities issued by the employer or a member of the employer's controlled group of corporations that are readily tradable on an established securities market.[7]

A "one-participant retirement plan" will not be considered an applicable defined contribution or individual account plan.

Divestiture rights

According to the IRS,[8] it is permissible for the plan to limit the time for divestment of employer securities and reinvestment to periodic opportunities occurring at least quarterly. However, it is not permissible for a plan to impose restrictions on these rights that differ from restrictions on the divestment of other types of plan assets, or to offer benefits conditioned on investment in employer securities. For example, a plan cannot give applicable individuals the opportunity to divest other types of investments more frequently than employer securities, nor can it give those who divest employer securities a lower rate of matching employer contributions than those who choose not to divest themselves of employer securities. It is permissible for a plan, for example, to restrict the percentage of a participant's account balance which can be invested in employer securities, as long as the limitations apply without regard to a prior exercise of rights to divest employer securities. It is not permissible, however, to restrict a participant for a period of time from reinvesting in employer securities after divestment, because this limitation takes into account a prior exercise of rights to divest employer securities.

Notice of right to divest employer securities

Under the PPA, a plan administrator must provide a notice to applicable individuals who are eligible to exercise the right to direct the proceeds from the divestment of employer securities with respect to any type of contribution. The notice must be provided not later than 30 days before the first date on which the applicable participant becomes eligible to divest employer securities. The notice must set out the right to direct the divestment of employer securities and must describe the importance of diversifying retirement account assets in investments.[9]

The notices must be written in a manner calculated to be understood by the average plan participant. It may be delivered in written, electronic, or other appropriate form to the extent that the form used is reasonably accessible to the recipient of the notice.

Plan administrators that fail to comply with the requirement to provide the diversification rights notice may be assessed a penalty of up to $100 a day from the date of noncompliance. Plan administrators are subject to a separate penalty for each individual participant or beneficiary to whom notice has not been provided.

IRS final regs. The IRS issued final regulations implementing the diversification requirements in May 2010.[10] The final rules apply to plan years beginning on or after January 1, 2011.

For more information, see CCH PENSION PLAN GUIDE ¶ 4472.

---

[1] Code Sec. 401(a)(35), as added by the Pension Protection Act of 2006 (P.L. 109-280).

[2] ERISA Sec. 204(j)(1), as added by P.L. 109-280.

[3] Code Sec. 401(a)(35)(B) and ERISA Sec. 204(j)(2), as added by P.L. 109-280.

[4] Code Sec. 401(a)(35)(G)(i) and ERISA Sec. 204(j)(6)(A), as added by P.L. 109-280.

[5] Code Sec. 401(a)(35)(C) and ERISA Sec. 204(j)(3), as added by P.L. 109-280.

[6] Code Sec. 401(a)(35)(D)(i) and ERISA Sec. 204(j)(4), as added by P.L. 109-280.

[7] Code Sec. 401(a)(35)(G)(v) and ERISA Sec. 204(j)(6)(E)ERISA Sec. 204(j)(6)(E), as added by P.L. 109-280 (Pension Protection Act of 2006). "Readily tradable on an established securities market" is defined in IRS Reg. § 1.401(a)(35)-1(f)(5)(ii).

[8] IRS Notice 2006-107, IRB 2006-51, December 18, 2006.

[9] ERISA Sec. 101(m), as added by P.L. 109-280.

[10] IRS Reg. § 1.401(a)(35)-1.

¶ 2365

FIDUCIARY DUTIES: Selection of Annuity Provider

Pension plans purchase benefit distribution annuities for several purposes. Annuities typically are purchased for participants and beneficiaries in connection with the termination of a plan or for participants who are retiring or separating from service with accrued vested benefits.

The selection of an annuity provider is a fiduciary decision and the DOL has brought several actions against fiduciaries who have failed to follow adequate procedures in selecting the safest available annuity provider. The DOL has provided guidance for fiduciaries to follow when selecting an annuity provider for purposes of benefit distribution where the plan intends to transfer liability for benefits to the annuity provider.[1]

Safest available annuity

In selecting an annuity provider for purposes of benefit distribution, fiduciaries must take steps calculated to select the safest annuity available, unless it would be in the interest of participants and beneficiaries to do otherwise. Fiduciaries may not select an annuity provider without an "objective, thorough, and analytical" search and an evaluation of factors relating to the annuity provider's credit worthiness and ability to pay claims.[2]

Factors to be considered. The fiduciary may not rely solely on ratings provided by insurance ratings services, but must consider:[3]

1. the quality and diversification of the annuity provider's investment portfolio;

2. the size of the insurer relative to the proposed contract;

3. the level of the insurer's capital and surplus;

4. the lines of business of the annuity provider and other indications of an insurer's exposure to liability;

5. the structure of the annuity contract and guarantees supporting the annuities, such as the use of separate accounts; and

6. the availability of additional protection through state guaranty associations and the extent of those guarantees.

EBSA interim final regulations released in 2007 require only defined benefit plans offering an annuity option to meet the higher "safest available annuity" standard. The proposed regulations provide a new safe harbor applicable to annuity provider selection by fiduciaries of defined contribution individual plan accounts, such as 401(k) plan accounts.[4]

PPA clarification

Final EBSA regulations issued in 2008 provide a safe harbor for the selection of annuity providers for the purpose of benefit distributions from individual account plans such as 401(k) plans. The final regulations require the fiduciary to engage in an objective, thorough, and analytical search for the purpose of identifying and selecting providers from which to purchase annuities. The fiduciary responsible for the selection of the annuity provider is required to consider information sufficient to assess the ability of the annuity provider to make all future payments under the annuity contract. Further, the final rule adds a requirement directing the fiduciary to consider "fees and commissions" as part of the decisionmaking process.

EBSA clarifies that the safe harbor does not establish minimum requirements or the exclusive means for satisfying responsibilities with regard to the selection of an annuity provider or contract for benefit distributions.

Specifically, the regulations provide guidance regarding how a fiduciary can meet the requirements of the safe harbor.[5] For example, the regulations address the consideration of:

1. the ability of the annuity provider to administer the payment of benefits under the annuity to participants and beneficiaries;

2. the cost of the annuity contract in relation to the benefits and administrative services being offered;

3. the annuity provider's experience and financial expertise in providing annuities of the type selected or being offered;

4. the structure of the annuity contract and benefits provided and the use of separate accounts to underwrite the provider's benefit obligations;

5. the annuity provider's level of capital, surplus, and reserves available to make payments under the annuity contract;

6. the annuity provider's rating by insurance rating services; and

7. the availability of additional protections through state guaranty associations and the extent of their guarantees.

Costs may be considered

Under certain circumstances, the selection of the safest available annuity may not be in the interests of participants and beneficiaries. Such an instance may arise where the safest available annuity is only marginally safer, but disproportionately more expensive than competing annuities, and the participants, and beneficiaries are likely to bear a significant portion of that increased cost.[6]

Cost considerations, however, may never allow a fiduciary to put the benefits of annuitized participants and beneficiaries at risk by purchasing an unsafe annuity. Thus, a fiduciary may not purchase a riskier annuity solely because there are insufficient funds to purchase a safer annuity. In such a case, the fiduciary may be required to condition the purchase of annuities on additional employer contributions sufficient to purchase the safest available annuity.[7]

In addition, the fiduciary may not purchase a riskier, lower-priced annuity in order to ensure or maximize an employer's reversion following the termination of an overfunded plan.[8] The safest available annuity must still be purchased.

---

[1] ERISA Reg. § 2509.95-1; PWBA Interpretive Bulletin 95-1, 3-6-95 (60 FR 12328), CCH Pension Plan Guide ¶ 19,972C.

[2] *Ibid.*

[3] *Ibid.*

[4] ERISA Reg. § 2509.95-1(c).

[5] ERISA Reg. § 2550.404a-4(c)(2).

[6] ERISA Reg. § 2509.95-1(d).

[7] *Ibid.*

[8] *Ibid.*

¶ 2370

FIDUCIARY DUTIES: Adherence to Plan Documents

Plan fiduciaries must act in accordance with plan documents and instruments to the extent that they are consistent with the requirements established by ERISA.[1]

Generally, trustees do not breach their fiduciary duties by interpreting the plan in good faith, even if it is later determined that the interpretation was wrong.[2] However, where plan terms are clear, a violation of plan terms will lead to a determination of a fiduciary duty breach. For example, the use of plan funds to pay expenses of outside investment managers in violation of plan terms is a breach of fiduciary duties.[3]

The fiduciary duties under ERISA require plan administrators to communicate plan contents to employees. See the discussion at ¶ 2220.

[1] ERISA Sec. 404(a)(1)(D).

[2] See, e.g., *Morgan v. Independent Drivers Association Pension Plan*, CA-10 (1992), 975 F2d 1467.

[3] *In re Gulf Pension Litigation*, DC Tex (1991), 764 FSupp 1149.

¶ 2375

FIDUCIARY DUTIES: Pre-PPA Participant-Directed Accounts

The Pension Protection Act of 2006 has substantially changed the rules dealing with investment advice (see ¶ 2312) and with default investment alternatives (see ¶ 2376). Prior to the PPA, a pension plan may provide for individual accounts and permit a participant or beneficiary to exercise control over assets in his or her account.[1] This type of plan is sometimes referred to as an "ERISA Sec. 404(c) plan." Under this type of plan, a participant or beneficiary who exercises such control is not deemed to be a fiduciary. Moreover, no person who is otherwise a fiduciary is liable under the fiduciary responsibility rules for any loss or for any breach that results from the participant's or beneficiary's exercise of control over his or her account.[2]

In order to qualify as an individual account plan, a plan must give participants the opportunity to: choose from a broad range of investment alternatives, receive investment instruction with appropriate frequency, diversify investments, and obtain sufficient information to make informed investment decisions. Fiduciaries are not relieved of their duty to consider the prudence of the investment alternatives made available to participants under the plan and to maintain oversight over the investment options.[3]

Broad range of investment alternatives

To provide a broad range of investment alternatives, a plan must offer participants the opportunity to exercise control over investments that materially affect the potential return on assets. In addition, it must also allow participants to choose from at least three investment alternatives, each of which is diversified and has materially different risk and return characteristics. Finally, a plan must give participants the opportunity to diversify investments so as to minimize the risk of large losses.[4]

Charges for reasonable expenses. A plan may charge the account of a participant or a beneficiary for reasonable expenses incurred in carrying out investment instructions.[5] However, the plan must inform participants and beneficiaries of the actual expenses associated with their individual accounts.

Fiduciary may reject investment instructions. A fiduciary may refuse to implement investment instructions that would jeopardize the tax qualified status of the plan, result in a prohibited transaction, or generate income taxable to the plan.[6]

Restrictions on frequency of investment instructions. A plan may impose reasonable restrictions on the frequency with which participants may give investment instructions to the plan administrator. To be considered reasonable, the restrictions must offer participants the right to give investment instructions with appropriate frequency, considering the market volatility of the investment. For the three core investments, which are intended to constitute a broad range of investment alternatives, participants must be allowed to give investment instructions at least quarterly.[7]

Opportunity to exercise control requires information

Participants will be considered as exercising control over their accounts only if they are provided with enough information about the plan and available investment alternatives to be able to make *informed* investment decisions.[8] Items that must be provided to participants include:[9]

1. an explanation that the plan is intended to comply with ERISA Sec. 404(c), and that plan fiduciaries may be relieved of liability for losses resulting from participants' investment directions;

2. a description of the investment alternatives, including a general description of the investment objectives and risk and return characteristics of each alternative;

3. identification of any designated investment managers;

4. an explanation of the circumstances under which participants and beneficiaries may give investment instructions and of any limitations placed on those instructions set forth in the plan;

5. a description of any transaction fees or expenses which are charged to the participants' accounts;

6. the name, address, and phone number of the fiduciary who is responsible for providing certain documents upon request and a description of those documents;

7. in the case of plans that offer an investment alternative designed to permit a participant or beneficiary to acquire or sell any employer security, a description of the procedures relating to the confidentiality of information regarding the purchase, holding, and sale of the securities and to the exercise of voting rights; and the name, address, and phone number of the fiduciary responsible for monitoring compliance with the procedures;

8. a copy of the most recent prospectus provided immediately prior to or immediately following a participant's initial investment in a mutual fund or security in which he or she has no assets invested; and

9. subsequent to an investment, any materials provided to the plan relating to the exercise of voting, tender, or similar rights (which are incidental to the ownership interests held in the account) to the extent that the rights are passed through to the participant, and a description of or reference to plan provisions describing these rights.

Additionally, certain information must be provided on request to participants, including a description of the annual operating expenses of investment alternatives, copies of any prospectuses, financial statements and reports, and a list of assets comprising the portfolio of an investment alternative.[10]

Investment education and fiduciary liability

Participants and beneficiaries in a 404(c) plan must have access to sufficient information to enable them to make informed investment decisions. ERISA Sec. 404(c) does not require a plan sponsor to provide investment advice or educational information, materials, or programs to participants in order to preserve its exemption from fiduciary liability.[11] However, a Labor Department Interpretive Bulletin allows plan sponsors to provide certain types of investment information without incurring fiduciary liability as investment advisers.[12] The Interpretive Bulletin describes several "safe harbors" or types of information and materials that can be provided to participants without giving "investment advice" under ERISA. These include:

1. **Plan information**—information about plan participation, the benefits of increasing plan contributions, the impact of preretirement withdrawals on retirement income, the terms and operation of the plan, investment alternatives, such as a description of investment objectives and philosophies, risk and return characteristics, historical return information, and investment prospectuses.

2. **General financial and investment information**—information about general financial and investment concepts, historic differences in rates of return between different asset classes, effects of inflation, estimating future retirement income needs, determining investment time horizons, and assessing risk tolerance.

3. **Asset allocation models**—information and materials, such as pie charts, graphs, or case studies, that provide models of asset allocation portfolios for hypothetical individuals with different time horizons and risk profiles.

4. **Interactive investment materials**—questionnaires, worksheets, software, and similar materials that provide a participant or beneficiary with the means to estimate future retirement income needs and assess the impact of different asset allocations on retirement income.

¶2375

Tax-free retirement planning services. Employers sponsoring qualified plans are able to provide qualified retirement planning services to employees and their spouses as a tax-free fringe benefit.[13] Qualified retirement planning services would include advice and information regarding retirement income planning, but would not encompass tax preparation, accounting, legal, or brokerage services.

Exercising control following automatic rollover of cash-out distributions. Under the Economic Growth and Tax Relief Reconciliation Act of 2001, a plan that provides for a cash-out distribution of a nonforfeitable account balance that does not exceed $5,000 must use a direct rollover as the default option for involuntary distributions that exceed $1,000.[14] Thus, employers may no longer cash-out a participant whose account balance is under $5,000 but over $1,000. The distribution must be rolled over automatically to a designated IRA, unless the participant affirmatively elects to have the distribution transferred to a different IRA or to receive it directly.

In the event that an automatic direct rollover complies with regulations promulgated by the DOL governing the designation of institutions to receive rollovers and the investment of funds, a participant will be treated as exercising control over the assets in the IRA upon the earlier of: (1) the rollover of all or a portion of the assets to another IRA; or (2) one year after the automatic rollover.[15] Once the participant is treated as exercising control over the retirement account, the plan sponsor and trustee are relieved of fiduciary liability for losses incurred by the participant. The language of the statute further suggests that participants will be treated as exercising control over accounts, even if they do not take conscious actions with respect to their accounts following the automatic rollover.

EBSA final regulations issued. Final regulations issued by the EBSA provide, effective March 28, 2005, a safe harbor for fiduciaries involved in the selection of a financial institution as an individual retirement plan provider and in the investment of the funds in connection with the automatic rollover.[16] A fiduciary's rollover of mandatory distributions to an individual retirement plan, in accordance with the conditions of the final regulations, will be treated as a transfer that is made in a manner consistent with EBSA guidance. Thus, immediately following the rollover, a participant will be viewed as exercising control over the assets of the individual retirement plan for purposes of ERISA Sec. 404(c)(3).[17]

SIMPLE plans relieve employer of fiduciary liability

An employer maintaining a SIMPLE plan (¶ 170), or other fiduciary associated with the plan, is relieved of fiduciary liability for actions taken by participants and beneficiaries who exercise control over assets in the SIMPLE account.[18]

---

[1] ERISA Sec. 404(c).

[2] *Ibid.*

[3] ERISA Reg. § 2550.404c-1(b)(2)(i).

[4] ERISA Reg. § 2550.404c-1(b)(3)(i).

[5] ERISA Reg. § 2550.404c-1(b)(2)(ii)(A).

[6] ERISA Reg. § 2550.404c-1(b)(2)(ii)(B).

[7] ERISA Reg. § 2550.404c-1(b)(2)(ii)(C).

[8] ERISA Reg. § 2550.404c-1(b)(2)(i)(B).

[9] ERISA Reg. § 2550.404c-1(b)(2)(i)(B)(1).

[10] ERISA Reg. § 2550.404c-1(b)(2)(i)(B)(2).

[11] ERISA Reg. § 2550.404c-1(c)(4).

[12] PWBA Interpretive Bulletin 96-1, 6-11-96, CCH PENSION PLAN GUIDE ¶ 19,972D.

[13] Code Sec. 132(a)(7), as added by P.L. 107-16 (Economic Growth and Tax Relief Reconciliation Act of 2001), Act. Sec. 665(a)(1).

14 Code Sec. 401(a)(31)(B), as added by P.L. 107-16 (Economic Growth and Tax Relief Reconciliation Act of 2001), Act. Sec. 657(a).

15 Code Sec. 404(c)(3), as added by P.L. 107-16 (Economic Growth and Tax Relief Reconciliation Act of 2001), Act. Sec. 657(c)(1).

16 ERISA Reg. § 2550.404a-2.

17 Preamble to ERISA Reg. § 2550.404a-2, 69 FR 58017, September 28, 2004, CCH PENSION PLAN GUIDE ¶ 24,806P.

18 ERISA Sec. 404(c)(2).

¶ 2376

FIDUCIARY DUTIES: Default Investment Elections

A participant in an individual account plan is deemed to have exercised actual control over assets in his or her account if the plan's fiduciaries make default investments for the participant in accordance with final rules provided by the Department of Labor.

Under the Pension Protection Act of 2006, effective for plan years beginning after December 31, 2006, a participant in an individual account plan who does not submit investment instructions to the plan administrator will be treated as exercising actual control over the assets in his or her account if the plan's fiduciaries default investments are made in accordance with regulations prescribed by the Department of Labor.[1]

Qualified default investment alternatives

The Employee Benefits Security Administration (EBSA) has issued final regulations implementing PPA provisions that provide relief to plan fiduciaries who invest the assets of participants in "qualified default investment alternatives" in the absence of participant investment direction.[2] The final rules are designed to make it easier for fiduciaries of 401(k) plans and other participant-directed defined contribution plans to adopt automatic enrollment design features.

Conditions for relief. Under the final regulations, fiduciary relief is conditioned on compliance with certain conditions.

(1) *Assets invested in QDIAs.* Assets must be invested in qualified default investment alternatives.

(2) *Participant must fail to exercise opportunity to direct investments.* Participants or beneficiaries on whose behalf assets are being invested in a QDIA must have had the opportunity to direct the investment of assets in the individual account and failed to direct the investment of assets.

(3) *Advance and annual notice.* Participants and beneficiaries must receive an advance initial notice and an annual notice regarding the investments to be made on their behalf. The final rules allow the initial notice to be provided: (1) at least 30 days in advance of the date of plan eligibility, or at least 30 days in advance of any first investment in a QDIA on behalf of a participant or beneficiary, or (2) on or before the date of plan eligibility, provided that the participant has the opportunity to make the withdrawals authorized under Code Sec. 414(w).

Under the final rules the specified information must be disclosed in a notice that is separate from the SPD or SMM. However, the initial advance or annual notice may be distributed with the SPD or other materials that are provided to participants and beneficiaries.

The regulations provide relief from fiduciary liability stemming from the investment of a participant's account in any QDIA. Fiduciaries, therefore, are not required to determine which of the approved QDIAs is the "most prudent" for a participant or a plan.

(4) **Pass-through information rules.** Materials provided to the plan relating to a participant's or beneficiary's investment in a QDIA (e.g., account statement, prospectus, proxy voting rights) must be provided to the participant or beneficiary. A fiduciary may comply with the pass-through disclosure requirements under the safe harbor by satisfying the pass-through requirement under the ERISA § 404(c) regulations. In addition, the DOL notes that the required information may be furnished directly to the participant or beneficiary by the provider of the investment alternative or a third party.

(5) **Transfer rights.** A participant whose assets are invested in a QDIA must be afforded the opportunity to transfer such assets to any other investment alternative under the plan without financial penalty. Specifically, the final regulations empower a participant or beneficiary with the right to transfer, in whole or in part, assets invested in a QDIA to any other investment alternative available under the plan with a frequency consistent with (but no greater than) that afforded participants and beneficiaries who affirmatively elect to invest in the QDIA, but no less frequently than once within a 3-month period.

The final rules further prohibit the imposition of any restrictions, fees, or expenses (other than investment management or similar types of fees and expenses) during the first 90 days (beginning on the date of the participant's first elective contribution) of a defaulted participant's or beneficiary's investment in the QDIA. Any transfer or permissible withdrawal during the 90-day period may not be subject to any restrictions, fees, or expenses (other than the fees and expenses that are charged on an ongoing basis for the investment itself such as investment management fees, distribution and service fees (12b-1 fees)), and are not imposed and do not vary based on the participant's decision to withdraw, sell, or transfer assets out of the investment alternative.

Investment in QDIAs. The centerpiece of the fiduciary relief afforded by the final regulations is the requirement that assets be invested in qualified default investment alternatives. A QDIA must satisfy specified requirements:

(1) **Restriction on holding employer securities.** The QDIA may generally not hold or permit the acquisition of employer securities. However, exceptions are provided, such as for employer securities acquired as matching contributions from the employer/ plan sponsor or at the direction of the participant or beneficiary.

(2) **Transfer rights may not be restricted or subject to penalty.** The QDIA may not impose financial penalties or otherwise restrict the ability

of a participant or beneficiary to transfer investments from the QDIA to another investment option (see above).

(3) **QDIA must be managed by investment manager or registered investment company.** The QDIA must be managed by an investment manager (as defined by ERISA § 3(38) or a registered investment company.

The final rules authorize plan sponsors who are named fiduciaries (under ERISA § 402(a)(2) to manage QDIAs. The plan sponsor may utilize asset allocation models to manage investments and allocate assets. The plan sponsor may also employ an investment consultant. However, the investment consultant would be subject to ERISA's fiduciary responsibility standards.

A QDIA may be a life cycle or targeted-retirement-date fund, a balanced fund, or a professionally managed account.

Scope of regulation clarified. Labor Department Field Assistance Bulletin (FAB) 2008-03 clarifies that when a plan sponsor chooses to create and manage a QDIA using a mix of the plan's available investment alternatives, the plan sponsor will not qualify for the QDIA safe harbor unless it is a named fiduciary of the plan. The plan sponsor would remain liable for the management and monitoring of the QDIA.

The QDIA regulations provide that for a 90-day period following the first investment in a QDIA (the time period during which those who opt out of the plan are most likely to do so), any transfer or withdrawal of assets from the QDIA by a participant cannot be subject to any restrictions, fees, or expenses. The FAB clarifies that payment of such fees during this period by the plan sponsor or a service provider are not prohibited, because such payment would not inhibit a participant's decision to opt out of the plan. The FAB also clarifies that the 90-day restriction on fees and expenses does not apply to participants with existing assets invested in the plan prior to the effective date of the QDIA regulations.

---

[1] ERISA Sec. 404(c)(5)(A), as added by the Pension Protection Act of 2006 (P.L. 109-280).

[2] ERISA Reg. § 2550.404c-5.

¶ 2377
FIDUCIARY DUTIES: Plan Termination

ERISA provides elaborate rules for the allocation of assets upon plan termination (see ¶ 2800). A fiduciary that fails to follow the asset allocation rules may incur liability. Upon the termination of a pension plan that is not subject to the plan termination insurance provisions of ERISA at the time of termination but which is covered by the fiduciary responsibility requirements of ERISA, plan assets are to be allocated according to the regular allocation rules (¶ 2838). In other words, the allocation rules apply as if the plan was covered by termination insurance.[1] This rule does not apply to a plan to which no employer contributions have been made.

---

[1] ERISA Sec. 403(d)(1).

¶ 2378

FIDUCIARY DUTIES: Termination of Abandoned Individual Account Plans

Effective May 22, 2006, a process has been created to terminate abandoned individual account plans so that benefit distributions can be made to participants and beneficiaries. The Abandoned Plan Coordinator in EBSA's Office of Enforcement administers the Abandoned Plan Program.

EBSA has established standards for determining when a plan is abandoned, simplify procedures for winding up the plan and distributing benefits to participants and beneficiaries, and provide guidance on who may initiate and carry out the winding-up process.[1] This offers guidance to custodians of 401(k) or other individual account pension plans after their sponsors abandon the plans due to employer bankruptcies, mergers and the like. Prior to the EBSA guidance, custodians, such as banks, insurers and mutual fund companies, were left holding the assets of these abandoned plans without the authority to terminate such plans and make benefit distributions in response to participant requests.

Plan abandonment defined

EBSA has set forth the circumstances under which a plan will be considered abandoned and the financial institution holding the plan assets can terminate the plan and distribute benefits to the plan's participants and beneficiaries, with limited liability. A plan generally will be considered abandoned if no contributions to or distributions from the plan have been made for a period of at least 12 consecutive months and, following reasonable efforts to locate the plan sponsor, it is determined that the sponsor no longer exists, cannot be located, or is unable to maintain the plan.

A finding that the plan is abandoned must be done by a "qualified termination administrator" (QTA). To be a QTA, an entity must hold the plan's assets and be eligible as a trustee or issuer of an individual retirement plan under the Internal Revenue Code (that is, a bank, trust company, mutual fund group, or insurance company).

The regulations include model notices for the plan custodian to use to notify the sponsor of its intent to terminate the plan, to notify participants and beneficiaries of the termination of the plan, and to notify EBSA of the plan's abandonment, the custodian's intent to serve as a QTA, and the completion of the termination.

Fiduciary safe harbor provided

The final regulations also provide a fiduciary safe harbor when making distributions from terminated plans on behalf of participants and beneficiaries who fail to make an election regarding the form of benefit distribution.[2] A QTA does not have an obligation to conduct an inquiry or review to determine whether or what breaches of fiduciary responsibility may have occurred with regard to the plan prior to it's becoming a QTA. In most cases, the account of a missing participant will be transferred directly to an individual retirement plan.

[1]ERISA Reg. Sec. 2578.1.   [2]ERISA Reg. Sec. 2550.404a-3.

¶ 2380
FIDUCIARY LIABILITY: Personal Liability of Fiduciary

A plan fiduciary who breaches any of the fiduciary responsibilities, obligations or duties imposed by ERISA is personally liable to the plan for any losses the plan suffers because of such breach. The fiduciary must also restore to the plan any profits which he has made through the use of any plan asset.[1]

Timing of liability

Generally, a plan fiduciary is not liable for any breach of fiduciary duty that occurred before he became a fiduciary or after he is no longer a fiduciary.[2]

Fiduciary liability limited to specific responsibilities

If a plan allocates specific duties to named fiduciaries, each fiduciary is responsible only for those assigned responsibilities.[3] Absent an allegation of cofiduciary liability (see ¶ 2385), personal liability of a fiduciary is limited to the fiduciary role performed for the plan.[4] Named fiduciaries are not liable for acts or omissions properly allocated to other fiduciaries.[5]

Forms of relief

A fiduciary who breaches his duty is subject to various types of relief, including restitution and other equitable or remedial relief a court may deem appropriate.[6] In other words, courts are given the discretion to fashion appropriate relief.

Individual relief for fiduciary breach. ERISA Sec. 409(a) explicitly states that a fiduciary is liable *to the plan* for plan losses stemming from a breach of fiduciary duty. In addition, profits realized by the fiduciary from the use of plan assets must be restored *to the plan*. The United States Supreme Court in *Massachusetts Mutual Life Insurance Company v. Russell* ruled that neither ERISA Sec. 409(a), nor its companion remedial provision, ERISA Sec. 502(a)(2), authorize a plan participant to bring suit for compensatory and punitive damages against a plan administrator that wrongfully delayed payment of a claim.[7] In addition, according to the Court, because ERISA Sec. 409(a) is designed to protect the entire plan, the statute's authorization of other appropriate equitable or remedial relief does not provide relief other than for the plan itself.

Russell was brought under ERISA Sec. 502(a)(2), which empowers a participant to bring suit for appropriate relief under ERISA Sec. 409. The Supreme Court subsequently held that plan participants and beneficiaries may seek *individual* equitable relief for breach of fiduciary duty under ERISA Sec. 502(a)(3).[8] ERISA Sec. 502(a)(3) does not cross-reference ERISA Sec. 409 and authorizes appropriate equitable relief to redress any act or practice that violates the plan or ERISA.

The Court rejected the contention that ERISA Sec. 409 provides the exclusive remedy for breach of fiduciary duty. According to the Court, its interpretation of ERISA Sec. 502(a)(3) as a "catch-all" remedy was consistent with ERISA's general purpose of protecting the interests of plan participants and beneficiaries, especially participants who may be left without a remedy for a breach of fiduciary duty.

However, in 2008, 23 years after the *Russell* case, the U.S. Supreme Court, in a decision that reflects the sea change in the employee benefits landscape over the last generation away from defined benefit plans to 401(k) plans, has unanimously ruled that ERISA allows participants to bring suit to recover losses from fiduciary breaches that impair the value of plan assets held in their individual accounts.[9] The Court acknowledged in *LaRue v. DeWolff, Boberg & Associates, Inc.* that ERISA affords an avenue of relief for injuries sustained by individual plan participants holding accounts under defined contribution plans, even if the financial solvency of the entire plan is not threatened by the alleged fiduciary breach.

The U.S. Supreme Court initially noted that the emphasis in *Russell* on protecting the "entire plan" from the consequences of fiduciary misconduct, reflected an employee benefit plan landscape dominated by defined benefit plans. Under a defined benefit plan, the Court explained, fiduciary misconduct would not affect an individual's entitlement to benefits, unless it creates or enhances the risk of default by the entire plan. Accordingly, the Court in *Russell* inferred the Congressional intention underlying ERISA as being to protect the entire plan rather than the rights of individual beneficiaries.

In the years since *Russell* was decided, however, the employee benefit plan landscape has come to be dominated by defined contribution plans, which feature individual accounts. Participants in DC plans with individual accounts are subject to individual losses resulting from a fiduciary breach that would not directly affect individuals in DB plans exclusive of all other plan participants. Fiduciary misconduct, the Court explained "need not threaten the solvency of the entire plan to reduce benefits below the amounts that participants would otherwise receive." Thus, the focus on a loss to or recovery by the entire plan (which remains a condition for relief under a DB plan) is not relevant with respect to a DC plan.

The essence of the Court's opinion, is that a fiduciary breach that diminishes plan assets payable to participants with individual accounts is as redressable under ERISA as an injury to plan assets that are payable to all participants and beneficiaries. Accordingly, while ERISA Sec. 502(a)(2) does not provide a remedy for individual injuries that are distinct from plan injuries, it does authorize recovery for a fiduciary breach that impairs the value of plan assets in a participant's individual account.

Offset of fiduciary's plan benefits. Despite the general rule against the alienation of vested benefits, a plan may offset a judgment for breach of fiduciary duty against the vested benefits of the fiduciary.[10]

Additional civil penalty

A fiduciary can be subject to a special civil penalty whenever the plan recovers an amount through a settlement agreement or a judicial proceeding involving a

¶2380

violation of ERISA's fiduciary responsibility rules.[11] This penalty also applies to persons who knowingly participate in fiduciary responsibility violations.

[1] ERISA Sec. 409.

[2] ERISA Sec. 409(b).

[3] ERISA Reg. § 2509.75-8, FR-16.

[4] ERISA Reg. § 2509.75-8, FR-13.

[5] ERISA Reg. § 2509.75-8, D-4.

[6] ERISA Sec. 409(a).

[7] *Massachusetts Mutual Life Insurance Company v. Russell*, US Sup Ct (1985), 473 US 134, rev'g, CA-9 (1983), 704 F2d 482.

[8] *Howe v. Varity Corp.*, US Sup Ct (1996), 516 US 489.

[9] *LaRue v. DeWolff, Boberg & Associates, Inc., et al.*, United States Supreme Court, No. 06-856, February 20, 2008.

[10] ERISA Sec. 206(d)(4); Code Sec. 401(a)(13)(C)(i). This is effective for judgments, orders, and decrees issued and settlement agreements entered into on or after August 5, 1997.

[11] ERISA Sec. 502(l).

¶ 2385
FIDUCIARY LIABILITY: Co-Fiduciary and Nonfiduciary Liability

In addition to the responsibility a plan fiduciary bears for his own conduct, he may also be liable for a breach of fiduciary responsibility by another fiduciary with respect to the same plan.[1]

A fiduciary is liable for a co-fiduciary's breach if:

1. he participates knowingly in, or knowingly undertakes to conceal, an act or omission of the other fiduciary, knowing the act or omission to be a breach;

2. by his failure to comply with the fiduciary duties, he has enabled the other fiduciary to commit a breach; or

3. having knowledge of a breach by the other fiduciary, he makes no reasonable efforts under the circumstances to remedy the breach.

Knowing participation

Under the knowing participation rule stated in (1) above, the fiduciary must know that the other person is a fiduciary with respect to the plan, must know that the other fiduciary participated in the act that constituted a breach, and must know that it was a breach.[2]

Example 1: A and B are co-trustees, and the terms of the trust provide that they are not to invest in commodity futures. If A suggests to B that B invest part of the plan assets in commodity futures, and B does so, A, as well as B, is liable for the breach.

Knowing concealment

A fiduciary may be liable for the breach of fiduciary responsibility by another fiduciary of the plan if he knowingly undertakes to conceal a breach committed by the other. For the nonbreaching fiduciary to be liable, he must know that the other is a fiduciary with respect to the plan, must know of the act, and must know that it is a breach.[3]

Example 2: A and B are co-trustees, and B invests in commodity futures in violation of the trust agreement. If B tells his co-trustee A of this investment, A would be liable with B for breach of fiduciary responsibility if A concealed this investment.

Actions that enable co-fiduciary to commit breach

A fiduciary also is liable for the loss caused by another plan fiduciary if he enables the other fiduciary to commit a breach through his failure to exercise prudence, or otherwise comply with the basic fiduciary duties under ERISA.[4]

Example 3: A and B are co-trustees who jointly manage plan assets. A improperly allows B to have the sole custody of the plan's assets and makes no inquiry concerning his conduct. B is thereby enabled to sell the property and to embezzle the proceeds. A is liable for a breach of fiduciary responsibility.

Duty to remedy breach

If a fiduciary knows that another fiduciary of the plan has committed a breach, the first fiduciary must take reasonable steps under the circumstances to remedy the breach.[5]

If, in Example (1), A has the authority to do so, and if it is prudent under the circumstances, A may be required to dispose of the commodity futures acquired by B in violation of fiduciary duties. Alternatively, the most appropriate steps in the circumstances may be to notify the plan's sponsor of the breach, or to proceed to an appropriate federal court for instructions, or bring the matter to the attention of the Secretary of Labor. The proper remedy is to be determined by the facts and circumstances of the particular case, and it may be affected by the relationship of the fiduciary to the plan and to the co-fiduciary, the duties and responsibilities of the fiduciary in question, and the nature of the breach.[6]

Reasonable steps. Where a majority of trustees appear ready to take action which would clearly be contrary to the prudence requirement of ERISA, it is incumbent on the minority trustees to take all reasonable and legal steps to prevent the action. If, having taken all reasonable and legal steps to prevent the imprudent action, the minority trustees have not succeeded, they will not incur liability for the action of the majority.[7]

Although a fiduciary may not be liable for the acts of predecessor fiduciaries under ERISA Sec. 409, if he knows of a breach of fiduciary responsibility committed by a predecessor, he would be obligated to take whatever action is reasonable under the circumstances to remedy the breach. Failure to take appropriate action to remedy the breach would constitute a separate breach of fiduciary responsibility by the successor fiduciary.[8]

Participation of nonfiduciaries

The U.S. Supreme Court has ruled that plan participants may not recover money damages from a nonfiduciary who knowingly participates in a fiduciary's breach of fiduciary duty.[9] Although plan participants are authorized by ERISA Sec. 502(a)(3) to file suits for "appropriate equitable relief," that relief is limited to the types of relief that are typically available in equity, such as injunction, mandamus, and restitution.

Violations of ERISA prohibited transaction rules

The U.S. Supreme Court has ruled that the authority of a plan participant, beneficiary, or fiduciary to bring a civil action for "appropriate equitable relief" under ERISA Sec. 502(a)(3) (see ¶ 2702) extends to a suit against a nonfiduciary party in interest (see ¶ 2406) to a prohibited transaction barred under ERISA Sec. 406(a).[10] Thus, in seeking to redress a prohibited transaction, a fiduciary, participant, or beneficiary is not limited to suing the fiduciary who caused the plan to enter into the transaction.

---

[1] ERISA Sec. 405(a).

[2] ERISA Sec. 405(a)(1); P.L. 93-406 (ERISA), Conference Committee Report.

[3] P.L. 93-406 (ERISA), Conference Committee Report.

[4] ERISA Sec. 405(a)(2); P.L. 93-406 (ERISA), Conference Committee Report.

[5] ERISA Sec. 405(a)(3); P.L. 93-406 (ERISA), Conference Committee Report.

[6] P.L. 93-406 (ERISA), Conference Committee Report.

[7] ERISA Reg. § 2509.75-5, FR-10 (ERISA Interpretive Bulletin 75-5).

[8] ERISA Opinion Letter 76-95, 10-30-76.

[9] *Mertens v. Hewitt Associates,* US Sup Ct (1993), 508 US 248.

[10] *Harris Trust and Savings Bank v. Salomon Smith Barney Inc.*, US Sup Ct (2000), 530 US 238.

¶ 2390

FIDUCIARY LIABILITY: Effect of Agreement to Relieve Fiduciary of Liability

Generally, exculpatory provisions in an agreement or instrument that purport to relieve a fiduciary of liability for breach of the fiduciary responsibility rules are void.[1]

Insurance for fiduciaries

However, a plan may purchase insurance for itself and for its fiduciaries to cover liability or losses resulting from their acts or omissions if the insurance permits recourse by the insurer against the fiduciaries in case of a breach of fiduciary responsibility. Additionally, a fiduciary may purchase insurance to cover his own liability, and an employer or union may purchase liability insurance for plan fiduciaries. It is not necessary, however, that policies in these latter instances provide the insurer with recourse against fiduciaries.[2]

Indemnification agreements

An indemnification agreement that leaves the fiduciary fully responsible and liable, but which permits another party to satisfy any liability incurred by the fiduciary in the same manner as insurance is also allowed.[3] However, any arrangement for indemnification of a plan fiduciary by the plan following a breach of duties is void. Such an arrangement would have the same result as an exculpatory clause in that it would, in effect, relieve the fiduciary of responsibility and liability to the plan by abrogating the plan's right to recovery from the fiduciary for breaches of fiduciary obligations.[4]

---

[1] ERISA Sec. 410(a).

[2] ERISA Sec. 410(b); ERISA Reg. §2509.75-4 (ERISA Interpretive Bulletin 75-4).

[3] ERISA Reg. §2509.75-4 (ERISA Interpretive Bulletin 75-4).

[4] ERISA Sec. 410(a); ERISA Reg. §2509.75-4 (ERISA Interpretive Bulletin 75-4).

¶ 2391

FIDUCIARY LIABILITY: Fiduciary Liability During Blackout Periods

For plans that give participants and beneficiaries control over the investment of assets in their accounts, plan fiduciaries may become subject to liability during periods when participants' rights to direct investments under the plan are suspended, unless the suspension, or "blackout period," meets the requirements of this provision. Plan fiduciaries will have relief from potential liability if they make qualified changes in investment options in accordance with the requirements of this provision.

The Pension Protection Act of 2006 creates a new exception to the relief from fiduciary liability that ERISA Sec. 404(c) grants to fiduciaries under circumstances where the plan permits participants and beneficiaries to exercise control over the investment of assets in their accounts (see ¶ 2375). Such relief will not be available under circumstances where a participant or beneficiary is unable to direct the investment of assets due to a suspension of this right by the plan sponsor or fiduciary (a "blackout period"), which does not meet ERISA Sec. 101(i)(7) requirements.[1]

This provision applies to plan years beginning after 2007. A later effective date applies to collectively bargained plans.

Qualified changes in investment options

If a "qualified change in investment options" is made to a self-directed plan, fiduciary liability will not accrue to plan administrators or other fiduciaries as long as:

- at least thirty and not more than sixty days prior to the effective date of the change, the administrator furnishes written notice of the change to the participants and beneficiaries containing a comparison of the existing and new investment options and a description of the default investments that will be made absent contrary instructions from the participant or beneficiary;

- the participant or beneficiary has not provided the plan, prior to the effective date of the change, investment instructions that are contrary to the proposed reallocation of investments in their account; and

- the investment of the participant or beneficiary's account immediately before the effective date of the proposed reallocation of investments was the result of the participant or beneficiary exercising control over the investment of assets in the account.[2]

---

[1] ERISA Sec. 404(c)(1), as amended by the Pension Protection Act of 2006 (P.L. 109-280).

[2] ERISA Sec. 404(c)(4)(C), as amended by P.L. 109-280.

¶ 2392

FIDUCIARY LIABILITY: Bonding Requirements

As a general rule, every fiduciary of an employee benefit plan and every person who handles funds or other property of the plan (referred to as a "plan official") must be bonded.[1] It is unlawful for any plan official who is subject to the bonding requirements to receive, handle, disburse, or otherwise exercise custody or control of any employee benefit plan's funds or other property without being bonded. It likewise is unlawful for a plan official to permit a person that is not bonded to handle plan funds.[2]

However, various exceptions apply to the bonding requirements.

Pre-2008 amount of bond rules

For plan years beginning before 2008, the amount of the bond required for nonexempt fiduciaries and plan officials must be fixed at the beginning of each fiscal year of the plan. The amount of the bond is required to be $1,000 or 10% of the amount of funds handled, whichever is greater. The bond amount may not exceed $500,000, except that the Secretary of Labor, after notice and hearing, may prescribe an amount in excess of $500,000. However, a bond amount that is in excess of $500,000 cannot exceed 10% of the funds handled.[3]

Determining the amount of the bond. In fixing the amount of the bond, the amount of funds handled must be determined by looking at the funds handled by the person, group, or class to be covered by the bond and by any predecessors during the preceding reporting year. If the plan had no preceding reporting year, the amount of funds handled would be estimated based on the nonreported experience of the previous year. Where a plan does not have sufficient experience to allow it to estimate the amount of funds handled, the amount to be handled for the current reporting year is the amount initially required to fund or set up the plan, plus the amount of required contributions for the current year.[4]

Post-2007 bonding amount rules

The maximum bond amount required of fiduciaries of employee benefit plans holding employer securities is raised from $500,000 to $1 million.[5] For benefit plans that do not hold employer securities, the $500,000 maximum bond amount remains unchanged. This increased bond limit applies to plan years beginning after December 31, 2007.

Other bonding rules

A bond must furnish protection to the plan against loss through fraud or dishonesty on the part of a plan official, directly or through connivance with others.

It is required to have as surety a corporate surety company which is an acceptable surety on federal bonds under authority granted by the Secretary of the Treasury.[6] The bond must be in a form or of a type approved by the Secretary. Examples include individual bonds or schedule or blanket forms of bonds which cover a group or class.

Restrictions. ERISA prohibits any person from procuring any required bond from any surety in which the plan has any control or significant financial interest.[7] Individuals who must be bonded under these rules because they handle funds or other property of an employee benefit plan are not subject to other bonding requirements.[8]

Prohibited transactions. The purchase by a plan of a bond covering plan officials will not be considered a prohibited transaction under ERISA.[9]

Exceptions to bonding requirements

If the Secretary of Labor determines that the plan administrator offers adequate evidence of the financial responsibility of the plan, or that other bonding arrangements would provide adequate protection of the participants and beneficiaries, the plan may be exempted from the above-prescribed bonding requirements of ERISA.[10]

Investment advice. A person who renders investment advice, but who does not exercise, or have the right to exercise, discretionary authority over plan assets, is not required to be bonded solely because he or she renders investment advice. Such a person is not considered to be "handling" funds.[11]

Exception for certain corporate fiduciaries. No bond is required of a fiduciary (or of any director, officer, or employee of such fiduciary) if the fiduciary:[12]

1. is a corporation organized and doing business under federal or state law;

2. is authorized under such laws to exercise trust powers or to conduct an insurance business;

3. is subject to supervision or examination by federal or state authorities; and

4. at all times has a combined capital and surplus of at least $1,000,000.

A corporate fiduciary must meet all four requirements in order to qualify for the exception.

Banks or other financial institutions that are authorized to exercise trust powers, but whose deposits are not insured by the Federal Deposit Insurance Corporation, may qualify for the exception only if they also meet bonding or similar requirements under state law which the Secretary of Labor determines to be at least equivalent to those imposed on banks by federal law.[13] However, because the DOL has not made any determinations as to whether any state bonding or similar requirements are "at least equivalent" to those imposed on banks by federal law, the statutory exemption authorized by ERISA Sec. 412(a)(2) is not available to any bank or other financial institution authorized to exercise trust powers that has deposits that are not insured by the FDIC. By contrast, banks and other financial institutions that have no deposits are not subject to this additional condition. Accordingly, a subsidiary of a bank holding company that was authorized to exercise trust powers under a non-deposit bank charter, and that satisfied the other conditions set forth in ERISA Sec. 412(a)(2), was exempt from the fidelity bonding requirements.[14]

Limited exemption under proposed rules

Proposed Labor Department regulations would provide relief from ERISA's bonding rules for:[15]

1. any broker-dealer registered under the Securities Exchange Act of 1934; and

2. any investment adviser registered under the Investment Advisers Act of 1940 who (a) controls, is controlled by, or is under common control with a broker-dealer registered under the Exchange Act, (b) does not maintain actual custody or possession of the assets of employee benefit plans, and (c) is named as an additional insured on the registered broker-dealer's bond.

EBSA clarification. The Employee Benefits Security Administration (EBSA) has issued Field Assistance Bulletin 2008-04 that provides guidance on fidelity bonding requirements under ERISA Sec. 412 For instance, EBSA makes it clear that fiduciaries must be bonded only if they "handle" funds or other property of an employee benefit plan and do not fall within one of the exemptions in ERISA Sec. 412 or the regulations. A bond can insure more than one plan. An "omnibus clause" may be used as an alternative way to identify multiple plans as insureds on one bond, rather than specifically naming on the bond each individual plan in a group of plans, according to the Labor Department.

According to the EBSA guidance, the $1 million bond amount for plans that hold employer securities does not apply to every plan that holds employer securities. It is the DOL's view that a plan is not considered to be holding employer securities, for purposes of the increased bonding requirement, merely because the plan invests in a broadly-diversified common or pooled investment vehicle that holds employer securities, but which is independent of the employer and any of its affiliates.

---

[1] ERISA Sec. 412(a).

[2] ERISA Sec. 412(b).

[3] ERISA Sec. 412(a); ERISA Temp. Reg. § 2580.412-11.

[4] ERISA Sec. 412(a); ERISA Temp. Reg. §§ 2580.412-14 and 2580.412-15.

[5] ERISA Sec. 412(a), as amended by the Pension Protection Act of 2006 (P.L. 109-280).

[6] ERISA Sec. 412(a).

[7] ERISA Sec. 412(c).

[8] ERISA Sec. 412(d).

[9] ERISA Reg. § 2509.75-5, FR-9 (ERISA Interpretive Bulletin 75-5).

[10] ERISA Sec. 412(e).

[11] ERISA Reg. § 2509.75-5, FR-8 (ERISA Interpretive Bulletin 75-5).

[12] ERISA Sec. 412(a)(2).

[13] ERISA Sec. 412(a).

[14] ERISA Opinion Letter 2004-07A, 7-1-04, CCH PENSION PLAN GUIDE ¶ 19,990H.

[15] ERISA Prop. Reg. § 2580.412-33.

¶ 2395
For More Information

☐ For more information on ERISA fiduciary rules, see ¶ 4400-4535 and ¶ 7526A-7526C of the CCH PENSION PLAN GUIDE.

Prohibited Transactions

¶ 2400
Overview of Prohibited Transaction Rules

The prohibited transaction rules bar a fiduciary from engaging in certain transactions, such as dealing with plan assets, for the fiduciary's own interest. These prohibited transaction rules apply to a party in interest (called a disqualified person by the Internal Revenue Code). A person who participates in a prohibited transaction is subject to a 15% excise tax on the amount involved. If the prohibited transaction is not timely corrected, an excise tax of 100% of the amount involved is imposed. The discussion in this chapter describes various types of prohibited activities, who these rules apply to, and how a prohibited transaction can be corrected.

Exemptions from the prohibited transaction rules are available. A number of exemptions are provided by statute. Individual exemptions from the prohibited transaction rules have been granted for various types of transactions. Unlike individual exemptions, which offer relief only to the specific parties requesting an exemption, class exemptions furnish relief to any parties who engage in transactions of the type covered by the class exemption, if the parties meet stated terms and conditions.

With only a few exceptions, requests for administrative exemptions from the prohibited transaction provisions are handled through the Labor Department. Any party in interest or disqualified person with respect to a plan may initiate an application for exemption, as may the Labor Department itself. In some situations, an association or organization that represents disqualified persons or parties in interest may apply for an exemption. The discussion in this chapter sets forth Labor

Department guidelines on who may apply for a prohibited transaction exemption, the contents of the application, special information required for individual exemptions, stages of the application process, and the effect of a successful exemption application.

¶ 2402

GENERAL RULES: Definition of Prohibited Transaction

A plan fiduciary may not cause a plan to engage in any transaction which he or she knows, or should know, constitutes a direct or indirect:[1]

1. sale, exchange, or lease of any property between the plan and a party in interest;

2. loan of money or other extension of credit between the plan and a party in interest;

3. furnishing of goods, services, or facilities between the plan and a party in interest;

4. transfer of any plan assets to, or use by or for the benefit of, a party in interest;

5. acquisition, on behalf of any plan, of any employer security or employer real property in violation of the 10% limitation imposed by ERISA on the acquisition and holding of employer securities and employer real property.

A fiduciary with respect to the plan is also prohibited from:[2]

1. dealing with plan assets in the fiduciary's own interest or for the fiduciary's own account;

2. acting, in any transaction involving the plan, on behalf of a party whose interests are adverse to the interests of the plan or the interests of its participants or beneficiaries;

3. receiving any consideration for his or her personal account from any party dealing with the plan in connection with a transaction involving the income or assets of the plan.

---

[1] ERISA Sec. 406(a).   [2] ERISA Sec. 406(b).

¶ 2404

GENERAL RULES: Application of the Prohibited Transaction Rules

All qualified plans, as well as qualified annuity plans, bond purchase plans, and IRAs, are subject to the prohibited transaction rules. Governmental plans and church plans that have not elected to be subject to the participation, vesting, and funding rules of ERISA are excluded from the prohibited transaction rules.

Prohibited transaction rules are included in the labor and tax provisions of ERISA and the Internal Revenue Code, respectively. The labor prohibitions affect "parties in interest," and the tax prohibitions affect "disqualified persons." The two terms are substantially the same in most respects, but the labor term includes a somewhat broader range of persons (see ¶ 2406).[1]

The labor and tax provisions governing prohibited transactions and their exceptions are nearly identical. However, under the labor provisions, a fiduciary is liable only if the fiduciary knew or should have known that he or she engaged in a prohibited transaction. This knowledge requirement has not been incorporated by the tax provisions of the Code.

In addition, the prohibited transaction rules under the labor provisions apply to all plans to which the general labor fiduciary rules apply (see ¶ 2325). Under the labor provisions, a fiduciary is liable for losses to a plan from a prohibited transaction in which he or she engaged if a prudent person would have known that the transaction involving the party in interest was prohibited. In the case of a significant transaction, a prudent fiduciary must make a thorough investigation of the other party's relationship to the plan to determine if he or she is a party in interest. In the case of a normal or day-to-day transaction, it may be sufficient for the fiduciary to check the identity of the other party against a roster of parties in interest that is periodically updated.

Although ERISA calls for the coordinated action of the Internal Revenue Service and the Labor Department in the administration of the prohibited transaction rules, duplicate efforts have resulted in delays, especially in the granting of prohibited transaction exemptions. As a result, under the ERISA Reorganization Plan, the Secretary of the Treasury has transferred to the Secretary of Labor the general authority to issue regulations, rulings, opinions, and exceptions under Code Sec. 4975, concerning the tax on prohibited transactions.

---

[1] Code Sec. 4975; ERISA Sec. 3(14).

¶ 2406

GENERAL RULES: Parties in Interest/Disqualified Persons

Under labor law provisions, the prohibited transaction rules affect a "party in interest." The tax law prohibited transaction rules affect a "disqualified person." The two terms are substantially the same in most respects, but the labor term includes a somewhat broader range of persons.

Party in interest

ERISA specifically defines a party in interest with respect to an employee benefit plan to include:[1]

1. any fiduciary;

2. a person providing services to the plan;

3. an employer, any of whose employees are covered by the plan;

4. an employee organization, any of whose members are covered by the plan;

5. an owner, direct or indirect, of 50% or more of: (i) the combined voting power of all classes of stock entitled to vote or the total value of shares of all classes of stock of a corporation, (ii) the capital interest or the profits interest of a partnership, or (iii) the beneficial interest of a trust or unincorporated enterprise, which is an employer or employee organization described in (3) or (4) above;

6. a relative of any individual described in (1), (2), (3), or (5);

7. a corporation, partnership, or trust or estate of which (or in which) 50% or more of: (i) the combined voting power of all classes of stock entitled to vote or the total value of shares of all classes of stock of such corporation, (ii) the capital interest or profits interest of such partnership, or (iii) the beneficial interest of such trust or estate is owned directly or indirectly, or held by persons described in (1)—(5);

8. an employee, officer, director (or an individual having powers or responsibilities similar to those of officers or directors), or a 10%-or-more shareholder, directly or indirectly, of a person described in (2), (3), (4), (5), or (6), or of the employee benefit plan; or

9. a 10% or more (directly or indirectly in capital or profits) partner or joint venturer or a person described in (2), (3), (4), (5), or (6).

Fiduciaries. The definition of a fiduciary is very broad and includes any person who has any discretionary authority regarding the management of the plan or its assets. It also includes any person who renders investment advice to the plan for a fee or who has authority or responsibility to render such advice, as well as anyone who has any discretionary authority in the administration of the plan. A person designated by a fiduciary (under ERISA Sec. 405(c)(1)(B)) to carry out fiduciary responsibilities (other than trustee responsibilities) is also considered a fiduciary.[2]

Disqualified persons

Under the Internal Revenue Code, the prohibited transaction rules apply to disqualified persons. A disqualified person includes:[3]

1. a fiduciary. However, a fiduciary is not liable for the excise tax unless he or she participates in the transaction in a role other than, or in addition to, his or her fiduciary capacity;

2. a person who provides services to the plan;

3. an employer whose employees are covered by the plan;

4. any employee organization whose members are covered by the plan;

5. any owner, direct or indirect, of 50% or more of (i) the combined voting power of all classes of stock entitled to vote or the total value of shares of all classes of stock; (ii) the capital or profits interest of a partnership; or (iii) the beneficial interest of a trust or unincorporated enterprise, which is an employer or employee organization;

6. a member of the family of an individual described in (1), (2), (3), or (5) above, including the spouse, ancestor, lineal descendant, and any spouse of a lineal descendant;

7. a corporation, partnership, or trust or estate of which, or in which, 50% or more of the combined voting power of all classes of stock or the total value of all classes of stock, the capital interest of a partnership, or the beneficial interest of a trust is owned, directly or indirectly, or held by a person described in (1)-(5) above. The Treasury Secretary may reduce the 50% ownership requirement by regulation after consultation with the Secretary of Labor;

8. an officer, director, or an individual having similar powers, a 10%-or-more shareholder, or a highly compensated employee (earning 10% or more of the annual wages of an employer) of a person described in (3), (4), (5), and (7) above. The Treasury Secretary can reduce the 10% requirement by regulation after consultation with the Secretary of Labor; or

9. a 10% or more (in capital or profits) partner or joint venturer of a person described in (3), (4), (5), or (7).

Only highly compensated can be disqualified persons. The Code's definition of a disqualified person effectively includes parties in interest. However, note that an employee is a party in interest but is not a disqualified person unless the employee is highly compensated which, for this purpose, means that the employee earns 10% or more of the aggregate wages paid by the employer.

---

[1] ERISA Sec. 3(14).

[2] Code Sec. 4975(e)(2)(A) and (e)(3); IRS Reg. § 54.4975-9; ERISA Reg. § 2510.3-21.

[3] Code Sec. 4975(a), (b), (e), and (g).

¶ 2408

GENERAL RULES: Excise Taxes on Prohibited Transactions

A disqualified person or party in interest who participates in a prohibited transaction is subject under the Internal Revenue Code to a two-level excise tax. The tax is aimed at bringing about the correction of the prohibited transaction.

Two-tier excise tax

The first level of the prohibited transaction excise tax is a tax of 15% of the amount involved in each prohibited transaction for each year or part of a year in the taxable period.[1] The 15% tax is imposed automatically even if the violation is inadvertent.

The second level of the prohibited transaction excise tax is a tax of 100% of the amount involved in each transaction.[2] The second tier 100% excise tax is assessed unless the prohibited transaction is corrected (see ¶ 2412) during the period beginning with the date on which the prohibited transaction occurs and ending 90 days after the date on which a notice of deficiency for the penalty tax on the prohibited transaction was mailed.[3] If the transaction is corrected, amounts assessed will be abated and amounts collected will be credited or refunded as overpayment.[4]

CCH Pointer: The party in interest or disqualified person participating in the prohibited transaction is personally liable for the excise tax. A plan may not pay the excise tax imposed on the party in interest or the disqualified person. However, a qualified trust will not lose its qualified status under Code Sec. 401 as a result of the prohibited transaction.

Joint and several liability. If more than one person is liable for the 15% or 100% excise tax, all persons are jointly and severally liable for the excise tax.[5]

Amount involved

The amount involved in a prohibited transaction (and, thus, the amount subject to tax), except in cases involving services, is the greater of (a) the amount of money and the fair market value of property given by the disqualified person, or (b) the amount of money and the fair market value of property received by the disqualified person.[6]

The excise tax imposed for the failure to timely deposit deferrals to a 401(k) plan is assessed only on interest on the untimely deferrals. Essentially the fiduciary is assessed a 15% excise tax on the value of the use of the funds.[7]

For purposes of the 15% excise tax, property is valued as of the date of the transaction.[8] In the case of the 100% excise tax, the value of the property will be the highest market value registered during the taxable period.

Taxable period

The "taxable period" is the period beginning with the date the prohibited transaction occurs and ending on the earlier of the date the IRS mails a notice of deficiency to the taxpayer regarding the 15% tax, the date the 15% tax is assessed, or the date on which the prohibited transaction is corrected.[9]

Welfare plans and nonqualified plans

The Secretary of Labor is authorized to assess civil penalties against parties in interest who engage in prohibited transactions with plans, including welfare and nonqualified pension plans, that are not subject to the excise tax imposed by Code Sec. 4975. The amount of the civil penalty may not exceed 5% of the "amount involved" in the transaction, except that, if a prohibited transaction is not "corrected" within 90 days, the penalty may be up to 100% of the "amount involved." [10]

¶ 2408

Report prohibited transaction and excise tax on Form 5330

Prohibited transactions and the attendant excise taxes must be reported by the disqualified person or party in interest on Form 5330 (Return of Excise Taxes Related to Employee Benefit Plans). Failure to file Form 5330 will subject the taxpayer to an additional penalty tax, unless the failure to file was due to reasonable cause.

---

[1] Code Sec. 4975(a).

[2] Code Sec. 4975(b).

[3] Code Sec. 4963(e)(1); IRS Reg. §53.4963-1; ERISA Sec. 502(i).

[4] Code Sec. 4961(a).

[5] Code Sec. 4975(f)(1).

[6] Code Sec. 4975(f)(4).

[7] Rev. Rul. 2006-38, I.R.B. 2006-29, CCH PENSION PLAN GUIDE ¶ 19,948Z-155.

[8] Code Sec. 4975(f)(4).

[9] Code Sec. 4975(f)(2).

[10] ERISA Sec. 502(i); ERISA Reg. §2560.502i-1(a).

¶ 2410

GENERAL RULES: Multiemployer Plans

The prohibited transaction rules under Code Sec. 4975 apply to withdrawal liability funds established under Code Sec. 501(c)(22). A withdrawal liability fund is a fund established by sponsors of multiemployer plans to pay withdrawal liabilities under certain circumstances (see ¶ 2906).[1]

Disqualified persons (including disqualified persons with respect to any plan participating in the fund) who participate in prohibited transactions with the fund are subject to the 15% excise tax.[2] In addition, under ERISA, any person who is an interested party to a plan to which a tax-exempt withdrawal liability payment fund is permitted to make payments is to be treated as an interested party with respect to the fund. Interested parties include fiduciaries, employees, employers, and employee organizations.[3]

Withdrawal liability

An exemption to the prohibited transaction provisions of ERISA is provided for (1) any transaction under the employer withdrawal liability provisions of ERISA, (2) a merger of multiemployer plans, or (3) the transfer of assets or liabilities under the ERISA Sec. 4231 rules governing the merger or transfer of plan assets or liabilities among multiemployer plans. However, the exemption does not apply to an act by a disqualified person who is a fiduciary and who deals with the income or assets of a plan in his own interest or for his own account. The exemption also does not apply to the receipt of consideration by a fiduciary for his or her own personal account from any party dealing with the plan in connection with a transaction involving the income or assets of the plan.[4]

---

[1] Withdrawal liability payment funds are described in ERISA Sec. 4223.

[2] Code Sec. 4975(e)(9); P.L. 96-364 (Multiemployer Pension Plan Amendments Act of 1980), Sec. 210(c).

[3] ERISA Sec. 3(14).

[4] Code Sec. 4975(d)(14) and (15); ERISA Sec. 408(b)(10) and (11).

¶ 2412

GENERAL RULES: Correcting Prohibited Transactions

One of the main purposes of the prohibited transactions excise tax is to bring about the correction of the transaction. A prohibited transaction is corrected if it is undone to the extent possible. However, at a minimum, a correction must place the plan in a financial position that is no worse than that in which it would have been if the disqualified person had acted under the highest fiduciary standards.[1]

Coordinated IRS and DOL correction effort

Under the ERISA Reorganization Plan, the Secretary of the Treasury generally transferred to the Secretary of Labor authority to issue regulations, rulings, opinions, and exceptions concerning prohibited transactions. However, an exception to this transfer of authority was made for rules involving the correction or undoing of a prohibited transaction.[2] Thus, the correction of a prohibited transaction may involve the coordinated efforts of the IRS and the Department of Labor.[3]

Correction period

Internal Revenue Code. The period during which a prohibited transaction may be corrected begins with the date on which the prohibited transaction occurs and ends on the 90th day after the IRS mails the notice of deficiency with respect to the 100% tax, extended by any period in which a deficiency may not be assessed under Code Sec. 6213(c), and any other period determined by the IRS to be reasonable or necessary to bring about the correction of the prohibited transaction.[4]

If the taxable event is corrected during the correction period, the 100% second-tier tax will not be assessed.[5] If the prohibited transaction is not corrected at the end of this period, the 100% tax is imposed. However, the tax will not be assessed if the taxpayer files a petition with the Tax Court for a redetermination of that tax and the prohibited act is corrected by the time the Tax Court's decision becomes final.

The correction period may be extended beyond the date that the Tax Court decision becomes final if the IRS determines that the extension is reasonable and necessary to bring about the correction. Thus, where the taxpayer petitions the Tax Court to redetermine the 100% tax, the tax may not be assessed unless the court decides that the taxpayer has engaged in an act giving rise to the 15% tax and that the act was not timely corrected.[6]

The collection of any 100% excise tax which was assessed is suspended until the taxpayer completes its administrative and judicial refund procedures. As a result, a taxpayer may have issues involving the 100% tax reviewed before a U.S. district court or the U.S. Claims Court without first being required to pay the 100% tax.[7]

ERISA. ERISA Sec. 502(i) allows a party in interest to correct a prohibited transaction within 90 days after notice from the Secretary of Labor and thereby avoid the 100% second-tier penalty. In general, the correction period begins on the date the prohibited transaction occurs and ends 90 days after final DOL action on the transaction.[8] However, the party in interest must respond to a notice of the DOL's intent to impose a sanction within 30 days, or the notice will become a final order and the initial 15% penalty will be automatically imposed.[9] The correction period would end 90 days after the expiration of the 30-day period.[10]

Correction period for securities and commodities. The correction period for prohibited transactions involving securities and commodities is 14 days after the party discovers or should have discovered that the transaction was prohibited.[11] The provision applies to any transaction which the fiduciary or disqualified person discovers, or reasonably should have discovered, after August 17, 2006, constitutes a prohibited transaction.

The 14-day correction period applies for certain transactions that occur by mistake between a plan and a party in interest. The transaction must be in connection with the acquisition, holding, or disposition of a security or commodity.

The correction period is the 14-day period beginning on the date on which the disqualified person, fiduciary or party in interest discovers, or reasonably should have discovered, that the transaction would constitute a prohibited transaction.[12]

Voluntary Fiduciary Correction Program

Fiduciaries may avoid civil actions and civil penalties for specified breaches of fiduciary duty by voluntarily undertaking required corrective actions under the Employee Benefits Security Administration's Voluntary Fiduciary Correction (VFC) Program. For more information about the VFC program and about relief from prohibited transaction excise taxes for fiduciaries that use the VFC Program, see ¶ 2487 and ¶ 2737.

[1] Code Sec. 4975(f)(5); ERISA Sec. 502(i).

[2] Sec. 102, ERISA Reorganization Plan.

[3] ERISA Sec. 3003(b).

[4] Code Sec. 4963(e); IRS Reg. § 53.4963-1(e).

[5] Code Sec. 4961(a); IRS Reg. § 53.4961-1.

[6] Code Sec. 4961(b); IRS Reg. § 53.4961-2.

[7] Code Sec. 4961(c).

[8] ERISA Reg. § 2560.502i-1(d)(1).

[9] ERISA Reg. § 2570.5.

[10] ERISA Reg. §§ 2560.502i-1(d)(3)(i) and 2570.5.

[11] Code Sec. 4975(d)(23) and ERISA Sec. 408(b)(20), as added by P.L. 109-280 (Pension Protection Act of 2006), Act Sec. 612.

[12] Code Sec. 4975(f)(11) and ERISA Sec. 408(b)(20)(D), as added by P.L. 109-280 (Pension Protection Act of 2006), Act Sec. 612.

¶ 2414

GENERAL RULES: Statute of Limitations

For purposes of assessing the excise tax under Code Sec. 4975, the filing of Form 5500 starts the statute of limitations running where a prohibited transaction is indicated on the form.[1]

In cases involving discrete transactions, if the plan discloses the prohibited transaction on Form 5330 or 5500 (whichever is applicable), the three-year statute of limitation under Code Sec. 6501(a) applies. However, if a transaction is not disclosed, the six-year statute of limitation under Code Sec. 6501(e)(3) applies. If

Form 5330 or 5500 is never filed, or the return is fraudulently filed with respect to the excise tax due, no statute of limitations applies, and the tax may be assessed at any time.

Recurring prohibited transactions

A prohibited transaction that is of a continuing nature, such as a loan or a lease, is deemed to reoccur on the first day of each taxable year subsequent to the taxable year in which the act first occurred.[2] In this circumstance, the filing of the applicable return for the plan year in which the prohibited transaction first occurred commences the statute of limitations running for transactions occurring in that year only. However, the filing of the return does not begin the statute of limitations for transactions occurring in subsequent years, assuming the prohibited transaction has not been corrected. Thus, the expiration of the statute of limitations must be determined separately for each taxable year.[3]

---

[1] IRS General Counsel's Memorandum 39475, 8-16-85, CCH PENSION PLAN GUIDE ¶ 17,512.

[2] ERISA Reg. § 2560.502i-1(e).

[3] IRS General Counsel's Memorandum 38846, 2-26-82, CCH PENSION PLAN GUIDE ¶ 17,471.

¶ 2416

TYPES OF PROHIBITED TRANSACTIONS: Sale, Exchange, or Lease of Property

The direct or indirect sale, exchange, or leasing of any property between the plan and a party in interest (or disqualified person)[1] is a prohibited transaction.[2] The prohibition encompasses sales, exchanges, or leases of property from the party in interest to the plan and also from the plan to the party in interest. The property at issue need not actually be owned by the plan or by a party in interest in order for a prohibited transaction to occur.

A sale or exchange of property includes a transfer of property to a plan in which:[3]

1. the plan assumes a mortgage or similar lien; or

2. the property is subject to a mortgage or similar lien which a disqualified person has placed on the property within a ten-year period ending with the date of the transfer to the plan.

Thus, a disqualified person may not circumvent the prohibition on the sale of property by mortgaging it before transferring it to the plan.

Noncash plan contributions

The U.S. Supreme Court has ruled that an employer's contribution of unencumbered property to a defined benefit plan to satisfy its minimum funding obligation is a sale or exchange between a qualified plan and a disqualified person that is a prohibited transaction.[4] The Court clarified that Code Sec. 4975(f)(3) was intended by Congress to expand the scope of the prohibited transaction provision to include contributions of encumbered property that do not satisfy funding obligations. The provision was not meant to restrict the concept of what was considered a sale or exchange, according to the Court.

CCH Pointer: The Supreme Court in *Keystone* did not address in-kind contributions to defined contribution or welfare plans. However, the EBSA will treat an in-kind contribution to a defined contribution plan or a welfare plan as a prohibited sale or exchange of property if it is used to reduce or satisfy a funding obligation that is measured in cash.[5]

Excess contributions. The reasoning of *Keystone* has also been extended to in-kind contributions that exceed the amount needed to satisfy the plan's funding requirement for the year.[6] Because an in-kind contribution to a defined benefit plan is credited to the plan's funding standard account, it is a transfer made in order to reduce the employer's funding obligation and, therefore, constitutes a prohibited transaction. Excess contributions that are not used to reduce the accumulated funding deficiency for the year would also be prohibited because they are used as a credit against future funding obligations.

---

[1] For purposes of this discussion, the term "party in interest" includes disqualified persons, unless otherwise indicated.

[2] Code Sec. 4975(c)(1)(A) and (f)(3).

[3] ERISA Sec. 406(c). A parallel provision, for purposes of the IRS excise taxes on prohibited transactions, is contained in Code Sec. 4975(f)(3).

[4] *Commissioner v. Keystone Consolidated Industries, Inc.,* US Sup Ct (1993), 508 U.S. 152.

[5] PWBA Interpretive Bulletin 94-3, 12-28-94, CCH PENSION PLAN GUIDE ¶ 19,972.

[6] *Ibid.*

¶ 2418

TYPES OF PROHIBITED TRANSACTIONS: Loans Between Plan and Disqualified Person

Any lending of money or other extension of credit between a plan and a disqualified person or a party in interest is prohibited.[1] In such a loan agreement, it is the contract to loan and not the disbursal of funds which constitutes the prohibited transaction. Thus, a loan between a plan and a fiduciary constitutes a prohibited transaction even if the plan does not incur damages.

Exceptions for certain plan loans

A plan may loan money to disqualified persons or parties in interest who are participants or beneficiaries of the plan if the loans:[2]

1. are available to all participants and beneficiaries on a reasonably equivalent basis;

2. do not discriminate in favor of highly compensated employees;

3. are made in accordance with specific plan provisions;

4. bear a reasonable rate of interest; and

5. are adequately secured.[3]

Suspension of loan during employee's military service. A plan will not engage in a prohibited transaction merely by suspending an employee's obligation to repay a plan loan during the period of the employee's military service (even if the individual is not entitled to reemployment).[4]

---

[1] Code Sec. 4975(c)(1)(B); ERISA Sec. 406(a)(1)(B) and (b)(1); ERISA Reg. §§ 2550.408b-1 and 2550.408c-2(b)(4).

[2] Code Sec. 4975(d)(1); ERISA Reg. § 2550.408b-1(a)(1).

[3] See Rev. Rul. 80-269, 1980-2 CB 191, CCH Pension Plan Guide ¶ 19,541 and IRS Letter Ruling 7944001, 5-22-79, CCH Pension Plan Guide ¶ 17,370E (inadequately secured plan loan to em-

ployer was a prohibited transaction) and Rev. Rul. 81-145, 1981-1 CB 350, CCH Pension Plan Guide ¶ 19,590, superseding Rev. Rul. 73-609, 1973-2 CB 187 (failure of trustees to promptly demand payment of the interest due on an adequately secured loan from an exempt employees' trust to the trust's employer-creator was a prohibited transaction).

[4] Code Sec. 414(u)(4).

¶ 2420

TYPES OF PROHIBITED TRANSACTIONS: Provision of Goods, Services, or Facilities

The providing of goods, services, or facilities between a plan and a disqualified person or party in interest is prohibited.[1] However, this general prohibition does not prevent a plan from entering into a contract or a reasonable arrangement with a disqualified person or party in interest for office space or for services necessary to the establishment or operation of the plan, such as legal and accounting services (see ¶ 2438).

---

[1] Code Sec. 4975(c)(1)(C); ERISA Sec. 408(b)(2).

¶ 2422

TYPES OF PROHIBITED TRANSACTIONS: Transfer or Use of Assets

A transfer of plan assets or income to a disqualified person or the use of plan assets or income by or for the benefit of a disqualified person is prohibited.[1] Thus, an employer and a plan trustee could not use a plan checking account as an expense account or use plan assets to repay debts of the employer.[2]

Quid pro quo exchanges

An employer may, however, use plan assets to purchase liability releases from employees in exchange for enhanced pension benefits offered under an early retirement program.[3] According to the U.S. Supreme Court, ERISA does not bar a quid pro quo exchange between fiduciaries and plan participants in which the plan pays out benefits to the participants pursuant to its terms.

---

[1] Code Sec. 4975(c)(1)(D).

[2] IRS Letter Ruling 9424001, 2-8-94, CCH Pension Plan Guide ¶ 17,387U.

[3] *Lockheed Corp. v. Spink*, US Sup Ct (1996), 517 US 882.

¶ 2424

TYPES OF PROHIBITED TRANSACTIONS:
Acquisition of Employer Securities and Real Property

No fiduciary with authority or discretion to control or manage the assets of a plan, other than an eligible individual account plan, may permit the plan to acquire or hold any employer security which is not a "qualifying employer security" and any employer real property which is not "qualifying employer real property." [1]

CCH Pointer: *Post-2006 diversification rules for investments in employer securities.* For plan years beginning after 2006 (with delayed effective dates for collectively bargained plans and for certain securities held in an ESOP), the Pension Protection Act of 2006 has added a provision that defined contribution plans must meet diversification requirements with regard to any portion of employee contributions, elective deferrals and employer contributions invested in employer securities (see ¶ 2362). With regard to employee contributions and elective deferrals invested in employer securities, an individual must be allowed to elect to direct the plan to divest employer securities into other investment options.

Ten-percent restriction

A plan (other than an eligible individual account plan) may not acquire any qualifying employer security or qualifying employer real property if, immediately after such acquisition, the aggregate fair market value of employer securities and employer real property held by the plan exceeds 10% of the fair market value of the assets of the plan.[2] The acquisition rules apply not only to the purchase of employer securities or real property, but also to acquisition by exercise of warrants or on default of a loan where the stock is made security for the loan.

Exception for ESOPs. The 10% restriction on investments in employer securities and real property does not apply to employee stock ownership plans.[3]

Statutory exemption

Notwithstanding the prohibited transaction rules, qualifying employer securities and qualifying employer real property can generally be acquired for "adequate consideration" if no commission is charged and the acquisition is allowed by the employer securities rules.[4] However, except in the case of individual account plans, the acquisition and holding of qualifying employer securities and qualifying employer property must also meet fiduciary standards, such as prudence and diversification (see ¶ 2355 and ¶ 2362). Thus, less than 10% of plan assets must be held in employer securities and employer real property if required by the diversification and prudence rules.

Further, while a plan may be able to acquire employer securities or real property under the employer securities rules, the acquisition must be for the exclusive benefit of participants and beneficiaries. Thus, real property acquired primarily to finance the employer would not be proper.

Adequate consideration. Adequate consideration for assets other than securities (see ¶ 2450) for which there is a generally recognized market is fair market value as determined in good faith by the trustee or named fiduciary.[5] Adequate consideration for securities for which there is a generally recognized market is the price of the security prevailing on a national securities exchange.[6] If the security is not traded on national securities exchange, adequate consideration would be a price not less favorable to the plan than the offering price for the security as established by the current bid and asked prices quoted by persons who are independent of the issuer and parties in interest.

Eligible individual account plan

The above restrictions do not apply to any acquisition or holding of qualifying employer securities or qualifying employer real property by an eligible individual account plan.[7] An "eligible individual account plan" is an individual account plan that is:[8]

1. a profit-sharing, stock bonus, thrift, or savings plan;

2. an employee stock ownership plan; or

3. a money purchase plan that was in existence on September 2, 1974, and that, on such date, invested primarily in qualifying employer securities.

This definition does not include individual retirement accounts (IRAs) or annuities.

Limit on investment in employer securities by individual accounts

An individual account plan that requires elective deferrals of over 1% of an employee's eligible compensation to be invested in qualifying employer securities and qualifying employer real property, at the direction of a person other than the participant, is not an eligible individual account plan.[9] In the event that the 1% threshold is exceeded, the portion of the plan that consists of elective deferrals (and earnings thereon) will be treated as a separate plan subject to the 10% limit on investments in employer securities and real property.[10] However, the restriction does not apply to an individual account plan for a plan year if the fair market value of the assets of all individual account plans maintained by the employer, on the last day of the preceding plan year, does not exceed 10% of the value of the assets of all pension plans (other than multiemployer plans) maintained by the employer.[11]

Floor-offset arrangements. An individual account plan will not be eligible if the plan's benefits were taken into account in determining the benefits payable to a participant under any defined benefit plan.[12] In addition, such a "floor-offset" arrangement (see ¶ 103), is treated as a single plan for purposes of the rule limiting a plan's investment in employer securities and employer real property to 10% of the plan's assets.[13]

Qualifying employer real property

The term "qualifying employer real property" (property that can be held by the plan) refers to parcels of employer real property:[14]

1. if a substantial number of the parcels are dispersed geographically;

2. if each parcel of real property and the improvements on such property are suitable (or adaptable without excessive cost) for more than one use;

3. even if all of such real property is leased to one lessee (which may be the employer or an affiliate of the employer); and

4. if the acquisition and retention of such property comply with the fiduciary responsibility provisions of ERISA, other than the diversification requirements, the prudent man rule (to the extent it requires diversification), the prohibited transaction restrictions, and the restriction on a plan's acquisition of employer securities and real property.

Qualifying employer security

The term "qualifying employer security" denotes an employer security which is stock or a marketable obligation.[15] In the case of a plan other than an eligible individual account plan, stock will be considered a qualifying employer security that the plan can hold only if, immediately following the acquisition:[16]

1. not more than 25% of the aggregate amount of stock of the same class issued and outstanding at the time of acquisition by the plan is held by the plan, and

2. at least 50% of the aggregate amount of the stock is held by persons independent of the issuer.

If readily tradable common stock is not available, common stock issued by the employer having a combination of voting power and dividend rights equal to or in excess of that class of common stock of the employer that has the greatest voting power and that class of common stock having the greatest dividend rights, will be treated as qualifying employer securities. Noncallable preferred stock is also considered a qualifying employer security if the stock may be converted at any time into the readily tradable common stock, or the alternative to readily tradable common stock, and if the conversion is at a reasonable conversion price. Preferred stock is noncallable if, after the call, there is a reasonable opportunity for a conversion.

---

[1] Code Sec. 4975(e)(8); ERISA Secs. 406(a)(1), 407(a)-(e), and 408(b); P.L. 100-203 (Omnibus Budget Reconciliation Act of 1987), Act Sec. 9345(a) and (b).

[2] ERISA Sec. 407(a)(2).

[3] ERISA Sec. 407(b)(2)(B)(iii), as added by P.L. 105-34 (Taxpayer Relief Act of 1997).

[4] Code Sec. 4975(d)(13); ERISA Sec. 408(e); ERISA Reg. § 2550.408e.

[5] ERISA Sec. 3(18)(B).

[6] ERISA Sec. 3(18)(A).

[7] ERISA Sec. 407(b)(1).

[8] ERISA Sec. 407(d)(3)(A).

[9] ERISA Sec. 407(b)(2)(B)(iv), as added by P.L. 105-34 (Taxpayer Relief Act of 1997).

[10] ERISA Sec. 407(b)(2)(A).

[11] ERISA Sec. 407(b)(2)(B)(ii).

[12] ERISA Sec. 407(d)(3)(C).

[13] ERISA Sec. 407(d)(9).

[14] ERISA Sec. 407(d)(4).

[15] ERISA Sec. 407(d)(5).

[16] ERISA Sec. 407(f)(1).

¶ 2426

TYPES OF PROHIBITED TRANSACTIONS: Fiduciary Dealing with Plan Assets in Own Interest

A plan fiduciary (see ¶ 2305) may not:[1]

1. deal with plan assets in the fiduciary's own interest or for the fiduciary's own account;

2. act in any capacity, in any transaction involving the plan on behalf of any party whose interests are adverse to the interests of the plan or the interests of its participants or beneficiaries; or

3. receive any consideration for the fiduciary's personal account from any party dealing with such plan in connection with any transaction involving the assets of the plan.

CCH Pointer: The statutory exemption that allows a plan to contract with a party in interest for office space or services necessary for the establishment or operation of the plan (see ¶ 2438), will not shield from liability a fiduciary who exercises authority to cause a plan to enter into a transaction in which the fiduciary has an interest that may affect his or her judgment.[2]

---

[1] Code Secs. 4975(c)(1)(E) and (F); ERISA Sec. 406(b)(1), (2), and (3).

[2] ERISA Reg. § 2550.408b-2(e)(1).

¶ 2428

TYPES OF PROHIBITED TRANSACTIONS: Permissible Actions for Fiduciaries

Despite the prohibited transaction rules, fiduciaries are permitted to engage in a wide range of activities. Under ERISA, a fiduciary is allowed to:[1]

1. Receive any benefit to which the fiduciary may be entitled as a plan participant or beneficiary, as long as the benefit is computed and paid on a basis consistent with the terms of the plan as applied to all other participants and beneficiaries;

2. Receive reasonable compensation or a reimbursement of expenses for services rendered to the plan. However, a fiduciary who is receiving full-time pay from an employer or association of employers (with employees covered by the plan) or from a union (with members covered by the plan) may be reimbursed only for expenses properly and actually incurred; and

3. Serve as a fiduciary in addition to being an officer, employee, agent, or other representative of a party in interest.

---

[1] ERISA Sec. 408(c); ERISA Reg. § 2550.408(c)-2.

¶ 2430

EXEMPTIONS TO PROHIBITED TRANSACTION RULES: General Procedures

The IRS and the Department of Labor have established general procedures for the processing of applications for exemption from the prohibited transaction rules.[1] An exemption may be granted only if it is administratively feasible, in the interest of the plan and its participants and beneficiaries, and protective of the rights of participants and beneficiaries.

Before an exemption can be granted, adequate notice must be provided to interested persons and the pendency of the exemption must be published in the *Federal Register*. In addition, interested persons are to be allowed an opportunity to present their views on the pending exemption.

Procedures for obtaining exemptions

☐ The procedures for obtaining prohibited transaction exemptions are covered at ¶ 2506 and following.

---

[1] Code Sec. 4975(c)(2); ERISA Sec. 408(a).

¶ 2432

EXEMPTIONS TO PROHIBITED TRANSACTION RULES: Types of Exemptions

There are three types of exemptions granted from the prohibited transaction rules of ERISA: individual exemptions, class exemptions, and statutory exemptions.

Individual exemptions

Individual exemptions have been granted for various types of transactions. The most common exemptions involve plan loans or the sale of real property to disqualified persons or parties in interest, a plan lease of real property to an employer, and the plan purchase of trust interests for parties in interest.

Class exemptions

Unlike individual exemptions, which offer relief only to the specific parties requesting the exemption, class exemptions furnish relief to all parties who engage in transactions of the type covered by the class exemption, provided the parties meet stated terms and conditions.

☐ Class exemptions granted by the Labor Department are discussed beginning at ¶ 2460.

Statutory exemptions

In addition to individual and class exemptions, a number of transactions are exempt from the prohibited transaction rules by statute.

☐ These statutory exemptions are discussed beginning at ¶ 2436.

¶ 2436

STATUTORY EXEMPTIONS: Participant Loans

In general, under the prohibited transaction rules, any lending of money or other extension of credit between a plan and a disqualified person or a party in interest is prohibited. However, plan loans to disqualified persons or parties in interest are permitted under certain circumstances.

Under this exception, a plan may loan money to disqualified persons or parties in interest who are participants or beneficiaries of the plan if the loans:[1]

1. are available to all participants and beneficiaries on a reasonably equivalent basis;

2. do not discriminate in favor of highly compensated employees;

3. are made in accordance with specific plan provisions;

4. bear a reasonable rate of interest; and

5. are adequately secured.

Reasonably equivalent basis

Loans must be available to all plan participants and beneficiaries without regard to any individual's race, color, religion, sex, age, or national origin. Moreover, consideration must be given only to those factors that would be considered in a normal commercial setting, including the applicant's creditworthiness and financial need. Finally, an evaluation of all relevant facts and circumstances must indicate that, in actual practice, loans are not unreasonably withheld from any applicant.

---

[1] Code Sec. 4975(d)(1); ERISA Sec. 408(b)(1); ERISA Reg. §§ 2550.408b-1 and 2550.408c-2(b)(4).

¶ 2438

STATUTORY EXEMPTIONS: Contracting for Reasonable Office Space or Services

A plan may contract or make reasonable arrangements with a party in interest, including a fiduciary, for office space or for legal, accounting, or other services necessary for the establishment or operation of the plan.[1] However, no more than reasonable compensation may be paid for the office space or services.[2]

Necessary service

A service is necessary for the establishment or operation of a plan if it is appropriate and helpful to the plan in carrying out its purposes. A service provider also may furnish goods that are necessary for the establishment or operation of the plan in the course of furnishing services to the plan.[3]

Reasonable contract or arrangement

A reasonable contract or arrangement is one which permits termination of services on reasonably short notice by the plan without penalty. For example, a long-term lease that may be terminated prior to its expiration without penalty to the plan on reasonably short notice is not an unreasonable arrangement simply because of its long term. A provision in a contract that reasonably compensates the service provider for loss upon early termination is not a penalty.[4]

> **CCH Pointer:** The EBSA has issued interim final regulations that are designed to provide plan fiduciaries with sufficient information to evaluate the reasonableness of compensation and fees directly and indirectly paid to certain service providers (including affiliates), and assess the potential for conflicts of interest that may affect the performance of a service provider.[5] A service contract or arrangement would not be reasonable unless covered service providers (including fiduciary service providers, banks, consultants, investment providers, and third-party administrators) comply with a series of new disclosure requirements.
>
> Absent compliance by the service provider with the disclosure requirements, the plan fiduciary would be subject to liability for engaging in a prohibited transaction. However, the DOL has incorporated a class exemption into the final regulations that would relieve a fiduciary of liability for a prohibited transaction resulting from a service provider's failure to comply with the notice requirements.[6] The fiduciary may not have had knowledge of the service provider's compliance failure and would be required to take actions upon discovering the failure, including notification to the DOL.
>
> In order to allow parties sufficient time to address the new rules and establish procedures to ensure compliance with the regulations and the class exemption, the rules were set to be effective July 16, 2011.[7] However, the EBSA has extended the effective date of the rules to April 1, 2012.[8]
>
> For more details, see ¶ 2945.

Reasonable compensation

Payment by a plan to a party in interest for services rendered is not reasonable compensation if it is made to a fiduciary who is already receiving full-time pay from an employer whose employees are participants in the plan unless the payment is reimbursement of direct expenses properly and actually incurred.[9] An expense is not a direct expense if it would have been sustained had the service not been provided or if it represents an allocable portion of overhead expenses.

If a fiduciary provides services to a plan without receiving compensation, the provision of these services does not, by itself, constitute a prohibited act.[10] Allowance of a tax deduction to an employer under Code Secs. 162 or 212 for the expense incurred in furnishing office space or services to a plan by the employer does not constitute compensation or other consideration for this purpose.

Fiduciary may not receive "additional" fees. Fiduciaries may not use their authority, control, or responsibility as a fiduciary to cause a plan to pay additional fees to the fiduciary to provide a service.[11] Nor may a fiduciary cause an additional fee to be paid by a company or entity in which the fiduciary has an interest which may affect the exercise of the fiduciary's best judgment. Similarly, a fiduciary may not use his authority, control, or responsibility as a fiduciary to cause a plan to enter into a transaction involving plan assets whereby the fiduciary would receive consideration from a third party in connection with the transaction. A fiduciary who engages in any of these acts has violated ERISA Sec. 406(b), which prohibits acts involving conflicts of interests by fiduciaries.

---

[1] Code Sec. 4975(d)(2); ERISA Sec. 408(b)(2); ERISA Reg. § 2550.408b-2.

[2] ERISA Reg. § 2550.408b-2(a).

[3] ERISA Reg. § 2550.408b-2(b).

[4] ERISA Reg. § 2550.408b-2(c).

[5] EBSA interim final regulations, 75 FR 41600, July 16, 2010, CCH Pension Plan Guide ¶ 24,808T; ERISA Reg. § 2550.408b-2(c).

[6] EBSA class exemption, 75 FR 41600, July 16, 2010, CCH Pension Plan Guide ¶ 24,808T; ERISA Reg. § 2550.408b-2(c)(1)(ix).

[7] ERISA Reg. § 2550.408b-2(c)(1)(xii).

[8] EBSA final regulations, 76 FR 42539, July 19, 2011, CCH Pension Plan Guide ¶ 24,809B; ERISA Reg. § 2550.408b-2(c)(1)(xii).

[9] ERISA Reg. §§ 2550.408b-2(d) and 2550.408c-2(b)(3).

[10] ERISA Reg. § 2550.408b-2(e)(3).

[11] ERISA Reg. § 2550.408b-2(e)(1).

¶ 2439
STATUTORY EXEMPTIONS: Service Providers

The Pension Protection Act of 2006 (P.L. 109-280) added an exemption for service providers who are not fiduciaries with respect to the assets involved.[1] The exemption applies only if, in connection with a sale or exchange, lease, extension of credit, or transfer of plan income or assets transaction, the plan receives no less, nor pays no more, than adequate consideration.

"Adequate consideration" for this purpose means:

1. For a security where there is a generally recognized market, the price of the security on a national securities exchange. If the security is not traded on such an exchange, a price not less favorable to the plan than the offering price for the security as established by the current bid and asked prices quoted by persons independent of the issuer and of the disqualified person/party in interest. Factors such as the size of the transaction and marketability of the security must be taken into account for all securities.

2. For an asset other than a security where there is a generally recognized market, the fair market value of the asset as determined in good faith by a fiduciary.[2]

This exemption applies for transactions occurring after August 17, 2006.

---

[1] Code Sec. 4975(d)(20) and ERISA Sec. 408(b)(17), as added by P.L. 109-280 (Pension Protection Act of 2006), Act Sec. 611(d)(2)(A). Code Sec. 4975(d)(20), as amended by P.L. 110-458 (Worker, Retiree, and Employer Recovery Act of 2008), Act Sec. 106(b)(2)(B).

[2] Code Sec. 4975(f)(10) and ERISA Sec. 408(b)(17)(B), as added by P.L. 109-280 (Pension Protection Act of 2006), Act Sec. 611(d)(2)(B).

¶ 2440
STATUTORY EXEMPTIONS: ESOP Loans

A fiduciary must not receive any consideration for the fiduciary's own account from any party dealing with the plan in connection with a transaction involving the income or assets of the plan. However, a loan made by a disqualified person to an ESOP may be exempt if certain conditions are met.[1]

☐ The special rules on ESOP loans are discussed at ¶ 3035.

---

[1] IRS Reg. § 54.4975-7(b)(2)(i), (b)(3)-(14), and (b)(15)(i).

¶ 2441
STATUTORY EXEMPTIONS: Block Trading

A statutory exemption is provided for block trading. To achieve better execution, reduce costs and provide for more efficient plan asset transactions, pension assets may be included in block trades.[1] This exemption from the prohibited transaction rules includes any transaction involving the purchase or sale of securities between a plan and a disqualified person/party in interest (other than a fiduciary with respect to the plan) if:

1. the transaction involves a block trade;

2. at the time of the transaction, the interest of the plan (together with the interests of any other plans maintained by the same plan sponsor) does not exceed 10% of the aggregate size of the block trade;

3. the terms of the transaction, including the price, are at least as favorable to the plan as an arm's-length transaction; and

4. the compensation associated with the purchase and sale is not greater than an arm's-length transaction.

A "block trade" is any trade of at least 10,000 shares or with a market value of at least $200,000 that will be allocated across two or more unrelated client accounts of a fiduciary.[2]

This statutory exemption is effective for transactions occurring after August 17, 2006.

---

[1] Code Sec. 4975(d)(18) and ERISA Sec. 408(b)(15), as added by P.L. 109-280 (Pension Protection Act of 2006), Act Sec. 611(a)(2)(A). Code Sec. 4975(d)(18), as amended by P.L. 110-458 (Worker, Retiree, and Employer Recovery Act of 2008), Act Sec. 106(b)(2).

[2] Code Sec. 4975(f)(9) and ERISA Sec. 408(b)(15)(B), as added by P.L. 109-280 (Pension Protection Act of 2006), Act Sec. 611(a)(2)(B).

¶ 2442
STATUTORY EXEMPTIONS: Bank Deposits

Plan funds may be invested in deposits, which bear a reasonable rate of interest, in a bank (or similar financial institution) supervised by the federal or a state government, even if the bank is a fiduciary of the plan or other party in interest, if:[1]

1. the plan covers only employees of the bank or its affiliate; or
2. the investment is expressly authorized by a plan provision or by a fiduciary, other than the bank, that is expressly empowered by the plan to so instruct the trustee with respect to the investment.

With regard to (2), above, if the investment is authorized by a fiduciary (other than the bank or other institution which is to hold the deposit) that is empowered by the plan to direct that the investment be made, there is no conflict of interest involving the bank fiduciary upon the making of the deposit.

---

[1] Code Sec. 4975(d)(4); ERISA Sec. 408(b)(4).

¶ 2443

STATUTORY EXEMPTIONS: Electronic Communications Networks

There is an exemption from the prohibited transaction rules for any transaction involving the purchase and sale of securities between a plan and a disqualified person/party in interest if:[1]

1. the transaction is executed through an electronic communication network, alternative trading system, or similar execution system or trading venue subject to the applicable federal or foreign regulating entity;
2. either:
   a. the transaction is made under rules designed to match purchases and sales at the best price available through the execution system in accordance with the applicable rules of the Securities and Exchange Commission or other related governmental authority, or
   b. neither the execution system nor the parties to the transaction take into account the identity of the parties in the execution of trades;
3. the price and compensation associated with the purchase and sale is at least as favorable as an arm's-length transaction;
4. if the disqualified person/party in interest has an ownership interest in the system or venue, the system or venue has been authorized by the plan sponsor or other independent fiduciary; and
5. not less than 30 days prior to the initial transaction executed through any system or venue, a plan fiduciary is provided written or electronic notice of the execution.

This statutory exemption applies to transactions occurring after August 17, 2006.

---

[1] Code Sec. 4975(d)(19) and ERISA Sec. 408(b)(16), as added by P.L. 109-280 (Pension Protection Act of 2006), Act Sec. 611(c)(2). Code Sec. 4975(d)(19), as amended by P.L. 110-458 (Worker, Retiree, and Employer Recovery Act of 2008), Act Sec. 106(b)(2)(B).

¶ 2444
STATUTORY EXEMPTIONS: Purchase of Insurance from Employer

A statutory exemption is provided for any contract for life insurance, health insurance, or annuities with one or more insurers that are qualified to do business in a state, if the plan pays no more than adequate consideration, and if each insurer is:[1]

1. the employer maintaining the plan; or
2. a party in interest or disqualified person or entity that is wholly owned (directly or indirectly) by the employer establishing the plan or by any party in interest or disqualified person with respect to the plan.

Five-percent limit

The exception applies only if the total premium and annuity considerations written by the insurer for life insurance, health insurance, or annuities for all plans and their employees, with respect to which the insurer is a disqualified person, do not exceed 5% of the total premium and annuity considerations written for lines of insurance in that year by the insurer.[2]

In computing this 5% figure, all premiums and annuity considerations written by an insurance company for a plan which it maintains are to be excluded from consideration. This exemption is also allowed only if no more than adequate consideration is paid for the insurance.

---

[1] Code Sec. 4975(d)(5); ERISA Sec. 408(b)(5).

[2] Code Sec. 4975(d)(5)(B); ERISA Sec. 408(b)(5)(B).

¶ 2446
STATUTORY EXEMPTIONS: Ancillary Bank Services

Ancillary services provided by a bank or similar financial institution to a plan for which it acts as a fiduciary are exempt from certain prohibited transaction rules.[1]

The provision of any ancillary service by a bank (or similar financial institution) is permissible if:[2]

1. this service is provided at not more than reasonable compensation;
2. the bank is a fiduciary of the plan;
3. the bank has adopted adequate internal safeguards to assure that the provision of these services is consistent with sound banking and financial practice, as determined by federal or state supervisory authorities; and
4. specific guidelines issued by the bank or financial institution stipulate that the service may not be provided in an excessive

or unreasonable manner, or in a manner that would be inconsistent with the best interests of the plan participants and beneficiaries.

[1] Code Sec. 4975(d)(6); ERISA Sec. 408(b)(6); ERISA Reg. § 2550.408b-6(b). [2] *Ibid.*

¶ 2447

STATUTORY EXEMPTIONS: Cross Trading

There is an exemption from the prohibited transaction rules for any transaction involving the purchase and sale of a security between a plan and any other account managed by the same investment manager if:[1]

1. the transaction is a purchase or sale, for no consideration other than cash payment against prompt delivery of a security for which market quotations are readily available;

2. the transaction is made at the independent current market price of the security;

3. no brokerage commission, fee, or other remuneration is paid in connection with the transaction;

4. a fiduciary for each plan participating in the transaction authorizes in advance of any cross trades the investment manager to engage in cross trades at the investment manager's discretion;

5. each plan participating in the transaction has assets of at least $100,000,000, except that if the assets of a plan are invested in a master trust containing the assets of plans maintained by employers in the same controlled group the master trust has assets of at least $100,000,000;

6. the investment manager provides to the plan fiduciary who authorized cross trading a quarterly report detailing all cross trades executed by the investment manager in which the plan participated during the quarter;

7. the investment manager does not base its fee schedule on the plan's consent to cross trading, and no other service is conditioned on the plan's consent to cross trading;

8. the investment manager has adopted, and cross trades are made in accordance with, written cross-trading policies and procedures; and

9. the investment manager has designated an individual responsible for periodically reviewing these purchases and sales to ensure compliance with the written policies and procedures.

CCH Pointer: The Employee Benefits Security Administration (EBSA) has issued final rules that address the content of the written policies and procedures that must be adopted before parties can engage in cross-trading, as exempted under the Pension Protection Act of 2006.[2] The investment manager's policies and procedures must be fair and equitable to all accounts participating in its cross-trading program and must provide for appointment of a compliance officer who is responsible for periodically reviewing purchases and sales of securities made pursuant to the exemption to ensure compliance with the written policies and procedures. This final rule is effective on February 4, 2009.

This statutory exemption applies to transactions occurring after August 17, 2006.

---

[1] Code Sec. 4975(d)(22) and ERISA Sec. 408(b)(19), as added by P.L. 109-280 (Pension Protection Act of 2006), Act Sec. 611(g)(2).

[2] ERISA Reg. § 2550.408b-19.

¶ 2448
STATUTORY EXEMPTIONS: Transactions Involving Owner-Employees

The statutory exemptions to the prohibited transaction rules generally do not apply to a transaction involving a plan that covers an owner-employee in which:[1]

1. the plan directly or indirectly loans any part of its corpus or income to the owner-employee;

2. the plan directly or indirectly pays any compensation to the owner-employee for services; or

3. the plan acquires any property from, or sells any property to, any person who is (a) an owner-employee with regard to the plan, (b) a member of the family of the owner-employee, or (c) a corporation controlled by the owner-employee. For this purpose "control" means direct or indirect ownership of 50% or more of the total combined voting power of all classes of stock entitled to vote, or 50% or more of the total value of shares of all classes of stock of the corporation.

"Members of the family" include brothers and sisters (whether by the whole or half blood), the spouse, ancestors, and lineal descendants.[2]

Loans to owner-employees. Despite the foregoing rules limiting the statutory exemptions from the prohibited transaction rules for owner-employees, owner-employees and 50%-shareholders are permitted under ERISA to qualify for the exemption from the prohibited transaction rules relating to plan loans (see ¶ 2436) if a special exemption is approved by the Labor Department.[3]

EGTRRA authorizes loans to shareholder employees. Plans may be amended for years beginning after 2001, to authorize loans to all plan participants, including owner-employees and shareholder-employees.[4] Thus, beginning in 2002, plan loans to Subchapter S shareholders, partners in partnerships, and sole proprietors of unincorporated businesses are exempt from treatment as prohibited transactions. However, the statutory and regulatory requirements governing loans must still be satisfied.[5]

IRAs subject to restrictions. The loan restrictions imposed on IRA participants and beneficiaries and employers maintaining IRAs continue to apply.

ESOP purchase of stock from shareholder-employees of S corp.

The sale of employer securities to an ESOP maintained by an S corporation by a shareholder-employee, family member of the shareholder-employee, or a corporation in which the shareholder owns at least 50% of the stock, is permitted.[6] A shareholder-employee is an employee or officer of the S corporation who owns, or is considered as owning, more than 5% of the outstanding stock of the corporation on any day during the corporation's tax year.[7]

---

[1] Code Sec. 4975(f)(6)(A); ERISA Sec. 408(d)(1).

[2] Code Sec. 267(c)(4).

[3] ERISA Sec. 408(a) and (d).

[4] Code Sec. 4975(f)(6)(B)(iii), as added by P.L. 107-16 (Economic Growth and Tax Relief Reconciliation Act of 2001), Act Sec. 612(a). ERISA Sec. 408(d)(2)(C), as added by P.L. 107-16 (Economic Growth and Tax Relief Reconciliation Act of 2001), Act Sec. 612(b).

[5] Note that EGTRRA's Conference Committee Report expressed the intent of Congress that the DOL and IRS waive any penalty or excise tax in situations where: (1) a loan made prior to 2002 was exempt when initially made (treating refinancing as new loans) and, (2) the loan would have been exempt throughout the period of the loan if the new rule had been in effect during the period of the loan.

[6] Code Sec. 4975(f)(6)(B); ERISA Sec. 408(d)(2).

[7] Code Sec. 4975(f)(6)(C); ERISA Sec. 408(d)(3).

¶ 2449

STATUTORY EXEMPTIONS: Foreign Exchange Transactions

An exemption from the prohibited transaction rules has been added for certain foreign exchange transactions.[1] The exemption applies to any foreign exchange transaction between a bank or broker-dealer (or affiliate of either), and a plan, where the bank or broker-dealer is a trustee, custodian, fiduciary, or other disqualified person/party in interest, if:

1. the transaction is in connection with the purchase, holding, or sale of securities or other investment assets;

2. at the time the foreign exchange transaction is entered into, the terms of the transaction are not less favorable to the plan than the terms generally available in comparable arm's-length foreign exchange transactions, or the terms provided by the bank or broker-dealer in comparable foreign exchange transactions;

3. the exchange rate used by the bank or broker-dealer for an exchange does not deviate by more than 3% from the inter-bank bid and asked rates at the time of the transaction as displayed on an independent service that reports rates of exchange in the foreign currency market for the currency; and

4. the bank or broker-dealer does not have investment discretion, or provide investment advice, with respect to the transaction.

This statutory exemption applies to transactions occurring after August 17, 2006.

---

[1] Code Sec. 4975(d)(21) and ERISA Sec. 408(b)(18), as added by P.L. 109-280 (Pension Protection Act of 2006), Act Sec. 611(e)(2). Code Sec. 4975(d)(21), as amended by P.L. 110-458 (Worker, Retiree, and Employer Recovery Act of 2008), Act Sec. 106(b).

¶ 2450
STATUTORY EXEMPTIONS: Conversion of Securities

A plan may exercise a privilege to convert securities if the plan receives no less than adequate consideration.[1]

Adequate consideration for securities traded in a generally recognized market is the price prevailing on a national securities exchange.[2] If the security is not traded on a national securities exchange, adequate consideration is a price not less favorable to the plan than the offering price for the security as established by the current bid and asked prices quoted by persons independent of the issuer and parties in interest.[3] For assets other than securities for which there is a generally recognized market, adequate consideration is defined as fair market value determined in good faith by a plan trustee under Labor Department regulations.

Under proposed Labor Department regulations, the fair market value assigned to a plan would be the price at which an asset changes hands between a willing buyer and a willing seller without any compulsion and where both parties are able and willing to trade and are well-informed about the asset and the market for the asset.[4] The valuation of the asset would have to be made on the date of the transaction in which it is involved, and would have to be documented in writing.

A fiduciary would be required to determine the fair market value in good faith, as determined by a prudent investigation of circumstances prevailing at the time of the valuation and the application of sound business principles. The fiduciary would also have to either (1) be independent of all parties to the transaction, or (2) rely on the report of an independent appraiser.

---

[1] Code Sec. 4975(d)(7) and ERISA Sec. 408(b)(7).

[2] ERISA Sec. 3(18)(A)(i).
[3] ERISA Sec. 3(18)(A)(ii).
[4] ERISA Prop. Reg. § 2510.3-18.

¶ 2452
STATUTORY EXEMPTIONS: Pooled Investment Funds

A transaction between a plan and a common trust fund or pooled investment fund maintained by a bank is allowed if:[1]

1. the transaction is a purchase of an interest in the fund;

2. the bank receives no more than reasonable compensation; and

3. the transaction is expressly permitted by the instrument under which the plan is maintained, or by a fiduciary (other than the bank or trust company) that has authority to manage and control plan assets.

Furthermore, a fiduciary does not violate ERISA if it does not use any of its authority, control, or responsibility to cause the plan to pay additional fees for a service furnished by the fiduciary or to pay a fee for a service furnished by a person or entity, in which the fiduciary has an interest and which may affect the exercise of its best judgment.

¹ Code Sec. 4975(d)(8); ERISA Sec. 408(b)(8);
ERISA Reg. § 2550.408b-2(e)(2).

¶ 2454
STATUTORY EXEMPTIONS: Receipt of Benefits

A disqualified person may receive any benefit to which he or she may be entitled as a participant or beneficiary of the plan.[1] In addition, a disqualified person may receive compensation for services rendered or reimbursement of expenses.[2]

The benefits paid must be computed and paid on the same basis that benefits are computed and paid to other participants and beneficiaries.

¹ Code Sec. 4975(d)(9) and (10); ERISA Sec. 408(c).   ² ERISA Opinion Letter 89-09A, 6-13-89.

¶ 2456
STATUTORY EXEMPTIONS: Termination Distributions

A fiduciary must distribute the assets of the trust in accordance with the terms of the plan. The decision to terminate a retirement plan is exempt from ERISA's fiduciary standards.[1] Thus, the prohibited transaction provisions are not applicable to a fiduciary's distribution of assets in accordance with the plan's provisions if the assets are distributed as part of the termination of the plan.

¹ Code Sec. 4975(d)(12); ERISA Sec. 408(b)(10).

¶ 2457
STATUTORY EXEMPTIONS: Investment Advice Provided by Fiduciary Advisers

Under a new prohibited transaction exemption, effective for investment advice provided after December 31, 2006, qualified "fiduciary advisers" can offer personally tailored professional investment advice to help employees manage their 401(k) and other plans.[1] Fiduciary advisers may provide investment advice pursuant to "eligible investment advice arrangement" under which (1) portfolio recommendations are generated for a participant based on an unbiased computer model that has been certified and audited by an independent third party, or (2) fiduciary advisers provide their investment advice services by charging a flat fee that does not vary depending on the investment option chosen by the participant.[2]

If the applicable requirements are satisfied, the following are exempt from prohibited transaction treatment:[3]

- providing investment advice to a participant or beneficiary regarding any security or property available as a plan investment;

- an investment transaction (i.e., a sale, acquisition, or holding of a security or other property) pursuant to the investment advice; and

- the direct or indirect receipt of fees or other compensation by a fiduciary adviser or its affiliates (or any employee, agent, or registered representative of the fiduciary or adviser or its affiliates) in connection with the providing investment advice or an investment transaction pursuant to the investment advice.

A number of stringent safeguards must be met in order to be eligible for the prohibited transaction exemption for investment advice.

CCH Pointer: *DOL issues final rules on investment advice under 401(k)s and IRAs.* The EBSA has issued final regulations implementing provisions of the Pension Protection Act of 2006 (PPA) that authorize fiduciary advisers to provide individualized investment advice to participants and beneficiaries in individual account plans, such as 401(k) plans, and beneficiaries of IRAs.[4] The final regulations define the scope of the fee leveling requirements under an eligible investment advice arrangement; specify the requirements for the certification of model investment advice programs; set forth the conditions under which a fiduciary adviser may elect to be the sole plan fiduciary; explain the circumstances under which an auditor will be deemed sufficiently independent to review an investment arrangement; and provide a voluntary Model Fiduciary Adviser Form for the disclosure of fees, compensation and services.

The new regulations contains certain safeguards and conditions to prevent investment advisers from providing biased advice that is not in a participant's best interest. To qualify for the exemption in the final regulations, investment advice must be given through the use of a computer model that is certified as unbiased by an independent expert or through an adviser compensated on a "level-fee" basis, meaning that the fees do not vary based on investments selected. Both types of arrangements must also satisfy several other conditions, including the express authorization of the arrangement by a separate plan fiduciary, the disclosure of the adviser's fees and other information to participants and beneficiaries, a disclosure to fiduciaries authorizing the arrangement, an annual audit of the arrangement for compliance with the regulation, and the retention of records.

Note that the final regulations clarify that the conditions of the rules apply only to investment advice that would constitute a prohibited transaction. In addition, the final regulations stress that a plan fiduciary is not statutorily obligated to offer, provide, or otherwise make available investment advice to a participant or beneficiary.

For more information about the requirements for the provision of investment advice by fiduciary advisors, see ¶ 2312.

---

[1] Code Sec. 4975(d)(17), as added by P.L. 109-280 (Pension Protection Act of 2006), Act Sec. 601(b)(1)(C); ERISA Sec. 408(b)(14), as added by P.L. 109-280, Act Sec. 601(a)(1).

[2] Code Sec. 4975(f)(8), as added by P.L. 109-280 (Pension Protection Act of 2006), Act Sec. 601(b)(2); ERISA Sec. 408(g), as added by P.L. 109-280 (Pension Protection Act of 2006), Act Sec. 601(a)(2).

³ Code Sec. 4975(d)(17) and ERISA Sec. 408(b)(14), as added by P.L. 109-280 (Pension Protection Act of 2006).

⁴ ERISA final regulations, 76 FR 66136, October 25, 2011, CCH PENSION PLAN GUIDE ¶ 24,809D; ERISA Reg. § 2550.408g-1. The rules are effective December 27, 2011.

¶ 2458

STATUTORY EXEMPTIONS: Merger of Multiemployer Plans

The merger of multiemployer plans and the transfer of assets and liabilities are permissible, provided the requirements of ERISA Sec. 4231 are met (see ¶ 2931).[1] Thus, a fiduciary may act in any transaction involving the plan on behalf of a party whose interests are adverse to the interests of the plan or interests of its participants and beneficiaries in a merger or transfer of assets.

The exemptions, however, do not apply to an act by a disqualified person who is a fiduciary and who deals with the income or assets of a plan in his or her own interest or for his or her own account. These exemptions also do not apply to a fiduciary's receipt of consideration for his or her own personal account from a party dealing with the plan in connection with a transaction involving the income or assets of the plan.

¹ Code Sec. 4975(d)(14) and (15); ERISA Sec. 408(b)(11). Under ERISA Sec. 4231, a merger or transfer of plan assets or liabilities is acceptable if (1) the multiemployer plan's sponsor notifies the PBGC of the merger or transfer of assets at least 120 days before the merger or asset transfer; (2) no participant's or beneficiary's accrued benefit is reduced by the merger or asset transfer; (3) the participants' benefits are not expected to be subject to ERISA Sec. 4245 suspension; and (4) an actuarial valuation of the assets and liabilities of each of the affected plans has been performed during the plan year preceding the effective date of the merger or transfer. See ¶ 2931-2932.

¶ 2459

STATUTORY EXEMPTIONS: Sale of Bank Stock in IRA Relating to S Corp. Election

A statutory exemption is provided, effective October 22, 2004 (the date of enactment of P.L. 108-357, American Jobs Creation Act of 2004), for the sale by an IRA to the IRA beneficiary of bank stock held by the IRA on October 22, 2004.[1]

The sale will be exempt from treatment as a prohibited transaction if:

1. the sale is made pursuant to an S Corporation election by the bank;
2. the stock is sold at fair market value at the time of the sale (as determined by an independent appraiser);
3. the terms of the sale are otherwise at least as favorable to the trust as the terms that would apply on a sale to an unrelated party;
4. the IRA does not pay any commission, cost, or other expenses in connection with the sale; and

5. the stock is sold in a single transaction for cash not later than 120 days after the S Corporation election is made.[2]

[1] Code Sec. 4975(d)(16), as added by P.L. 108-357 (American Jobs Creation Act of 2004), Act Sec. 233(c).

[2] *Ibid.*

¶ 2460

CLASS EXEMPTIONS: Broker-Dealers, Reporting Dealers, and Banks

Specified agency transactions and services, principal transactions, underwritings, market-making, and deals involving the extension of credit between employee benefit plans and certain broker-dealers, reporting dealers, and banks are exempt from the prohibited transaction rules, under a Labor Department class exemption. A plan may engage in certain transactions with broker-dealers, reporting dealers and banks that are plan fiduciaries as long as the institutions and their affiliates do not have investment authority over or provide investment advice with regard to the plan's assets involved in the transaction.[1]

Lending of securities by plans

The lending of securities by employee benefit plans to banks and broker-dealers who are parties in interest with respect to the plan are also exempt, provided that neither the borrower nor an affiliate possesses discretionary authority with regard to the investment of the plan assets involved in the transaction. Further, on the day of the loan, the plan must receive from the borrower collateral having a market value (as of the preceding business day) of not less than 100% of the market value of the loaned securities. The plan must also receive a reasonable fee related to the value of the borrowed securities and the duration of the loan and be able to terminate the loan at any time.[2]

CCH Pointer: A prohibited transaction class exemption amends and incorporates PT Exemptions 81-6 and 82-63, effective January 2, 2007.[3] PT Exemption 2006-16 expands the relief provided in PT Exemptions 81-6 and 82-63 to include additional parties and additional forms of collateral, subject to specified conditions. The categories of permissible borrowers will now include certain foreign broker-dealers and banks, such as those of the United Kingdom and Canada. For securities lending transactions, the types of collateral that may be offered to employee benefit plans have been broadened under the new PTE to include negotiable certificates of deposits payable in the United States, mortgage backed securities, the British pound, the Canadian dollar, the Swiss franc, the Japanese yen, the Euro, securities issued by Multilateral Development Banks, rated foreign sovereign debt, and irrevocable letters of credit issued by certain foreign banks.

The Class PTE also provides that compensation must be reasonable, and must be paid to the lending fiduciary in accordance with the terms of a written instrument, which may be in the form of a master agreement covering a series of securities lending transactions.

[1] PT Exemption 75-1 (40 FR 50845), CCH PENSION PLAN GUIDE ¶ 16,601 (as amended by 71 FR 5883, CCH PENSION PLAN GUIDE ¶ 16,649Q).

[2] PT Exemption 81-6 (46 FR 7527, amended by 52 FR 18754), CCH PENSION PLAN GUIDE ¶ 16,621. PT Exemption 2002-13 defines the term "employee benefit plan," as it is used in PTE 81-6, to include plans described in Code Sec. 4975(e)(1).

These plans include qualified plans, qualified annuity plans, IRAs, and individual retirement annuities. The exemption was issued to address uncertainty regarding the scope of this PTE (PT Exemption 2002-13 (67 FR 9483), CCH PENSION PLAN GUIDE ¶ 16,649E).

[3] PT Exemption 2006-16 (71 FR 63786), CCH PENSION PLAN GUIDE ¶ 16,649V.

¶ 2462

CLASS EXEMPTIONS: Foreign Exchange Transactions

A class exemption allows for the purchase and sale of foreign currencies for employee benefit plans by banks and broker-dealers and their affiliates which are parties in interest to the plans. The exemption applies to transactions "directed" by independent plan fiduciaries if certain conditions are met, including a "general" arm's-length test and a "particular" arm's-length test.[1]

Foreign exchange transactions pursuant to standing instructions

A class exemption has been approved for stipulated foreign exchange transactions between employee benefit plans and certain banks and broker-dealers that are parties in interest with respect to such plans, pursuant to standing instructions.[2] The exemption applies to income item conversions (e.g., repatriation of dividend or interest payments routinely generated by foreign securities) or de minimis purchase or sale transactions, occurring after January 12, 1999, between a bank and a broker-dealer and an employee benefit plan with respect to which the bank or broker-dealer is a trustee, custodian, fiduciary, or other party in interest, pursuant to standing instructions. Among the conditions that must be met in order for the exemption to apply is that each transaction may not involve more than $300,000.

[1] PT Exemption 94-20 (59 FR 8022), CCH PENSION PLAN GUIDE ¶ 16,641.

[2] PT Exemption 98-54 (63 FR 63503), CCH PENSION PLAN GUIDE ¶ 16,649.

¶ 2464

CLASS EXEMPTIONS: Securities Transactions by Plan Fiduciaries

Fiduciaries for employee benefit plans (other than discretionary plan trustees, plan administrators, or sponsoring employers) may effect or execute securities transactions under stipulated conditions designed to protect the interests of plan participants and beneficiaries.[1] The class exemption also allows sponsors of pooled separate accounts and other pooled investment funds, under certain circumstances, to use their affiliates to effect or execute securities transactions for the accounts.

The exemption requires that a person engaging in securities transactions on behalf of a plan receive written authorization, executed in advance, from an independent fiduciary. In addition, persons effecting or executing securities transactions on behalf of plans under this exemption must periodically disclose certain information to the authorizing plan fiduciary.

A fiduciary may execute or effect securities transactions for a plan if he or she credits all profits earned in connection with the transaction to the plan. Persons generally excluded from coverage under the exemption (i.e., plan trustees, plan administrators, and sponsoring employers) may engage in such securities transactions on behalf of plans in these situations.

Discretionary plan trustees. The EBSA adopted an amendment that allows employee benefit plan fiduciaries that are also discretionary plan trustees to effect or execute securities transactions on behalf of those plans.[2] This relief is limited to trustees of plans with net assets valued at more than $50 million. Also, discretionary trustees are required to furnish the "authorizing fiduciary" with information, such as certain commissions paid by the plan to brokerage firms both affiliated and unaffiliated with the trustee. In addition, the amendment allows sponsors of pooled separate accounts and other pooled investment funds that are also discretionary trustees of these accounts and funds to effect or execute security transactions for such accounts if certain conditions are met.

CCH Pointer: PTE 86-128 does not define the term "fiduciary." However, the DOL has explained that the relief provided by the exemption extends to any person who qualifies as a fiduciary under ERISA Sec. 3(21)(A), including a person who is a fiduciary solely by reason of rendering investment advice.[3]

---

[1] PT Exemption 86-128 (51 FR 41686), CCH PENSION PLAN GUIDE ¶ 16,631. This exemption replaces two class exemptions, PT Exemption 79-1 (44 FR 5963), CCH PENSION PLAN GUIDE ¶ 16,612,

and 84-46 (49 FR 22157), CCH PENSION PLAN GUIDE ¶ 16,629.

[2] Amendment to PT Exemption 86-128 (67 FR 64137), CCH PENSION PLAN GUIDE ¶ 16,649H.

[3] EBSA Advisory Opinion 2011-08A, June 21, 2011, at CCH PENSION PLAN GUIDE ¶ 19,992T.

¶ 2466

CLASS EXEMPTIONS: Purchase and Sale of Life Insurance

Two class exemptions authorize the purchase and sale of insurance policies by a plan and its participants under certain conditions.

A plan may acquire an individual life insurance or annuity contract from a plan participant on whose life the contract was issued or from an employer whose employees are covered by the plan.[1]

A plan is also permitted to sell an individual life insurance or annuity contract to the participant covered by the policy, one of the participant's relatives, a sponsoring employer, or another plan for the cash surrender value of the policy.[2] A plan may also sell a similar contract to a personal or private trust established by or for the benefit of the participant.[3]

---

[1] PT Exemption 92-5 (57 FR 5019), amending and redesignating PT Exemption 77-7 (42 FR 31575), CCH PENSION PLAN GUIDE ¶ 16,636.

[2] PT Exemption 92-6 (57 FR 5189), amending and redesignating PT Exemption 77-8 (42 FR 31574), CCH PENSION PLAN GUIDE ¶ 16,637.

[3] Amendment to PT Exemption 92-6, May 2003, CCH PENSION PLAN GUIDE ¶ 16,649J.

¶ 2468

CLASS EXEMPTIONS: Insurance Agents and Brokers

Insurance agents and brokers, pension consultants, insurance companies, investment companies, and investment company principal underwriters who are parties in interest may invest plan assets in insurance contracts or mutual fund shares or receive sales commissions subject to certain requirements. Among these requirements are that the transaction be on terms at least as favorable to the plan as an arm's-length transaction with an unrelated party and that the combined fees, commissions, and other consideration received by the agent or broker in connection with the purchase of insurance or annuity contracts or securities issued by an investment company not exceed "reasonable compensation," as defined by ERISA Sec. 408(b)(2) and (c)(2) or Code Sec. 4975(d)(2) and (d)(10).[1]

Insurance companies that are related to employers through substantial stock or partnership interests are also permitted to sell life insurance, health insurance, or annuity contracts designed to provide funding for employee benefit plans established or maintained by the employers.[2] The exemption applies only if the insurance company has undergone a financial examination either by a state insurance commission within the last five years or by an independent certified public accountant for its last taxable year. Further, the gross premiums and annuity considerations received by an insurer for these contracts may not exceed 50% of the payments received for all lines of insurance by the insurer during the taxable year.

A class exemption has also been provided to authorize the sale of insurance or annuity contracts to employee benefit plans and the receipt of commissions from these sales by agents or brokers who are also the employers maintaining the plans or who are related to the plans.[3] This exemption pertains to an employer whose employees are covered by a plan that will purchase insurance or to a partner having a 10% or greater share in the capital or profits of the employer. The exemption limits the total commissions an agent or broker can receive in one taxable year from the sale of insurance for employees to 5% of the total insurance premiums for that year.

Another class exemption amendment extends relief to transactions involving the sales of insurance and mutual fund products and the receipt of related commissions to insurance agents and brokers, pension consultants, and investment company principal underwriters whose affiliates exercise investment discretion over plan assets that are not involved in the transaction.[4]

Insurance company pooled separate accounts

A transaction between a party in interest to a plan and an insurance company pooled separate account in which the plan has an interest, or any acquisition or holding by the pooled separate account of employer securities or employer real property, is permissible, if at the time of the transaction, acquisition, or holding:[5]

1. (a) the assets of the plan in the pooled separate account do not exceed 10% of the total of all assets or (b) the pooled separate account is a specialized account, which, as a matter of policy, invests substantially all of its assets in short-term obligations, and

2. the party in interest is not the insurance company which holds the plan assets in its pooled separate account, any other account of the insurance company, or any affiliate of the insurance company.

Multiple-employer plan exemption

Any transaction between an employer or employees covered by a multiple-employer plan and an insurance company pooled separate account in which the plan has an interest, or any acquisition or holding by the pooled separate account of employer securities or employer real property may also be allowed. The exemption applies if at the time of the transaction, acquisition, or holding:[6]

1. the assets of the multiple-employer plan in the pooled separate account do not exceed 10% of the total assets in the account and the employer is not a "substantial employer" with respect to the plan, as defined in ERISA Sec. 4001(a)(2), or

2. the assets of the multiple-employer plan in the pooled separate account exceed 10% of the total assets in the account, but the employer is not a substantial employer and would not be a substantial employer with respect to the plan if, under ERISA Sec. 4001(a)(2), its contributions to the plan for each plan year constituting either the two immediately preceding plan years or the first two of the immediately preceding plan years totaled an amount greater than or equal to 5% of any contributions required to be paid to or under the plan for that year.

Insurance company pooled separate accounts, however, may engage in transactions involving the lease of real property and the incidental furnishing of goods in excess of the previously discussed limits.

---

[1] PT Exemption 77-9 (42 FR 32395, amended by PT Exemption 84-24, 44 FR 13209), CCH Pension Plan Guide ¶ 16,607.

[2] PT Exemption 79-41 (44 FR 46365), CCH Pension Plan Guide ¶ 16,616.

[3] PT Exemption 79-60 (44 FR 59018), CCH Pension Plan Guide ¶ 16,617.

[4] PT Exemption 84-24 (49 FR 13209), CCH Pension Plan Guide ¶ 16,607 (as amended by 71 FR 5887, CCH Pension Plan Guide ¶ 16,649R).

[5] PT Exemption 90-1 (55 FR 2391), amending and redesignating PT Exemption 78-19 (43 FR 59915), CCH Pension Plan Guide ¶ 16,633.

[6] *Ibid.*

¶ 2470

CLASS EXEMPTIONS: Insurance Company General Accounts

Insurance company general accounts that hold plan assets may transact business with parties related to employee benefit plans for which the insurer is a fiduciary.[1] The exemption (retroactive to January 1, 1975) is designed to counter the potential effects of the decision of the U.S. Supreme Court in *John Hancock Mutual Life Insurance Co. v. Harris Trust & Savings Bank*,[2] that funds allocated to an insurer's general account, under a contract with a plan, that vary with investment experience, are plan assets. Insurance companies had feared that they would be exposed to unanticipated fiduciary liabilities.

> **CCH Pointer:** In light of the *Harris Trust* decision, the Labor Department has issued regulations clarifying the ERISA status of plan assets held in insurance company general accounts. See ¶ 2330.

Exempt parties and transactions

The exemption covers transactions between a party in interest and an insurance company general account in which the plan has an interest as an account holder. Thus, an insurance company may make a loan to a company that has a party in interest relationship with a plan that has purchased a general account contract from the insurer.

The exemption will further allow the acquisition and holding of employer securities and real property by the general account and also permit an insurer to aggregate qualifying employer securities with employer securities held by its general account, in which the plan has an interest.

Reserves may not exceed 10% of liabilities in general account

The exemption will not apply unless, at the time of the transaction, acquisition, or holding, the amount of reserves and liabilities for the general account contracts held by or on behalf of the plan, combined with the reserves and liabilities for the general account contracts held by the employer's other plans, do not exceed 10% of the total reserves and liabilities of the general accounts.

Service providers for general accounts

Plans may engage in transactions with persons who provide services to an insurance company general account in which the plan has an interest as a contract holder or as the beneficial owner of a contract.

Asset pool investment trusts

Certificates of interest owned by the general account are generally considered, under *Harris Trust*, to be assets of the plan contracting with the insurer. However, the exemption enables a plan, under stipulated conditions, to invest in asset-based pass-through certificates representing interests in pooled investment trusts, even though an insurance company general account may also invest in the same pool.

The insurance company may also invest in a different class of security backed by the same asset pool.

The exemption covers persons who are deemed to be parties in interest as a result of providing services to a plan solely because of the plan's ownership of certificates issued by a pooled investment trust.

---

[1] PT Exemption 95-60 (60 FR 35925), CCH Pension Plan Guide ¶ 16,643. PT Exemption 2002-13 defines the term "employee benefit plan," as it is used in PTE 95-60, to include plans described in Code Sec. 4975(e)(1). These plans include qualified plans, qualified annuity plans, IRAs, and individual retirement annuities. The exemption was issued to address uncertainty regarding the scope of this PTE (PT Exemption 2002-13 (67 FR 9483), CCH Pension Plan Guide ¶ 16,649E).

[2] *John Hancock Mutual Life Insurance Co. v. Harris Trust & Savings Bank*, US Sup Ct (1993), 510 US 86.

¶ 2472

CLASS EXEMPTIONS: Investment Advisory Firms

Investment advisory firms may continue to invest the assets of employee benefit plans that they advise in open-end mutual funds that they may manage.[1] A plan may also purchase and sell shares of a registered open-end investment company even where a fiduciary to the plan (i.e., an investment manager) is also the investment manager for the investment company. However, the plan may not: pay a sales commission in connection with the purchase or sale of the shares; pay a redemption fee in connection with the sale by the plan to the investment company, unless the fee is paid only to the investment company and the fee is disclosed in the investment company prospectus; or pay an investment management, investment advisory, or similar fee with respect to plan assets invested in the shares for the entire period of the investment.

A second independent fiduciary must approve all sales and purchases. In order to exercise this role, the second fiduciary must receive a current prospectus issued by the investment company, full and detailed written disclosure of the fees charged to or paid by the plan and the company, and an explanation by the investment adviser as to why the purchase is appropriate for the plan.

---

[1] PT Exemption 77-4 (42 FR 18732), CCH Pension Plan Guide ¶ 16,604. See also, ERISA Opinion Letter 93-26A, 10-9-93 (individual retirement arrangements (IRAs) are considered "employee benefit plans" for purposes of meeting the requirements of PTE 77-4).

¶ 2473

CLASS EXEMPTIONS: Cross-Trades of Securities Among Index, Model-Driven Funds

Cross-trades of securities among index and model-driven funds managed by investment managers and among such funds and certain large accounts that engage such managers to carry out a specific portfolio restructuring program or to otherwise act as a "trading advisor" for the programs are permitted.[1] The exemption affects employee benefit plans whose assets are invested in index or model-driven funds, and large pension plans and other large accounts involved in portfolio restructuring programs.

The exemption provides relief from the restrictions in ERISA for (1) the purchase and sale of securities between an index or model-driven fund and another such fund, at least one of which holds "plan assets" subject to ERISA; and (2) the purchase and sale of securities between such funds and certain large accounts pursuant to portfolio restructuring programs of large accounts. The exemption also applies to cross-trades between two or more large accounts if such cross-trades occur as part of a single cross-trading program involving both funds and large accounts pursuant to which securities are cross-trades solely as a result of the objective operation of the program. The term "large accounts" is defined to include certain large employee benefit plans or other large institutional investors with at least $50 million in total assets.

Certain conditions must be met. For example, any cross-trade of securities by a fund must occur as a direct result of a "triggering event" and must be executed no later than the close of the third business day following the "triggering event." Also, if the cross-trade involves a model-driven fund, the cross-trade must not take place within three business days following any change made by the manager to the model underlying the fund.

The exemption does not address cross-trades of securities among "actively-managed" accounts.

---

[1] PT Exemption 2002-12 (67 FR 6613), CCH PENSION PLAN GUIDE ¶ 16,649D.

¶ 2474

CLASS EXEMPTIONS: Mutual Fund "In-House" Plans

A mutual fund "in-house" plan may invest the assets of its employee benefit plan in its own open-end mutual fund.[1] An "in-house" plan covers only employees of the mutual fund, employees of the mutual fund's investment adviser or principal underwriters, or of any of their affiliates. Under the exemption, the plan is prohibited from paying:

1. any investment management, investment advisory, or similar fee to the investment adviser, principal underwriter, or their affiliates;

2. a sales commission for the acquisition or sale of shares; or

3. a redemption fee for the sale of shares by the plan to the investment company unless the fee is paid only to the investment company and the fee is disclosed in the investment company prospectus.

In-kind exchange of plan assets for mutual fund shares

The relief afforded by PTE 77-3 applies to both cash purchases of investment company shares and to transactions involving the exchange of securities held on behalf of a plan for shares of a mutual fund.

---

[1] PT Exemption 77-3 (42 FR 18734), CCH PENSION PLAN GUIDE ¶ 16,603.

¶ 2476

CLASS EXEMPTIONS: Multiemployer and Multiple-Employer Plans

A class exemption addressing delinquent employer contributions to multiemployer and multiple-employer plans authorizes:[1]

1. an extension of time for making contributions;

2. acceptance of less than the full amount of a contribution owed in satisfaction of the employer's obligation to pay the entire amount; and

3. the termination of efforts to collect contributions that are deemed uncollectible in whole or in part.

The exemption further permits construction loans to be made by a multiemployer or multiple-employer plan to a participating employer if the decision to make the loan is made for the plan by a bank, insurance company, or loan association. However, in the period immediately following the loan, the aggregate amount of investments (including loans) of the plan in the participating employer must not exceed 10% of the fair market value of the plan's assets and the aggregate amount of plan investments in loans to all participating employers may not exceed 35% of the fair market value of the plan's assets.

A multiemployer or multiple-employer plan may also share office space and administrative services and goods, lease office space, provide administrative services, or sell or lease goods to a participating employee organization, participating employer, participating employer organization, or to another multiple-employer plan. The arrangement must provide the plan reasonable compensation and allow the plan to terminate the transaction on reasonably short notice.[2]

---

[1] PT Exemption 76-1 (41 FR 12740), CCH PENSION PLAN GUIDE ¶ 16,602.

[2] PT Exemption 76-1 (41 FR 12740), CCH PENSION PLAN GUIDE ¶ 16,602, and PT Exemption 77-10 (42 FR 33918), CCH PENSION PLAN GUIDE ¶ 16,608.

¶ 2478

CLASS EXEMPTIONS: Multiple-Employer Apprenticeship Plans

Collectively bargained multiple-employer apprenticeship plans may purchase or lease personal or real property from employers who contribute to the plan.[1] The leasing of real property from sponsoring employee organizations is also allowed.

The exemption requires that the transaction be on terms at least as favorable to the plan as would result from an arm's-length transaction with an unrelated party and satisfy the purposes for which the plan was established and maintained.

[1] PT Exemption 78-6 (43 FR 23024), CCH PEN-
SION PLAN GUIDE ¶ 16,609.

¶ 2480
CLASS EXEMPTIONS: Customer Note Sales

Employee benefit plans may acquire, hold, accept in-kind contributions of, and sell customer notes of employers.[1] Customer notes are installment instruments backed by security agreements negotiated with the customers of plan sponsors in connection with the sale of tangible personal property by sponsors as part of their ordinary business activities.

In order for the exemption to apply, an independent fiduciary must approve in advance the acquisition of the notes and monitor the investments to ensure that payments are timely received. In addition, the acquisition of the customer note must not result in the plan holding, immediately following the acquisition, more than 50% of the current value of the plan assets in customer notes or more than 10% of the current value of plan assets in the notes of any one customer. Finally, the notes must be secured by the property being financed, the maximum term of the notes may not exceed five years, and the employer must guarantee in writing the repayment of notes that become more than 50 days delinquent.

[1] PT Exemption 85-68 (50 FR 13293), CCH PEN-
SION PLAN GUIDE ¶ 16,630.

¶ 2482
CLASS EXEMPTIONS: Closed-End Investment Companies

The shares of registered closed-end investment companies may be acquired and sold by employee benefit plans covering employees of the investment company, its investment adviser, or an affiliate of either.[1]

[1] PT Exemption 79-13 (44 FR 25533), CCH PEN-
SION PLAN GUIDE ¶ 16,614.

¶ 2484
CLASS EXEMPTIONS: Court-Ordered Transactions

Any transaction or activity authorized or required by an order of a United States District Court or by a settlement of litigation approved by that court is permitted. The transaction or activity must be specifically described in the order or settlement and the Secretary of Labor or the IRS must be a party to the litigation at the time of the order or settlement.[1]

[1] PT Exemption 79-15 (44 FR 26979), CCH PEN-
SION PLAN GUIDE ¶ 16,615. PTE 2002-13 defines the
term "employee benefit plan," as it is used in PTE
79-15, to include plans described in Code Sec.

4975(e)(1). These plans include qualified plans, qualified annuity plans, IRAs, and individual retirement annuities. The exemption was issued to ad-dress uncertainty regarding the scope of this PTE (PT Exemption 2002-13 (67 FR 9483), CCH PENSION PLAN GUIDE ¶ 16,649E).

¶ 2485

CLASS EXEMPTIONS: Settlement of Litigation

Parties in interest may engage in certain transactions associated with the settlement of litigation.[1] The class exemption permits:

1. the release by a retirement plan of a claim against a party in interest in exchange for consideration given by the party in interest to the plan in settlement of the claim, and

2. permits a plan, under terms of a settlement, to provide an extension of credit to a party in interest whereby the party in interest would repay, in installments, the settlement amounts owed to the plan.

The exemption affects all employee benefit plans, the participants and beneficiaries of such plans, and parties in interest with respect to those plans engaged in the described transactions.

CCH Pointer: The Employee Benefits Security Administration (EBSA) has finalized an amendment of PT Exemption 2003-39 that expands the types of allowable consideration to permit a plan, in settlement of litigation, to acquire, hold, and dispose of employer securities, including stock rights or warrants on employer securities, and clarifies the duties of the independent fiduciary charged with settling litigation on behalf of a plan.[2]

---

[1] PT Exemption 2003-39 (68 FR 75632), CCH PENSION PLAN GUIDE ¶ 16,649L.

[2] Amendment to PT Exemption 2003-39 (75 FR 33830), CCH PENSION PLAN GUIDE ¶ 16,649X. The amendment is effective for settlements occurring on or after June 15, 2010.

¶ 2486

CLASS EXEMPTIONS: Transactions Authorized by DOL Settlement Agreements

Parties in interest may conduct transactions with employee benefit plans that have been authorized by the DOL pursuant to a settlement agreement with the DOL.[1] The relief is limited to transactions specifically authorized under settlement agreements that result from DOL investigations and does not cover transactions or activities that gave rise to the investigations and were cited as violations in Voluntary Compliance Letters.

In addition, the following conditions must be met before a transaction will be considered exempt:

1. the nature of the transaction must be specifically described in writing by the terms of the settlement agreement;

2. the parties in interest must provide advance written notice of the transaction to all affected participants in a manner designed to ensure receipt at least 30 days before the parties enter into the settlement agreement;

3. the DOL office that negotiated the settlement must approve in advance a copy of the notice and the method of distribution; and

4. the notice must contain an objective description of the transaction, the approximate date on which the transaction will occur, the address of the DOL office that negotiated the settlement, and a statement informing participants and beneficiaries of their right to forward comments to the DOL office.

---

[1] PT Exemption 94-71 (59 FR 51216), CCH PENSION PLAN GUIDE ¶ 16,642.

¶ 2487

CLASS EXEMPTIONS: Excise Taxes for Prohibited Transactions Corrected Under VFC Program

The excise taxes imposed under Code Sec. 4975(a) and (b) will not apply to the following eligible transactions described in the Voluntary Fiduciary Correction (VFC) Program (see ¶ 2737) provided certain conditions are met:

1. the failure to transmit participant contributions to a pension plan within the time frames in DOL regulations or the failure to transmit participant loan repayments to a pension within a reasonable time after withholding or receipt by the employer;

2. making a loan at a fair market interest rate to a party in interest with respect to a plan;

3. the purchase or sale of an asset (including real property) between a plan and a party in interest at fair market value; and

4. the sale of real property to a plan by the employer and the leaseback of the property to the employer at fair market value and fair market rental value.[1]

The class exemption was amended, effective May 19, 2006, to include two additional transactions: (5) the plan's acquisition and/or subsequent sale of an asset later determined to be illiquid and (6) the use of plan assets to pay expenses which are properly characterized as "settlor" expenses.[2]

There are conditions specific to each of the above transactions. There are also conditions applicable to all above transactions, such as that the applicant has met all of the pertinent requirements of the VFC Program and that the EBSA has issued a no-action letter to the applicant under the VFC Program concerning a transaction listed above.[3] Also, written notice of the transaction and the method for correcting it must have been provided to interested persons within 60 calendar days following the date of the submission of an application under the VFC Program. Furthermore, a copy of the notice must have been provided to the EBSA within the same 60-day period. Plan assets must not have used to pay for the notice.

---

[1] PT Exemption 2002-51 (67 FR 70623), CCH PENSION PLAN GUIDE ¶ 16,649I.

[2] Amendment to Prohibited Transaction Class Exemption 2002-51 (71 FR 20135), CCH PENSION PLAN GUIDE ¶ 16,649T.

[3] Prohibited Transaction Class Exemption 2002-51 (67 FR 70623), CCH PENSION PLAN GUIDE ¶ 16,649I. Amended by 71 FR 20135, CCH PENSION PLAN GUIDE ¶ 16,649T.

¶ 2488

CLASS EXEMPTIONS: Interest-Free Loans Between Plans and Parties in Interest

Interest-free loans (and the repayment of those loans) between plans and parties in interest are authorized if:[1]

1. no interest or other fee is charged to the plan and no discount for payment in cash is relinquished by the plan in connection with the loan;

2. the proceeds of the loan or extension of credit are used only for the payment of ordinary expenses (including the payment of benefits and periodic premiums), or for a purpose incidental to the ordinary operation of the plan;

3. the loan or extension of credit is unsecured; and

4. the loan or extension of credit is not directly or indirectly made by an employee benefit plan.

---

[1] PT Exemption 80-26 (45 FR 28545), CCH PENSION PLAN GUIDE ¶ 16,618. Amended by 71 FR 17917, CCH PENSION PLAN GUIDE ¶ 16,649S. PT Exemption 2002-13 defines the term "employee benefit plan," as it is used in PTE 80-26, to include plans described in Code Sec. 4975(e)(1). These plans include qualified plans, qualified annuity plans, IRAs, and individual retirement annuities. The exemption was issued to address uncertainty regarding the scope of this PTE (PT Exemption 2002-13 (67 FR 9483), CCH PENSION PLAN GUIDE ¶ 16,649E).

¶ 2490

CLASS EXEMPTIONS: Bank Collective Investment Funds

Bank collective investment funds (CIFs) may engage in certain transactions with parties in interest if the plan's participation in the CIF does not exceed 10% of the fund's total assets.[1]

The exemption permits:

1. transactions between an employer of employees covered under a multiple-employer plan and a CIF in which the plan has an interest greater than the percentage limitation which would normally apply;

2. transactions involving short-term CIFs;

3. transactions between bank CIFs and a party in interest whose participation in the CIF is limited to being a service provider;

4. the leasing of real property and the incidental furnishing of goods by bank CIFs to a party in interest; and

5. the acquisition or holding by a plan of qualifying employer securities or qualifying employer real property in excess of the 10% limitation imposed by ERISA, if the limitation would be violated solely because the employer securities and real property were aggregated with employer securities and real property held by a bank CIF in which the plan has an interest.

Conversion of bank CIF

An employee benefit plan may purchase shares of a registered investment company, even where the bank or plan adviser that serves as the investment adviser for the fund is also a fiduciary of the plan, in exchange for plan assets transferred in-kind to the fund from a CIF maintained by the bank or plan adviser.[2] The transfer or purchase must be made in connection with the complete withdrawal of the plan's assets from the CIF.

The exemption effectively allows a bank or plan adviser that serves as a fiduciary to an employee benefit plan as well as an adviser to an investment company fund to convert the plan's assets currently managed through a CIF into a fund by transferring the assets out of the CIF and into the fund without running the risk of dealing with the plan's assets in their own interest. A bank or plan adviser that complies with the stipulated requirements may be able to receive investment management and investment advisory fees from the fund and the employee benefit plan with respect to the plan assets invested in the shares of the fund.

> **CCH Pointer:** The exemption only covers the purchase of fund shares by an employee benefit plan in exchange for assets that are transferred in-kind from a CIF. The exemption does not provide relief for any prohibited transactions that may arise in connection with the termination of a CIF or the liquidation or transfer of plan assets held by the CIF.

---

[1] PT Exemption 91-38 (56 FR 31966), CCH PENSION PLAN GUIDE ¶ 16,634, amending and redesignating PT Exemption 80-51 (45 FR 49709). PT Exemption 2002-13 defines the term "employee benefit plan," as it is used in PTE 91-38, to include plans described in Code Sec. 4975(e)(1). These plans include qualified plans, qualified annuity plans, IRAs, and individual retirement annuities. The exemption was issued to address uncertainty regarding the scope of this PTE (PT Exemption 2002-13 (67 FR 9483), CCH PENSION PLAN GUIDE ¶ 16,649E).

[2] PT Exemption 97-41 (62 FR 42830), CCH PENSION PLAN GUIDE ¶ 16,648.

¶ 2491

CLASS EXEMPTIONS: Receipt by Banks of Automatic Rollovers from Their Employees

A fiduciary of a pension plan that is also the employer maintaining the plan may establish an individual retirement plan at a bank or other regulated financial institution which is the employer or an affiliate, on behalf of its separated employees, to receive a mandatory distribution.[1] The exemption permits plan fiduciaries to select a proprietary product as the initial investment for an individual retirement plan, and also provides relief from what would otherwise be a prohibited transaction for the receipt of certain fees by individual retirement plan providers in connection with the establishment or maintenance of the individual retirement plan and the initial investment of a mandatory distribution, provided that required conditions are met.

Final regs granting safe harbor issued concurrently

This final prohibited transaction class exemption was issued concurrently with final regulations providing a fiduciary responsibility safe harbor for automatic rollovers (see ¶ 2375) and affects plan sponsors, plan fiduciaries, and individual retirement plan providers and account holders. The class exemption is effective for mandatory distributions made on or after March 28, 2005.

---

[1] PT Exemption 2004-16 (69 FR 57964), CCH PENSION PLAN GUIDE ¶ 16,649O.

¶ 2492

CLASS EXEMPTIONS: Plan Purchase of Securities to Reduce or Retire Indebtedness Owed to Party in Interest

An employee benefit plan may purchase securities in a public offering where the proceeds from the sale may be used by the issuer to reduce or retire indebtedness owed to a party in interest with respect to the plan.[1] Under the exemption, the price paid by the plan fiduciary may not exceed the offering price described in an effective registration statement. In addition, the fiduciary must maintain, for a period of six years from the date of the transaction, the records necessary to verify that the conditions of the exemption have been satisfied.

---

[1] PT Exemption 80-83 (45 FR 73189), CCH PENSION PLAN GUIDE ¶ 16,620. PT Exemption 2002-13 defines the term "employee benefit plan," as it is used in PTE 80-83, to include plans described in Code Sec. 4975(e)(1). These plans include qualified plans, qualified annuity plans, IRAs, and individual retirement annuities. The exemption was issued to address uncertainty regarding the scope of this PTE (PT Exemption 2002-13 (67 FR 9483), CCH PENSION PLAN GUIDE ¶ 16,649E).

¶ 2494

CLASS EXEMPTIONS: Transactions Involving Mortgage Pool Investment Trusts

Transactions related to the origination, maintenance, and termination of mortgage pool investment trusts and the acquisition and holding of certain mortgage-backed pass-through certificates of mortgage pools by employee benefit plans are permissible.[1]

In these arrangements, sponsors and others form investment pools consisting of first mortgage notes originated by the sponsor of the pool or purchased from mortgage lenders. The mortgage loans are then transferred to a trustee who returns certificates representing a beneficial interest in the mortgages to the pool. These certificates are subsequently issued to investors, including employee benefit plans.

The exemption allows the sale, exchange, or transfer of certificates between an employee benefit plan and the pool sponsor, trustee, or insurer who is a fiduciary with respect to the investing plan. However, the total value of the certificates purchased cannot exceed 25% of the amount at issue and at least 50% of the issue must be acquired by persons independent of the pool sponsor, trustee, or insurer.

Pools containing loans secured by mortgages or deeds of trust, other than first lien loans and contracts for the purchase or sale of one or more certificates which are to be determined at an agreed future settlement date, have also been granted an exemption.[2]

Residential mortgage financing arrangements

In addition, employee benefit plans are authorized to provide mortgage financing to purchasers of certain residential construction and to later honor this commitment by:[3]

1. making mortgage loans to purchasers of the units;

2. the direct acquisition, sale, or exchange of real estate mortgage loans; and

3. the acquisition or disposal of a participation interest in the mortgages.

---

[1] PT Exemption 81-7 (46 FR 7520), CCH PENSION PLAN GUIDE ¶ 16,622.

[2] PT Exemption 83-1 (48 FR 895), CCH PENSION PLAN GUIDE ¶ 16,627. PT Exemption 2002-13 defines the term "employee benefit plan," as it is used in PTE 83-1, to include plans described in Code Sec. 4975(e)(1). These plans include qualified plans, qualified annuity plans, IRAs, and individual retirement annuities. The exemption was issued to address uncertainty regarding the scope of this PTE (PT Exemption 2002-13 (67 FR 9483), CCH PENSION PLAN GUIDE ¶ 16,649E).

[3] PT Exemption 88-59 (53 FR 24811), CCH PENSION PLAN GUIDE ¶ 16,632 amending and redesignating PT Exemption 82-87 (47 FR 21331). PT Exemption 2002-13 defines the term "employee benefit plan," as it is used in PTE 88-59, to include plans described in Code Sec. 4975(e)(1). These plans include qualified plans, qualified annuity plans, IRAs, and individual retirement annuities. The exemption was issued to address uncertainty regarding the scope of this PTE (PT Exemption 2002-13 (67 FR 9483), CCH PENSION PLAN GUIDE ¶ 16,649E).

¶ 2495

CLASS EXEMPTIONS: Trust REIT Shares

A class exemption authorizes the acquisition, holding, and sale of specified publicly traded shares of beneficial interest in a real estate investment trust (REIT) that is structured under state law as a business trust (Trust REIT) by individual account plans sponsored by the Trust REIT or its affiliates.[1] Retroactive and prospective relief is provided for transactions that meet required conditions.

Covered transactions

The class exemption authorizes: the purchase or sale of "qualifying REIT shares," on behalf of an individual account at the direction of a participant; the purchase or sale of qualifying REIT shares on behalf of a plan at the direction of an independent fiduciary; the contribution in-kind of qualifying REIT shares by an employer, or the purchase of qualifying REIT shares pursuant to plan terms requiring that employer cash contributions be used to purchase qualifying REIT shares; and the holding of qualifying REIT shares by the plan.[2]

Qualifying REIT shares

Qualifying REIT shares are the shares of beneficial interest in a Trust REIT that are: (1) publicly traded (i.e., traded on the New York Stock Exchange, the American Stock Exchange, or the National Association of Securities Dealers Automated Quotation System National Market); and (2) are not subject to trading restrictions other than those necessary to qualify for REIT status or to otherwise satisfy securities law or applicable exchange or market system trading rules.[3]

No specified limit on percentage of Trust REIT shares in account

The exemption does not impose a single percentage limitation on investments in qualifying REIT shares by individual account plans maintained by the Trust REIT or employer affiliates. The plan fiduciary, however, must determine the appropriate level of investment in qualifying REIT shares, consistent with its fiduciary duties under ERISA.[4]

---

[1] PT Exemption 2004-07 (69 FR 23220), CCH Pension Plan Guide ¶ 16,649M.

[2] PT Exemption 2004-07, Sec. I, (69 FR 23220), CCH Pension Plan Guide ¶ 16,649M.

[3] PT Exemption 2004-07, Sec. III(j), (69 FR 23220), CCH Pension Plan Guide ¶ 16,649M.

[4] Preamble to PT Exemption 2004-07, (69 FR 23220), CCH Pension Plan Guide ¶ 16,649M.

¶ 2496

CLASS EXEMPTIONS: Short-Term Plan Investments

Employee benefit plans may engage in four types of short-term investments: banker's acceptances, commercial paper, repurchase agreements, and certificates of deposit.[1]

A plan may invest in banker's acceptances issued by a federal-or state-supervised bank that have a stated maturity rate of one year or less and neither the bank nor its affiliates have discretionary authority over the plan's assets.

A plan is permitted to invest in commercial paper provided it is not issued by an employer who has employees covered by the plan and it has a stated maturity rate of nine months or less from the date of issue.

Investments in repurchase agreements are exempt if the agreement has a duration of one year or less and its terms are at least as favorable to the plan as would be those from an arm's-length transaction with an unrelated third party.

Finally, a plan is allowed to invest in a certificate of deposit in a federal- or state-supervised bank if neither the bank nor an affiliate of the bank has discretionary control or authority over the investment of plan assets involved in the transaction. Plans may also invest in securities issued by a bank where the bank is a party in interest with respect to the plan only by reason of the furnishing of a checking account or related services to the plan.

---

[1] PT Exemption 81-8 (46 FR 7511, as amended by 50 FR 14043), CCH PENSION PLAN GUIDE ¶ 16,623.

¶ 2500

CLASS EXEMPTIONS: Qualified Professional Asset Managers

Plans managed by qualified professional asset managers (QPAMs), such as banks, insurance companies, or regulated investment advisers, may engage in a wide variety of party in interest transactions with entities associated with the plan, if certain conditions are met.[1] The exemption is intended to expand the investment alternatives available to pension plans while protecting the benefits of fund participants and beneficiaries.

The QPAM must retain full authority over the terms of the transaction, and investment decisions and transactions among the managerial fund, the QPAM, and parties empowered to appoint or terminate the QPAM are prohibited. Further, the exemption applies only if a plan's assets represent no more than 20% of all plan assets, including client-managed assets, under the management of the QPAM.

More specific exemptions provide that plan sponsors and their affiliates can furnish limited amounts of goods and services to managed funds under stipulated conditions. Each employer and its affiliates, however, can derive no more than 1% of their gross receipts (from the previous year) from transactions with a related QPAM managed fund.

A QPAM or its affiliates may also lease minimal amounts of office or commercial space from an investment fund managed by the QPAM. However, the QPAM is prohibited from receiving commissions from the leasing arrangements.

> **CCH Pointer:** In 2005, the EBSA amended PT Exemption 84-14 in response to recent industry consolidation and the difficulties presented by the large resulting institutions in complying with conditions of the QPAM exception requiring the monitoring of corporate affiliates.[2] The amendments focused on the portions of PT Exemption 84-14 that address power of appointment and parties that are related to the QPAM. The amendments narrowed the restrictions on transactions with parties in interest that have the power to invest a plan's assets in a pooled fund managed by a QPAM and increased the pool of related parties with which plans are allowed to engage. In addition, the EBSA clarified that the Section I(a) power of appointment provision refers only to the power to appoint the QPAM as manager of the assets involved in the transaction, as opposed to other plan assets.
>
> Additional limited relief was provided for certain employers to furnish restricted amounts of goods and services to a managed fund in the ordinary

course of business, for leases of office or commercial space between managed funds and QPAMs or contributing employers, and for transactions involving places of public accommodation owned by a managed fund.

In 2010, the EBSA amended PTE 84-14 to permit a financial institution to act as a QPAM for its own plan under certain circumstances.[3] The exemption is effective on November 3, 2010.

---

[1] PT Exemption 84-14 (49 FR 9494), amended by (50 FR 41430), CCH PENSION PLAN GUIDE ¶ 16,628. PT Exemption 2002-13 defines the term "employee benefit plan," as it is used in PTE 84-14, to include plans described in Code Sec. 4975(e)(1). These plans include qualified plans, qualified annuity plans, IRAs, and individual retirement annuities. The exemption was issued to address

uncertainty regarding the scope of this PTE (PT Exemption 2002-13 (67 FR 9483), CCH PENSION PLAN GUIDE ¶ 16,649E).

[2] Amendment to PT Exemption 84-14 (70 FR 49305), CCH PENSION PLAN GUIDE ¶ 16,649P. The amendment is effective August 23, 2005.

[3] Amendment to PT Exemption 84-14 (75 FR 38837), CCH PENSION PLAN GUIDE ¶ 16,649Y.

¶ 2502
CLASS EXEMPTIONS: In-House Asset Managers

The portion of a plan managed by an in-house asset manager may engage in transactions prohibited by ERISA Sec. 406(a)(1)(A)—(D) (sales, loans, provision of services, and transfers) with most party in interest service providers, except for the in-house asset manager or a party related to the in-house asset manager.[1] The exemption enables a plan to lease commercial and office space to the employer and covers the furnishing of services to a party in interest by plan-owned hotels and motels managed by an in-house asset manager.

In-house asset manager defined

An in-house asset manager is an organization that is:

1. either (a) a direct or indirect wholly-owned subsidiary of an employer or of a parent organization of the employer or (b) a member of a nonprofit corporation, a majority of whose members are officers or directors of such an employer or parent corporation; and

2. a registered investment adviser that, as of the last day of the most recent fiscal year, has under its management and control total assets attributable to plans maintained by affiliates of the in-house asset manager in excess of $50 million.

CCH Pointer: The EBSA has issued an amendment to PT Class Exemption 96-23, which allows in-house asset managers (INHAMs) to engage in a variety of transactions with parties in interest, provided that the conditions of the exemption are met.[2] Among other things, EBSA has expanded the definition of INHAM and the relief provided by PTE 96-23 relating to the leasing of office or commercial space owned by a plan managed by an INHAM to an employer with respect to the plan or an affiliate of the employer. In addition, the amendment eases the restrictions on parties in interest to engage in transactions with the plan if the parties are "co-joint venturers" and changed the exemption audit requirements.

As to the definition of INHAM, EBSA has expanded the definition to include a subsidiary that is directly or indirectly 80% or more owned by the employer or by the parent company of the employer. The amount of assets that must be managed by an INHAM that is an investment adviser has been increased from $50 million to $85 million as of the last day of the first fiscal year of the investment adviser beginning on or after April 1, 2011.

---

[1] PT Exemption 96-23 (61 FR 15975), CCH PENSION PLAN GUIDE ¶ 16,644. Prior to April 10, 1996, in-house asset managers who wished to engage in transactions prohibited by ERISA were required to either seek an individual exemption from the La-

bor Department, hire a qualified professional asset manager, or forego the investment opportunity.

[2] Amendment to PT Exemption 96-23 (76 FR 18255), CCH PENSION PLAN GUIDE ¶ 16,649Z. The amendment is generally effective April 1, 2011.

¶ 2503
CLASS EXEMPTIONS: QTAs of Abandoned Individual Account Plans

In connection with final regulations that provide procedures and requirements for the termination of abandoned individual account plans, a class exemption exempts a "qualified termination administrator" (QTA) from certain prohibited transactions arising in connection with its activities as a QTA, including providing services in connection with terminating and winding up the abandoned plan, for services rendered to the plan prior to its becoming a QTA, and for distributions from abandoned plans transferred to IRAs or other accounts maintained by the QTA.[1]

A QTA must determine that a plan has been abandoned. To be a QTA, an entity must hold the plan's assets and be eligible under IRS rules to be a trustee or issuer of an individual retirement account plan. Thus, QTAs will generally be a bank, trust company, mutual fund group or insurance company.[2]

In particular, the exemption allows a QTA to select itself or an affiliate to provide services to the plan in connection with the termination of the plan, to pay itself or an affiliate fees for those services, and to pay itself for services provided prior to the plan's deemed termination.[3] The exemption also permits a QTA to: (1) designate itself or an affiliate as the provider of an individual retirement plan or other account for the distribution of a participant or beneficiary who fails to make an election regarding the disposition of such benefits; (2) select a proprietary investment product as the initial investment for such plan or account; (3) provide a federally insured bank or savings association account for small distributions; and (4) pay itself or its affiliate fees in connection these activities.

CCH Pointer: The EBSA has issued an amendment to PT Exemption 2006-06 that requires, as a condition of relief under the exemption, that benefits for a missing, designated nonspouse beneficiary be directly rolled over into an inherited IRA that fully complies with Code requirements. The EBSA also clarifies that the exemption provides relief to a QTA that designates itself or an affiliate as the provider of an inherited IRA for a missing, designated non-spouse beneficiary pursuant to the exemption's conditions.[4]

For more information about requirements for terminating abandoned individual account plans, see ¶ 2803.

[1] PT Exemption 2006-06 (71 FR 20856), CCH Pension Plan Guide ¶ 16,649U.

[2] ERISA Reg. § 2578.1(g) (April 21, 2006, 71 FR 20820). These final regulations were effective May 22, 2006.

[3] PT Exemption 2006-06 (71 FR 20856), CCH Pension Plan Guide ¶ 16,649U.

[4] Amendment to PT Exemption 2006-06 (73 FR 58629), October 7, 2008.

¶ 2504
CLASS EXEMPTIONS: IRAs

The Labor Department has issued class exemptions that allow banks to provide small gifts or free or reduced cost services to individuals who maintain IRAs (including SIMPLE IRAs and education IRAs) and Keogh plans.[1] Registered broker-dealers may also provide services at reduced fees or no cost to IRA (including SIMPLE IRA, Roth IRA, and education IRA), SEP, or Keogh plan customers.[2] For details, see ¶ 3208.

[1] PT Exemption 93-1 (58 FR 3567), CCH Pension Plan Guide ¶ 16,638; PT Exemption 93-33 (58 FR 31053), CCH Pension Plan Guide ¶ 16,640,

amended 3-8-99 (64 FR 11044), CCH Pension Plan Guide ¶ 16,649B.

[2] PT Exemption 97-11 (62 FR 5855), CCH Pension Plan Guide ¶ 16,647, amended 3-8-99 (64 FR 11042), CCH Pension Plan Guide ¶ 16,649A.

¶ 2506
PROCEDURES FOR OBTAINING PROHIBITED TRANSACTION EXEMPTIONS: Applications for Exemption

The Labor Department has general authority to grant exemptions to the prohibited transaction rules. Thus, other than the three exceptions noted below, all requests for administrative exemptions from the prohibited transactions provisions of Part 4 of Subtitle B of Title I of ERISA and/or Code Sec. 4975 should be submitted only to the Department of Labor.[1]

CCH Pointer: The EBSA has issued final regulations that update the procedures governing the filing and processing of applications for exemptions from the prohibited transaction provisions of ERISA.[2] The final rules consolidate existing policies, clarify the types of information and documentation required to submit a complete filing, provide expanded opportunities for the electronic submission of information and comments relating to an exemption, and require a summary statement designed to make complex exemptions more understandable to participants and other interested parties. These rules govern the filing and processing of applications for both individual and class exemptions.

In addition, an accelerated exemption procedure is available to certain applicants (see below).

Certain applications to be filed with IRS

The following requests for exemptions from the prohibited transaction rules should be made to the Treasury Department, rather than the Labor Department:

1. all requests regarding individual retirement accounts and individual retirement annuities;

2. all requests regarding directed investments that are exempt from the prohibited transaction provisions by virtue of ERISA Sec. 404(c); and

3. all requests for employee stock ownership plans described in Code Sec. 4975(e)(7) (i.e., "leveraged" ESOPs).

Initiating an application

Any party in interest or disqualified person with respect to the plan may initiate an application (see ¶ 2508). In addition, the Secretary of Labor may initiate exemption proceedings.

In the case of an exemption applicable to a class of fiduciaries, disqualified persons, or a class of transactions, an association or organization that represents parties in interest or disqualified persons may apply.[3]

Filing addresses

Exemption applications directed to the Labor Department may be mailed via first-class mail to: Employee Benefits Security Administration, Office of Exemption Determinations, U.S. Department of Labor, Room N-5700, 200 Constitution Avenue NW., Washington, DC 20210.[4] Alternatively, applications may be emailed to the Department at e-OED@dol.gov, or transmitted via facsimile at (202) 219-0204. Notwithstanding the above transmission methods, applicants are also required to submit one paper copy of the application for the Department's file.

Oral requests and advice

The Labor Department does not propose or issue exemptions upon oral request, nor does the DOL grant exemptions orally. An exemption applicant may ask for and receive oral advice from Labor Department employees in preparing its exemption application. However, this oral advice does not constitute part of the record and is not binding on the Labor Department in its processing of the exemption application or in its examination or audit of a plan.[5]

Reasons for granting exemptions

Exemptions are not allowed unless the transaction is in the interest of the plan and its participants and beneficiaries, does not present administrative problems, and adequate safeguards are provided for participants and beneficiaries.

Notice and hearing

Before an exemption will be allowed, adequate notice (including publication in the *Federal Register*) must be provided to interested persons, who are to have an opportunity to present their views.[6] In the case of an exemption from the prohibition against a fiduciary dealing with plan assets for his own account, acting on behalf of an adverse party to the plan, or receiving consideration for his personal account, any interested person who may be adversely affected by an exemption may request a hearing.

Accelerated exemption procedures

A prohibited transaction class exemption allows for accelerated approval of certain prospective transactions that are generally prohibited but that are substantially similar to at least two individual exemptions issued by the DOL in the five years prior to the application for relief under the class exemption.[7] Parties to the transaction must submit information to the DOL and provide notice to interested persons regarding the transaction. In addition, the party requesting the exemption must demonstrate that the transaction poses little, if any, risk of abuse or loss to plan participants and beneficiaries.

> **CCH Pointer:** The EBSA has adopted an amendment that expands the accelerated procedure for receiving approval of transactions that would otherwise be prohibited to allow applicants to cite either two substantially similar individual exemptions granted by the DOL within the previous five years, or one individual exemption granted by the DOL within the last ten years and one transaction authorized under the accelerated procedure within the past five years.[8]

---

[1] IRS Announcement 79-6, I.R.B. 1979-4, 43.

[2] EBSA final regulations, 76 FR 66637, October 27, 2011, CCH PENSION PLAN GUIDE ¶ 24,809E, ERISA Reg. § 2570.30 and following. These regulations are effective December 27, 2011 and apply to all applications filed after that date.

[3] ERISA Reg. § 2570.32, as amended by EBSA final regulations, 76 FR 66637, October 27, 2011.

[4] ERISA Reg. § 2570.36, as amended by EBSA final regulations, 76 FR 66637, October 27, 2011.

[5] ERISA Reg. § 2570.30(e), as amended by EBSA final regulations, 76 FR 66637, October 27, 2011.

[6] ERISA Reg. §§ 2570.43 and 2570.46, as amended by EBSA final regulations, 76 FR 66637, October 27, 2011.

[7] PT Exemption 96-62 (61 FR 39988), CCH PENSION PLAN GUIDE ¶ 16,645. PT Exemption 2002-13 defines the term "employee benefit plan," as it is used in PTE 96-62, to include plans described in Code Sec. 4975(e)(1). These plans include qualified plans, qualified annuity plans, IRAs, and individual retirement annuities. The exemption was issued to address uncertainty regarding the scope of this PTE (PT Exemption 2002-13 (67 FR 9483), CCH PENSION PLAN GUIDE ¶ 16,649E).

[8] Amendment to PT Exemption 96-62 (67 FR 44622), CCH PENSION PLAN GUIDE ¶ 16,649G.

¶ 2508

PROCEDURES FOR OBTAINING PROHIBITED TRANSACTION EXEMPTIONS: Persons Who May Apply for PT Exemptions

Any party in interest with respect to the plan may initiate an application for a prohibited transaction exemption. A plan which is a party to the exemption transaction may also initiate an application.[1] An association or organization that represents parties in interest may apply for a prohibited transaction exemption covering a class of fiduciaries, parties in interest, or transactions. In addition, the Department of Labor may initiate exemption proceedings on its own motion.[2]

An exemption application may be submitted either by an applicant or by that applicant's authorized representative. If an application is submitted by a representative for the applicant, however, the representative must submit proof of his authority in the form of:[3]

1. a power of attorney; or
2. a written certification from the applicant that the representative is authorized to file the application.

If an authorized representative submits an exemption application and submits proper proof of authority, the Labor Department will direct all correspondence and inquiries regarding the application to the representative, unless otherwise requested to do so by the applicant.[4]

Shared representation

The Labor Department requires disclosure of the identity of any representatives for the affected plan(s) and parties in interest and what individuals or entities they represent.[5] Shared representation of a plan and parties in interest could raise questions under the ERISA exclusive benefit and prudence rules and the prohibited transaction rules under both the Code and ERISA.[6]

Cost of obtaining an exemption

The payment by a plan of the cost of obtaining an exemption may raise questions under ERISA's rule prohibiting a fiduciary from causing a plan to engage in a transaction that results in a plan's assets being used to benefit a party in interest.[7] Accordingly, an individual application must disclose the identity of the person who will bear the cost of an exemption application[8] and also of the person who will bear the cost of any fee payable to an independent fiduciary with regard to the exemption transaction.[9]

Under certain conditions it may be appropriate for a plan to pay all or part of the costs incurred incident to obtaining an exemption, such as where it is necessary to ensure the independence of an independent fiduciary or third-party expert. However, the Labor Department believes that the propriety of such payments by a plan is an inherently factual determination that can be made on a case-by-case basis.[10]

---

[1] ERISA Reg. § 2570.32(a), as amended by EBSA final regulations, 76 FR 66637, October 27, 2011.

[2] ERISA Reg. § 2570.30(c), as amended by EBSA final regulations, 76 FR 66637, October 27, 2011.

[3] ERISA Reg. § 2570.32(b), as amended by EBSA final regulations, 76 FR 66637, October 27, 2011.

[4] ERISA Reg. § 2570.32(c), as amended by EBSA final regulations, 76 FR 66637, October 27, 2011.

[5] ERISA Reg. § 2570.34(a)(3), as amended by EBSA final regulations, 76 FR 66637, October 27, 2011.

[6] Preamble to ERISA Reg. §§ 2570.30—2570.52, 55 FR 32839, August 10, 1990.

[7] Preamble to ERISA Reg. §§ 2570.30—2570.52, 55 FR 32839, August 10, 1990.

[8] ERISA Reg. § 2570.35(a)(18), as amended by EBSA final regulations, 76 FR 66637, October 27, 2011.

[9] ERISA Reg. § 2570.35(a)(19), as amended by EBSA final regulations, 76 FR 66637, October 27, 2011.

[10] Preamble to ERISA Reg. §§ 2570.30—2570.52, 55 FR 32839, August 10, 1990.

¶ 2510

PROCEDURES FOR OBTAINING PROHIBITED TRANSACTION EXEMPTIONS: Special Rules Precluding Exemptions in Certain Cases

Under the following circumstances, the Department of Labor will not consider a prohibited transaction exemption application.

Class exemption under consideration

The DOL generally does not consider an application for an individual exemption relating to a specific transaction if it is already considering a class exemption relating to the same type of transaction.[1] However, the DOL may waive the general rule in certain instances.

Investigated transactions

The DOL does not consider applications involving transactions that are the subject of an investigation of possible violations of ERISA's reporting and disclosure rules or fiduciary responsibility rules.[2] Similarly, the DOL does not consider applications involving a party in interest who is the subject of such an investigation or who is a defendant in an action brought by the DOL or the IRS to enforce ERISA's reporting and disclosure or fiduciary responsibility rules.

Incomplete applications

The DOL typically does not consider exemption applications that fail to include all required information (see ¶ 2512 and ¶ 2514) or otherwise fail to conform with the procedures for obtaining prohibited transaction exemptions.[3]

CCH Pointer: In certain cases, the Labor Department may exercise its discretion to consider exemption applications in situations where, for example, deficiencies in the exemption application are merely technical or where an enforcement matter is clearly unrelated to the exemption transaction.[4]

DOL notification

If the Labor Department decides not to consider an exemption application, it must inform the applicant in writing of its decision and explain the reasons underlying its decision.[5]

[1] ERISA Reg. § 2570.33(b), as amended by EBSA final regulations, 76 FR 66637, October 27, 2011.

[2] ERISA Reg. § 2570.33(a)(2), as amended by EBSA final regulations, 76 FR 66637, October 27, 2011.

[3] ERISA Reg. § 2570.33(a)(1), as amended by EBSA final regulations, 76 FR 66637, October 27, 2011.

[4] Preamble to ERISA Reg. §§ 2570.30—2570.52, 55 FR 32839, August 10, 1990.

[5] ERISA Reg. § 2570.33(d), as amended by EBSA final regulations, 76 FR 66637, October 27, 2011.

¶ 2512

PROCEDURES FOR OBTAINING PROHIBITED TRANSACTION EXEMPTIONS: Contents of Exemption Application

All applications for exemptions must disclose:[1]

1. the name of the applicant;

2. a detailed description of the exemption transaction, including the identification of all parties in interest involved, a description of any larger integrated transaction of which the exemption transaction is a part, and a chronology of the events leading up to the transaction;

3. the identify of any representatives for the affected plan(s) and parties in interest and what individuals or entities they represent;

4. reasons a plan would have for entering into the exemption transaction;

5. the prohibited transaction provisions from which the exemptive relief is requested and the reason why the transaction would violate each such provision;

6. whether the transaction is customary for the industry or class involved;

7. whether the transaction is or has been the subject of a Labor Department or IRS investigation or enforcement action;

8. the hardship or economic loss that would result from a denial of the exemption;

9. why the requested exemption would be administratively feasible, in the interests of affected plans and their participants and beneficiaries, and protective of the rights of participants and beneficiaries of affected plans; and

10. a signed declaration by the applicant that the application is accurate.

As applicable, applications must include specialized statements from qualified, independent appraisers and fiduciaries, and other independent, third-party experts.[2]

Notice requirements

The application must also contain a description of the interested persons to whom the applicant intends to provide notice, the manner in which notice will be provided, and an estimate of the time the applicant will need to furnish notice to all interested persons (following publication of a notice of the proposed exemption in the Federal Register). See also ¶ 2528.[3]

Draft of exemption

An application for exemption may include a draft of the requested exemption. The draft exemption would define the transaction and parties in interest for which exemptive relief is sought and the specific conditions under which the exemption would apply.[4]

> **CCH Pointer:** Although an applicant is not required to submit a draft of the proposed exemption, the Labor Department encourages applicants to do so. The Labor Department indicates that a draft submission which explains the requested exemption in a clear and concise manner and focuses on what the applicant considers to be the essential features of the exemption transaction and the critical safeguards supporting the requested relief is likely to facilitate the DOL's administrative review.[5]

Individual exemptions

In addition to the information required for all prohibited transaction exemption applications, each application for individual exemptions must contain the information detailed at ¶ 2514.

---

[1] ERISA Reg. § 2570.34(a)-(b), as amended by EBSA final regulations, 76 FR 66637, October 27, 2011.

[2] ERISA Reg. § 2570.34(c)-(e), as amended by EBSA final regulations, 76 FR 66637, October 27, 2011.

[3] ERISA Reg. § 2570.34(b)(2), as amended by EBSA final regulations, 76 FR 66637, October 27, 2011.

[4] ERISA Reg. § 2570.34(f), as amended by EBSA final regulations, 76 FR 66637, October 27, 2011.

[5] Preamble to ERISA Reg. §§ 2570.30—2570.52, 55 FR 32839, August 10, 1990.

¶ 2514

PROCEDURES FOR OBTAINING PROHIBITED TRANSACTION EXEMPTIONS: Special Rules for Contents of an Individual Exemption Application

In addition to the information required for every PT exemption application (see ¶ 2512), each application for individual exemption must disclose:[1]

1. the name, address, telephone number, and type of plan to which the requested exemption applies;

2. the employer identification number and the plan number;

3. whether the plan has ever been found to have violated the exclusive benefit rule or engaged in a prohibited transaction;

4. whether any relief from the prohibited transaction rules has been requested or provided to the applicant or any of the parties on behalf of whom the exemption is sought;

5. whether the applicant or parties in interest are or were (in the past five years) defendants in any lawsuit or criminal action concerning such person's conduct as a fiduciary or party in interest (other than lawsuits relating solely to routine benefit claims);

6. whether the applicant has been convicted (within the last 13 years) of any crime described in ERISA Sec. 411 and in section I(g) of PTE 84-14, including robbery, bribery, or extortion;

7. whether, within the last five years, any plan or party in interest involved in the exemption transaction has been under investigation or examination by, or engaged in a continuing controversy with, the Labor Department, IRS, Pension Benefit Guaranty Corporation, or other specified agencies;

8. whether the plan has experienced any reportable events under ERISA Sec. 4043 (see ¶ 2810);

9. whether a notice of intent to terminate has been filed;

10. names, addresses, and taxpayer identification numbers of all parties in interest involved in the transaction;

11. the estimated number of participants and beneficiaries in each plan affected by the requested exemption;

12. the percentage of the fair market value of the total assets of each affected plan;

13. whether the exemption transaction has been consummated or will be consummated only if the exemption is granted;

CCH Pointer: If the transaction has already been consummated, the applicant must explain the circumstances which resulted in plan fiduciaries causing the plan to engage in the transaction before obtaining an exemption. In addition, the applicant must indicate: (a) whether the transaction has been terminated; (b) whether the transaction has been corrected; (c) whether Form 5330 (Return of Excise Taxes Related to Employee Benefit Plans) has been filed; and (d) whether any excise taxes or civil penalties due have been paid.

14. the name of every person who has investment discretion over any assets involved in the transaction;

15. information on plan loans or property leased to a party in interest, or on securities issued by any party in interest involved in the exemption transaction;

CCH Pointer: In the event that plan assets are invested in loans or property leased to a party in interest, or in securities issued by any party in interest, the applicant must provide a statement for each of these three types of investments, which indicates: (a) the type of investment to which the statement pertains; (b) the aggregate fair market value of all investments of this type as reflected in the plan's most recent annual report; (c) the approximate percentage of the fair market value of the plan's total assets (as shown in the annual report) that is represented by all investments of this type; and (d) the statutory or administrative exemption covering these investments, if any.

16. the approximate aggregate fair market value of the total assets of each plan;

17. the person(s) who will bear the costs of the exemption application and of notifying interested persons;

18. information on any independent fiduciary involved;

19. true copies of all contracts, deeds, trust agreements, and related documents;

20. a discussion of the facts relevant to the exemption transaction that are reflected in these documents;

21. a copy of the most recent financial statements of the plan affected by the requested exemption; and

22. a net worth statement of any party in interest that is providing a personal guarantee with respect to the exemption transaction.

CCH Pointer: In general, an application for an exemption relating to an individual transaction will not ordinarily be considered separately if a class exemption that would encompass the individual transaction is presently under consideration or has already been considered (see ¶ 2510).[2]

Individual exemptions involving pooled funds

Applications for individual exemptions involving pooled funds are subject to special informational requirements.[3] For example, such exemptions involving pooled funds need not furnish information required by items 8 through 12, above. In addition, information required by items 1 through 7, above, and items 13 through 18, above, must be furnished with reference to the pooled fund, rather than by reference to the plans participating in the pooled funds. For information involving item 15, above (relating to investments in plan loans, property leases, or security issuances involving parties in interest), information should be provided only about other pooled fund transactions with, and investments in, parties in interest involved in the exemption transaction which are also sponsors of plans which invest in the pooled fund.

For individual exemption applications involving pooled funds, the following information must also be furnished:[4]

1. an estimate of the number of plans that are participating (or will participate) in the pooled fund; and

2. the minimum and maximum limits imposed by the pooled fund (if any) on the portion of the total assets of each plan that may be invested in the pooled fund.

More stringent informational requirements apply to applications involving one or more pooled funds in which any participating plan (1) invests more than 20% of the total assets of the pooled fund or (2) covers employees of (a) the party sponsoring or maintaining the pooled fund (or any affiliate of such party) or (b) any fiduciary with investment discretion over the pooled fund's assets (or any affiliate of such fiduciary).[5]

Inapplicability to mere investment by plan. The special requirements applicable to pooled funds do not apply to an individual exemption request solely for the investment by a plan in a pooled fund.[6] Plans merely investing in pooled funds need only provide the general application information (see ¶ 2512) and the regular information applicable to individual exemption requests (see 1 through 22, above).

---

[1] ERISA Reg. § 2570.35(a)-(b), as amended by EBSA final regulations, 76 FR 66637, October 27, 2011.

[2] ERISA Reg. § 2570.33(b), as amended by EBSA final regulations, 76 FR 66637, October 27, 2011.

[3] ERISA Reg. § 2570.35(c), as amended by EBSA final regulations, 76 FR 66637, October 27, 2011.

[4] ERISA Reg. § 2570.35(c)(3), as amended by EBSA final regulations, 76 FR 66637, October 27, 2011.

[5] ERISA Reg. § 2570.35(c)(4), as amended by EBSA final regulations, 76 FR 66637, October 27, 2011.

[6] ERISA Reg. § 2570.35(c)(5), as amended by EBSA final regulations, 76 FR 66637, October 27, 2011.

¶ 2516

PROCEDURES FOR OBTAINING PROHIBITED TRANSACTION EXEMPTIONS: Amending and Supplementing Exemption Applications

An applicant for a PT exemption must promptly notify the DOL in writing if the applicant discovers, while the exemption application is pending, that any material fact or representation contained in the application, or in any documents or testimony provided in support of the application, is inaccurate.[1] Similarly, an applicant has a duty to notify the DOL if any material fact or representation in the application changes while the application is pending, if anything occurs that might affect the continuing accuracy of any material fact or representation, or if it learns that a material fact or representation has been omitted from the exemption application.

Inform DOL if party in interest is subject to investigation

While the exemption application is pending, an applicant must notify the DOL if the applicant or any party in interest who would participate in the exemption transaction becomes the subject of an investigation or enforcement action involving ERISA or the employee benefit provisions of the Code.[2] This duty to notify extends to investigations or enforcement actions by the DOL, IRS, Justice Department, PBGC, or Federal Retirement Thrift Investment Board.

[1] ERISA Reg. § 2570.37(a), as amended by EBSA final regulations, 76 FR 66637, October 27, 2011.

[2] ERISA Reg. § 2570.37(b), as amended by EBSA final regulations, 76 FR 66637, October 27, 2011.

¶ 2518

PROCEDURES FOR OBTAINING PROHIBITED TRANSACTION EXEMPTIONS: Retroactive Exemptions

The DOL will favorably consider retroactive exemptions for transactions already consummated, but only where the safeguards necessary for the grant of a prospective exemption were in place at the time of the transaction.[1]

Good faith necessary

Where the DOL grants retroactive exemptions, applicants must be able to document that they acted in good faith by taking reasonable and appropriate steps to protect the plan from abuse and unnecessary risk. Among the factors that the DOL will take into account in determining whether the applicant has acted in good faith are:

1. the participation of an independent fiduciary acting on behalf of the plan who is qualified to negotiate, approve, and monitor the transaction;

2. the existence of contemporaneous appraisal by a qualified independent appraiser or reference to an objective third-party source, such as a stock or bond index;

3. the existence of a bidding process or evidence of comparable fair market transactions with unrelated third parties;

4. the submission of an accurate and complete application for exemption containing documentation of all necessary and relevant facts and representations upon which the applicant relied, presented in a manner that is susceptible to review by the DOL (Additional weight is given to facts and representations that are prepared and certified by independent sources.);

5. the submission of evidence that the fiduciary did not engage in an act or transaction knowing that it was prohibited (The DOL will give appropriate weight to the submission of contemporaneous, reasoned legal opinion of counsel upon which the fiduciary relied in good faith before entering into the act or transaction.);

6. the submission of a statement of the circumstances prompting the submission of the application and the steps the applicant took with regard to the transaction upon discovery of the violation;

7. the submission of a statement prepared and certified by an independent person familiar with the types of transactions for which relief is requested demonstrating that the transaction's terms and conditions were at least as favorable as those obtainable in a similar transaction with an unrelated party; and

8. any other undertakings and assurances with respect to the plan and its participants that may be offered by the applicant that are relevant to the criteria under ERISA Sec. 408(a) and Code Sec. 401(a).

As a general matter, the Labor Department will not favorably consider retroactive exemption requests where transactions or conduct with regard to which an exemption is requested resulted in a loss to the plan. In addition, the DOL does not favorably consider requests for exemptions where the transactions are inconsistent with general fiduciary responsibility provisions[2] or the Code's exclusive benefit requirements.[3]

---

[1] ERISA Reg. § 2570.35(d), as amended by EBSA final regulations, 76 FR 66637, October 27, 2011. The final regulations incorporate the standards for retroactive relief for past prohibited transactions issued in ERISA Technical Release 85-1, 1-22-85, CCH PENSION PLAN GUIDE ¶ 19,956.

[2] ERISA Secs. 403 and 404.

[3] Code Sec. 401(a).

¶ 2520

PROCEDURES FOR OBTAINING PROHIBITED TRANSACTION EXEMPTIONS: Tentative Denial of Application

If the DOL decides not to propose or grant the prohibited transaction exemption, it will notify the applicant in writing of its tentative denial.[1] This letter of tentative denial will be accompanied by a short statement of the DOL's reasons for the tentative denial.

The applicant then has 20 days from the date of the tentative denial letter to request a conference or notify the DOL of its intent to submit additional information in writing.[2] If the DOL receives neither a conference request nor a notice of intent to submit additional information within 20 days, it will issue a final denial letter. An applicant is entitled to only one conference with respect to any exemption application.

Opportunities to submit additional information

An applicant may notify, either by telephone, letter, or email, the DOL of its intent to submit additional information in support of its exemption application.[3] If a letter or email is sent, it should be sent to the relevant address furnished in the applicant's tentative denial letter. When notifying the DOL of an intent to submit additional information, the applicant should generally indicate the type of information that he or she will submit.

An applicant must submit the additional information intended to support an exemption application, in writing, within 40 days from the date of the tentative denial letter.[4] All additional information must be accompanied by a dated and signed declaration testifying to the truth and correctness of the information.

Extensions of time. An applicant who, for reasons beyond his control, cannot submit all additional information within the 40-day period may request an extension of time to furnish the information.[5] A request for extension must be made before the 40-day period expires. Additional time within which to submit additional information is granted only in unusual situations and only for limited periods of time.

Withdrawal of applications. If an applicant cannot submit all of the additional information intended to provide support for the exemption application within the required 40-day period (or within any additional DOL-granted time period), the applicant may withdraw the exemption application before the applicable time period expires.[6] An applicant may later reinstate such a withdrawn application (see ¶ 2530).

Final denial letters

The DOL will issue, without further notice, a final denial letter denying the requested exemption if:[7]

1. the DOL has not received the additional information that the applicant indicated would be submitted within the 40-day period or within any additional DOL-granted period of time;

2. the applicant did not request a conference; and

3. the applicant has not withdrawn the application, as permitted.

[1] ERISA Reg. § 2570.38(a), as amended by EBSA final regulations, 76 FR 66637, October 27, 2011.

[2] ERISA Reg. § 2570.38(b), as amended by EBSA final regulations, 76 FR 66637, October 27, 2011.

[3] ERISA Reg. § 2570.39(a), as amended by EBSA final regulations, 76 FR 66637, October 27, 2011.

[4] ERISA Reg. § 2570.39(b), as amended by EBSA final regulations, 76 FR 66637, October 27, 2011.

[5] ERISA Reg. § 2570.39(c), as amended by EBSA final regulations, 76 FR 66637, October 27, 2011.

[6] ERISA Reg. § 2570.39(d), as amended by EBSA final regulations, 76 FR 66637, October 27, 2011.

[7] ERISA Reg. § 2570.39(e), as amended by EBSA final regulations, 76 FR 66637, October 27, 2011.

¶ 2522

PROCEDURES FOR OBTAINING PROHIBITED TRANSACTION EXEMPTIONS: Conferences on Requested Exemptions

Prohibited transaction exemption applicants are entitled to no more than one conference with the Labor Department regarding any exemption application.[1] However, an applicant is not entitled to a conference where the DOL has held a hearing on the exemption.

DOL-applicant conferences on requested exemptions are held in Washington, DC, unless an applicant requests a telephone conference.

CCH Pointer: In addition to the formal conference, the DOL maintains a policy of informally contacting applicants regarding their applications, as the DOL deems appropriate.[2]

Additional information

Within 20 days after a conference, an applicant may submit a written record to the Labor Department of any additional data, arguments, or precedents discussed at the conference but not previously or adequately presented in writing.[3]

[1] ERISA Reg. § 2570.40(b), as amended by EBSA final regulations, 76 FR 66637, October 27, 2011.

[2] Preamble to ERISA Reg. §§ 2570.30—2570.52, 55 FR 32839, August 10, 1990.

[3] ERISA Reg. § 2570.40(h), as amended by EBSA final regulations, 76 FR 66637, October 27, 2011.

¶ 2524

PROCEDURES FOR OBTAINING PROHIBITED TRANSACTION EXEMPTIONS: Final Denial Letters

Once a tentative denial has been issued and an applicant has not (a) requested a conference within 20 days, or (b) notified the Department of Labor of an intent to submit additional information within 40 days, the DOL will issue a final denial letter.[1]

The DOL will also issue a final denial letter where, after issuing a tentative denial letter and considering the entire record of the case (including any additionally submitted information), it decides not to propose an exemption or to withdraw an exemption already proposed.

In addition, the DOL will issue a final denial letter if, after proposing an exemption, conducting a hearing, and considering the entire record in the case, it decides to withdraw the proposed exemption. In this instance, the Labor Department will not issue a tentative denial letter because it considers that the hearing will have already provided the applicant and other proponents of the exemption application an adequate opportunity to present their views and other evidence in support of the exemption.[2]

[1] ERISA Reg. § 2570.41, as amended by EBSA final regulations, 76 FR 66637, October 27, 2011.

[2] Preamble to ERISA Reg. §§ 2570.30—2570.52, 55 FR 32839, August 10, 1990.

¶ 2526

PROCEDURES FOR OBTAINING PROHIBITED TRANSACTION EXEMPTIONS: Publication of Notice of Proposed Exemption

If the DOL tentatively decides to grant the exemption, it will publish a notice of the proposed exemption in the *Federal Register*.[1] The notice must explain the exemption transactions and summarize the information and reasons in support of proposing the exemption. In addition, the notice must describe the scope of relief and any conditions under which the exemption is proposed.

The notice must also inform interested persons of their right to submit comments electronically or in writing to the DOL relating to the proposed exemption. A deadline for the receipt of such comments is also included in the notice.

If the proposed exemption includes one or more transactions between a plan and a fiduciary, the notice must also provide that any interested party may request that a hearing be held on the matter.

[1] ERISA Reg. § 2570.42, as amended by EBSA final regulations, 76 FR 66637, October 27, 2011.

¶ 2528

PROCEDURES FOR OBTAINING PROHIBITED TRANSACTION EXEMPTIONS: Notification of Interested Persons

If notice has been published in the *Federal Register*, the applicant must give adequate notice to interested persons of the pendency of the exemption.[1] If the DOL determines that the notification (as set forth in the exemption application—see ¶ 2512) is inadequate, the applicant must obtain the DOL's consent as to the manner and time period of providing the notice to interested persons.

Interested persons

An applicant is required, as part of the exemption application, to include a description of the interested persons to whom the applicant intends to give notice. However, the regulations do not specify which individuals or organizations constitute "interested persons" for purposes of these notification rules.

According to the DOL, the persons or organizations to be treated as "interested persons" depends on nature of the exemption being requested. As a result, the DOL will determine whether the range of persons to be notified (and the method of notification) is adequate. The Labor Department believes that this approach provides the necessary flexibility to accommodate the varied types of exemption applications, as well as circumstances unique to a particular applicant.[2]

Method of delivery

The method used to furnish notice to interested persons must be reasonably calculated to ensure that interested persons actually receive the notice.[3] Both personal delivery and delivery by first-class mail generally are considered reasonable methods of furnishing notice. If applicants elect to provide notice electronically, they must provide satisfactory proof of electronic delivery to the entire class of interested persons.

Confirmation of notice

After furnishing the required notice, an applicant must submit a written statement to the Labor Department confirming that notice was furnished to interested persons and that notice was adequate and timely.[4] A declaration under oath attesting to the truth of the information provided and signed by a qualified person must also be provided to the Labor Department. No exemption is granted by the Labor Department until such a statement and its accompanying declaration have been furnished to the Labor Department.

---

[1] ERISA Reg. § 2570.43(a), as amended by EBSA final regulations, 76 FR 66637, October 27, 2011.

[2] Preamble to ERISA Reg. §§ 2570.30—2570.52, 55 FR 32839, August 10, 1990.

[3] ERISA Reg. § 2570.43(b), as amended by EBSA final regulations, 76 FR 66637, October 27, 2011.

[4] ERISA Reg. § 2570.43(c), as amended by EBSA final regulations, 76 FR 66637, October 27, 2011.

¶ 2530

PROCEDURES FOR OBTAINING PROHIBITED TRANSACTION EXEMPTIONS: Withdrawal of Exemption Application

An applicant may withdraw an application for an exemption at any time by informing the Labor Department, orally or in writing (including electronically), of the intent to withdraw.[1]

Individual exemptions

After receiving an applicant's notice of intent to withdraw an application for an individual exemption, the Labor Department will confirm the withdrawal by letter to the applicant. The Labor Department will also terminate all proceedings relating to the application. If a notice of proposed exemption has been published in the *Federal Register,* the Labor Department will publish a notice withdrawing the proposed exemption.[2]

Class exemptions

Upon receiving an applicant's notice of intent to withdraw an application for a class exemption, or for an individual exemption that is being considered with other applications as a request for a class exemption, the Labor Department will inform any other applicants for the exemption of the withdrawal. The Labor Department will continue to process other applications for the same exemption. If all applicants for a particular class exemption withdraw their applications, the Labor Department may either terminate all proceedings relating to the exemption or propose the exemption on its own motion.[3]

Reinstatement of application

If, after the withdrawal of an exemption application, an applicant decides to reapply for the same exemption, the applicant may contact the Labor Department in writing (including electronically), requesting that the application be reinstated and referring to the application number assigned to the original application.[4]

If any additional information is not yet submitted when the original application is withdrawn, the additional information must accompany the letter requesting reinstatement of the application.[5] However, an applicant need not resubmit information previously furnished to the Labor Department in connection with a withdrawn application unless the applicant is requesting a reinstatement more than two years after the earlier application was withdrawn.

---

[1] ERISA Reg. § 2570.44(a), as amended by EBSA final regulations, 76 FR 66637, October 27, 2011.

[2] ERISA Reg. § 2570.44(b), as amended by EBSA final regulations, 76 FR 66637, October 27, 2011.

[3] ERISA Reg. § 2570.44(c), as amended by EBSA final regulations, 76 FR 66637, October 27, 2011.

[4] ERISA Reg. § 2570.44(d), as amended by EBSA final regulations, 76 FR 66637, October 27, 2011.

[5] *Ibid.*

¶ 2532

PROCEDURES FOR OBTAINING PROHIBITED TRANSACTION EXEMPTIONS: Requests for Reconsideration of Denied Applications

An applicant for a prohibited transaction exemption that has been denied with finality by the Labor Department may make one request for reconsideration. However, in order for the request for reconsideration to be considered by the Labor Department, the applicant must present significant new facts or arguments which, for good reason, could not have been submitted for the Labor Department's consideration during its initial review of the exemption application.[1]

Form of request for reconsideration

A request for reconsideration of a previously denied application must be made within 180 days after issuance of a final denial letter. A copy of the Labor Department's final letter denying the exemption and a statement setting forth the new information and/or arguments that provide the basis for reconsideration must accompany the request for reconsideration.[2] A request for reconsideration must also include a declaration, signed by a qualified person, attesting to the truth of the new information.[3]

Labor Department's options

If, after reviewing the request for reconsideration, the Labor Department decides that the facts and arguments presented do not warrant reversal of its original decision to deny the exemption, it will send a letter to the applicant reaffirming the original decision.[4]

However, if the Labor Department decides, based on the new facts or arguments submitted, to reconsider its denial letter, it will notify the applicant of its intent to reconsider the application in light of the new information presented. The Labor Department will then take whatever steps that remained at the time it issued its final denial letter to process the exemption application.[5]

If, at any point during its subsequent processing of the application, the Labor Department decides again that the exemption is unwarranted, it will issue a letter affirming its final denial.[6]

---

[1] ERISA Reg. § 2570.45(a), as amended by EBSA final regulations, 76 FR 66637, October 27, 2011.

[2] ERISA Reg. § 2570.45(b), as amended by EBSA final regulations, 76 FR 66637, October 27, 2011.

[3] ERISA Reg. § 2570.45(c), as amended by EBSA final regulations, 76 FR 66637, October 27, 2011.

[4] ERISA Reg. § 2570.45(d), as amended by EBSA final regulations, 76 FR 66637, October 27, 2011.

[5] ERISA Reg. § 2570.45(e), as amended by EBSA final regulations, 76 FR 66637, October 27, 2011.

[6] ERISA Reg. § 2570.45(f), as amended by EBSA final regulations, 76 FR 66637, October 27, 2011.

¶ 2534

PROCEDURES FOR OBTAINING PROHIBITED TRANSACTION EXEMPTIONS: Hearings on Exemption Applications

Any interested person who might be adversely affected by a proposed exemption from the restrictions on fiduciary self-dealing[1] may request a hearing before the Labor Department within the time period specified in the *Federal Register* notice of the proposed exemption.[2]

Form of request for hearing

Any request for a hearing in opposition to the exemptions from restrictions on fiduciary self-dealing must state:[3]

> 1. the name, address, telephone number, and email address of the person making the request;
>
> 2. the nature of the person's interest in the exemption and the manner in which the person would be adversely affected by the exemption; and
>
> 3. a statement of the issues to be addressed and a general description of the evidence to be presented at the hearing.

Where a hearing is necessary to fully explore material factual issues identified by the person requesting the hearing, the Labor Department will grant a request for a hearing and publish a notice of the hearing in the *Federal Register*. However, the Labor Department may decline to hold a hearing where:[4]

> 1. the request for the hearing does not meet the requirements stated above;
>
> 2. the only issues identified for exploration at the hearing are matters of law; or
>
> 3. the factual issues identified can be fully explored through the submission of written (including electronic) evidence.

Notification of interested persons

An applicant for an exemption must notify interested persons if the Labor Department schedules a hearing on the exemption. This notification must be given in the form, time, and manner prescribed by the Labor Department. Ordinarily, however, adequate notification can be given by providing interested persons with a copy of the notice of hearing published by the Labor Department in the *Federal Register* within 10 days of its publication.[5] Notification must be done so as to reasonably ensure that interested persons actually receive the notice. Generally, personal delivery and delivery by first-class mail are considered reasonable methods of furnishing notice.[6] In addition, notification may be provided electronically if the applicant supplies satisfactory proof of electronic delivery to the entire class of interested persons.

After furnishing the required notice, an applicant must submit a statement confirming that notice was given in the form, manner, and time prescribed by the Labor Department.[7] This statement must be accompanied by a signed statement attesting to its truth under penalty of perjury.

Other hearings

In its discretion, the Labor Department may schedule a hearing on its own motion where it determines that issues relevant to the exemption can be fully or expeditiously explored at a hearing.[8] The Department will publish notice of the hearing in the *Federal Register*.

As with hearings involving restrictions on fiduciary self-dealing, an applicant for exemption must notify interested persons of any hearing on an exemption scheduled by the Labor Department.[9] Once again, notification must be provided as outlined above in the **Notification of interested persons**. An applicant must also submit a statement attesting to its truth under penalty of perjury.

---

[1] Under ERISA Sec. 406(b) or Code Sec. 4975(c)(1)(E) or (F).

[2] ERISA Reg. § 2570.46(a), as amended by EBSA final regulations, 76 FR 66637, October 27, 2011.

[3] *Ibid.*

[4] ERISA Reg. § 2570.46(b), as amended by EBSA final regulations, 76 FR 66637, October 27, 2011.

[5] ERISA Reg. § 2570.46(c), as amended by EBSA final regulations, 76 FR 66637, October 27, 2011.

[6] ERISA Reg. § 2570.43(b) (as referenced by ERISA Reg. § 2570.46(c)), as amended by EBSA final regulations, 76 FR 66637, October 27, 2011.

[7] ERISA Reg. § 2570.46(d), as amended by EBSA final regulations, 76 FR 66637, October 27, 2011.

[8] ERISA Reg. § 2570.47(a), as amended by EBSA final regulations, 76 FR 66637, October 27, 2011.

[9] ERISA Reg. § 2570.47(b), as amended by EBSA final regulations, 76 FR 66637, October 27, 2011.

¶ 2536

PROCEDURES FOR OBTAINING PROHIBITED TRANSACTION EXEMPTIONS: DOL's Decision to Grant Exemption

If the Labor Department determines that the exemption should be granted, it will publish a notice in the *Federal Register* granting the exemption.[1] A decision to grant an exemption is made only after considering all the facts and circumstances submitted by an applicant in support of its exemption application, all the comments received in response to a notice of proposed exemption, the record of any hearing held in connection with the proposed exemption, and determining that the exemption is administratively feasible, in the interests of the plan and its participants and beneficiaries, and protective of the rights of the plan participants and beneficiaries.

The *Federal Register* notice granting the exemption summarizes the transaction and specifies the conditions under which the exemptive relief is available.[2]

---

[1] ERISA Reg. § 2570.48(a), as amended by EBSA final regulations, 76 FR 66637, October 27, 2011.

[2] ERISA Reg. § 2570.48(b), as amended by EBSA final regulations, 76 FR 66637, October 27, 2011.

¶ 2538

PROCEDURES FOR OBTAINING PROHIBITED TRANSACTION EXEMPTIONS: Reliance on the Exemption

An exemption does not take effect with regard to the exemption transaction unless the material facts and representations contained in the application (and in any materials and documents submitted in support of the application) were true and complete.[1]

In addition, an exemption is effective only for the period of time specified and only under the conditions set forth in the exemption.[2]

Only the specific parties to whom an exemption grants relief may rely on the exemption. If the notice granting the exemption does not limit exemptive relief to specific parties, all parties to the exemption transaction may rely on the exemption.[3]

Revocation or modification

The Labor Department may take steps to modify or revoke the exemption if, after the exemption takes effect, changes in circumstances call into question the continuing validity of the Labor Department's original conclusions concerning the exemption.[4] A "change in circumstances" includes a change in law or in policy.

Before revoking or modifying an exemption, however, the Labor Department will publish a notice of its proposed action in the *Federal Register* and provide interested persons with a chance to comment on the proposed revocation or modification. Prior to the publication of the notice, the Labor Department will provide applicants with notice of the proposed revocation or modification and its reasons for considering such a revocation or modification. After the publication of the notice, applicants will have the opportunity to comment on the revocation or modification.[5]

Ordinarily, the revocation or modification of an exemption has a prospective effect only.[6] However, in rare cases, where there has been a substantial change in a material fact, an omission of a material fact, or a misstatement, the revocation or limitation be given retroactive effect.[7]

Exemption applications open for public inspection

All applications for exemption (including documents submitted in support of such applications) and all comments and records of hearings and conferences (if any) are open to public inspection.[8]

---

[1] ERISA Reg. § 2570.49(a), as amended by EBSA final regulations, 76 FR 66637, October 27, 2011.

[2] ERISA Reg. § 2570.49(b), as amended by EBSA final regulations, 76 FR 66637, October 27, 2011.

[3] ERISA Reg. § 2570.49(c), as amended by EBSA final regulations, 76 FR 66637, October 27, 2011.

[4] ERISA Reg. § 2570.50(a), as amended by EBSA final regulations, 76 FR 66637, October 27, 2011.

[5] ERISA Reg. § 2570.50(b), as amended by EBSA final regulations, 76 FR 66637, October 27, 2011.

[6] ERISA Reg. § 2570.50(c), as amended by EBSA final regulations, 76 FR 66637, October 27, 2011.

[7] ERISA Proc. 75-1 (40 FR 18471); Rev. Proc. 75-26 (Secs. 9.02 and 9.03), 1975-1 CB 722, CCH PENSION PLAN GUIDE ¶ 17,243.

[8] ERISA Reg. § 2570.51, as amended by EBSA final regulations, 76 FR 66637, October 27, 2011.

¶ 2546
For More Information

☐ For more information on the prohibited transaction rules, see ¶ 4538-4775 and ¶ 5505-5515 of the CCH PENSION PLAN GUIDE.

Interference With Protected Rights Under ERISA

¶ 2550
Scope of Protection Under ERISA Sec. 510

ERISA Sec. 510 prohibits discrimination against and interference with rights under employee benefit plans. The section makes it unlawful for any person to "discharge, fire, suspend, expel, discipline, or discriminate" against a participant or beneficiary either for exercising any right to which he or she is entitled under the provisions of an employee benefit plan or ERISA or for the purpose of interfering with a participant's attainment of such a right.[1] Courts have equitable power under ERISA to put an employee back in the position he or she would have been in, absent illegal retaliation or interference.[2]

If the interference with employee benefit rights takes the form of fraud, force, violence, threats, or intimidation, then the perpetrator may be subject to a fine of $100,000 or a maximum term of imprisonment of 10 years, or both, effective for violations occurring on and after August 17, 2006.[3] For violations occurring before August 17, 2006, the penalty was a fine of up to $10,000, imprisonment for up to one year, or both.[4]

CCH Pointer: Note that the vesting requirements imposed by ERISA limit the extent to which employees with prior service can be deprived of benefits. For more information on vesting, see ¶ 800 and following.

Independent contractors. A plan participant who consented to classification as an independent contractor could not recover for interference with the attainment of a benefit under ERISA Sec. 510. [5]

ERISA protects pension and welfare benefits

ERISA Sec. 510 prevents interference with the attainment of any right to which a participant may become entitled under a "plan." ERISA further defines a "plan" as including both welfare and pension plans. In addition, the U.S. Supreme Court held that the plain language of ERISA Sec. 510 does not distinguish between rights that vest under ERISA and those that do not (such as welfare benefits).[6]

Parties alleging violations of ERISA Sec. 510 must establish a specific intent on the part of the employer to interfere with the attainment of pension eligibility.[7] For example, simply closing a plant does not establish intent to interfere with ERISA rights.

Prohibition on retaliation against employers exercising their rights

ERISA's prohibition against retaliation has been extended to provide protection to employers who contribute to multiemployer plans. A plan sponsor or any other person may not discriminate against a contributing employer for exercising rights under ERISA or for giving information or testifying in any inquiry or proceeding relating to ERISA before Congress.[8]

Exhaustion of remedies

Courts are divided as to whether a party bringing an action under ERISA Sec. 510 must first exhaust a plan's administrative claims procedures.[9] See ¶ 2645 for a further discussion of the exhaustion of remedies doctrine.

Civil enforcement

Actions to redress violations of ERISA Sec. 510 must comply with ERISA's provisions on civil procedure.[10] Hence, the court must have jurisdiction over the action, the plaintiff must have standing, etc. See ¶ 2700 for more on ERISA's civil enforcement provisions.

ERISA preemption. State wrongful discharge claims fall squarely within the ambit of ERISA Sec. 510 and thus are preempted by ERISA. Thus, federal district courts are given exclusive jurisdiction over such actions.[11]

Double taxation eliminated. Effective for attorneys' fees and court costs paid after October 22, 2004, with respect to any judgment or settlement occurring after such date, there is a tax deduction for attorneys' fees and court costs incurred by, or on behalf of, an individual in connection with any action involving lawsuits filed under ERISA Sec. 510.[12]

AIDS cases

Some employers seeking to reduce health care costs associated with AIDS have modified their plans to reduce the lifetime limit on health benefits. Two federal courts of appeal have ruled that such retroactive modifications are legal and do not violate ERISA's anti-discrimination provision.[13]

---

[1] ERISA Sec. 510.

[2] See, e.g., *Browning v. Gutchess,* CA-6 (1988), 843 F2d 1390, aff'g w/o opinion, DC Ohio (1987), Nos. 87-3420, 87-3460.

[3] ERISA Sec. 511, as amended by the Pension Protection Act of 2006 (P.L. 109-280).

[4] ERISA Sec. 511, prior to amendment by P.L. 109-280.

[5] *Benders v. Bellows and Bellows,* CA-7 (2008).

[6] *Inter-Modal Rail Employees Association v. Atcheson, Topeka, and Santa Fe Railway Co.,* US Sup Ct (1997), 520 U.S. 510. Lower courts had ruled that ERISA Sec. 510 bars interference only with

vested rights. See, e.g., *Stiltner v. Beretta U.S.A. Corp.* CA-4 (1996), 74 F3d 1473.

[7] See, e.g., *Abbott v. Pipefitters Local Union No. 522,* CA-6 (1996), 94 F3d 236; *Rogers v. International Marine Terminals, Inc.*, CA-5 (1996), 87 F3d 755, *Crawford v. TRW Automotive U.S. LLC*, CA-6 (2009).

[8] ERISA Sec. 510, as amended by the Pension Protection Act of 2006 (P.L. 109-280).

[9] Compare, for instance, *Gavalik v. Continental Can Company,* CA-3 (1987), 812 F2d 834, *cert. denied,* 12-7-87 (exhaustion of remedies not required) with *Powell v. AT & T Communications,*

Inc. CA-7 (1991), 938 F2d 823 (exhaustion of remedies required).

[10]Under ERISA Sec. 502(a)(3), a participant, beneficiary, or fiduciary may bring an action to enjoin any act or practice that violates any provision of ERISA Title I or may obtain equitable relief to redress such violations or to enforce any provisions of ERISA Title I. ERISA Sec. 510 appears under Title I.

[11] *Ingersoll-Rand Co. v. McClendon,* US Sup Ct (1990), 498 US 133.

[12] Code Sec.62(a)(1), as added by P.L. 108-357.

[13] *McGann v. H & H Music Co.,* CA-5 (1991), 946 F2d 401, *cert. denied* 11/9/92; *Owens v. Storehouse, Inc.,* CA-11 (1991), 984 F2d 394.

¶ 2555
Effect of Other Anti-Discrimination Statutes

While ERISA Sec. 510 provides the primary means by which individuals may sue for interference with their pension rights, other federal statutes provide avenues of recovery as well.

A brief overview of other relevant federal anti-discrimination statutes appears below. Parties seeking relief may bring causes of action under these other federal statutes either independently of or in conjunction with ERISA Sec. 510 actions.

Sex discrimination laws

Title VII of the *1964 Civil Rights Act* prohibits discrimination in compensation, terms, and conditions or privileges of employment on the basis of race, color, national origin, religion, and sex. The issue of sex discrimination has figured most prominently in the pension area because of the widespread (and now illegal) use of gender-based annuity tables.

Under the *Pregnancy Discrimination Act*, Title VII was amended to prohibit discrimination on the basis of pregnancy, childbirth, or other related condition.

☐ For more on sex discrimination and employee benefits, see ¶ 10,160 and following of the CCH PENSION PLAN GUIDE and ¶ 36,010 and following of CCH EMPLOYEE BENEFITS MANAGEMENT.

Age discrimination laws

The *Age Discrimination in Employment Act*, enacted in 1967, prohibits discrimination in compensation, terms, and conditions or privileges of employment on the basis of age. The *Older Workers Benefit Protection Act of 1990* (P.L. 101-433) clarified that the ADEA encompasses all employee benefits, including those provided under a *bona fide* employee benefit plan.

☐ For more on age discrimination and benefits, see ¶ 10,144 and following of the CCH PENSION PLAN GUIDE.

Disability discrimination laws

Under the *Americans with Disabilities Act,* an employer may not discriminate against a qualified person on the basis of a disability. The Act allows differentials in cost or coverage of health benefits if justified on the principles of risk classification, as long as the differentials are not a subterfuge to evade the purposes of the law.

☐ For more on the *Americans with Disabilities Act* as it affects employee benefits, see ¶ 10,174 of the CCH PENSION PLAN GUIDE.

¶ 2560

Participant's Plan Interest in Personal Bankruptcy

Generally, plan provisions and applicable law[1] prevent an individual's creditors from reaching his or her interest in a qualified pension plan. As we have seen, interference with this right is actionable at law. Does this protection change in the context of bankruptcy?

Generally, under the U.S. Bankruptcy Code, an individual debtor's bankruptcy estate includes all property in which the debtor has a legal or equitable interest at the time the bankruptcy proceedings begin.[2] However, there are two important exceptions to this general rule of inclusion. One is the "applicable nonbankruptcy law" exclusion and the other is the federal pension plan exemption.

Applicable nonbankruptcy law exclusion

The Bankruptcy Code excludes interests in a trust from a debtor's bankruptcy estate to the extent the interests are subject to a transfer restriction that is enforceable under "applicable nonbankruptcy law."[3] For these purposes, nonbankruptcy law includes ERISA Sec. 206(d)(1), which requires that a qualified plan must prohibit the assignment or alienation of plan benefits.

In a 1992 decision, the U.S. Supreme Court unanimously ruled that a debtor's interest in an ERISA-qualified plan was excluded from his bankruptcy estate under the Bankruptcy Code's "applicable nonbankruptcy law" exception.[4] The decision, *Patterson v. Shumate*, settled a long-standing split of authority among the federal appellate courts.

The Court found that the plain language of the Bankruptcy Code and ERISA makes it clear that an antialienation provision in a qualified plan constitutes a restriction on transfer enforceable under applicable nonbankruptcy law. The Court pointed out that the Bankruptcy Code contains no limitation on "applicable nonbankruptcy law," nor does it suggest that the phrase relates exclusively to state law.

CCH Pointer: The *Patterson v. Shumate* decision only addressed those plan benefits that are subject to restrictions on transfer under ERISA. Other plans or arrangements, such as IRAs or church plans, are not protected by this decision (though they may be under the federal pension plan exemption). See ¶ 3212 for a discussion on assignment and alienation of funds deposited in an IRA.

Federal pension plan exemption

An individual debtor may exempt from the bankruptcy estate his or her right to receive a payment under a stock bonus, pension, profit-sharing, annuity, or similar plan or contract on account of illness, disability, death, age, or length of service, to the extent reasonably necessary for the support of the debtor and any dependent of the debtor (unless prohibited by state law).[5]

However, the debtor may not exempt the property if:

1. the plan is not qualified under Code Sec. 401(a), 403(a), 403(b), or 408,

2. the plan or contract was established under the auspices of an insider that employed the debtor at the time the debtor's rights under such plan or contract arose, and

3. the payment is on account of age or length of service.

If the debtor is an individual, an "insider" includes a relative of the debtor or of a general partner of the debtor, a partnership in which the debtor is a general partner, a general partner of the debtor, and a corporation where the debtor is a director, officer, or person in control.[6]

The law provides a more specific standard (the "reasonably necessary" standard) for determining the extent of the exemption for pensions. Under this standard, a debtor's right to receive a payment under a stock bonus, pension, profit-sharing, annuity, or similar plan may be exempt property to the extent reasonably necessary for the support of the debtor and any dependent.[7]

CCH Pointer: The federal pension plan exemption exempts a broader category of interests than the applicable nonbankruptcy law exclusion. For instance, IRAs and church plans are not subject to the antialienation provisions of the Code and ERISA. Although a debtor's interest in these plans could not be excluded under the applicable nonbankruptcy law exclusion, his or her interest nevertheless could generally be exempted under the federal pension plan exemption.

BAPCPA expands bankruptcy protection for retirement assets

Effective for bankruptcy cases commenced on or after October 17, 2005, the Bankruptcy Abuse Prevention and Consumer Protection Act of 2005 (BAPCPA) (P.L. 109-8), significantly expanded the bankruptcy protection afforded retirement assets held in plans that are not covered by ERISA (e.g., IRAs). The Act amends the Bankruptcy Code to authorize an exemption from the bankruptcy estate for retirement assets held in funds or accounts that are exempt from taxation regardless of whether the funds are held in ERISA qualified plans. Thus, the Act shields funds in traditional and Roth IRAs (including rollover amounts) from a debtor's creditors, regardless of whether the funds are reasonably necessary for the support of the debtor.[8]

In addition, the Act creates a new exclusion from the bankruptcy estate for employee contributions to: ERISA Title I plans, Code Sec. 414(d) governmental plans, 457 plans, 403 tax-deferred annuities, and state regulated health insurance plans.[9] The exclusion will protect employee deferrals to 401(k) plans and other employee contributions to plans from the reach of creditors prior to the deposit of the funds in the plan's separate trust fund.

---

[1] Code Sec. 401(a)(13); ERISA Sec. 206(d).

[2] 11 U.S.C. § 541(a)(1).

[3] 11 U.S.C. § 541(c)(2).

[4] *Patterson v. Shumate,* US Sup Ct (1992), No. 91-913, aff'g CA-4 (1991), 943 F2d 362.

[5] 11 U.S.C. § 522(d)(10).

⁶11 U.S.C. § 101(31).
⁷11 U.S.C. § 522(d)(11)(E).

⁸11 U.S.C. Secs. 522(b)(3)(C) and 522(d)(12), as added by P.L. 109-8, Act Sec. 224(a).
⁹11 U.S.C. Sec. 541(b)(7), as added by P.L. 109-8, Act Sec. 323.

¶ 2565
For More Information

☐ For more on the rules barring interference with plan participants' rights under ERISA, see ¶ 5705-5720 of the CCH PENSION PLAN GUIDE.

Claims Procedures Under ERISA

¶ 2600

Reasonable Plan Rules Required

A plan must set up reasonable rules for a participant to file a claim and describe the rules, either in the summary plan description (see ¶ 2220), or in a separate document that accompanies the SPD. (In that case, the SPD must state that claims procedures are available from the plan administrator in a separate document, automatically, and at no charge.) [1]

CCH Pointer: Different claims processing procedures exist for claims under group health plans and plans providing disability benefits.[2] In July 2010, the IRS, Employee Benefits Security Administration (EBSA), and Department of Health and Human Services (HHS) issued interim final regulations regarding health plans that added new requirements for internal claims procedures and appeals. The new rules implement the claims appeals requirements in Public Health Service Act Sec. 2719, as added by the Patient Protection and Affordable Care Act (PPACA) (P.L. 111-148). In June 2011, the IRS, EBSA, and HHS amended the 2010 rules.[3]

Adherence to a plan's claim procedures, known as "exhaustion of remedies," is often *required* before an action may be brought in federal court. See ¶ 2645.

---

[2] ERISA Reg. § 2560.503-1. See ¶ 2640.

[1] ERISA Reg. § 2520.102-3(s).

[3] 75 FR 43350; 76 FR 37208.

¶ 2605
Notification to Claimant of Plan's Decision

The plan administrator has only a reasonable amount of time to decide whether or not to pay benefits. The regulations limit this period to 90 days from the date the claim is filed. If more time is required for a special case, the administrator may take up to an additional 90 days, but the participant or beneficiary must be notified and the administrator must explain the special circumstances which require more time as well as indicate the date by which a final decision is expected.[1]

If a participant or beneficiary who files a claim document gets no answer within 90 days (or within 180 days in certain cases) the claim is considered to be denied and the claimant can proceed to the review procedure (see ¶ 2615).

CCH Pointer: Group health plans and those plans providing disability benefits are subject to more stringent requirements concerning the time frames for notice of a plan's claims determination.[2] See ¶ 2640.

[1] ERISA Reg. § 2560.503-1(f)(1).   [2] ERISA Reg. § 2560.503-1(f)(2).

¶ 2610
Contents of Notice—Reasons for Denial

If a claim for benefits is denied, the plan administrator (or insurance company if applicable) must provide in written or electronic form the following information to the claimant:[1]

1. The specific reason or reasons for the denial;
2. Specific reference to the plan provisions on which the denial is based;
3. A description of any additional material or information needed by the administrator to decide the participant's claim; and
4. Information explaining the steps to be taken if the participant or beneficiary wishes to submit the claim for review.

[1] ERISA Sec. 503(1); ERISA Reg. § 2560.503-1(g).

¶ 2615
Full and Fair Review of Claim Denial

Every plan must set up rules for a full and fair review of denied claims.[1]

Period for making appeals claim

The plan must allow a reasonable period for written presentation of the appeals claim. Generally, in no event can it be less than 60 days from receipt by the claimant of written notice of denial. Where a notice fails to adequately inform an employee of his or her rights of appeal under a plan, the notice will not trigger the 60-day time restriction for filing an administrative appeal.[2]

Special rules apply to group health plans and disability plans. See ¶ 2640.

Appeal procedures

The claimant or his or her representative must have the opportunity to appeal the denied claim to "an appropriate named fiduciary." This person may be the plan administrator or another person identified in the plan. In any event, it must be a person with authority to make a final decision on the appeals claim.[3]

Standards for review

Labor Department regulations set forth standards for what constitutes a full and fair review of a claim denial. The rules require, among other things, that:[4]

1. The review of an adverse benefit determination be conducted by an appropriate named fiduciary who is neither the initial claims reviewer nor the subordinate of that party,

2. The review not defer to the facts and conclusions in the initial adverse benefit determination, and

3. The review take into account all comments, documents, records, and other information submitted by the claimant without regard to whether this information was submitted or relied on in the initial determination.

[1] ERISA Sec. 503(2).

[2] ERISA Reg. § 2560.503-1(h).

[3] ERISA Sec. 503; ERISA Reg. § 2560.503-1(h).

[4] ERISA Reg. § 2560.503-1(h)(2); Preamble to final regulations (65 FR 70246).

¶ 2620
Decision on Claim Review

The claimant is entitled to a written decision of the appeal that is clear and understandable. Specific reasons must be given for the decision. General statements will not suffice. Also, the written decision must furnish specific references to pertinent plan provisions on which the decision is based.[1]

The decision must be made promptly and ordinarily not later than 60 days after receipt of the request for review. In special cases the plan may take an additional 60 days before making the decision regarding the appeal, but the participant must be notified of the delay and the special circumstances requiring delay.

If a collectively-bargained plan provides for review by a committee or a board that meets at least four times a year (about every 90 days), the 60-day limit does not apply. Instead, the board must decide the matter at its first meeting after the request is filed. However, if the request for appeal is filed less than 30 days before a meeting, the decision can be delayed until the following meeting.

CCH Pointer: Claims involving group health benefits are governed by shorter time frames, including expedited notification for claims involving urgent care.[2] See ¶ 2640.

[1] ERISA Sec. 503; ERISA Reg. § 2560.503-1(i) and (j).

[2] ERISA Reg. § 2560.503-1, as amended.

¶ 2625

Insured Plans

Under claim procedure rules applicable to insurance companies administering group health plans, claim denials must be reviewed by an "independent medical reviewer" who is neither responsible for the initial denial nor a subordinate of such individual.[1] The reviewer need not be unaffiliated with the health plan in question.

---

[1] ERISA Reg. § 2560.503-1(h).

¶ 2630

Collectively Bargained Plans

In an effort to preserve the integrity of collectively bargained grievance and arbitration procedures, the Department of Labor has relieved plans which are the product of a collective bargaining agreement from full compliance with the claims procedure regulations. In order to take advantage of this, the collective bargaining agreement must set forth or incorporate by specific reference:[1]

1. Provisions concerning the filing of benefit claims and the initial disposition of benefit claims, and

2. A grievance and arbitration procedure for denied claims.

If the grievance or arbitration procedure does not specifically provide a procedure for handling a claim up to and including the denial, a plan must establish procedures to comply with filing, notification, and reasons for denial, but it need not establish additional procedures concerning the items at ¶ 2620 relating to claims review.[2]

"Taft-Hartley" plans administered by a joint board of employer and union representatives—multiemployer plans—are not subject to the exception above for collectively bargained plans and must establish a claims procedure that follows the general rules set forth in the regulations.[3]

---

[1] ERISA Reg. § 2560.503-1(b)(6). This exception for single-employer collectively-bargained plans was retained in final regulations otherwise amending ERISA Reg. § 2560.503-1. See preamble at

CCH PENSION PLAN GUIDE ¶ 24,805O (65 FR 70246).

[2] Ibid.

[3] Ibid.

¶ 2635

Apprenticeship Plans

Employee benefit plans that solely provide apprenticeship training benefits are not covered by the claims procedure regulations.[1]

---

[1] ERISA Reg. § 2560.503-1(n).

¶ 2640
Group Health Plans

Special claims procedures apply to claims under group health plans.[1] Highlights of those special rules are outlined below.

Notification to claimant of plan's decision. Generally, the group health plan must notify the claimant of its decision not later than 30 days after receipt of the claim. More rapid notification is required in cases of pre-service approvals and "urgent care" claims.[2]

Period for appeal of claims denial. Generally, group health plans must provide claimants at least 180 days to appeal a claims denial.[3]

Timing of decision on claim review. Generally, the group health plan must notify the claimant of the decision upon review not later than 60 days after receipt of the claimant's request for review. More rapid notification is required in the case of pre-service approvals and "urgent care" claims.[4]

Exhaustion of administrative remedies. Group health plans (and plans providing disability benefits) may not require a claimant to file more than two appeals of an adverse benefits determination before filing a civil action under ERISA Sec. 502.[5]

Disability plans. Special claim procedure rules also apply to disability plans.[6]

Impact of health care reform legislation. Pursuant to the health care reform legislation package signed by President Obama in March 2010, group health plans and health insurers must implement an effective process for appeals of coverage determinations and claims, including an internal claims appeal process and employee notification. In July 2010, the IRS, EBSA, and HHS issued interim final regulations regarding health plans that, among other changes, added new requirements for internal claims procedures and appeals. In June 2011, the IRS, EBSA, and HHS amended the 2010 rules.[7]

---

[1] ERISA Reg. § 2560.503-1.

[2] ERISA Reg. § 2560.503-1(f)(2).

[3] ERISA Reg. § 2560.503-1(h)(3).

[4] ERISA Reg. § 2560.503-1(i)(2).

[5] ERISA Reg. § 2560.503-1(c)(2).

[6] ERISA Reg. § 2560.503-1.

[7] § 2719 of the Public Health Service Act (PHSA), as added by P.L. 111-148 (Patient Protection and Affordable Care Act), Sec. 1001(5), and amended by P.L. 111-152 (Health Care and Education Reconciliation Act of 2010), Sec. 10101(g). 75 FR 43350; 76 FR 37208.

¶ 2645
Exhaustion of Administrative Remedies

ERISA itself does not expressly require a beneficiary to exhaust a plan's internal review procedures before bringing an action for benefits. This requirement—where it is imposed—is the product of court decisions.

Whether exhaustion will be required usually depends on the *basis* of the claim. Where the claim is based on terms of the plan, exhaustion is generally required.

Conversely, where the claim is based on a specific provision of ERISA, courts are split on whether exhaustion is required prior to filing suit.[1]

[1]Compare, for instance, *Springer v. Wal- Mart Associates Group Health Plan*, CA-11 (1990), 908 F2d 897, with *Zipf v. American Telephone and Telegraph Co.*, CA-3 (1986), 799 F2d 889.

¶ 2650
For More Information

☐ For more information on plan participants' claims procedures under ERISA, see ¶ 5723-5770 of the CCH PENSION PLAN GUIDE.

ERISA Civil Enforcement and Procedure

¶ 2700
Overview of ERISA Enforcement Rules

The Employee Retirement Income Security Act of 1974 (ERISA) sets forth a comprehensive framework for the federal regulation of employee benefit plans. Toward that end, ERISA Title I provides for the protection of employee benefit rights. This chapter covers Part 5 of Title I, dealing with the administration and enforcement provisions of ERISA.

☐ Interference with protected rights under ERISA Sec. 510 is covered at ¶ 2550 and following.

☐ ERISA claims procedures are discussed beginning at ¶ 2600.

ERISA civil procedure

ERISA expressly authorizes various causes of action. Plan participants or beneficiaries may bring civil actions to recover benefits, enforce rights, or clarify future rights to plan benefits. Such parties may also sue plan administrators who fail to comply with notice requirements under ERISA. Suits to redress violations of ERISA's fiduciary responsibility rules may be brought by participants, beneficiaries, plan fiduciaries, or the Secretary of Labor. Participants, beneficiaries, and fiduciaries may sue for an injunction or other equitable relief.

Specific procedural rules govern ERISA causes of action. These rules control such matters as jurisdiction, venue, the availability of trial by jury, punitive damages, and attorneys' fees.

Preemption of state laws

Since a major objective of ERISA is to provide a uniform remedy for covered employees, the statute gives federal courts exclusive jurisdiction over ERISA claims. To this end, all state laws that "relate to" an employee benefit plan are preempted by ERISA. There are, however, specific exceptions to the broad reach of ERISA preemption.

Judicial standard of review

ERISA does not explicitly define a standard for courts to use when reviewing the benefit decisions of plan administrators and fiduciaries. The standard of care is therefore defined by case law. The *Firestone* case, decided by the U.S. Supreme Court in 1989, in effect created two standards of review:

1. if the administrator or fiduciary lacks discretionary authority, the court will apply a *de novo* review;

2. if the administrator or fiduciary has discretionary authority, the court will only overturn the decision if the denial is arbitrary or capricious or there is an abuse of discretion.

Under *de novo* review, a court will examine the judgment of the fiduciary or administrator and not grant the high degree of deference that it would under the arbitrary and capricious standard.

Labor Department enforcement actions

Under ERISA, the Secretary of Labor has the broad authority to investigate whether any person has violated or is about to violate any provision of ERISA Title I. In connection with the investigation, the Labor Department may require the submission of books, records, reports, and the filing of supporting data.

ERISA permits the Labor Department to bring civil lawsuits in a variety of situations. The DOL is also permitted to intervene in existing lawsuits brought by private litigants. In addition, ERISA contains criminal provisions covering willful violations of its reporting and disclosure requirements and coercive interference with protected rights.

¶ 2702
ERISA CIVIL PROCEDURE: Causes of Action Available Under ERISA

ERISA expressly authorizes various causes of action. Plan participants or beneficiaries may bring civil actions to recover benefits, enforce rights, or clarify future rights to plan benefits. Such parties may also sue plan administrators who fail to comply with notice requirements under ERISA. Suits to redress violations of ERISA's fiduciary responsibility rules may be brought by participants, beneficiaries, plan fiduciaries, or the Secretary of Labor. Participants, beneficiaries, and fiduciaries may sue for an injunction or other equitable relief. The Labor Department may also ask for an injunction in certain cases.

Actions to enforce or clarify rights under a plan

A plan participant or beneficiary may bring a civil action to:[1]

1. recover benefits due under the terms of a plan,

2. enforce rights under the terms of the plan, or

3. clarify rights to future benefits under the terms of the plan.

Actions to redress ERISA's fiduciary responsibility provisions

Civil actions to redress violations of ERISA's fiduciary responsibility rules (see ¶ 2300) may be brought by participants, beneficiaries, plan fiduciaries, or the Secretary of Labor.[2]

Actions for injunctions or other equitable relief

Under ERISA Sec. 502(a)(3), a plan participant, beneficiary, or fiduciary may bring a civil action to:

1. enjoin any act or practice that violates ERISA Title I (protection of employee benefit rights);
2. enjoin any act or practice that violates the terms of the plan; or
3. obtain other "appropriate equitable relief" to redress such violations.

Individualized equitable claims allowed. According to the U. S. Supreme Court, ERISA Sec. 502(a)(3) is a "catch all" provision that authorizes individualized equitable relief.[3] Therefore, an individual plan participant or beneficiary can obtain equitable relief under ERISA for an employer's breach of fiduciary duty. See ¶ 2380 for further discussion.

Legal relief not available. ERISA does not authorize legal relief. The U. S. Supreme Court has ruled that relief is limited to the types of remedies that are traditionally available in equity, such as injunction, mandamus, and restitution.[4] Compensatory and punitive damages are not equitable relief.

Actions to redress failure to provide individual statements

A plan participant, beneficiary, or the Secretary of Labor may bring a civil action for appropriate relief in case of a violation of ERISA Sec. 105(c).[5] ERISA Sec. 105(c) requires a plan administrator to furnish individual benefit statements to participants.

Other actions involving the Secretary of Labor

The Secretary of Labor, under certain conditions, may bring a civil action to enjoin or to seek equitable relief for acts or practices that violate ERISA Title I (see ¶ 2736).[6] The DOL is also authorized to bring a civil action in two other circumstances:

1. to collect civil penalties for violations of prohibited transaction provisions[7] and
2. to collect civil penalties in cases where a breaching fiduciary or a person who knowingly participates in the breach is required to make restitution to the plan.[8]

Suits against the Labor Department

ERISA permits a plan administrator, fiduciary, participant, or beneficiary of an employee benefit plan to bring an action in federal court to review a final order of the Department of Labor, restrain the Department from taking any action in violation of ERISA, or compel the Department to take action required by ERISA.[9]

Suits involving purchase of an annuity

The Department of Labor or a plan participant, beneficiary, or fiduciary can bring an action for appropriate relief if the purchase of an insurance contract or annuity for a terminating pension plan participant violates fiduciary standards or terms of the plan. Appropriate relief includes damages for benefits lost under the insurance or annuity contract.[10]

---

[1] ERISA Sec. 502(a)(1)(B).

[2] ERISA Sec. 502(a)(2).

[3] *Howe v. Varity Corp.*, US Sup Ct (1996), 516 U.S. 489. See also, *CIGNA Corp., et al. v. Amara*, US Sup Ct (2011), No. 09-804, where the Court found that ERISA Sec. 502(a)(3) could provide appropriate authority for the equitable relief ordered by the district court in a case involving a plan administrator's notice failures concerning the conversion of a defined benefit plan to a cash balance plan. On the contrary, ERISA Sec. 502(a)(1)(B) was not the proper authority for the provided relief of reforming the terms of the cash balance plan and enforcing the plan as reformed. The decision of the lower court was vacated and the case remanded for further proceedings. Certiorari was granted on a petition submitted by plan participants.

[4] *Mertens v. Hewitt Associates*, US Sup Ct (1993), 508 U.S. 248. See also *Great-West Life & Annuity Insurance Co. v. Knudson*, US Sup Ct (2002), No. 99-1786 and *Sereboff v. Mid Atlantic Medical Services, Inc.*, US Sup Ct (2006), No. 05-260.

[5] ERISA Sec. 502(a)(4).

[6] ERISA Sec. 502(a)(5).

[7] ERISA Sec. 502(i).

[8] ERISA Sec. 502(l).

[9] ERISA Sec. 502(k).

[10] ERISA Sec. 502(a)(9).

¶ 2704
ERISA CIVIL PROCEDURE: Standing to Sue

In order to assert a claim under ERISA, the party bringing suit must have "standing." In other words, it must be a party entitled to bring an action under ERISA.

ERISA authorizes civil actions to be brought by:[1]

1. participants,

2. beneficiaries,

3. fiduciaries, and

4. the Secretary of Labor.

Courts have tended to strictly limit standing to these four classes.

A plan participant is any employee or former employee who is or may become eligible to receive benefits under the employer's plan.[2] The United States Supreme Court has identified two categories of ERISA participants:[3]

1. employees in, or reasonably expected to be in, covered employment, or

2. former employees who have a reasonable expectation of returning to covered employment and/or colorable claims to vested benefits.

In order to establish that they may become eligible for benefits, claimants must have a "colorable" claim that:

1. they will prevail in suit for benefits, or

2. eligibility requirements will be fulfilled in the future.

---

[1] ERISA Sec. 502.

[2] ERISA Sec. 3(7).

[3] *Firestone Tire & Rubber Co. v. Bruch*, US Sup Ct (1989), 489 U.S. 101.

¶ 2706

ERISA CIVIL PROCEDURE: Subject Matter Jurisdiction

ERISA generally vests the United States district courts with exclusive jurisdiction over all actions brought under Title I (protection of employee benefit rights).[1] Federal district courts have jurisdiction over ERISA's civil enforcement provisions without regard to the amount in controversy or the citizenship of the parties.[2] If federal subject matter jurisdiction is lacking, the case will be remanded to state court.

Concurrent federal/state jurisdiction

Actions brought under ERISA Sec. 502(a)(1)(B) to recover benefits due under the terms of a plan may be filed in *either* a federal court or a state court of competent jurisdiction.[3] This is known as *concurrent jurisdiction*. Typically, such actions are brought to resolve or apply the terms of a plan, rather than a particular provision of ERISA.

Declaratory relief against Department of Labor

A plan administrator, fiduciary, participant, or beneficiary of an employee benefit plan may bring suit in federal court to review a final order of the Secretary of Labor, restrain the Department from taking any action in violation of ERISA, or compel the Department to take action required by ERISA.[4]

[1] ERISA Sec. 502(e)(1).
[2] ERISA Sec. 502(f).
[3] ERISA Sec. 502(e)(1).
[4] ERISA Sec. 502(k).

¶ 2708

ERISA CIVIL PROCEDURE: Venue

An action under ERISA may be brought in any federal judicial district where:[1]

1. the plan is administered,
2. the breach has occurred, or
3. a defendant resides or may be found.

[1] ERISA Sec. 502(e)(2).

¶ 2710

ERISA CIVIL PROCEDURE: Personal Jurisdiction— Service of Process

In addition to obtaining subject matter jurisdiction under ERISA, a court must acquire jurisdiction over the person of the defendant. This is acquired once "service of process" is made on that defendant.

Service of process

Normally, service of process is effective only within the boundaries of the state in which the federal court sits. However, actions under ERISA may be brought in any district where the defendant "resides or may be found."[1] A defendant may be found for venue purposes where "minimum contacts" exist between the defendant and the forum district. In effect, this provision authorizes a nationwide service of process.

Service of process can be made on a plan by serving the trustee or plan administrator in its respective capacity.[2] A plan's summary plan description is required to identify the plan's agent for service of legal process.[3] However, if a plan's summary plan description designates no agent for service, service of process may be made on the Secretary of Labor.[4]

Removal from state to federal court

The civil enforcement provisions of ERISA are intended to take precedence over similar state common law causes of action. Thus, if such claims are brought in state court, they are removable (i.e., transferable) to federal court.[5]

The Federal Rules of Civil Procedure provide that an action may be removed to federal court where a federal question exists. Under the "well pleaded complaint rule," a federal question must be presented on the face of the plaintiff's properly pleaded complaint and not be based on a federal defense that is anticipated in the plaintiff's complaint. In the benefits context, the federal claim must relate to ERISA.

---

[1] ERISA Sec. 502(e)(2).

[2] ERISA Sec. 502(d)(1).

[3] ERISA Reg. § 2520.102-3(g).

[4] ERISA Sec. 502(d)(1).

[5] 28 U.S.C. § 1441; *Metropolitan Life Insurance Co. v. Taylor,* US Sup Ct (1987), 481 U.S. 58, rev'g CA-6 (1987), 763 F2d 216.

¶ 2712

ERISA CIVIL PROCEDURE: Jury Trial

ERISA does not expressly provide for trial by jury for any of the causes of action that it creates. Most courts have held that a jury trial is not required in an ERISA civil enforcement action, since such actions are equitable in nature.[1] However, in actions under ERISA to enforce legal rights, such as suits to recover benefits, a jury trial may be required.[2]

---

[1] See e.g., *Tischman v. ITT/Sheraton Corp.,* CA-2 (1997), 145 F3d 561; *Sullivan v. LTV Aerospace and Defense Co.,* CA-7 (1996), No. 95-7527; *Cox v. Keystone Carbon Co.,* CA-3 (1990), 894 F2d 647, *cert. denied,* 10-1-90; *Haeffele v. Hercules Inc.,* DC Del (1989), 703 FSupp 326; *Wardle v. Central States, Southeast & Southwest Areas Pension Fund,* CA-7 (1980), 627 F2d 820, *cert. denied,* US Sup Ct (1981), 449 US 1112.

[2] See e.g., *Sheet Metal Workers Local 19 v. Keystone Heating and Air Conditioning,* CA-3 (1991), 934 F2d 35; *Katsaros v. Cody,* CA-2 (1984), 744 F2d 270.

¶ 2714
ERISA CIVIL PROCEDURE: Equitable Claims— Promissory Estoppel

ERISA permits individuals to bring actions in court to enforce rights or recover benefits. The remedies sought are usually "legal." That is, they are based on a specific provision in the law or the benefit plan. However, the courts will also entertain "equitable" claims; that is, claims not based on a specific provision in the law or plan, but on the concept of fairness or justice. For this reason, courts may recognize a claim based on a promise made by the employer that is relied on by the employee. This avenue of recovery is referred to as "promissory estoppel" or "detrimental reliance."

A promise of pension payments may be enforceable under the doctrine of promissory estoppel if there is:[1]

1. a promise,

2. a detrimental reliance on that promise, and

3. an injustice that can be avoided only by enforcement of the promise.

Oral modification of plan

Promissory estoppel does not permit a plan to be modified by oral representations. To allow an ERISA plan to be modified by oral representations based on the common law doctrine of estoppel is inconsistent with the statutory requirement that ERISA plans be maintained in writing.[2] However, while an ERISA plan may not be modified by an oral promise, promissory estoppel may permit recovery where the representation relied on reflects an *interpretation* of a plan about which reasonable persons could disagree.[3]

---

[1] See e.g., *Vastoler v. American Can Company*, CA-3 (1983), 700 F2d 916; *Stutleberg v. Farrell Lines, Inc.*, DC NY (1982), 529 FSupp 566; *National Companies Health Benefit Plan v. St. Joseph's Hospital of Atlanta, Inc.*, CA-11 (1991), 929 F2d 1558; *Cucio v. John Hancock Mutual Life Insurance Co.*, CA-3 (1994), 33 F3d 226.

[2] See e.g., *Pruitt v. Westinghouse Electric Corp.*, DC Fla (1989), 719 FSupp 1061; *Meadows v. Cagles, Inc.*, CA-11 (1992), 954 F2d 686.

[3] *Kane v. Aetna Life Insurance Co.*, CA-11 (1990), 893 F2d 1283, cert. denied 10/1/90; *Production and Maintenance Employees' Local 504 v. Roadmaster Corp.*, CA-7 (1992), 954 F2d 1397.

¶ 2716
ERISA CIVIL PROCEDURE: Injunctive Relief

A court grants an injunction in order to forbid a party from committing an act which it is threatening or attempting to commit. An injunction can also be issued to restrain the party from continuing certain acts. Injunctions can be *final* or *preliminary*. A final injunction is granted when the rights of the parties are determined. A preliminary injunction is granted to restrain certain acts pending the outcome of the litigation. *Permanent injunctions* can be issued to redress serious misconduct.

Elements of an injunction

Generally, a party requesting an injunction must show that:[1]

1. no adequate remedy at law exists and irreparable injury will result if the injunction does not issue;

2. the threatened injury to plaintiffs outweighs the threatened harm the injunction may inflict on the defendant;

3. there is a reasonable likelihood of success on the merits (for preliminary injunctions); and

4. the grant of the injunction is not adverse to the public interest.

[1]See, e.g., *Musto v. American General Corp.*, DC Tenn (1985), 615 FSupp 1483; *Central States, Southeast and Southwest Areas Pension Fund v.* *Jack Cole-Dixie Highway Co., Inc. and Admiral Merchants Motor Freight, Inc.*, CA-8 (1981), aff'g DC Minn (1980), 642 F2d 1122.

¶ 2718

ERISA CIVIL PROCEDURE: Punitive and Extracontractual Damages

When a beneficiary sues a plan to recover benefits, the beneficiary may recover all benefits to which he or she is contractually entitled. However, a beneficiary is not ordinarily entitled to "extracontractual" relief, such as punitive damages.

The U. S. Supreme Court has ruled that an ERISA fiduciary cannot be held personally liable to a plan beneficiary for extracontractual compensatory or punitive damages in actions brought under ERISA Sec. 502(a)(2) for the improper or untimely processing of a claim.[1] Subsequent to the Court's holding, the vast majority of lower courts have denied punitive damages. However, some courts have allowed punitive damages under ERISA Sec. 502(a)(3), which authorizes courts to award "appropriate equitable relief." [2]

[1] *Massachusetts Mutual Life Insurance Co. v. Russell*, 473 US 134 (1985).

[2]See e.g., *Warren v. Society National Bank*, CA-6 (1990), 905 F2d 975, cert. denied 6/3/91. For a contrasting view, see *Donkenny, Inc. v. Virginia Financial and Insurance Services, Inc.* DC Va (1990), 739 FSupp 290.

¶ 2720

ERISA CIVIL PROCEDURE: Attorneys' Fees

ERISA provides for two types of attorneys' fees: discretionary and mandatory fees.

Discretionary attorneys' fees

In an action brought under ERISA Title I by participants, beneficiaries, or fiduciaries, a court in its discretion *may* allow reasonable attorneys' fees as well as the costs of an action.[1] Attorneys' fees may be awarded to *either* party.

Factors in awarding attorneys' fees. In cases where the award of attorneys' fees is discretionary, the courts tend to consider the following factors:[2]

1. the degree of the opposing parties' culpability or bad faith;

2. the ability of the opposing party to satisfy an award of fees;

3. whether an award of fees against the opposing parties would deter others from acting in the same way under similar circumstances;

4. whether the parties requesting fees seek to benefit all participants and beneficiaries of an ERISA plan or to resolve a significant legal question regarding ERISA; and

5. the relative merits of the parties' positions.

Mandatory attorneys' fees

In an action brought by a fiduciary, for or on behalf of a plan, to collect delinquent multiemployer plan contributions, in which a judgment is awarded in favor of the plan, the court *must* award reasonable attorneys' fees and costs of the action.[3]

Calculating the amount of the fee

In calculating the amount of the attorneys' fees to award, courts typically use the "lodestar method." Under this method, the number of reasonable hours spent on the case is multiplied by a reasonable hourly rate.

CCH Pointer: In making this calculation, a court may consider certain relevant factors, such as the complexity of the case, the fact that one party prevailed on all issues of the case, and the attorney's customary hourly fee.

---

[1] ERISA Sec. 502(g)(1).

[2] See e.g., *Arizona State Carpenters Pension Trust Fund v. Citibank (Arizona)* CA-9 (1997), 125 F3d 715; *Ironworkers Local # 272 v. Bowen*, CA-11 (1983), 695 F2d 531; *Clouatre v. Lockwood*, DC La (1984), 593 FSupp 1136; *McKnight v. Southern Life and Health Insurance Company*, CA-11 (1985), 758 F2d 1566; *Hummell v. S.E. Rykoff & Co.*, CA-9 (1980), 634 F2d 446; *Corder v. Howard Johnson & Co.*, CA-9 (1994), 37 F3d 550.

[3] ERISA Sec. 502(g)(2).

¶ 2722

ERISA CIVIL PROCEDURE: Statute of Limitations

ERISA provides a specific time limit by which suits to enforce fiduciary standards may be brought. In other types of suits, ERISA does not provide an express time limit for bringing actions.

Suits involving fiduciary violations

In suits involving a breach of fiduciary responsibility, duty, or obligation,[1] ERISA provides a specific statute of limitations. Under this limit, no action may be brought after the *earlier of:*[2]

1. Six years after (a) the date of the last action which was part of the breach or violation or (b) in the case of an omission, the

latest date on which the fiduciary could have cured the breach of violation; *or*

2. Three years after the earliest date on which the party bringing suit had actual knowledge of the breach or violation.

However, in the case of *fraud or concealment*, fiduciaries remain vulnerable to suit for a period of six years from the discovery of their breach or violation.

Other civil actions

ERISA does not contain a statute of limitations for bringing civil actions other than those referred to above. In civil actions that involve causes of action other than fraud, concealment, or breach of fiduciary duty, courts have generally applied the limitation period that is contained in the most analogous state statute of limitations.[3]

---

[1] ERISA Title I, part 4.

[2] ERISA Sec. 413.

[3] See e.g., *Lumpkin v. Envirodyne Industries, Inc.*, CA-7 (1991), 933 F2d 449. *cert. denied* 11/4/91; *Jenkins v. Local 705 International Brotherhood of Teamsters Pension Plan*, CA-7 (1983), 713 F2d 247.

¶ 2724

ERISA CIVIL PROCEDURE: Special Remedies for Multiemployer Plans

A plan fiduciary, employer, plan participant, or beneficiary who is adversely affected by the act or omission of any party under ERISA's special provisions for multiemployer plans[1] may bring an action for appropriate legal or equitable relief. Such an action can also be brought by an employee organization that represents a participant or beneficiary. However, an action against the Secretary of the Treasury, the Secretary of Labor, or the PBGC is not authorized.[2] The PBGC may also bring a civil action against any person failing to provide any notice required under the special provisions for multiemployer plans.[3]

Jurisdiction and venue

The United States district courts have jurisdiction of civil actions under the multiemployer plan provisions.[4] Process may be served in any district where a defendant resides, does business, or may be found.[5] A copy of any complaint in a civil suit must also be served upon the PBGC by certified mail. The PBGC may intervene in any such action.[6]

Removal from state to federal court

In any state court suit, action, or proceeding in which the PBGC is a party or intervenes, the PBGC may remove the suit, action, or proceeding from the state court to a federal district court.[7]

Attorneys' fees

The court has the discretion to award all or a portion of the costs and expenses incurred in connection with the action, including reasonable attorneys' fees, to the prevailing party.[8]

However, in an action brought by a fiduciary, for or on behalf of a plan, to collect delinquent multiemployer plan contributions,[9] and in which a judgment is awarded in favor of the plan, the court *must* award reasonable attorneys' fees and costs of the action to the plan (see ¶ 2720).[10]

Statute of limitations

An action to enforce ERISA's multiemployer plan provisions must be brought within the later of:[11]

1. six years after the date on which the cause of action arises, or
2. three years after the earliest date on which the plaintiff acquires or should have acquired actual knowledge of the existence of the cause of action.

The three-year period is extended to six years after the date of discovery in the case of fraud or concealment.

Liquidated damages—Prejudgment interest

In actions by a fiduciary to recover delinquent contributions under a multiemployer plan where a judgment in favor of the plan is awarded, the court must award interest on the unpaid contributions.[12] In addition, the court must award (1) the greater of interest on the unpaid contributions or liquidated damages provided for under the plan and (2) reasonable attorneys' fees and costs of the action. The liquidated damages are limited to 20% of the delinquency.[13]

Failure to make withdrawal liability payment

In an action to compel an employer to pay withdrawal liability, in addition to the unpaid liability plus interest, the court must award an amount equal to the greater of interest or liquidated damages payable to the plan, and reasonable attorneys' fees and costs of the action.[14] In an action to compel an employer to pay withdrawal liability, failure of the employer to make any withdrawal liability payment within the time prescribed is treated in the same manner as a delinquent contribution, thus making the above remedies available.

---

[1] ERISA Title IV.
[2] ERISA Sec. 4301(a).
[3] ERISA Sec. 4302.
[4] ERISA Sec. 4301(c).
[5] ERISA Sec. 4301(d).
[6] ERISA Sec. 4301(g).
[7] ERISA Sec. 4003(f).
[8] ERISA Sec. 4301(e).
[9] ERISA Sec. 515.
[10] ERISA Sec. 502(g)(2).
[11] ERISA Sec. 4301(f).
[12] ERISA Sec. 502(g)(2)(B).
[13] ERISA Sec. 502(g)(2)(C).
[14] ERISA Sec. 4301(b).

¶ 2726

ERISA PREEMPTION OF STATE LAWS: Breadth of ERISA Preemption

Since a major objective of ERISA is to provide a uniform remedy for covered employees, the statute preempts all laws affecting ERISA claims with certain stated exceptions. To this end, all state laws that "relate to" an employee benefit plan are preempted by ERISA.[1] An employee benefit plan must be established or maintained by an employer or employee organization.[2]

State laws

"State laws" encompass all laws, decisions, rules, regulations, or other state actions having the effect of law.[3] A "state" includes an agency, instrumentality, or subdivision of a state.[4]

Law must relate to a plan

The Supreme Court has repeatedly held that a law relates to an employee benefit plan "if it has any connection with or reference to such a plan." [5] Thus, the reach of ERISA preemption is quite broad.[6] A law relates to an ERISA plan if it acts "immediately and exclusively" upon the plan,[7] or if the existence of the plan is essential to the law's operation.[8] The Court looks to the objectives of ERISA as a guide to the scope of the state law that Congress understood would survive and to the nature of the law's effect on ERISA plans.[9]

Federal laws and regulations

ERISA supersedes state laws, not other federal laws and regulations. Under ERISA's "savings clause," ERISA is not to be construed to "alter, amend, modify, invalidate, impair, or supersede" any federal laws or regulations.[10]

---

[1] ERISA Sec. 514(a).

[2] ERISA Sec. 3(1) and 3(2).

[3] ERISA Sec. 514(c)(1).

[4] ERISA Sec. 514(c)(2).

[5] *Shaw v. Delta Air Lines*, US Sup Ct (1983), 463 US 85; *Ingersoll-Rand Co. v. McClendon*, US Sup Ct (1990), 498 US 133; *District of Columbia v. Greater Washington Board of Trade*, US Sup Ct (1992), 113 SCt 580.

[6] See CCH Pension Plan Guide ¶ 5905 for a list of cases in which state laws or actions have been held to be preempted.

[7] *Mackey v. Lanier Collection Agency & Service, Inc.*, US Sup Ct (1988), 486 US 825.

[8] *District of Columbia v. Greater Washington Board of Trade*, US Sup Ct (1992), 506 US 125.

[9] *California Division of Labor Standards Enforcement v. Dillingham Construction, N.A., Inc.*, US Sup Ct (1997), 117 SCt 832.

[10] ERISA Sec. 514(d).

¶ 2728

ERISA PREEMPTION OF STATE LAWS: Exceptions to ERISA Preemption

State laws that do not "relate to" employee benefit plans are not preempted by ERISA. In addition, there are specific exceptions to the broad reach of ERISA preemption. ERISA does not preempt:

1. state laws that regulate insurance, banking, or securities;[1]

2. any generally applicable criminal law of a state;[2]

3. state laws that regulate certain multiple employer welfare arrangements;[3]

4. qualified domestic relations orders and qualified medical child support orders;[4]

5. any state cause of action for Medicaid recoupment;[5] and

6. the Hawaii Prepaid Health Care Act.[6]

Numerous state laws or actions have been ruled not preempted by ERISA because they were found not to relate to employee benefit plans or because they dealt with one of the exempt categories listed above.[7]

State regulation of insurance

According to the U.S. Supreme Court, a law "regulates" insurance if it is specifically directed towards the insurance industry instead of merely having an impact on the industry.[8]

A state law involves the business of insurance if it:

1. has the effect of spreading the policyholder's risk,

2. is an integral part of the policy relationship between the insurer and the insured, and

3. is limited to entities within the insurance industry.

An ERISA-governed employee benefit plan is not "deemed" to be an insurance company. Hence, such a plan does not fit within the exception to ERISA preemption.[9]

CCH Pointer: The Supreme Court has restated the standard used for determining, for ERISA preemption purposes, whether a state law regulates insurance. Under the restated standard, a state law will be deemed to be a law that regulates insurance if it:

1. is specifically directed toward entities engaged in insurance; and

2. substantially affects risk pooling arrangements between the insurer and the insured.[10]

Multiple employer welfare arrangements (MEWAs)

Multiple employer welfare arrangements (MEWAs) are specifically exempted from the ERISA preemption provisions.[11] Thus, such plans are subject to state insurance regulation.[12] A MEWA is any plan or other arrangement established to offer welfare benefits, such as health insurance, to the employees of two or more employers.[13]

In the case of a fully insured MEWA, any state insurance law may apply to such arrangement to the extent that the law provides standards requiring the maintenance of specified levels of reserves and contributions in order for such an arrangement to be considered adequately funded. This is also true with respect to MEWAs that are not fully insured that have been exempted from ERISA by the Secretary of Labor. The Secretary's determination of the exemption may be made on a case-by-case basis or on a class basis.[14] A MEWA is considered fully insured only if the terms of the arrangement provide for benefits the amount of all of which the Secretary of Labor determines are guaranteed under a contract or a policy of insurance, issued by an insurance company, insurance service, or insurance organization, qualified to conduct business in a state.[15]

Domestic relations law

ERISA does not preempt qualified domestic relations orders (QDROs) and qualified medical child support orders (QMCSOs).[16] A QDRO is a judgment, decree, or order entered into under a state domestic relations law, including a community property law.[17] The order must relate to the provision of child support, alimony payments, or marital property rights to a spouse, former spouse, child, or other dependent of a participant, and must meet certain other rules (see ¶ 1600 and following). A QMCSO is a medical child support order. A child who is the subject of such an order is treated as a beneficiary under a group health plan.[18]

Hawaii Prepaid Health Care Act

The Hawaii Prepaid Health Care Act[19] is partially exempted from preemption by ERISA.[20] The Act is exempted from preemption as it existed when ERISA became effective. However, preemption is continued for any amendment of the Hawaii Prepaid Health Care Act enacted after September 2, 1974 (to the extent it provides for more than the effective administration of the Act as in effect on September 2, 1974).

State garnishment laws

The U.S. Supreme Court has held that general state garnishment procedures are not preempted by ERISA.[21] Congress did not intend to prohibit the use of state law mechanisms of executing judgments against ERISA welfare plans even when those mechanisms prevent plan participants from receiving their benefits, the Court explained.

[1] ERISA Sec. 514(b)(2)(A).

[2] ERISA Sec. 514(b)(4).

[3] ERISA Sec. 514(b)(6).

[4] ERISA Sec. 514(b)(7).

[5] ERISA Sec. 514(b)(8).

[6] ERISA Sec. 514(b)(5).

[7] See CCH PENSION PLAN GUIDE ¶ 5910 for a list of cases in which ERISA did not preempt a state law or action.

[8] *Pilot Life Insurance Company v. Dedeaux,* US Sup Ct (1987), 481 US 41.

[9] ERISA Sec. 514(b)(2)(B).

[10] *Kentucky Assn. of Health Plans v. Miller,* US Sup Ct, No. 00-1471, April 2, 2003. In *Miller* the Court held that ERISA did not preempt Kentucky's "any willing provider" law, the Kentucky Health Care Reform Act.

[11] ERISA Sec. 514(b)(6).

[12] ERISA Opinion Letter 93-17A, 7-7-93.

[13] ERISA Sec. 3(40); ERISA Opinion Letter 87-11A, 12-21-87.

[14] ERISA Sec. 514(b)(6)(A) and (B).

[15] ERISA Sec. 514(b)(6)(D).

[16] ERISA Sec. 514(b)(7).

[17] ERISA Sec. 206(d)(1).

[18] ERISA Sec. 609(a)(2)(A).

[19] Haw. Rev. Stat. § § 393-1 through 393-51.

[20] ERISA Sec. 514(b)(5), enacted under the Periodic Payment Settlement Act of 1982 (P.L. 97-473) in order to reverse the U.S. Supreme Court decision *Agsalud v. Standard Oil Company,* US Sup Ct (1981), 102 SCt 79, aff'g CA-9 (1980), 633 F2d 760.

[21] *Mackey v. Lanier Collection Agency & Service, Inc.,* US Sup Ct (1988), 486 US 825.

¶ 2730

JUDICIAL STANDARD OF REVIEW: De Novo Review vs. Arbitrary and Capricious Standard

ERISA does not explicitly define a standard for courts to use when reviewing the benefit decisions of plan administrators and fiduciaries. The standard of care is therefore defined by case law. The U.S. Supreme Court set forth the judicial standard of review in its landmark *Firestone* decision, rendered in 1989.[1]

According to the Supreme Court, a benefit denial challenged under ERISA Sec. 502(a)(1)(B) is to be reviewed under a *de novo* standard unless the plan gives the administrator or fiduciary discretionary authority to determine eligibility for benefits or to construe the plan's terms. Where the plan does grant such authority, deferential review under the "arbitrary and capricious standard" is appropriate.

Under a *de novo* review, the case will be considered anew, on its merits. Thus, the court will examine the judgment of the fiduciary or administrator and not grant the high degree of deference that it would have under the arbitrary and capricious standard. Under this standard, the benefits-related decisions of administrators and fiduciaries are accorded great deference.

The *Firestone* decision in effect created two standards of review:

1. if the administrator or fiduciary lacks discretionary authority, the court will apply a *de novo* review;

2. if the administrator or fiduciary has discretionary authority, the court will only overturn the decision if the denial is arbitrary or capricious or there is an abuse of discretion.[2]

While the general principles are clear enough, many questions remain. The Court failed to provide specific guidance as to what plan language is necessary to grant discretionary authority to an administrator or fiduciary, thus insuring that their decisions are accorded deference by the courts. Case law developed since the *Firestone* decision has helped to fill in some of the gaps.[3]

---

[1] *Firestone Tire & Rubber Co. v. Bruch*, US Sup Ct (1989), 489 US 101.

[2] In determining whether a fiduciary's actions were arbitrary and capricious, courts consider whether the fiduciary has acted "rationally" or "reasonably," there was fraud or bad faith, the fiduciary acted impartially in rendering its decision, established review procedures were followed, there was a consistent application of the terms of a plan or ERISA, or the fiduciary's actions were based on "substantial evidence." See CCH PENSION PLAN GUIDE ¶ 5915 and ¶ 5925.

[3] See CCH PENSION PLAN GUIDE ¶ 5925.

¶ 2732

LABOR DEPARTMENT ENFORCEMENT ACTIONS: DOL Investigative Authority—In General

The Secretary of Labor has the broad authority to investigate whether any person has violated or is about to violate any provision of ERISA Title I.[1] Title I addresses, among other things, reporting and disclosure requirements, participation, funding, vesting, fiduciary responsibility, civil suits, and prohibited transactions.

In connection with the investigation, the Labor Department may require the submission of books, records, reports, and the filing of supporting data,[2] though plans cannot be required to submit such information more than once a year unless the Department has "reasonable cause" to believe that a violation exists.[3] The DOL is also authorized to enter places and inspect records and accounts and to question persons if there is reason to believe that a violation of the ERISA Title I may exist.[4]

EBSA authority

The DOL's enforcement arm with respect to Title I is the Employee Benefits Security Administration (EBSA). The EBSA has developed a detailed enforcement strategy with the aim of:[5]

1. providing protection for the largest number of plan participants and amount of plan assets, given the available resources,

2. identifying and investigating areas with the most potential for abuse,

3. detecting and obtaining correction of ERISA violations,

4. establishing a presence in the regulated community,

5. disseminating information and promoting voluntary compliance, and

6. responding to participant complaints, public inquiries, and referrals from other government agencies, such as the PBGC.

PBGC authority

Separate powers are granted to the Pension Benefit Guaranty Corporation to enforce the termination insurance provisions of ERISA. See ¶ 2800 and following.

---

[1] ERISA Sec. 504(a).

[2] ERISA Sec. 504(a)(1).

[3] ERISA Sec. 504(b).

[4] ERISA Sec. 504(a)(2).

[5] *ERISA Enforcement Strategy Implementation Plan*, U.S. Department of Labor, Pension and Welfare Benefits Administration, September 1990, pp. 1-2.

¶ 2734

LABOR DEPARTMENT ENFORCEMENT ACTIONS: Subpoena Powers

For purposes of conducting its investigations, the Secretary of Labor has the power to issue administrative subpoenas to compel the production of materials.[1] If a party who receives a subpoena refuses to comply, the DOL must file an action in federal court to enforce the subpoena. At that time, the subpoenaed party may raise certain objections to the subpoena. For instance, the subpoena can be challenged on the ground that it is overly broad or unduly burdensome. Courts have generally given the DOL wide latitude in the type of documents that can be sought under a subpoena.[2]

[1] ERISA Sec. 504(c).

[2]See *Donovan v. National Bank of Alaska*, CA-9 (1983), 696 F2d 678.

¶ 2736

LABOR DEPARTMENT ENFORCEMENT ACTIONS: Civil Actions

ERISA permits the Labor Department to bring civil lawsuits in a variety of situations. The DOL is also permitted to intervene in existing lawsuits brought by private litigants. Suits brought by the Labor Department are generally subject to the general civil procedure rules outlined at ¶ 2702 and following.

In civil actions under ERISA, the Secretary of Labor is to be represented by attorneys appointed by the Secretary (except for litigation before the Supreme Court and Court of Claims). All such civil litigation is subject to the direction and control of the Attorney General.[1]

Suits to enforce ERISA Title I

The Secretary of Labor can sue to enjoin any act or practice which violates Title I of ERISA or to obtain any other appropriate relief to enforce rules under Title I.[2] In the case of a qualified plan (or a plan which has a pending application for qualification), the Secretary of Labor may not bring an action to enforce the participation, vesting, or funding rules unless requested to do so by the Secretary of the Treasury.[3]

Requests submitted to Labor Secretary

All requests by participants, beneficiaries, and fiduciaries for the Secretary of Labor to exercise his or her enforcement authority with respect to a violation of, or the enforcement of the participation, vesting, and funding rules must be in writing and contain information sufficient to form a basis for identifying the participant, beneficiary, or fiduciary and the plan involved. All such requests are considered filed if they are directed to and received by any office or official of the Labor Department or referred to and received by any party to whom such writing is directed.[4]

In bringing any actions and in exercising authority with respect to participation, vesting, and funding under Title I of ERISA and, with respect to any definitions, the Secretary of Labor is bound by the regulations, rulings, opinions, variances, and waivers issued by the Secretary of the Treasury.[5]

Judicial review. Department of Labor decisions enforcing the participation, vesting, and funding standards under the regulatory provisions of ERISA may be subject to judicial review. A plan administrator, fiduciary, participant, or beneficiary may bring a suit to review a final order of the Secretary of Labor, to restrain the Secretary of Labor from taking any action contrary to ERISA, or to compel the Secretary of Labor to take action to enforce the regulatory portions of ERISA.[6]

Suits to require disclosure of individual benefit statements

The Secretary of Labor (as well as participants or beneficiaries) may bring a civil action for appropriate relief in case of a violation of ERISA Sec. 105(c).[7] ERISA Sec. 105(c) requires a plan administrator to furnish individual benefit statements to participants.

DOL intervention in existing suits

In any action brought by a participant, beneficiary, or fiduciary alleging a violation of ERISA, a copy of the complaint must be served upon the Secretary of Labor (and the Secretary of the Treasury) by certified mail. Either Secretary has the right in his or her discretion to intervene in any action; however, the Secretary of the Treasury may not intervene in any plan termination insurance action.[8]

Enforcement of fiduciary violations

The Secretary of Labor may sue a plan fiduciary to make restitution to the plan for any losses resulting from a breach of fiduciary duty, including the improper handling of plan assets.[9]

In addition, the Secretary of Labor has the same powers to sue for violations of the fiduciary responsibility rules as he or she has for violations of the reporting and disclosure and participation, vesting, and funding rules. However, the Secretary of Labor may not initiate an action for delinquent employer contributions.[10]

Seeking voluntary compliance with ERISA's provisions is the Labor Department's preferred method of correcting transactions or practices that are found to be in violation of ERISA.[11] However, some cases by their nature might require immediate court action to preserve plan assets or protect participants' rights. The method and time of informing officials of the DOL's findings vary with individual cases. Some cases might involve matters that could be easily remedied and could be taken care of by a discussion between plan officials and the compliance officers before the matter leaves the plan's offices. Other situations might involve fiduciary breaches and could require substantial analysis, evaluation, and legal advice before a decision could be made concerning what violations existed and what remedy is appropriate. There may be some situations that require immediate court action without prior notification to plan officials.

Statute of limitations

The DOL's rights to bring an action are governed by the general ERISA statute of limitations (see ¶ 2722). Thus, actions must be brought within the earlier of (1) six years after the date of the breach or (2) three years after the earliest date on which the plaintiff (in this case, the Secretary of Labor) had actual knowledge of the breach or violation. The three-year statute of limitations will not commence to run against the DOL for the purpose of barring its action against the fiduciary until the Department actually becomes aware of the breach of fiduciary duty.[12]

Suits to collect civil penalties

The Labor Department is authorized to bring suit against a plan administrator who fails or refuses to file an annual report as required by ERISA Sec. 101(b)(4).[13] The DOL can assess a civil penalty of up to $1,100 per day from the date of the failure or refusal to file. An annual report that has been rejected by the Labor Department for failing to provide material information is treated as not having been filed for purposes of this penalty.[14]

Also, the DOL is authorized to bring a civil action:

1. to collect civil penalties for violation of prohibited transaction provisions[15] and

2. to collect civil penalties in cases where a breaching fiduciary or a person who knowingly participates in the breach is required to make restitution to the plan.[16]

DOL consent decrees

The parties to a Department of Labor action may enter into a settlement agreement with the DOL under which they agree to undertake certain actions to remedy ERISA violations. For instance, plan trustees might agree to make restitution to plan participants. These agreements are known as consent orders. Although they are founded on the agreement of the parties, consent orders are nevertheless judicial acts enforceable by sanctions.

[1] ERISA Sec. 502(j).

[2] ERISA Sec. 502(a)(5). ERISA Title I addresses, among other things, reporting and disclosure requirements, participation, funding, vesting, fiduciary responsibility, civil suits, and prohibited transactions.

[3] ERISA Sec. 502(b).

[4] ERISA Reg. § 2560.502-1.

[5] ERISA Reorganization Plan, Sec. 104.

[6] ERISA Sec. 502(k).

[7] ERISA Sec. 502(a)(4).

[8] ERISA Sec. 502(h).

[9] ERISA Sec. 502(a)(2).

[10] ERISA Sec. 502(b)(2).

[11] DOL News Release, USDL 77-222, 3-11-77.

[12] ERISA Sec. 413(a)(2).

[13] ERISA Sec. 502(a)(6) and 502(c)(2).

[14] ERISA Sec. 502(c)(2).

[15] ERISA Sec. 502(a)(6) and 502(i).

[16] ERISA Sec. 502(a)(6) and 502(l).

¶ 2737

LABOR DEPARTMENT ENFORCEMENT ACTIONS:
Voluntary Fiduciary Correction Program

In order to encourage the full correction of breaches of fiduciary duty and the restoration to participants and beneficiaries of losses resulting from such breaches, the Employee Benefits Security Administration has adopted the Voluntary Fiduciary Correction (VFC) Program.[1] Similar to the Employee Plans Compliance Resolution System (EPCRS) maintained by the IRS for redressing qualification defects (see ¶ 360), the VFC Program is a remedial mechanism that allows fiduciaries to avoid civil actions and civil penalties for specified breaches of fiduciary duty by voluntarily undertaking stipulated corrective actions.

Limited scope of VFC program

The VFC Program is limited to the following five types of breach of fiduciary duty under ERISA Title I:

1. failure to timely remit employee contributions to the plan;[2]

2. loans to parties in interest that do not comply with ERISA (e.g., loans below market interest rates);

3. purchase of assets (including real property) by a plan from a party-in- interest, for which no prohibited transaction exemption applies;

4. payment of benefits without proper valuation of the plan assets on which the payment was based; and

5. payment of duplicative, excessive, or unnecessary compensation to a service provider.

Relief from prohibited transaction excise taxes

The Labor Department has finalized a class exemption designed to encourage use of the VFC Program.[3] The class exemption provides limited relief from excise taxes for employers who use the VFC Program to correct certain transactions. See ¶ 2487.

---

[1]EBSA Adoption of Updated Voluntary Fiduciary Correction Program, April 19, 2006, CCH Pension Plan Guide ¶ 19,953D. The VFC Program was established on an interim basis as of April 14, 2000 and was made permanent as of April 29, 2002. The VFC Program was revised and the newest release supersedes earlier versions, effective May 19, 2006, CCH Pension Plan Guide ¶ 19,953D.

[2]The EBSA has issued a set of questions and answers offering clarification on how to calculate earnings on delinquent participant contributions under the VFC program. Frequently asked questions related to late plan contributions, small delinquent contributions, and rate of return calculations are provided. In addition, hypothetical examples of acceptable calculations of lost earnings in specific situations are offered. See Voluntary Fiduciary Correction Program FAQs, July 31, 2002, CCH Pension Plan Guide ¶ 19,953B.

[3]Prohibited Transaction Class Exemption 2002-51, November 25, 2002 (67 FR 70623), CCH Pension Plan Guide ¶ 16,649I, amended April 19, 2006 (71 FR 20135), CCH Pension Plan Guide ¶ 16,649T.

¶ 2738

LABOR DEPARTMENT ENFORCEMENT ACTIONS: Criminal Enforcement

ERISA includes criminal provisions covering:

1. willful violations of the reporting and disclosure requirements and

2. coercive interference with protected rights.

In addition, ERISA disqualifies individuals convicted of certain crimes from holding positions with ERISA plans for a specified period following conviction. There are also several provisions of the U.S. Criminal Code which proscribe certain conduct relating to ERISA-covered plans.

Under a Memorandum of Understanding between the Justice Department and Labor Department, all cases involving criminal provisions of ERISA will be prosecuted by the Department of Justice. The Secretary of Labor will investigate matters that may form the basis for possible criminal action under ERISA Sec. 501. These matters include reporting and disclosure violations. The Justice Department will investigate those criminal matters under ERISA Sec. 411, relating to the prohibition of certain persons holding certain positions and ERISA Sec. 511, relating to the interference with the rights of a participant by fraud or coercion.[1] The EBSA obtains investigative leads for criminal investigations from many sources, including reviews of Forms 5500, civil investigations, contacts with other law enforcement agencies, including U.S. attorneys, informants, and the media.[2]

Reporting and disclosure violations

Any person who *willfully* violates any of the reporting and disclosure provisions of ERISA is subject to a maximum fine of $100,000 ($500,000 if the violator is an entity other than an individual) or imprisonment for not more than 10 years, or both.[3]

Good faith defense. A good faith reliance on a regulation or written ruling of the Secretary of Labor is a defense which, if established, will bar prosecution for a violation of the plan description, annual reporting, or bonding requirements of ERISA.[4]

Coercive interference with protected rights

It is a crime for any person to use fraud, force, violence, or threats of force or violence to restrain, coerce, intimidate, or attempt to restrain, coerce, or intimidate any participant or beneficiary for the purpose of interfering with or preventing the exercise of any right to which that person is or may be entitled to under ERISA, an ERISA-covered plan, or the Welfare and Pension Plans Disclosure Act of 1958.[5] Any person who *willfully* violates this provision is subject to a $100,000 fine or imprisonment for not more than 10 years, or both.

Certain persons barred from holding plan positions

No person who has been convicted of certain crimes or offenses, or who has been imprisoned as a result of a conviction, is permitted to serve as an administrator, fiduciary, officer, trustee, custodian, agent, counsel, or employee of, or consultant or advisor to, or representative in any capacity of any employee benefit plan, or to serve in any capacity that involves decisionmaking authority or custody or control of the moneys, funds, assets, or property of any employee benefit plan, during or for thirteen years after the conviction or after the end of the term of imprisonment, whichever is later. A consultant or advisor to an employee benefit plan includes, but is not limited to, any entity whose activities are, in whole or substantial part, devoted to providing goods or services to any employee benefit plan.[6]

The offenses enumerated in this provision include:

1. Robbery;

2. Bribery;

3. Extortion;

4. Embezzlement;

5. Fraud;

6. Grand larceny;

7. Burglary;

8. Arson;

9. Murder;

10. Rape;

11. Kidnapping;

12. Perjury;

13. Assault with intent to kill;

14. A felony violation of federal or state law involving "controlled substances" as defined in the Comprehensive Drug Abuse Prevention and Control Act of 1970;

15. Any crime described in section 9(a)(1) of the Investment Company Act of 1940;

16. A violation of Ch. 63 of Title 18 of the U.S. Code (relating to mail fraud);

17. A violation of 18 USC § 874 (relating to kickbacks from public works employees);

18. A violation of 18 USC § 1027 (relating to false statements and concealment of facts concerning documents required under the Welfare and Pension Plans Disclosure Act of 1958, which was repealed and replaced by ERISA);

19. A violation of 18 USC § 1503 (relating to influencing or injuring an officer, juror, or witness generally in any federal court or before a federal magistrate);

20. A violation of 18 USC § 1505 (relating to the obstruction of proceedings before federal departments, agencies, or committees);

21. A violation of 18 USC § 1506 (relating to the theft or alteration of records and process, and false bail, in any federal court);

22. A violation of 18 USC § 1510 (relating to the obstruction of investigations of violations of any federal criminal statute);

23. A violation of 18 USC § 1951 (relating to interference with commerce by threats and violence);

24. A violation of 18 USC § 1954 (relating to the offer, acceptance, or solicitation to influence operations of employee benefit plans);

25. A violation of section 302 of the Labor-Management Relations Act of 1947;

26. A violation of the Labor-Management Reporting and Disclosure Act of 1959;

27. A violation of any provision of ERISA; and

28. Any felony involving abuse or misuse of such person's position or employment in a labor organization or employee benefit plan to seek or obtain an illegal gain at the expense of the members of the labor organization or the beneficiaries of the employee benefit plan.

The same prohibition applies to persons convicted of a conspiracy to commit any of the above-listed crimes or any crime in which any of the above-listed crimes is an element.

Any person who *intentionally* violates this provision is subject to a fine of up to $10,000 or imprisonment of not more than five years, or both.[7]

ERISA requires disqualification immediately upon conviction; the person cannot remain in office pending the outcome of an appeal.[8] The individual's salary will continue to be paid, but it will be placed into an escrow account. If the person's conviction is overturned on appeal, the amounts will be paid to him. If the person's conviction is sustained on appeal, the amounts will be returned to the individual or organization responsible for paying his salary.[9]

Restoration of right to serve as fiduciary. The above-mentioned prohibition against acting in certain capacities with or for an employee benefit plan may be lifted before the end of the prescribed thirteen-year period in two situations. The first is when a person's citizenship rights have been revoked as a result of the conviction, and are later fully restored. Second, if the offense is federal, the sentencing judge, or, if the offense is state, a United States district court, may determine that a person serving in any capacity referred to in the prohibition would not be contrary to ERISA's provisions relating to the protection of employee benefit rights.

Prior to making such a determination, the court is required to hold a hearing and give notice of the proceeding by certified mail to the state, county, and federal prosecuting officials in the jurisdiction or jurisdictions in which the person's conviction took place. No corporation or partnership may be precluded from acting as an administrator, fiduciary, officer, trustee, custodian, agent, counsel, or employee of, or consultant to, an employee benefit plan without a notice, hearing, and determination by the court that such service would be inconsistent with the intention of this provision.[10]

U.S. Criminal Code provisions

While ERISA provides for a system of administrative penalties, civil actions, and criminal sanctions, there are a number of provisions in the U.S. Criminal Code under which violations relating to employee benefit plans can be prosecuted. For example:

1. thefts or embezzlements from employee benefit plans are covered by 18 U.S.C. Sec. 664,

2. the making of false statements and concealment of facts in relation to documents required by ERISA are covered by 18 U.S.C. Sec. 1027, and

3. the offer, acceptance, or solicitation of funds to influence the operation of employee benefit plans is covered by 18 U.S.C. Sec. 1954.

It should also be noted that, in addition to the ERISA proscriptions, the acceptance of kickbacks by a plan trustee might cause the trustee to run afoul of the Racketeer Influenced and Corrupt Organizations Act (RICO).[11]

---

[1]Memorandum of Understanding between the Departments of Labor and Justice, February 8, 1975; Comprehensive Crime Control Bill of 1984.

[2] *ERISA Enforcement Strategy Implementation Plan*, U.S. Department of Labor, Pension and Welfare Benefits Administration, September 1990, p. 21.

[3] ERISA Sec. 501, as amended by P.L. 107-204 (Sarbanes-Oxley Act of 2002), Act Sec. 904.

[4] ERISA Sec. 108.

[5] ERISA Sec. 511, as amended by P.L. 109-280 (Pension Protection Act of 2006), Act Sec. 623(a)(1)-(2). Prior to August 17, 2006, willful violations were subject to a fine of $10,000 or imprisonment for not more than a year, or both.

[6] ERISA Sec. 411(a).

[7] ERISA Sec. 411(b).

[8] ERISA Sec. 411(c)(1).

[9] ERISA Sec. 411(d).

[10] ERISA Sec. 411(a).

[11]18 U.S.C. §§1961-1968. See, e.g., *U.S. v. Pieper*, CA-7 (1988), 854 F2d 1020.

¶ 2740

ACTIONS INVOLVING THE PENSION BENEFIT GUARANTY CORPORATION: Authority of PBGC

ERISA established the Pension Benefit Guaranty Corporation, within the Department of Labor, with the Secretary of Labor serving as chairman of the Corporation's board of directors.[1] Its purpose is to insure participants and beneficiaries of employee benefit plans against loss of benefits arising from complete or partial termination of the plan. The Director of the PBGC is appointed by the President, by and with the advice and consent of the Senate.[2]

The Pension Benefit Guaranty Corporation also issues opinion letters to advise the public of its views of the meaning of Title IV of ERISA. While the opinion letters are not binding on the public or the courts, they may be used for guidance.[3]

---

[1] ERISA Sec. 4002(a).

[2] ERISA Sec. 4002(a), as amended by P.L. 109-280 (Pension Protection Act of 2006), Act Sec. 411(a)(1).

[3]PBGC Opinion Letter No. 87-7, 7-21-87.

¶ 2742

ACTIONS INVOLVING THE PENSION BENEFIT GUARANTY CORPORATION: PBGC Investigative Power

The Pension Benefit Guaranty Corporation can make investigations it deems necessary to enforce the termination insurance provisions.[1] The PBGC Director, members of the board of directors and those appointed by the Director or the board may conduct investigations, subpoena witnesses, and require the production of books, papers, correspondence and any other records relevant to an investigation.[2]

[2] ERISA Sec. 4003(b), as amended by P.L. 109-280 (Pension Protection Act of 2006), Act Sec. 411(a)(2)(A)-(B).

[1] ERISA Sec. 4003(a).

¶ 2744

ACTIONS INVOLVING THE PENSION BENEFIT GUARANTY CORPORATION: Enforcement Authority Relating to Single-Employer Plan Terminations

Specific authority has been given to a person who is, with respect to a single-employer plan, a fiduciary, contributing sponsor, member of the contributing sponsor's controlled group, participant, beneficiary, or an employee organization representing a participant or beneficiary for plan purposes to enforce certain plan termination provisions. If the person or entity is adversely affected by certain acts or practices of any party (other than the PBGC), it may bring an action to enjoin such act or practice or to obtain other appropriate equitable relief to redress the violation or to enforce such provision.[1]

These acts or practices include violations of ERISA Secs. 4041 on voluntary single employer plan terminations, 4042 on terminations by the Pension Benefit Guaranty Corporation, 4062 on liability for the termination of a single-employer plan, 4063 on liability of a substantial employer for withdrawal from single-employer plans under multiple controlled groups, 4064 on liability on termination of single-employer plans under multiple controlled groups, or 4069 on transactions to avoid liability.

A copy of the complaint or notice of appeal in any action under this provision must be served on the PBGC by certified mail, and the PBGC has discretion to intervene in the suit.

Jurisdiction and venue

The federal district courts have exclusive jurisdiction of civil actions under ERISA Sec. 4070 relating to the terminations of single-employer plans.[2] The actions may be brought in the district where the plan was administered, where the violation took place, or where a defendant resides or may be found. Process may be served in any other district where a defendant resides or may be found. The federal district courts have jurisdiction, without regard to the amount in controversy or the citizenship of the parties, to grant relief.

Status of plan as party to action

A single-employer plan may be sued as an entity.[3] Service of summons, subpoena, or other legal process of a court upon a trustee or a plan administrator in the trustee's or administrator's capacity as such constitutes service upon the plan. If the plan in the summary plan description has not designated an agent for the service of process, service upon any contributing sponsor constitutes service. Any money judgment against a single-employer plan is enforceable only against the plan as an entity and is not enforceable against any other person unless liability against such person is established in such person's individual capacity.

Costs and expenses

In any action brought under ERISA Sec. 4070, the court in its discretion may award all or a portion of the costs and expenses incurred in connection with the action, including reasonable attorneys' fees, to any party that prevails or substantially prevails in the action.[4] Notwithstanding this provision, no plan is required to pay any costs and expenses, including attorneys' fees.

Statute of limitations

An action under ERISA Sec. 4070, on enforcement of plan termination provisions, may not be brought after the later of (1) six years after the date on which the cause of action arose or (2) three years after the earliest date on which the plaintiff acquired or should have acquired actual knowledge of the existence of the cause of action.[5]

In the case of a plaintiff who is a fiduciary bringing the case, the three-year period begins when the plaintiff becomes a fiduciary with respect to the plan if that date is after the date when the plaintiff acquired or should have acquired actual knowledge of the cause of action. In the case of fraud or concealment, a six- year period is substituted in place of the three-year period.

Penalty for failure to provide required information

The PBGC may assess penalties for failure to provide information required by the plan termination insurance provisions (except for the special provisions for multiemployer plans under ERISA Secs. 4201-4281).[6]

☐ The single-employer plan termination provisions are discussed beginning at ¶ 2800.

---

[1] ERISA Sec. 4070(a).

[2] ERISA Sec. 4070(c).

[3] ERISA Sec. 4070(b).

[4] ERISA Sec. 4070(e).

[5] ERISA Sec. 4070(f).

[6] ERISA Sec. 4071.

¶ 2746

ACTIONS INVOLVING THE PENSION BENEFIT GUARANTY CORPORATION: Civil Actions Brought by the PBGC

The Pension Benefit Guaranty Corporation may sue in a federal district court for appropriate legal and/or equitable relief to enforce the termination insurance provisions of ERISA.[1]

A plan fiduciary, employer, plan participant, or beneficiary who is adversely affected by the act or omission of any party under the subtitle in ERISA on special provisions for multiemployer plans, or an employee organization that represents such a plan participant or beneficiary may bring an action for appropriate legal or equitable relief. However, this provision does not authorize an action against the Secretary of the Treasury, the Secretary of Labor, or the PBGC.[2] For suits brought *against* the PBGC, see the discussion at ¶ 2748.

The PBGC may intervene in a Tax Court declaratory judgment instituted by an employee, plan administrator, or employer.[3] The PBGC can, itself, file a petition for declaratory judgment (to the Tax Court) to appeal an IRS ruling relating to plan qualification, plan amendments, terminations, and other matters.

Jurisdiction and venue

The United States District Courts have jurisdiction of civil actions under the multiemployer plan provisions. State courts have concurrent jurisdiction over an action brought by a plan fiduciary to collect withdrawal liability.[4] The proper venues for bringing civil actions under the multiemployer plan provisions are the districts where the plan is administered or where a defendant resides or does business. Process may be served in any district where a defendant resides, does business, or may be found.[5] A copy of any complaint in a civil suit must be served upon the PBGC by certified mail. The PBGC may intervene in any such action.[6]

In any state court suit, action, or proceeding under the multiemployer plan provisions in which the PBGC is a party or intervenes, the PBGC may remove the suit, action, or proceeding from the state court to a federal district court.[7]

☐ The multiemployer plan termination rules are discussed beginning at ¶ 2868.

---

[1] ERISA Sec. 4001(e)(1).

[2] ERISA Sec. 4301(a).

[3] ERISA Sec. 3001(c).

[4] ERISA Sec. 4301(c).

[5] ERISA Sec. 4301(d).

[6] ERISA Sec. 4301(g).

[7] ERISA Sec. 4003(f).

¶ 2748

ACTIONS INVOLVING THE PENSION BENEFIT GUARANTY CORPORATION: Civil Actions Brought Against the PBGC

Except with respect to multiemployer plan withdrawal liability disputes, a fiduciary, employer, contributing sponsor, member of a contributing sponsor's controlled group, participant, or beneficiary that is adversely affected by any action of the PBGC with respect to a plan in which the person or organization has an interest may bring actions against the PBGC for appropriate equitable relief.[1] Any organization that represents a participant or beneficiary for purposes of collective bargaining with respect to the plan is also authorized to bring actions against the PBGC.

The court may award all or a portion of the costs and expenses incurred in connection with the action to any party who prevails or substantially prevails.[2] The PBGC insurance trust funds have been specifically authorized to be credited with the attorneys' fees awarded to the PBGC.

---

[1] ERISA Sec. 4003(f)(1).

[2] ERISA Sec. 4003(f)(3).

¶ 2750

ACTIONS INVOLVING THE PENSION BENEFIT GUARANTY CORPORATION: Jurisdiction and Venue

The proceedings described at ¶ 2748 are the exclusive means for bringing actions against the PBGC under the plan termination provisions of ERISA, including actions against the PBGC in its capacity as trustee.[1] The federal district courts have jurisdiction of these actions without regard to the amount in controversy.[2]

The appropriate court to bring such an action is the federal district court where plan termination proceedings are being conducted.[3] If no termination proceedings are being conducted, the appropriate court is the federal district court where the plan has its principal office, or the federal district court for the District of Columbia.[4]

In any action or proceeding in which the PBGC is a party or intervenes in a state court, it may remove the action or proceeding to the federal district court for the district or division where the action or proceeding is pending.[5] No bond or security is necessary for the removal of the suit.

---

[1] ERISA Sec. 4003(f)(4).

[2] ERISA Sec. 4003(f)(6).

[3] ERISA Sec. 4003(f)(2)(A).

[4] ERISA Sec. 4003(f)(2)(B) and (C).

[5] ERISA Sec. 4003(f)(7).

¶ 2752

ACTIONS INVOLVING THE PENSION BENEFIT GUARANTY CORPORATION: Statute of Limitations on Actions Brought Against the PBGC

No action may be brought against the PBGC under the above provisions after the later of:[1]

1. six years after the date on which the cause of action arose, or

2. three years after the plaintiff acquired or should have acquired actual knowledge of the existence of such cause of action.

In the case of a fiduciary bringing the action in the exercise of fiduciary duties, the three-year period begins when the plaintiff becomes a fiduciary with respect to the plan if that date is later than the date the plaintiff acquired or should have acquired actual knowledge of the cause of action.[2]

In the case of fraud or concealment, a six-year period is substituted in place of the three-year period.[3]

---

[1] ERISA Sec. 4003(f)(5)(A) and (B)(i).

[2] ERISA Sec. 4003(f)(5)(B)(ii).

[3] ERISA Sec. 4003(f)(5)(C).

¶ 2754

ACTIONS INVOLVING THE PENSION BENEFIT GUARANTY CORPORATION: Statute of Limitations on Actions Brought by the PBGC

The law provides for statutes of limitations on actions brought by the PBGC that are similar to the limitations periods for actions to enforce plan termination provisions and for actions against the PBGC.

An action may not be instituted by the PBGC after the later of six years after the cause of action arose or three years after the PBGC acquired or should have acquired actual knowledge of the existence of the cause of action.[1] If the PBGC brings the action as a trustee, the three-year period begins to run on the date that the PBGC became a trustee with respect to the plan if this date is later than the date on which the PBGC acquired or should have acquired actual knowledge of the existence of the cause of action. In the case of fraud or concealment, a six-year period is substituted in place of the three-year period.

---

[1] ERISA Sec. 4003(e)(6).

¶ 2756

ACTIONS INVOLVING THE PENSION BENEFIT GUARANTY CORPORATION: Review of PBGC Determinations

ERISA provides that plan participants, beneficiaries, plan administrators, or employees may seek judicial review of PBGC actions that adversely affect them.[1] However, such parties generally may not challenge PBGC determinations in court until they have exhausted the administrative remedies provided for under PBGC rules (see below).[2] These rules cover the issuance of initial determinations by the PBGC and the procedures for requesting and obtaining administrative review by the PBGC.[3]

Any person "aggrieved" by an initial determination covered by the rules may request reconsideration or an appeal of the determination. An "aggrieved person" means any participant, beneficiary, plan administrator, contributing sponsor, controlled group member, plan sponsor, or employer adversely affected by an initial determination of the PBGC for a pension plan in which such participant, beneficiary, etc., has an interest. A "beneficiary" includes an alternate payee under a qualified domestic relations order. A "contributing sponsor" includes only a person entitled to receive a deduction for required contributions to a single-employer plan. In addition, the term "controlled group" takes into account all persons under common control with a contributing sponsor, while the term "employer" includes all trades or businesses under common control.[4]

Most determinations by the PBGC that have an actual impact on plan participants or on employers who maintain plans are covered by the administrative review rules. Specifically, the rules apply to nine types of determinations, four of which are subject to the reconsideration procedures and five of which are subject to the appeals procedures described below. Where the PBGC determines that it would be appropriate to do so, it will review, upon request or on its own initiative, determinations that are not covered by these rules.[5]

Requirements for initial determinations

All initial determinations covered by the administrative review rules must be in writing, state the reason for the determination, contain notice of the right to seek reconsideration or to appeal the determination, and briefly describe the procedures for requesting review.[6]

In general, the PBGC will stay the effectiveness of any determination covered by the rules until requested review is completed and a decision on review is issued.[7] If no request for review is filed, the determination will become effective when the prescribed time for filing a request has elapsed (see below). However, the PBGC reserves the right to make an initial determination effective on the date it is issued. In that event, an "aggrieved person" will not be required to seek administrative review of the determination, but rather may seek judicial review at the outset.[8] Aggrieved persons may still request that the PBGC review the determinations in such cases. However, the basic administrative review provisions will not apply to this request.[9]

Reconsideration of initial determinations

Any person aggrieved by a PBGC initial determination covered by the rules may request reconsideration of the determination. Reconsideration may be requested for initial determinations on the following matters:[10]

1. Determinations that a plan is covered by the termination insurance provisions under ERISA Sec. 4021.

2. Determinations regarding premiums, interest, and late payment penalties.

3. Determinations regarding voluntary terminations, including a determination that the requirements pertaining to either the notice of intent to terminate or the certification of final asset distribution have not been met, a determination as to the sufficiency of plan assets for benefit liabilities or guaranteed benefits, and a determination that a contributing sponsor does not satisfy the distress termination requirements.

4. Determinations regarding allocation of assets, including distribution of excess assets.

A request for reconsideration must be written. It must be clearly designated as a request for reconsideration, state the grounds for the request and the relief sought, and refer to all pertinent information already in the possession of the PBGC and include any relevant additional information.[11] It must be filed within 30 days after the date of the initial determination unless an extension of time is requested and granted.[12] The PBGC will grant an extension upon good cause, provided the request for an extension is filed before the expiration of the prescribed period of time. The request must be submitted to the Director of the office within the PBGC that issued the initial determination.[13] However, a request for reconsideration of a determination that the distress termination criteria have not been met must be submitted to the Executive Director.[14]

Requests for reconsideration will be handled by the office that made the initial determination. Generally, the decision on reconsideration will be made by a higher ranking official than the individual who made the initial decision. However, reconsideration of an initial determination issued by an Office Director will be performed by the same Office Director (or his or her delegate). In the case of a determination involving a distress termination, the Executive Director (or a designated official) will issue the decision on a request for reconsideration.

Decisions on requests for reconsideration must be in writing, must specify the relief granted (if any), and must state that the person has exhausted his or her administrative remedies.[15] All decisions are final.

¶2756

Administrative appeals

Any person aggrieved by an initial determination covered by the administrative procedure rules may file an appeal. Further, a third party who may be aggrieved by a PBGC appeals decision granting the relief requested, in whole or part, may participate in the appeal.[16]

The administrative appeals procedure applies only to the following determinations by the PBGC:[17]

1. Determinations that a plan is not covered by plan termination insurance provisions under ERISA Sec. 4021.

2. Determinations of benefit entitlement of participants and beneficiaries (taking into account outstanding benefit liabilities) under covered plans and determinations as to whether a domestic relations order is a qualified domestic relations order.

3. Determinations of the amount of guaranteed benefits of participants and beneficiaries (taking into account outstanding benefit liabilities) under covered plans.

4. Determinations of the amount of money subject to recapture.

5. Determinations as to employer liability for termination of a single-employer plan under a distress termination or termination by the PBGC, as to employer liability upon termination of a single-employer plan under a multiple controlled group, and as to the liability of a substantial employer for withdrawal from a single-employer plan under a multiple controlled group.

Note that agency determinations of employer liability for unfunded benefit liabilities do not include net worth decisions (an aggrieved person may still request review of a net worth decision).[18]

Appeals must be filed within 45 days after the date of the initial determination being appealed, unless the appellant requests an extension of time to file and the request is granted.[19] The request must be made before the expiration of the 45-day filing period. An extension will be granted by the PBGC upon a showing of good cause.[20]

An appeal must be written. It must state the grounds on which it is based and the relief sought. The appeal must include additional information or data which the appellant believes is relevant. The appellant may request the opportunity to appear in person or through a representative before the Appeals Board and to present witnesses to testify before the Board.[21] If the appellant desires to call witnesses, he or she must state why the presence of witnesses will further the decision-making process. The opportunity to appear and to present witnesses will be permitted at the discretion of the Appeals Board.[22] In any case where the appellant believes that another person (third party) may be aggrieved if the PBGC grants the relief sought, the appeal must also include the name and address of such other person (or persons).

¶2756

Multiple appeals. When multiple appeals are filed that arise out of similar facts and seek similar relief, the Appeals Board may consolidate the appeals.[23]

Decision of appeals board. The decision of the Appeals Board constitutes the final decision of the PBGC with regard to the determination which was the subject of the appeal and is binding on all parties who participated in the appeal and who were notified of their right to participate in the appeal. The decision must be in writing. It must specify the relief granted (if any), state the bases for the decision (including a brief statement of the facts or legal conclusions supporting the decision), and state that the appellant has exhausted administrative remedies.[24]

[1] ERISA Sec. 4003(f).

[2] Title 5, U.S. Code Sec. 704; *Myers v. Bethlehem Shipbuilding Co.*, US Sup Ct (1938), 303 US 41.

[3] PBGC Reg. § 4003.1(a).

[4] PBGC Reg. § 4003.2.

[5] PBGC Reg. § 4003.1(a) and (b).

[6] PBGC Reg. § 4003.21.

[7] PBGC Reg. § 4003.22(a).

[8] PBGC Reg. § 4003.22(b).

[9] Preamble to PBGC final rule, published in the *Federal Register* on June 4, 1993 (58 FR 35377).

[10] PBGC Reg. § 4003.1(a) and (b) and § 4003.31.

[11] PBGC Reg. § 4003.34.

[12] PBGC Reg. § 4003.32.

[13] PBGC Reg. § 4003.33.

[14] PBGC Reg. § 4003.33.

[15] PBGC Reg. § 4003.35(b).

[16] PBGC Reg. § 4003.51.

[17] PBGC Reg. § 4003.1(a) and (b).

[18] Preamble to PBGC final rule, published in the *Federal Register* on June 4, 1993 (58 FR 35377).

[19] PBGC Reg. § 4003.52.

[20] PBGC Reg. § 4003.4.

[21] PBGC Reg. § 4003.54.

[22] PBGC Reg. § 4003.55.

[23] PBGC Reg. § 4003.56.

[24] PBGC Reg. § 4003.59.

¶ 2758
For More Information

□ For more information on ERISA civil procedure and enforcement provisions, see ¶ 5773-6005 of the CCH PENSION PLAN GUIDE.

Single-Employer Plan Terminations—Plan Mergers

¶ 2800

Overview of Single-Employer Plan Terminations and Plan Mergers

This chapter discusses the rules governing terminations of single-employer defined benefit and defined contribution plans. The nature of these rules vary considerably depending on the type of plan involved. For instance, the requirements and procedures for terminating a defined benefit plan are much more complicated than those applicable to a defined contribution plan.

Employers have fairly broad latitude in terminating retirement plans. Once a plan is terminated, however, plan participants become totally vested in their ac-

¶2800

crued benefits, as of the date of termination or partial termination, to the extent the benefits are funded. In addition, ERISA imposes requirements on sponsors of terminating plans that are designed to further protect the benefits of plan participants and beneficiaries.

☐ For rules on the termination of multiemployer plans, see ¶ 2868 and following.

Plan mergers and consolidations

The benefits of participants in qualified pension, profit-sharing, or stock bonus plans are also protected following the merger or consolidation of the plans, or the transfer or assets or liabilities from one plan to another. Essentially, a plan participant's benefit after a merger or consolidation must equal or exceed the benefit before the merger. Employers should be aware that plans involved in corporate mergers or reorganizations may encounter problems in retaining their qualified status.

¶ 2803
GENERAL RULES: Termination of Single-Employer Plans

Employers looking to terminate a single-employer retirement plan are subject to restrictions that are designed to protect plan participants.[1] The nature of these restrictions depends on whether the plan is a defined benefit or defined contribution arrangement.

Defined benefit plans

Single-employer defined benefit plans may be terminated voluntarily by the plan sponsor or involuntarily by the PBGC.

Voluntary terminations. There are two types of voluntary terminations:

1. standard terminations (see ¶ 2812—2819); and
2. distress terminations (see ¶ 2820—2831).[2]

A plan may be terminated in a standard termination only if plan assets are sufficient to cover liabilities. In the event plan assets are not sufficient to cover benefit liabilities, the plan sponsor may terminate the plan, if specified conditions of financial distress (e.g., bankruptcy) are met.

Involuntary termination by PBGC. In order to protect the interests of plan participants, the PBGC may take it upon itself to terminate a single- employer defined benefit plan under specified circumstances (e.g., failure to meet minimum funding standards) (see ¶ 2833).[3]

Defined contribution plans

An employer may terminate a defined contribution plan more easily than a defined benefit plan because ERISA's termination provisions do not apply to defined contribution plans. Typically, an employer merely adopts a resolution terminating the plan. ERISA's goal of protecting plan participants from employers that want to terminate a plan in order to recover excess assets does not apply to defined contribution plans because specific amounts are allocated to employees' accounts under these plans. Upon termination of a defined contribution plan, employees are simply entitled to all amounts in their respective accounts.[4]

Note participants in qualified 401(k) plans must fully vest in amounts credited to their accounts upon the final or partial termination of the plan, irrespective of the participant's years of service or vesting status.[5] Thus, there is no need for premium payments to provide for guaranteed benefits. However, participants in defined contribution plans are also not entitled to PBGC insurance coverage.

CCH POINTER: *Termination of abandoned 401(k) plans.* Participants in plans abandoned by a plan sponsor may encounter difficulty in gaining access to money held in individual accounts under plans that have been abandoned (e.g., no contributions to or distributions from the plan for the preceding continuous 12-month period) by the employer. Regulations issued by the Employee Benefits Security Administration address this problem by authorizing a qualified termination administrator (QTA) to determine that a plan has been abandoned and undertake action to terminate the plan, including the distribution of benefits.[6] The QTA must make a reasonable effort to locate the known sponsor and must provide the sponsor with a notice of intent to terminate the plan and distribute benefits. The EBSA has provided a model notice that a QTA may use to comply with this requirement.[7]

Deemed termination. Once a QTA determines that a plan has been abandoned, the plan would be deemed to be terminated on the 90th day following the date on which the QTA provides notice of its decision and its election to serve as a QTA to the Department of Labor.[8] EBSA has provided a Model Notice that may be used by a QTA to satisfy the notice requirement.[9]

Fiduciary safe harbor. The governing rules clarify and limit a QTA's responsibilities (and potential liability) incident to the termination of an abandoned plan. The rules require a QTA to roll over the benefits of a participant or beneficiary who fails to elect a form of benefit distribution to an individual retirement plan. However, the EBSA has also provided a safe harbor that will shield the QTA from fiduciary liability incident to the rollover, if among other specified requirements, the QTA and the individual retirement plan provider enter into a written agreement governing the investment of assets.[10]

Class Exemption allows QTA to provide termination services to abandoned plans. EBSA has also issued a Prohibited Transaction Class Exemption that would permit the QTA of an abandoned plan to select itself or one of its affiliates to provide termination services to the plan and pay itself or the affiliate for those services.[11]

The exemption would apply if the fees and expenses of the QTA: (1) were consistent with industry rates for similar services and (2) did not exceed the rates charged by the QTA for similar services provided to customers that were not plans terminated pursuant to the procedures authorized by proposed regulations discussed above. The QTA would be required to notify participants and beneficiaries that their account balances could be invested in the QTA's proprietary investment product. However, the investment product would need to preserve the principal and provide a reasonable rate of return and liquidity. In addition, the holder of the individual retirement plan would need to be able to transfer his or her account balance to different investments offered by either the QTA or an individual retirement plan sponsored by a different financial institution within a reasonable period of time after making a request to do so.

EBSA rules allow for distributions from terminating plans to missing nonspouse beneficiaries. The Employee Benefits Security Administration EBSA has issued an interim final rule, which, effective for distributions made on or after March 19, 2007, will allow for distributions from the accounts in terminated abandoned plans of nonspousal beneficiaries. The final rules reconcile provisions under the Pension Protection Act of 2006 authorizing rollover distribution on behalf of nonspousal beneficiaries into rollover IRAs with the existing regulations that provide fiduciaries under terminating plans and qualified termination administrators (QTAs) of abandoned plans with a safe harbor from liability for distributions made on behalf of missing participants and beneficiaries.[12]

Amended rule allows for rollovers to IRA of nonspousal beneficiary. As amended, the regulations require that a deceased participant's benefit be directly rolled over to an inherited individual retirement plan established to receive the distribution on behalf of a missing, designated nonspouse beneficiary. These amendments eliminate the prior safe harbor condition that required a distribution on behalf of a missing nonspouse beneficiary to be made only to an account other than an individual retirement plan. Therefore, under the new rules, a distribution on behalf of a missing nonspouse beneficiary would satisfy this condition of the safe harbor only if directly rolled into an individual retirement plan that satisfies the requirements of 402(c)(11), as added by PPA.[13]

PTE amended concurrently to allow QTA to use proprietary plans for nonspouse beneficiaries. Concurrent with the issuance of the interim final regulations, the DOL is publishing proposed amendments to PTE 2006-06, which provides relief to a QTA that selects itself as the provider of an inherited individual retirement plan under the safe harbor. The EBSA has clarified that the exemption permits a QTA to designate not only itself, but also an affiliate as the provider of an inherited individual retirement plan for a nonspouse beneficiary who has not returned a distribution election.[14]

Termination date

When a plan terminates a termination date must be established. If the plan is underfunded and terminates in a distress or involuntary termination, the termination date is the date agreed upon by the plan administrator and PBGC. If the parties don't agree, the date is set by a United States District Court.

The termination date determines the date from which a plan sponsor's liability to the PBGC is calculated. Under the law prior to the enactment of the Pension Protection Act of 2006, the plan's termination date also determined the amount of benefits participant in the terminated plan would receive, including the benefits guaranteed by the PBGC and the amount of additional benefits payable from the plan's assets. However, under current law, and pursuant to regulations effective July 14, 2011, in the event a PBGC-insured plan terminates while a contributing sponsor is in bankruptcy, the PBGC guaranteed benefit (see¶ 2811) and the amount of benefits entitled to Priority Class 3 in the allocation of the plan's assets (see ¶ 2838) are determined as of the date that the plan sponsor filed the bankruptcy petition. [15] This rule applies even if the plan continues in existence and participants continue to accrue benefits.

Full vesting on plan termination

Upon the termination (or partial termination (see below)) of a plan, the rights of all participants to benefits, accrued to the date of the termination, vest, to the extent funded (see ¶ 2804).[16] In the case of a plan that maintains individual accounts for participants (i.e., money purchase, profit-sharing, 401(k), and stock bonus plans), the amount credited to a participant's account must vest.[17]

Partial plan termination

Under certain circumstances, a defined contribution plan or defined benefit plan will be considered partially terminated (see ¶ 2806).[18] The major difference between a partial termination and a full termination is that, in the case of partial termination, vesting is required only for the part of the plan that is terminated.[19]

Required allocation

A qualified plan must provide (either at the time the plan is adopted or by an amendment made prior to the termination or discontinuance of contributions) for the allocation of any previously unallocated funds to employees upon the termination or partial termination of the plan or, in the case of profit-sharing or stock bonus plans, upon the complete discontinuance of contributions (see ¶ 2838).[20] The allocation of assets to participants from a terminated plan may not be discriminatory in favor of officers, stockholders, and other highly compensated employees.[21]

Notice and reporting requirements

Plan administrators of single-employer defined benefit plans that are terminating through a standard or distress termination are required to provide notice to various affected parties as well as to file numerous forms with the IRS and the PBGC.[22] In order to begin the termination process, a notice of intent to terminate a defined benefit plan in a standard or distress termination must be given to plan participants at least 60 days (and no more than 90 days) prior to the proposed termination date.[23] See ¶ 2813 and ¶ 2822.

The PBGC must also provide notice to the plan if it institutes involuntary plan termination proceedings (see ¶ 2833). In addition, the plan administrator of a plan that has received notice of the involuntary termination from the PBGC must furnish affected parties with information that was provided to the PBGC, generally within 15 days of request.

Notification of request for determination letter. Plan participants and beneficiaries must be notified if the plan applies to the IRS for a determination letter regarding the qualification of the plan upon termination.[24] This rule also applies to terminating defined contribution plans.

☐ Notice rules under a standard termination are discussed at ¶ 2814 and ¶ 2816. The notice rules applicable in distress terminations are detailed at ¶ 2823 and ¶ 2825.

☐ A Plan Termination Reporting Table highlighting the applicable reporting requirements is at ¶ 2859.

[1] ERISA Secs. 4001—4070.

[2] ERISA Sec. 4041(b) and (c).

[3] ERISA Sec. 4042(a).

[4] IRS Reg. § 1.401-6(a)(1).

[5] Code Sec. 411(d)(3);IRS Reg. § IRS Reg. § § 1.401-6(a) and 1.411(d)-2(a)(1).

[6] ERISA Reg. § 2578.1.

[7] ERISA Reg. § 2578, Appendices A and C.

[8] ERISA Reg. § 2578.1(c).

[9] ERISA Reg. § 2578, Appendix B.

[10] ERISA Reg. § 2578.1(e).

[11] PT Class Exemption 2006-6, 4-21-06 (71 FR 20856), at CCH Pension Plan Guide ¶ 16,649U.

[12] ERISA Reg. § 2578.1; Preamble to ERISA Reg. § 2578.1 (72 FR 7516), at CCH Pension Plan Guide ¶ 24,807I.

[13] *Ibid.*

[14] Proposed Amendment to PTE 2006-6, Application No.D-11404, 2-15-07 (72 FR 7461), at CCH Pension Plan Guide ¶ 16,710.

[15] ERISA Sec. 4044(e), as added by P.L. 109-289 (Pension Protection Act of 2006), Act Sec. 404(b).

[16] Code Sec. 411(d)(3).

[17] IRS Reg. § 1.401-6(b)(2).

[18] IRS Reg. § 1.411(d)-2(b)(1).

[19] IRS Reg. § 1.401-6(b)(2).

[20] IRS Reg. § 1.411(d)-2(a)(2)(i).

[21] IRS Reg. § 1.401(a)(4)-5(b).

[22] ERISA Sec. 4041(a)(2), (b)(2), and (c)(2).

[23] ERISA Sec. 4041(a)(2); PBGC Reg. § 4041.23(a).

[24] ERISA Sec. 3001(a); IRS Reg. § 1.7476-1 and 1.7476-2; Rev. Proc. 2001-6, Sec. 18, I.R.B. 2001-1, CCH Pension Plan Guide ¶ 17,299P-56.

¶ 2804

GENERAL RULES: Vesting on Termination of Plan

A plan will not be treated as qualified unless it provides that, in the event of the termination or partial termination of the plan, the rights of each "affected employee" to (a) benefits *accrued* to the date of termination or partial termination, *to the extent funded*, as of such date, or (b) the amounts credited to the employee's account, are nonforfeitable.[1] Affected employees include former employees who were eligible for benefits on the plan's termination date, but do not include all plan participants.[2]

Accrued benefits

Accrued benefits to which an employee is entitled upon termination or partial termination of a plan refer to: (1) the benefits determined under a defined benefit plan, expressed as an annual benefit commencing at normal retirement age, or (b) the balance of an employee's account under a defined contribution plan.[3] Employees are not entitled, upon the termination of the plan, to unaccrued benefits based on future years of service. Employees must be eligible for benefits as of the plan's termination date.

Individual accounts

If a plan maintains individual accounts for participants, the amount credited to a participant's account must vest.[4]

Surplus assets

Employers may recover surplus plan assets following the termination of a single-employer plan if all plan liabilities have been met and the reversion is authorized by the plan (see ¶ 2839).[5] In addition, surplus assets remaining after a partial termination are not, absent plan authorization, required to be distributed to plan participants.[6]

Merger or corporate acquisition may require vesting

In the event that a plan is terminated in a corporate merger or acquisition (such as when the purchasing corporation does not adopt the acquired corporation's plan and contributions are discontinued), the vesting rules apply and employees are entitled to accrued benefits. However, if the plan is maintained following the merger or acquisition, vesting is not required.[7] See discussion beginning at ¶ 2861.

Conversion of money purchase plans. The IRS has ruled that the conversion of a money purchase pension plan (see ¶ 109) into a profit-sharing plan, does not, under approved conditions, constitute a partial termination requiring full vesting.[8] In the scenario approved by the IRS, the assets and liabilities of the money purchase plan, following the conversion or merger, retained their characterization under the profit-sharing plan and employees vested in the continuing profit-sharing plan under the same vesting schedule that applied under the money purchase plan.

---

[1] Code Sec. 411(d)(3); IRS Reg. § 1.411(d)-2(a)(1); Rev. Rul. 73-450, 1973-2 CB 140, CCH Pension Plan Guide ¶ 19,275.

[2] *Flanagan v. Inland Empire Electrical Workers Pension Plan & Trust,* CA-9 (1993), F3d 1246; *Borda v. Hardy, Lewis, Pollard & Page, P.C.,* CA-6 (1998), No. 97-1004; *Ailor v. PBGC,* CA-7 (1993), No. 92-4012 (*unpublished opinion*).

[3] Code Sec. 411(a)(7).

[4] Code Sec. 411(d)(3); IRS Reg. § 1.411(d)-2; Rev. Rul. 73-450, 1973-2 CB 140, CCH Pension Plan Guide ¶ 19,275.

[5] ERISA Sec. 4044(d).

[6] *Borst v. Chevron Corp.,* CA-5 (1994), 36 F3d 1308; *Outzen v. FDIC,* CA-10 (1991), 948 F2d 1184; *Chait v. Bernstein,* CA-3 (1987), 835 F2d 1017.

[7] IRS Reg. § 1.401-6(b)(1).

[8] Rev. Rul. 2002-42, I.R.B. 2002-28, 7-15-2002, at CCH Pension Plan Guide ¶ 19,946Z.

¶ 2805

GENERAL RULES: Complete Discontinuation of Contributions and Suspension of Contributions

Plans that are not subject to the minimum funding rules (i.e., profit-sharing and stock bonus plans) must, as a condition of qualification, also provide for vesting in the event of the complete discontinuation of contributions.[1] Defined benefit plans need not provide for vesting upon the discontinuation of contributions.

CCH POINTER: A profit-sharing plan should specifically provide that employees' account balances become nonforfeitable upon the complete discontinuance of plan contributions in order to be qualified, even if contributions are made during that year.[2]

Factors that constitute complete discontinuation

The IRS will determine whether a complete discontinuation of contributions (rather than a temporary suspension of contributions) has occurred without regard to the amount of any employee contributions. The IRS will consider whether contributions are recurring and substantial and whether there is a reasonable probability that the lack of contributions will continue indefinitely.[3]

Date when considered terminated

In the case of the complete discontinuation of contributions under a profit-sharing or stock bonus plan, the plan will be treated as having been terminated on the day on which the plan administrator notifies the IRS that contributions have been discontinued.[4]

---

[1] Code Sec. 411(d)(3); IRS Reg. § 1.411(d)-2(a).

[2] Rev. Rul. 89-53, 1989-1 CB 116, CCH Pension Plan Guide ¶ 19,723.

[3] IRS Reg. § 1.411(d)-2(d).

[4] Code Sec. 411(d)(3).

¶ 2806

GENERAL RULES: Partial Plan Termination

Unlike full termination, in the event of a partial plan termination, only employees who are affected by the termination fully vest in their benefits.[1] Whether or not a plan has been partially terminated will be determined on the basis of applicable facts and circumstances.[2] For example, a partial termination may occur when a group of employees is excluded from coverage through amendment or discharge, when benefits or employer contributions are reduced, or when eligibility or vesting requirements are made less generous.[3] Plan amendments that adversely affect the rights of employees to vest in benefits under the plan may also establish a partial termination.[4]

Significant percentage of employees test

A partial termination occurs if a "significant percentage" of employees is excluded from participation in the plan either by reason of plan amendment or by discharge from employment (i.e., "vertical plan termination"). For example, a partial termination of a qualified plan occurs when an employer discharges 95 of the 165 participants in the plan in connection with the dissolution of one division of its business.[5]

The determination of whether an employer's reduction of its work force constitutes a partial termination, however, depends on all relevant facts and circumstances. A partial termination is not based on a threshold termination number that reflects the number of participants leaving a plan as a percentage of individuals retaining employment.[6]

Rebuttable presumption of partial termination from 20 percent reduction in participation. The Seventh Circuit has adopted a rebuttable presumption that a 20 percent or greater reduction in plan participation is a partial termination, while a reduction under that threshold is not a partial termination.[7] The Seventh Circuit's position assumes a "band" around 20 percent in which consideration of tax motives or consequences can be used to rebut the presumption created by a reduction in participation. Under this band, a reduction in coverage below 10 percent would be conclusively presumed not to be a partial termination. By contrast, a reduction in coverage above 40 percent would be conclusively presumed to be a partial termination.

Vested and nonvested participants counted in determination of partial termination. The 20% calculation is based on the ratio of participants who lose coverage, whether or not vested, to all participants, whether or not vested.[8] The IRS subsequently stated that a turnover ratio of at least 20% will support the presumption that a partial termination has occurred.[9]

The turnover ratio is determined by dividing the number of participating employees who had an employer-initiated severance from employment during the applicable period (i.e., plan year or longer period) by the sum of all participating employees at the start of the applicable period and the employees who became participants during the applicable period.

Facts and circumstances test. All participating employees (vested and nonvested) are taken into account in calculating the turnover ratio. However the determination of whether a partial termination based on participant turnover has occurred is based on all applicable facts and circumstances, including the extent to which participating employees had a severance from employment (and whether the termination was voluntary or initiated by the employer).[10] Facts and circumstances indicating that the turnover rate for the applicable period is routine for the employer may suggest that a partial termination has not occurred. By contrast, a turnover rate in excess of 20% would support the presumption of a partial termination when the severance from employment was due to a shutdown of one of the employer's business locations (and not as result of a routine turnover).

Partial termination of 401(k) plan. In ascertaining whether a 401(k) plan has experienced a decrease in population sufficient to result in a partial termination, the determinative factor is the number of employees who are eligible to make elective deferrals, and not the number of participants who actually make deferrals.[11]

CCH POINTER: File Form 5300 for determination of partial termination. An employer or a plan administrator may file Form 5300 (Application for Determination of Employee Benefit Plan) in order to request a determination letter from the IRS regarding whether a partial termination has occurred and whether applicable qualification requirements have been met.[12]

Reduction in benefit accruals

A corporate event that effects a substantial reduction in future benefit accruals, thereby increasing the potential for a reversion of plan assets upon termination of

¶2806

the plan, is considered to be a partial termination. This type of termination is known as a "horizontal termination." [13]

[1] IRS Reg. § 1.401-6(b)(2).

[2] IRS Reg. § 1.411(d)-2(b)(1).

[3] IRS Reg. § 1.401-6(b)(2).

[4] IRS Reg. § 1.411(d)-2(b)(2).

[5] Rev. Rul. 81-27, 1981-1 CB 228, CCH PENSION PLAN GUIDE ¶ 19,560.

[6] *Haliburton Co. v. Commissioner*, TC (1993), 100 TC 216, CCH Dec. 48,914; *Baker v. Commissioner*, TC (1994), 68 TCM 48, CCH Dec. 49,953(M); *Administrative Committee of the Sea Ray Employees' Stock Ownership and Profit-Sharing Plan v. Robinson*, CA-6 (1999), 164 F. 3d 981, at CCH PENSION PLAN GUIDE ¶ 23,950X (percentage of excluded plan participants is only one factor to consider in making a determination of partial termination).

[7] *Matz v. Household International Tax Reduction Investment Plan*, CA-7 (2004), 388 F.2d 570, at CCH PENSION PLAN GUIDE ¶ 23,989S.

[8] See *Weil v. Retirement Plan Administrative Committee of the Terson Co., Inc.*, CA-2 (1991), 933 F2d 106, vacating opinion at 913 F2d 1045 (1990).

[9] Rev. Rul 2007-43, I.R.B. 2007-28, 7-9-0-7, at CCH PENSION PLAN GUIDE ¶ 19,948Z-194.

[10] *Ibid.*

[11] *Matz v. Household International Tax Reduction Investment Plan*, CA-7 (2004), 388 F.2d 570, at CCH PENSION PLAN GUIDE ¶ 23,989S.

[12] Form 5300 (Application for Determination of Employee Benefit Plan), Instructions.

[13] *In re Gulf Pension Litigation*, DC Tex (1991), 764 FSupp 1149 *aff'd* as *Borst v. Chevron Corp.*, CA-5 (1994), 36 F.3d 1208.

¶ 2807

PLAN TERMINATION INSURANCE PROGRAM: Role of Pension Benefit Guaranty Corporation

The Pension Benefit Guaranty Corporation (PBGC) is a nonprofit corporation within the Department of Labor that insures participants and beneficiaries of private defined benefit plans against the loss of pension benefits following plan termination.[1]

☐ *Annual insurance premiums.* Single-employer defined benefit plans that are covered under ERISA's termination insurance provisions (see ¶ 2808) must pay annual insurance premiums to the PBGC. Required PBGC premium payments are discussed at ¶ 2809.

☐ *Reportable events.* Plan administrators must notify the PBGC when they know or have reason to know of certain areas of potential abuse (i.e., reportable events) involving the plan. The rules covering reportable events are discussed at ¶ 2810.

☐ *Guaranteed benefits.* The PBGC is required to guarantee a certain of amount of benefits for participants of underfunded terminating plans. However, the PBGC guarantee extends only to nonforfeitable benefits. The PBGC benefit guarantee is discussed at ¶ 2811.

☐ *Termination by PBGC.* The PBGC is empowered to terminate single-employer plans. The procedures governing such involuntary terminations are set forth at ¶ 2833-2834.

☐ The responsibilities and powers of the PBGC are covered in detail at CCH PENSION PLAN GUIDE ¶ 6447-6459.

[1] ERISA Sec. 4002(a).

¶ 2808
PLAN TERMINATION INSURANCE PROGRAM:
Covered Plans

The issue of whether a plan is covered under ERISA's termination insurance provisions determines whether employers are required to pay insurance premiums and whether employees are guaranteed a minimum level of benefits upon termination of an underfunded plan.

PBGC insurance generally covers all defined benefit plans

ERISA requires mandatory termination insurance coverage of defined benefit employee pension plans (and successor defined benefit plans) that:

1. are maintained by employers and or employee organizations engaged in commerce or in any industry or activity affecting commerce and, in the case of nonqualified plans, have met the standards applicable to qualified plans for five years; or

2. are qualified under Code Sec. 401(a) or, in the case of the purchase of retirement annuities, meet the requirements of Code Sec. 404(a)(2).[1]

Excluded plans

ERISA specifically excludes the following plans from mandatory termination insurance coverage: individual account plans (e.g., 401(k), money purchase, profit-sharing, and stock bonus plans); plans maintained by substantial owners (defined as ownership of more than 10 percent of the capital or profits of a partnership or more than 10 percent of a corporation's stock); plans of professional service employees that do not have more than 25 active participants; unfunded plans (e.g., plans maintained primarily to provide deferred compensation for management or highly compensated employees or to provide benefits in excess of the Code Sec. 415 limits on contributions and benefits); plans that do not provide for employer contributions; unwritten plans; IRAs; target benefit plans (see ¶ 103) that do not guarantee a benefit upon the occurrence of inadequate contributions; and welfare benefit plans.[2]

The following plans are also excluded from termination coverage: governmental plans, church plans that do not elect coverage, non-U.S. plans for nonresidential aliens, plans of tax-exempt international organizations, and (effective for years beginning on or after August 17, 2006) certain plans established and maintained by an Indian Tribal government or its subdivisions, agencies, or instrumentalities, in which all plan participants are tribal government employees performing noncommercial essential government functions (e.g., plans covering teachers in tribal schools, but not plans for workers in casinos operated by a tribal government).[3]

Plans funded through insurance policies and annuities are covered

Pension plans that are funded through insurance policies issued by private insurance companies are not excluded from mandatory insurance coverage. Such plans are not exempt from premium payments to the PBGC.[4] A tax qualified plan, other than a separate account plan or an individual account plan, that provides for a fixed annual annuity beginning at retirement age and that is funded through the purchase of individual retirement policies and retirement annuity contracts is subject to ERISA's termination insurance rules.[5]

☐ Additional information on plans that are excluded from ERISA's termination rules, including government and church plans and non-U.S. plans maintained for nonresident aliens, is at CCH Pension Plan Guide ¶ 6459.

---

[1] ERISA Sec. 4021(a).

[2] ERISA Sec. 4021(b), PBGC Opinion Letter 76-86, 6-25-76, PBGC Opinion Letter 75-43, 6-25-75, PBGC Opinion Letter 90-6, 10-31-90, PBGC Opinion Letter 75-14, 1-15-75, PBGC Opinion Letters 77-171, 12-16-77, 74-24, 12-12-74, and 81-8, 4-17-81, PBGC Opinion Letters 75-55, 11-10-75 and 76-56, 1-19-76, PBGC Opinion Letter 75-13, 1-6-75, PBGC Opinion Letter 74-17, PBGC Opinion Letter 75-40, 8-12-75; PBGC Opinion Letter 76-7, 1-14-76.

[3] ERISA Sec. 4021(b)(2), as amended by P.L. 109-280 (Pension Protection Act of 2006), Act Sec. 906(a)(2)(B).

[4] PBGC News Release No. 75-4, 11-15-74.

[5] PBGC Opinion Letter 75-4, 1-14-75.

¶ 2809
PLAN TERMINATION INSURANCE PROGRAM:
Premium Payments

Single-employer defined benefit plans that are covered by ERISA's termination insurance provisions (see ¶ 2808) must pay annual termination insurance premiums to the PBGC.[1] In addition, plans that terminate under a distress or involuntary termination (after 2005 and before 2010) are subject to a termination premium for a period of three years after termination.

Flat rate premium

All covered single-employer defined benefit plans must pay an annual flat rate premium.[2] The premium is based on the number of participants in the plan as of the last day of the plan year preceding the premium payment year.[3]

The statutorily specified flat rate premium is $30 per participant. [4] However the flat rate premium is indexed for cost-of-living increases in the same manner as Social Security benefits are adjusted.[5] The inflation adjusted flat rate premium for plan years beginning in 2012 is $35 per participant (unchanged from 2011).[6]

Additional premium for terminated plans in bankruptcy. Single-employer plans that are terminated under ERISA Sec. 4041(c)(2)(B)(ii) or (iii) or ERISA Sec. 4042(distress termination where the PBGC takes over as trustee of the terminated plan) are subject to an additional premium of $1,250 multiplied by the number of participants in the plan immediately before the termination date.[7]

Variable rate premium

Single-employer defined benefit plans with unfunded vested benefits, as of the close of the preceding year, must pay an additional variable rate premium.[8] Thus, the premium does not apply to fully funded plans. In addition, multiemployer plans are not required to pay variable rate premiums (see¶ 2870).

Determining the variable rate premium. The variable rate premium is based on the amount of potential liability that the plan creates for the PBGC. A plan's per-participant variable rate premium (VRP) is generally $9.00 for each $1000 (or fraction thereof) of unfunded vested benefits under the plan, as of the end of the preceding year.[9] A reduced per-participant VRP of $5 times the participant count applies to plans of small employers (see below).

The per-participant VRP is multiplied by the number of plan participants during the plan year to yield the total VRP.

Unfunded vested benefits. The amount of a plan's unfunded vested benefit, for purposes of determining the variable rate premium, prior to amendments implemented by the Pension Protection Act of 2006, had been the excess of the plan's vested benefits over the value of the plan's assets.[10] Thus, unfunded vested benefits generally represented the amount that would be the unfunded current liability (within the meaning of ERISA Sec. 302(d)(8)(A)) if only vested benefits were taken into account.

The rules governing the determination of unfunded vested benefits prior to 2008 are set forth at CCH PENSION PLAN GUIDE ¶ 6471.

New rules for calculating variable rate premium after 2007. The variable rate premium will be calculated under new rules, effective for plan years beginning after 2007. Specifically, the determination of unfunded vested benefits will conform to the new funding rules implemented by the Pension Protection Act of 2006 (see ¶ 1400 and discussion beginning at ¶ 1493). Accordingly, unfunded vested benefits for a plan year will be the excess (if any) of (1) the funding target of the plan (including at-risk assumptions) as determined under ERISA Sec. 303(d) for the plan year by taking into account only vested benefits and using a specified interest rate, over (2) the fair market value of plan assets for the plan year which are held by the plan on the valuation date.[11] See below for further information on the determination of unfunded vested benefits.

Premium funding target. In order to distinguish the funding target used for premium purposes from that used for funding purposes (see ¶ 1493B), PBGC regulations would designate a "premium funding target," which would be the funding target determined by taking only vested benefits into account and using the special segment rates described in ERISA § 4006(a)(3)(E)(iv) (see ¶ 1493D) (i.e., the "standard premium funding target").[12]

Alternative premium funding target. The PBGC final regulations also permit filers to use an "alternative premium funding target," which would be the vested portion of the plan's funding target under ERISA Sec. 303(d)(1) that is used in determining the plan's minimum contribution under ERISA Sec. 303 for the premium payment year.[13] Once elected for the plan, the alternative premium funding target, would be irrevocable for a period of five years. As financial markets fluctuate, the averaged rates used for the alternative premium funding target would fluctuate above and below the spot rates used for the standard premium funding target. Requiring the election to be locked in for five years would prevent plans from calculating the premium funding target both ways each year and using the smaller number.

CCH POINTER: *Election of alternative premium funding target.* The election to use the alternative premium funding target (APFT) must be made by the due date for calculating the variable rate premium for the first plan year to which the election applies. The election is made by checking Box 5 in Part II (Alternative Premium Funding Target Election) of the comprehensive premium filing for that plan year.

Relief for plans failing to properly execute election. The PBGC has provided relief for plans for which the plan administrator intended to elect to use the alternative premium funding target to calculate the variable rate premium but neglected to check Box 5 on the comprehensive premium filing for the plan year.[14] Under the relief, the failure to check Box 5 would not preclude use of the APFT, if specified conditions are satisfied.

The relief is generally limited to plan years commencing in 2008. However, the relief will apply to plan years beginning in 2009, if the comprehensive premium filing for the plan year was due on or before July 15, 2010.

Among the applicable conditions: the comprehensive premium filing must have been made on time; the APFT must have been used to determine the plan's variable rate premium; and "Alternative" must have been checked in Line 7(d)(1) of Part II (Premium Information) of the comprehensive premium.

Notice to PBGC. The plan must also provide a notice to the PBGC's Financial Operations Department (FOD) stating that the plan intended to elect APFT effective for the first day of the applicable plan year and that the specified conditions for relief have been met. In addition, the plan must disclose (among other information) the filing date for the last timely comprehensive premium filing for the applicable plan year.

If the FOD, after reviewing the plan's comprehensive premium filing for the applicable plan year, verifies that the specified conditions for relief have been met, the plan will be deemed to have made a valid election to use the APFT.

The PBGC further notes that the relief will be available, even if the plan has amended its comprehensive premium filing for the applicable plan year to use the standard premium funding target. The PBGC will disregard the amended filing if the relief is authorized.

Election irrevocable for 5 years. Once elected for the plan, the alternative premium funding target is irrevocable for a period of five years (beginning with the first plan year to which the election applies).

Note, as financial markets fluctuate, the averaged rates used for the alternative premium funding target will fluctuate above and below the spot rates used for the standard premium funding target. Requiring the election to be locked in for five years prevents plans from calculating the premium funding target both ways each year and using the smaller number.

¶2809

Interest rate. The interest rate to be used in calculating the funding target of the plan will be the first, second, and third segment rates under the new funding rules implemented by the Pension Act (see ¶ 1493D) for the month preceding the month in which the plan year begins, determined by using the monthly yields for the month preceding the month the plan year begins on investment grade bonds with varying maturities, and in the top 3 quality levels, rather than on the average of such yields for a 24-month period.[15]

CCH POINTER: *Variable rate premium not increased.* Note, although the rules for calculating the amount of unfunded vested benefits for determining the variable rate premium have been modified, the variable rate premium has not been changed, and will remain $9 per $1000 of unfunded vested benefits.

Evolution of required interest rate. The interest rate to be used in valuing vested benefits for purposes of the variable rate premium had been the "applicable percentage" of the annual yield on 30-year Treasury securities for the month preceding the beginning of the plan year for which the premiums were being paid. Each month the PBGC issued the required interest rate to be used in determining the variable rate premium for the premium payment year. The interest rate reflected the applicable percentage of the yield figure for the preceding month (see CCH PENSION PLAN GUIDE ¶ 6465).[16]

Determining unfunded vested benefits. Schedule A of PBGC Form 1 had been used, prior to 2008, by single-employer plans to determine the amount owed with respect to the variable rate portion of the PBGC premium.

Effective for plan years after 2007, the amount of a plan's unfunded vested benefits, for a given premium payment year, is the excess (if any) of the plan's premium funding target over the fair market value of the plan's assets. [17]

Valuation date. UVBs must be determined as of the plan's valuation date for the premium payment year, based on plan provisions and the plan's population as of that date.[18]

Premium funding target. A plan may determine its premium funding target using either the standard method or an alternative method. [19]

Standard Premium Funding target. In general, a plan's funding target for premium purposes is determined the same way as it is for funding purposes. Thus, the standard premium funding target is generally the plan's funding target for the premium payment year using the same assumptions that are used for funding purposes (see ¶ 1493B). However, two exceptions apply. First, when determining the premium funding target, only vested benefits are taken into account. Second, the interest rates to be used are the special segment rates described in ERISA Sec. 4006(a)(3)(E)(iv). Those special segment rates are "spot rates" (i.e., based on bond yields for a single recent month), rather than the 24-month average segment rates used for funding purposes. [20]

Alternative premium funding target. The alternative premium funding target is calculated using the same assumptions used to calculate the plan's funding target under the funding rules, except that the calculation is based only on vested benefits, rather than all benefits. Thus, the alternative premium funding target is the vested portion of the plan's funding target under ERISA Sec. 303(d) that is used to determine the plan's minimum contribution under ERISA Sec. 303 for the premium payment year. [21]

Once the alternative funding target is elected for a plan, the election is irrevocable for a period of five years. [22]

☐ The methods for determining unfunded vested benefits are discussed at CCH Pension Plan Guide ¶ 6468-6480.

Variable rate premium cap for small employers. The variable rate premium for employers with 25 or fewer employees on the first day of the plan year will be capped, effective for plan years beginning after December 31, 2006. The variable rate premium may not exceed $5.00 multiplied by the number of participants in the plan as of the close of the preceding plan year.[23] Specifically, the variable rate premium may not exceed $5 multiplied by the square of the number of participants in the plan on the last day of the plan year preceding the premium payment year.[24]

Aggregate number of employees determines application of cap. In determining whether an employer has 25 or fewer employees on the first day of the plan year, all the employees of all members of the contributing sponsor's controlled group must be taken into account.[25] In the event a plan is maintained by two or more contributing sponsors, the employees of all contributing sponsors and their controlled groups must be aggregated in applying the 25 employee limit. Thus, the applicability of the cap is determined on a plan-by-plan, and not on an employer-by-employer basis.

In addition, note that the employee count, for purposes of the cap, is determined without regard to the minimum coverage rules of Code Sec. 410(b), which an employer might otherwise apply to exclude collective bargaining employees, employees not meeting a plan's age and service requirements, and employees in separate lines of business.[26]

☐ The PBGC variable rate premiums are reproduced at CCH Pension Plan Guide ¶ 71.

Participant notice of funded status: Pre-2008

The administrators of plans required to pay the variable rate premium were required, prior to 2008, to notify plan participants, beneficiaries, alternate payees, and employee organizations of the plan's funded status (including the funded current liability percentage) and of the limits on the PBGC's benefit guarantee should the plan terminate while underfunded.[27]

CCH POINTER: *Participant notice of funding status repealed after 2007.* ERISA Sec. 4011, which had set forth the requirements to provide participants with a notice of the plan's current liability funding percentage, was repealed, effective for plan years beginning after 2006, by the Pension Protection Act of 2006.[28] Sponsors of single employer defined benefit plans are subject, generally effective for plan years beginning after December 31, 2007, to an expanded annual funding notice.[29] The notice, which must be provided within 120 days after the end of the plan year, must, among other information, disclose: (1) whether the plan's funding target attainment percentage for the plan year (and the two prior plan years) is at least 100 percent (or the actual percentage) and (2) the total assets and liabilities of the plan for the plan year for which the last report was filed and the two preceding plan years, and the value of the plan's assets and liabilities for the plan year to which the notice relates as of the last day of the plan year, determined using fair market value and the interest rate used in determining variable rate premiums.[30]

The previously applicable participant notice requirement at discussed at CCH PENSION PLAN GUIDE ¶ 6465

Plans exempt from variable rate premium

The following types of single-employer plans are not required to determine or report vested benefits, assets, or unfunded vested benefits on PBGC Form 1 and do not have to pay the variable rate portion of the PBGC insurance premium.[31]

1. *Plans without vested benefit liabilities,* (i.e., plans with no vested participants as of the last day of the plan year preceding the premium payment year).

2. *Insurance contract plans,* as defined under Code Sec. 412(i). In order to qualify for this exemption, the plan must be considered an insurance contract plan on the last day of the plan year preceding the premium payment year.

3. *Plans terminating in a standard termination,* if the plan issues a notice of intent to terminate in a standard termination, setting forth a proposed date of termination on or before the last day of the plan year preceding the premium payment year, and ultimately makes a final distribution of assets in full satisfaction of its obligations under a standard termination.[32]

Due dates for filing premium payment form

The date by which a plan must file the premium payment form depends on the number of plan participants required to be reported on the Form 1 for the plan year preceding the plan year for which the filing is made. [33]*Note,* the participant count date for purposes of determining the filing due date is different from the participant count date used for computing the premium.

CCH POINTER: The PBGC has replaced Form 1, Schedule A and Form 1-ES with one comprehensive premium filing which is filed electronically. For plan years beginning with 2010 premium year filings the PBGC has combined the estimated flat rat premium filing (formerly Form 1-ES) with the comprehensive premium filing package [34]

3-tiered due date structure. The PBGC's due date structure is based on three categories:

Large plans –plans that owed premiums for 500 or more participants for the plan year preceding the premium payment year;

Mid-sized plans –plans that owed premiums for 100-499 participants;

Small plans –all other plans not included in the "large" or "mid-size" categories.[35]

Small plans (less than 100 participants). For small plans, the same due date will apply to both the flat-rate premium and the variable rate premium. All premiums will be due on the last day of the 16th full calendar month that begins on or after the first day of the premium payment year. For example, for plan year 2010, the due date is April 30, 2011. [36]

Mid-size (100-499 participants). For mid-size plans, the same due date will apply to both the flat-rate premium and the variable rate premium. All premiums will be due on the 15th day of the 10th full calendar month that begins on or after the first day of the premium payment year. For example, for plan year 2010, the due date is October 15, 2011. [37]

Penalty-free "true-up" period . The PBGC permits mid-sized plans to make variable rate premium filings based on estimated liabilities, providing a "true-up" period in which corrections may be made without incurring a penalty. However, note that interest is not suspended.

The waiver of the penalty covers the period from the variable rate premium due date until the small plan due date, or, if earlier, the filing of the final variable rate premium. For example, for plan year 2010, penalties may be waived until April 30, 2011.[38]

Large plans (500 or more participants). For large plans, different due dates apply to the flat-rate and the variable rate premiums.

Flat-rate premium. For the flat-rate premium, single-employer plans with 500 or more participants reported on the preceding year's Form 1 are required to pay the flat-rate per participant premium by the last day of the second full calendar month after the close of the prior plan year ("first filing due date"), using the estimated flat rate premium filing (formerly PBGC Form 1-ES). Thus, for calendar year plans, the due date is February 28 of the premium payment year.[39]

Flat rate premium safe harbor. If the participant count is not known in time to meet the February 28 filing deadline, a large plan may delay filing for a certain period. A reconciliation filing containing the participant count, along with the flat-rate premium payment must be made by October 15 of the premium payment year. [40] The PBGC will waive any underpayment penalty that would otherwise have been due for the period ending on the reconciliation due date if either:

1. fewer than 500 participants are reported for the plan year preceding the premium payment year; or

2. the flat-rate premium due date for the plan year preceding the premium payment year is later than the flat-rate premium due date for the premium payment year. [41]

Variable rate premium. The due dates and penalty structure for large plan variable rate premiums are the same as those applicable to mid-size plans [42]

¶2809

CCH POINTER: *When is PBGC Form 1 considered filed?* PBGC Form 1 is considered to be filed on the date it is postmarked if certain requirements are met.[43] If the requirements are not met, the filing date is the date the PBGC receives the submission. A submission made through the PBGC's website is considered to have been sent when the plan administrator has performed the last act necessary to indicate that the submission is filed and cannot be further edited or withdrawn. [44]

Plans filing for the first time

New and newly covered plans are not required to pay an estimated premium by the first filing date.[45]

For new and newly covered plans (regardless of the number of participants) that have not previously been required to make a comprehensive premium filing, the filing due date for both the flat rate and the variable rate premium is the latest of the following dates:

1. the last day of the 16th full calendar month that began on or after the first day of the premium payment year (for a newly-covered plan) or that began on or after the plan's effective date (in the case of a new plan) or

2. 90 days after the plan adoption date.[46]

EXAMPLE: A new calendar-year plan was adopted and became effective on January 1, 2010, and had 650 participants on that date. Although there are more than 500 participants, the plan is not considered a large plan for 2010 because plan size is based on the number of participants for whom 2009 premiums were required to be paid. Because the plan is a new plan, the 2010 flat-rate premium is not due on February 28, 2010 (the due date applicable for pre-existing large plans). Instead, the plan would be required to pay its flat-rate and variable rate premiums by April 30, 2011. As a new plan, its 2010 participant count date is January 1, 2011 (the first day of the plan year), so the 2010 flat-rate premium is based on a participant count of 650 as of January 1, 2010.

In 2011, this plan will be considered a large plan because the participant count for the 2010 premium payment year was above 500. As a large plan, the 2011 flat-rate premium will be due on March 2, 2011. Note that this date is before the date 2010 premium payments are due (April 30, 2011). The 2011 variable rate premium will be due on October 15, 2011.

> **EXAMPLE:** A new plan is adopted on December 1, 2010 and has a July 1-June 30 plan year. The plan became effective on December 1, 2010. The filing due date for the plan's first year (December 1, 2010 through June 30, 2011) is March 31, 2012, regardless of the participant count on the participant count date (December 1, 2010).

CCH POINTER: *First day of year for premium purposes.* The first day of a new plan's first plan year for premium purposes is the effective date of the plan. [47] Accordingly, plan administrators are not required to choose between the effective date and the adoption date as the first day of the plan year for the premium filing.

¶2809

Plans that change plan years

For a plan that changes its plan year, the filing due dates for the short year are unaffected by the change in plan year. For the first plan year under the new cycle, the due date is whichever is the later of (1) 30 days following the date on which a plan amendment changing the plan year was adopted or (2) the date the filing would otherwise be done [48]

Proration for short plan years

Each plan year's premium filing(s) and payment(s) must reflect and be based on a full 12-month plan year. The premium may generally not be prorated for the short plan year.

The PBGC provides for premium refunds for plans with "short plan years." The annual premium is prorated by months. However, the plan administrator is required to pay the full 12- month premium and then file for a refund or claim a credit against future premium payments. Plan administrators of plans with short plan years are afforded the option of paying a prorated premium for the short year, instead of paying a nonprorated premium and then requesting a refund or claiming a credit against a future premium payment [49]

The premium is prorated by the number of months in the short plan year. For purposes of this provision, a part of a month is treated as a month. [50]

Short plan year. The short plan year relief applies where: (1) a new or newly covered plan goes into effect for premium purposes on a date other than the first day of its first plan year, (2) a plan amendment changes the plan year, but only if the plan does not merge into or consolidate with another plan or otherwise cease its independent existence during the short plan year or at the beginning of the full plan year following the short plan year; (3) the plan's assets (other than excess assets) are distributed pursuant to the plan's termination; and (4) the plan is a single-employer plan and a plan trustee is appointed under ERISA Sec. 4042. [51]

Safe harbor for underpayment of premium following change in plan year. A plan administrator may anticipate the adoption of a plan amendment that shortens the plan year (or the distribution of plan assets in connection with the plan's termination). However, if the plan year is longer than expected, the plan administrator must make up any premium underpayment (including interest and penalties from the due date forward). The PBGC has authorized safe harbor penalty relief for the underpayment of the flat rate premium that is due by the early filing due date (end of February for calendar year plans). The safe harbor applies where a plan amendment that changes the plan year has been adopted, but the short year has not ended, by the early filing due date, and later events result in the plan year being longer than anticipated because the expected change in plan year does not occur (e.g., the amendment changing the plan year is rescinded before the end of the short year provided for in the amendment). Under such circumstances, the safe harbor rule authorizes the waiver of the underpayment penalty accruing between the flat rate payment due date and the due date for the reconciliation filing (October 15 for calendar year plans) when the penalty arises from reliance on the short year amendment. [52]

¶2809

File premium payment forms until plan terminates

The obligation to file the PBGC estimated flat rate premium filing and the comprehensive premium filing continues until the end of the plan year in which either the plan's assets are distributed pursuant to a plan termination or a trustee (usually, the PBGC) is appointed for the terminating plan, whichever is earlier.[53]

Proration and refunds. Required premium payments are charged for a full plan year and, generally, may not be prorated. However, the PBGC authorizes premium refunds for plans with short plan years.[54]

☐ See below for discussion of the termination premium that is assessed to single–employer plans that terminate (before 2010) in a distress or involuntary termination.

Determining number of participants

In determining whether an individual is a participant for premium purposes, the determinative factor is whether the plan has benefit liabilities for the individual. Specifically, an individual is considered to be a participant on any date if the plan has benefit liabilities with respect to the individual on that date.[55] Accordingly, individuals who are earning or retaining credited service, but who on the premium snapshot date, have no accrued benefit (and for whom the plan has no other benefit liabilities) may be excluded from the participant count, relieving employers of the need to pay premiums for the individuals. [56]

Loss or distribution of benefits excludes employees from participant count. Under the prior rules governing premium rates, a participant qualified as an active participant if he or she earned or retained credited service under the plan, without reference to whether the plan was obligated to provide benefits to the person. [57] Under the current PBGC regulations, the participant count will exclude plan participants who work in permanent part-time jobs but who do not perform sufficient hours to meet the plan's service requirement for accrual; individuals who participate in a plan that has been frozen for benefit accruals prior to their participation or before they have had time to accrue benefits; individuals without vested accrued benefits who incur a one-year break in service; nonvested individuals whose entire "zero dollar" vested accrued benefits are deemed distributed under the plan; and deceased nonvested individuals. [58] In addition, a living individual whose accrued benefit is fully or partially vested, or a deceased individual whose accrued benefit was fully or partially vested at the time of death will not be considered a participant after: (1) an insurer makes an irrevocable commitment to pay all benefit liabilities with respect to the individual, or (2) all benefit liabilities with respect to the individual are otherwise distributed [59]

Determination date for participant count. The participant count to be entered on PBGC Form 1, for purposes of determining the amount due for the premium payment year, generally is the number of plan participants as of the last day of the preceding plan year.[60]

☐ Different determination date rules apply to new or newly covered plans and to plans involved in a merger or spinoff (see CCH PENSION PLAN GUIDE ¶ 6501).

¶2809

Electronic filing of premium payment forms

Plans must submit premium filings (estimated or final) to the PBGC electronically.[61]

Filings may be submitted through the PBGC's online e-filing application, My Plan Administration Account (My PAA).[62] Before a filing may be submitted under MY PAA, however, the plan administrator must provide a certification using a prescribed authentication process that establishes the identity of the person making the certification. See CCH PENSION PLAN GUIDE ¶ 6503.

Paper filing generally not acceptable. Absent an exemption, premium filings on paper or in any manner other than the prescribed electronic method, will not satisfy the filing requirements.[63] Thus, the applicable penalty may be imposed until the filing is made electronically, even if a timely paper filing is made.

Administrator and sponsor liable for premiums and penalties

The plan administrator and the plan's contributing sponsor are liable for premium payments. If the contributing sponsor is a member of a controlled group, each member of the controlled group is jointly and severally liable for the required premiums.[64] Any entity that is liable for required premiums is also liable for any interest and penalties assessed on the premiums.

Recordkeeping requirements

Plan administrators are required (for six years after the premium payment date) to retain all plan records prepared by an enrolled actuary or insurer from which the insurance contracts were purchased that are necessary to support or validate PBGC premium payments (e.g., records establishing the number of plan participants and that support the calculation of unfunded vested benefits).[65] The records must also include calculations and other data prepared by the plan's actuary or for a 412(i) plan by the insurance company from which the insurance contracts are purchased.

Electronic record management. Electronic media may be used to maintain and retain records.[66] However, the electronic record must be maintained in reasonable order and in a safe and accessible place that allows for ready inspection or examination. In addition, the employer or plan administrator must implement adequate record management practices that provide for the retention of paper copies of records.[67]

PBGC may request records supporting filing. Plan administrators must also, subject to a penalty of $1,100 per day, submit plan records supporting premium filings within 45 days of the PBGC's written request.[68] However, plan administrators may apply for an automatic extension of the 45-day period.

PBGC audits

The PBGC may audit any premium payment. If the PBGC determines upon audit that the full amount of the premium due was not paid, late payment interest charges and late payment penalty charges may be assessed on the unpaid balance from the premium due date to the date of payment.[69]

Late payment penalty

The PBGC may assess a penalty for the late payment or underpayment of premiums. The penalty equals the greater of 5% of the unpaid amount each month, or $25, but may never exceed 100% of the unpaid premium.[70]

Two-tiered penalty for late premium payments. A reduced penalty of 1% per month is assessed if the premium is paid on or before the date that the PBGC provides written notice (e.g., a premium bill, a letter initiating an audit, or a letter questioning a failure to make a premium filing) to any person liable for the plan's premium, indicating that there is or may be a premium delinquency.[71] If the premium is paid after the PBGC has provided such notice, the penalty will continue to be assessed at the rate of 5% per month. The minimum total penalty will remain at $25, and the penalty will continue to be limited to 100% of the imposed premium.

Waiver of late payment penalty charge. In addition to the safe harbor relief discussed above, the PBGC may waive the late payment penalty charge under stipulated circumstances, including substantial hardship or a demonstration of reasonable cause.[72] The PBGC may also waive the penalty for the period ending on a date that a reconciliation filing is due if less than 500 participants are reported for the plan year preceding the premium payment year.[73]

CCH POINTER: The PBGC will continue to guarantee basic benefits for participants in single employer (or multiemployer) plans even if a plan administrator fails to pay any premium when due.[74]

Termination premium: Pre-2010

Single-employer plans that terminated after 2005 and before 2010 in a distress or involuntary termination were subject to an additional "termination premium" for a three year period following the termination.[75] The premium was generally equal to $1,250 multiplied by the number of individuals participating in the plan immediately before the termination date (i.e., the day before the termination date under ERISA Sec.4048).[76] However, the termination premium rate was $2,500 per participant for commercial passenger airlines or airline catering services that elected specified funding relief (see ¶ 1413) for a frozen plan, if the plan (absent extraordinary circumstances) (e.g., terrorist attack)) terminated during the first 5 years of the funding relief period.[77]

---

[1] ERISA Sec. 4006.

[2] ERISA Secs. 4006(a)(1) and 4006(a)(3)(A)(i).

[3] PBGC Reg. § 4006.3(a).

[4] ERISA Sec. 4006(a)(3)(A)(i), as amended by P.L. 109-171 (Deficit Reduction Act of 2005), Act Sec. 8101(a)(1)(A). The flat rate premium in effect prior to 2006 was $19 per participant.

[5] ERISA Sec. 4006(a)(3)(F), as added by P.L. 109-171 (Deficit Reduction Act of 2005), Act Sec.

8101(a)(1)(B). The inflation adjustment is set forth in PBGC Reg. 4000.3(d) (effective January 16, 2008), which explains that adjustments are based on changes in the national average wage index, as defined in Social Security Act Sec. 209(k)(1), with a two year lag. Thus, for 2007, the 2005 index will be compared to the baseline (the 2004 index). Premium rates are rounded to nearest whole dollar.

[6] PBGC Website, Oct. 25, 2011.

[7] ERISA Sec. 4006(a)(7)(a), as added by P.L. 109-171 (Deficit Reduction Act of 2005), Act Sec. 8101(b).

[8] ERISA Sec. 4021(a).

[9] ERISA Sec. 4006(a)(3)(E)(i) and (ii); PBGC Form 1, Instructions.

[10] PBGC Reg. 4006.4(b).

[11] ERISA Sec. 4006(a)(3)(E)(iii), as added by P.L. 109-280 (Pension Protection Act of 2006), Act. Sec. 401(a)(1). PBGC Reg. § 4006.4(a).

[12] PBGC Reg. § 4006.4(b).

[13] PBGC Reg. § 4006.4(g).

[14] PBGC Technical Update 10-2, June 6, 2010, at ¶ 19,975Z-27.

[15] ERISA Sec. 4006(a)(3)(E)(iv), as added by P.L. 109-280 (Pension Protection Act of 2006), Act. Sec. 401(a)(1).

[16] ERISA Sec. 4006(a)(3)(E)(iii)(II); PBGC Reg. 4006.4(b)(1).

Increased interest rate for determining unfunded vested benefits for 2002 and 2003 plan years. The interest rate to be used in determining the amount of unfunded vested benefits for purposes of calculating the variable rate premium was increased, effective for plan years beginning after December 31, 2001 and before January 1, 2004, to 100% of the interest rate on 30-year Treasury securities for the month preceding the month in which the plan year began (ERISA Sec. 4006(a)(3)(E)(IV), added by P.L. 107-147 (Job Creation and Worker Assistance Act of 2002), Act Sec. 405(c)) However, the relief was only effective for plan years beginning after December 31, 2002 and before January 1, 2004. Accordingly, the temporary increase in the required interest rate expired in 2003.

Interest rate for determining interest rate for 2004 and 2005. The Pension Funding Equity Act of 2004 subsequently modified the rules for determining the required interest rate for premium payment years beginning after December 31, 2003 and before January 1, 2006. Specifically, for premium payment years beginning in 2004 or 2005, the required interest rate was to be the applicable percentage (85%) of the annual rate of interest determined by the Treasury Secretary on amounts conservatively invested in long-term investment grade corporate bonds for the month preceding the beginning of the plan year for which the premiums are being paid (ERISA Sec. 4006(a)(3)(e)(iii)(V), as added by P.L. 108-218 (Pension Funding Equity Act of 2004), Act Sec. 101(1)(4)).

Interest rate for valuing unfunded vested benefits in 2006 and 2007. The temporary rules for determining unfunded vested benefits set forth in

ERISA Sec. 4006(a)(3)(E)(iii)(V) (see above) were extended for 2006 and 2007 plan years. Accordingly, for 2006, the interest rate used in determining the amount of unfunded vested benefits for purposes of calculating the variable rate premium was 85 percent of the annual rate of interest determined by the Treasury on amounts invested conservatively in long-term investment grade corporate bonds for the month preceding the month in which the plan year begins (ERISA Sec. 4006(a)(3)(E)(iii)(V), as amend by P.L. 109-280 (Pension Protection Act of 2006), Act Sec. 301(a)(3)).

Effect of revised mortality tables for 2007 on VRP interest rate. Under ERISA Sec. 4006(a)(3)(E)(iii), upon the release of revised mortality tables, the applicable percentage that was used to determine the required interest rate was to increase from 85% to 100% of the annual rate of interest determined on amounts conservatively invested in long-term investment grade corporate bonds. The IRS released the revised mortality tables in February 2007 in IRS Reg. § 1.412(l)(7)-1 (see CCH PENSION PLAN GUIDE ¶ 12,250X). Accordingly, in computing the variable rate premiums for the 2007 plan year, a plan was required to use a required interest rate of 100 percent of the annual rate of interest on amounts invested conservatively in long-term corporate bonds (i.e., composite corporate bond rate) (PBGC Technical Update 07-1, 2-13-07 (revised 2-15-07) at CCH PENSION PLAN GUIDE ¶ 19,975Z-14. Note, the PBGC advised that most plans would not use the new mortality table in determining 2007 premiums because the mortality table to be used to measure UVBs on the premium snapshot date was the table in effect for the plan year containing the premium snapshot date. For most plans, the PBGC explained, the premium snapshot date for the 2007 plan year was the last day of the plan year that began in 2006). In addition, the plan had to use the fair market value of assets, rather than the actuarial value of assets, in determining unfunded vested benefits.

Composite corporate bond rate. The composite corporate bond rate was determined on the basis of two or more indices that are periodically selected by the Treasury Secretary and that are in the top three quality levels available. The composite corporate bond rate for a month is determined by reference to designated corporate indices (IRS Notice 2004-34, I.R.B. 2004-18, at CCH PENSION PLAN GUIDE ¶ 17,128X). For each index, a monthly rate is determined based on the average of the daily values for the yield to maturity for the bonds that are included in the index. The composite corporate bond rate for the month is determined by computing the average of the monthly rates. The composite corporate bond rates are set forth in tables provided by the IRS that are updated monthly.

[17]ERISA Sec. 4006(a)(3)(iii)-(iv) , as amended by P.L 2009-280 (Pension Protection Act of 2006);PBGC Reg. § 4006.4.

[18]PBGC Reg. § 4006.4(a). A plan's valuation date for a plan year generally is the first day of the plan year. See Code Sec. 303(g)(2)(A).

[19]PBGC Reg. § 4006.4(b).

[20]PBGC Reg. § 4006.4(b)(2). Preamble to ERISA regulations (73 FR 15065; 3/21/2008) at CCH Pension Plan Guide ¶ 24,807R.

[21]PBGC Reg. § 4006.5(g) Preamble (73 FR 15065; 3/21/2008) at CCH Pension Plan Guide¶ 24,807R.

[22]PBGC Reg. § 4006.5(g)(1). According to the PBGC, the reason for permitting use of the alternative method is not to reduce premiums but to lessen the burden of computing premiums for the plan sponsor. The PBGC expects that as financial markets fluctuate, the averaged rates used for the alternative premium funding target will fluctuate above and below the spot rates used for the standard premium funding target but, over time, the two methods should produce approximately equal results. Requiring a five-year commitment to the use of the alternative premium funding target will give this averaging process a chance to work. See Preamble to ERISA regulations (73 FR 15065; 3/21/2008) at CCH Pension Plan Guide ¶ 24,807R..

[23] ERISA Sec. 4006(a)(3)(H)(i), as added by P.L. 109-280 (Pension Protection Act of 2006), Act Sec. 405(a)(2).

[24]PBGC Reg. § 4006.3(b)(2).

[25] ERISA Sec. 4006(a)(3)(H)(ii), as added by P.L. 109-280 (Pension Protection Act of 2006), Act Sec. 405(a)(2);PBGC Reg. § 4006.3(b)(3).

[26]PBGC Reg. § 4006.3(b)(4).

[27] ERISA Sec. 4011(a); PBGC Reg. § 4011.3.

[28] ERISA Sec. 4011, repealed by P.L. 109-280 (Pension Protection Act of 2006), Act Sec. 501(b); ERISA Sec. 101(f), as amended by P.L. 109-280 (Pension Protection Act of 2006), Act Sec. 501(a). P.L. 109-280 (Pension Protection Act of 2006), Act Sec. 501(d); Proposed Reg. § 4011.1, amended 1-22-07 (72 FR 2615).

[29]ERISA Sec. 101(f), as amended by P.L. 109-280 (Pension Protection Act of 2006), Act Sec. 501(a). P.L. 109-280 (Pension Protection Act of 2006), Act Sec. 501(d).

[30] ERISA Sec. 101(f)(2), as amended by P.L. 109-280 (Pension Protection Act of 2006), Act Sec. 501(a).

[31] PBGC Reg. § 4006.5(a).

[32] PBGC Reg. § 4006.5(a)(4); PBGC Form 1, Instructions.

[33] PBGC Reg. § 4007.11(a) and (b); PBGC Form 1, Instructions.

[34]2010 PBGC Premium Payment Instructions.

[35] PBGC Reg. § 4007.11.

[36] PBGC Reg. § 4007.11(a)(1).

[37] PBGC Reg. § 4007.11(a)(2)(i).

[38] PBGC Reg. § 4007.11(a)(2)(ii).

[39] PBGC Reg. § 4007.11(a)(3)(i).

[40] PBGC Reg. § 4007.11(a)(3)(iii).

[41] PBGC Reg. § 4007.8(f).

[42] PBGC Reg. § 4007.11(a)(3)(ii).

[43] PBGC Reg. § 4000.23.

[44] PBGC Reg. § 4000.23(a).

[45] PBGC Comprehensive Premium Filing Instructions: Form 1 Instructions.

[46] PBGC Reg. § 4007.11(c).

[47]Preamble to PBGC Reg. § 4007.11(c). at CCH Pension Plan Guide ¶ 24,807R

[48] PBGC Reg. § 4007.11(b);PBGC Comprehensive Premium Filing Instructions; PBGC Form 1 Instructions.

[49] PBGC Reg. § 4006.5(f).

[50]*Ibid.*

[51] *Ibid..*

[52] Preamble to PBGC Reg. § 4006.5(f).

[53] PBGC Reg. § 4007.11(d); PBGC Comprehensive Premium Filing Instructions, PBGC Form 1 Instructions.

[54] PBGC Reg. § 4006.5(f).

[55] PBGC Reg. § 4006.6(a).

[56] Preamble toPBGC Reg. § 4006.6.

[57]PBGC Reg. § 4006.2, prior to amendment on 12-2-2000 (65 FR 75160).

[58]PBGC Reg. § 4006.6(b)(1).

[59]PBGC Reg. § 4006.6(b)(2).

[60] PBGC Reg. § 4006.3.

[61] PBGC Reg. § 4000.3(b)(1) and 4007.3, as amended June 1, 2006 (71 FR 31077).

[62] PBGC Reg. § 4007.3, as amended June 1, 2006 (71 FR 31077); Preamble to PBGC Reg. § 4000.3(b)(1) and 4007.3, as amended June 1, 2006 (71 FR 31077), at CCH Pension Plan Guide ¶ 24,806Z.

[63]PBGC Reg. § 4007.3(b), as amended 3-3-08 (73 FR 15065).

[64] ERISA Sec. 4007(a) and (e)(1)(A); PBGC Reg. § 4007.12(a).

[65] PBGC Reg. § 4007.10(a).

[66] PBGC Reg. §§ 4007.10(a)(2) and 4000.53.

[67] PBGC Reg. § 4000.53.

[68] PBGC Reg. §§ 4007.10(c)(1) and 4071.3.

[69] PBGC Reg. § 4007.10(b).

[70] ERISA Sec. 4007(b); PBGC Reg. § 4007.8(a).

[71] PBGC Reg. § 4007.8(a)(1), codifying PBGC Statement of Policy 12-2-96 (61 FR 63874).

[72] PBGC Reg. § 4007.8(b)—(e).

[73] PBGC Reg. § 4007.8(f).

[74] ERISA Sec. 4007(d); PBGC Reg. § 4007.9(a).

[75] ERISA Sec.4006(a)(7)(A). See also PBGC Reg. § 4007.13(a)(1) and (4).

[76] PBGC Reg. § 4006.7(b).

[77] P.L. 109-280 (Pension Protection Act of 2006), Act Sec. 402(g)(2)(B); PBGC Reg. § 4006.7(b).

¶ 2810
PLAN TERMINATION INSURANCE PROGRAM: Reportable Events

Administrators and contributing sponsors of single-employer plans must notify the PBGC, generally within 30 days, after they have reason to know of certain areas of potential abuse involving the plan ("post-event reporting").[1] These areas of potential abuse are referred to as "reportable events." However, a waiver of post-event reporting is authorized under specified conditions.

☐ The reportable event rules do not apply to multiemployer plans.[2]

What is a reportable event?

Reportable events include:[3]

1. disqualification of the plan by the IRS or a determination by the Secretary of Labor that the plan is not in compliance with the regulatory provisions of ERISA;

2. plan amendments that would decrease a benefit of any participant that is payable from employer contributions;

3. a decrease in the number of active plan participants to fewer than 80% of those participating at the beginning of the current plan year or to fewer than 75% of those participating as of the beginning of the previous plan year;

4. termination or partial termination under the Tax Code;

5. failure to make required minimum funding payments;

6. current or projected inability to pay benefits when due;

7. a distribution to a substantial owner of a contributing sponsor;

CCH POINTER: A distribution to a substantial owner of a contributing sponsor is considered a reportable event if: (1) the total amount of distributions made to the substantial owner within the one-year period ending with the distribution exceeds $10,000; (2) the distributions were not made on account of the death of the substantial owner; (3) the distribution is not made because of the substantial owner's death; and (4) immediately after the distribution, the plan has nonforfeitable benefits that are not funded. [4]

Substantial owner. A substantial owner is an individual who: (1) owns the entire interest in an unincorporated trade or business; (2) is a partner who owns more than 10 percent of the capital interest or profits interest in the partnership; or (3) owns more than 10 percent in value of either the voting stock of a corporation or all the stock of a corporation. [5]

8. mergers and consolidations of plans or transfers of plan assets or liabilities;

9. a transaction that results in a change in the contributing sponsor or in persons discontinuing membership in the controlled group where the plan has less than $1 million in unfunded vested benefits or no unfunded vested benefits;

10. involvement by any member of the plan's controlled group in bankruptcy or similar proceedings;

11. liquidation of a contributing sponsor or a member of the sponsor's controlled group under federal bankruptcy law or any similar federal, state, or local law;

12. declaration of an extraordinary dividend or stock redemption above certain thresholds by a contributing sponsor or a member of the sponsor's controlled group;

13. the transfer, in any 12-month period, of an aggregate of 3% or more of the plan's total benefit liabilities to a person who is not a member of the contributing sponsor's controlled group or to a plan maintained by a person who is not a member of the contributing sponsor's controlled group;

14. application for a minimum funding waiver;

15. default by a member of the plan's controlled group on a loan with an outstanding balance of $10 million or more; and

16. any other event that is specified in the regulations and that is indicative of a need to terminate the plan.

Waiver of notice requirement

The PBGC has authorized an unconditional waiver of the 30-day post-event notice requirement for the following reportable events:

1. tax disqualification of the plan or a determination that the plan is not in compliance with Title I of ERISA;[6]

2. a plan amendment that decreases benefits;[7]

3. termination or partial termination;[8] and

4. plan merger or consolidation, or the transfer of assets or liabilities.[9]

Conditional waiver of notice requirement. Circumstances under which the 30-day post-event notice requirement may be waived on a conditional basis include the following: a reduction in the plan's rate of active participation (if, among other conditions, the plan has less than 100 participants as of the beginning of the current or previous plan year, no variable rate premium is required to be paid for the plan for the event year, or the plan has less than $1 million in unfunded vested benefits as of the testing date);[10] the required minimum funding payment is made within 30 days after its due date;[11] a distribution is made to a substantial owner (if, among other conditions, total distributions do not exceed the Code Sec. 415(b) limits (see ¶ 515), no variable rate premium is required for the event year, and the sum of all distributions to the substantial owner in the year is 1 percent or less of the end of the year current value of the plan's assets for either of the two preceding years);[12] a change in a controlled group of a *de minimis* 10% segment or a change limited to foreign entities;[13] liquidation by a *de minimis* 10% segment of the plan's controlled group;[14] an extraordinary dividend or stock redemption by a *de minimis* 5% segment of the plan's controlled group;[15] an inability to pay benefits when due unless the plan (in the preceding year) had 100 or fewer participants;[16] a loan default is cured, or waived by the lender, within 30 days or by the end of a stipulated period;[17] all of the plan's benefit liabilities and assets are transferred to another plan, or the value of the assets being transferred is less than 3 percent of the assets of the transferor plan;[18] or the member of the controlled group involved in bankruptcy or similar proceedings is a foreign entity, other than a foreign parent.[19]

Failure of small employer to make quarterly contributions. The PBGC has provided relief from reporting requirements for reportable events when a required quarterly contribution for the 2010 or 2011 plan year is not timely made by certain small plans and the failure is not due to financial inability. [20]

Initially, PBGC ruled that, for plans that had less than 25 participants for whom flat-rate premiums were payable for the 2008 plan year, the reporting requirement would be waived for a failure to make one or more required quarterly contribution for the 2009 plan year if financial inability was not the reason for the missed contribution(s). [21]

Subsequently, the PBGC provided that plans with less than 25 participants for whom flat rate premiums were payable in the 2009 plan year would not be subject to the reporting requirements for the failure to make one or more required quarterly contributions for the 2010 plan year, as long as the failure to make the contributions was not due to financial inability. [22] In December 2010, the PBGC further extended the relief to plans with less than 25 participants for whom flat rate premiums were payable for the 2010 plan year. [23] In December 2011, the PBGC again extended the relief to plans with less than 25 participants for whom flat rate premiums were payable for the 2012 plan year.[24] Thus, the reporting requirement may be waived with respect to a failure to make required quarterly contributions for the 2012 plan year, if financial inability to make the contributions was not the cause of the failure to make the contributions.

Plans with 25 or more participants. With respect to plans that had 25 or more participants, but less than 100 participants, for whom flat-rate premiums were payable for the 2008 plan years, the PBGC initially stated that the reporting requirement would be considered satisfied if financial inability was not the reason for the missed contribution(s) and if certain information was reported to the PBGC by the time the first missed quarterly reportable event report for the 2009 plan year would otherwise be due. [25] The PBGC extended this relief to plans subject to the flat rate premiums for the 2009 and 2010 plan years that failed to make one or more quarterly contributions for the 2010 and 2011 plan years (for reasons other than financial inability), as long as the required notice was provided to the PBGC by the date by which the first missed quarterly reportable event report would have been due. [26] In December 2011, the PBGC again extended the relief to plans that failed to make a required contribution for the 2012 plan year.[27]

Required information. The information that must be reflected in the notices includes: the plan name, employer identification number, and plan number most recently reported in a PBGC premium filing; the beginning date of the 2009, 2010, 2011, or 2012 plan year; statements that a quarterly contribution for the 2009, 2010, 2011, or 2012 plan year has not been (or will not be) timely made and that financial inability is not the reason for the missed contribution(s); the last day for satisfying the plan's minimum funding requirement for the 2009, 2010, 2011, or 2012 plan year; a statement that the filer understands that if the minimum funding requirement is not satisfied by the final payment date, a reportable event notice must be filed under the reportable events regulations; and the name, telephone number, and email address of a person whom the PBGC may contact for more information. [28]

> **CCH POINTER:** *Proposed regulations would require reporting of missed contributions for all plans.* Proposed regulations issued by PBGC in November 2009 would eliminate most automatic waivers and extensions and would require the reporting of a missed quarterly contribution without regard to plan size or the motivation for missing the contribution. [29] The proposed rules would further create two new reportable events based on PPA provisions dealing with funding-based limits and with asset transfers to retiree health accounts.

The proposed amendments would apply to post-event reports for reportable events occurring on or after the effective date of the final regulations and to advance reports due on or after the effective date of the final rules. As we went to press, PBGC has not issued final rules.

Note: PBGC Technical Update 09-4 (see CCH PENSION PLAN GUIDE ¶ 19,975Z-25) provided interim guidance for 2010 as to compliance with the existing unamended regulations for reportable events to which the final rules would not apply. In order to provide interim guidance for 2011 and 2012, the PBGC extended the guidance in PBGC Technical Update, until the amendments to the reportable events regulations become effective. [30]

30-day advance notice

The contributing sponsor (but not the plan administrator) of a defined benefit plan is required to provide at least 30 days *advance* notice of certain reportable events, including: a change in the contributing sponsor or controlled group; liquidation of a member of a plan's controlled group; declaration of an extraordinary dividend, or stock redemption above stipulated thresholds by a member of the plan's controlled group; transfer in a 12-month period of 3 percent or more of the plan's total benefit liabilities; application for a minimum funding waivers; default by a member of the plan's controlled group on a loan with an outstanding balance of $10 million or more; or involvement by any member of the plan's controlled group in bankruptcy or similar proceedings.[31]

Reporting limited to private companies with underfunded plans. The advance notice requirement only applies to privately held companies that are members of a controlled group that maintains a plan with (1) aggregate unfunded vested benefits over $50 million as of the close of the preceding plan year (disregarding plans with no vested benefits), and (2) an aggregate funded vested benefit percentage (i.e., ratio of assets to vested benefits to vested benefits) of less than 90%.[32]

Determining vested benefits. Vested benefits for purposes of determining the $50 million and 90% funding percentage threshold tests are computed using the variable rate premium interest rate as of the testing date for the plan year that includes the effective date of the reportable event.[33]

Effect of Pension Protection Act of 2006 on advance and post-event reporting. The value of assets and vested benefits and the amount of unfunded vested benefits as of the testing date for an event year are to be determined for purposes of advance and post-event reporting in the same manner as for premiums for the plan year preceding the event year under the applicable premium regulations. [34] The PBGC explains that the VRP values as of the testing date to be used for an event year beginning in 2011 or 2012 are those determined for premium purposes for the plan year preceding the event year under the premium regulations. [35] Thus, with respect to a calendar year plan with a January 1 valuation date, the VRP values determined as of January 1, 2011 for purposes of the 2011 variable rate premium are also to be used in applying the $50 million advance reporting threshold test for events becoming effective in 2012.

Waivers of advance notice requirements. The advance notice requirement may be waived under circumstances that generally offer relief to smaller plans and smaller members of a plan's controlled group (e.g., liquidation or stock redemption by *de minimis* 5 percent member of plan's controlled group).[36]

Extension of advance notice. The date by which the advance notice must be provided is also extended until 10 days after the application for a minimum funding waiver, loan default, or involvement by a controlled group member in a bankruptcy settlement.[37]

Contents of notice

The 30-day notice must include, in addition to basic information about the plan and the plan sponsor, a brief statement of the facts relating to the reportable event; a copy of the current plan document; a copy of the most recent actuarial statement and opinion; and a statement of any material change in the assets or liabilities of the plan occurring after the actuarial statement or opinion has been rendered.[38] Additional information is required for specified reportable events (e.g., reduction in active participants; failure to make required minimum funding contributions; distributions to a substantial owner).[39]

PBGC Form 10 (Post-Event Notice of Reportable Events) and PBGC Form 10-Advance (Advance Notice of Reportable Event), may be used by a contributing sponsor and administrator of single -employer plans, as applicable, to comply with the notice requirements.

Penalty for failure to file

The failure to file a required notice or provide required information subjects each person who is required to provide the notice to a penalty of $1,100 per day for each day that the failure continues.[40]

Additional information required by PBGC

Contributing sponsors, and each member of a contributing sponsor's controlled group, that maintain substantially underfunded plans must submit annual financial and actuarial reports to the PBGC.[41] The information requirement is designed to alert the PBGC to transactions that may reduce corporate assets available to pay pension benefits and to further enable the PBGC to act more quickly to negotiate agreements, provide additional funding, or take other measures to protect pension assets.

Mandatory electronic filing of annual financial and actuarial information. The annual financial and actuarial information specified under ERISA Sec. 4010 must be filed in a standardized electronic format. [42]

Pension Protection Act of 2006 changes criteria for persons required to file information with PBGC. Each contributing sponsor for a single-employer plan, and each member of the contributing sponsor's controlled group, must file annual actuarial and financial information with the PBGC if the funding target attainment percentage at the end of the preceding plan year is less than 80 percent. [43]

Additional information required in section 4010 report. The information submitted to the PBGC in the section 4010 report must include: the amount of benefit liabilities under the plan determined utilizing the assumptions used by the PBGC in determining liabilities; the funding target of the plan, determined as if the plan has been in at-risk status for at least five plan years; and the funding target attainment percentage of the plan. [44]

Final regulations implement PPA statutory changes. Final regulations implement PPA statutory changes. The PBGC issued final regulations in March 2009 governing annual financial and actuarial information reporting that, effective April 15, 2009, provide guidance on how to determine whether reporting is required based on a plan's funding target attainment percentage. [45] The regulations also make conforming changes to address the PPA changes affecting ERISA Sec. 4010 reporting triggers based on the imposition of certain liens or on the granting of certain minimum funding waivers.

¶2810

In addition, the regulations waive reporting in certain cases for controlled groups with aggregate underfunding of $15 million or less; modify the standards for determining which plans are exempt from reporting actuarial information; and provide guidance on reporting requirements for sponsors of multiple-employer plans

80% FTAP Gateway Test. Reporting is required (unless otherwise waived) if any plan within the controlled group has a funding target attainment percentage (FTAP) of less than 80 percent for the plan year ending within the information year (the "80% FTAP Gateway Test"). [46]

Funding target attainment percentage. ERISA Sec. 4010 requires reporting if the funding target attainment percentage at the end of the preceding plan year of a plan maintained by the contributing sponsor or any member of its controlled group is less than 80 percent. The funding target attainment percentage (for purposes of the 80% FTAP Gateway Test) is to be determined as of the valuation date for the plan year ending within the information year –generally, the first day of the plan year that ends within the information year. [47]

Information year. The PBGC found no indication that the PPA altered the use of the concept of the "information year" that has been integral to the process of reporting under ERISA Sec. 4010. Therefore, reporting will continue to be based on the concept of "information year." [48] The final regulations clarify that the gateway tests apply only to plans maintained as of the end of the "information year" and, thus, exclude plans no longer maintained by the controlled group as of the end of the information year. [49]

Identifying information. Each filer is required to provide identifying information with respect to each plan (including exempt plans) maintained by any member of the filer's controlled group (including exempt entities). [50] In the case of a multiple employer plan, a list of the contributing sponsors as of the end of the plan year ending within the filer's information year, including the name, employer identification number, contact information, fiscal year, and a statement as to whether each contributing sponsor is a publicly-traded company, must be provided. [51]

Actuarial information. PPA specifies three items of actuarial information that are required to be filed with the PBGC: (1) the amount of benefit liabilities under the plan determined using the assumptions utilized by the PBGC in determining liabilities; (2) the funding target of the plan determined as if the plan has been in at-risk status for at least five plan years; and (3) the funding target attainment percentage of the plan. The final regulations provide detailed guidance on how to determine benefit liabilities for ongoing plan. [52]

The final regulations further clarify that the assumptions used to determine the minimum required contribution for the plan year ending within the filer's information year, other than assumptions for decrements, interest, and expenses, must be used when determining benefit liabilities. The types of assumptions in this category include form of payment, cost-of-living increases, and marital status. [53]

CCH POINTER: *PBGC provides alternative form-of-payment assumption for determining benefit liabilities.* For information years starting on or after January 1, 2008, filers may determine benefit liabilities using the form-of-payment assumption described in PBGC Reg. 4044.51, which governs the allocation of assets in single-employer plans.[54] Thus, according to the PBGC if a benefit is not in pay status and no valid election with respect to the form of benefit has been made, the filer may use the form of benefit that, under the terms of the plan, is payable in the absence of a valid election (generally an annuity form of payment). Filers who use the alternative form-of-payment assumption under PBGC Reg. § 4044.51 must report that fact to the PBGC using the comment feature of the e-4010 filing application.

In addition, the actuarial reporting requirements are modified to require filers to report information regarding the funding target of the plan determined as if the plan has been in at-risk status for at least five plan years, the funding target attainment percentage of the plan, and whether the plan, at any time during the plan year, was subject to any of the limitations described in ERISA Sec. 206(g)) (e.g., funding-based limits on benefits and benefit accruals) and, if so, which limitations applied, when such limitations applied, and when such limitations were lifted (if applicable). [55] Also, certain information must be reported concerning liens and outstanding minimum funding waivers. [56]

Exempt plans. Under the final rules, actuarial information is not required if (1) the plan has fewer than 500 participants as of the end of the plan year ending within the filer's information year or as of the valuation date for that plan year, and (2) the plan's 4010 funding shortfall does not exceed $15 million. [57]

Waiver for controlled groups with aggregate plan underfunding not exceeding $15 million. Reporting is waived for a filer for an information year if, for a plan year ending within the information year, the aggregate plan underfunding for all plans (including any exempt plans) maintained by the filer's controlled group does not exceed $15 million (disregarding those plans with no underfunding). [58] The waiver does not apply if reporting is required for any reason other than having a funding target attainment percentage below 80%.

The final rules clarify that the entire underfunding (i.e., 4010 funding shortfall) of a multiple employer plan is counted when determining whether the $15 million waiver applies to any employer that is a contributing sponsor of the multiple employer plan. [59]

The final rules are detailed at CCH Pension Plan Guide ¶ 6518, which also discusses the information disclosure requirements applicable under prior law.

[1] ERISA Sec. 4043(a): PBGC Reg. § 4043.20.

[2] PBGC Reg. § 4043.4(b).

[3] ERISA Sec. 4043(c)(1)-(13); PBGC Reg. §§ 4043.21—4043.35.

[4] PBGC Reg. § 4043.27(a).

[5] ERISA Sec. 4021(d).

[6] PBGC Reg. § 4043.21.

[7] PBGC Reg. § 4043.22.

[8] PBGC Reg. § 4043.24.

[9] PBGC Reg. § 4043.28.

[10] PBGC Reg. § 4043.23(c).

[11] PBGC Reg. § 4043.25(c).

[12] PBGC Reg. § 4043.27(c).

[13] PBGC Reg. § 4043.29(c).

[14] PBGC Reg. § 4043.30(c).

[15] PBGC Reg. § 4043.31(c).

[16] PBGC Reg. § 4043.26(c).

[17] PBGC Reg. § 4043.34(c).

[18] PBGC Reg. § 4043.32(c).

[19] PBGC Reg. § 4043.35(c).

¶2810

[20] PBGC Technical Update 09-3, 4-30-09, at CCH PENSION PLAN GUIDE ¶ 19,975Z-24; PBGC Technical Update 09-4, 11-23-09, at CCH PENSION PLAN GUIDE ¶ 19,975Z-25; PBGC Techncial Update 10-4, 12-03-10, at CCH PENSION PLAN GUIDE ¶ 19,975Z-29.

[21] PBGC Technical Update 09-3, 4-30-09, at CCH PENSION PLAN GUIDE ¶ 19,975Z-24.

[22] PBGC Technical Update 09-3, 4-23-09, at CCH PENSION PLAN GUIDE ¶ 19,975Z-25.

[23] PBGC Technical Update 10-4, 12-03-10, at CCH PENSION PLAN GUIDE ¶ 19,975Z-29.

[24] PBGC Technical Update 111-1, 12-07-11, at CCH PENSION PLAN GUIDE ¶ 19,975Z-30.

[25] PBGC Technical Update 09-3, 4-30-09, at CCH PENSION PLAN GUIDE ¶ 19,975Z-24.

[26] PBGC Technical Update 09-3, 4-23-09, at CCH PENSION PLAN GUIDE ¶ 19,975-25 and PBGC Technical Update 10-4, 12-03-10, at CCH PENSION PLAN GUIDE ¶ 19,975Z-29.

[27] PBGC Technical Update 11-1, 12-07-11, at CCH PENSION PLAN GUIDE ¶ 19,975-25Z-30.

[28] *Ibid.*

[29] PBGC Proposed Reg. 4043.4, (74 FR 61248), at CCH PENSION PLAN GUIDE ¶ 20,537U.

[30] PBGC Technical Update 11-1, 12-07-11, at CCH PENSION PLAN GUIDE ¶ 19,975Z-30; PBGC Technical Update 10-4, 12-03-10, at CCH PENSION PLAN GUIDE¶ 19,975-29.

[31] PBGC Reg. § 4043.61—68.

[32] ERISA Sec. 4043(b)(1) and (3); PBGC Reg. § 4043.61(b);

[33] PBGC Reg. § 4043.61(c)(3).

[34] PBGC Technical Update 09-1, 1-9-09, at CCH PENSION PLAN GUIDE ¶ 19,975Z-22.

[35] PBGC Technical Update 11-1, 12-07-11, at CCH PENSION PLAN GUIDE ¶ 19,975Z-30; PBGC Technical Update 10-4, 12-03-10, at CCH PENSION PLAN GUIDE ¶ 19,975Z-29. Similar rules applied for event years beginning in 2010 under PBGC Technical Update 09-4, 11-23-09, at CCH PENSION PLAN GUIDE ¶ 19,975Z-22.

[36] ERISA Sec. 4043(b)(4); PBGC Reg. §§ 4043.62—4043.65.

[37] PBGC Reg. §§ 4043.66—4043.68.

[38] PBGC Reg. § 4043.3(b).

[39] PBGC Reg. § 4043.23(b), 4043.25(b), 4043.26(b), 4043.27(b), 4043.29(b), and 4043.35(b).

[40] ERISA Sec. 4071; PBGC Reg. § 4043.3(e).

[41] ERISA Sec. 4010; PBGC Reg. § 4010.4-4010.11; PBGC Technical Update 96-3, 3-15-96, CCH PENSION PLAN GUIDE ¶ 19,974C.

[42] PBGC Reg. § 4000.3(b) and 4010.3(a).

[43] ERISA § 4010(b)(1), as amended by P.L. 109-280 (Pension Protection Act of 2006), Act Sec. 505(a). *Note,* under the rules in effect prior to the enactment of the PPA, filing was required if: the aggregate unfunded vested benefits of all underfunded plans (including fully funded plans that were not required to pay the variable rate premium) maintained by members of the controlled group exceeded $50 million at the end of the preceding year; any member of the controlled group failed to make a required installment, resulting in aggregate unpaid contributions of $1 million, and the contributions were not paid within 10 days after the due date; or any plan maintained by a member of a controlled group had been granted one or more minimum funding waivers that were in excess of $1 million and remained unpaid at the end of the plan year.

[44] ERISA § 4010(d)(1), as amended by P.L. 109-280 (Pension Protection Act of 2006), Act Sec. 505(b).

[45] Preamble to PBGC Final Regulations (74 FR 11022), at CCH PENSION PLAN GUIDE ¶ 24,808D,

[46] PBGC Reg. § 4010.4(a),

[47] Preamble to PBGC Final Regulations (74 FR 11022), at CCH PENSION PLAN GUIDE ¶ 24,808D; PBGC Reg. § 4010.4(a) and (b).

[48] PBGC Reg. § 4010.5,

[49] Preamble to PBGC Final Regulations (74 FR 11022), at CCH PENSION PLAN GUIDE ¶ 24,808D

[50] PBGC Reg. § 4010.7(b).

[51] PBGC Reg. § 4010.7(b)(1)(vi),

[52] PBGC Reg. § 4010.8(d)(2),

[53] PBGC Reg. § 4010.8(d)(2),

[54] PBGC Technical Update 09-2, 3-25-09, at CCH PENSION PLAN GUIDE¶ 19,975Z-23.

[55] PBGC Reg. § 4010.8(a)(5), PBGC Reg. § 4010.8(a)(6), and PBGC Reg. § 4010.8(a)(8)

[56] PBGC Reg. § 4010.8(a)(9) and PBGC Reg. § 4010.8(a)(10).

[57] Preamble to PBGC Final Regulations (74 FR 11022), at CCH PENSION PLAN GUIDE ¶ 24,808D: PBGC Reg. § 4010.8(c)

[58] PBGC Reg. § 4010.11(a),

[59] PBGC Reg. § 4010.11(c)(3),

¶ 2811

PLAN TERMINATION INSURANCE PROGRAM:
Guaranteed Benefits

In the event that an underfunded single-employer plan terminates, the PBGC will guarantee payment of "pension benefits" that are "nonforfeitable" on the date of termination and to which the "participant is entitled." [1] However, the PBGC will not guarantee a benefit that vests solely because of the plan's termination.[2] In addition, the PBGC will not guarantee a benefit beyond a maximum monthly amount.

Nonforfeitable benefits

A benefit is nonforfeitable if, on the date of plan termination, the participant has satisfied all of the plan conditions entitling him or her to benefits, except submission of a formal application, retirement, or the completion of a required waiting period.[3]

Pension benefits

The PBGC only guarantees pension benefits. A pension benefit generally refers to a benefit that is payable as an annuity to a participant who has permanently left covered employment or to a surviving beneficiary. These payments must, by themselves or in combination with Social Security, Railroad Retirement, or workers' compensation benefits, provide a substantially level income to the recipient.[4]

Annuity payable for total disability is pension benefit. An annuity that is payable under the terms of the plan on account of the total and permanent disability of a participant is considered to be a pension benefit if the disability is expected to last for the life of the participant and began on or before the termination date.[5]

Entitlement to benefits

A participant or beneficiary is *entitled* to a benefit if:

1. the benefit was in pay status on the date of the plan termination;

2. a benefit payable at normal retirement age is an optional form of payment of the benefit otherwise payable at such age, and the participant elected the benefit before the plan's termination date;

3. except for a benefit payable in (2) above, before the date of plan termination the participant had satisfied the plan requirements necessary to establish the right to receive the benefit prior to that date, other than application for the benefit, satisfaction of a waiting period described in the plan, or retirement; or

4. the benefit is payable upon retirement, absent an election by the participant.[6]

Right to benefits continues after plan termination. A participant who is entitled, on the date of termination, to a certain guaranteed benefit payable beginning at an age that has not yet been attained (i.e., retirement age), is guaranteed payment of that benefit when the required age is attained.[7]

> **CCH POINTER:** The PBGC is required to guarantee a certain amount of benefits for participants of terminating plans that are underfunded. Under PBGC Reg. § 4022.3, a benefit is only guaranteed if the participant satisfies the conditions for entitlement to the benefit as of the plan's termination date. USERRA provides that an individual who leaves a job to serve in the uniformed services is generally entitled to reemployment by the previous employer and, upon reemployment, to receive credit for benefits, including employee pension plan benefits, that would have accrued but for the employee's absence due to the military service.

> The PBGC, effective December 17, 2009, amended the governing regulations to provide that a participant is deemed to have satisfied the reemployment condition for entitlement to benefits as of the plan's termination date, for purposes of the PBGC's guarantee, even if the reemployment occurred after the plan's termination date. [8] For instance, if a participant had 14 years of pension service at the time he or she entered military service, and had spent one year in the military as of the plan's termination date, the participant would be considered to have 15 years of service, for guarantee purposes, so long as he or she returns to his or her former employment within the limits set by USERRA.

Time of payment

A participant is eligible to begin receiving an annuity benefit from the PBGC on the participant's "earliest PBGC retirement date," or, if later, the plan's termination date.[9] The earliest PBGC retirement date is the earliest date on which a participant could "retire" for certain purposes.[10] The method for determining this date depends on the earliest age at which the participant is entitled to an annuity.

Immediate annuity on or after age 55. The earliest PBGC retirement date will be the earliest annuity date if the participant's earliest annuity date is on or after the date that the participant attains age 55.[11] Thus, the earliest PBGC retirement date will be the earliest date on which the participant could separate from service with the right to receive an immediate annuity.

Immediate annuity before age 55. The earliest PBGC retirement date will be the date that the participant attains age 55 if the participant's earliest annuity occurs before that date.[12]

Maximum guaranteed benefit

The maximum benefit guaranteed by the PBGC upon plan termination to each participant is determined under formulas contained in ERISA and PBGC regulations. The maximum amount is adjusted on a yearly basis for changes in the cost of living. For plans terminating in 2012, the maximum monthly benefit guarantee will be $4,653.41 per month ($55,840.92 per year) for individuals retiring at age 65. [13] The maximum amount will be higher for individuals who retire later than age 65 and higher for those who retire earlier or elect survivor benefits.

Note, the increase is not retroactive. In addition, if a plan ends in 2012, but a retiree does not begin collecting benefits until a future year, the 2012 rates continue to apply. Furthermore, in the event a plan terminates because of bankruptcy, the applicable maximum yearly rate will be that in effect on the date the bankruptcy started, and not on the date the plan ended.

Calculating the maximum benefit. Benefits payable to a participant under a plan are guaranteed only to the extent that they do not exceed the actuarial value of a benefit in the form of a life annuity payable in monthly installments, commencing at age 65 which is equal to the lesser of the following:

1. 1/12 of the participant's average annual gross income from his employer during either his highest-paid five consecutive calendar years in which he was an active participant under the plan or, if he was not an active participant throughout that period, then the lesser number of calendar years within that period during which he was an active participant; or [14]

2. $750 multiplied by the fraction, x/$13,200, where "x" is the Social Security contribution and benefit base in effect at the date of termination of the plan. [15]

Maximum monthly guaranteed benefits table. Maximum monthly guaranteed benefits table. A table of maximum guaranteed benefits for the current year and previous years is set forth at CCH PENSION PLAN GUIDE ¶ 6534

See ¶ 1493H for discussion of the present value of the maximum PBGC guaranteed benefit for purposes of the restrictions on lump-sum benefits applicable to plans with an adjusted funding target attainment percentage of between 60 and 80 percent.

Bankruptcy filing date determines guaranteed benefits. Generally, the PBGC benefit guarantee is based on the participant's benefit on the date of plan termination (see ¶ 2836). However, if a plan terminates after an employer enters bankruptcy, effective for bankruptcy proceedings initiated on or after September 16, 2006, the amount of the PBGC guarantee (and the amount of benefits entitled to priority 3 in the hierarchy for allocating the assets of a terminated plan will be based on benefits on the date of the bankruptcy filing, rather than the date of plan termination.[16] The effect of this rule is to freeze the amount of the PBGC guaranteed benefit when the contributing sponsor enters bankruptcy, thereby preserving plan assets for the payment of nonguaranteed benefits.

Final regulations, effective July 14, 2011, further stress that:

1. The maximum guaranteeable benefit, the phase-in limit, and the accrued-at-normal limit (i.e., the benefit payable at a straight-life annuity beginning at normal retirement age) are all determined as of the bankruptcy filing date.

2. Only benefits that are nonforfeitable as of the bankruptcy filing date are guaranteed. Thus, early retirement subsidies and disability benefits to which a participant became entitled after the bankruptcy filing date are not guaranteed.

3. Participants who retired under a subsidized early retirement or disability benefit to which they became entitled between the bankruptcy filing date and the

¶2811

termination date will continue in or go into pay status. However, the amount of the benefit is reduced to reflect that the subsidy or other benefit is not guaranteed.

4. The benefits in priority category 3 under ERISA Sec. 4044(a) are benefits in pay status, or that could have been in pay status, three years before the bankruptcy filing date, generally taking into account only benefit increases that were effective throughout the period beginning five years before the bankruptcy filing date and ending on the termination date (see ¶ 2838). [17]

The PBGC notes that, although the monthly amount of guaranteed benefits and benefits in priority category 3 are determined as of the bankruptcy filing date, the value of the those benefits continues to be determined as of the plan's termination date. In addition, the value of the terminated plan's assets is determined as of the termination date.

CCH POINTER: *Determination of USERRA benefits following bankruptcy.* The bankruptcy filing date is also treated (under final regulations effective December 17, 2009) as the plan's termination date for purposes of determining USERRA benefits. Accordingly, if a participant is performing military service as of the bankruptcy filing date (on or after September 16, 2006), any benefit relating to the period of military service that is accrued and vested through the bankruptcy filing date would be considered nonforfeitable if the participant becomes reemployed pursuant to USERRA after the bankruptcy filing date.[18]

Benefits payable other than as a monthly benefit. If the benefit under the plan is payable in any manner other than as a monthly benefit payable for life commencing at age 65, the maximum guaranteeable monthly amount of the benefit must be adjusted. [19]Basically, the adjustment factors are applied to the monthly amount guaranteeable in the following manner: each percentage point increase or decrease must be added to or subtracted from a base of 1.00, with the resulting amount multiplied by the maximum benefit guaranteeable. [20] The adjustment factors involve variances such as the annuitant's age, factors for benefits payable in a form other than as a life annuity and for several of the more common benefit forms payable in monthly installments (for example, period certain and continuous annuity, joint and survivor annuity (contingent basis), joint and survivor annuity (joint basis), factors for differences in the beneficiary's and participant's ages, and step-down annuities). The adjustment factors needed for computing the maximum monthly guaranteeable amount are found in the regulations.[21]

Adjust benefits payable before age 65. If benefits are payable under the plan in any manner other than as a monthly benefit payable for life beginning at age 65, the maximum guaranteeable monthly benefit must be adjusted.[22] For example, if a nondisabled participant or the beneficiary of a deceased participant elects to receive his or her benefit prior to age 65, the maximum monthly guaranteed benefit will be reduced.[23]

Example: Earl retires in 2012 at age 65. He is entitled to a maximum PBGC guaranteed monthly benefit of $4,653.41. Wilma retires at age 64 and is entitled to 93% of the maximum monthly benefit ($4,328). Bill retires at age 62 and is entitled to 79% of the maximum monthly benefit ($3,676). Gina retires at age 59 and is entitled to 61% of the maximum monthly benefit ($2,838). Sam retires at age 55 and is entitled to 45% of the maximum monthly benefit ($2,094).

Disability benefits. The maximum guaranteed benefits will not be reduced for a participant under age 65 who is receiving disability benefits under a plan if the participant is entitled to social security benefits on account of a disability that occurred on or before the plan's termination date. This exception applies to a disability benefit that is in the form of an annuity payable because of permanent and total disability. The participant must show that the Social Security Administration determined that he or she falls under the definition of disability under the Social Security Act and relevant regulations.[24]

Benefit increases that are guaranteed

The PBGC guarantees new or increased benefits attributable to a new plan, the adoption of a new benefit under an existing plan, or an increase in benefits resulting from an amendment of a plan (i.e., liberalized participation or vesting rules).[25]

Phase-in of PBGC guarantee of benefit increase in effect under 5 years. The PBGC guarantee is phased in where a plan or amendment has not been in effect for at least five years (i.e., 60 months) prior to termination of the plan. Benefit increases that have been in effect for less than five years are phased in under the following formula: (1) number of years the benefit increase has been in effect (not to exceed 5) multiplied by (2) the greater of (a) 20 percent of the monthly increase or $20 per month.[26] By contrast, benefits provided to a substantial owner (i.e., ownership of 10 percent or more of the voting stock of a corporation or all of the stock of a corporation) are phased in over a 30-year period, often resulting in a smaller PBGC-guaranteed benefit for the business owner.[27]

Modified phase-in rule for substantial owners. The Pension Protection Act modified the phase-in rule applicable to owner/participants in terminated plans by basing the phase-in on the amount of the ownership interest. Under the amendment, the 60 month phase-in rule that applies to non-owner participants will also apply to substantial owners.[28] Substantial owners are defined as owning the entire interest in an unincorporated trade or business; more than 10 percent of the capital interest or the profits of a partnership; or more than 10 percent in value of either the voting stock or all of the stock of a corporation.[29]

Stricter phase-in rule for majority owners. A stricter phase-in rule will apply to majority owners who own: the entire interest in an unincorporated trade or business; 50 percent or more of either the capital interest or the profits of a partnership; or 50 percent or more in value of either the voting stock or all of the stock of a corporation.[30] Under this rule, the amount of benefits guaranteed is determined by multiplying:

1. a fraction (which may not exceed one), the numerator of which is the number of years from the later of (a) the effective date or (b) the adoption date of the plan, to the termination date, and the denominator of which is 10, by

2. the amount of benefits that would be guaranteed under the phase-in rules for participants who are not majority owners.

Thus, not only will the phase-in occur over a 10-year period, but the guaranteed benefit of a majority owner may not exceed the amount phased-in over 60 months for other participants.[31]

Certain payments not guaranteed.The PBGC will not guarantee that part of an installment payment which exceeds the dollar amount payable as a straight life annuity commencing at normal retirement age, or thereafter, to which a participant would have been entitled under the provisions of the plan in effect on the date of the plan termination, on the basis of his credited service to such date. Thus, the PBGC will not guarantee benefits payable to a participant who retires before normal retirement age. If the plan does not provide a straight life annuity either as its normal form of retirement benefit or as an option to the normal form, the PBGC will convert the plan's normal form benefit to a straight life annuity of equal actuarial value as determined by the PBGC.[32]

Exceptions to limitation The above limitation does not apply to: (1) a survivor's benefit payable as an annuity on account of the death of a participant which occurred on or before the plan's termination date and before the participant retired; (2) a disability pension; or (3) a benefit payable in non-level installments which in combination with Social Security, Railroad Retirement, or workmen's compensation benefits yields a substantially level income if the projected income from the plan benefit over the expected life of the recipient does not exceed the value of the straight life annuity.[33]

The PBGC, however, will not guarantee: (a) the payment of that part of any benefit which exceeds the limitations set forth in ERISA Sec. 4022(b), (b) a benefit payable in a single installment (or substantially so) upon the death of a participant or his surviving beneficiary unless that benefit was substantially derived from a reduction in the pension benefit payable to the participant or surviving beneficiary, or (c) a benefit payable to other than natural persons, or a trust or estate for the benefit of one or more natural persons.[34]

Note: Termination insurance payments to a participant may not exceed the limits regardless of the number of plans in which he participated. The benefit limit will be determined on the date of the most recent plan termination. The limitations do not apply to guaranteed nonbasic benefits.

Benefits not guaranteed after plan disqualification

Benefits that accrue after a plan has been disqualified by the IRS are not guaranteed by the PBGC.[35]

Plant shutdown and other contingent event benefits

The PBGC's guarantee of pension benefits under a new plan, or of a new benefit or benefit increase under an amendment to an existing plan, is phased in based on the number of full years the benefit increase has been provided for in the plan. [36] The time period that a benefit increase has been provided under a plan is measured from the later of the adoption date of the provision creating the benefit increase or the effective date of the benefit increase. Generally, 20% of a benefit increase is guaranteed after one year, 40% after two years, etc., with full phase-in of the guarantee after five years.

The PBGC provides a limited guarantee for benefits that become payable due to a plant shutdown and other contingent events (i.e., unpredictable contingent event benefits). The guarantee will be calculated using the method currently applied to benefits associated with plan amendments implemented within 5 years of plan termination. The guarantee will apply to unpredictable contingent event benefits as if the plan amendment had been adopted on the date that the event giving rise to the benefit *occurred* (rather than the actual adoption date).[37] Accordingly, the guarantee for such contingent event benefits (excluding benefits payable following the attainment of any age, performance of any service, receipt of compensation, or death or disability) is phased-in over a 5-year period at the rate of 20 percent of the guaranteed benefit per year. As a result of ERISA Sec.4022(b)(8), the guarantee of benefits arising from plant shutdowns and other unpredictable contingent events that occur within 5 years of plan termination (or the date the plan sponsor entered bankruptcy, if applicable) will generally be lower than under pre-PPA law.

Proposed rules issued by PBGC in March 2011 would further provide that the guarantee of an unpredictable contingent event benefit be phased in from the latest of the date the benefit provision is adopted, the date the benefit is effective, or the date the unpredictable contingent event that makes the benefit payable occurs.[38] Where a plan provides that an unpredictable contingent event benefit is payable only upon the occurrence of more than one unpredictable contingent event, the proposed regulations would also allow the guarantee to be phased in from the latest date when all such unpredictable contingent events have occurred.

See ¶ 1493H for discussion of the rules that restrict payment of unpredictable contingent event benefits under plans that are less than 60 percent funded for the plan year in which the event occurs.

Insurance benefits under plan in effect less than five years

The PBGC will not pay insurance benefits in full where the plan is terminated less than five years after it comes into existence or a plan amendment increasing benefits was adopted and took effect less than five years immediately preceding plan termination (subject to the phase-in rule discussed above).[39]

Benefits payable in single installment not guaranteed

Benefits that are otherwise guaranteed, but that are payable in a single installment under plan terms, will not generally be guaranteed by the PBGC. Rather, the PBGC will guarantee any alternative benefit that provides for the payment of equal periodic installments for the life of the recipient.[40]

Lump-sum payment of $5,000 or less. In the event that the lump-sum value of a benefit payable by the PBGC is $5,000 or less, and the benefit is not yet in pay status, the benefit may be paid in a lump-sum.[41] In determining whether the lump-sum value of a benefit is $5,000 or less, the PBGC may disregard: lump-sum benefits previously paid by the plan or the PBGC; benefits previously paid by the plan through the purchase of an annuity contract; benefits derived from certain mandatory employee contributions that are returned to the employee; and the value of benefits not yet determined by the PBGC with respect to payments in excess of unfunded guaranteed benefits.[42]

See CCH PENSION PLAN GUIDE ¶ 6544 for discussion of the determination of a lump-sum payment.

Form of payment where benefits not in pay status

If a participant's benefit is already in pay status, the PBGC will generally continue to pay the benefit in the form being paid. If a participant's benefit is not already in pay status, participants may choose an annuity benefit form or, if the participant has not chosen an optional form of benefit, the PBGC will pay the benefit in an "automatic" PBGC form of benefit.[43]

Automatic PBGC forms of benefit include the form of benefit to which a participant would have been entitled absent an election or a qualified pre-retirement survivor annuity (QPSA) for the spouse of a deceased participant.[44] Optional forms of benefit that may be elected by participants include a straight life annuity, a 5-10-or 15 year certain and continuous annuity, or a joint and 50%-75% or 100% survivor annuity.[45]

The method by which the PBGC determines the amount of a benefit in an optional form elected by a participant is detailed at CCH PENSION PLAN GUIDE ¶ 6544.

Recovery of payments in excess of unfunded guaranteed benefits

The PBGC may recover additional benefits (unfunded benefit liabilities and unpaid employer contributions) from the plan sponsor. Participants, beneficiaries, and alternate payees may recover a percentage of unfunded benefit liabilities in excess of PBGC guaranteed benefits in the event the PBGC recovers amounts from the employer. The amount to be paid is determined by multiplying the outstanding amount of benefit liabilities by the applicable recovery ratio.[46] The "outstanding amount of benefit liabilities" is: (1) the value of the benefit liabilities under the plan (see ¶ 2812), less (2) the value of the benefit liabilities which would be determined by only taking into account benefits which are guaranteed or to which assets of the plan are allocated pursuant to ERISA allocation rules (see ¶ 2838). [47] The method to be used for calculating the applicable "recovery ratio" is determined by whether the outstanding amount of benefit liabilities for the terminated plan exceeds $20,000,000.[48]

Recovery ratio for unfunded benefit liabilities. The recovery ratio for terminated plans with benefit liabilities under $20 million is the average ratio of (a) the value of the recovery of the PBGC under the plan sponsor liability rules for prior plan terminations, over (b) the amount of unfunded benefit liabilities under the plan as of the termination date for the prior plan termination.[49] The Pension Protection Act changed the period used to determine the recovery ratio for unfunded benefit liabilities. Specifically, the recovery ratio that applies to plans will include the PBGC's actual recovery experience for plan terminations in the 5-

Federal fiscal year period ending with the "third fiscal year" preceding the fiscal year in which occurs the notice of intent to terminate for the plan termination for which the recovery ratio is being determined.[50]

With respect to terminated plans with outstanding benefit liabilities over $20 million, the recovery ratio is the ratio of: (1) the value of the recovery by the PBGC under the plan sponsor liability rules for the terminated plan, over (2) the amount of unfunded benefit liabilities under the plan as of the termination date.[51]

Recovery ratio for unpaid employer contributions. Amounts to be recovered from terminated plans that are attributable to unpaid employer contributions are determined on a plan-specific basis, rather than on prior PBGC experience.[52] The Pension Protection Act created a recovery ratio for determining amounts recovered for unpaid employer contributions owed to the plan. The PBGC will determine the recovery amount by multiplying: (1) the amount of liability under ERISA Sec. 4062(c) as of the date of plan termination by (2) the ERISA Sec. 4062(c) recovery ratio.[53] The ERISA Sec. 4062 recovery ratio is the ratio which (1) the sum of all PBGC recoveries of unpaid employer contributions in connection with plan terminations during the applicable 5-year period bears to (2) the sum of all the liabilities associated with unpaid employer contributions during the same 5-year period.[54]

Recouping benefit overpayments

Because the calculation of guaranteed benefits after plan termination may be delayed, it is likely that some payments to a participant or beneficiary may exceed the benefits guaranteed by the PBGC. Congress did not intend such delays to create a windfall for beneficiaries.[55] Accordingly, the PBGC may recoup net overpayments.[56] However, interest is not assessed on the amount of the net overpayment.[57] In addition, the PBGC may elect not to recoup de minimis net overpayments.[58]

Recoupment of benefits following death of participant. The death of a participant will not prevent the PBGC from recovering overpayments. The PBGC may recoup benefit overpayments from either the surviving beneficiary or the estate of a deceased participant, depending on whether the participant was entitled to future annuity payments.[59]

Reduction of future benefits. The PBGC recoups net overpayments of benefits by reducing the amount of each future benefit to which a participant or beneficiary is entitled. The amount of the future benefit reduction is determined by (a) dividing the amount of the benefit overpayment by the present value of benefits payable to the participant (as determined by the PBGC as of the termination date) and (b) multiplying that amount by the future benefit to which the participant is entitled.[60] The reduction in benefits may not exceed the greater of: (a) 10 percent per month or (b) the amount of benefits per month in excess of the minimum guaranteeable benefit, determined without an adjustment for age and form of benefits.[61]

Recoupment stops benefit reduction. The reduction of future benefit payments ceases when the amount of the net overpayment (without interest) is recouped.[62] Benefit recoupment will also be discontinued one month early if the amount remaining to be recouped in the final month is less than the amount of the monthly reduction.[63]

Notice to participants and beneficiaries. The PBGC, prior to implementing a benefit reduction, must notify a participant or beneficiary in writing of the amount of the benefit overpayment and of the amount of the reduced benefit.[64]

Reimbursement of benefit underpayments

In the event that net benefits paid to a participant in a PBGC-trusteed plan are less than the amount to which the participant or his or her beneficiary is entitled to under ERISA, the PBGC will reimburse the participant or beneficiary for the net underpayment with interest.[65] Interest on the underpayment will be paid in a single payment.

Payments owed upon death

PBGC regulations govern who will receive benefits that are owed to deceased participants where: (1) the benefit is not in the form of a joint and survivor or other type of annuity under which payments may be continued after the participant's death; (2) the benefit is in the form of a joint and survivor annuity, but the person designated to receive the survivor benefit predeceases the participant; or (3) the benefit is in the form of an annuity where payments may continue after the participant's death, but the participant dies with no payments owed for future periods.[66]

Under the regulations, the PBGC will pay benefits to persons who have been designated to receive them by the participant. The person must be designated with the PBCC at any time on or after the date that the plan is taken over by the PBGC.[67]

CCH POINTER: The PBGC rules govern the recipient of benefits owed at a participant's death, even if contrary provisions are contained in the plan or in a participant's will.[68] However, if a participant dies within 180 days after the PBGC assumes trusteeship, without having made a designation with the PBGC, benefits generally will be paid to persons who are designated by or under the plan.[69]

---

[1] ERISA Sec. 4022(a); PBGC Reg. § 4022.3.

[2] PBGC Reg. § 4022.4(a).

[3] PBGC Reg. § 4022.4(a).

[4] PBGC Reg. § 4022.2.

[5] PBGC Reg. § 4022.7(a).

[6] PBGC Reg. § 4022.6(a).

[7] PBGC Opinion Letter 76-69, 5-19-76.

[8] PBGC Reg. § 4022.11; Preamble to PBGC Final Regulations (74 FR 59093), at CCH PENSION PLAN GUIDE ¶ 24,808I.

[9] PBGC Reg. § 4022.9(a).

[10] PBGC Reg. § 4022.10.

[11] PBGC Reg. § 4022.10(a).

[12] PBGC Reg. § 4022.10(b).

[13] PBGC Reg. § 4022.83. PBGC News Release 12-07. Note, the maximum monthly benefit guarantee in 2011 was $4,500 per month ($54,000 per year).

[14] ERISA Sec. 4022(b)(3); PBGC Reg. § 4022.22.

[15] PBGC Reg. § 4022.22(b). The benefit base is determined under SSA § 230. Note that while the Social Security Amendments of 1977 changed the base for Social Security purposes, the Amendments limited PBGC's maximum guaranteed benefit to the increased level the base would have been if the Amendments had not been enacted.

[16] ERISA Sec. 4022(g), as added by P.L. 109-280 (Pension Protection Act of 2006), Act Sec. 404(a).

17 PBGC Reg. §4001.2., PBGC Reg. §4022.3, PBGC Reg. §4022.51, ¶4022.62, and PBGC Reg. §4044.13.

18 PBGC Reg. §4011.2 and PBGC Reg. §4022.11(d).

19 PBGC Reg. §4022.23(a).

20 PBGC Reg. §4022.23(b).

21 PBGC Reg. §4022.23(c)-(e).

22 PBGC Reg. §4022.23(a).

23 PBGC Reg. §4022.23(c); PBGC News Release 04-11, 11-13-2003, at CCH Pension Plan Guide ¶19,980G.

24 PBGC Reg. §4022(b).

25 PBGC Reg. §4022.24.

26 ERISA Sec. 4022(b)(7); PBGC Reg. §4022.25.

27 ERISA Sec. 4022(b)(5); PBGC Reg. §4022.6.

28 ERISA Sec. 4021(d), as added by P.L. 109-280 (Pension Protection Act of 2006), Act Sec. 407(c)(1); ERISA Sec. 4022(b)(5), as amended by P.L. 109-280 (Pension Protection Act of 2006), Act Sec. 407(a). Note, the rules under ERISA Sec. 4021(d) are effective for plan terminations with respect to which notices of intent are provided, or for which the PBGC provides notices of determination with respect to involuntary terminations, after December 31, 2005 (P.L. 109-280 (Pension Protection Act of 2006), Act Sec. 407(d)(1)).

29 ERISA Sec. 4021(d), as added by P.L. 109-280 (Pension Protection Act of 2006), Act Sec. 407(c)(1). Note, the provision takes effect on January 1, 2006 (P.L. 109-280 (Pension Protection Act of 2006), Act Sec. 407(d)(2)).

30 ERISA Sec. 4022(b)(5), as added by P.L. 109-280 (Pension Protection Act of 2006), Act Sec. 407(a).

31 ERISA Sec. 4022(b)(5)(B), as added by P.L. 109-280 (Pension Protection Act of 2006), Act Sec. 407(a).

32 PBGC Reg. §4022.21(a)(1).

33 PBGC Reg. §4022.21(a)(2).

34 PBGC Reg. §4022.21(b)-(d).

35 ERISA Sec. 4022(b)(6).

36 ERISA Sec. 4022(b)(7).

37 ERISA Sec. 4022(b)(8), as added by P.L. 109-280 (Pension Protection Act of 2006), Act Sec. 403(a). The rule is effective for benefits that become payable as a result of events occurring after July 26, 2006.

38 PBGC Proposed Reg. §4022.27.

39 ERISA Sec. 4022(b)(1).

40 PBGC Reg. §4022.7(a).

41 PBGC Reg. §4022.7(b)(1)(i).

42 PBGC Reg. §4022.7(d)(1).

43 PBGC Reg. §4022.8(a)(1) and (2).

44 PBGC Reg. 4022.8(b)(1) and (2).

45 PBGC Reg. 4022.8(b)(1).

46 ERISA Sec. 4022(c).

47 ERISA Sec. 4001(a)(19).

48 ERISA Secs. 4022(c)(3)(A) and (C).

49 ERISA Sec. 4022(c)(3)(A).

50 ERISA Sec. 4022(c)(3)(B)(ii), as amended by P.L. 109-280 (Pension Protection Act of 2006), Act Sec. 408(a), effective for plan terminations for which a notice of intent to terminate is provide on or after September 16, 2006. Under prior law, the period used for purposes of the benefit recovery ratio was the 5-federal fiscal year period that ended with the fiscal year immediately prior to the fiscal year in which a notice of intent to terminate was dated with respect to a plan.

51 ERISA Sec. 4022(c)(3)(C).

52 ERISA Sec. 4062(c).

53 ERISA Sec. 4044(e)(1)(B)(ii), as added by P.L. 109-280 (Pension Protection Act of 2006), Act Sec. 408(b)(2).

54 ERISA Sec. 4044(e)(2), as added by P.L. 109-280 (Pension Protection Act of 2006), Act Sec. 408(b)(2).

55 *Bechtel v. PBGC*, CA-DC (1985), 781 F2d 906.

56 PBGC Reg. §4022.81(a).

57 PBGC Reg. §4022.81(c)(4).

58 PBGC Reg. §4022.82(a)(4).

59 PBGC Reg. §4022.81(d)(1).

60 PBGC Reg. §4022.82(a)(1).

61 PBGC Reg. §4022.82(a)(2).

62 PBGC Reg. §4022.82(a).

63 PBGC Reg. §4022.82(a)(5).

64 PBGC Reg. §4022.82(a)(3).

65 PBGC Reg. §§4022.81(b) and 4022.83.

66 4022.91—4022.95.

67 4022.94(a).

68 PBGC Reg. §4022.91(d).

69 PBGC Reg. §4022.93(c).

¶ 2812
STANDARD PLAN TERMINATION: General Requirements for Standard Termination

An employer maintaining a single-employer defined benefit plan may terminate a plan in a standard termination only if the assets in the plan are sufficient to satisfy all benefit liabilities, as of the termination date.[1] A single-employer plan will satisfy benefit liabilities if there are no unfunded benefit liabilities under the plan.[2]

Benefit liabilities

The plan's benefit liabilities are the present value of all benefits due under the plan. Thus, "termination liability" includes all fixed and contingent obligations, vested and unvested, owed to employees and their beneficiaries.[3] Present value is determined pursuant to interest and mortality assumptions prescribed by the PBGC.

General standard termination procedures

A single-employer plan may terminate under a standard termination only if:

1. the plan administrator provides a notice of intent to terminate (NOIT) to plan participants at least 60 days, but no more than 90 days prior to the proposed termination date (see ¶ 2813);

2. the plan administrator files a standard termination notice with the PBGC no later than 180 days after the proposed termination date (see ¶ 2814);

3. the plan administrator provides notices of plan benefits to plan participants and beneficiaries no later than the day on which the standard termination notice is filed with the PBGC (see ¶ 2816);

4. the PBGC does not issue a notice of noncompliance (see ¶ 2817); and

5. by the later of 180 days following the end of the PBGC's review period, or 120 days after receipt of a determination letter from the IRS, the plan administrator distributes all plan assets in satisfaction of all benefit liabilities under the plan (see ¶ 2818).[4]

CCH POINTER: A special valuation rule applies to certain financially health companies involved in acquisitions or other transactions occurring on or after August 17, 2006. Under the rules, in the event a fully funded defined benefit plan is sponsored by a financially healthy employer that is sold as part of an acquisition or sales transaction (or a series of such transactions), the interest rate to be used in determining whether the plan has sufficient assets to meet benefit liabilities under the standard termination rules, must not be less than the interest rate used for determining whether the plan is fully funded.[5] Note, however, the interest rate will apply only to a transaction in which the employer maintaining the plan immediately before or after the transaction meets specified criteria with respect to (1) its investment rating and (2) the compensation of its domestic workforce.[6]

Amendment to stop benefit accruals not required

An employer typically terminates a plan by adopting a resolution of its board of directors. Employers are not required, prior to terminating the plan, to adopt a separate amendment to stop benefit accruals.[7]

☐ Plans that do not meet the requirements of a standard termination may elect a distress termination. See ¶ 2820—¶ 2830.

---

[1] ERISA Secs. 4001(a)(16) and 4041(b)(1)(D).

[2] ERISA Sec. 4041(d)(1).

[3] ERISA Sec. 4001(a)(16); Code Sec. 401(a)(2).

[4] ERISA Sec. 4041(b)(1); PBGC Reg. §4041.21(a).

[5] ERISA Sec. 4041(b)(5), as added by P.L. 109-280 (Pension Protection Act of 2006), Act Sec. 409(a).

[6] ERISA Sec. 4041(b)(5)(B), as added by P.L. 109-280 (Pension Protection Act of 2006), Act Sec. 409(a).

[7] *Aldridge v. Lily-Tulip, Inc. Salary Retirement Plan Benefits Committee*, CA-11 (1994), 40 F3d 1202.

¶ 2813

STANDARD PLAN TERMINATION: Notice of Intent to Terminate

The plan administrator of a terminating single-employer plan must issue a written notice of intent to terminate (NOIT) to all affected parties at least 60 days but no more than 90 days before the proposed termination date.[1] The PBGC will not extend the 60-day time limit.

Omission of affected parties

Failure to provide the required notice within the stipulated time period will nullify the proposed termination. However, if the plan administrator discovers additional affected parties after the expiration of the time period for issuing the notice, the notice will not be untimely if the administrator could not reasonably have been expected to know of the additional parties and notice is promptly distributed to them.[2]

Affected party

An "affected party" is a participant, a beneficiary of a deceased participant, and a beneficiary who is an alternate payee under a domestic relations order. Affected parties also include any person designated in writing to receive notice on behalf of an affected party, each employee organization that currently represents any group of participants, and the organization that last represented a group that is not currently represented within the five-year period preceding the issuance of the NOIT.[3]

PBGC is not an affected party. A notice of intent to terminate a plan in a standard termination need not be provided to the PBGC.

¶2813

Individual notice required

The required NOIT must be issued to each person who is an affected party as of the proposed termination date. Notice may be provided to each individual either by hand delivery or by first-class mail or courier service to the affected party's last-known address.[4] A plan administrator may also provide the notice by electronic means reasonably calculated to ensure actual receipt by the affected party.[5]

Contents of notice of intent to terminate

The NOIT must contain a specific proposed termination date or a termination date that is dependent on the occurrence of some future event.[6] In addition, the NOIT must include: identifying information regarding the plan and the employer; a statement that benefit accruals will stop on the date the plan terminates; information on how to obtain the latest updated summary plan description; a statement that the PBGC will not guarantee a participant's or a beneficiary's benefits after plan assets have been distributed in satisfaction of plan benefits; and information regarding the level of protection offered by a state guaranty association.

☐ Additional information that must be disclosed in the NOIT is set forth at CCH Pension Plan Guide ¶ 6564.

Methods for issuing notice

The NOIT may be provided to affected parties by any method of issuance (e.g., hand, mail, commercial delivery service) that is reasonably calculated to ensure actual receipt of the material by the intended recipient.[7]

Electronic delivery of notice. A plan administrator may also provide the notice by electronic means reasonably calculated to ensure actual receipt by the affected party.[8] PBGC rules set forth an electronic safe harbor, which requires an employer to adopt measures to protect confidential information and provide intended recipients with access to information in a non-electronic format.[9]

Date of issuance. An issuance may be treated as furnished on the date it was sent, provided specified conditions are satisfied.[10] The applicable conditions depend on the method by which the issuance is provided. For example, electronic issuances must satisfy the safe harbor conditions specified in PBGC Reg. § 4000.14 and must identify in an e-mail issuance, the name and telephone number of the person to contact in the event that the intended recipient requires the issuance to be re-submitted.[11]

---

[1] PBGC Reg. § 4041.23(a).

[2] PBGC Reg. § 4041.3(c)(3).

[3] ERISA Sec. 4001(a)(21); PBGC Reg. § 4001.2.

[4] PBGC Reg. § 4041.3(c)(1).

[5] PBGC Reg. § 4041.3(c)(1)(iii).

[6] PBGC Reg. § 4041.23(b).

[7] PBGC Reg. § 4001.13(a) and 4041.3(c)(4).

[8] PBGC Reg. § 4041.3(c)(1)(iii).

[9] PBGC Reg. § 4000.14.

[10] PBGC Reg. § 4000.21 and 4041.3(c)(1).

[11] PBGC Reg. § 4000.29(b).

¶ 2814

STANDARD PLAN TERMINATION: Termination Notice to PBGC

In a standard termination, the plan administrator must file PBGC Form 500 (Standard Termination Notice, Single-Employer Plan Termination) along with Schedule EA-S (Standard Termination Certification of Sufficiency) with the PBGC within 180 days after the proposed termination date.[1] The forms certify to the PBGC that the plan will have sufficient assets to met its benefit liabilities.

If the termination notice is not timely filed, the PBGC will issue a notice of noncompliance and the plan sponsor will have to select a new termination date and restart the termination process (see ¶ 2817).

Filing methods

The termination notice (and other submissions) may be filed with the PBGC by hand, mail, or commercial delivery service, or through electronic media.[2]

Notice filed when sent. Most submissions will be treated as filed when they are sent, provided specified requirements are met.[3] The applicable requirements depend on the method used to submit the filing to the PBGC.

Electronically filed documents treated as filed when sent. Documents that are submitted electronically will be treated as filed when transmitted, if specified requirements are satisfied.[4] The PBGC website (http://www.pbgc.gov) contains the technical requirements applicable to each type of filing.[5]

Supplemental notice for purchase of annuities

If benefits of the terminating plan are to be provided through the purchase of irrevocable commitments (i.e., annuities) from an insurer who is not identified in the standard termination, or is different from the insurer identified in the NOIT, the plan administrator must file a supplemental notice with the PBGC, no later than 45 days before the date of distribution, identifying the insurer.[6]

Schedule EA-S

Schedule EA-S contains an enrolled actuary's certification that a plan terminating in a standard termination will have sufficient assets to pay all benefit liabilities as of the proposed distribution date.[7]

---

[1] PBGC Reg. § 4041.25.

[2] PBGC Reg. § 4000.3 and PBGC Reg. § 4041.3(b)(1).

[3] PBGC Reg. § 4000.21 and 4041.3(b)(1).

[4] PBGC Reg. § 4000.29.

[5] PBGC Reg. § 4000.29(b)(1).

[6] PBGC Reg. § 4041.27(d).

[7] ERISA Sec. 4041(b)(2)(A); PBGC Form 500, Instructions.

¶ 2815

STANDARD PLAN TERMINATION: Plan Administration During Standard Termination

The plan administrator of the terminating plan must carry out normal plan operations from the date the NOIT is issued until the last day of the PBGC review period.[1] Thus, plan administrators must continue to put participants into pay status, collect contributions due the plan, invest plan assets, and make loans to qualified participants. However, during the pendency of the termination proceedings, the plan administrator may not (1) purchase irrevocable commitments to provide any plan benefits, or (2) pay benefits attributable to employer contributions, other than death benefits, in a form other than an annuity.[2] However, the plan administrator may pay benefits that are attributable to employer contributions through the purchase of irrevocable commitments or in a form other than an annuity if the participant has separated from service and the arrangement is consistent with prior plan practice and not reasonably expected to jeopardize the plan's sufficiency for benefit liabilities.[3]

---

[1] PBGC Reg. § 4041.22(a).

[2] *Ibid.*

[3] PBGC Reg. § 4041.22(b).

¶ 2816

STANDARD PLAN TERMINATION: Notice of Plan Benefits to Participants and Beneficiaries

A plan administrator must provide each affected party (other than an employee organization) with a notice of that individual's plan benefits by the date on which the plan administrator files the standard termination notice (i.e., on or before the 180th day after the proposed termination date). The notice of plan benefits may not be filed later than the date that the standard termination notice is filed.[1] The plan administrator may provide the required notice by using any method (e.g., hand, mail, or commercial delivery or electronic media) that is reasonably expected to ensure actual receipt of the notice (other than posting). [2]

Contents of notice of plan benefits

The notice of plan benefits must include identifying information regarding the plan and the contributing plan sponsor (including the employer identification number) disclose the proposed termination date;[3] and provide the personal data used to calculate the benefits of an affected party (other than a party who has been in pay status for more than one year).[4]

Persons in pay status. For participants or beneficiaries who are in pay status as of the proposed termination date, the notice of plan benefits must include:

1. the amount and form of the participant's plan benefits payable as of the proposed termination date;

2. the amount and form of benefit, if any, payable to a beneficiary upon the participant's death and the name of the beneficiary; and

3. the amount and date of any increase or decrease in the benefit scheduled to occur after the proposed termination date (or that has already occurred) and an explanation of the increase or decrease, including, where applicable, a reference to the pertinent plan provision.[5]

Persons not in pay status. For participants or beneficiaries who are not in pay status as of the proposed termination date, but who, as of that date, have elected the form and the starting date of the benefit, or with respect to whom the plan administrator has determined that a lump-sum distribution will be made, the plan administrator must disclose: (1) the amount and form of the participant's plan benefits payable as of the projected benefit starting date; (2) the projected benefit starting date; (3) the amount and form of benefit payable to a beneficiary upon the participant's death and the name of the beneficiary; (4) the amount and date of any increase or decrease in the benefit scheduled to occur after the proposed termination date; (5) age and form adjustment factors, in the event that benefits will be paid in form other than a lump-sum and the age at which, or form in which, the benefits will be paid differs from the normal retirement benefit; and (6) information regarding plan benefits that will be paid in a lump-sum, such as the interest rate and mortality table used to convert the lump sum, and the plan's applicable consent rules.[6]

---

[1] PBGC Reg. § 4041.24(a).

[2] PBGC Reg. § 4000.13 and PBGC Reg. § 4041(c)(1).

[3] PBGC Reg. § 4041.24(b).

[4] PBGC Reg. § 4041.24(b)(4).

[5] PBGC Reg. § 4041.24(c).

[6] PBGC Reg. § 4041.24(d).

¶ 2817

STANDARD PLAN TERMINATION: PBGC Notice of Noncompliance

If the PBGC determines that plan assets, as of the distribution date proposed in the standard termination notice, will not be sufficient to satisfy all benefit liabilities under the plan, it must issue a notice of noncompliance.[1] The PBGC has discretion as to whether to issue a notice of noncompliance when the plan administrator fails to satisfy the notice and other procedural rules applicable in a standard termination.[2]

60-day review period

The PBGC has 60 days from the date after it receives the standard termination notices to issue a notice of noncompliance.[3] If the PBGC does not issue a notice of noncompliance by the end of the 60-day review period, the plan administrator must close out the plan (see ¶ 2818).

Extension of review period. The PBGC and a plan administrator may reach a written agreement before the close of the 60-day period to extend the review period for an additional 60 days.[4] More than one extension may be executed.

Notice of noncompliance ends standard termination process

A notice of noncompliance ends the standard termination proceeding, nullifies all actions taken to terminate the plan, and renders the plan an ongoing plan.[5] Once a notice is issued, the plan administrator must take no further action to terminate the plan, except by initiation of a new termination.

Request for reconsideration. After receiving a notice of noncompliance, a plan administrator may request a reconsideration. Such a request automatically stays the effectiveness of the notice of noncompliance until the PBGC issues its decision on reconsideration.[6]

The plan administrator, upon receiving the decision of the PBGC on reconsideration affirming the notice of noncompliance, or, if earlier, upon the administrator's decision not to request termination, must notify the affected parties (other than the PBGC) in writing that the plan is not going to terminate [7]

---

[1] ERISA Sec. 4041(b)(2)(C)(i); PBGC Reg. § 4041.31(a)(1)(iv).

[2] ERISA Sec. 4041(b)(2)(C)(i)(III); PBGC Reg. § 4041.31(a)(1)(v) and 4041.31(b)(1).

[3] PBGC Reg. § 4041.26(a)(1).

[4] ERISA Sec. 4041(b)(2)(C)(ii); PBGC Reg. § 4041.26(a)(1).

[5] PBGC Reg. § 4041.31(e)(1).

[6] PBGC Reg. § 4041.31(d).

[7] PBGC Reg. § 4041.31(g).

¶ 2818

STANDARD PLAN TERMINATION: Final Distribution of Assets Under Standard Termination

If the PBGC does not issue a notice of noncompliance, the plan administrator is required to distribute all plan assets by the later of (a) 180 days following the end of the PBGC's 60-day review period or any extended period, or (b) 120 days after receipt of a favorable determination letter from the IRS regarding the plan's qualified status upon termination.[1] For the latter provision to apply, the plan administrator's request for a determination letter must have been made by the time the standard termination notice was filed.[2]

Assets must be sufficient for benefit liabilities prior to distribution

Prior to distributing plan assets incident to a close out, the plan administrator must determine that plan assets, as of the termination date, are sufficient to satisfy all benefit liabilities.[3] A participant's or beneficiary's plan benefits are determined under the plan provisions in effect on the termination date. [4]

All liabilities must be considered, including benefit payments due before the distribution date, PBGC premiums for all plan years through and including the plan year in which assets are distributed, expenses, and fees and other administrative costs. In the event plan assets are insufficient to meet all benefit liabilities, no distribution of assets may occur. The plan administrator must also promptly notify the PBGC of the insufficiency.

Distribution date is annuity starting date. The distribution date is the annuity starting date for purposes of calculating the present value of plan benefits (absent evidence of another annuity starting date). [5] This factor applies in determining the interest rate to be used in valuing a lump-sum distribution. [6]

Thus, although the minimum lump-sum value of a participant's accrued benefit is calculated using the definition of applicable interest rate and applicable mortality table based on the plan provisions reflecting the law in effect on the plan's termination date, PBGC explains that the time for determining the specific assumptions is based on the distribution date.

Application of assumptions to terminating plans. The Pension Protection Act significantly modified the interest rates and mortality tables used in calculating minimum lump-sum amounts. Generally, PPA changed the applicable interest rate under Code Sec. 417(e)(3) to the adjusted first, second, and third segment rates derived from a corporate bond yield curve, similar to the rates used to determine minimum funding requirements under PPA (see ¶ 1493D).

Effective date of new rules. The PBGC confirmed that plan provisions that incorporate changes mandated by the Pension Protection Act of 2006, with respect to the valuation of benefits, cannot take effect, for purposes of ERISA Sec. 4041, before the first plan year beginning on or after January 1, 2008. [7] However, PBGC Technical Update 07-3 did not address how the PPA 2006 changes apply to a plan that terminates after the effective date of the changes and makes a distribution in a plan year subsequent to the plan year the plan terminated (e.g., a plan that terminates in its 2008 plan year, and pays lump sums in its 2009 plan year). PBGC Technical Update 08-4 addressed such issues.

Applicable interest rate. Because the applicable phase-in percentages for years 2008-2011 apply to plan years beginning after December 31, 2007, if a plan terminates during the period 2008 through 2011, the applicable interest rate will be determined based on the applicable phase-in percentage in effect for the plan year in which the lump sum is paid (and not for the plan year in which the plan terminates).

EXAMPLE: XYZ maintains a calendar year plan that is amended in 2008 to reflect PPA 2006 minimum lump sum assumptions. The plan terminates on July 1, 2009. [8]The plan has a one-year stability period and a two-month lookback period. Accordingly, a lump sum paid in 2010 will be calculated based on the phase-in percentage for the plan year beginning in 2010 and the November 2009 rates. Under this formula, a lump sum paid in 2010 would be determined using a blended rate based on a 60 percent weighting of the November 2009 segment rates and a 40 percent weighting of the November 2009 30-year Treasury rate.

Applicable mortality table. For a plan with a termination date on or after the first day of the first plan year beginning in 2008, a lump sum would be determined based on the applicable mortality table as specified by the Secretary of Treasury on the plan's termination date, taking into account projected mortality improvements under the table through the plan year containing the distribution. [9]

The interest rate and mortality tables used in determining the present value of lump-sum distribution under post-2007 rules are discussed at ¶ 869

Failure to distribute assets nullifies termination

The failure to distribute plan assets within the stipulated time period because of an insufficiency of plan assets, or for any other reason, nullifies the termination.[10] Accordingly, the plan will be treated as ongoing. The plan administrator must notify affected parties in writing that the plan will not terminate or, if applicable, that a new NOIT will be issued.[11]

In addition, note that an employer may not recover excess assets unless the plan formally terminates in accordance with specified ERISA procedures (see ¶ 2839).

Discretionary extension of distribution deadline. A plan administrator who is otherwise unable to complete the distribution within the 180-day (or extended) period may apply to the PBGC for a discretionary extension.[12]

☐ The distribution of plan assets to missing participants is discussed at ¶ 2831.

Post-distribution certification

Following the distribution of plan assets, the plan administrator must certify to the PBGC that the participants have received all of the benefits to which they were entitled and that all assets have been properly distributed.[13] PBGC Form 501 (Post-Distribution Certification for Standard Terminations) must be filed by the plan administrator within 30 days after the distribution of plan assets is completed. If benefits are to be provided in an annuity, the plan administrator must certify that benefit liabilities have been met through the purchase of irrevocable commitments.

90-day grace period to file certification. In the event that the post-distribution certification is not filed within 30 days, the PBGC may impose a penalty of up to $1,100 per day for each day that the failure continues.[14] The 30-day deadline may not be extended.[15] However, the PBGC will assess a penalty only if the certification is filed more than 90 days after the distribution deadline (i.e., the date 180 days after the PBGC's 60-day period for review of the standard termination notice) including extensions.[16] Thus, if the distribution deadline is March 1 and the final distribution of assets is made by January 15, the PBGC will not assess a penalty if the post-distribution certification is filed by May 30 (90 days after March 1).

---

[1] PBGC Reg. § 4041.28(a)(1).

[2] PBGC Reg. § 4041.25(c).

[3] PBGC Reg. § 4041.28(b).

[4] PBGC Reg. § 4041.8(a).

[5] PBGC Reg. § 4041.28(c)(2).

[6] PBGC Technical Update 07-3, 12-3-07, at CCH PENSION PLAN GUIDE ¶ 19,975Z-16.

[7] PBGC Technical Update 07-3, 12-3-07, at CCH PENSION PLAN GUIDE ¶ 19,975Z-16.

Applicable mortality table. For a plan with a termination date on or after the first day of the first plan year beginning in 2008, a lump sum would be determined based on the applicable mortality table as specified by the Secretary of Treasury on the plan's termination date, taking into account projected mortality improvements under the table through the plan year containing the distribution.

[8] PBGC Technical Update 08-4, 12-31-08, at CCH PENSION PLAN GUIDE ¶ 19,975Z-21.

[9] *Ibid.*

[10] PBGC Reg. § 4041.31(e)(1). See also, *Jensen v. Moore Wallace North America, Inc.*, CA-6 (2007), No. 06-4388, at CCH PENSION PLAN GUIDE ¶ 24,000V (employees were not entitled to surplus assets under a plan that had been discontinued,

but had not been terminated in accord with ERISA's specified procedures and continued to pay plan benefits).

[11] PBGC Reg. § 4041.31(g).

[12] PBGC Reg. § 4041.30(a).

[13] PBGC Reg. § 4041.29(a).

[14] ERISA Sec. 4071; PBGC Reg. § 4041.6.

[15] PBGC Reg. § 4041.30(d)(2).

[16] PBGC Reg. § 4041.29(b).

¶ 2819

STANDARD PLAN TERMINATION: Annuity Requirement Under Standard Termination

When a plan is closed out, a plan administrator must distribute assets in satisfaction of plan benefits by purchasing an irrevocable commitment from an insurer or in another permitted form that fully provides for benefit liabilities under the plan.[1] The plan administrator must select the insurer from which the irrevocable commitments will be purchased in accordance with ERISA's fiduciary standards.[2] The PBGC will audit the selection of insurers for compliance with ERISA's fiduciary requirements.

Notice of annuity contract

Where plan benefits are distributed through annuity contracts, the plan administrator must provide each participant and beneficiary with a copy of the annuity contract or a certificate indicating the insurer's name and address and clearly reflecting the insurer's obligation to provide the benefit.[3] The information must be provided within 30 days after it is available.

If the contract or certificate is not provided by the date on which the post-distribution certification is required to be filed in order to avoid penalty (see ¶ 2818), the plan administrator must, no later that date, provide each participant and beneficiary with written notice stating that the obligation to provide plan benefits has been transferred to the insurer.[4]

[1] ERISA Sec. 4041(b)(3); PBGC Reg. § 4041.28(c). Note, the Ninth Circuit has ruled that the purchase of irrevocable commitments from an insurer is not a requirement under ERISA, but that alternative methods of termination are permitted as long as they are sufficient to cover plan liabilities. In addition, the court explained that a merger into a multiemployer plan is a permissible means of terminating a plan under ERISA. Accordingly, an employer breached its fi-

duciary duties to plan participants when it elected to purchase an annuity to make a final distribution terminating a plan, rather than adequately consider a union proposal to merge the plan into an existing multiemployer plan. (*Beck v International Union*, CA-9 (2005), Nos. 03-15303 and 03-15331, at CCH PENSION PLAN GUIDE ¶ 23,933Q.)

[2] PBGC Reg. § 4041.28(c)(1).

[3] PBGC Reg. § 4041.28(d)(1).

[4] PBGC Reg. § 4041.28(d)(2).

¶ 2820

DISTRESS TERMINATION: General Requirements for Distress Termination

Single-employer defined benefit plans that do not qualify for a standard termination may be voluntarily terminated through a distress termination if the contributing plan sponsor and each member of its controlled group satisfy one of the following criteria.[1]

1. ***Liquidation in bankruptcy.*** The liquidation petition must have been filed by (or against the employer) as of the proposed termination date.[2]

2. ***Reorganization in bankruptcy or insolvency proceeding.*** The reorganization petition must have been filed by (or against the employer) as of the proposed date of termination.[3] The employer must notify the PBGC of any request to the bankruptcy court (or other appropriate court) for approval of the plan termination by concurrently filing with the PBGC a copy of the motion requesting court approval.[4] In addition, the bankruptcy court (or other appropriate court) must determine that, unless the plan is terminated, the employer will be unable to pay all its debts pursuant to a reorganization plan and will be unable to continue in business outside the reorganization process. The court must also approve the plan termination.[5]

3. ***Inability to continue in business.*** An employer must demonstrate that, absent a distress termination, it will be unable to pay its debts when due and to continue in business.[6]

4. ***Unreasonably burdensome pension costs.*** An employer must establish that its costs of providing pension coverage have become unreasonably burdensome solely as a result of declining covered employment under all single-employer plans for which that employer is a contributing sponsor.[7]

Note, plans that terminate in a distress or involuntary termination after 2005 and before 2010 are subject to a termination premium (see ¶ 2809).

---

[1] ERISA Sec. 4041(c)(1) and 4041(c)(2)(B); PBGC Reg. § 4041.41(a)(3).

[2] ERISA Sec. 4041(c)(2)(B)(i); PBGC Reg. § 4041.41(c)(1).

[3] PBGC Reg. § 4041.41(c)(2).

[4] *Ibid.*

[5] PBGC Reg. § 4041.41(c)(2)(iv). See *In re: Kaiser Aluminum Corp.*, CA-3 (2006), 456 F. 3d 328, at

CCH Pension Plan Guide ¶ 23,996X (Bankruptcy Court, in determining whether a company in Chapter 11 bankruptcy may terminate multiple pension plans under the reorganization test, must apply the reorganization test to all of the company's plans in the aggregate, rather than on a plan-by-plan basis).

[6] PBGC Reg. § 4041.41(c)(3).

[7] PBGC Reg. § 4041.41(c)(4).

¶ 2821

DISTRESS TERMINATION: Procedural Requirements for Distress Termination

A single-employer plan may be terminated in a distress termination only if:[1]

1. the plan administrator provides a notice of intent to terminate (NOIT) to each affected party and the PBGC at least 60 days and no more than 90 days before the proposed termination date (see ¶ 2822);

2. the plan administrator files a distress termination notice with the PBGC no later than 120 days after the proposed termination date (see ¶ 2823); and

3. the PBGC determines that the contributing sponsor and each member of its controlled group has met at least one of the necessary distress criteria (see ¶ 2820).

Failure to meet requirements ends termination

If the PBGC determines that all of the requirements of a distress termination have not been met, any actions taken to effect the termination will be null and void and the plan will be treated as an ongoing plan.[2] Each contributing sponsor or plan administrator of a plan terminated in a distress termination (or a standard termination) must maintain all records necessary to demonstrate compliance with the governing rules of ERISA Sec. 4041 for 6 years after the post-distribution certification has been filed with the PBGC.[3] Electronic media may be used to maintain and retain the required records.[4]

Notice required when asset are adequate to provide guaranteed benefits

If the PBGC determines that the plan has sufficient assets to provide at least guaranteed benefits, it will issue a distribution notice. In that case, the plan administrator must: (1) issue a notice of benefit distribution to each participant/ beneficiary within 60 days after receiving the distribution notice; (2) file a certification with the PBGC (within 15 days after issuance of the notices is completed) that the notices of benefit distribution were issued; (3) distribute plan assets by the later of the date on which the issuance of the notices of benefit distribution is completed, or 120 days after receipt of a favorable determination letter from the IRS; and (4) file a post-distribution certification with the PBGC within 30 days after the distribution of assets is completed.[5]

---

[1] ERISA Sec. 4041(c)(1); PBGC Reg. § 4041.41(a).

[2] PBGC Reg. §§ 4041.41(b)(1) and 4041.46(c)(1).

[3] PBGC Reg. § 4041.5.

[4] PBGC Reg. § 4041.5(a)(3).

[5] PBGC Reg. § 4141.47(c).

¶ 2822
DISTRESS TERMINATION: Notice of Intent to Terminate

At least 60 days, but no more than 90 days, before the proposed termination date, the plan administrator must issue a written notice of intent to terminate (NOIT) to all "affected parties" (i.e. plan participants, beneficiaries, employee organizations representing participants and the PBGC). [1] The NOIT to all affected parties other than the PBGC is to be issued at or before the time the administrator files the notice with the PBGC.

The notice to the PBGC must be filed on Form 600 (Distress Termination Notice of Intent to Terminate). [2] There is no prescribed form for the NOIT that must be issued to other affected parties. However, the plan administrator must include information specified by the PBGC in the NOIT provided to parties other than the PBGC, including identifying information (e.g., EIN of the contributing plan sponsor and the plan number), a statement as to whether plan assets are sufficient to pay all guaranteed benefits, a description of the benefits guaranteed by the PBGC, and a statement (if applicable) that benefits may be subject to reduction. [3]

Filing rules. The required NOIT may be provided by hand, mail, or commercial delivery service or by electronic media. [4] The method of issuance must be calculated to ensure actual receipt of the material. Thus, posting of a NOIT at an employee work site is not a permissible method of delivery. [5] In addition, issuances provided by electronic media must satisfy the safe harbor conditions specified in PBGC Reg. § 4000.14 (see CCH PENSION PLAN GUIDE¶ 6564).

Failure to provide NOIT nullifies proposed termination

An administrator's failure to issue the NOIT within the prescribed time period will nullify the proposed termination. [6] In addition, the PBGC may assess a penalty of up to $1,100 per day for each day that the failure continues. [7]

CCH POINTER: ***Enhanced disclosure of termination information.*** Plan administrators that have filed a NOIT provide affected parties with any information provided to the PBGC no later than 15 days after receipt of a request from an affected party for the information or the provision of new information to the PBGC relating to a previous request. [8]

Note, similar requirements apply to plan sponsors and administrators under PBGC-initiated terminations (see ¶ 2834).

Disclose information provided to PBGC after NOIT. The plan sponsor or administrator must provide an affected party with any information under ERISA Sec. 4041(c)(2)(A) (or the regulations under ERISA Sec.4041(a)(2)) that was required to be submitted to the PBGC pursuant to the termination. [9] Thus, the information to be disclosed to an affected party includes information that is required to be disclosed to the PBGC at the time the written notice of intent to terminate the plan is given, as well as information that must be disclosed to the PBGC thereafter.

Procedures for disclosing termination information

PBGC rules further specify that the request for information: be submitted in writing to the plan administrator; provide the name of the plan and state that the request is for information submitted to the PBGC with respect to applications for distress termination; furnish the name of the person making the information request and indicate the person's relationship to the plan (e.g., plan participant), stating that the relationship qualifies the person as an affected party under PBGC Reg. 4001.2; and be signed by the person making the request [10]

Confidentiality requirements. A plan administrator may not, under ERISA Sec. 4041(c)(2)(D), provide information pursuant to a request from an affected party in a form that includes any information that may directly or indirectly be associated with, or otherwise identify, an individual participant or beneficiary. In addition, a court may limit disclosure of confidential information (as described under the Freedom of Information Act) to any authorized representative of the participants or beneficiaries that agrees to ensure the confidentiality of such information. The final rules stress that , with respect to confidential information, the plan administrator is not only not required to provide information that may directly or indirectly identify an individual plan participant or beneficiary, but is prohibited from furnishing such information.[11]

---

[1] ERISA Secs. 4001(a)(21) and 4041(c)(2); PBGC Reg. § 4041.43(a).

[2] PBGC Reg. § 4041.43(a)(4).

[3] PBGC Reg. § 4041.43(b).

[4] PBGC Reg. § 4000.3.

[5] PBGC Reg. § 4000.13(a).

[6] PBGC Reg. § 4041.44(c) and PBGC Reg. § 4041.3(b).

[7] PBGC Reg. § 4041.6.

[8] ERISA Sec. 4041(c)(2)(D), as added by P.L. 109-280 (Pension Protection Act of 2006), Act Sec. 506(a)(1).

[9] ERISA Sec. 4041(c)(2)(D)(i), as amended by P.L. 110-458 (Worker, Retiree, and Employer Recovery Act of 2008), Act Sec. 105(e)(1).

[10] PBGC Reg. § 4041.51(a)(2).

[11] PBGC Reg. § 4041.51(b)(5)(i).

¶ 2823

DISTRESS TERMINATION: Distress Termination Notice

Within 120 days after the proposed termination date (including extensions), the plan administrator must file with the PBGC, Form 601 (Distress Termination Notice, Single-Employer Plan Termination) with Schedule EA-D (Distress Termination Enrolled Actuary Certification).[1]

Unless the enrolled actuary certifies that the plan is sufficient for guaranteed benefits or for benefit liabilities, the participant and benefit information required by Form 601 must be filed with the PBGC by the later of the 120th day after the proposed termination date, or 30 days after receipt of the PBGC's determination that the distress termination requirements have been satisfied.[2] The plan administrator's failure to provide the required information will allow the PBGC to void the distress termination.[3]

---

[1] PBGC Reg. § 4041.45(a). PBGC Form 601 is reproduced at CCH PENSION PLAN GUIDE ¶ 10,816.

[2] PBGC Reg. § 4041.45(b)(1).

[3] PBGC Reg. § 4041.45(b)(3).

¶ 2824

DISTRESS TERMINATION: PBGC Determination of Sufficiency of Plan Assets

If the PBGC determines that the plan is sufficient for guaranteed benefits, but not for benefit liabilities, or is sufficient for benefit liabilities, it will issue a notice allowing the plan administrator to: (1) issue notices of benefit distribution (see ¶ 2825); (2) close out the plan (see ¶ 2830); and (3) file a timely post-distribution certification with the PBGC (see ¶ 2825).[1]

Insufficiency for guaranteed benefits

If the PBGC is unable to determine that a plan's assets are sufficient to cover guaranteed benefits, it will issue a "notice of inability to determine sufficiency" and advise the plan administrator that the plan will continue to be administered under the restrictions imposed on plans terminating under a distress termination (see ¶ 2827). The termination will be completed under the provisions permitting the PBGC to involuntarily terminate a plan.[2]

---

[1] PBGC Reg. § 4041.47(c).

[2] PBGC Reg. § 4041.47(b).

¶ 2825

DISTRESS TERMINATION: Notice of Benefit Distribution

After receiving a distribution notice from the PBGC, the plan administrator must issue a notice of benefit distribution to each affected party (except the PBGC and any employee organization) within 60 days.[1] Within 15 days after completion of the notice of benefit distribution, the plan administrator is required to file with the PBGC a certification that the notices were properly issued.[2]

Notice of annuity information

The notice of benefit distribution must generally contain the information discussed at ¶ 2816 applicable to plans undergoing a standard termination.[3] In addition, unless the plan distributes Title IV benefits in the form of a nonconsensual lump-sum, the plan administrator must provide a notice of annuity information to each affected party, other than the PBGC and an affected party whose Title IV benefits will be distributed in the form of a nonconsensual lump-sum.[4]

The notice must:[5]

1. disclose the name and address of the insurer or insurers from whom or from among whom the annuity contracts will be purchased;[6]

2. inform affected parties that, if the plan administrator subsequently decides to select a different insurer, the affected parties will receive a supplemental notice no later than 45 days from the distribution date;[7]

3. contain information that may not have been previously provided regarding state guaranty coverage (see ¶ 2813);[8] and

4. include a statement that the PBGC will no longer guarantee a participant's Title IV benefits once plan assets have been distributed, either by the purchase of annuity contracts or by an alternative form of distribution authorized by the plan.[9]

The notice of annuity information must be issued to each affected party within 45 days before the party's distribution date.[10]

---

[1] PBGC Reg. § 4041.48(a)(1).

[2] PBGC Reg. § 4041.48(b).

[3] PBGC Reg. §§ 4041.24(b)—(e) and 4041.48(a).

[4] PBGC Reg. § 4041.48(c)(1).

[5] PBGC Reg. § 4041.48(c)(4).

[6] PBGC Reg. § 4041.27(b)(1).

[7] PBGC Reg. § 4041.27(b)(2).

[8] PBGC Reg. § 4041.27(b)(3).

[9] PBGC Reg. § 4041.23(b)(9).

[10] PBGC Reg. § 4041.27(d)(1) and § 4041.48(c)(5).

¶ 2826

DISTRESS TERMINATION: Verification of Plan Sufficiency by Plan Administrator

Before distributing plan assets, the plan administrator must verify that the assets are sufficient to provide for the benefit liabilities or guaranteed benefits.[1]

Subsequent insufficiency for guaranteed benefits

If the plan administrator finds that a plan is no longer sufficient for guaranteed benefits, the plan administrator must promptly notify the PBGC in writing and may take no further action to implement the plan termination pending a PBGC determination.[2]

If the PBGC agrees that the plan is insufficient for guaranteed benefits, the distribution notice becomes void and the PBGC will require the plan administrator to submit a new valuation certified by an enrolled actuary.[3] Alternatively, if the PBGC does not agree that the plan is insufficient to pay guaranteed benefits, it will notify the plan administrator in writing and the distribution notice will remain in effect.[4]

Insufficient for benefit liabilities

In the event that the plan administrator determines that the plan is sufficient for guaranteed benefits, but is no longer sufficient for benefit liabilities, the PBGC must be notified, but the plan administrator must continue with the distribution of assets.[5]

Subsequent PBGC finding that plan is insufficient for guaranteed benefits

If the PBGC finds on its own initiative that the plan is insufficient for guaranteed benefits, the distribution notice becomes void.[6] The plan administrator will then be required to submit a new valuation certified by an enrolled actuary.

[1] PBGC Reg. § 4041.49(a).

[2] PBGC Reg. § 4041.49(b).

[3] PBGC Reg. § 4041.49(b)(1).

[4] PBGC Reg. § 4041.49(b)(2).

[5] PBGC Reg. § 4041.49(c).

[6] PBGC Reg. § 4041.49(d).

¶ 2827

DISTRESS TERMINATION: Plan Administration During Distress Period

While the termination proceedings are pending, the plan administrator must continue to carry out normal operations of the plan, including placing participants in pay status, collecting contributions due the plan, and investing plan assets.[1]

From the date that plan administrator first issues a NOIT, however, loans may not be made to plan participants.[2] In addition, from the date the plan administrator first issues a NOIT until the plan administrator is authorized to distribute plan assets, the plan administrator may not:

1. distribute assets or take any other actions to carry out the proposed distress termination;

2. pay benefits attributable to employer contributions (except death benefits) in any form other than as an annuity; or

3. purchase irrevocable commitments to provide benefits from an insurer.[3]

Reduced benefit levels

Beginning on the proposed termination date, the plan administrator is required to reduce benefit levels to no more than the accrued benefit payable at normal retirement age or the maximum guaranteeable benefit (see ¶ 2828).[4]

[1] ERISA Sec. 4041(c)(3)(D); PBGC Reg. § 4041.42(a).

[2] PBGC Reg. § 4041.42(b).

[3] *Ibid.*

[4] PBGC Reg. § 4022.61(b) and (c) and § 4041.42(c).

¶ 2828

DISTRESS TERMINATION: Required Reduction of Benefits

Benefit payments made by plan administrators of single-employer plans ending in distress terminations will be reduced if the portion of the monthly benefit payable to a participant exceeds the participant's accrued benefit payable at normal retirement age or the maximum guaranteeable benefit.[1] A plan administrator must include in the Notice of Intent to Terminate in a distress termination a statement that benefit reductions may be required.[2]

Four-step procedure

The reduction of benefits is part of a four-step benefit limitation and estimation procedure applicable to plans ending in a distress termination.

Step 1. Reduce benefits to the amount accrued for retirement at normal retirement age.[3]

Step 2. Reduce the monthly benefit that exceeds the maximum guaranteeable benefit.[4]

Step 3. Estimate the phase-in of PBGC guaranteed benefit increases resulting from plan amendments, scheduled increases, or the establishment of a new plan.[5]

Step 4. Estimate the Title IV benefits of participants whose benefit and plan asset levels are treated as assets sufficient to pay the non-guaranteed portion of benefits allocated to priority categories 3 and 4 under ERISA Sec. 4044.[6] The PBGC will pay benefits in excess of guaranteed levels if those benefits are funded by plan assets on the date of plan termination.

[1] PBGC Reg. § 4022.61.
[2] PBGC Reg. § 4041.43(b)(9).
[3] PBGC Reg. § 4022.61(b).
[4] PBGC Reg. § 4022.61(c).
[5] PBGC Reg. § 4022.62.
[6] PBGC Reg. § 4022.63(b).

¶ 2830

DISTRESS TERMINATION: Closeout of Plan in a Distress Termination

If the plan administrator receives a distribution notice from the PBGC and neither the plan administrator nor the PBGC make a finding of insufficiency (see ¶ 2826), the plan administrator must distribute the plan assets by the later of (1) the day on which the plan administrator completes the issuance of the notices of benefit distribution (see ¶ 2825); or (2) 120 days after receipt of a favorable determination letter from the IRS.[1]

Request for IRS determination letter

In order to qualify for the later distribution deadline, the plan administrator must submit to the IRS a valid request for a determination of the plan's qualification status upon termination.[2] The request for the determination letter must be made by the day on which the plan administrator completes the issuance of the notices of benefit distribution.

Annuity requirement

As is the case with a standard termination, the plan administrator in a distress termination must distribute plan assets through the purchase of irrevocable commitments from an insurer, or in another permitted form.[3]

Notice of annuity contract

Where benefit liabilities are being distributed through annuity contracts, the plan administrator must provide each participant and beneficiary with a copy of the annuity contract or certificate within 30 days after it is available.[4] This copy must indicate the insurer's name and address and clearly reflect the insurer's obligation to provide the benefit.

If a copy of the annuity contract or certificate is not provided to the participant or beneficiary by the date on which the post-distribution certification (see below) is required to be filed, the plan administrator must issue a notice informing participants and beneficiaries that the obligation for providing Title IV benefits has been transferred to the insurer.[5] In addition, the notice must include: the name and address of the insurer; the name, address, and telephone number of the person designated by the insurer to answer questions regarding the annuity; and a statement that the participant or beneficiary will receive from the plan administrator or the insurer a copy of the annuity contact or a certification showing the insurer's name and address and reflecting the insurer's obligation to provide the participant's or beneficiary's Title IV benefits.[6] Generally, these notice requirements are the same as those that apply in a standard termination.

Post-distribution certification

Within 30 days after the distribution of plan assets is completed, the plan administrator must file a post-distribution certification (PBGC Form 602 (Post Distribution Certification For Distress Termination)).[7]

A penalty for the late filing of a post-distribution certification will be assessed only if the certification is filed more than 90 days after the deadline for distributing plan assets described above.[8]

---

[1] PBGC Reg. § 4041.28(a) and § 4041.50.

[2] PBGC Reg. § 4041.48(d) and § 4041.50(c).

[3] PBGC Reg. § 4041.28(c) and § 4041.50.

[4] PBGC Reg. § 4041.28(d) and § 4041.50.

[5] PBGC Reg. § 4041.28(d)(2) and § 4041.50.

[6] *Ibid.*

[7] PBGC Reg. § 4041.29 and § 4041.50.

[8] PBGC Reg. § 4041.29(b).

¶ 2831

DISTRESS TERMINATION: Missing Participant Program

ERISA sets forth specific time limits as to when distributions from a terminating defined benefit plan must be made. However, a problem arises when a participant cannot be located.

The administrator of a terminating single-employer defined benefit plan may distribute benefits for missing participants only by:

    1. purchasing an annuity from an insurer (that satisfies the requirements discussed at ¶ 2819 and 2830), or

2. paying a "designated benefit" to the PBGC, which will then assume responsibility for locating the missing participants and paying benefits to individuals who are located.[1]

CCH POINTER: *PBGC Missing Participant Program extended to 401(k) plans*. The PBGC Missing Participant Program does not currently apply to 401(k) plans or other defined contribution plans. However, the Pension Protection Act of 2006 authorized (but did not require) the administrators of 401(k) plans to elect, to transfer missing participant's benefit to the PBGC upon plan termination.[2] The option is available to plans that, at the time assets are to be distributed upon termination: (1) have missing participants and (2) have not provided for the transfer of assets to pay the benefits of all missing participants to another retirement plan.[3]

In the event benefits of a missing participant are transferred, the PBGC, upon locating the participant or beneficiary, will pay the amount transferred in a lump-sum (plus interest), or such other form as will be specified by the PBGC. [4]

Missing Participant Program limited to qualified plans. The Worker, Retiree, and Employer Recovery Act of 2008 clarifies that the Missing Participant Program is available only to plans that have at no time provided for employer contributions. In addition, the program is limited to qualified plans.[5]

Diligent search for missing participants

A plan administrator must make a "diligent search" for each missing participant, including those for whom the plan administrator purchases an annuity, before information about the missing participant or payment is submitted to the PBGC.[6] The diligent search may not begin more than six months before the Notice of Intent to Terminate is issued.[7] In order to perform a diligent search, the plan administrator must question beneficiaries of the missing participant whose names and addresses are known to the administrator and must utilize a commercial locator service.[8] The cost of the commercial locator service may not be charged to the missing participant or used to reduce the participant's benefits.[9]

CCH POINTER: Participants who refuse to sign or return an election form are not treated as "missing participants." With respect to such a non-responsive participant, the plan administrator must purchase an irrevocable commitment from an insurer which preserves all of the participant's benefit options.[10]

Participant's designated benefit

The amount of a missing participant's designated benefit varies in accord with whether the participant was to receive a lump sum payment as of the deemed distribution date.[11] Generally, the designated benefit is the greater of the lump sum (under plan assumptions) or the value of the annuity (under the PBGC's missing participant assumptions).

¶2831

Missing participant forms

Plan administrators wishing to participate in the Missing Participant Program must complete PBGC Forms 501 and 602 and Schedule MP.[12]

☐ The rules governing the missing participant program (including the assumptions used in calculating a designated benefit, filing deadlines, the payment of lump-sum benefits, and payments to beneficiaries of missing participants) are discussed in detail at CCH PENSION PLAN GUIDE ¶ 6800.

---

[1] ERISA Sec. 4050; PBGC Reg. § 4050.3.

[2] ERISA Sec. 4050(d)(1), as added by P.L. 109-280 (Pension Protection Act of 2006), Act Sec. 410(a).

[3] ERISA § 4050(d)(4)(B), as added by P.L. 109-280 (Pension Protection Act of 2006), Act Sec. 410(a).

[4] ERISA § 4050(d)(3), as added by P.L. 109-280 (Pension Protection Act of 2006), Act Sec. 410(a).

[5] ERISA § 4050(d)(4)(A), as amended by P.L. 110-458 (Worker, Retiree, and Employer Recovery Act of 2008), Act Sec. 104(e).

[6] PBGC Reg. § 4050.4(a).

[7] PBGC Reg. § 4050.4(b)(1).

[8] PBGC Reg. § 4050.4(b)(2).

[9] PBGC Reg. § 4050.4(b)(3).

[10] "Employee Plan News," Volume 5, Spring 2005.

[11] PBGC Reg. § 4050.5.

[12] PBGC Reg. § 4050.2.

¶ 2833

INVOLUNTARY TERMINATION BY PBGC: PBGC Termination Proceedings

The PBGC may institute termination proceedings in the United States District Court for the district in which the plan administrator resides or does business, or in which any of the plan's trust property is located.[1] The PBGC may bring an action to terminate if:[2]

1. the plan has not met the minimum funding standards;
2. the plan sponsor is deficient in paying the tax for failure to meet the minimum funding standards;
3. the plan will not be able to pay benefits when due;
4. a distribution exceeding $10,000 that is a reportable event under ERISA (¶ 2810) is made to a substantial owner; or
5. the loss to the PBGC will increase unreasonably if the plan is not terminated.

As soon as practicable, the PBGC is required to institute court proceedings to terminate a single-employer plan whenever it determines that the plan does not have assets available to pay benefits that are currently due under the plan.[3]

Required notice to plan and affected parties

The PBGC must provide notice to the plan administrator of its decision to institute involuntary plan termination proceedings.[4] Upon receiving the notice of involuntary plan termination from the PBGC, the plan sponsor or administrator must (generally effective for plan terminations with respect to which an ERISA Sec. 4042 notice of determination occurred after August 17, 2006) also provide any affected party with information furnished to the PBGC in connection with the plan termination.[5]

The information must be provided to the affected party not later than 15 days after receipt of a request from the affected party for such information or the provision of any new information to the PBGC relating to a previous request by an affected party.[6] In addition, the PBGC is required, within 15 days, to provide a copy of the administrative record, including the trusteeship decision record in connection with a plan termination.

Affected party. An "affected party" is defined as each plan participant, beneficiary of a deceased participant, alternate payees under anapplicable qualified domestic relations order (QDRO), employee organizations that represent any group of participants, and the PBGC [7]

Confidentiality requirements. The plan sponsor and administrator must not provide information pursuant to a request from an affected party in a form that includes any information that may directly or indirectly be associated with, or otherwise identify, an individual participant or beneficiary. [8] In addition, a court may limit disclosure of confidential information (as described under the Freedom of Information Act) to authorized representatives of the participants or beneficiaries that agree to ensure the confidentiality of such information.

> **CCH POINTER:** The Worker, Retiree, and Employer Recovery Act of 2008 extends to the PBGC to the requirement to provide information to affected parties. In addition, the Act applies the confidentiality rules that prohibit plan sponsors or administrators from disclosing the information in a manner that identifies an individual participant or beneficiary to the PBGC [9]

Procedures for disclosing termination information. Final regulations issued by PBGC in November 2008, effective for information requests made on or after 12-18-08, further clarify the procedures for the disclosure of information in a termination initiated by the PBGC. [10]

Under the final regulations, an affected party may, beginning on the third business day after the PBGC has issued a Notice of Determination that a plan should be terminated, submit the request to the plan sponsor and/or the plan administrator for information that was submitted to the PBGC with respect to the termination. [11] Note, an affected party may request termination information only after the plan administrator has received the Notice of Determination.

The request must be in writing; state the name of the plan and that the request is for termination information submitted to the PBGC; name the person requesting the information, stating the person's relationship to the plan (e.g., participant) and that the relationship qualifies the prison as an affected party. [12]

The plan administrator or plan sponsor must provide the requested information no later the 15th business day after receipt of the request.[13] In addition, the plan administrator or plan sponsor must provide information furnished to the PBGC in connection with the termination to any affected party that has previously made a request, no later than the 15th business day after the information is submitted to the PBGC. [14]

¶2833

With respect to confidential information, the plan administrator and plan sponsor are prohibited from providing information that may, directly or indirectly, identify an individual participant or beneficiary. [15] In addition, a plan administrator or sponsor may seek a court order, pursuant to which information that would be confidential under the Freedom of Information Act will be disclosed only to authorized representatives that agree to ensure the confidentiality of the information, and will not be disclosed to other affected parties.[16]

Reasonable fees may be assessed. The plan administrator or plan sponsor may assess a "reasonable" fee for information that is provided in other than an electronic format. [17] However, the PBGC has not established a fee schedule, nor has it prescribed a minimum fee.

Disclosure of administrative record by PBGC

An affected party may submit a request to the PBGC, beginning on the third business day after the PBGC has issued the Notice of Determination, for the administrative record of the PBGC's determination that the plan should be terminated. The written request, identifying the plan and person making the request, and signed by the person requesting the information, must be sent to the PBGC's Disclosure Officer. [18]

The PBGC, upon request of the Administrative Record Request, must "promptly" (i.e., no later than the second business day after receipt of the request) (a)notify the plan administrator and the plan sponsor that it has received the request and (b) state the date by which it will provide the information to the affected party. [19] The PBGC must send the administrative record to the affected party submitting the request no later than 15 business day after receipt of the request.[20] Finally, the information must be provided pursuant to measures that are calculated to ensure actual receipt of the material by the intended recipient. [21]

Confidentiality protections. The PBGC may not disclose any portion of the administrative record that is subjec to prohibted disclosure under the Privacy Act. [22] In addition, the plan administrator and or plan sponsor may seek a court order pursuant to which portions of the administrative record that contain information that is confidential under the Freedom of Information Act will only be disclosed to authorized representatives that agree to ensure the confidentiality of the information. In the event the PBGC receives the court order before the 15th business day after it has received the Administrative Record Request, it may disclose only the portion of the administrative record containing confidential information as authorized by the order.[23]

The PBGC will interpret the above provision as requiring it to disclose any part of the administrative record that contains confidential information (including trade secrets), except as limited by court order. [24]

Note, further, the PBGC is not authorized, in lieu of a court order, to rely on a confidentiality agreement between private parties, in determining its obligations to persons who are not parties to the agreement.

¶2833

The valuation of assets in a terminating plan are discussed at ¶ 2838.

[1] ERISA Sec. 4042(g).

[2] ERISA Sec. 4042(a).

[3] *Ibid.*

[4] ERISA Sec. 4042(c).

[5] ERISA Sec. 4042(c)(3)(A), as added by P.L. 109-208 (Pension Protection Act of 2006), Act Secs. 506(b)(1)(C) and 506(c).

[6] ERISA Sec. 4042(c)(3)(B), as added by P.L. 109-208 (Pension Protection Act of 2006), Act Sec. 506(b)(1)(C).

[7] ERISA Sec. 4001(a)(21); PBGC Reg. § 4001.2

[8] ERISA Sec.4042(c)(3)(C), as added by P.L. 109-280 (Pension Protection Act of 2006), Act Sec. 506(b)(1)(C).

[9] ERISA Sec. 4042(c)(3)(C)(i), as amended by P.L. 110-458 (Worker, Retiree, and Employer Recovery Act of 2008), Act Sec. 105(e)(2)..

[10] PBGC Reg. § 4042.1—4042.5.

[11] PBGC Reg. § 4042.4(a)(1).

[12] PBGC Reg. § 4042.4(a)(2).

[13] PBGC Reg. § 4042.4(b)(1).

[14] PBGC Reg. § 4042.4(b)(2).

[15] PBGC Reg. § 4042.4(b)(3)(i).

[16] PBGC Reg. § 4042.4(b)(3)(ii).

[17] PBGC Reg. § 4042.4(b)(4).

[18] PBGC Reg. § 4042.5(a).

[19] PBGC Reg. § 4042.5(b)(1).

[20] PBGC Reg. § 4042.5(b)(3).

[21] PBGC Reg. § 4042.5(b)(4).

[22] PBGC Reg. § 4042.5(b)(2).

[23] PBGC Reg. § 4042.5(b)(2)(iii).

[24] Preamble to PBGC Reg. § 4042.5.

¶ 2834

INVOLUNTARY TERMINATION BY PBGC: Powers and Duties of Trustees

The PBGC may institute termination proceedings if: the plan has not met its minimum funding obligations, the plan sponsor is deficient in paying the tax assessed for failure to meet the minimum funding standards, the plan will not be able to pay benefits when due, or the plan has made a distribution exceeding $10,000 to a substantial owner. In addition the PBGC may bring termination proceedings if the failure to terminate the plan will unreasonably increase the potential loss to the PBGC. [1]

Once the PBGC has instituted proceedings to terminate a plan, it may, after notifying the plan, apply to the appropriate District Court for the appointment of a trustee to administer the plan pending the issuance of a court decree to terminate the plan.[2] The court may then appoint a trustee, subject to the plan administrator's consent.

Powers of trustee

A trustee that has been appointed in connection with an involuntary plan termination may:[3] perform any act authorized by the plan or by Title IV of ERISA which may be performed by the plan administrator or any trustee of the plan; require the transfer of part or all of the plan's assets and records to himself as trustee; invest any assets of the plan which the trustee holds in accordance with the plan's provisions, PBGC regulations, and applicable rules of law; limit payment of the plan's benefits to basic benefits or continue payment of some or all of the benefits which were being paid prior to his appointment; in the case of a multiemployer plan, reduce benefits or suspend benefit payments under the plan, give appropriate notices, amend the plan, and perform other acts required or authorized by the plan sponsor or administrator of the multiemployer plan; execute any other acts deemed necessary to continue the plan's operation without increasing the potential liability of the PBGC, as allowed under the plan; and require the plan sponsor, the plan administrator, any contributing or withdrawn employer, and any employee organization representing plan participants to furnish any information on the plan that the trustee may reasonably need in order to administer the plan.

PBGC subject to fiduciary rules

The PBGC is subject to ERISA's fiduciary rules when it serves as the trustee of a terminated plan. Accordingly, the PBGC was subject to suit, as a trustee, for breaches of fiduciary duty that allegedly occurred: (1) when it failed to timely issue final benefits determinations to participants in a terminated plan[4] and (2) incident to its calculation of guaranteed benefits.[5]

Notice to interested parties

The appointed trustee must give notice as soon as practicable to interested parties of the initiation of proceedings to determine whether a plan should be terminated or to terminate the plan.[6]

The notice requirement does not apply, however, if the PBGC and the plan administrator have agreed to terminate the plan.[7]

[1] ERISA Sec.4042(a).

[2] ERISA Sec. 4042(b)(1).

[3] ERISA Sec. 4042(d)(1)(A).

[4] *Pineiro v. PBGC*, DC NY (1997), No. 96 Civ. 7392 (LAP).

[5] *Pineiro v. PBGC*, DC NY (1999), No. 96 Civ. 7392, aff'd on rehearing DC NY (2000).

[6] ERISA Sec. 4042(d)(2).

[7] *Jones & Laughlin Hourly Pension Plan v. LTV Corp.*, CA-2 (1987), Nos. 87-6100 and 87-6102.

¶ 2835

RESTORATION OF PLANS: Restoration of Terminated Plans

The PBGC is empowered to restore a plan that has terminated in a standard, distress, or PBGC-instituted termination to its pre-termination status. In such a situation, control of part or all of remaining assets and liabilities of the plan may be transferred to the employer or to the plan administrator.[1]

Restoration payment schedule

Whenever the PBGC issues a plan restoration order under ERISA, it will provide the plan sponsor with a restoration repayment schedule that will set forth a schedule of payments (for not more than 30 years) sufficient to amortize the initial restoration amortization base.[2] This amortization base consists of the unfunded liability of the plan at the valuation date for the plan year in which the initial post-restoration valuation date falls, based upon the assets and liabilities returned by the PBGC. The amortization base replaces all other amortization bases that previously existed for the plan.

Restoration funding method

The restoration of a terminated plan retroactively reinstates benefit accruals under the plan because ERISA requires the plan to be restored to pre-termination status.[3] In addition, the funding standard account (see ¶ 1415) must be reestablished and maintained for all subsequent plan years. However, because the plan will have been underfunded upon termination and because the plan sponsor will generally not have made any contributions to the plan while it was in terminated status, the plan will be even more underfunded upon restoration. Accordingly, a "restoration funding method" *must* be used by all plans that have been or are being terminated and restored under ERISA.[4] The restoration method provides for the funding of a restored plan under a "restoration payment schedule order" issued by the PBGC that specifies the timing and amount of contributions required to amortize plan liabilities that arise prior to the plan's first valuation date after restoration. The restoration method must be used by a plan until the initial amortization base has been fully restored.[5]

☐ The restoration funding method is discussed further at ¶ 1445.

---

[1] ERISA Sec. 4047.

[2] PBGC Reg. § 4047.1(a) and (b).

[3] ERISA Sec. 4047.

[4] IRS Reg. § 1.412(c)(1)-3.

[5] IRS Reg. § 1.412(c)(1)-3(f).

¶ 2836

TERMINATION DATE: Plan Termination Date

The date on which a plan terminates determines the benefits guaranteed by the PBGC and the employer's liability to the PBGC for plan underfunding. Different termination dates apply to single-employer plans depending upon whether the termination is a standard, distress, or involuntary termination.

Standard termination

For a plan terminated in a standard termination, the termination date is the date specified in the notice of intent to terminate.[1]

Distress termination

For a plan terminated in a distress termination, the termination date is the date established by the plan administrator and agreed to by the PBGC.[2]

Involuntary termination

When a plan terminates as a result of an involuntary termination by the PBGC, the termination date is the date established by the PBGC and agreed to by the plan administrator.[3]

Note: The use of the bankruptcy filing date of the plan sponsor as the termination date for purposes of determining guaranteed benefits is discussed at ¶ 2811.

Court-ordered termination date

In the event that the plan administrator and the PBGC cannot reach an agreement on the termination date of a plan terminating in a distress or involuntary termination, a court will impose a termination date.[4]

---

[1] ERISA Sec. 4048(a)(1).   [3] ERISA Sec. 4048(a)(3).

[2] ERISA Sec. 4048(a)(2).   [4] ERISA Sec. 4048(a)(4).

¶ 2838

ASSET ALLOCATION RULES: Allocation of Assets Upon Plan Termination

Plan participants may receive more than their guaranteed benefits (see ¶ 2811) from the PBGC, depending on the amount of plan assets and whether the benefits are entitled to priority under the allocation structure of ERISA Sec. 4044.

Upon the termination of a single-employer defined benefit plan, the benefits of all participants are distributed. The plan administrator allocates the plan assets available to pay for benefits under the plan among six priority categories.[1] Plan assets available to pay for benefits include all plan assets remaining after the subtraction of all liabilities, other than liabilities for future benefit payments, payable from plan assets under plan terms. Liabilities include expenses, fees, and other administrative costs, and benefits due before the allocation date. Benefits payable by an insurer under an irrevocable commitment are excluded from the allocation process.

Order of priorities

Plan assets will be allocated in the following order upon the termination of a single-employer defined benefit plan:[2]

Class 1 benefits. Accrued benefits derived from voluntary employee contributions.

Class 2 benefits. Accrued benefits derived from accumulated mandatory employee contributions.

Class 3 benefits. Annuity benefits that were in pay status before the beginning of the 3-year period ending on the termination date, and those annuity benefits that could have been in pay status (then or as of the next payment date under the plan's rules for starting benefit payments) for participants, who, before the beginning of the 3-year period ending on the termination date, had reached their earliest retirement date (under ERISA Reg. § 4022.10) based on plan provisions in effect on the day before the beginning of the 3-year period ending on the termination date. Benefit increases that were in effect during the 5-year period ending on the termination date, including automatic increases during that period are also included in Priority Class 3.

CCH POINTER: *Bankruptcy filing date as termination date*. In the event the plan sponsor has filed (or has had filed against it) a bankruptcy petition, Priority Class 3 benefits will be determined as if the bankruptcy filing date was

¶2838

the termination date of the plan. [3] Thus, benefits in Priority Class 3 will include benefits in pay status, or that could have been in pay status, 3 years before the bankruptcy filing date.

Class 4 benefits. All other guaranteed benefits (including benefits that would be guaranteed, except for the aggregate benefit limitations on a participant in more than one plan and the stricter phase-in limits that apply to a "substantial owner").

CCH POINTER: The PBGC is required to determine the amount of a participant's monthly benefit in Priority Class 4 by reference to the bankruptcy filing date, rather than the termination date. Accordingly, the guaranteed benefit in Priority Class 4 will be the plan benefits that were both accrued and nonforfeitable as of the bankruptcy filing date, based on the guaranteed limits as of that date. [4]

Class 5 benefits. All other nonforfeitable (uninsured) benefits under the plan, as of the termination date. Note, the change effected by ERISA Sec. 4044(e), requiring benefits to be determined as of the bankruptcy filing date does not affect Priority Class 5 benefits. A benefit that is not guaranteed because it was forfeitable as of the bankruptcy filing date will be treated as nonforfeitable for purposes of Priority Class 5 if the participants satisfied conditions for entitlement to benefits between the participant's filing date and the plan's termination date [5]

Class 6 benefits. All other benefits, whether forfeitable or nonforfeitable.

Application of asset allocation rules to substantial owners. The asset allocation rules apply to substantial owners (see ¶ 2811) in the same manner as they do to other participants.[6]

Allocate assets as of date of distribution

If a plan closes out pursuant to a Notice of Sufficiency, assets must allocated as of the date plan assets are to be distributed.[7] For plans that did not receive a Notice of Sufficiency and, thus, were placed in trusteeship, assets must be allocated as of the date of plan termination.

Assignment of plan assets

In allocating plan assets to pay for benefits, basic benefits (i.e., guaranteed benefits) and nonbasic benefits payable for each participant in a terminated plan must first be assigned by the plan administrator to one or more of the priority classes described above. The amount of benefit payable for each participant is determined as of the date of plan termination. [8]

Valuation of benefits and plan assets

After the benefits of participants have been assigned to the applicable priority class or classes, the benefits of participants and the assets of the terminated plan (as of the termination date) must be valued. Once the plan benefits and assets are valued the assets are poured through the priority classes.

The value of a participant's benefits assigned to each priority class is determined as of the allocation date.[9] Benefits initially assigned to each priority class are computed by first determining all of a participant's benefits of a type (i.e., basic or nonbasic) assigned to that priority class. A participant's benefits of each type are then valued and reduced by the value of the same type of benefit assigned to a higher priority class.

It is important to note that participant benefits and plan assets will be valued as of the plan's termination date, and not as of the bankruptcy filing date. The requirement to treat the bankruptcy filing date as the termination date for purposes of Priority Class 3 is limited to a determination of the kind of benefit that falls into Class 3, and not the time or manner of valuing the benefits or plan assets. Benefits and plan assets under all of the priority classes will continue to be valued as of the plan's termination date.

Allocation of assets to priority classes. Assets available to pay for plan benefits are allocated to each priority class in succession, beginning with priority class 1. If the plan has sufficient assets to pay for all benefits in a priority class, the remaining assets are then allocated to the next lower priority class. This process is repeated until all benefits in priority categories 1 through 6 are provided or until all available plan assets are allocated. Any assets remaining after satisfaction of all benefits in priority classes 1 through 6 may be distributed to the employer if certain requirements are met (see ¶ 2839).[10]

CCH POINTER: *Class 3 benefits have priority over guaranteed Class 4 benefits.* Benefits in Priority Class 3 have priority over guaranteed benefits in Class 4. The PBGC explains that if a terminated plan's assets are sufficient to cover all benefits in Class 3, these benefits will be paid, even if they are not guaranteed [11]

Valuing assets of terminating plans

The PBGC has provided standards for valuing the assets of terminating defined benefit plans for purposes of determining whether plan assets are sufficient to discharge all insured benefits and of computing the current value of plan assets in connection with employer liability.[12] Separate rates are provided for trusteed and non-trusteed plans. [13]

Plan assets are to be valued at their fair market value as determined under the valuation method that most accurately reflects the fair market value.[14] In the event that a plan terminates in a distress or an involuntary termination, the PBGC values the plan's benefits in order to allocate assets to benefits in accordance with the priority categories specified in ERISA Sec. 4044 (see ¶ 2838). The valuation and allocation affect the amount the PBGC's employer liability claim and the benefit to which a participant is entitled beyond guaranteed benefits.

The method for valuing benefits of a trusteed plan (i.e., a plan closed out by the PBGC because plan assets are not sufficient to provide guaranteed benefits) differs from the method applicable to a non-trusteed plan (i.e., a plan that receives a Notice of Sufficiency from the PBGC and that is able to close out by purchasing annuities in the private sector).[15]

Mechanics of valuation: Mortality and interest rate assumptions: Trusteed plans

The plan administrator initially must determine the form of each benefit to be valued (i.e., benefit in pay status or not in pay status on valuation date) using specified assumptions as to the timing of the benefit. [16] The plan administrator must then value all benefits as of the valuation date by using mortality assumptions and interest rate assumptions specified by the PBGC. [17] The interest rates are applied in conjunction with the PBGC's mortality and other assumptions to value annuity benefits.

Mortality assumptions. The mortality assumptions reflect the probability that a participant or beneficiary will survive to each expected benefit payment date. The PBGC prescribes mortality assumptions for nondisabled healthy participants, Social Security disabled participants, and non-Social Security disabled participants. [18] Separate tables apply to female and male participants.

Prescribed mortality tables. Effective for plans with termination dates on or after January 1, 2006, the mortality assumptions used to value benefits for nondisabled healthy participants will be taken from the 1994 Group Annuity Mortality Basic (GAM-94) Table. [19] The mortality tables under PBGC Reg. § 4044.75, Appendix A, are reproduced at CCH PENSION PLAN GUIDE ¶ 15,476E.

Projected mortality table. The PBGC regulations prescribe a projected mortality table that is intended to reflect expected improvement in mortality. The regulations do not provide a full generational mortality table, but specify the use of mortality tables projected to the year of valuation, plus 10 years, as an approximation for the duration of liabilities in plans that terminate in distress or involuntary terminations. [20]

Determination of expected retirement age. Plan administrators must determine the expected retirement age (XRA) of a participant who is required to retire in order to begin receiving an early retirement benefit. [21] The administrator is required to determine whether a participant is in the high, medium, or low retirement rate category using a prescribed Selection of Retirement Rate Category Table, based on the participant's monthly benefit payable at unreduced retirement age and the year in which the participant reaches unreduced retirement age. [22]

The plan administrator is also required to determine XRA for a participant who is not required to retire in order to begin receiving early retirement benefits. [23] The plan administrator determines XRA by using Table II-C of the Retirement Rate Category Table, using the participant's unreduced retirement age and earliest retirement age at the termination date.

In the event of a facility closing, the XRA of a participant is determined as equal to the earliest retirement age at valuation [24]

Table to determine expected retirement age. The expected retirement age for participants in plans terminated in either a distress termination or an involuntary termination by the PBGC is determined under a Selection of Retirement Rate Category Table (Table I-08) prescribed by the PBGC. [25] The table, which is used to compute the value of early retirement benefits and, thus, the total value of benefits under the plan, is reproduced at CCH Pension Plan Guide ¶ 15,476H.

Interest rate assumptions. Benefits under a PBGC-trusteed plan are valued using interest rates set forth by the PBGC. [26] Because the rates and factors must reflect the investment market, the rates and factors are updated periodically. The PBGC sets forth the rates and factors on a prospective basis, before the period of time for which they are applicable, rather than on a retrospective basis for the preceding period of time.

The interest rates are reproduced at CCH Pension Plan Guide ¶ 52 and ¶ 15,476A

☐ The mechanics of valuation, including the use of the prescribed mortality and interest rate assumptions, are discussed in detail at CCH Pension Plan Guide ¶ 6714.

Valuation rules: Non-trusteed plans

The value of a benefit which is to be paid as an annuity is the cost of purchasing the annuity on the date of distribution from an insurer under the qualifying bid. [27] The form of the annuity to be valued varies, under the rules of PBGC Reg. § 4044.72, depending on such factors as whether the participant and beneficiary are alive on the date of distribution, and whether the participant or beneficiary die after plan termination, but before or after the date of distribution.

Lump-sum benefit payable in lieu of annuity. In the event a lump-sum distribution is provided in lieu of an annuity, the value of the lump-sum is the present value of the normal form of benefit provided by the plan payable at normal retirement age, determined as of the date of distribution using reasonable actuarial assumptions as to interest and mortality. [28]

[1] PBGC Reg. § 4044.3(a).

[2] ERISA Sec. 4044(a)(1); PBGC Reg. § 4044.11—4044.16.

[3] ERISA Sec. 4044(e), as added by P.L. 109-280 (Pension Protection Act of 2006), Act Sec. 404(b).

[4] ERISA Sec.4044(e); PBGC Reg. § 4044.14.

[5] Preamble to PBGC Reg. § 4044.14.

[6] ERISA Secs. 4044(a)(4) and 4044(b)(3), as added by P.L. 109-280 (Pension Protection Act of 2006), Act Sec. 407(b).

[7] PBGC Reg. § 4044.3(b).

[8] PBGC Reg. § 4044.10(b).

[9] PBGC Reg. § 4044.10(c).

[10] PBGC Reg. § 4044.10(d).

[11] Preamble to PBGC Reg. § 4044.10(d).

[12] PBGC Reg. § 4044.41.

[13] PBGC Reg. §§ 4044.51--4044.57 and 4044.71–4044.75.

[14] PBGC Reg. §§ 4044.3(a) and 4044.41(b).

[15] PBGC Reg. §§ 4044.51-4044.75.

[16] PBGC Reg. § 4044.51.

[17] PBGC Reg. § 4044.52, Appendix A; PBGC Reg. § 4044.52, Appendix B; PBGC Reg. § 4044.53 See, e.g., *Erven v. Blandin Paper Company, a Minnesota Corporation* (CA-8 2007), Dkt. No. 05-1695, at CCH Pension Plan Guide ¶ 23,998W (a plan administrator's calculation of lump-sum payments from a defined benefit plan was incorrect, because the calculations were made using an obsolete PBGC mortality table, resulting in less favorable benefits for the plan's participants).

[18] PBGC Reg. § 4044.53, Appendix A.

[19] PBGC Reg. § 4044.53(c).

[20] *Ibid.*

[21] PBGC Reg. § 4044.55.

[22] PBGC Reg. § 4044.55(c); PBGC Reg. § 4044.75, Appendix D.

[23] PBGC Reg. § 4044.56.

[24] PBGC Reg. § 4044.57.

[25] PBGC Reg. § 4044.75, Appendix D. Note, the revised table applies to plans with valuation dates after December 31, 2010 and before January 1, 2012.

[26] PBGC Reg. § 4044.75, Appendix B.   [28] PBGC Reg. § 4044.73.

[27] PBGC Reg. § 4044.71.

¶ 2839

ASSET ALLOCATION RULES: Recovery of Excess Assets by Employer

Employers, subject to restrictions, may recover excess assets following the termination of a single-employer plan. ERISA, however, does not authorize the distribution of excess plan assets to contributing employers upon the termination of a multiemployer plan.[1]

Recovery of excess assets

Any residual assets of a single-employer plan may be distributed to the employer only if:[2]

1. all liabilities of the plan to participants have been satisfied;

2. the distribution does not contravene any provision of law; and

3. the plan authorizes the distribution.

Plan must terminate. An employer may not recover excess assets unless the plan formally terminates.

Plan may be amended to provide for recovery of excess assets. A plan must specifically empower an employer to recover excess assets. A plan may be amended either to authorize the reversion of excess assets to the employer, or increase the amount of a reversion. Generally, the amendment may not take effect before the end of the fifth calendar year following the date the amendment was adopted.[3] However, if a plan has been in effect for less than five years and the plan has provided for the distribution of residual assets to the employer since the effective date of the plan, such a distribution will be allowed.[4]

☐ A nondeductible excise tax is imposed on the amount of a reversion from a terminating plan. The excise tax is discussed at ¶ 2841.

Allocate assets attributable to employee contributions

Plan assets attributable to employee contributions that remain after all liabilities of the plan to participants and their beneficiaries have been satisfied must be equitably distributed, in the event that the plan actually terminates, to the employees who made such contributions or to their beneficiaries (including alternate payees).[5]

Employees have no right to unaccrued benefits. Employees are not entitled, at plan termination, to unaccrued benefits for future years of service.[6]

---

[1] ERISA Sec. 4044(d); ERISA Opinion Letter 94-39A, 11-28-94.

[2] ERISA Sec. 4044(d)(1).

[3] ERISA Sec. 4044(d)(2)(A).

[4] ERISA Sec. 4044(d)(2)(B).

[5] ERISA Sec. 4044(d)(3). However, where the amendment of a contributory defined benefit plan to add a noncontributory benefit structure did not affect the capacity of the plan to fund preexisting obligations and, thus, did not effectively terminate the plan (under the theory of "wasting trust"),

participants were not entitled to surplus assets existing in the plan that were attributable to the investment growth of the employee's contributions. (*Hughes Aircraft Co. v. Jacobson*, U.S. Sup Ct (1999), 525 U.S. 432, CCH Pension Plan Guide¶ 23,950Q, *rev'g* CA-9 (1998), 128 F3d 1305.) Participants in the plan had no protected interest in the plan's surplus, according to the U.S. Supreme Court (see discussion beginning at ¶ 845). Subsequently, the Ninth Circuit further ruled that the contributory defined benefit plan participants did not have a right to surplus assets. Participants in defined benefit plans are only entitled to a fixed periodic payment from an unsegregated pool of assets, the court explained, and the employer bears the investment risk and is responsible for any underfunding. (*Jacobson v. Hughes Aircraft Co.*, CA-9 (1999), 20 EBC 2393, CCH Pension Plan Guide¶ 23,952L.)

[6] *Blessit v. Retirement Plan for Employees of Dixie Engine Co.,* CA-11 (1988), 848 F2d 1164.

¶ 2841

ASSET ALLOCATION RULES: Excise Tax Imposed on Reversions

An employer that terminates a defined benefit plan and recovers excess assets is liable for a nondeductible 50% excise tax on the amount of the reversion in addition to ordinary income tax.[1] The employer may reduce the excise tax to 20% by:[2]

1. establishing a qualified replacement plan; or

2. amending the terminating plan to provide for pro rata benefit increases for all qualified participants.

Transfer of excess assets to retiree health accounts. An employer may avoid the excise tax on reversions by transferring excess assets to a retiree health account. Specifically, effective through 2013, qualified transfers of excess assets in a defined benefit plan (other than a multiemployer plan) to a Code Sec. 401(h) retiree health account will not result in plan disqualification or be subject to excise tax as a prohibited transaction or a reversion.[3] However, no more than one qualified transfer may be made in any tax year. Amounts that are not used to pay qualified current retiree health liabilities for the tax year of the transfer must be returned to the general assets of the plan and will be subject to the 20 percent excise tax as an employer reversion.

☐ The rules governing the transfer of excess assets to retiree health accounts (including the minimum cost requirements applicable to qualified transfers and collectively bargained transfers under Code Sec. 420(f)) are detailed at CCH Pension Plan Guide ¶ 6770—¶ 6786.

Due date and payment of excise tax

The excise tax is due on the last day of the month following the month in which the reversion occurs.[4] The excise tax is paid on Form 5330 (Return of Excise Taxes Related to Employee Benefit Plans).[5]

☐ The excise tax imposed on employer reversions from terminating plans and the requirements for qualified replacement plans and pro rata benefit increases are discussed in greater detail at CCH Pension Plan Guide ¶ 5525-5535 and ¶ 6768.

[1] Code Sec. 4980(a) and (d)(1).

[2] Code Sec. 4980(d)(1).

[3] Code Sec. 420(a) and(b), as amended by P.L. 108-281 (Pension Funding Equity Act of 2004), Act Sec. 204(a); ERISA Secs. 403(a) and 408(b)(13), as amended by P.L. 108-218 (Pension Funding Equity Act of 2004), Act Sec. 204(b). Note the authorization to transfer excess pension assets to retiree health accounts had been scheduled to expire in 2006.

[4] Code Sec. 4980(c)(4).

[5] IRS Form 5330 is reproduced at CCH PENSION PLAN GUIDE ¶ 10,781.

¶ 2845

ASSET ALLOCATION RULES: Recapture by PBGC of Plan Payments

The PBGC may recover from a plan participant payments from the plan which began within three years prior to termination.[1] ERISA provides for the recapture of any excess over an aggregate of $10,000 (or the amount a plan participant would have received as a monthly benefit under a lifetime annuity beginning at age 65, if greater) distributed to a plan participant in any 12-month period in the three years preceding termination.

The PBGC may not recover payments made on account of death or disability. In addition, the PBGC may waive the recovery of certain amounts if recovery would cause substantial hardship to participants or their beneficiaries.[2]

[1] ERISA Sec. 4045.

[2] ERISA Sec. 4045(c).

¶ 2851

LIABILITY UNDER DISTRESS OR PBGC TERMINATIONS: Liability to PBGC

Following a distress termination or an involuntary termination by the PBGC, contributing plan sponsors and members of their controlled groups are jointly and severally liable to the PBGC for the total amount of the unfunded benefit liabilities of all participants and beneficiaries under the plan, plus interest.[1]

The amount of unfunded liabilities, determined as of the termination date, is the value of the benefit liabilities *less* the current value of the plan's assets.[2] The assessed rate of interest must be reasonable and must be calculated from the termination date.[3]

Benefit liabilities

Benefit liabilities include both fixed and contingent liabilities, as well as benefits provided by the plan at termination for vested and nonvested participants.[4]

Pay liability on termination date

Generally, payment is due to the PBGC as of the termination date in cash or securities.[5] Liability (including interest) that exceeds 30% of the collective net worth of persons liable in connection with the plan termination is to be paid under commercially reasonable terms prescribed by the PBGC. Up to 50% of any amount of liability otherwise payable for any year may be deferred if no plan sponsors or contributing members have individual pre-tax profits for the fiscal year.[6]

Submissions may be made to the PBGC by hand, mail, or commercial delivery service or through electronic media.[7] Payments of liability must be clearly designated and include the name of the plan. A submission will be treated as filed with the PBGC on the date it is sent, provided specified requirements are satisfied.[8]

PBGC lien authority

If any person liable to the PBGC neglects or refuses to pay the amount of assessed liability (plus interest) after demand, the PBGC may impose a lien upon that person's real and personal property. The amount of the lien may not exceed 30% of the collective net worth of all persons liable for the payment.[9] The lien arises on the date of the termination of the plan and continues until the liability is satisfied or becomes unenforceable due to the lapse of time.[10]

Notification and demand for payment

Generally, the PBGC is required to provide written notification to persons subject to termination liability of the amount of the liability.[11] The notification must also include a statement disclosing the right to appeal the liability assessment. If the liability is not paid, the PBGC will issue a demand letter for the amount as long as an unresolved appeal is not outstanding.

Six-year statute of limitations applies to collection actions. The PBGC may bring an action in federal court to collect liability within six years after the date of plan termination, or prior to the expiration of any period for collection agreed upon by the employer and the PBGC before the close of the 6-year period.[12]

Liability for withdrawal under multiple controlled group

The plan administrator of a single employer plan that has two or more contributing sponsors, at least two of whom are not under common control, is required to notify the PBGC within 60 days of the withdrawal of a substantial employer from the plan.[13] As soon as practicable thereafter, the PBGC must determine whether there is liability resulting from the withdrawal and notify parties of their liability. Liability is allocated under ERISA Sec. 4063(b) to the withdrawing employer based upon a ratio of the employer's required contributions to all required contributions for the 5 years preceding withdrawal.

Liability upon substantial cessation of operations

In the event an employer ceases operations at a facility in any location, resulting in the separation from employment of more than 20 percent of the total number of employees participating in a plan established and maintained by the employer (i.e., a "Section 4062(e) event") the employer will be treated as a substantial employer under a plan pursuant to which more than one employer makes contributions.[14]

CCH POINTER: *Proposed rules amend requirements governing reporting and liability.* The PBGC has issued proposed regulations that would amend the current rules under ERISA Sec. 4062(e) governing the reporting requirements and liability attendant the substantial cessation of operations by employers that maintain single-employer defined benefit plans. [15]

Cessation of operations. The proposed regulations would apply ERISA Sec. 4062(e) to an employer's cessation of operations at any facility in any location, even if the employer continued or resumed operations at another facility in another location. [16] An employer's cessation of operations at a facility would be considered to occur only if the employer voluntarily discontinued all "significant" activity at the facility in furtherance of the purpose of the operations. [17] Separate rules would apply to the involuntary discontinuation of operations.

In determining whether 20 percent of more of the employer's employees are "separated from employment" as the result of the cessation of operations at a facility, the proposed regulations would focus on the discontinuance of active performance, pursuant to the employee's employment relationship with the employer, of activities in furtherance of the employer's operations, rather than separation from employment in the operations. [18]

An employee's separation could, under the proposed regulations, result from the cessation of operations at a facility even if the employee's employment had been in another operation or even at another facility.[19] The PBGC would specify four presumptions that would apply in determining whether a separation from employment has been the result of an employer's cessation of operations.

Enforcement provisions. The proposed rules would prescribe recordkeeping requirements and authorize waivers in appropriate circumstances.[20]

Computing liability. ERISA Sec. 4062(c) does not specify how total liability is to be apportioned when an employer ceases operations. In the event a substantial owner withdraws from a multiple employer plan, liability is allocated under ERISA Sec. 4063(b) to the withdrawing employer based upon a ratio of the employer's required contributions to all required contributions for the 5 years preceding the withdrawal. However, because the ERISA Sec. 4063(b) allocation formula is impractical for single employer plans, the PBGC utilizes a formula under which an employer's liability will be its liability under ERISA Sec. 4062(b). Generally, liability will be the total amount of unfunded benefit liabilities as of the termination date (plus interest), multiplied by the following fraction: number of employer's employees who are participating in the plan and separated from employment as a result of the cessation of operations/ total number of employer's employees who were participating in the plan immediately before the cessation of operations.[21]

---

[1] ERISA Secs. 4062(a) and (b)(1)(A); PBGC Reg. § 4062.3(a).

[2] ERISA Sec. 4001(a)(18).

[3] ERISA Sec. 4062(b)(1)(A).

[4] ERISA Sec. 4001(a)(16). **Note:** The Tenth Circuit has ruled that PBGC claims for unpaid contributions and unfunded benefit liabilities resulting from the underfunding of a plan were not entitled to tax or administrative priority in bankruptcy (*In re: CFI Fabricators of Utah, Inc.,* CA-10 (1998), 150 F3d 1293, CCH Pension Plan Guide ¶ 23,940). Similarly, the Sixth Circuit has held that the PBGC was not entitled to administrative expense priority in bankruptcy for unpaid post-petition minimum funding contributions accrued by a bankrupt employer between the time it filed for bankruptcy and the date the plan terminated (*PBGC v. Sunarhauserman,* CA-6 (1997), 126 F3d 811).

[5] ERISA Sec. 4062(b)(2)(A).

[6] ERISA Sec. 4062(b)(2)(B); PBGC Reg. §4062.8(c).

[7] PBGC Reg. §4000.3 and 4062.9(a).

[8] PBGC Reg. §4000.27 and PBGC Reg. §4062.9(b).

[9] ERISA Sec. 4068(a); PBGC Reg. §4068.4.

[10] ERISA Sec. 4068(b).

[11] PBGC Reg. §4068.3.

[12] ERISA Sec. 4068(d).

[13] ERISA Sec.4063(a)(1); PBGC Reg. §4063.1.

[14] ERISA Sec. 4064(a); PBGC Reg. §4064.1.

[15] PBGC Proposed Reg. §§4062.21—4062.35 (71 FR 48283), at CCH PENSION PLAN GUIDE ¶ 20,537X.

[16] PBGC Proposed Reg. §4062.24-25, at CCH PENSION PLAN GUIDE ¶ 20,537X.

[17] PBGC Proposed Reg. §4062.26, at CCH PENSION PLAN GUIDE ¶ 20,537X.

[18] PBGC Proposed Reg. §§4062.27, at CCH PENSION PLAN GUIDE ¶ 20,537X.

[19] PBGC Proposed Reg. §4062.28, at CCH PENSION PLAN GUIDE ¶ 20,537X.

[20] PBGC Proposed Reg. §4062.30—35, at CCH PENSION PLAN GUIDE ¶ 20,537X.

[21] PBGC Reg. §4062.8.

¶ 2853

LIABILITY UNDER DISTRESS OR PBGC TERMINATIONS: Liability to Section 4042 Trustee

If a plan terminates in a distress termination or in a termination instituted by the PBGC, and the plan is subject to PBGC trusteeship proceedings, each contributing sponsor and each member of its controlled group may also be subject to liability to the trustee appointed under ERISA Sec. 4042 (see ¶ 2834).[1]

Amount of liability

The amount of liability is the outstanding balance of the accumulated funding deficiencies, the outstanding balance of the amount of waived funding deficiencies that was waived before the termination date, and the outstanding balance of the amount of decreases in the minimum funding standard allowed before the termination date together with interest from the termination date.[2]

Liability payable on termination date

The assessed liability is due and payable to the trustee as of the termination date in cash or securities.[3]

[1] ERISA Sec. 4062(a) and (c).

[2] ERISA Sec. 4062(c)(1)-(3).

[3] ERISA Sec. 4062(c)(3).

¶ 2854

LIABILITY UNDER DISTRESS OR PBGC TERMINATIONS: Deduction for Liability Payments

Payments under a standard, distress, or PBGC-instituted termination, withdrawal liability payments of a substantial employer from single-employer plans under multiple controlled groups, and payments under terminations of single-employer plans under multiple controlled groups are deductible when paid.[1] The maximum amount that is deductible is capped by the amount of the full funding limitation for the year.

Payments subject to limits on employer contribution deductions

Payments to terminate a plan under a standard termination are treated as an employer contribution to a qualified plan under Code Sec. 404 for tax deduction purposes. These payments are subject to the Code Sec. 404 limitations (see discussion beginning at ¶ 600) on employer deductions for contributions to the extent that the payments result in the plan assets being in excess of the total amount of benefits under the plan that are guaranteed by the PBGC.[2]

Similarly, liability payments to a Sec. 4042 trustee are subject to the Code Sec. 404 limitations on employer deductions for contributions. The payments are deductible at a time prescribed by regulation.[3]

CCH POINTER: *Maximum deduction limit.* In the event that a single employer plan terminates during the year, the maximum deductible amount is generally not less than the amount needed to make the plan assets sufficient to fund benefit liabilities (i.e., unfunded termination liability).

For 2006 and 2007, the maximum deductible amount for contributions to a single employer plan may not be less than the excess of: (1) 150% of the plan's current liability, over (2) the value of plan assets.[4]

For tax years after 2007, the maximum deductible amount will be the greater of (1) the excess of the sum of the plan's funding target, the plan's target normal cost, and a specified "cushion" amount for a plan year, over the value of plan assets (as determined under the minimum funding rules applicable after 2007 (see discussion beginning at ¶ 1493), and (2) the minimum required contribution for the plan year.[5] However, larger deduction limits apply to plans that are not at-risk.

In addition, note, the maximum deductible amount for contributions to a single employer plan that terminates during the year will continue to be generally no less than the amount needed to make plan assets sufficient to fund unfunded termination liability.

---

[1] Code Sec. 404(g)(1) and (3)(A).

[2] Code Sec. 404(g)(3)(B).

[3] Code Sec. 404(g)(3)(C).

[4] Code Sec. 404(a)(1)(D)(i), as amended by P.L. 109-280 (Pension Protection Act of 2006), Act Sec. 801(a).

[5] Code Sec. 404(o), as added by P.L. 109-280 (Pension Protection Act of 2006), Act Sec. 801(a).

¶ 2855

LIABILITY UNDER DISTRESS OR PBGC TERMINATIONS: Transactions to Evade Liability

If a person or organization enters into a transaction in order to evade liability owed to the PBGC, and the transaction becomes effective within five years before the termination date, the person or organization and any controlled group member are subject to liability in connection with the termination as if it were a contributing sponsor of the terminated plan as of the termination date.[1] The rule also applies to transactions designed to avoid liability to participants and beneficiaries for benefit liabilities.

However, a person or organization will not be liable in connection with a plan termination for any increases or improvements in the plan benefits that were adopted after the date on which the evasive transaction became effective. Nevertheless, the transferor may still be held liable for benefits that were adopted prior to the date of the transaction if plan participants did not become eligible for the benefits until after the date of the transaction.[2]

---

[1] ERISA Sec. 4069(a).

[2] P.L. 99-272 (Consolidated Omnibus Budget Reconciliation Act), Sec. 11013(b).

¶ 2859
REPORTING REQUIREMENTS: Plan Termination Reporting Table

Terminating plans that are subject to the plan termination insurance rules must comply with numerous reporting and notice obligations that require information to be provided to the IRS and DOL, the PBGC, and plan participants. The following table presents a step-by-step guide to the reports, forms, notices, and other documents that are to be filed with the government or furnished to other interested parties when a plan terminates.

Under the table, items to be furnished to the IRS (i.e., application for determination of tax qualification, notice of plan termination, and the filing of the annual report) and notices to interested parties apply to defined benefit, money purchase, profit-sharing, and stock bonus plans.

Items to be furnished directly to or by the PBGC and notices to employees, as set forth in the chart below, apply to single-employer defined benefit plans that are covered by plan termination insurance and voluntarily terminated by the plan administrator.

The rules applicable to missing participants are discucssed at ¶ 2831.

The reporting requirements for terminated defined benefit plans are summarized at CCH Pension Plan Guide ¶ 6798.

The reporting rules governing terminating defined contribution plans are discussed at CCH Pension Plan Guide ¶ 6801.

IRS

DOCUMENT	PURPOSE	FURNISHED BY	FURNISHED TO	WHEN DUE
(1) Forms 5310 (plus attachments) and 6088	Request IRS determination as to plan's qualification status upon termination	Employer, plan administrator (if designated) or fiduciary trustee (or custodian)	Internal Revenue Service	Any time determination of qualification is desired
(2) Form 1099-R (Plan distributions)	Report amount of plan distributions	Payor of plan administrator	IRS and recipients	To IRS: February 28 following the year of distribution—To participants: January 31 following the year of distribution

DOL

DOCUMENT	PURPOSE	FURNISHED BY	FURNISHED TO	WHEN DUE
(1) Notice of plan termination	Report plan termination information on appropriate line of annual return/report (Form 5500 series)	Plan administrator	Employee Benefits Security Administration	Seven months after end of plan year in which termination occurred
(2) Form 5500 (Final annual return/report)	Provide information required by applicable form for year in which complete distribution is made or plan assets are brought under PBGC control	Plan administrator	Employee Benefits Security Administration	Seven months after end of plan year (plan year ends upon complete distribution or PBGC control of plan assets)
(3) Terminal report. The final Form 5500 acts as the terminal report				

PBGC

DOCUMENT	PURPOSE	FURNISHED BY	FURNISHED TO	WHEN DUE
(1) PBGC Form 500 and Schedule EA-S (Standard termination notice and enrolled actuary certification)	Provide standard termination notice containing termination information and plan administrator's certification (Form 500); also provide enrolled actuary's certification of plan sufficiency for benefit liabilities (Schedule EA-S)	Plan administrator of a single-employer plan terminating in a standard termination	Pension Benefit Guaranty Corporation	No later than 180 days after the proposed termination date
(2) PBGC Form 600 (Distress Termination Notice of intent to terminate)	Provide notice of intent to terminate in a distress termination	Plan administrator of a single-employer plan terminating in a standard termination	Pension Benefit Guaranty Corporation[1]	At least 60, but no more than 90, days prior to the proposed termination date
(3) PBGC Form 601 and Schedule EA-D (Distress termination notice enrolled actuary certification)	Provide notice containing distress criteria information and plan administrator's certification (Form 601); also provide certification by enrolled actuary as to plan's funding level (Schedule EA-D)	Plan administrator of a single-employer plan terminating in a distress termination	Pension Benefit Guaranty Corporation	Within 120 days after proposed termination date. However, if a plan is insufficient for guaranteed benefits, participant and benefit information must be filed by the later of 120 days after the proposed termination date, or 30 days after receipt of the PBGC determination that distress termination requirements have been met.

DOCUMENT	PURPOSE	FURNISHED BY	FURNISHED TO	WHEN DUE
(4) Notice of reduced benefits	Provide certification regarding reduction in the benefits paid to participants where benefits exceed the PBGC maximum guarantee	Plan administrator of a single-employer plan terminating in a distress termination	Pension Benefit Guaranty Corporation	Within 30 days after payment of reduced benefits has begun
(5) PBGC Form 602 (Post-distribution certification)	Provide certification that assets have been properly distributed	Plan administrator of a single-employer plan terminating in a distress termination	Pension Benefit Guaranty Corporation	Within 30 days after plan asset distribution is completed
(6) Notice of noncompliance[2]	Advise that certain standard termination requirements have not been met or that there is reason to believe that plan is not sufficient for benefit liabilities	Pension Benefit Guaranty Corporation	Plan administrator of single-employer plan terminating in a standard termination	Within 60 days of receipt of standard termination notice
(7) Notice to plan administrator as to satisfaction of distress criteria	Notify whether plan meets one of necessary distress criteria to qualify for a distress termination	Pension Benefit Guaranty Corporation	Plan administrator of a single-employer plan terminating in a distress termination	As soon as practicable
(8) Notification that plan which meets distress criteria requirements is sufficient to pay liabilities	Advise that plan administrator is to make final distribution of assets, to make certification to PBGC that plan assets have been distributed so as to pay all benefit liabilities, and to proceed as if termination were a standard termination	Pension Benefit Guaranty Corporation	Plan administrator of plan terminating in a distress termination	As soon as practicable after determinations are made
(9) Notification that plan which meets distress criteria requirements is sufficient for guaranteed benefits but not or benefit liabilities	Advise that plan administrator is to make final distribution of assets, to make certification to PBGC that the distribution has occurred, and to take appropriate steps to terminate the plan	Pension Benefit Guaranty Corporation	Plan administrator of plan terminating in a distress termination	As soon as practicable after determinations are made
(10) Notification that plan is no longer sufficient for guaranteed benefits	Appraise PBGC of a finding of insufficiency	Plan administrator of a single-employer plan terminating in a distress termination	Pension Benefit Guaranty Corporation	Plan administrator must promptly notify PBGC of finding
(11) Notification that plan is sufficient for guaranteed benefits, but no longer sufficient for benefit liabilities	Appraise PBGC of a finding of insufficiency	Plan administrator of single-employer plan terminating in a distress termination	Pension Benefit Guaranty Corporation	Plan administrator must immediately notify PBGC of finding

DOCUMENT	PURPOSE	FURNISHED BY	FURNISHED TO	WHEN DUE
(12) PBGC Form 501 (Post-distribution Certification for Standard Termination)	Certify that assets and benefit liabilities were distributed in accordance with specified requirements	Plan administrator of a plan terminating in a standard termination	Pension Benefit Guaranty Corporation	No later than 30 days after completion of final distribution of assets (see ¶ 2818 as to when final distribution must be made)
(13) Certification to PBGC of issuance of notice of benefit distribution in distress termination	Insure that notices of benefit distribution were provided to affected parties	Plan administrator	Pension Benefit Guaranty Corporation	No later than 15 days after the date on which the plan administrator completes issuance of notices of benefit distribution
(14) Notice to plan not qualifying for distress termination	Advise plan administrator that requirements for a distress termination have not been met and that the proposed termination is null and void	Pension Benefit Guaranty Corporation	Plan administrator of single-employer plan requesting distress termination	As soon as practicable after determining that plan does not qualify for distress termination
(15) Schedule MP (Missing Participant Information)	Provide information to PBGC to assist plan administrators participating in PBGC Missing Participant Program to close out plans and enable missing participants to obtain their benefits	Plan administrator of terminating single-employer plan	Pension Benefit Guaranty Corporation	No later than 30 days after final distribution of assets

PARTICIPANTS AND BENEFICIARIES

DOCUMENT	PURPOSE	FURNISHED BY	FURNISHED TO	WHEN DUE
(1) Notice of intent to terminate (see also PBGC Form 600-Distress Termination Notice of Intent to Terminate)	Notification that a termination of a PBGC-covered pension plan is intended and the proposed termination date	Plan administrator of a single-employer plan terminating in a standard or distress termination	Participant, beneficiary of deceased participant, alternate payee under a qualified domestic relations order, any employee organization currently representing employees, any employee organization that formerly represented participants without current representation, any person designated in writing to receive notice	At least 60, but no more than 90, days before proposed termination date

DOCUMENT	PURPOSE	FURNISHED BY	FURNISHED TO	WHEN DUE
(2) Notice to interested parties of determination letter request	Notification that determination letter on plan termination is being requested	Employer or plan administrator	All present employees with accrued benefits, all former employees with vested benefits, and all beneficiaries of deceased employees currently receiving benefits	Not less than 10 or more than 24 days before a request for determination is made, regardless of the form of delivery
(3) Notice of benefit amount	Furnish the amount of each person's plan benefits and information used in determining those benefits	Plan administrator of a single-employer plan terminating in a standard termination	Each participant and beneficiary	No later than 180 days after the proposed termination date
(4) Notice of benefit distribution	Advise participants of distribution of benefits	Plan administrator of a single-employer plan terminating in a distress termination	Each affected party, except PBGC and any employee organization	No later than 60 days after receipt of distribution notice from PBGC
(5) Notice of annuity information	Provide information regarding annuity and insurer and PBGC obligation	Plan administrator	Each affected party, other than the PBGC and an affected party whose title IV benefits will be distributed as a nonconsensual lump-sum	Within 45 days before the affected party's distribution date
(6) Notice of plan amendment significantly reducing benefit accruals	Notify interested persons that future benefit accruals will be reduced due to plan termination	Plan administrator	Plan participants, alternate payees, and representative employee organizations.	At least 15 days before effective date of the amendment
(7) Notice of annuity contract	Inform participants and beneficiaries that plan benefits will be distributed through annuity contracts, identify insurer, and clarify insurer's obligation to provide benefits	Plan administrator	Each affected party and beneficiary	Within 30 days of availability of information
(8) Participant notice of plan's funded status	Inform participants in plans required to pay the variable rate premium of the plan's funded status (including the funded current liability percentage) and of the limits on the PBGC's benefit guarantee should the plan terminate while underfunded	Plan administrators of plans required to pay variable rate premium	Plan participants, beneficiaries, alternate payees, and employee organizations	Two months after the due date (including extensions) for the prior year's Form 5500

[1] The NOIT must also be furnished to affected parties other than the PBGC before Form 600 is furnished to the PBGC. However, there is no prescribed form for this purpose.

[2] In the event that the notice of noncompliance is not received by the plan administrator within 60 days of notice to the PBGC, the administrator must close out the plan.

¶ 2861

PLAN MERGERS AND CONSOLIDATIONS: Benefits After Merger, Consolidation, or Transfer

The accrued benefits of plan participants following the merger or consolidation of plans, or the transfer of assets or liabilities from one plan to another, must be equal to or greater than the benefits to which the participants would have been entitled immediately before the transaction.[1] However, plan participants are not entitled to residual assets remaining in the trust following the merger, but only to accrued benefits.[2] In addition, an employer that transfers pension assets and liabilities does not have a fiduciary duty to guarantee future nonvested benefits or to ensure that benefits will increase at the same rate as if they had not been transferred.[3]

Failure to provide equal benefits may negate qualified status

A trust which is part of a plan will not be a qualified trust, and the plan will not be qualified unless, in the event of merger, consolidation, or transfer of assets or liabilities, each participant would receive, upon termination of the plan, benefits immediately after the merger, consolidation, or transfer which are equal to or greater than the benefits to which the participants would have been entitled had the plan been terminated immediately before the merger, consolidation, or transfer.[4]

In addition, Code Sec. 401(a)(12) requires a plan by its terms to entitle each participant to a benefit after the merger, consolidation, or transfer that is at least equal to the value of the benefit to which the participant would have been entitled before the merger. This requirement is not limited to plans which experience such a restructure. Code Sec. 401(a)(12), unlike Code Sec. 414(l), requires a plan to provide for such benefits regardless of whether a merger, consolidation, or transfer of assets or liabilities ever occurs.

---

[1] Code Secs. 401(a)(12) and 414(l)(1); IRS Reg. § 1.401(a)-12; ERISA Sec. 208.

[2] *Malia v. General Electric Co.*, CA-3 (1994), 23 F3d 828, *cert. denied* 513 U.S. 956. See also, *Brillinger v. General Electric Co.*, CA-2 (1997), 130 F2d 61 (participants in a contributory defined benefit plan were not entitled, following a plan merger, to an increase in benefits that would reflect surplus plan assets attributable to employee contributions).

[3] *Dougherty v. Chrysler Motors Corporation*, CA-6 (1988), 840 F2d 2.

[4] Code Sec. 414(l)(1); IRS Reg. § 1.414(l)-1(a)(2).

¶ 2862

PLAN MERGERS AND CONSOLIDATIONS: Merged Plan

A merger or consolidation refers to the combining of two or more plans into a single plan.[1] A plan is a single plan only if, on an ongoing basis, all of the plan assets are available to pay benefits to employees who are covered by the plan and their beneficiaries.[2] A merger or consolidation does not occur if two plans are not combined into a single plan.[3] Nor does a merger or consolidation occur simply because one or more corporations undergo a reorganization (whether or not taxable). Plans will not fail to be merged if separate accounting is maintained for purposes of cost allocation but not for purposes of providing benefits under the plan. However, the plans will not be merged if a portion of the plan assets is not available to pay some of the benefits.

Transfer of assets or liabilities

A transfer of assets or liabilities occurs when there is a diminution of assets or liabilities in one plan and the acquisition of these assets or the assumption of these liabilities by another plan.[4] The shifting of assets between several funding media used for a single plan (for example, between trusts, between annuity contracts, or between trusts and annuity contracts) is not treated as a transfer of assets or liabilities.

[1] IRS Reg. § 1.414(l)-1(b)(2).

[2] IRS Reg. § 1.414(l)-1(b)(1).

[3] IRS Reg. § 1.414(l)-1(b)(2).

[4] IRS Reg. § 1.414(l)-1(b)(3).

¶ 2863
PLAN MERGERS AND CONSOLIDATIONS: Merger of Defined Contribution Plans

If two or more defined contribution plans merge, the following requirements apply:[1]

1. the sum of the account balances in each plan must equal the fair market value (determined as the date of the merger) of the entire plan assets;

2. the assets of each plan must be combined to form the assets of the merged plan; and

3. immediately after the merger, each participant in the merged plan must have an account balance equal to the sum of the account balances he or she had in the plans immediately prior to the merger.

Participant notice requirement

An employer is not required to provide notice to plan participants prior to the merger or spinoff of a plan.

[1] IRS Reg. § 1.414(l)-1(d).

¶ 2864
PLAN MERGERS AND CONSOLIDATIONS: Merger of Defined Benefit Plans

Generally, in the case of a merger of defined benefit plans, benefits on a termination basis before and after the merger must be compared.[1] "Benefits on a termination basis" are the benefits that would be provided exclusively by plan assets pursuant to ERISA Sec. 4044, which prescribes the allocation of assets to various priority categories (see ¶ 2838).[2] In the event that the total assets of all of the plans are not less than the present value of the accrued benefits (vested and nonvested), the assets must be combined and each participant's accrued benefits preserved.[3]

The benefits provided on a termination basis under the merged plan may be different from benefits provided on a termination basis under the plans prior to merger, where the assets are merely combined and each participant retains an accrued benefit.[4] In this situation, some participants would receive smaller (or greater) benefits after the merger than they would receive before the merger. Accordingly, the Code Sec. 414(l) requirements would not be met unless the distribution of benefits on termination was modified to prevent any participant from receiving smaller benefits on a termination basis as a result of the merger. Therefore, the application of ERISA Sec. 4044 is modified through the use of a special schedule of benefits.[5] The schedule must be used for up to 5 years after the merger.[6]

However, the special schedule need not be established if data sufficient to create the schedule is maintained.[7] An enrolled actuary must certify to the plan administrator that each element of data necessary to determine the schedule as of the date of the merger is maintained. The data need not be maintained for more than 5 years after the merger if the plan is not terminated or spun-off within 5 years.[8]

Merger of defined benefit and defined contribution plans

Prior to a merger between a defined benefit plan and a defined contribution plan, one of the plans should be converted into the other type of plan.[9] The above rules would apply if the defined contribution plan were converted to a defined benefit plan. If the defined benefit plan were converted to a defined contribution plan, the rules at ¶ 2863 would apply.

CCH Pointer: The application of the 25% deduction limit of Code Sec. 404 to 401(k) profit-sharing plans (see ¶ 670) has caused many employers to reevaluate the continuing necessity of maintaining separate money purchase (MP) plans. Prior to executing a merger of a 401(k) plan and a money purchase plan, an employer needs to aware that: the merger does not divest the MP assets of their attributes as MP assets; merged assets remain subject to the distribution restrictions applicable to MP plans; an ERISA 204(h) notice (see ¶ 866) must be provided to affected plan participants; and an amendment must be adopted freezing the MP contribution formula.[10]

☐ The rules governing the conversion of a money purchase plan to a profit-sharing plan are discussed in detail at CCH PENSION PLAN GUIDE ¶ 1453.

Joint and survivor annuity requirements. Money purchase plans must provide benefits in the form of a qualified joint and survivor annuity (QJSA) unless the participant or his spouse consents to the receipt of benefits in an alternative form. 401(k) plans are not generally required to provide a QJSA. However, a 401(k) plan will be subject to the joint and survivor annuity requirements if (with respect to the participant) the plan has received a transfer of benefits from a plan to which the joint and survivor annuity requirements apply and the plan does not separately account for the transferee assets. Employers that are considering merging a MP plan and a 401(k) plan, thus, need to ensure that the profit-sharing plan applies the joint and survivor annuity requirement to the MP assets.

[1] IRS Reg. § 1.414(l)-1(e).

[2] IRS Reg. § 1.414(l)-1(b)(5).

[3] IRS Reg. § 1.414(l)-1(e)(1).

[4] IRS Reg. § 1.414(l)-1(e)(2).

[5] IRS Reg. § 1.414(l)-1(f).

[6] IRS Reg. § 1.414(l)-1(j).

[7] IRS Reg. § 1.414(l)-1(i).

[8] IRS Reg. § 1.414(l)-1(j).

[9] IRS Reg. § 1.414(l)-1(l).

[10] Rev. Rul. 2004-12, I.R.B. 204-7, 2-17-04, at CCH PENSION PLAN GUIDE ¶ 19,948Z-45.

¶ 2865

PLAN MERGERS AND CONSOLIDATIONS: Maintaining Qualified Status After Merger

Plans involved in corporate mergers or reorganizations may encounter problems in retaining their qualified status. For example, the absorption of the employees of an acquired corporation into the qualified plan of the acquiring corporation will raise nondiscrimination issues.

A qualified plan must meet certain coverage requirements, based either on a percentage-of-employees test or an average-benefits test (see ¶ 1050—1080). A change in the number of employees covered by the plan, or a change in the classes of employees included in, or excluded from, the plan as a consequence of a merger may result in the plan's being declared discriminatory. Accordingly, the plan may have to be amended in order to eliminate its discriminatory aspects. Caution should also be exercised when including the predecessor's employees in the successor's plan so that the changes do not result in discrimination in contributions or benefits.

If the acquiring corporation does not have a plan of its own, but simply takes over the operation of the predecessor's plan along with the employment of the predecessor's employees, the makeup of the plan's participants, when related to the makeup of the successor's employees, may also result in discriminatory coverage. However, an employer may designate several trusts, or several trusts and an annuity plan or plans, as constituting one single plan that is intended to meet the coverage requirements.[1] Consequently, if the successor corporation already has a plan that covers its own employees, both plans may be considered as a unit in determining whether or not the coverage requirements are satisfied.

CCH Pointer: *Elimination of optional forms of benefit.* In addition to coverage concerns, an acquiring employer that is attempting to reconcile plans with different terms and conditions must be cautious not to eliminate optional forms of benefit, such as the right to an immediate lump-sum distribution. Under such circumstances, the merged or spun-off plan would have to be amended in order to retain qualified status.

In-service distribution restrictions continue to apply. The in-service distribution restrictions that apply to 401(k) plans may not be avoided through a merger or transfer of benefit. The distribution limits generally continue to apply to amounts attributable to elective contributions that are transferred to another plan of the same or another employer. Accordingly, if incident to a merger of a 401(k) and a qualified non-401(k) plan, elective contributions are transferred, the merged plan may not allow for immediate lump-sum in-service distributions.

---

[1] Code Secs. 401(a)(3) and 410(b).

¶ 2866
PLAN MERGERS AND CONSOLIDATIONS: Plan Spin-Offs

In the event that a single plan splits, or is "spun-off," into two or more plans, plan participants are entitled to benefits equal to or greater than those to which they would have been entitled prior to the transaction.[1] Different rules apply in the event of a spin-off of defined contribution and defined benefit plans.

Defined contribution plans

In the case of a spin-off of a defined contribution plan, the no-reduction rule is satisfied if, after the spin-off:[2]

1. the sum of the account balances for each of the participants in the resulting plans equals the participant's account balance in the plan prior to the spin-off, and

2. the value of the assets in each resulting plan, immediately after the spin-off, equals the sum of the account balances of all participants in that plan.

Defined benefit plans

In the event that a defined benefit plan is spun off, the no-reduction rule is satisfied if:[3]

1. all of the accrued benefits of each participant are allocated to only one of the resulting plans, and

2. the value of the assets allocated to each resulting plan is not less than the present value of the pre-spin-off benefits (determined on a termination basis) of the individuals participating in that resulting plan.

De minimis spin-off. The no-reduction rule will be considered to be satisfied if:

1. the value of the assets spun off equals the present value of the accrued benefits (vested and unvested) spun off, and

2. the value of the assets spun off, when combined with any assets transferred in other spin-offs during the same plan year, is less than 3% of the assets of the pre-spin-off plan on at least one day in that plan year.[4]

Excess assets allocated among spun-off plans

In the case of spin-offs and similar transactions involving defined benefit plans (within a controlled group), excess assets are to be allocated proportionately among spun-off plans.[5]

Excess assets are the (1) the fair market value of the assets of the original plan immediately before the spin-off, over (2) the amount of assets required to be allocated after the spin-off to all plans (determined without regard to the spin-off rule for allocation of assets).

Excess assets are to be allocated to each spun-off plan in the proportion that (1) the excess of the full funding limitation for the spun-off plan over the amount of assets required to be allocated after the spin-off (determined without regard to the spin-off rule for allocation of assets) *bears to* (2) the sum of excesses calculated separately under (1) for each of the spun-off plans.

Employees not entitled to excess assets. Employees participating in defined benefit plans are only entitled to receive the same level of benefits under the plan after the spin-off as they would have received before the spin-off. Thus, because defined benefit plan participants have no ownership interest in the assets of the plan, they have no right to increased benefits under the plan, in the event that the plan's assets grow significantly because of successful investment practices, or to a pro rata share of excess residual assets.[6]

Spinoff to bridge depository institution. A bridge depository institution is a bank established by the Federal Deposit Insurance Corporation to assume the deposits and other liabilities of a closed bank and continue banking operations. A spinoff to a bridge depository institution is subject to the allocation rule.[7] However, the provision only applies with respect to 50 percent of the excess assets. A bridge depository institution would also be authorized to cause the plan maintained by the closing bank to spin off assets to a defined benefit plan maintained by the bridge depository institution in accordance with the allocation rule within 180 days after the closing of the bank.

---

[1] IRS Reg. § 1.414(l)-1(m) and (n) and IRS Reg. § 1.414(l)-1(b)(4).

[2] ERISA Sec. 208; IRS Reg. § 1.414(l)-1(m).

[3] ERISA Sec. 208; IRS Reg. § 1.414(l)-1(n)(1).

[4] IRS Reg. § 1.414(l)-1(n)(2).

[5] Code Sec. 414(l)(2)(C).

[6] *Systems Council EM-3 v. AT&T Corp.*, CA-DC (1998), 159 F3d 1376, 22 EBC 2492, CCH Pension

Plan Guide ¶ 23,949H. See also, *Malia v. General Electric Co.*, CA-3 (1994), 23 F3d 828, 18 EBC 1113 (plan participants were not entitled to surplus assets following plan merger).

[7] Code Sec. 414(l)(2)(G), as amended by P.L. 110-289 (Federal Housing Finance Regulatory Reform Act of 2008), Act Sec. 1604(b)(4) (substituting "bridge depository institution" for "bridge bank").

¶ 2867
For More Information

☐ For more information on single-employer plan terminations, see ¶ 6400-6804 of the CCH Pension Plan Guide. For more information on plan mergers, see ¶ 1443-1459 of the CCH Pension Plan Guide.

Multiemployer Plans and Withdrawal Liability

¶ 2868

Overview of Multiemployer Plans and Withdrawal Liability

The rules governing multiemployer plans focus on four major topics: plan termination, withdrawal liability, mergers and transfers, and plans in reorganization.

Multiemployer plan termination

Multiemployer plans may be terminated by:

1. amendment;

2. the withdrawal of every employer; or

3. through proceedings instituted by the PBGC.

Premium payments

As with single-employer plans (see ¶ 2809), multiemployer plans are required to make annual premium payments for plan participants. The PBGC, in turn, guarantees a limited amount of the nonforfeitable benefits offered under the multiemployer plan, if the plan becomes insolvent.

Withdrawal liability

An employer that totally or partially withdraws from a multiemployer plan is required to continue funding a proportional share of the plan's unfunded vested benefits by making annual withdrawal liability payments to the plan. The plan determines the amount of liability in accord with stipulated methods. The employer must make level annual payments as dictated by a payment schedule formula. Disputes regarding the withdrawal liability assessment generally must be arbitrated.

Reorganization of multiemployer plans

Financially troubled multiemployer plans are subject to special rules regarding funding and adjustments in accrued benefits.

Mergers, transfers, and partition

A multiemployer plan may merge with one or more multiemployer plans or transfer assets or liabilities to or from another multiemployer plan. Mergers or transfers may also be made with single-employer plans.

The PBGC is empowered to order to partition a multiemployer plan so that a portion of its assets and liabilities is segregated and held as a separate plan.

☐ The rules for single-employer plan terminations are covered at ¶ 2800 and following.

☐ The minimum funding rules applicable to multiemployer plans and significantly underfunded multiemployer plans are discussed at ¶ 1493K and ¶ 1493L.

¶ 2869
Multiemployer Plan Defined

A multiemployer plan is a plan: (1) to which more than one employer is required to contribute; (2) which is maintained under a collective bargaining agreement between an employee organization and more than one employer and; (3) which satisfies additional requirements that may be specified by the Secretary of Labor (see ¶ 185).[1] Note, PBGC regulations finalized in 2008, further define a multiemployer plan as a plan the elects to be a multiemployer plan under ERISA Sec. 3(37) and Code Sec. 414(f)(6) (discussed below). [2]

Multiemployer plan status after termination. A plan is considered a multiemployer plan on and after its termination date if it was a multiemployer plan for the plan year preceding its termination date.[3]

Special election rules

Single-employer plans that had paid PBGC premiums for the three plan years preceding September 26, 1980 as a single employer plan were allowed a one-year window in which they could elect to continue to be treated as a single-employer plan.[4] The election to be treated as single-employer plan was to be irrevocable. However, the Pension Protection Act of 2006 provided plans that made a prior election with a new one year opportunity to revoke the existing election.[5]

Special procedures for implementing the election, including applicable participant and PBGC notice requirements are detailed at see CCH PENSION PLAN GUIDE ¶ 6905.

Plans covered by termination insurance

As a general rule, multiemployer plans that are defined benefit plans are covered under ERISA's termination insurance provisions.[6] Hybrid multiemployer plans that require fixed contributions, but that also promise a fixed pre-determined benefit, are generally not treated as individual account plans and, therefore, are covered by termination insurance.[7]

---

[1] ERISA Sec. 4001(a)(3). See IRS Letter Ruling 200734022, 5-29-07, at CCH PENSION PLAN GUIDE at ¶ 17,428F, in which the IRS privately ruled that a transferee plan did not become a multiemployer plan following the transfer of accrued benefits and liabilities of another plan where the former parent company retained responsibility for the administration, funding, and other aspects of the transferee plan. In addition, the former subsidiary had no responsibility for the maintaining or funding the plan. Therefore, the transferee plan was maintained by only one employer and did not become a multiemployer plan as a result of the transfer.

[2] PBGC Reg. § 4001.2.

[3] ERISA Sec. 4001(a)(3).

[4] Code Sec. 414(f)(5); ERISA Sec. 3(37)(E).

[5] Code Sec. 414(f)(6)(A), as added by P.L. 109-280 (Pension Protection Act of 2006), Act Sec. 1106(a); ERISA Sec. 3(37)(G)(i), as added by P.L. 109-280 (Pension Protection Act of 2006), Act Sec. 1106(a). The following special election rules applied. The new election, which is irrevocable, must be made within one year of the August 17, 2006 date of enactment of the Pension Act. In addition, the plan must satisfy the requirements of a multiemployer plan for each of the three plan years before August 17, 2006. *Election to be treated as a multiemployer plan.* Certain plans to which tax-exempt employers contribute are allowed, under Code Sec. 414(f)(6)(ii) and ERISA Sec. 3(37)(G)(i)(II)) an opportunity to elect, within one year of August 17, 2006, to be treated as a multiemployer plan. Thus, the election must

be made before August 17, 2007. A plan is eligible to make the election if for the plan year ending after August 17, 2006, and for each of the 3 plan years ending immediately before the first plan year for which the plan elects multiemployer status: (a) more than one employer is required to contribute to the plan and (b) the plan is maintained pursuant to one or more collective bargaining agreements between one or more employee organizations and more than one employer. In addition, substantially all of the plan's employer contributions for each of the 3 plan years immediately preceding the first plan year for which multiemployer status is elected must have been made or required to have been made by organizations that were exempt from tax under Code Sec. 501; and (3) the plan must have been established prior to September 2, 1974.

Under the U.S. Troop Readiness, Veterans' Care, Katrina Recovery, and Iraq Accountability Appropriations Act of 2007 (P.L. 110-28), a plan may designate the plan year in which the revocation of the election to be treated as a single-employer plan is to take effect, rather than having to use the plan year beginning right after August 17, 2006, as originally mandated by the Pension Protection Act of 2006. A plan may select an effective date starting with any plan year beginning on or after January 1, 1999, and ending before January 1, 2008.

[6] ERISA Sec. 4021(a) and (b).

[7] *Connolly v. PBGC*, CA-9 (1978), 581 F2d 729, cert. denied 2-26-79; *PBGC v. Defoe Shipbuilding*, CA-6 (1981), 639 F2d 311.

¶ 2870

PREMIUM PAYMENTS: Premium Payment Rules

The rules governing multiemployer plan terminations, similar to the rules controlling single employer plan terminations, require employers to pay premiums and the PBGC to guarantee benefits.

Premium payment amount

Multiemployer plans covered by the termination insurance provisions are required to pay an annual per participant premium to the PBGC. The provision is subject to cost-of-living adjustments. The flat-rate premium for 2012 is $9 (unchanged from 2011) per participant. [1] This premium amount is significantly less than the flat-rate premium that applies to single-employer plans (see ¶ 2809). In addition, variable rate premiums do not apply to multiemployer plans.

Due dates for filing premium payment form

Multiemployer plans, like single-employer plans, are required to make premium payments.

The PBGC has replaced the previously applicable Form 1, Schedule A and Form 1-EZ with one comprehensive premium filing, which must be made electronically. For plan years beginning with the 2010 plan year premium filings, the PBGC has combined the estimated flat rate premium filing (formerly Form 1-ES) with the comprehensive premium filing package.[2]

The due date for making the PBGC Comprehensive Premium Filing and paying the premium owed depends on whether the plan has 500 or more participants.

In determining whether a multiemployer plan has 500 or more participants, the plan administrator looks to the first day of the first plan year (if the premium payment year is the plan's second plan year), or the last day of the second preceding plan year (if the premium payment year is the plan's third or subsequent plan year).[3] Note that the participant count date for purposes of determining the filing due date is different from the participant count date used in computing the premium.

Plans with 500 or more participants. Multiemployer plans with 500 or more participants are required to make an estimated payment of the entire flat- rate premium on the estimated flat rate premium filing (formerly PBGC Form 1-ES) by the last day of the second full calendar month following the close of the preceding plan year (i.e., the first filing due date).[4]

EXAMPLE: A multiemployer plan has 750 participants and its plan year begins on January 1. For the 2012 plan year, an estimated premium payment on PBGC Form 1-ES must be made by February 28, 2012.

Reconciliation filing. In the event that the number of plan participants on the last day of the plan year preceding the premium payment year is not known by the first filing date, plans with at least 500 participants must make a reconciliation filing by the 15th day of the 10th full calendar month following the end of the plan year preceding the premium payment year (i.e., the final filing date).[5] For calendar year plans, the filing date is October 15.

If all of the information needed to make a comprehensive filing is known before the first filing date, a plan administrator should make that filing instead of the estimated flat-rate premium filing (formerly PBGC Form 1-ES).[6] Plans that file the estimated flat rate premium filing (formerly Form 1-ES) will be required to make a final filing by the applicable due date.

Safe harbor rules for late premium payments. In the event that the full amount is not paid by the required filing date (i.e., February 28 of the premium payment year), the plan will be subject to late payment interest charges and late payment penalty charges. However, because plan administrators may not know the exact participant count for the premium payment year by February 28 of the premium payment year, the PBGC provides a safe harbor, pursuant to which the late payment penalty charges (but not the late payment interest charge) will not be assessed if the plan administrator, by February 28 of the premium payment year, pays at least the lesser of (1) 90% of the flat rate premium due for the premium payment year, or (2) 100% of the flat rate premium that would be due for the premium payment year if the number of participants for that year were the lesser of (a) the actual number of participants for the prior year; or (b) the number of participants reported on the prior year's PBGC Form 1 or amended PBGC Form 1, filed by February 28 of the premium payment year.[7] See also ¶ 2809.

Plans with fewer than 500 participants. The filing due dates for plans with less than 500 participants depends on whether the plan is a small plan or a mid-size plan. [8] For small plans (less than 100 participants), flat-rate premiums are due on the last day of the 16th full calendar month that begins on or after the first day of the premium payment year. For mid-size plans (100-499 participants) flat-rate premiums are due on the 15th day of the 10th full calendar month that begins on or after the first day of the premium payment year.

When premium payment filings are considered filed. In general, a premium filing is considered to be filed on the date it is postmarked if certain requirements are met [9] If the requirements are not met, the filing date is the date the PBGC receives the submission. If the 15th day is a weekend or federal holiday, the due date is extended to the next business day. However, late payment interest and penalty charges include a weekend or federal holiday if either falls on the due date.

Electronic filings. A submission made through the PBGC's website is considered to have been sent when the plan administrator has performed the last act necessary to indicate that the submission is filed and cannot be further edited or withdrawn. [10]

Premium may be waived

The PBGC may waive or reduce premiums for a multiemployer plan for any plan year during which it provides financial assistance to the plan. However, any amount waived or reduced will be treated as part of the financial assistance.[11] See also ¶ 2809.

---

[1] ERISA Sec. 4006(a)(3)(A)(iii), as amended by P.L. 100-171 (Deficit Reduction Act of 2005), Act Sec. 8181(a)(2)(A), effective for plan years after December 31, 2005; ERISA Sec. 4006(a)(3)(G), as added by P.L. 109-171 (Deficit Reduction Act of 2005), Act Sec. 8101(a)(2)(B). PBGC Website, October 25, 2011.

[2] 2010 PBGC Premium Payment Instructions.

[3] PBGC Reg. § 4007.11(b)(2); 2010 Premium Payment Instructions.

[4] PBGC Reg. § 4007.11(a)(2)(i); 2010 Premium Payment Instructions.

[5] PBGC Reg. § 4007.11(a)(2)(ii), as amended 12-14-98 (63 FR 68684).

[6] 2010 Premium Payment Instructions.

[7] PBGC Reg. § 4007.8(g).

[8] PBGC Reg. §§ 4007.11(a)(1) and 4007.11(a)(2)(i), as amended 12-14-98 (63 FR 68684). Prior to the 1999 premium payment year, the final filing date was the 15th day of the 8th full calendar month following the month in which the plan year began (September 15 for calendar year plans).

[9] PBGC Reg. § 4000.23.

[10] PBGC Reg. § 4000.23(a).

[11] ERISA Sec. 4007(a); PBGC Reg. §§ 4007.8(b)—(g).

¶ 2871

PREMIUM PAYMENTS: Liability for Premiums and Late Payment Penalties

The plan administrator of a multiemployer plan is generally liable for the payment of premiums, even if another party is designated by the plan administrator to file the PBGC forms and submit the premium payments.[1]

Interest and penalty charges

In the event that any premium payment due is not paid by the last day prescribed for payment, interest and penalties will be charged on the unpaid amount.[2] However, the PBGC may authorize a waiver of the penalty where warranted by reasonable cause or hardship.[3] See also ¶ 2809.

[1] ERISA Sec. 4007(e)(1)(B); PBGC Reg. § 4007.12(a).

[2] PBGC Reg. § 4007.7(a) and Appendix A; PBGC Reg. § 4007.8(a).

[3] PBGC Reg. § 4007.8(b) and (c).

¶ 2872

GUARANTEED BENEFITS: Benefits Guaranteed for Insolvent Plans

The PBGC guarantees a multiemployer plan's nonforfeitable benefits only if the plan is insolvent.[1] A multiemployer plan is insolvent if its "available resources" are not sufficient to pay benefits (at least equal to the PBGC's maximum guaranteed benefit—see ¶ 2873) under the plan when due for the plan year.[2] Available resources include the plan's cash, marketable assets, contributions, withdrawal liability payments, and earnings, less reasonable administration expenses and amounts for the plan year owed to the PBGC for financial assistance.[3]

Insolvency following benefit reduction

If a plan is terminated by the withdrawal of all employers, and if the value of nonforfeitable benefits exceeds the value of plan assets, the plan sponsor must amend the plan to reduce benefits, but only to the extent necessary to pay all of the nonforfeitable benefits when due and to the extent that those benefits are not eligible for the PBGC's guarantee. If, after the implementation of the reduction, the plan's available resources are not sufficient to pay benefits when due, the plan is considered insolvent.[4]

Benefits in effect less than 60 months not guaranteed

The PBGC will not guarantee a benefit or benefit increase that has been in effect under a multiemployer plan for less than 60 months.[5] In addition, the PBGC will not guarantee a benefit or benefit increase in effect for less than 60 months before the first day of the plan year in which a plan amendment reducing the increase is taken into account. The 60-month period does not include any month of a plan year during which the plan is insolvent or any month after the plan is terminated by mass withdrawal of employers.[6]

Forfeitable benefits are not guaranteed

Forfeitable benefits are generally not guaranteed by the PBGC. In addition, benefits that become nonforfeitable solely on account of plan termination are not guaranteed by the PBGC.[7]

Financial assistance for insolvent plans

A plan sponsor who has determined that a resource benefit level for an insolvency year is below the level of basic benefits, must apply for financial assistance from the PBGC.[8] The financial assistance is provided in the form of a loan.

---

[1] ERISA Sec. 4022A(a).

[2] ERISA Sec. 4245(b)(1).

[3] ERISA Sec. 4245(b)(3).

[4] ERISA Sec. 4281(d)(2).

[5] ERISA Sec. 4022A(b)(1).

[6] ERISA Sec. 4022A(b)(1)(A).

[7] ERISA Sec. 4022A(a).

[8] ERISA Sec. 4245(f); ERISA Sec. 4261; Code Sec. 418E(f).

¶ 2873

GUARANTEED BENEFITS: Amount of Guaranteed Benefits

In order to create an incentive for multiemployer plans to avoid insolvency while reducing the risk of excessive costs, benefits guaranteed by the PBGC are lower than those to which a recipient would be entitled under the plan.[1]

The monthly benefit of a participant or beneficiary that is guaranteed by the PBGC is the product of (1) 100% of the monthly benefit accrual rate up to $11 plus 75% of the lesser of $33 or the accrual rate, if any, in excess of $11 and (2) the number of the participant's years of credited service.[2]

Example: John completes 30 years of service and has a benefit accrual rate of $23 per month. The maximum benefit guarantee for John is $600 per month ($7,200 per year), determined as follows:

1. [($100% multiplied by $11) + (75% multiplied by 12)] multiplied by 30 years = $600 per month.

2. $600 multiplied by 12 months = $7,200 per year.

Guaranteed monthly benefits

The monthly benefits eligible for the guarantee are limited to retirement benefits which would otherwise be subject to guarantee, are not greater than the plan benefit payable at normal retirement age as a life annuity, and are determined without regard to reductions permitted on account of cessation of contributions by an employer. The accrual rate is determined by dividing a participant's monthly benefits eligible for the guarantee by the number of full and fractional years of service credited to the participant.[3]

Year of credited service

A year of credited service is a year in which the participant completed a full year of participation in the plan or any period of service before participation that is credited for purposes of benefits accrual as the equivalent of a full year of participation.[4]

Aggregate limit on guaranteed benefits

ERISA imposes a limit on the aggregate present value of benefits that may be paid to a participant who is eligible for benefits under more than one plan. The aggregate present value of benefits is limited to an amount that is not in excess of the actuarial value of a monthly benefit in the form of a life annuity commencing at age 65 equal to $750 multiplied by the following fraction:[5]

$$\frac{\text{contribution and benefit base in effect upon termination}}{\$13,200}$$

---

[1]P.L. 96-364 (Multiemployer Pension Plan Amendments Act of 1980), Senate Committee Report.

[2] ERISA Sec. 4022A(c)(1).

[3] ERISA Sec. 4022A(c)(3).

[4] ERISA Sec. 4022A(c)(4).

[5] ERISA Sec. 4022B, cross-referencing ERISA Sec. 4022 (b)(3)(B).

¶ 2874

GUARANTEED BENEFITS: Reduction of Guaranteed Benefits

In the event a participant's benefits are reduced because of circumstances, such as a cessation of employer contributions or the amendment of a plan in reorganization, the amount of the PBGC guarantee will also be reduced.

CCH POINTER: Under prior law, if a multiemployer plan became insolvent before year 2000 and was required to reduce or suspend benefits, the level of benefits guaranteed by the PBGC was reduced.[1] The maximum guarantee for monthly base benefits for each year of credited service under such a plan was 100% of the first $5 of benefit accrual plus 65% (rather than 75%) of the accrual rate greater than $5, but not exceeding $15.

The Consolidated Appropriations Act of 2001 (P.L. 106-554) eliminated the provisions of ERISA requiring the reduction in guaranteed benefits for plans that became insolvent before 2000. The amendment applies to multiemployer plans that did not receive financial assistance from the PBGC within the one-year period ending on December 21, 2000. The prior law rules apply to participants in multiemployer plans that received financial assistance from the PBGC in 2000.[2]

☐ Applicable transition rules are discussed at CCH PENSION PLAN GUIDE ¶ 6963.

Cessation of employer contributions

A multiemployer plan may provide that benefits accrued as a result of service with an employer before the employer had an obligation to contribute under the plan are not payable if the employer ceases to contribute to the plan. The PBGC will guarantee only the lesser of this reduced benefit or the benefit calculated under the basic-benefit limitations.[3]

Plans in reorganization

Generally, plan amendments are not permitted to reduce benefits already accrued by an employee. However, amendments to a multiemployer plan in reorganization may reduce accrued benefits attributable to employer contributions under certain circumstances.[4] Benefits that have been in effect for less than 60 months and are not eligible for guarantee by the PBGC are subject to this reduction.[5]

Active and inactive participants. Benefits of inactive participants may not be reduced in greater proportions than those of active participants. Benefits attributable to employer contributions (other than accrued benefits) and the rate of future benefit accruals are to be decreased to the same extent as the accrued benefits of inactive participants.[6]

Change in benefit form or eligibility requirements. Benefit reductions that are effected through a change in form or eligibility requirements do not apply to any participant or beneficiary in pay status on the effective date of the amendment. In addition, the reduction does not apply to any participant who has attained normal retirement age or who is within five years of attaining normal retirement age on the effective date of the amendment.[7]

Rate of contributions. The rate of employer contributions for the plan year in which the amendment becomes effective and for all future years while the plan is in reorganization must at least equal the greater of:[8]

1. the rate of employer contributions (without regard to the amendment) for the plan year in which the amendment becomes effective; or

2. the rate of employer contributions for the preceding plan year.

Notice of reduction in accrued benefits. At least six months before the first day of the plan year in which the amendment is adopted, plan participants, beneficiaries, and their collective bargaining representatives, and each employer who must contribute under the plan, must be notified that the plan is in reorganization and that, if contributions are not increased, accrued benefits will be reduced or an excise tax will be imposed on the employers.[9] Note, a plan that provides an ERISA Sec.4244A(b) notice will be treated as timely providing any required ERISA Sec. 204(h) notice.[10]

---

[1] ERISA Sec. 4022A(c)(2), prior to amendment by P.L. 106-554.

[2] PBGC Technical Update 00-7, 12-26-2000, CCH Pension Plan Guide ¶ 19,974S.

[3] ERISA Sec. 4022A(d).

[4] ERISA Sec. 4244A(a); Code Sec. 418D(a).

[5] ERISA Secs. 4244A(a) and 4022A(b)(1)(A); Code Sec. 418D(a).

6 ERISA Sec. 4244A(b)(1)(B)(i) and (ii); Code Sec. 418D(b)(1)(B)(i) and (ii).

7 ERISA Sec. 4244A(b)(1)(B)(iii); Code Sec. 418D(b)(1)(B)(iii).

8 ERISA Sec. 4244A(b)(1)(C); Code Sec. 418D(b)(1)(C).

9 ERISA Sec. 4244A(b)(1)(A); Code Sec. 418D(b)(1)(A).

10 IRS Reg. §IRS Reg. 54.4980F-1, A-9(g)(3)(ii)(D).

¶ 2875

GUARANTEED BENEFITS: Suspension of Nonbasic Benefits by Insolvent Plan

An insolvent multiemployer plan must suspend the payment of nonbasic benefits which exceed the highest level of monthly benefits that the plan could pay out of its available resources, as determined by the plan sponsor (i.e., the "resource benefit level").[1]

If a plan sponsor determines a resource benefit level which is below the basic benefit level for a plan year, the payment of all nonbasic benefits must be suspended for that year. Alternatively, if the plan sponsor determines by the end of the plan year that benefits may be paid above the resource benefit level, the benefits must be distributed. Where benefits up to the resource benefit level have not been paid, the amount necessary to bring benefits up to that level must be distributed, if the plan's available resources permit.[2]

☐ For additional discussion, see ¶ 2930.

---

1 ERISA Secs. 4245(a) and (b) and 4281(d); Code Sec. 418E(a) and (b).

2 ERISA Sec. 4245(c)(5); Code Sec. 418E(c)(5).

¶ 2876

GUARANTEED BENEFITS: Insolvency Notices

The sponsor of an insolvent multiemployer plan is generally required to file a notice of insolvency and a notice of insolvency benefit level with the PBGC. Specifically, the sponsor of a multiemployer plan in reorganization must notify both the PBGC and interested persons when it determines that the plan's available resources are or may be insufficient to pay benefits when due for a plan year (i.e., "notice of insolvency"). In addition, the plan sponsor is required to notify the PBGC and interested parties of the level of benefits expected to be paid during each insolvency year (i.e., "notice of insolvency benefit level").[1] Note, a plan that provides an ERISA Sec. 4245(e) notice will be treated as timely providing any required ERISA Sec. 204(h) notice.[2]

CCH POINTER: *Multiemployer Plan Funding Notice.* The administrators of multiemployer defined benefit plans are also required to furnish an annual funding notice to participants and beneficiaries, labor organizations, contributing employers, and the PBGC detailing the financial status of the plan.[3] The notice requirements were significantly changed by the Pension Protection Act of 2006, effective for plan years beginning after 2007.[4] In addition to expanded information requirements, the time by which the notice must be provided has been accelerated. See ¶ 1493L.

Multiemployer financial plan information provided upon request. Upon written request, each multiemployer plan administrator must furnish specified financial information for the plan to any plan participant or beneficiary, employee representative, or any employer that has an obligation to make contributions. [5] The information that must be made available includes: a copy of any periodic actuarial report (including any sensitivity testing) received by the plan for any plan year that has been in the plan's possession for at least 30 days; a copy of any quarterly, semiannual, or annual financial report prepared for the plan by any plan investment manager or advisor, or other fiduciary that has been in the plan's possession for at least 30 days; and a copy of any application requesting an extension of amortization periods concerning multiemployer plan funding (filed with the Secretary of the Treasury under Code Sec. 431(d) or ERISA Sec. 304, as well as any determination made upon this application by the Treasury Secretary (see ¶ 2220).

Confidentiality limits. Any actuarial or financial report required to be provided under this provision is subject to confidentiality limits. These required reports may not (a) include any individually identifiable information regarding any plan participant, beneficiary, employee, fiduciary, or contributing employer; or (b) reveal any proprietary information about the plan, any contributing employer, or entity providing services to the plan. [6] Note, the Worker, Retiree, and Employer Recovery Act of 2008 clarified that a plan is not prohibited from disclosing the identity of an investment manager or adviser, or any person preparing a financial report (other than an employee of the plan) whose performance is the subject of the report or evaluation. [7]

Contents of notice of insolvency

In addition to identifying plan information specified in the governing PBGC regulations, the notice of insolvency filed with the PBGC must disclose: the plan year or years for which the plan sponsor has determined that the plan is or may be insolvent; a copy of the plan document, including the last restatement of the plan and all subsequent amendments in effect (or due to become effective) during the insolvency year or years; a copy of the most recent actuarial valuation for the plan and a copy of the most recent Schedule M (Form 5500) filed for the plan, if the Schedule contains more recent information than the actuarial valuation (unless the information was previously submitted to the PBGC); the estimated amount of annual benefit payments under the plan (determined without regard to the insolvency) for each insolvency year; and the estimated amount of the plan's available resources for each insolvency year.[8]

Notice to interested parties. The notice of insolvency required to be furnished to interested parties (i.e., participants and beneficiaries, contributing employers, and employee organizations representing participants) must further contain a statement that explains that, during the insolvency year, benefits above the amount that can be paid from available resources or the level guaranteed by the PBGC, whichever is greater, will be suspended.[9] The statement must also explain the benefits that are guaranteed by the PBGC. PBGC Reg. § 4254.4(b)(5) provides model language that may be used as an explanation of PBGC guaranteed benefits.

Note, the plan sponsor must certify in writing that notices of insolvency containing the required information have been provided to interested parties.

Time for delivering notice. A plan sponsor must generally deliver the notices of insolvency no later than 30 days after it determines that the plan is or may become insolvent.[10]

Contents of notice of insolvency benefit level

A notice of insolvency benefit level filed with the PBGC is generally required to include the same information as the notice of insolvency.[11] However, the notice of insolvency benefit level must further include the amount of any financial assistance requested from the PBGC.[12]

Notice to pay status participants and nonpay status participants. Different requirements apply to the notices provided to pay status participants and beneficiaries and to the notices furnished to other interested parties.[13] The notice of insolvency benefit level required to be provided to contributing employers, employee organizations, and participants and beneficiaries who are not in pay status (or reasonably expected to enter pay status during the insolvency year) must include the estimated amount of the annual benefit payments under the plan for the insolvency year, the estimated amount of the plan's available resources for the insolvency year, and the amount of any financial assistance requested from the PBGC.

The notice furnished to pay status participants and beneficiaries must set forth the monthly benefit expected to be paid to the participant or beneficiary during the insolvency year and include a statement cautioning that, in subsequent plan years, depending on the plan's available resources, the monthly benefit level may be modified, but not below the level guaranteed by the PBGC.[14]

Notice due 60 days before insolvency year. The plan sponsor must generally mail or otherwise deliver the required notice of insolvency benefit level, at least 60 days before the beginning of the insolvency year.[15]

Delivery of notices

The notice of insolvency and the notice of insolvency benefit level may be delivered pursuant specified to methods.

Delivery to PBGC. The notice of insolvency and notice insolvency benefit level required to be filed with the PBGC may be provided by hand, mail, or commercial delivery service or through electronic media.[16]

Generally, a submission is treated as filed on the date that it is sent, provided specified conditions are satisfied.[17] The applicable conditions are determined by the method pursuant to which the submission is filed. For example, electronic filings must comply with specified technical requirements, satisfy the safe harbor rules of PBGC Reg. § 4000.14, and identify a contact person for the re-submission of a filing.[18]

¶ 2876

Delivery to interested parties. The notice of insolvency or notice of insolvency benefit level may be provided to interested parties pursuant to any method (e.g., hand, mail, or commercial delivery service or electronic media) that is reasonably calculated to ensure actual receipt of the material to the intended recipient.[19]

Posting of notice. Posting of the notice in the workplace is, generally, not an acceptable method for providing the notice.[20] However, the plan sponsor may notify interested parties, other than participants and beneficiaries who are in pay status, when the notice is required to be delivered (for the notice of insolvency) or during the insolvency year for which the notice is given (for the notice of insolvency benefit level), by posting the notice at participants' work sites or publishing the notice in a union newsletter or in a newspaper of general circulation in the area and areas in which participants reside.[21]

Notice issued when sent. The notice of insolvency and the notice of insolvency benefit level are treated as having been issued on the date sent, if specified conditions are satisfied.[22]

[1] ERISA Sec. 4245(e); PBGC Reg. §§ 4245.3-4245.5(a).

[2] IRS Reg. § 54.4980F-1, A-9(g)(3)(ii)(E).

[3] ERISA Sec. 101(f), as added by P.L. 108-218 (Pension Funding Equity Act of 2004), Act Sec. 103(a) and 103(d).

[4] ERISA Sec. 101(f), as added by P.L. 108-280 (Pension Protection Act of 2006), Act Sec. 501(a) and (d).

[5] ERISA Sec. 101(k)(1), as added by P.L. 109-280 (Pension Protection Act of 2006), Act Sec. 502(a)(1)(B).

[6] ERISA Sec.101(k)(2)(C), as added by P.L. 109-280 (Pension Protection Act of 2006), Act Sec. 502(a)(1)(B).

[7] ERISA Sec.101(k)(2), as amended by P.L. 110-458 (Worker, Retiree, and Employer Recovery Act of 2008), Act Sec. 105(b)(1).

[8] PBGC Reg. § 4245.4(a).

[9] PBGC Reg. § 4245.4(b).

[10] PBGC Reg. § 4245.3(b).

[11] PBGC Reg. § 4245.6.

[12] PBGC Reg. § 4245.6(a)(12).

[13] PBGC Reg. § 4245.6(b) and 4245.6(c).

[14] PBGC Reg. § 4245.6(c).

[15] PBGC Reg. § 4245.5(c).

[16] PBGC Reg. § 4000.3; 4245.3(c); and PBGC Reg. § 4245.5(d).

[17] PBGC Reg. § 4000.23; 4245.3(c)(2); and 4245.5(d)(2).

[18] PBGC Reg. § 4000.29.

[19] PBGC Reg. § 4000.13; 4245.3(d); and 4245.5(e).

[20] PBGC Reg. § 4000.13(a).

[21] PBGC Reg. § 4245.3(d) and PBGC Reg. § 4245.5(e).

[22] PBGC Reg. § 4000.21; 4245.3(d)(2); and 4245.5(e)(12).

¶ 2877
TERMINATION OF MULTIEMPLOYER PLANS:
Methods of Termination

Multiemployer plans may be terminated by:

1. the withdrawal of every employer from the plan (i.e., "mass withdrawal") (see ¶ 2878);

2. an amendment of the plan that denies participants credit under the plan for any period of service with the employer after a specific date or that converts the plan into defined contribution plan (see ¶ 2882); or

3. proceedings instituted by the PBGC (see ¶ 2882A).

¶ 2878

TERMINATION OF MULTIEMPLOYER PLANS:
Termination by Mass Withdrawal

A plan from which every employer has withdrawn is terminated on the earlier of the date the last employer withdraws or the first day of the first plan year for which no employer contributions are required under the plan.[1]

File termination notice with PBGC

A notice of termination must be filed with the PBGC by a multiemployer plan that is terminated by mass withdrawal (or plan amendment).[2] The notice is to be filed by the plan sponsor or a duly authorized representative of the sponsor.

The Notice of Termination may be filed with the PBGC by hand, mail, or commercial delivery service or through electronic media.[3] Generally, a submission is treated as filed when it is sent, provided specified requirements are satisfied.[4] The applicable requirements vary, depending on the method of delivery elected. For example, electronic filings must comply with technical requirements set forth by the PBGC.[5]

☐ Information that must be provided in the notice of termination is discussed at CCH PENSION PLAN GUIDE ¶ 6980.

Plan amendment reducing benefits

If a plan is terminated by mass withdrawal, the value of nonforfeitable benefits and the value of the assets of the plan must be determined in writing as of the end of the plan year of the termination and each plan year thereafter.[6] In the event that the value of nonforfeitable benefits exceeds the value of plan assets, the plan sponsor must amend the plan to reduce benefits under the plan. Benefits need be reduced only to the extent necessary to pay all of the nonforfeitable benefits when due and to the extent that those benefits are not eligible for the PBGC's guarantee.[7]

Notice of benefit reduction

If a plan amendment that reduces benefits is adopted by a multiemployer plan terminated by mass withdrawal, the plan sponsor must notify the PBGC and plan participants and beneficiaries whose benefits are reduced by the amendment.[8] The notice must be delivered no later than the earlier of 45 days after the amendment is adopted or the date of the first reduced payment.

Notices of benefit reduction are to be delivered in the manner and within the time period prescribed by the PBGC.[9] The Notice of benefit reduction may be filed with the PBGC by hand, mail, or commercial delivery service or through electronic media, pursuant to requirements specified by the PBGC.[10] The notice may be provided to interested parties pursuant to any method (including electronic media) that is reasonably calculated to ensure actual receipt by the intended recipient.[11]

Note, a plan that provides an ERISA Sec. 4281 notice will be treated as timely providing any required ERISA Sec. 204(h) notice. [12]

☐ Information that must be provided in the notice is discussed at CCH PENSION PLAN GUIDE ¶ 6986.

Restoration of benefits

The sponsor of a plan that has been amended to reduce benefits must amend the plan to restore those benefits before adopting any amendment increasing benefits under the plan.[13] The plan must notify the PBGC in writing of the restoration of benefits.[14] A plan, however, is not required to make retroactive benefit payments for any benefit was reduced and subsequently restored.

Annual and other insolvency determinations

In the event that a multiemployer plan terminated by mass withdrawal is amended to eliminate all benefits subject to reduction, the plan sponsor must determine in writing whether the plan is expected to be insolvent for the first plan year beginning after the effective date of the amendment and for each plan year thereafter.[15]

If no benefits are subject to reduction as of the date of plan termination, the plan sponsor must determine in writing whether the plan is expected to be insolvent for the second plan year beginning after the first plan year for which it is determined that the value of nonforfeitable benefits exceeds the value of the plan's assets. The determination must also be made for each plan year thereafter.[16]

Suspension of benefits

In the event that the plan is expected to be insolvent for a plan year, the sponsor must suspend benefits to the extent necessary to reduce the benefits to the greater of the resource benefit level (see ¶ 2875) or the level of guaranteed benefits.[17]

Notice of insolvency

A plan sponsor of a multiemployer plan terminated by mass withdrawal that determines that the plan is, or is expected to be, insolvent for a plan year must issue notices of insolvency to the PBGC and to plan participants and beneficiaries.[18] Generally, the notices of insolvency must be delivered no later than 30 days after the plan sponsor determines that the plan is or may be insolvent.[19]

☐ Information required in the notice of insolvency is discussed at CCH PENSION PLAN GUIDE ¶ 6994.

Annual updates

After issuing a notice of insolvency, the plan sponsor must issue annual updates to the PBGC and to participants and beneficiaries for each plan year beginning after the plan year for which the notice of insolvency was issued. The annual update must generally be delivered no later than 60 days before the beginning of the year for which the annual update is issued.[20]

¶2878

Notice of insolvency benefit level

For each insolvency year, the sponsor of a multiemployer plan terminated by mass withdrawal must issue a notice of insolvency benefit level to the PBGC and to plan participants and beneficiaries in pay status (or reasonably expected to enter pay status during the insolvency year).[21] Generally, the notice of insolvency benefit level must be provided no later than 60 days before the beginning of the insolvency year.[22]

The notice of insolvency benefit level may be provided to the PBGC by hand, mail, or commercial delivery service or (pursuant to rules effective beginning November 28, 2003) electronic media.[23] The notice of insolvency benefit level provided to plan participants and beneficiaries in pay status (or reasonably expected to enter pay status during the insolvency year) may be delivered pursuant to any method that is reasonably calculated to ensure actual receipt of the material by the intended recipient.[24] The final rules further provide a safe harbor method that will allow the notice to be delivered to interested parties electronically.[25]

☐ Information required in the notice of insolvency benefit level is discussed at CCH PENSION PLAN GUIDE ¶ 6996.

Application for financial assistance

If the plan sponsor of a multiemployer plan terminated by mass withdrawal determines that the plan's resource benefit level (i.e., the highest level of monthly benefits that can be paid out of the plan's available resources) for an insolvency year is below the level of benefits guaranteed by the PBGC or that the plan will be unable to pay guaranteed benefits when due for any month during the year, the plan sponsor must apply to the PBGC for financial assistance.[26]

☐ Information that must be included in the application for financial assistance is at CCH PENSION PLAN GUIDE ¶ 6998.

---

[1] ERISA Sec. 4041A(a) and (b).

[2] PBGC Reg. § 4041A.11.

[3] PBGC Reg. § 4000.3 and 4041A.3(a).

[4] PBGC Reg. § 4000.23 and 4041A.3(a).

[5] PBGC Reg. § 4000.29(b(1).

[6] ERISA Sec. 4281(b).

[7] ERISA Sec. 4281(c).

[8] PBGC Reg. § 4281.32.

[9] PBGC Reg. § 4281.32.

[10] PBGC Reg. § 4000.3 and 4281.3(a).

[11] PBGC Reg. § 4000.13 and 4281.32(c).

[12] IRS Reg. § 54.4980F-1, A-9(g)(3)(ii)(F).

[13] PBGC Reg. § 4281.33(a).

[14] PBGC Reg. § 4281.33(b).

[15] PBGC Reg. § 4041A.25(a).

[16] *Ibid.*

[17] PBGC Reg. § 4281.41.

[18] PBGC Reg. § 4281.43-4281.44.

[19] PBGC Reg. § 4281.43(c).

[20] PBGC Reg. § 4281.43(d).

[21] PBGC Reg. § § 4281.45-4281.46.

[22] PBGC Reg. § 4281.45(b).

[23] PBGC Reg. § 4000.3; 4281.3(a); and PBGC Reg. § 4281.45.

[24] PBGC Reg. § 4000.13 and 4281.45(c).

[25] 4281.45(c).

[26] PBGC Reg. § 4281.47.

¶ 2879

TERMINATION OF MULTIEMPLOYER PLANS: Annual Plan Valuation and Monitoring

The plan sponsor of a multiemployer plan terminated by mass withdrawal must, no later than 150 days after the end of the plan year, determine the value of nonforfeitable benefits under the plan and the value of the plan's assets.[1] This valuation must be made as of the end of the plan year in which the plan terminates and each plan year thereafter (excluding any plan year for which the plan receives financial assistance from the PBGC) up to but not including the plan year in which the plan is closed out with sufficient assets.

Benefits exceeding assets

The plan sponsor, upon receipt of the annual valuation, must determine whether the value of nonforfeitable benefits exceeds the value of the plan's assets, including claims for withdrawal liability owed to the plan.[2] If benefits exceed assets, the plan sponsor must:

1. *if plan benefits are subject to reduction,* amend the plan to reduce the benefits to the extent necessary to ensure that the plan's assets are sufficient to discharge, when due, all of the plan's obligations for nonforfeitable benefits; or

2. *if plan benefits are not subject to reduction,* make periodic determinations of plan solvency (see ¶ 2878).

---

[1] PBGC Reg. § 4041A.24(a).   [2] PBGC Reg. § 4041A.24(b).

¶ 2880

TERMINATION OF MULTIEMPLOYER PLANS: Plan Sponsor's Duties During Mass Withdrawal

The plan sponsor of a multiemployer plan terminated in a mass withdrawal must continue to administer the plan in accordance with the applicable law, regulations, and plan provisions until a trustee is appointed or, in the case of plans with sufficient assets, the assets are distributed.[1] In addition, the plan sponsor is responsible for duties described below.

Payment of benefits

Generally, the plan sponsor must pay benefits attributable to employer contributions, other than death benefits, only in the form of an annuity.[2] However, the plan sponsor may pay benefits in a non-annuity form if: the plan assets are distributed in full satisfaction of all nonforfeitable benefits under the plan; the PBGC approves the payment of benefits in an alternative form; or the value of the entire nonforfeitable benefit does not exceed $1,750.[3] The PBGC may further authorize the plan to pay benefits valued at over $1,750 in a form other than an annuity.[4]

Imposition and collection of withdrawal liability

Until plan assets are distributed in accordance with the rules for closing out sufficient plans (see ¶ 2881) or until the end of the plan year in which the PBGC determines that plan assets (not counting claims for withdrawal liability) are sufficient to satisfy all nonforfeitable benefits, the plan sponsor is responsible for determining, imposing, and collecting withdrawal liability.[5]

☐ Withdrawal liability is discussed at ¶ 2883 and following.

---

[1] PBGC Reg. § 4041A.21.

[2] PBGC Reg. § 4041A.22(a).

[3] ERISA Sec. 4041A(c)(2) and (f)(1); PBGC Reg. § 4041A.22(b).

[4] PBGC Reg. § 4041A.27.

[5] PBGC Reg. § 4041A.23.

¶ 2881

TERMINATION OF MULTIEMPLOYER PLANS: Procedures for Closing Out Sufficient Plans

The plan sponsor of a "sufficient" multiemployer plan terminated by mass withdrawal may close out the plan by distributing plan assets in full satisfaction of all nonforfeitable benefits provided under the plan.[1] A plan is "sufficient" if it has enough plan assets, excluding any claim of the plan for unpaid withdrawal liability, to satisfy all obligations for nonforfeitable benefits under the plan.

Distribution method

The plan sponsor must distribute plan assets by purchasing contracts from an insurer to provide all required benefits in annuity form and by paying in a lump sum (or other alternative elected by the participant) all other benefits.[2]

CCH POINTER: The PBGC's Missing Participant Program (see ¶ 2831), under which plan administrators may purchase an annuity and transfer a missing participant's benefit to the PBGC, has been extended to multiemployer plans.[3]

Form of benefit

Generally, the sponsor of a plan that is closed out must provide for the payment of benefits attributable to employer contributions only in the form of an annuity.[4] However, the plan sponsor may pay benefits attributable to employer contributions in a form other than an annuity if: the present value of the participant's entire nonforfeitable benefit does not exceed $5,000; the payment is for death benefits provided under the plan; or the participant elects an alternative form of distribution.[5]

---

[1] PBGC Reg. § 4041A.41.

[2] PBGC Reg. § 4041A.42.

[3] ERISA Sec. 4050(c), as added by P.L. 109-280 (Pension Protection Act of 2006), Act. Sec. 410.

[4] PBGC Reg. § 4041A.43(a).

[5] PBGC Reg. § 4041A.43(b) and (c).

¶ 2882

TERMINATION OF MULTIEMPLOYER PLANS:
Termination by Plan Amendment

Amendments of a multiemployer plan that either deny participants credit for any period for service with an employer after a date specified by the amendment or change the plan into a defined contribution arrangement will (as of the later of the date the amendment is adopted or effective) terminate the plan.[1]

Continued maintenance of terminated plan

An employer may continue to maintain a plan terminated by amendment. However, the employer must make contributions at a rate no less than the highest rate applicable during the period of the five preceding years ending on or before the date of termination. This rate may be reduced if the PBGC finds that the plan is or soon will be fully funded.[2]

Termination notice

A multiemployer plan that is terminated by plan amendment must file a termination notice with the PBGC.[3] The notice must contain identifying information about the plan and the sponsor, including the plan's most recent Form 5500 and schedules, all of which must be certified as accurate by the sponsor.[4] However, a greater amount of information must be provided in the termination notice that is required when a multiemployer plan is terminated by mass withdrawal (see ¶ 2878).

The plan sponsor or its authorized representative is required to file the notice within 30 days after the later of the date on which the amendment is adopted or takes effect.[5]

---

[1] ERISA Sec. 4041A(b)(1).

[2] ERISA Sec. 4041A(e).

[3] PBGC Reg. § 4041A.11(a).

[4] PBGC Reg. § 4041A.12(a) and (c).

[5] PBGC Reg. § 4041A.11(c).

¶ 2882A

TERMINATION OF MULTIEMPLOYER PLANS:
Termination by the PBGC

A multiemployer plan may be terminated through proceedings instituted by the PBGC. The PBGC may initiate termination proceedings if the plan has not met the minimum funding standards or will not be able to pay benefits when due.[1] In addition, a plan may be terminated in order to shield the PBGC from an unreasonably large loss.

The PBGC may petition a federal court for the appointment of a trustee to administer the plan pending issuance of court decree terminating the plan.[2]

□ The rules governing terminations by the PBGC are discussed at ¶ 2833 and 2834. The rules generally apply to involuntary terminations of both single employer and multiemployer plans.

[1] ERISA Sec. 4042(a).

[2] ERISA Sec. 4042(b).

¶ 2883
WITHDRAWAL LIABILITY: General Rules

An employer that totally or partially withdraws from a multiemployer pension plan is required to continue funding a proportional share of the plan's unfunded vested benefits by making specified annual withdrawal liability payments to the plan.[1] A complete withdrawal occurs when an employer permanently ceases to have an obligation to contribute under the plan or permanently ceases all covered operations under the plan (see ¶ 2888).[2] A partial withdrawal occurs where the employer does not completely withdraw from the plan, but where a specific event significantly reduces the employer's plan contribution obligations (see ¶ 2890).[3]

The plan sponsor determines the amount of the withdrawing employer's liability, determines whether the withdrawal is partial or complete, and collects the amount on behalf of the plan.[4] An employer that withdraws from a plan must comply within 30 days with a request from the plan sponsor for information necessary to enable the sponsor to compute and collect withdrawal liability.[5]

[1] ERISA Secs. 4201-4225.

[2] ERISA Sec. 4203(a).

[3] ERISA Sec. 4205.

[4] ERISA Sec. 4202.

[5] ERISA Sec. 4219(a).

¶ 2884
WITHDRAWAL LIABILITY: Employers Subject to Withdrawal Liability

An "employer" that withdraws from a multiemployer plan is liable for withdrawal liability. ERISA's broad definition of the term employer that applies for purposes of Title I does not apply for purposes of withdrawal liability. Accordingly, courts generally find that officers and controlling shareholders of a company are not personally subject to withdrawal liability.[1]

Contractual obligation to contribute creates liability

A company may be subject, under the "contributing obligor" test, to withdrawal liability as an employer if it has a contractual obligation to contribute to the plan.[2] Accordingly, an employee leasing firm that was obligated under a collective bargaining agreement to make pension contributions, for which it was reimbursed by a trucking firm, was solely responsible for withdrawal liability payments. The trucking firm, the Seventh Circuit explained, was not obligated to contribute to the fund and was not an employer subject to withdrawal liability.[3]

Commonly controlled businesses are a single employer

All trades or businesses under common control are to be treated as a single employer for withdrawal liability purposes.[4] Thus, trades or businesses under common control are jointly and severally liable for each other's withdrawal liability.[5] Similarly, a partnership will be responsible for the withdrawal liability of a corporation with which it is under common control.

The governing rules are detailed at CCH Pension Plan Guide ¶ 7046.

[1] See, e.g., *Debrecini v. Graf Bros. Leasing, Inc.,* CA-1 (1987) 828 F2d 877, *cert. denied* 2-22-88; *Scarborough v. Perez, Inc.,* CA-6 (1989), 870 F2d 1079, *aff'g* DC Tenn (1987), 683 FSupp 659.

[2] See, e.g., *Tampa Bay International Terminals, Inc. v. Tampa Bay Maritime Association-International Longshoremen's Association Pension Plan and Trust,* CA-11 (1996), No. 95-2776; *Rheem Manufacturing Co. v. Central States Southeast and Southwest Areas Pension Fund,* CA-8 (1995), 63 F3d 703, *cert. denied,* 116 S.Ct 1016 (1996); *Seaway Port Authority v. Duluth-Superior ILA Marine,* CA-8 (1990), 920 F2d 503.

[3] *Transpersonnel, Inc. v. Roadway Express, Inc.,* CA-7 (2005), No. 04-2321, at CCH Pension Plan Guide ¶ 23,992Z.

[4] ERISA Sec. 4001(b)(1).

[5] *In re Cardon Realty Corporation,* DC NY (1991), No. CIV-90-564C, 124 B.R. 630; *Board of Trustees of the Western Conference of Teamsters Pension Trust Fund v. Lafrenz,* CA-9 (1988), 837 F2d 892. See also *The Retirement Plan of the UNITE HERE National Retirement Fund v. Kombassan Holding A.S.,* CA-2 (2010), No. 07-4143-cv, at CCH Pension Plan Guide ¶ 24,009A, in which a Turkish company was liable for a bankrupt U.S. company's withdrawal liability as the alter ego of the company, even though it had assigned its stock holdings to other corporations. The court rejected the argument that intent to evade obligations or an anti-union animus were necessary for imposition of alter-ego status.

¶ 2885

WITHDRAWAL LIABILITY: Statute of Limitations

An action to collect withdrawal liability must be brought within the later of:[1]

1. six years after the date on which the cause of action arose, or

2. three years after the earliest date on which the claimant acquired or should have acquired actual knowledge of the existence of the cause of action.

The three-year period is extended to six years after the date of discovery in the case of fraud or concealment.

Statute of limitations triggered by failure to make scheduled payment

According the United States Supreme Court, the six-year statute of limitations period governing a plan's action to collect unpaid withdrawal liability does not begin to run until the employer fails to make payments on a schedule set by the fund.[2] The Court rejected the holding of the Ninth Circuit, that the statute of limitations begins to run from the date of the employer's withdrawal from the plan. The statute of limitations is not triggered, the Court explained, until the plan: (1) calculates the employer's withdrawal liability, sets a payment schedule, and demands payment from the employer and (2) the employer defaults on an installment due and payable under the withdrawal.

Each missed installment payment carries own limitations period. The Court further ruled that each missed installment payments creates a separate cause of action that carries its own six year limitations period.[3]

---

[1] ERISA Sec. 4301(f).

[2] *Bay Area Laundry & Dry Cleaning Pension Trust Fund v. Ferbar Corporation of California,*

Inc., US Sup Ct (1997), 118 S.Ct 542, *rev'g* CA-9 (1996), 73 F3d 971.

[3] *Ibid.* See also, *Board of Trustees of District 15 Machinists' Pension Fund v. Kahle Engineering Corp.,* CA-3 (1994), 43 F3d 852.

¶ 2886

WITHDRAWAL LIABILITY: "Free Look" Rule

An employer first entering a plan will be allowed a "free look" during which it can withdraw from the plan without incurring withdrawal liability.[1] The "free look" rule applies to complete or partial withdrawals (but not to mass withdrawals) if:

1. the employer was required to contribute to the plan for no more than the lesser of six consecutive plan years preceding the date on which the employer withdrew or the number of years required for vesting under the plan;

2. the employer's required contributions for each plan year were less than 2% of all employer contributions to the plan for the plan year;

3. the employer did not previously use the "free look" exception;

4. the plan does not primarily cover employees in the building and construction industry;

5. the plan provides or is amended to provide that the benefits of employees accrued on the basis of service for the employer before it was required to contribute to the plan may not be payable if it ceases contributions to the plan;

6. the ratio of plan assets to benefit payments for the plan year preceding the first plan year for which the employer was required to contribute was at least 8 to 1; and

7. the plan is amended to provide for application of the exception.

CCH POINTER: Multiemployer plans that primarily cover employees in the building and construction industries may (effective for withdrawals occurring on or of after January 1, 2007), adopt the free look rule [2]

---

[1] ERISA Sec. 4210.

[2] ERISA Sec.4210(b), as amended by P.L. 109-280 (Pension Protection Act of 2006), Act Sec. 204(c)(1).

¶ 2887

WITHDRAWAL LIABILITY: Specific Industry Exceptions

The construction and entertainment industries are afforded a partial exemption from the employer withdrawal liability rules. For an employer that is obligated to contribute for work performed in the building and construction industry, a complete withdrawal occurs only if the employer ceases to be required to contribute to the plan, and: (1) continues to perform work in the jurisdiction of the CBA of the type for which contributions were previously required, or (2) resumes such work in the jurisdiction within 5 years (3 years for plans terminated by mass withdrawal) after the date that the employer's obligation to contribute ceased, without resuming the obligation.[1] Plan withdrawal liability is similarly limited in the case of an employer in the entertainment industry where the withdrawing employer stays in the area of the plan and continues to work or resumes work without continuing or resuming contributions under the plan [2]

Trucking, household moving, and public warehousing industries

A limited exemption also applies to plans in which substantially all of the required contributions are made by employers in the long-and short-haul trucking industry, the household moving industry, or the public warehousing industry.[3]

Other industries may seek PBGC approved exceptions

Multiemployer plans covering employers in industries other than the construction and entertainment industries may request PBGC approval of plan amendments establishing special withdrawal liability rules.[4] The amendment will not be effective unless approved by the PBGC. In determining whether to approve special withdrawal liability rules, the PBGC looks to the effect of the cessation of contributions by employers in the industry on the plan's contribution base.

Applicable procedures by which multiemployer plans may request PBGC approval of plan amendments establishing special withdrawal liability rules are set forth at CCH PENSION PLAN GUIDE ¶ 7058.

---

[1] ERISA Sec. 4203(b) and (c).

[2] ERISA Sec. 4203(c).

[3] ERISA Sec. 4203(d)(2).

[4] PBGC Reg. §§ 4203.3-4203.5 and 4220.3.

¶ 2888

COMPLETE WITHDRAWAL: What Constitutes a Complete Withdrawal

A complete withdrawal from a multiemployer plan occurs when an employer permanently ceases to have an obligation to contribute under the plan or permanently ceases all covered operations under the plan.[1]

Cessation of obligation to contribute

An employer "ceases to have an obligation to contribute" when it is no longer required to make contributions under the terms of the collective bargaining agreement.[2]

Cessation of covered operations

An employer completely withdraws from a multiemployer plan for purposes of the withdrawal liability calculation when it totally ceases all operations covered by the collective bargaining agreement, and not when operations are reduced to a minimum.[3]

Minimal continued business operations and the continuation of an employer's corporate form do not postpone withdrawal liability from attaching on the date the employer ceases the usual business activity that gave rise to contributions to a plan.[4]

Sale of corporate assets

The transfer of an employer's operations to another employer in connection with a bona fide arm's length sale of assets will not cause a complete (or partial) withdrawal, if certain conditions are satisfied (see ¶ 2896).

Exception for change in corporate structure

A complete withdrawal of an employer does not occur if the employer ceases to exist solely because of a change in corporate structure (for example, a corporate reorganization, such as a merger or consolidation) as long as the employer is replaced by a successor employer and there is no interruption in the employer's required contributions to the plan.[5] In this case, a successor or parent corporation or other entity resulting from such a change is considered the original employer. These rules also apply to a change in form, such as a change to an unincorporated form of business.

Labor dispute exception

A complete withdrawal does not occur solely because an employer *suspends* (as opposed to permanently ceases) plan contributions during a labor dispute involving its employees.[6]

---

[1] ERISA Sec. 4203(a).

[2] *Parmac, Inc. v. I.A.M. National Pension Fund Benefit Plan*, CA D of C (1989), 872 F 2d 1069, 10 EBC 2670.

[3] *Trustees of the Iron Workers Local 473 v. Allied Products Corp.*, CA-7 (1989), 872 F2d 208, *cert. denied* 10-2-89.

[4] *ILGWU National Retirement Fund v. Weatherall Fashions, Inc.*, DC NY (1986), No. 84 Civ. 0772.

[5] ERISA Sec. 4218(1).

[6] ERISA Sec. 4218(2); *T.I.M.E.-DC, Inc. v. Trucking Employees of North Jersey Welfare Fund, Inc.*, DC NY (1983), 560 FSupp 294.

¶ 2889

COMPLETE WITHDRAWAL: Abatement of Complete Withdrawal Liability

An eligible employer that has completely withdrawn from a multiemployer plan, but later reenters the plan, may apply to the plan for abatement of its complete withdrawal liability.[1]

Bond/escrow requirement

An employer that reenters the plan may, in lieu of making withdrawal liability payments, provide the plan with a bond or escrow account pending the plan sponsor's determination of abatement.[2] The bond or escrow must equal 70% of the withdrawal liability payment that would otherwise be due and must be furnished before the date of payment.[3]

Abatement determination relieves employer of liability payments

If the plan sponsor determines that the employer satisfies the requirements for abatement of its complete withdrawal liability:[4]

1. the employer ceases to have an obligation to make further withdrawal liability payments to the plan with respect to its complete withdrawal;

2. any bond or escrow relating to withdrawal liability payments due during the pendency of the abatement determination provided by the employer to the plan must be canceled or refunded; and

3. any withdrawal liability payments due after the reentry that are made to the plan by the employer must be refunded without interest.

Effects of nonabatement determination

In the event that the plan sponsor determines that the employer does not satisfy the requirements for abatement of its complete withdrawal liability:[5]

1. the bond or escrow paid to the plan pending determination of abatement must be paid to the plan within 30 days after the plan sponsor's notice to the employer of its nonabatement determination;

2. the employer is required to pay to the plan (within 30 days after the plan sponsor's notice of nonabatement) the amount of its withdrawal liability payment or payments which is in excess of the applicable bond or escrow;

3. the employer must resume making its withdrawal liability payments to the plan as they fall due; and

4. the employer will be treated as a new employer for purposes of any future application of the withdrawal liability rules with respect to its participation in the plan after its reentry.

[1] PBGC Reg. §4207.3(a).

[2] PBGC Reg. §4207.4(a).

[3] PBGC Reg. §4207.4(b).

[4] PBGC Reg. §4207.3(c).

[5] PBGC Reg. §4207.3(d).

¶ 2890

PARTIAL WITHDRAWAL: Events That Trigger Partial Withdrawal

Under a partial withdrawal, the employer does not completely withdraw from the plan, but experiences a specified event that significantly reduces its obligation to make plan contributions.[1]

Specified trigger events

Specified events that trigger a partial withdrawal are:[2]

1. a 70% decline in contribution base units (for example, hours worked, tons of coal mined, etc.) (see ¶ 2891); or

2. a partial cessation of an employer's obligation to contribute to a plan (see ¶ 2892).

[1] ERISA Sec. 4205.

[2] ERISA Sec. 4205(a).

¶ 2891

PARTIAL WITHDRAWAL: 70% Decline in Contributions

A 70% decline in contribution base units takes place if, during the plan year and in each of the preceding two plan years (referred to as the "three-year testing period"), the number of contribution base units for which the employer was required to make plan contributions did not exceed 30% of the number of such units for the "high base year." [1] The "high base year" is determined by averaging the employer's contribution base units for the two plan years for which such units were the highest within the five plan years preceding the 3-year testing period.[2]

Example: An employer's contribution base units for 2009, 2010, and 2011 (the three-year testing period) are 25,000, 26,000, and 27,000 hours, respectively. The employer's contribution base units for 2005, 2006, 2007, 2008, and 2009 (the five- year base period) are 102,000, 98,000, 95,000, 91,000 and 85,000 hours, respectively. Thus, contribution base units are the highest in the five-year base period in 2005 and 2006 when the units are 102,000 hours and 98,000 hours, respectively. In order to ascertain whether a partial withdrawal occurs in 2012, a determination must first be made as to whether the number of contribution base units for each year of the three-year testing period—2009, 2010, and 2012—exceed 30% of 100,000 (the average number of such units in 2005 and 2006). Because the contribution base units do not exceed 30,000 hours (30% × 100,000) for any year in the three-year testing period, a partial withdrawal takes place as of the close of 2012.

---

[1] ERISA Sec. 4205(b)(1).   [2] ERISA Sec. 4205(b)(1)(B)(ii).

¶ 2892

PARTIAL WITHDRAWAL: Partial Cessation of Employer's Obligation

A partial cessation of an employer's obligation to a plan occurs if an employer that is required to contribute to a plan under multiple collective bargaining agreements permanently ceases to have an obligation to contribute under at least one (but not all) of the agreements, but continues a specific type of work. That is, a partial cessation will result if the employer continues to work in the jurisdiction of the agreement for which contributions were previously required or transfers such work to another location.[1] A partial cessation will also occur if the employer out sources the work to another party that is owned or controlled by the employer.[2] By contrast, an employer that permanently ceases covered work under one of its collective bargaining agreements and instead contracts to buy the service or product from an independent third party does not transfer such work to another location for purposes of this rule.[3]

A partial withdrawal also occurs if an employer permanently ceases to have an obligation to contribute under the plan for work performed at one or more (but not all) of its facilities covered under the plan, but continues to perform work at the facility of the type for which the obligation to contribute ceased. However, a cessation is not deemed to take place if there is merely a substitution of an agreement with one collective bargaining agent for an agreement with another collective bargaining agent under the same plan.[4]

---

[1] ERISA Sec. 4205(b)(2)(A).

[2] ERISA Sec. 4205(b)(2)(A), as amended by P.L. 109-280 (Pension Protection Act of 2006), Act Sec.

204(b), effective for work transferred on or after August 17, 2006.

[3] PBGC Opinion Letter 86-17.

[4] ERISA Sec. 4205(b)(2)(B).

¶ 2893

PARTIAL WITHDRAWAL: Pro Rata Determination of Partial Withdrawal Liability

The amount of liability assessed for a partial withdrawal is calculated on a pro rata basis. Specifically, the amount of withdrawal liability is determined by multiplying the amount of withdrawal liability that would have applied in the case of a complete withdrawal by a stipulated fraction. The date of partial withdrawal and elements of the fraction are determined by whether the partial withdrawal is caused by the partial cessation of an employer's obligation or by a 70% decline in employer contributions.

Partial cessation of employer's obligation

If a partial withdrawal occurs because of the partial cessation of an employer's obligation, withdrawal liability is determined by multiplying the withdrawal liability that would have applied in the case of complete withdrawal *on the date of the partial withdrawal,* by the following fraction:[1]

$$1 \text{ minus} \quad \frac{\text{Employer's contribution base units for plan year following the plan year of the partial withdrawal}}{\text{Average of the employer's contribution base units for the 5 plan years preceding the plan year of partial withdrawal}}$$

70% decline in contributions

In the event that a partial withdrawal occurs because of a 70% decline in employer contributions, the date for determining withdrawal liability is the *last day of the first plan year in the 3-year testing period.*[2] This figure is multiplied by the following fraction:[3]

$$1 \text{ minus} \quad \frac{\text{Employer's contribution base units for the plan year of the partial withdrawal}}{\text{Average of the employer's contribution base units for the 5 plan years immediately preceding the 3-year testing period}}$$

[1] ERISA Sec. 4206(a)(2).

[2] ERISA Sec. 4206(a)(1)(B).

[3] ERISA Sec. 4206(a)(2)(B).

¶ 2894

PARTIAL WITHDRAWAL: Credit Against Future Withdrawal Liability

In order to protect a withdrawing employer from being charged twice for the same unfunded vested benefits of the plan, current or prior withdrawal liability can be credited against future withdrawal liability. Specifically, the amount of partial withdrawal liability, as reduced by abatement or reduction of the liability, will be applied as a credit against withdrawal liability for any future partial or complete withdrawal from the plan.[1]

Note, the amount of the credit may also be reduced so as to prevent other employers from being responsible for unfunded vested benefits properly allocable to withdrawing employers.

[1] ERISA Sec. 4206(b); PBGC Reg. § 4206.1-9.

¶ 2895

PARTIAL WITHDRAWAL: Abatement of Partial Withdrawal Liability

All or part of an employer's partial withdrawal liability arising from a 70% contribution decline may be abated in the event of:[1]

1. a two-year 90% restoration of contributions;[2]

2. a one-year complete restoration of contributions;

3. a two-year reversal of the reduction of contributions which triggered the liability;

4. a 10% contribution increase; or

5. the restoration of withdrawn work.

---

[1] ERISA Sec. 4208(a)-(c).

[2] PBGC Reg. § 4208.4.

¶ 2896

TRANSFEROR LIABILITY: Sale of Assets

Continuing withdrawal liability is generally imposed on a transferring employer that transfers corporate assets. A complete or partial withdrawal will not occur solely because an employer transfers covered operations to an unrelated party in connection with a bona fide arm's-length sale of assets.[1] However, an employer will not escape withdrawal liability following a transfer of corporate assets unless the conditions discussed below are satisfied at the time that the assets are sold.[2]

Buyer must make contributions to plan

The buyer must be a party unrelated to the employer. In addition, the buyer must be required to contribute to the plan for substantially the same number of contribution base units (hours worked, tons of coal mined, etc.) for which the seller was required to contribute to the plan.[3]

Buyer must provide bond or escrow

The buyer must provide to the plan for a period of five plan years, starting with the first plan year beginning after the sale of assets, a bond, or escrow in an amount equal to the greater of:[4]

1. the average annual contribution required to be made by the seller to the plan for the three plan years preceding the plan year in which the sale of assets occurs; or

2. the annual contribution that the seller was required to make to the plan for the last plan year before the plan year in which the sale of the assets occurs.

If the buyer withdraws from the plan or fails to make a contribution to the plan when due at any time during the first five plan years, the bond or escrow must be paid to the plan.[5]

Seller must post bond

The seller must also post a bond or escrow in the event that it distributes all or substantially all of its assets or liquidates within a five-year period following the sale.[6] The withdrawal liability of any seller or any buyer furnishing a bond or escrow is to be reduced by the amount of any payment made under the bond or escrow.[7]

Seller is secondarily liable for withdrawal liability

The contract for sale must provide that, if the buyer withdraws in a complete or partial withdrawal during the first five plan years and fails to pay the liability due, the seller is secondarily liable for any withdrawal liability it would have had but for the asset sale rules.[8]

The secondary liability rule is also an affirmative duty imposed on the seller.[9]

Waiver of bond/escrow and sales contract requirements

The bond/escrow and sales contract requirements may be waived if:[10]

1. the amount of the bond does not exceed the lesser of $250,000 or 2% of the average total annual contributions paid to the plan by all employers for the three plan years preceding the date of determination;[11]

2. the buyer's average net income after taxes for its three most recent fiscal years before the sale (reduced by any interest expense incurred with respect to the sale, payable in the fiscal year following the date of determination) equals or exceed 150% of the amount of the bond/ escrow;[12] or

3. The buyer's net tangible assets indicate an ability to pay its potential withdrawal liability.[13]

An employer that cannot meet the above standard criteria may apply to the PBGC for an individual or class variance or exemption from the sale of assets rule.[14]

The exemption procedures are discussed at CCH Pension Plan Guide ¶ 7119.

Sale to related party is beyond exception

If the seller and the purchaser are not "unrelated parties," the seller will not be able to avoid withdrawal liability extending from the sale of assets.[15] The PBGC does not have the authority to grant an individual variance with regard to the unrelated party requirement.

Sale to avoid liability may be disregarded

The sale of an incorporated or unincorporated division by an employer may result in the imposition of withdrawal liability, even though the requirements of the exemption are met, if the principal purpose of the sale is to avoid liability (e.g., sale of a failing subsidiary for significantly less than market value).[16] Under such circumstances, the transaction will be voided and employer liability will be assessed and collected according to the substance of the transaction and without regard to the sham transaction.

[1] ERISA Sec. 4204(a)(1).

[2] *Lear Siegler Diversified Holdings Corp. v. Regal Beloit Corp.*, DC Ill (1999), No. 97C4018.

[3] ERISA Sec. 4204(a)(1)(A).

[4] ERISA Sec. 4204(a)(1)(B).

[5] ERISA Sec. 4204(a)(1)(B)(ii).

[6] ERISA Sec. 4204(a)(3)(A).

[7] ERISA Sec. 4204(a)(4).

[8] ERISA Sec. 4204(a)(1)(C).

[9] ERISA Sec. 4204(a)(2).

[10] PBGC Reg. § 4204.11(a).

[11] PBGC Reg. § 4204.12.

[12] PBGC Reg. § 4204.13(a)(1).

[13] PBGC Reg. § 4204.13(a)(2).

[14] PBGC Reg. §§ 4204.1(a) and 4204.21.

[15] PBGC Opinion Letter 88-7. "Unrelated party" is defined at Code Sec. 267(b).

[16] ERISA Sec. 4212(c); PBGC Opinion Letter 85-15, 5-31-85. See *Supervalu, Inc., v. Board of Trustees of the Southwestern Pennsylvania and Western Maryland Area Teamsters and Employers Pension Fund*, CA-3 (2007), No. 06-3829, at CCH PENSION PLAN GUIDE at ¶ 24,001I, (a termination agreement between an employer that had withdrawn from a multiemployer fund and a union that was designed to relieve the employer of withdrawal liability in exchange for severance payments and salary enhancements did not prevent the imposition of withdrawal liability because the principal purpose of the agreement was to enable the employer to avoid paying it's share of existing unfunded benefit liability). Contrast, *Central States, Southeast and Southwest Areas Pension Fund v. Georgia Pacific LLC*, CA-7 (2011), No. 10-2489, at CCH PENSION PLAN GUIDE ¶ 24,009H (employer did not owe withdrawal liability because its sale of one division to a buyer that was able to make all pension contributions was not the culmination of multi-year scheme to evade liability by withdrawing in stages from the plan).

¶ 2898
COMPUTING WITHDRAWAL LIABILITY:
Computation Methods

A withdrawing employer's share of a multiemployer plan's unfunded vested benefits is computed under one of four prescribed statutory methods or an alternative PBGC-approved method.

Presumptive method

The basic statutory method for computing withdrawal liability is the presumptive method (see ¶ 2899). This method requires an employer that withdraws from a plan to fund a share of the increase in the plan's unfunded vested benefits during the period of the employer's required contributions to the plan.[1] A plan's unfunded vested benefits are generally the amount by which the plan's vested (nonforfeitable) benefits exceed plan assets.

Alternative statutory methods

The presumptive method is generally used to determine withdrawal liability. However, a plan may be amended to authorize use of an alternative method. The three alternative methods pursuant to which plans may compute withdrawal liability: the modified presumptive method (see ¶ 2900), the rolling-5 method (see ¶ 2901), and the direct attribution method (see ¶ 2902). The presumptive method generally applies unless a plan adopts one of the alternative methods.

The statutory alternative methods may be adopted without PBGC approval. However, an alternative method may not be applied to an employer without its consent if it withdrew from the plan before the adoption of the alternative calculation method.[2]

Note: The surcharge assessed to plans in critical funding status is excluded from the allocation fraction under the presumptive, modified presumptive, and rolling-5 methods. See ¶ 2903A.

Plans without unfunded benefits may assess withdrawal liability

A plan has the right to assess withdrawal liability under any statutory allocation method even when it has no unfunded vested benefits at the end of the year preceding withdrawal.[3]

Withdrawal following merger

In the event that an employer withdraws following a merger of multiemployer plans, withdrawal liability may be computed under the statutory allocation methods, a nonstatutory allocation method adopted by the plan and approved by the PBGC, or one of the allocation methods specifically prescribed by the PBGC for use by merged multiemployer plans.[4]

---

[1] ERISA Sec. 4211.

[2] ERISA Sec. 4214(a); *Jos. Schlitz Brewing Co. v. Milwaukee Brewery Workers' Pension Plan*, CA-7 (1993), U.S. App LEXIS 20658.

[3] PBGC Withdrawal of Notice of Interpretation, 3-22-91 (56 FR 12288) (withdrawing PBGC Notice of Interpretation, 12-31-86 (51 FR 47342); *Wise v. Ruffin*, CA-4 (1990), 914 F2d 570; *Ben Hur Construction Co. v. Goodwin*, CA-8 (1986), 784 F2d 876; ERISA Opinion Letter 83-19, 8-11-83.

[4] ERISA Sec. 4211(f); PBGC Reg. § 4211.31-4211.37.

¶ 2899

COMPUTING WITHDRAWAL LIABILITY: Presumptive Method

The presumptive method is generally used to determine withdrawal liability. Under the presumptive method, the amount of unfunded vested benefits (UVBs) allocable to a withdrawing employer is the sum of the employer's proportional share of:

- the unamortized amount of the change in the plan's unfunded vested benefits for each plan year ending after September 25, 1980, for which the employer has an obligation to contribute under the plan (i.e., multiple-year liability pools) ending with the plan year preceding the plan year of employer's withdrawal;

- the unamortized amount of the unfunded vested benefits at the end of the last plan year ending before September 26, 1980, with respect to employers who had an obligation to contribute under the plan for the first plan year ending after such date; and

- the unamortized amount of the reallocated unfunded vested benefits (i.e., amounts the plan sponsor determines to be uncollectible or unassessable) for each plan year ending before the employer's withdrawal.

Each of the amounts described above is reduced by 5 percent for each plan year after the plan year for which it arose. An employer's proportional share is based on a fraction equal to the sum of the contributions required to be made under the plan by the employer over total contributions made by all employers who had an obligation to contribute under the plan, for the five plan years ending with the plan year in which such change arose, the five plan years preceding September 26, 1980, and the five plan years ending with the plan year such reallocation liability arose, respectively (i.e., the "allocation fraction"). [1]

Adjustments in allocation formula. The PBGC has prescribed changes that a plan may adopt (without PBGC approval) in the denominator of the allocation fraction that is used to determine a withdrawing employer's share of unfunded vested benefits under the presumptive method (and the rolling 5 method) (see ¶ 2901).

Fresh start option. PBGC has implemented a "fresh start" option that will enable plans using the presumptive method of determining withdrawal liability to substitute a plan year designated in a plan amendment and for which the plan has no UVBs for the plan year ending before September 26, 1980 (see ¶ 2903).

Computing liability for reallocated unfunded vested benefits

Under the presumptive method, liability also must be computed with respect to unfunded vested benefits that are reallocated under the plan because they are uncollectible or not assigned to an employer under certain relief provisions.[2]

☐ The procedures for computing an employer's withdrawal liability for reallocated unfunded vested benefits are illustrated at CCH PENSION PLAN GUIDE ¶ 7130.

---

[1] ERISA Sec. 4211(b)(1)—(3).　　　　　[2] ERISA Sec. 4211(b)(4).

¶ 2900
COMPUTING WITHDRAWAL LIABILITY: Modified Presumptive Method

The modified presumptive method, unlike the presumptive method, bases an employer's withdrawal liability on the aggregate change in unfunded vested benefits for plan years ending after September 25, 1980, instead of on the change in unfunded vested benefits for each separate plan year for which the employer was required to contribute to the plan.[1]

Specifically, under the modified presumptive method, a withdrawing employer is liable for a proportional share of:

- the plan's unfunded vested benefits as of the end of the plan year preceding the withdrawal (less outstanding claims for withdrawal liability that can reasonably be expected to be collected and the amounts set forth in the item below allocable to employers obligated to contribute in the plan year preceding the employer's withdrawal and who had an obligation to contribute in the first plan year ending after September 26, 1980); and

- the plan's unfunded vested benefits as of the end of the last plan year ending before September 26, 1980 (amortized over 15 years), if the employer had an obligation to contribute under the plan for the first plan year ending on or after such date. [2]

An employer's proportional share is based on the employer's share of total plan contributions over the five plan years preceding the plan year of the employer's withdrawal and over the five plan years preceding September 26, 1980, respectively.

Plans that use the modified presumptive method fully amortize their first pool as of 1995. Employers that withdraw after 1995 are subject to the allocation of unfunded vested benefits as if the plan used the "rolling-5 method" discussed at ¶ 2901.

Fresh start option. A fresh start option that will allow plans using the modified presumptive method to designate a plan year that could be substituted for the last plan year ending before September 26, 1980 is discussed at ¶ 2903.

☐ The modified presumptive method is detailed at CCH PENSION PLAN GUIDE ¶ 7132.

---

[1] ERISA Sec. 4211(c)(1).   [2] *Ibid.*

¶ 2901
COMPUTING WITHDRAWAL LIABILITY: Rolling-5 Method

Under the rolling-5 method, the employer's withdrawal liability is computed with reference to all of the plan's unfunded vested benefits. An employer's withdrawal liability is determined under the following formula:[1]

Plan's unfunded vested benefits, as of the end of the plan year preceding the plan year of withdrawal, *less* the value as of the end of such year of all outstanding claims which can be reasonably expected to be collected from employers who withdrew before such year

×

Total contributions required of withdrawing employer for the last 5 plan years ending before withdrawal

―――――――――――――――――

Total contributions made by all employers for the same 5 plan years *plus* employer contributions owed for earlier period that are collected during the 5 plan years *less* contributions by any employer who withdrew during the 5 plan years

――――――――

[1] ERISA Sec. 4211(c)(3).

¶ 2902
COMPUTING WITHDRAWAL LIABILITY: Direct Attribution Method

Under the direct attribution method, the portion of the plan's unfunded vested benefits that is attributable to the service of plan participants with the employer, rather than the employer's share of plan contribution during a period of time, is computed. Portions of the unfunded vested benefits are attributed to each employer. Unfunded vested benefits that are not attributable to any present employer are also computed.[1]

A portion of these "unattributable benefits" is then allocated to the withdrawing employer. An employer's withdrawal liability is the sum of:[2]

1. the portion of the plan's unfunded vested benefits that is attributable to plan participants' service with the employer; and

2. the portion of "unattributable benefits" that is allocated to the employer.

All determinations are made as of the end of the plan year preceding the plan year of withdrawal.

An employer remains subject to withdrawal liability under the attribution method of determining liability even if the pension plan as a whole has no unfunded vested benefits.[3]

――――――――

[1] ERISA Sec. 4211(c)(4).

[2] ERISA Sec. 4211(c)(4)(A).

[3] *Ben Hur Construction Co. v. Goodwin*, CA-8 (1986), 784 F2d 876. Also see, PBGC Withdrawal of Notice of Interpretation, 3-22-91 (56 FR 12288).

¶ 2903

COMPUTING WITHDRAWAL LIABILITY:
Nonstatutory Alternative Allocation Methods

The three statutory alternative allocation methods explained at ¶ 2900—¶ 2902 may be adopted without the approval of the PBGC.[1] Non-statutory alternative allocation methods, however, may be adopted with PBGC approval provided they do not significantly increase the risk of financial loss to plan participants, beneficiaries, or the PBGC.[2]

Generally, an alternative allocation method (or modification of an allocation method) must satisfy three conditions:

1. the plan's total unfunded vested benefits must be allocated, on both a current and prospective basis, to the same extent as any of the statutory allocations or permitted modifications;

2. the amount allocated to an employer must be calculated either on the basis of that employer's share of total contributions to the plan over a specified period, or on the basis of unfunded vested benefits attributable to employers; and

3. all unfunded vested benefits that cannot be collected from withdrawn employers, or that are not assessed against withdrawn employers because of the *de minimis* rules, the 20-year cap, and the insolvent employer provision (see ¶ 2904), must be fully reallocated among employers that have not withdrawn.[3]

CCH POINTER: *Building and construction industry plans.* A multiemployer plan that primarily covers employees in the building and construction industry must use the presumptive method (see ¶ 2899) to allocate unfunded vested benefits to construction industry employers.[4] However, construction industry plans may adopt a different allocation method for non-construction industry employers who contribute to the plan. Use of any other method, including the statutory allocation method is subject to PBGC approval. However, a construction industry plan may adopt modifications to the presumptive method (see ¶ 2900) without PBGC approval.[5]

Fresh start option

A fresh start option enables a plan (including construction industry plans) to make amendments regarding the application of the presumptive method of computing withdrawal liability.[5] Effective for plan withdrawals occurring on or after January 1, 2007, the fresh start option will allow a multiemployer plan, including plans that primarily cover the building and construction industries, to be amended to provide that the presumptive method of computing withdrawal liability prescribed in ERISA Sec. 4211(b) be applied by using a plan year specified in the amendment and for which there was no unfunded vested benefits, instead of the plan year that ended before September 26, 1980.

¶2903

For plan years ending before the designated plan year and for the designated plan year, the plan will be relieved of the burden of calculating changes in UVBs separately for each plan year and allocating those changes to the employers that contributed to the plan in the year of the change. As the plan must have no UVBs for the designated plan year, employers withdrawing from the plan after the modification is effective will have no liability for UVBs arising in plan years ending before the designated plan year, thereby enabling the plan to "start fresh" with liabilities that arise in plan years after the designated plan year.

> **CCH POINTER:** *Fresh start option does not increase UVBs.* The fresh start option merely allows a plan to amend the method for allocating substantially all of a plan's UVBs among employers who are obligated to contribute under the plan. The option does not allow for an increase the amount of the UVBs to be allocated.

PBGC final regulations issued in 2008 (effective for employer withdrawals occurring on or after January 1, 2007) allow plans to substitute a new plan year for the plan year ending before September 26, 1980, without regard to the amount of a plan's UVBs at the end of the newly designated plan year. [6] This change permits plans using the presumptive method to aggregate the multiple liability pools attributable to prior plan years and the designated plan year. The new rules will, thus, enable such plans to allocate the plan's UVBs as of the end of the designated plan year among the employers who have an obligation to contribute under the plan for the first plan year ending on or after such date, based on the employer's share of the plan's contributions for the five-year period ending before the designated plan year. Thereafter, the plan would apply the regular rules under the presumptive method to segregate changes in the plan's UVBs by plan year and to allocate individual plan year liabilities among the employers obligated to contribute under the plan in that plan year.

> **CCH POINTER:** The modification to the presumptive method is designed to ease the administrative burdens of plans that lack the actuarial and contributions data necessary to compute each employer's allocable share of annual changes in UVBs occurring in plan years as far back as 1980. Note, however, that this modification does not apply to a construction industry plan, because PBGC may prescribe only adjustments in the denominators of the allocation fractions for such plans. [7]

Fresh start option under modified presumptive method. The PBGC final rules extend the regulatory fresh start option by allowing plans using the modified presumptive method to designate a plan year that may be substituted for the last plan year ending before September 26, 1980. Such an amendment would allow for the allocation of substantially all of a plan's UVBs among employers who have an obligation to contribute under the plan, while enabling plans to split a single liability pool for plan years ending after September 25, 1980 into two liability pools: one based on the plan's UVBs as of the end of the newly designated plan year, allocated among employers who have an obligation to contribute under the plan for the plan year immediately following the designated plan year, and a second based on the UVBs as of the end of the plan year prior to the withdrawal (offset in the manner described above for the modified presumptive method). [8] For a period of time, this modification would reduce new employers' liability for UVBs of the plan before the employer's participation, which could assist plans in attracting new employers and preserving the plan's contribution base.

Note, the amendment would not require PBGC approval in order to be adopted.

UVBs reduced by outstanding withdrawal liability claims. A plan's unfunded vested benefits, determined with respect to plan years ending after the plan year designated in the plan amendment, must, under the fresh start option, be reduced by the value of the outstanding claims for withdrawal liability that may reasonably be expected to be collected from employers who withdrew from the plan in or before the designated plan year. [9]

---

[1] PBGC Reg. § 4211.11.

[2] ERISA Sec. 4211(c)(5); PBGC Reg. § 4211.23(a).

[3] PBGC Reg. § 4211.23(b).

[4] ERISA Sec. 4211(c)(2).

[5] ERISA Sec. 4211(c)(5)(E), as amended by P.L. 109-280 (Pension Protection Act of 2006), Act Sec. 204(c)(2).

[5] PBGC Reg. § § 4211.3(a) and 4211.11(b).

[6] PBGC Reg. § 4211.12(c)(2).

[7] PBGC Reg. § 4211.12(c)(3).

[8] PBGC Reg. § 4211.12(d)(1).

[9] PBGC Reg. § 4211.12(d)(2).

¶ 2903A

COMPUTING WITHDRAWAL LIABILITY: Calculating Withdrawal Liability for Plans in Critical Status

The Pension Protection Act of 2006 implemented additional funding rules for multiemployer plans in endangered or critical status (see ¶ 1493L). Under the funding rules, the sponsor of a plan in critical status (i.e., a plan that is less than 65 percent funded and/or meets any of the other defined tests) is required to adopt a rehabilitation plan that will enable the plan to cease to be in critical status within a specified period of time. [1] The rehabilitation plan may include reductions to adjustable benefits. However, any benefit reductions must be disregarded in determining a plan's unfunded vested benefits for purposes of an employer's withdrawal liability [2]

A plan is also limited in its payment of lump sums and similar benefits after a notice of the plan's critical status is sent [3] However, such benefit limits must be disregarded in determining a plan's UVBs for purposes of determining an employer's withdrawal liability.

Note, Employers are not required under FASB rules to disclose estimated withdrawal liability (see ¶ 1493L).

Adjustable benefits. Adjustable benefits include benefits, rights, and features under the plan, such as post-retirement death benefits, 60-month guarantees, disability benefits not yet in pay status; certain early retirement benefits, retirement-type subsidies, and benefit payment options; and benefit increases that would not be eligible for a guarantee on the first day of the initial critical year because the increases were adopted (or, if later, took effect) less than 60 months before such date. [4]

An amendment reducing adjustable benefits may not affect the benefits of any participant or beneficiary whose benefit commencement date is before the date on which the plan provides notice that the plan is or will be in critical status for a plan year. The level of a participant's accrued benefit at normal retirement age also is protected.

Actuarial assumptions. A plan actuary must use actuarial assumptions that, in the aggregate, are reasonable and, in combination, offer the actuary's best estimate of anticipated experience in determining the UVBs of a plan for purposes of determining an employer's withdrawal liability (absent regulations setting forth such methods and assumptions). For purposes of determining withdrawal liability, UVBs are the amount by which the value of nonforfeitable benefits under the plan exceeds the value of plan assets.

Benefit reductions disregarded. Reductions in benefits under a rehabilitation plan are disregarded in determining a plan's unfunded vested benefits (i.e., amount by which the value of nonforfeitable benefits under the plan exceeds the value of plan assets) for purposes of determining an employer's withdrawal liability. [5] PBGC final rules issued in December 2008 reflect this PPA provision. Specifically, the definitions of nonforfeitable vested benefits and unfunded vested benefits have been revised to include adjustable benefits that have been reduced by the plan sponsor pursuant to ERISA Sec. 305(e)(8) or Code Sec. 432(e)(8), but that would otherwise have been nonforfeitable benefits. [6]

Simplified method for disregarding benefit reduction in calculating withdrawal liability. The PBGC was charged with providing specific means by which withdrawal liability may be calculated in such circumstances [7] The PBGC regulations issued in December 2008 did not provide such simplified methods. However, a Technical Update released by the PBGC in July 2010 furnished the following simplified method for applying the requirement to disregard benefit reductions in determining withdrawal liability [8]

Determining value of benefit reductions. In the event that a plan, as part of a rehabilitation plan, reduces benefits, the amount of unfunded vested benefits allocable to an employer that withdraws after the last day of the plan year in which the reduction occurred will be equal to the sum of : (a) the amount determined in accordance with ERISA Sec.4211 under the method in use by the plan, and (b) the employer's proportional share determined as of the end of the plan year prior to withdrawal of the unamortized balance of the value of the reduced nonforfeitable benefits (i.e., affected benefits).

The PBGC explains that, under this simplified method:

(1) the value of the affected benefits (i.e., benefit reductions which are to be disregarded under Code Sec. 432(e)(9)(A) in determining a plan's unfunded vested benefits for purposes of determining an employer's withdrawal liability) will be determined pursuant to the same assumptions that are used by the plan to determine unfunded vested benefits for purposes of ERISA Sec. 4211, and

(2) the unamortized balance of the affected benefits as of a plan year will be the value of that amount as of the end of the year in which the reductions took effect (base year), reduced as if that amount were being fully amortized in level annual installments over 15 years, at the plan's valuation interest rate, beginning with the first plan year after the base year.

An employer's proportional share of the unamortized balance of the affected benefits will be the product of:

(i) the unamortized balance as of the end of the plan year preceding the withdrawal, and

(ii) the following fraction: the sum of all contributions required to be made by the employer under the plan for the last 5 plan years ending before withdrawal/ the total amount contributed under the plan by all employers for the last 5 plan years ending before the withdrawal, increased by any employer contributions owed with respect to earlier periods which were collected in those plan years, and decreased by any amount contributed to the plan during those plan years by employers who ceased to be obligated to contribute or ceased covered operations.

EXAMPLE: Plan X is certified to be in critical status for the plan year beginning January 1, 2008. On April 1, 2008, Plan X provides notice of the plan's certified status to the required parties, including notice that certain benefits under the plan will be reduced for participants and beneficiaries whose benefit commencement date is on or after April 1, 2008. Plan X adopts a rehabilitation plan on October 1, 2008, followed by schedules to the bargaining parties reflecting reductions in benefits and increases in contributions.

Employer A withdraws from Plan X during the 2013 plan year. The plan uses the rolling-5 method for allocating unfunded vested benefits to withdrawn employers. The Plan's actuary first determines the amount of Employer A's withdrawal liability using the rolling-5 method (i.e., based on the plan's unfunded vested benefits as of the end of 2012, excluding the value of any benefits that were reduced under the rehabilitation plan, and disregarding any surcharges under Code Sec. 432(e)(7). In accordance with Code Sec. 432(e)(9)(A), the actuary then adds to this amount the employer's proportional share of the affected benefits.

The actuary determines the value as of December 31, 2008 (base year) of the affected benefits (which are to be disregarded under Code Sec.432(e)(9)(A) in determining a plan's unfunded vested benefits for purposes of determining an employer's withdrawal liability), using the same assumptions used by Plan X to determine unfunded vested benefits under ERISA Sec. 4211. This value is then reduced in accordance with a 15-year amortization schedule beginning in 2009. Assuming the value of the affected benefits as of December 31, 2008, was $20 million, and the valuation interest rate for the base year was 7.5%, the unamortized balance as of December 31, 2012 (the end of the plan year before Employer A's withdrawal) is $16.575 million (the principal balance on $20 million at 7.5% after four annual payments).

¶2903A

Employer A's proportional share of $16.575 million is determined by applying a fraction equal to Employer A's required contributions for the last 5 plan years ending before the withdrawal over all employer contributions for the same period (adjusted as appropriate).

Disregard employer surcharges in calculating withdrawal liability

Each employer otherwise obligated to make contributions for the initial plan year and any subsequent plan year that a plan is in critical status must pay a surcharge to the plan for such plan year, until the effective date of a collective bargaining agreement that includes terms consistent with the rehabilitation plan adopted by the plan sponsor. [9] Employer surcharges are generally disregarded in determining an employer's withdrawal liability. However, the surcharges are include for purposes of determining the UVBs attributable to an employer under the direct attribution method or a comparable approved method. [10]

As noted at ¶ 2899—2901, the presumptive, modified presumptive, and rolling-five methods of allocating UVBs allocate the liability pools among participating employers based on the employers' contribution obligations for the five-year period preceding the date the liability pool was established, or the plan year immediately preceding the plan year of the employer's withdrawal (depending on the method or liability pool). The numerator of the allocation fraction is the total amount required to be contributed by the withdrawing employer for the five-year period, and the denominator of the allocation fraction is the total amount contributed by all employers under the plan for the five-year period. [11] The PBGC final regulations issued in 2008 (effective for employer withdrawals occurring in plan years beginning on or after January 1, 2008) exclude amounts attributable to the employer surcharge from the contributions that are otherwise includible in the numerator and the denominator of the allocation fraction under the presumptive, modified presumptive, and rolling-five methods. [12]

Simplified method for calculating withdrawal liability. The Pension Benefit Guaranty Corporation is required to prescribe simplified methods for calculating withdrawal liability in these situations [13] The PBGC final rules provide a simplified method for the application of this principle in the form of an illustration of the exclusion of employer surcharge amounts from the allocation fraction. [14]

EXAMPLE: Plan X is a multiemployer plan that has vested benefit liabilities of $200 million and assets of $130 million as of the end of its 2015 plan year. During the 2015 plan year, there were three contributing employers. Two of three employers were in the plan for the entire five-year period ending with the 2015 plan year. One employer was in the plan during the 2014 and 2015 plan years only. Each employer had a $4 million contribution obligation each year under a collective bargaining agreement. In addition, for the 2011, 2012, and 2013 plan years, employers were liable for the automatic employer surcharge under section ERISA Sec. 305(e)(7) and Code Sec. 432(e)(7), at a rate of 5% of required contributions in 2011 and 10% of required contributions in 2012 and 2013.

¶2903A

Employers A, B and C contributed $48 million during the five-year period, excluding surcharges, and $50 million including surcharges. Under the rolling-5 method, the unfunded vested benefits allocable to an employer are equal to the plan's unfunded vested benefits as of the end of the last plan year preceding the withdrawal, multiplied by a fraction equal to the amount the employer was required to contribute to the plan for the last five plan years preceding the withdrawal over the total amount contributed by all employers for those five plan years (other adjustments are also required).

Employer A's share of the plan's unfunded vested benefits in the event it withdraws in 2016 is $29.17 million determined by multiplying $70 million (the plan's unfunded vested benefits at the end of 2015) by the ratio of $20 million to $48 million. Employer B's allocable unfunded vested benefits are identical to Employer A's, and the amount allocable to Employer C is $11.66 million ($70 million multiplied by the ratio of $8 million over $48 million). The $2.0 million attributable to the automatic employer surcharge is excluded from contributions in the allocation fraction.

---

[1]ERISA Sec. 305(a)(2), as added by P.L 109-280 (Pension Protection Act of 2006), Act Sec 202(a); Code Sec. 432(a)(2), as added by P.L. 109-280 (Pension Protection Act of 2006), Act Sec. 212(a).

[2]ERISA Sec. 305(e)(9), as added by P.L 109-280 (Pension Protection Act of 2006), Act Sec 202(a); Code Sec.432(e)(9), as added by P.L. 109-280 (Pension Protection Act of 2006), Act Sec. 212(a).

[3]ERISA Sec. 305(f), as added by P.L 109-280 (Pension Protection Act of 2006), Act Sec 202(a); Code Sec. 432(f), as added by P.L. 109-280 (Pension Protection Act of 2006), Act Sec. 212(a).

[4]ERISA Sec. 305(e)(8), as added by P.L 109-280 (Pension Protection Act of 2006), Act Sec 202(a); Code Sec. 432(e)(8), as added by P.L. 109-280 (Pension Protection Act of 2006), Act Sec. 212(a).

[5]ERISA Sec. 305(e)(9)(A), as added by P.L 109-280 (Pension Protection Act of 2006), Act Sec 202(a); Code Sec. 432(e)(9)(A), as added by P.L. 109-280 (Pension Protection Act of 2006), Act Sec. 212(a).

[6]PBGC Reg. § 4211.2.

[7]ERISA Sec. 305(e)(9)(C), as added by P.L 109-280 (Pension Protection Act of 2006), Act Sec 202(a); Code Sec. 432(e)(9)(C), as added by P.L. 109-280 (Pension Protection Act of 2006), Act Sec. 212(a).

[8]PBGC Technical Update 103, July 15, 2010 at ¶ 19,975Z-28.

[9]ERISA Sec. 305(e)(7), as added by P.L 109-280 (Pension Protection Act of 2006), Act Sec 202(a); Code Sec. 432(e)(7), as added by P.L. 109-280 (Pension Protection Act of 2006), Act Sec. 212(a).

[10]ERISA Sec. 305(e)(9), as added by P.L 109-280 (Pension Protection Act of 2006), Act Sec 202(a); Code Sec. 432(e)(9), as added by P.L. 109-280 (Pension Protection Act of 2006), Act Sec. 212(a).

[11]ERISA Sec. 4211.

[12]PBGC Reg. § 4211.4.

[13]ERISA Sec. 305(e)(9)(c), as added by P.L 109-280 (Pension Protection Act of 2006), Act Sec 202(a); Code Sec. 432(e)(9)(C), as added by P.L. 109-280 (Pension Protection Act of 2006), Act Sec. 212(a).

[14]Preamble to PBGC Reg. § 4211.4, at ¶ 24,808A.

¶ 2904

COMPUTING WITHDRAWAL LIABILITY: Adjustments of Withdrawal Liability

An employer's withdrawal liability amount for a complete or partial withdrawal may be reduced or limited under the following rules.[1]

De minimis rules

An employer's withdrawal liability may be reduced (but not below zero) by an amount computed under *de minimis* rules, which cannot be waived by a plan. Under the de minimis rule, unfunded vested benefits allocable to an employer that withdraws from the plan are reduced. Specifically, the amount of unfunded vested benefits allocable to an employer must be reduced by lesser of (1) $50,000 or (2) ¾ of 1% of the plan's unfunded vested benefits determined as of the close of the plan year ending before the date of withdrawal.[2] However, the limitation is reduced by the amount by which the unfunded vested benefits attributable to an employer exceeds $100,000.

Discretionary de minimis rule. A plan may be amended to provide for a reduction in an employer's withdrawal liability (but not below zero) equal to the greater of (1) the amount of the reduction determined under the mandatory *de minimis* rule or (2) the lesser of (a) ¾ of 1% of the plan's unfunded vested benefits determined as of the close of the plan year ending before the date of withdrawal or (b) $100,000.[3] The *de minimis* amount is to be phased out, dollar- for-dollar, to the extent that the employer's withdrawal liability exceeds $150,000.

De minimis rules do not apply in mass withdrawal. The de minimis rules do not apply to employers involved in a mass withdrawal from the plan.[4]

50% insolvency rule

An insolvent employer undergoing liquidation or dissolution is minimally liable for the first 50% of its normal withdrawal liability (i.e., 50% of the unfunded vested benefits allocable to the employer).[5] The employer is then liable only for that portion of the next 50% of the allocable unfunded vested benefits that does not exceed the liquidation or dissolution value of the employer determined as of the beginning of the liquidation or dissolution and reduced by the first 50% of its normal withdrawal liability.

An insolvent employer need not undergo a formal liquidation or dissolution in order to qualify for relief. However, the employer must be insolvent and wind up its business affairs. An employer is insolvent if the liabilities of the employer, including withdrawal liability determined before application of these special rules, exceed the employer's assets determined as of the beginning of the liquidation or dissolution.[6]

Asset sales to unrelated parties

An employer's withdrawal liability may be limited following the sale of all or substantially all of the assets of the employer in a bona fide, arm's-length transaction to an unrelated party.

In the event the liquidation or dissolution value of the employer (determined after the sale or exchange of such assets) does not exceed $5 million, the employer's withdrawal liability will be limited to the greater of:

1. 30% of the liquidation or dissolution value of the employer; or

2. in situations where a plan calculates withdrawal liability under the attributable method, the unfunded vested benefits attributable to the employer's employees.[7]

In the event the liquidation value of the employer exceeds $5 million, the 30% limitation is gradually increased until it reaches 80% for sales exceeding $25 million.

---

[1] ERISA Sec. 4201(b).

[2] ERISA Sec. 4209(a). See also, *Ben Hur Construction Co. v. Goodwin*, CA-8 (1986), 784 F2d 876 (withdrawal liability could not be reduced by application of de minimis rules where the plan as a whole had no unfunded vested benefits, making the de minimis reduction zero).

[3] ERISA Sec. 4209(b).

[4] ERISA Sec. 4209(c) and (d).

[5] ERISA Sec. 4225(b).

[6] ERISA Sec. 4225(d).

[7] ERISA Sec. 4225(a), as amended by P.L. 109-280, Act Sec. 204(a), effective for sales occurring on or after January 1, 2007. *Pre-2007 sales rules.* With respect to sales occurring before 2007, if the liquidation or dissolution value of the employer after the sale or exchange of such assets does not exceed $2 million, the employer's withdrawal liability will be limited to the greater of: (1) 30% of the liquidation or dissolution value of the employer; or (2) the unfunded vested benefits attributable to the employer's employees. In the event that an employer's liquidation or dissolution value exceeds $2 million, the 30% limitation will be gradually increased so that it will reach 80% for sales exceeding $10 million.

¶ 2906
PAYMENT OF WITHDRAWAL LIABILITY: Schedule for Payment of Withdrawal Liability

Following an employer's complete or partial withdrawal from a multiemployer plan, the plan sponsor must notify the employer, as soon as practicable, of the amount of withdrawal liability and the schedule for paying the liability. The plan sponsor must also demand withdrawal payments in accordance with the payment schedule.[1] Withdrawal liability is collectible once notice and the demand for payment have been made (see ¶ 2907).

CCH POINTER: *Notice of potential withdrawal liability* Upon written request, a multiemployer plan sponsor or administrator must (generally within 180 days of the request) provide, to any employer who has an obligation to contribute to the plan, a notice of: the estimated amount of what the employer's withdrawal liability would be if the employer withdrew on the last day of the plan year preceding the date of the request; and an explanation of how this estimated withdrawal liability amount was determined, including (a) the actuarial assumptions and methods used to determine the value of plan liabilities and assets; (b) the data regarding employer contributions, unfunded vested benefits, and annual changes in the plan's unfunded vested benefits, and (c) the application of any relevant limits on the estimated withdrawal liability. [2]

The employer may not require the estimate more than once in a 12-month period and the plan may charge a reasonable fee for the cost of providing the notice.

Penalties. A penalty of up to $1,000 per day may be imposed for any failure to provide the notice of potential withdrawal liability to any employer that has an obligation to make contributions.

Final rules provide procedural framework for assessment of penalties for failure to furnish financial plan information and notice of potential withdrawal liability. Final rules issued by the EBSA set forth rules for the computation of the maximum penalty amount, identify circumstances under which a penalty may be assessed, establish procedural rules for service and filing, and provide plan administrators with a mechanism by which to contest a penalty assessment and request an administrative hearing. [3] The final regulations stress that the penalty is a personal liability of the plan administrator that may not be transferred to the plan as a reasonable expense of plan administration. However, the rules also authorize the DOL to waive or reduce the penalty assessment upon a showing by the plan administrator, in a written reasonable cause statement, of compliance or mitigating circumstances regarding the degree or willfulness of noncompliance. The rules are detailed at CCH PENSION PLAN GUIDE ¶ 4306.

Payment schedule formula

The payment schedule under which the withdrawing employer is required to pay its withdrawal liability is determined by the plan sponsor under the following formula:[4]

Annual amount of withdrawal liability payment =

Average annual number of contribution base units (e.g., hours worked) for the 3 consecutive plan years during the 10-year plan period ending before the plan year of withdrawal, in which the number of such units was the highest	×	Highest contribution rate (e.g., cents an hour) for required contributions of the employer during the 10-year plan period ending with plan year of withdrawal

The amount determined under this formula is the level annual payment which is to be paid over a period of years necessary to amortize the liability, subject to the "20-year cap" described below. The amount is calculated as if the first payment was made on the first day of the plan year following the plan year in which the withdrawal occurs and as if each subsequent payment was made on the first day of each subsequent plan year.[5] Thus, even though the liability of an employer is based on the plan's calculation of unfunded benefits at the end of the previous year, the first payment is not due until the beginning of the plan year after the year of withdrawal.

Quarterly and nonquarterly payments

Payments are generally made in four equal quarterly installments.[6] The plan may allow payments to be made at other intervals. However, payments that are made other than quarterly should be adjusted to the actuarial equivalent of the quarterly payments specified in ERISA Sec. 4219 if the plan receives payment earlier or later than it would have on a quarterly schedule.[7]

20-year payment cap

An employer generally is required to make level annual payments to the plan for the lesser of the number of years it would take to amortize its withdrawal liability (determined under the actuarial assumptions used in the most recent actuarial valuation of the plan) or 20 years.[8] However, the 20-year payment cap does not apply where a multiemployer plan terminates because of the withdrawal of all employers from the plan or if substantially all of the employers in the plan withdraw under an agreement or arrangement to withdraw.[9]

In the case of a partial withdrawal, the annual amount payable will be the amount determined under the payment schedule formula multiplied by the fraction used for the pro rata determination of partial withdrawal liability (see ¶ 2893).[10]

Withdrawal liability payment fund

Plan sponsors of multiemployer plans may establish or participate in a private withdrawal liability payment fund for the purpose of paying withdrawal liabilities.[11] The tax-exempt fund is funded by amounts paid by plans which participate in the funds. In the event that an employer withdraws from a plan participating in the withdrawal liability payment fund, the fund will pay the employer's liability to the plan.[12]

---

[1] ERISA Sec. 4219(b)(1).

[2] ERISA Sec. 101(l), as added by P.L. 109-280 (Pension Protection Act of 2006), Act Sec. 502(b)(1). *Note,* similar information was also required under ERISA Sec. 4221(e). However, ERISA Sec. 4221(e) was repealed by the Worker, Retiree, and Employer Recovery Act of 2008 (P.L. 110-458), Act Sec 105(b)(2).

[3] ERISA Reg. § 2560.502c-4.

[4] ERISA Sec. 4219(c)(1)(C)(i).

[5] ERISA Sec. 4219(c)(1)(A)(i).

[6] ERISA Sec. 4219(c)(3).

[7] PBGC Opinion Letter 85-1, as clarified by PBGC Opinion Letter 85-18.

[8] ERISA Sec. 4219(c)(1)(A) and (B).

[9] ERISA Sec. 4219(c)(1)(D).

[10] ERISA Sec. 4219(c)(1)(E).

[11] ERISA Sec. 4223; Code Sec. 501(c)(22).

[12] ERISA Sec. 4223(c).

¶ 2907

PAYMENT OF WITHDRAWAL LIABILITY: When Payment Is Due

Payment of withdrawal liability must begin no later than 60 days after the date on which the plan sponsor demands payment.[1] Payment is not due until demanded by the plan. However, if a payment is not made when due, interest will accrue on the unpaid amount.[2]

Default on payments

An employer generally defaults on payment of withdrawal liability when it fails to make any payment of its withdrawal liability when due and then fails to make payment within 60 days after receiving written notice from the plan sponsor of such failure.[3]

60-day grace period. No default for nonpayment may be declared until the 61st day after the later of the date:[4]

1. the period for requesting plan review expires (see ¶ 2910);
2. the period for requesting arbitration, if the employer requests a review, expires (see ¶ 2918); or
3. issuance of the arbitrator's final decision, if arbitration is timely initiated by the plan or the employer.[5]

Plan may require immediate payment. A plan may authorize a plan sponsor, in the event that an employer defaults on payment of its withdrawal liability, to require immediate payment of all or a portion of the balance of the withdrawal liability, plus any interest accrued from the date on which the first payment in default was due.[6] If the plan sponsor accelerates only a portion of the balance of an employer's withdrawal liability, the sponsor must establish a new schedule of payments for the remaining amount of the liability.[7]

Arbitration delays accelerated payments. A plan's right to seek accelerated payments is conditioned on the employer not seeking arbitration.[8]

Cessation of payments when plan terminates

When a multiemployer plan terminates, each employer's obligation to make future withdrawal liability payments ceases at the end of the plan year in which plan assets (not counting outstanding withdrawal liability claims) are sufficient to meet all of its obligations, as determined by the PBGC.[9]

---

[1] ERISA Sec. 4219(c)(2).

[2] ERISA Sec. 4219(c)(6).

[3] PBGC Reg. § 4219.31(b)(1)(i).

[4] PBGC Reg. § 4219.31(c).

[5] PBGC Reg. § 4219.31(c)(2)(iii).

[6] ERISA Sec. 4219(c)(5); PBGC Reg. §§ 4219.31(b)(2) and 4219.32.

[7] PBGC Reg. § 4219.31(b)(2).

[8] ERISA Sec. 4221(b)(1); *Chicago Truck Drivers, Helpers, and Warehousemen Union (Independent) Pension Fund v. Century Motor Freight*, CA-7 (1997), 125 F3d 526.

[9] ERISA Sec. 4219(c)(8).

¶ 2908

PAYMENT OF WITHDRAWAL LIABILITY: Refund of Overpayment

An overpayment of withdrawal liability may be refunded to the employer within six months after the date on which the overpayment is determined. ERISA authorizes a refund of overpayment of withdrawal liability to an employer within 6 months after the date of such determination.[1]Similarly, ERISA and the Internal Revenue Code allow a multiemployer plan to return overpayments of withdrawal liability that are attributable to mistakes of fact or law (other than mistakes regarding the qualification of the plan) to be returned to the employer within 6 months after the determination by the plan administrator that the payment was made by mistake.[2] Such refunds will not be considered a prohibited return of assets inuring to the benefit of the employer.

Lump-sum payment with interest. The overpayment of withdrawal liability must be returned to the employer, with interest, in a lump-sum.[3] The overpayment may not be applied to future payments.

Include interest in employer's gross income. Any interest credited or paid on a refund of mistaken withdrawal liability payments must be included in the employer's gross income.[4]

Interest rate. Interest will be credited on the overpayment from the date of the overpayment to the date on which the overpayment is refunded to the employer at the rate that is specified for overdue withdrawal liability payments.[5]

The applicable withdrawal liability interest rates are set forth at CCH PENSION PLAN GUIDE¶ 79.

Request for refund not required. A multiemployer plan may refund an overpayment regardless of whether the employer has requested the refund or initiated a review of the initial withdrawal liability assessment or whether the assessment is subject to arbitration under ERISA Sec. 4221.[6]

CCH POINTER: The return of an overpayment of withdrawal liability will not result in a violation of the exclusive benefit rule of Code Sec. 401(a)(2), if the overpayment is returned to the employer with interest, in accord with the governing PBGC regulations.[7]

---

[1] ERISA Sec. 403(c)(3).

[2] ERISA Sec. 403(c)(2)(A)(ii); Code Sec. 401(a)(2).

[3] PBGC Reg. § 4219.31(d).

[4] IRS Reg. § 1.401(a)(2)-1(c).

[5] PBGC Reg. § 4219.31(d).

[6] ERISA Opinion Letter 95-24A, 9-8-95.

[7] IRS Reg. § 1.401(a)(2)-1(b)(2)(ii)(B).

¶ 2909

PAYMENT OF WITHDRAWAL LIABILITY: Deduction for Withdrawal Liability Payments

Withdrawal liability payments are deductible as employer contributions to a stock bonus, pension, profit-sharing, or annuity plan.[1] The deduction is allowed without regard to the usual limitation on employer deductions for contributions to a tax-qualified plan. However, withdrawal liability payments are included in the employer's total plan contributions for purposes of the maximum deduction allowable under the full funding limitation.

Note, the deduction limitation for contributions to multiemployer plans, for plan years may not be less than 140 percent (as opposed to 100 percent under prior law) of the current liability of the plan, minus the value of the plan's assets.[2] See ¶ 1404.

---

[1] Code Sec. 404(g)(1).

[2] Code Sec. 404(a)(1)(D), as amended by P.L. 109-280 (Pension Protection Act of 2006), Act

Secs. 801(d) (applicable to years before 2007) and 802(a) (applicable to years beginning after 2007).

¶ 2910
PAYMENT OF WITHDRAWAL LIABILITY: Request for Review of Plan Sponsor's Determinations

An employer may request the plan sponsor to review any item relating to the calculation of withdrawal liability and the payment schedule within 90 days after the employer receives the initial notice and demand for payment of liability.[1] During this period the employer may identify errors in the determination of withdrawal liability and furnish the plan sponsor with any additional relevant information.

The plan sponsor must conduct a reasonable review of any matter raised and notify the employer of its decision, the basis for its decision, and the reason for any modification in the determination of the employer's liability or the payment schedule.

> **CCH POINTER:** An employer that does not make a request for review within 90 days of receiving the notice of liability forfeits its right to challenge the withdrawal liability assessment. The employer does not have the right to extend the 90-day deadline.[2]

---

[1] ERISA Sec. 4219(b)(2).

[2] *Reliable Liquors, Inc. v. Truck Drivers and Helpers Local Union No. 355 Pension Fund*, DC MD

(2003), No. JFM-02-3854, CCH PENSION PLAN GUIDE ¶ 23,982Z.

¶ 2911
MASS WITHDRAWAL: Mass Withdrawal Liability

Special rules apply for redetermining an employer's withdrawal liability and for fully allocating the total unfunded vested benefits in either of two "mass withdrawal" situations. These situations are:

1. the termination of a plan by the withdrawal of every employer; and

2. the withdrawal of substantially all employers pursuant to an agreement or arrangement to withdraw.[1]

Following withdrawal, the total unfunded vested benefits of the plan must be fully allocated among all employers. In order to ensure that all unfunded vested benefits are fully allocated among all liable employers, the plan's unfunded vested benefits as of end of the plan year in which the plan terminates, must be determined.[2] The calculation is based on the value of the plan's nonforfeitable benefits as of that date, less the value of plan assets (benefits and assets valued in accordance with assumptions specified by PBGC), less the outstanding balance of any initial withdrawal liability (i.e., assessments made without regard to mass withdrawal) and redetermination liability (assessments made for de minimis and 20-year cap reduction amounts) that can reasonably be expected to be collected.

The plan sponsor must then notify each employer of the amount of the initial withdrawal liability and collect it from each employer.

---

[1] PBGC Reg. §§ 4219.11-4219.19.

[2] PBGC Reg. § 4219.15(b).

¶ 2912

MASS WITHDRAWAL: Employers Subject to Liability

An employer that was afforded relief by the *de minimis* rule in determining its initial withdrawal liability will be subject to redetermination liability for this amount if it:[1]

1. withdrew from a plan in the plan year in which the plan terminated because of the withdrawal of every employer; or

2. withdrew pursuant to an agreement or arrangement to withdraw from a multiemployer plan from which substantially all employers withdrew pursuant to an agreement or arrangement to withdraw.

If the employer was afforded relief by the 20-year limitation on annual payments in the assessment of its initial withdrawal liability, the employer will be liable for redetermination liability for such amount if it withdrew from a plan that terminated because of the withdrawal of every employer, or withdrew pursuant to an agreement or arrangement as described in 2. above.[2] Thus, an employer's redetermination liability is the sum of any liability for de minimis amounts and any liability for 20-year limitation amounts.

An employer that withdraws within a period of three consecutive plan years during which substantially all employers withdraw will be presumed to have withdrawn pursuant to an agreement or arrangement to withdraw.[3]

Liability for reallocation liability

An employer will be liable for the amount of unfunded vested benefits allocated to the employer in the event of a mass withdrawal, if the employer withdrew pursuant to an agreement or an arrangement as described in 2. above. An employer will also be liable if it withdrew after the beginning of the second full plan year preceding the date of plan termination from a plan that terminated because of the withdrawal of every employer, *and,* as of the reallocation record date:[4]

1. the employer has not been completely liquidated or dissolved;

2. the employer is not the subject of a bankruptcy proceeding (and the plan sponsor does not determine that the employer is liable for reallocation liability because the employer is reasonably expected to be able to pay its initial withdrawal liability and its redetermination liability in full and on time to the plan); and

3. the plan sponsor has not determined that the employer's initial withdrawal liability or redetermination liability is limited under the dollar limitations on withdrawal liability.[5]

Calculation of reallocation liability. Each liable employer's share of reallocation liability is equal to the amount of the reallocation liability multiplied by the following fraction:[6]

sum of the employer's initial withdrawal liability and any redetermination liability/sum of all initial withdrawal liabilities and all the redetermination liabilities of all liable employers

The PBGC final rules modify the current allocation fraction for reallocation liability in order to address situations in which employers, who would otherwise be liable for reallocation liability, have little or no initial withdrawal liability or redetermination liability and, therefore, have a zero (or understated) reallocation liability. According to PBGC, such situations may arise where an employer withdraws from the plan before the mass withdrawal valuation date, but has no withdrawal liability under the modified presumptive and rolling-5 methods because either: (1) the plan has no unfunded vested benefits as of the end of the plan year preceding the plan year in which the employer withdrew, or (2) the plan did not require the employer to make contributions for the five-year period preceding the plan year of withdrawal. Under such circumstances, if the employer's withdrawal is later determined to be part of a mass withdrawal for which reallocation liability applies, the employer would not be liable for any portion of the reallocation liability.

In order to ensure that reallocation liability is allocated broadly among all liable employers, the PBGC amended, effective for terminations by mass withdrawal occurring on or after January 25, 2009, PBGC Reg. 4219.15(c) to replace the current allocation fraction based on initial withdrawal liability with a new allocation fraction for determining an employer's allocable share of reallocation liability. Under the new fraction, the plan's unfunded vested benefits will be allocated based on the average of the employer's contribution base units relative to the combined averages of the plan's total contribution base units for the three plan years preceding the employer's withdrawal from the plan.

The fraction would be:[7]

withdrawing employer's average contribution base units during the three plan years preceding the withdrawal (i.e., the employer's total contribution base units over the three plan years divided by three)/sum of the averages of all the employer's contribution base units during the three plan years preceding each employer's withdrawal

Contribution base unit. A contribution base unit is a unit with respect to which an employer has an obligation to contribute under a multiemployer plan (e.g., a hour worked or a unit of production) or with respect to which the employer would have an obligation to contribute if the contribution requirement with respect to the plan were greater than zero [8]

---

[1] ERISA Sec. 4219(c)(1)(D); PBGC Reg. § 4219.12(a).

[2] ERISA Sec. 4219(c)(1)(D); PBGC Reg. § 4219.12(b).

[3] PBGC Reg. § 4219.12(g).

[4] The reallocation date is a date selected by the plan sponsor that falls on or after the date of the plan's actuarial report for the year of mass withdrawal, but not later than one year after the last day of the plan year in which the plan terminates (mass withdrawal valuation date) (PBGC Reg. § 4210.2(b)).

[5] PBGC Reg. § 4219.12(c).

[6] PBGC Reg. § 4219.15(c)(1).

[7] PBGC Reg. § 4219.15(c)(1), as amended 1-29-09 (73 FR 79628).

[8] ERISA Sec.4001(a)(11); PBGC Reg. § 4219.15(c)(3).

¶ 2913

MASS WITHDRAWAL: Notice to Employers and PBGC

The plan sponsor of a multiemployer plan is required to provide various types of notices to other employers participating in the plan and to the PBGC in connection with a mass withdrawal.

Notice of mass withdrawal

A notice that a mass withdrawal has occurred must be sent within 30 days after the mass withdrawal valuation date (the last day of the plan year in which the mass withdrawal occurs) to each employer that the plan sponsor reasonably expects may be liable upon mass withdrawal.[1] The notice must include the mass withdrawal valuation date, provide a description of the consequences of mass withdrawal, and advise each employer obligated to make initial withdrawal liability payments to continue making those payments in accordance with its schedule.

Notice of redetermination liability

Within 150 days after the mass withdrawal date (i.e., the last day of the plan year in which the plan terminates or the last day of the plan year as of which substantially all employers have withdrawn), the plan sponsor must determine the liability of withdrawing employers for *de minimis* amounts and for 20-year limitation amounts.[2] Subsequently, the plan sponsor must issue a notice of redetermination liability to each employer liable for *de minimis* amounts or 20-year-limitation amounts, within 30 days after determining such liability. The notice must specify the amount of the employer's liability for *de minimis* amounts and for 20-year-limitation amounts, include a schedule for payment of the liability, and demand payment of the liability.

Notice of reallocation liability

Within 30 days after the date on which the plan sponsor is required to have determined the reallocation liability of employers (the date one year after the reallocation record date), the plan sponsor is to issue a notice of reallocation liability to liable employers.[3] The notice of reallocation liability must include the amount of the liability, a schedule for payment, and a demand for payment of the liability in accordance with the schedule.

Notice to employers without liability

The plan sponsor is required to notify an employer that receives a notice of mass withdrawal of any subsequent determination relieving the employer of liability for mass withdrawal liability or any component of such liability.[4] The notice must be issued no later than the notice of reallocation liability.

Reporting to the PBGC

The plan sponsor must notify the PBGC that mass withdrawal has occurred and provide separate certifications that determinations of redetermination liability and reallocation liability have been made with notices provided to employers.[5]

The notice of mass withdrawal and the certification may be filed with the PBGC by hand, mail, or commercial delivery service or through electronic media.[6] The notice or certification will generally be treated as filed on the date it is sent, if requirements specified by the PBGC are met.[7] For example, electronic filings must satisfy the applicable technical requirements specified by the PBGC (see http://www.pbgc.gov) and must identify the person to be contacted in the event the filing needs to be resubmitted.[8]

---

[1] PBGC Reg. § 4219.16(a).

[2] PBGC Reg. §§ 4219.2(b) and 4219.16(b).

[3] PBGC Reg. § 4219.16(c).

[4] PBGC Reg. § 4219.16(d).

[5] PBGC Reg. § 4219.17.

[6] PBGC Reg. § 4000.3 and 4219.17(a)(2).

[7] PBGC Reg. § 4000.21 and PBGC Reg. § 4219.17(e).

[8] PBGC Reg. § 4000.29.

¶ 2914
MASS WITHDRAWAL: Payment Schedules

A multiemployer plan must establish schedules for payment of an employer's mass withdrawal liability.[1]

Employers with existing payment schedules

If an employer owes initial withdrawal liability as of the mass withdrawal valuation date, the plan sponsor must amend the existing schedule of payments in order to amortize the additional liability (redetermination liability and reallocation liability) being assessed.

In order to determine the amended payment schedule for redetermination liability, the plan sponsor must add the amount of that liability to the employer's total initial withdrawal liability and then determine a payment schedule in accordance with ERISA Sec. 4219(c)(1), excluding application of the 20-year limitation rule (see ¶ 2906).

In amending the payment schedule to reflect the reallocation of liability, the plan sponsor must add that liability to the present value (as of the date following the mass withdrawal valuation date) of the unpaid portion of the payment schedule as amended for redetermination liability. A new payment schedule of level annual payments must be determined, calculated as if the first payment had been made on the day following the mass withdrawal valuation date.

Employers without existing payment schedules

Where an employer had no initial withdrawal liability or had fully paid that liability by the mass withdrawal valuation date, a payment schedule is determined for the redetermination liability in the same manner that the schedule for initial withdrawal liability was (or would have been) determined, using the same interest assumptions. This schedule is then amended to include the reallocation liability following the procedure described above for reallocation liability for an employer having an existing payment schedule.

---

[1] PBGC Reg. § 4219.16(f).

¶ 2915

MASS WITHDRAWAL: Refund of Mass Withdrawal Liability

If a plan sponsor determines, after it has imposed mass withdrawal liability, that a mass withdrawal has not actually occurred, all payments already made for mass withdrawal liability must be refunded to the employer, with interest.[1] Interest accrues from the date the payment was received by the plan until the date of refund.

---

[1] PBGC Reg. § 4219.16(i).

¶ 2916

MASS WITHDRAWAL: Withdrawal by Substantially All Employers in a Plan Year

Separate rules govern the determination and imposition of liability for *de minimis* amounts when substantially all employers withdraw from a plan in a single plan year. Rules relating to the withdrawal of substantially all employers in a plan year are addressed separately because, for an ongoing plan, this type of withdrawal gives rise to liability for *de minimis* amounts independently of a mass withdrawal.

The procedures and rules follow closely the procedures applicable to the determination of *de minimis* amounts in a plan that experiences a mass withdrawal (see ¶ 2912). Employers that withdraw in a single plan year are liable for *de minimis* amounts if their initial withdrawal liability was reduced under the *de minimis* rule.[1] The amount of this liability is calculated under the rules for determining liability for *de minimis* amounts.

The plan sponsor, within 30 days after the determination of liability, must issue a notice of liability that includes the employer's liability for *de minimis* amounts, a payment schedule, and a demand for payment. The notice may be delivered by any method that is reasonably calculated to ensure actual receipt of the material by the intended recipient.[2] The PBGC also provides a safe harbor method, pursuant to which the notice may be issued electronically.[3] The issuance is generally treated as filed on the date sent, provided requirements specified by the PBGC are satisfied.[4]

---

[1] PBGC Reg. § 4219.18(a).

[2] PBGC Reg. § 4000.13 and 4219.19.

[3] PBGC Reg. § 4000.13(b) and 4000.14.

[4] PBGC Reg. § 4000.23 and 4219.19.

¶ 2917

MASS WITHDRAWAL: Valuation of Benefits and Assets

A multiemployer plan from which all contributing employers have withdrawn, or from which substantially all contributing employers have withdrawn pursuant to an agreement to withdraw, must allocate vested benefits among the withdrawing employers.[1] A multiemployer plan that *terminates* because of the withdrawal of all employers or the cessation of all employers' obligations to contribute must value its assets and vested benefits each year to determine whether and to what extent benefits must be reduced.[2] In valuing plan assets, outstanding claims for withdrawal liability must be considered.[3]

> **CCH POINTER:** *Use mortality assumptions for single-employer plans when valuing multiemployer plan assets.* Plan administrators valuing multiemployer plan assets following mass withdrawal must use the mortality rates and tables prescribed by the PBGC for use by terminating single-employer plans.[4]

Generally, the valuation date where the plan does not terminate is the end of the plan year in which the mass withdrawal occurs. Where the plan terminates because of the complete withdrawal of every employer from the plan (or the cessation of the obligation of all employers to contribute under the plan), the valuation date is the last day of the plan year in which the plan terminates[5] Subsequent valuation dates fall on the anniversaries of the first valuation date. Where substantially all the employers withdraw from the plan pursuant to an agreement or arrangement to withdraw, the valuation date is the last day of the plan year in which substantially all employers have withdrawn.

The regulations reflect a recognition that a multiemployer plan's usual valuation methods cannot be applied without modification in such significantly changed circumstances and a further recognition that fairness to all parties demands consistency in valuing plan assets and liabilities. The principle that plan assets and benefits should reflect current market rates is fundamental to the valuation rules in the regulations. When valuations are required in mass withdrawal situations, they must conform to the requirements of the regulations. To a great extent, the particular valuation methods used for terminated single-employer plans are incorporated in the regulations.

Special valuation rule for plans closing out. The annual valuation is no longer required when a terminated plan satisfies all liabilities for nonforfeitable benefits and cease operations.[6]

---

[1] ERISA Sec. 4219(c)(1)(D).

[2] ERISA Sec. 4281(b); PBGC Reg. §§ 4281.11-4281.18.

[3] PBGC Reg. § 4281.18(a)-(c).

[4] PBGC Reg. § 4281.14, as amended by 71 FR 75115 (12-14-06).

[5] PBGC Reg. § 4281.11.

[6] PBGC Reg. § 4281.16.

¶ 2918
RESOLUTION OF DISPUTES: Arbitration Requirement

A dispute between an employer and the plan sponsor relating to the determination of withdrawal liability must be resolved through an arbitration proceeding.[1] Note, for purposes of withdrawal liability, all trades or businesses under common control are treated as a single employer.

60-day period to initiate arbitration

The employer or the plan sponsor may initiate arbitration within a 60-day period following the earlier of:[2]

      1. the date the plan sponsor notifies the employer of its decision after a reasonable review of any matter raised; or

      2. 120 days after the date the employer requests a review of the plan sponsor's determination of withdrawal liability.

The parties may also jointly initiate arbitration within the 180-day period following the date of the plan sponsor's initial notice and demand.[3] The parties may, however, by mutual agreement at any time, waive or extend the prescribed time limits.[4]

Notice of initiation of arbitration

The party that unilaterally initiates arbitration is responsible for establishing that the notice of initiation of arbitration was received by the other party within the time limit for one-party initiation (taking into account any waiver or extension).[5] If the employer initiates arbitration, it must include in the notice of initiation a statement that it disputes the plan sponsor's determination of its withdrawal liability and is initiating arbitration.[6]

A party must object promptly to an incomplete initiation agreement or a notice of initiation of arbitration or lose its right to subsequently object to any deficiencies in the agreement.[7]

Payment due upon failure to arbitrate

If an employer fails to initiate arbitration within the required 60-day period, it waives the right to contest the withdrawal liability assessment and the amount demanded by the plan sponsor becomes immediately due and owing.[8]

Selection of arbitrator

An employer and plan sponsor must select the arbitrator within 45 days after the arbitration is initiated (or within such other period as is mutually agreed upon).[9] The parties must mail a notice of appointment to the arbitrator and the arbitrator must make a written acceptance of the appointment within 15 days.

Prior to accepting the appointment, the arbitrator must disclose to the parties any circumstances likely to affect its impartiality, including any bias or any financial or personal interest in the result of the arbitration and any past or present relationship with the parties or their counsel.[10]

In addition, after an arbitrator has been selected, a party may ask an arbitrator to withdraw from the proceedings at any point before a final award is rendered on the ground that it is unable to render an impartial award.[11]

Presumption that withdrawal liability determination is correct

For purposes of arbitration, a plan sponsor's determination of withdrawal liability is presumed to be correct unless the party seeking to contest the determination shows by a preponderance of the evidence that the determination is unreasonable or clearly erroneous.[12] The determination of the plan as to the amount of its unfunded vested benefits for a plan year is also to be presumed correct, unless a party seeking to contest the determination shows by a preponderance of the evidence that:

1. the actuarial assumptions and methods used in the determination were unreasonable in the aggregate; or

2. a significant error was made by the plan's actuary in applying actuarial assumptions or methods.

Disputes regarding transactions to evade liability

Plan sponsors may disregard any transaction that they believe was undertaken to evade or avoid the assessment of withdrawal liability. Generally, employers disputing a withdrawal liability assessment must pay the assessed amount pending the outcome of arbitration.[13] However, employers that wish to dispute a sponsor's assessment that a transaction was intended to evade liability may delay or reduce payments pending the outcome of arbitration or litigation, if certain requirements are met.[14]

With respect to a transaction occurring after December 31, 1998, if: (1) the plan sponsor finds that a complete or partial withdrawal occurred or that the employer is liable for withdrawal liability payments, and (2) the sponsor's finding of withdrawal liability is due to transactions that occurred on or after December 31, 1998, and at least 5 years (2 years for a small employers) prior to the withdrawal, and the transaction's purpose was to evade or avoid withdrawal liability, the person liable for withdrawal liability imposed by the plan sponsor may contest the plan sponsor's determination through an arbitration proceeding or in court. The effect of the rule is to relieve the contesting employer of the obligation to pay withdrawal liability until a final decision has been reached by an arbitrator or court.[15]

In order to avoid the obligation of making withdrawal liability payments until a final arbitration or court decision upholds the plan sponsor's withdrawal liability determination, the electing person: (1) must provide notice to the plan sponsor of the election within 90 days after the plan sponsor notifies the electing person of its withdrawal liability, and (2) may need to provide a surety bond or deposit amounts in escrow in the amount of the withdrawal liability payment that would otherwise be due.[16]

Note, PBGC final rules issued in 2008 (effective for ERISA Sec. 4219(b)(1) notices received on or after August 17, 2007 with respect to transactions occurring after 1998) further provide that an employer that complies with the procedures under ERISA Sec. 4221(g) will not be considered in default of withdrawal liability under ERISA Sec. 4219(c)(5). [17]

Arbitrate dispute before going to court

Withdrawal liability disputes must generally be arbitrated before the parties may proceed to court.[18] However, the DC, Second, Fifth, Sixth, Seventh, and Ninth Circuits hold that arbitration is not a jurisdictional prerequisite to federal court review.[19] According to these Circuits, federal courts retain subject matter jurisdiction over all disputes arising under ERISA.

☐ Any party to arbitration may bring an action to enforce, vacate, or modify the award. Post-arbitration actions are discussed at ¶ 2921.

---

[1] ERISA Sec. 4221(a)(1).

[2] ERISA Sec. 4221(a)(1); PBGC Reg. § 4221.3(a).

[3] ERISA Sec. § 4221(a)(1)(B).

[4] PBGC Reg. § 4221.3(b).

[5] PBGC Reg. § 4221.3(c).

[6] PBGC Reg. § 4221.3(d).

[7] PBGC Reg. § 4221.3(e).

[8]See, e.g., *Robbins v. Admiral Merchants Motor Freight, Inc.,* CA-7 (1988), 846 F2d 1054.

[9] PBGC Reg. § 4221.4(a).

[10] PBGC Reg. § 4221.4(b).

[11] PBGC Reg. § 4221.4(c).

[12] ERISA Sec. 4221(a)(3). See *Concrete Pipe and Products of California, Inc., v. Construction Laborers Pension Trust for Southern California,* US Sup Ct (1993), 508 U.S. 602 (presumption favoring the withdrawal liability determination and calculation made by plan sponsors and trustee did not violate an employer's due process rights).

[13] ERISA Sec. 4221(d).

[14] ERISA Sec. 4221(f); ERISA Sec. 4221(g), as added by P.L. 109-280 (Pension Protection Act of 2006), Act Sec. 204(d), applicable to persons who receive a notification under ERISA Sec. 4219(b)(1) on or after August 17, 210-06 with respect to trans-action that occurred after December 31, 1998, redesignated as ERISA Sec. 4221(f) by P.L. 110-458 (Worker, Retiree, and Employer Recovery Act of 2008), Act. Sec. 105(b)(2).

[15] ERISA Sec.4221(f)(1), as added by P.L. 109-280 (Pension Protection Act of 2006), Act Sec. 204(d). Note, rules applicable to transactions occurring before January 1, 1999, are set forth at ERISA Sec. 4221(e).

[16] ERISA Sec.4221(f)(2), as added by P.L. 109-280 (Pension Protection Act of 2006), Act Sec. 204(d).

[17] PBGC Reg. § 4219.1(c).

[18] See, e.g., *Connors v. Brady-Cline Coal Co.,* DC D of C (1986), 668 FSupp 5; *Central States, Southeast and Southwest Areas Pension Fund v. MGS Transportation,* DC Ill (1987), 661 FSupp 54; *Robbins v. Griffith Motor Express,* DC Ill (1987), No. 86 C 0700; *Grand Union Company v. Food Employers Labor Relations,* CA D of C (1987), 808 F2d 66.

[19] *I.A.M. National Pension Fund v. Clinton Engines Corp.* CA-DC (1987), 825 F2d 415; *ILGWU National Retirement Fund v. Levy Bros. Frocks, Inc.,* CA-2 (1988); *Central States Southeast & Southwest Areas Pension Fund v. T.I.M.E.-DC,* CA-5 (1987), 826 F2d 320; *Central States Southeast & Southwest Areas Pension Fund v. Chatham Properties,* CA-6 (1991), 929 F2d 260; *Robbins v. Admiral Merchants Motor Freight, Inc.* CA-7 (1988), 846 F2d 1054; *Board of Trustees of the Construction Laborers Pension Trust for Southern California v. M.M. Sundt Construction Co.,* CA-9 (1994), 37 F3d 1419.

¶ 2919

RESOLUTION OF DISPUTES: Interim Withdrawal Liability

Generally, an employer is required to make withdrawal liability payments even if the assessment is the subject of ongoing arbitration [1] or the employer is undergoing bankruptcy.[2] Interim payments must be made in accordance with the existing payment schedule, together with interest on past-due installments.[3] A plan may sue to recover interim withdrawal liability.

An employer may avoid interim payments if the claim for withdrawal liability is frivolous or not colorable.[4] However, employers have been ordered to make withdrawal liability payments pending arbitration even where the assessment was clearly erroneous.[5] Payments will be adjusted for any overpayments or underpayments arising out of the arbitrator's decision regarding the withdrawal liability assessment.[6]

---

[1] ERISA Sec. 4219(c)(2). See, e.g., *Central States, Southeast and Southwest Areas Pension Fund v. National Cement Products Co.,* DC Ill (1998), No. 97CV4031; *Central States Southeast and Southwest Areas Pension Fund v. Tom Boy, Inc.,* DC Ill (1988); and *Trustees of the Amalgamated Cotton Garment and Allied Industries v. Baltimore Sportswear, Inc.,* DC NY (1986), 632 FSupp 1142.

[2] See, e.g., *Marvin Hayes Lines v. Central States, Southeast and Southwest Areas Pension Fund,* CA-6 (1987), 814 F2d 297; *Central States Southeast and Southwest Areas Pension Fund v. Chatham Properties,* CA-6 (1991), 929 F2d 260.

[3] See, e.g., *Debreceni v. Merchants Terminal Corporation,* CA-1 (1989), 889 F2d 1.

[4] *Trustees of the Plumbers and Pipefitters National Pension Fund v. Mar-Len, Inc.,* CA-5 (1994), 30 F3d 621; *NYSA-ILA Pension Trust Fund v. Lykes Bros. Inc.,* DC NY (1997), No. 96 Civ. 5616 (DLC).

[5] *Marvin Hayes Lines, Inc. v. Central States Southeast and Southwest Areas Pension Fund,* CA-6 (1987), 814 F2d 297, rev'g DC Tenn (1985), No. 3-84-0906.

[6] ERISA Sec. 4221(d).

¶ 2921

RESOLUTION OF DISPUTES: Awards and Costs

The arbitrator must render a written award resolving the withdrawal liability dispute. The award must generally be rendered no later than 30 days after the proceedings close and must:[1]

1. state the basis for the award, including such findings of fact and conclusions of law (without explicitly characterizing his statements as such) as are necessary to resolve the dispute;

2. adjust (or provide a method for adjusting) the amount or schedule of withdrawal liability payments to be made after the award to reflect overpayments or underpayments made before the award was rendered or require the plan sponsor to refund overpayments; and

3. provide for an allocation of costs.

Reconsideration of award

A party may seek modification or reconsideration of the arbitrator's award by filing a written motion with the arbitrator and all opposing parties within 20 days after the award is rendered.[2] A motion for modification or reconsideration may be granted only if:[3]

1. there is a numerical error or a mistake in the description of any person, thing, or property referred to in the award;

2. the arbitrator has rendered an award upon a matter not submitted to the arbitrator and the matter affects the merits of the decision; or

3. the award is imperfect in a matter of form not affecting the merits of the dispute.

The arbitrator must deny the motion for modification or reconsideration or render an opinion within 20 days after the request is filed with the arbitrator. [4]

Court review of arbitration award. A party may bring suit in federal court to enforce, vacate, or modify an arbitrator's award within 30 days after the award is issued.[5] The filing of a motion of reconsideration with the arbitrator, however, suspends the 30-day period for requesting court review.

Costs and attorneys' fees

Each party is to bear the costs of its own witnesses.[6] If only one party requests a transcript of the record of the arbitration, it must bear the costs of transcription and copying. However, the parties must share the other costs of the arbitration proceedings equally unless the arbitrator determines otherwise.[7]

Ordinarily, each party will bear its own attorneys' fees. However, the arbitrator may require a party that initiates or contests an arbitration in bad faith or engages in vexatious conduct during the course of the arbitration to pay the reasonable attorneys' fees of other parties.[8] In the absence of bad faith or misconduct, an arbitrator may not award attorneys' fees.[9]

[1] PBGC Reg. § 4221.8(a) and (b).

[2] PBGC Reg. § 4221.9(a).

[3] PBGC Reg. § 4221.9(b).

[4] PBGC Reg. § 4221.9(c).

[5] ERISA Sec. 4221(b)(2).

[6] PBGC Reg. § 4221.10(a).

[7] PBGC Reg. § 4221.11(b).

[8] PBGC Reg. § 4221.11(c).

[9] *Rootberg v. Central States, Southeast and Southwest Areas Pension Fund,* CA-7 (1988), 856 F2d 796.

¶ 2922

RESOLUTION OF DISPUTES: PBGC-Approved Alternative Procedure

Arbitration may be conducted under an alternative procedure approved by the PBGC rather than under the procedures prescribed by the regulations.[1] A plan may require the use of a PBGC-approved procedure for all arbitrations of withdrawal liability disputes, or the parties may agree to the use of a PBGC- approved procedure in a particular case.

Alternative procedure

An alternative procedure, the Multiemployer Pension Plan Arbitration Rules sponsored by the International Foundation of Employee Benefit Plans and administered by the American Arbitration Association, has been approved by the PBGC.

□ The approved alternative procedure is at CCH PENSION PLAN GUIDE ¶ 7237.

[1] PBGC Reg. § 4221.14(a).

¶ 2923

REORGANIZATION OF MULTIEMPLOYER PLANS: Special Rules for Multiemployer Plans in Reorganization

Financially troubled multiemployer plans in a state of "reorganization" are subject to special rules regarding funding and adjustments in accrued benefits.

A multiemployer plan is in reorganization for a year if the plan's "reorganization index" is greater than zero.[1] The reorganization index is the amount of the "vested benefits charge" of the plan, less the net charge to the plan's funding standard account for the year.[2] The reorganization index is calculated anew for each plan year.

Note, additional funding rules apply to significantly underfunded plans. Specifically, multiemployer plans that are so underfunded as to be in endangered or critical status are required to adopt funding improvement and rehabilitation plans and take prescribed actions to improve their funding status over a multi-year period. The applicable rules are detailed at ¶ 1493L.

Vested benefits charge

The "vested benefits charge" is the amount needed to amortize in equal annual installments the unfunded vested benefits of the plan determined as of the end of the "base plan year" over a period of:[3]

1. 10 years, to the extent such benefits are attributable to persons in pay status (generally, current retirees); and

2. 25 years, to the extent such benefits are attributable to other participants.

Base plan year. The base plan year for any plan year is the last plan year ending at least six months before the earliest effective date of any relevant collective bargaining agreement.[4] If there is no relevant bargaining agreement, the base plan year is the last plan year ending at least one year before the beginning of the plan year in which the determination of the vested benefits charge is made.

Net charge to funding standard account

The net charge to the plan's funding standard account is:[5]

1. the sum of the charges to the account for the plan's normal pension cost for the plan year and annual amounts necessary to

amortize initial past service costs, an increase in past service costs, experience losses, changes in actuarial assumptions resulting in a loss, waived funding deficiency, and "switchback liability;" *less*

2. the sum of the credits to the account for annual amounts necessary to amortize a decrease in past service costs, experience gains, and changes in actuarial assumptions resulting in a gain.

Switchback liability. "Switchback liability" refers to the amount of the excess of charges over credits built up in the funding standard account when the alternative minimum funding standard account is used and the plan later switches back to the funding standard account.

Credits not counted. The following credits are not counted in computing the net charge to the funding standard account for purposes of determining the reorganization index:

1. credit for actual contributions to the plan for the year;

2. credit for any waived funding deficiency for the year; and

3. credit for "switchback liability."

---

[1] ERISA Sec. 4241(a); Code Sec. 418(a).

[2] ERISA Sec. 4241(b)(1); Code Sec. 418(b)(1).

[3] ERISA Sec. 4241(b)(3); Code Sec. 418(b)(3).

[4] ERISA Sec. 4241(b)(5); Code Sec. 418(b)(5).

[5] ERISA Sec. 4241(b)(2); Code Sec. 418(b)(2).

¶ 2924

REORGANIZATION OF MULTIEMPLOYER PLANS: Annuity Payment Requirement

While a plan is in reorganization, a participant's vested benefits that are derived from employer contributions and that have a value over $1,750 must be distributed as an annuity that provides substantially level payments over the life of the participant.[1]

---

[1] ERISA Sec. 4241(c); Code Sec. 418(c).

¶ 2925

REORGANIZATION OF MULTIEMPLOYER PLANS: Minimum Contribution Requirement

Under the minimum contribution requirement, the funding target for each year that a plan is in reorganization must be set at a level that is sufficient to fund the unfunded vested benefits attributable to participants in pay status over ten years and the unfunded vested benefits attributable to all other participants over 25 years, plus an additional amount for increases in normal cost made while a plan is in reorganization.[1]

Cash flow requirement

In the case of a plan that has a very large number of retirees and few assets, the minimum contribution requirement may not be adequate to ensure that the plan will be able to meet its benefit commitments. Accordingly, if the plan's vested benefits charge is less than the plan's cash flow amount for a plan year, the minimum contribution requirement is determined by substituting the "cash flow amount" for the vested benefits charge. In this case, no adjustments are made for reductions in contribution base units.[2]

The "cash flow amount" refers to the amount of benefits payable under the plan for the base plan year increased by the plan's administration expenses for the base plan year and decreased by the value of available plan assets for the base plan year.

---

[1] ERISA Sec. 4243; Code Sec. 418B.

[2] ERISA Sec. 4243(b)(3); Code Sec. 418B(b)(3).

¶ 2926

REORGANIZATION OF MULTIEMPLOYER PLANS:
Accumulated Funding Deficiency

For any plan year for which a plan is in reorganization, the plan must continue to maintain its funding standard account. The plan's accumulated funding deficiency under ERISA Sec. 304 is the sum of the minimum contribution requirement for the plan year (taking into consideration any overburden credit (see ¶ 2928)) and the plan's accumulated funding deficiency for the preceding plan year. This sum is reduced by amounts considered contributed by employers for the plan year (increased by amounts waived (see below)). Sufficient employer contributions to eliminate the accumulated funding deficiency would eliminate the excise tax for failure to meet the minimum funding standard for the year.[1]

Note, the funding rules applicable to multiemployer plans are detailed at ¶ 1493K and ¶ 1493L.

Waiver of accumulated funding deficiency

If 10% or more of the employers contributing to a multiemployer plan are unable to make contributions that will satisfy the minimum funding standard for a plan year without substantial business hardship, the IRS may waive all or a portion of the contribution requirements of the minimum funding standard for the plan year. In addition, the IRS may waive any accumulated funding deficiency of a plan in reorganization.[2] This waiver is not to be treated as a waived funding deficiency that would be amortized over a 15-year period.

---

[1] ERISA Sec. 4243(a)(1); Code Sec. 418B(a)(1).

[2] ERISA Sec. 4243(f); Code Sec. 418B(f).

¶ 2927

REORGANIZATION OF MULTIEMPLOYER PLANS:
Limitation on Required Increases

The minimum contribution requirement does not exceed the greater of the funding standard requirement for the plan year, or 107% of the amount required for the preceding year plus an amount that takes into account certain benefit increases.[1] The funding standard requirement for any plan year is the net charge to the funding standard account for the plan year.[2] If the plan was not in reorganization in the preceding plan year, the 107% is multiplied by the funding standard requirement for the preceding plan year.

If the plan was in reorganization for the preceding plan year, the 107% is multiplied by the sum of the minimum contribution requirement for the preceding year (including the 107% limitation) plus an amount to take into account certain benefit increases for the preceding year.

---

[1] ERISA Sec. 4243(d)(1); Code Sec. 418B(d)(1).   [2] ERISA Sec. 4243(d)(2); Code Sec. 418B(d)(2).

¶ 2928

REORGANIZATION OF MULTIEMPLOYER PLANS:
Overburden Credit

For some plans, industry declines have resulted in the number of retirees in the plan exceeding the number of active workers. Required contribution increases in such cases may be pushed to intolerable levels. Where a plan is considered to be financially overburdened, the plan is required to apply an "overburden credit" against its minimum contribution requirement for the plan year.[1] The overburden credit reduces the additional funding needed to satisfy the minimum contribution requirement.

The overburden credit does not permanently forgive a portion of a plan's underfunding. Rather, it eliminates a portion of the plan's underfunding for that year for purposes of determining whether the funding standards have been violated. The underfunding will be reflected in subsequent computations of the vested benefits charge.

Calculation of overburden credit

The amount of the overburden credit is the product of one-half of the average guaranteed benefit paid in the base plan year and the overburden factor for the plan year.[2] The amount of the overburden credit may not exceed the amount of the minimum contribution requirement for the year.

---

[1] ERISA Sec. 4244; Code Sec. 418C.   [2] ERISA Sec. 4244(c); Code Sec. 418C(c).

¶ 2929

REORGANIZATION OF MULTIEMPLOYER PLANS:
Reduction of Benefits

Generally, plan amendments are not permitted to reduce benefits already accrued by an employee. However, amendments to a multiemployer plan in reorganization may reduce accrued benefits attributable to employer contributions if certain conditions are met. Benefits that may be reduced are those that have been in effect for less than 60 months and that are not guaranteed by the PBGC.[1]

Limit on benefit reductions

Benefits of inactive participants may not be reduced in greater proportions than those of active participants.[2] Benefits attributable to employer contributions (other than accrued benefits) and the rate of future benefit accruals are to be decreased to the same extent that the accrued benefits of inactive participants are decreased.

A benefit may be reduced by changing its form and eligibility requirements. However, the reduction will not apply to participants or beneficiaries in pay status on the effective date of the amendment or to participants who have attained normal retirement age (or are within 5 years of attaining normal retirement age), on the effective date of the amendment.

[1] ERISA Sec. 4244A(a); Code Sec. 418D(a).

[2] ERISA Sec. 4244A(b)(1)(B); Code Sec. 418D(b)(1)(B).

¶ 2930

REORGANIZATION OF MULTIEMPLOYER PLANS:
Suspension of Nonbasic Benefits by Insolvent Plans

The plan sponsor of a multiemployer plan that is in reorganization must determine the plan's resource benefit level (i.e., the highest level of monthly benefits the plan could pay from reliable sources) for each insolvency year no later than 3 months before the beginning of the plan year.[1] If the resource benefit level is below the basic benefit level for a plan year, the payment of all nonbasic benefits must be suspended for that year.[2] The suspension does not apply where the PBGC guarantees supplemental benefits.

Assess plan assets every 3 years

A plan sponsor is required, at least every three years during a plan's reorganization, starting with the end of the first plan year in reorganization, to compare the value of plan assets with the total amount of benefit payments.[3] Unless plan assets are greater than three times the benefit payments, the sponsor must determine whether the plan will become insolvent during any of the next five plan years.[4] If the sponsor of plan in reorganization reasonably determines, taking into account the plan's recent and anticipated financial experience, that the plan's available resources are not sufficient to pay benefits under the plan when due for the next plan year, the plan sponsor must make this determination available to interested parties.

Annual assessment. In the event the plan sponsor determines that the plan has the potential to become insolvent in any of the next five plan years, the sponsor will have to complete the solvency determination annually, rather than every three years. The solvency determination must be conducted on an annual basis until the sponsor can make the determination that the plan will not be insolvent in any of the next five plan years.

Notice requirements

A determination that the plan is insolvent or that it may become insolvent any time within the next three plan years requires the sponsor to notify the IRS, the PBGC, plan participants and beneficiaries, each employer required to contribute to the plan, and each affected employee organization of the potential insolvency.[5] The plan sponsor must also notify these parties of the plan's resource benefit level within 2 months before the final day of the plan year for which the plan is insolvent. Moreover, the sponsor must notify the parties that, in the event of insolvency, payments in excess of basis benefits will be suspended, but that basic benefits will be paid.

Insolvency notices

A plan sponsor of an insolvent multiemployer plan is generally required to file a notice of insolvency and a notice of insolvency benefit level with the PBGC.[6] The administrators of multiemployer defined benefit plans are further required to provide an annual funding notice to participants and beneficiaries, labor organizations, contributing employers, and the PBGC detailing the financial status of the plan.[7]

---

[1] Code Sec. 418E(c); ERISA Sec. 4245(c).

[2] Code Sec. 418E(c)(3); ERISA Sec. 4245(c)(3).

[3] ERISA Sec. 4245(d); Code Sec. 418E(d).

[4] ERISA Sec. 4245(d)(1), as amended by P.L. 109-280 (Pension Protection Act of 2006), Act Sec. 203(a); Code Sec. 418E(d)(1), as amended by P.L. 109-280 (Pension Protection Act of 2006), Act Sec. 213(a). Note, prior to 2008, plan sponsors were

required to determine whether the plan would become insolvent during any of the next three plan years.

[5] ERISA Sec. 4245(e); Code Sec. 418E.

[6] PBGC Reg. §§ 4245.3(a) and 4245.5(a).

[7] ERISA Sec. 101(f), as added by P.L. 108-218 (Pension Funding Equity Act of 2004), Act Sec. 103(a) and 103(d).

¶ 2931

MERGERS, TRANSFERS, AND PARTITIONS:
Mergers and Transfers Between Multiemployer Plans

A multiemployer plan is permitted to merge with one or more other multiemployer plans, or to engage in a transfer of assets or liabilities to or from another multiemployer plan if:[1]

   1. the plan sponsor notifies the PBGC of the merger or transfer at least 120 days before the effective date of the merger or transfer;

2. the accrued benefit of any participant or beneficiary is not lower after the effective date of a merger or transfer than it was immediately before that date;

3. the benefits of participants and beneficiaries are not reasonably expected to be suspended under the insolvency provisions; and

4. an actuarial valuation of assets and liabilities of each of the affected plans for the plan year preceding the effective date of the merger or transfer has been performed.

Accrued benefits must be preserved

A plan that assumes an obligation to pay benefits for a group of participants as the result of a merger or transfer must preserve accrued benefits.[2]

Actuarial valuation requirement

A merger or transfer of assets between multiemployer plans generally requires an actuarial valuation of the assets and liabilities of each of the affected plans to have been performed during the plan year preceding the effective date of the merger or transfer.[3]

The actuarial valuation must generally be based on the most recent data available as of the day before the start of the plan year. However, in the case of a plan that is "significantly affected" by a merger or transfer, other than a plan that is significantly affected only because the merger or transfer involves a plan that has terminated by mass withdrawal under ERISA Sec. 4041A(a)(2), the actuarial valuation must have been based on the plan's assets and liabilities as of a date not earlier than the first day of the last plan year ending before the proposed effective date of the transaction.[4] The valuation must separately identify the assets, contributions, and liabilities being transferred, and must be based on the actuarial assumptions and methods that are expected to be used for the first plan year beginning after the transfer.

By contrast, if a plan is not significantly affected by a merger or transfer, or is significantly affected only because the merger or transfer involves a plan that has terminated by mass withdrawal, the actuarial valuation must be based on the plan's assets and liabilities as of a date no more than *three years* before the date on which the notice of merger is filed.[5]

Significantly affected plans. A plan is significantly affected by merger or transfer if the plan:

1. transfers assets equal to or in excess of 15% of its assets before the transfer;

2. receives a transfer of unfunded accrued benefits that is equal to or in excess of 15% of the its assets before the transfer;

3. is created by a spinoff from another plan; or

4. engages in a merger or transfer (other than a de minimis merger or transfer either after the plan has terminated by mass

withdrawal under ERISA Sec. 4041A(a)(2) or with another plan that has so terminated.[6]

Plan solvency tests

A merger or transfer of assets or liabilities between multiemployer plans may not occur if the benefits of participants and beneficiaries would reasonably be expected to be subject to suspension under ERISA's insolvency rules.[7] An actuary must determine solvency for each plan that exists after the transaction, but not for each plan involved in the transaction.[8] In determining whether the plan solvency requirement is met, two separate tests, based on whether or not a plan is significantly affected by a merger or transfer, are applied.[9]

Non-significantly affected plans. If a plan is not significantly affected by a merger or transfer, the plan solvency rules require that:

1. the expected fair market value of plan assets immediately after the merger or transfer equal or exceed five times the benefit payments for the last plan year ending before the proposed effective date of the merger or transfer; or

2. expected plan assets, expected contributions, and investment earnings equal or exceed expected expenses and benefit payments in each of the first five plan years beginning on or after the proposed effective date of the merger or transfer.[10]

Significantly affected plans. In the event that a plan is significantly affected by a merger or transfer, the plan solvency rules require that:

1. expected contributions equal or exceed the estimated amount necessary to satisfy the minimum funding requirements (including reorganization funding, if applicable) for the five plan years beginning on or after the proposed effective date of the transaction;

2. the expected fair market value of plan assets immediately after the transfer equal or exceed the total amount of expected benefit payments for the first five plan years beginning on or after the proposed effective date of the transaction;

3. expected contributions for the first plan year beginning on or after the proposed effective date of the transaction equal or exceed expected benefit payments for that plan year; and

4. expected contributions for the amortization period (see below) equal or exceed unfunded accrued benefits plus expected normal costs.[11]

Amortization period. An actuary may select as the amortization period, either:

1. the first 25 plan years beginning on or after the proposed effective date of the transaction; or

2. the amortization period for the resulting base when the combined charge base and the combined credit base are offset under Code Sec. 412(b)(4).[12]

Request for compliance determination

The plan sponsor (or sponsors) of one or more plans involved in a merger or transfer *may* request a ruling from the PBGC that the transaction complies with the notice requirements and other rules relating to mergers or transfers between multiemployer plans.[13]

Actuarial calculations and assumptions

All calculations required by the rules governing mergers and transfers between multiemployer plans must be based on the most recent actuarial valuation as of the date that the notice of the transaction is filed with the PBGC, updated to reflect any material changes.[14] In addition, calculations must be based on methods and assumptions that are reasonable in the aggregate.[15]

[1] ERISA Sec. 4231(b).

[2] PBGC Reg. § 4231.4.

[3] ERISA Sec. 4231(b)(4).

[4] PBGC Reg. § 4231.5(b).

[5] PBGC Reg. § 4231.5(a).

[6] PBGC Reg. § 4231.2.

[7] ERISA Sec. 4231(b)(3); PBGC Reg. § 4231.3(a)(3)(i)

[8] PBGC Reg. § 4231.3(a)(3).

[9] PBGC Reg. § 4231.6.

[10] PBGC Reg. § 4231.6(a).

[11] PBGC Reg. § 4231.6(b).

[12] PBGC Reg. § 4231.6(b)(4).

[13] PBGC Reg. §§ 4231.3(b) and 4231.9(a).

[14] PBGC Reg. § 4231.10(a).

[15] PBGC Reg. § 4231.10(b).

¶ 2932

MERGERS, TRANSFERS, AND PARTITIONS: Notice to the PBGC

Plan sponsors of all plans involved in a merger or transfer of assets between multiemployer plans must file notice of the proposed merger or transfer with the PBGC at least 120 days before the effective date of the transaction.[1] In addition to information identifying the plans involved in the merger or transfer, the notice to the PBGC must indicate: whether the transaction is a merger or transfer, whether it involves a plan that has terminated by mass withdrawal, whether any significantly affected plan is involved in the transaction (identifying each plan), and whether the transaction is de minimis (as indicated by an enrolled actuary's certification).[2] The notice must also disclose the proposed effective date of the transaction and provide a copy of each plan provision stating that no participant's or beneficiary's accrued benefit will be lower immediately after the effective date of the merger or transfer than the benefit immediately before that date. Additional requirements apply to significantly affected plans (see ¶ 2931) that exist after the transaction.[3]

Filing the notice. The notice may be filed with the PBGC by hand, mail, or commercial delivery service or through electronic media.[4] The notice is generally treated as filed when it is sent.[5] However, a notice will not be considered filed until all required information has been submitted.[6]

PBGC may waive notice

The PBGC may waive the notice requirement if the plan sponsor demonstrates that failure to complete the merger or transfer in less than 120 days after filing the notice will cause harm to the participants or beneficiaries of the plans involved in the transaction, the PBGC determines that the transaction complies with the requirements of ERISA Sec. 4231, or the PBGC completes its review of the transaction.[7]

☐ The required PBGC notice is further discussed at CCH PENSION PLAN GUIDE ¶ 7295.

---

[1] PBGC Reg. § 4231.8(a).

[2] PBGC Reg. § 4231.8(e).

[3] PBGC Reg. § 4231.8(e)(7).

[4] PBGC Reg. § 4000.3 and 4231.8(a)(2).

[5] PBGC Reg. § 4000.23 and 4231.8(d).

[6] PBGC Reg. § 4231.8(d).

[7] PBGC Reg. § 4231.8(f).

¶ 2933

MERGERS, TRANSFERS, AND PARTITIONS: Transfers Between Multiemployer and Single-Employer Plans

In the case of a transfer of assets or liabilities between a multiemployer plan and a single-employer plan, or the merger of such plans, the accrued benefits of any participant may not be lower immediately after the transfer or merger than they were immediately before the transaction.[1]

Liability for terminating single-employer plan

In general, if a multiemployer plan transfers liabilities to a single employer plan, the multiemployer plan will be liable to the PBGC if the single employer plan terminates within 60 months after the transfer.[2]

The amount of the liability is the lesser of:[3]

1. the amount of the plan asset insufficiency of the terminated single-employer plan, less 30% of the net worth of the employer maintaining the single-employer plan; or

2. the value, at the time of the transfer, of the unfunded benefits transferred to the single-employer plan and guaranteed by the PBGC.

The PBGC must make a determination of liability within 180 days after receipt of an application from the sponsor of the multiemployer plan for such a determination. However, the multiemployer plan will not be liable if the PBGC determines that the interests of the participants and beneficiaries are otherwise adequately protected or if the PBGC fails to make a determination within 180 days.[4]

Exception to liability

An exception to multiemployer plan liability is available to multiemployer plans that merge with, but later spin off, single-employer plans. Under the "in-and-out rule," a multiemployer plan is not liable because of the transfer of liabilities to a single-employer plan if:[5]

1. the liabilities had previously accrued under a single-employer plan that merged with the multiemployer plan;

2. the value of the liabilities transferred to the single employer plan does not exceed the value of liabilities for benefits which accrued before the single-employer plan merged with the multiemployer plan; and

3. the value of the assets transferred to the single-employer plan is substantially equal to the value of the assets which would have been in the single-employer plan if the employer had maintained and funded it as a separate plan under which no benefits accrued after the merger.

Asset transfer rules

A multiemployer plan must provide rules for the transfer of assets to another plan. These rules may not unreasonably restrict the transfer of plan assets in connection with the transfer of plan liabilities.[6] A plan will not unduly restrict the transfer of plan assets by following the requirements of ERISA Sec. 4232(c)(3) described above.

[1] ERISA Sec. 4223(b).
[2] ERISA Sec. 4232(c)(1).
[3] ERISA Sec. 4232(c)(2).

[4] *Ibid.*
[5] ERISA Sec. 4232(c)(3).
[6] ERISA Sec. 4234(a).

¶ 2934

MERGERS, TRANSFERS, AND PARTITIONS:
Transfers Relating to Change in Bargaining Representative

If an employer completely or partially withdraws from a multiemployer plan as a result of a certified change in the employees' collective bargaining representative, a transfer of assets and liabilities may be required. Specifically, if participants of the old plan who are employed by the employer will, because of the change, participate in another multiemployer plan, the old plan must transfer assets and liabilities to the new plan.[1]

[1] ERISA Sec. 4235(a).

¶ 2935

MERGERS, TRANSFERS, AND PARTITIONS:
Partition of Multiemployer Plan

The PBGC may, on its own initiative, or upon the request of the plan sponsor, order the partition of a multiemployer plan so that a portion of its assets and liabilities is segregated and held as a separate plan.[1]

A plan may be partitioned only if the PBGC finds that:[2]

1. a federal bankruptcy proceeding (whether or not pending) involving an employer has caused or will cause a substantial reduction in the aggregate amount of contributions to the plan;

2. the plan is likely to become insolvent;

3. contributions will have to be increased significantly in reorganization to meet the minimum contribution requirement and prevent insolvency; and

4. the partition would significantly reduce the risk that the plan will become insolvent.

The PBGC's order for partition must provide for the transfer of no more than the nonforfeitable benefits directly attributable to service with the bankrupt employer and an equitable share of the plan's assets.[3]

The partition also may not occur unless notice is provided to the plan sponsor and to participants and beneficiaries whose vested benefits will be affected.

---

[2] ERISA Sec. 4233(b)(1)-(4) and (c).

[1] ERISA Sec. 4233(a) and (b).

[3] ERISA Sec. 4233(d).

¶ 2936

ENFORCEMENT OF MULTIEMPLOYER PLAN RULES: Parties That May Bring an Action

A plan fiduciary, employer, plan participant, or beneficiary who is adversely affected by an act or omission of any party under the multiemployer provisions of ERISA (Subtitle E of Title IV), or an employee organization that represents such a plan participant or beneficiary, may bring an action for appropriate legal or equitable relief.[1] However, ERISA preempts state law actions for the collection of withdrawal liability.[2]

☐ The ERISA civil enforcement rules governing multiemployer plans are discussed at ¶ 2724.

---

[2] *Central States Southeast and Southwest Areas Pension Fund v. Melody Farms, Inc.*, DC Mich (1997), No. 94-72846.

[1] ERISA Sec. 4301(a).

¶ 2937

ENFORCEMENT OF MULTIEMPLOYER PLAN RULES: Penalties and Remedies

Any person who fails without reasonable cause to provide any notice required under the multiemployer plan rules is liable to the PBGC in an amount up to $110 for each day that the failure continues.[1]

Remedies

In an action to compel an employer to pay withdrawal liability, failure of the employer to make any withdrawal liability payment within the time prescribed is treated in the same manner as a delinquent multiemployer plan contribution. The remedies for a delinquent contribution include liquidated damages.[2]

Attorney's fees. A court may further award all or a portion of the costs and expenses incurred in connection with an action to collect withdrawal liability, including attorney's fees.[3]

[2] ERISA Sec. 4301(b).

[1] ERISA Sec. 4302; PBGC Reg. § 4302.3.

[3] ERISA Sec. 4301(e).

¶ 2938
For More Information

☐ For more information on multiemployer plans and withdrawal liability, see CCH PENSION PLAN GUIDE ¶ 6900-¶ 7312.

401(k) Plans—Special Rules

¶ 2940
Overview of 401(k) Plan Rules

401(k) plans are cash or deferred arrangements under which eligible employees make an election to either receive current compensation or to defer compensation by having their employer contribute a limited portion to a qualified profit-sharing or stock bonus plan. An employer may further enhance an employee's account by making a contribution that matches all or a portion of the employee's elective deferral. The employee is not subject to current income tax on the amount of the elective deferral or on the employer's matching contribution. The amounts in the account are not taxed until they are distributed, at which time the employee may be in a lower tax bracket.

A 401(k) plan participant also has a nonforfeitable right to elective deferrals once they are made. However, an employee's right to a distribution from the account prior to retirement or the termination of employment is limited.

Qualification rules apply

401(k) plans are subject to the rules that generally apply to qualified plans. However, 401(k) plans must also comply with additional requirements that are primarily designed to assure that the plan does not discriminate in favor of highly compensated employees as to plan coverage or as to contributions and benefits.

Roth 401(k) plan. 401(k) plans may incorporate a "qualified Roth contribution program," pursuant to which participants may elect to have all or a portion of their elective deferrals (but not matching contributions or nonelective contributions) to the plan designated as after-tax "Roth contributions." Qualified distributions (including earnings) from a designated Roth account will not be subject to tax. In addition, provided that a 5-year nonexclusion period has been satisfied, earnings on the contributed amounts will grow tax-free and will not be subject to tax upon distribution. However, Roth contributions must be allocated to a separate account for each participant. In addition, Roth contributions are subject to annual deferral limits and to strict conditions that govern excess contributions, distributions, rollovers, and reporting (see¶ 2941A).

CCH POINTER: *Tax credit for employers establishing new plans.* Employers, especially small employers, may be reluctant to provide retirement plans for their employees due to the costs associated with setting up and administering plans. Such costs include fees to change the payroll system, set up an investment vehicle and obtain advice from various consultants.

Some tax incentives for starting retirement plans are available for employers. For example, costs incurred in creating and maintaining an employee retirement plan are generally deductible as ordinary and necessary business expenses. [1] In addition, small employers with no more than 100 employees are eligible to receive a tax credit for up to 50 percent of the costs of establishing new retirement plans (up to $500). [2] The credit may be claimed for qualified costs incurred in each of the three years beginning with the tax year in which the plan becomes effective. [3]

Plan fees

Accompanying the surge in the growth of 401(k) plans and the attendant increase in investment options and investment services is the concern that associated investment management and administrative fees may inappropriately reduce the account balance of plan participants or at least temper the potential growth of retirement account savings. Increasingly diverse investment options and new investment services, such as daily valuation of a participant's account, carry costs that are imposed increasingly on the plan participant alone. In addition, the expenses of operating and maintaining an investment portfolio that are charged against a plan participant's account exact an "opportunity cost" in the form of foregone investment in every contribution period. A small reduction in a participant's potential investment, because of the diversion of account assets to pay an investment or administrative fee, can develop into a large loss over the period in which the employee participates in the plan. Plan fees and the fiduciary obligation to monitor fees are discussed at ¶ 2945.

---

[1] Code Sec. 162.

[2] Code Sec. 45E(a).
[3] Code Sec. 45E(b).

¶ 2940A
CASH OR DEFERRED ARRANGEMENTS: Cash or Deferred Elections

Generally, a cash or deferred election is any election, or modification of an earlier election, by an employee to have an employer either:

1. provide an amount to the employee in the form of cash or some other taxable benefit that is not currently available on the date of the election; or

2. contribute an amount to a trust or provide an accrual or other benefit under a deferred compensation plan. [1]

CCH POINTER: The IRS has privately ruled that an arrangement pursuant to which an employee could make an election to either forfeit unused vacation pay or allow the employer to contribute an amount equal to the value of the unused forfeitable vacation time to a qualified defined contribution plan was not a cash or deferred arrangement. Employees did not have the option to elect cash or any other taxable benefit in lieu of the additional employer contribution to the plan and, thus, the IRS explained, the employee's choice among the plan's options did not create a cash or deferred arrangement. [2]

Note, as a consequence of the ruling, an employer may make a direct contribution of unused vacation pay to an employee's 401(k) account, without subjecting the employee to tax. The employer's contribution would not be treated as deferred compensation, but would be viewed as a profit-sharing contribution. However, employers that elect this option need to be aware that the contributions are subject to nondiscrimination and minimum coverage testing (see ¶ 2950 and ¶ 2950A).

Compensation may not be currently available

A cash or deferred election may only be made with regard to: (1) an amount that is not "currently available" to the employee on the date of the election (i.e., paid to the employee or not subject to restriction) and (2) amounts that would be (but for the cash or deferred election) currently available after the later of the date on which the employer adopts the cash or deferred arrangement or the date on which the arrangement first becomes effective (see below).[3]

Pre-funded contributions may not be deducted. Contributions may only be made after the election is made. In addition, contributions will be treated as made pursuant to a cash or deferred election only if they are made after the employee's performance of services which relate to the compensation that would have been paid to the employee absent the election. [4] Amounts contributed in anticipation of the future performance of services are not treated as elective contributions. Thus, employers may not pre-fund elective contributions in order to accelerate the deduction for elective contributions.

Negative elections: Automatic enrollment

An employer may generally not defer amounts for an employee without the employee's election. However, employers looking to increase participation in their plans may adopt "negative" or automatic elections (or enrollment) under which the employer unilaterally and without an affirmative election by the employee deducts a stipulated percentage of compensation from an employee's paycheck, but affords the employee the opportunity to make an election to discontinue the deferral at any time. The IRS has approved a negative election arrangement in which newly hired employees were provided with an effective opportunity to elect to receive amounts in cash and were informed of their right to discontinue deferrals, [5] and the application of a similar arrangement to current employees pursuant to a plan amendment. [6] In addition, the IRS had formally designated negative election provisions as available features in prototype 401(k) plans that are pre-approved by the IRS. [7]

¶2940A

Automatic contribution arrangements.

The Pension Protection Act of 2006, generally effective for plan years beginning after December 31, 2007, provides statutory authorization for automatic enrollment under an "automatic contribution arrangement." [8] Similar to negative elections and automatic enrollment features under prior law, an automatic enrollment arrangement will allow an employer to unilaterally deduct a specified percentage from an employee's compensation to be contributed to a 401(k) plan, absent an election by the employee not to participate in the plan or change the percentage at which contributions are made.

The Act authorizes automatic contribution arrangements (which will provide an ERISA preemption shield from state garnishment laws and other restrictions) and Eligible Automatic Contribution Arrangements (see ¶ 2940B), which allow for participant withdrawals of automatic contributions. Note, plans that implement automatic enrollment provisions may also satisfy the ADP and ACP nondiscrimination tests and avoid the top heavy rules by making specified contributions under a qualified automatic contribution arrangement (QACA). See ¶ 2976.

Preemption of state laws restricting automatic contribution arrangements. ERISA preempts any state law that directly or indirectly prohibits or restricts the inclusion of automatic contribution arrangements in a plan. [9]

An automatic contribution arrangement to which the ERISA preemption provision would apply would (1) allow a participant to elect to have the plan sponsor make payments as contributions under the plan on behalf of the participant or the plan in cash; (2) treat a participant as having elected to have the plan sponsor make such contributions in an amount equal to a uniform percentage of compensation, until the participant elects not to have such contributions made (or elects to have contributions made at a different percentage); and (3) invest contributions under the arrangement in accord with DOL regulations governing default investments (see ¶ 2375). [10]

Preemption requires compliance with notice requirement. In addition, the plan administrator must (subject to a penalty of up to $1000 per day) issue an annual notice to each participant: (a) explaining the participant's rights under the arrangement not to have elective contributions made or to have contributions made at a different percentage; (b) providing the participant with a reasonable period of time after the receipt of the notice and before the first elective contribution is made, to make the election; and (c) explaining how contributions will be invested absent an election by the participant. [11]

Proposed rules clarify calculation and administration of penalty. Plan administrators are subject to a penalty of up to $1000 per day for each violation of the notice requirement. [12] Note, proposed regulations issued by the EBSA in December 2007 would impose joint and several liability for the penalty and stress that the penalty is a personal liability which may not be transferred to the plan as a reasonable expense of plan administration. [13] The proposed regulations, however, would authorize the EBSA to waive or reduce the penalty upon a showing (in a written reasonable cause statement) by the administrator of compliance with the notice

¶2940A

requirements or mitigating circumstances regarding the degree or willfulness of the noncompliance

> **CCH POINTER:** *Does preemption require compliance with default investment rules?* ERISA preempts any state law that prohibits or restricts the inclusion in ERISA plans of an automatic contribution arrangement. However, as defined in ERISA Sec. 514(e)(2), automatic contribution arrangements require contributions to be invested in accordance with the regulations under ERISA Sec. 404(c)(5). Thus, the issue emerged as to whether ERISA preemption requires compliance with the default investment rules.

The final regulations resolved the issue by stating that ERISA supersedes state laws that would directly or indirectly prohibit or restrict the inclusion of an automatic contribution arrangement in a pension plan, regardless of whether the plan includes an automatic contribution arrangement as defined in (i.e., maintained in compliance with) the final regulations. The DOL has expressly declined to condition preemption on compliance with the default investment requirements. Accordingly, state laws may not prohibit or restrict automatic contribution arrangements that allow for default investment that are not qualified default investment alternatives (QDIAs) or that do not otherwise comply with the final regulations. [14]

One-time elections are not cash or deferred elections

An employee does not make a cash or deferred election by making upon first becoming eligible under any plan of the employer, a one-time irrevocable election to have a specified amount or percentage of compensation (including zero compensation) contributed by the employer on the employee's behalf for the duration of employment. [15]

---

[1] IRS Reg. § 1.401(k)-1(a)(3)(i).

[2] IRS Letter Ruling 200311043, 12-18-2002. See also, IRS Letter Ruling 9635002, 11-9-95 (National Office Technical Advice Memorandum), CCH PENSION PLAN GUIDE ¶ 17,395.

[3] IRS Reg. § 1.401(k)-1(a)(3)(iii).

[4] IRS Reg. § 1.401(k)-1(a)(3)(iii)(B) and (C).

[5] Rev. Rul. 98-30, I.R.B. 1998-24, 6-22-98, CCH PENSION PLAN GUIDE ¶ 19,911.

[6] Rev. Rul. 2000-8, I.R.B. 2000-7, CCH PENSION PLAN GUIDE ¶ 19,943G. Note, IRS Reg. § 1.401(k)-1(a)(3)(ii), generally effective after 2005, further provides that, for purposes of determining whether an election is a cash or deferred election, it is irrelevant that the default that applies absent an affirmative election is the employer contributing an amount to a trust or providing an accrual or other benefit under a plan deferring the receipt of compensation.

[7] IRS Announcement 2000-60, I.R.B. 2000-31, CCH PENSION PLAN GUIDE ¶ 17,097Q-80.

[8] Code Sec. 414(w)(3), as added by P.L. 109-280 (Pension Protection Act of 2006), Act Sec. 902(d).

[9] ERISA Sec. 514(e)(1), as added by P.L. 109-280 (Pension Protection Act of 2006), Act Sec. 902(f); P.L. 109-280 (Pension Protection Act of 2006), Act Sec. 902(g).

[10] ERISA Sec. 514(e)(2), as added by P.L. 109-280 (Pension Protection Act of 2006), Act Sec. 902(f).

[11] ERISA Sec. 514(e)(3), as added by P.L. 109-280 (Pension Protection Act of 2006), Act Sec. 902(f); ERISA Sec. 502(c)(4), as amended by P.L. 109-280 (Pension Protection Act of 2006), Act Sec. 902(f).

[12] ERISA Sec. 502(c)(4), as amended by P.L. 109-280 (Pension Protection Act of 2006), Act Sec. 902(f).

[13] DOL Proposed Reg. § 2560.502c-4(j).

[14] ERISA Sec. 2550.404c-5(f).

[15] IRS Reg. § 1.401(k)-1(a)(3)(iv).

¶ 2940B

CASH OR DEFERRED ARRANGEMENTS: Eligible
Automatic Contribution Arrangements

The Pension Protection Act of 2006 expanded upon the automatic enrollment arrangements that had been approved by the IRS by, effective for plan years beginning after December 31, 2007, authorizing an eligible automatic contribution arrangement (EACA) that will enable employers to unilaterally enroll employers in their 401(k) plans at a specified percentage of compensation and invest contributions in DOL-approved default investment funds without fear of fiduciary liability, and without being subject to state garnishment law restrictions. [1] However, employees must receive an annual notice of their rights under the arrangement including the right not to participate in the arrangement or the right to elect to make contributions at a different percentage of compensation. [2] In addition, employees are allowed a 90-day window within which to request refunds of automatic contributions made under the arrangement. The distributions will be subject to income tax (but not penalty tax) and matching contributions will be forfeited.

The IRS has issued final regulations governing permissible withdrawals and other issues relating to EACAs. [3] The final rules apply to plan years beginning on or after January 1, 2010. However, a plan may comply with the requirement to be operated in accordance with the good faith interpretation of the rules under Code Sec. 414(w) by adhering to the final regulations. Note, the final regulations do not apply to automatic enrollment arrangements established prior to the enactment of the Pension Protection Act of 2006. [4]

Qualified automatic contribution arrangements (including the effect of final regulations that are generally effective for plan years beginning on or after January 1, 2008) are discussed in detail at ¶ 2976.

Time period for establishing EACA. The rules under Code Sec. 414(w) governing EACAs do not specifically address the time period during which an EACA may be established. By contrast, regulations implementing Qualified Automatic Contribution Arrangements require the QACA safe harbor for an existing qualified cash or deferred arrangement to be adopted before the first day of the plan year. [5] Thus, the final regulations do not allow for EACAs (or QACAs) to be established mid-year. [6]

Required plan amendments. A plan may be amended to implement EACAs (or QACAs) by the last day of the plan year. Practitioners advise employers to maintain documentation evidencing the intention to maintain the EACA or QACA and comply in operation with the notice rules and other governing requirements. [7] The plan must further remain in operational compliance with the governing rules. [8]

IRS provides sample amendments for adoption of automatic contribution arrangements. The IRS has issued two sample plan amendments that will enable employers to add automatic contribution features to their 401(k) plans. [9] Sample Amendment One may be used to add an automatic contribution arrangement to a 401(k) plan. Sample Amendment Two may be used to add an eligible automatic contribution arrangement (authorizing withdrawals of elective deferrals) to a 401(k) plan.

Time period for adopting amendments. The IRS advises that plan sponsors wishing to adopt an amendment must do so by the later of: (1) the end of the plan year in which the amendment is effective (pursuant to the deadline for adopting a discretionary amendment set forth in Rev. Proc. 2007-44, Sec. 5.05(2)); or (2) the last day of the first plan year beginning on or after January 1, 2009 (2011 for governmental plans), as specified in The Pension Protection Act of 2006 (Act Sec. 1107).

Eligible employees

An EACA, under the final rules, need not cover all employees who are eligible to elect to have contributions made on their behalf under the plan. [10] The EACA, the IRS explains, applies only to those employees specified in the plan as being covered by the EACA, and not to all employees eligible to make a deferral election under the plan.

Automatic enrollment at uniform percentage of compensation

Under an eligible automatic contribution arrangement, as under a traditional 401(k) plan, an employee may affirmatively elect to participate in the plan by having the employer make salary reduction contributions to the plan. However, absent such an election, the employee will be treated as having elected to have the employer make a salary reduction contribution to the 401(k) plan at a uniform percentage of compensation. The contribution will be made until the participant specifically elects not to have the contribution made or specifically elects to have the contribution made at a different percentage. [11] Note, the uniformity requirement does not apply to automatic contribution arrangements that are not intended to be EACAs or QACAs.

Automatic increases in participant deferrals. A plan may authorize an automatic annual increase in the amount of a participant's deferral. For example, a plan may provide for an increase that is tied to an annual date, annual review, salary adjustment, or some other triggering event. Such plan provisions will require vigilance on the part of the employer and coordination between the third party vendors and payroll departments to ensure compliance with the terms of the plan. [12]

Variation in contribution rates. IRS rules that allow for variations in the elective deferral percentage under a QACA also apply to contribution rates under EACAs, without regard to whether the arrangement is intended to be a QACA. [13] Thus, although the default deferral percentage must generally be applied uniformly to all employees eligible to make a cash or deferred election (i.e., existing employees and new hires), contribution rates under the EACA may vary based on the number of years an employee has participated in the automatic contribution arrangement.

CCH POINTER: *Application of escalator provision in automatic contribution arrangements.* The IRS has issued guidance clarifying the use of escalator provisions in automatic contribution arrangements that allow for an adjustment in the amount of an employee's default contributions based on increases in pay. [14]

¶2940B

Aggregation of all EACAs under plan. Separate EACAs may be established for different groups under a plan (e.g., collectively bargained and non-collectively bargained employees). However, for purposes of the requirement that default elective contributions under an EACA be a uniform percentage of compensation, all automatic contribution arrangements within a plan that are intended to be EACAs must be aggregated. [15]

A plan subject to the minimum contribution requirements of Code Sec. 410(b) may provide for separate EACAs for different groups of collectively bargained employees or different employers in a multiple employer plan and use a different percentage for each EACA. However, the disaggregation rules of IRS Reg. § 1.401(k)-1(b)(4) apply. Accordingly, the plan may not apply different default percentages to different groups of employees that, following application of the disaggregation rules, are in the same plan.

> **Example:** ABC Co. sponsors a 401(k) plan that includes two EACAs: one covering Division A with a default rate of 3% and the other covering Division B with a default rate of 5%. A is comprised exclusively of collectively-bargained employees, and B is comprised of noncollectively-bargained employees.
>
> Because collectively-bargained employees are disaggregated under Code Sec. 410(b) both EACAs satisfy the uniformity requirement.
>
> Alternatively, assume Division A hires a group of nonunion employees that cannot be disaggregated for any other reason. Because nondisaggregated employees are now being covered by two EACAs with nonuniform default rates, the plan no longer satisfies the uniformity requirement. [16]

Annual notice requirement

The benefits of an eligible automatic contribution arrangement to an employer and an employee are conditioned on compliance with an annual notice requirement. Specifically, the administrator of a plan containing an eligible automatic contribution arrangement must, within a reasonable period of time before each plan year provide each employee to whom the arrangement applies with notice of the employee's rights and obligations under the arrangement. [17] The notice must be sufficiently accurate and comprehensive to apprise employees of their rights and be written in manner that is calculated to be understood by the average employee to whom the arrangement applies. [18] Note, the notice must be in writing, but may be distributed through electronic media, in compliance with the requirements of IRS Reg. § 1.414(w)-1(b)(3)(i).

Contents of notice. The notice must include an explanation of the employee's rights under the arrangement to elect (1) not to have elective contributions made on his or her behalf, or (2) to have the elective contributions made at a different time. [19] The notice must also explain the manner in which contributions under the eligible automatic contribution arrangement will be invested absent an investment election by the employee. [20]

IRS final rules further require the notice to accurately describe: (1) the level of elective contributions that would be made on the employee's behalf, absent an affirmative election; and (2) the employee's right to make permissible withdrawals and the procedures for electing a withdrawal. [21].

Timing rules. The notice must be provided within a reasonable period of time before the beginning of each plan year. The notice due an employee who becomes eligible in a give year (including an employee who first becomes covered under the arrangement as a result of a change in employment) must be furnished within a reasonable period of time before the employee becomes eligible. [22]

Deemed timing rules. The final rules allow for the deemed satisfaction of the timing rules, if the notice is provided (to each employee covered under the arrangement for the plan year) at least 30 days and no more than 90 days before the beginning of each year. [23] Thus, for a calendar year plan, the notice must be provided by December 1, but no earlier than October 2.

In the event an employee becomes eligible (or becomes covered under the arrangement as a result of a change in employment status) after the 90th day before the beginning of the plan year (and thus, does not receive the notice within the specified time period), the timing requirement would be deemed satisfied if the notice is provided no more than 90 days before the employee becomes eligible (or becomes covered under the arrangement as a result of a change in employment status), but no later than the date the employee actually becomes eligible.

Coordinated EACA and QACA notices. The IRS, in the Preamble to the proposed rules, suggested that the varying notice requirements applicable to automatic contribution arrangements under the Internal Revenue Code and ERISA could be satisfied in a single document. In coordination with the DOL, the IRS "anticipated" that a single document would be able to satisfy all of the applicable notice requirements, as long as the document contained all of the required information and satisfied the timing requirements applicable to each of the notices. [24]

The Sample Automatic Enrollment Notice provided by the IRS for use by sponsors of QACAs that authorize eligible EACA withdrawals to satisfy the applicable notice requirements, would seem to serve this purpose. The sample notice is set forth at CCH PENSION PLAN GUIDE ¶ 17,203Y-12.

Penalty for failure to provide notice. In the event the required notice is not provided in a timely manner, a penalty of $1,000 per day for each day the notice is late may be imposed. [25] Thus, if a notice to one participant due December 1 was delivered December 15, the sponsor could incur $14,000 in penalties. That amount could double if two participants failed to receive the opt-out notice within the permissible 30-90 day time period. [26]

Final rules provide procedural framework for assessment of penalties for failure to provide automatic contribution notice. Final rules issued by EBSA, effective March 3, 2008, set forth rules for the computation of the maximum penalty amount, identify circumstances under which a penalty may be assessed, establish procedural rules for service and filing, and provide plan administrators with a mechanism by which to contest a penalty assessment and request an administrative hearing. [27]

¶2940B

Joint and several liability. The final regulations stress that the liability for the penalty is applied on a joint and several basis among the persons responsible as plan administrators (including the plan sponsor) for the compliance failures. In addition, the penalty is treated as a personal liability of the plan administrator (including the plan sponsor) that may not be transferred to the plan as a reasonable expense of plan administration. However, the rules also authorize the EBSA to waive or reduce the penalty assessment upon a showing by the plan administrator, in a written reasonable cause statement, of compliance or mitigating circumstances regarding the degree or willfulness of noncompliance.

Employee must be allowed reasonable time to make opt out election. The employee must be allowed a reasonable period of time after receiving notice (and before the first elective contribution is made) to make an election not to participate or to change the deferral [28]

Withdrawal of automatic contributions

An eligible automatic contribution arrangement may allow employees to elect "permissible" withdrawals of amounts that were automatically contributed to the plan on behalf of the employee. The election must be made with 90 days after the date of the first automatic contribution made for the employee under the arrangement. [29] The distribution of such contributions will not be treated as a violation of any of the distribution restrictions generally applicable to 401(k) plans. [30] Thus, while the distribution is subject to income tax, the 10 percent premature distribution penalty tax is not imposed.

Employers not required to offer withdrawal option. An employer is not required to include the Code Sec.414(w)(2) withdrawal provision in the plan. In the event the plan does authorize withdrawals, the option need not be made available to all employees eligible under the EACA. Accordingly, the IRS explains an employer may restrict the withdrawal option to employees for whom no elective contribution has been made under the CODA (or predecessor CODA) before the EACA is effective. [31]

Withdrawal within 90 days of first elective contribution under the EACA. A covered employee must make the election to withdraw default elective contributions no later than 90 days after the date of the first default elective contribution under the EACA. [32] The date of the first default elective contribution is the date that the compensation subject to the cash or deferred election would otherwise have been included in gross income (and not the date the first contribution is received by the plan (i.e., trust) for the participant).

CCH POINTER: *Failure to provide timely notice negates withdrawal.* The annual notice (see above) must describe an employee's right under the arrangement to make withdrawals and the procedures for electing a withdrawal. The IRS stresses that if the required notice is not provided in a timely manner, the contributions will fail to be an EACA. As a consequence, the employee contributions will remain in the plan. [33]

Deadline for election may be less than 90 days. The IRS allows for flexibility in application of the rule by allowing a plan to limit the period during which the election may be made to less than 90 days. However, the election period for covered employees must be no less than 30 days. [34]

Rehired employees. The permissible withdrawal clock is reset for an employee who did not have a default deferral withheld during the plan year immediately preceding their rehire. [35] Accordingly, any withdrawal requirement would be applicable only to newly withheld automatic deferrals and not to any deferrals that were contributed during the participant's prior period of employment. [36]

Latest effective date of election. The effective date of the election, under the proposed rules, could have been no later than the last day of the payroll period that begins after the date of the election. The final regulations, however, provide that the latest effective date of the election may not be later than the earlier of: (1) the pay date for the second payroll period beginning after the election is made, or (2) the first pay date that occurs at east 30 days after the election is made. Alternatively, the IRS notes, a plan may authorize an earlier effective date.

Amount of refund distribution. The amount of the refund distribution may not exceed the amount of the default elective contribution made with respect to first payroll period to which the eligible automatic contribution applies to the employee and any succeeding payroll period beginning before the date of the election (and attributable earnings). [37]

Account balance adjusted for gains and losses. As noted, the amount of the distribution is generally the employee's account balance attributable to the default elective contributions, adjusted for gains and losses. In the event default elective contributions are accounted for separately in the participant's account, the distribution will be equal to the total amount in the account. However, if default contributions are not separately accounted for, the amount of allocable gains and loss will be determined under the rules of IRS Reg. § 1.401(k)-2(b)(2)(iv), governing the distribution of excess contributions. [38]

Fees may be assessed. The distribution may be reduced for generally applicable fees. However, the plan may not assess a greater fee for the refund distribution under Code Sec. 414(w) than it would impose on other distributions. [39] Thus, a plan may charge a reduced fee for such distributions.

Distribution taxable income in year of receipt. The withdrawn amounts will be includable in the gross income of the employee as compensation for the tax year in which the distribution is made. [40] However, the distribution will not be subject to the 10 percent penalty tax generally imposed on premature distributions. [41]

1099-R reporting of withdrawal. The amount of the withdrawal is reported on Form 1099-R. [42]

Income tax withholding. Permissible withdrawals are subject to income tax withholding under Code Sec. 3405.

Penalty tax does not apply. The distribution of erroneous automatic contributions will not be subject to the 10-percent penalty tax generally imposed on premature distributions.

¶2940B

Withdrawal distribution may not be rolled over. The proposed regulations would provide that the withdrawal distribution is not an eligible rollover distribution. [43]

Forfeiture of matching contributions. Employer matching contributions on the erroneous contributions (including attributable earnings) will be forfeited). [44] The IRS explains that the forfeited matching contribution is not a mistaken or erroneous contribution. Accordingly, the distribution may not be returned to the employer (or distributed to the employee, as is the case with excess aggregate contributions). The forfeited contribution must remain in the plan and be treated in the same manner under plan terms as any other forfeiture under the plan.

The final regulations clarify that the forfeiture rule applies to any matching contributions that have been allocated to a participant's account, adjusted for allocable gain or loss. In addition, the final rules allow a plan to provide that matching contributions will not be made with respect to any withdrawal that is made prior to the date on which the match would otherwise be allocated. [45] Thus, as long as an employer is not otherwise required to allocate the match earlier (e.g., each pay period), the final regulations do not require an allocation or immediate forfeiture of matching contributions related to automatic deferrals that are permissibly withdrawn. [46]

Excise tax on excess contributions and excess aggregate contributions. The excise tax imposed under Code Sec. 4979 will not apply to excess contributions or excess aggregate contributions under an EACA which are distributed or forfeited (with allocable income) within 6 months after the end of the plan year. [47] Generally, such excess contributions must be corrected within 2 ½ months of the following plan year.

Application of nondiscrimination rules. Default elective contributions that are refunded to an employee will not be taken into account in applying the ADP and ACP nondiscrimination tests (or for purposes of the Code Sec. 402(g) elective deferral limits). [48]

---

[1] Code Sec. 414(w)(3), as added by P.L. 109-280 (Pension Protection Act of 2006), Act Sec. 902(d).

[2] Code Sec. 414(w)(4), as added by P.L. 109-280 (Pension Protection Act of 2006), Act Sec. 902(d).

[3] IRS Reg. § 1.414(w)-1

[4] Preamble to IRS Reg. § 1.414(w)-1.

[5] IRS Reg. § 1.401(k)-3.

[6] IRS Reg. § 1.401(k)-3(e) and IRS Reg. § 1.414(w)-1(b)(3)(iii).

[7] Adam C. Pozek, Sentinel Financial Group, ASPPA Webcast: "Automatic Enrollment Redux: The Final Regulations Have Arrived," April 14, 2009.

[8] Rhonda Migdail, IRS, ASPPA Webcast: "Automatic Enrollment Redux: The Final Regulations Have Arrived," April 14, 2009.

[9] IRS Notice 2009-65, I.R.B. 2009-39, 9-28-09, at CCH Pension Plan Guide ¶ 17,143G.

[10] IRS Reg. § 1.414(w)-1(b)(2)(iii).

[11] Code Sec. 414(w)(3)(B) as added by P.L. 109-280 (Pension Protection Act of 2006), Act Sec. 902(d); IRS Reg. § 1.414(w)-1(b)(2).

[12] EP Team Audit (EPTA) Program-EPTA Compliance Trends and Tips- 401(k) Plan Trends, April 2009.

[13] IRS Reg. § 1.414(w)-1(b)(2)(ii), cross-referencing IRS Reg. § 1.401(k)-3(j)(2).

[14] Revenue Ruling 2009-30, I.R.B. 2009-39, 9-28-09, at CCH Pension Plan Guide ¶ 19,948Z-266.

[15] IRS Reg. § 1.414(w)-1(b)(2)(iii).

[16] "Automatic Enrollment Redux: The Final Regulations Have Arrived," Adam C. Pozek, CCH Journal of Pension Benefits, Vol 16, No. 4, Summer 2009.

[17]Code Sec. 414(w)(4) as added by P.L. 109-280 (Pension Protection Act of 2006), Act Sec. 902(d).

[18]Code Sec. 414(w)(4)(A) as added by P.L. 109-280 (Pension Protection Act of 2006), Act Sec. 902(d).

[19]Code Sec. 414(w)(4)(B) as added by P.L. 109-280 (Pension Protection Act of 2006), Act Sec. 902(d).

[20]*Ibid.*

[21]IRS Reg. § 1.414(w)-1(b)(3)(ii)(B).

[22]IRS Reg. § 1.414(w)-1(b)(3)(iii)(A).

[23]IRS Reg. § 1.414(w)-1(b)(3)(iii)(B).

[24]Preamble to IRS Proposed Reg. § 1.414(w)-1.

[25]ERISA Sec. 502(c)(4); ERISA Reg. § 2560.502c-4.

[26]James Farley, CCH Benefit Practice Portfolio, "Automatic Enrollment: Some Unintended Plan Sponsor Consequences," August 2008.

[27]ERISA Reg. § 2560.502c-4.

[28]Code Sec.414(w)(4)(B)(ii) as added by P.L. 109-280 (Pension Protection Act of 2006), Act Sec. 902(d).

[29]Code Sec.414(w)(2)(B) as added by P.L. 109-280 (Pension Protection Act of 2006), Act Sec. 902(d).

[30]Code Sec.414(w)(1)(C) as added by P.L. 109-280 (Pension Protection Act of 2006), Act Sec. 902(d).

[31]Preamble to IRS Proposed Reg. § 1.414(w)-1.

[32]IRS Reg. § 1.414(w)-1(c)(2)(ii).

[33]EP Team Audit (EPTA) Program-EPTA Compliance Trends and Tips-401(k) Plan Trends, April 2009.

[34]IRS Reg. § 1.414(w)-1(c)(2)(i).

[35]"Automatic Enrollment Redux: The Final Regulations Have Arrived," Adam C. Pozek, CCH Journal of Pension Benefits, Vol. 16, No. 4, Summer 2009.

[36]IRS Reg. § 1.414(w)-1(c)(2)(iv)(A).

[37]Code Sec. 414(w)(2)(C) as added by P.L. 109-280 (Pension Protection Act of 2006), Act Sec. 902(d).

[38]IRS Reg. § 1.414(w)-1(c)(3)(i).

[39]IRS Reg. § 1.414(w)-1(c)(3)(iii).

[40]Code Sec. 414(w)(1)(A) as added by P.L. 109-280 (Pension Protection Act of 2006), Act Sec. 902(d).

[41]Code Sec. 414(w)(1)(A) as added by P.L. 109-280 (Pension Protection Act of 2006), Act Sec. 902(d).

[42]IRS Reg. § 1.414(w)-1(d).

[43]*Ibid.*

[44]*Ibid.*

[45]IRS Reg. § 1.414(w)-1(d)(2).

[46]Adam C. Pozek, Sentinel Financial Group, ASPPA Webcast: "Automatic Enrollment Redux: The Final Regulations Have Arrived," April 14, 2009

[47]Code Sec. 4979 as added by P.L. 109-280 (Pension Protection Act of 2006), Act Sec. 902.

[48]Code Sec. 414(w)(6) as added by P.L. 109-280 (Pension Protection Act of 2006), Act Sec. 902(d), as amended by P.L. 110-458 (Worker, Retiree, and Employer Recovery Act of 2008), Act Sec. 109(b)(6); IRS Reg. § 1.401(k)-2(a)(5)(vi) and IRS Reg. § 1.401(m)-1(a)(6)(ii).

¶ 2941
CASH OR DEFERRED ARRANGEMENTS: Types of 401(k) Plans

A 401(k) plan may be included in a profit-sharing, stock bonus, pre-ERISA money purchase plan, or a rural cooperative plan.[1] Generally, 401(k) plans are structured as profit-sharing or bonus-type plans or salary reduction or thrift-type plans. Post-ERISA money purchase or defined contribution pension plans may not be established as 401(k) arrangements.

Bonus-type plans. Under a bonus-type plan, contributions are not usually made until the end of the year when a traditional bonus is declared for all employees. After the bonus is declared, each employee may then elect to receive the bonus distribution in cash or defer the amounts by having them contributed to the plan.

Some plans have an all-or-nothing approach, requiring that an employee take the entire amount as either a cash bonus or as a plan contribution. In other plans, however, an employee is allowed to split the bonus and take part of the distribution in cash and part as a plan contribution.

Salary reduction plans. Under a salary reduction, or thrift-type plan, an employee has the option of receiving a reduced salary (or foregoing a salary increase) and having the difference contributed to the plan on the employee's behalf. Under such a plan, the 401(k) contribution—a fixed percentage of salary—is deducted from each paycheck and contributed to the plan. Typically, employees may change their contribution levels once or twice a year, but there are no legal restrictions on how often the amount of the contributions may be changed.

Participant-directed account plans. An employer may give employees the right to direct the investment of their own accounts. Plan fiduciaries who choose to comply with participant-directed account regulations issued by the Labor Department may be relieved of fiduciary responsibility for investment losses when participants exercise independent control over the assets in their individual accounts.[2]

Under these participant-directed account rules, a participant must have the opportunity to choose from a broad range of investment alternatives, receive investment instruction with appropriate frequency, diversify investments, and obtain sufficient information to make informed investment decisions.[3] However, fiduciaries are not relieved of their duty to consider the prudence of the investment alternatives made available to participants under the plan.

☐ The rules governing participant-directed accounts are discussed in detail at ¶ 2375.

SIMPLE 401(k) plans. Certain small employers may establish "SIMPLE" 401(k) plans.[4] The acronym "SIMPLE" stands for "Savings Incentive Match Plan for Employees." SIMPLE plans may be sponsored by employers that (1) have up to 100 employees who earned at least $5,000 in compensation during the prior year and (2) do not maintain another qualified plan. See ¶ 2994 and ¶ 2995 for more information on SIMPLE 401(k) plans.

☐ Also note that SIMPLE plans may be provided as IRAs, instead of 401(k)s. See ¶ 3224 for more information on SIMPLE IRAs.

One-person 401(k) plans

One-person 401(k) plans, which are also commonly referred to as "one-participant 401(k)," "solo 401(k)," "individual 401(k)," or "uni-401(k)" plans, are retirement arrangements that allow the sole owner of a business (and the owner's spouse) to make greater tax-deferred and tax deductible contributions than would be permitted under an IRA, SEP, SIMPLE plan, or even a profit-sharing plan, while avoiding the complex nondiscrimination testing associated with larger 401(k) plans, the requirements of ERISA Title I, and the expense of also maintaining a money purchase plan (i.e., combination plan).

A one participant plan is specifically defined as a plan that, on the first day of the plan year: (1) covers only one individual (or the individual and the individual's spouse) and the individual (or the individual and the individual's spouse) owned

100 percent of the plan sponsor (whether or not incorporated), or (2) covered only one or more partners (or partners and their spouses) in the plan sponsor. [5]

One-person 401(k) plans effectively enable sole owners (e.g., sole proprietorships, partnerships, Limited Liability Corporations, S Corporations and C Corporations) that do not retain common law employees or hire only employees that may be excluded from coverage (i.e., part time employees and individuals under age 21) to both: (1) accumulate maximum retirement savings for themselves and their spouses and (2) shelter otherwise taxable income, by making tax deductible contributions as an owner and tax deferred contributions as an employee. As with a traditional 401(k) plan, earnings would grow on a tax-deferred basis and would not be subject to income tax until distribution. In addition to the tax advantages, one-person 401(k) plans may allow for participant loans (unlike IRAs) and enable an owner to consolidate retirement assets by rolling over funds from IRAs, SEPs, and traditional 401(k) plans.

While one-person 401(k) plans are subject to annual contribution and deduction limits and many of the other requirements applicable to qualified 401(k) plans (e.g., annual reporting), the administrative requirements are substantially reduced.[6] For example, nondiscrimination testing, which can be a complex undertaking for large 401(k) plans and top-heavy testing, which can be costly for an employer, are not concerns in a 401(k) plan that does not cover employees, but is limited to an owner and his or her spouse. In addition, one participant plans are exempt from the diversification requirements that generally apply to defined contribution plans. [7]

Finally, one-person 401(k) plans are not subject to the fiduciary requirements or other rules of ERISA Title I.

Partnership 401(k) plan

A partnership may establish and maintain a 401(k) plan covering partners. The partnership 401(k) plan may also match elective contributions to participating partners (see ¶ 2942).

KSOPs

401(k) plans may be combined with ESOPs. Under the resulting KSOP, an employer may make contributions in the form of company stock and may take a deduction for dividend payments of company stock held by the KSOP.

An employer may deduct dividends paid in cash on securities held by an ESOP if the dividends are: paid in cash to the plan participants or their beneficiaries; (2) paid to the plan and distributed in cash to participants or their beneficiaries no later than 90 days after the close of the plan year in which paid; (3) at the election of the participants or their beneficiaries, payable as provided in (1) or (2), or paid to the plan and reinvested in qualifying employer securities; or (4) used to make payments on certain loans, the proceeds of which were used to acquire employer securities (whether or not allocated to participants) with respect to which the dividend is paid.[8]

¶2941

Nonqualified plans

A nonqualified cash or deferred arrangement is an unfunded plan that is designed to benefit highly compensated employees and is not subject to the coverage, nondiscrimination, vesting, or distribution restrictions applicable to qualified 401(k) plans.[9] Elective contributions under a nonqualified CODA are includable in the employees's gross income at the time the employee would have received the contribution but for the deferral election.[10]

> **CCH POINTER:** Code Sec. 409A provides for the first time specific rules for elections and distributions under nonqualified deferred compensation plans. Individual participants who defer compensation under plans that fail to comply with the rules are subject to current taxation on all deferrals and enhanced penalties (see ¶ 3345).

Deemed IRAs

Employers maintaining a qualified plan may allow employees to make voluntary employee contributions to a separate individual retirement account or annuity established under the plan. An account or annuity that meets the requirements under Code Sec. 408 for traditional IRAs or Code Sec. 408A for Roth IRAs will be "deemed" to be an IRA, and not a qualified plan.[11] The amounts in a deemed IRA and contributions made to the deemed IRA are not taken into account in applying the limits on contributions under the qualified plan and a qualified plan will not lose its qualified status as a consequence of establishing and maintaining a deemed IRA program.[12]

> **CCH POINTER:** A 401(k) plan is not required to accept deemed IRA contributions. [13] In addition, a 401(k) plan that does not accept deemed IRA contributions is not required to make the option available to all participants, as the deemed IRA contribution option is not a benefit, right, or feature under Code Sec. 401(a)(4). [14]
>
> The amounts in a deemed IRA and contributions made to the deemed IRA are not taken into account in applying the limits on contributions under the qualified plan. Nor will a qualified plan lose its qualified status as a consequence of establishing and maintaining a deemed IRA program. [15]

☐ Deemed IRAs are discussed further at ¶ 3202.

Combined defined benefit/401(k) (DB/K) plan

Employers with 500 or fewer (but no less than two) employees are authorized, effective for plan years beginning after 2009, to establish a combined plan, consisting of a defined benefit (DB) plan and an automatic enrollment 401(k) plan.[16] The arrangement is designed to provide employees the guaranteed employer-provided retirement benefit offered by a DB plan supplemented by tax deferred elective employee contributions under a 401(k) plan.

The DB/K plan only requires the filing of a single Form 5500 annual report. However, the assets of the plan must be held in a single trust and must be clearly identified and allocated to the DB plan and the 401(k) plan, to the extent necessary for the separate application of the rules of the Internal Revenue Code and ERISA.[17]

The plan must meet specified benefit, contribution, vesting, and nondiscrimination requirements. All contributions, benefits, and other rights and features that are provided under the DB plan or 401(k) component of the DB/K plan must be provided uniformly to all participants. [18] A plan that satisfies the applicable requirements will be deemed (a) not to be top-heavy and (b) to satisfy the ADP/ ACP tests.

Defined benefit plan requirements. The defined benefit component of the DB/K plan would be required to provide each participant with a benefit of not less than the "applicable percentage" of the participant's final average pay. The applicable percentage would be the lesser of (1) one percent of final average pay multiplied by the participant's years of service with the employer, or (2) 20 percent.[19] Final average pay would be determined using the consecutive-year period (not exceeding 5 years) during which the participant earns the highest aggregate compensation.[20]

Participants 100 percent vested after 3 years. Any benefits provided under the DB components of the DB/K plan (including benefits provided in addition to required benefits) must be fully vested after the participant completes 3 years of service.[21]

Cash balance component. As an alternative to the 1 percent of pay final average pay formula for 20 years of service, the DB component of the DB/K plan may be a cash balance plan, under which the accrued benefit is calculated as the balance of a hypothetical account or an accumulated percentage of the participant's average compensation, and which meets the applicable interest credit requirements of Code Sec. 411(b)(5)(B)(i). The plan would be treated as meeting the benefit requirements if each participant received a pay credit for the year which is not less than a specified percentage of compensation, based on the participant's age. For participants who are age 30 or less at the beginning of the year, the percentage is 2. The applicable percentage increases to 4 for participants older than 30, but younger than 40; 6 for participants older than 40, but younger than 50; and 8 for participants who are age 50 or older.[22]

Defined contribution plan requirements. The 401(k) component of the DB/K plan must provide for automatic employee contributions at a specified enrollment rate and for a fully vested matching contribution.

Automatic contribution arrangement. The cash or deferred arrangement under the DB/K plan must constitute an automatic contribution arrangement, pursuant to which each eligible employee is treated as having elected to make an elective contribution of 4 percent of compensation. However, an eligible employee may elect to not make such contributions or elect contributions at a different enrollment rate.[23]

Notice requirement. Each employee eligible to participate in the automatic contribution arrangement must receive a notice explaining his or her right not to make contributions or to make contributions at a different rate. Participants must be afforded a reasonable period of time after receipt of the notice (and before the first elective contribution is made) to make the election. [24]

Eligible participants must further receive an annual notice, within a reasonable period prior to the beginning of the year, informing them of their rights and obligations under the automatic contribution arrangement. [25]

Employer matching contribution. In addition to incorporating an automatic contribution arrangement, the 401(k) component of the DB/K plan must provide for an employer matching contribution on behalf of each employee eligible to participate in the arrangement. The matching contribution must be equal to 50 percent of the employee's elective deferrals, up to 4 percent of compensation. [26]

Nondiscriminatory rate of matching contribution. The rate of matching contribution with respect to any elective deferrals for highly compensated employees may not exceed the matching contribution rate for nonhighly compensated employees.[27] However, consistent with the rules generally applicable to matching contributions under a 401(k) plan, matching contributions may be provided at a different rate, if (1) the rate of matching contributions does not increase as the rate of elective deferrals increases, and (2) the aggregate amount of matching contributions with respect to each rate of elective deferral is not less than the amount that would be provided under the general rules.[28]

Separate termination of DB and DC components of plan. In the event of the termination of the defined benefit plan and the applicable defined contribution plan forming part of the eligible combined plan, the plan administrator must terminate the individual account and defined benefit components of the plan separately.[29]

[1] Code Sec. 401(k)(2).

[2] ERISA Reg. § 2550.404c-1.

[3] ERISA Sec. 404(c)(1); ERISA Reg. § 2550.404c-1(a).

[4] Code Secs. 401(k)(11) and 408(p).

[5] Code Sec. 401(a)(35)(E), as amended by P.L. 110-458 (Worker, Retiree, and Employer Recovery Act of 2008), Act Sec. 109(a); ERISA Sec. 101(i)(8)(B), as amended by P.L 110-458 (Worker, Retiree, and Employer Recovery Act of 2008), Act Sec. 105(g).

[6] IRS Reg. § 1.401(k)-1(a)(6).

[7] Code Sec. 401(a)(35).

[8] Code Sec. 404(k)(2)(A); IRS Notice 2002-2, I.R.B. 2002-2, 1-24-2002, CCH PENSION PLAN GUIDE ¶ 17,122X.

[9] IRS Reg. § 1.401(k)-1(a)(5)(i).

[10] IRS Reg. § 1.401(k)-1(a)(5)(iii).

[11] Code Sec. 408(q)(1), as added by P.L. 107-16 (Economic Growth and Tax Relief Reconciliation Act of 2001), Act Sec. 602(a).

[12] Code Sec. 408(q)(2), as added by P.L. 107-16 (Economic Growth and Tax Relief Reconciliation Act of 2001), Act Sec. 602(a).

[13] Code Sec. 408(a)(1).

[14] IRS Reg. § 1.408(a)-1(f)(6).

[15] Code Sec. 408(q)(2) as added by P.L. 107-16 (Economic Growth and Tax Relief Reconciliation Act of 2001), Act Sec. 602(a).

[16] Code Sec. 414(x), as added by P.L. 109-280 (Pension Protection Act of 2006), Act Sec. 903(a); ERISA Sec. 210(e), as added by P.L. 109-280 (Pension Protection Act of 2006), Act Sec. 903(b).

[17] Code Sec. 414(x)(2)(A), as added by P.L. 109-280 (Pension Protection Act of 2006), Act Sec. 903(a); ERISA Sec. 210(e)(2)(A)), as added by P.L. 109-280 (Pension Protection Act of 2006), Act Sec. 903(b).

[18] Code Sec. 414(x)(2)(E), as added by P.L. 109-280 (Pension Protection Act of 2006), Act Sec. 903(a); ERISA Sec. 210(e)(2)(A)), as added by P.L. 109-280 (Pension Protection Act of 2006), Act Sec. 903(b).

[19] Code Sec. 414(x)(2)(B)(ii), as added by P.L. 109-280 (Pension Protection Act of 2006), Act Sec. 903(a); ERISA Sec. 210(e)(2)(B)(ii)), as added by P.L. 109-280 (Pension Protection Act of 2006), Act Sec. 903(b).

[20]Code Sec. 414(x)(2)(B)(i), as added by P.L. 109-280 (Pension Protection Act of 2006), Act Sec. 903(a); ERISA Sec. 210(e)(2)(B)(i)), as added by P.L. 109-280 (Pension Protection Act of 2006), Act Sec. 903(b).

[21]Code Sec. 414(x)(2)(D)(i), as added by P.L. 109-280 (Pension Protection Act of 2006), Act Sec. 903(a); ERISA Sec. 210(e)(2)(D)), as added by P.L. 109-280 (Pension Protection Act of 2006), Act Sec. 903(b).

[22]Code Sec. 414(x)(2)(B)(iii), as added by P.L. 109-280 (Pension Protection Act of 2006), Act Sec. 903(a); ERISA Sec. 210(e)(2)(B)(iii)), as added by P.L. 109-280 (Pension Protection Act of 2006), Act Sec. 903(b).

[23]Code Sec. 414(x)(2)(C)(i)(I), as added by P.L. 109-280 (Pension Protection Act of 2006), Act Sec. 903(a); ERISA Sec. 210(e)(2)(C)(i)(I)), as added by P.L. 109-280 (Pension Protection Act of 2006), Act Sec. 903(b); ERISA Sec. 210(e)(4), as added by P.L. 109-280 (Pension Protection Act of 2006), Act Sec. 903(b).

[24]Code Sec. 414(x)(5)(B)(ii), as added by P.L. 109-280 (Pension Protection Act of 2006), Act Sec.

903(a); ERISA Sec. 210(e)(4)(B)(ii), as added by P.L. 109-280 (Pension Protection Act of 2006), Act Sec. 903(b).

[25]Code Sec. 414(x)(5)(B)(iii), as added by P.L. 109-280 (Pension Protection Act of 2006), Act Sec. 903(a); ERISA Sec. 210(e)(4)(B)(iii), as added by P.L. 109-280 (Pension Protection Act of 2006), Act Sec. 903(b).

[26]Code Sec. 414(x)(2)(C)(i)(II), as added by P.L. 109-280 (Pension Protection Act of 2006), Act Sec. 903(a); ERISA Sec. 210(e)(2)(C)(i), as added by P.L. 109-280 (Pension Protection Act of 2006), Act Sec. 903(b).

[27]*Ibid.*

[28]Joint Committee on Taxation, Technical Explanation of Pension Protection Act of 2006 (JCX-38-06).

[29]Code Sec. 414(x)(1), as amended by P.L. 110-458 (Worker, Retiree, and Employer Recovery Act of 2008), Act Sec. 109; ERISA Sec. 210(e)(1), as amended by P.L. 110-458 (Worker, Retiree, and Employer Recovery Act of 2008), Act Sec. 109.

¶ 2941A

CASH OR DEFERRED ARRANGEMENTS: Qualified Roth Contribution Program: Roth 401(k) Plans

401(k) plans and 403(b) plans (but not SIMPLE plans, SARSEPs, or 457 plans) are authorized (but not required) to incorporate a "qualified Roth contribution program," pursuant to which participants may make an irrevocable election to have all or a portion of their elective deferrals to the plan designated as after-tax "Roth contributions." The participant is subject to income tax (as well as FICA and Medicare payroll taxes) on the contributions at the time of deferral and the contribution is reported on the participant's W-2 Form for the year of the contribution. Thus, the Roth 401(k) contributions do not reduce a participant's taxable income. However, "qualified distributions" from a designated Roth account are not included in adjusted gross income and are not subject to income tax.[1] Similar to Roth IRAs, earnings on amounts contributed to such "Roth 401(k) plans" (or "Roth 403(b) plans") grow tax-free and are not subject to income tax upon distribution, provided a five-year participation or nonexclusion period has been satisfied. Roth 401(k) accounts, therefore, may be attractive to low income employees who do not pay federal income tax (e.g., those eligible for the earned income tax credit); young employees who expect to be in a higher tax bracket as their salaries increase; older employees who, because of their accumulated retirement assets, do not expect to be in a lower tax bracket upon retirement or who because of their income are not eligible to contribute to a Roth IRA; Social Security recipients looking to avoid the taxation of benefits that is applied to when adjusted gross income exceeds specified thresholds.

In addition, Roth 401(k) plans do not subject an individual taxpayer's ability to make designated contributions to an income ceiling. Roth contributions, however, are subject to annual deferral limits and tax-favored treatment is subject to strict conditions governing excess contributions, distributions, rollovers, conversion to Roth IRAs, and reporting.

Sample Roth 401(k) plan amendment. Plan sponsors wishing to allow for Roth 401(k) contributions, must adopt a discretionary amendment by the end of the plan year in which the amendment is to be effective. The timely adoption of the amendment must be evidenced by a written document that is signed and dated by the employer (including an adopting employer of a pre-approved plan). Thus, a calendar year plan that allows participants to begin making Roth 401(k) contributions on January 1, 2011, must be amended by December 31, 2010, in order to implement the Roth 401(k) feature.

The IRS has provided a sample amendment that may be used by individual plan sponsors and sponsors of pre-approved plans in order to comply with the plan amendment requirement.[2] The sample amendment is reproduced at CCH PENSION PLAN GUIDE ¶ 17,133R.

Roth contribution election

Under a qualified Roth contribution program, an employee elects to make a "designated Roth contribution" in lieu of all or a portion of the elective deferrals that the employee is otherwise eligible to make under the applicable retirement plan (i.e., 401(k) or 403(b) plan).[3] A contribution may not be made to a Roth 401(k) account absent an election by the participant.

Roth contribution may not be stand-alone arrangement. An employer may not offer only the Roth contribution option. In order to provide for Roth 401(k) contributions, the cash or deferred arrangement must also offer pre-tax elective contributions. [4] Roth contributions are made in lieu of all or a portion of the pre-tax elective contributions that an employee is otherwise eligible to make under the plan. According to the IRS, if a CODA offered only designated Roth contributions, participants would not be electing to make such contributions in lieu of elective contributions that they were otherwise eligible to make under the plan.[5]

Roth election is irrevocable. The Roth 401(k) contribution, to the extent permitted by the plan must be designated irrevocably by the employee at the time of the cash or deferred election.[6]

Restrictions on election changes. The rules under IRS Reg. § 1.401(k)-1(e)(2)(ii), governing the frequency of elections with respect to pre-tax elective contributions, also apply to Roth 401(k) contributions. [7] Under these rules, an employee must be afforded the effective opportunity to make or change a Roth contributions election at least once during each plan year. Thus, a plan may restrict employees to one election per year.

Automatic enrollment. Plans that provide for both pre-tax elective deferrals and designated Roth contributions may implement automatic enrollment. However, the plan must set forth the extent to which default contributions will be pre-tax elective contributions or designated Roth contributions.[8]

Roth deferral as default election. In the event default contributions are designated Roth contributions, an employee who has not made an affirmative election will be deemed to have irrevocably designated the contributions as Roth contributions.[9]

Designated Roth 401(k) contribution. A designated Roth contribution is basically an elective deferral that would have been excludable from the individual's income but for the individual's election to designate the contribution as not being excludable.[10] Thus, elective contributions to a cash or deferred arrangement that are designated as Roth contributions are included in an employee's gross income. [11] In addition, Roth 401(k) contributions are subject to FICA tax.[12]

Pre-tax deferrals may not be recharacterized as Roth contributions. Because Roth contributions must be designated irrevocably at the time of the cash or deferred election, Roth 401(k) contributions may not be recharacterized and elective deferrals (including those made prior to 2006) may not (unlike IRA contributions) be converted to Roth contributions.

Roth contributions subject to tax, but treated as elective deferrals. Roth 401(k) contributions are treated by the employer as includible in the employee's gross income at the time the employee would have received the contribution in cash, if the employee had not made the cash or deferred election.[13] However, although Roth contributions are includible in an employee's current gross income, designated Roth contributions are treated as elective deferrals. Accordingly, the contributions fully and immediately vest.

Required minimum distribution rules apply to Roth deferrals. The final IRS rules further clarify that designated Roth 401(k) contributions are subject to the required minimum distribution rules of Code Sec. 401(a)(9)(A) and (B) in the same manner as pre-tax elective contributions.[14] Thus, a Roth 401(k) participant will be required to begin distributions by the later of age 70 ½ , or upon termination of employment for those owning 5% or less of a company, unless the amounts are rolled over. A plan can specify that a required minimum distribution first come from taxable sources; from the Roth 401(k); or that it be taken proportionately between sources. The plan may further allow a participant to elect (on a year by year or other basis), the source of the required minimum distribution.[15]

Roth contributions limited to elective deferrals. Designated Roth contributions are limited to a participant's elective deferrals (including catch-up contributions).[16] Thus, forfeitures may not be allocated to the designated Roth 401(k) account. [17]

Matching contributions. Because only an employee's designated Roth contribution can be allocated to a Roth 401(k) account, employer matching contributions and nonelective contributions may not be designated as after-tax Roth contributions. An employer may match Roth 401(k) contributions. However, the matching contribution will made on pre-tax basis, must be held in a separate account, and will

¶2941A

be taxable to the participant upon distribution. Note, by contrast, an employer may not match contributions to a Roth IRA.

Roth contributions aggregated with all elective deferrals for purposes of ADP test. Designated Roth contributions are treated as elective deferrals (and thus, taken into account with pre-tax deferrals) for purposes of the ADP nondiscrimination test applicable to 401(k) plans.[18] Although after-tax employee contributions are generally not included in the ADP test, after-tax Roth contributions are combined with pre-tax elective deferrals in applying the ADP test. However, because after-tax Roth 401(k) contributions are treated as elective deferrals, the contributions are not aggregated with after-tax contributions and need not satisfy the ACP test.

Separate accounting and recordkeeping for Roth contributions

Because of the different tax treatment of Roth and 401(k) contributions and distributions, the 401(k) plan under which the qualified Roth contribution program is maintained must establish, for each participating employee, a separate "designated Roth account" that will hold designated Roth contributions and earnings allocable to the contributions.[19] The plan must also provide for separate recordkeeping for each designated Roth account.[20] The separate accounting requirement applies at the time the designated Roth contribution is made to the plan. In addition, the separate account must be maintained until amounts in the Roth account are completely distributed.[21]

Pooled accounts permissible. The separate accounting rule does not require an employer to maintain two separate brokerage accounts or to otherwise physically house the Roth contributions and pre-tax deferrals in separate accounts. Thus, a plan may operate a "pooled account," under which a single brokerage account is maintained for a participant, while separately accounting for the source of the contributions.

Annual limit on elective deferrals to Roth contribution accounts

The amount of an individual's designated Roth contributions (as an elective deferral) is subject to the Code Sec. 402(g) annual limit on elective deferrals ($16,500 in 2011 and $17,000 in 2012), reduced by the amount of the participant's other elective deferrals under the 401(k) or 403(b) plan.[22] Thus, the Code Sec. 402(g) limit applies to the total of the employee's pre-tax elective deferrals (including contributions to a SEP and elective employer contributions to a SIMPLE plan) and after-tax Roth contributions. For example, a participant who defers $13,000 to a 401(k) plan may only make a designated Roth 401(k) contribution of $3,500 for 2011.

Note, however, participant contributions to a Roth 401(k) account are not limited by contributions to a Roth IRA. Thus, for 2012, a participant under age 50 may contribute up to $17,000 to a Roth 401(k) (or a Roth 401(k) and a traditional 401(k) plan) and $5,000 to a Roth IRA.

Catch-up contributions. Catch-up contributions are limited to elective deferrals and are not available for after-tax contributions (see ¶ 2982). However, a

¶2941A

participant's catch-up contributions may either be pre-tax elective deferrals or designated Roth contributions.[23]

Note, catch-up eligible participants may contribute up to $5,500 to the Roth 401(k) plan for 2012 (unchanged from 2011). Thus, catch-up eligible participants may be allowed to make a total Roth contribution of up to $22,500 in 2012.

Qualified distributions of Roth contributions excludable from participant's income

A "qualified distribution" from a participant's designated Roth contribution account is not includible in an individual's gross income and will not subject the participant to the 10 percent penalty that is generally imposed on pre-retirement distributions. A participant must complete a 5-tax year period of participation before being eligible for a qualified Roth distribution.[24] In addition, similar to qualified Roth IRA distributions, a distribution from a designated Roth contribution account will not be qualified unless it is: (1) made on or after the date on which the participant attains age 59 ½ , (2) made to a beneficiary (or to the estate of the participant) on or after the death of the participant, or (3) attributable to the participant's being disabled.[25] Corrective distributions of excess deferrals (and allocable income) and corrective distributions of excess contributions are expressly not treated as qualified distributions (see below).[26] In addition, note that distributions from a Roth 401(k) that are made because of the death or disability of the participant are subject to tax if they are made within 5 years of the first contributions to the account.

5-year participation period. Distributions from a Roth 401(k) that are made because of the death or disability of the participant are subject to tax if they are made within 5 years of the first contribution to the account.

Under the 5-year participation or nonexclusion rule, a payment or distribution from a designated Roth account will not escape tax as a qualified distribution if it is made within a period of 5 consecutive tax years beginning with the first tax year for which the participant made a designated Roth contribution to any designated Roth account established for the individual under the same applicable retirement plan.[27]

The final rules clarify that the 5-year period begins on the first day of first tax year in which the employee makes a designated Roth contribution to the plan.[28] The first tax year for which an employee makes a designated Roth contribution is the year in which the contribution is includible in the employee's gross income. Accordingly, the nonexclusion period for an employee who began making Roth contributions on October 1, 2012, would be January 1, 2012.

The nonexclusion period ends at the completion of 5 "consecutive" years of participation.[29] Thus, a new 5-year period is not triggered every time the participant makes a contribution in subsequent years.

Redetermination of 5-year period not required. The final rules explain that the beginning of the 5 tax year period of participation is not redetermined for any portion of an employee's designated Roth account.[30] Accordingly, the 5-year period will not be redetermined even if the entire designated Roth account is distributed during the 5 year period and the employee subsequently makes additional designated contributions under the plan.

Rollover does not restart 5-year period of participation. An employee's 5-year period of participation is generally determined separately for each plan in which the employee participates.[31] Thus, for example, an employee who contributes to a Roth account one year after beginning contributions to a separate Roth account under a separate plan (e.g., following a change in employment) would be subject to two different 5-year periods of participation.

Rollovers between Roth 401(k) accounts and with Roth IRAs

A Roth 401(k) plan may authorize (or be amended to authorize) a participant, in compliance with the rules of Code Sec. 402(c), to directly roll over a distribution from a designated Roth contribution account to: (1) another Roth contribution account maintained for the individual, or (2) a Roth IRA of the individual.[32] The amount rolled over would not be included in the distributee's gross income. [33] The recipient plan, however, must also provide for Roth accounts and be authorized to accept rollover Roth 401(k) or Roth 403(b)) contributions.

Roth IRA may not be rolled over to Roth 401(k). Distributions from a Roth IRA may not be rolled over to a Roth 401(k) (or a Roth 403(b)) plan. This rule applies even if all of the amounts in the Roth IRA are attributable to rollover contributions from a Roth 401(k). Thus, a participant who rolls over a Roth 401(k) distribution to a Roth IRA may not subsequently roll the amount back to a Roth 401(k) plan.[34]

Rollovers between Roth 401(k) and traditional 401(k) plans. Participants in a 401(k) and other qualified plan may roll over distributions directly to a Roth IRA (thereby avoiding the need for an intervening rollover to a non-Roth IRA followed by a conversion to a Roth IRA).[35] In addition, after-tax contributions may be rolled over in a trustee-to-trustee transfer from a qualified plan to a DB plan or a 403(b) plan (as well as to a defined contribution plan or an IRA).[36]

Participants in a Roth 401(k) plan, however, may not roll over distributions to a traditional 401(k) plan. Thus, if an employee terminates employment with a company that maintains a Roth 401(k) plan in which he participated, he may: (1) roll over the account to the Roth 401(k) of his new employer or, (2) roll the account to his own Roth IRA.

Participants in a traditional 401(k) plan could not, under prior law, roll over distributions to a Roth 401(k) plan. However, effective for distributions after September 27, 2010, funds may be rolled over 401(k) to Roth 401(k) accounts. [37]

The rollover rules are discussed in detail at ¶ 2993.

Income tax reporting requirements

In addition to the reporting and recordkeeping requirements discussed above, the amount of a participant's designated Roth contributions must be reported on the individual's Form W-2 as elective deferrals.[38] Distributions from a Roth 401(k) plan are to be reported on Form 1099-R.

Roth 401(k) plans are discussed in detail at CCH PENSION PLAN GUIDE ¶ 7432.

[1] Code Sec. 402A, as added by P.L. 107-16, (Economic Growth and Tax Relief Reconciliation Act of 2001), Act Sec. 617(a).

[2] IRS Notice 2006-44, I.R.B. 2006-20, 5-15-06, at CCH PENSION PLAN GUIDE ¶ 17,133R.

[3] Code Sec. 402A(b)(1) and 402A(e), P.L. 107-16, (Economic Growth and Tax Relief Reconciliation Act of 2001) as added by Act Sec. 617(a).

[4] IRS Reg. § 1.401(k)-1(f)(1).

[5] Preamble to IRS Reg. § 1.401(k)-1(f)(1).

[6] IRS Reg. § 1.401(k)-1(f)(1)(i).

[7] IRS Reg. § 1.401(k)-1(f)(5)(i).

[8] IRS Reg. § 1.401(k)-1(f)(5)(ii)(A).

[9] IRS Reg. § 1.401(k)-1(f)(5)(ii)(B).

[10] Code Sec. 401A(c)(1).

[11] IRS Reg. § 1.401(k)-1(a)(4)(iii).

[12] Code Sec.3121(v)(1)(A), as amended by P.L. 100-172 (Tax Technical Corrections Act of 2007), Act Sec. 8

[13] IRS Reg. § 1.401(k)-1(f)(1)(ii).

[14] IRS Reg. § 1.401(k)-1(f)(4)(i).

[15] Richard Perlin, CCH Benefit Practice Portfolio, "The Nuts and Bolts of Roth 401(k) Programs," September-October 2006.

[16] IRS Reg. §§ IRS Reg. §§ 1.401(k)-1(f)(1) and 1.401(k)-6.

[17] IRS Reg. §§ IRS Reg.§ 1.401(k)-1(f)(3).

[18] Code Sec. 402A(a)(1), as added by P.L. 107-16, (Economic Growth and Tax Relief Reconciliation Act of 2001), Act Sec. 617(a); IRS Reg. § 1.401(k)-1(f)(4)(i).

[19] Code Sec. 402A(b)(2)(A), as added by P.L. 107-16, (Economic Growth and Tax Relief Reconciliation Act of 2001), Act Sec. 617(a).

[20] Code Sec. 402A(b)(2)(B), as added by P.L. 107-16, (Economic Growth and Tax Relief Reconciliation Act of 2001), Act Sec. 617(a).

[21] IRS Reg. § 1.401(k)-1(f)(3).

[22] Code Sec. 402A(c)(2), as added by P.L. 107-16, (Economic Growth and Tax Relief Reconciliation

Act of 2001), Act Sec. 617(a). Code Sec. 402(g)(1), as amended by P.L. 107-16, (Economic Growth and Tax Relief Reconciliation Act of 2001), Act Sec. 617(b). IRS Reg. § 1.401(k)-1(f)(4).

[23] IRS Reg. § 1.401(k)-1(f).

[24] Code Sec. 402A(d), as added by P.L. 107-16, (Economic Growth and Tax Relief Reconciliation Act of 2001), Act Sec. 617(a). IRS Reg. § 1.402A-1, Q-2.

[25] Code Sec. 402A(d)(2)(A), as added by P.L. 107-16, (Economic Growth and Tax Relief Reconciliation Act of 2001), Act Sec. 617(a); IRS Reg. § 1.402A-1, Q-2.

[26] IRS Reg. § 1.402A-1, Q-11.

[27] Code Sec. 402A(d)(2)(B)(i), as added by P.L. 107-16 (Economic Growth and Tax Relief Reconciliation Act of 2001), Act Sec. 617(a); IRS Reg. § 1.402A-1, Q-2 and Q-4.

[28] IRS Reg. § 1.402A-1, Q-4.

[29] *Ibid.*

[30] IRS Reg. § 1.402A-1, Q-4(c).

[31] IRS Reg. § 1.402A-1, Q-4(b).

[32] Code Sec. 402A(c)(3)(A), as added by P.L. 107-16, (Economic Growth and Tax Relief Reconciliation Act of 2001), Act Sec. 617(a). IRS Reg. § 1.401(k)-1(f)(4)(ii); IRS Reg. § 1.408A-10, Q-1.

[33] IRS Notice 2009-75, Q-1(b), I.R.B. 2009-39, 9-28-09, at CCH PENSION PLAN GUIDE ¶ 17,143L.

[34] IRS Reg. § 1.408A-10, Q-5.

[35] Code Sec. 408A(e); IRS Reg. § 1.408A-10, Q-5; IRS Notice 2008-30, I.R.B. 2008-12, 3-24-08, at CCH PENSION PLAN GUIDE¶ 17,138X, amplified and clarified by IRS Notice 2009-75, I.R.B. 2009-39, 9-28-09, at CCH PENSION PLAN GUIDE ¶ 17,143L.

[36] Code Sec. 402(c)(2)(A), as amended by P.L. 109-280 (Pension Protection Act of 2006), Act Sec. 822(a).

[37] P.L. 111-240 (Small Business Jobs Act of 2010), Act Sec. 2112).

[38] Code Sec. 6051(a)(8).

¶ 2942

CASH OR DEFERRED ARRANGEMENTS: 401(k) Plan Sponsors

Generally, any employer, including sole proprietors and partnerships, may adopt a 401(k) plan. In addition, tax-exempt organizations,[1] Indian tribal governments,[2] rural cooperatives[3], and colleges or universities that sponsor a qualified football coaches plan[4] may adopt 401(k) plans. However, state and local governments may not adopt 401(k) plans (or maintain plan that were adopted after May 6, 1986).[5] For additional discussion, see CCH Pension Plan Guide ¶ 7425.

☐ As an alternative to a 401(k) plan, state and local government may adopt nonqualified deferred compensation arrangements, called "457 plans" (see ¶ 180).

Partnerships

A partnership may establish and maintain a 401(k) plan that covers partners. Individual partners may make 401(k) elections with regard to compensation (i.e., earned income as defined in Code Sec. 401(c)(2)) attributable to services rendered to the partnership. The same rules generally apply to partnership 401(k) plans as apply to other 401(k) plans, but some special rules apply to contributions and the time for electing deferrals.[6]

Partner's power to vary contributions. A partnership 401(k) plan includes any arrangement that directly or indirectly permits individual partners to vary the amount of contributions made on their behalf.[7] The elective contributions will not be included in the participant's income and may be deductible by the employer if they are made under a qualified cash or deferred arrangement and the contributions do not exceed the applicable Code Sec. 402(g) limit.

An arrangement is not qualified, however, if a partnership allows employees (including partners) to make a one-time irrevocable election upon the commencement of employment or initial eligibility under any plan of the employer.[8] If a partnership allows its employees to have a specified amount or percentage of compensation contributed by the employer throughout the employee's period of employment, the arrangement is not qualified.

Time for electing deferral. For purposes of the "currently available" rule (see ¶ 2940A), a partner's compensation is considered to be currently available on the last day of the partnership's tax year. Thus, a partner's election to defer compensation may be made at any time before the end of the partnership's tax year because that is the date on which, except for the election, the compensation would be includible in the partner's taxable income. As a result, a partner may not make an elective contribution of any portion of the partner's compensation attributable to a particular partnership tax year after the last day of that tax year.[9]

CCH POINTER: The IRS has privately ruled that a partnership may allow partners to make elective contributions to plans from periodic advances of earnings received during the year.[10] Under the scenario approved by the IRS, the advances, which were designed to be equivalent to periodic payments of compensation, were not currently available to the individual partners. Accordingly, the IRS concluded that contributions to the plans made by partners from periodic advances received during the year qualified as elective contributions under Code Sec. 401(k).

Matching contributions. Matching contributions made to 401(k) plans for self-employed persons are not treated as elective contributions and are, therefore, not subject to the limit on elective contributions (see ¶ 2981).[11]

Deductions for contributions. A partnership must allocate the deduction for all contributions to a defined contribution plan on behalf of a partner to that partner. Therefore, it is, in effect, almost impossible for a partnership to make matching contributions for a partner.

Multiemployer 401(k) plans

Several employers may, pursuant to a collective bargaining agreement with a labor union, adopt and contribute to a single multiemployer or "union" (i.e., "Taft-Hartley") 401(k) plan. Multiemployer plans (unlike collectively bargained single-employer plans) typically do not provide for employer matching contributions and do not authorize participants to direct the investment of assets in their accounts.

Multiple employer plans

In contrast to a multiemployer plan, a "multiple employer plan" is a single plan maintained by two or more unrelated employers that is not operated pursuant to a collective bargaining agreement.[12] Multiple employer plans are typically adopted by employers that share common ownership that falls short of controlled group status (e.g., automobile dealerships).

Administrative advantage. The administrative advantage afforded by a multiple employer plan is that a plan sponsor is required to file only a single determination letter application (on Form 5330) and one Form 5500 (although a separate Schedule T must be filed for each employer).[13]

---

[1] Code Sec. 401(k)(4)(B)(i).

[2] Code Sec. 401(k)(7)(B)(iii).

[3] Code Sec. 401(k)(7)(B).

[4] P.L. 104-188 (Small Business Job Protection Act), Sec. 704(k).

[5] Code Sec. 401(k)(4)(B); IRS Reg. § 1.401(k)-1(e)(4)(i).

[6] IRS Reg. § 1.401(k)-1(a)(6)(i).

[7] IRS Reg. § 1.401(k)-1(a)(6)(i).

[8] IRS Reg. § 1.401(k)-1(a)(6)(i).

[9] IRS Reg. § 1.401(k)-1(a)(6)(iii).

[10] IRS Letter Ruling 200247052, 8-28-2002, at CCH PENSION PLAN GUIDE ¶ 17,414Q.

[11] Code Sec. 402(g)(8); IRS Reg. § 1.401(k)-1(a)(6)(ii).

[12] IRS Reg. § 1.413-2(a)(2).

[13] Instructions for Form 5300 (Application for Determination for Employee Benefit Plan); Rev. Proc. 2011-8, Sec. 6.05, I.R.B. 2011-1, at CCH PENSION PLAN GUIDE ¶ 17,299T-58.

¶ 2944

CASH OR DEFERRED ARRANGEMENTS: Types of 401(k) Plan Contributions

Varying types of contributions can be made to 401(k) plans. Each type of contribution may be subject to different vesting and distribution rules.

Elective contributions

Elective contributions (or, elective deferrals) are the pre-tax contributions that an employer makes to a plan pursuant to its employees' elections, instead of paying the employees cash. Employees are not subject to current income tax on elective deferrals that do not exceed the applicable dollar limit for the year ($16,500 in 2009 (see ¶ 2981)). In addition, elective contributions and their earnings must be fully vested at all times (see ¶ 2979). However, amounts in a participant's account are subject to withdrawal restrictions (see ¶ 2989).

Catch-up contributions

Employers *may* allow employees who (a) will attain age 50 by the end of the tax year and (b) are prohibited by applicable plan or statutory limits from making other elective deferrals to the plan for the plan or other applicable year, to make additional "catch-up" contributions to the 401(k) plan in which they participate.[1] Catch-up contributions are made *in addition* to elective deferrals to the plan.

Catch-up contributions are discussed further at ¶ 2982.

Voluntary after-tax contributions

A plan may allow employees to make additional after-tax contributions at a fixed percentage of salary through payroll deductions. After-tax contributions are included in an employee's income, but the plan earnings attributable to them are not taxed until distribution. In addition, after-tax contributions must be fully vested when made and may be withdrawn at any time.

After-tax "Roth" contributions

401(k) plans (and 403(b) plans) may incorporate a "qualified Roth contribution program," pursuant to which participants may elect to have all or a portion of their elective deferrals (but not matching contributions or nonelective contributions) to the plan designated as after-tax "Roth contributions." Similar to Roth IRAs, earnings on the contributed amounts would also grow tax-free and would not be subject to tax upon distribution (see ¶ 2941A).[2]

Matching contributions

Most employers sponsoring 401(k) plans also make additional contributions to the plan in order to match amounts that employees elect to contribute. A qualified 401(k) plan is not required to provide for matching contributions. In addition, no particular matching formula is required as long as the formula does not result in discrimination or contributions in excess of statutory maximums.

Plans may require employers to provide a "fixed match" for employee contributions (i.e., $.25 per $1.00 up to 6% of pay); a "graded match" (i.e., $1.00 per $1.00 on the first 3% of pay and $.50 per $1.00 on the next 3% of pay); or a match based on the participant's length of service.

Matching contributions may be subject to deferred vesting and are subject to restrictions on withdrawal. However, these restrictions are far less stringent than those that apply to elective contributions.

Employees are not currently taxed on matching contributions made by their employers.

CCH POINTER: Employers may make matching contributions in the form of company stock. Companies typically also require employer contributions to be invested in employer stock. ERISA generally does not impose restrictions on matching contributions made in the form of employer stock, as long as the stock constitutes qualifying employer securities and the plan is an individual account plan.

Nonelective contributions

Nonelective contributions are made irrespective of any election or contribution by the employee. These contributions are generally computed on the basis of the employer's profits and are allocated to employees in proportion to their salaries. The contributions are subject to restrictions on withdrawal and may be subject to deferred vesting as well.

Like elective contributions and employer matching contributions, nonelective contributions are not currently taxable to employees.

QNECs and QMACs

Qualified Nonelective Contributions (QNECs) and Qualified Matching Contributions (QMACs) are contributions made to a participant by an employer in order to satisfy the ADP or ACP nondiscrimination tests (see ¶ 2951 and 2952). The contributions are fully vested and are subject to withdrawal restrictions.

> **CCH POINTER:** Of the possible 401(k) contributions, only elective contributions are required in order for an arrangement to constitute a 401(k) plan. The other options may be added by employers to make the plans more attractive to employees and to increase the amounts that can be sheltered from current taxation, but they are not required.

[1] Code Sec. 414(v), as amended by P.L. 107-147 (Job Creation and Worker Assistance Act of 2002), Act Sec. 411(o).

[2] Code Sec. 402A, as added by P.L. 107-16 (Economic Growth and Tax Relief Reconciliation Act of 2001), Act Sec. 617(a).

¶ 2945
CASH OR DEFERRED ARRANGEMENTS: 401(k)
Plan Fees

Plan sponsors incur numerous costs in adopting, maintaining, and administering a 401(k) plan. Initially, the sponsor will absorb legal and consulting expenses incident to the design of the plan and the drafting of plan documents. Additional set up costs could include user fees assessed by the IRS for a determination of a plan's tax qualified status. A plan will also incur ongoing administrative costs, such as trustee and custodial fees, compliance costs (e.g., preparation and filing of Form 5500, nondiscrimination testing, and penalties for noncompliance), recordkeeping and communication expenses, and account maintenance fees. The fee may be assessed as a fixed dollar amount or as a percentage of plan assets and will vary with the size and complexity of the plan.

Plan sponsors and participants may also be assuming investment management fees (e.g., transaction fees, wrap fees, surrender charges, and 12b-fees) of which they may not be fully aware. The surge in the growth of 401(k) plans and the attendant increase in investment options and services have resulted in investment expenses comprising the largest proportion of costs incurred by most plans. However, this factor has also highlighted the concern that investment management and administrative fees may inappropriately reduce the account balance of plan participants or at least temper the potential growth of retirement account savings.

Plan expenses that are paid directly by the employer are a deductible business expense.[1] However, employers are increasingly passing plan costs on to plan participants by paying the expenses from plan assets. Increasingly diverse investment options and new investment services, such as daily valuation of a participant's account, carry costs that are imposed increasingly on the plan participant alone. In addition, the expenses of operating and maintaining an investment portfolio that are charged against a plan participant's account exact an "opportunity cost" in the form of foregone investment in every contribution period.

Fiduciary obligation to monitor fees

Plan sponsors and administrators need to be aware of their fiduciary duty to evaluate and monitor fees that may adversely affect participants' retirement assets.

Prescribed procedures for evaluating fees. Pursuant to the fiduciary duty to evaluate fees, employers should:

1. establish a prudent process for selecting investment alternatives and service providers;

2. ensure that fees paid to service providers and other expenses of the plan are reasonable in light of the level and quality of services provided;

3. select prudent and adequately diversified investment alternatives; and

4. monitor investment alternatives and service providers once they have been selected to assure that they continue to be appropriate.

Fee and investment disclosure obligations of plan administrators under participant-directed plans

The Department of Labor has issued final regulations that require plan administrators, in satisfaction of their fiduciary duties under ERISA, to provide participants and beneficiaries in participant-directed plans with plan and investment-related information (including details of fees and expenses assessed to and deducted from their individual accounts) on an annual and quarterly basis. [2] The final rules generally require the disclosure of investment-related fee and expense information (e.g., sales loads, deferred sales charges, redemption fees, service charges, exchange fees, account fees, purchase fees, and the expense ratio for the total operating expenses of the investment) to be made in a chart or similar format that would allow for a comparison of the plan's investment options.

Uniform regulatory framework. The rules effectively extend the disclosure requirements applicable to ERISA Sec. 404(c) plans to all 401(k) plans. Thus, the regulations represent an effort by the DOL to establish a uniform disclosure framework for all participant-directed individual account plans that will allow for effective comparisons of plan investment options.

Fiduciary liability shield for plan administrators. The regulations impose administrative burdens on plan administrators, who will be responsible for providing and ensuring the accuracy of the required information. However, the DOL has developed a model chart that will facilitate compliance with the disclosure requirement. In addition, the rules provide plan administrators with protection from liability related to the completeness and accuracy of information furnished by service providers if they reasonably and in good faith rely on the information.

Delayed effective date. The final rules will be effective on December 20, 2010 and apply to covered individual account plans for plan years beginning on or after November 1, 2011. Calendar year plans will be required to be in compliance with the new rules by January 1, 2012. Under a limited transition rule, plan administrators are further allowed up to 60 days after the applicability date of the regulations to furnish the required disclosures to participants and beneficiaries who, as of the applicability date, have the right to direct the investment of assets held in or contributed to their individual accounts.[3]

Proposed extension of transition rule. Proposed rules issued by EBSA in May 2011 would allow plans 120 days (rather than 60) after the applicability date to furnish the initial disclosures that are otherwise required to be provided before the date on which participants or beneficiaries can first direct their investments.[4] Accordingly, a calendar year plan would be required, under the proposed rules, to furnish the initial disclosures by April 30, 2012. The quarterly statement of fees/expenses actually deducted (required under ERISA Reg. § 2550.404a-5(c)(2)(ii) and (c)(3)(ii)) would also need to be furnished no later than May 15, 2012.

EBSA further advises that, under the proposed transition rule, the initial disclosures would need to be provided to all participants and beneficiaries who have the right to direct their investment when such disclosures are furnished, and not just to individuals who had the right to direct their investment on the applicability date. This rule is designed to ensure that individuals who become plan participants in between the applicable date and the end of the 120-day transition period receive the required disclosures.

Plan administrators subject to disclosure rules. The final regulations clarify that the plan administrator (as defined in ERISA Sec. 3(16)) is the fiduciary responsible for complying with the new disclosure requirements. [5]

Disclosure requirements limited to "covered" individual account plans. The final rules are limited to participant-directed individual account plans (as defined in ERISA Sec. 3(34)).[6] However, the new requirements expressly do not apply to IRAs or IRA-based plans (e.g., SEPs and SIMPLE plans). Nor have the rules been expanded to cover defined contribution plans that do not allow for participant direction.

No small plan exception. The disclosure rules apply to all covered individual account plans, regardless of size.

Disclosures must be made to all employees eligible to participate in plan. Plan administrators must make the required disclosures to all employees eligible to participate under the terms of the plan, without regard to whether the individual has actually enrolled (i.e., "participates") in the plan. In addition, employees must receive both the initial disclosure and annual disclosures, regardless of whether they enroll in the plan, make contributions, or direct investments. The DOL, however, does clarify that disclosures only need to be provided to beneficiaries who have the right to direct the investment of assets held in, or contributed to, their accounts. [7] Typically, such rights arise incident to the death of a participant or pursuant to a QDRO.

Plan-related information. The final rules require disclosure of three types of plan-related information that will basically illustrate the structure and mechanics of the plan and its attendant expenses. [8]

General operational and plan identification information. Plan administrators will need to inform participants and beneficiaries of the: procedures for providing investment instructions; limitations applicable to investment instructions (including restrictions on the transfer of assets to or from a designated investment alternative); procedures for the exercise of voting, tender, and similar rights with respect to a designated investment alternative (including restrictions on those rights); the specific designated investment alternatives offered under the plan; and the designated investment managers to whom participants and beneficiaries may give investment instructions.[9]

Provide information on date participant may first direct investments. The general plan information must be based on the latest information available to the plan and be furnished to individuals on or before the date of on which they can first direct their investments and on an at least an annual basis thereafter. [10]

Administrative expenses. Participants and beneficiaries will need to be furnished (on or before the date they can direct investments and at least annually thereafter) with an explanation of any fees and expenses assessed for plan administrative services (e.g., legal, accounting, and recordkeeping) that may be charged against their individual accounts (whether through the liquidation of shares or the deduction of dollar amounts). [11] Participants would further need to be informed as to whether the charges would be allocated to, or affect the balance of, their individual accounts, on a pro rata or a per capita basis.

Individual expenses. Participants and beneficiaries would need to be provided (on or before the date they can direct investments and at least annually thereafter) with information relating to expenses that may be assessed on an individual, rather than on a plan-wide basis. [12] Accordingly, participants would need to be informed of expenses that may be incurred incident to obtaining qualified domestic relations orders, plan loans, or investment advice services. In addition, participants would be entitled to information on fees for brokerage windows, commissions, front or back-end loads or sales charges, redemption fees, transfer fees, and option rider charges in annuity contracts. However, fees reflected in the total annual operating expenses of a designated investment alternative would not need to be disclosed again.

Participants and beneficiaries must be informed of any change in the disclosed information at least 30 days but not more than 90 days in advance of the effective date of the change. However, exceptions are authorized for situations where notice cannot be provided because of unforeseeable events or circumstances beyond the control of the plan administrator.[13]

Disclosure before first investment by new participant. In order to provide new participants with the required disclosure of plan related information on or before the date the participant or beneficiary can first direct investments, the plan administrator may furnish the new participant or beneficiary with the most recent annual disclosures furnished to other participants and beneficiaries.[14]

Quarterly disclosure statements. In addition to the annual disclosure of expenses that might be charged to an individual account, plan administrators will need to provide a quarterly statement that (a) discloses the dollar amount of plan-related fees and expenses (administrative or individual) actually assessed to or deducted from the account and (b) identifies the service to which the expense relates. [15]

Disclosure of revenue sharing. The quarterly statement must include an explanation that, in addition to the other fees and expenses disclosed in the statement, some of the plan's administrative expenses for the preceding quarter were paid from the total operating expenses of one or more of the plan's designated investment alternatives (e.g., through revenue sharing arrangements, Rule 12b-1 fees, or sub-transfer agent fees). [16]

Investment-related information. On or before the date they first have the ability to direct their investments, and at least annually thereafter, participants and beneficiaries must be furnished by the plan administrator with basic information regarding each designated investment alternative offered under the plan. [17]

Identifying information. Information that would need to be disclosed for each designated investment alternative would include: (1) the name of the investment and (2) the type or category of investment (e.g., money market, balanced fund (stocks and bonds), large cap stock fund, employer stock fund, and employer securities). [18]

Performance data for investment alternatives. The specific investment performance data that must be disclosed varies depending on whether the designated investment alternative provides a fixed return (e.g., guaranteed investment contract) or does not offer a fixed return (e.g., equity index fund).

Investment without fixed return. With respect to investment alternatives that do not provide a fixed return (e.g., mutual funds), the fiduciary would need to disclose the average annual total return (expressed as percentage) of the investment for 1-year, 5-year, and 10-year periods (or for the life of the alternative, if shorter), ending on the date of the most recently completed calendar year. [19] The disclosure would further need to include a statement cautioning participants that the investment's past performance is not necessarily indicative of the investment's future performance.

Average annual return. Average annual return is defined as the average annual compounded rate of return that would equate an initial investment in a designated investment alternative to the ending redeemable value of that investment calculated with the before tax methods of computation prescribed in SEC Form N-1A, N-3, or

N-4 (as appropriate). [20] Plan administrators, however, could exclude any front-end, deferred, or other sales loads that are not actually charged to plan participants and beneficiaries.

Fixed return investments. With respect to investment alternatives for which the return is fixed or stated for the term of the investment, the fiduciary would be required to disclose both the fixed or stated annual rate of return and the term of the investment. [21] In addition, the disclosure would need to include a statement advising participants and beneficiaries if an issuer has reserved the right to adjust the rate of return prospectively during the term of the contract or the arrangement. Participants would need to be further informed of the means (e.g., telephone or Web site) by which to obtain the most recent rate of return information available.

Investment risks of fixed return investments borne by entity other than participant. Fixed return investments, for purposes of the regulations, are limited to designated investment alternatives that provide a fixed or stated rate of return to the participant, for a stated duration, and with respect to which the investment risks are borne by an entity other than the participant. Thus, fixed return investments would include certificates of deposit, guaranteed insurance contracts, variable annuity fixed accounts, and other similar interest bearing contracts from banks or insurance companies, but not money market mutual funds and stable value funds.

Benchmark standard. In providing performance data for an investment alternative that does not provide a fixed return, the plan administrator must also provide performance data from an appropriate broad-based benchmark (i.e., securities market index) over the 1, 5, and 10 calendar year time periods (or life of the alternatives, if shorter). [22] The securities market index selected as a benchmark, however, could not be administered by an affiliate of the investment provider, its investment adviser, or a principal underwriter, unless the index was widely recognized and used.

Fee and expense disclosures. The centerpiece of the final regulations may be the rules governing the disclosure of fees and expenses that arise attendant to the purchase, holding, and sale of each of the plan's designated investment alternatives.

Disclosures required when return is not fixed. A plan administrator must disclose for each designated investment alternative for which a return is not fixed: 1. the amount and a description of: (a) each shareholder-type fee (i.e., fees charged directly against a participant's or beneficiary's investment, such as commissions, sales loads, sales charges, deferred sales charges, redemption fees, surrender charges, exchange fees, account fees, and purchase fees, which are not included in the total operating expenses of any designated investment alternative), and (b) any restriction or limitation that may be applicable to a purchase, transfer, or withdrawal of the investment in whole or in part (e.g., roundtrip, equity wash, or other restriction); 2. total annual operating expenses of the investment expressed as a percentage (e.g., expense ratio); 3. the total annual operating expenses of the investments for a one-year period expressed as a dollar amount per $1000 investment (assuming no returns and based on the total annual operating expenses percentage); 4. a statement indicating that fees and expenses are only one of several factors that participants and beneficiaries should consider when making investment decisions; and 5. a statement informing participants and beneficiaries that the cumulative effect of fees and expenses can substantially reduce the growth of a retirement account and advising them to visit the EBSA website for an example demonstrating the long-term effects of fee and expenses on account balances. [23]

Shareholder-type fees under alternatives with a fixed rate of return. Fiduciaries would also need to disclose, with respect to investment alternatives that provide a fixed return, the amount and description of any shareholder-type fees and a description of any restriction or limitation that may be applicable to a purchase, transfer, or withdrawal of the investment in whole or in part. [24]

Internet Web site address. Plan administrators will be required to ensure the availability of an Internet Web site address that is sufficiently specific to provide participants and beneficiaries with access to specified additional information about the investment options for employees who want more or more current information. [25] The information that must be included on the Web site is: the name of the investment's issuer; the objectives or goals of the investment alternative (consistent with SEC Form N-1A or N-3); the alternative's principal strategies (including a general description of the types of assets held by the investment) and principal risks; the alternative's portfolio turnover rate (i.e., the rate at which securities are being bought and sold); the alternative performance date (updated at least quarterly); and the alternative's fee and expense information.

Special disclosure rules applicable to investments in employer securities. The final regulations continue to require the disclosure of information regarding investments in employer securities. However, the final rules authorize limited exceptions to the generally applicable disclosure requirements that recognize the unique nature of company stock as a plan investment option. [26]

Glossary . Participants and beneficiaries would also need to be provided with a general glossary of terms to assist them in understanding the plan's investment options. [27] Alternatively, the Internet Web site address must be sufficiently specific to provide access to such a glossary.

Annuity options. The final regulations impose specific disclosure requirements with respect to a designated investment alternative that consists of a contract, fund or product that affords participants or beneficiaries the option to allocate contributions towards the current purchase of a stream of retirement income payments guaranteed by an insurance company.[28] The regulations apply to fixed-deferred annuities (under which participant contributions purchase a fixed stream of income, typically commencing at retirement age) and variable annuities (under which participants and beneficiaries purchase an annuity with accumulated savings at a rate specified in the contract). Under the rules, the plan administrator must provide each participant or beneficiary with basic information about the benefits and costs of the annuity. This condition would require disclosure of: (1) any limitation on the ability of participants or beneficiaries to withdraw or transfer amounts allocated to the option (e.g., "lock-ups") and any fees or charges applicable to withdrawals or transfers; and (2) any fees that will reduce the value of amounts allocated by participants or beneficiaries to the option (e.g., surrender, charges, market value adjustments, and administrative fees). [29]

Disclosures in comparative format. Much of the information that must be disclosed under the final regulations is currently required of ERISA Sec. 404(c) compliant plans. However, the rules implementing ERISA Sec. 404(c) do not require investment-related information to be provided in a comparative format that allows for a review of investment options by participants and beneficiaries. By contrast, the final regulations under ERISA Sec. 404(a) require the specified investment-related information to be furnished in a chart or similar format that is designed to facilitate a comparison of the information provided for each designated investment alternative under the plan. [30]

The chart must prominently display the date and must include a statement that identifies the plan administrator (and other contact resources for plan information) and a statement informing participants and beneficiaries that more current information (i.e., fee, expense, and performance information) may be available on the Web site for the investment alternative. The comparative disclosure must also inform participants and beneficiaries of the procedures for requesting and obtaining free of charge, paper copies of the information required to be maintained on a Web site (including that related to annuity options and fixed return investments).

Model Comparative Chart. The DOL has developed a Model Comparative Chart that *may* be used by fiduciaries to satisfy the disclosure requirements. [31] The Model Comparative Chart is comprised of three parts. Part 1 provides information about the past performance of the plan's investment options that do not have fixed or stated rate of return. Part 2 furnishes fee and expense information for investment options, including total annual operating expenses that are expected to reduce the rate of return and shareholder-type fees. Part 3 provides information on annuity options under the plan, including pricing factors, restrictions, and fees.

CCH POINTER: Certain fee and expense information described in ERISA Reg. §2550.404a-5(e)(1) and (2) may be included in the quarterly pension benefit statement required under ERISA Sec. 105(a)(1)(A)(i). The information (e.g., investment instructions, current list of plan investment options, and fee information) must be given to participants or beneficiaries on or before the date that they can first direct their investments and then annually thereafter. Pension benefit statements are discussed in detail at ¶2220.

Fiduciary liability shield. Plan administrators are responsible for ensuring that the information contained in the required disclosures is complete and accurate. However, the final regulations expressly shield plan administrators from liability with respect to the completeness and accuracy of information provided to participants and beneficiaries if the plan administrator has reasonably and in good faith relied upon information furnished by a service provider or the issuer of a designated investment alternative. [32]

Fiduciary duty to prudently select and monitor service providers . The final regulations under ERISA Sec. 404(a) stress the DOL position that a fiduciary in compliance with the new disclosure requirements remains subject to a duty under ERISA to prudently select and monitor providers of services to the plan or designated investment alternatives under the plan. [33]

ERISA 404(c) amendment. In order to further stress the fiduciary duty to prudently select and monitor service providers, the DOL has amended ERISA Reg. § 2550-404c-1 to emphasize that compliance with ERISA Sec. 404(c) does not relieve a fiduciary of the duty to prudently select and monitor a designated investment manager or designated investment alternative under the plan. [34] The amendment reflects the DOL view that ERISA Sec. 404(c) does not shield a fiduciary from liability for an investment loss incurred in connection with the plan's selection of a designated investment alternative even where the loss is not the result of the participant's or beneficiary's exercise of control.

Uniform disclosure rules encompass non-ERISA 404(c) plans. The DOL has integrated the disclosure requirements under ERISA Reg. § 2550.404a-5 with the disclosure rules under the ERISA Sec. 404(c) regulations. [35] Accordingly, DOL explains, a uniform disclosure framework applies to all participant-directed individual account plans, whether or not the plan is designed to be in compliance with ERISA Sec. 404(c).

Fee disclosures by service providers to fiduciaries

A 401(k) plan may contract or make reasonable arrangements with a party in interest, including a fiduciary, for office space or legal, accounting, or other services necessary for the establishment or operation of the plan. [36] However, no more than reasonable compensation may be paid for this office space or services and the exemption does not apply where a plan fiduciary has an interest in the transaction that may affect its judgment as a fiduciary. [37]

In July 2010, EBSA released interim final regulations, effective July 16, 2011, pursuant to which a service contract or arrangement would not be reasonable, for purposes of the prohibited transaction exemption authorized under ERISA for necessary plan services, unless covered service providers (including fiduciary service providers, banks, consultants, investment providers, and third party administrators) have complied with a series of new disclosure requirements. [38]

Absent compliance by the service provider with the disclosure requirements, the plan fiduciary would be subject to liability for engaging in a prohibited transaction. However, the DOL has incorporated a Class Exemption into the final regulations that would relieve a fiduciary of liability for a Prohibited Transaction resulting from a service provider's failure to comply with the notice requirements. The fiduciary may not have had knowledge of the service provider's compliance failure and would be required to take actions upon discovering the failure, including notification of the DOL.

CCH POINTER: *April 1, 2012 effective date.* The EBSA subsequently extended the applicability date of the final rules to January 1, 2012. [39] Proposed rules issued by EBSA in May 2011 would have implemented the extension announced in February 2011. [40] Final rules issued in July further extended the effective date of the 408(b)(2) regulations to April 1, 2012. [41] Thus, covered service providers are not required to make initial disclosures prior to April 1, 2012.

Covered service providers . Not every entity providing services to the plan would be covered by the new rules. Accordingly, the threshold determination under the final rules will be whether a service provider is subject to the disclosure requirements.

$1000 threshold. Service providers subject to the disclosure requirements would be restricted to those who have entered into a contract or arrangement with a covered plan and reasonably expect $1000 or more in compensation (direct or indirect) to be received in connection with the provision of specified services. The rules would apply whether or not the services will be performed, or whether such compensation is actually received by the covered service provider, affiliate or subcontractor. [42]

Service provider categories. The final regulations designate the following three categories of service providers as being subject to the disclosure requirements: [43]

1. *Fiduciary and investment services.* Service providers who provide services directly to the plan as a fiduciary under ERISA Sec. 3(21) (e.g., plan trustee or investment adviser) or as an investment adviser registered under the Investment Advisers Act of 1940 or any state law.

2. *Recordkeeping and brokerage services.* Providers of recordkeeping or brokerage services to covered individual account plans that permit participants or beneficiaries to direct the investment of their accounts, if one or more designated investment alternatives will be made available through a platform of investment options or a similar mechanism, in connection with the recordkeeping or brokerage services. [44] Affected service providers will include third party recordkeepers, service providers who furnish recordkeeping or brokerage services that include designated investment alternatives independently selected by the responsible fiduciary and later added to the cover plan's platform. [45]

3. *Service providers receiving indirect compensation.* Service providers (including an affiliate or subcontractor) who receive indirect compensation or compensation from related parties in connection with accounting, auditing, actuarial, appraisal, banking, consulting, custodial insurance, investment advisory (whether or not the service provider is registered), legal, recordkeeping, securities or other investment brokerage, third party administration, or valuation services provided to the covered plan.[46] Indirect compensation includes compensation from anyone other than the plan or the plan sponsor (e.g., 12b-1 fees)

Disclosure of compensation and fees. The primary focus of the final rules is on highlighting the compensation or fees received by service providers and their affiliates in connection with services provided to the plan. The regulations specify the following four categories of compensation to be disclosed. [47]

1. Direct compensation (either in the aggregate or by service (i.e., itemized basis)) that the service provider, affiliate or subcontractor reasonably expect to directly receive from the plan.

¶2945

2. Indirect compensation that the service provider, affiliate or subcontractor reasonably expect to receive from a source other than the plan, plan sponsor, service provider, affiliate or subcontractor in connection with the services to be provided pursuant to the contract, including the services for which the indirect compensation will be received and the payor of the indirect compensation.

3. Compensation paid among related parties (i.e., covered service providers, affiliates and subcontractors) that is: (a) set on a transaction basis (e.g., commissions, soft dollars, finder's fees or other similar incentive compensation based on business placed or retained), or (b) charged directly against the covered plan's investments and reflected in the net value of the investment (e.g., 12b-1 fees). In addition, the service provider must identify the services for which compensation will be paid, the recipients of the compensation, and the status of each payer or recipient as an affiliate or subcontractor. However, the disclosure requirement does not extend to compensation received by employees from their employers for work performed by the employee.

4. Compensation that the service provider, affiliate, or subcontractor reasonably expect to receive in connection with the termination of the contract and the means by which any pre-paid amount will be calculated and refunded upon such termination.

Compensation defined. Compensation would include "anything of monetary value" (e.g., money, gifts, awards, and tips) with the exception of non-monetary compensation valued at $250 or less, in the aggregate, during the term of contract.[48] Note, however, compensation that is paid to the service provider by the plan sponsor, but that is not reimbursed by the plan, need not be disclosed.

Format for disclosing compensation. A description or estimate of compensation may be expressed as a monetary amount, formula, percentage of the covered plan's assets, or a per capita charge for each participant or beneficiary. In the event the compensation cannot be reasonably expressed in such terms, any other reasonable method may be used. However, the compensation or fees must be described in a manner and with sufficient detail (e.g., by disclosing assumptions used in a formula) that will allow the responsible plan fiduciary to determine whether the fees are reasonable.

Disclosure of recordkeeping services. The final regulations (unlike the proposed rules) require a covered service provider to furnish a description of all direct and indirect compensation that the provider, affiliate or subcontractor reasonably expects to receive in connection with recordkeeping services. [49] In the event the service provider reasonably expects recordkeeping services to be furnished in whole or in part without explicit compensation for the services or when compensation for the services is offset or rebated based on other compensation received by the provider, affiliate or subcontractor, the service provider must furnish a reasonable and good faith estimate of the cost to the covered plan of the recordkeeping services. The methodology and assumptions used in preparing the estimate must be explained and services to be provided must be disclosed in detail.

¶2945

Manner of payment of compensation. The service provider must disclose the manner in which compensation and payments for recordkeeping services will be received.[50] For example, the provider must indicate whether the plan will be billed or the compensation will be deducted directly from the plan's account(s) or investments.

Investment disclosure. Covered service providers who furnish services as a fiduciary to an investment contract, product, or entity that holds plan assets and in which the plan has a direct equity investment must (in addition to compensation covering the services provided) disclose compensation regarding the investment with respect to which they are a fiduciary (or provide recordkeeping or brokerage services).[51] The information to be disclosed includes: (1) compensation to be charged directly against the amount invested in connection with the acquisition, sale, transfer of an withdrawal from an investment contract, product, or entity (e.g., sales loads, sales charges, deferred sales charges, redemption fees, surrender charges, exchange fees, account fees, and purchase fees; (2) annual operating expenses (e.g., expense ratio) if the return is not fixed; and (3) ongoing expenses in addition to annual operating expenses (e.g., wrap fees, mortality and expense fees).

Timing of disclosure requirements . Covered service providers must provide the required disclosures to the responsible plan fiduciary "reasonably in advance" of the date that the contract or arrangement is entered into, extended, or renewed. [52]

Class Exemption provides fiduciary relief from PT resulting from service provider's compliance failure. In the event that a service provider fails to comply with the disclosure requirements, the service contract will not qualify for the exemptive relief under ERISA Sec. 408(b)(2), and the plan fiduciary would be liable for a prohibited transaction under ERISA Sec. 406. The DOL, concurrently with the issuance of the proposed disclosure regulations, released a Proposed Prohibited Transaction Class Exemption that would relieve a plan fiduciary of liability for a prohibited transaction that results from the failure by a service provider to comply with the disclosure regulations. The DOL has now adopted the Class Exemption, with modifications, and incorporated it into the final rules as a statutory exemption.[53]

Class Exemption conditions. The Class Exemption shields a responsible plan fiduciary from the restrictions of ERISA Sec. 406(a)(1)(C) and (D) following the failure of a covered service provider to comply with the disclosure requirements if: (1) the fiduciary did not know that the covered service provider failed or would fail to make a required disclosure and reasonably believed that the provider made the required disclosure; (2) the responsible plan fiduciary, upon discovering the failure of the covered service provider to disclose the required information, makes a written request for the information to the service provider; and (3) the fiduciary notifies the DOL of the service provider's failure to comply with the written request for information within 90 days.

Fiduciary may not receive "additional" fees. The statutory exemption that allows reasonable compensation to be provided for office space and services necessary for the establishment or operation of the plan, does not apply to transactions under

ERISA Sec. 406(b) that involve a conflict of interest on the part of fiduciaries. [54] A fiduciary that uses the authority, control, or responsibility which makes it a fiduciary to cause the plan to enter into a transaction involving the provision of services, where the fiduciary has an interest in the transaction that may affect the exercise of its best judgment as a fiduciary, may not claim an exemption under ERISA Sec. 408(b)(2). Thus, fiduciaries may not use their authority, control, or responsibility as a fiduciary to cause a plan to pay additional fees to the fiduciary to provide a service. [55] This also applies to an additional fee caused to be paid by a person in which the fiduciary has an interest which may affect the exercise of the fiduciary's best judgment. Nor may a fiduciary use his authority, control, or responsibility as a fiduciary to cause a plan to enter into a transaction involving plan assets whereby the fiduciary would receive consideration from a third party in connection with the transaction.

[1] IRS Reg. § 1.404(a)-3(d).

[2] ERISA Reg. § 2550.404a-5.

[3] ERISA Reg. § 2550.404a-5(j).

[4] Proposed ERISA Reg. § 2550.404a-5(j)(3)(i).

[5] ERISA Reg. § 2550.404a-5(a).

[6] ERISA Reg. § 2550.404a-5(b)(2).

[7] ERISA Reg. § 2550.404a-5(b)(1).

[8] ERISA Reg. § 2550.404a-5(c).

[9] ERISA Reg. § 2550.404a-5(c)(1).

[10] ERISA Reg. § 2550.404a-5(c)(1)(i).

[11] ERISA Reg. § 2550.404a-5(c)(2)(i)(A).

[12] ERISA Reg. § 2550.404a-5(c)(3).

[13] ERISA Reg. § 2550.404a-5(c)(3)(B).

[14] ERISA Reg. § 2550.404a-5(c)(4).

[15] ERISA Reg. § 2550.404a-5(c)(2)(ii).

[16] ERISA Reg. § 2550.404a-5(c)(2)(ii)(C).

[17] ERISA Reg. § 2550.404a-5(d)(1).

[18] ERISA Reg. § 2550.404a-5(d)(1)(i).

[19] ERISA Reg. § 2550.404a-5(d)(1)(ii)(A).

[20] ERISA Reg. § 2550.404a-5(h)(3.

[21] ERISA Reg. § 2550.404a-5(d)(1)(ii)(B).

[22] ERISA Reg. § 2550.404a-5(d)(1)(iiii).

[23] ERISA Reg. § 2550.404a-5(d)(1)(iv)(A).

[24] ERISA Reg. § 2550.404a-5(d)(1)(iv)(B).

[25] ERISA Reg. § 2550.404a-5(d)(1)(v).

[26] ERISA Reg. § 2550.404a-5(i)(1).

[27] ERISA Reg. § 2550.404a-5(d)(1)(vi).

[28] ERISA Reg. § 2550.404a-5(d)(1)(vii).

[29] ERISA Reg. § 2550.404a-5(i)(2).

[30] ERISA Reg. § 2550.404a-5(d)(2)(i).

[31] ERISA Reg. § 2550.404a-5(e)(3); Appendix to ERISA Reg. § 2550.404a-5.

[32] ERISA Reg. § 2550.404a-5(b)(1).

[33] ERISA Reg. § 2550.404a-5(f).

[34] ERISA Reg. § 2550.404c-1(d)(2)(iv).

[35] ERISA Reg. § 2550.404c-1(b)(2)(i)(B)(2); ERISA Reg. § 2550.404c-1(c)(1)(ii)..

[36] Code Sec. 4975(d)(2); ERISA Sec.408(b)(2); ERISA Reg. § 2550.408b-2.

[37] ERISA Reg. § 2550.408b-2(a).

[38] ERISA Reg. § 2550.408b-2(c)(1) and (c)(1)(xii).

[39] DOL News Release, February 11, 2011.

[40] ERISA Proposed Reg. § 2550.408b-2(c)(1)(xii), 75 FR 31544, June 1, 2001.

[41] ERISA Reg. § 2550.408b-2(c)(1)(xii).

[42] ERISA Reg. § 2550.408b-2(c)(1)(iii).

[43] ERISA Reg. § 2550.408b-2(c)(1)(iii)(A).

[44] ERISA Reg. § 2550.408b-2(c)(1)(iii)(B).

[45] Preamble to ERISA Reg. § 2550.408b-2.

[46] Preamble to ERISA Reg. § 2550.408b-2(c)(1)(iii)(C).

[47] ERISA Reg. § 2550.408b-2(c)(1)(iv)(C).

[48] *Ibid.*

[49] ERISA Reg. § 2550.408b-2(c)(1)(iv)(D).

[50] ERISA Reg. § 2550.408b-2(c)(1)(iv)(E).

[51] ERISA Reg. § 2550.408b-2(c)(1)(iv)(F).

[52] ERISA Reg. § 2550.408b-2(c)(1)(v)(A).

[53] ERISA Reg. § 2550.408b-2(c)(1)(x).

[54] ERISA Reg. § 2550.408b-2(a).

[55] ERISA Reg. § 2550.408b-2(e)(1).

¶ 2946

QUALIFICATION RULES: General Qualification Requirements

A 401(k) plan must be part of an underlying qualified profit-sharing, stock bonus, pre-ERISA money purchase plan, or rural cooperative plan. As a result, 401(k) plans must generally meet the same requirements applicable to qualified plans. For example, plan assets must be held in a trust that is created or organized in the United States and administered at all times as a domestic trust in the United States.

In addition, 401(k) plans are subject to special nondiscrimination requirements governing benefits and contributions and to rules covering eligibility, elective deferrals, distributions, and accounting for benefits and contributions.

In order to meet the general qualification requirements, a 401(k) plan must:[1]

1. be a written plan that is communicated to employees,

2. be maintained for the exclusive benefit of employees or their beneficiaries,

   CCH POINTER: The exclusive benefit rule prevents an employer from allowing independent contractors or consultants to participate in the plan. The IRS will generally not make a determination regarding the existence of an employee/employer relationship when determining the qualified status of a plan. However, the IRS will make a determination as to the existence of an employer/employee relationship if requested to do so by the determination letter applicant.[2]

3. not discriminate in favor of highly compensated employees (in coverage or as to contributions and benefits) (see¶ 2950—¶ 2978),

4. meet the minimum vesting rules (see ¶ 2979),

5. provide that an employee's entire interest be paid out by April 1 of the year after the employee retires or reaches age 70½, whichever is later, or provide that periodic payments begin no later than the above-mentioned dates and generally be paid over the lifetime of the employee (other alternatives are available) (see ¶ 2989—¶ 2990,

6. provide for a qualified joint and survivor annuity (if applicable),

   CCH POINTER: A 401(k) plan that is subject to the survivor annuity requirement must afford each participant with an opportunity to elect to waive the QJSA or qualified preretirement survivor annuity (QPSA). In addition, participants who elect to waive the QJSA or QPSA may elect a qualified optional survivor annuity (see ¶ 1700).

7. contain a provision prohibiting plan benefits from being assigned or alienated, and

8. file various reports with the IRS and the Department of Labor.

☐ See ¶ 300 and following for the general plan qualification requirements.

Qualified plan must be permanent

A qualified 401(k) plan must be established as a permanent program. However, an employer may reserve the right to change or terminate the plan and to discontinue contributions to the plan at any time.[3]

---

[1] Code Sec. 401(a).

[2] Rev. Proc. 2011-6, I.R.B. 2011-1, Sec. 6.13, at CCH Pension Plan Guide ¶ 17,299T-56.

[3] IRS Reg. § 1.401-1(b)(2).

¶ 2948

QUALIFICATION RULES: Special Qualification Rules for 401(k) Plans

In addition to meeting the general plan qualification rules, special requirements relating to elective deferrals, vesting, and distributions, and nondiscrimination rules governing coverage and benefits and contributions, a 401(k) plan must meet certain additional rules.

Eligibility requirement may not exceed one year

No employee may be required to complete a period of service longer than one year (not in excess of 1000 hours) with the employer maintaining the plan in order to make an election under the 401(k) arrangement.[1] An employee, including a part-time employee, who completes 12 months of service is eligible to participate in a 401(k) plan. Note, however, an employer may condition an employee's eligibility to participate in the 401(k) plan upon the attainment of age 21.[2]

> **CCH POINTER:** Employees eligible to participate in a 401(k) plan (i.e., make elective deferrals and receive matching contributions) are limited to individuals who "perform services" for an employer and who are either common law employees of the employer, self-employed individuals who are treated as employees, or leased employees who are treated as employees of the employer.[3] An individual ceases to be an employee of the employer when he or she discontinues performing services as an employee for the employer.[4] Accordingly, individuals who are no longer active employees and have discontinued performing services for the employer (including terminated employees receiving severance payments and disabled employees) may not make elective deferrals or receive matching contributions under a qualified plan.

Deferrals must be available in cash

The plan must provide that the amount that each eligible employee may defer as an elective contribution is available to the employee in cash.[5] Thus, a plan will not be qualified if an employee is provided with an option to receive a taxable benefit (other than cash) or to have the employer contribute an amount equal to the taxable benefit to a profit-sharing plan on the employee's behalf. Note, the cash availability requirement also applies to 401(k) arrangements maintained under a cafeteria plan.

Transmission of deferrals to the plan

Although not a condition of tax qualified status, ERISA requires that a plan participant's elective deferrals must be paid to the plan trustee by the earliest date on which the contributions can be reasonably segregated from the employer's general assets, but no later than the 15th business day of the month following the month in which contributions would otherwise have been payable in cash to the participant (see ¶ 2330).[6] The 15-day time period by which elective contributions must be transmitted to the plan, however, is not a safe harbor. In ascertaining the earliest date by which contributions may be reasonably segregated from an employer's general assets, an employer's past practices or deposit history will generally be determinative.

> **CCH POINTER:** *Safe harbor allows employers maintaining small plans 7 days in which to deposit employee contributions.* The EBSA has amended the governing plan asset regulations to provide employers maintaining plans with less than 100 participants at the beginning of the plan year a 7-day safe harbor in which to deposit employee contributions (and loan repayments (see ¶ 2025) to the plan. Under the safe harbor, participant contributions and loan repayments that are deposited within 7 business days from the date the funds are received or withheld from the participant would be deemed to comply with the requirement to deposit contributions on the earliest date on which contributions can be reasonably segregated from the employer's general assets.[7]

> **EXAMPLE:** ABC sponsors a 401(k) plan. There are 30 participants in the 401(k) plan. ABC has one payroll period for its employees and uses an outside payroll processing service to pay employee wages and process deductions. ABC has established a system under which the payroll processing service provides payroll deduction information to ABC within 1 business day after the issuance of paychecks. ABC checks this information for accuracy within 5 business days and then forwards the withheld employee contributions to the plan. The amount of the total withheld employee contributions is deposited with the trust that is maintained under the plan on the 7th business day following the date on which the employees are paid. Under the safe harbor, when the participant contributions are deposited with the plan on the 7th business day following a pay date, the participant contributions are deemed to be contributed to the plan on the earliest date on which such contributions can reasonably be segregated from ABC's general assets.[8]

> *Contributions deposited when placed in participant's account.* Participant contributions would continue to be considered deposited when placed in an account of the plan without regard to whether the contributed amounts have been allocated to the accounts of participants or directed to the investments selected by the participants.

> *Safe harbor may be used on deposit-by-deposit basis.* The safe harbor is available on a deposit-by deposit basis. Accordingly, the failure to meet the safe harbor during one payroll period will not result in the required

application of the general rules (i.e., preclude use of the safe harbor) for the entire plan year.

Safe harbor is optional. Use of the safe harbor is not mandatory. [9] Nor is the safe harbor the exclusive means by which an employer may comply with the deposit requirements. Employers that elect not to conform to the safe harbor, however would still need to establish that participant contributions have been deposited as of the earliest date on which the contributions could reasonably have been segregated from the employer's general assets, and manage all the uncertainty attendant compliance with that standard. In addition, in the event the employer fails to timely deposit contributions, losses and interest on the late payments must be calculated from the actual date the contribution could have been reasonably segregated from the employer's general assets. Thus, EBSA cautions loss and interest may not be computed from the end of the safe harbor period.

Trustees have fiduciary obligation to collect delinquent plan contributions. The collection of contributions is a trustee responsibility under ERISA. [10] In addition, the requirement under ERISA Sec. 404 that fiduciaries discharge their duties prudently and solely in the interests of plan participants and beneficiaries carries the attendant obligation to collect contributions. While the steps necessary to discharge a duty to collect contributions will depend on the applicable facts and circumstances, the failure of a plan to make systematic, reasonable, and diligent efforts to collect delinquent employer contributions is treated as a prohibited transaction. Similarly, the failure to collect delinquent contributions because of an arrangement, agreement or understanding (express or implied) between the plan and a delinquent employer would be deemed a PT.

Named fiduciary must allocate responsibility for collection of contributions. The plan's named fiduciary is responsible for ensuring that the obligation to collect contributions has been appropriately assigned either to a trustee, a directed trustee, or to an investment manager. This duty does not preclude a fiduciary from entering into a trust agreement that relieves a particular trustee of responsibility for monitoring and collecting contributions. However, in guidance intended to highlight the responsibility of named fiduciaries and trustees of 401(k) plans for the collection of delinquent employer and employee contributions, the EBSA cautions that, if the responsibility to collect contributions is not allocated to a trustee or investment manager, the fiduciary with the authority to hire trustees will be subject to liability for a failure to collect contributions. [11]

Trustees have residual fiduciary duty to remedy breach of duty to collect contributions. The EBSA further advises that trustees who are relieved under the trust agreement from monitoring and collecting contributions have a continuing fiduciary obligation under ERISA to take appropriate steps to remedy a situation where they have knowledge that no party has assumed responsibility for the collection and monitoring of contributions and that delinquent contributions are not being collected. [12] Under such circumstances, the trustee may be liable for the breach of duty by another fiduciary by either: (1) knowingly participating in the breach, or (2) enabling the fiduciary to commit a breach by not complying with its own obligations under ERISA Sec. 404(a). Thus, a trustee's failure to act prudently to redress a fiduciary's failure to collect delinquent contributions would subject the trustee to liability for the breach of duty by the fiduciary.

Correction of failure to timely deposit deferrals under EPCRS. In the event an employer fails to make a timely deposit of elective deferrals, the failure may constitute an operational error that could result in plan disqualification for failure to follow plan terms (if the plan specifies a date by which elective deferrals must be deposited by the employer) and a prohibited transaction. The operational error of not operating the plan in accordance with the plan document may be corrected under EPCRS.

Correction of late deposits under EPCRS requires: (1) a determination of the amount of late deposits and calculation of lost earnings, and (2) deposit of missed elective deferrals (and lost earnings) into the trust.

Voluntary Fiduciary Correction Program. The failure to timely remit employee contributions to the plan is a fiduciary breach that may be corrected under the Voluntary Fiduciary Correction Program.[13]

Prescribed correction mechanisms. The VFC Program provides the exclusive means by which a stipulated breach of fiduciary duty may be corrected.[14]

Unpaid contributions. In the event that participant contributions have not been paid to the plan, the principal amount (i.e., unpaid participant contributions), plus the greater of (1) lost earnings on the principal amount or (2) restoration of profits resulting from the employer's use of the principal amount, must be paid to the plan.[15]

Late contributions. By contrast, if participant contributions have been paid to the plan, but were transmitted outside of the required time period, the employer must remit to the plan only the greater of (1) lost earnings or (2) restoration of profits resulting from the employer's use of the principal amount.[16]

Loss date. For purposes of the above calculations, the loss date for each participant contribution is the earliest date on which the contributions could reasonably have been segregated from the employer's general assets. [17] However, the loss date may not be later than the 15 day period specified in ERISA Reg. § 2510.3-102 (see above).

The correction of delinquent contributions under VFCP (including the calculation of lost earnings) is illustrated at CCH PENSION PLAN GUIDE ¶ 7526.

Class exemption provides relief from excise taxes for failure to timely remit participant contributions. In the event an employer fails to transmit elective deferrals, it is considered to be using plan assets for its own purposes and will be subject, under Code Sec. 4975(a) , to a 15 percent prohibited transaction excise tax on the value of the use of the funds. However, a class exemption provides limited relief from excise taxes for transactions involving the failure to timely remit participant contributions to the plan.[18] In order for the relief to apply: (1) contributions must be transmitted to the plan within 180 calendar days from the date the amounts were received by the employer or the date the amounts otherwise would have been payable to the participant in cash; (2) the transaction may not have been part of a broader overall agreement, arrangement, or understanding designed to benefit a party in interest; and (3) the applicant must not have taken advantage of relief provided by the VFC Program or the exemption for a similar type of transaction identified in the application during the 3-year period prior to the submission of the application.

Notice to interested persons and EBSA. The class exemption requires applicants to provide notice to interested persons (within 60 calendar days following the date of the submission of the application under the VFC Program) that: (a) provides an objective description of the transaction and corrective measures taken and (b) is written in a manner calculated to be understood by the average plan participant or beneficiary.[19] The notice, which may be provided by any means reasonably calculated to ensure receipt (e.g., posting, regular mail, electronic mail, or any combination thereof), must specifically indicate the applicant's participation in the VFCP and the intention to claim relief under the class exemption.

Reporting on Form 5500, Schedules H and I. An employer that fails to transmit participant contributions to a plan by the earliest date by which the contributions can be reasonably segregated from the employer's general assets must report the aggregate amount of all late contributions for the year on Form 5500, Schedule H (for plans with 100 or more participants as of the beginning of the plan year) or Schedule I (for plans with less than 100 participants as of the beginning of the plan year).[20] Form 5330 (Return of Excise Taxes Related To Employee Benefit Plans) must also be filed with the IRS, paying the applicable excise tax.

Maximum deferrals

A plan under which elective deferrals may be made for any individual during a calendar year will not be qualified unless the plan provides that the amount of the participant's combined deferrals under the plan and all other plans, contracts, or arrangements of the employer maintaining the plan (and all related employers) cannot exceed the amount of the annual limitation for taxable years beginning in such calendar year.[21]

In general, the maximum amount that an employee can elect to defer for any tax year under all 401(k) plans in which the employee participates is limited to $17,000 (for 2012) (see ¶ 2981). However, employees age 50 or above may make additional catch-up contributions (see ¶ 2982).

CCH POINTER: 401(k) plans may allow veterans returning to employment from military service to make up employee contributions and elective deferrals that were not made during the employee's period of military service, without risking disqualification of the plan for violating the applicable contribution limits.[22] Make-up contributions made by an employer or an employee to a 401(k) plan on behalf of reemployed veterans are not subject to the generally

¶2948

applicable plan contribution limits or the limits on deductible contributions, with respect to the year in which the contributions are made.[23] However, the make-up contributions may not exceed the aggregate amount of contributions that would have been permitted under the limits for the year for which the contributions are made if the individual had continued to be employed by the employer during the period of military service.[24]

Differential wage payments. Differential wage payments (effective for remuneration paid after December 31, 2008) will be treated as compensation for purposes of the USERRA requirements.[25] Prior to amendment, differential wage payments were not treated as wages, thereby precluding individuals from making elective deferrals to 401(k) plans (or 403(b) plans and 457(b) plans) from the payments.

Differential wage payments are defined as payments that: (1) are made by an employer to an individual with respect to any period during which the individual is performing services in the uniformed military service, while on active duty for a period of more than 30 days; and (2) represent all or a portion of the wages that the individual would have received from the employer if the individual were performing services for the employer. [26]

Deferrals from differential wage payments. Under the amended rules, an individual receiving a differential wage payment is treated as an employee of the employer making the payment, and the payment is treated as compensation. [27] Treating the payment as compensation will enable the employee to make contributions to the 401(k) plan from the differential wage payment. However, employees should be cautioned that making deferrals from the differential wage payments will reduce the amount of contributions that they may be able to make upon resuming employment.

Limit on annual additions to an employee's account

A separate limit restricts all additions (contributions) to a participant's 401(k) account, including elective deferrals, employer matching contributions, after-tax employee contributions, and forfeitures allocable to the employee's account following the departure of nonvested employees, to the lesser of 100 percent of the employee's compensation (net of deferrals) or $50,000 (in 2012).[28] See ¶ 2985.

A plan may correct excess annual additions by authorizing the distribution of elective deferrals or the return of voluntary or mandatory employee contributions and gain attributable to those contributions.[29]

Compensation limit

In computing plan contributions or benefits for each 401(k) plan participant, the amount of annual compensation that may be taken into account by a plan for any plan year is subject to an inflation-adjusted limit ($250,000 in 2012, up from $245,000 in 2011).[30] Thus, a plan may not base contributions or benefits on compensation in excess of the annual limit. In addition, the amount of a participant's compensation that is taken into account in applying the nondiscrimination rules is subject to the annual limitation.[31]

Benefits contingent upon elective deferrals

A 401(k) plan may not condition, either directly or indirectly, any other benefit (other than matching contributions under Code Sec. 401(m)) upon an employee's elective deferrals.[32] Other benefits include benefits under a defined benefit plan; nonelective employer contributions under a defined contribution plan; the availability, cost, or amount of health benefits; vacations or vacation pay; life insurance; dental plans; legal services plans; loans; financial planning services; subsidized retirement benefits; stock options; dependent care assistance; and salary increases or bonuses.[33]

Nonqualified deferred compensation plans. Participation in a *nonqualified* deferred compensation plan is treated as contingent upon an employee's elective deferral if the employee could receive additional deferred compensation only if elective contributions were made.[34] However, deferred compensation under a nonqualified CODA that is dependent on an employee's having made the maximum permitted elective deferral or contribution under the terms of the plan is *not* treated as contingent.

Separate accounting

A 401(k) plan must provide a separate account for each participant and must separately account for contributions that are subject to the vesting and distribution rules governing 401(k) plans. Gains, losses, withdrawals, forfeitures from other plan participants, and other credits and charges must be separately allocated on a reasonable and consistent basis to the participant's account.[35]

See ¶ 2941A for discussion of the separate accounting rules applicable to Roth 401(k) plans.

---

[1] IRS Reg. § 1.401(k)-1(e)(5).

[2] Code Sec.410(a)(1)(A).

[3] IRS Reg. § 1.410(b)-9, cross-referenced by IRS Reg. § 1.401(k)-1(g)(4) and (5).

[4] IRS Reg. § 1.410(b)-9.

[5] IRS Reg. § 1.401(k)-1(e)(2).

[6] ERISA Reg. § 2510.3-102(a) and (b).

[7] ERISA Reg. § 2510.3-102(a)(2).

[8] ERISA Reg. § 2510.3-102(f).

[9] ERISA Reg. § 2510.3-102(a)(2)(ii).

[10] *Central States Southeast and Southwest Areas Pension Fund v. Central Transport*, US Sup Ct (1985), 472 U.S. 559.

[11] EBSA Field Assistance Bulletin 2008-01, 2-1-08, at CCH PENSION PLAN GUIDE ¶ 19,981U.

[12] *Ibid.*

[13] EBSA Adoption of VFCP, April 19, 2006 (71 FR 20261).

[14] EBSA Adoption of Voluntary Fiduciary Correction Program, Sec. 7, April 19, 2006 (71 FR 20261).

[15] EBSA Adoption of Voluntary Fiduciary Correction Program, Sec. 7.1(a)(2)(i), April 19, 2006 (71 FR 20261).

[16] EBSA Adoption of Voluntary Fiduciary Correction Program, Sec. 7.1(a)(2)(ii), April 19, 2006 (71 FR 20261).

[17] EBSA Adoption of Voluntary Fiduciary Correction Program, Sec. 7.1(a)(2)(i), April 19, 2006 (71 FR 20261).

[18] Prohibited Transaction Class Exemption 2002-51, November 25, 2002 (67 FR 70623), amended April 19, 2006 (71 FR 20135).

[19] Prohibited Transaction Class Exemption 2002-51, Sec. IV, November 25, 2002 (67 FR 70623), amended April 19, 2006 (71 FR 20135).

[20] Form 5500, Instructions,

[21] Code Sec. 401(a)(30); IRS Reg. § 1.401(a)-30(a).

[22] Code Sec. 414(u).

[23] Code Sec. 414(u)(1)(A).

[24] Code Sec. 414(u)(1)(B).

[25] Code Sec. 414(u)(12)(A), as added by P.L. 110-245 (Heroes Earnings Assistance and Tax Relief Act of 2008), Act Sec. 105(b)(1).

[26] Code Sec. 3401(h)(2), as added by P.L. 110-245 (Heroes Earnings Assistance and Tax Relief Act of 2008), Act Sec. 105(b)(1).

[27] Code Sec. 414(u)(12)(A), as added by P.L. 110-245 (Heroes Earnings Assistance and Tax Relief Act of 2008), Act Sec. 105(b)(1).

[28] Code Sec. 415(c)(1), as amended by P.L. 107-16 (Economic Growth and Tax Relief Recon-

ciliation Act of 2001), Act Secs. 611(b)(1) and 632(a)(1).

[29] IRS Reg. § 1.415-6(b)(6).

[30] Code Sec. 401(a)(17).

[31] IRS Reg. § 1.401(a)(17)-1(a)(1).

[32] IRS Reg. § 1.401(k)-1(e)(6)(i).

[33] Code Sec. 401(k)(4)(A); IRS Reg. § 1.401(k)-1(e)(6)(ii).

[34] IRS Reg. § 1.401(k)-1(e)(6)(iv).

[35] IRS Reg. § 1.401(k)-1(e)(3).

¶ 2950

NONDISCRIMINATION RULES: Nondiscrimination Rules for 401(k) Plans

Like other qualified plans, a 401(k) plan must not discriminate in favor of highly compensated employees as to plan coverage or as to contributions and benefits (see ¶ 2950A).

Highly compensated employees

An employee is considered highly compensated if he or she:

1. was a more than 5% owner at any time during the current plan year or the preceding plan year, or

2. earned compensation from the employer in excess of $80,000 (adjusted to $115,000 in 2012 (up from $110,000 in 2011)) during the preceding year, and, if the employer so elects, was in the top-paid group (i.e., top 20% of employees by compensation) of employees for the preceding year.[1]

☐ See ¶ 1035 for additional information on highly compensated employees.

Compensation for testing purposes. In determining whether an employee is highly compensated, the definition of compensation under Code Sec. 415(c)(3) applies (see ¶ 1172).[2] In addition to W-2 wages, the Code Sec. 415(c)(3)(C) definition of compensation also includes:

1. elective deferrals to 401(k) plans and other similar arrangements (such as employer contributions under a salary reduction arrangement to purchase a Code Sec. 403(b) annuity and employer contributions to SEPs and SIMPLE 401(k) plans);

2. elective contributions to Code Sec. 457 nonqualified deferred compensation plans; and

3. salary reduction contributions to a cafeteria plan and to a plan for qualified transportation benefits.[3]

Period during which compensation is determined. The period used to determine an employee's compensation for a plan year must be either (1) the plan year or (2) the calendar year ending within the plan year.[4] The period selected must be applied uniformly to determine the compensation of every eligible employee under the plan for that plan year.

Nondiscriminatory plan coverage

In order to satisfy the nondiscrimination in coverage requirement, a 401(k) plan must, *as a condition of qualification*, satisfy minimum coverage rules. A 401(k) plan will automatically satisfy the minimum coverage rules if the plan: allows all of the employer's employees to participate without satisfying age and service conditions; covers only highly compensated employees; benefits only nonhighly compensated employees; or benefits only collectively bargained employees.[5]

Plans that do not automatically satisfy the minimum coverage tests must meet one of the following tests (detailed at ¶ 1050—¶ 1075).[6]

Ratio percentage test. Under the ratio percentage test, the percentage of NHCEs benefiting under the plan (i.e., eligible to make an elective deferral or receive matching contributions) must be at least 70 percent of the percentage of HCEs benefiting under the plan.[7]

Average benefits test. A plan with a ratio percentage under 70 percent may still satisfy the minimum coverage requirement by meeting an average benefits test. Under the average benefit test (1) the plan must benefit those employees who qualify under a classification set up by the employer that is found by the IRS not to be discriminatory in favor of highly compensated employees (nondiscriminatory classification test), and (2) the average benefit percentage for nonhighly compensated employees of the employer must be at least 70 percent of the average benefit percentage for highly compensated employees of the employer (average benefit percentage test).[8]

Excludable employees

Generally, all current and former employees of the employer are taken into account in applying the coverage tests (see ¶ 1020). However, employees who do not meet age and service requirements prescribed by the plan as a condition for plan participation; employees covered by collective bargaining agreements (CBA); nonresident aliens without U.S. source income; airline pilots not covered by a CBA; and certain terminating and former employees may be excluded from the coverage tests.[9] Excludable employees are not taken into account for purposes of the coverage tests, even if they are benefiting under the plan.[10] However, employees who are eligible to make elective contributions are treated as benefiting under the plan, even if they do not actually make contributions (see ¶ 1025).

Plan disaggregation and aggregation

An employer may elect to treat two or more separate plans (with the same plan year) as a single plan for purposes of the ratio percentage test or the nondiscriminatory classification test.[11] However, certain plans must be disaggregated.[12] For example, the 401(k) and 401(m) portions of a plan may not be combined with the rest of the plan.[13] See ¶ 1040—1045.

CCH POINTER: *Aggregation of DB and DC plans.* Defined benefit and defined contribution plans may be aggregated for purposes of satisfying the minimum coverage test of Code Sec. 410(b) and the nondiscrimination test of Code Sec. 401(a)(4). [14] For example, if aggregated plans pass the average benefit percentage test of Code Sec. 410(b), the plans may be aggregated in order to comply with the Code Sec. 401(a)(4) nondiscrimination requirements. However, the requirement of IRS Reg. § 1.410(b)-7(d)(5), that aggregated plans must have the same plan year in order to be treated as a single plan, may prove problematic where, for example, an employer maintains a defined benefit plan with a December 29 plan year and a defined contribution plan with a December 31 plan year. Under such circumstances, the employer could aggregate, based on plan years in same calendar year (i.e., December 29, 2008 and December 31, 2008).

Separate lines of business

An employer that operates qualified separate lines of business (see ¶ 1300) for a year may apply the minimum coverage requirements separately to employees in each separate line of business, unless the plan is tested on an employer-wide basis.[15]

Retroactive correction of coverage defects

Highly compensated employees who participate in a plan that fails to comply with the coverage requirements and, thus, loses qualified status, are subject to tax on their elective deferrals. However, a plan will be treated as complying with the coverage requirements, as of the last day of the plan year if amendments retroactively correcting the coverage defects are adopted by the 15th day of the 10th month following the close of the plan year (e.g., October 15, 2009 for a plan year ending December 31, 2008).[16]

EPCRS correction requires employees to be compensated for missed deferral opportunity. Employers may voluntarily correct the failure to provide employees with the opportunity to make elective deferrals under EPCRS. The prescribed correction method requires the employee to make a QNEC to the plan on behalf of the employee to replace the missed deferral opportunity. The missed deferral opportunity is equal to 50 percent of the employee's missed deferral, determined by multiplying the employee's elected deferral percentage by the employee's compensation. [17]

---

[1] Code Secs. 414(q)(1)(i).

[2] Code Sec. 414(a)(4).

[3] Code Sec. 415(c)(3)(D).

[4] IRS Temporary Reg. § 1.414(q)-1T, Q&A-14.

[5] IRS Reg. § 1.410(b)-2(b)(5)–(7).

[6] Code Secs. 401(k)(3)(A) and 410(b)(1) and (2); IRS Reg. §§ 1.401(k)-1(b)(1) and 1.410(b)-2.

[7] Code Sec. 410(b)(1)(A); IRS Reg. § 1.410(b)-2(b)(2).

[8] Code Sec. 410(b)(2)(A); IRS Reg. § 1.410(b)-4 and 5.

[9] Code Sec. 410(b)(4)(A); IRS Reg. § 1.410(b)-6(a)(1).

[10] IRS Reg. § 1.410(b)-6(a)(1).

[11] Code Sec. 410(b)(6)(B); IRS Reg. § 1.410(b)-7(d)(1).

[12] IRS Reg. § 1.410(b)-7(d)(2).

[13] IRS Reg. § 1.410(b)-7(c)(1).

[14] IRS Reg. § 1.401(c)(4)-1(c)(4) and IRS Reg. § 1.410(b)-7(d)

[15] Code Sec. 410(b)(5)(A).

[16]   IRS   Reg.   §§ 1.401(a)(4)-11(g),   [17] Rev Proc. 2008-50, Appendix A, I.R.B. 2008-35,
1.401(k)-1(b)(1), and 1.410(b)-8(a)(1).   9-2-08 at ¶ 17,299S-66.

¶ 2950A

NONDISCRIMINATION RULES: Nondiscrimination in Benefits and Contributions

A qualified 401(k) plan may not discriminate in favor of highly compensated employees as to benefits or contributions. Basically, a qualified 401(k) plan must satisfy on an annual basis an Actual Deferral Percentage (ADP) test (see ¶ 2951), which compares the rate at which highly compensated employees and nonhighly compensated employees make elective deferrals to the plan. A highly compensated employee is not prohibited from making elective contributions to a plan at a greater rate than nonhighly compensated employees. However, a plan will pass the ADP test only if the average of the actual deferral ratios (i.e., elective contributions for the plan year divided by compensation for the plan year) of highly compensated employees does not exceed the ADP of nonhighly compensated employees by more than a specified percentage. In addition, employer matching contributions and after-tax employee contributions must meet an Actual Contribution Percentage (ACP) test (see ¶ 2952), which is essentially the same as the ADP test that applies to elective deferrals.

> **CCH POINTER:** Plans must specify the nondiscrimination testing method and the optional choices being used under that method. For example, a plan must specify whether the current year or prior year ADP testing method was being used. A plan that uses the safe harbor method must specify whether the safe harbor contribution will be the nonelective safe harbor contribution or the matching safe harbor contribution. In addition, plans that use the safe harbor nondiscrimination method may not reserve the right to use the ADP method in the event that the safe harbor conditions are not met.[1]

Safe harbor alternative

Complying with the ADP and the ACP tests, and implementing the required corrections, may prove to be very difficult for plan sponsors. In order to alleviate this burden, safe harbor alternatives to the ADP test and the employer matching contribution portion of the ACP test have been authorized (see ¶ 2975).

> ***Corrective measures.*** The failure to meet the ADP or the ACP test may not result in disqualification of the plan if stipulated corrective measures are adopted. These corrective mechanisms are discussed at ¶ 2977—2978.

> **CCH POINTER:** Employers that incorporate automatic enrollment provisions into their 401(k) plan will be further able to comply with the ADP and ACP nondiscrimination tests (and avoid the top-heavy rules) by making specified contributions under a "qualified automatic contribution arrangement." Similar to the 401(k) safe harbor under Code Secs. 401(k)(12) and 401(m)(11), a qualified automatic contribution arrangement would provide an additional safe harbor for compliance with the nondiscrimination tests to employers maintain-

ing an eligible automatic enrollment arrangement that provides for a minimum automatic employee contribution and a minimum employer matching or nonelective contribution.[2]

Employers would be required to make a matching contribution on behalf of nonhighly compensated employees equal to 100 percent of elective contributions up to 1 percent of compensation, plus 50 percent of the next 5 percent of compensation deferred (i.e., 2-6 percent of compensation).[3] Alternatively, the employer could make a nonelective contribution, equal to at least 3 percent of compensation, to the 401(k) plan or another defined contribution plan on behalf of each nonhighly compensated employee who is eligible to participate in the plan.[4] However, unlike safe harbor 401(k) plans, which offer immediate vesting, employees would vest in the matching contributions under the automatic enrollment safe harbor after two years of service.

Employers must also comply with an annual notice requirement. The notice must explain the employee's right not to have elective contributions made on his or her behalf or to elect to have contributions made in a different amount.

Availability of benefits, rights, and features

In addition to the satisfying the ADP and the ACP tests, a plan may not discriminate as to the availability of benefits, rights, and features. Benefits, rights, and features include the right of a plan participant to make each rate of elective contributions and after-tax contributions authorized under the plan and the right to receive each level of matching contributions.[5] The benefits, rights, and features must satisfy a dual current availability and an effective availability requirement (see ¶ 1140).

[1] IRS Reg. § 1.401(k)-1(e)(7).

[2] Code Sec. 401(k)(13), as added by P.L. 109-280 (Pension Protection Act of 2006), Act Sec. 902(a).

[3] Code Sec. 401(k)(13)(d)(i)(I), as added by P.L. 109-280 (Pension Protection Act of 2006), Act Sec. 902(a).

[4] Code Sec. 401(k)(13)(D)(i)(II), as added by P.L. 109-280 (Pension Protection Act of 2006), Act Sec. 902(a).

[5] IRS Reg. §§ 1.401(k)-1(a)(4)(iv) and 1.401(m)-1(a)(2).

¶ 2951

NONDISCRIMINATION RULES: Actual Deferral Percentage (ADP) Test

A qualified 401(k) plan must not only be nondiscriminatory on paper but also in actual operation. Accordingly, a plan must be nondiscriminatory with respect to actual deferrals.

CCH POINTER: Satisfaction of the ADP test is a qualification requirement. A 401(k) plan must specifically state that it will meet the requirements of the ADP test.[1] Plans that fail the ADP test risk losing qualified status. However, an employer may adopt corrective measures that will allow the plan to pass the ADP test and remain qualified. See ¶ 2977.

Actual deferral percentage

A plan satisfies the nondiscrimination requirement if the actual deferral percentage (ADP) of highly compensated employees does not exceed the ADP of all other "eligible employees" by more than a specified amount.[2] Note, that a plan in which only HCEs or only NHCEs participate is deemed to satisfy the ADP test.[3]

Eligible employee. An "eligible employee" is an employee who has satisfied the plan's age and service requirements and is authorized to make an elective deferral to the plan, even if the employee elects not to make deferrals or is prohibited from making deferrals because he or she has received a hardship distribution (see ¶ 2989). Once an employee is eligible, the employee remains eligible for the entire plan year and, absent plan amendment, subsequent plan years.

ADP limits. The ADP for a group of eligible HCEs for the current plan year may not be more than 125 percent of the ADP of eligible NHCEs for the preceding plan year (see below). Under an alternative limitation test, the ADP of the group of eligible HCEs for the current plan year may not be more than 2 percentage points higher than the ADP of NHCEs for the preceding plan year and may not be more than 2 times the ADP of NHCEs for the preceding plan year.[4] Thus, under the alternative limitation, if the ADP for NHCEs is 2 percent or less, the ADP for HCEs may be 4 percent. Similarly, if the ADP of the NHCE group is 6 percent, the ADP of the HCE group may not exceed 8 percent (see chart below). By contrast, if the ADP or the NHCE group is over 8 percent, the ADP for the HCE group may not be more than 125 percent of the NHCE ADP. Thus, if the ADP for the NHCE group is 12 percent, the ADP for the HCE group may not exceed 15 percent.

Chart of permissible ADPs for HCEs. The following chart illustrates the range of permissible ADP ratios.

Chart of Permissible ADPs for HCEs

ADP for Non-HCE	ADP for HCE
1	2
2	4
3	5
4	6
5	7
6	8
7	9
8	10
9	11.25
10	12.50
11	13.75
12	15

¶2951

Actual deferral ratio

The ADP for a group of eligible HCEs or NHCEs for the plan year is the average of actual deferral ratios (ADR), calculated to the nearest one-hundredth of a percentage point for each employee in the group.[5] The ADR for an individual employee is equal to the employee's total elective contributions (excluding catch-up contributions (see ¶ 2982)) for the plan year divided by his compensation for the plan year.[6] For example, the ADR of an employee whose compensation is $100,000 and whose elective contributions for year are $6,000 is 6 percent ($6,000 ÷ by $100,000). The ADR of an eligible employee who makes no elective contributions is zero.[7]

Once the individual ADRs have been determined the next step is to determine the average of these individual ADRs (expressed as a percentage) for the group. For example, if there are three HCEs with individual ratios of 5%, 6%, and 7%, the average is 6% (5% + 6% + 7% ÷ 3). This process is repeated for eligible non-HCEs.

> **Example:** June Tek Inc. maintains a 401(k) plan for its employees on a calendar-year basis. Compensation, elective contributions, and individual ADPs for the year were as follows:

Employee	Compensation	Elective contributions	Individual ADP
W. Clauser	$108,000	$9,828	9.1 %
P. Fike	107,000	9,095	8.5
S. Webster	103,000	8,446	8.2
N. Fields	48,000	2,976	6.2
R. Jovin	34,000	1,530	4.5
C. Randum	29,000	1,479	5.1

The highly compensated group consists of Clauser, Fike, and Webster. The average ADP for this group is 8.6% ((9.1% + 8.5% + 8.2%) ÷ 3). The average ADP of the low-paid group (Fields, Jovin, and Randum) is 5.27% ((6.2% + 4.5% + 5.1%) ÷ 3).

Under these facts, the plan fails the ADP test.

> ***Employees eligible under more than one 401(k) plan.*** If a HCE is eligible to participate in more than one 401(k) plan maintained by the same employer, the actual deferral ratio of the employee will be generally calculated by treating (1) all of the employer's 401(k) plans as one plan and (2) all of the contributions with respect to the HCE (including matching and after-tax contributions) as being made under the plan being tested.[8] The ADR of the HCE under each plan would be computed by dividing the employee's total elective contributions under the plan by the employee's compensation.

> **Example:** George earns $120,000 in compensation and is eligible to make elective contributions under two separate 401(k) plans of his employer. During the current plan year, George makes elective deferrals of $7,000 to Plan A and $4,000 to Plan B. His actual deferral ratio under each 401(k) plan is calculated by dividing his total elective contributions under both arrangements by

$120,000. Accordingly, George's ADR under each plan is 8.33% ($11,000/$120,000).

Aggregation restriction. Plans that may not generally be aggregated, such as an ESOP and a 401(k) plan, may not be aggregated for purposes of calculating the actual deferral ratio.

Compensation

Compensation, for purposes of the ADP test, is defined by Code Sec. 414(s).[9] Code Sec. 414(s) allows an employer to select from among four safe harbor definitions of compensation, including traditional Code Sec. 415(c)(3) compensation, modified Code Sec. 415(c)(3) compensation, and W-2 wages (see ¶ 1172). Code Sec. 415(c)(3) compensation also includes elective deferrals.

☐ The annual compensation limit of Code Sec. 401(a)(17) ($250,000 in 2012) (see ¶ 545) applies for purposes of the ADP test.

Use of prior year data

The ADP for highly compensated employees in the current year must generally be compared to the ADP for nonhighly compensated employees for the preceding year.[10] Accordingly, the current year ADP for HCEs is compared to the prior year ADP for NHCEs. The use of prior year data enables a plan sponsor to perform the ADP test before the close of the testing year.

Determine NHCE status as of prior year. The status of a NHCE is determined as of the prior year. Thus, an individual who was a NHCE in the prior year is included in the calculation as a NHCE, even if the individual has become a HCE for the current year or has terminated service with the employer.[11]

Option to use current year data for NHCEs. An employer has the option of electing to use current year ADP data for nonhighly compensated employees.[12] The governing plan document must indicate whether the plan utilizes the current year testing method or the prior year testing method for a testing year. In addition, the plan must be amended by end of the prescribed GUST remedial amendment period (see ¶ 316).[13]

ADP determined without regard to changes in eligible NHCEs. Generally, the ADP for NHCEs for the prior year under a plan is determined without regard to changes in the group of NHCEs who are eligible employees under the plan in the testing year.[14] Accordingly, under the prior year testing method, the prior year ADP for NHCEs may be used even if some NHCEs first become eligible employees in the testing year, and even if individuals who were eligible under the plan and NHCEs in the prior year are no longer employed by the employer or have become HCEs in the testing year.

CCH POINTER: Under Code Sec. 401(k)(3), the actual deferral ratio (ADR) of a highly compensated employee (HCE) who is eligible to participate in two or more CODAs of the same employer is determined by treating all of the plans in which the employee is eligible to participate as one CODA. The ADR for each HCE participating in more than one CODA must be determined by aggregating the elective contributions of the HCE that are made within the plan year of the CODA being tested. The rule is designed to ensure that each of the employer's CODAs will use 12 months of elective contributions and 12 months of compensation in determining the ADR for an HCE who participates in multiple plans, even if the plans have different plan years. Similar rules apply to the determination of the actual contribution ratio under the ACP test for an HCE who receives matching contributions on employee contributions under two or more plans.

Determining ADP for new plan's first year

In the first plan year of a plan (other than a successor plan) that uses the prior year testing method, the ADP of nonhighly compensated employees for the preceding plan year is 3 percent.[15] Alternatively, the employer may elect to actually calculate the ADP for the NHCEs for the first plan year.

Alternative ADP test for early participants

Employers may choose to provide coverage for employees who do not meet the plan's age and service requirements. In the event that such employees are covered, the plan must consider the employees in applying the ADP nondiscrimination test. However, plans may disregard nonhighly compensated employees (but not highly compensated employees) who are eligible to participate in the plan before the satisfaction of the age and service requirements, if the plan, accounting for only those employees, satisfies the minimum coverage rules under Code Sec. 410(b) (see ¶ 1050—1075 and ¶ 2950).[16]

Thus, instead of applying two separate ADP tests for nonhighly compensated employees, a plan may adopt a single ADP test that compares the ADP for highly compensated employees who are eligible to participate with the ADP for nonhighly compensated employees who are eligible to participate and who have met the plan's minimum age and service requirements.

☐ The alternative test will also apply for purposes of the ACP test (see ¶ 2952).[17]

☐ A safe harbor alternative to the ADP test that relieves employers of the need to actually test contributions is discussed at ¶ 2975.

Governmental plans

All governmental plans are treated, effective for years beginning after August 17, 2006, as complying with the ADP test.[18]

[1] Code Sec. 401(k)(3).

[2] Code Sec. 401(k)(3).

[3] IRS Reg. § 1.401(k)-2(a)(1)(ii).

[4] Code Sec. 401(k)(3); IRS Reg. § 1.401(k)-2(a)(1)(i).

[5] IRS Reg. § 1.401(k)-2(a)(3)(i).

[6] Code Sec. 401(k)(3)(B).

[7] IRS Reg. § 1.401(k)-2(a)(3)(i).

[8] Code Sec. 401(k)(3)(A); IRS Reg. § 1.401(k)-2(a)(3)(ii).

[9] Code Sec, 401(k)(9); IRS Reg. § 1.401(k)-6.

[10] Code Sec. 401(k)(3)(A).

[11] IRS Notice 97-2, I.R.B. 1997-2, 1-13-97, CCH Pension Plan Guide ¶ 17,111X.

[12] Code Sec. 401(k)(3)(A).

[13] IRS Notice 98-1, I.R.B. 1998-3, 1-20-98, Sec. IX, CCH Pension Plan Guide ¶ 17,113N-5; Rev. Proc.

2001-55, I.R.B. 2001-49, at CCH Pension Plan Guide ¶ 17,299P-83, modifying Rev. Proc. 2000-27, I.R.B. 2000-20, 6-26-2000, Sec. 4.01, CCH Pension Plan Guide ¶ 17,299P-34.

[14] IRS Notice 98-1, I.R.B. 1998-3, 1-20-98, Sec. VI(A), CCH Pension Plan Guide ¶ 17,113N-5.

[15] Code Sec. 401(k)(3)(E).

[16] Code Sec. 401(k)(3)(F).

[17] Code Sec. 401(m)(5)(C).

[18] Code Sec. 401(k)(3)(G), as amended by P.L. 109-280 (Pension Protection Act of 2006), Act Sec. 861(a)(2).

¶ 2951A

NONDISCRIMINATION RULES: Elective Contributions Taken Into Account

In applying the ADP test, an elective contribution may be taken into account only if it satisfies the following two requirements.[1]

Allocation within plan year

The elective contribution must be allocated to the employee as of a date within the plan year. An elective contribution is considered to be allocated as of a date within the plan year only if:

1. the allocation is not contingent upon the employee's participation in the plan or performance of services on any later date, and

2. the elective contribution is actually paid to the plan no later than the end of the 12-month period immediately following the plan year to which it relates.[2]

The considerably shorter time period within which the DOL requires elective deferrals to be paid to the plan is discussed at ¶ 2948.

Contribution must relate to compensation received in plan year

The elective contribution must relate to compensation that either (1) would have been received by the employee in the plan year but for the employee's deferral election, or (2) is attributable to services performed by the employee during the plan year, and, but for the employee's election to defer, would have been received by the employee within 2½ months after the close of the plan year.[3]

Elective contributions that are not taken into account

Elective contributions that do not satisfy the requirements discussed above may not be taken into account in applying the ADP test for the plan year for which they are made or for any other plan year. Instead, they must satisfy the Code Sec. 401(a)(4) nondiscrimination test (without application of the ADP test) for the plan year for which they are allocated as if they were the only employer contribution for that plan year.[4]

Elective contributions that are not to be taken into account for purposes of the ADP test include the following.

Excess deferrals of NHCEs. Elective contributions of a NHCE do not include excess deferrals, but only if the excess deferrals are prohibited under Code Sec.

401(a)(30). Excess deferrals that are not prohibited under Code Sec. 401(a)(30) will be included in a NHCE's elective contributions, even if distributed.[5]

Catch-up contributions. Elective contributions that are treated as catch-up contributions are not taken into account for purposes of the ADP test for the plan year for which the contributions were made, or for any other plan year.[6]

Contributions by reemployed veterans. Additional elective contributions authorized under Code Sec. 414(u) by veterans returning to employment from military service are not taken into account for purposes of the ADP test for the plan year for which the contributions are made or for any other plan year.[7]

---

[1] IRS Reg. § 1.401(k)-2(a)(4)(i).

[2] IRS Reg. § 1.401(k)-2(a)(4)(i)(A).

[3] IRS Reg. § 1.401(k)-2(a)(4)(i)(B).

[4] IRS Reg. § 1.401(k)-2(a)(5)(i).

[5] IRS Reg. § 1.401(k)-2(a)(5)(ii).

[6] IRS Reg. § 1.401(k)-2(a)(5)(iii).

[7] IRS Reg. § 1.401(k)-2(a)(5)(v).

¶ 2951B

NONDISCRIMINATION RULES: QNECs and QMACs as Elective Contributions

In applying the ADP test, all or any part of qualified nonelective employer contributions (QNECs) and qualified matching employer contributions (QMACs) made to any plan of the employer on behalf of those employees eligible under the 401(k) plan being tested may, at the plan's option, be treated as elective contributions in calculating actual deferral ratios.[1]

CCH POINTER: QNECs and QMACs must satisfy the distribution and vesting requirements imposed on elective contributions. Thus, QNECs and QMACs must be 100 percent vested and must meet the in-service distribution requirements at the time of contribution, regardless of whether they are actually taken into account as elective contributions for purposes of the ADP test (or the ACP test) for the year.[2] Accordingly, a QNEC may not be an unrestricted profit-sharing contribution that is recharacterized as a QNEC merely because it is needed in order for the plan to pass the ADP test (or the ACP test).[3]

Conditions for treating QNECs and QMACs as elective contributions

In determining whether QNECs or QMACs may be considered elective contributions, the following conditions apply.[4]

1. The QNEC or QMAC must be allocated to the NHCE's account no later than the end of the 12-month period immediately following the year to which the contribution relates. Thus, if a plan uses the prior year testing method, a QNEC or QMAC must be contributed no later than the end of the 12-month period immediately following the applicable year, in order to use contributions in calculating ADP for eligible NHCEs even though the applicable year is different than the plan year being

tested.[5] Contributions made later than the specified date may not be used in calculating ADP for eligible NHCEs.

2. The nonelective contributions, including the QNECs treated as elective contributions for ADP purposes, must not discriminate in favor of highly compensated employees.

3. As required by Code Sec. 401(a)(4), nonelective contributions, excluding (a) those QNECs that are treated as elective contributions for ADP purposes and (b) those QNECs that are treated as matching contributions under the ACP test, must not discriminate in favor of highly compensated employees.

4. The plan that includes the 401(k) feature and the plans to which the QNECs and QMACs are made may be aggregated for purposes of the Code Sec. 410(b) coverage tests (other than the average benefit percentage test). If the plan year of the plan that includes the 401(k) arrangement is changed to satisfy the requirement that aggregated plans have the same plan year, the qualified nonelective contributions and the qualified matching contributions may be taken into account in the resulting short plan year only if the contributions could be taken into account under the ADP test for plans with the same short plan year.

QNECs and QMACs may be limited to NHCEs

A plan may limit QNECs or QMACs to NHCEs, or, alternatively, to a select number of NHCEs. However, QNECs and QMACs that are provided exclusively to NHCEs will be discriminatory if they are needed to help other nonelective contributions satisfy the Code Sec. 401(a)(4) nondiscrimination requirements or to help other employee or matching contributions satisfy the ACP test.[6]

Use of QNECs and QMACs in both ADP and ACP tests

QNECs may be used to satisfy the ADP test even if they are also used to satisfy the ACP test. However, if QMACs are considered to be elective contributions in order to meet the ADP test, they may not also be used again to satisfy the ACP test.[7]

Restrictions on bottom-up QNECs. The final rules limit the use of the "bottom-up leveling" technique, pursuant to which employers attempt to pass the ADP test by targeting high percentage QNECs to a small number of part-time, terminated, or other short-service NHCEs with the lowest compensation during the year (raising that NHCE's ADR), rather than providing compensation to a broad group of NHCEs.[8] The bottom-up leveling method enables an employer to pass the ADP test by contributing a small amount of money to select NHCEs, which because the ADP test is based on the unweighted average of ADRs, has the effect of increasing the average contribution for NHCEs.

Permissible targeted contributions. Under the final rules, QNECs may not be taken into account in determining the ADP of an NHCE to the extent the contributions exceed the product of the NHCE's compensation and the greater of

5% or two times the plan's "representative contribution rate." An exception is provided for QNECs made by an employer in order to comply with prevailing wage obligation under the Davis Bacon Act, to the extent contributions do not exceed 10% of the NHCE's compensation.[9]

Note, a QNEC taken into account under the ACP test may not be taken into account in the determination of ADR for purposes of the ADP test (including the determination of the representative contribution rates).

Representative contribution rate. The plan's representative contribution rate is the greater of: (1) the lowest applicable contribution rate of any eligible NHCE among a group of eligible NHCEs that consists of one-half of all eligible NHCEs for the plan year, or (2) the lowest applicable contribution rate of an eligible NHCE in the group of all eligible NHCEs for the plan year and who is employed by the employer on the last day of the plan year.[10]

Applicable contribution rate. The applicable contribution rate for an eligible NHCE is the sum of the qualified matching contributions taken into account in calculating the ADR of a NHCE for the plan year and the QNECs made for the eligible NHCE for the plan year, divided by the eligible NHCE's compensation for the same plan year.[11]

---

[1] IRS Reg. § 1.401(k)-2(a)(6).

[2] IRS Reg. § 1.401(k)-1(g)(13)(i)-(iii).

[3] IRS Announcement 94-101, I.R.B. 1994-35, CCH PENSION PLAN GUIDE ¶ 17,097N-44.

[4] IRS Reg. § 1.401(k)-2(a)(6)(i)-(vi).

[5] IRS Reg. § 1.401(k)-2(a)(6)(i).

[6] IRS Announcement 94-101, I.R.B. 1994-35, CCH PENSION PLAN GUIDE ¶ 17,097N-44.

[7] IRS Reg. § 1.401(k)-2(a)(6).

[8] IRS Reg. § 1.401(k)-2(a)(6)(iv)(A).

[9] IRS Reg. § 1.401(k)-2(a)(6)(iv)(D).

[10] IRS Reg. § 1.401(k)-2(a)(6)(iv)(B).

[11] IRS Reg. § 1.401(k)-2(a)(6)(iv)(C).

¶ 2952

NONDISCRIMINATION RULES: Actual Contribution Percentage (ACP) Test

Employer matching contributions and after-tax employee nonelective contributions to a plan must satisfy an actual contribution percentage (ACP) test.[1] The ACP test is essentially the same as the actual deferral percentage (ADP) test that applies to elective deferrals under a 401(k) plan (see ¶ 2951), except that it is applied to after-tax employee nonelective contributions and employer matching contributions, rather than to elective contributions.

The ACP test is the exclusive method of satisfying Code Sec. 401(a)(4).[2] The plan must specifically provide that the ACP test will be met.[3] The plan must also specify the method by which it will be tested for compliance with the rules of Code Sec. 401(m) and identify the options being used under that method. For example, a plan must indicate whether it will apply the ADP or ACP test or safe harbor rules and must state whether the current year or the prior year testing method is to be used.

Applying the ACP test

Under the ACP test, the "actual contribution percentage" of eligible highly compensated employees (HCEs) for the plan year may not exceed the greater of:

1. 125 percent of the ACP of all eligible nonhighly compensated employees (NHCEs) for the *preceding* plan year; or

2. the lesser of 200 percent of the ACP of eligible NHCEs for the preceding plan year, or the ACP of the NHCEs for the preceding plan year plus two percentage points.[4]

☐ The chart at ¶ 2951 illustrating the maximum ADP for HCEs may also be used to determine the maximum ACP for HCEs.

Actual contribution percentage. The actual contribution percentage for a group of employees for the plan year is the average of the "actual contribution ratios" (ACRs) of the "eligible employees" in the group for that year.[5] Thus, if a company employs three HCEs with individual ACRs of 10%, 6%, and 5%, respectively, the average ratio (or ACP) is 7% (10% plus 6% plus 5%, divided by 3).

The ACR and ACP for the group are calculated to nearest one hundredth of a percentage point.[6]

Actual contribution ratio. An employee's actual contribution ratio is the sum of the after-tax employee and employer matching contributions allocated to the employee's account for the plan year, including qualified nonelective contributions (QNECs) and elective contributions treated as matching contributions for the year (and recharacterized excess contributions), divided by the employee's compensation for the plan year.[7] However, matching contributions under the ADP test are not taken into account for purposes of the ACP test (see below).[8]

ACR may be zero. In the event an eligible employee makes no after-tax employee contributions and no QNECs, or matching or elective contributions are taken into account in applying the ACP test for the employee, the ACR of the employee is zero.

Eligible employees

Only "eligible employees" are taken into consideration under the ACP test. An eligible employee is an employee who is directly or indirectly eligible to make an employee contribution (or an elective deferral, if the employer takes elective deferrals into account) or receive an allocation of matching contributions, including matching contributions derived from forfeitures, under the plan for a plan year.[9] Note, an eligible employee will be included in the ACP test, even if the employee has not made a required employee contribution. However, employees who are eligible to make rollover contributions, but not to receive matching contributions, are not eligible employees for purposes of the ACP test.[10]

Early participants. Employers may choose to provide coverage for employees who do not meet the age and service requirements. In the event that such employees are covered, the plan must generally consider the employees in applying the ACP test. However, plans may disregard nonhighly compensated employees (but not HCEs) who are eligible to participate in the plan before the satisfaction of the age and service requirements, if the plan, accounting for only those employees, satisfies the minimum coverage rules under Code Sec. 410(b).[11]

This rule also applies under the ADP test. See also ¶ 2951.

Compensation

Compensation, for purposes of the ACP test, is defined by Code Sec. 414(s) (see ¶ 1172 and ¶ 2951).[12] The amount of compensation used in determining ACP may not exceed the Code Sec. 401(a)(17) dollar limit ($250,000 in 2012).

After-tax employee contributions

An employee contribution is any mandatory or voluntary contribution to the plan that is treated, at the time of the contribution, as an after-tax employee contribution and that is allocated to a separate account to which attributable earnings and losses are allocated.[13] A contribution is treated as an after-tax employee contribution at the time of contribution if it is reported as taxable income subject to applicable withholding requirements.

Employee contributions do not include designated Roth contributions, loan repayments, rollover contributions, repayment of distributions under Code Sec. 411(a)(7)(C), or employee contributions that are transferred to the plan from another plan.[14]

Matching contributions

A matching contribution is any employer contribution made to a defined contribution plan (including contributions made at the employer's discretion) that is made on account of an employee contribution or an elective deferral (including a catch-up contribution (see ¶ 2982)).[15] Matching contributions also include any forfeiture allocated on the basis of employee contributions, matching contributions, or elective contributions.[16]

In order to be taken into account for a plan year, the matching contribution must be allocated to the employee's account within the year and actually paid to the trust no later than 12 months after the close of the plan year.[17]

Aggregation rules

A plan must generally apply a single ACP test with respect to all employee contributions and matching contributions and all eligible employees under the plan.[18] Thus, if two groups of employees are eligible for matching contributions, all employee contributions and matching contributions under the plan must be subject to a single test, even if different rates of match or other variant features apply.

If two or more plans to which matching contributions, employee contributions, or elective deferrals are made are treated by the employer as one plan for coverage purposes, the plan must also be treated as one plan for ACP testing.[19]

¶2952

Use of previous and current year data

The ACP for highly compensated employees is compared to the ACP for nonhighly compensated employees for the preceding year.[20] Accordingly, the current year ACP for HCEs is compared to the prior year ACP for NHCEs. In making this comparison, the status of a NHCE is determined as of the prior year. Thus, an individual who was a NHCE in the prior year is included in the calculation as a NHCE, even if the individual has become a HCE for the current year or has terminated service with the employer.[21] The prior year's ACP for NHCEs may be calculated as soon as the required data on prior year status, contributions, and compensation become available.

Employer may elect to use current year data. An employer has the option of using current year ACP data for nonhighly compensated employees.[22]

Determining ACP for new plan's first year

In the first plan year of a plan (i.e., first year in which plan provides for employee contributions or matching contributions), other than a successor plan, an employer may treat the ACP of nonhighly compensated employees for the preceding plan year as 3 percent.[23] Alternatively, the employer may elect to actually calculate the ACP for the NHCEs for the first plan year.

ACP determined without regard to changes in eligible NHCEs

Generally, the ACP for NHCEs for the prior year under a plan is determined without regard to changes in the group of NHCEs who are eligible employees under the plan in the testing year.[24] Accordingly, under the prior year testing method, the prior year ACP for NHCEs may be used even though some NHCEs may have first become eligible employees in the testing year.

Collectively bargained plans

A plan established and maintained under a collective bargaining agreement is considered to automatically satisfy the coverage requirements and, thus, is not required to satisfy the ACP test.[25]

Governmental plans

All governmental plans are treated as complying with the ACP test.[26]

Safe harbor alternative to ACP test

A safe harbor alternative to the matching contributions part of the ACP test is available to employers. The safe harbor is discussed at ¶ 2975.

---

[1] Code Sec. 401(m)(1).

[2] IRS Reg. § 1.401(m)-1(a)(1).

[3] IRS Reg. § 1.401(m)-1(b)(2).

[4] Code Sec. 401(m)(2).

[5] IRS Reg. § 1.401(m)-2(a)(2).

[6] *Ibid.*

[7] IRS Reg. § 1.401(m)-2(a)(2) and (3).

[8] IRS Reg. § 1.401(m)-1(b)(4)(ii)(B).

[9] Code Sec. 401(m)(5); IRS Reg. § 1.401(m)-5.

[10] Rev. Rul. 96-48, 1996-2 C.B. 31, CCH PENSION PLAN GUIDE ¶ 19,844.

[11] Code Sec. 401(m)(5)(C).

[12] IRS Reg. § 1.401(m)-5.

[13] IRS Reg. § 1.401(m)-1(f)(6).

[14] IRS Reg. § 1.401(m)-1(a)(3)(ii).

15 Code Sec. 401(m)(4)(A); IRS Reg. § 1.401(m)-1(a)(2).

16 IRS Reg. § 1.401(m)-1(a)(2)(i)(C).

17 IRS Reg. § 1.401(m)-2(a)(4)(iii).

18 IRS Reg. § 1.401(m)-1(b)(4)(ii).

19 Code Sec. 401(m)(2)(B); IRS Reg. § 1.401(m)-1(b)(4)(iii)(A).

20 Code Sec. 401(m)(2)(A).

21 IRS Reg. § 1.401(m)-2(a)(2)(ii).

22 Code Sec. 401(m)(2)(A).

23 Code Sec. 401(m)(3).

24 IRS Notice 98-1, I.R.B. 1998-3, Sec. VI(A), CCH PENSION PLAN GUIDE 17,113N-5.

25 IRS Reg. § 1.401(m)-1(b)(2).

26 Code Sec. 414(d), as amended by P.L. 109-280 (Pension Protection Act of 2006), Act Sec. 906(a)(1).

¶ 2954

NONDISCRIMINATION RULES: Qualified Nonelective Contributions and Elective Contributions Under the ACP Test

A plan may satisfy the ACP test on the basis of total employee contributions and matching contributions alone. However, if the ACP test cannot be satisfied on that basis, the plan has the option, under stipulated conditions, of treating all or any part of QNECs and elective contributions as matching contributions.[1] If the ACP test is met for the employee contributions and matching contributions as so augmented, the plan qualifies under Code Sec. 401(a)(4) as to the amount of employee contributions and matching contributions.

CCH POINTER: QNECs may be used to satisfy the ACP test and ADP test for elective contributions under a 401(k) plan. However, the same QNECs may not be used to satisfy both the ACP and ADP tests.[2]

Required conditions

In order be treated as matching contributions, QNECs and elective contributions must satisfy (to the extent applicable) the following requirements.[3]

1. The QNECs must be allocated to the employee as of a date within the plan year that is not contingent on the employee's participation in the plan or the performance of services subsequent to that date.[4] The QNECs must also actually be paid to the plan within 12 months after the close of the plan year. Thus, in calculating the ACP for a group of eligible NHCEs for the applicable year under the prior year testing method, a QNEC must be contributed no later than the end of the 12-month period following the applicable year. This rule controls even where the applicable year is different than the plan year being tested.

   In addition, the elective contributions must relate to compensation that either would have been received by the employee in the plan year, but for the deferral election, or that is attributable to services performed by the employee in the plan year, and that would have been received by the employee within 2½ months after the close of the plan year, but for the election.[5]

2. The CODA to which the elective contribution is made must satisfy the ADP test. Elective contributions may not be taken into account under the ACP test unless the CODA under which the elective contributions are made is subject to the ADP test and satisfies the test for the plan year or applicable year. Accordingly, elective contributions made to a 403(b) plan or a safe harbor plan may not be taken into account under the ACP test, as such plans are not subject to the ADP test.

3. The nonelective contributions, including QNECs treated as matching contributions for purposes of the ACP test, must satisfy the Code Sec. 401(a)(4) requirement that a plan not discriminate in favor of highly compensated employees.[6] Thus, the QNECs used to pass the ACP test are part of a separate plan for purposes of nondiscrimination testing.

4. The nonelective contributions, excluding QNECs treated as matching contributions for purposes of the ACP test and QNECs treated as elective contributions for purposes of the ADP test, must satisfy the Code Sec. 401(a)(4) rule that a plan not discriminate in favor of HCEs.[7]

5. The plan that takes QNECs and elective contributions into account and the plan to which those contributions are made must be plans that are, or could be, aggregated for purposes of the Code Sec. 410(b) coverage requirements (other than the average benefit percentage test).[8]

Restrictions on targeted QNECs. QNECs may not be taken into account for an applicable year for a NHCE to the extent the contributions exceed the product of the NHCE's compensation and the greater of 5% of compensation and 2 times the plan's representative contribution rate.[9] In addition, QNECs taken into account under the ADP test may not be taken into account for purposes of the ACP test (including the determination of the representative contribution rate).

---

[1] IRS Reg. § 1.401(m)-2(a)(6).

[2] IRS Reg. § 1.401(m)-1(b)(4)(ii)(B).

[3] IRS Reg. § 1.401(m)-2(a)(6).

[4] IRS Reg. § 1.401(m)-2(a)(6)(i).

[5] *Ibid.*

[6] IRS Reg. § 1.401(m)-2(a)(6)(iii).

[7] IRS Reg. § 1.401(m)-2(a)(5)(iii).

[8] IRS Reg. § 1.401(m)-2(a)(6)(iv).

[9] IRS Reg. § 1.401(m)-2(a)(6)(v).

¶ 2955

NONDISCRIMINATION RULES: Use of QNECs and QMACs Under the Prior Year Testing Method

As previously noted at ¶ 2951 and ¶ 2952, plans must generally use prior year data in determining ADP and ACP for NHCEs, while continuing to use current year data for HCEs. A plan, however, may continue to take QNECs and QMACs made in the current year into account in calculating ADP and ACP under the prior year testing method and, thereby, pass the ADP or ACP test.[1]

Contribute QNEC or QMAC by end of testing year

In order to be considered in the calculation of the ACP or ADP for a year under the prior year testing method, a QNEC or QMAC must be allocated within the year and must be paid to the trust no later than the end of the year to which the contribution relates. Thus, under the prior year testing method, in order to be considered in calculating the ACP or ADP for NHCEs for the prior year, the QNEC or QMAC must be contributed by the end of the testing year.[2] For example, if the prior year testing method is used in 2011, QNECs or QMACs that are allocated to the accounts of NHCEs for the 2010 plan year must be contributed to the plan by the end of the 2011 plan year in order to be treated as elective contributions for the ADP test for the 2011 testing year. By contrast, a plan using the current year testing method would not be required to contribute the QNECs or QMACs to the accounts of NHCEs until the end of the 2012 plan year in order to factor them into the determination of the NHCEs' ADP or ACP for 2011.

Changing from current year to prior year testing method

Once an employer elects to use the current year testing method (see ¶ 2951 and ¶ 2952) its ability to change that election is limited. However, a plan may change from the current year testing method to the prior year testing method without notifying the IRS under any of the following circumstances.[3]

1. The plan is not the product of the aggregation of two or more plans, and the current year testing method was used for either (a) each of the five plan years preceding the plan year of the change or (b) if lesser, the number of plan years the plan has been in existence, including years in which the plan was part of another plan.

2. The plan is the product of the aggregation of two or more plans, and each of the plans being aggregated used the current year testing method for either (a) each of the five plan years preceding the plan year of change, or (b) if lesser, the number of plan years that the aggregating plan has been in existence, including years in which the aggregating plan was part of another plan.

3. As the result of the acquisition or disposition under Code Sec. 410(b)(6)(C)(i) and IRS Reg. §1.410(b)-2(f), the employer maintains a plan using the prior year testing method and a plan using the current year testing method; and the change from the current year testing method to the prior year testing method occurs within the Code Sec. 416(b)(6)(C)(ii) transition period (i.e., the period beginning on the date of the change in the members of a group and ending on the last day of the first plan year beginning after the date of the change).

4. The change in testing method occurs during the plan's GUST remedial amendment period (see ¶ 316).

¶2955

Plan amendment required. In the event an employer changes the testing method, the plan must be amended, within the applicable remedial amendment period, to reflect the change.[4]

[1] IRS Notice 98-1, I.R.B. 1998-3, 1-20-98, Sec. IV, CCH Pension Plan Guide ¶ 17,113N-5.

[2] IRS Notice 98-1, I.R.B. 1998-3, 1-20-98, Sec. IV(A), CCH Pension Plan Guide ¶ 17,113N-5.

[3] IRS Notice 98-1, I.R.B. 1998-3, 1-20-98, Sec. VII(A), CCH Pension Plan Guide ¶ 17,113N-5.

[4] IRS Notice 98-1, I.R.B. 1998-3, 1-20-98, Sec. IX, CCH Pension Plan Guide ¶ 17,113N-5.

¶ 2966

NONDISCRIMINATION RULES: Plan Aggregation

Various aggregation rules are used in applying Code Sec. 401(k) and 401(m) and the special nondiscrimination rules applicable to 401(k) plans.

Two or more 401(k) plans included in a plan

Generally, all 401(k) plans included in a plan are treated as a single 401(k) plan. For example, if two groups of employees are eligible for separate 401(k) plans under the same plan, the two 401(k) plans are treated as a single 401(k) plan, even if they have significantly different features such as greatly different limits on elective contributions.[1]

Aggregation of plans

Plans that are aggregated for purposes of the Code Sec. 410(b) coverage requirements (other than for purposes of satisfying the average benefit percentage test) are treated as a single plan for purposes of the actual deferral percentage, actual contribution percentage, and multiple use (see ¶ 2976) tests, as well as other Code Sec. 401(k) and 401(m) rules.[2]

☐ The mandatory disaggregation rules and the permissive aggregation rules under Code Sec. 410(b) (see ¶ 2950) also apply for purposes of the ADP and ACP tests.

Exception for union employees. A plan that covers employees covered by a collective bargaining agreement and employees not covered by the agreement is treated as comprising separate plans.[3] However, an employer may treat union employees covered by separate collective bargaining agreements separately or as members of single collective bargaining unit.

Special disaggregation rule. An employer may not restructure a plan, and thereby apply the ADP and ACP test, on an employee group basis. However, an employer may separately test the portion of a plan benefiting employees who have not satisfied the greatest minimum age and service requirements permitted under Code Sec. 410(a) (i.e., completion of one year of service and attainment of age 21). Accordingly, a plan may separately test these "otherwise excludable" employees under the ADP or ACP test without violating the prohibition on restructuring because this separate testing does not constitute restructuring. Thus, an employer may treat a plan that benefits employees including otherwise includable employees as two separate plans (one for the otherwise excludable employees and one for other eligible employees).[4]

---

[1] IRS Reg. § 1.401(k)-1(b)(4)(i).

[2] Code Sec. 401(k)(3)(A).

[3] IRS Reg. § 1.401(k)-1(b)(4)(v)(B).

[4] IRS Reg. §§ 1.401(k)-1(b)(4)(iv)(a) and 1.401(m)-1(b)(4)(iv)(A)

¶ 2975

NONDISCRIMINATION RULES: Safe Harbor Alternatives to ADP and ACP Tests

Safe harbor alternatives to the ADP test and the employer matching contributions part of the ACP test enable a 401(k) plan to automatically pass the tests as long as stipulated notice and contributions requirements are met during the *entire plan year.*[1]

The adoption of the design-based safe harbors eliminates the need to actually test some plan contributions. However, employers are not required to adopt the safe harbors or to use a safe harbor for a minimum number of years.

CCH POINTER: Plans that satisfy the safe harbor rules detailed below will not be considered top heavy (see ¶ 905).

ADP test safe harbor

Under the safe harbor alternative to the ADP test, a plan must make either:

1. a nonelective contribution to a defined contribution plan on behalf of a nonhighly compensated employee (NHCE), or

2. a stipulated matching contribution to each NHCE.[2]

The nonelective or matching contribution must be made pursuant to plan terms and the employer must reveal, prior to the beginning of the plan year, the contribution that will be made. Thus, matching contributions, for purposes of the safe harbor, may not be made at the employer's discretion.[3]

The type of contribution specified in the plan may not be changed mid-year. In the event an employer elects to change the 3 percent nonelective contribution, the plan must be amended prior to the first day of the plan year in which the safe harbor will be effective.

An employer may reserve the right to decide whether to make a nonelective contribution (by adopting a plan amendment) for up to 30 days before the end of the plan year.[4] Employees must be provided with: (1) an initial notice informing them that the plan may be amended to allow for the nonelective contribution and, (2) a supplemental notice (30 days prior to the last day of the plan year) informing them of amendment authorizing the contribution.

Nonelective contribution. The nonelective contribution to the defined contribution plan must equal at least 3 percent of the compensation of the NHCE eligible to participate in the plan.[5] The contribution must be made whether or not the employee actually makes elective contributions under the plan.

Matching contributions. The required safe harbor contribution may be determined under a basic matching formula or an enhanced matching formula.[6]

Basic contribution formula. The "basic" matching contribution safe harbor requires an employer to make a matching contribution on behalf of each eligible NHCE who makes elective deferrals to the plan equal to:

1. 100 percent of the employee's elective contributions, up to 3 percent of the employee's compensation, *and*

2. 50 percent of the employee's elective contributions that exceed 3 percent, but that are not more than 5 percent, of the employee's compensation.[7]

Alternative "enhanced" matching contribution option. In the event that the rate of a matching contribution, at any rate of elective contribution, does not meet the specified percentages discussed above, a plan will still satisfy the matching contribution requirement of the safe harbor if:

1. the rate of the employer's matching contribution does not increase as the employee's rate of elective contributions increases, and

2. the aggregate amount of matching contributions, at that rate of elective contribution, at least equals the aggregate amount of matching contributions that would have been provided under the basic matching formula.[8]

CCH POINTER: The safe harbor nonelective and matching contributions under the basic or enhanced matching contribution formula may not be restricted to employees who are still employed on the date that the contributions are allocated (i.e. "last day rule") or that work a specified number of hours (e.g., 1000 hours) during the plan year.

Compensation for purposes of the safe harbor contribution. A uniform and nondiscriminatory definition of compensation must be used in determining the amount of the safe harbor contributions. Basically, the definition of compensation set forth in IRS Reg. § 1.401(k)-6, which incorporates the rules of Code Sec. 414(s). A plan may not, for purposes of the safe harbor contribution, exclude compensation earned by a nonhighly compensated employee in excess of a stipulated dollar amount, as is generally permitted under IRS Reg. § 1.414(s)-1(d)(2)(iii).[9] However, compensation in excess of the Code Sec. 401(a)(17) annual compensation limit is not factored into the safe harbor calculation.

Compensation earned by employee prior to plan eligibility may be ignored. An employer may limit the period used to determine compensation for any year to the portion of the plan year in which an employee is eligible to make deferrals, as long as the restriction is applied uniformly to all eligible employees under the plan for the plan year. Thus, compensation earned by employees before they begin participating in the plan by making elective deferrals need not be considered in determining the amount of a safe harbor contribution.[10]

¶2975

Elective deferrals, bonuses, overtime pay. A plan may exclude bonus or overtime pay or elective deferrals in evaluating compensation for purposes of calculating the amount of the safe harbor contribution.[11] However, as noted below, a plan may not impose limits on the type of compensation or the amount of elective contributions that prevent an eligible NHCE from making contributions sufficient to receive the maximum amount of matching contributions available under the plan.

Restrictions on elective contributions by NHCEs. Elective contributions by NHCEs may be subject to restrictions regarding the frequency and duration of cash or deferred election periods, the amount of elective contributions, and types of compensation that may be deferred. [12]

Nonelective and matching contributions are nonforfeitable

Employer matching and nonelective contributions that are used to satisfy the contribution requirements of the safe harbor (unlike traditional matching contributions) are nonforfeitable.[13] However, the contributions are subject to the restrictions that apply under Code Sec. 401(k)(2)(B) and (C) to withdrawals of an employee's elective deferrals (see discussion beginning at ¶ 2989).

Restrictions on in-service withdrawals. Matching and nonelective contributions are subject to the restrictions on in-service withdrawals of an employee's elective deferrals that apply under Code Sec. 401(k)(2)(B). Thus, safe harbor contributions may not be distributed prior to a participant's retirement, death, disability, separation from service, attainment of age 59½ , or the occurrence of a plan termination or other event stipulated by the IRS.

Employees must receive advance notice of rights

The ADP (or ACP) safe harbor may not be adopted unless the employer provides advance written notice to all employees who are eligible to participate in the plan of their rights and obligations under the plan.[14] The notice, which must be provided within a reasonable period (generally within 90 days) before the beginning of **each** plan year, must be: (a) sufficiently accurate and comprehensive to inform employees of their rights and obligations and (b) written in a manner calculated to be understood by the average employee eligible to participate in the plan.

Notice provided through electronic media. The IRS will allow the safe harbor notice to be provided to an employee through an electronic medium that is reasonably accessible to the employee.[15] However, at the time the electronic notice is provided, an employee must be advised that he or she may request and receive the notice on a written paper document at no charge.

Rules governing electronic transmission of notice. Final rules issued by the IRS in October 2006, applicable to notices provided on or after January 1, 2007, could allow for the electronic transmission of the safe harbor notice under Code Sec. 401(k)(12) and 401(m)(11).[16]

Under the prescribed rules, the electronic system must:

1. be reasonably designed to provide the information to a recipient in a manner that is not less understandable to the recipient than a written paper document; and

2. be designed to alert the recipient, at the time the notice is provided, to the significance of the information in the notice (including identification of the subject matter of the notice) and provide any instructions needed to access the notice in a manner that is readily understandable.

Notice deemed timely if provided 30-90 days before beginning of the plan year. According to the IRS, notice will be deemed to have been provided within a reasonable period of time if it is furnished to each eligible employee for the plan year at least 30 days (and no more than 90 days) before the beginning of each plan year.[17] If an employee does not become eligible to participate in the plan until after the 90th day before the beginning of the plan year, the notice will be deemed timely if it is provided no more than 90 days before the employee becomes eligible (and no later than the date that the employee becomes eligible).[18]

ACP test safe harbor

Under the ACP test safe harbor, a plan is treated as satisfying the ACP test with respect to employer matching contributions if, for the entire plan year, (1) each NHCE eligible to receive an allocation of matching contributions is also an eligible employee under a 401(k) plans that satisfies the ADP test safe harbor and (2) the plan satisfies matching contribution limitations under a basic matching, enhanced matching, or other matching contribution formula.[19] The employer must also satisfy the notice requirements of Code Sec. 401(k)(12)(D) (see above).

Basic matching formula. A plan meets the matching contribution limits if: (1) the plan satisfies the matching contribution requirement of the ADP test safe harbor using the basic matching formula and (2) no other matching contributions are provided under the plan.[20]

Enhanced matching formula. A plan satisfies the matching contribution limits if (1) the plan meets the matching contribution requirement of the ADP test safe harbor, using an enhanced matching formula under which matching contributions are made only with respect to elective deferrals that do not exceed 6 percent of the employee's compensation, and (2) no other matching contributions are provided under the plan.[21] The plan may not condition the contributions on satisfaction of a last day or minimum hours of service requirement.

Other matching contribution formula. The matching contribution limits of the safe harbor may be made under any other matching formula, if under the terms of the plan, the following requirements are met.

1. *6 percent limit on additional matching contributions.* Matching contributions with respect to after-tax employee contributions or elective deferrals do not exceed 6 percent of the employee's compensation.[22] Thus, if a matching contribution applies to elective deferrals in excess of 6% of pay (or to elective deferrals

and after-tax contributions in excess of 6% of pay), the ACP test must be performed.

4 percent limit on discretionary matching contributions. Note, plans may not, under the ACP test safe harbor, authorize an employer to make a discretionary matching contribution on behalf of any employee that would, in the aggregate, exceed 4 percent of the employee's compensation.[23]

2. *Rate of matching contribution may not increase with rate of elective deferral.* The rate of an employer's matching contribution does not increase as the rate of an employee's after-tax contributions or elective deferrals increases.[24]

3. *Matching contributions may not be greater for HCEs.* The rate of matching contributions for eligible HCEs, at any rate of after-tax employee contributions or elective deferrals is not greater than the rate of matching contributions for eligible NHCEs who have the same rate of employee contributions or elective deferrals.[25]

The final regulations retain the limitation on the rate of the matching contribution, but provide that the "ratio" of matching contributions for an HCE to the HCE's elective deferrals and/or employee contributions for the plan year may not be greater than the "ratio" of matching contributions to elective deferrals and/or employee contributions that would apply to NHCEs for whom the elective deferrals or employee contributions are the same percentage of compensation.[26]

Matching contributions on aggregate elective deferrals and after-tax contributions. A safe harbor plan may authorize matching contributions on both elective deferrals and after-tax employee contributions. However, the plan must state that the matching contributions made on an employee's elective deferrals may not be affected by the amount of the employee's after-tax contributions. Alternatively the plan must require that matching contributions be made with respect to the sum of an employee's elective deferrals and after-tax contributions under the same terms that apply to matching contributions made with respect to elective contributions.[27]

Matching contributions may be provided separately for each payroll period. Plans are authorized to provide matching contributions separately for each payroll period (or for all payroll periods ending with or within each month or quarter of a plan year) taken into account under the plan for the plan year.[28] However, matching contributions with respect to elective deferrals or employee contributions made during a plan year quarter must be contributed to the plan by the last day of the immediately following plan year quarter.

ACP safe harbor does not apply to after-tax employee contributions. A plan that satisfies the ACP test safe harbor with respect to matching contributions remains subject to a modified ACP test for after-tax employee contributions made under the plan.[29] The modified ACP test also applies to a plan that meets the safe harbor requirement of the ADP safe harbor, but fails to meet the ACP test safe harbor for matching contributions.

Modified ACP test. Generally, plans subject to the ACP test must satisfy the test using the current year testing method.[30] However, an employer may elect to disregard, for all eligible employees: (1) all matching contributions (if the ACP test safe harbor is satisfied); or (2) matching contributions up to 4 percent of each employee's compensation (if the matching contribution requirement of the ADP test safe harbor is met).

In addition, in applying the ACP test, (a) matching contributions may not be treated as elective contributions to a CODA that satisfies the ADP test safe harbor (and is, thus, excluded from the ACP test under Code Sec. 401(m)(3)) and (b) elective contributions under a CODA that meets the ADP test safe harbor may not be treated as matching contributions under Code Sec. 401(m)(3).[31] However, QNECs may generally be treated as matching contributions, to the extent permitted under IRS Reg. § 1.401(m)-1(b)(5) (see ¶ 2954).

Time for making matching and nonelective contributions

Matching and nonelective contributions required to be made under the safe harbor rules must be made to the plan no later than 12 months after the close of the plan year. Thus, the contributions must be made to the plan within the same period that would apply if the contributions were made to a plan using the current year testing method for purposes of the ADP or ACP test.[32]

Contributions may be based on compensation for payroll period. The safe harbor contributions may be made throughout the plan year, instead of at one time after the close of the plan year.[33] In addition, 401(k) safe harbor plans may authorize the contributions to be based on compensation for a payroll period.[34] The "payroll period method" relieves employers of the need to make additional contributions at the end of the year to account for an employee's total amount of compensation for the plan year.

Contributions may not be used as QNECs or QMACs

Matching contributions and nonelective contributions that are made in order to pass the ADP test safe harbor may not be used as QMACs and QNECs under any plan for any plan year.[35]

Safe harbor contributions to other defined contribution plans

Safe harbor matching or nonelective contributions may be made to the plan that contains the CODA or to another qualified defined contribution plan.[36] In the event that safe harbor contributions are made to another defined contribution plan, the contribution requirements of the ADP test safe harbor must be met in the same manner as if the contributions were made to the plan containing the CODA. In addition, safe harbor contributions may generally not be made to another defined contribution plan unless that plan has the same plan year as the plan containing the CODA.[37]

¶ 2975

The final regulations further require that, if safe harbor contributions are made to another defined contribution plan, the safe harbor plan must specify the plan to which the contributions are to be made.[38] In addition, while confirming that the plan to which contributions are made must have the same plan year as the plan containing the cash or deferred arrangement, the final rules note that the plan to which the safe harbor contributions are made need not be a plan that can be aggregated with the plan that contains the CODA.

Plan aggregation rules

Under the plan aggregation rules (see ¶ 2966), all CODAs included in a plan are treated as a single CODA that must satisfy the contribution and notice requirements of the ADP test safe harbor.[39] Two plans that are treated as a single plan under the permissive aggregation rules are also treated as a single plan for purposes of the safe harbor.

Exception for plans providing for early participation. In the event that an employer applies the coverage rules of Code Sec. 410(b) separately to a portion of the plan that benefits only employees who satisfy age and service conditions that are lower than the maximum age and service conditions permitted under Code Sec. 410(a), (i.e., age 21 and one year of service) the plan is treated as two separate plans, and the ADP test safe harbor need not be satisfied for both plans in order for one plan to use the ADP safe harbor.[40] Thus, a plan that uses one of the 401(k) safe harbor methods is not required to provide safe harbor matching or nonelective contributions to participants who have not yet attained age 21 and completed one year of service. However, in addition to authorizing the exception to the safe harbor contribution, the plan must specifically provide that elective contributions and matching contributions made on behalf of those employees that the employer has elected to treat separately for coverage purposes must satisfy the ADP and ACP tests.[41]

Aggregating contributions for highly compensated employees

Elective or matching contributions made on behalf of a highly compensated employee who is eligible to participate in more than one plan of the same employer providing such contributions must generally be aggregated and treated as if made under each of the plans, even if one or more of the plans is intended to satisfy the ADP or ACP test safe harbor.[42] Application of this rule could prevent satisfaction of the safe harbor requirements.

CCH POINTER: The final rules do not require that elective or matching contributions on behalf of an HCE who is eligible to participate in more than one plan of the same employer be aggregated for purposes of the ADP safe harbor.

Plan year may not be less than 12 months

A plan will not generally satisfy the ADP or ACP test safe harbors for a plan year unless the plan year is at least 12 months long.[43] In addition, the final rules emphasize that the safe harbor provisions of the plan must be adopted before the first day of the plan year and remain in effect for the entire 12 month plan year (see below).[44]

Initial plan year may be less than 12 months. A newly established plan (other than a successor plan) may have a plan year that is less than 12 months long.[45] The plan year must be at least 3 months long. However, the plan year may be less than 3 months long if the plan is established by a new employer as soon as is administratively feasible after the plan comes into existence.

Addition of safe harbor to existing profit-sharing plan. A CODA that is added to an existing profit-sharing, stock bonus, or pre-ERISA money purchase pension plan for the first time during a plan year may adopt a 401(k) safe harbor method for that plan year, if: (1) the plan is not a successor plan; (2) the CODA is effective no later than three months prior to the end of the plan year; and (3) the safe harbor requirements are otherwise satisfied for the entire period from the effective date of the CODA (including retroactive effective dates) to the end of the plan year.[46] Accordingly, an existing calendar year profit-sharing plan that does not contain a CODA may be amended as late as October 1 to add a CODA that utilizes a 401(k) safe harbor method for that plan year. The final regulations incorporate the provisions of Notice 2000-3, governing the addition of a CODA to an existing plan. However, the final rules do not expressly include condition (3).[47]

Reduction or suspension of safe harbor contributions. A plan using the safe harbor matching contribution method may be amended during the plan year to reduce or eliminate matching contributions on future elective and employee contributions during the plan year, and instead use current year ADP and ACP (if applicable) nondiscrimination testing for the plan year. [48] In addition to other requirements, the employer must provide employees with a written notice of the suspension of matching contributions.

Termination of safe harbor plans. A safe harbor plan must generally satisfy the requirements of Code Sec. 401(k)(12) and Code Sec. 401(m)(11) and the governing regulations for an entire 12 month plan year. However, the final rules authorize the termination of a safe harbor plan during the plan year (i.e., before the expiration of the 12 month period). The plan would be able to remain a safe harbor arrangement for the year of termination if it: (1) satisfied the governing rules through the date of termination and (2) was terminated in connection with a merger or acquisition under Code Sec. 410(b)(6)(C) or in response to a substantial business hardship incurred by the employer.[49] A safe harbor plan could also be terminated for other reasons as long as the plan satisfied the ADP test for the entire plan year and the employer satisfied the applicable funding obligations through the date of termination, among other conditions.

CCH POINTER: *Proposed Rules Would Allow for Reduction or Suspension of Safe Harbor Nonelective Contributions.* An employer, under current rules, is not (short of terminating the plan) allowed to reduce or suspend the safe harbor nonelective contribution during the plan year. An employer that reduces or suspends the nonelective contribution risks the disqualification of the plan. However, the IRS has issued proposed regulations that would allow employers sponsoring a safe harbor 401(k) plan, including a qualified automatic contribution arrangement (QACA) under Code Sec. 413 (see ¶ 2976) to reduce or suspend required nonelective contributions, in the event they have incurred a "substantial business hardship" during the plan year. [50] In addition, taxpayers may rely on the proposed regulations for guidance pending the issuance of the final regulations.

Requirements for reducing safe harbor nonelective contributions under proposed rules. The proposed rules would allow for the reduction or suspension of safe harbor nonelective contributions, including those under a QACA, in accordance with the following conditions.

1. The employer incurs a "substantial business hardship." Factors contributing to a determination of substantial business hardship would, under Code Sec. 412(c), include whether: the employer is operating at an economic loss, there is substantial unemployment or underemployment in the employer's trade or business and in the industry; the sales and profits of the industry are depressed or declining; and it is reasonable to expect that the plan will be continued only if the relief is granted. It is important to understand that the determination of substantial business hardship is not made by the IRS (absent an audit), but by the plan fiduciary.

Note, the requirement that an employer incur a substantial business hardship does not apply to the reduction or suspension of safe harbor matching contributions.

2. The amendment implementing the reduction or suspension must be adopted after May 18, 2009.

3. All eligible employees are provided a supplemental notice of the reduction or suspension of the contributions (see below).

4. The reduction or suspension of the nonelective contributions is effective no earlier than the later of 30 days after eligible employees are provided the supplemental notice and the date the amendment is adopted.

5. Eligible employees are given a reasonable opportunity (including a reasonable opportunity after receipt of the supplemental notice), prior to the reduction or suspension of the safe harbor nonelective contributions, to change their cash or deferred elections (and after-tax contributions, if applicable).

6. The plan is amended to provide that the ADP (or ACP test, if applicable) will be satisfied for the entire plan year in which the reduction or suspension occurs, using the current year testing method (i.e., using current plan year participant salary deferrals and matching contributions).

7. The plan satisfies the safe harbor nonelective contribution requirement with respect to safe harbor compensation paid through the effective date of the amendment reducing or suspending the contributions.

Supplemental notice. The supplemental notice would need to explain: (1) the consequences of the amendment reducing or suspending future safe harbor nonelective contributions; (2) the procedures for changing cash or deferred elections and employee contribution elections (if applicable); and (3) the effective date of the amendment.

Note, the proposed rules do not require the notice to describe the allocation of profit-sharing contributions or to set forth a vesting schedule.

Factors to consider in reducing safe harbor nonelective contributions. The proposed rules would allow an employer to reduce or suspend safe harbor nonelective contributions without terminating the plan. However, in addition to the conditions specified above, employers need to consider the following factors in exercising the relief.

1. An employer may not reduce or suspend safe harbor contributions during a year by adopting the amendment at the end of the plan year. The reduction may not be effective earlier than 30 days after the notice is provided to all eligible employees and the date the amendment is adopted.

2. A plan that is amended during the year to reduce or suspend nonelective or matching contributions must prorate the applicable Code Sec. 401(a)(17) compensation limit.

3. The plan, as amended to reduce or suspend safe harbor contributions, is subject to the top heavy rules of Code Sec. 416 and the possible requirement to make a 3 percent minimum contribution for all participants employed on the last day of the plan year.

Effect of reduction or suspension of nonelective contribution. Once the nonelective contribution is reduced or suspended, the plan is no longer a safe harbor plan and must run the ADP test on a current year basis. In the event the plan fails the test, the plan may need to refund deferrals to HCEs.

Plan must adopt safe harbor before plan year

A plan sponsor must generally adopt the safe harbor before the first day of the plan year.[51]

Employers may delay adoption of nonelective contribution safe harbor until December 1 of the calendar year. An employer that sponsors an existing 401(k) plan that uses the current year ADP or ACP testing method may reserve the right, in the initial notice provided to employees, to amend the plan to adopt the safe harbor nonelective contribution method for the plan year.[52] The plan sponsor must, no later than 30 days before the end of the plan year (December 1 for calendar year plans) (1) amend the plan to adopt the safe harbor nonelective contribution method and (2) provide all eligible employees with a supplemental notice stating that a 3 percent safe harbor nonelective contribution is to be made for the plan year. In addition, the plan must otherwise satisfy the ADP and or ACP safe harbor for the plan year, including the applicable notice requirements.

Notice requirements. The safe harbor notice that is provided to employees within a reasonable period of time before the beginning of the plan year need not state the amount of the safe harbor nonelective contribution to be made under the plan. However, the notice must provide that (1) the plan may be amended during the plan year to allow the employer to make a safe harbor nonelective contribution of at least 3 percent to the plan for the plan year, and (2) if the plan is so amended, a supplemental notice will be provided to eligible employees 30 days prior to the last day of the plan year informing them of the amendment.[53] Note, the final rules incorporate the existing notice requirements. However, the final rules refer to the initial notice as a "contingent notice."

Supplemental notice. The supplemental notice must be provided to all eligible employees no later than 30 days prior to the last day of the plan year (i.e., December 1 for calendar year plans), and must state that a 3 percent safe harbor nonelective contribution will be made for the plan year. The supplemental notice may be provided separately, or as part of the safe harbor notice for the following plan year.

The final rules refer to the supplemental notice as a "follow-up" notice.[54] The follow up notice may be provided in writing or in such other form as may be prescribed by the Commissioner (e.g., electronically). In addition, the final rules, consistent with IRS Notice 2000-3, allow the follow up notice to be combined with the content notice for the next plan year.

[1] Code Secs. 401(k)(12) and 401(m)(11); IRS Reg. §§ 1.401(k)-3 and 1.401(m)-3.

[2] Code Sec. 401(k)(12)(A); IRS Reg. § 1.401(k)-3(b).

[3] IRS Notice 98-52, Sec. VI.B.4, I.R.B. 1998-46, 11-16-98, CCH Pension Plan Guide ¶ 17,115B.

[4] IRS Reg. § 1.401(k)-3(f).

[5] Code Sec. 401(k)(12)(C); IRS Notice 98-52, Sec. V.B.2, I.R.B. 1998-46, 11-16-98, CCH Pension Plan Guide ¶ 17,115B.

[6] IRS Reg. § 1.401(k)-3(c)(1).

[7] Code Sec. 401(k)(12)(B)(i); IRS Reg. § 1.401(k)-3(c)(2); IRS Notice 98-52, Sec. V.B.1(a)(i), I.R.B. 1998-46, 11-16-98, CCH Pension Plan Guide ¶ 17,115B.

[8] Code Sec. 401(k)(12)(B)(iii); IRS Reg. § 1.401(k)-3(b)(3); IRS Notice 98-52, Sec. V.B.1(a)(ii), I.R.B. 1998-46, 11-16-98, CCH Pension Plan Guide ¶ 17,115B.

[9] IRS Notice 98-52, Sec. IV.B at CCH Pension Plan Guide ¶ 17,115B; IRS Reg. § 1.401(k)-3(b)(2).

[10] IRS Reg. § 1.401(k)-3(b).

[11] IRS Reg. § 1.414(s)-1(d)(2).

[12] IRS Notice 98-52, Sec. V.B.1(c), I.R.B. 1998-46, 11-16-98, at CCH Pension Plan Guide ¶ 17,115B; IRS Reg. § 1.401(k)-3(c)(6).

[13] Code Sec. 401(k)(12)(E)(i).

[14] Code Secs. 401(k)(12)(D) and 401(m)(11)(A); IRS Reg. § 1.401(k)-3(d).

[15] IRS Notice 2000-3, Sec. III, Q&A-7, I.R.B. 2000-3, 1-24-2000, CCH Pension Plan Guide ¶ 17,117R.

[16] IRS Reg. § 1.401(a)-21.

[17] IRS Notice 98-52, Sec. V.C.2(b), I.R.B. 1998-46, 11-16-98, CCH Pension Plan Guide ¶ 17,115B; IRS Reg. § 1.401(k)-3(d)(3).

[18] *Ibid.*

[19] Code Sec. 401(m)(11); IRS Reg. § 1.401(m)-3(c) and (d); IRS Notice 98-52, Secs. I and VI, I.R.B. 1998-46, 11-16-98, CCH Pension Plan Guide ¶ 17,115B.

[20] IRS Notice 98-52, Sec. VI.B.1, I.R.B. 1998-46, at CCH Pension Plan Guide ¶ 17,115B; IRS Reg. § 1.401(m)-3(b).

[21] IRS Notice 98-52, Sec. VI.B.2, I.R.B. 1998-46, at CCH Pension Plan Guide ¶ 17,115B; IRS Reg. § 1.401(m)-3(d).

[22] Code Sec. 401(m)(11)(B)(i); IRS Notice 98-52, Sec. VI.B.3, I.R.B. 1998-46, at CCH Pension Plan Guide ¶ 17,115B.

[23] IRS Notice 98-52, Sec. VI.B.4(b), I.R.B. 1998-46, at CCH Pension Plan Guide ¶ 17,115B; IRS Reg. § 1.401(m)-3(d).

[24] Code Sec. 401(m)(11)(B)(ii); IRS Reg. § 1.401(m)-3(d)(2).

[25] Code Sec. 401(m)(11)(B)(iii); IRS Notice 98-52, Sec. VI.B.3, I.R.B. 1998-46, at CCH Pension Plan Guide ¶ 17,115B.

[26] IRS Reg. § 1.401(m)-3(d)(4).

[27] IRS Notice 2000-3, Sec. III, Q&A-5, I.R.B. 2000-3, at CCH Pension Plan Guide ¶ 17,117R.

[28] IRS Reg. § 1.401(m)-3(d)(4).

[29] IRS Notice 98-52, Sec. VIII.F, I.R.B. 1998-46, 11-16-98, CCH Pension Plan Guide ¶ 17,115B; IRS Reg. § 1.401(m)-3(j)(6).

[30] IRS Notice 98-52, Sec. VIII.F.3, I.R.B. 1998-46, 11-16-98, CCH Pension Plan Guide ¶ 17,115B.

¶2975

[31] *Ibid.*

[32] IRS Notice 98-52, Sec. VII.A, I.R.B. 1998-46, 11-16-98, CCH PENSION PLAN GUIDE ¶ 17,115B; IRS Reg. § 1.401(k)-3(h); IRS Reg. § 1.401(m)-3(j).

[33] *Ibid.*

[34] IRS Notice 2000-3, Sec. III, Q&A-2, I.R.B. 2000-3, 1-24-2000, CCH PENSION PLAN GUIDE ¶ 17,117R; IRS Reg. § 1.401(k)-3(c)(5)(ii).

[35] IRS Notice 98-52, Sec. VIII.D, I.R.B. 1998-46, 11-16-98, CCH PENSION PLAN GUIDE ¶ 17,115B.

[36] IRS Notice 98-52, Sec. IX.A.2, I.R.B. 1998-46, 11-16-98, CCH PENSION PLAN GUIDE ¶ 17,115B.

[37] IRS Notice 98-52, Sec. IX.A.2, I.R.B. 1998-46, 11-16-98, CCH PENSION PLAN GUIDE ¶ 17,115B.

[38] IRS Reg. §§ 1.401(k)-3(h)(4) and 1.401(m)-3(j)(4).

[39] IRS Notice 98-52, Sec. IX.B.1, I.R.B. 1998-46, 11-16-98, CCH PENSION PLAN GUIDE ¶ 17,115B.

[40] *Ibid.*

[41] IRS Notice 2000-3, Sec. III, Q&A-10, I.R.B. 2000-3, 1-24-2000, CCH PENSION PLAN GUIDE ¶ 17,117R.

[42] Code Sec. 401(m)(2)(B); IRS Reg. § 1.401(m)-3(d)(5);IRS Notice 98-52, Sec. IX.B.2, I.R.B. 1998-46, 11-16-98, CCH PENSION PLAN GUIDE ¶ 17,115B.

[43] IRS Notice 98-52, Sec. X, I.R.B. 1998-46, 11-16-98, CCH PENSION PLAN GUIDE ¶ 17,115B.

[44] IRS Reg. §§ 1.401(k)-3(e)(1) and 1.401(m)-3(f)(1).

[45] IRS Reg. §§ 1.401(k)-3(e)(2) and 1.401(m)-3(f)(2).

[46] IRS Notice 2000-3, Sec. III, Q&A-11, I.R.B. 2000-3, 1-24-2000, CCH PENSION PLAN GUIDE ¶ 17,117R.

[47] IRS Reg. §§ 1.401(k)-3(e)(2) and 1.401(m)-3(f)(2).

[48] IRS Notice 2000-3, Sec. III, I.R.B. 2000-3, 1-24-2000, at CCH PENSION PLAN GUIDE ¶ 17,117R.

[49] IRS Reg. §§ 1.401(k)-3(e) and 1.401(m)-3(f)(4).

[50] IRS Proposed Reg. §§ 1.401(k)-3 and IRS Proposed Reg. § 1.401(m)-3.

[51] IRS Notice 98-52, Sec. X.A.1, I.R.B. 1998-46, 11-16-98, CCH PENSION PLAN GUIDE ¶ 17,115B; IRS Reg. §§ 1.401(k)-3(e)(4) and 1.401(m)-3(f)(4).

[52] IRS Notice 2000-3, Sec. III, Q&A-1, I.R.B. 2000-3, 1-24-2000, CCH PENSION PLAN GUIDE ¶ 17,117R; IRS Reg. §§ 1.401(k)-3(f) and 1.401(m)-3(g).

[53] IRS Reg. §§ 1.401(k)-3(f) and 1.401(m)-3.

[54] IRS Reg. § 1.401(k)-3(f)(3).

¶ 2976

NONDISCRIMINATION RULES: Automatic Enrollment Safe Harbor: Qualified Automatic Contribution Arrangement

401(k) plan sponsors that implement automatic enrollment provisions will be further able to comply with the ADP and ACP nondiscrimination tests by making specific contributions under qualified automatic contribution arrangements. Similar to 401(k) safe harbor plans (see ¶ 2975), a qualified automatic contribution arrangement would provide an additional safe harbor for compliance with the nondiscrimination tests to employers maintaining an eligible automatic enrollment arrangement (see ¶ 2940B) that provides for a minimum automatic employee contribution and a minimum employer matching or nonelective contribution.[1] However, unlike safe harbor 401(k) plans, which offer immediate vesting, employees would not vest in the matching contributions under the automatic enrollment safe harbor until completing two years of service.[2]

Employers must also comply with an annual notice requirement. The notice must explain the employee's right under the arrangement not to have elective contributions made on his or her behalf or to elect to have contributions made in a different amount. In addition, the notice must disclose how contributions will be invested in the absence of an investment election by the employee.

Adoption of QACA before plan year

As with traditional safe harbor plans, the plan provision implementing a QACA for an existing qualified cash or deferred arrangement must be adopted before the first day of the plan year and remain in effect for an entire 12-month plan year. [3]

Automatic deferral at specified "qualified percentage"

Under a qualified automatic contribution arrangement, an eligible employee, absent a contrary election is treated as having elected to have the employer make elective contributions in an amount equal to a "qualified percentage" of compensation, not to exceed 10 percent.[4] The default election is the specified qualified percentage multiplied by the employee's compensation from which elective contributions are permitted to be made. [5]

Annually escalating percentage. The qualified percentage must be equal to at least: 3 percent of compensation during the first year of the employee's automatic enrollment, increase to 4 percent during the second year, 5 percent during the third year, and 6 percent during the fourth year and thereafter.[6]

CCH POINTER: *Application of escalator provision in automatic contribution arrangements.* The IRS has issued guidance clarifying the use of escalator provisions in automatic contribution arrangements that allow for an adjustment in the amount of an employee's default contributions based on increases in pay. [7]

The scenario outlined by the IRS concerns a profit-sharing plan that is intended to be a QACA and an EACA, under which, for plan years after the first plan year of an employee's participation, the default contribution percentage is automatically increased, beginning with the first period that begins on or after April 1. The increase in the default contribution percentage is equal to 1 percentage point, but may not exceed 10 percent.

The IRS concluded that the default contribution percentage for each plan year after the first plan year satisfies the applicable minimum default contribution requirements. The increased default contribution percentage of 4 percent applies earlier than required under the governing regulations, the IRS explained, as it begins with the first pay period that begins on or after April 1 of the plan year following the first plan year.

Length of periods of participation. A new period generally begins immediately following the last day of the preceding period. However, the initial period of participation in a QACA for an employee may last for two years.

Minimum qualified percentage. An employee must be allowed to make elective contributions in an amount that is at least sufficient to receive the maximum amount of matching contributions available under the plan for the plan year. The employee may also elect a lesser amount of elective contributions. However, the minimum qualified percentages specified by statute do not prevent a QACA from authorizing higher contribution percentages (or an escalation beyond the 5th year), as long as the qualified percentage does not exceed 10 percent of compensation.[8]

Uniform application of qualified percentage. The qualifying percentage must be applied uniformly to all eligible employees. [9] However, the following considerations apply.

Mid-year increase in default percentage. The elective deferral percentages under a QACA may vary based on the number of years an employee has participated in the automatic contribution arrangement. The final regulations further provide that the default percentage may vary based on portions of years since the date the employee first had contributions made to the QACA pursuant to a default election.[10] Accordingly, a plan may, as an alternative to a year-end increase, provide for a mid-year increase in the default percentage, thereby allowing the employer to coordinate the increased deferral with mid-year performance evaluations and salary increases. [11]However, the IRS cautions, the percentage must be uniform, based on the number of years or portions of years since an employee first had contributions made pursuant to the default election, and must satisfy the minimum percentage requirement throughout the plan year.

Prior deferral rate need not be reduced. A QACA is not required to reduce the rate of elective deferral under a participant's prior cash or deferred election that was in effect when the QACA became effective.

Contribution limited to comply with statutory caps. The QACA may also limit the amount of elective contributions so as not to exceed the applicable statutory limits on compensation, elective deferrals, or benefits and contributions (i.e., Code Sec. 402(g) (excluding catch-up) and Code Sec. 415).

Contributions not required during hardship suspension. A plan would not fail the uniformity requirement merely because an employee was not automatically enrolled during the 6 month period following a hardship distribution in which he or she was suspended from making elective contributions. However, the plan would be required to allow the employee, at the end of the 6 month suspension period, to resume elective contributions at the level (i.e., percentage) that would be applicable if the suspension had not occurred. [12]

Excludable employees. An employer may limit participation in the QACA to employees hired after the effective date on which the provision was adopted. Thus, an employer may exclude from participation not only those who have opted out of the arrangement, but employees hired before the effective date of the QACA provision. The employer is further not required to provide the annual participant notice (see below) to employees who have opted out or are not eligible to participate in the arrangement.

Matching and nonelective contributions

An employer, under a qualified automatic contribution arrangement is required to make either a specified matching contribution on behalf of NHCEs or a nonelective contribution to the 401(k) plan or another defined contribution plan on behalf of each NHCE who is eligible to participate in the plan.[13]

Matching contribution at specified percentage of NHCE compensation. The employer's matching contributions must equal 100 percent of the elective contributions of the NHCE, up to 1 percent of pay, plus 50 percent of elective deferrals that exceed 1 percent of pay, but do not exceed 6 percent of compensation (i.e., deferrals between 2–6 percent of compensation).[14]

Limit on rate of matching contributions. The rate of matching contributions may not increase as the rate of an employee's elective deferrals increase. In addition, the rate of matching contributions with respect to any rate of elective deferral of a HCE may not exceed the rate of matching contributions with respect to the same rate of deferral of a NHCE.[15]

> **CCH POINTER:** *Deemed satisfaction of ACP test.* A plan including an automatic enrollment feature that provides for matching contributions will, similarly, be deemed to satisfy the ACP test if: matching contributions are not provided with respect to elective deferrals in excess of 6 percent of compensation; the rate of matching contributions does not increase as the rate of an employee's elective deferrals increases; and the rate of matching contributions with respect to any rate of elective deferrals of a HCE is not greater than the rate of matching contributions with respect to the same rate of deferrals of a NHCE.[16]

Nonelective contribution equal to 3 percent of compensation. An employer, as an alternative to the matching contributions, may make nonelective contributions, equal to at least 3 percent of compensation, to a defined contribution plan on behalf of each NHCE who is eligible to participate in the qualified automatic contribution arrangement.[17]

Note, that an employer is not required to make the 3 percent nonelective contribution to a 401(k) plan. The contribution may be made to any defined contribution plan maintained by the employer.

> **CCH POINTER:** *Proposed rules would allow for reduction or suspension of QACA nonelective contributions.* The IRS has issued proposed regulations that would allow employers sponsoring a safe harbor 401(k) plan, including a qualified automatic contribution arrangement, to reduce or suspend required nonelective contributions, in the event they have incurred "substantial business hardship" during the plan year (see ¶ 2975).[18] Employers may rely on the proposed regulations for guidance pending the issuance of the final regulations.

> *Two-year cliff vesting.* Matching or other employer contributions under the qualified automatic contribution arrangements vest at least as rapidly as under 2-year cliff vesting. Accordingly, employees will have a nonforfeitable right to 100 percent of the employee's accrued benefit derived from the contributions after two years of service.[19]

Annual notice requirement

The application of the safe harbor is conditioned on each employee eligible to participate in the qualified automatic contribution arrangement receiving, within a reasonable period of time before each plan year, written notification of the employee's rights and obligations under the arrangement.[20] The notice must be: (1)

sufficiently accurate and comprehensive to apprise the employee of such rights and obligations under the arrangement, and (2) written in manner calculated to be understood by the average employee to whom the arrangement applies.

Content requirements. The notice must provide the information required by Code Sec. 401(k)(12) under safe harbor plans (see ¶ 2975). In addition, the notice, similar to the notice that must be provided under an eligible automatic contribution arrangement, pursuant to Code Sec. 401(k)(13)(E)(i) (see ¶ 2940B), must explain the employee's rights under the qualified automatic contribution arrangement to elect not to have elective contributions made on the employee's behalf or to elect to have such contributions made at a different percentage of compensation.[21]

The final regulations further require the notice to disclose the level of elective contributions that would be made on the employee's behalf, absent an affirmative election. The final rules also clarify that the requirement to explain how contributions will be invested under the automatic contribution arrangement applies even if the plan does not allow an employee to make an election among two or more investment options.[22]

Sample automatic enrollment notice. The IRS has provided a sample "Automatic Enrollment Notice" that may be used by sponsors of qualified automatic contribution arrangements (QACAs) to satisfy the applicable notice requirements.

Detailed description of QACA matching contribution. The notice requires disclosure of the amount of the matching contribution to be made by the employer under the QACA. Specifically, the notice must explain that the company match is determined by the amount contributed by the employee each pay period and caution employees that they will receive no matching contributions if they elect not to make contributions for the pay period.

The sample notice is reproduced at CCH PENSION PLAN GUIDE ¶ 17,023Y-12.

Cross-reference to SPD does not satisfy notice requirement. The IRS cautions that the additional notice requirements may not be satisfied by reference to the plan's summary plan description.[23]

CCH POINTER: *Reasonable period of time to make elections.* An employee must be afforded a reasonable period of time after the receipt of the notice and before the first contribution is made, to make an election not have contributions made or to have contributions made at a different percentage, or to make investment elections.[24] However, the plan may not allow the default election to be effective later than the earlier of: (1) the pay date for the second payroll period that begins after the date the notice is provided; and (2) the first pay date that occurs at least 30 days after the date the notice is provided.[25]

The final regulations specify that if it is not practicable for the notice to be provided on or before the eligibility date specified in the plan, the notice will be treated as timely if: (a) it is provided as soon as practicable after that date, and (b) the employee is allowed to elect to defer from all types of compensation that may be deferred under the plan, earned beginning on the date the employee becomes eligible.[26] Thus, according to the IRS, the notice must be provided to the employee prior to the pay date for the payroll period that includes the date the employee becomes eligible.

[1] Code Sec. 401(k)(13), as added by P.L.109-280 (Pension Protection Act of 2006) Act Sec. 902(a); Code Sec. 401(m)(12), as added by P.L.109-280 (Pension Protection Act of 2006) Act Sec. 902(b).

[2] IRS Reg. § 1.401(k)-3.

[3] IRS Reg. § 1.401(k)-3(e) and IRS Reg. § 1.401(m)-3(f).

[4] Code Sec. 401(k)(13)(C), as added by P.L.109-280 (Pension Protection Act of 2006) Act Sec. 902(a); IRS Reg. § 1.401(k)-3(j)(2)(i).

[5] IRS Reg. § 1.401(k)-3(j)(i)(i).

[6] Code Sec. 401(k)(13)(C)(iii), as added by P.L.109-280 (Pension Protection Act of 2006) Act Sec. 902(a); IRS Reg. § 1.401(k)-3(g)(2)(ii).

[7] Revenue Ruling 2009-30, I.R.B. 2009-39, 9-28-09, at CCH PENSION PLAN GUIDE ¶ 19,948Z-266.

[8] IRS Reg. § 1.401(k)-3(j)(2)(i)(B).

[9] Code Sec. 401(k)(13)(C)(iii).

[10] IRS Reg. § 1.401(k)-3(j)(2)(iii).

[11] SeeRev. Rul. 2009-30, I.R.B. 2009-30, 9-28-09, at CCH PENSION PLAN GUIDE ¶ 19,948Z-266 (default contributions exempt from uniformity requirements where increases apply in the same manner to all eligible employees for whom the same number of years or portions of years have elapsed since the default contributions were first made for them).

[12] IRS Reg. § 1.401(k)-3(j)(2)(iii)(D).

[13] Code Sec. 401(k)(13)(D)(i), as added by P.L.109-280 (Pension Protection Act of 2006) Act Sec. 902(a).

[14] Code Sec. 401(k)(13)(D)(i)(I), as added by P.L.109-280 (Pension Protection Act of 2006) Act Sec. 902(a); IRS Reg. § 1.401(k)-3(k)(2).

[15] Code Sec. 401(k)(13)(D)(ii) (cross-referencing Code Sec. 401(k)(12)(B)) as added by P.L.109-280 (Pension Protection Act of 2006) Act Sec. 902(a).

[16] Code Sec.401(m)(12), as added by P.L.109-280 (Pension Protection Act of 2006) Act Sec. 902(b).

[17] Code Sec. 401(k)(13)(D)(ii), as added by P.L.109-280 (Pension Protection Act of 2006) Act Sec. 902(a).

[18] IRS Proposed Reg. § 1.401(k)-3.

[19] Code Sec. 401(k)(13)(D)(iii)(I), as added by P.L.109-280 (Pension Protection Act of 2006) Act Sec. 902(a).

[20] Code Sec. 401(k)(13)(E), as added by P.L.109-280 (Pension Protection Act of 2006) Act Sec. 902(a).

[21] Code Sec. 401(k)(13)(E)(ii)(I), as added by P.L.109-280 (Pension Protection Act of 2006) Act Sec. 902(a); IRS Reg. § 1.401(k)-3(k)(4)(ii).

[22] IRS Reg. § 1.401(k)-3(k)(4)(ii)(A).

[23] Preamble to IRS Reg. § 1.401(k)-3.

[24] Code Sec. 401(k)(13)(E)(ii)(iiI), as added by P.L.109-280 (Pension Protection Act of 2006) Act Sec. 902(a).

[25] IRS Reg. § 1.401(k)-3(k)(4)(iii).

[26] IRS Reg. § 1.401(k)-3(k)(4)(ii).

¶ 2977

NONDISCRIMINATION RULES: Correction of Excess Contributions

In the event that the elective contributions of highly compensated employees to a 401(k) plan exceed the elective contributions of nonhighly compensated employees by more than specified percentages (i.e., the plan fails the ADP test), an "excess contribution" is the result. The failure of the ADP test subjects the employer to a 10 percent excise tax on the amount of the excess contributions and could result in the loss of the plan's qualified status (see below). However, a plan may allow an employer to correct a violation of the ADP test by adopting one, or a combination, of the following corrective measures.

QNECs and QMACs

An employer may make QNECs or QMACs that are treated as elective contributions and that, in combination with other elective contributions made to the plan, satisfy the ADP test. The use of QNECs and QMACs under the ADP (and ACP) test are discussed at ¶ 2951B, 2954, and 2955.[1]

Corrective distributions

The excess contribution (and income allocable thereto) may be returned to the employee within 12 months after the close of the plan year in which the excess contribution arose.[2] Corrective distributions made within 2½ months after the end of the plan year for which the excess contributions were made are generally taxable to HCEs in the year prior to distribution, or in an earlier year. Any reasonable, nondiscriminatory method may be used to determine income allocable to excess contributions.[3]

Corrective distributions of excess contributions are implemented through a 4-step process[4]: calculation of the total amount of excess contributions that must be distributed under the plan; apportionment of the total amount of excess contributions among HCEs; determination of income allocable to excess contributions; and distribution of the apportioned excess contributions and allocable income.

Gap period income not included in corrective distribution. Corrective distributions of excess contributions need not include earnings from the end of the plan year in which the contribution was made through the date of distribution (i.e., gap period income). [5]

Recharacterization of excess contributions

As an alternative to making a corrective distribution, a plan may, within 2½ months after the close of the plan year in which an excess contribution occurred, recharacterize the excess contribution as an after-tax employee contribution.[6] The recharacterized amount is treated as if it was received by the employee during the plan year and contributed to the plan on an after-tax basis. Accordingly, excess contributions that are recharacterized are includible in the employee's income on the earliest date any elective contribution would have been paid to the employee had the employee elected to receive the amounts in cash.[7] In addition, the recharacterized contributions are treated as after-tax employee contributions for purposes of the general nondiscrimination rules of Code Sec. 401(a)(4) and the ACP test.[8]

One-to-one correction method

The IRS has formally approved a "one-to-one" correction method, pursuant to which an excess contribution (adjusted for earnings) is (1) either distributed to or forfeited from the account of HCEs, and (2) contributed to the plan and allocated to NHCEs.[9] This correction method is available when excess contributions are not corrected during the plan year following the plan year of the ADP/ACP failure.

Leveling method for determining excess contributions of HCEs

In applying the recharacterization and distribution correction methods, the share of a HCE's excess contributions that will be decreased so as to enable a plan to pass the ADP test must be determined under a "leveling" method.[10] The elective contributions of the HCE who has deferred the greatest dollar amount will be reduced before contributions made by other HCEs are reduced. The IRS has provided a method for allocating the excess contributions for a plan year among highly compensated employees.[11]

Correction methods may be used in combination. A plan may use any of the authorized correction methods, limit elective contributions so as to prevent excess contributions from being made, or use a combination of these methods in order to avoid or correct excess contributions.[12] For example, if a highly compensated employee has made excess contributions, a portion of the excess contributions may be recharacterized and the remaining portion may be distributed.

HCE may elect correction mechanism. A plan may require or permit a highly compensated employee to make an election as to whether any excess contributions are to be recharacterized or distributed.[13]

Impermissible correction methods

Excess contributions for a given plan year may not remain unallocated or be allocated to a suspense account for allocation to one or more employees in any future year.[14] Nor may an employer use the retroactive correction method that is available to correct minimum coverage defects (see ¶ 2950) in order to correct excess contributions. Thus, an employer may not correct excess contributions by granting QNECs to NHCEs who were not eligible employees for the plan year.

Taxation of corrective distributions

A corrective distribution of excess contributions and allocable income that is made within 2½ months after the end of the plan year for which the excess contributions were made is generally includible in the employee's gross income on the earliest date that the employee would have received any elective contributions during the plan year if the employee had elected to receive the amounts in cash.[15] Thus, the distributions are generally taxable or partly taxable in the year prior to the distribution (and in an even earlier year).

A corrective distribution of excess contributions and allocable income that is made more than 2½ months after the end of the plan year for which the contributions were made is includible in the employee's gross income in the tax year of the employee in which the distribution occurred.[16] Note, in the event excess contributions and allocable income are distributed later than 2½ months after the close of the plan year, the employer is subject to a 10 percent excise tax (see below).

10 percent excise tax on employer

In the event excess contributions and allocable income are distributed later than 2½ months (75 days) after the close of the plan year (but before the end of the following plan year) the employer is subject to a 10 percent excise tax.[17] The tax is not assessed if the excess contribution and allocable income are distributed within 2½ months after the end of the plan year.

Corrective distributions taxed in year of contribution before 2008. Excess contributions that are distributed within 2½ months after the close of the plan year (with the exception of distributions under $100) are treated as received and earned by the recipient in the tax year for which the contributions (and not the distributions) were made.[18]

Corrective distributions taxed in year of distribution after 2007. The provision under current law allowing corrective distributions made within 2½ months after the end of the year of the excess contribution to be included in the recipient's taxable income for the prior year will no longer apply in plan years after 2007. The Pension Protection Act of 2006 amended Code Sec. 4979(f)(2) to provide that corrective distributions of excess contributions (under a traditional 401(k) plan or an automatic enrollment arrangement) that are made within the time frame required to avoid the excise tax will be treated as earned and received (and, thus, taxable) to the recipient in the year in which the distribution (and not the contribution) is made.[19]

6-month period of time to distribute excess contributions under automatic contribution arrangement. The distribution of excess contributions under an eligible automatic contribution arrangement (see ¶ 2940B), effective for plan years after 2007, will not be subject to the excise tax if made within 6 months after the end of the plan year.[20]

Voluntary correction of excess contributions under EPCRS

A plan may avoid the loss of qualified status for failing to make a corrective distribution during the 12-month period following the plan year in which the excess contribution arose, by voluntarily correcting the error, prior to IRS audit. The IRS has provided approved methods by which a plan sponsor may voluntarily correct excess contributions under the SCP and VCP components of the Employee Plans Compliance Resolution System (EPCRS).[21] The approved correction methods include: (1) making QNECs for nonhighly compensated employees and (2) a one-to-one correction method pursuant to which an excess contribution is either distributed to highly compensated employees or forfeited from their accounts and contributed to the plan and allocated to nonhighly compensated employees.

Note, however, voluntary correction under EPCRS requires full correction and will subject the employer to fees (under VCP) as well as the costs of correction, including applicable excise taxes.

[1] IRS Reg. § 1.401(k)-2(b)(1)(i)(A).

[2] IRS Reg. § 1.401(k)-2(b)(2)(v).

[3] IRS Reg. § 1.401(k)-2(b)(2)(iv)(B).

[4] IRS Reg. § 1.401(k)-2(b)(2)(ii)–(v).

[5] Code Sec. 401(k)(8)(A)(i); IRS Proposed Reg. § 1.401(k)-2(b)(2)(iv)(A).

[6] IRS Reg. § 1.401(k)-2(b)(5)(ii).

[7] IRS Announcement 94-101, I.R.B. 1994-35.

[8] IRS Reg. § 1.401(k)-2(b)(3)(ii).

[9] Rev. Proc. 2006-27, I.R.B. 2006-22 at CCH PENSION PLAN GUIDE ¶ 17,299R-86.

[10] IRS Reg. § 1.401(k)-2(b)(2)(ii).

[11] IRS Notice 97-2, 1997-1 C.B. 348, CCH PENSION PLAN GUIDE ¶ 17,111X.

[12] IRS Reg. § 1.401(k)-2(b)(1)(ii).

[13] *Ibid.*

[14] IRS Reg. § 1.401(k)-2(b)(1)(iii).

[15] IRS Reg. § 1.401(k)-2(b)(2)(vi)(A).

[16] *Ibid.*

[17] Code Sec. 4979(f); IRS Reg. §§ 1.401(k)-2(b)(5)(i) and 54.4979-1.

[18] Code Sec. 4979(f)(2).

[19] Code Sec. 4979(f)(2), as amended by P.L. 109-280 (Pension Protection Act of 2006), Act Sec. 902(e)(2); IRS Proposed Reg. § 1.401(k)-2(b)(2)(vi)(A).

[20]Code Sec. 4979(f)(1), as amended by P.L. 109-280 (Pension Protection Act of 2006), Act Sec. 902(e)(1); IRS Proposed Reg. §54.4979-1(c).

[21]Rev. Proc. 2008-50, I.R.B. 2008-35, 9-2-08 at CCH PENSION PLAN GUIDE ¶ 17,299S-66.

¶ 2978

NONDISCRIMINATION RULES: Correction of Excess Aggregate Contributions

The fact that the aggregate amount of after-tax employee contributions and matching contributions (including QNECs and elective deferrals taken into account for the ACP test) made on behalf of highly compensated employees for a plan year exceeds the maximum level permitted under the ACP test will not cause the plan to lose qualified status if corrective measures are taken. A plan may generally correct such excess aggregate contributions by making QNECs for nonhighly compensated employees, treating elective contributions as matching contributions, making corrective distributions (including allocable income) to highly compensated employees, or making forfeitures.

QNECs and elective contributions

A plan may authorize an employer to make QNECs or elective contributions that, in combination with employee and matching contributions, satisfy the ACP test.[1] However, QNECs and elective contributions may not correct an ACP violation if they have been used for purposes of the ADP test.

Determination of excess aggregate contributions

The amount of excess aggregate contributions is determined under a method that requires the actual contribution ratio (ACR) of the HCE with the highest ACR to be reduced so as to equal either the ACR of the HCE with the next highest ACR, or if a lesser amount, that needed to pass the ACP test.[2]

Corrective distribution of excess aggregate contributions

A plan may correct excess aggregate contributions by distributing the excess amounts to highly compensated employees.[3] The corrective distribution is made pursuant to a four-step process that requires the distribution of the total amount of excess aggregate contributions and allocable income to highly compensated employees within 12 months of the close of the plan year.

The first step is to determine the aggregate amount by which the matching and employee contributions of HCEs must be reduced in order for the ACP of the HCE group to pass the ACP test.[4] The second step is the allocation of excess aggregate contributions (based on the amount of matching contributions and employee contributions beginning with the HCE with largest amount of contributions).[5] The third step is to determine the income allocable to the excess aggregate contributions).[6]

CCH POINTER: The income allocable to excess aggregate contributions is the sum of the allocable gain or loss for the plan year. However, effective for plan years beginning after 2007, corrective distributions of excess aggregate contributions need not include "gap period" earnings.[7]

The final step in the correction of excess aggregate contributions through a corrective distribution is to actually distribute the apportioned contributions and allocable income, or, alternatively, forfeit the apportioned matching contributions (to the extent the amounts are forfeitable).[8] The excess aggregate contributions and allocable income must be distributed to the appropriate HCE within 12 months after the close of the plan year in which the excess aggregate contribution arose.[9]

Note, a plan may not forfeit vested matching contributions.[10] However, a plan may forfeit nonvested excess aggregate contributions within 12 months after the end of the plan year in which excess aggregate contribution arose.[11]

One-to-one correction method

The IRS has formally approved a "one-to-one" correction method, pursuant to which an excess contribution amount (adjusted for earnings) is (1) either distributed to or forfeited from the account of HCEs, and (2) contributed to the plan and allocated to NHCEs.[12]

The method authorized by the plan for distributing excess aggregate contributions must satisfy the nondiscrimination rules. Thus, after the correction of excess aggregate contributions, each level of matching contributions must be currently and effectively available to a group of employees that satisfies the minimum coverage requirements of Code Sec. 410(b).[13] For example, a plan that provides the same rate of matching contributions to all employees will be considered discriminatory if after-tax employee contributions are distributed to highly compensated employees in order to pass the ACP test, while matching contributions attributable to those employee contributions remain allocated to the accounts of highly compensated employees. This rule applies, the IRS explains because the level of matching contributions will be higher for a group of employees that consists entirely of HCEs.[14]

Impermissible correction methods

An employer may not correct excess aggregate contributions by: (1) forfeiting *vested* matching contributions; (2) recharacterizing matching contributions (although this option may be used to pass the ADP test (see ¶ 2977)); or (3) not making matching contributions required under the terms of the plan.[15]

Tax treatment of corrective distributions

A corrective distribution of excess aggregate contributions and allocable income that is made to an employee within 2 ½ months after the end of the plan year for which the excess contributions were made is includible in the employee's gross income for the tax year ending with or within the plan year for which the excess aggregate contributions were made.[16] However, corrective distributions of excess aggregate contributions (under a traditional 401(k) plan or an automatic enrollment arrangement) that are made within the time frame required to avoid the excise tax will be treated as earned and received (and thus, taxable) to the recipient in the year in which the distribution (and not the contribution) is made.[17]

A corrective distribution that is made more than $2\frac{1}{2}$ months after the end of the plan year for which the excess aggregate contributions were made remains taxable to the employee in the year in which it is distributed.[18]

Distribution of Roth 401(k) contributions. A distribution of excess aggregate contributions that represent a distribution of Roth 401(k) contributions will not be included in the participant's gross income.[19] However, income allocable to the corrective distribution of excess aggregate contributions that are Roth 401(k) contributions will be taxed in the same manner as income allocable to a corrective distribution of excess aggregate contributions that are not designated Roth contributions.

10 percent excise tax imposed on employer. An employer is liable for a 10 percent excise tax on excess aggregate contributions that are not corrected within $2\frac{1}{2}$ months after the close of the year in which the contributions were made.[20] If excess aggregate contributions are not corrected within 12 months after the close of the year in which they were made, the plan will lose it qualified status for the plan year for which the excess aggregate contributions were made and for all subsequent years in which the excess aggregate contributions remain in the plan.[21]

Voluntary correction of excess aggregate contributions under EPCRS

A plan may avoid the loss of qualified status for failing to make a corrective distribution during the 12-month period following the plan year in which the excess aggregate contribution arose by voluntarily correcting the error, prior to IRS audit. The IRS has provided approved methods by which a plan sponsor may voluntarily correct excess aggregate contributions under the SCP and VCP components of the Employee Plans Compliance Resolution System (EPCRS).[22] The approved correction methods include: (1) making QNECs for nonhighly compensated employees and (2) a one-to-one correction method pursuant to which an excess contribution is either distributed to highly compensated employees or forfeited from their accounts and contributed to the plan and allocated to nonhighly compensated employees.

Note, however, voluntary correction under EPCRS requires full correction and will subject the employer to fees as well as the costs of correction, including applicable excise taxes.

---

[1] IRS Reg. § 1.401(m)-2(a)(6).

[2] IRS Reg. § 1.401(m)-2(b)(2)(ii).

[3] IRS Reg. §§ 1.401(m)-2(b)(1)(b) and 1.401(m)-2(b)(2).

[4] IRS Reg. § 1.401(m)-2(b)(2)(ii).

[5] IRS Reg. § 1.401(m)-2(b)(2)(iii).

[6] IRS Reg. § 1.401(m)-2(b)(2)(iv).

[7] Code Sec. 401(m)(6)(A), as amended by P.L. 109-280 (Pension Protection Act of 2006), Act Sec. 9802(e)(3); IRS Proposed Reg. § 1.401(m)-2(b)(2)(iv).

[8] IRS Reg. §§ 1.401(m)-2(b)(2)(i) and 1.401(m)-2(b)((2)(v).

[9] *Ibid.*

[10] IRS Reg. § 1.410(m)-2(b)(1)(iii).

[11] IRS Reg. § 1.401(m)-2(b)(2)(v).

[12] Rev. Proc. 2008-50, I.R.B. 2008-35, at CCH PENSION PLAN GUIDE ¶ 17,299S-66.

[13] IRS Reg. § 1.401(m)-2(b)(3)(v)(B).

[14] *Ibid.*

[15] IRS Reg. § 1.401(m)-2(b)(1)(iii).

[16] IRS Reg. § 1.401(m)-2(b)(2)(vi)(A).

[17]Code Sec. 4979(f)(2), as amended by P.L. 109-280 (Pension Protection Act of 2006), Act Sec. 902(e)(2); IRS Proposed Reg. § 1.401(m)-2(b)(2)(vi).

[18]IRS Reg. § 1.401(m)-2(b)(2)(vi)(A).

[19]IRS Reg. § 1.401(m)-2(b)(2)(vi)(C).

[20] IRS Reg. § 1.401(m)-2(b)(4)(i).

[21] IRS Reg. § 1.401(m)-2(b)(4)(ii).

[22]Rev. Proc. 2008-50, I.R.B. 2006-22, 5-30-06, at CCH PENSION PLAN GUIDE ¶ 17,299S-66.

¶ 2979

VESTING RULES: Vesting Rules for 401(k) Plans

Full and immediate vesting is required for the following types of contributions to a 401(k) plan:

1. contributions made by an employer pursuant to an employee's election (elective contributions or deferrals);[1]

2. contributions made by an employee (voluntary after-tax contributions);[2]

3. any other contributions taken into account in computing an employee's actual deferral percentage (i.e., QNECs and QMACs) for purposes of the ADP test (see ¶ 2951);[3] and

4. rollovers;

5. deemed IRA contributions; and[4]

6. nonelective and matching contributions under a safe harbor 401(k) plan or a SIMPLE 401(k) plan.[5]

Vesting not contingent on age or length of service. An employee's elective contributions (unlike matching contributions) are nonforfeitable and totally vested, regardless of the employee's age and length of service or whether the employee is employed on a specific date.[6] In addition, any earnings allocable to these types of contributions are required to be fully and immediately vested.

Elective contributions may not be forfeited upon death. A 401(k) plan (unlike other qualified plans) may not forfeit elective contributions following the death of a participant.[7]

Deferred vesting schedules for nonelective and matching contributions

Nonelective contributions and employer matching contributions (including earnings) to a 401(k) plan (other than a SIMPLE 401(k) or a safe harbor 401(k) plan) that are not taken into account for purposes of the ADP test vest under a deferred vesting schedule. Note, deferred vesting does not apply to elective contributions. For example, if a plan provides that 50% of an employee's account is vested in a given year, only the matching and nonelective contributions are subject to the 50% vesting schedule. Elective contributions must be fully vested.

Two alternative vesting schedules

An accelerated vesting schedule applies to employer matching contributions.[8]

Matching contributions. Employer matching contributions must vest at least as rapidly as under one of the following two alternative minimum vesting schedules:

1. ***Three-year cliff vesting,*** under which a participant acquires a nonforfeitable right to 100 percent of employer matching contributions upon completion of three years of service; or

2. ***Two-to six-year graded vesting,*** under which a participant will have a nonforfeitable right to 20 percent of employer matching contributions upon the completion of two years of service and will fully vest in the employer matching contributions after six years of service, in accord with the following schedule:

Years of Service	Nonforfeitable percentage
2	20
3	40
4	60
5	80
6 or more	100

Uniform schedule applies to all employer contributions. Nonelective employer contributions to a 401(k) plan vest under the schedule that applies to matching contributions (and top-heavy contributions (see below)).[9] Thus, if a plan uses three-year cliff vesting, an employee who has completed at least three years of service will have a nonforfeitable right to 100 percent of the accrued benefit derived from employer contributions, including nonelective contributions.[10] Similarly, if a 401(k) plan utilizes graduated vesting, benefits derived from all employer contributions, including nonelective contributions, must vest with a participant at the rate of 20 percent per year, beginning with the second year of service (20 percent after 2 years, 40 percent after 3 years, 60 percent after 4 years, 80 percent after 5 years, and 100 percent after 6 years).[11]

One-hour service requirement. The accelerated vesting schedule that applies to all employer contributions will not apply to any employee before the date on which the employee has completed one hour of service under the plan in any plan year to which the amended schedules apply.[12]

Year of service. A year of service is a calendar year, plan year, or any other consecutive 12-month period designated by the plan during which a participant is required to complete no more than 1,000 hours of service.[13] Any consecutive 12-month period that the plan designates as the vesting computation period, in lieu of the plan year or the calendar year (such as the 12-month period beginning on the employee's date of hire and ending on the anniversary of the employee's date of hire), must apply equally to all participants. [14]

Full vesting upon attainment of normal retirement age and plan termination

A qualified 401(k) plan must provide a plan participant with a nonforfeitable right to the entire plan interest upon the participant's attainment of normal retirement age. [15] Normal retirement age is the earlier of: (1) the time defined by the plan, or (2) the later of (a) age 65 or (b) 5 years after the time the participant begins participating in the plan. [16]

A qualified 401(k) plan must also expressly provide that, upon full or partial termination of the plan, or the complete discontinuation of contributions, the right of each participant to the amount credited to the participant's account at such time fully vests, regardless of the participant's years of service or vesting status.[17] Thus, an employee participating in a plan with a 6-year vesting schedule would be fully vested in all funds in the matching account at plan termination, even if the employee had not completed 6 years of service.

Top-heavy plans

A 401(k) plan is "top-heavy" if, as of the last day of the preceding plan year, the sum of the account balances of "key employee" participants (see ¶ 925) for the plan year exceeds 60 percent of the sum of the account balances of all employees under the plan (see ¶ 905).[18] Accelerated vesting schedules apply to employer- provided benefits under top-heavy plans.[19]

☐ The vesting rules applicable to top-heavy plans are discussed in detail at ¶ 930.

Forfeitures

Elective contributions and nonelective and matching contributions in which an employee is vested may not be forfeited, regardless of the employee's age or length of service.[20] However, an employee who terminates employment will forfeit the nonvested portion of the account balance that is attributable to employer contributions.

Forfeitures may reduce matching contributions. Amounts forfeited by departing employees may be applied to reduce employer contributions or may be allocated among remaining employees as additional nonelective contributions.

☐ The vesting rules generally applicable to qualified plans are discussed beginning at ¶ 800.

---

[1] Code Sec. 401(k)(2)(C).

[2] Code Sec. 411(a)(1).

[3] Code Sec. 401(k)(3)(D)(ii).

[4] Code Sec. 408(q).

[5] Code Sec. 401(k)(12)(E).

[6] IRS Reg. § 1.401(k)-1(c)(2).

[7] IRS Reg. § 1.401(k)-1(c)(2).

[8] Code Sec. 411(a)(12), prior to removal by P.L. 109-280 (Pension Protection Act of 2006), Act Sec. 904(a)(2); ERISA Sec. 203(a)(2), prior to removal by P.L. 109-280 (Pension Protection Act of 2006), Act Sec. 904(b)(2); Code Sec. 411(a)(2) (post-2006), as amended by P.L. 109-280 (Pension Protection Act of 2006), Act Sec. 904(a)(1); ERISA Sec. 203(a)(2) (post-2006), as amended by P.L. 109-280 (Pension Protection Act of 2006), Act Sec. 904(b)(1).

[9] Code Sec. 411(a)(2), as amended by P.L. 109-280 (Pension Protection Act of 2006), Act Sec. 904(a); ERISA Sec. 203(a)(2), as amended by P.L. 109-280 (Pension Protection Act of 2006), Act Sec. 904(b).

[10] Code Sec. 411(a)(2)(B)(ii), as added by P.L. 109-280 (Pension Protection Act of 2006), Act Sec. 904(a)(1); ERISA Sec. 203(a)(2)(B)(ii), as added by P.L. 109-280 (Pension Protection Act of 2006), Act Sec. 904(b)(1).

[11] Code Sec. 411(a)(2)(B)(iii), as added by P.L. 109-280 (Pension Protection Act of 2006), Act Sec. 904(a)(1); ERISA Sec. 203(a)(2)(B)(iii), as added by P.L. 109-280 (Pension Protection Act of 2006), Act Sec. 904(b)(1).

[12] P.L. 109-280 (Pension Protection Act of 2006), Act Sec. 904(c)(3).

[13]Code Sec. 411(a)(5)(A).

[14]ERISA Reg. § 2530.203-2(a).

[15] IRS Reg. § 1.411(a)-1(a)(1).

[16] Code Sec.411(a)(8); IRS Reg. § 1.411(a)-7(b).

[17] Code Sec.411(d)(3); IRS Reg. § 1.411(d)-2(a)(1).

[18] Code Sec. 416(g)(1)(A)(ii).

[19] Code Sec. 416(b).

[20] IRS Reg. § 1.401(k)-1(c)(1).

¶ 2981

CONTRIBUTION AND DEFERRAL LIMITS: Limits on 401(k) Plan Contributions

Employees may exclude from gross income elective deferrals to a 401(k) plan that fall within statutorily prescribed limits (see ¶ 2983).[1] Deferrals in excess in of the limits, however, subject participants to tax in the year for which the amount was contributed and in the year in which the amount is distributed. See ¶ 2984.

Elective deferral limit is a qualification requirement

The limit on elective deferrals is a condition of qualification.[2] Accordingly, a 401(k) plan that permits excess deferrals risks disqualification.

Elective deferrals. The elective deferral limit applies only to "elective deferrals" (and not to employer matching contributions). A participant's elective deferrals for the tax year are the sum of: (1) elective contributions under a 401(k) plan, to the extent not includible in gross income for the tax year under Code Sec. 402(e)(3) (before application of the Code Sec. 402(g) limits); (2) employer contributions to a SEP under Code Sec. 402(h)(1)(B); (3) employer contributions to a Code Sec. 403(b) tax-sheltered annuity under a salary reduction agreement, to the extent excludable from gross income for the tax year under Code Sec. 403(b); and (4) elective contributions to a SIMPLE plan.[3]

Note, participants age 50 and older who are prohibited by plan or statutory limits from making deferrals for the year are authorized to make additional "catch-up" contributions to the plan (see ¶ 2982).

CCH POINTER: *Contribution of unused vacation pay to 401(k) plan as means of avoiding elective deferral limit.* The IRS has issued private letter rulings in which contributions of unused and otherwise forfeitable vacation pay to a 401(k) plan and a qualified defined contribution plan were treated as employer nonelective contributions, and not as elective deferrals under cash or deferred arrangements.[4] The rulings provide a potentially effective means of avoiding the Code Sec. 402(g) ceiling on elective deferrals.

Expanded conditions under which unused PTO may be contributed to plan. The IRS issued two Revenue Rulings in 2009 that clarified its position and expanded the scope of the option by specifying the conditions under which a qualified plan may require or allow for an annual contribution of the dollar equivalent of an employee's unused paid time off to the plan.[5] The IRS also detailed the circumstances under which qualified plans may require or allow for the contribution of the dollar equivalent of unused paid time off to the plan upon the termination of a participant's employment.

Matching contributions for self-employed individuals. Matching contributions made to 401(k) plans for self-employed persons are not treated as elective contributions and, therefore, are not subject to the limit on elective contributions. [6] However, total contributions to an employee's account are subject to an annual additions limit.[7] See ¶ 2985

Annual dollar limit on elective deferrals

The aggregate annual amount that may be deferred by an employee under all qualified 401(k) plans in which the employee participates is subject to an annual statutorily prescribed dollar limit that is adjusted for changes in the cost of living. The applicable dollar limitation in 2012 is $17,000 ($11,500 for contributions to a SIMPLE 401(k) plan (see ¶ 2994)).[8]

Dollar limit applies to participants, not plans. The limit on elective deferrals applies to plan participants and not to the plan. Thus, an individual taxpayer may not (exclusive of catch-up contributions (see ¶ 2982)) defer more than $17,000 in the 2012 tax year, even if he or she participates in separate plans of separate employers.

Plan-specific limit on elective deferrals. Many employers impose a plan-specific limit on elective deferrals. The limit is typically expressed as a uniform maximum percentage of each employee's compensation (e.g., 10 percent of compensation).

[1] Code Sec. 402(e)(3); IRS Reg. § 1.402(a)-1(d)(2).

[2] Code Sec. 401(a)(30); IRS Reg. § 1.401(a)-30(a).

[3] Code Sec. 402(g)(3); IRS Reg. § 1.402(g)-1(b).

[4] IRS Letter Ruling 200311043, 12-18-02; Technical Advice Memorandum 9635002, 11-9-95.

[5] Revenue Ruling 2009-31 , I.R.B. 2009-30, 9-28-09, at CCH PENSION PLAN GUIDE ¶ 19,948Z-267; Revenue Ruling 2009-32, I.R.B. 2009-30, 9-28-09, at CCH PENSION PLAN GUIDE ¶ 19,948Z-268.

[6] Code Sec. 402(g)(8).

[7] Code Sec. 415(c); IRS Reg. § 1.415-6.

[8] Code Sec. 402(g)(1), as amended by P.L. 107-16 (Economic Growth and Tax Relief Reconciliation Act of 2001), Act Sec. 611(d).

¶ 2982

CONTRIBUTION AND DEFERRAL LIMITS: Catch-Up Contributions to 401(k) Plans

Employers *may* allow employees who (a) will attain age 50 by the end of the tax year and (b) are prohibited by applicable plan or statutory limits from making other elective deferrals to the plan for the plan or other applicable year to make additional "catch-up" contributions to the 401(k) plan (or SIMPLE plan, SARSEP, 403(b), or governmental 457 plan) in which they participate.[1] Catch-up contributions are made *in addition* to elective deferrals to the plan. Accordingly, catch-up contributions are not subject to the Code Sec. 402(g) limits on elective deferrals and are not taken into account in applying other contribution limits applicable to qualified plans or the deduction limit for employer contributions.

CCH POINTER: The catch-up contribution provision is limited to elective deferrals and is not available for after-tax contributions. In addition, catch-up contributions may only be made to a 401(k), SIMPLE 401(k), SIMPLE IRA, SARSEP, 403(b), or governmental plan. Thus, catch-up contributions may not be made to defined benefit plan.[2]

Catch-up eligible participants

A plan may authorize catch-up contributions by individuals who will attain (or would have attained) age 50 by the end of the tax year.[3] Similarly, IRS final rules provide that a participant who is eligible to make elective deferrals under a 401(k) plan or other applicable employer plan is eligible to make catch-up contributions for a tax year if the employee's 50th birthday would occur before the end of the tax year.[4] Thus, all participants who will attain age 50 during a calendar year will be treated the same beginning January 1 of that year, regardless of whether the participant actually attains age 50, dies, or terminates employment during the year and without regard to the employer's plan year. For example, an employer with a fiscal year plan ending July 30, 2012 could allow participants who will not attain age 50 until December 31, 2012 to make contributions for the fiscal year.

Non-calendar year plans. Participants in non-calendar year plans are treated as catch-up eligible participants beginning on January 1 of the calendar year in which the participant attain age 50, without regard to the plan year.[5]

Eligible participant need not have made excess deferrals before making catch-up contribution. An employee who has attained age 50 is eligible to make catch-up contributions if the employee is barred by applicable statutory or plan limits from making further elective deferrals to the plan for the plan year or other applicable year (e.g., calendar year).[6] A participant is not required to have actually made elective deferrals in excess of an otherwise applicable limit before making catch-up contributions. Catch-up contributions may be made at the start of the plan year. For example, a plan that authorizes catch-up contributions of $5,500 in 2012 could allow an eligible participant to make elective deferrals in an amount projected to exceed the otherwise applicable limit by $5,500 at any time during 2012.[7]

Applicable statutory and plan limits

Elective deferrals made by catch-up eligible participants may be treated as catch-up contributions if they exceed "applicable limits" for the plan or other applicable year (and do not exceed the specified catch-up contribution limit for the year (see below)). Applicable limits include: statutory limits (e.g., the Code Sec. 402(g) elective deferral limit and the Code Sec. 415 annual additions limit); employer-provided limits that are contained in the terms of the plan but are not required under the Internal Revenue Code (e.g., cap on elective deferrals by highly compensated employees of 10 percent of compensation); and the actual deferral percentage (ADP) limit (e.g., highest dollar amount of elective deferrals that may be retained in the plan by a highly compensated employee after application of the Code Sec. 401(k)(8)(C) corrections).[8]

Employer-provided limit must be specified in the plan. An employer-provided limit that will trigger catch-up contributions must be specified in the plan.[9] However, an employer may comply with the requirement by imposing limits in "accordance with plan terms." For example, a limit on elective deferrals by highly compensated employees (e.g., 10% of compensation), or another limit that is "otherwise permissible under Code Sec. 401(k)" that is imposed by the plan administrator in accordance with plan terms is an employer-provided limit contained in the plan.[10]

Amount of excess deferral determined at end of plan year. The amount of elective deferrals in excess of the applicable limit is determined as of the end of the plan year by comparing the total elective deferrals for the plan year with the applicable limit for the plan year.[11]

Payroll-by-payroll determinations of catch-up contributions. A plan may impose separate employer-provided limits on elective deferrals of separate portions of plan compensation within the plan year. For example, a plan may impose a monthly limit on deferrals that is based on a percentage of compensation earned during the month. However, the final rules stress that the applicable limit for the plan year is the sum of the dollar amounts of the limits for the separate portions of the plan compensation, determined at the end of the year.[12] Thus, plans that provide for payroll-by payroll limits, or similar limits that apply to a portion of the plan year, may not determine amounts in excess of the applicable limits based on the payroll period for which the limits are applied.

Alternative method: Time-weighted average of employer limits. A plan may limit elective deferrals for separate portions of the plan year. In determining amounts in excess of an employer-provided limit under such plans, the applicable limit for the plan year is the product of the employee's plan year compensation and the time-weighted average of the deferral percentage limits.[13] Thus, the employer-provided limit is not calculated as the sum of the limits for the separate portion of the year. For example, the applicable limit under a plan that limits deferrals by HCEs to 8% of compensation during the first half of the plan year and 10% during the second half of the plan year would be 9% of each employee's plan year compensation.

Catch-up contribution limit

Elective deferrals made by an eligible participant may be treated as catch-up contributions if they exceed an applicable statutory or plan limit, but only to the extent that the deferrals do not exceed the "catch-up contribution limit" for the tax year, reduced by elective deferrals previously treated as catch-up contributions for the tax year. The catch-up contribution limit for a tax year is the lesser of: (a) the applicable dollar catch-up contribution for the tax year, or (b) the participant's compensation for the year (as defined under Code Sec. 415(c)(3)), reduced by any other elective deferrals made by the participant for the year.[14] In addition, a participant's elective deferrals will not be treated as a catch-up contribution if the individual's total elective deferrals for the year exceed compensation.

Applicable dollar catch-up limit. The applicable dollar catch-up limit varies depending on the type of plan in which the eligible individual participates. For plans, other than SIMPLE 401(k) plans under Code Sec. 401(k)(11) and SIMPLE IRAs, the applicable dollar limit (for 2012) is $5,500.[15] Thus, in 2012 an eligible individual participating in a 401(k) plan may (subject to plan limits) be able to make a maximum elective deferral of $22,500 ($17,000 elective deferral plus $5,500 catch-up contribution).

Catch-up contributions for SIMPLE plans. The limit for catch-up elective deferrals under a SIMPLE plan is $2,500 for 2012 (see ¶ 2994).[16]

Timing rules

In calculating the maximum catch-up contribution that may be made by an eligible participant during a tax year, the determination of whether an elective deferral is a catch-up contribution is made as of the last day of the plan year (or the last day of the limitation year for purposes of the Code Sec. 415 limits). However, because the maximum catch-up contribution is based on a participant's tax year, IRS proposed rules prescribe a timing rule, under which the determination of whether elective deferrals that exceed an applicable limit that is tested on a tax year or a calendar year basis may be treated as catch-up contributions is made at the time the amounts are deferred.[17]

Catch-up contributions not subject to other limits

Catch-up contributions are not taken into account in applying the limits of Code Secs. 401(a)(30) (applying elective deferral limits), 402(h) (SEP contributions), 403(b) (TSA contributions), 408 (IRAs, SEPs, and SIMPLE IRAs), 415(c) (contribution limits for defined contribution plans), or 457(b)(2) (maximum deferrals under a 457 plan without regard to the special catch-up rules of Code Sec. 457(b)(3)) to other contributions or benefits under the plan offering catch-up contributions or any other plan of the employer.[18]

> **CCH POINTER:** Note that, because catch-up contributions are treated as elective deferrals, the amounts are subject to the distribution (see ¶ 2989) and vesting (see ¶ 2979) restrictions generally applicable under 401(k) plans.[19]

Nondiscrimination requirements inapplicable

A plan will not be treated as failing to satisfy the nondiscrimination requirements of Code Secs. 401(a)(4), 401(k)(3), 401(k)(11), 403(b)(12), 408(k), 410(b), or 416 merely by authorizing catch-up contributions.[20] However, catch-up contributions are subject to the Code Sec. 401(a)(26) minimum participation requirements, Code Sec. 401(k)(12) alternative Code Sec. 401(k) nondiscrimination rules, and Code Sec. 408(p) SIMPLE plan requirements.

Catch-up contributions excluded from ADP test

Elective deferrals that are treated as catch-up contributions because they exceed a statutory or employer-provided limit are, under proposed rules, subtracted from the participant's elective deferrals for the plan year in determining the actual deferral ratio of the participant for purposes of the ADP test (see ¶ 2951).[21]

Excess deferrals treated as catch-up contributions retained by plan. A 401(k) plan that satisfies the ADP test by taking corrective actions prescribed in Code Sec. 401(k)(8) must retain any elective deferrals that are treated as catch-up contributions because they exceed the ADP limit.[22] Retaining such excess deferrals will not cause the plan to violate the correction requirements of Code Sec. 401(k)(8). However, the residual excess contributions (i.e., deferrals in excess of the applicable catch-up contribution limit) would need to be corrected pursuant to the prescribed correction mechanisms (e.g., corrective distributions or recharacterization of excess contributions).

Catch-up contribution not included in top-heavy determination. Catch-up contributions for the "current" plan year are not taken into account in determining whether a plan is top-heavy under Code Sec. 416 (see ¶ 905).[23] Accordingly, if catch-up contributions are the only contributions made for key employees for the plan year, no top-heavy minimum contribution is required for the year. However, catch-up contributions for "prior" years are included in the account balances that are used in determining whether a plan is top-heavy.[24]

Effect of catch-up contributions on average benefits percentage test

Catch-up contributions for the "current" year are not taken into account for purposes of Code Sec. 410(b). Thus, catch-up contributions are not considered in determining the average benefit percentage under IRS Reg. § 1.410(b)-5 for the year if benefit percentages are based on current year determinations.[25]

By contrast, catch-up contributions for "prior" years would be included in the account balances that are used in determining the average benefit percentage, if allocations for prior years are taken into account (i.e., accrued-to-date allocations are used).[26]

Matching formula for catch-up contributions

An employer is permitted (but not required) to make matching contributions with respect to catch-up contributions.[27] A plan may apply a single matching formula for catch-up contributions and elective deferrals that do not qualify as catch-up contributions. The matching formula applicable to participants who are eligible to make catch-up contributions will not be treated as a separate benefit, right, or feature (see ¶ 1140) from the matching formula applied to other participants. However, the matching contribution on a catch-up contribution must satisfy the ACP test, taking into account all matching contributions, including matching contributions on catch-up contributions.[28]

Universal availability requirement

Employers are not required to allow eligible participants to make catch-up contributions, even if the plan provides for elective deferrals. Similarly, plans that do not provide for elective deferrals are not required to authorize catch-up contributions. However, an employer that provides for catch-up contributions must allow all eligible participants to make the same election.[29]

Effective opportunity to make catch-up contributions. A plan that offers catch-up contributions complies with the nondiscrimination requirements of Code Sec. 401(a)(4) only if all catch-up eligible participants who participate in an applicable employer plan maintained by the employer are provided with the "effective opportunity" to make the same dollar amount of catch-up contributions.[30]

Different limits may apply to employees. A plan may set forth different employer-provided limits for different groups of employees, consistent with the nondiscriminatory availability rules of IRS Reg. § 1.401(a)(4)-4. Thus, a plan could authorize an employer-provided limit that applies only to highly compensated employees. However, a plan may not establish lower employer-provided limits for catch-up eligible participants.[31]

Exclusion of collectively bargained employees. A plan may deny collectively bargained employees (and other employee described in Code Sec. 410(b)(3)) the opportunity to make catch-up contributions without violating the universal availability requirement.[32]

Multiple plans of related employers treated as one plan. For purposes of the universal availability rule, all plans maintained by related employers will be treated as one plan if the employers are treated as a single employer under Code Sec. 414 (e.g., employers that are members of a controlled group, trades or business under common control, or affiliated service groups).[33] Thus, plans maintained by employers in a controlled group that authorize elective deferrals must generally also provide catch-up eligible participants with an effective opportunity to make catch-up contributions.

Participants in multiple plans: Aggregation of catch-up contributions

In applying the catch-up contribution limit, elective deferrals by a participant under all plans maintained by the same employer (other than governmental 457 plans) are aggregated. As a result, the total amount of catch-up contributions made by a participant under all applicable plans of a single employer (other than governmental 457 plans) may not exceed the applicable dollar catch-up limits for the tax year.[34] Thus, if an employer sponsors a 401(k) and a 403(b) plan, a catch-up eligible participant may not defer more than $22,500 to the plans for 2012 ($17,000 Code Sec. 402(g) deferral limit plus $5,500 catch-up contribution). Amounts deferred in excess of $22,500 may not be treated as a catch-up contribution and must be distributed pursuant to specified allocation rules.

Coordinating employer-provided limits for participants in multiple plans

A plan may permit catch-up eligible participants to defer an amount in addition to the amount allowed under the employer-provided limit, without regard to whether the employee has made a catch-up contribution under another plan of the same employer (as determined by the aggregation rules).[35] However, if elective deferrals made under another plan maintained by the employer have been treated as catch-up contributions during the tax year, the elective deferrals that may be treated as catch-up contributions may not exceed the remaining catch-up limit for the year. Any other elective deferrals that exceed the employer-provided limit may not be treated as catch-up contributions and must satisfy the applicable nondiscrimination rules (i.e., the benefits, rights and features rules of IRS Reg. § 1.401(a)(4)-4.

¶2982

In addition, excess contributions that are not catch-up contributions must be included in the ADP test.[36]

Allocation rules determine plans under which excess deferrals are treated as catch-up contributions

In the event that a catch-up eligible participant makes additional elective deferrals in excess of the applicable limit under more than one applicable employer plan maintained by the same employer (as determined by the aggregation rules), the plan under which the excess contribution will be treated as a catch-up contribution may be determined in any manner that is not inconsistent with the manner in which the amounts were actually deferred under the plan.[37]

Income tax exclusion for catch-up contributions

The amount of elective deferrals that eligible participants may exclude from their taxable income is increased by the maximum catch-up contribution allowed for the tax year.[38]

Participants in multiple plans. An eligible participant may exclude from gross income elective deferrals in excess of the applicable Code Sec. 402(g) limit to the extent that the total amount of elective deferrals does not exceed the applicable catch-up limit for the tax year, without regard to the treatment of the elective deferrals by the plan under the catch up rules.[39] Thus, the total amount that an eligible participant may exclude from income as a catch-up contribution for a year may not exceed the catch-up contribution limit for that year, without regard to whether that participant made catch-up contributions under plans maintained by more than one employer.[40]

A catch-up eligible participant who participates in plans of two or more unrelated employers may further exclude from taxable income elective deferrals that in total exceed the Code Sec. 402(g) limit by an amount that does not exceed the dollar catch-up limit under either plan.[41] The exclusion applies even if neither plan treats the elective deferrals as catch-up contributions. Thus, a catch-up eligible participant who participates in plans of two or more employers may exclude from income elective deferrals that exceed the Code Sec. 402(g) limit, even if, when considered separately, the elective deferrals do not exceed an applicable limit for either employer's plan. In addition, the tax treatment of the participant's elective deferrals will not affect the qualified status or have any effect on the plan of either employer.[42]

[1] Code Sec. 414(v), as added by P.L. 107-16 (Economic Growth and Tax Relief Reconciliation Act of 2001), Act Sec. 631(a).

[2] Conference Committee Report to P.L. 107-16 (Economic Growth and Tax Relief Reconciliation Act of 2001) and Conference Committee Report to P.L. 107-147 (Job Creation and Worker Assistance Act of 2002).

[3] Code Sec. 414(v)(5)(A). **Note:** Prior to amendment by P.L. 107-147, Code Sec. 414(v)(5)(A), as enacted by EGTRRA, required a catch-up eligible

participant to have attained age 50 before the end of the "plan" year.

[4] IRS Reg. § 1.414(v)-1(g)(3).

[5] Preamble to IRS Reg. § 1.414(v)-1.

[6] Code Sec. 414(v)(5)(B). **Note:** Prior to amendment by P.L. 107-147, Code Sec. 414(v)(5)(B), as enacted by EGTRRA, required a catch-up eligible participant to have been barred by applicable limits from making further elective deferrals for the "plan" year.

[7] Preamble to IRS Reg. § 1.414(v)-1.

8 Code Sec. 414(v)(5)(B); IRS Reg. § 1.414(v)-1(b)(1) and (2)(i).

9 IRS Reg. § 1.414(v)-1(b)(1)(ii).

10 *Ibid.*.

11 IRS Reg. § 1.414(v)-1(b)(2)(i)(A).

12 *Ibid.*

13 IRS Reg. § 1.414(v)-1(b)(2)(i)(B)(1).

14 Code Sec. 414(v)(2)(A), as added by P.L. 107-16 (Economic Growth and Tax Relief Reconciliation Act of 2001), Act Sec. 631(a). IRS Reg. § 1.414(v)-1(b) and (c).

15 Code Sec. 414(v)(2)(B)(i), as added by P.L. 107-16 (Economic Growth and Tax Relief Reconciliation Act of 2001), Act Sec. 631(a).

16 Code Sec. 414(v)(2)(B)(ii), as added by P.L. 107-16 (Economic Growth and Tax Relief Reconciliation Act of 2001), Act Sec. 631(a).

17 IRS Reg. § 1.414(v)-1(c)(3).

18 Code Sec. 414(v)(3)(A).

19 IRS Reg. § 1.414(v)-1(a)(2).

20 Code Sec. 414(v)(3)(B).

21 IRS Reg. § 1.414(v)-1(d)(2).

22 IRS Reg. § 1.414(v)-1(d)(2)(iii).

23 Code Sec.414(v)(3)(B), as added by P.L. 107-16 (Economic Growth and Tax Relief Reconciliation Act of 2001), Act Sec. 631(a); IRS Reg. § 1.414(v)-1(d)(3)(i).

24 IRS Reg. § 1.414(v)-1(d)(3)(i).

25 IRS Reg. § 1.414(v)-1(d)(3)(ii).

26 Code Sec.414(v)(3)(B); IRS Reg. § 1.414(v)-1(d)(3)(ii).

27 Conference Committee Report to P.L. 107-16 (Economic Growth and Tax Relief Reconciliation Act of 2001).

28 Preamble to IRS Reg. § 1.414(v)-1.

29 Code Sec. 414(v)(4)(A), as added by P.L. 107-16 (Economic Growth and Tax Relief Reconciliation Act of 2001), Act Sec. 631(a).

30 IRS Reg. § 1.414(v)-1(e)(1).

31 IRS Reg. § 1.414(v)-1(e)(1)(i)(A).

32 IRS Reg. § 1.414(v)-1(e)(2).

33 Code Sec.414(v)(4)(B), as added by P.L. 107-16 (Economic Growth and Tax Relief Reconciliation Act of 2001), Act Sec. 631(a).

34 IRS Reg. § 1.414(v)-1(f)(1).

35 IRS Reg. § 1.414(v)-1(f)(2).

36 *Ibid.*

37 IRS Reg. § 1.414(v)-1(f)(3).

38 IRS Reg. § 1.402(g)-2(a).

39 Code Sec.402(g)(1)(C), as amended by P.L. 107-147 (Job Creation and Worker Assistance Act of 2002), Act Sec. 411(o)(1).

40 Conference Committee Report to P.L. 107-147 (Job Creation and Worker Assistance Act of 2002).

41 IRS Reg. § 1.402(g)-2(b).

42 Preamble to IRS Reg. § 1.414(v)-1.

¶ 2983

CONTRIBUTION AND DEFERRAL LIMITS: Tax Treatment of Elective Contributions

Elective contributions to a qualified 401(k) plan that fall within the stipulated dollar limits (see ¶ 2981) may be excluded from a plan participant's gross income.[1] The amounts are not included in the participant's gross income either at the time they could have been received in cash, but for the election, or at the time they are contributed to the plan. Rather, they are taxed only when distributed to the participant.[2]

Currently available amounts are taxable

Amounts contributed to a 401(k) plan that are currently available (i.e., paid to the employee or not subject to restriction (see ¶ 2940A)) to the participant at the time of the election are includible in the employee's gross income at the time they are contributed to the plan.[3]

FICA and FUTA tax withholding

Elective contributions and additional voluntary contributions in excess of the deferral limit are subject as wages to FICA and FUTA taxes (as well as state unemployment insurance taxes) at the time of the contribution.[4] However, nonelective and matching contributions are exempt from FICA and FUTA taxes at the time of contribution and at the time of distribution (see ¶ 2993).[5]

No income tax withholding

Deferred amounts do not constitute wages and are not subject to income tax withholding.[6]

Elective contributions to nonqualified plans are taxable

Elective contributions to a cash or deferred arrangement that is not qualified are includible in the participant's gross income at the time they would have been received by the employee but for the election.[7] The contribution will be taxable even if the election was made before the year in which the amount was earned by the employee or before the year in which the amount became currently available to the employee.

Saver's credit for elective deferrals

Lower and middle income taxpayers participating in 401(k) plans (including SIMPLE 401(k) plans) may qualify for a temporary nonrefundable tax credit (i.e., "saver's credit") for elective deferrals (up to $2,000 per year) to the plan.[8] The credit is provided in addition to the exclusion from gross income afforded participants making elective deferrals and allows eligible taxpayers to use plan (and IRA and Roth IRA) contributions (including those contributed pursuant to negative elections (see ¶ 2940A)) up to $2,000 to reduce their federal income tax on a dollar-for-dollar basis.[9] However, the credit does not entitle an employee to an income tax refund.

Credit for after-tax contributions. The saver's credit extends to voluntary after-tax contributions to a qualified plan or 403(b) plan. However, the saver's credit is not available for an employee contribution that is required as a condition of employment. [10]

Eligible taxpayers. The saver's credit is limited to taxpayers who are: age 18 or older, not full-time students, and not claimed as a dependent by another taxpayer.[11] In addition, the credit is not available to taxpayers with adjusted gross income in excess of a specified inflation-adjusted level of AGI (see below).

Maximum contribution eligible for credit. The maximum annual contribution that is eligible for the saver's credit is $2,000. Married taxpayers who are filing jointly are each entitled to a credit for contributions up to $2,000.[12]

Distributions reduce credit. The amount of a contribution eligible for the saver's credit is reduced by the aggregate distributions received from a retirement plan or IRA by the taxpayer (or the taxpayer's spouse) during a specified testing period.[13]

Testing period. The testing period consists of: the year for which the credit is claimed; the period after the end of the year for which the credit is claimed and before the due date (including extensions) of the taxpayer's income tax return for that year; and the two tax years preceding the year for which the credit is claimed.[14]

¶2983

Thus, for 2011, a taxpayer will subtract distributions received from January 1, 2009 through April 15, 2012 from the total 2011 contributions, then multiply the result (up to $2,000) by the applicable saver's credit rate.[15]

Spousal distributions reduce credit. Distributions received by a taxpayer's spouse will be considered to be distributions to the taxpayer, and, thus, will reduce the contributions used in calculating the credit, if a joint return is filed for the tax year in which the spouse received the distribution. [16]

Distributions that do not reduce credit. The saver's credit will not be reduced by: loans treated as distributions under Code Sec. 72(p); distributions of excess contributions under Code Sec. 401(k)(8); excess aggregate contributions distributed before the end of the of the following plan year under Code Sec. 401(m)(6); distributions of excess deferrals under Code Sec. 402(g)(2); or deductions for dividends paid on certain employer securities under Code Sec. 404(k).[17]

Rollover distribution. Distributions may be rolled over from another plan without affecting the amount of the saver's credit. However, distributions from a Roth IRA that are not rolled over will reduce the amount of the saver's credit, even if the distributions are not subject to tax under Code Sec. 25B(d)(2)(A).

Saver's credit rate. The amount of the saver's credit for a year is equal to the "applicable percentage" times the amount of qualified retirement savings contributions (not to exceed $2,000) made by an eligible individual in the tax year to the plan. The applicable percentage is determined by the taxpayer's filing status and adjusted gross income for the tax year for which the credit is claimed.[18]

Saver's credit rate adjustments. The threshold AGI used to calculate the amount of the saver's credit is adjusted for inflation.[19] The applicable percentage will be applied to AGI as adjusted in amounts rounded to nearest multiple of $500.

Under the AGI thresholds applicable beginning in 2012, the credit will be completely phased out at AGI levels of $57,500 for joint filers, $43,125 for head of household filers, and at $28,750 for single and married filing separately filers. [20]

The credit rate applicable to joint filers has been modified slightly. Accordingly, in 2012, a married taxpayer filing jointly with AGI of $34,500 or less would be entitled to a credit rate of 50 percent. The credit rate would drop to 20 percent for married taxpayers filing jointly with AGI between $34,501 and $37,500, and to 10 percent for joint filers with AGI between $37,501 and $57,500. [21]

Similarly, the applicable percentages for head of household filers and single taxpayers are not changed, but will apply to an adjusted level of income. [22] The income limit for a head of household filer would be 75 percent of the dollar amount for married taxpayers filing joint returns. [23] The income limits applicable to single taxpayers (and to married taxpayers not filing a joint return) would be 50 percent of the adjusted dollar amount for married taxpayers filing jointly.

Thus, under the adjusted thresholds, a head of household filer with AGI of $25,875 or less would be entitled to a credit rate of 50 percent. The credit rate would decrease to 20 percent for head of household filers with AGI between

$25,876 and $28,125, and to 10 percent for head of household filers with AGI between $28,126 and $43,125. [24]

A single or married filing separately filer with AGI of $17,250 would be entitled to a credit rate of 50 percent. The credit rate would decline to 20 percent for such taxpayers with AGI between $17,251 and $18,750, and to 10 percent for those with AGI between $18,751 and $28,750. [25]

[1] Code Sec. 402(e)(3); IRS Reg. § 1.402(a)-1(d)(2).

[2] IRS Reg. §§ 1.401(k)-1(a)(4)(iii) and 1.402(a)-1(d)(2)(i).

[3] IRS Reg. §§ 1.401(k)-1(a)(3)(ii) and 1.402(a)-1(d)(1).

[4] Code Secs. 3121(v)(1)(A) and 3306(b)(5)(A).

[5] Code Secs. 3121(a)(5) and 3306(r)(1)(A).

[6] Code Sec. 3401(a)(12)(A).

[7] IRS Reg. §§ 1.401(k)-1(a)(5)(iii) and 1.402(a)-1(d)(1).

[8] Code Sec. 25B, as added by P.L. 107-16 (Economic Growth and Tax Relief Reconciliation Act of 2001), Act Sec. 618(a).

[9] IRS Announcement 2001-106, Q&A-11, I.R.B. 2001-44, October 20, 2001, at CCH PENSION PLAN GUIDE ¶ 17,097R-52.

[10] Code Sec. 25B(d)(1)(C), as added by P.L. 107-16 (Economic Growth and Tax Relief Reconciliation Act of 2001), Act Sec. 618(a).

[11] Code Sec. 25B(c), as added by P.L. 107-16 (Economic Growth and Tax Relief Reconciliation Act of 2001), Act Sec. 618(a). IRS Announcement 2001-106, Q&A-2, I.R.B. 2001-44, October 20, 2001, at CCH PENSION PLAN GUIDE ¶ 17,097R-52.

[12] Code Sec. 25B(a), as added by P.L. 107-16 (Economic Growth and Tax Relief Reconciliation Act of 2001), Act Sec. 618(a). IRS Announcement 2001-106, Q&A-9, I.R.B. 2001-44, October 20, 2001, at CCH PENSION PLAN GUIDE ¶ 17,097R-52.

[13] Code Sec. 25B(d)(2)(A), as added by P.L. 107-16 (Economic Growth and Tax Relief Reconciliation Act of 2001), Act Sec. 618(a).

[14] Code Sec. 25B(d)(2)(B), as added by P.L. 107-16 (Economic Growth and Tax Relief Reconciliation Act of 2001), Act Sec. 618(a). IRS Announcement 2001-106, Q&A-4, I.R.B. 2001-44, October 20, 2001, at CCH PENSION PLAN GUIDE ¶ 17,097R-52.

[15] IRS News Release IR-2001-107, November 7, 2001.

[16] Code Sec. 25B(d)(2)(D), as added by P.L. 107-16 (Economic Growth and Tax Relief Reconciliation Act of 2001), Act Sec. 618(a).

[17] Code Sec. 25B(d)(2)(C), as added by P.L. 107-16 (Economic Growth and Tax Relief Reconciliation Act of 2001), Act Sec. 618(a).

[18] Code Sec. 25B(b), as added by P.L. 107-16 (Economic Growth and Tax Relief Reconciliation Act of 2001), Act Sec. 618(a).

[19] Code Sec. 25B(b), as amended by P.L. 109-280 (Pension Protection Act of 2006), Act Sec. 833(a).

[20] IR- 2011-103, 11-20-11, at CCH PENSION PLAN GUIDE ¶ 17,037Q.

[21] Code Sec. 25B(b)(1), as amended by P.L. 109-280 (Pension Protection Act of 2006), Act Sec. 833(a); IR-2011-103, 10-20-11, at CCH PENSION PLAN GUIDE ¶ 17,037Q.

[22] Code Sec. 25B(b), as amended by P.L. 109-280 (Pension Protection Act of 2006), Act Sec. 833(a).

[23] Code Sec. 25B(b)(2), as amended by P.L. 109-280 (Pension Protection Act of 2006), Act Sec. 833(a).

[24] IR 2011-103, 10-20-11, at CCH PENSION PLAN GUIDE ¶ 17,037Q.

[25] *Ibid.*

¶ 2984

CONTRIBUTION AND DEFERRAL LIMITS: Taxation and Correction of Excess Deferrals

An excess deferral is the amount by which the sum of a participant's elective deferrals exceeds the applicable limit for the tax year. The tax consequences of an excess deferral are the following:

1. the excess deferral is includible in the employee's gross income for the year in which it was contributed to the plan,[1]

2. earnings on the excess deferral are taxed in the year of distribution, [2]

3. an excess deferral that is not returned to the participant (by April 15 of the year following the year of deferral), but that is retained in the plan, is *taxed again* when it is eventually distributed,[3] and

4. any excess deferral that is retained in the plan after the first April 15 following the tax year in which it occurred is subject to the same withdrawal restrictions as any other elective contribution.[4]

Penalty taxes. Excess deferrals that are distributed in a timely manner are not subject to the 10 percent early distribution tax or to 20 percent withholding. However, untimely distributions are subject to penalty tax.

Correction of excess deferrals

A plan *may* allow a participant to avoid the potential double taxation caused by an excess deferral by authorizing a corrective distribution (by April 15 of the following year) of the amount of the excess deferral and income allocable to the excess deferral. A corrective distribution may not be made unless it is specifically authorized by the terms of the plan.

A plan is not required to provide for the distribution of excess deferrals.[5] However, an excess deferral may not be corrected by a means other than distribution. [6] In addition, a qualified plan must provide for the distribution of excess deferrals if the deferrals are made to the plan of the same employer.

Making the corrective distribution. Two steps must be followed in order for a corrective distribution to be made:[7]

1. *Employee notification of plan.* No later than the first April 15 (or an earlier date specified by the plan) of the year following the year in which the excess deferral was made, the participant must notify each plan under which deferrals were made of the amount of the excess deferral (and the portion comprised of designated Roth contributions) contributed to the plan. A plan may, alternatively, require the employer to notify the plan on the participant's behalf of the excess deferrals.

2. *Distribution of excess deferral and earnings.* No later than the first April 15 following the close of the tax year in which the excess deferral was made, the plan must distribute to the participant the amount of the excess deferral and income allocable to the excess deferral through the end of the year.

Corrective distribution during tax year of deferral

A plan may authorize a corrective distribution of an excess deferral to be made during the same year in which it arose. Such a distribution may be made only if the following conditions are satisfied:[8]

1. the participant designates the distribution as an excess deferral (and identifies the extent to which the excess deferrals are comprised of Roth contributions);

2. the corrective distribution is made after the date on which the plan received the excess deferral; and

3. the plan designates the distribution as a distribution of excess deferrals.

Income allocable to excess deferrals

The corrective distribution must include income that is allocable to the excess deferral for the tax year.[9] Allocable income is equal to the sum of the allocable gain or loss in the participant's tax year.

Gap period income. Under pre-2008 law, the corrective distribution was to include allocable gain or loss for the "gap period" between the end of the tax year and the date of distribution.[10] Accordingly, to the extent excess deferrals were or would be credited with gain or loss during the gap period if the total account were to be distributed, the allocable gain or loss during that period was to be included in the distribution.

The IRS had also prescribed a safe harbor method for allocating gap period income, pursuant to which income on excess deferrals for the gap period was equal to 10 percent of the income allocable to excess deferrals for the tax year, multiplied by the number of calendar months that had passed since the end of the tax year.[11]

Repeal of requirement to include gap period income in distribution. The Worker, Retiree, and Employer Recovery Act of 2008, effective for plan years after 2007, repealed the requirement that gap period income be included in the corrective distribution. The income to be distributed, under the modified rule, is the income allocable to the excess deferral through the end of the year. [12]

Reasonable method for allocating income. A plan may use any reasonable method for computing the income allocable to excess deferrals, provided that the method: does not violate the general nondiscrimination rules of Code Sec. 401(a)(4) (see discussion beginning at ¶ 1100); is used consistently for all participants and for all corrective distributions under the plan for the plan year; and is used by the plan for allocating income to participant accounts.[13]

Corrective distribution reduced by prior distributions

The amount of excess deferrals that may be included in a corrective distribution is reduced by excess contributions that have previously been distributed or recharacterized (in order to correct violations of the ADP test (see ¶ 2977)) for the plan year beginning with or within the tax year.[14] In addition, the amount by which the corrective distribution is reduced will also reduce the amount of excess contributions included in the participant's income and reported by the employer as a distribution of excess contributions for the plan year.[15]

¶2984

Corrective distribution does not require participant consent

A 401(k) plan may make a corrective distribution of excess deferrals and allocable income without first notifying or acquiring the consent of the participant or the participant's spouse.[16]

Taxation of timely corrective distributions

A corrective distribution of an excess deferral that is made on or before the first April 15 following the close of the tax year may be excluded from the participant's gross income for the distribution year (and will not be subject to the early distribution tax).[17] However, income allocable to the excess deferral is included in the participant's gross income for the tax year in which it is distributed.[18]

Double tax imposed on late corrective distributions. Although excess deferrals are included in a participant's income in the tax year of the deferral, in the event that a corrective distribution of excess deferrals and allocable income for a tax year is not made on or before the first April 15 following the close of the tax year, the distribution is also included in the participant's gross income in the tax year in which it is distributed.[19]

Distribution of excess deferrals from designated Roth account

The rules governing the distribution of excess deferrals after the correction period also apply to distributions of excess deferrals from designated Roth accounts. Accordingly, if a designated Roth account includes excess deferrals, the distribution of amounts attributable to those excess deferrals will be included in the participant's income, without adjustment for any return of investment in the contract under Code Sec. 72(e)(8).[20] Such distributions, further, will not be treated as qualified distributions eligible rollover distributions.

Correction of excess deferrals under EPCRS

In the event an excess deferral is not corrected by the first April 15 following the close of the year, the plan sponsor may correct the excess deferral under EPCRS. Such an operational error may be corrected under SCP for no fee or under VCP for a specified fee.

The prescribed correction method under EPCRS requires the plan to distribute the excess deferral to the employee and report the amount as taxable in both the year of deferral and in the year distributed.[21] The amount of the distribution will be reported on Form 1099-R. In addition, unlike the tax treatment under IRS Reg. § 1.402(g)-1(e), corrective distributions made though the EPCRS remain subject to the 10% premature distribution penalty tax under Code Sec. 72(t).

Distributions of excess deferrals made after April 15 to a highly compensated employees are included in the ADP test for the year of deferral. However, distributions to a NHCE are not included in the ADP test.

---

[1] Code Sec. 402(g)(1).

[2] Code Sec. 402(g)(2)(C)(ii).

[3] Code Sec. 402(g)(7).

[4] Code Sec. 401(k)(2)(B).

[5] IRS Reg. § 1.402(g)-1(e)(4).

[6] Code Sec. 401(k)(2)(B).

[7] Code Sec. 402(g)(2)(A); IRS Reg. § 1.402(g)-1(e)(2).

[8] IRS Reg. § 1.402(g)-1(e)(3).

[9] IRS Reg. § 1.402(g)-1(e)(2).

[10] IRS Reg. § 1.402(g)-1(e)(5)(i).

[11] IRS Reg. § 1.402(g)-1(e)(5)(iv).

The following rules applied prior to repeal of the gap period requirement.

Plan restatement submitted in Cycle B. A restated plan submitted to the IRS in Cycle B (February 1, 2007 through January 31, 2008) or Cycle C (February 1, 2008 through January 31, 2009) must provide for the distribution of gap period earnings. In the event a plan submitted before March 24, 2008 did not provide for the distribution of gap period earnings, the plan sponsor will not receive a determination letter until the plan is amended to include the distribution of gap period earnings (IRS Notice 2008-30, Q-19, I.R.B. 2008-12, 3-24-08, at CCH PENSION PLAN GUIDE, ¶ 17,141E).

Interim plan amendment. An interim plan amendment providing for the inclusion of gap period earnings in the distribution of excess deferrals will not need to be adopted until the last day of the first plan year beginning on or after January 1, 2009 (IRS Notice 2008-30, Q-20, I.R.B. 2008-12, 3-24-08, at CCH PENSION PLAN GUIDE, ¶ 17,141E).

Plan must include gap period earnings in corrective distributions before 2009. The IRS cautions that, although interim plan amendments implementing the gap period earnings rules, need not be adopted before the last day of the first plan year beginning on or after January 1, 2009, plans must include gap period earnings in the distribution of excess deferrals, effective for excess deferrals attributable to tax years beginning on or after January 1, 2007. (IRS Notice 2008-30, Q-21, I.R.B. 2008-12, 3-24-08, at CCH PENSION PLAN GUIDE, ¶ 17,141E).

[12] Code Sec. 402(g)(2)(A)(ii), as amended by P.L. 110-458 (Worker, Retiree, and Employer Recovery Act of 2008), Act Sec. 109(b)(3).

[13] IRS Reg. § 1.402(g)-1(e)(5)(ii).

[14] IRS Reg. § 1.402(g)-1(e)(6).

[15] *Ibid.*

[16] IRS Reg. § 1.402(g)-1(e)(7).

[17] Code Sec. 402(g)(2)(C)(i); IRS Reg. § 1.402(g)-1(e)(8)(i).

[18] Code Sec. 402(g)(2)(C)(ii); IRS Reg. § 1.402(g)-1(e)(8)(i).

[19] Code Sec. 402(g)(7); IRS Reg. § 1.402(g)-1(e)(8)(iii).

[20] IRS Reg. § 1.402(g)-1(e)(8)(iv).

[21] Rev. Proc. 2008-50, I.R.B. 2008-35, 9-2-08 at CCH PENSION PLAN GUIDE ¶ 17,299S-66.

¶ 2985

CONTRIBUTION AND DEFERRAL LIMITS: Limits on Annual Additions to a Participant's Account

The calendar year dollar limit on elective deferrals (see ¶ 2981) does not apply to other types of employer contributions to the plan or to an employee's after tax-contributions. However, under a completely separate plan year limit, known as the "415 limit," the total of all additions (contributions) to an employee's account in a 401(k) plan (including elective deferrals, employer matching contributions, after-tax employee contributions, and forfeitures allocated to the employee's account following the departure of nonvested employees) may not in a limitation year exceed the lesser of $50,000 (in 2012) or 100 percent of the employee's compensation (net of deferrals).[1] Thus, in 2012 an employer may make additional contributions on behalf of an employee to the extent that such contributions when aggregated with elective deferrals made by the employee during the limitation year do not exceed the overall limit of the lower of $50,000 or 100 percent of the participant's compensation.

Application of Code Sec. 401(a)(17) compensation limit

A plan may not base allocations under a defined contribution plan on compensation in excess of the annual limitation under Code Sec. 401(a)(17) ($250,000 in

2012).[2] Accordingly, compensation used by a plan in applying the 415 limits may not exceed the applicable Code Sec. 401(a)(17) limit for the year.

Limitation year

The limitation year, for purposes of determining whether annual additions comply with the 415 limits, is generally the calendar year. Alternatively, the plan may specify the use of any other consecutive 12 month period as the limitation period.[3]

Employer may maintain multiple plans with different limitation years. An employer may maintain more than one qualified plan, each of which provide for different limitation years.[4] In the event a participant is credited with annual additions in more than one defined contribution plan, each plan will satisfy Code Sec. 415 only if the applicable limits are satisfied with respect to annual additions for the limitation year with respect to the participant, plus amounts credited to the participant's account under all other plans required to be aggregated with the plan under Code Sec. 415(f) that would have been considered annual additions for the limitation year under the plan if they had been credited under the plan rather than the aggregated plan. [5]

Change in limitation year. The limitation year may be changed only by a plan amendment. [6] Any change in the limitation year must be changed to a 12-month period beginning with any day within the current limitation year. [7]

Pro rate 415 limit in short limitation year. A change in the limitation year will result in a short limitation year. Under the final regulations, the 415 limits are to be separately applied to a limitation period that begins with the first day of the current limitation year and that ends on the day before the first day of the limitation year for which the change is effective.[8]

Annual additions

Annual additions for purposes of the Code Sec. 415 limits include elective deferrals (other than catch-up contributions); employer matching contributions; employer nonelective contributions; employee after-tax contributions (mandatory and voluntary); forfeitures allocated to a participant's individual account following the termination of nonvested or partially vested participants; and employer contributions to other defined contribution plans, such as profit-sharing plans, money purchase plans, and ESOPs.[9]

Medical benefits. Annual additions also include: (1). amounts allocated to an individual medical account that are offered under an employer's qualified pension plan; [10] and (2) employer contributions for a key employee that are allocated to a separate account under a welfare benefit plan for post-retirement medical benefits. [11]

Funds not included as annual additions

Annual additions do not include earnings on participant's accounts, amounts directly transferred or rolled over from another plan, or excess deferrals that are distributed in timely corrective distributions.[12] However, excess contributions and excess aggregate contributions that cause a failure of the ADP/ACP nondiscrimination tests will be treated as annual additions, even if they are corrected through distribution (or forfeited).

Catch-up contributions. Catch-up contributions made under Code Sec. 414(v) by participants age 50 and over do not give rise to annual additions.[13]

Loan repayments. Mandatory employee contributions are treated as annual additions. However, repayments of loans made to a plan participant are not annual additions.[14]

Restorative payments are not annual additions. The allocation of restorative payments to a participant's account does not give rise to an annual addition for any limitation year. Restorative payments are generally payments made to restore losses to a plan resulting from actions by a fiduciary for which there is a reasonable risk of liability for breach of fiduciary duty, where similarly situated plan participants are treated similarly with respect to the payments. Under the final rules, payments made in order to restore some or all of the plan's losses due to an action (or a failure to act) that creates a reasonable risk of liability for such breach of fiduciary duty under ERISA or under other applicable federal or state law (e.g., payments made pursuant to a DOL order or court-approved settlement or under the DOL's Voluntary Fiduciary Correction Program) may also be treated as restorative payments.[15]

Timing rules for annual additions

An annual addition (i.e., contribution or forfeiture) is credited to a participant's account for a limitation year if it is allocated to the participant's account, under the terms of the plan, as of any date within the limitation year.[16]

Date employer contributions treated as annual additions. Employer contributions will be treated as credited to a participant's account (and as annual additions) for the limitation year if they are actually made to the plan within 30 days after the plan year. [17] However, a contribution by a tax-exempt employer will be taken into account for the limitation year as an annual addition if it is credited to a participant's account no later than the 15th day of the 10th calendar month following the end of the calendar or fiscal year with or with which the limitation year ends.

Date employee contributions are treated as annual additions. Employee contributions, whether voluntary or mandatory, are not treated as annual additions for a limitation year unless the contributions are actually made to the plan within 30 days after the close of the limitation year. [18]

Contributions made pursuant to veterans' reemployment rights. Employer contributions to an employee account with respect to a prior limitation year, that are made in accordance with a veteran's reemployment rights under Code Sec. 414(u) will be treated as an annual addition for the limitation year to which the contributions relate, rather than the year in which it is made. [19]

Annual additions limit is an aggregate limit

¶2985

A participant's annual additions for purposes of the 415 limit include all contributions made for the participant under all defined contribution plans maintained by the employer, including plans maintained by members of a controlled group or an affiliated service group. [20]

Aggregation rules

Under Code Sec. 415(f), all defined contribution plans (without regard to whether the plan has been terminated) that have ever been maintained by the employer (or predecessor employer) are treated as one defined contribution plan. [21] The controlled group rules, the affiliated service group rules, and the leased employee rules all apply for purposes of determining whether a plan that is maintained by an entity other than the employer is considered to be maintained by the employer under the aggregation rules.

Plans of predecessor employer. An employer's plan must be aggregated with all plans maintained by a predecessor employer (as defined under Code Sec. 414(a)). The aggregation rule applies whether or not the plan is assumed by the employer. A former employer will be treated as a predecessor employer with respect to a participant in a plan maintained by an employer if the employer maintains a plan under which the participant has accrued a benefit while performing services for the former employer. However, the benefit must have been provided under the plan maintained by the employer. [22]

Compensation for purposes of the annual additions limit

A participant's compensation, for purposes of the Code Sec. 415 limits is not limited to salary, but, under Code Sec. 415(c)(3)(C) and (D), includes elective deferrals and such items as moving expenses, salary reduction contributions to a cafeteria plan, and qualified transportation fringe benefit elections. However, not all remuneration for services will be treated as compensation for Code Sec. 415 purposes.

Includible compensation. A participant's total 415 compensation includes[23]: wages, salary, fees for professional services, and other amounts received (including non-cash amounts) for personal services rendered in the course of employment with the employer maintaining the plan, to the extent the amounts are includible in gross income (e.g., sales commissions, tips, bonuses, fringe benefits, and reimbursements under nonaccountable plans); earned income (under Code Sec. 401(c)(2) of a self-employed person, plus elective deferrals; employer contributions to a Code Sec. 403(b) tax-sheltered annuity, whether or not the amounts are excludable from an employee's gross income; employer-provided accident and health insurance benefits and medical reimbursement plan benefits that are includible in the gross income of the employee; amounts paid or reimbursed by an employer for an employee's moving expenses to the extent that, at the time of payment, it is reasonable to believe that the amounts are not deductible by the employee; the value of nonqualified stock options granted to an employee to the extent that the value of the options is includible in the employee's gross income in the tax year in which granted; the amount includible in an employee's gross income following an election under Code Sec. 83(b) to be taxed on the value of property transferred in connection with the performance of services; and amounts includible in the gross income of an employee under Code Sec. 409A or Code Sec. 457(f)(1)(A), or because the amounts were constructively received. [24]

Elective deferrals are included in compensation. An employee's compensation, for purposes of the Code Sec. 415 limits, includes any elective deferrals.[25] In addition, amounts deferred by a participant under a 403(b) plan, 457 plan, SARSEP and to a SIMPLE plan will be viewed as compensation.

Salary reduction contributions to a cafeteria plan. Salary reduction contributions made to a cafeteria plan are included in a participant's compensation for purposes of the Code Sec. 415(c) limits on contributions and benefits.[26] Because salary reduction contributions to a cafeteria plan do not reduce an employee's Code Sec. 415 compensation, such contributions will effectively increase the amount that may be contributed to a defined contribution plan on behalf of nonhighly compensated employees.

Qualified transportation benefits. Qualified transportation benefits that are provided pursuant to salary reduction arrangement and that are not included in a participant's income are treated as compensation under Code Sec.415(c)(3). [27]

Items not treated as compensation. Compensation, for purposes of the annual additions limit, does not include: (1) employer contributions (other than elective deferrals) to qualified plans, 403(b) plans, simplified employee pension plans (SEPs), or SIMPLE plans, to the extent not includible in the gross income of the employee for the tax year in which contributed; (2) distributions from a deferred compensation plan (whether or not qualified) , even if the amounts are includible in the gross income of the employee when distributed; (3) amounts realized from the exercise of a nonqualified stock option, or when restricted stock (or property) held by an employee becomes freely transferable or is no longer subject to a substantial risk of forfeiture; (4) distributions from a deferred compensation plan (other than an unfunded nonqualified plan), even if the amounts are includible in the gross income of the employee when distributed; (5) amounts realized from the exercise of a nonqualified stock option, or when restricted stock (or property) held by an employee becomes freely transferable or is no longer subject to a substantial risk of forfeiture; (6) amounts realized from the sale, exchange, or other disposition of stock acquired under a qualified stock option; (7). amounts that receive special tax benefits, such as premiums for group-term life insurance, but only to the extent the premiums are not includible in an employee's gross income; and (8) items that are "similar" to other specified excluded remuneration. [28]

Safe harbor definitions of compensation. A plan that defines compensation as including only the items specified in IRS Reg. § 1.415(c)-2(b)(1) and (2) (i.e., taxable wages, salary, commissions, and bonuses), and excluding the amounts listed in IRS Reg. § 1.415(c)-2(c) (see above) will automatically be considered to be using a definition of compensation that satisfies Code Sec. 415(c)(3).[29]

Alternatively, a plan may automatically satisfy 415(c)(3) by defining compensation as:

1. Wages and payments of compensation that are required to be reported on Form W-2 (i.e., W-2 definition). Note, amounts paid or reimbursed by an employer for employee moving expenses may be excluded if the expenses were deductible by the employee.[30]

2. Wages subject to federal income tax withholding under Code Sec. 3401(a).[31]

Note, for purposes of the safe harbor, rules that limit the remuneration included in wages based on the nature or location of the employment or services provided, are disregarded.

Compensation paid during the limitation year. Compensation, for purposes of the Code Sec. 415 limits, will not be taken into account for a limitation year, unless it is actually paid or made available to the employee (or includible in the employee's gross income, if earlier) during the limitation year.[32] In addition, compensation, for purposes of Code Sec. 415, must generally be paid (or treated as paid) to the employee before the employee's severance from employment with the employer maintaining the plan.[33]

Note, a plan may treat as compensation amounts earned during the limitation year, but not paid during that year, solely because of the timing of pay periods and pay dates. However, in order for this treatment to apply, the amounts must be paid during the first few weeks of the next limitation year, the amounts with respect to all similarly situated employees must be treated uniformly and consistently, and no compensation may be included in more than one limitation year.[34]

Post-severance compensation. Although payments received by an employee following severance from employment are generally not treated as compensation, specified post-severance payments may be included in a participant's compensation if paid by the later of 2½ months after severance from employment or the end of the limitation year that includes the date of severance from employment.

CCH POINTER: It is important at this point to remember the requirement under IRS Reg. § 1.401(k)-1(e)(8) that elective deferrals may only be made from Code Sec. 415(c) compensation. Pursuant to this rule, an employee, under a qualified 401(k) plan may not make a cash or deferred election with respect to an amount paid after severance from employment, unless the amount is paid by the later of 2 ½ months after severance from employment or the end of the year that includes the date of severance from employment.[35]

Payments included in 415 compensation. Post-severance payments that may be included in Code Sec. 415 compensation under IRS Reg. § 1.415(c)-2(e)(3) include: payments of regular compensation for services provided during the employee's regular working hours, overtime and shift differential pay, commissions, and bonuses, or similar payments that would have been paid to the employee prior to severance, if the employee had continued employment with the employer.[36] In addition, the plan may authorize the following amounts to be included in Code Sec. 415 compensation: (1) payments for unused accrued bona fide sick, vacation or other leave, but only if the employee would have been able to use the leave if the employee had continued employment with the employer; (2) payments under a nonqualified unfunded deferred compensation plan, but only if the payments would have been paid to the employee at the same time if the employee had continued employment, and only to the extent that the payments are includible in the employee's gross income. [37]

Severance pay and parachute payments. Compensation paid after severance from employment with the employer maintaining the plan will not, absent statutory authorization, be treated as 415 compensation, even if it is paid within the specified 2½ month period after the severance from employment or the end of the limitation year. Accordingly, severance payments and parachute payments that are paid after an employee severs employment will not be 415 compensation. Similarly, post-severance payments under a nonqualified deferred compensation plan will not be treated as 415 compensation unless the payments would have been paid at that time irrespective of the employee's severance from employment.[38]

Military continuation pay. Post-severance payments made to individuals in qualified military service may, if the plan provides, be treated as compensation for purposes of Code Sec. 415. However, the payments may not exceed the pay the individual would have received if he or she had continued to work for the employer rather than entering qualified military [39]

Deemed disability payments. The final regulations provide an additional exception to the post-severance timing rule for compensation paid to a permanently and totally disabled participant that is designed to allow the employer to continue to make contributions for such employees. Such deemed disability payments will be treated as compensation if: (1) the participant is not highly compensated immediately before becoming disabled, or the plan provides for the continuation of contributions on behalf of all participants who are permanently and totally disabled for a fixed or determinable period; (2) the plan explicitly provides for the treatment of the payments to disabled participants as compensation; and (3) contributions made with respect to the deemed disability payments that are treated as compensation are nonforfeitable when made. [40]

Excess deferrals and excess contributions. Excess deferrals, excess contributions, and excess aggregate contributions are treated as annual additions.[41] Excess contributions and excess aggregate contributions are considered annual additions even if they are corrected by distribution or recharacterization. However, excess deferrals that are returned in a corrective distribution are not annual additions.

Correction of excess annual additions

Excess annual additions may be corrected under the procedures specified and approved by the IRS in the Employee Plans Compliance Resolution System (EPCRS). The final regulations applicable to limitation years beginning on or after July 1, 2007 eliminate the procedures provided under previously applicable IRS Reg. §415-6(b)(6) that allowed for the correction of excess annual additions through the allocation and reallocation (i.e., refund) of the excess amounts or though the distribution of elective deferrals and voluntary or mandatory employee contributions.[42] The eligibility rules and other conditions applicable under EPCRS are more flexible and not as severe as those under IRS Reg. § 1.415-6(b)(6), which should simply the process for correcting excess annual additions.

The IRS notes that the methods specified in the deleted regulations are generally permitted under the Employee Plans Compliance Resolution System (EPCRS).[43]

IRS correction methods

The correction method specified under the IRS Voluntary Correction Program (see ¶ 369) for redressing a plan's failure to limit annual additions that are elective deferrals or employee contributions (even if the excess did not result from a reasonable error in the determination of the maximum elective deferral or employee contribution that could be made under the Code Sec. 415 limits) is to distribute the elective deferrals or employee contributions under a method similar to that prescribed by the previously applicable procedures under IRS Reg. § 1.415-6(b)(6)(iv).[44]

Forfeited matching contributions. Elective deferrals and after-tax employee contributions that are matched may be returned to the employee, provided that the matching contributions relating to such contributions are forfeited (which will also reduce excess annual additions for the affected individuals). The forfeited matching contributions are to be placed into an unallocated account to be used as an employer contribution, other than elective deferrals, in succeeding periods. [45]

EPCRS prescribed overpayment correction mechanism. For limitation years beginning on or after January 1, 2009, the failure to limit annual additions (other than elective deferrals and after-tax contributions (i.e., nonelective and matching contributions)) allocated to participants in a defined contribution plan as required under Code Sec. 415 must be corrected in accordance with the overpayment correction methods specified under EPCRS.[46]

Forfeiture correction method. An additional correction method approved by the IRS authorizes: (1) the forfeiture of nonvested employer contributions for certain nonhighly compensated terminated employees who have received a distribution of elective deferrals, and (2) the repayment of the previously paid excess amounts to the plan.[47]

> **CCH POINTER:** *Fail-safe plan language ensures 415 limits are not violated.* A plan should contain "fail-safe" language to address inadvertent violations of the 415 limits. For example, under the previously applicable regulations, a plan could state that: "Amounts in excess of the limit will be reallocated to the remaining participants. To the extent every participant in the plan has reached his or her limit, any remaining amounts shall be placed in a suspense account and reallocated in the next year."[48] The final regulations authorize plan provisions that automatically freeze or reduce the amount of annual additions to ensure that the 415 limits are not exceeded, as long as the determination does not involve employer discretion.

---

[1] Code Sec. 415(c) as amended by P.L. 107-16 (Economic Growth and Tax Relief Reconciliation Act of 2001), Act Sec. 611(b).

[2] IRS Reg. § 1.415(c)-2(f).
[3] IRS Reg. § 1.415(j)-1(a) and (b).
[4] IRS Reg. § 1.415(j)-1(c).

[5] IRS Reg. § 1.415(j)-1(c)(2).

[6] IRS Reg. § 1.415(j)-1(d)(1).

[7] IRS Reg. § 1.415(j)-1(d).

[8] IRS Reg. § 1.415(j)-1(d)(3).

[9] Code Sec. 415(c)(2).

[10] Code Sec. 415(l); IRS Reg. § 1.415(c)-1(a)(2).

[11] Code Sec.419A(d)(2); IRS Reg. § 1.415(c)-1(a)(2).

[12] IRS Reg. §§ 1.415(c)-1(b)(1)(ii) and 1.415(b)(3)(i).

[13] IRS Reg. § 1.415(c)-1(b)(2)(ii)(B).

[14] IRS Reg. § 1.415(c)-1(c)(3).

[15] IRS Reg. § 1.415(c)-1(b)(2)(ii)(C).

[16] IRS Reg. § 1.415(c)-1(b)6)(i)(A).

[17] IRS Reg. § 1.415(c)-1(b)6)(i)(B).

[18] IRS Reg. § 1.415(c)-1(b)6)(i)(C).

[19] IRS Reg. § 1.415(c)-1(b)6)(ii)(D).

[20] Code Sec. 415(f).

[21] IRS Reg. § 1.415(f)-1(a)(2)..

[22] IRS Reg. § 1.415(f)-1(a)(2).

[23] IRS Reg. § 1.415(c)-2(b).

[24] IRS Reg. § 1.415(c)-2(b).

[25] Code Sec. 415(c)(3)(D).

[26] Code Sec. 415(c)(3)(D)(ii).

[27] Code Sec. 415(c)(3)(D)(ii), as amended by P.L. 106-554 (Community Renewal Tax Relief Act of 2000), Act Sec. 314(e)(1).

[28] IRS Reg. § 1.415(c)-2(c).

[29] IRS Reg. § 1.415(c)-2(d).

[30] IRS Reg. § 1.415(c)-2(d)(4).

[31] IRS Reg. § 1.415(c)-2(d)(3).

[32] IRS Reg. § 1.415(c)-2(e)(1)(i).

[33] IRS Reg. § 1.415(c)-2(e)(1)(ii).

[34] IRS Reg. § 1.415(c)-2(e)(2).

[35] IRS Reg. § 1.401(k)-1(e)(8).

[36] IRS Reg. § 1.415(c)-2(e)(3)(ii).

[37] IRS Reg. § 1.415(c)-2(e)(3)(iii).

[38] IRS Reg. § 1.415(c)-2(e)(3)(iv).

[39] IRS Reg. § 1.415(c)-2(e)(4)).

[40] IRS Reg. § 1.415(c)-2(e)(4; IRS Reg. § 1.415(c)-2(g)(4)(ii).

[41] IRS Reg. § 1.415(c)-1(b)(1).

[42] IRS Reg. §§ 1.415(c)-1; 1.401(a)-2(b); 1.401(a)(9)-5,A-9(b)(1); and 1.402(c)-2, A-4(a).

[43] Preamble to IRS Reg. § 1.415(c)-1 (72 FR 16878), April 5, 2007.

[44] Rev. Proc. 2008-50 Appendix A, Sec. 08, I.R.B. 2008-35, at CCH PENSION PLAN GUIDE ¶ 17,299S-66.

[45] *Ibid.*

[46] Rev. Proc. 2008-50 Sec. 6.06(2) and (3), I.R.B. 2008-35, at CCH PENSION PLAN GUIDE ¶ 17,299S-66.

[47] Rev. Proc. 2008-50, Appendix B, Sec. 2.04(2)(a)(ii), I.R.B. 2008-35, at CCH PENSION PLAN GUIDE ¶ 17,299S-66.

[48] *401(k) Answer Book*, Steven Franz, Joan C. McDonagh, and Lisa R. Richardson, Aspen Publishers.

¶ 2987

CONTRIBUTION AND DEFERRAL LIMITS: Employer's Deductions for Contributions

An employer may, within limits, deduct elective, nonelective, and matching contributions to a 401(k) plan. Specifically, the maximum deductible contribution that an employer may make to a profit-sharing or a stock bonus plan in a year may not exceed the greater of:

1. 25 percent of the compensation paid or accrued by the employer during the tax year to plan participants; or

2. the amount an employer maintaining a SIMPLE 401(k) plan is required to contribute under Code Sec. 401(k)(11) (see ¶ 2994).[1]

CCH POINTER: An employer may not avoid the annual deduction limit by adopting more than one profit-sharing or stock bonus plan. In the event that an employer sponsors two or more profit-sharing plans, the plans are treated as a single plan for purposes of the deduction limit.[2] Thus, for example, the amount an employee may defer under an employer's 401(k) plan will be affected by the amount of the employer's discretionary nonelective contributions to a separate profit-sharing plan, as well as elective FSA or health plan contributions made by employees.

All compensation paid or accrued to plan participants

Compensation, for purposes of the deduction limits, will encompass amounts treated as compensation under Code Sec. 415(c)(3).[3] Thus, compensation taken into account in applying the employer deduction limits includes elective deferrals to a 401(k) plan (as well as a SEP, SIMPLE plan, or 403(b) plan). In addition, compensation includes amounts excludable from gross income that are contributed under a Code Sec. 125 cafeteria plan or a Code Sec. 132(f) qualified transportation fringe benefit plan.

Plan's definition of compensation does not control amount of employer deduction. The plan's definition of compensation does not determine the maximum amount of the employer's deduction.[4] For example, assume a plan does not allow participants to defer any portion of a bonus, and bonuses are not taken into account in allocating nonelective contributions. The employer pays compensation (exclusive of bonuses) of $1 million. The employer also pays bonuses for the year of $500,000. The employer's maximum deduction for the tax year is $375,000 ($1,500,000 x 25%) and not $250,000 ($1,000,000 x 25%).[5]

Elective deferrals are not taken into account in applying deduction limit. Elective deferrals are not taken into account in determining the limit on an employer's deductible contributions. Elective deferrals to a 401(k) plan, SARSEP, 403(b), or a SIMPLE plan are not deemed employer contributions and are therefore, not subject to the employer deduction limits.[6] Thus, in determining whether an employer's contribution falls within the 25 percent of compensation limit, an employee's elective deferrals are not taken into account as employer contributions and the employer deduction will not be reduced by the amount of elective deferrals.

Maximum compensation limit. The maximum amount of compensation that may be taken into account for each employee, for purposes of the deduction limits, is subject to the Code Sec. 401(a)(17) limit of $250,000 in 2012.[7]

10 percent excise tax on excess contributions

An employer that makes contributions in excess of the deductible amount is subject to an excise tax equal to 10 percent of the nondeductible contribution.[8] The tax is assessed for the year in which the excess contribution was made.

Return of nondeductible contributions. The 10 percent excise tax is imposed on nondeductible contributions, determined as of the close of the employer's tax year.[9] In determining the amount of nondeductible contributions for the tax year, amounts returned to the employer because of a mistake of fact, the failure of the plan to qualify, or the failure of the contributions to be deductible, are not counted as nondeductible contributions if they are returned on or before the due date (including extensions) for the employer's tax return.[10]

Combined limit for defined benefit and defined contribution plans

In the event that an employer contributes to both a defined benefit plan and a defined contribution plan (such as a profit-sharing plan) the total amount deductible in a tax year under both plans may not exceed the greater of:

1. 25 percent of compensation paid or accrued during the tax year to participants in the plans, or

2. the amount of the contribution made to the defined benefit plan in order to satisfy the minimum funding standard (but not less than the amount of the plan's unfunded current liability).[11]

Application of combined deduction limit to DC plans. The combined deduction limit of 25% of compensation does not apply if the only amounts contributed to the DC plan are elective deferrals. In addition, the overall deduction limit for contributions to combination plans applies to contributions to one or more DC plans only to the extent that the contributions exceed 6 percent of compensation otherwise paid or accrued to the beneficiaries under the plans for the tax year.[12]

Combined limit applicable to matching and nonelective contributions. The IRS has clarified that a plan that contains a qualified cash or deferred arrangement under Code Sec. 401(k) is taken into account for purposes of applying the combined limit.[13] Elective deferrals to a 401(k) plan are not taken into account, pursuant to Code Sec. 404(n), for purposes of the combined limit. However, the IRS explains that matching contribution and nonelective contributions are considered in applying the limit. Thus, if the only contributions to a defined contribution plan are elective deferrals, the plan is not taken into account in applying the combined limit.

Exception to application of combined limit. The IRS had stated in IRS Notice 2007-28 that, in the event DC contributions were less than 6 percent of compensation, contributions to the DB plan remained subject to the deduction limit of the greater of 25 percent of compensation or the minimum required contributions. However, the Worker, Retiree, and Employer Recovery Act of 2008 reversed the IRS position, amending Code Sec. 404(a)(7)(C)(ii) to provide that, if employer contributions to one or more DC plans do not exceed 6 percent of compensation, the overall deduction limit will not apply to employer contributions to the DB plan.[14] In addition, in the event that DC contributions exceed 6 percent of compensation, the deduction limit will apply only to the excess contributions.[15]

Deduction limit for self-employed

Self-employed persons may deduct contributions to their own account. The generally applicable deduction limit of 25% of compensation is not reduced. However, the compensation of a self-employed person, for purposes of calculating the deduction, must be reduced by the amount of the contributions. In calculating the limit on deductible contributions for self-employed persons, compensation refers to net earnings from self-employment (including elective deferrals to a 401(k) plan).

Net earnings from self-employment are stated as gross income (net earnings) from the individual's business minus allowable deductions for that business. Allowable deductions include the deduction allowed for one-half of self-employment tax.[16]

Carryover of excess contributions

Employer contributions to a plan that exceed the deduction limit for the tax year may be carried over and deducted in succeeding tax years. However, the total of the carryover amount and regular contributions in the carryover year may not exceed 25 percent of compensation paid or accrued during that tax year (or the amount required under Code Sec. 401(k)(11), applicable to SIMPLE 401(k) plans (see ¶ 2994)).[17]

Note, for purposes of the exception to the deduction limit applicable where DC contributions do not exceed 6 percent of compensation, amounts carried over from preceding tax years are treated as employer contributions to one or more DC plans, to the extent attributable to such plans in the preceding tax years. [18]

Contributions deductible in tax year in which paid

With the exception of contributions that may be carried over to a later year, employer contributions are deductible only for the tax year in which they are paid, regardless of whether the employer uses the cash or accrual method of accounting.[19]

"Grace period" for contributions made after end of tax year. A grace period set forth in Code Sec. 404(a)(6) provides a limited exception to the general rules, under which an employer that makes contributions after the end of its tax year is deemed to have made a payment on the last day of the preceding tax year. However, the grace period applies only if: (a) the payment is made on account of that tax year and, (b) is not made later than the time prescribed by law for filing the return for the tax year, including extensions.[20]

The sole effect of Code Sec. 404(a)(6) is to deem a payment to have been made on the last day of the preceding tax year. Code Sec. 404(a)(6) merely provides a grace period during which accrual basis taxpayers that may have difficulty in gathering information about the tax year by the close of the tax year may compute the amount of the contribution. The provision does not allow an employer to deduct a contribution in a tax year if that contribution could not otherwise have been deducted in that tax year if it had actually been paid on the last day of the tax year.[21] Thus, elective contributions to a 401(k) plan and employer matching contributions are not deductible by an employer for a tax year if they are attributable to compensation earned by plan participants after the end of that year.[22] Compensation cannot be deferred or contributed to a plan as elective deferrals, and matching contributions cannot be made to the plan with respect to elective deferrals, until the underlying compensation has actually been earned.[23]

Grace period does not cover contributions attributable to compensation earned after year. An employer may not deduct grace period elective deferrals or matching contributions made to a 401(k) plan for a tax year if the contributions are attributable to compensation earned by the plan participants after the end of that tax year, even if the employer's liability to make a minimum contribution is fixed before the close of that tax year.[24]

Tax-shelter disclosure statement. Corporate taxpayers that claim tax deductions for contributions to 401(k) plans, or matching contributions to defined contribution plans, that are attributable to compensation earned by plan participants after the end of the tax year may be required to report such a "tax avoidance" transaction on an information statement filed with their federal income tax returns.[25] A separate disclosure statement for each reportable transaction must be attached to the taxpayer's federal income tax return for each year for which the taxpayer's federal income tax liability is affected by participation in the transaction.

[1] Code Sec. 404(a)(3)(A), as amended by P.L. 107-16 (Economic Growth and Tax Relief Reconciliation Act of 2001), Act Sec. 616(a).

[2] Code Sec. 404(a)(3)(A)(iv).

[3] Code Sec. 404(a)(12), as added by P.L. 107-16 (Economic Growth and Tax Relief Reconciliation Act of 2001), Act Sec. 616(b).

[4] Rev. Rul. 80-145, 1980-1 C.B. 89.

[5] *401(k) Answer Book*, Steven Franz, Joan C. McDonagh, Lisa R. Richardson, Aspen Publishers, Inc.

[6] Code Sec. 404(n), as added by P.L. 107-16 (Economic Growth and Tax Relief Reconciliation Act of 2001), Act Sec. 614(a).

[7] Code Sec. 401(a)(17) and Code Sec. 404(l).

[8] Code Sec. 4972(a) and (b).

[9] Code Sec. 4972(a).

[10] Code Secs. 4972(c)(3) and 4980 (c)(2)(B)(ii)(II) and (III).

[11] Code Sec. 404(a)(7)(A).

[12] Code Sec. 404(a)(7)(C)(iii), as added by P.L. 109-280 (Pension Protection Act of 2006), Act Sec. 803(a) and (d).

[13] IRS Notice 2007-28, Q&A-7, I.R.B. 2007-14, 4-2-07, at CCH Pension Plan Guide ¶ 17,136F.

[14] Code Sec. 404(a)(7)C)(iii), as amended by P.L. 110-458 (Worker, Retiree, and Employer Recovery Act of 2008), Act Sec. 108(c).

[15] *Ibid.*

[16] IRS Pub. 560, Retirement Plans for Small Business.

[17] Code Sec. 404(a)(3)(A)(ii); IRS Reg. § 1.404(a)-9(e).

[18] Code Sec. 404(a)(7)(C)(iii), as amended by P.L. 110-458 (Worker, Retiree, and Employer Recovery Act of 2008), Act Sec. 108(c).

[19] Code Sec. 404(a).

[20] Code Sec. 404(a)(6);IRS Reg. § 1.404(a)-9(a).

[21] IRS Coordinated Issue Paper, UIL No. 404-11-00, 10-23-96, at CCH Pension Plan Guide ¶ 17,202E. See also, *Lucky Stores v. Commissioner*, CA-9 (1998), 153 F3d 964, *aff'g* TC (1996) 107 T.C. No. 1, *cert denied*, No. 98-1279 (corporation could not deduct contributions to collectively bargained multiemployer defined benefit plans that were made during an 8 month extension for filing its 1986 tax return because the contributions were not made during or on account of the 1986 tax year).

[22] Rev. Rul. 90-105, 1990-2 C.B. 69, CCH Pension Plan Guide ¶ 19,739.

[23] *Ibid.*

[24] Rev. Rul. 2002-46, I.R.B. 2002-29, July 22, 2002, at CCH Pension Plan Guide ¶ 19,947D, modified by Rev. Rul. 2002-73, I.R.B. 2002-45, 11-12-2002, at CCH Pension Plan Guide ¶ 19,947Q.

[25] IRS Reg. § 1.6011-4.

¶ 2989

DISTRIBUTIONS: 401(k) Plan Distribution Rules

Elective deferrals held in a 401(k) plan may generally not be distributed prior to the participant's retirement, death, disability, severance from employment, or the occurrence of another event stipulated by the IRS, such as employee hardship.[1]

Severance from employment

Participants may receive distributions from their 401(k) plans upon severance from employment (rather than separation from service) with the employer maintaining the plan.[2] Accordingly, employees participating in a 401(k) plan are not prevented by statute from receiving distributions in the event that they continue on the same job for a different employer following a liquidation, merger, consolidation, or other corporate transaction.

> **CCH POINTER:** *What constitutes severance from employment?* An employee will not be treated as having experienced a severance from employment if, in connection with a change of employment, the employee's new employer maintains the 401(k) in which the employee participated (e.g., by assuming sponsorship of the plan or by accepting a transfer of plan assets and liabilities with respect to the employee).[3]

> *Change in status to leased employee is not a severance from employment.* A distribution is not authorized for an individual whose employment status has changed from that of a common law employee to a leased employee, where the individual continues to provide services for the same employer. [4]

> *Severance pay does not prevent distribution upon severance from employment.* Individuals who have severed employment may receive a distributions from the 401(k) plans in which they participate, even if the individuals continue to receive compensation from their former employers pursuant to a severance agreement.[5]

Hardship distributions

Unlike other qualified plans, a 401(k) plan (including SIMPLE 401(k) plans (see ¶ 2994)) may authorize hardship distributions if:[6]

1. the participant has an immediate and heavy financial need ("needs test"), and
2. the distribution is necessary to satisfy the participant's financial need ("events test").

Note, hardship distributions subject the recipient to the 10 percent early distribution tax under Code Sec. 72(t) (see ¶ 2993).

Immediate and heavy financial need under objective standards. Whether a participant has experienced an immediate and heavy financial need is a facts and circumstances determination. The plan must set forth nondiscriminatory and objective standards for determining whether the specified need is present and the amount necessary to satisfy that need.[7] As an alternative means of complying with the events and needs tests, a plan may adopt safe harbors prescribed by the IRS.

Deemed immediate and heavy financial need. A distribution is deemed, under a prescribed safe harbor, to be made on account of an immediate and heavy financial need if it is made in order to pay for one of the following expenses.[8]

1. Medical expenses previously incurred by the employee, the employee's spouse or dependents, or amounts necessary for these persons to obtain medical care.

> **CCH Pointer:** *Extension of hardship rules to beneficiaries other than spouses and dependents.* The safe harbor rules authorize a distribution

upon a hardship incurred by a participant's spouse or dependent. Accordingly, if a beneficiary other than a spouse or dependent of the participant (e.g., sibling or same-sex domestic partner) incurred medical expenses or experienced another event that would constitute hardship if experienced by the participant, spouse, or dependent, the plan could not make a hardship distribution, in accordance with the safe harbor. The Pension Protection Act of 2006 (P.L. 109-280) requires the Treasury to modify the governing regulations to provide that, if an event (including the occurrence of a medical expense) would constitute a hardship if it occurred with respect to the participant's spouse or dependent, the event will, to the extent permitted by the plan, constitute a hardship if it occurs with respect to a person who is a beneficiary under the plan.

The IRS has clarified that a 401(k) plan that authorizes hardship distributions of elective contributions to a participant only for expenses described in IRS Reg. § 1.401(k)-1(d)(3)(iii)(B) may, beginning on August 17, 2006, permit distributions for medical, tuition (and related educational fees and room and board expenses), and burial and funeral expenses for an individual who is named as a beneficiary under the plan and who has an unconditional right to all or a portion of the participant's account balance under the plan upon the death of the participant (i.e., primary beneficiary).[9] Note, however, that while the distributable event may have been incurred by the participant's beneficiary, the distribution from the plan is actually made to the participant and not to the beneficiary.

Mid-year plan amendments. The IRS has confirmed that a 401(k) safe harbor plan may be amended mid-year in order to implement the new hardship withdrawal rules described in Notice 2007-7, even if the required safe harbor notice does not address the provision.[10]

2. Costs directly related to the employee's purchase of a principal residence (not including mortgage payments other than to prevent foreclosure)

3. Payment of tuition and related educational fees and room and board expenses for up to the *next* (i.e., prospective, not prior) 12 months of post-secondary education for the employee, the employee's spouse, children or dependents.

4. Payments necessary to prevent the eviction of the employee from his or her principal residence or to avoid foreclosure on the mortgage on that residence.

5. Burial or funeral expenses for an employee's deceased parents, spouse, children, and dependents.[11]

6. Expenses incurred for the repair of damage to the employee's principal residence that would qualify as a deductible casualty expense under Code Sec. 165 (determined without regard to whether the loss exceeds 10% of adjusted gross income).[12]

Distribution necessary to satisfy financial need. A hardship distribution is not treated as necessary to satisfy an immediate and heavy financial need to the extent that it exceeds the amount required to relieve the need, or to the degree the need may be satisfied by other resources that are reasonably available to the employee, such as a plan loan, or the assets of the employee's spouse and minor children.[13]

Note, the amount distributed to meet an immediate and heavy financial need may include funds necessary to pay any federal, state, or local income tax and penalties resulting from the distribution. [14]

Distribution necessary to satisfy financial need: Safe Harbor. A plan may deem a distribution to be necessary to satisfy a financial need (without requiring the employee to exhaust other remedies) if the following requirements are met.[15]

1. The distribution is not in excess of the amount of the immediate and heavy financial need of the employee (including federal, state, or local income taxes or penalties reasonably expected to result from the distribution).

2. The employee has obtained all currently available distributions, other than hardship distributions, and all nontaxable (at the time of the loan) loans available under all plans maintained by the employer.

3. The plan, or an otherwise legally enforceable agreement, prohibits an employee from making elective contributions (and after-tax employee contributions) to the plan and all other plans maintained by the employer (including qualified and nonqualified deferred compensation plans (e.g., stock option and stock purchase plans)) for at least 6 months after receipt of the hardship distribution.[16]

Hardship distribution limited to amount of elective contributions. The amount available for hardship withdrawal is generally limited to the employee's total elective contributions as of the date of the distribution, reduced by the amount of any prior hardship distribution.[17]

CCH POINTER: Hardship distributions from a 401(k) plan may not be made at the discretion of the employer, but must be authorized by the plan and made in accordance with plan terms. An employer that allows hardship distributions that are not authorized by the plan risks disqualification of the plan.

In the event a plan sponsor determines that (due in large measure to the absence of written policies and procedures for reviewing applications) hardship distributions have been made on discriminatory basis or to parties that have not experienced a hardship, the mistake may be corrected under the VCP component of EPCRS. The mistake of discriminatory distributions may not be corrected pursuant to a retroactive corrective amendment, but must be redressed in a manner reasonably designed to facilitate compliance in accordance with the principles of EPCRS. [18]

☐ See CCH PENSION PLAN GUIDE ¶ 7660-7673 for more detailed information on hardship distributions.

Note, special relief from the generally applicable distribution restrictions applies to victims of certain hurricanes and other severe storms. See ¶ 2003 and ¶ 2020.

Distributions upon termination of 401(k) plan

Distributions may be made from a 401(k) plan upon the actual full (and not partial) termination of the plan, if the employer does not establish or maintain an alternative defined contribution plan (other than an ESOP, SEP, SIMPLE IRA, 403(b) plan, or plan under Code Sec. 457(b) and (f)) that exists at the time of termination or within the 12-month period following the distribution of plan assets.[19]

Attainment of age 59½

A 401(k) plan that is part of profit-sharing or stock bonus plan may authorize distributions to a participant who has attained age 59½.[20]

Distribution upon merger or acquisition

Amounts attributable to elective contributions that are transferred from a 401(k) plan to another plan incident to a merger may not be distributed before the occurrence of an authorized distributable event.[21]

Cash-out distribution

A 401(k) plan may make a lump-sum distribution to a participant of a vested account balance that does not exceed $5,000 without the participant's consent.[22] However, if the present value of the vested account balance (as adjusted for any outstanding balance) exceeds $5,000, the cash-out distribution may not be made without the participant's consent if the distribution is immediately distributable (see ¶ 869).[23]

Valid consent requires participant notice. Consent to a distribution will not be valid unless the participant, no less than 30 days and no more than 180 days before the distribution, receives a general description of the material features, and an explanation of the relative value of, the optional forms of benefit provided under the plan.

The distribution notice must inform the participant of the right to defer the receipt of the distribution or to have the distribution directly transferred to another retirement plan or IRA, and under rules to be issued by the Treasury, explain to participants the consequences of failing to defer the receipt of the distribution.[24].

CCH POINTER: *Proposed rules specify content of required notice.* Proposed rules issued by the IRS in October 2008 would require a participant to be provided with the following: (1) a description of the federal tax implications of failing to defer a distribution, including: differences in the timing of inclusion in taxable income of an immediately commencing distribution that is not rolled over (or not eligible to be rolled over) and a distribution that is deferred until it is no longer immediately distributable (including differences in the taxation of distributions of designated Roth contributions); application of the 10 percent penalty tax imposed on distributions before the participant attains age 59½; and the loss of opportunity under a 401(k) plan upon commencement of a distribution for future tax-favored treatment of earnings if the distribution is not rolled over (or not eligible to be rolled over) to an eligible retirement plan; (2) a statement indicating that some currently available investment options in the plan may not be generally available on similar terms outside the plan and contact information for obtaining additional information on the general availability outside the plan of currently available investment options in the plan; (3) a statement that fees and expenses (including administrative or investment related fees) outside the plan may differ from fees and expenses that apply to the participant's account and contact information for obtaining additional information on the fees and expenses that apply to the participant's account; and (4) an explanation of any provisions of the plan (and provisions of an accident or health plan maintained by the employer) that could be reasonably expected to materially affect a participant's decision whether to defer receipt of the distribution (e.g., plan terms under which the benefits of a rehired participant who failed to defer may be adversely affected by the decision not to defer) and plan terms under which undistributed benefits that are otherwise nonforfeitable become forfeitable upon the participant's death. [25]

Safe harbor allows for reasonable compliance with new requirements. The IRS explains that a description that is written in a manner that is reasonably calculated to be understood by the average participant and that describes the investment options available under the plan (including fees) will constitute a reasonable attempt to comply with the new requirements. Note, however, the IRS stresses that the description must include the portion of the summary plan description that contains any rules that might materially affect a participant's decision to defer receipt of a distribution.[26]

Rollover contributions excluded from $5,000 threshold. The present value of a participant's plan benefit may be determined without including amounts received by the distributing plan that are attributable to rollover contributions and earnings allocable to rollover contributions.[27]

Automatic rollover of cash-out distributions. A plan that provides for a cash-out distribution of a nonforfeitable account balance that does not exceed $5,000 must use a direct rollover as the default option for involuntary distributions that exceed $1,000.[28] Thus, employers will no longer be permitted to cash-out a participant whose account balance is under $5,000 but over $1,000. Note, the automatic rollover rules apply to eligible rollover distributions over $1000 that are made without a participant's consent and are made before the participant attains the later of age 62 or normal retirement age.[29]

Participant may elect to receive distribution in cash. A participant may affirmatively elect to have the distribution transferred to an IRA other than that designated by the employer or to receive the funds directly.[30] In addition, participants must be informed in writing that they possess the right to elect to receive the distribution in cash.

CCH POINTER: Final regulations issued by EBSA provide fiduciaries with a safe harbor that covers both the selection of an institution to receive a mandatory distribution rollover and the initial investment choice for the rolled-over funds made before the regulations' effective date.[31]

[1] Code Sec. 401(k)(2)(B); IRS Reg. § 1.401(k)-1(d)(1).

[2] Code Sec. 401(k)(2)(B)(i)(I), as amended by P.L. 107-16 (Economic Growth and Tax Relief Reconciliation Act of 2001), Act Sec. 646(a)(1)(A).

[3] IRS Notice 2002-4, Sec. III, I.R.B. 2002-2, January 14, 2002 at CCH PENSION PLAN GUIDE ¶ 17,122Z.

[4] Preamble to IRS Reg. § 1.401(k)-1.

[5] Joint Committee on Employee Benefits, Q & A with Treasury and IRS, 5-12-2000.

[6] Code Sec. 401(k)(2)(B)(i)(I).

[7] IRS Reg. § 1.401(k)-1(d)(3)(i).

[8] IRS Reg. § 1.401(k)-1(d)(3)(iv)(A).

[9] IRS Notice 2007-7, Sec. III, Q&A-5, I.R.B. 2007-5, 1-29-07, at CCH PENSION PLAN GUIDE ¶ 17,135R.

[10] IRS Announcement 2007-59, I.R.B. 2007-25, 6-18-07, at CCH PENSION PLAN GUIDE ¶ 17,097T-10

[11] IRS Reg. § 1.401(k)-1(d)(3)(iii)(B)(5).

[12] IRS Reg. § 1.401(k)-1(d)(3)(iii)(B)(6).

[13] IRS Reg. § 1.401(k)-1(d)(3)(iv)(B).

[14] IRS Reg. § 1.401(k)-1(d)(3)(iv).

[15] IRS Reg. § 1.401(k)-1(d)(3)(iv). Note, plans are no longer required, as condition of the safe harbor to limit an employee's elective contributions for the year following a hardship distribution to the applicable Code Sec. 402(g) deferral limit minus the employee's elective deferrals for the year of contribution.

[16] P.L.107-16 (Economic Growth and Tax Relief Reconciliation Act of 2001), Act Sec. 636(a)(1). IRS Reg. § 1.401(k)-1(d)(3)(iv)(F).

[17] IRS Reg. § 1.401(k)-1(d)(3)(i).

[18] "401(k) Plan Potential Mistakes," IRS Website.

[19] Code Secs. 401(k)(2)(B)(i)(II) and 401(k)(10)(A); IRS Reg. § 1.401(k)-1(d)(4)(i).

[20] IRS Reg. § 1.401(k)-1(d)(1)(ii).

[21] IRS Reg. § 1.401(k)-1(d)(5)(iv).

[22] Code Sec. 411(a)(11); IRS Reg. § 1.411(a)-11(c)(3).

[23] Code Sec.411(a)(11); IRS Reg. § 1.411(a)-11(c)(4).

[24] P.L. 109-280 (Pension Protection Act of 2006), Act Sec. 1102(b).

[25] IRS Proposed Reg. § 1.411(a)-11(c)(2)(vi)(A).

[26] IRS Notice 2007-7, Sec. VIII, Q-33, I.R.B. 2007-5, 1-29-07, at CCH PENSION PLAN GUIDE ¶ 17,135R.

[27] Code Sec. 411(a)(11)(D), as added by P.L. 107-16 (Economic Growth and Tax Relief Reconciliation Act of 2001), Act Sec. 648(a). ERISA Sec. 203(e)(4), as added by P.L. 107-16 (Economic Growth and Tax Relief Reconciliation Act of 2001), Act Sec. 648(a).

[28] Code Sec. 401(a)(31)(B), as added by P.L. 107-16 (Economic Growth and Tax Relief Reconciliation Act of 2001), Act Sec. 657(a).

[29] IRS Notice 2005-5, Q&A 1-2, I.R.B. 2005-3, at CCH PENSION PLAN GUIDE ¶ 17,130N.

[30] Code Sec. 401(a)(31)(B)(i)(II), as added by P.L. 107-16 (Economic Growth and Tax Relief Reconciliation Act of 2001), Act Sec. 657(a).

[31] ERISA Reg. § 2550.404a-2.

¶ 2990

DISTRIBUTIONS: Required Distributions from a 401(k) Plan

Participants in 401(k) plans (other than 5 percent owners) must begin receiving distributions by April 1 of the calendar year following the later of either:

1. the calendar year in which the participant attains age 70½, or

2. the calendar year in which the participant retires from employment with the employer maintaining the plan.[1]

CCH POINTER: *Temporary waiver of required minimum distributions for 2009.* The Worker, Retiree, and Employer Recovery Act of 2008 provides a temporary waiver of the minimum distributions from 401(k) plans that are required for 2009. [2] Under the relief, any minimum distribution that would otherwise be required for 2009 need not be made. The next required minimum distribution would be for 2010.

For example, if an individual attains age 70½ in 2009, a required minimum distribution would not need to be made by April 1, 2010. However the distribution would need to be made by the end of 2010. Similarly, individuals who have been receiving required minimum distributions, because they attained age 70½ or retired in an earlier year, may waive the distribution for 2009 without incurring excise tax.

Thus, a beneficiary receiving distribution over a 5-year period could waive the distribution for 2009, effectively taking distributions over a 6-year period. A participant or beneficiary may also take a withdrawal in 2009 and roll over the funds to an IRA or other eligible retirement plan, as long as the amount is not a RMD for 2008. [3] However, note, the previously untaxed portion of the withdrawal that is not rolled over must be included in gross income.

The applicable rules are discussed at CCH PENSION PLAN GUIDE ¶ 7649

5 percent owners must receive distributions by age 70½

More than 5 percent owners (see ¶ 1805) must begin receiving distributions no later than April 1 of the calendar year following the calendar year in which they attain age 70½.[4]

Form of distribution

If a 401(k) plan participant's entire interest is not distributed in a lump-sum distribution by the required beginning date, distributions must begin no later than that date and must be made: over the life of the employee; over the life of the employee and his or her designated beneficiary; over a period that does not extend beyond the life expectancy of the employee; or over a period that does not extend beyond the joint life and last survivor expectancy of the employee and his or her designated beneficiary.[5]

Determining minimum distribution amount

Final rules provide a uniform and simplified method for determining a participant's required minimum distributions. Generally, the required minimum distribution from an individual account is to be determined by dividing the employee's account balance by a distribution period.[6] For lifetime required minimum distributions, the rules provide a uniform distribution period for all employees of the same age. Note, the required minimum distribution may never exceed the value of the account balance on the date of the distribution.

Uniform Lifetime Distribution Table. The IRS provides a Uniform Lifetime Distribution Table that must be used in determining the distribution period for lifetime distributions to an employee (unless the employee's spouse is the sole beneficiary).[7]

Specifically, for *each calendar year* the required distribution calculation is determined by dividing (1) the participant's account balance as of the last valuation date in the calendar year immediately preceding the distribution calendar year (i.e., valuation year) by (2) an age-based factor from the Uniform Lifetime Distribution Table that is based on the joint life and last survivor expectancy of an individual and a hypothetical beneficiary 10 years younger.[8]

☐ The Uniform Lifetime Distribution Table is reproduced at ¶ 1835.

Distribution period for surviving spousal beneficiary. In the event that an employee's sole beneficiary is his or her spouse, and the spouse is no more than 10 years younger than the employee, the applicable distribution period for distributions during the employee's lifetime is the longer of (1) the distribution period determined under the Uniform Lifetime Distribution Table or (2) the joint life and last survivor life expectancy of the employee and the spouse (based on the Joint and Last Survivor Table set forth at IRS Reg. § 1.401(a)(9)-9, A-3) using the employee's and the spouse's attained age as of their birthdays in the distribution calendar year.[9] The spouse must be the sole beneficiary of the employee's entire interest at all times during the distribution calendar year.

Calculating life expectancy

The uniform table prescribed for the calculation of required minimum distributions during an employee's life relieves employees of the need to recalculate their life expectancy each year.

CCH POINTER: The life expectancy tables adopted by the final rules account for increased longevity and, by extending the period over which minimum distributions must be taken, will produce smaller required distributions, and allow employees and beneficiaries to spread out payments and, thereby, effectively lessen their tax.

Determination of designated beneficiary

The designated beneficiary is an individual entitled, upon the death of the participant, to any portion or all of a participant's interest in the plan. A participant is not required to make an affirmative election specifying a beneficiary in order for a person to be considered a designated beneficiary.[10] The plan may specify a beneficiary. Under such circumstances, the person specified by the plan will be treated as if designated by the participant.

Period for determining designated beneficiary

The designated beneficiary is determined as of September 30 of the calendar year following the calendar year of the plan participant's death.[11] However, the individual must have been designated as a beneficiary before the participant's death.[12]

Estate or trust may not be designated beneficiary. Generally, only individuals may be designated as beneficiaries. An employee's estate may not be a designated beneficiary for purposes of the required minimum distribution rules.[13]

A trust may also not be designated beneficiary, for RMD purposes, even if the trust is named as the beneficiary.[14] However, the beneficiaries of the trust may be treated as if they were the designated beneficiaries of the employee if the trust is valid under state law and specified documentation requirements are met.[15]

Death of participant after distribution has begun

In the event that a participant dies after the distribution of his or her interest has begun (i.e., after the required beginning date), the remaining portion of that interest must be distributed at least as rapidly as under the method of distribution being used on the participant's date of death.[16] In applying this rule, the distribution of a participant's interest is considered to begin on the required beginning date, even if the payments have actually begun before that date.[17]

Participant without designated beneficiary. In the event a participant does not have a designated beneficiary as of September 30 of the calendar year following the calendar year of death, the distribution period will be measured by the remaining life expectancy of the participant, using the age of the participant as of the participant's birthday in the calendar year of death. [18] In subsequent calendar years, the distribution period will be reduced by one for each calendar year that has elapsed after the year in which the employee died.

Participant with designated beneficiary. Alternatively, if the participant has a designated beneficiary as of September 30 of the calendar year following the calendar year of death, the distribution period is the longer of the remaining life expectancy of the designated beneficiary or the remaining life expectancy of the participant. [19]

Note: The application of the RMD rules to nonspousal beneficiaries is discussed in detail at CCH Pension Plan Guide ¶ 7649.

Distributions beginning after participant's death

If a participant dies before required distributions have begun, (i.e., before the required beginning date) the participant's interest is distributed under a 5-year rule or a life expectancy rule.

5-year rule. Under the 5-year rule, the entire interest of a participant in the 401(k) plan must be distributed within 5 years of the participant's death, regardless of who or what entity receives the distribution.[20]

CCH POINTER: *Effect of RMD waiver for 2009 on distributions under 5-year rule.* The 5-year period over which distributions are to be made is determined, in accordance with the RMD waiver implemented by the Worker, Retiree, and Employer Recovery Act of 2008 (see above), without regard to 2009. [21] For example, assume a plan participant died in 2008, prior to the time the plan required him to begin taking distributions. The participant left his plan interest to his estate. Under the generally applicable 5-year rule, the participant's entire interest would need to be distributed by December 31, 2013. However, reflecting the RMD waiver of 2009, the 5-year period for making the distribution will end on December 31, 2014. [22]

Life expectancy rule. Under an exception to the 5-year rule (known as the life expectancy rule or, alternatively, the designated beneficiary rule), any portion of a participant's interest which is payable to or for the benefit of a designated beneficiary (including trust beneficiaries who are treated as designated beneficiaries) must be distributed beginning within one calendar year of the participant's death, over the life of the designated beneficiary, or over a period not extending beyond the life expectancy of the beneficiary [23] Distributions must begin on or before the end of the calendar year immediately following the calendar year in which the employee dies. [24]

Minimum required distributions are not eligible rollover distributions

Amounts distributed by one plan and rolled over to another plan are treated as distributions by the distributing plan, notwithstanding the rollover.[25] However, minimum required distributions under Code Sec. 401(a)(9) are not eligible rollover distributions.[26] Thus, all amounts distributed from a qualified plan, including a 401(k) plan, during any calendar year in which a minimum distribution is required are counted towards that year's minimum required distribution, until the amount equals or exceeds the required minimum.[27] Note, RMDs for 2009 may be rolled over under the temporary relief enacted by the Worker, Retiree, and Employer Recovery Act of 2008 (see above).

Transfers between plans

The transfer of an employee's benefit from one plan to another is not treated as a distribution by the transferor plan for minimum distribution purposes. [28] Rather, the benefit of the employee under the transferor plan is decreased by the amount transferred. However, if any portion of an employee's benefit is transferred in a distribution calendar year, the amount of the required minimum distribution for the employee must be determined by the transferor plan using the employee's benefit under the transferor plan before the transfer.

50 percent excise tax for violation of minimum distribution rules

If a participant fails to receive a required minimum distribution for any tax year, or received an amount less than the required minimum distribution, the *participant* is subject to an excise tax equal to 50 percent of the required amount that was not distributed.[29] However, the IRS may waive the 50 percent excise tax if the taxpayer can establish that any shortfall in minimum required distributions is attributable to reasonable error and that steps are being taken to remedy the shortfall.[30]

☐ The required minimum distribution rules, including the treatment of distributions occurring before and after an employee's death, are discussed in greater detail beginning at ¶ 1800.

---

[1] Code Sec. 401(a)(9)(C).

[2] Code Sec. 401(a)(9)(H), as added by P.L. 110-458 (Worker, Retiree, and Employer Recovery Act of 2008), Act Sec. 201.

[3] IRS Notice 2009-9, I.R.B. 2009-5, at CCH Pension Plan Guide ¶ 17,141Y.

[4] Code Sec. 401(a)(9)(C)(ii).

[5] Code Sec. 401(a)(9)(A); IRS Reg. § 1.401(a)(9)-2.

[6]IRS Reg. § 1.401(a)(9)-5, A-1—4.

[7]IRS Reg. § 1.401(a))(9)-9, A-2.

[8] IRS Reg. § 1.401(a)(9)-5, A-4(a).

[9] IRS Reg. § 1.401(a)(9)-5, A-4(b).

[10] IRS Reg. § 1.401(a)(9)-4, A-1 and A-2.

[11] IRS Reg. § 1.401(a)(9)-4, A-4.

[12]IRS Reg. § 1.401(a)(9)-4, A-4.

[13] IRS Reg. § 1.401(a)(9)-4, A-3(a).

[14] IRS Reg. § 1.401(a)(9)-4, A-5.

[15] *Ibid.*

[16]Code Sec. 401(a)(9)(B)(i); IRS Reg. § 1.401(a)(9)-2, A-5.

[17]IRS Reg. § 1.401(a)(9)-2, A-6(a).

[18]IRS Reg. § 1.401(a)(9)-5, A-5(a) and (c).

[19]IRS Reg. § 1.401(a)(9)-5, A-5(a).

[20]Code Sec. 401(a)(9)(B)(ii); IRS Reg. § 1.401(a)(9)-3, A-1 and A-2.

[21]Code Sec. 401(a)(9)(H)(ii)(II), as added by P.L. 110-458 (Worker, Retiree, and Employer Recovery Act of 2008), Act Sec. 201.

[22]IRS Notice 2009-9, I.R.B. 2009-2, 2-2-2009; "WRERA Waives RMDs for 2009," Eric Paley and Steven Mindy, CCH Journal of Pension Benefits, Vol. 16, No. 4, Summer 2009.

[23]Code Sec. 401(a)(9)(B)(iii); IRS Reg. § 1.401(a)(9)-3, A-3(a).

[24]IRS Reg. § 1.401(a)(9)-3, A-3.

[25] IRS Reg. § 1.401(a)(9)-7, A-1.

[26] Code Secs. 402(c)(4)(B) and 408(d)(3)(E).

[27] IRS Reg. § 1.401(a)(9)-7.

[28] IRS Reg. § 1.401(a)(9)-7, A-3.

[29] Code Sec. 4974(a); IRS Reg. § 54.4974-2, Q&A-1.

[30] Code Sec. 4974(d); IRS Reg. § 54.4974-2, Q&A 7.

¶ 2991

DISTRIBUTIONS: Loans to 401(k) Plan Participants

An important feature of many 401(k) plans is a provision that allows employees to borrow against their account balances. A loan provision is particularly useful in encouraging low-paid employees to participate in a 401(k) plan. Without such a provision, these employees may be reluctant to tie up funds that they may need to purchase a car, for medical expenses, or for other large or unexpected expenses.

Before adopting a loan program, however, an employer needs to be aware of several restrictions. Generally, the loan terms must be set forth in a written and legally enforceable agreement; the amount of the loan may not exceed the lesser of $50,000 (reduced by previous outstanding loans) or one-half of the present value of the participant's nonforfeitable accrued benefit; the terms of the loan (other than principal residence loans), must require repayment within 5 years; and the loan must be amortized on a substantially level basis with payments made no less frequently than quarterly.[1] The loan program must meet several additional requirements set forth by ERISA in order to ensure that plan loans do not constitute prohibited transactions.

□ The governing rules are discussed in detail, beginning at ¶ 2000.

[1]Code Secs. 72(p) and 4975(d); IRS Reg. § 1.72(p)-1.

¶ 2993

DISTRIBUTIONS:Taxation of 401(k) Plan Distributions

Elective contributions to a qualified 401(k) plan that are not currently available to participant at the time of the election are not taxed until they are distributed to the participant.[1] Generally, distributions from 401(k) plans are taxed in the same

manner as distributions from other qualified plans (see discussion beginning at
¶ 1900). The applicable tax treatment depends on whether the distributions are
paid in a lump-sum or in an annuity over the life of the employee.

Lump-sum distributions

Lump-sum distributions made within one tax year of the balance to the credit
(i.e., vested account balance) of an employee, may qualify for favorable tax treatment if made on account of the death, separation from service, disability, or
attainment of age 59½ of an employee who has participated in the plan for 5 or
more years. The distribution is generally taxed as ordinary income, but may be
eligible for averaging, or capital gains treatment, depending on the age of the
recipient and the year in which the distribution is made.[2]

☐ The tax rules applicable to lump-sum distributions are discussed beginning
at ¶ 1940.

Annuity distributions

Participants in 401(k) plans may receive distributions of their accounts over a
number of years through installment or periodic distributions. Typically, periodic
payments are made through an annuity that is paid over the life of the participant or
over the lives of the participant and a designated beneficiary. Annuity payments are
taxed as ordinary income when they are received.[3] However, if an employee has an
investment in contract (or cost basis), a portion of each annuity payment is treated
as the recovery of employee contributions and is not taxed. For example, the
payments corresponding to after-tax contributions would not be subject to tax. In
determining the portion of each monthly payment that is excludable from gross
income as recovery of basis, the basis is divided by the anticipated number of
payments, using tables prescribed by the IRS.[4]

Nonperiodic distributions. Amounts not received as an annuity (nonperiodic distributions) that are received on or after the annuity starting date are fully
includible in the recipient's gross income.[5] Nonperiodic distributions received
before the annuity starting date are not included in gross income to the extent they
are allocable to the recipient's investment in contract.

☐ The taxation of annuity distributions is discussed beginning at ¶ 1922.

In-service distributions

A distribution made to a participant during the course of employment that is
attributable to after-tax contributions is excluded from income. The remaining
amount is taxable as ordinary income (and subject to penalty tax) when received.[6]

In-service distributions to military personnel. Plan distributions made to
an individual will not, effective for remuneration paid after 2008, be treated as an in-
service distribution during any period in which the individual is performing military
service while on active duty for a period of more than 30 days.[7]

Eligible rollover distributions

Employees may defer tax on a lump-sum distribution from a 401(k) plan by rolling the entire amount or a portion of the distribution over to another eligible retirement plan (see below) within 60 days or receipt. Alternatively, employees may elect to have the distribution directly rolled over to an eligible retirement plan. Eligible rollover distributions that are not directly rolled over into a retirement plan or IRA (including a Roth IRA) are included in the recipient's gross income and are subject to mandatory 20% withholding.[8]

Distributions not eligible for rollover. Generally, any amount distributed to an employee from a qualified plan is an eligible rollover distribution (see ¶ 1954). However, required minimum distributions, distributions that are part of a series of substantially equal periodic payments, corrective distributions of excess deferrals and excess employer contributions, returns of deferrals in excess of the Code Sec. 415 limits, and loans that are treated as deemed distributions are not eligible rollover distributions. In addition, hardship distributions from a 401(k) plan that are attributable to elective deferrals and employer matching and nonelective contributions, are not eligible rollover distributions and thus, may not be rolled over to an eligible retirement plan or to an IRA (or converted to an Roth IRA).[9]

Spousal beneficiary rollovers. The surviving spouse of a deceased 401(k) plan participant may make a tax-free rollover of a distribution from the participant's plan in the same manner as if the spouse were the participant.[10] Thus, the funds may be rolled over to an IRA, qualified plan, 403(b) plan, or governmental 457(b) plan. Under such circumstances, the surviving spouse is not required to begin receiving minimum distributions until he or she attains age 70½.

Nonspousal beneficiary rollovers. Distributions from a 401(k) plan to a nonspouse beneficiary (e.g., children, siblings, domestic partners) may be directly rolled over to an IRA (but not to a qualified plan, 403(b) plan or 457(b) plan) via a trustee-to-trustee transfer.[11] The transfer will be treated as an eligible rollover distribution (as long as the amount is not actually received by the nonspouse beneficiary).[12] In addition, the transferred amounts will not be included in the nonspouse beneficiary's gross income in the year of distribution.

> **CCH POINTER:** *Plans required to provide for nonspousal beneficiary rollovers beginning in 2010.* Plans were authorized, but were not required by the Pension Protection Act to provide for the direct rollover of a distribution to a nonspousal beneficiary. [13] The IRS stated, in the 2007 List of Interim and Discretionary Amendments, that nonspousal beneficiary rollovers would be required for plan years beginning on or after January 1, 2008. However, administrators and employers remained unclear of the application of the requirement, especially since the IRS action was taken in response to technical corrections legislation that was introduced in 2007 but never enacted.
>
> The Worker, Retiree, and Employer Recovery Act of 2008 resolved the issue, clarifying that nonspousal rollover transfers are eligible rollover distributions and, thereby, requiring that plans allow for direct rollovers by nonspousal beneficiaries (pursuant to the mandatory rollover rules of Code Sec.

401(a)(31)).[14] Note, however, plans were not required to provide for non-spousal beneficiary rollovers before 2010. [15]

IRA will be treated as inherited IRA of nonspousal beneficiary. The IRA to which the funds are transferred must have been established in the name of the plan participant, payable to the nonspousal beneficiary (e.g., "Tom Smith as beneficiary of John Smith").[16] The beneficiary may not transfer the inherited amounts to his or her own IRA. In addition, because the nonspouse beneficiary will not be treated as the owner of the rolled over assets, the inherited IRA may not be subsequently rolled over to his or her own IRA.

Application of required minimum distribution rules. Distributions from the inherited IRA must be made in accordance with the required minimum distribution rules applicable to nonspousal beneficiaries when the participant dies before the entire interest has been distributed.[17] The calculation of the amount that is not eligible for rollover (i.e., the required minimum distribution) is determined by whether the employee died before on or after his or her required beginning dates.[18]

Death of employee before required beginning date. In the event the employee dies before the required beginning date, the required minimum distribution for purposes of determining the amount eligible for rollover with respect to the nonspouse beneficiary is determined under the 5-year rule or the life expectancy rule. The IRS notes, however, that under either rule, no amount will be a required minimum distribution for the year in which the employee dies.[19]

Death of employee on or after required beginning date. In the event the employee dies on or after his required beginning date, the required minimum distribution in the year of the employee's death that is not eligible for rollover is the amount that would have applied if the employee were still alive and had elected the direct rollover.[20]

The IRS has issued an example illustrating the application of the required minimum distribution rules.[21] The IRS also issued a private letter ruling that illustrates the means by which a decedent's interest may be transferred via a trustee-to-trustee transfer to a retitled IRA for a nonspousal beneficiary and the calculation of required minimum distributions from the IRA to the beneficiary.[22]

Eligible retirement plans. In order to avoid tax, the eligible rollover distribution must be transferred to an eligible retirement plan. An eligible retirement plan includes an: (1) individual retirement account, (2) individual retirement annuity, (3) qualified trust, (4) 403(a) annuity and 403(b) plan, and (5) a government 457(b) plan.[23] Note, however, the fact that an arrangement is an eligible retirement plan does not obligate it to accept rollover contributions.

Rollovers between 401(k) plans and 403(b) plans. An employee participating in a 403(b) plan may roll over an eligible rollover distribution to a 401(k) plan.[24] In addition, eligible rollover distributions from a 401(k) plan may be rolled over tax-free to a 403(b) plan.

Rollovers between 401(k) plans and 457 plans. An employee participating in a governmental deferred compensation plan under Code Sec. 457 may roll over an eligible rollover distribution tax free to a 401(k) plan. In addition, an eligible rollover distribution from a 401(k) plan may be rolled over tax free to a governmental 457 plan.[25]

Rollovers from IRAs to 401(k) plans. An eligible rollover distribution from an IRA may be rolled over into a 401(k) plan, even if the IRA is not a conduit IRA.[26]

Rollover of after-tax contributions through direct trustee-to-trustee transfer. Employees may roll over the entire amount of any qualified distribution received from a 401(k) plan, including the portion of the distribution that represents after-tax contributions, to another qualified plan, IRA, or to a defined benefit plan or tax-sheltered annuity.[27] The rollover of after-tax contributions, however, may be executed only through a direct trustee-to-trustee transfer.[28] A qualified plan must also separately account for the contributions and related earnings.[29]

Rollovers between Roth 401(k) and traditional 401(k) plan.

A Roth 401(k) plan may authorize a participant to directly roll over a distribution to another Roth 401(k) account or to a Roth IRA. However, distributions from a Roth IRA may not be rolled over to a Roth 401(k).[30] Similarly, participants in a Roth 401(k) plan may not roll over distributions to a traditional 401(k) plan.

Direct rollover of 401(k) plan distributions to Roth IRAs.

A 401(k) plan participant may directly roll over a 401(k) plan distribution to a Roth IRA via a trustee-to-trustee transfer. A rollover may be made through a direct rollover from a 401(k) plan to the Roth IRA, or an amount may be distributed from the plan and contributed (i.e., rolled over) to the Roth IRA within 60 days. Under either scenario: (1) the amount must be an eligible rollover distribution, and (2) the 401(k) plan participant would need to include in gross income the amount that would have been included in income if the distribution were not rolled over. [31]

401(k) rollovers to Roth 401(k) accounts: In-plan conversions.

Distributions made from traditional 401(k) plans prior to September 28, 2010, could not be rolled over to Roth 401(k) accounts. However, effective for distributions after September 27, 2010, rollovers may be made from 401(k) plans (as well as 403(b) plans and governmental 457(b) plans) to designated Roth accounts. [32]

Rollovers to Roth 401(k) account. Under the new rollover rules, if a 401(k) plan (403(b) plan or governmental 457(b)) plan includes a qualified designated Roth contribution program, a distribution to an employee or surviving spouse from an account under the plan that is not a designated Roth account will be permitted to be rolled over into a designated Roth account under the plan for the individual. [33] However, a plan that does not otherwise have a designated Roth program will not be allowed to establish a designated Roth account solely to accept these rollover contributions. Thus, a profit-sharing or other type of plan that does not include a qualified cash or deferred arrangement with a designated Roth program may not authorize rollover contributions from non-Roth accounts to designated Roth accounts established solely for purposes of accepting the rollover contributions.

Retroactive plan amendments authorized. A plan amendment providing for in-plan Roth rollovers is a discretionary amendment that generally must be adopted by the last day of the plan year in which the amendment is effective. However, in order to enable plan participants to make in-plan Roth rollovers before the end of the 2010 plan year, the IRS is extending the deadline for adopting plan amendments (including amendments to provide for in-plan Roth rollovers in a 401(k) plan) to the later of the last day of the plan year in which the amendment is effective or December 31, 2011. [34] Thus, a plan may be amended retroactively to allow for in-plan Roth rollovers. However, amendments must be effective as of the date the plan first operates in accordance with the amendment.

Note: IRS cautions that the extension does not apply to a plan amendment that is adopted to add a 401(k) cash or deferred arrangement to the plan. [35]

Safe harbor 401(k) plans. The extended time by which a plan may adopt amendments authorizing in-plan Roth rollovers also applies to safe harbor 401(k) plans. However, the amendment of the safe harbor 401(k) plan must be made by the later of the day before the first day of the plan year in which the safe harbor provisions are effective (rather than the last day of the plan year in which the amendment is effective) or December 31, 2011. [36]

Qualified Roth contribution program "in place". A plan must have a qualified Roth contribution program in place at the time a rollover contribution to a designated Roth account is made in an in-plan Roth rollover. [37] IRS further advises that, although a plan may be amended retroactively to add a qualified Roth contribution program, a program will be "in place" on a date only if, with respect to compensation that could be deferred beginning with that date, eligible employees are allowed the opportunity to elect on that date to have designated Roth contributions made to the plan (or would have such an opportunity but for a statutory or plan limitation on the amount of an employee's elective deferrals). [38]

Written explanation (402(f) rollover notice) of in-plan Roth rollover option. A plan that offers in-plan Roth rollovers must include a description of this feature in the written explanation (402(f) Notice) that the plan furnishes to participants who receive an eligible rollover distribution. [39] The IRS has produced two safe harbor explanations that may be provided to individuals receiving an eligible rollover distribution that highlights the tax consequences of the rollover and subsequent distributions from the Roth account (see CCH PENSION PLAN GUIDE¶ 17,146D).

Conversion limited to eligible rollover distributions. In a significant limitation on the potential application of the Roth in-plan conversion option, an amount may not be rolled over unless it is an eligible rollover distribution under the terms of the plan. Accordingly, amounts (elective deferrals and safe harbor contributions) in a 401(k) plan subject to distribution restrictions (i.e., the limitation on in-service distributions before age 59½) may not be rolled over to a designated Roth account.[40]

In-plan rollover of amounts not distributable under plan. An employer may elect to expand distribution options beyond those currently allowed under the plan, such as by authorizing in-service distributions or distributions prior to normal retirement age, in order to allow employees to make the newly authorized rollover contributions. Under such circumstances, the plan may condition eligibility for the new distribution on the employee's election to have the distribution directly rolled over to the designated Roth account within the plan.

¶2993

In addition, the plan would not be required, by implementing the amendment, to allow for any other rollover or distribution option for the amounts. [41] Thus, IRS explains, a plan that does not currently allow for in-service distributions from a participant's pre-tax elective deferral account may be amended to permit in-plan Roth direct rollovers from the account by participants who have attained age 59½, while not otherwise permitting distribution of the funds. However, IRS cautions that a plan may not impose such a restriction on a pre-existing distribution option without violating Code Sec. 411(d)(6).

Direct rollover. The rollover contribution may be executed at the election of the employee (or surviving spouse) through a direct rollover. However, such a direct rollover would be allowed only if the employee (or surviving spouse) was eligible for a distribution in that amount and in that form (if property is transferred) and the distribution is an eligible rollover distribution.

In-plan Roth rollover by alternate payee. An in-plan Roth rollover may be executed by a beneficiary only if he or she is a surviving spouse and by an alternate payee only if he or she is spouse or former spouse of the plan participant. [42] This restriction extends from the fact that in-plan Roth rollovers are limited to eligible rollover distributions. Under the applicable rules, eligible rollover distributions may be made to a spousal beneficiary and to an alternate payee who is a spouse or former spouse, but not to a nonspousal beneficiary.

Note: Code Sec. 402(c)(11), which allows for nonspousal beneficiary rollovers to an IRA or Roth IRA, does not, the IRS stresses, allow for rollovers to qualified plans.

Tax considerations. Individuals who roll over contributions to a Roth 401(k) account would be required to include the distribution in gross income in the same manner as if the distribution were rolled over into a Roth IRA. In the event a participant rolls over an eligible rollover distribution into a designated Roth account, IRS advises that the participant must include any previously untaxed portion of the distribution in gross income.[43]

Taxable amount of in-plan Roth 401(k) rollover. The taxable amount of an in-plan Roth rollover is included in a participant's gross income. The taxable amount is the fair market value of the distribution reduced by any basis the participant has in the distribution. [44] Accordingly, IRS explains, the fair market value of a distribution that includes employer securities must reflect net unrealized appreciation. In addition, IRS notes, if an outstanding loan is rolled over in the in-plan Roth rollover, the balance of the loan is included in gross income.

20 percent withholding does not apply. In-plan Roth rollovers are not subject to the 10 percent early withdrawal penalty tax. Nor will mandatory 20 percent withholding apply to in-plan Roth direct rollovers. However, IRS cautions that a participant electing an in-plan Roth rollover may need to increase withholding or make estimated tax payments to avoid an underpayment penalty. [45]

Special tax rules for 2010 rollovers and conversions. The taxable amount of a distribution that is rolled over in a in-plan Roth 401(k) rollover is generally included in gross income in the tax year in which the distribution occurs. [46] However, under a special rule applicable for 2010 rollovers and conversions, a taxpayer may include the distribution in income in equal parts in 2011 and 2012. [47] Note, the 2-year income deferral may not be available unless the distribution is made by December 31, 2010 and the plan has a designated Roth account in place at the time the distribution is rolled over. [48]

Alternatively, an employee may elect to include the entire taxable amount of the rollover in 2010 gross income. However, a participant who elects to include the rolled over amount in 2010 gross income may not revoke that election after the due date (including extensions) of his or her 2010 federal income tax return. The IRS further cautions that the participant may also: (1) owe estimated tax on the taxable amount of the rollover for the year or years it is included in gross income or (2) may incur an underpayment penalty. [49]

In-plan Roth 401(k) rollover may not be recharacterized. A participant who has elected an in-plan Roth rollover may not undo or recharacterize the in-plan Roth rollover. [50] The recharacterization rule of Code Sec. 408A(d)(6), the IRS advises, applies only to IRA contributions.

Income acceleration of distribution allocable to 2010 in-plan Roth rollovers. Special income acceleration rules apply when a participant receives a distribution of any amount of the taxable portion of the in-plan Roth rollover in 2010 or 2011 that would not have been included in gross income until 2011 and 2012. [51] Under such circumstances, the participant's gross income for the year of the distribution will be increased by the amount of the distribution that would not otherwise be includible in gross income until a later year. However, the amount that would otherwise be includible in the participant's gross income in 2012 would be reduced by the income accelerated. Similarly, if a distribution is made in 2010, the amount that would otherwise be includible in the participant's gross income in 2011 is reduced by the amount that the income accelerated to 2010 exceeds the amount that would otherwise be includible in income in 2012.

> **Example:** Jack makes an in-plan Roth rollover in 2010, but defers the taxable amount of the rollover to 2011 and 2012. Assume, Jack takes a distribution from the Roth account in 2010 that consists of $5,000 allocable to the taxable amount of the 2001 in-plan Roth rollover. Under such circumstances, the $5,000 would be included in Jack's 2010 gross income. The remaining taxable amount of the 2010 in-plan rollover ($3,000) would be included in his 2011 gross income. [52]

Recapture rule for Roth distributions within 5 years. In the event an amount allocable to the taxable amount of an in-plan Roth rollover is distributed within the 5-year taxable period beginning with the first day of the participant's taxable year in which the rollover was made, the distribution will be subject to the 10 percent penalty tax assessed on early distributions under Code Sec. 72(t). [53] For example, if a participant withdraws an amount that includes $5,000 allocable to the taxable amount of an in-plan Roth rollover made within the preceding 5 years, the $5,000 would be includible in the participant's gross income and subject to a tax of $500 under Code Sec. 72(t).

The 5-year recapture rule will not apply to a distribution that is rolled over to another designated Roth account of the participant or to a Roth IRA owned by the participant. However, the rule will apply to subsequent distributions from the rolled over account or IRA within the 5-taxable year period.

Ordering rule for allocating taxable distributions. The IRS has prescribed ordering rules for purposes of allocating the taxable amount of a distribution from a Roth account to which a participant has made an in-plan rollover. [54] Solely for purposes of the income acceleration rule and the 5-year recapture rule, a distribution from an in-plan Roth rollover account will be treated as attributable to an in-plan Roth rollover to the extent the distribution constitutes recovery of basis (determined under the rules of Code Sec.72 and IRS Reg. § 1.402A-1, Q-9).

Similarly, a distribution from a designated Roth account that, under the terms of the plan, is not paid from an in-plan Roth rollover account, will be treated as attributable to an in-plan Roth rollover to the extent the portion of the distribution that represents recovery of basis exceeds the basis in the designated Roth account other than the basis resulting from in-plan Roth rollovers.

Finally, the IRS explains, a distribution that is treated as attributable to an in-plan Roth rollover will be attributed to an in-plan Roth rollover on fist-in-first-out basis. Under this rule, any amount attributed to the rollover will be allocated first to the taxable amount of the rollover.

Reporting in- plan rollovers to Roth accounts. The IRS advises that the amounts rolled over must be reported on Form 1099-R in Box 1 (Gross Distribution).[55] The taxable amount of the rollover would be reported in Box 2a and any basis in the rollover would be reported in Box 5 (Employee Contributions). Distribution Code G should be used in completing Box 7 on Form 1099-R.

Separate 1099-R required to report 2010 Roth distributions. The IRS cautions that distributions made to plan participants in 2010 from designated Roth accounts must be reported on a separate Form 1099-R. In addition, the portion of a Roth distribution that is allocable to an in-plan Roth rollover must be reported on 1099-R. The distribution should be reported as any other distribution from a designated Roth account. However, IRS advises that the amount of the distribution allocable to the in-plan Roth rollover should be entered in the blank box to left of Box 10. [56]

Rollovers between SIMPLE plans and 401(k) plans. Distributions from a SIMPLE 401(k) plan may be rolled over to a qualified employer sponsor plan or to an IRA.[57] However, distributions from a SIMPLE 401(k) plan may not be rolled over to a SIMPLE IRA (see ¶ 2994).

Early distributions subject to penalty

Pre-retirement distributions that are not rolled over are subject to a 10% penalty (assessed on the taxable portion of the distribution) unless they are made after the employee attains age 59½, dies, becomes disabled, or retires after reaching age 55. The 10% penalty on early distributions applies to hardship distributions (see ¶ 2989), but does not apply to distributions made: to a beneficiary after the employee's death; because the employee is totally and permanently disabled; as part of a series of substantially equal periodic payments over the life (or life expectancy) of the employee or the joint lives (or joint life expectancies) of the employee and his or her beneficiary; to an employee on account of medical expenses that exceed 7.5% of the employee's adjusted gross income; or to an alternate payee under a QDRO.[58] The penalty also does not apply to an employee who has exercised an option under the plan to separate from service after attaining age 55. [59]

Corrective distributions are not subject to penalty tax. Excess deferrals (and income) returned to a plan participant through a corrective distribution are not subject to the 10-percent tax on premature distributions. [60]

A corrective distribution made to a highly compensated employee of the employee's share of excess elective contributions made to a 401(k) plan also is not subject to the premature distribution tax. [61] Similarly, a distribution of excess aggregate contributions made to meet the nondiscrimination requirements applicable to matching contributions is exempt from the additional 10-percent tax. [62]

Qualified reservist distributions. An exemption to the 10-percent premature distribution penalty applies to distributions from a 401(k) plan that are attributable to elective deferrals and made to "qualified reservists" who are called up to active duty during a specified period for a minimum period of time. The exemption is available to an individual who (1) is a reservist or guardsman (as defined in 37 U.S.C. 101(24)) and (2) has been ordered or called to active duty for a period *in excess* of 179 days or for an indefinite period. In addition, the distribution must be made during the period beginning on the date of the order or call to duty, and ending at the close of the active duty period.

FICA and FUTA tax withholding

401(k) distributions are not subject to FICA or FUTA tax.

☐ The FICA and FUTA tax withholding rules applicable to elective deferrals and nonelective and matching contributions are discussed at ¶ 2983.

Income tax withholding

The taxable portion of a distribution from a 401(k) plan (as contrasted to elective deferrals) is subject to income tax withholding. Plan administrators are generally responsible for withholding on 401(k) distributions.[63]

Income tax is withheld on periodic payments, such as annuities, as if the payments were wages. However, a recipient may elect to not have income tax withheld.[64]

Income tax withholding is imposed at a 20% rate on any nonperiodic distribution that is eligible for rollover but that is not transferred directly to an eligible transferee plan.[65]

¶2993

Estate tax

Distributions made upon the death of a 401(k) plan participant may be subject to federal estate tax. However, the spousal beneficiary of a participant's 401(k) plan assets will not be subject to estate tax until his or her own death.

Report distributions on From 1099-R

Taxable distributions from a 401(k) plan (including installment distributions, in-service distributions, and premature distributions) are reported to participants and the IRS on Form 1099-R (see ¶ 2205).

☐ See ¶ 1900 and following for more information on the taxation of qualified plan distributions.

---

1 Code Sec. 402(e)(3); IRS Reg. §§ 1.401(k)-1(a)(4)(iii) and 1.402(a)-1(d)(2).

2 Code Sec. 402(d).

3 Code Secs. 72(a)-(c), 402(a), and 403(a)(1); IRS Reg. § 1.72-4(d)(1).

4 Code Secs. 72(b) and (d).

5 Code Sec. 72(e)(2)(A).

6 Code Sec. 72(d) and (e).

7 Code Sec. 414(u)(12)(B)(i), as added by P.L. 110-245 (Heroes Earnings Assistance and Relief Tax Act of 2008), Act Sec. 105(b); Code Sec. 3401(h)(2)(A) , as added by P.L. 110-245 (Heroes Earnings Assistance and Relief Tax Act of 2008), Act Sec. 105(a)(1).

8 Code Secs. 401(a)(31) and 402(c).

9 Code Sec. 402(c)(4), as amended by P.L. 107-16 (Economic Growth and Tax Relief Reconciliation Act of 2001), Act Sec. 636(b).

10 Code Sec. 402(c)(9).

11 Code Sec. 402(c)(11), as added by P.L. 109-280 (Pension Protection Act of 2006), Act Sec. 829(a)(1).

12 Code Sec. 402(c)(11)(A)(i), as added by P.L. 109-280 (Pension Protection Act of 2006), Act Sec. 829(a)(1).

13 IRS Notice 2007-7, I.R.B. 2007-5, at CCH PENSION PLAN GUIDE ¶ 17,135R.

14 Code Sec. 402(c)(11), as added by P.L. 110-458 (Worker, Retiree, and Employer Recovery Act of 2008), Act Sec. 108(f).

15 P.L. 110-458 (Worker, Retiree, and Employer Recovery Act of 2008), Act Sec. 108(f)(2)(C).

16 Code Sec. 402(c)(11)(A)(ii), as added by P.L. 109-280 (Pension Protection Act of 2006), Act Sec. 829(a)(1); IRS Notice 2007-7, I.R.B. 2007-5, 1-29-07, at CCH PENSION PLAN GUIDE ¶ 17,135R.

17 Code Sec. 402(c)(11)(A)(iii), as added by P.L. 109-280 (Pension Protection Act of 2006), Act Sec. 829(a)(1).

18 *Ibid.*

19 *Ibid.*

20 *Ibid.*

21 IRS Employee Plans News, February 13, 2007.

22 IRS Letter Ruling 200717023, 2-10-07, at CCH PENSION PLAN GUIDE ¶ 17,427J.

23 Code Sec. 402(c)(8)(B); IRS Reg. § 1.402(c)-2, Q&A-2

24 Code Secs. 402(c)(8)(B)(vi) and 403(b)(8)(A)(ii), as amended by P.L. 107-16 (Economic Growth and Tax Relief Reconciliation Act of 2001), Act Sec. 641(b)(1) and (2).

25 Code Secs. 402(c)(8)(B) and 457(e)(16)(A), as amended by P.L. 107-16 (Economic Growth and Tax Relief Reconciliation Act of 2001), Act Sec 641(a).

26 Code Sec. 408(d)(3)(A), as amended by P.L. 107-16 (Economic Growth and Tax Relief Reconciliation Act of 2001), Act Sec. 642(a).

27 Code Sec. 402(c)(2), as amended by P.L. 107-16 (Economic Growth and Tax Relief Reconciliation Act of 2001), Act Sec. 643(a).

28 Code Sec. 401(a)(31), as amended by P.L. 107-16 (Economic Growth and Tax Relief Reconciliation Act of 2001), Act Sec. 643(b).

29 Code Sec. 402(c)(2), as amended by P.L. 107-16 (Economic Growth and Tax Relief Reconciliation Act of 2001) Act Sec. 643(a).

30 IRS Reg. § 1.408A-10, Q&A-5.

31 Code Sec. 408A(e); IRS Notice 2008-30, Q-1, I.RB. 2008-12, 3-24-08, at CCH PENSION PLAN GUIDE ¶ 17,138X.

32 P.L. 111-240 (Small Business Jobs Act of 2010), Act Sec. 2112.

33 Code Sec. 402A(C)(4)(B), as amended by P.L. 111-240 (Small Business Jobs Act of 2010), Act Sec. 2112.

34 IRS Notice 2010-84, Q-15, I.R.B. 2010-51, at CCH PENSION PLAN GUIDE ¶ 17,146D.

35 IRS Notice 2010-84, Q-17, I.R.B. 2010-51, at CCH Pension Plan Guide ¶ 17,146D.

36 IRS Notice 2010-84, Q-18, I.R.B. 2010-51, at CCH Pension Plan Guide ¶ 17,146D.

37 IRS Notice 2010-84, Q-19, I.R.B. 2010-51, at CCH Pension Plan Guide ¶ 17,146D.

38 IRS Notice 2010-84, Q-20, I.R.B. 2010-51, at CCH Pension Plan Guide ¶ 17,146D.

39 IRS Notice 2010-84, Q-5, I.R.B. 2010-51, at CCH Pension Plan Guide ¶ 17,146D.

40 IRS Notice 2010-84, Q-2, I.R.B. 2010-51, at CCH Pension Plan Guide ¶ 17,146D.

41 IRS Notice 2010-84, Q-4, I.R.B. 2010-51, at CCH Pension Plan Guide ¶ 17,146D.

42 IRS Notice 2010-84, Q-14, I.R.B. 2010-51, at CCH Pension Plan Guide ¶ 17,146D.

43 IRS Website, October 1, 2010, "New Law Allows In-Plan Rollovers to Designated Roth Accouts."

44 IRS Notice 2010-84, Q-7, I.R.B. 2010-51, at CCH Pension Plan Guide ¶ 17,146D.

45 IRS Notice 2010-84, Q-8, I.R.B. 2010-51, at CCH Pension Plan Guide ¶ 17,146D.

46 IRS Notice 2010-84, Q-9, I.R.B. 2010-51, at CCH Pension Plan Guide ¶ 17,146D.

47 Code Sec. 402A(c)(4)(A)(iii), as amended by P.L. 111-240 (Small Business Jobs Act of 2010), Act Sec. 2112.

48 IRS Notice 2010-84, Q-19, I.R.B. 2010-51, at CCH Pension Plan Guide ¶ 17,146D.

49 IRS Website, October 1, 2010, "New Law Allows In-Plan Rollovers to Designated Roth Accounts."

50 IRS Notice 2010-84, Q-6, I.R.B. 2010-51, at CCH Pension Plan Guide ¶ 17,146D.

51 IRS Notice 2010-84, Q-11, I.R.B. 2010-51, at CCH Pension Plan Guide ¶ 17,146D.

52 IRS Notice 2010-84, Q-11, I.R.B. 2010-51, at CCH Pension Plan Guide ¶ 17,146D.

53 IRS Notice 2010-84, Q-12, I.R.B. 2010-51, at CCH Pension Plan Guide ¶ 17,146D.

54 IRS Notice 2010-84, Q-13, I.R.B. 2010-51, at CCH Pension Plan Guide ¶ 17,146D.

55 IRS Website, November 21, 2010.

56 *Ibid.*

57 Code Sec. 401(k)(11)(B)(i)(III); IRS Reg. § 1.401(k)-4(e)(1).

58 Code Sec. 72(t). Note, the IRS has approved three methods by which a distributin may be made in a seirs of substnaily equl periodc pamtn for the life of a distirutee who has separed from servies (see Rev. Rul. 2002-62, I.R.B. 2002-42, 10-21-2002 at CCH Pension Plan Guide ¶ 19,947L.

59 See *Williams v. Commissioner*, TC (2008), No. 2008-53, at CCH Pension Plan Guide ¶ 24,002X (a distribution to a taxpayer that was made after the individual attained age 55 did not fall within the exception because he had retired at age 53. The application of the exception is conditioned on the age of the employee at the time of separation for service and not on the time the distribution is made or the benefits are received).

60 Code Sec. 402(g)(2)(C); IRS Reg. § 1.402(g)-1(e)(8)(i).

61 Code Sec. 401(k)(8)(D); IRS Reg. § 1.401(k)-1(f)(4)(v).

62 Code Sec. 401(m)(7)(A); IRS Reg. § 1.401(m)-1(e)(3)(v).

63 Code Sec. 3405(d)(2).

64 Code Secs. 3405(a)(2) and (b)(2) See IRS Notice 2008-30, I.R.B. 2008-12, 3-24-08, at CCH Pension Plan Guide ¶ 17,138X.

65 Code Sec. 3405(c)(1).

¶ 2994

SIMPLE 401(k) PLANS: Contributions and Distributions

Employers (other than governmental employers) that employ 100 or fewer employees (applying the aggregation rules of Code Sec. 414(r)) who earned at least $5,000 (unadjusted for inflation) in compensation during the prior year and that do not maintain another qualified plan may adopt a Savings Incentive Match Plan for Employees (SIMPLE plan) as part of a 401(k) arrangement.[1] The advantage of a SIMPLE 401(k) is that the nondiscrimination tests applicable to elective deferrals and employer matching contributions under a 401(k) plan will be deemed satisfied if the plan provides a specified level of matching or nonelective contributions in which employees are 100 percent vested (see ¶ 2995). However, the arrangement (unlike a SIMPLE IRA—see ¶ 3224) must satisfy the other rules governing qualified plans, as well as all other requirements applicable to 401(k) plans.[2]

General contribution rule

Contributions under a SIMPLE 401(k) are limited to:

1. employee deferrals (salary reduction contributions made by an employer at the election of employees)[3] and
2. employer matching contributions or nonelective contributions.[4]

Employee deferrals. Employee deferrals (salary reduction contributions) are made on the employee's behalf to a trust under the SIMPLE 401(k) plan.[5] The maximum annual amount of a salary reduction contribution that may be made on behalf of any employee under a SIMPLE 401(k) plan in 2012 is $11,500 (compared to $17,000 under a traditional 401(k) plan).[6]

Cost of living adjustment. The annual limit on elective deferrals under a SIMPLE 401(k) is adjusted to reflect changes in the cost of living. The $10,000 limit on deferrals to a SIMPLE plan will be indexed in $500 increments.[7]

Saver's credit for elective deferrals. Lower and middle income taxpayers participating in a SIMPLE 401(k) plan may qualify for a temporary nonrefundable tax credit (i.e., saver's credit) for salary reduction contributions (up to $2,000 per year) to the plan.[8] See ¶ 2983.

"Catch-up" contributions. Individuals who: (1) who will attain at least age 50 by the end of the tax year and (2) are prohibited by applicable plan or statutory limits from making other elective deferrals to the plan for the plan or calendar year, may make additional "catch-up" contributions to a SIMPLE 401(k) plan.[9] The applicable dollar limit for catch-up elective deferrals under a SIMPLE 401(k) plan is $2,500 (for 2012).[10] The limit on catch-up contributions to a SIMPLE 401(k) plan is adjusted for inflation in $500 increments.[11]

☐ Catch-up contributions are discussed in detail at ¶ 2982.

Limit on annual additions to income. In addition to the dollar limits on elective deferrals, a separate limit applies to all additions (contributions) to an employee's account in a 401(k) plan, including a SIMPLE 401(k) plan. The annual additions limit (for 2012) is the lesser of $50,000 or 100% of an employee's compensation (see ¶ 2985).[12]

Matching employer contributions. An employer under a SIMPLE 401(k) plan is generally required to match employee deferrals on a dollar for dollar basis, up to (and not in excess of) a limit of 3% of the employee's compensation for the entire calendar year.[13]

Annual limit on compensation. The amount of the employer's matching contribution is subject to the annual limit on compensation applicable to qualified plans ($250,000 in 2012). Accordingly, the maximum employer match to a SIMPLE 401(k) account for 2012 is $7,500 (3% × $250,000).

Nonelective contributions. As an alternative to matching contributions, an employer may make across-the-board "nonelective" contributions equal to 2% of compensation for each eligible employee with at least $5,000 of compensation from the employer for the entire calendar year.[14] The 2% nonelective contribution is subject to the annual compensation limit ($250,000 in 2012) on compensation that applies to qualified plans.[15] Thus, the maximum nonelective employer match for 2012 is $5,000 (2% × $250,000).

Matching contribution may not be reduced to less than 3 percent of compensation. An employer maintaining a SIMPLE 401(k) plan must either match employee deferrals dollar-for-dollar or provide a nonelective contribution of 2 percent of each eligible employee's compensation. The employer does not have the option available to employers maintaining SIMPLE IRAs of reducing the matching contribution to less than 3 percent of an employee's compensation.

Contributions are fully vested. All contributions (including employer matching contributions) under a SIMPLE 401(k) plan are fully vested and nonforfeitable when made.[16]

Employer deduction for contributions

An employer may deduct contributions to a SIMPLE 401(k) that are required to be made under Code Sec. 401(k)(11)(B). An employer's deduction for contributions to a SIMPLE 401(k), unlike contributions to a traditional 401(k) plan, is not limited to 25% of the total compensation of plan participants for the year. Rather, the employer's deduction is limited to the greater of 25% of the compensation paid or accrued during the tax year to beneficiaries under a stock bonus or profit-sharing plan, or the amount that the employer is required to contribute to a SIMPLE 401(k) plan for the year.[17] Thus, an employer may deduct contributions to a SIMPLE 401(k) that are in excess of 25% of the compensation otherwise paid or accrued during the year.

Note, for purposes of determining the employer's deduction, salary reduction contributions to the SIMPLE plan are not treated as employer contributions (see ¶ 2987).[18]

Deduct contributions in year paid. Generally, an employer may deduct contributions to a SIMPLE 401(k) plan in the tax year in which they are paid.[19] The employer may deduct matching or nonelective contributions no later than the due date, including extensions, of its tax return for the tax year for which it makes contributions.[20]

Carryover deductions. Employer contributions that exceed the applicable deduction limit may be carried over and deducted in succeeding years. The deduction may not exceed the greater of 25% of the compensation otherwise paid or accrued during the tax year to beneficiaries under the stock or bonus plan or the amount that employer is required to contribute to the SIMPLE 401(k) plan.[21]

Employees not taxed on employer contributions

Employees are not required to include in income any amount contributed by the employer to a SIMPLE 401(k), as long as the contributions do not exceed the prescribed dollar limits.[22]

¶2994

Elective deferrals counted for withholding. An employee's elective deferrals are included in the Social Security (FICA) and unemployment insurance (FUTA) wage bases for withholding purposes and for purposes of determining the employer's contributions to those taxes.[23]

Contribution deposit rules

Employer contributions to the SIMPLE 401(k) plan become plan assets and must, therefore, be paid to the plan on the earliest day they can reasonably be segregated from the employer's general assets, but in no event later than the 15th business day of the month following the month in which the contributions were withheld or received by the employer.[24] Note, contributions to a SIMPLE IRA may be made up to 30 days after the month in which the amounts would otherwise have been payable to the employee (see ¶ 3224).

Employee elections

An employer maintaining a SIMPLE 401(k) plan must allow employees to make a salary reduction election to participate in the arrangement and must notify eligible employees, within a reasonable period of time, of their right to participate in the arrangement and to make or modify salary reduction contributions.[25]

Generally, each eligible employee may make or modify a salary reduction election (elective deferral) during the 60-day period immediately preceding each January 1.[26] For the year an employee becomes eligible to make elective deferrals, the 60-day election period requirement is deemed to be satisfied if the employee may make or modify a salary reduction election during a 60-day period that includes either the date the employee becomes eligible or the day before that date.[27]

> **Example:** LAN Co. maintains a SIMPLE 401(k) plan. For the 2012 calendar year, employees of LAN must have been allowed to make a salary reduction election during the period between November 2 to December 31, 2011.

Notification of election period. An employer (not the SIMPLE 401(k) plan trustee) must notify each employee eligible to participate in the arrangement of the employee's right during the governing 60-day period to make or modify a salary reduction contribution to the plan. The notice must be provided within a reasonable period of time prior to each 60-day election period, or on the day the election period start.[28] The notice must further indicate whether the employee will make matching contributions or nonelective contributions.

Termination of participation. An employee participating in a SIMPLE 401(k) plan may terminate a salary reduction election at any time during the year. However, if an employee terminates a salary reduction election, the plan may refuse to allow the employee to resume participation until the beginning of the next calendar year.

Distributions from a SIMPLE 401(k)

A SIMPLE 401(k) is subject to general restrictions on withdrawals that apply to all 401(k) plans. [29] See ¶ 2989.

¶2994

Hardship withdrawals. Hardship withdrawals may be made from a SIMPLE 401(k) plan if the participant has an immediate and heavy financial need and other resources are not reasonably available to meet that need (see ¶ 2989).[30]

Taxation of distributions. Contributions to a SIMPLE 401(k), and the earnings on those contributions, accumulate tax-free until the funds are withdrawn. Withdrawn funds are taxed at ordinary income tax rates.

Early withdrawal tax. Early distributions from a SIMPLE 401(k) are subject to a 10% additional income tax.[31]

Rollovers and transfers. An employee who receives a distribution from a SIMPLE 401(k) plan may defer tax on the distribution by rolling over all or part of the distribution within 60 days of receipt to another qualified employer- sponsored plan, IRA, or to a 403(b) plan or governmental 457 plan.[32] Similarly, a distribution from a qualified plan may be rolled over to a SIMPLE 401(k) plan. However, distributions from a SIMPLE 401(k) plan may not be rolled over to SIMPLE IRA plan. Contributions to a SIMPLE IRA are restricted to employee elective contributions, employer matching or nonelective contributions, and rollover contributions from a SIMPLE IRA.[33] Similarly, amounts received under a SIMPLE 401(k) plan may be rolled over to a qualified plan but may not be rolled over to another SIMPLE 401(k) plan because a SIMPLE 401(k) plan may only receive elective and matching contributions. [34] However, distributions from qualified plans may be rolled over into a SIMPLE 401(k) plan.

Top-heavy exemption

A SIMPLE 401(k) plan that authorizes only contributions necessary to satisfy the requirements of Code Sec. 401(k)(11) is exempt from the top-heavy plan rules of Code Sec. 416 that apply to traditional 401(k) plans (see ¶ 905 and ¶ 2979).[35] Note, an employer may avoid the top-heavy restrictions by converting a 401(k) plan to a SIMPLE 401(k) plan.

Plan year must be calendar year

The plan year of a plan containing the SIMPLE 401(k) feature must be the calendar year. Thus, a SIMPLE 401(k) plan may only be established on January 1, and may only be terminated on December 31. A 401(k) plan that is maintained on a fiscal year basis must be converted to a calendar year in order to adopt the SIMPLE arrangement.[36]

Form 5500 reporting

A Form 5500 annual report must be filed for each year that the SIMPLE 401(k) plan has assets.

Model amendment

The IRS has issued a model amendment (see CCH PENSION PLAN GUIDE ¶ 17,299N-95) that may be used by certain employers in order to adopt a SIMPLE plan as part of a 401(k) arrangement.[37] The model amendment may be adopted only by sponsors of M&P regional prototype, volume submitter specimen, and individually designed plans that contain cash or deferred arrangement provisions and that have received favorable letters from the IRS. Eligible plan sponsors may adopt the model amendment without filing an application or paying a user fee to the IRS.

[1] Code Secs. 401(k)(11) and 408(p).

[2] Rev. Proc. 97-9, I.R.B. 1997-2, 1-13-97, CCH PENSION PLAN GUIDE ¶ 17,299N-95.

[3] Code Sec. 401(k)(11)(B)(i)(I).

[4] Code Sec. 401(k)(11)(B)(i)(II) and (III).

[5] Code Sec. 401(k)(11)(B)(i)(I).

[6] Code Sec. 401(k)(11)(B)(i)(I), as amended by P.L. 107-16 (Economic Growth and Tax Relief Reconciliation Act of 2001), Act Sec. 611(f)(3). Code Sec. 408(p)(2)(E)(i), as amended by P.L. 107-16 (Economic Growth and Tax Relief Reconciliation Act of 2001), Act Sec. 611(f).

[7] Code Sec. 408(p)(2)(E)(ii), as amended by P.L. 107-16 (Economic Growth and Tax Relief Reconciliation Act of 2001), Act Sec. 611(f).

[8] Code Sec. 25B, as added by P.L. 107-16 (Economic Growth and Tax Relief Reconciliation Act of 2001), Act Sec. 618(a). IRS Announcement 2001-106, I.R.B. 2001-44, 10-29-2001, at CCH PENSION PLAN GUIDE ¶ 17,097R-52.

[9] Code Sec. 414(v), as amended by P.L. 107-16 (Economic Growth and Tax Relief Reconciliation Act of 2001), Act Sec. 631(a).

[10] Code Sec. 414(v)(2)(B)(ii), as amended by P.L. 107-16 (Economic Growth and Tax Relief Reconciliation Act of 2001), Act Sec. 631(a). IRS Reg. § 1.414(v)-1(c)(2)(ii).

[11] Code Sec. 414(v)(2)(C), as amended by P.L. 107-16 (Economic Growth and Tax Relief Reconciliation Act of 2001), Act Sec. 631(a).

[12] Code Sec. 415(c)(1), as amended by P.L. 107-16 (Economic Growth and Tax Relief Reconciliation Act of 2001), Act Sec. 611(b).

[13] Code Sec. 401(k)(11)(B)(i)(II).

[14] Code Sec. 401(k)(11)(B)(ii).

[15] Code Sec. 408(p)(2)(B)(ii).

[16] Code Sec. 401(k)(11)(A)(ii); Code Sec. 408(p)(3).

[17] Code Sec. 404(a)(3)(A)(i), as amended by P.L. 107-16 (Economic Growth and Tax Relief Reconciliation Act of 2001), Act Sec. 616(A).

[18] Code Sec. 404(n), as added by P.L. 107-16 (Economic Growth and Tax Relief Reconciliation Act of 2001), Act Sec. 614(a).

[19] Code Sec. 404(a)(3)(A)(i).

[20] Code Sec. 404(a)(6).

[21] Code Sec. 404(a)(3)(A)(ii).

[22] Code Sec. 402(e)(3).

[23] Code Sec. 3121(v)(1)(A); Code Sec. 3306(r)(1)(A).

[24] ERISA Sec. 2510.3-102(b).

[25] IRS Reg. § 1.401(k)-4(d)(3).

[26] Rev. Proc. 97-9, I.R.B. 1997-2, 1-13-97, CCH PENSION PLAN GUIDE ¶ 17,299N-95.

[27] *Ibid.*

[28] IRS Reg. § 1.401(k)-4(d)(3).

[29] Rev. Proc. 97-9, I.R.B. 1997-2, 1-13-97, CCH PENSION PLAN GUIDE ¶ 17,299N-95.

[30] IRS Reg. § 1.401(k)-1(d)(2).

[31] Code Sec. 72(t).

[32] Code Sec. 402(c)(8)(B), as amended by P.L. 107-16 (Economic Growth and Tax Relief Reconciliation Act of 2001), Act. Secs. 617(c) and 641.

[33] Code Sec.408A(p)(2)(A)(iv); IRS Notice 98-4, Q-A D-1, I.R.B. 1998-2, at CCH PENSION PLAN GUIDE ¶ 17,113O.

[34] Code Sec. 401(k)(11)(B)(i)(III); IRS Reg. § 1.401(k)-4(e)(1).

[35] Code Sec. 401(k)(11)(D)(ii).

[36] Rev. Proc. 97-9, I.R.B. 1997-2, 1-13-97, CCH PENSION PLAN GUIDE ¶ 17,299N-95.

[37] *Ibid.*

¶ 2995

SIMPLE 401(k) PLANS: Nondiscrimination Rules

Under a SIMPLE 401(k) plan, the nondiscrimination rules generally applicable to elective deferrals (the actual deferral percentage (ADP) test) and employer matching contributions (the actual contribution percentage (ACP) test) are deemed to be met if:

1. an employee's elective deferrals for the year, expressed as a percentage of compensation, do not exceed an inflation ad-

justed amount specified under Code Sec. 408(p)(2)(A)(ii) ($11,500 in 2012);

2. the employer makes contributions matching the employee's elective deferrals, up to 3% of the employee's compensation for the year, or alternatively, makes a nonelective contribution of 2% of compensation for each eligible employee who has earned at least $5,000 in compensation from the employer for the year; and

3. no other contributions are made under the arrangement.[1]

Notice of nonelective contribution election

Employers that decide to make the 2% nonelective contribution must notify employees of the election within a reasonable period of time before the 60th day before the beginning of the year.[2]

Contributions are fully vested

Contributions to the SIMPLE 401(k) plan must be 100% vested.[3] Thus, the contributions are not subject to a vesting schedule.

Contributions to other plans prohibited

A SIMPLE 401(k) plan will not satisfy the applicable nondiscrimination tests if contributions were made or benefits were accrued during the year for any employee eligible for the plan under any other qualified plan of the employer.[4]

☐ See ¶ 3224 for a discussion of SIMPLE IRAs.

---

[1] Code Sec. 401(k)(11)(B) as amended by P.L. 107-16 (Economic Growth and Tax Relief Reconciliation Act of 2001), Act Sec. 611(f)(3)(A).

[2] Code Sec. 401(k)(11)(B)(ii).
[3] Code Sec. 401(k)(11)(A)(iii).
[4] Code Sec. 401(k)(11)(C).

¶ 2996
For More Information

☐ For more information on 401(k) plans, see the CCH PENSION PLAN GUIDE ¶ 7400—¶ 7740.

ESOPs—Special Rules

¶ 3000
Overview of Special Rules for ESOPs

Employee stock ownership plans (ESOPs) may be either stock bonus plans or a combination of stock bonus plans and money purchase plans. They must qualify for tax purposes under Code Sec. 401(a), must be designed to invest primarily in employer securities, must meet ERISA's reporting and disclosure requirements, and must satisfy the special requirements outlined below. ESOPs can be divided into two main types: the nonleveraged or "basic" ESOP and the leveraged ESOP.

Establishing an ESOP

In deciding whether to establish an ESOP, employers should take both tax and non-tax considerations into account. On the non-tax side of the ledger, ESOPs are a technique for making employees shareholders in the company. If the employer sees this as a means of encouraging employee motivation, then the establishment of an ESOP may be a sound business decision. ESOPs have also been accorded favorable tax treatment and this has been a prime reason for the phenomenal growth of such plans over the past two decades.

Special ESOP requirements

In order to take advantage of the preferred tax treatment accorded to ESOPs, the ESOP must meet certain special requirements in addition to the general qualification requirements of the. Code. These requirements govern the types of securities issued to ESOPs, voting rights of ESOP stock, the offering of put options and a right of first refusal, diversification, allocation, and distribution. There are also special rules governing minimum coverage under an ESOP and limits on contributions. An ESOP loan must meet certain requirements relating to duration, interest rate, collateral, and use of loan proceeds.

Tax treatment

ESOPs are accorded advantageous tax treatment. The limit on the amount of a deduction for a contribution to an ESOP is higher than the usual limit for defined contribution plans. Leveraged ESOPs offer employers several tax incentives, such as the deduction for dividends paid in cash, tax-free rollover treatment on the sale of qualified securities, and an exception from the unrelated business income tax and the asset reversion tax.

Fiduciary rules

ESOP trustees are subject to the general fiduciary duty rules of ERISA. Thus, when making investment decisions, ESOP fiduciaries, just as fiduciaries of other kinds of plans, are governed by the exclusive benefit and prudence tests of ERISA. However, a company's board of directors does not breach its fiduciary duties to corporate shareholders by using an ESOP as a device to thwart a hostile takeover.

ESOPs are exempt from the ERISA rules prohibiting sales and exchanges of property between plans and parties in interest and the lending of money or extension of credit between plans and parties in interest. However, the sale or acquisition of employer stock must be for adequate consideration, as defined in ERISA and Labor Department regulations, in order for trustees to receive the exemption from the prohibited transaction rules.

¶ 3005
CHARACTERISTICS OF ESOPs: What is an ESOP?

Employee stock ownership plans (ESOPs) are defined as stock bonus plans — or a combination of stock bonus plans and money purchase plans—that are qualified under Code Sec. 401(a) and designed to invest primarily in employer securities.[1]

ESOPs provide a means for employees to have an ownership interest in the companies for which they work. Leveraged ESOPs also provide companies with an important financing tool: the ability to sell employer stock to employees in return for funds obtained as loans from banks or other institutions. This type of arrangement can provide an employer with much needed capital.

Distinction between leveraged ESOP and stock bonus plan

A stock bonus plan is a plan established and maintained by an employer to provide benefits similar to those of a profit-sharing plan. However, contributions by the employer are not necessarily dependent upon profits and the benefits are distributable in stock of the employer company.[2] By contrast, a "leveraged" ESOP is used as a financing vehicle for the employer corporation.

Operation of an ESOP

An ESOP is operated through a trust created for the benefit of employees. The trustees are typically appointed by the sponsoring corporation's board of directors. The employer contributes stock to the trust (or makes cash contributions with which the trustees purchase company stock) and the employer receives a tax deduction for the contribution.[3] If the ESOP is "leveraged," the employer makes or arranges for a loan that is used to purchase stock.

Formal designation as ESOP

To be an ESOP, a plan must be formally designated as such in the plan document.[4]

Addition to other plan

An ESOP may be part of a plan that includes a qualified pension, profit-sharing, or stock bonus plan that is not an ESOP.[5]

Conversion of existing plan to an ESOP

If an existing pension, profit-sharing, or stock bonus plan is converted into an ESOP, the fiduciary requirements of ERISA Sec. 404 (see ¶ 2300 and following) and the exclusive benefit rule of Code Sec. 401(a) (see ¶ 321) continue to apply to the converted plan.[6] A conversion may constitute a termination of an existing plan.[7]

Integration prohibited

A plan designated as an ESOP must not be integrated directly or indirectly with contributions or benefits under Title II of the Social Security Act or any other state or federal law.[8] ESOPs established and integrated before November 1, 1977, may remain integrated. However, such plans must not be amended to increase the integration level or the integration percentage.

☐ Integration of plans with Social Security is discussed in detail beginning at ¶ 1200.

---

[1] ERISA Sec. 407(d)(6); Code Sec. 4975(e)(7).

[2] IRS Reg. § 1.401-1(b)(1)(iii).

[3] Code Sec. 404(a)(3) and (9).

[4] IRS Reg. § 54.4975-11(a)(2).

[5] IRS Reg. § 54.4975-11(a)(5).

[6] IRS Reg. § 54.4975-11(a)(6).

[7] *Ibid.*

[8] IRS Reg. § 54.4975-11(a)(7)(ii).

¶ 3010
CHARACTERISTICS OF ESOPs: Types of ESOPs

Employee stock ownership plans can be divided into two main types: the nonleveraged or "basic" ESOP and the leveraged ESOP.

Basic ESOP

A basic or nonleveraged ESOP is essentially a stock bonus plan that qualifies as an eligible individual account plan under ERISA. As such, it operates like a profit-sharing plan with one significant limitation: benefits must be invested primarily in securities of the employer.

Under the basic ESOP, the employer deposits into a trust either company stock or cash to buy company stock. The employer receives a tax deduction for the contribution to the ESOP and employees do not pay tax until they receive and sell their shares. Unlike the leveraged ESOP (see below), the plan cannot borrow money to acquire the employer securities.

Leveraged ESOP

When an ESOP is leveraged, the plan borrows money (usually from a commercial lender) with which to purchase the employer's stock. This loan is secured by the stock and is typically guaranteed by the employer corporation. The borrowed money is then paid to the employer or its shareholders for its stock. The plan repays its loan to the lender with cash contributions made each year to the plan by the employer. Contributions are ordinarily not based on profits, but rather are fixed (as in money purchase plans). This insures that the loan can be repaid with tax-deductible dollars even though the employer may be without profits in a particular year. Each year, as employer contributions are made to pay off the loan, the stock purchased by the plan is assigned to the employee participants. After a participant retires or dies, he or she is entitled to the full value of the account.

Today, most ESOPs are leveraged. Leveraged ESOPs can serve several employer needs, such as:

1. raising funds for business expansion,

2. serving as a vehicle for repurchasing employer stock, and

3. defending against a hostile takeover.

☐ In addition to meeting the general ESOP rules, leveraged ESOPs are subject to additional requirements governing loan transactions. The rules for making ESOP loans are covered at ¶ 3035.

¶ 3015

CHARACTERISTICS OF ESOPs: General Qualification Rules

The Internal Revenue Code specifies that an ESOP is a defined contribution plan that is qualified under Code Sec. 401(a).[1] Hence, it must meet the general qualification requirements of the Code (see ¶ 303) along with the special requirements outlined in this chapter.

Application of the vesting rules

A leveraged ESOP will not fail to meet the requirement that an accrued benefit not be decreased by amendment merely because it modifies distribution options by eliminating or retaining the right to eliminate a lump-sum option or installment payment option in a nondiscriminatory manner.[2]

CCH Pointer: The Pension Protection Act of 2006 (P.L. 109-280) provides faster vesting for employer contributions to defined contribution plans (see ¶ 2979). The rules are generally effective for plan years beginning after December 31, 2006. However, if an ESOP incurred a loan for the purpose of acquiring qualifying employer securities and that loan is still outstanding on September 26, 2005, the faster vesting schedule does not apply to any plan year beginning before the earlier of: (1) the date the loan is fully repaid, or (2) the date on which the loan was scheduled to be fully repaid as of September 26, 2005.

Application of nondiscrimination rules

In testing for nondiscrimination (see ¶ 1100 and following), ESOPs may not use the safe harbor for allocation formulas that use an age or service factor set out in IRS regulations under Code Sec. 401(a)(4). Nor may ESOP allocations be tested on a benefit basis.[3]

Application of joint and survivor rules

The requirement that a qualified plan provide for the payment of benefits to an employee or his or her surviving spouse in the form of a joint and survivor annuity or preretirement survivor annuity unless the employee, with the consent of his or her spouse, elects otherwise, does *not* apply to distributions of stock or dividends from ESOPs.[4]

Minimum funding requirements

An ESOP or a stock bonus plan is *not required* to meet the IRS minimum funding rules[5] or the plan termination provisions of ERISA.[6]

[1] ERISA Sec. 407(d)(6).

[2] Code Sec. 411(d)(6)(C); ERISA Sec. 204(g)(3).

[3] IRS Reg. §§ 1.401(a)(4)-2(a)(2) and 1.401(a)(4)-8(b).

[4] Code Sec. 401(a)(11)(C); ERISA Sec. 205(b)(2).

[5] Code Sec. 412(h)(1); ERISA Sec. 301(a)(8).

[6] ERISA Sec. 4021(b)(1).

¶ 3020

ESTABLISHING AN ESOP: Applying to the IRS

An employer who has established a plan intended to meet the qualification requirements under Code Secs. 409 (for the basic ESOP) or under Code Sec. 4975(a)(7) (for a leveraged ESOP) may file Form 5309 (Application for Determination of Employee Stock Ownership Plan) for IRS confirmation that the applicable requirements have been met.[1]

Form 5309 should be attached to Form 5300 (Application for Determination for Employee Benefit Plan), plus a copy of all documents and statements required by such forms, should be filed for either initial determination or amendment of a plan intended to qualify.[2]

[1] Instructions to IRS Form 5309.

[2] Rev. Proc. 2012-6 , I.R.B. 2012-1, Sec. 7.02, CCH PENSION PLAN GUIDE ¶ 17,299T-86.

¶ 3025

ESTABLISHING AN ESOP: Nontax Considerations

The decision to establish an ESOP can impact employee motivation and, hence, corporate growth. ESOPs can create a ready market for employer stock, which is an important consideration for small companies. In addition, leveraged ESOPs can play an important role in corporate takeovers (see ¶ 3097).

Employee motivation

Proponents of ESOPs contend that ESOPs have a positive impact on employee motivation and productivity, because stock ownership gives employees a stake in the operation of the company. However, the establishment of an ESOP also transfers increased risks to employees, since a substantial part of an employee's retirement nest egg would be tied to company stock.

Company growth

If ESOPs increase employee motivation, then increased corporate growth should follow. Indeed, a number of studies have demonstrated that companies with ESOPs outperform companies that do not have ESOPs. However, other studies have found no correlation between ESOPs and productivity growth. ESOPs can also enable the employer to conserve needed working capital, rather than making cash contributions to a conventional plan.

Market for minority interests

An ESOP can create a ready market for minority interests in employer stock, including those of retiring employees who will ordinarily wish to convert their stock into cash. It can also solve the post-death liquidity problems of substantial stockholders.

Anti-takeover device

Due to its borrowing ability, a leveraged ESOP can be used to purchase a large block of employer stock immediately. Thus, a corporation seeking to place a large amount of its stock in friendly hands can implement an ESOP. The use of ESOPs to thwart unfriendly corporate takeovers is discussed further at ¶ 3097.

Corporate recapitalization tool

A leveraged ESOP can be used as a vehicle to recapitalize a company since ESOP debt can be repaid with pretax dollars. The ESOP borrows from a lender and purchases treasury stock or newly issued stock. The sponsoring company can then either pay out stock dividends or exchange existing shares for cash and securities of the newly recapitalized company.

¶ 3030
ESTABLISHING AN ESOP: Tax Considerations

Leveraged ESOPs offer employers several significant tax incentives, such as the partial interest exclusion on ESOP loans (generally for loans made on or before August 20, 1996) and the dividends paid deduction (see the discussion beginning at ¶ 3087). The tax incentives were significantly reduced by the Omnibus Budget Reconciliation Act of 1989 (P.L. 101-239). However, ESOPs are still viewed as an attractive employee benefit and as a tax-efficient means of financing 401(k) matching contributions and profit-sharing allocations.

¶ 3035
SPECIAL ESOP REQUIREMENTS: Terms of the ESOP Loan

The IRS sets forth three general requirements for a loan to a leveraged ESOP:[1]

1. The loan must be made primarily for the benefit of participants and beneficiaries of the plan.

2. The loan must be made at a reasonable rate of interest.

3. Qualifying employer securities must be the only collateral given by the ESOP to the lender.

In addition, the loan must be made for a specific term[2] and must be made to a plan that is an ESOP at the time of the loan.[3]

Primary benefit requirement

In general, an ESOP loan must be primarily for the benefit of the ESOP participants and their beneficiaries.[4] All the surrounding facts and circumstances will be considered in determining whether the loan satisfies this requirement. Factors the IRS will consider include the net effect of the loan on plan assets, the terms of the loan, the use of the loan proceeds, the liability and collateral of the ESOP for the loan, and the default provisions of the loan. The IRS will also examine whether the loan provides employee ownership of employee stock, whether contributions to the ESOP are recurring and substantial, and the extent to which the loan repayment method benefits employees.

Net effect on plan assets. At the time that a loan is made, the interest rate for the loan and the price of securities to be acquired with the loan proceeds should not have the effect of "draining off" plan assets.[5]

Arm's-length standard. The terms of a loan, whether or not between independent parties, must, at the same time the loan is made, be at least as favorable to the ESOP as the terms of a comparable loan resulting from arm's-length negotiations between independent parties.[6]

Use of loan proceeds

The proceeds of an exempt loan must be used within a reasonable time after their receipt by the borrowing ESOP for *only* the following purposes:[7]

1. to acquire qualifying employer securities,

2. to repay such loan, or

3. to repay a prior exempt loan.

Liability and collateral of ESOP for loan

An exempt loan must be "without recourse" against the ESOP. This means that if the ESOP defaults on the loan, the lender cannot collect from the ESOP's other assets. Furthermore, the only assets of the ESOP that may be given as collateral on the loan are qualifying employer securities of two classes:[8]

1. those acquired with the proceeds of the loan, and

2. those that were used as collateral on a prior exempt loan repaid with the proceeds of the current exempt loan.

☐ For more on "qualifying securities," see ¶ 3040.

No person entitled to payment under the loan may have any right to assets of the ESOP other than:[9]

1. collateral given for the loan,

2. contributions (other than contributions of employer securities) that are made under an ESOP to meet its obligations under the loan, and

3. earnings attributable to such collateral and the investment of such contributions.

Reasonable rate of interest

Factors considered in determining a reasonable rate of interest include:[10]

1. the amount and duration of the loan,

2. the security and guarantee (if any) involved,

3. the credit standing of the ESOP and the guarantor (if any), and

4. the interest rate prevailing for comparable loans.

When these factors are considered, a *variable interest rate* may be reasonable.

Default

In the event of default upon an exempt loan, the value of plan assets transferred in satisfaction of the loan cannot exceed the amount of default.[11]

If the lender is a disqualified person,[12] the loan must provide for a transfer of plan assets upon default only upon and to the extent of the failure of the plan to meet the payment schedule of the loan.[13]

---

[1] Code Sec. 4975(d)(3).

[2] IRS Reg. § 54.4975-7(b)(13).

[3] IRS Reg. § 54.4975-7(b)(14). However, a loan to a plan formally designated as an ESOP at the time of the loan that fails to be an ESOP because it does not comply with section 401(a) of the Code or IRS Reg. § 54.4975-11 will be exempt as of the time of such loan if the plan is amended retroactively.

[4] IRS Reg. § 54.4975-7(b)(3)(i).

[5] IRS Reg. § 54.4975-7(b)(3)(ii).

[6] IRS Reg. § 54.4975-7(b)(3)(iii).

[7] IRS Reg. § 54.4975-7(b)(4).

[8] IRS Reg. § 54.4975-7(b)(5).

[9] *Ibid.*

[10] IRS Reg. § 54.4975-7(b)(7).

[11] IRS Reg. § 54.4975-7(b)(6).

[12] A "disqualified person" is defined at Code Sec. 4975(e). See discussion at ¶ 2406.

[13] IRS Reg. § 54.4975-7(b)(6).

¶ 3040

SPECIAL ESOP REQUIREMENTS: Types of Securities Issued to ESOPs

An ESOP is defined as a defined contribution plan that is designed to invest "primarily in qualifying employer securities." [1] The term "qualifying employer securities" is generally defined as common stock issued by the employer (or by a corporation which is a member of the same controlled group) which is readily tradable on an established securities market.[2]

Where there is no readily tradable common stock, an ESOP may invest in common stock issued by the employer (or by a corporation which is a member of the same controlled group) having a combination of voting power and dividend rights equal to or in excess of:[3]

1. that class of common stock of the employer (or of any other such corporation) having the greatest voting power, and

2. the class of common stock of the employer (or of any other such corporation) having the greatest dividend rights.

Employees of a partnership may not participate in an ESOP of a related corporation.[4] This is because a partnership cannot be part of a controlled group of corporations and cannot be connected to other corporations through stock ownership.

Noncallable preferred stock can be treated as employer securities if it is convertible at any time into stock which meets the requirements mentioned above and if such conversion is at a conversion price which (as of the date of the acquisition by the ESOP) is reasonable.[5]

---

[1] Code Sec. 4975(e)(7). For information on what constitutes "primarily," see the discussion of prohibited transaction rules at ¶ 3095.

[2] Code Sec. 409(l)(1). NOTE: The meaning of the term "readily tradable on an established securities market" as defined by the regulations under Code Sec. 401(a)(35) (see ¶ 2362) also applies for purposes of the rules on qualifying employer se-

curities under Code Sec. 409(l), generally effective for plan years beginning on or after January 1, 2012. See IRS Notice 2011-19, I.R.B. 2011-11, 3-14-11, CCH PENSION PLAN GUIDE ¶ 17,146Z.

[3] Code Sec. 409(l)(2).

[4] IRS General Counsel's Memorandum 39880, 5-12-92, CCH PENSION PLAN GUIDE ¶ 17,530.

[5] Code Sec. 409(l)(3).

¶ 3045

SPECIAL ESOP REQUIREMENTS: Voting Rights

ESOP participants and beneficiaries of deceased participants must be given the right to direct the plan as to the voting of securities of the employer corporation which are entitled to vote and which are allocated to the participant's account.[1]

Employers with registration-type class of securities

In the case of an employer with a registration-type class of securities, the power to direct voting must apply to any matter on which the securities are entitled to vote.[2] A registration-type class of securities is a class of securities that is required to be registered under section 12 of the Securities Exchange Act of 1934 or that would be required to be registered except for the exemption in section 12(g)(2)(H) of that Act.

Employers without registration-type class of securities

In the case of an employer without a registration-type class of securities, the power to direct must relate to approval or disapproval of a "major change" (corporate merger or consolidation, recapitalization, reclassification, liquidation, dissolution, or sale of substantially all assets of a trade or business).[3]

Some plans permit participants to vote on matters involving the employer corporation on the basis of one-man-one-vote. The "major change" voting rule is satisfied if the vote on a corporate matter is conducted on that basis and if the plan trustee votes the shares in proportion to the outcome of that vote.[4] For example, if

67% of the participants vote for a merger, the trustee would be required to vote 67% of the voting power of the stock held by it in favor of the merger.

Trustees may vote non-directed shares

An ESOP will not fail to comply with the pass-through voting rules if the ESOP trustee votes shares of stock that have been allocated to the accounts of participants or beneficiaries for which no directions are timely received from the participants or beneficiaries.[5] Trustees may vote allocated but non-directed shares regardless of whether the employer securities are of a registration-type class or not.

☐ The fiduciary rules applicable to ESOP trustees under ERISA are discussed at ¶ 3094.

---

[1] Code Sec. 409(e).

[2] Code Sec. 409(e)(2).

[3] Code Sec. 409(e)(3).

[4] Code Sec. 409(e)(5).

[5] Rev. Rul. 95-57, 1995-2 CB 62, CCH PENSION PLAN GUIDE ¶ 19,812.

¶ 3050

SPECIAL ESOP REQUIREMENTS: ESOP Contribution Limits

The contribution limits that apply to an ESOP are the same as those that apply to any other qualified defined contribution plan, except that certain requirements are not included as annual additions. However, there is a special, higher deduction limit than the usual limit for contributions to a defined contribution plan.

The general limitation on annual contributions to a defined contribution plan under Code Sec. 415 also applies to ESOPs. Thus, the limit on annual additions to the account of an ESOP participant is the lesser of:[1]

1. $50,000 for 2012 ($49,000 for 2011), or

2. 100% of a participant's compensation.

Annual additions are based on the amount of contributions used for loan payments, not on the value of the stock allocated to participants' accounts.[2]

Excludable contributions

Contributions that are applied by an ESOP to the payment of interest on its loan, as well as any forfeitures of employer securities purchased with loan proceeds, are excluded for purposes of computing the limitation on annual additions to a defined contribution plan.

This applies only if contributions allocated to "highly compensated employees" are not more than one-third of the employer contributions for the year.[3]

---

[1] Code Sec. 415(c)(1); IR-2011-103, 10-20-11, CCH PENSION PLAN GUIDE ¶ 17,037Q.

[2] IRS Reg. §54.4975-11(a)(8)(ii).

[3] Code Sec. 415(c)(6).

¶ 3055

SPECIAL ESOP REQUIREMENTS: ESOP Coverage Rules

As outlined at ¶ 3015, an ESOP must meet the general qualification rules of the Code. This includes the requirement under Code Sec. 410(b) that a plan cover a minimum number of employees (for a discussion of the minimum coverage rules, see ¶ 1000 and following).

Separate testing

IRS regulations require ESOPs to be tested separately for Code Sec. 410(b) coverage purposes.[1] The separate testing requirement gives some assurance that an ESOP covers a minimum coverage group, while preventing the employer from using another plan to dilute the number of nonhighly compensated employees that must be covered under the plan.

KSOPs

Where a 401(k) plan includes an ESOP feature (a so-called "KSOP"), the ESOP portion of the plan must be tested for discrimination separately from the rest of the 401(k) plan. Thus, in applying the ADP and ACP tests, the ESOP and 401(k) features of the plan are tested separately.[2]

> **CCH Pointer:** Final regulations issued in December 2004 eliminate mandatory disaggregation of the ESOP and non-ESOP portions of a Code Sec. 414(l) plan for purposes of ADP and ACP testing and allow an employer to permissively aggregate two Code Sec. 414(l) plans, one that is an ESOP and one that is not.[3] The regulations are generally effective for plan years beginning on or after January 1, 2006. However, a plan may implement this provision before this effective date where the plan applies all of the conditions of the final regulations for the plan year and all subsequent plan years. Mandatory disaggregation continues to apply for purposes of the Code Sec. 410(b) coverage rules.

---

[1] IRS Reg. § 54.4975-11(e). This position is reaffirmed in IRS Reg. § 1.410(b)-7(c)(2) and (e)(2).

[2] IRS Reg. §§ 1.401(k)-1(g)(11)(i), 1.401(m)-1(f)(14), and 1.401(m)-2(b).

[3] IRS Reg. § 1.401(k)-1(b)(4)(v), as added by T.D. 9169, 12-29-04 (69 FR 78144).

¶ 3060

SPECIAL ESOP REQUIREMENTS: Allocations to Participants' Accounts

All assets acquired by an ESOP with the proceeds of an exempt loan must be added to and maintained in a suspense account.[1] As the loan is repaid, the shares are released from the suspense account and allocated to the individual accounts of participants in accordance with methods prescribed by the IRS.[2]

Release of ESOP shares

The IRS provides two methods for releasing shares from a suspense account:

1. The general rule provides for a release of shares on the basis of principal and interest paid during the year.[3]

2. A special rule provides for a release of shares based on principal payments only, but only if the loan is amortized at a rate that is "not less rapid at any time than level annual payments of such amounts for ten years." [4]

Stock allocations to individual accounts

At the end of each plan year, the ESOP must consistently allocate to the participants' accounts non-monetary units representing participants' interests in assets withdrawn from the suspense account.[5] Income with respect to securities acquired with the proceeds of an exempt loan must be allocated as income of the plan except to the extent that the ESOP provides for the use of income from such securities to repay the loan or income is distributed to participants.[6]

Forfeitures

If a portion of a participant's account is forfeited, qualifying employer securities allocated under the allocation rules described above must be forfeited only after other assets. If interests in more than one class of qualifying employer securities have been allocated to the participant's account, the participant must be treated as forfeiting the same proportion of each such class.[7]

Valuation of securities

Valuation of securities must be made in good faith and based on all relevant factors for determining fair market value.[8] Generally, a determination of fair market value based on at least an annual appraisal independently arrived at by a person who customarily makes such appraisals and who is independent of any party to a transaction will constitute a good faith determination of value.[9] However, an independent appraisal will not in itself constitute a good faith determination of value in the case of a transaction between a plan and a disqualified person.

☐ For the definition of a disqualified person, see ¶ 2406.

---

[1] IRS Reg. § 54.4975-11(c).

[2] IRS Reg. § 54.4975-7(b)(8) and (15).

[3] IRS Reg. § 54.4975-7(b)(8)(i).

[4] IRS Reg. § 54.4975-7(b)(8)(ii).

[5] IRS Reg. § 54.4975-11(d)(2).

[6] IRS Reg. § 54.4975-11(d)(3).

[7] IRS Reg. § 54.4975-11(d)(4).

[8] IRS Reg. § 54.4975-11(d)(5).

[9] Code Sec. 401(a)(28)(C).

¶ 3065
SPECIAL ESOP REQUIREMENTS: Distribution Requirements

The payment of benefits under an ESOP must begin no later than one year after the later of the close of the plan year:[1]

1. in which the participant terminates employment due to attainment of normal retirement age under the plan, disability, or death, or

2. which is the fifth plan year following the plan year in which the participant otherwise separates from service (provided the participant is not reemployed by the employer before the distribution is required to commence).

These rules apply only if the participant, with the consent of the participant's spouse (if applicable under the rules relating to joint and survivor annuities—see ¶ 1700 and following), so elects.

An exception to the above general rule applies if any portion of a participant's account balance includes employer securities which were acquired in connection with a loan that has not been repaid in full. Under this exception, distributions are not required to be made available to a participant under the general rule until the close of the plan year following the plan year in which the loan is fully repaid.[2]

The general qualification rules require that, if the participant does not otherwise elect, benefits must begin being paid to the participant no later than the 60th day after the close of the latest plan year in which (a) the participant attains the earlier of age 65 or the normal retirement age under the plan, (b) the tenth anniversary of the participant's participation in the plan occurs, or (c) the participant terminates employment.[3]

Duration of distributions

Unless the plan provides that a participant may elect a longer distribution period, the plan is to provide distributions of the participant's account balance in substantially equal periodic payments (not less frequently than annually) over a period not longer than five years.[4] However, if the participant's account balance exceeds $1,015,000 (for 2012; $985,000 for 2011) this distribution period is extended by one year (up to an additional 5 years) for each $200,000 (for 2012; $195,000 for 2011) (or fraction of that amount) by which the amount exceeds $1,015,000.[5] These dollar amounts are adjusted for cost-of-living increases at the same time and in the same manner as are the dollar limits under Code Sec. 415(d).[6]

☐ An ESOP is also subject to the minimum distribution rules of Code Sec. 401(a)(9). For details, see ¶ 1800 and following.

---

[1] Code Sec. 409(o)(1)(A).

[2] Code Sec. 409(o)(1)(B).

[3] Code Sec. 401(a)(14).

[4] Code Sec. 409(o)(1)(C).

[5] Code Sec. 409(o)(1)(C), as amended by P.L. 107-147 (Job Creation and Worker Assistance Act of 2002). IR-2011-103, 10-20-11, CCH PENSION PLAN GUIDE ¶ 17,037Q.

[6] Code Sec. 409(o)(2).

¶ 3070
SPECIAL ESOP REQUIREMENTS: Taxation of ESOP Distributions

Distributions from ESOPs are subject to the general rules governing the taxation of distributions from qualified plans. The direct rollover option permitting direct rollovers to an IRA or to another qualified plan also applies to ESOPs.

Deferral of the tax on net unrealized appreciation in employer securities is available for distributions of employer stock.[1]

Cash dividend distributions from an ESOP are exempt from the 10% penalty tax on early distributions.[2]

Lump-sum distributions

When a lump-sum distribution includes securities of the employer, the fair market value of the securities less unrealized appreciation, is includible in the employee's gross income.[3] A stock's net unrealized appreciation is the excess of the fair market value of the stock on the date it is distributed over the stock's cost or other basis to the plan's trustee.[4] The appreciation in the value of the stock is not taxable until the employee disposes of the stock. The remainder of the fair market value of the securities distributed is included in the employee's gross income to the extent it exceeds his after-tax contributions.[5]

> **CCH Pointer:** *Net unrealized appreciation of S corporation stock.* In the event that an ESOP participant receives a distribution of S corporation stock, the stock's net unrealized appreciation (NUA) is determined using the ESOP's adjusted basis in the stock.[6] For example, if the market value of S corporation stock when distributed is $580 and the ESOP's adjusted basis in the stock is $550, the amount of NUA in the corporation's stock would be $30.

Withholding

Distributions of employer securities are exempt from the withholding requirements that generally apply to employee plans.[7] Cash dividend distributions from an ESOP are also exempt from the withholding.[8]

☐ The taxation of distributions from qualified plans is discussed in detail beginning at ¶ 1900 and following.

☐ The direct rollover rules are discussed at ¶ 1970.

☐ Lump-sum distributions are covered beginning at ¶ 1940.

☐ The taxation of net unrealized appreciation in employer securities is discussed at ¶ 1916.

☐ Withholding from employee plans is discussed beginning at ¶ 2100.

---

[1] Code Sec. 402(e)(4) and (j).

[2] Code Sec. 72(t)(2)(A)(vi).

[3] Code Sec. 402(e)(4)(B).

[4] IRS Reg. § 1.402(a)-1(b)(2)(i).

[5] Code Sec. 72(e); IRS Reg. § 1.72-11(d).

[6] Rev. Rul. 2003-27, 2003-11 CB 597, 3-17-2003, CCH PENSION PLAN GUIDE ¶ 19,948L.

[7] Code Sec. 3405(e)(8).

¶ 3075

SPECIAL ESOP REQUIREMENTS: Cash Distribution Option

Distributions of benefits from an ESOP may be in the form of cash or employer securities or may be made partly in cash and partly in employer securities. However, a participant may demand that his benefit be distributed in employer securities.[1] This right is waived to the extent that the employee elects to diversify his account (see ¶ 3086).

Right to demand employer stock

The participant or beneficiary must be advised in writing of his right to demand employer securities before the plan may distribute cash to him. An ESOP may preclude a participant from demanding a distribution in the form of employer securities if the employer's corporate charter or bylaws restrict the ownership of substantially all outstanding employer securities to employees or the ESOP.[2]

If employer securities distributed to a participant are not readily tradable on an established market, the participant has the right to require the employer to repurchase them under a fair valuation formula (see ¶ 3080).

ESOPs maintained by S corporations

ESOPs may be shareholders of S corporations (see ¶ 3093). However, ESOPs established or maintained by S corporations are not required to allow participants to demand their distributions in the form of employer securities, if the employees have the right to receive such distributions in cash. The plan may distribute employer securities if the employee retains the right to resell the securities to the employer in the event that the securities are not readily tradable on an established market.[3]

> **CCH Pointer:** *Rollover by ESOP participant of distribution of S corporation stock to IRA.* An ESOP that holds S corporation stock and permits distributions in the form of employer securities must permit participants to elect to have any distribution of S corporation stock that is an eligible rollover distribution to be paid in a direct rollover to an eligible retirement plan specified by the distributee. An eligible retirement plan includes an IRA, even though an IRA trustee or custodian is not a permissible S corporation shareholder.[4] The IRS has provided guidelines under which a corporation's subchapter S election will not be terminated when an ESOP distributes the entity's stock to a participant's IRA in a direct rollover.[5]

---

[1] Code Sec. 409(h)(1)(A).

[2] Code Sec. 409(h)(2)(last sentence).

[3] Code Sec. 409(h)(2)(B).

[4] Rev. Proc. 2003-23, 2003-1 CB 599, 3-17-03, CCH PENSION PLAN GUIDE ¶ 17,299Q-68.

[5] See Rev. Proc. 2004-14, 2004-1 CB 489, CCH PENSION PLAN GUIDE ¶ 17,299R-14.

¶ 3080

SPECIAL ESOP REQUIREMENTS: Put Option

If the securities of an employer corporation distributed to a participant are not readily tradable on an established market, the participant must have the right to require the employer to repurchase them under a fair valuation formula.[1] In other words, the distributee has a "put option" that he may exercise.

The put option permits a participant to "put" the security to the employer. Under no circumstances may the put option bind the ESOP. However, it may grant the ESOP an option to assume the rights and obligations of the employer at the time that the put option is exercised.

If it is known at the time a loan is made that federal or state law will be violated by the employer's honoring of such a put option, the put option must permit the security to be put, in a manner consistent with federal or state law, to a third party (for example, to an affiliate of the employer or a shareholder other than the ESOP) that has substantial net worth at the time the loan is made and whose net worth is reasonably expected to remain substantial.[2]

Definition of readily tradable

Stock that is not "readily tradable" is stock that is not publicly traded or that is subject to a trading limitation.[3] A security is "publicly traded" if it is listed on a registered national securities exchange or is quoted on a system sponsored by a registered national securities exchange.[4] A "trading limitation" is a restriction under any federal or state securities law or regulation or an agreement that makes the security not as freely tradable as one not subject to the restriction.[5]

Deferred corporate payment for the securities under a put option must be adequately secured.[6]

Put option period

The period during which the distributee may exercise the put option commences with the date following the date of distribution and ends with the 60th day thereafter. If the put option is not exercised in that period, the employer must provide that it may be exercised during an additional 60-day period in the following plan year.[7]

Fair acquisition formula

If a distributee receives the entire balance to the credit of his account within one taxable year and exercises his put option, the acquisition formula is considered to be fair if the purchase price to be paid by the employer is paid in substantially equal periodic payments (at least annually) over a period beginning not more than 30 days after the exercise of the put option and not exceeding five years.[8] In addition, there must be adequate security for the unpaid purchase price and the payment of reasonable interest on such unpaid price.[9]

Installment payments. If a distributee receives a distribution of employer securities in installments and exercises his put option with respect to any installment, the acquisition formula is considered to be fair if the amount to be paid by the employer for the securities is paid within 30 days after the exercise of the put option with respect to that installment.[10]

CCH Pointer: An employer's repurchase liability will increase in proportion to the appreciation in the company's stock. Other factors affecting repurchase liability include the level of contributions, the employee turnover rate, and the demographics of the employee group.

Exercise of put option

In general, a put option must be exercisable at least during a 15-month period which begins on the date the security subject to the put option is distributed by the ESOP.[11]

Manner of exercise. A put option is exercised by the holder notifying the employer in writing that the put option is being exercised.[12]

Price. The price at which a put option must be exercisable is the value of the security as of the ESOP's most recent valuation date.[13] The valuation must be made in good faith and based on all relevant factors for determining the fair market value of securities.[14]

---

[1] Code Sec. 409(h)(1)(B). NOTE: The meaning of the term "readily tradable on an established securities market" as defined by the regulations under Code Sec. 401(a)(35) (see ¶ 2362) also applies for purposes of the rules on qualifying employer securities under Code Sec. 409(h)(1)(B), generally effective for plan years beginning on or after January 1, 2012. See IRS Notice 2011-19, I.R.B. 2011-11, 3-14-11, CCH Pension Plan Guide ¶ 17,146Z.

[2] IRS Reg. § 54.4975-7(b)(10).

[3] *Ibid.*

[4] IRS Reg. § 54.4975-7(b)(1)(iv).

[5] IRS Reg. § 54.4975-7(b)(10).

[6] IRS Reg. § 54.4975-7(b)(12)(iv).

[7] Code Sec. 409(h)(4).

[8] Code Sec. 409(h)(5)(A); IRS Reg. § 54.4975-7(b)(12)(iv).

[9] Code Sec. 409(h)(5)(B).

[10] Code Sec. 409(h)(6).

[11] IRS Reg. § 54.4975-7(b)(11).

[12] IRS Reg. § 54.4975-7(b)(12)(i).

[13] IRS Reg. § 54.4975-7(b)(12)(iii).

[14] IRS Reg. § 54.4975-11(d)(5).

¶ 3085

SPECIAL ESOP REQUIREMENTS: Right of First Refusal of ESOP Stock

Qualifying employer securities acquired with proceeds of an exempt loan may, but need not, be subject to a right of first refusal giving the employer or ESOP the first opportunity to repurchase stock.

However, securities subject to this right must meet the following rules:[1]

1. Securities subject to a right of first refusal must be employer stock or an employer equity security, or a debt security convertible into stock or an equity security. Also, the securities must not be publicly traded at the time the right may be exercised.

2. The right of first refusal must be in favor of the employer, the ESOP, or both in any order of priority. The selling price and other terms must not be less favorable to the seller than the greater of the value of the security,[2] or the purchase price and other terms offered by a buyer, other than the employer or the ESOP, making a good faith offer to purchase the security.

3. The right of first refusal must lapse no later than 14 days after the security holder gives written notice to the holder of the right that an offer by a third party to purchase the security has been received.

---

[1] IRS Reg. § 54.4975-7(b)(9).

[2] The value of the security must be determined under IRS Reg. § 54.4975-11(d)(5)— i.e., the valuation must be made in good faith and based on all relevant factors for determining the fair market value of securities.

¶ 3086

SPECIAL ESOP REQUIREMENTS: Diversification Requirement

An ESOP must provide qualified participants with an annual diversification election period for the 90-day period following the close of the ESOP plan year. This requirement reflects Congress's concern that employees who depend on ESOPs as a major source of retirement savings, may find those savings jeopardized if they are invested exclusively in employer securities.[1]

Consequently, within 90 days after the end of a plan year, an ESOP must permit an election by those "qualified participants" who become or remain eligible to make a diversification election during the plan year.[2] Any participant who has attained age 55 and completed 10 years of participation in the ESOP is a qualified participant.[3]

CCH Pointer: These diversification requirements do not apply to "applicable defined contribution plans."[4] These plans are subject to a different set of diversification requirements under Code Sec. 401(a)(35). See ¶ 2941.

Qualified election period

For an employee who has 10 years of service when he attains age 55, the "qualified election period" consists of the plan year in which he attains age 55 and the five succeeding plan years. If the employee does not have 10 years of service when he attains age 55, the qualified election period consists of the plan year in which the employee completes 10 years of service and the five succeeding plan years. Thus, there are six plan years in the qualified election period, and the diversification election may be made, modified or revoked during the 90-day period following the close of those six years.[5]

Example 1: Alpha Corporation maintains an ESOP that uses the calendar year as the plan year. Ben Barker, a participant in Alpha Corporation's ESOP, has participated in the ESOP for 10 years before reaching age 55. He reaches age 55 in 2006 and thus becomes a qualified participant eligible to direct diversification during the 90-day election period beginning January 1, 2007. He will remain eligible to direct diversification during the annual election periods in 2008, 2009, 2010, 2011, and 2012.

Example 2: Beta Corporation maintains an ESOP that uses the calendar year as the plan year. Tom Brown completes 10 years of participation in the ESOP in 2006 when he is age 58. Thus, he becomes a qualified participant in the plan year beginning January 1, 2006. He will be eligible to direct diversification during the election periods in 2007, 2008, 2009, 2010, 2011, and 2012.

Partial diversification

The annual diversification election permits only a partial diversification of the amount in an ESOP participant's account balance. For any participant who has reached at least age 55 and completed 10 years of participation in the ESOP, the amount of the participant's account balance subject to the diversification election (other than the last diversification election) at the end of the year of the plan year is 25% of the participant's account balance at the end of the year, reduced by amounts previously diversified. When the election year in which the participant can make his or her election is the last election year, the amount eligible for diversification is 50%, rather than 25%, less amounts previously diversified. Thus, since these rules do not permit diversification to exceed a cumulative amount, the scope of each year's election depends, in part, on prior elections.

Example: Mary Barnes, who has 10 years of participation in the Omega Corporation ESOP, reaches age 55 during the 2006 plan year. The ESOP uses a calendar plan year. During the 90-day period beginning on January 1, 2007, and ending on March 31, 2007, Mary may direct the trustee to diversify up to 25% of her account balance. If she elects to direct diversification of the 25% maximum amount, the only amounts of which she may elect diversification during the 2008, 2009, 2010, and 2011 election periods are amounts attributable to increases in her account balance, whether attributable to growth or additional employer contributions. From January 1, 2012, to March 31, 2012, Mary must be given the opportunity to direct diversification to bring the total amount subject to the diversification election to a cumulative 50% of her account balance at the end of the 2011 plan year.

If Mary did not elect diversification during the 2007 election period, a similar election would be available during the 2008, 2009, 2010, and 2011 election periods. In each year, she could elect to direct diversification for that portion of her account balance that, when aggregated with prior amounts for which diversification was elected, did not exceed 25% of the account balance at the end of that year. If Mary did not elect any diversification during the 2007-2011 election periods, she could make a final election in 2012 (the last election period in which she is entitled to make a diversification election) to direct diversification of as much as 50% of her account balance.

Trustee action on participant's election

ESOP plan trustees must complete diversification in accordance with the participant's election no later than 90 days after the close of the election period. The trustees may satisfy this requirement:

1. by distributing to the participant an amount of employer securities equal to the amount for which the participant elected diversification,

2. by substituting for the amount of the employer securities for which the participant elects diversification an equivalent amount of other assets, in accordance with the participant's investment direction, or

3. by providing the option of transferring the portion of the account for which diversification is elected into a qualified plan that provides for employer-directed investments.[6]

The ESOP must offer at least three investment options not inconsistent with regulations prescribed by the IRS to each participant making the election. Within 90 days after the period during which the election may be made, the plan must invest the portion of the participant's account covered by the election in accordance with the participant's instructions.[7] Of course, if a participant chooses not to elect a distribution of the portion of the account subject to the diversification election, the diversification election requirement is nevertheless satisfied.

Independent appraiser

Any valuation of employer securities not readily tradable on an established market that are contributed or purchased by the plan must be determined by an "independent appraiser." [8]

ESOPs and Code Sec. 409(a) plans

The diversification and independent appraiser requirements apply to basic and leveraged ESOPs (within the meaning of Code Sec. 4975(e)(7)) and to plans that meet the tax credit ESOP requirements under Code Sec. 409(a).[9]

---

[1] *General Explanation of the Tax Reform Act of 1986*, prepared by the staff of the Joint Committee on Taxation, p. 833. The diversification rules apply to stock acquired after 1986 (P.L. 99-514 (Tax Reform Act of 1986), Sec. 1140(a)(2)). However, employer securities acquired by, or contributed to, an ESOP on or before December 31, 1986, but allocated to participant accounts after that date are not subject to the diversification requirements (IRS Notice 88-56, 1988-1 CB 540, CCH Pension Plan Guide ¶ 17,101K).

[2] Code Sec. 401(a)(28)(B)(i).

[3] Code Sec. 401(a)(28)(B)(iii).

[4] Code Sec. 401(a)(28)(B)(v), as amended by P.L. 109-280 (Pension Protection Act of 2006).

[5] Code Sec. 401(a)(28)(B)(iv).

[6] Code Sec. 401(a)(28)(B)(ii).

[7] P.L. 99-514 (Tax Reform Act of 1986), Conference Committee Report.

[8] Code Sec. 401(a)(28)(C). NOTE: The meaning of the term "readily tradable on an established securities market" as defined by the regulations under Code Sec. 401(a)(35) (see ¶ 2362) also applies for purposes of the rules on qualifying employer securities under Code Sec. 401(a)(28)(C), generally effective for plan years beginning on or after January 1, 2012. See IRS Notice 2011-19, I.R.B. 2011-11, 3-14-11, CCH Pension Plan Guide ¶ 17,146Z.

[9] Code Sec. 401(a)(28)(A).

¶ 3087

TAXATION OF ESOPs: Deduction of Loan Principal and Interest

For leveraged ESOPs, contributions applied to the payment of the principal of a loan used to acquire employer securities may be deducted in an amount not exceeding 25% of compensation paid to or accrued by all employees under the ESOP during the tax year.[1] In addition, an unlimited deduction is permitted for amounts applied to interest on the loan.[2]

An employer is not entitled to any deduction or credit for any amount transferred to an ESOP if the special exception to the reversion tax applies to the transfer (see ¶ 330).[3]

Aggregation of contributions

An employer may maintain a leveraged ESOP and another qualified plan. Generally, contributions to two or more stock bonus or profit-sharing trusts are aggregated for purposes of the compensation limit.[4]

Contribution by S corporation

The increased deduction limit of Code Sec. 404(a)(9)(B) does not apply to S corporations.[5] Contributions to an ESOP by an S corporation are deductible subject to the limits of Code Sec. 404(a)(1) and 404(a)(3).

---

[1] Code Sec. 404(a)(9)(A).

[2] Code Sec. 404(a)(9)(B).

[3] Code Sec. 4980(c)(3)(F).

[4] Code Sec. 404(a)(3)(A)(iv).

[5] Code Sec. 404(a)(9)(C).

¶ 3088

TAXATION OF ESOPs: Deduction of Dividends Paid

An employer may deduct dividends paid in cash on securities held by an ESOP if the dividends are:[1]

1. paid in cash to the plan participants or their beneficiaries,

2. paid to the plan and distributed in cash to participants or their beneficiaries no later than 90 days after the close of the plan year in which paid,

3. at the election of the participants or their beneficiaries, payable as provided in (1) or (2) above, or paid to the plan and reinvested in qualifying employer securities,[2] or

4. used to make payments on certain loans, the proceeds of which were used to acquire employer securities (whether or not allocated to participants) with respect to which the dividend is paid. These dividends are known as "applicable dividends."

Item (3) above is generally effective for tax years beginning after December 31, 2001.

Reinvested dividends. As stated in (3) above, a corporation may deduct dividends that are paid to an ESOP and reinvested in qualified employer securities, at the election of the plan participants or their beneficiaries. Thus, employers may deduct dividends that an employee voluntarily reinvests back into the ESOP in exchange for more of the employer's stock.

The IRS has issued specific guidance[3] on the deductibility of these reinvested ESOP dividends, including the effective date of the amended deduction rules, the possible reduction of the deductible amounts by investment losses attributable to the dividends, vesting requirements applicable to eligible dividends, and participant elections.

In order for such reinvested dividends to be deductible, participants must be offered the choice of electing (a) that the dividends be paid to them in cash (or that the dividends be paid to the ESOP and subsequently distributed to them in cash, depending on the plan's terms), or (b) that the dividends be paid to the ESOP and reinvested in employer securities. A number of other conditions apply. Participants must be given a reasonable opportunity before a dividend is paid or distributed in which to make their elections, for example. Also, participants must have a reasonable opportunity to change a dividend election at least once every year.

Redemption of stock. As stated in (2) above, an employer may deduct dividends where the dividends are paid to the plan and distributed in cash to participants within 90 days after the close of the plan year in which they were paid. The scope of this provision was tested in 2001 in an IRS ruling[4] involving stock redemption. In an ESOP, participants may be permitted to take distributions in cash, rather than stock, at their retirement or termination of employment. In the ruling, a corporation redeemed a large number of shares in the ESOP accounts of a large group of terminating employees. The corporation contended that the redemptions should be treated as dividends and that they would be deductible by the company pursuant to (2), above. The IRS ruled that Code Sec. 404(k) does not apply to amounts paid for the redemption of stock held by an ESOP and that the corporation was barred from taking a deduction for such payments by Code Sec. 162(k)(1), which prohibits deductions for amounts paid in connection with a company's reacquisition of its stock.

CCH Pointer: Final regulations reaffirm the IRS' position that payments made to redeem stock held by an ESOP are not deductible under Code Sec. 404(k) because such payments do not constitute applicable dividends.[5]

Vesting requirements. A participant must be fully vested in any dividend with respect to which the participant is offered a dividend reinvestment.[6]

Dividends used to pay loan

An employer may deduct dividends that are used to repay an acquisition loan only if the dividends are made on employer securities acquired with the loan. If dividends are used to repay a loan, securities with a fair market value of no less than the amount of the dividend must be allocated to participant's accounts for the year.[7]

Applicable employer securities

Securities upon which deductible dividends are paid are determined as of the record date for such dividend by an ESOP maintained by the paying corporation or any controlled group of corporations which includes the payor corporation.[8]

Timing of employer deduction

Employer deductions for dividends paid on employer stock held by an ESOP are to be permitted *only* in the taxable year of the employer in which the dividend is paid or distributed to the participant or beneficiary.[9] Moreover, a corporation will be allowed a deduction for dividends paid on stock held by an ESOP whether such dividends are passed through to beneficiaries of plan participants or to the plan participants themselves.

Reinvested dividends may be deducted in the later of the tax year of the corporation in which (1) the dividends are reinvested in employer securities at the participant's election or (2) the election is made by the plan participant to have the dividends paid to the plan and reinvested in qualifying employer securities.[10]

Dividends paid under separate contract

Dividends paid on employer stock held by an ESOP are treated as paid under a contract separate from the contract under which the stock is held.[11]

Distribution is not prohibited transaction

Current distributions of dividends paid on employer stock allocated to a participant's account under an ESOP will not be treated as violating the requirements of Code Secs. 401, 409, or Code Secs. 4975(e)(7), or as engaging in a prohibited transaction, and consequently will not be disqualifying distributions.[12]

Dividends must be reasonable

The IRS can disallow deductions for dividends paid on stock held by an ESOP if payment of the dividends constitutes, in substance, the avoidance or evasion of tax.[13] Hence, to be deductible, dividends must be "reasonable." The IRS has ruled that a reasonable dividend is one "normally paid in the ordinary course of business."

Dividends paid by S corporation

The special rules relating to ESOPs do not apply to S corporations. Thus, no deduction is allowed for a dividend paid by an S corporation to an ESOP.[14]

Reporting 404(k) dividends

Code Sec. 404(k) dividends paid in cash from ESOPs in 2009 or later years must be reported on a Form 1099-R that does not report any other distributions.[15]

---

[1] Code Sec. 404(k)(2)(A); IRS Notice 90-6, 1990-1 CB 304, CCH PENSION PLAN GUIDE ¶ 17,102Z. This rule is generally effective for securities acquired by an ESOP after August 4, 1989.

[2] Code Sec. 404(k)(2)(A)(iii), as added by P.L. 107-16 (Economic Growth and Tax Relief Reconciliation Act of 2001), Act Sec. 622.

[3] IRS Notice 2002-2, 2002-1 CB 285, January 14, 2002, CCH PENSION PLAN GUIDE ¶ 17,122X.

[4] Rev. Rul. 2001-6, 2001-1 CB 491, February 5, 2001, CCH PENSION PLAN GUIDE ¶ 19,944V. Further guidance in this area may be found in IRS Chief Counsel Notice CC-2004-038, CCH PENSION PLAN GUIDE ¶ 17,203L.

[5] IRS Reg. §§ 1.162(k)-1 and § 1.404(k)-3, adopted under T.D. 9282 (71 FR 51471). The Ninth Circuit has held that payments made by a corporation to redeem its stock held by its ESOP were deductible as dividends paid under Code Sec. 404(k). See *Boise Cascade v. United States*, CA-9 (1983), CCH Pension Plan Guide ¶ 23,985E. However, the IRS has stated that, in light of the holding by CA-9, the IRS will continue to assert in any matter in controversy outside CA-9 that Code Sec. 162(k) and Code Sec. 404(k) disallow a deduction for payments to reacquire employer securities held by an ESOP. For any matter in controversy within CA-9, the IRS advises agents or district counsel attorneys to consult the National office. In addition, it should be noted that the U.S. Tax Court, the Third Circuit, and the Eighth Circuit have declined to follow the Ninth Circuit's holding in *Boise Cascade*. See *Conopco v. United States* , CA-3 (2009), CCH PENSION PLAN GUIDE ¶ 24,005N; *General Mills, Inc. and Subsidiaries v. United States*, CA-8 (2009), CCH PENSION PLAN GUIDE ¶ 24,004G; *Nestle Purina v. Commissioner*, CA-8 (2010), No. 09-13, CCH PENSION PLAN GUIDE ¶ 24,006R, aff'g TC (2008), 131 TC No. 4, CCH Dec. 57,534, cert. denied 10/4/10.

[6] Code Sec. 404(k)(7), as amended by P.L. 107-147 (Job Creation and Worker Assistance Act of 2002).

[7] Code Sec. 404(k)(2)(B).

[8] Code Sec. 404(k)(3).

[9] Code Sec. 404(k)(4); IRS Temp. Reg. § 1.404(k)-1T.

[10] Code Sec. 404(k)(4)(B), as added by P.L. 107-147 (Job Creation and Worker Assistance Act of 2002). See also IRS Notice 2002-2, 2002-1 CB 285, CCH PENSION PLAN GUIDE ¶ 17,122X.

[11] Code Sec. 72(e)(5)(D).

[12] Code Sec. 404(k)(5)(B).

[13] Code Sec. 404(k)(5)(A).

[14] Code Sec. 404(k)(1).

[15] IRS Announcement 2008-56, I.R.B. 2008-26, 6-30-08, CCH PENSION PLAN GUIDE ¶ 17,097T-31.

¶ 3089

TAXATION OF ESOPs: Lender's Partial Exclusion of Interest on ESOP Loans

Prior to August 20, 1996, a bank, insurance company, commercial lender, or regulated investment company (such as a mutual fund) could exclude 50% of the interest received on loans to an ESOP, or to an employer corporation, from income when the proceeds of the loans were used to acquire employer securities from the plan. This exclusion has now been eliminated.[1] However, the interest exclusion will continue to apply to loans made pursuant to written binding contracts in effect prior to June 10, 1996, under the rules detailed below. In addition, lenders may exclude 50% of the interest on loans made after August 20, 1996 to refinance loans made before August 20, 1996 (see below).[2]

The 50% interest exclusion will continue to apply to loans made after August 20, 1996, to refinance loans made on or before August 20, 1996, if:

1. the refinancing loan meets the requirements of Code Sec. 133, prior to repeal;

2. immediately after the refinancing, the outstanding principal amount of the loan is not increased; and

3. the term of the refinancing loan does not extend beyond the term of the original ESOP loan.

Securities acquisition loan

The exclusion of the interest received by the lender must be made "with respect to a securities acquisition loan." This includes any loan used to refinance loans made to acquire employer securities. However, the partial interest exclusion for ESOP loans is available to lenders only where the ESOP owns more than 50% of the employer-corporation's stock (see "50% requirement" below).

The exclusion is also available for a loan to a corporation to the extent that, within 30 days, employer securities are transferred to the plan in an amount equal to the proceeds of the loan and such securities are allocable to participants' accounts within one year after the date of the loan.[3]

For a loan used to refinance an original securities acquisition loan, the partial exclusion applies only to interest accrued during the excludable period with respect to the original securities acquisition loan (generally for the first seven years of the loan).[4]

Qualifying lender

To be eligible for the 50% partial interest exclusion, the loan must be made by a "qualifying lender." A qualifying lender is:

1. a bank,

2. an insurance company,

3. a corporation actively and regularly engaged in the business of lending money, or

4. a regulated investment company.

A lender is not considered to be "actively and regularly engaged in the business of lending money" if the predominant share of the value of the loans it makes are ESOP loans.[5]

Loans between related parties

Any loans made between corporations that are members of the same controlled group of corporations do not qualify for this partial exemption of interest on a securities acquisition loan. In addition, any loan made between an ESOP and any person that is either the employer of employees covered by the plan or a member of a controlled group of corporations that includes such an employer does not qualify for the exclusion.[6]

Repayment terms of securities acquisition loan

A loan to a corporation does not fail to be treated as a securities acquisition loan merely because the loan proceeds are loaned to an ESOP sponsored by the corporation (referred to as a "back to back loan"). Such a loan must include repayment terms that are substantially similar to the terms of the loan between a commercial lender and the sponsoring corporation. Alternatively, the loan may contain repayment terms that provide for more rapid repayment of principal or interest, but only if:[7]

¶3089

1. the allocations under the ESOP attributable to such repayment do not discriminate in favor of highly compensated employees, and

2. the repayment period of the loan from the commercial lender is not more than seven years.

In proposed and temporary regulations, the IRS has indicated that the test for determining whether the terms of the loan to the employer by a lender and the loan from the employer to the ESOP are substantially similar will be met only if the actual rate of allocation of shares under the ESOP based upon the terms of the loan from the employer to the ESOP would be substantially the same if the ESOP loan terms were identical to the terms of the securities acquisition loan made to the employer.[8]

Limit on term of securities acquisition loan

The partial interest exclusion will apply only to those loans with a term that does not exceed 15 years.[9]

More than 50% requirement

The 50% income exclusion of interest paid on loans made to ESOPs by banks, insurance companies, and other corporate entities is available to lenders only if the ESOP owns (immediately after any stock acquisition by, or transfers to, the ESOP) more than 50% of:

1. each class of outstanding stock of the corporation using the employer securities, or

2. the total value of all outstanding stock of the corporation.

The partial interest exclusion does not apply to interest allocable to any post-acquisition or post-transfer period during which the ESOP does not meet the more-than-50% requirement. However, the IRS is authorized to issue regulations that would allow for after-the-fact compliance where the ESOP acquires enough stock to meet the 50% requirement within 90 days of the ownership test failure (or such longer period not to exceed 180 days).

The more-than-50% rule may be satisfied by counting all stock in any ESOP maintained by the employer (or other member of the employer's controlled group). The IRS is also generally authorized to issue regulations that would treat warrants, options, contracts to acquire stock, convertible debt interests, and other similar stock rights as stock for purposes of the 50% requirement.[10]

Voting rights

For the partial interest exclusion to apply, participants in the ESOP must generally be entitled to direct how the employer securities acquired with the loan (or transferred to the ESOP)—and allocated to their account—are to be voted. No preferred stock may be acquired by, or transferred to, the ESOP in connection with the loan unless such stock has voting rights equivalent to the stock to which it may be converted.[11]

[1] Code Sec. 133, repealed by P.L. 104-188 (Small Business Job Protection Act), Sec. 1602(a).

[2]P.L. 104-188 (Small Business Job Protection Act), Sec. 1602(c)(2) and (3).

[3] Code Sec. 133(b)(1)(B).

[4] Code Sec. 133(e).

[5] IRS Reg. § 1.133-1T, Q&A-2.

[6] Code Sec. 133(b)(2).

[7] Code Sec. 133(b)(3) and (e)(2)(B).

[8] IRS Reg. § 1.133-1T, Q&A-1.

[9] Code Sec. 133(b)(1).

[10] Code Sec. 133(b)(6).

[11] Code Sec. 133(b)(7).

¶ 3091

TAXATION OF ESOPs: Tax-Free Rollover on Sale of "Qualified Securities" to ESOP

A shareholder of an employer-corporation that establishes an ESOP is allowed to defer any gain on the sale of his shares to the ESOP if the proceeds of the sale are reinvested in "qualified replacement property" within a specified "replacement period." The gain will be recognized only to the extent that the amount realized on the sale exceeds the cost to the taxpayer of the qualified replacement property.[1]

Requirements for nonrecognition of gain

To be eligible for nonrecognition treatment:[2]

1. the qualified securities must be sold to an ESOP,

2. the ESOP must own, immediately after the sale, at least 30% of each class of outstanding stock of the corporation that issued the qualified securities or at least 30% of the total value of all outstanding stock of the corporation disregarding the shares or value of nonvoting preferred stock,

3. the shareholder must provide certain information in a written statement to the IRS, and

4. the shareholder must have held the securities for at least three years (determined as of the time of the sale) before the sale of the stock to the ESOP.

In addition, in order for the nonrecognition-of-gain election to be available, the income from replacement securities, for the taxable year preceding the year of purchase, must not consist of more than 25% passive investment income. Qualified replacement property is limited to securities issued by a domestic operating corporation other than the corporation that issued the securities involved in the nonrecognition transaction.

Qualified securities

The transaction must involve the sale of "qualified securities" to the ESOP. Qualified securities are employer securities that:[3]

1. are issued by a domestic corporation that does not have out-standing any securities that are traded on an established securities market, and

2. were not obtained by the shareholder as a distribution from a qualified plan, statutory stock option plan, or a restricted property transfer.

Reinvestment period

The reinvestment of the proceeds from the sale of the qualified securities to the ESOP must take place within a period of three months prior to the sale to the ESOP or within the 12-month period after the sale.

Qualified replacement property

The reinvestment must be made in securities issued by a domestic corporation (other than the employer or a member of a controlled group of corporations that includes the employer) that does not, for the taxable year in which stock is issued, have passive investment income exceeding 25% of the gross receipts of the corporation for such year. The holding period of the employer's share sold to the ESOP is added to the holding period of the qualified replacement property. The basis of the qualified replacement property is adjusted to reflect the tax-deferred gain.[4]

Disposition of qualified replacement property

Generally, gain realized upon the disposition of qualified replacement property must be recognized at the time of the disposition, to the extent of gain previously deferred.[5] However, the recapture rules do not apply to the transfer of qualified replacement property that occurs:[6]

1. in any reorganization, unless the person making the election owns a controlling interest in the acquiring or acquired company and such property is substituted basis property in the hands of the transferee;

2. by reason of the death of the person making the election;

3. by gift; or

4. in any transaction to which Code Sec. 1042(a) applies.

Contribution of qualified replacement property. Generally, the contribution of property to a partnership in exchange for an interest in the partnership will not cause gain or loss to be recognized by the partnership or any of its partners.[7] However, the transfer of qualified replacement property to a partnership in exchange for a partnership interest by a taxpayer who has elected to defer the recognition of gain is a disposition of qualified replacement property. In addition, the exceptions stipulated in Code Sec. 1042(e)(3) do not treat the contribution of qualified replacement property to a partnership in exchange for an interest in the partnership as a transfer exempt from the recapture rules. Accordingly, the contribution of qualified replacement property in exchange for a partnership interest required a recapture of gains that were deferred by a taxpayer from the sales of shares to an ESOP.[8]

Restrictions on allocations of employer securities

Specifically, an ESOP must provide that no portion of the assets of the plan attributable to securities acquired by the plan to which the nonrecognition-of- gain provisions of Code Sec. 1042 apply may accrue during a specified nonallocation period for the benefit of:[9]

1. a taxpayer seeking nonrecognition treatment under Code Sec. 1042(a),

2. any person who is related to that taxpayer or that decedent,[10]

3. any other person who owns (after application of the attribution rules of Code Sec. 318(a)) more than 25% of (a) any class of outstanding stock of the corporation that issued employer securities or of any corporation which is a member of the same controlled group of corporations as such corporation or (b) the total value of any class of outstanding stock of such corporation.

This restriction also applies to prohibit any direct or indirect accrual of benefits under any qualified plan of an employer or an allocation of assets to the employer securities involved in a nonrecognition-of-gain transaction under Code Sec. 1042.

An individual is to be treated as a 25% shareholder only if the individual is a 25% shareholder:[11]

1. at all times during the one-year period ending on the date of the sale of the securities to an ESOP, or

2. on the date on which any of the securities sold to the ESOP are allocated.

Excise tax on prohibited allocation

A prohibited allocation is a prohibited transaction subject to a 50% excise tax on the amount of the prohibited allocation.[12]

Sale of S corporation stock

The special rules relating to ESOPs do not apply to S corporations. Thus, an S corporation shareholder cannot obtain tax-free rollover treatment for sales of S corporation stock to an ESOP.[13]

[1] Code Sec. 1042(a).

[2] Code Sec. 1042(b).

[3] Code Sec. 1042(c)(1). NOTE: The meaning of the term "readily tradable on an established securities market" as defined by the regulations under Code Sec. 401(a)(35) (see ¶ 2362) also applies for purposes of the rules on qualifying employer securities under Code Sec. 1042(c)(1)(A), dealing with the definition of "qualified securities" involving the sale of stock to an ESOP, generally effec-

tive for plan years beginning on or after January 1, 2012. See IRS Notice 2011-19, I.R.B. 2011-11, 3-14-11, CCH PENSION PLAN GUIDE ¶ 17,146Z.

[4] Code Sec. 1042(d).

[5] Code Sec. 1042(e)(1).

[6] Code Sec. 1042(e)(3).

[7] Code Sec. 721(a).

[8] Rev. Rul. 2000-18, 2000-1 CB 847, CCH PENSION PLAN GUIDE ¶ 19,943N.

[9] Code Sec. 409(n)(1).

[10] As described in Code Sec. 267(b).

[11] Code Sec. 409(n)(3).

[12] Code Sec. 409(n)(2)(B).

[13] Code Sec. 1042(c)(1)(A).

¶ 3092

TAXATION OF ESOPs: Excise Tax on Dispositions Reducing Number or Value of Employer Securities

A 10% excise tax is imposed on the employer maintaining an ESOP if, within three years after certain employer securities are acquired (or transferred), a disposition of stock by the ESOP occurs in which:[1]

1. the total number of shares held by the ESOP after the disposition is less than the total number of employer securities held after the acquisition (or transfer), or

2. the value of the employer securities held by the ESOP after the disposition is less than 30% of the total value of all employer securities as of the time of the dispositions, unless provided otherwise in IRS regulations.

The excise tax applies to the disposition of employer securities acquired by (or transferred to) the ESOP in a transaction involving a tax-free rollover (¶ 3091).

The 10% excise tax is also imposed where employer securities are disposed of before being allocated to the accounts of plan participants or beneficiaries and the proceeds from such a disposition are not allocated to the appropriate accounts. However, certain distributions to employees (e.g., upon death, retirement, disability or separation from service), exchanges of employer securities in the course of various reorganizations, dispositions to meet qualified plan diversification requirements, and other forced dispositions occurring by operation of state law are not taken into account for purposes of the excise tax provisions.

The excise tax is equal to 10% of the amount realized on the disposition to the extent allocable to the transaction in question. Where the amount realized cannot be readily determined because a given disposition does not amount to a "sale or exchange," the amount realized on the disposition is the fair market value of the security in question at the time of disposition.

A disposition of employer securities will be treated as having been made in the following order for purposes of the excise tax:[2]

1. from qualified employer securities acquired during the three-year period ending on the date of such disposition, beginning with the securities first acquired; and

2. from any other employer securities.

[1] Code Sec. 4978(a).

[2] Code Sec. 4978(b)(2).

¶ 3093

TAXATION OF ESOPs: ESOPs Maintained by S Corporations

ESOPs are permitted to own S corporation stock.[1] S corporation income allocable to an ESOP is not subject to current taxation. In 2001, in the Economic Growth and Tax Relief Reconciliation Act of 2001 (P.L. 107-16) (EGTRRA), Congress acted on a perception it had that the exemption from tax for S corporation income flowing through to ESOPs was being abused and that ESOPs were being used by S corporation owners to obtain inappropriate tax deferral or tax avoidance. In an effort to stem some perceived abuses of this tax provision, Congress enacted specific provisions in EGTRRA limiting the tax deferral opportunities in S corporation ESOPs (see below). Also, the IRS and Treasury Department have made abusive transactions involving S corporation ESOPs "listed transactions" for tax shelter purposes.[2]

Prohibited allocations

General rule. If there is a "nonallocation year" with respect to an ESOP maintained by an S corporation:

1) the amount allocated in a "prohibited allocation" to someone who is a "disqualified person" is treated as distributed to the individual (and included in his or her gross income) and

2) a 50% excise tax is imposed on the S corporation with respect to the amount of the prohibited allocation or any "synthetic equity" owned by a disqualified person.[3]

Prohibited allocation defined. A prohibited allocation for purposes of this provision is defined as an accrual (or direct or indirect allocation under any qualified plan of the S corporation) of any portion of the assets of the ESOP that are attributable to (or allocable in lieu of) the employer's S corporation stock if the accrual or allocation is for the benefit of a disqualified person during a "nonallocation year."[4]

Nonallocation year for an ESOP. A nonallocation year is any plan year of an S corporation's ESOP holding shares in the S corporation if, at any time during the plan year, disqualified persons own at least 50% of the S corporation's total outstanding shares.[5]

Disqualified persons. A person is a disqualified person, for S corporation ESOP purposes, if a person is a member of a "deemed 20% shareholder" or is himself a "deemed 10% shareholder."[6] A person is a deemed 20% shareholder if the total number of deemed-owned shares of the person and the person's family members is at least 20% of the S corporation's deemed-owned shares of stock.[7]

Any person having deemed-owned shares who is a member of the family of a deemed 20% shareholder, if not otherwise treated as a disqualified person, is treated as a disqualified person.[8]

Example: Fred Miller owns 51% of the shares of ABC Corp. ABC is an S corporation that has an ESOP for its employees. Income on the S corporation stock held by ABC's ESOP is allocated to Fred's account. Fred is a disqualified person because he owns more than 20% of the plan's deemed-owned shares and, therefore, the allocation is a prohibited allocation.

A person is a deemed 10% shareholder if the person's deemed-owned shares are at least 10% of the deemed-owned shares of stock in the corporation and the person is not a deemed 20% shareholder.[9]

Deemed owned shares. Deemed-owned shares, with respect to any person, include (1) S corporation stock constituting employer securities of an ESOP that is allocated to that person under the plan and (2) the person's share of the S corporation's stock which the plan holds but has not yet allocated to the plan participants.[10]

A person's share of unallocated S corporation stock is the amount of unallocated stock which would be allocated to the person if all unallocated stock were allocated to each participant in the same proportion as the most recent stock allocation under the plan.[11]

Synthetic equity in S corporation ESOPs. Synthetic equity is any stock option warrant, restricted stock, deferred issuance stock right, or similar interest that gives the holder the right to acquire or receive the S corporation's stock in the future. Except to the extent provided in regulations, synthetic equity also includes a stock appreciation right, phantom stock unit, or similar right to a future cash payment based on the value of such stock or appreciation in such value.[12]

CCH Pointer: Temporary and proposed regulations issued in December 2004 provide guidance on the definition and effects of a prohibited allocation, identification of disqualified persons and determination of a nonallocation year, calculation of synthetic equity, and standards for determining whether a transaction is an avoidance or evasion of Code Sec. 409(p).[13] Final regulations under Code Sec. 409(p) were issued in December 2006, generally applicable to plan years beginning on or after January 1, 2006.[14] The 2004 regulations remain applicable to plan years beginning before January 1, 2006.

The 2006 final regulations retain the rule of the 2004 temporary regulations concerning prohibited allocations under which there is an impermissible accrual to the extent employer securities consisting of S corporation stock are held under the ESOP for the benefit of a disqualified person during a nonallocation year. Thus, in the event of a nonallocation year, S corporation shares held in a disqualified person's account and all other ESOP assets attributable to S corporation stock, including distributions, sales proceeds, and earnings, are treated as an impermissible accrual whether attributable to contributions in the current year or a prior year.

The final regulations follow the rules for synthetic equity that were set forth in the prior regulations. Thus, the person who is entitled to the synthetic equity is treated as owning a number of shares of stock in the S corporation equal to the present value of the synthetic equity divided by the fair market value of a share of the S corporation's stock as of the same date. The final regulations also retain the triennial method set forth in the 2004 regulations that permits the ESOP to treat the number of synthetic equity shares owned on a determination date as remaining constant for a three-year period.

Excise taxes imposed on prohibited allocations. If the S corporation ESOP makes a prohibited allocation, the S corporation is liable for an excise tax equal to 50% of the amount allocated to the account of a disqualified person.[15]

A special rule applies for the first nonallocation year, regardless of whether there is a prohibited allocation.[16] In that year, the 50% excise tax also applies to the fair market value of the deemed-owned shares of any disqualified person, even though the ESOP holds those shares and they have not yet been allocated to the disqualified person in that year.

The S corporation is also liable for the 50% excise tax with respect to any synthetic equity interest owned by any disqualified person in any nonallocation year.[17]

Effective date and sunset provision. Generally, the provision relating to prohibited allocation of stock in an ESOP maintained by an S corporation applies to plan years beginning after December 31, 2004. However, for ESOPs established after March 14, 2001, or for ESOPs established on or before such date if the employer securities held by the plan consist of stock in a corporation that has made an S corporation election that is not in effect on such date, the provisions apply to plan years ending after March 14, 2001.[18]

☐ Prohibited allocations of S corporation stock and the applicable excise tax are discussed in detail in the CCH PENSION PLAN GUIDE at ¶ 7922.

[1] Code Sec. 514(e).

[2] See Rev. Rul. 2004-4, I.R.B. 2004-6, CCH PENSION PLAN GUIDE ¶ 19,948Z-38. Transactions described in Rev. Rul. 2004-4 are eligible for settlement under a special IRS initiative. Under this initiative, taxpayers may resolve abusive transactions by paying any taxes owed, plus interest and a penalty, but avoid lengthy litigation and criminal investigations. See IRS Announcement 2005-80, 10-11-2005, CCH PENSION PLAN GUIDE ¶ 17,097S-80.

[3] Code Sec. 4979A, as amended by P.L. 107-16 (Economic Growth and Tax Relief Reconciliation Act of 2001).

[4] Code Sec. 409(p)(1), as added by P.L. 107-16 (Economic Growth and Tax Relief Reconciliation Act of 2001).

[5] Code Sec. 409(p)(3)(A), as added by P.L. 107-16 (Economic Growth and Tax Relief Reconciliation Act of 2001).

[6] Code Sec. 409(p)(4), as added by P.L. 107-16 (Economic Growth and Tax Relief Reconciliation Act of 2001).

[7] Code Sec. 409(p)(4)(A)(i), as added by P.L. 107-16 (Economic Growth and Tax Relief Reconciliation Act of 2001).

[8] Code Sec. 409(p)(4)(B), as added by P.L. 107-16 (Economic Growth and Tax Relief Reconciliation Act of 2001).

[9] Code Sec. 409(p)(4)(A)(ii), as added by P.L. 107-16 (Economic Growth and Tax Relief Reconciliation Act of 2001).

[10] Code Sec. 409(p)(4)(C)(i), as added by P.L. 107-16 (Economic Growth and Tax Relief Reconciliation Act of 2001).

[11] Code Sec. 409(p)(4)(C)(ii), as added by P.L. 107-16 (Economic Growth and Tax Relief Reconciliation Act of 2001).

[12] Code Sec. 409(p)(6)(C), as added by P.L. 107-16 (Economic Growth and Tax Relief Reconciliation Act of 2001).

[13] Temp. Reg. § 1.409(p)-1T.

[14] Reg. § 1.409(p)-1, as issued under T.D. 9302, 12-20-06 (71 FR 76134).

[15] Code Sec. 4979A(a)(3), as added by P.L. 107-16 (Economic Growth and Tax Relief Reconciliation Act of 2001).

[16] Code Sec. 4979A(e)(2)(C), as added by P.L. 107-16 (Economic Growth and Tax Relief Reconciliation Act of 2001).

[17] Code Sec. 4979A(c)(4), as added by P.L. 107-6 (Economic Growth and Tax Relief Reconciliation Act of 2001).

[18] P.L. 107-16 (Economic Growth and Tax Relief Reconciliation Act of 2001), Act Sec. 656(d). See

also IRS Notice 2002-2, 2002-1 CB 285, CCH PENSION PLAN GUIDE ¶ 17,122X. The IRS has made it clear that ESOPs marketed to evade the nonallocation rules are not eligible for the delayed (2005) effective date. Such plans are therefore subject to the rules of Code Sec. 409(p), effective for plan years ending after March 14, 2001. See Rev. Rul. 2003-6, I.R.B. 2003-2, CCH PENSION PLAN GUIDE ¶ 19,948B.

¶ 3094

FIDUCIARY REQUIREMENTS AND REPORTING RULES: Fiduciary Requirements for ESOP Trustees and Administrators

ESOPs are generally governed by the same fiduciary rules that control the administration and operation of other employee benefit plans. Accordingly, the assets of an ESOP must be held in trust and the ESOP trustee must have the exclusive authority to manage and control assets, unless:[1]

1. the plan expressly provides that the trustee is subject to the direction of named fiduciary who is not a trustee; or

2. the authority to manage, acquire, or dispose of plan assets is delegated to one or more investment managers.

Trustees may also be subject to the direction of plan participants regarding the management of assets allocated to their accounts (see below).

ERISA also requires that plan fiduciaries discharge their duties:[2]

1. solely in the interests of the participants and beneficiaries,

2. for the exclusive purpose of providing benefits to participants and beneficiaries and defraying the reasonable expenses of administering the plan, and

3. with the care, skill, prudence, and diligence that a prudent man would use under similar circumstances.

☐ General fiduciary requirements are discussed in detail beginning at ¶ 2300.

Fiduciary implications of plan investment decisions

The fiduciary requirements of ERISA are not violated when an ESOP acquires qualifying employer securities (see ¶ 3095). Nonetheless, a number of courts have ruled that, when making investment decisions, ESOP fiduciaries, like fiduciaries of other plans, are governed by the exclusive benefit and prudence tests of ERISA.[3]

Fiduciary responsibility during tender offer: Pass-through rules

A trustee's decision whether to tender employer stock held by a plan with regard to a tender offer for the plan sponsor, and the voting of proxies incident to the employer stock held by the plan, are fiduciary acts of plan management.[4] Because such decisions involve the management of plan assets, they are generally subject to the exclusive authority and responsibility of the plan trustee.[5] However, a trustee must follow the instructions of participants in a plan that has empowered the participants to direct the trustee with respect to the management of the assets *allocated* to their accounts. Thus, under such circumstances, ESOP trustees must solicit the plan's participants and vote as directed, even if the trustees believe that their fiduciary duty requires them to override the directions of the participants.[6]

Participant directions may not violate ERISA. The participant directions must be made in accordance with plan terms and must not violate ERISA. According to the DOL, a trustee can assure that the instructions it receives from participants with respect to *allocated* shares do not violate ERISA by following procedures that ensure that: the plan's provisions are fairly implemented, the participants are not subject to coercion or undue pressures in making decisions, that necessary information is provided, and that false or misleading information is not distributed.

Pass-through rule does not apply to unallocated or non-voted shares. Trustees are not required to follow plan provisions requiring unallocated shares of employer securities or non-voted allocated shares to be voted in accordance with participant instructions if they believe that following such instructions would violate ERISA. Thus, the trustee must diligently investigate and determine whether the participant's directions would lead to an imprudent result. For example, with respect to a tender offer, the trustee should weigh the prospect that the proceeds would be reinvested against the likelihood that a higher share value would be produced by current management and the long-term value of the company.

---

[1] ERISA Sec. 403(a).

[2] ERISA Sec. 404(a)(1).

[3] E.g., see *Eaves v. Penn,* CA-10 (1978), 587 F2d 453; *Dimond v. Retirement Plan for Employees of Michael Baker Corp.,* DC Pa (1983), 582 FSupp 892.

[4] ERISA Sec. 3(21); PWBA Private Letter, 9-28-95, CCH PENSION PLAN GUIDE ¶ 19,976B.

[5] ERISA Sec. 403(a).

[6] PWBA Private Letter, 9-28-95, CCH PENSION PLAN GUIDE ¶ 19,976B.

¶ 3095

FIDUCIARY REQUIREMENTS AND REPORTING RULES: Prohibited Transaction Rules

ERISA prohibits plan fiduciaries from engaging in certain transactions and imposes a special excise tax on other persons who are parties to such transactions.[1] Among the prohibited transactions are a sale, exchange, or leasing of any property between the plan and a "disqualified person" or a "party in interest," the lending of money or other extension of credit between a plan and a disqualified person or a party in interest, and the transfer to or use by or for the benefit of a disqualified person or party in interest of the income or assets of the plan. (See ¶ 2406 for more on "parties in interest.")

Exceptions for ESOPs

Under ERISA, however, an exception is made for employees who transact business with stock bonus plans and ESOPs.[2] Thus, an employer may guarantee loans obtained by the plan or may sell stock to the plan on an installment basis—

actions that would ordinarily be considered prohibited extensions of credit. Furthermore, there is no barrier to sales and exchanges of securities between the plan and parties in interest. The IRS rules on plan qualification are not violated where a plan borrows for purposes of investing the securities of an employer corporation.[3]

A loan made by a disqualified person to an ESOP is exempt from the excise tax on prohibited transactions.[4] However, a fiduciary must not receive any consideration for his own account from any party dealing with the plan in connection with a transaction involving the income or assets of the plan. In addition, in order to be exempt from ERISA's prohibited transaction provisions, ESOPs must meet the special loan requirements set out at ¶ 3035 [5] as well as other general requirements.[6]

A loan to an ESOP does not lose its exemption from ERISA's prohibition against the extension of credit between a plan and a party in interest solely because the plan's fiduciary repays the loan with proceeds from the sale of stock acquired by the loan.[7] Persons entitled to a repayment of an exempt loan do not have a right to assets of an ESOP other than collateral given for the loan, contributions made to an ESOP to meet the obligations of the loan, and earnings attributable to the collateral and investment of the contributions.[8]

CCH Pointer: The exception to the prohibited transaction rules for ESOPs did not apply to owner-employees prior to 2002. However, for post-2001 years, plans may be amended to authorize loans to all plan participants including owner-employees and shareholder-employees.[9]

Use of stock proceeds and dividends to repay loan . An ESOP of a C Corporation is not treated as engaging in a prohibited transaction merely because a dividend paid with respect to qualifying employer securities held by the ESOP is used to make payment on a loan (interest and principal) that was used to acquire employer securities, whether or not allocated to participants.[10] The relief does not apply to a dividend paid with respect to an employer security that is allocated to participants unless the plan provides that employer securities with a fair market value of no less than the amount of the dividend is allocated to the participant for the year for which the dividend would have been allocated to the participant.[11]

Similarly, (effective for distributions made with respect to S Corporation stock after 1997) an ESOP maintained by a S Corporation (see ¶ 3093) is not treated as engaging in a prohibited transaction merely because, in accordance with plan provisions, a distribution made with respect to S Corporation stock that constitutes qualifying employer securities held by the ESOP is used to make payments on a loan that was used to acquire the securities, whether or not allocated to participants.[12] However, the relief will not apply to a distribution with respect to S Corporation stock that is allocated to a participant unless the plan provides employer stock with fair market value of not less than the amount of the distribution allocated to the participant for the year in which distributions would have been allocated to the participant.

Acquisition of "qualifying employer securities." The acquisition or sale by an ESOP of "qualifying employer securities" is not a prohibited transaction if the sale is for adequate consideration (see ¶ 3096), no commission is charged in connection with the acquisition or sale, and the plan is an eligible individual account plan.[13] ERISA defines a qualifying employer security as stock, a marketable obligation, or an interest in a publicly traded partnership.[14] By contrast, where there is readily tradable common stock, the Internal Revenue Code defines a qualifying employer security as common stock issued by the employer having voting power and dividend rights equal to or in excess of that class of common stock having the greatest dividend right (see ¶ 3040).[15]

Purchase of stock from shareholder-employees of S corporation. Generally, a qualified plan that provides contributions or benefits for employees, some of whom are owner-employees, may not acquire property from or sell property to a shareholder-employee of an S corporation, a member of the family of the shareholder, or a corporation controlled by the shareholder-employee.[16] However, the sale of employer securities to an ESOP maintained by an S corporation by a shareholder-employee, family member of the shareholder-employees, or corporation in which the shareholder owns at least 50% of the stock, is permitted.[17] A shareholder-employee refers to an employee or officer of an S corporation who owns, or is considered as owning, more than 5% of the outstanding stock of the corporation on any day during the corporation's tax year.[18]

ESOP investment "primarily" in employer securities

As noted at ¶ 3000, an ESOP must be designed to invest "primarily" in qualifying employer securities.[19] Although the Labor Department regulations do not define the term "primarily," the regulations do state that a stock bonus plan or a money purchase pension plan constituting an ESOP may invest part of its assets in securities other than qualifying employer securities. The DOL has stated in advisory opinions that neither ERISA nor its regulations contain maximum or minimum percentages of plan assets which must be invested in qualifying employer securities over the life of the ESOP in order to satisfy the "primarily" requirement.[20] The DOL has concluded that a plan provision requiring the plan to invest more than 50% of its assets in qualifying employer securities would not, in itself, contravene the requirement that an ESOP invest primarily in qualifying employer securities.

Adequate consideration

In addition, the sale or acquisition of employer stock must be for adequate consideration, as defined in ERISA, in order for trustees to receive automatic exemption from the prohibited transaction rules. This requirement, which pertains to situations where an ESOP is dealing with a party in interest, is discussed further at ¶ 3096.

☐ The prohibited transaction rules are generally covered at ¶ 2400 and following.

---

[1] Code Sec. 4975; ERISA Sec. 406.

[2] Code Sec. 4975(d)(3) and (13); ERISA Sec. 408(b)(3) and (e).

[3] Rev. Rul. 71-311, 1971-2 CB 184, CCH PENSION PLAN GUIDE ¶ 19,064.

[4] IRS Reg. § 54.4975-7(b)(2)(i).

[5] ERISA Reg. § 2550.408b-3. This regulation mirrors relevant portions of IRS Reg. §§ 54.4975-7 and -11.

[6] ERISA Reg. § 2550.407d-6. This regulation mirrors relevant portions of IRS Reg. §§ 54.4975-7 and -11.

¶3095

[7]ERISA Opinion Letter 93-35A, 12-23-93.

[8] IRS Reg. §54.4975-7(b)(5); ERISA Reg. §2550.408b-3(e).

[9] Code Sec. 4975(f)(6)(B)(iii) and ERISA Sec. 408(d)(2)(C) as added by P.L. 107-16 (Economic Growth and Tax Relief Reconciliation Act of 2001).

[10] Code Sec. 404(k)(5)(B).

[11] Code Sec. 404(k)(2)(B).

[12] Code Sec. 4975(f)(7), as added by P.L. 108-357 (American Jobs Creation Act of 2004).

[13] Code Sec. 4975(d)(13); ERISA Sec. 408(e).

[14] ERISA Sec. 407(d)(5).

[15] Code Sec. 409(l)(2).

[16] Code Sec. 4975(d), prior to amendment by P.L. 105-34 (Taxpayer Relief Act of 1997); Code Sec. 4975(f)(6); ERISA Sec. 408(d)(1).

[17] Code Sec. 4975(f)(6)(B); ERISA Sec. 408(d)(2).

[18] Code Sec. 4975(f)(6)(C); ERISA Sec. 408(d)(3).

[19] ERISA Sec. 407(d)(6); ERISA Reg. §2550.407d-6(b).

[20]ERISA Opinion Letter 83-6A, 1-24-83; ERISA Opinion Letter 90-05A, 3-29-90.

¶ 3096

FIDUCIARY REQUIREMENTS AND REPORTING RULES: Valuing ESOP Stock

The sale or acquisition of employer stock must be for adequate consideration, as defined in ERISA, in order for trustees to receive automatic exemption from the prohibited transaction rules.[1] Proposed regulations, issued by the Labor Department in 1988, establish a two-part test for determining the adequacy of consideration paid for assets other than publicly traded securities:[2]

1. the consideration must reflect fair market value, and

2. the valuation must be made in good faith.

Fair market value

Fair market value is defined in the proposed regulations as the price at which an asset would change hands between a willing buyer and a willing seller when neither party is under any compulsion to enter into the transaction.[3]

The proposed DOL rules embody standards of fair market value previously set forth by the IRS.[4] These include:

1. the nature of the business and the history of the enterprise from its inception.

2. the economic outlook in general and the condition and outlook of the specific industry in particular.

3. the book value of the stock and the financial condition of the business.

4. the earning capacity of the company.

5. the dividend-paying capacity of the company.

6. whether or not the enterprise has goodwill or other intangible value.

7. sales of the stock and the size of the block of stock to be valued.

8. the market price of stocks of corporations engaged in the same or a similar line of business that have their stocks actively

traded in a free and open market, either on an exchange or over-the-counter.

Good faith standard

The good faith standard requires the fiduciary to apply sound business principles when valuing securities and to conduct a prudent investigation of the circumstances prevailing at the time of the valuation. Either the fiduciary making the valuation must itself be independent of all parties to the transaction or the fiduciary must rely on the report of an independent appraiser.[5]

---

[1] ERISA Sec. 408(e).

[2] ERISA Sec. 3(18)(B); ERISA Prop. Reg. § 2510.3-18(b)(1)(i).

[3] ERISA Prop. Reg. § 2510.3-18(b)(1)(ii).

[4] Rev. Rul. 59-60, 1959-1 CB 237.

[5] ERISA Prop. Reg. § 2510.3-18(b)(3)(ii).

¶ 3097

FIDUCIARY REQUIREMENTS AND REPORTING RULES: Use of Leveraged ESOPs to Prevent Corporate Takeovers

An ESOP can quickly acquire large blocks of employer stock because of its ability to buy shares with borrowed funds. This makes an ESOP an ideal vehicle for a company to use to prevent a hostile corporate takeover. The more stock the ESOP holds, the better the chances of thwarting a corporate raider, since the stock is in the hands of employees and officers of the company. These parties are presumably more likely to favor the existing management in a tender offer.

Limits on use of ESOPs in takeover

ESOPs are subject to close scrutiny when used as anti-takeover devices. In a landmark decision, *Shamrock Holdings, Inc. v. Polaroid Corp.*, the Delaware Chancery Court upheld the use of ESOPs to thwart takeover attempts.[1] In that case, the target company significantly increased the number of its shares owned by the ESOP shortly after receiving a tender offer. The employees, voting as a block, were able to prevent the takeover. A subsequent decision, however, rendered by a federal district court in Ohio, held that an ESOP created *primarily* to prevent a hostile takeover was invalid.[2] The court distinguished this case from the *Polaroid* decision, finding that, while the Polaroid plan was only "partly" defensive, the plan in this case was adopted with the "overwhelming" purpose of thwarting a tender offer. Thus, where the purpose of the ESOP is primarily or overwhelmingly to prevent a takeover, employee benefits are not the primary concern of the plan, and, hence, the plan may be found invalid.

□ See ¶ 3094 for a discussion of fiduciary responsibility rules in connection with a tender offer.

---

[1] *Shamrock Holdings, Inc. v. Polaroid Corporation,* Del Chanc Ct (1989), 559 A2d 257.

[2] *NCR Corp. v. American Telephone and Telegraph Co.,* DC Ohio (1991), 761 FSupp 475.

¶ 3098
FIDUCIARY REQUIREMENTS AND REPORTING RULES: ERISA Reporting and Disclosure

Because an ESOP is a stock bonus plan, it is subject to the ERISA reporting and disclosure requirements that apply to such plans. These include reports to the IRS, the Department of Labor, and to participants and beneficiaries under the plan.

A special Schedule E (ESOP Annual Information) must be filed as an attachment with the Form 5500 annual report. Schedule E must be filed by every employer or plan administrator that contains ESOP benefits.[1]

CCH Pointer: IRS-only forms and schedules are being removed from the Form 5500 Annual Return/Report as a result of the move to a wholly electronic filing system.[2] Schedule E will be removed for the 2009 plan year and thereafter. Three questions from Schedule E have been moved to the 2009 Schedule R.

☐ The general plan reporting and disclosure rules are discussed at ¶ 2200.

---

[1] Instructions to IRS Form 5500, Schedule E.

[2] EBSA, IRS, and PBGC Notice of Adoption of Revisions to the Annual Information Returns/Reports, 72 FR 64731, 11-16-07, CCH PENSION PLAN GUIDE ¶ 19,981P. See also ERISA Reg. § 2520.103-1.

¶ 3099
For More Information

☐ For more information on ESOPs, see ¶ 7800-7960 of the CCH PENSION PLAN GUIDE.

Tax-Sheltered Annuities— Special Rules

¶ 3100

Tax-Sheltered Annuities—An Overview

A tax-sheltered annuity, also commonly referred to as a "403(b) plan," "TSA," or "tax-deferred annuity," is a deferred compensation retirement arrangement that may be purchased *only* on behalf of employees of specified employers. Thus, individual taxpayers (including self-employed ministers) may not establish 403(b) accounts for themselves. Specifically, 403(b) plans may be maintained for employees by: a 501(c)(3) tax-exempt organization organized and operated exclusively for religious, charitable, scientific, educational or other specified purposes (see

¶ 3135); an educational organization (see ¶ 3130); or a state (including an Indian tribal government (see ¶ 3137), or political subdivision of a state, or an agency or instrumentality thereof.[1] A TSA may also be maintained for a duly ordained or licensed minister by the minister's employer (see ¶ 3160). [2] However, different rules apply to 403(b) plans maintained by churches and those maintained by tax-exempt organizations, educational organizations, and state governments.

TSAs are funded primarily through salary reduction agreements whereby employees reduce their salaries by a fixed amount or forgo a future increase in salary. The employee's taxable compensation for the year is the compensation *after* it is reduced by the salary reduction. Often employers will make contributions to the TSA either as a fixed percentage of employee compensation or as a "matching" contribution. An example of a matching contribution would be an employer contribution of 50 cents for each dollar an employee contributes through salary reduction. A properly maintained TSA will hold these contributions and accumulate earnings that are tax-free until they are later distributed.

Final rules codify 40 years of 403(b) guidance

The IRS in July 2007 issued long awaited final regulations governing 403(b) plans.[3] The final regulations update prior rules last adopted in 1964 and reflect legislative and regulatory developments released over the past 40 years, including amendments made by ERISA, the Small Business Job Protection Act of 1996 (SBJPA), the Economic Growth and Tax Relief Reconciliation Act of 2001 (EGTRRA), and the Pension Protection Act of 2006 (PPA; P.L. 109-280), which have had the effect of diminishing the differences between 403(b) plans and other salary reduction arrangements, such as 401(k) plans and 457(b) plans. The regulations also provide guidance on Code Sec. 414(c) common control rules for certain tax-exempt organizations. **The final regulations generally apply for tax years beginning after December 31, 2008.** Thus, because individuals will almost uniformly be on a calendar tax year, the regulations generally apply on January 1, 2009. There are later dates of application for collectively bargained and church plans. In addition, the regulations are subject to a number of explicit transition rules. Taxpayers may generally rely on the final regulations prior to the applicable date provided they do so on a "consistent and reasonable" basis.

403(b) plan sponsors have until end of 2009 to adopt written plan. The IRS provided relief in 2009 for compliance with the January 1, 2009 written plan requirement for 403(b) plans.[4] A 403(b) plan will not be treated as failing to satisfy Code Sec. 403(b) and the final regulations during the 2009 calendar year if:

1) on or before December 31, 2009, the plan sponsor adopts a written plan document that is intended to satisfy Code Sec. 403(b) and the final regulations effective as of January 1, 2009;

2) during 2009, the plan sponsor operates the plan in accordance with a reasonable interpretation of Code Sec. 403(b) and the final regulations; and

¶3100

3) before the end of 2009, the plan sponsor makes its best efforts to retroactively correct any operational failure during the 2009 calendar year to conform with the written plan.

Similarly, the IRS has announced a remedial amendment period and reliance for employers that, under upcoming IRS guidance, either adopt a pre-approved 403(b) plan with a favorable opinion letter or apply for an individual determination letter for a 403(b) plan when available. An employer that first establishes a 403(b) plan after December 31, 2009, will also have reliance beginning on the effective date of the plan, provided the employer either adopts a pre-approved plan with a favorable opinion letter or applies for an individual determination letter and corrects any defects in the form of the plan retroactive to the plan's effective date. Revenue procedures will include this remedial amendment provision and will address the time-frames for adopting a pre-approved plan or applying for a determination letter and other details regarding the remedial amendment period. In addition, employers may rely on the IRS announcement prior to publication of the revenue procedure for pre-approved 403(b) plans.[5]

---

[1] Code § 403(b)(1).

[2] Code Sec. 403(b)(i); Code Sec. 414(e)(5)(A).

[3] IRS Reg. § 1.403(b)-0—IRS Reg. § 1.403(b)-11; preamble at CCH PENSION PLAN GUIDE ¶ 24,508U.

[4] IRS Notice 2009-3, I.R.B. 2009-2, 1-12-2009, at CCH PENSION PLAN GUIDE ¶ 17,141S.

[5] Announcement 2009-89, I.R.B. 2009-52, 12-28-2009, at CCH PENSION PLAN GUIDE ¶ 17,097T-45.

¶ 3105

Benefits of Providing a TSA

403(b) plans afford advantages for both employers and employees. A TSA offers an employee a tax-advantaged means of supplementing both benefits under qualified plans and Social Security benefits. Contributions made by a participant to a 403(b) plan pursuant to a salary reduction are not taxable to the individual until the amounts are withdrawn from the plan. Earnings and gains on the amount in an individual 403(b) account are also not taxed until withdrawn. Finally, in addition to the benefits of tax deferral, elective deferrals to a 403(b) plan may enable a taxpayer to further reduce income tax liability through a "saver's credit" (see ¶ 3177).

403(b) plans offer a stable retirement savings vehicle, as elective deferrals contributed to the plan are immediately nonforfeitable[1] and assets held in a 403(b) plan may be excluded from an employee's bankruptcy estate.[2] Within limits, life insurance protection for an employee's beneficiaries can be provided under a TSA. And repayable loans may be made to employees from a TSA, again with specific restrictions.

---

[1] Code Sec. 403(b)(1)(C) and 403(b)(6).

[2] 11 U.S.C. § 541(b), as added by P.L. 109-8 (Bankruptcy Abuse Prevention and Consumer Protection Act of 2005), Act Sec. 323.

¶ 3110

Funding a TSA

A TSA is typically funded through a combination of pre-tax employee and employer contributions.

Elective deferrals. The primary way in which contributions are made to a TSA is by a salary reduction agreement with the employer through either a pre-tax salary reduction or the foregoing of salary increases. Contributions made pursuant to a salary reduction agreement are treated as employer contributions for income tax purposes.

> **Example:** Archie is an employee of a tax-exempt employer. He participates in a TSA and, pursuant to a salary reduction agreement with his employer, receives a monthly $2,000 paycheck, reduced by 10%. Therefore, Archie receives taxable monthly income of $1,800, and $200 is withheld from his paycheck. The amount withheld is paid over to the insurance company which maintains the TSA. The employer's monthly matching contribution is 10% of whatever Archie contributes by salary reduction. Here, that would be $20 (10% of $200), which is also paid over to the insurance company. The matching employer contribution is not taxable to Archie until it is later distributed.

☐ A detailed discussion of contributions to TSAs pursuant to salary reduction agreements is at ¶ 3165.

Nonelective contributions. Nonelective contributions include employer contributions that are not made pursuant to a salary reduction agreement, such as matching contributions, discretionary contributions, and mandatory contributions. As with elective deferrals, the taxpayer is not taxed on the contributions until they are withdrawn.

Nonelective contributions for former employees. An advantage of 403(b) plans over qualified plans, from an employee perspective, is that nonelective contributions may be made for an employee for up to five years after the employee has retired and, thus, is not receiving current compensation from the employer.[1] The amount of compensation is based on the employee's includible compensation (see ¶ 3183) in the last year of service before retirement.

After-tax contributions. TSAs, less frequently, allow employees to make after-tax contributions. After-tax contributions are not excluded from a participant's income and may not be deducted on the participant's tax return.

Roth 403(b) plan. 403(b) plans may incorporate a "qualified Roth contribution program," pursuant to which participants may elect to have all or a portion of their elective deferrals to the plan designed as after-tax Roth contributions. Qualified distributions from a designated Roth account would not be subject to tax, provided that a five-year "nonexclusion" or holding period has been satisfied. See ¶ 3163.[2]

CCH Pointer: The final regulations provide rules on designated Roth contributions under 403(b) plans, but do not address the taxation of distributions from Roth 403(b) plans.

Voluntary employee contributions. Employees are not permitted to make deductible voluntary employee contributions to a TSA.[3] However, voluntary employee contributions may remain in the employee account until distributed in accordance with the terms of the TSA. The contributions will be includible in gross income when they are distributed unless the employee elects a rollover or direct transfer of the funds.

---

[1] Code § 403(b)(3).

[2] Code Sec. 402A.

[3] Code § 72(o)(5).

¶ 3115
Who Holds the Contributions?

The money contributed to a TSA is not held by the employer or the employee. Whether contributions are made by salary reduction alone or together with employer contributions, the employer acts merely as a conduit for transferring funds to the insurance company or custodian. Either of those entities will hold and invest the funds in separate tax-deferred accounts for the employees until such time as the employees request a distribution in accordance with the terms of the TSA.

A plan that is arranged so that salary reduction or non-salary reduction contributions are placed in a savings account for employees to purchase annuity contracts for themselves at retirement is not a TSA and invites adverse tax consequences for employers and employees.[1]

---

[1] IRS Reg. § 1.403(b)-8.

¶ 3120
Restrictions on Contributions—General Rules

There are two restrictions on the amount of contributions that can be made to a TSA, each of which must be taken into account on an annual basis:

1. The amount of "elective deferrals" to a TSA is subject to a limit under Code Sec. 402(g)(4). Elective deferrals under a TSA are employer contributions made under a salary reduction agreement to the extent the contributions are not includable in gross income for the taxable year. The annual limitation on elective deferrals to a TSA is $17,000 for 2012.[1] See ¶ 3177. Unless corrected, excess deferrals are included in the employee's gross income.[2]

2. A separate limitation on employer contributions for each limitation year applies under Code Sec. 415.[3] The contributions and other additions by the employer may be excluded from an employee's gross income for the tax year to the extent that the aggregate of such contributions and additions does not exceed

the applicable limit under Code Sec. 415 ($50,000 in 2012).[4] See ¶ 3183.

Joint application of contribution limits. In the event that elective deferrals and nonelective contributions are made to a participant's account, the maximum annual contribution is the annual additions limit. By contrast, if only elective deferrals under a salary reduction agreement are made, the contribution ceiling is the lesser of the elective deferral limit or the annual additions limit. Similarly, if only nonelective contributions are made to the 403(b) account, the limit on annual additions applies. [5]

Exception to limits for reemployed veterans

TSAs may allow veterans returning to employment from military service to make up elective deferrals and employee contributions that were not made during the employee's period of military service. Significantly, these "make-up contributions" are *not* subject to the limitations on contributions described above.[6] The employer is required, however, to match any additional elective deferrals and employee contributions at the same rate that would have been required had the contributions been made during the period of uniformed service.[7] These overall rules allow employers to comply with the Uniformed Services Employment and Reemployment Rights Act of 1994 (USERRA) without the loss of tax-favored Code Sec. 403(b) status.[8]

To comply with USERRA, TSAs must permit reemployed veterans to make additional elective deferrals or employee contributions during the period that begins on the date of reemployment and that extends for the lesser of five years or the period of the individual's military service multiplied by three.[9]

☐ See ¶ 1645 and ¶ 8120 of the CCH PENSION PLAN GUIDE for a discussion of USERRA.

---

[1] Code Sec. 402(g).

[2] Code Secs. 403(b)(1).

[3] Code Sec. 415(a)(2)(B).

[4] Code § 403(b)(1).

[5] IRS Publication 571 (Tax-Sheltered Annuity Plans (403 (b) Plans)), at CCH PENSION PLAN GUIDE ¶ 17,005.

[6] Code Sec. 414(u)(1).

[7] Code Sec. 414(u)(2).

[8] These requirements also apply to qualified retirement plans.

[9] Code Sec. 414(u)(2)(A).

¶ 3125
Establishing a Tax-Sheltered Annuity

Only the following employees and individuals may participate in a TSA:

1. employees of public educational systems,

2. employees of organizations described in Code Sec. 501(c)(3) that are exempt from taxation under Code Sec. 501(a), and

3. self-employed ministers (see ¶ 3160).

☐ Independent contractors may not participate in a TSA maintained by an eligible employer (see ¶ 3140).

¶ 3130

Employees of Public Educational Systems

The two key questions that arise here, for purposes of establishing and participating in a TSA, are (1) whether there is a qualified employer, and (2) whether an individual performs services for that employer as an employee.

Qualified employer

Only a state, a political subdivision of a state, or an agency or instrumentality of a state constitutes a qualified employer for employees of a public "educational organization." [1] However, the regulations broaden this definition to include "federal public-supported schools." To be an educational organization, several criteria must be met:[2]

1. The primary function of the institution must be the presentation of formal instruction.

2. A regular faculty and curriculum must be maintained.

3. A regular enrolled body of pupils or students must be in attendance at a site where educational activities are regularly carried on.

"Educational organization" includes primary, secondary, preparatory, and high schools, as well as colleges and universities. If the organization engages in both educational and noneducational activities, it will qualify as an educational organization only if the noneducational activities are *incidental* to the primary educational purpose.[3]

Eligible employees

An individual performs services for an educational organization "if he is performing services as an employee directly or indirectly for such an institution." This test applies equally to the teaching staff and those who are in other positions, without regard to title or salary range.[4]

Direct services. The university president, principal, teacher, clerical employee, or football coach would all be considered to provide direct services to the educational institution as employees.[5] A state employee whose duties are to assist in developing and promoting programs to expand educational programs at all academic levels is eligible to participate in a TSA.[6]

Indirect services. An employee who performs services involving the operation or direction of a state's, or political subdivision's, educational program as carried on through educational institutions provides indirect services. An employee participating in an "in-home" teaching program provides indirect services because the program is an extension of the services provided at the institution as does an individual whose primary activity is to plan, direct, and administer a statewide program of licensure, inspection, and advisory services to private schools.[7]

¶3130

Employees holding elective or appointed office

As a general rule, an individual holding an elective or appointed office is not considered an employee performing services, directly or indirectly, for an educational institution. However, if the individual has received training in, or is experienced in the field of education, he may be considered to be an employee performing services for an educational institution. For example, a regent or trustee of a state university or a member of a board of education is not usually considered to be an employee of an educational institution, whereas a commissioner or superintendent of education will generally be considered an employee.[8]

[1] Code Sec. 403(b)(1)(A)(ii).

[2] Code Sec. 170(b)(1)(A)(ii) and IRS Reg. § 1.170A-9(b).

[3] IRS Reg. § 1.170A-9(b)(1).

[4] IRS Reg. § 1.403(b)-1.

[5] *Ibid.*

[6] IRS Letter Ruling 7747057, 8-25-77.

[7] IRS Reg. § 1.403(b)-1; IRS Letter Ruling 7801019, 10-7-77. Alternatively, see Rev. Rul. 72-390, 1972-2 CB 227, CCH PENSION PLAN GUIDE ¶ 19,175; Rev. Rul. 80-139, 1980-1 CB 88, CCH PENSION PLAN GUIDE ¶ 19,526.

[8] IRS Reg. § 1.403(b)-1.

¶ 3135

Employees of Section 501(c)(3) Organizations

The second group of employees that may participate in a TSA are employees of specific tax exempt organizations listed under Code Sec. 501(c)(3).[1] A wide range of charitable, religious, scientific, public safety, and educational organizations qualify for tax-exempt purposes.[2]

To be exempt, the organization must (1) be *organized* and *operated* exclusively for the tax-exempt purpose for which it was established, (2) not have its net income inure to the benefit of any individual, and (3) not have, as any substantial part of its activities, a program to influence legislation by propaganda or other means (except for certain lobbying activities).[3]

Government instrumentalities

As a general rule, state and municipal agencies and instrumentalities do not qualify as 501(c)(3) organizations. However, if an organization serves the exclusive purposes described in Code Sec. 501(c)(3) *and is a separate entity from the government,* then it may establish a TSA for its employees.[4]

[1] Code Sec. 403(b)(1)(A)(i).

[2] Code Sec. 501(c)(3) defines this class of favored tax-exempt organizations.

[3] Code Sec. 501(c)(3).

[4] Rev. Rul. 60-384, 1960-2 CB 172, CCH PENSION PLAN GUIDE ¶ 18,232.

¶ 3137

Employees of Indian Tribal Governments

Indian tribal governments, including political subdivisions, are treated as states for purposes of being able to establish TSAs.[1] Therefore, educational organizations associated with Indian tribal governments (as defined under Code Sec. 7701(a)(40)) are employers eligible to establish a TSA.

---

[1] Code Sec. 7871(a)(6)(B) and (d).

¶ 3140
Employer-Employee Relationship

A TSA may only be purchased by or on behalf of, an *employee* of an eligible employer. Contributions made to a TSA from an independent contractor will be immediately taxable to the individual.[1] Accordingly, it may be necessary to determine whether an employer-employee relationship actually exists between the organization and individual providing services. This question is more likely to arise in the relationship between Code Sec. 501(c)(3) hospitals and professionals, such as physicians and radiologists who often work with a greater degree of independence than other employees.

Employer-employee or independent contractor

The Supreme Court in *Nationwide Mutual Insurance Company v. Darden*, held that a common-law test determines who qualifies as an employee under ERISA.[2] In Rev. Rul. 87-41 (cited with approval in *Nationwide Mutual*), the IRS identified 20 factors to be weighed in determining whether an employer-employee or independent contractor relationship exists. [3] The factors, which are set forth at CCH PENSION PLAN GUIDE ¶ 8140, are primarily designed to determine the extent to which an employer has control over the performance of an individual's services.

> **CCH Pointer:** Whether a physician is an employee of a hospital depends on the amount of supervision and control exercised by the hospital of the services performed by the physician.[4] Factors that determine whether a physician is an employee of a hospital include whether the individual: furnishes services to other hospitals without the employer's consent; pays an associate or substitute; is allowed to privately practice medicine; is entitled to regular employee fringe benefits; or is subject to the general rules that apply to the hospital's other employees.

---

[1] Rev. Rul. 66-274, 1966-2 CB 446, CCH PENSION PLAN GUIDE ¶ 18,530; Rev. Rul. 70-136, 1970-1 CB 12, CCH PENSION PLAN GUIDE ¶ 18,806.

[2] *Nationwide Mutual Insurance Company v. Darden*, US SupCt (1992), 112 S.Ct. 1344.

[3] Rev. Rul. 87-41, 1987-1 CB 296. While the revenue ruling deals with technical service personnel, such as engineers, designers, drafters, computer programmers, system analysts, and similarly skilled employees, the principles discussed therein should be applicable to this discussion.

[4] For a discussion of the physician as an employee, see *Haugen v. Commissioner*, TC (1971),

TC Memo. 1971-294, CCH Dec. 31,081(M); (pathologist was an employee of a hospital, even though the doctor was not treated as employee of the hospital for FICA and FUTA purposes and a W-2 Wage and Earnings Statement was prepared for only one year, where the doctor could be fired without cause or notice, could not engage in private practice, and did not maintain an office outside the hospital); Rev. Rul. 84, 1953-1 CB 404; Rev. Rul. 57-21, 1957-1 CB 317; Rev. Rul. 66-274, 1966-2 CB 446, CCH PENSION PLAN GUIDE ¶ 18,530; Rev. Rul. 70-269, 1970-2 CB 228; Rev. Rul. 72-203, 1972-1 CB 324; and Rev. Rul. 73-417, 1973-2 CB 332.

¶ 3145
Types of TSA Arrangements

Three different types of funding vehicles—each of which has its own requirements and each of which shares common requirements—may be used to provide retirement benefits for a TSA:

1. annuity contracts (see ¶ 3150);

2. custodial accounts (see ¶ 3155); and

3. retirement income accounts for churches (see ¶ 3160).

¶ 3150
Annuity Contracts

Annuity contracts, which must be purchased from an insurance company, can be individual contracts for each particular employee or a group contract under which each employee has his or her own separate account.[1] With annuity contracts, contributions are invested with an insurance company generally with a guaranteed interest rate or at a variable rate.[2] However, a wide range of investment options can be made available to employees under TSA-annuity contracts and TSA-retirement income accounts.

Features of a TSA-annuity

To be a TSA-annuity contract, an annuity contract must satisfy the requirements of Code Sec. 403(b)(1)(A)-(E). If the annuity contract meets these requirements, then amounts contributed by the employer (both through salary reductions and direct employer contributions) for the contract are excluded from gross income for the taxable year of the employee to the extent that the amounts are excludable from gross income to the extent they do not exceed the limit on annual additions under Code Sec. 415. See ¶ 3183.

These requirements are:

1. Only employees of (1) tax-exempt employers described in Code Sec. 501(c)(3) and (2) public educational institutions described in Code Sec. 170(b)(1)(A)(ii); and self-employed ministers may establish TSAs.[3]

2. The insurer must be under a contractual obligation to provide annuity payments and the amounts contributed may not be used for any other purposes (e.g., contributions to an investment fund maintained by a custodian where no annuity obligation is incurred).

3. The annuity must be nontransferable. This means that the insurance contract cannot be sold, assigned, or pledged as security or collateral to any person other than the issuer of the contract.[4] However, loans (assignments or pledges which are treated as loans) may be made from a TSA within specific

limitations; and amounts held under a TSA may be transferred tax-free from one insurance company to another (a transfer of TSAs) and may be rolled over to another TSA or IRA. Rollovers may also be made to a qualified plan or governmental 457 plan. See ¶ 3187.

4. Except for the failure to pay future premiums, employees' rights under an annuity contract to their own elective deferrals must be nonforfeitable. Note, employee salary reduction contributions that are treated as employer contributions are always nonforfeitable.[5]

5. Contribution limits apply in the year that contributions are made, without regard to when the contributions become vested.[6] Specifically, contributions and other additions by an employer to a 403(b) annuity contract will be excluded from an employee's gross income for tax years to the extent that the aggregate of such contributions and additions (when expressed as an annual addition under Code Sec. 415(c)) do not exceed the applicable Code Sec. 415 limits.[7]

6. A TSA (with the exception of certain church plans) must be purchased under a plan that satisfies specified nondiscrimination requirements.[8] The nondiscrimination rules apply to a TSA even if the only contributions are elective deferrals. See ¶ 3185.

7. Elective deferrals may not exceed a specified annual limit.[9] Individuals age 50 and older may make additional "catch-up" contributions. Each TSA contract—rather than the TSA-plan— must provide that elective deferrals cannot exceed the annual limitation.[10] See ¶ 3177.

☐ Applicable distribution restrictions are discussed at ¶ 3187.

Life insurance under a TSA

An individual annuity contract issued after December 31, 1962, or a group annuity contract can provide life insurance protection for the employee. However, the life insurance benefit must be "incidental" to the benefit provided by the retirement annuity and the employee is subject to tax on the cost of the life insurance.[11] The rules for qualified plans regarding whether life insurance protection is incidental to the retirement benefit are equally applicable to TSAs. Separate life insurance policies can be purchased as part of a TSA so long as the death benefit provided is incidental to the retirement benefit.[12]

---

[1] Code Sec. 403(b)(1) and IRS Reg. § 1.403(b)-1.

[2] Rev. Rul. 68-116, 1968-1 CB 177.

[3] Code Secs. 403(b)(1)(A)(i), (ii), and (iii), as amended by P.L. 105-34 (Tax Relief Act of 1997), 1601(d)(1)(5)(B).

[4] Code Sec. 401(g) and IRS Reg. § 1.401-9.

[5] Code Sec. 403(b)(1)(C).

[6] Code Sec. 401(b)(1), as amended by P.L. 107-147 (Job Creation and Worker Assistance Act of 2002), Act Sec. 411(p)(1).

[7] P.L. 107-147 (Job Creation and Worker Assistance Act of 2002), Act Sec. 411(p)(2), repealing Code Sec. 403(b)(6).

[8] Code Sec. 403(b)(1)(D) and 403(b)(12).

⁹ Code Secs. 403(b)(1)(E), 401(a)(30), and 402(g).

¹⁰ Code Sec. 403(b)(1)(E), as amended by P.L. 104-188 (Small Business Job Protection Act).

¹¹ IRS Reg. §1.403(b)-1. See also Rev. Rul. 74-115, 1974-1 CB 100, CCH Pension Plan Guide ¶19,308; Rev. Rul. 68-31, 1968-1 CB 151, CCH

Pension Plan Guide ¶18,606; Rev. Rul. 61-121, 1961-1 CB 65, CCH Pension Plan Guide ¶18,405; Rev. Rul. 70-611, 1970-2 CB 89; and Rev. Rul. 69-146, 1969-1 CB 132, CCH Pension Plan Guide ¶18,709.

¹² IRS Letter Ruling 9324042, March 25, 1993, CCH Pension Plan Guide ¶17,384H.

¶3155

Custodial Accounts

TSAs can be placed in custodial accounts so long as the funds are invested in mutual funds. Therefore, only one type of investment is permissible with TSA custodial accounts—regulated investment company stock (e.g., mutual funds).[1] Amounts contributed to a TSA-custodial account will be treated as contributed by an employer for an annuity contract if the following requirements are met.

Custodial account

The assets must be held by a bank or any other party that can fulfill certain IRS requirements. A bank is (1) any bank described in Code Sec. 581, (2) an insured credit union within the meaning of section 101(6) of the Federal Credit Union Act, and (3) a corporation which under the state law of its incorporation is subject to state supervision and examination.[2]

Nonbank custodian. The IRS provides a specific procedure (including payment of a user fee) for receiving approval as a nonbank custodian of a Code Sec. 403(b)(7) custodial account.[3]

Limitations on distributions

With the exception of qualified reservist distributions, amounts may be paid or made available from a custodial account only upon the occurrence of specified events: death, attainment of age 59½, severance from employment, and disability (within the meaning of Code Sec. 72(m)(7)); and only from salary reduction contributions in the event of financial hardship.[4] Unlike 401(k) plans (see ¶2989), distributions on account of plan termination cannot be made from a TSA. A custodial account-TSA that pays dividends as distributions before the employee has satisfied any of the access restrictions, rather than reinvesting these dividends, violates this rule and causes the TSA to lose its tax-deferred status.

CCH Pointer: The final regulations provide that a severance from employment occurs when an employee ceases to be employed by an eligible employer, even if the employee may continue to be employed by an entity that is part of the same controlled group but is not an eligible employer. A severance from employment also occurs when an employee ceases working for a public school, but continues to work for the same state employer.

Financial hardship. Salary reduction contributions may be distributed from a custodial account in the event a participant incurs a financial hardship. However, earnings on salary reduction contributions cannot be distributed for financial hardship.[5]

Loans

The IRS has ruled that custodians may make loans from a TSA custodial account and hold the note as a plan asset.[6] TSA loans must comply with the requirements applicable to loans from qualified plans (e.g., repayment within five years (see ¶ 2000—¶ 2030). In addition, plans subject to ERISA (see ¶ 3192) must satisfy the conditions specified for exemption from the prohibited transaction rules (see ¶ 2029).

General requirements for TSAs

Because a custodial account is treated as an annuity contract for purposes of the exclusion allowance under Code Sec. 403(b), the general requirements applicable to annuity contracts are equally applicable. Therefore, a custodial account must satisfy the requirements of Code Sec. 403(b)(1)(A)-(E), as noted above.[7]

Required distributions

The same rules regarding when minimum distributions are required to begin that apply to annuity contracts apply to custodial accounts.[8] See ¶ 1800 and following for a discussion of required distributions from qualified plans.

Exempt status of custodial account

Amounts contributed to a custodial account and the earnings on those contributions are treated as if they were contributed to a qualified retirement plan and trust under Code Sec. 401(a) solely for purposes of exempting them from taxation.[9]

Excise tax

The excise tax under Code Sec. 4973 applies to excess contributions to TSA custodial accounts.

[1] Code Secs. 403(b)(7) and 403(b)(7)(A)(i). A "regulated investment company" is defined in Code Sec. 851(a), and must be a domestic corporation.

[2] Code Secs. 403(b)(7)(A) and 408(n).

[3] Rev. Proc. 2011-4, Sec. 3.09, I.R.B. 2011-1, 1-3-11, at CCH Pension Plan Guide ¶ 17,299T-54. The applicable user fee is set forth in Rev. Proc. 2011-8, Sec. 6.01(6), I.R.B. 2011-1, 1-3-11, at CCH Pension Plan Guide ¶ 17,299T-58.

[4] Code Sec. 403(b)(7)(A)(ii). Prior to 2002, distributions were authorized for "separation from service."

[5] H. Rpt. No. 99-841, 99th Cong., 2d Sess. at II-453 and 455.

[6] IRS Letter Ruling 9107027, 11-20-90.

[7] Code Sec. 403(b)(7)(A).

[8] Code Sec. 403(b)(10).

[9] Code Sec. 403(b)(7)(B).

¶ 3160

Retirement Income Accounts of Churches

Separate rules apply to churches and certain church organizations that allow contributions to be made on behalf of their employees to purchase annuity contracts and custodial accounts under Code Sec. 403(b).[1] Like the custodial account, a retirement income account will be treated as a tax-sheltered annuity contract if it satisfies the requirements highlighted below.

☐ Self-employed ministers and church employees are generally subject to the same annual additions limit (i.e., lesser of $50,000 (for 2012) or 100% of includible compensation) that applies to other 403(b) plan participants. However, church employees may elect an alternative limit. See ¶ 3183.

Retirement income account defined

A retirement income account must be a defined contribution program established and maintained by a church, or a convention or association of churches, to provide retirement benefits under a TSA for its employees or beneficiaries.[2] Under the program each employee must have his own separate account to which contributions are made.

> **CCH Pointer:** A retirement income account differs from a TSA annuity contract or TSA custodial account because it does not have to be maintained by an insurance company or custodian.

A life annuity can generally only be provided from an individual account by the purchase of an insurance annuity contract. However, in light of the special rules applicable to church retirement income accounts, the final regulations permit a life annuity to be paid from such an account if certain conditions are satisfied.

Self-employed ministers

Ministers who are self-employed in the exercise of their ministry or who are employed by entities other than a 501(c)(3) tax-exempt organization and with which the minister shares common religious bonds can participate in retirement income accounts.[3] A self-employed minister is treated as employed by a tax-exempt organization that is a qualified employer.

> **CCH Pointer:** Self-employed ministers (like all other individual taxpayers) may not establish a 403(b) account for their own benefit. Only the organization (denomination) with which the self-employed minister is associated may set up the account.[4]

Commingling of assets

The assets of a retirement income account can be commingled in a common fund with other amounts devoted exclusively to church purposes, such as a fund maintained by a church pension board, if the following three criteria are satisfied:

1. The common trust fund must be able to separately record the assets of each account so that at any given time it is possible to determine the account's interest in the fund.

2. Investment performance is based on gains and losses on those assets.

3. The common trust fund, and therefore each separate account, cannot be used or diverted for any purpose other than the

exclusive benefit of the employees (and their beneficiaries) covered by the account.[5]

Administrative costs

The reasonable expenses of administering a retirement income account may be charged against the account, including the allocable expense of participating in a common fund.[6]

Exceptions to general annuity requirements

Even though a retirement income account is treated like an annuity contract under Code Sec. 403(b), not all the requirements of Code Sec. 403(b)(1)(A)-(E) (see ¶ 3150) must be satisfied. Specifically, the following two exceptions to the annuity requirements apply:

1. Retirement income accounts can only be purchased by employers that are church and church-related associations.

2. The nondiscrimination requirements that are applicable to TSAs do not apply to all retirement income accounts, but clearly apply to some.[7]

Distributions

The rules relating to the required beginning date for minimum distributions, the restrictions on the events that trigger permissible distributions, transfers and rollovers, and taxability of distributions are the same as for Code Sec. 403(b)(1) annuity contracts. See ¶ 3187.

Compensation

Once a minister's compensation is taken into account for purposes of determining contributions under a retirement income account, the same compensation cannot be taken into account under a non-church plan.[8]

---

[1] Code Sec. 403(b)(9).

[2] Code Sec. 403(b)(9)(B). This includes an organization described in Code Sec. 414(e)(3)(A).

[3] Code Secs. 414(e)(5)(A) and (B), and 404(a)(10).

[4] IRS Publication 571 (Tax-Sheltered Annuity Plans (403(b) Plans), at CCH Pension Plan Guide ¶ 17,005.

[5] IRS Reg. § 1.403(b)-9(a)(2). See also the *General Explanation of the Revenue Provisions of the Tax Equity and Fiscal Responsibility Act of 1982,* H.R. 4961, 97th Cong. at 329-333. P.L. 97-248 (Tax Equity and Fiscal Responsibility Act of 1982), Sec. 251(e)(5).

[6] *Ibid.*

[7] Code Secs. 403(b)(1)(D) and 403(b)(12)(B).

[8] Code Sec. 414(e)(5)(D).

¶ 3163
Roth 403(b) Plans

403(b) plans may incorporate a "qualified Roth contribution program," pursuant to which participants may elect to have all or a portion of their elective deferrals to the plan designated as after-tax "Roth contributions." A participant will be subject to income tax on the contribution at the time of deferral. However, qualified distributions from a designated Roth account are not subject to tax.[1] Similar to Roth

IRAs, earnings on amounts contributed to Roth 403(b) plans grow tax-free and are not subject to income tax upon distribution, provided a five-year nonexclusion period has been satisfied.

The rules for Roth 403(b) arrangements, including those governing the amount of annual deferrals, rollovers, conversions to Roth IRAs, and the separate accounting of Roth and 403(b) contributions, are similar to those that apply to Roth 401(k) arrangements. See ¶ 2941.

> **CCH Pointer:** The July 2007 final regulations do not address the taxation of a distribution of designated Roth contributions from a 403(b) plan. The final rules, however, relating to elective deferrals under a 403(b) plan that are designated Roth contributions are substantially unchanged from the proposed regulations that were issued in January 2006 regarding designated Roth accounts under a 403(b) plan.[2]

---

[1] Code Sec. 402A.

[2] Preamble to final regulations at CCH PENSION PLAN GUIDE ¶ 24,508U.

¶ 3165
Salary Reduction Agreements

The primary method by which employees contribute to TSAs is through a reduction in salary or the agreement to forego future salary increases, both of which are referred to as "salary reduction arrangements." TSAs are purchased by the employer for its employees.[1] What this means, as a practical matter, is that the employer brings its employees and the provider together and gives the provider the opportunity to sell its annuity product to the employees, thereby allowing for the insurance company or mutual fund to hold and invest the TSA contributions. Often the employer will select the provider for the employees. The employer then becomes the conduit for the transfer of the employees' deferred salary. Election forms, which are generally provided by the insurer or custodian, are used to provide the terms of the salary reduction agreement.

> **CCH Pointer:** The prerequisite conditions for the exclusion from gross income for 403(b) contributions must be satisfied in form and operation in the 403(b) contract. The IRS final regulations retain the requirement from the 2004 proposed rules that a 403(b) contract be maintained pursuant to a written plan which, in both form and operation, satisfies the requirements of Code Sec. 403(b).[2] However, in response to comments, the final rules clarify the requirement that the plan include all of the material provisions by permitting the plan to incorporate by reference other documents, including the insurance policy or custodial account, which as a result of such reference would become part of the plan. As a result, a plan may include a wide variety of documents. For example, the 403(b) contract must expressly include the Code Sec. 402(g) deferral limit. However, a single plan document would not be required.

Tax-deferred contributions

Under a salary reduction arrangement, an employee contributes what otherwise would have been compensation to a TSA. Amounts contributed to a TSA by salary reduction are also referred to as elective deferrals.[3] The effect of the salary reduction agreement is that the contributed amounts are not included in current compensation of the employee, and they remain tax-deferred in the TSA until distributed at a later date.[4] The agreement should spell out the terms of the salary reduction.

FICA taxation of 403(b) contributions under salary reduction agreements

Elective deferrals to a 403(b) plan, like contributions to a 401(k) plan, are subject to FICA tax withholding. However, final IRS regulations issued in November 2007 subject a wider variety of 403(b) contributions to FICA tax by expanding the definition of 403(b) salary reduction agreements beyond the definition of elective deferrals that applies for income tax purposes. The final regulations adopt without change temporary and proposed rules issued in November 2004 that apply to agreements requiring employers to reduce employee salaries and make contributions to a 403(b) tax-sheltered annuity.

Specifically, the IRS has clarified that a salary reduction agreement, subject to FICA tax withholding, includes a plan or arrangement under which a payment will be made if the employee elects to reduce compensation pursuant to a one-time irrevocable election made at or before the time of initial eligibility to participate in the plan or arrangement. FICA withholding will also be required of mandatory salary reduction contributions that are made by an employee as a condition of employment. The final regulations apply to contributions made to 403(b) plans on or after November 15, 2007. The temporary regulations, which were prospective only, apply to contributions made on or after November 16, 2004.

One-time irrevocable election

Contributions made pursuant to a one-time irrevocable election by the employee at the time of initial eligibility to participate in the salary reduction agreement are *not* elective deferrals.[6] For example, if an employee is required to contribute a fixed percentage of compensation to a TSA as a condition of employment, the contribution will *not* be treated as an elective deferral unless the employer and employee enter into a temporary employment contract.[7]

> **Example:** Kim participates in a TSA. In order to receive employer contributions under the TSA, she is required to elect to defer 3% of salary in the form of mandatory contributions. Kim has the option of terminating this election at any time with respect to amounts not yet earned, although she never terminates her election. The mandatory contributions are elective deferrals because her election is revocable. These contributions are therefore included in applying the Code Sec. 402(g) annual deferral limit (see ¶ 3177). They may also be subject to employment taxes.

Automatic enrollment under salary reduction agreements

Contributions made by a tax-exempt employer to a TSA will not fail to be made under a salary reduction agreement merely because a fixed percentage (e.g., 4%) of a newly hired or current employee's compensation, absent an affirmative election by the employee to receive the amount in cash, is automatically contributed to the plan on the employee's behalf.[8]

Effective opportunity to elect deferred amount in cash. An employee must have an "effective opportunity" to elect to receive in cash the amount that would be automatically contributed to the plan. According to the IRS, an employee has an effective opportunity to elect to receive an amount in cash if the employee: (1) receives notice of the availability of the right to elect to have compensation reduction contributions made and (2) after receiving notice, is allowed a reasonable period before the cash is currently available to make the election to receive the cash.

Automatic enrollment is not a one-time irrevocable election. A contribution is not treated as made under a salary reduction agreement if it is made pursuant to a one-time irrevocable election made by the employee at the time of initial eligibility to participate in the agreement.[9] Under the automatic enrollment arrangement approved by the IRS, employees were notified annually of their compensation reduction percentage and of their right to change the percentage. The right of employees to change the election in the future, the IRS explained, indicated that the contributions were not made pursuant to a one-time irrevocable election.[10]

Eligible Automatic Contribution Arrangements (Post-2007 Rules)

The Pension Protection Act of 2006 expanded upon the automatic enrollment arrangements currently approved by the IRS by, effective for plan years beginning after December 31, 2007, authorizing an eligible automatic contribution arrangement that will enable employers to (1) unilaterally enroll employees in their 403(b) (or 401(k) and 457(b)) plans at a specified percentage of compensation and (2) invest contributions in DOL-approved default investment funds without fear of fiduciary liability and without being subject to state garnishment law restrictions.[11] However, employees must receive an annual notice of their rights under the arrangement including the right not to participate in the arrangement or the right to elect to make contributions at a different percentage of compensation.[12] In addition, employees are allowed a 90-day window within which to request refunds of automatic contributions made under the arrangement. The distributions will be subject to income tax (but not penalty tax) and matching contributions will be forfeited.

Default investment of contributions. Absent an investment election by the participant, contributions under the eligible automatic contribution arrangement will be invested in accord with regulations to be issued by the Department of Labor governing default investment funds.

Annual notice requirement. The benefits of an eligible automatic contribution arrangement to an employer and an employee are conditioned on compliance with an annual notice requirement. Specifically, the administrator of a plan containing an eligible automatic contribution arrangement must, within a reasonable period of time before each plan year provide each employee to whom the arrangement applies with notice of the employee's rights and obligations under the arrangement.[13] The notice must be sufficiently accurate and comprehensive to apprise employees of their rights and be written in manner that is calculated to be understood by the average employee to whom the arrangement applies.[14]

The notice must include an explanation of the employee's rights under the arrangement to elect: (1) not to have elective contributions made on his or her behalf, or (2) to have the elective contributions made at a different percentage.[15]

☐ Automatic enrollment is discussed in greater detail at ¶ 2940A.

Multiple salary reduction agreements

TSA participants may enter into more than one salary reduction agreement per year.[16] Participants may enter into salary reduction agreements with the same frequency as 401(k) plan participants.

[1] Code Sec. 403(b)(1).

[2] IRS Reg. § 1.403(b)-3.

[3] Code Sec. 402(g)(4).

[4] IRS Reg. § 1.403(b)-1.

[6] Code Sec. 402(g)(3) and IRS Reg. § 1.402(g)-1(c).

[7] H. Rpt. No. 841 at II-405.

[8] Rev. Rul. 2000-35, I.R.B. 2000-31, 7-31-2000, CCH Pension Plan Guide ¶ 19,944B.

[9] Code Secs. 402(g)(3) and 403(b)(12).

[10] Rev. Rul. 2000-35, I.R.B. 2000-31, 7-31-2000, CCH Pension Plan Guide ¶ 19,944B.

[11] Code Sec. 414(w)(3), as added by P.L. 109-280 (Pension Protection Act of 2006), Act Sec. 902(d).

[12] Code Sec. 414(w)(4), as added by P.L. 109-280 (Pension Protection Act of 2006), Act Sec. 902(d).

[13] Code Sec. 414(w)(4), as added by P.L. 109-280 (Pension Protection Act of 2006), Act Sec. 902(d).

[14] Code Sec. 414(w)(4)(A), as added by P.L. 109-280 (Pension Protection Act of 2006), Act Sec. 902(d).

[15] Code Sec. 414(w)(4)(B)(i), as added by P.L. 109-280 (Pension Protection Act of 2006), Act Sec. 902(d).

[16] P.L. 104-188 (Small Business Job Protection Act), Sec. 1450(a).

¶ 3177

Annual Limitation on Amount of Elective Deferrals

A TSA must specifically set forth language limiting the amount of elective deferrals that can be contributed annually to a TSA pursuant to a salary reduction agreement by each employee or the TSA will lose its status as a Code Sec. 403(b) plan.[1] Elective deferrals which exceed these limits are includable in gross income.[2] In determining whether this limitation is exceeded on an annual basis, an individual's elective deferrals include all elective deferrals in all plans in which the individual participates (e.g., TSAs, 401(k) plans, SIMPLE plans, and simplified employee pension plans (SEPs)). Thus, the dollar limitation for a taxable year of the employee covers the aggregate of these elective deferrals.[3]

☐ The annual additions limit that must also be applied in determining the total contributions that may be made to an individual account is detailed at ¶ 3183.

Dollar limitation on excludable elective deferrals

The annual dollar limitation on elective deferrals to a TSA is $17,000 for 2012.[4] Special catch-up contribution limits are provided for employees age 50 and older (see below).[5]

Special catch-up election rules for long-term employees

A special catch-up election allows employees who have completed 15 or more years of service with a qualified employer to catch up on funding of their TSA retirement benefits where they might not have been able to do so earlier. Any employee who has completed 15 years of service with an educational organization, hospital, home health service agency, health or welfare service agency, or church, convention, or association of churches may increase their elective deferral limit by the lesser of:[6]

1. $3,000. **Note:** In no year can the additional salary reductions be more than $3,000. Therefore, the $17,000 limit in 2012 may not be increased above $20,000.

2. $15,000 reduced by elective deferrals excluded from gross income in prior years under the catch-up rule.

3. The excess of (1) $5,000 multiplied by the employee's number of years of service with the qualified employer, less (2) all elective deferrals in prior years under plans of the qualified organization, including a 401(k), SEP, SIMPLE, or other 403(b) plan (but not a governmental 457 plan).

   CCH Pointer: Therefore, in no event can the catch-up election be used if an individual's life-time elective deferrals exceed the individual's life-time limit. Solely for purposes of the special catch-up election, an individual's life-time limit on elective deferrals is $5,000 multiplied by the number of years of service with the qualified organization.

Catch-up contributions for employees age 50 and over

Special "catch-up" contributions are authorized for employees age 50 and over.[7] Unlike the catch-up election described above, which applies only to employees who have provided services for 15 years to qualified organizations that maintain TSAs, catch-up contributions under Code Sec. 414(v) are permitted for any plan participant who will attain at least age 50 before the close of the tax year and for whom no other elective deferrals may otherwise be made to the plan for the plan or other applicable year because of the application of the annual elective deferral limit or any comparable limit or restriction contained in the terms of the plan.[8] It is important to note that catch-up contributions are not included in the elective deferral or annual additions limits. Thus, the maximum amount that may be contributed to a participant's account is the amount authorized under the elective deferral and/or annual additions limit *plus* the applicable catch-up contribution.

The additional amount of elective contributions that are permitted to be made by an eligible individual (under all plans of the employer) is limited to the lesser of (1) the applicable dollar amount (see below) or (2) the participant's compensation for the year reduced by any other elective deferrals of the participant for the year.

Applicable dollar amount. For 403(b) plans, the applicable dollar amount in 2012 is $5,500.[9]

¶3177

CCH Pointer: The IRS regulations governing catch-up contributions specify that, in determining elective deferral limits for a catch-up eligible participant, the otherwise applicable limits under Code Sec. 402(g)(1)(B) "as increased under section 402(g)(7)" shall be further increased by the applicable catch-up limit.[10]

The 2007 final IRS regulations, however, further impose an ordering rule, under which any catch-up contribution for an employee who is eligible for the Code Sec. 414(v) catch-up contribution and the Code Sec. 402(g)(7) catch-up, would be treated first as special 403(b) catch-up contribution and then as an amount contributed as an age 50- catch-up (to the extent an age 50 catch-up amount exceeds the maximum special 403(b) catch-up contribution). [11]

☐ The rules governing catch-up contributions, including the aggregation and universal availability requirements, are discussed in detail at ¶ 2982.

Saver's credit

Lower and middle income taxpayers participating in 403(b) plans may qualify for a nonforfeitable tax credit (i.e. "savers credit") for elective deferrals (up to $2,000 per year) to the plan.[12] The credit is provided in addition to the exclusion from gross income afforded participants making elective deferrals and allows eligible individuals with adjusted gross income below specified inflation adjusted threshold levels to use plan contributions (up to $2,000) to reduce their federal income tax on a dollar-for-dollar basis.

☐ For more detail on the saver's credit, which also applies to 401(k), SIMPLE plans, 457(b) plans, and IRAs, see ¶ 2983.

Correction of excess elective deferrals

Elective deferrals in excess of the annual limit are included in gross income in the year of deferral and will cause the TSA to lose its status as a Code Sec. 403(b) plan. Excess deferrals may be corrected by returning the excess amounts (and allocable income) to the taxpayer during the tax year or by April 15 of the following tax year.[13] The excess deferral (and allocable income) must be distributed no later than April 15 of the year following the year the excess deferral was made.

In the event the excess deferral is distributed by April 15 of the following year: (1) the amount will be included in the participant's income in the year contributed, and (2) earnings will be taxed in the year distributed. However, excess deferrals that are not timely corrected will also be taxed again when they are distributed from the plan. The applicable correction mechanisms are detailed at CCH PENSION PLAN GUIDE ¶ 8195.

---

[1] Code Sec. 401(a)(30).

[2] Code Sec. 402(g). IRS Reg. § 1.402(g)-1(a) refers to amounts in excess of the limits as an individual's excess deferrals.

[3] Code Sec. 402(g)(3) and IRS Reg. § 1.402(g)-1(b).

[4] Code Sec. 402(g)(1).

[5] Code Sec. 414(v).

[6] Code Sec. 402(g)(7).

[7] Code Sec. 414(v), as added by P.L. 107-16 (Economic Growth and Tax Relief Reconciliation Act of 2001).

[8] Code Sec. 414(v), as amended by P.L. 107-147 (Job Creation and Worker Assistance Act of 2002), Act Sec. 411(o).

[9] IRS Reg. § 1.414(v)-1(c)(2).

[10] IRS Reg. § 1.402(g)-2(a).

[11] IRS Reg. § 1.403(b)-4.

[12]Code Sec. 25B, as added by P.L. 107-16 (Economic Growth and Tax Relief Reconciliation Act of

2001), Act Sec. 618(a) and amended by P.L. 109-280 (Pension Protection Act of 2006), Act Sec. 833(a). IRS Announcement 2001-106, I.R.B. 2001-44, 10-29-2001, at CCH PENSION PLAN GUIDE ¶ 17,097R-52.

[13] IRS Reg. § 1.402(g)-1(e).

¶ 3180

The Exclusion Allowance

For years prior to January 1, 2002, an "exclusion allowance" limited the amount of TSA contributions that could be excluded from an employee's income.[1] If an annuity contract (including custodial accounts and retirement income accounts) satisfied all of the applicable requirements set forth in Code Sec. 403(b)(1)(A)-(E), as well as any requirements unique to the particular type of TSA, amounts contributed to the TSA were not includible in gross income for the taxable year, to the extent the contributions did not exceed the employee's exclusion allowance. Rollover contributions from another TSA or an IRA were not taken into account for purposes of calculating the exclusion allowance.

CCH Pointer: The elimination of the exclusion allowance had been scheduled to sunset after 2010, at which time the rules applicable prior to 2002 were to again apply.[2] However, the Pension Protection Act of 2006 repealed application of the EGTRRA sunset rule to retirement plans, thereby permanently eliminating the exclusion allowance.[3]

---

[1]Code Secs. 403(b)(2)(A)—(d), prior to repeal by P.L. 107-16 (Economic Growth and Tax Relief Reconciliation Act of 2001), Act Sec. 632(a)(2).

[2]P.L. 107-16 (Economic Growth and Tax Relief Reconciliation Act of 2001), Act Sec. 901.

[3]P.L. 109-280 (Pension Protection Act of 2006), Act Sec. 811.

¶ 3183

Code Sec. 415 Limitation on Employer Contributions

An additional limitation on the total amount of contributions that may be made to a TSA is based on "annual additions" to the TSA.[1] Annual additions subject to the Code Sec. 415 limits include elective deferrals, nonelective contributions, and after-tax contributions, but not rollovers.

General rule limiting employer contributions

For purposes of the Code Sec. 415 limits, a TSA is treated as a defined contribution plan (DC plan).[2] Accordingly, the limitation on the amount of contributions to an employee's account is the lesser of:[3]

1. $40,000 or

2. 100% of the employee's includible compensation for the most recent year of service.

The $40,000 figure is adjusted for inflation and is $50,000 in 2012.

415 limits apply in the year contributions are made. Unlike the exclusion allowance applicable prior to 2002, the Code Sec. 415 limit applies to contributions made to a TSA whether or not they are vested. The Job Creation and Worker Assistance Act of 2002 further clarified that the Code Sec. 415 limits apply to contributions to a TSA in the year that the contributions are made, without regard to when the contributions become vested. Specifically, contributions and other additions by an employer are excluded from an employee's gross income for the tax year, to the extent that the aggregate of such contributions and additions (when expressed as an annual addition under Code Sec. 415(c)(2)) does not exceed the applicable Code Sec. 415 limits.[4]

Limitation year

The 415 limit is determined on the basis of a limitation year.[5] Only compensation paid or made available during the limitation year is taken into account. The limitation year for TSAs is generally the employee's calendar year.

Treatment of excess contributions

Contributions in excess of the 415 limit are includable in gross income.[6] However, contributions in excess of the Code Sec. 415 limits do cause a TSA to lose its Code Sec. 403(b) status unless excess contributions are held in a separate account.[7]

Includible compensation

Includible compensation refers to compensation received from the employer for the most recent period (ending not later than close of the tax year) which may be counted as one year of service and which precedes the tax year by no more than five years.[8]

Compensation includes elective deferrals. Includible compensation (which is not the same as the income included on the employee's tax return) includes elective deferrals, but does not include employer contributions to the 403(b) account or compensation earned while an employer was not an eligible plan sponsor.[9] By including elective deferrals in the definition of compensation, an employee can make larger annual additions to a TSA before the 415 limit is exceeded.

Correction of excess Code Sec. 415 contributions

Annual additions to a TSA in excess of the 415-limits are generally includable in gross income. Amounts in excess of the annual additions limit that are due to elective deferrals may be distributed to the employee, if among other factors, the excess contributions were attributable to reasonable errors in determining the amount of deferrals that could be made or in estimating the employee's compensation.[10]

Excise tax for excess contributions

A six-percent nondeductible excise tax is assessed on contributions to TSA custodial accounts that exceed the 415 limits. The tax is imposed on the employee, not the employer, and must be paid in each year in which excess contributions are in the account.[11] In addition, Form 5330 (Return of Excise Taxes Related to Employee Benefit Plans) must be filed if an excess contribution has been made to a custodial account that has not been correct. Note, the excise tax does no apply to funds in annuity contracts or to excess deferrals.[12]

☐ See ¶ 8210-8236 of the CCH PENSION PLAN GUIDE for detailed and fully illustrated explanations of: the limitation year, excess annual additions and required corrections, a plan year, compensation, special elections for calculating the 415 limitation, methods for choosing among various election alternatives, aggregation of TSAs with other plans, and the applicable excise tax.

---

[1] Code Sec. 415.

[2] IRS Reg. § 1.415-6(e)(1). Code Sec. 415(a)(2)(B) makes the 415-limits applicable to TSAs.

[3] Code Sec. 415(c)(1).

[4] Code Sec. 403(b)(1), as amended by P.L. 107-147 (Job Creation and Worker Assistance Act of 2002), Act Sec. 411(p)(1).

[5] IRS Reg. § 1.415-6(e)(1)(iii).

[6] IRS Reg. § 1.415-6(e)(1)(ii).

[7] IRS Reg. § 1.403(b)-4(f)(2).

[8] Code Sec. 403(b)(3).

[9] Code Sec. 415(c)(3)(E), as added by P.L. 107-16 (Economic Growth and Tax Relief Reconciliation Act of 2001), Act. Sec. 632(a)(3)(D).

[10] IRS Publication 571 (Tax-Sheltered Annuity Plans (403(b) Plans)).

[11] Code Sec. 4973; IRS Publication 571 (Tax-Sheltered Annuity Plans (403(b) Plans)).

[12] IRS Publication 571 (Tax-Sheltered Annuity Plans (403(b) Plans)).

¶ 3185

Nondiscrimination Requirements

TSAs are subject to rules prohibiting discrimination in favor of highly compensated employees (HCEs).[1] The nondiscrimination rules apply to all TSAs purchased by eligible employers, with the exception of church plans and governmental plans.[2]

The rules apply to employer contributions, other than elective deferrals, and employee after-contributions. However, separate nondiscrimination requirements apply (1) to contributions *not* made pursuant to a salary reduction agreement (i.e., employer contributions), and (2) to contributions made pursuant to a salary reduction agreement. The nondiscrimination requirements do not apply to elective deferrals. Rather, a universal availability requirement applies to all Code Sec. 403(b) elective deferrals.

CCH Pointer: The IRS had provided in Notice 89-23 (see CCH PENSION PLAN GUIDE ¶ 17,102A), that the nondiscrimination requirements could be met through a reasonable good faith interpretation of the rules under Code Sec. 403(b)(12). The 2007 final regulations do not include the Notice 89-23 good faith standard. However, the Notice 89-23 good faith standard will continue to apply to state and local public schools and certain church entities for determining the controlled group.

Nonelective and matching contributions or benefits. For contributions not made pursuant to a salary reduction agreement,[3] the nondiscrimination requirements of Code Secs. 401(a)(4) (nondiscrimination in contributions), 401(a)(5) (permitted disparity), 401(a)(17) (limit on compensation), 401(a)(26) (minimum participation), 401(m) (matching employer contributions (i.e., ACP test)), and 410(b) (coverage) apply as if the plan was a qualified plan.

In determining whether nonelective contributions to a TSA are nondiscriminatory, employers may rely on three safe harbors specified by the IRS.[4] The safe harbors are based on the aggregate of all the 403(b) plans to which an employer contributes. In addition, note that the safe harbors do not apply in determining whether matching and employee contributions are discriminatory. However, a 403(b) plan will satisfy the matching contribution requirements under Code Sec. 401(m) by satisfying the ADP test safe harbor (see ¶ 2975), including the making of nonelective or matching contributions.

☐ Safe harbor rules for satisfying the nondiscrimination requirement are set forth at CCH PENSION PLAN GUIDE ¶ 8240.

Elective deferrals. The nondiscrimination rules are met with regard to salary reduction contributions under a plan if all employees of the employer may make elective deferrals in excess of $200.[7] Under the universal availability rule, generally, if any employee of the employer sponsoring the TSA may make elective deferrals (including catch-up contributions) under the TSA, the program will be considered discriminatory with respect to elective deferrals unless the opportunity to make elective deferrals of more than $200 is available to all employees on a basis that does not discriminate in favor of HCEs.[8]

CCH Pointer: The final regulations are substantially similar to those in the 2004 proposed rules. The final regulations clarify that the employee's right to make elective deferrals also includes the right to designate Code Sec. 403(b) elective deferrals as designated Roth contributions (if any employee of the eligible employer may elect to have the organization make 403(b) elective deferrals as designated Roth contributions).

Geographically distinct units treated as separate employers. If an employer has historically treated geographically distinct units separately for purposes of employee benefits, each unit may continue to be considered a separate organization under the safe harbor.[11] As a general rule, units that are located within the same Standard Metropolitan Statistical Area are not geographically distinct.

Excludable employees. In applying the nondiscrimination rules, an employer may disregard specified "excludable employees," including: participants in 457 plans; employees eligible to participate in a 401(k) or other 403(b) plan maintained by the same employer; employees who normally work less than 20 hours per week; nonresident aliens; student employees; and employees whose benefits are determined by collective bargaining agreements.[12]

CCH Pointer: The rules would allow employees who normally work less than 20 hours per week to be excluded only if, for the 12-month period beginning on the date of the employee's employment, the employer reasonably expects the employee to work less than 1000 hours, or the employee actually works less than 1000 hours in the preceding 12 month period.[13]

Employers should also be aware that, if an excludable employee is allowed under the plan to make elective deferrals, the proposed regulations would prevent any other comparably situated employee from being excluded. Under this rule, for example, if one non-resident alien or one student performing services for a school is allowed to participate in the plan, then all non-resident aliens and all such students must be allowed to make elective deferrals under the arrangement.[14]

Both elective deferrals and nonelective contributions. If a TSA provides for both elective deferrals and other contributions, the rules provided above apply separately to each class of contribution and the assets that are attributable to each.[15]

Ministers. In general, the nondiscrimination rules do not apply to retirement income account TSAs established and maintained by churches. See ¶ 3160.[16]

Government employers. Governmental plans, other than those maintained by state or local governments, were treated as satisfying the requirements of Code Secs. 401(a)(4), 401(a)(26), 401(k) (3), and 401(m) until the first plan year beginning on or after January 1, 2003.[17] The IRS subsequently indicated that such governmental plans will continue to be treated as satisfying the nondiscrimination requirements until the first day of the first plan year beginning on or after the issuance of final rules on the subject.[18]

Effective for years beginning after August 17, 2006, the moratorium on the application of the nondiscrimination requirements that was previously applicable only to state and local governments has been extended to all governmental plans (including retirement plans established and maintained by Indian tribal governments, subdivisions of Indian tribal governments, or an agency or instrumentality of either).[19]

---

[1] Code Sec. 403(b)(12).

[2] Code Secs. 403(b)(1)(D) and 403(b)(12).

[3] Code Sec. 403(b)(12)(A)(i).

[4] IRS Notice 98-52, Sec. V, 1998-46, 11-16-98, at CCH Pension Plan Guide ¶ 17,115B.

[7] Code Sec. 403(b)(12)(A)(ii).

[8] Code Sec. 403(b)(12)(A)(ii).

[11] IRS Notice 98-52, 1998-46, 11-16-98, at CCH Pension Plan Guide ¶ 17,115B.

[12] Code Sec. 403(b)(12)(A).

[13] IRS Reg. § 1.403(b)-5(b)(4)(ii)(E), CCH Pension Plan Guide ¶ 20,261H.

[14] IRS Reg. § 1.403(b)-5(b)(4)(i), CCH Pension Plan Guide ¶ 20,261H.

[15] IRS Notice 89-23, 1989-1 CB 654, Part I.

[16] IRS Notice 2001-46, IRB 2001-32, 8-6-01 at CCH Pension Plan Guide ¶ 17,121R.

[17] *Ibid.*

[18] IRS Notice 2003-6, I.R.B. 2003-3, 1-21-03, at CCH Pension Plan Guide ¶ 17,125P.

[19] Code Sec. 401(a)(5)(G), as amended by P.L. 109-280 (Pension Protection Act of 2006), Act Sec. 861(a)(1); Code Sec. 414(d), as amended by P.L. 109-280 (Pension Protection Act of 2006), Act Sec. 906(a); ERISA Sec. 4021(b)(2), as amended by P.L. 109-280 (Pension Protection Act of 2006), Act Sec. 906(a).

¶ 3187

Distributions and Taxability

The rules for distributions for TSAs and the taxability of those distributions are basically the same as for qualified plans. The following is a checklist of the some of the major considerations in taking a distribution from a tax-sheltered annuity:

1. ***Required minimum distributions.*** Distributions from a 403(b) plan must meet the required minimum distribution rules of Code Sec. 401(a)(9).[1] Specifically, the 403(b) plan participant must begin receiving a specified required minimum distribution from the plan by April 1 of the calendar year following the later of the calendar year in which the participant attains age 70 1/2 or the calendar year in which the participant retires. Pre-1987 accruals must begin to be distributed by the later of the end of the calendar year in which the participant attains age 75 or April 1 of the calendar year following retirement.

   In the event that the required minimum distribution is not made, the participant will be assessed a 50% excise tax on the difference between the required minimum distribution and the amount that was actually distributed.[2] However, the IRS is empowered with discretionary authority to waive the excise tax where the payee can establish that the shortfall was due to reasonable error (e.g., miscalculation of distribution formula) and that reasonable steps are being taken to correct the error.[3]

   CCH Pointer: For ***2009***, pursuant to the Worker, Retiree, and Employer Recovery Act of 2008 (P.L. 110-458), the required minimum distribution rules do not apply to any qualified tax-sheltered annuity plan under Code Sec. 403(b). As a result, plan participants and beneficiaries will not be required by law to take required minimum distributions for the year. The change in the law suspends, ***for 2009 only***, the requirement that covered plans and arrangements contain provisions requiring required minimum distributions. It does not require that any plan or arrangement actually eliminate the plan's distribution requirement for 2009. Plans and arrangements must be formally amended to eliminate the requirement.

   ☐ The required minimum distribution rules are detailed beginning at ¶ 1800.

2. ***Rollovers.*** Rollovers may be made between TSAs and between TSAs and IRAs without incurring tax liability. In addition, an employee participating in a 403(b) plan may roll over an eligible rollover distribution tax-fee to another eligible retirement account, including a qualified plan (e.g., 401(k) plan) and a governmental 457 plan, as well as to another 403(b) plan or IRA.[4] Similarly, eligible rollover distributions from a qualified plan,

IRA, or governmental 457 plan may be rolled over tax free to a 403(b) plan.[5]

Eligible rollover distributions. The rollover amount is limited to the sum that, except for the rollover, would be taxable. In addition, required minimum distributions, hardship distributions, corrective distributions of excess contributions or excess deferrals (and income allocable to the excess), and substantially equal payments made over the participant's life expectancy or the joint lives or life expectancy of the participant and beneficiary may not be rolled over.

After-tax contributions. After-tax contributions may be rolled over from a 403(b) plan to another 403(b) plan. However, prior to 2007, after-tax contributions from a qualified plan could not be rolled over to a 403(b) plan. Effective, beginning in 2007, distributions of after-tax contributions from a qualified plan may be rolled over to a 403(b) plan or a qualified defined benefit plan.[6] The rollover must be executed through a direct trustee-to-trustee transfer and the plan must separately account for the after-tax amounts (including related earnings).

Rollovers between Roth 403(b) and pre-tax 403(b) plans. A Roth 403(b) (see ¶ 3163) may authorize a participant to roll over a distribution to another Roth 403(b) plan or to a Roth IRA. However, a distribution from a pre-tax 403(b) plan may not be rolled over to a Roth 403(b) plan. Similarly, participants in a Roth 403(b) plan may not roll over distributions to a traditional 403(b) plan.

Direct rollover of 403(b) distribution to Roth IRAs. Prior to 2008, a 403(b) plan participant could not directly roll over a distribution to a Roth IRA. The funds had to be directly rolled over to a traditional IRA and then converted to a Roth IRA. However, effective for distributions made after 2007, the Pension Protection Act of 2006 authorizes the direct rollover of 403(b) plan assets to a Roth IRA via a trustee-to-trustee transfer.[7] The rollover of 403(b) assets to a Roth IRA is subject to the rules that apply to rollovers from a traditional IRA to a Roth IRA. Accordingly, for tax years prior to 2010, a rollover to a Roth IRA will be allowed only if, for the tax year of the distribution to which the contribution relates, the taxpayer's adjusted gross income does not exceed $100,000 and the taxpayer is not a married individual filing a separate return (see ¶ 3225).

Automatic rollover rules. The automatic rollover rules, which require cash out distributions of more than $1,000 and less than or equal to $5,000 from a qualified plan to be paid in a direct rollover to an IRA, absent an affirmative election by the distributee to have the amount rolled over to an eligible retirement plan or receive the distribution directly (see ¶ 1971), apply to 403(b) plans.[8]

Withholding on distributions that are not directly rolled over. Amounts that are not directly rolled over, but that are distributed to employees and then rolled over within 60 days, are subject to mandatory 20% withholding.

Hardship distributions. Hardship distributions from a 403(b) plan are not eligible rollover distributions.[9] Accordingly, hardship distributions are not subject to 20 percent withholding.

Spousal rollovers. The surviving spouse of a deceased 403(b) plan participant may make a tax-free rollover of a distribution from the participant's plan in the same manner as if the spouse were the participant.[10] Under such circumstances, the surviving spouse is not required to begin receiving minimum distributions until he or she attains age 70 ½.

Nonspousal beneficiary rollovers. Nonspousal beneficiaries (e.g., children, siblings, domestic partners) of 403(b) plan participants were not, prior to 2007, authorized to roll over distributions to an IRA or other plan. Nonspousal beneficiaries were generally required to take the distribution in a lump-sum, subjecting the beneficiary to an immediate tax liability. However, effective for distributions after 2006, distributions from a 403(b) plan to a designated nonspouse beneficiary may be directly rolled over to an IRA (but not to a 401(k) plan or 457(b)) plan via a trustee-to-trustee transfer.[11] The transfer will be treated as an eligible rollover distribution for purposes of Code Sec. 402(c)(11) (as long as the amount is not actually received by the nonspouse beneficiary). In addition, the transferred amounts will not be included in the nonspouse beneficiary's gross income in the year of distribution.[12]

CCH Pointer: The Worker, Retiree, and Employer Recovery Act of 2008 (P.L. 110-458) made several adjustments to the nonspouse beneficiary rollover provisions. Significantly, qualified retirement plans must allow direct rollovers for nonspouse beneficiary distributees, because such rollovers are no longer treated as eligible rollover distributions "only" for Code Sec. 402(c) rollover purposes. Thus, the mandatory rollover rules in Code Sec. 401(a)(31) apply. Additionally, 403(a) plans, 403(b) plans and 457 plans also must allow direct nonspouse beneficiary rollovers because these plans incorporate the Code Sec. 402(c)(11) rules for nonspouse beneficiary rollovers.

IRA will be treated as inherited IRA of nonspousal beneficiary. The IRA to which the funds are transferred must have been established in the name of the plan participant, payable to the nonspousal beneficiary (e.g., "Tom Smith as beneficiary of John Smith").[13] The beneficiary may not transfer the inherited amounts to his or her own

IRA. In addition, because the nonspouse beneficiary will not be treated as the owner of the rolled over assets, the inherited IRA may not be subsequently rolled over to his or her own IRA.

☐ The rules governing rollovers are detailed at ¶ 1950—1974.

3. *Loans.* Loans may be made from a TSA under the same rules that apply to qualified plans (see discussion beginning at ¶ 2000). The 2007 final rules adopted the loan provisions from the 2004 proposed regulations.

4. *Excess accumulations and contributions.* Excise taxes no longer apply to excess accumulations that result from the failure to make required minimum distributions, excess contributions, and excess distributions.

5. *Taxation of distributions.* Distributions from a 403(b) plan are taxable as ordinary income, generally under the same rules that apply to distributions from other retirement plans. In addition, TSA distributions are subject to the additional tax that is assessed on premature distributions made to a participant prior to attaining age 59½ or the occurrence of other specified events.

6. *Form of distribution.* The form that a distribution from a TSA can take is very similar to the form of a distribution from a qualified retirement plan. For example, a distribution can be in the form of a single sum, periodic payments for the life of the employee, or periodic payments for the life of the employee and co-annuitant, or as a joint and survivor annuity.

Restrictions on distributions

There are restrictions on the time before which distributions can be made from TSAs-annuity contracts and TSA-retirement income contracts.[14] These are generally the same restrictions that are applicable to custodial accounts under Code Sec. 403(b)(7) (see ¶ 3155). They limit the events upon which distributions can be made prior to separation from employment. These limitations only apply, however, to contributions made pursuant to a salary reduction agreement.[15] Therefore, nonelective contributions may be distributed without regard to the limitation.

Under these rules, salary reduction contributions can be distributed from an annuity contract or retirement income contract only when the employee dies, attains age 59½, has a severance from employment, becomes disabled (within the meaning of Code Sec. 72(m)(7)), or experiences financial hardship.[16]

CCH Pointer: *Hardship distributions to nonspousal beneficiaries.* The current safe harbor rules authorize a distribution upon a hardship incurred by a participant's spouse or dependent. The Pension Protection Act requires the Treasury to modify the governing regulations to provide that, if an event (including the occurrence of a medical expense) would constitute a hardship if it occurred with respect to the participant's spouse or dependent, the event will, to the extent permitted by the plan, constitute a hardship if it occurs with respect to a person who is a beneficiary under the plan with respect to the beneficiary.[17]

The IRS has clarified that a plan may, beginning on August 17, 2006, permit distributions for medical, tuition, and funeral expenses for an individual who is named as a beneficiary under the plan and who has an unconditional right to all or a portion of the participant's account balance under the plan upon the death of the participant.[18]

Nontaxable transfers between TSAs

There are a number of situations where TSA assets held on behalf of an employee will be "distributed" from the TSA, but the transaction will not be considered a distribution, but rather, a nontaxable transfer. The IRS, in a 1990 Revenue Ruling (now made obsolete by the 2007 final regulations), set forth those methods of transfer between different types of TSAs that it would treat as transfers and not taxable distributions.[19]

The following types of transfers between TSAs were considered nontaxable distributions, under the Revenue Ruling, regardless of whether a complete or partial interest was being transferred or whether the transferring individual was a current employee, a former employee, or a beneficiary of a former employee.

1. *403(b)(1) annuity to a 403(b)(1) annuity,* if the transferred funds are not subject to the Code Sec. 403(b)(11) restrictions on distributions because the TSA was purchased entirely with nonelective contributions.

2. *403(b)(1) annuity to a 403(b)(7) custodial account,* if the transferred funds are not subject to the early distribution restrictions.

3. *403(b)(7) custodial account to a 403(b)(7) custodial account,* if the transferred funds continue to be subject to the early distribution restrictions under Code Sec. 403(b)(7)(A)(ii).

4. *403(b)(7) custodial account to a 403(b)(1) annuity,* if the transferred funds were subject to Code Sec. 403(b)(7)(A)(ii) restrictions on distributions and will continue to be subject to identical early distribution restrictions.

5. *403(b)(1) annuity to a 403(b)(1) annuity,* if the transferred funds were subject to the early distribution restrictions under Code Sec. 403(b)(11) and continue to be subject to the restrictions after the transfer.

6. *403(b)(1) annuity to a 403(b)(7) custodial account,* if the transferred funds were subject to the Code Sec. 403(b)(11) restrictions on distributions and will continue to be subject to the same or more stringent restrictions after the transfer.

CCH Pointer: The 2007 final regulations, effective for tax years after December 31, 2008, provide for three kinds of nontaxable exchanges or transfers of amounts in 403(b) contracts: (1) a contract exchange (a change of investment within the same plan); (2) a plan-to-plan transfer, where another employer plan is receiving the exchange; or (3) a transfer to purchase permissive service credit. If an exchange or transfer does not constitute a contract exchange, plan-to-plan transfer, or purchase of permissive service credit, it is treated as a taxable distribution of benefits if the exchange occurs after a distributable event (unless it is rolled over to an eligible retirement plan) or as a taxable conversion to a nonqualified annuity if a distributable event has not occurred. The regulations generally allow contract exchanges with certain characteristics associated with Rev. Rul. 90-24, but under rules that are generally similar to those applicable to qualified plans.

Trustee-to-trustee transfer for purchase of permissive service credit. Amounts may be transferred, via a trustee-to-trustee transfer, from a 403(b) plan to a governmental defined benefit plan for the purchase of permissive service credit (as defined by Code Sec. 415(b)(3)(A)) or the repayment of a cashout under a governmental plan to which Code Sec. 415 does not apply under Code Sec. 415(k)(3).[22]

CCH Pointer: *Expansion of permissive service credit.* Permissive service credit has been defined as credit for a period of service, recognized by the plan for purposes of calculating the employee's plan benefit, which the employee has not received under the plan, but can receive only if he or she voluntarily contributes an amount (actuarially determined under the plan) that does not exceed the amount necessary to fund the benefit attributable to the service credit.[23]

The Pension Protection Act of 2006 expanded the permissive service credit rules to include services relating to benefits to which the plan participant is not otherwise entitled under the governmental plan, rather than service credit which the participant has not received under the plan. Specifically, permissive service credit may include service credit for periods for which there is no performance of service, subject to limits on nonqualified service.

In addition, the Act provided an exemption from the limitations on non-qualified service credit for trustee-to-trustee transfers from a 403(b) plan to a governmental defined benefit plan made in order to purchase permissive service credit. Accordingly, the failure of the transferee plan to satisfy the five years of nonqualified service credit or the five-year participation rule will not cause the transferred amounts to be included in the plan participant's gross income.[24] The special rules for trustee-to-trustee transfer apply regardless of whether the transfer is made between plans maintained by the same employer.

---

[1] Code Sec. 403(b)(10).

[2] IRS Publication 571 (Tax-Sheltered Annuity Plans (403(b) Plans)); Code Sec. 4974; IRS Reg. § 54.4974-2.

[3] Code Sec. 4974(d); IRS Reg. § 54.4974-2.

[4] Code Sec. 403(b)(8)(A)(ii).

[5] Code Sec. 402(c)(8)(B)(iv).

[6] Code Sec. 402(c)(2)(A), as amended by P.L. 109-280 (Pension Protection Act of 2006), Act Sec. 822(a).

[7] Code Sec. 408A(e), as amended by P.L. 109-280 (Pension Protection Act of 2006), Act Sec. 822(a).

[8] Code Sec. 401(a)(31)(B)(i), as added by P.L. 107-16 (Economic Growth and Tax Relief Reconciliation Act of 2001). IRS Notice 2005-5, I.R.B.,

2005-3, 1-18-05, at CCH Pension Plan Guide ¶ 17,130N.

[9] Code Sec. 403(b)(8)(B).

[10] Code Sec. 402(c)(9).

[11] Code Sec. 402(c)(11), as added by P.L. 109-280 (Pension Protection Act of 2006), Act Sec. 829(a)(1); Code Sec. 403(b)(8)(B), as amended by P.L. 109-280 (Pension Protection Act of 2006), Act Sec. 829(a)(3).

[12] Code Sec. 402(c)(11)(A)(i), as added by P.L. 109-280 (Pension Protection Act of 2006), Act Sec. 829(a)(1); IRS Notice 2007-7, Sec. V, Q&A-11, I.R.B. 2007-5, 1-29-07, at CCH Pension Plan Guide ¶ 17,135R.

[13] Code Sec. 402(c)(11)(A)(ii), as added by P.L. 109-280 (Pension Protection Act of 2006), Act Sec. 829(a)(1); IRS Notice 2007-7, Sec. V, Q&A-13, I.R.B. 2007-5, 1-29-07, at CCH Pension Plan Guide ¶ 17,135R.

[14] Code Sec. 403(b)(11).

[15] P.L. 99-514 (Tax Reform Act of 1986), Sec. 1123(c)(1).

[16] Code Sec. 403(b)(11).

[17] P.L. 109-280 (Pension Protection Act of 2006), Act Sec. 826.

[18] IRS Notice 2007-7, Sec. III, Q&A-5, I.R.B. 2007-5, 1-29-07, at CCH Pension Plan Guide ¶ 17,135R; modified by IRS Notice 2007-99 at CCH Pension Plan Guide ¶ 17,137T.

[19] Rev. Rul. 90-24, 1990-1 CB 97, CCH Pension Plan Guide ¶ 19,732 (made obsolete by the 2007 final regulations). See Rev. Rul. 2009-18, I.R.B. 2009-27, 7-6-09 at CCH Pension Plan Guide ¶ 19,948Z-259.

[22] Code Sec. 403(b)(13).

[23] Code Sec. 415(n)(3)(A).

[24] Code Sec. 415(n)(3)(D), as added by P.L. 109-280 (Pension Protection Act of 2006), Act Sec. 821(b).

¶ 3190
Estate and Gift Taxes

The Tax Reform Act of 1986 repealed the estate and gift tax exclusions that previously existed with regard to a TSA purchased on behalf of an employee. In addition, the IRS explains that, a participant who, through an election or the failure to make an election, provides an annuity for beneficiary after his death, may have made a taxable gift equal to the value of the annuity. [1] However, in the event that the gift is an interest in a joint and survivor annuity, under which only the participant and the spouse are entitled to payment, the gift will qualify for the unlimited marital deduction.

[1] IRS Publication 571 (Tax-Sheltered Annuity Plans (403(b) Plans)).

¶ 3192
ERISA Title I Considerations

Legislative and regulatory developments (discussed in the preceding paragraphs) that have effectively equalized the tax treatment of 403(b) plans and qualified 401(k) plans have encouraged eligible tax-exempt and governmental employers to adopt or consider adopting such arrangements. However, nongovernmental employers need to be aware that in adopting and administering a 403(b) arrangement they may be subjecting themselves to unanticipated administrative burdens and regulatory requirements, including fiduciary liability, under ERISA.

In the event that the 403(b) plan is subject to ERISA, the following factors (in addition to other ERISA requirements addressed above) apply.

1. The employer may not require an employee to complete more than one year of service, or to attain an age greater than 21, as a

condition of plan eligibility, unless the plan provides for full and immediate vesting (in which case, two years of service may be required) or is an educational institution (in which case, age 26 may be used as the age requirement).

2. The plan must file the Form 5500 annual report with the EBSA and must distribute summary plan descriptions and summary annual reports to participants and beneficiaries.

3. The plan must be established and maintained pursuant to a written instrument that fully complies with the requirements of ERISA Sec. 402 (including the requirement to provide for a named fiduciary).

4. Plan assets must be held in trust unless the assets are held by an insurer.

5. Fiduciary rules apply, pursuant to which the employer and plan fiduciaries must act prudently in investing plan assets or in electing investment options to be made available to participants.

Plans subject to ERISA

Not all TSAs are subject to the various requirements and standards of ERISA Title I. Plans maintained by governmental employers are exempt from Title I and non-electing church plans (including those maintained, for example, by church-affiliated hospitals). The determinative factor in the application of Title I is whether the TSA is an "employee benefit pension plan" as defined in ERISA. The coverage, reporting and disclosure, summary plan description, summary annual report, and joint and survivor annuity rules of ERISA, for example, apply only to employee benefit pension plans. Therefore, if a TSA does not qualify as a pension plan it is not subject to ERISA Title I.

A TSA, entered into pursuant to a salary reduction agreement, will not be considered an employee benefit pension plan that is established or maintained by an employer for ERISA Title I purposes, if all of the requirements specified under ERISA Reg. § 2510.3-2(f) are met (see CCH PENSION PLAN GUIDE ¶ 8145).[1]

Employer contributions subject plan to Title I coverage. Any employer contributions to a plan will subject a TSA to the requirements of ERISA Title I. Thus, if an employer makes matching contributions to the plan, it will need to comply with Title I.

Power to determine eligibility for distributions may subject employer to ERISA. A plan will need to comply with Title I if the employer is authorized to make determinations regarding an employee's eligibility for hardship or disability distributions (even if the employer makes no contributions to the plan). The exercise of discretion required to make such determinations would exceed the minimal employer involvement required to exempt a plan from Title I.

EPCRS submissions do not subject TSA to ERISA. Employers may correct defects in 403(b) plans through the Employee Plans Compliance Resolution

¶3192

System (EPCRS) (see ¶3194) without subjecting the plan, the employer and the plan administrator to ERISA Title I.

Employer involvement in correction triggers Title I issue. Despite the general rule, the level of an employer's involvement in correcting defects, especially where correction is the proper responsibility of another party, may trigger ERISA coverage. This possibility is particularly acute if the correction requires extensive involvement of the employer in the maintenance and operation of the plan.

> **CCH Pointer:** The preamble to the final regulations notes that the question of whether any particular employer, in complying with the 403(b) regulations, has established or maintained a plan covered under ERISA Title I, will be analyzed on a case-by-case basis, applying the criteria of ERISA Reg. § 2510.3-2(f) and ERISA § 3(2). To assist employers interested in offering their employees access to a TSA that would not be an ERISA-covered plan, the Labor Department issued, in conjunction with the final IRS regulations, a Field Assistance Bulletin to provide additional guidance on the interaction of the safe harbor and the final 403(b) rules.[2]

☐ See ¶8145 and ¶27,035 of the CCH PENSION PLAN GUIDE for a discussion of the ERISA Title I requirements applicable to TSAs.

---

[1] ERISA Reg. § 2510.3-2(f). These factors are detailed at CCH PENSION PLAN GUIDE ¶8145.

[2] Preamble to IRS Reg. § 1.403(b) at CCH PENSION PLAN GUIDE ¶24,508U; Field Assistance Bulle-

tin No. 2007-02, July 24, 2007, at CCH PENSION PLAN GUIDE ¶19,981M. See also Field Assistance Bulletin No. 2010-01, February 17, 2010, at CCH PENSION PLAN GUIDE ¶19,981Z-17.

¶3194
Employee Plans Compliance Resolution System for TSAs

The Employee Plans Compliance Resolution System (EPCRS) sets forth the IRS's voluntary compliance and administrative enforcement structure for 403(b) plans, qualified plans, and SEPs.[1] The EPCRS is a voluntary compliance and enforcement system (encompassing three IRS enforcement programs (Self-Correction Program, Voluntary Correction Program, and Audit Closing Agreement Program)). It addresses plans with failures that would ordinarily result in the loss of tax-deferred status and the resulting loss of tax-deferred benefits. Circumstances within the scope of EPCRS include the failure to comply with: the salary reduction contribution rules of Code Sec. 403(b)(12), the distribution restrictions of Code Sec. 403(b)(7) and 403(b)(11), the compensation limit of Code Sec. 401(a)(17), the required minimum distribution rules, and the direct rollover rules.

Plan sponsors of 403(b) plans with eligible failures as defined in the EPCRS have the option of choosing from among a variety of remedies prescribed by the IRS that will maintain the plan's tax-deferred status (or tax-deferred benefits for adversely affected participants). The type of 403(b) failure, the timeframe in which it was discovered, whether the plan sponsor or plan is under an IRS examination, and the plan sponsor's choice of remedy will determine the nature of correction and whether any fee or dollar sanction will be imposed.

Updated procedures. In September 2008, the IRS released a revenue procedure updating and expanding the EPCRS. The EPCRS has been expanded to cover additional plan failures and includes streamlined application procedures under the Voluntary Correction Program (VCP) for numerous categories of plan failures.

Full correction of failure and restoration of benefits. The prescribed correction methods are all designed to ensure full correction of a qualification failure (i.e., operational, demographic, or employer eligibility failures) and effectively restore the plan to the position it would have been in had the failure not occurred. In addition, the correction must restore (e.g., through corrective allocations and distributions) to current participants and beneficiaries the benefits and rights they would have had if the failure had not occurred.[2] Finally, the correction method should be "reasonable and appropriate" and the method selected should be consistently applied to all similar failures. 403(b) plans may use the corrective methodologies specified in Appendices A and B of the governing Revenue Procedure.[3]

> **CCH Pointer:** ***Exceptions to full correction.*** An exception to the general rule requiring full correction is authorized under limited circumstances where full correction is not possible. For example, full correction may not be required where the administrative cost of determining the exact allocation amount needed to restore a participant's benefit may exceed the actual amount that would be restored.[4]

Effect of correction under EPCRS

If the 403(b) plan sponsor corrects a failure in accordance with the applicable requirements of the SCP, VCP, or Audit CAP, the IRS will not pursue income inclusion for affected participants, or liability for income tax withholding, on account of the failures.[5] However, the correction of a failure may result in income tax consequences to participants and beneficiaries (e.g., participants may be required to include in gross income distributions of excess amounts in the year of distribution). In addition, the correction of a failure does not result in the waiver of any excise tax, FICA or FUTA taxes, or any corresponding withholding obligation that may result from a failure.

Voluntary Fiduciary Correction Program

Fiduciaries of 403(b) plans that are subject to ERISA (see ¶ 3192) and not under examination may also correct specified breaches of fiduciary duty (e.g., failure to timely remit employee contributions to the plan) under the DOL's Voluntary Fiduciary Correction Program. The specified correction methods generally require plan participants and benefits to be restored to the position they would have been in had the breach not occurred. The governing rules are discussed at ¶ 2737.

---

[1] Rev. Proc. 2008-50, I.R.B. 2008-35, 9-2-2008, at CCH PENSION PLAN GUIDE ¶ 17,299S-66, superseding Rev. Proc. 2006-27, I.R.B. 2006-22, 5-30-2006, at CCH PENSION PLAN GUIDE ¶ 17,299R-86.

[2] Rev. Proc. 2008-50, I.R.B. 2008-35, 9-2-2008, at CCH PENSION PLAN GUIDE ¶ 17,299S-66, superseding Rev. Proc. 2006-27, I.R.B. 2006-22, 5-30-2006, at CCH PENSION PLAN GUIDE ¶ 17,299R-86.

[3] Rev. Proc. 2008-50, I.R.B. 2008-35, 9-2-2008, at CCH PENSION PLAN GUIDE ¶ 17,299S-66, superseding Rev. Proc. 2006-27, I.R.B. 2006-22, 5-30-2006, at CCH PENSION PLAN GUIDE ¶ 17,299R-86.

[4] Rev. Proc. 2008-50, I.R.B. 2008-35, 9-2-2008, at CCH PENSION PLAN GUIDE ¶ 17,299S-66, supersed-

ing Rev. Proc. 2006-27, I.R.B. 2006-22, 5-30-2006, at CCH PENSION PLAN GUIDE ¶ 17,299R-86.

[5] Rev. Proc. 2008-50, I.R.B. 2008-35, 9-2-2008, at CCH PENSION PLAN GUIDE ¶ 17,299S-66, superseding Rev. Proc. 2006-27, I.R.B. 2006-22, 5-30-2006, at CCH PENSION PLAN GUIDE ¶ 17,299R-86.

¶ 3196
For More Information

☐ For more information on 403(b) tax-sheltered annuity plans, see ¶ 8100-8360 of the CCH PENSION PLAN GUIDE.

IRAs, SEPs, Keogh Plans— Special Rules

¶ 3200
Overview of Special Rules for IRAs, SEPs, and Keogh Plans

Almost anyone who receives compensation can open an individual retirement account (IRA). In general, a person may contribute no more than $5,000 in 2011 and 2012 (or, if less, 100% of compensation) to an IRA. Individuals age 50 or older will be allowed to make special "catch-up contributions." The deductibility of these IRA contributions depends on whether the individual is an active participant in an employer-sponsored plan; active participants are subject to phase-out rules. Nondeductible contributions may also be made. Although contributions must be made in cash up to the due date of the individual's tax return, IRAs may then invest in a broad array of investments. IRA owners may direct the investment of their IRA assets.

In general, amounts paid out of an IRA are includible in the gross income of the recipient (except for nondeductible contributions, which had been taxed previously). A person's entire interest in an IRA must begin to be distributed to him or her by April 1 of the year after the person reaches age 70½ (except for Roth IRAs—see ¶ 3225). Improper IRA distributions, such as premature or insufficient distributions, are subject to penalties. IRA assets may be rolled over to other IRAs; IRAs may also accept rollovers from qualified retirement plans.

Employers with 100 or fewer employees who received at least $5,000 in compensation from the employer in the preceding year may adopt a Savings Incentive Match Plan for Employees (SIMPLE plan), if they do not currently maintain another qualified plan. The SIMPLE plan, which may be structured as an IRA (or 401(k) (see ¶ 2994), relieves smaller employers of the need to perform complex nondiscrimination testing and to comply with burdensome top-heavy plan and reporting rules.

☐ The special rules for SIMPLE IRAs are discussed at ¶ 3224.

Another type of tax-favored IRA vehicle is the Roth IRA. Under a Roth IRA, contributions are nondeductible. However, "qualified" distributions from a Roth IRA are not includible in the taxpayer's gross income and are not subject to the 10% tax on early withdrawals. Roth IRAs are subject to income phase-out limits. Rollovers from Roth IRAs to ordinary IRAs are allowed under certain circumstances.

☐ The special rules for Roth IRAs are discussed at ¶ 3225.

Simplified Employee Pensions (SEPs), sanctioned by Congress in 1978, provide employers with an easy way to furnish retirement benefits for themselves or their employees. Sponsors of SEPs may contribute up to the lesser of 25% of compensation or $49,000 annually per participant with a minimum amount of administrative complexity and paperwork. A salary reduction SEP (SARSEP) allows employees to defer salary on a tax-favored basis, similar to a 401(k) plan. Starting in 1997, SARSEPs were replaced by SIMPLE plans. However, employers can continue to maintain SARSEPs that were established prior to 1997.

☐ The special rules for SEPs are discussed beginning at ¶ 3226.

Unincorporated businesses, such as sole-proprietorships and partnerships, may establish retirement plans that have nearly identical features to plans of corporations. These plans are popularly called "Keoghs" (named after the Senator who introduced legislation enabling such businesses to establish retirement plans). Keogh plans are similar to corporate plans.

☐ The special rules for Keogh plans are discussed beginning at ¶ 3242.

¶ 3202
INDIVIDUAL RETIREMENT ARRANGEMENTS: Types of IRAs

Ordinarily, an individual establishes his or her own IRA with a bank, savings and loan, brokerage firm, or insurance company. However, in addition to the ordinary kind of IRA set up by individuals, there are several other types of IRAs.

Individual retirement annuities

An individual retirement annuity is an annuity contract (including a joint and survivor contract for the benefit of an individual and a spouse) or an endowment contract issued by an insurance company.[1]

Required features. To be an individual retirement annuity, the annuity or endowment contract must meet the following requirements:

1. The owner's entire interest must be nonforfeitable (i.e., fully vested);

2. The contract must not be transferable by the owner and may not be used as collateral for a loan;

3. The premiums may not be fixed;

4. The annual premium on behalf of any individual must not exceed the applicable dollar limit for the year. Any refund of premiums must be applied, before the close of the calendar year following the year of the refunded premium, toward the payment of future premiums or the purchase of additional benefits; and

5. The owner's entire interest must be distributed (or begin to be distributed) by April 1 of the calendar year following the year in which the employee reaches age 70½. (Roth IRAs are not subject to these minimum distribution rules. See ¶ 3225.)

Employer-sponsored IRAs

Employers (including self-employed persons, labor unions, and other employee associations) can establish IRAs for the exclusive benefit of their employees or members and their beneficiaries.[2] These sponsors can also establish IRAs for the nonemployed spouse of an employee or member.

Also, any employee organization composed of two or more employees may establish an IRA trust for employees. An employee organization can include self-employed individuals. However, there must be some connection between the employees (for example, employees of the same employer, employees in the same industry, etc.) in order for an organization to qualify as an employee association.

Exclusive benefit requirement. The IRA trust or custodial account must meet the usual IRA trust requirements (see ¶ 3204). However, the trust must also make a separate accounting for the interest of each employee or member (or spouse of an employee or member). "Separate accounting" means that separate records must be maintained for the interest of each individual for whose benefit the trust (or custodial account) is maintained.[3]

The assets of the trust (or custodial account) may be held in a common trust fund, common investment fund, or common fund for the account of all individuals who have an interest in the trust (or custodial account). An employer- or union-sponsored IRA trust does not violate the exclusive benefit requirement even if it maintains an account for former employees or members and employees who are temporarily on leave.[4]

Contribution limits. Employer-sponsored IRAs are subject to the regular IRA contribution limits (see ¶ 3206).[5] If an employer provides an IRA for its employees, but does not contribute the maximum amount, the individual employees may contribute the difference.

> **CCH Pointer:** As a practical matter, employers should take care to keep employees informed about how much has been contributed to IRAs on their behalf. This action could help prevent employees from inadvertently exceeding their maximum annual IRA contribution limit.

Payroll deduction IRAs

Rather than sponsoring IRAs, employers may instead set up a payroll deduction IRA program for their employees.[6] In this situation, an employer collects employee IRA contributions by deducting amounts from paychecks of participating employees and by transferring withheld funds to the IRA sponsor.

A payroll deduction IRA is not considered a pension plan within the meaning of ERISA (and thus is not covered by its reporting requirements) if:

1. no contributions to the IRA are made by an employer or employee association;

2. participation of employees or members is completely voluntary;

3. without employer endorsement of the sponsor, the sole involvement of the employer or employee organization is (a) to permit

a sponsor to sponsor or publicize the program to employees or members, (b) to collect contributions through payroll deductions or dues checkoffs, and (c) to remit the contributions to the sponsor; and

4. the employer or employee organization receives no compensation other than reasonable compensation for services actually rendered in connection with payroll deductions or dues checkoffs.

CCH Pointer: Employers offering payroll deduction IRAs may display their corporate name or logo on material giving information about the payroll deduction system, answer employee queries about the payroll deduction, and forward queries about the IRA to the sponsor. They may also pay administrative fees to the IRA sponsor or collect reasonable compensation for operating the payroll deduction system. Also, employers may limit the number of investment vehicles funded through the payroll deduction system, provided certain conditions are met.[7] However, employers offering payroll deduction IRAs may not provide any additional benefit or promise any particular investment return. They may not endorse an IRA sponsor or its products, or fail to disclose costs or assessments associated with an employee's ability to transfer or roll over IRA contributions to another IRA sponsor. Finally, employers may not negotiate special terms for its employees that are not generally available to purchasers of the IRA and may not profit from the arrangement.

Deemed IRAs under employer plans

If a qualified plan allows employees to make voluntary employee contributions to a separate account or annuity under the plan and, under the terms of the plan, the account or annuity meets the requirements of Code Sec. 408 for traditional IRAs or Code Sec. 408A for Roth IRAs, then the account or annuity will be deemed to be an IRA and not a qualified plan.[8] Further, a qualified plan will not lose its qualified status solely as a result of establishing and maintaining a deemed IRA program. Qualified employer plans maintained by governmental employers are eligible to establish deemed IRAs.

CCH Pointer: This provision in effect allows employers to set up traditional or Roth IRAs on behalf of their employees without impacting any other qualified plans of the employer.

The trustee or administrator of an IRA must generally be a bank. However, nonbank trustees that have received approval of the IRS may also serve as IRA trustees or custodians. See ¶ 3204. Under IRS regulations, governmental units are permitted to serve as nonbank trustees of deemed IRAs. [9] Governmental plans, including 403(b) and 457 plans, are exempt from the net worth and other requirements generally applicable to nonbank trustees.[10]

The deemed IRA and contributions to it are subject to ERISA's administration and enforcement rules in a manner similar to their application to SEPs.[11]

Qualified plans and deemed IRAs are separate entities. Qualified employer plans and deemed IRAs are, generally, to be treated as separate entities that are subject to the separate rules applicable to qualified plans and IRAs. Thus, eligibility, participation, disclosure, nondiscrimination, contribution, distribution, investment, and plan administration issues that arise with respect to the qualified plan are to be resolved under the rules applicable to qualified employer plans and not under the rules governing IRAs.[12]

> **CCH Pointer:** *Separate trust need not be created for each deemed IRA.* Deemed IRAs may be held in separate individual trusts, a single trust separate from a trust maintained by the qualified plan, or in a single trust that includes the qualified plan. In the event, however, that deemed IRAs are held in single trust that includes the qualified employer plan, a separate account must be maintained for each deemed IRA.[13]

Sample plan amendments. The IRS has provided a sample plan amendment that constitutes a reasonable, good faith interpretation of EGTRRA and will, thus, enable plan sponsors to implement deemed IRAs.[14]

Conduit IRAs

Part or all of a distribution received from a qualified plan may be transferred to another qualified plan through the medium of an IRA. This type of IRA, known as a "conduit IRA," serves as a holding account between employer plans. However, the conduit IRA must have no assets (such as regular, nonrollover IRA contributions) other than those which were previously distributed to the individual from the qualified plan. Also, the transferee qualified plan must provide for the acceptance of the amounts. With the liberalization of the rollover rules beginning in the 2002 tax year, conduit IRAs will no longer be the only way to transfer assets betwen different types of employer plans.

☐ See ¶ 3218 for a discussion of rollovers from qualified plans.

SIMPLE IRAs

Employers with 100 or fewer employees who received at least $5,000 in compensation from the employer in the preceding year may adopt a Savings Incentive Match Plan for Employees (SIMPLE plan), if they do not currently maintain another qualified plan.[15] The SIMPLE plan, which may be structured as an IRA, allows employees to make elective contributions of up to $11,500 per year in 2012 (and 2011) and requires employers to make matching contributions. Individuals age 50 or over will be allowed to make special "catch-up contributions." Assets in the account are not taxed until they are distributed to an employee, and employers may generally deduct contributions to employees' accounts. In addition, the SIMPLE plan is not subject to the nondiscrimination rules (including top-heavy provisions) and other complex requirements applicable to qualified plans.

☐ The special rules for SIMPLE IRAs are discussed at ¶ 3224.

¶3202

Roth IRAs

Starting with the 1998 tax year, individuals may establish "Roth IRAs." Contributions to a Roth IRA are not deductible. Instead, the tax advantages are "backloaded." The buildup (e.g., dividends and interest) within the account may be tax free depending on how and when the taxpayer withdraws money from the account.[16]

☐ The special rules for Roth IRAs are discussed at ¶ 3225.

---

[1] Code Sec. 408(b); IRS Reg. § 1.408-3(b).

[2] Code Sec. 408(c); Reg. § 1.408-2(c).

[3] IRS Reg. § 1.408-2(c)(4)(i).

[4] IRS Reg. § 1.408-2(c)(1).

[5] Code Sec. 219(b).

[6] ERISA Reg. § 2510.3-2(d).

[7] PWBA Interpretive Bulletin 99-1, 6-17-99, CCH Pension Plan Guide ¶ 19,972I.

[8] Code Sec. 408(q).

[9] IRS Reg. § 1.408(q)-1(f)(1).

[10] IRS Reg. § 1.408-2(e)(8).

[11] ERISA Sec. 4(c), as amended by P.L. 107-147 (Job Creation and Worker Assistance Act of 2002), Act Sec. 411(i)(2).

[12] IRS Reg. § 1.408(q)-1(c) and (e)(1).

[13] IRS Reg. § 1.408(q)-1(f)(2).

[14] Rev. Proc. 2003-13, I.R.B. 2003-4, 1-27-2003, CCH Pension Plan Guide ¶ 17,299Q-61. NOTE: A plan may not merely operate in compliance with EGTRRA and then retroactively amend the plan by the close of the applicable EGTRRA remedial amendment period (see ¶ 316). In order for the EGTRRA remedial amendment period to apply, a good faith conforming amendment that reflects a reasonable interpretation of the statute must be adopted. Under IRS Notice 2001-57 (2001-2 CB 279, CCH Pension Plan Guide ¶ 17,122B), the good faith EGTRRA plan amendments must generally be adopted by the later of (1) the end of the GUST remedial amendment period or (2) the end of the plan year in which the amendments are required to be, or are optionally, put into effect. Adoption of the sample amendment contained in Rev. Proc. 2003-13 will enable a plan sponsor to satisfy the good faith amendment requirement.

[15] Code Sec. 408(p).

[16] Code Sec. 408A.

¶ 3204
INDIVIDUAL RETIREMENT ARRANGEMENTS: Establishing an IRA

Almost anyone who receives compensation can establish an individual retirement account.[1] Employees and self-employed persons who receive compensation can open IRAs for themselves, even if they already participate in tax-qualified, employer-sponsored plans. Participants in governmental plans are also eligible to open IRAs. As a result, individual employees, sole proprietors and their employees, partners and the partnership's employees, and corporate employees are eligible to open IRAs.[2] An individual may open more than one IRA, as long as each year's contribution limits are not exceeded.

Age restrictions

Age does not generally affect an individual's ability to open an IRA. However, no one over age 70½ may contribute to an IRA or set up a new IRA to receive contributions.[3] The age-70½ restriction does not apply to Roth IRAs (see ¶ 3225).

Retired persons are eligible to establish IRAs as long as they are under age 70½ at the end of the year in question and receive compensation (such as from part-time jobs). Individuals over age 59½ may maintain IRAs and withdraw funds from them as necessary without incurring penalties for early withdrawals.

Compensation requirement

In order to establish and contribute to an IRA, a person must receive compensation. For purposes of the IRA contribution and deduction rules, the term "compensation" includes wages, salaries, professional fees, and other amounts received for personal services actually rendered. Compensation also includes such items as sales commissions, compensation for services on the basis of a percentage of profits, commissions on insurance premiums, as well as tips and bonuses.[4] Taxable alimony and separate maintenance payments received by an individual under a decree of divorce or separate maintenance are considered compensation.[5] The term "compensation" does not, however, include earnings and profits from property, such as interest, rents, dividends, or other amounts not includible in gross income.[6]

Military personnel earning combat pay. Members of the armed forces serving in Iraq and Afghanistan and other combat-designated localities may count tax-free combat pay as earned income in determining the contribution amount to a traditional or Roth IRA beginning in 2004.[7]

Trust requirements

An IRA must be a domestic trust (or custodial account) created or organized by a written instrument for the exclusive benefit of an individual or that person's beneficiaries. The written IRA instrument must include limits on the trustee's authority to invest, commingle, and distribute the funds.[8]

In general, the trustee of an IRA can be a bank, savings and loan association, insurance company, or federally insured credit union.[9] IRAs can also be self-directed, which means that the trustee or custodian has no discretion in managing the assets of the account, but instead merely executes orders and keeps records of the transactions. However, an individual cannot be a trustee of his own IRA.

Another permissible option is the selection of a nonbank trustee. This choice allows a person (for this purpose, an entity that is not an individual) other than a bank to serve as a trustee of an IRA if that entity demonstrates to the satisfaction of the IRS that it will administer the IRA trust in a manner consistent with IRS rules.[10] A nonbank trustee must satisfy rules concerning continuity and diversity of ownership, permanency of location, fiduciary experience, fiduciary responsibility, financial responsibility, and fitness to handle funds. Certain rules of fiduciary conduct governing the proper exercise of fiduciary powers, adequacy of net worth, and requirement of periodic audits, must also be met.

Formal adoption of IRA trust. In order to adopt an IRA, Form 5305 (Individual Retirement Trust Account) should be completed. Alternatively, completion of Form 5305-A (Individual Retirement Custodial Account) will create an IRA custodial account. Prototype IRA submissions must use Form 5306 (Application for Approval of Prototype or Employer Sponsored IRA).

CCH Pointer: Guidance for drafters and users of prototype and model IRAs was issued by the IRS in December 2010.[11] The guidance relates to recent statutory changes and the amendment and opinion letter procedures for these pre-approved IRAs.

[1] Code Sec. 219(b)(1).

[2] IRS Publication 590.

[3] Code Sec. 219(d)(2); IRS Publication 590.

[4] IRS Reg. § 1.219-1(c).

[5] Code Sec. 219(f)(1); IRS Publication 590.

[6] IRS Reg. § 1.219-1(c).

[7] P.L. 109-227 (Heroes Earned Retirement Opportunities Act).

[8] Code Sec. 408(a); IRS Reg. § 1.408-2(b)(2).

[9] Code Secs. 408(a)(2) and (n); IRS Reg. § 1.408-2(b)(2).

[10] IRS Reg. § 1.401-12(n).

[11] Rev. Proc. 2010-48, I.R.B. 2010-50, 12-13-10, at CCH PENSION PLAN GUIDE ¶ 17,299T-38.

¶ 3206

INDIVIDUAL RETIREMENT ARRANGEMENTS: IRA
Contributions and Deductions

For 2012, an IRA holder's annual contribution to an IRA is limited to (1) $5,000, or (2) 100% of taxable compensation, whichever is less.[1] The limit is unchanged from tax year 2011.[2] The amount that can be contributed to an IRA is restricted to the individual's compensation for the year if less than the dollar limits. If an individual has more than one IRA, the limit applies to the total contributions made to the IRAs for the year.[3] As a result, the purchase of additional IRAs for a single tax year does not increase the contribution limit. The extent to which an IRA contribution may be deductible will depend on the income of the IRA holder and whether the holder is an active participant in an employer-sponsored retirement plan (see below).

Contributions to an IRA generally must be in the form of cash.[4] The term "cash" includes checks or money orders.

Catch-up contributions

For individuals age 50 and over, additional catch-up contributions will be allowed beginning with the 2002 tax year. If an individual has reached age 50 before the close of the tax year, the regular contribution limit is increased by $1,000 for tax years 2006 and thereafter.[5]

Cost-of-living adjustments

The $5,000 annual limit on contributions to an IRA are adjusted for inflation in $500 increments for tax years beginning in calendar years after 2008.[6]

Timing of IRA contributions

An IRA owner may make contributions to an IRA for a year at any time during the year or by the due date for filing the return for the year, not including extensions.[7] As a result, for most people, contributions to an IRA are to be made by April 15 of the year following the relevant tax year.

An IRA owner who contributes to an IRA between January 1 and April 15 (generally, the due date for filing individual tax returns) must tell the IRA sponsor the year for which the contribution is being made. If the IRA owner does not notify the sponsor as required, the sponsor may assume that the contribution is for the year in which the contribution is made.

CCH Pointer: Due to a District of Columbia holiday, the due date for filing 2011 individual income tax returns is April 17, 2012.

Example 1: Marsha Washington makes a contribution to her IRA on March 1, 2012. However, she does not inform the IRA sponsor whether the contribution is for 2011 or 2012. As a result, the sponsor may assume that Marsha made the contribution for 2012 and report the contribution as being made for 2012 to the IRS on Form 5498.

A tax return on which an individual is claiming an IRA contribution may be filed before the taxpayer has actually made the IRA contribution. However, the taxpayer must make the contribution by the due date of the return, not including extensions.

Example 2: Liz Schultz, a calendar year taxpayer earning $50,000, files her 2011 tax return on March 1, 2012. On her tax return, she claims a full $5,000 IRA deduction, even though she has not yet actually made the contribution. On April 10, 2012, Schultz sends a check for $5,000 to her bank, designating it as an IRA contribution for 2011. Schultz's IRA contribution was timely because she made it before April 17, 2012, the due date for her return.

Where an individual has already filed a tax return and has not taken the full deduction permitted for an IRA or has not yet established an IRA, the taxpayer can still add to an existing IRA or open up a new one by the filing deadline by subsequently filing an amended return. The amended return is filed on Form 1040X (Amended U.S. Individual Income Tax Return). Generally, Form 1040X must be filed within the later of (a) three years after the date the original return was due, or (b) three years after the date it was filed.

Spousal IRAs

Under the spousal IRA limits, deductible IRA contributions of up to the annual dollar limit ($5,000 in 2011 and 2012) may be made for each spouse, including a spouse who does not work outside the home, if the combined compensation of both spouses is at least equal to the contributed amount. In order to take advantage of the spousal IRA limits, the couple must file a joint return.[8] However separate IRAs must be set up for each spouse.

Thus, in 2012, the maximum deduction that can be taken by both spouses for the taxable year is limited to the lesser of:[9]

1. $10,000, or
2. the compensation includible in the individual's gross income for the year, plus the compensation includible in the gross income of the individual's spouse for the year, minus the amount allowed as a deduction to the spouse for the year, the amount of any designated nondeductible contribution on behalf of the spouse, and the amount of any contribution on behalf of the spouse to a Roth IRA for the year.

Reductions in maximum IRA deduction. For active participants whose incomes exceed the threshold level, the maximum amount of the spousal IRA deduction is reduced proportionately, using the phase-out formula described below.

Active participation

If an individual is an active participant in a tax-qualified retirement plan for a taxable year, the amount of an individual's deduction may be reduced or eliminated for such year.[10] Accordingly, the first step in determining the permissible IRA deduction for a year is to determine a taxpayer's active participant status for the taxable year.

Determining active participation. An individual is considered an active participant for a tax year if he or she is covered by:[11]

1. a qualified pension, profit-sharing, or stock bonus plan, including a 401(k) plan,

2. a qualified annuity plan,

3. a tax-sheltered annuity plan,

4. a simplified employee pension (SEP),

5. a SIMPLE plan,

6. a plan established by the United States, a state or political subdivision of a state, or by a federal or state instrumentality, or

7. an employee-only contributory plan that is exempt from tax under Code Sec. 501(c)(18).

Married persons. An individual is not considered an active participant merely because the individual's spouse is an active participant for any part of a plan year. Special income phase-out rules apply in situations where an individual is not an active participant, but whose spouse is an active participant (see below).

Phase-out rules for active participants

If an individual is not an active plan participant for any part of the year, he or she can take a full deduction for IRA contributions. If an individual is an active participant, the individual may be able to take only a partial deduction or no deduction at all, depending on filing status and income.[12]

Individuals who are below a certain income level, called the "threshold level" can make deductible IRA contributions. For 2012, the threshold level for single persons and heads of household is $58,000-$68,000; for joint filers, $92,000-$112,000. For 2011, the threshold level for single persons and heads of household is $56,000-$66,000; for joint filers, $90,000-$110,000. For individuals who are married and file a separate tax return, the threshold level is zero.[13]

The amount by which an individual's adjusted gross income exceeds the threshold level is referred to as "excess AGI." If an individual's excess AGI is less than $10,000, the individual is still able to make a deductible IRA contribution, but it is limited in amount.[14] An individual may calculate his deduction limit by using the formula below:

($10,000 − Excess AGI/$10,000) × maximum allowable deduction

Example: Joe, a single person, is an active participant in his employer's 401(k) plan and has AGI of $63,000 in 2012. As a single person, his threshold level is $58,000. His Excess AGI is $5,000 ($63,000 AGI minus $58,000 threshold level). Using the formula above, his IRA deduction limit is $2,500. [$5,000/$10,000 times $5,000 equals $2,500]

Starting in the 2007 tax year, the threshold level widened to $20,000 for married taxpayers filing jointly.[15]

Active participant rules for married couples. As noted above, an individual is not considered an active participant in an employer-sponsored plan merely because the individual's spouse is an active participant. Special income phase-out rules apply in situations where an individual is not an active participant, but whose spouse is an active participant. The maximum deductible IRA contribution for an individual who is not an active participant, but whose spouse is, is phased out at adjusted gross incomes between $173,000 and $183,000 in 2012 and $169,000 and $179,000 in 2011.[16]

Example 1: Ralph is covered by a 401(k) plan at work. His wife, Alice, is a full-time homemaker. They file jointly and have an AGI of $200,000. Neither Ralph nor Alice is entitled to make deductible contributions to an IRA for the year because they exceed the income threshold.

Example 2: Assume the same facts as Example (1), except that the combined AGI of Ralph and Alice is $125,000. Alice can make a deductible contribution to the IRA for the year because she is not an active participant and their combined AGI is below the threshold. But Ralph cannot make a deductible contribution because he exceeds the income threshold for active participants (see above).

Married persons who file separate income tax returns for any tax year and live apart at all times during the tax year are not treated as married persons for active participation purposes.[17]

Nondeductible contributions

Individuals may make nondeductible IRA contributions to the extent they are ineligible to make deductible IRA contributions.[18] This option would apply, for example, for individuals whose IRA deductions are reduced or eliminated because of the phase-out due to the adjusted gross income limitation. Thus, an individual who is above the "threshold level" may still contribute up to the lesser of 100% of compensation or $5,000 to an IRA in 2012. The amount of the contribution which is not deductible may be designated as a nondeductible contribution.[19] Form 8606 is used to report nondeductible IRA contributions.

CCH Pointer: Qualified individuals may make nondeductible contributions to Roth IRAs (see ¶ 3225). Distributions from Roth IRAs may be made tax-free under certain circumstances. However, in 2012 the ability to contribute to a Roth IRA is phased out for single taxpayers with AGI exceeding $110,000 and joint filers with AGI exceeding $173,000. An individual who cannot (or does not) make contributions to a deductible or Roth IRA can still make contributions to a nondeductible IRA.

Excess contributions and return of contributions

Generally, an excess contribution is the amount an individual contributes to an IRA that exceeds the contribution limit. In this instance, the excess is subject to a cumulative, nondeductible 6% excise tax.[20]

An individual who makes a contribution, including an excess contribution, to an IRA can avoid the excise tax on excess contributions and premature distributions by withdrawing the contribution (and any earnings on the contribution) on or before the due date (including extensions) of the individual's income tax return.[21]

CCH Pointer: An IRA contributor who timely withdraws the contribution does not have to include the contribution in gross income as long as no deduction is taken and the interest attributable to the contribution is returned. The interest, however, must be included in the person's income for the year in which the contribution is made.[22]

Calculation of "attributable net income." Under IRS regulations, the amount of net income attributable to a returned contribution is determined by allocating to the contribution a pro-rata portion of the IRA's earnings that accrued during the time the contribution was held in the IRA.[23]

SAVER's credit for making IRA contributions

For tax years beginning after 2001, a nonrefundable tax credit, known as the "SAVER's credit," is established for contributions to traditional or Roth IRAs.[24] The amount of the credit for a tax year will be equal to the applicable percentage times the amount of qualified retirement savings contributions (not to exceed $2,000) made by an eligible individual.[25] The applicable percentage is determined by the taxpayer's filing status and adjusted gross income.[26]

The saver's credit, which was initially set to expire for tax years beginning after 2006, is now a permanent credit. In addition, under the Pension Protection Act of 2006 (P.L. 109-280), the adjusted gross income amounts used to figure the amount of the saver's credit are indexed for inflation beginning in 2007. Under the indexed income limits, the income limit for single taxpayers is one-half of the amount for married taxpayers filing a joint return and the limit for heads of household is three-fourths of the amount for joint returns. Thus, for 2012, the saver's credit is 50% for joint filers earning $0 to $34,500, for heads of household earning $0 to $25,875, and for all other filers earning $0 to $17,250. The credit is 20% for joint filers earning over $34,500 to $37,500, for heads of household earning over $25,875 to $28,125, and for all other filers earning over $17,250 to $18,750, and the percentage is 10% for joint filers earning over $37,500 to $57,500, for heads of household earning over $28,125 to $43,125, and for all other filers earning over $18,750 to $28,750.[27]

Additional IRA contributions for individuals affected by an employer's bankruptcy (2007-2009)

Qualifying individuals who participated in a bankrupt employer's 401(k) plan and received at least 50% matching contributions made in the employer's stock are permitted to make additional contributions to an IRA of up to $3,000 for tax years 2007, 2008 and 2009.[28] Taxpayers who elect to make additional contributions to an IRA under this provision are precluded from making catch-up contributions to an IRA that may otherwise be allowed for taxpayers aged 50 and older.[29]

CCH Pointer: The provision for additional contributions for individuals affected by an employer's bankruptcy was enacted as part of the Pension Protection Act of 2006 (P.L. 109-280) and terminates for tax years beginning after December 31, 2009.[30]

Differential wage payments

Effective for years beginning after 2008, differential wage payments will be included in a taxpayer's compensation for purposes of the annual limits on contributions to traditional and Roth IRAs.[31] Differential wage payments are payments that: (1) are made by an employer to an individual with respect to any period during which the individual is performing services in the uniformed military service, while on active duty for a period of more than 30 days; and (2) represent all or a portion of the wages that the individual would have received from the employer if the individual were performing services for the employer.[32]

Direct deposit of tax refunds

The IRS is required to make available a form or modify existing forms so that a taxpayer can direct that all or a portion of his or her tax refund can be deposited into an IRA.[33] IRS Form 8888 will be used for this purpose. The form will give all individual filers the ability to split their refunds. Taxpayers will attach the new form to their returns indicating amounts of each allocation and providing account information. Refunds may be deposited with any U.S. financial institution so long as taxpayers provide valid routing and account numbers.

---

[1] Code Sec. 219(b)(1)(A) and (b)(5)(A); IRS News Release IR-2011-103, 10-20-11, CCH PENSION PLAN GUIDE ¶ 17,037Q.

[2] IRS News Release IR-2011-103, 10-20-11, CCH PENSION PLAN GUIDE ¶ 17,037Q.

[3] Code Sec. 219(a) and (e)(1).

[4] Code Sec. 219(e)(1).

[5] Code Sec. 219(b)(5)(B).

[6] Code Sec. 219(b)(5)(C).

[7] Code Sec. 219(f)(3).

[8] Code Sec. 219(c)(2)(B).

[9] Code Sec. 219(c)(1).

[10] Code Sec. 219(g).

[11] Code Sec. 219(g)(5).

[12] Code Sec. 219(g)(1).

[13] Code Sec. 219(g)(3)(B). Under Code Sec. 219(g)(8), enacted by P.L. 109-280 (Pension Protection Act of 2006), the income limits for determining eligibility for deductible IRA contributions are indexed for inflation beginning in the 2007 tax year. However, the phaseout ranges ($10,000 for an individual taxpayer and $20,000 for married taxpayers filing jointly) are not affected. The indexed amount will be rounded to the nearest multiple of $1,000. The 2011 inflation adjustments are contained in IRS News Release IR-2010-108, 10-28-10, CCH PENSION PLAN GUIDE ¶ 17,037O. The 2012 inflation adjustments are contained in IRS News Release IR-2011-103, 10-20-11, CCH PENSION PLAN GUIDE ¶ 17,037Q.

[14] Code Sec. 219(g)(2)(A).

[15] Code Sec. 219(g)(3)(B)(i) and (ii).

[16] Code Sec. 219(g)(7). Under Code Sec. 219(g)(8), enacted by P.L. 109-280 (Pension Protection Act of 2006), the income limits for determining eligibility for deductible IRA contributions are indexed for inflation beginning in the 2007 tax year. The indexed amounts will be rounded to the nearest multiple of $1,000. The 2011 inflation adjustments are contained in IRS News Release IR-2010-108, 10-28-10, CCH Pension Plan Guide ¶ 17,037O. The 2012 inflation adjustments are contained in IRS News Release IR-2011-103, 10-20-11, CCH Pension Plan Guide ¶ 17,037Q.

[17] Code Sec. 219(g)(4).

[18] Code Sec. 408(o)(1).

[19] Code Sec. 408(o)(2).

[20] Code Sec. 4973.

[21] Code Secs. 408(d)(4) and 4973(b).

[22] Code Sec. 408(d)(4); IRS Reg. § 1.408-4(c)(2).

[23] IRS Reg. § 1.408-11.

[24] Code Sec. 25B. See also IRS Announcement 2001-106, I.R.B. 2001-44, CCH Pension Plan Guide ¶ 17,097R-52.

[25] Code Sec. 25B(a).

[26] Code Sec. 25B(b).

[27] The 2012 inflation adjustments are contained in IRS News Release IR-2011-103, 10-20-11, CCH Pension Plan Guide ¶ 17,037Q.

[28] Code Sec. 219(b)(5)(C), as added by P.L. 109-280 (Pension Protection Act of 2006), Act Sec. 831(a).

[29] Code Sec. 219(b)(5)(C)(i), as added by P.L. 109-280 (Pension Protection Act of 2006), Act Sec. 831(a).

[30] Code Sec. 219(b)(5)(C)(v), as added by P.L. 109-280 (Pension Protection Act of 2006), Act Sec. 831(a).

[31] Code Sec. 219(f)(1), as added by P.L. 110-245 (Heroes Earnings Assistance and Tax Relief Act of 2008), Act Sec. 105(b)(2). See also IRS Notice 2010-15, Sec. III, I.R.B. 2010-6, CCH Pension Plan Guide ¶ 17,144L.

[32] Code Sec. 3401(h)(2), as added by P.L. 110-245 (Heroes Earnings Assistance and Tax Relief Act of 2008), Act Sec. 105(a)(4). See also IRS Notice 2010-15, Sec. III, I.R.B. 2010-6, CCH Pension Plan Guide ¶ 17,144L.

[33] P.L. 109-280 (Pension Protection Act of 2006), Act Sec. 830; IRS News Release IR-2006-85, 5-31-06.

¶ 3208

INDIVIDUAL RETIREMENT ARRANGEMENTS:
Investment of IRA Assets

A wide array of investments are available to IRAs. However, an IRA is prohibited from investing in "collectibles" [1] and life insurace contracts.[2] The term "collectibles" includes any work of art, rug, antique, metal, gem, stamp, coin, alcoholic beverage, or other item of tangible personal property specified by the IRS.[3] However, IRAs may invest in certain U.S.-minted gold and silver coins and any coin issued under the laws of any state. Also, IRAs may invest in certain platinum coins and any gold, silver, platinum, or palladium bullion of a specified fineness.[4]

An IRA participant may generally self-direct the investment of the assets in his or her account even though those assets are under the control of the IRA trustee or custodian. In short, self-directed IRAs let investors make their own investment decisions. For example, IRA investors may order purchases or sales and increase or reduce cash positions in much the same way as they could through regular brokerage accounts. Given an agreeable trustee, IRA investment alternatives are far-ranging.

CCH Pointer: While individuals have great latitude in investing IRA assets, it is important to note that IRAs are subject to the general prohibited transaction rules that apply to all tax-qualified plans. The penalty imposed on an IRA owner that engages in a prohibited transaction with his or her IRA is the disqualification of the IRA with unfavorable tax consequences. The prohibited transaction rules are covered beginning at ¶ 2400. Statutory and administrative exemptions from the prohibited transaction rules affecting IRA investments are discussed below.

Sale of bank stock to IRA beneficiary

Traditional or Roth IRA may be shareholders of banks that are S corporations.[5] However, an IRA may be an S corporation shareholder only to the extent of bank stock held by the IRA on October 22, 2004. Under a statutory prohibited transaction exemption, the sale by an IRA to an IRA beneficiary is permitted, effective October 22, 2004, if certain specified conditions are met. Among these conditions is that the sale is made for fair market value pursuant to an S corporation election by the bank and the IRA incurs no commissions, costs, or other expenses in connection with the sale.[6]

Payment of IRA fees and commissions

IRA participants often face brokerage commissions or other charges in connection with their IRAs. The determination of whether IRA fees and commissions are deductible and whether they count toward the IRA contribution limits depends on whether the fees are (1) trustee's or administrative fees, or (2) commissions.

The *separate payment* of IRA's trustee's fees or administrative fees (in addition to the ordinary Code Sec. 219 contributions to an IRA) has been held to be deductible under Code Sec. 212 to the extent that it is an expense incurred for the production or collection of income.[7] Unlike trustee's fees or other administrative expenses, however, broker's fees incurred in connection with a securities transaction are not deductible.[8]

Gifts for establishing IRAs

Many individuals are attracted to financial institutions for the establishment of their IRAs by the institutions' offers of premiums, such as cash bonuses or other gifts. However, the receipt of premiums or free or reduced cost bank services raised questions with regard to the prohibited transaction rules (see ¶ 2400). In response, the Labor Department has issued class exemptions to the prohibited transaction rules which allow for the receipt of small gifts or free or reduced cost bank services.

Banks, credit unions, and other financial institutions can offer cash or other premiums as incentives for opening or making additional contributions to IRAs, or transferring property from another plan, without violating the prohibited transaction rules.[9] The exemption limits the value of an incentive to $10 on deposits up to $5,000 and $20 on deposits over $5,000. These premiums may be paid to the person for whose benefit the IRA is established or to that person's family members.

CCH Pointer: Under the class exemption that allows for premiums to IRA depositors, financial institutions can also offer group-term life insurance annually at no cost to account holders. Where a financial institution takes into account an IRA balance in determining eligibility for life insurance, however, the amount of insurance that is attributable on a dollar for dollar basis to the IRA deposit balance may not exceed $5,000.

No-cost banking services

Another exemption allows banks to provide services at reduced cost or no cost to individuals with beneficial interests in IRAs. The services must be those normally offered to customers free or at reduced cost in the ordinary course of the bank's business.[10] Under this class exemption, any required deposit balance for the IRA must be equal to the lowest balance required for any other type of account used to determine eligibility to receive reduced or no-cost services. Similarly, the rate of return on the IRA investment cannot be less favorable than the rate of return on an identical investment made by a customer who is not eligible for reduced or no-cost services. This class exemption also applies to simplified employee pensions (SEPs) and SIMPLE IRAs that give participants the unrestricted authority to transfer account balances to IRAs or SIMPLE IRAs sponsored by different financial institutions.[11]

Broker-dealer services

A Labor Department exemption finalized in 1997 permits broker-dealers to provide services at reduced fees or at no cost to IRA (including SIMPLE IRA), SEP, or Keogh plan customers.[12] The exemption covers banking-type services, but is subject to several conditions. Services allowed at reduced or no fees under the exemption include financial planning, direct deposit/debit and automatic fund transfer privileges, enhanced account statements, and check writing privileges. Roth IRAs are covered under the exemption.[13] The exemption does not apply to IRAs that are employee benefit plans under ERISA. However, SEPs and SIMPLE IRAs that allow participants unrestricted authority to transfer account balances to IRAs or SIMPLE IRAs sponsored by different financial institutions are treated as IRAs for purposes of the exemption.

Fee arrangements between IRAs and banks

The Department of Labor's Employee Benefits Security Administration (EBSA) has stated in an advisory opinion that, where fees received by a bank or its affiliate, in connection with investments in certain mutual funds by IRAs, are offset against management fees charged by the bank to the IRAs, the receipt and offset would not violate the prohibited transaction rules.[14] The receipt of fees attributable to assets of participating IRAs would not violate the prohibited transaction rules, according to EBSA, if the management fees received by the bank were reduced by an amount equal to such fees and the receipt of the fees did not cause the bank's compensation to exceed the amount of the management fees agreed to by the IRA holder.

Loans between IRAs and disqualified persons or parties in interest

Code Sec. 4975(c)(1)(B) prohibits loans or extensions of credit between plans and disqualified persons or parties in interest (see ¶ 2418). In an advisory opinion, the Labor Department has ruled that the purchase by an IRA of a promissory note and a deed of trust held by a bank would be a prohibited transaction under Code Sec. 4975(c)(1)(B) because the IRA owner and his wife, as obligors on the note, would be disqualified persons, and the family trust, which held title to the real property encumbered by the deed of trust and of which the IRA owner and his wife were trustees and sole beneficiaries, would be a disqualified person. [15]

PT Class Exemption 80-26, which provides relief for interest-free loans between plans and parties in interest (see ¶ 2488) does not provide relief for an IRA owner from Code Sec. 4975(c)(1)(B) for an "extension of credit" in the form of an indemnification agreement that was required by a broker before opening a futures trading account and that secured the broker from certain investment losses and/or taxes related to the IRA owner investing IRA assets in a futures contract. [16] In an earlier opinion letter, the DOL ruled that the grant by an individual to a broker of a security interest in the individual's non-IRA accounts with the broker would be an impermissible extension of credit to the individual's IRA. [17]

> **CCH Pointer:** The Labor Department has advised the IRS that it is considering further action with respect to the issues described above, including consideration of an expected class exemption request. Accordingly, pending further action by the DOL and until issuance of further IRS guidance, the IRS has announced that it will determine the tax consequences relating to an IRA without taking into account the consequences that might otherwise result from a prohibited transaction under Code Sec. 4975 resulting from entering into any indemnification agreement or any cross-collateralization agreement similar to the agreements described in Advisory Opinions 2009-03A and 2011-09A, provided there has been no execution or other enforcement pursuant to the agreement against the assets of an IRA account of the individual granting the security interest or entering into the cross-collateralization agreement. [18]

Application of wash sale rules

If an individual sells stock or securities for a loss and causes his or her traditional or Roth IRA to purchase substantially identical stock or securities within a specified period, the loss on the sale of the stock or securities is disallowed for tax purposes under the wash sale rules of Code Sec. 1091 and the individual's basis in the IRA or Roth IRA is not increased. [19]

---

[1] Code Sec. 408(m).

[2] Code Sec. 408(a)(3).

[3] Code Sec. 408(m)(2).

[4] Code Sec. 408(m)(3).

[5] Code Sec. 1361(c)(2)(A)(vi), as added by P.L. 108-357 (American Jobs Creation Act of 2004).

[6] Code Sec. 4975(d)(16).

[7] Rev. Rul. 84-146, 1984-2 CB 61, CCH PENSION PLAN GUIDE ¶ 19,661.

[8] Rev. Rul. 86-142, 1986-2 CB 60, CCH PENSION PLAN GUIDE ¶ 19,696.

[9] Prohibited Transaction Class Exemption 93-1, 1-8-93 (58 FR 3567), CCH PENSION PLAN GUIDE ¶ 16,638.

[10] Prohibited Transaction Class Exemption 93-33, 5-28-93 (58 FR 31053), CCH PENSION PLAN GUIDE ¶ 16,640, originally released as Prohibited Transaction Class Exemption 93-2, 1-11-93 (58 FR 3561), CCH PENSION PLAN GUIDE ¶ 16,639.

[11] Prohibited Transaction Class Exemption 93-33, 5-28-93 (58 FR 31053), as amended 3-8-99 (64 FR 11044), CCH PENSION PLAN GUIDE ¶ 16,649B.

[12] Prohibited Transaction Class Exemption 97-11, 2-7-97 (62 FR 5855), CCH PENSION PLAN GUIDE ¶ 16,647, as amended 3-8-99 (64 FR 11042), CCH PENSION PLAN GUIDE ¶ 16,649A and 12-12-2002 (67 FR 76425), CCH PENSION PLAN GUIDE ¶ 16,649K.

[13] Prohibited Transaction Class Exemption 97-11, 2-7-97 (62 FR 5855), CCH PENSION PLAN GUIDE

¶ 16,647, as amended 3-8-99 (64 FR 11042), CCH Pension Plan Guide ¶ 16,649A and 12-12-2002 (67 FR 76425), CCH Pension Plan Guide ¶ 16,649K; ERISA Opinion Letter 98-03A, 3-6-98, CCH Pension Plan Guide ¶ 19,987A.

[14]EBSA Opinion Letter 2005-10A, 5-24-05, CCH Pension Plan Guide ¶ 19,990V.

[15]EBSA Opinion Letter 2011-04A, 2-3-11, CCH Pension Plan Guide ¶ 19,992P.

[16]EBSA Opinion Letter 2011-09A, 10-2-11, CCH Pension Plan Guide ¶ 19,992U.

[17]EBSA Opinion Letter 2009-03A, 10-27-09, CCH Pension Plan Guide ¶ 19,992J.

[18]IRS Announcement 2011-81, I.R.B. 2011-52, 12-27-11, CCH Pension Plan Guide ¶ 17,097T-60.

[19]Rev. Rul. 2008-5, I.R.B. 2008-5, 1-22-08, CCH Pension Plan Guide ¶ 19,948Z-218.

¶ 3210

INDIVIDUAL RETIREMENT ARRANGEMENTS: Required Distributions

An individual's entire interest in an IRA must be, or begin to be, distributed no later than April 1 of the calendar year after the year in which the taxpayer reaches age 70½. A further distribution must be made by December 31 of each year after the year in which the taxpayer reaches age 70½.[1]

☐ Many of the required beginning distribution rules for IRAs are similar to those for qualified plans. See ¶ 1800 and following for a discussion of these rules.

☐ There are penalties for taking premature distributions, penalties for taking insufficient distributions, and penalties for violating the minimum distribution rules. See ¶ 3222.

☐ The age 70½ restrictions do not apply to Roth IRAs. See ¶ 3225.

---

[1] Code Sec. 401(a)(9).

¶ 3212

INDIVIDUAL RETIREMENT ARRANGEMENTS: Taxation of IRA Distributions

In general, any amount paid or distributed out of an IRA is includible in the gross income of the recipient under rules similar to the rules for qualified plans set forth in Code Sec. 72. Additionally, certain special rules apply for IRAs. All IRAs of an individual are treated as one IRA contract. All distributions during the same taxable year are treated as one distribution. The value of the contract (calculated after adding back distributions during the year), income on the contract, and investment in the contract are determined as of the close of the calendar year in which the individual's tax year begins.[1]

A distribution of any contribution paid during a taxable year is not subject to tax if:

1. the amount is distributed to the individual on or before the due date (including extensions) for filing his tax return for that year,

2. no deduction has been allowed for the contribution, and

3. the distribution includes the net income attributable to the contribution.

This net income is deemed to have been earned and receivable in the taxable year when the contribution was made.[2]

CCH Pointer: *Calculating amount of net income attributable to contribution.* The net income attributable to a contribution made to an IRA that is distributed as a returned contribution under Code Sec. 408(d)(4) is determined by allocating to the contribution a pro rata portion of the earnings accrued by the IRA during the period that the contribution was in the IRA.[3]

Contributions returned before due date of return

Even if the time for filing his income tax return has passed, an individual can withdraw an excess contribution without liability for income tax or the 10% premature distribution penalty tax. To qualify, the total contribution (including the excess contribution) cannot exceed the annual dollar limit and no deduction must have been allowed for the excess contribution. However, earnings attributable to the excess contribution need not be withdrawn.[4]

Example: Fred Miller (a calendar year taxpayer, age 48) makes a $5,500 contribution to his IRA in 2011. He has made a $500 excess contribution for 2011. No deduction is allowed for the 2011 excess contribution. In July 2012, after Miller has filed his income tax return, he withdraws the $500 excess contribution. He does not have to include the $500 in his gross income for 2011, nor is it subject to the 10% premature distribution penalty tax. However, he is liable for a 6% excise tax of $30 (6% × $500) for 2011. He is not liable for the 6% penalty tax for 2012 (¶ 3222) since he has corrected the excess contribution before December 31, 2012. This example assumes that Miller is eligible to make deductible IRA contributions.

Excess rollover contributions may be withdrawn

To the extent that a rollover contribution (including an attempted rollover contribution) is an excess contribution as a result of erroneous information supplied to an IRA participant by a plan, trust, or institution making the distribution which was the subject of the rollover, the IRA participant can withdraw the excess rollover contribution, regardless of amount, without incurring liability for income tax or the 10% penalty tax.[5]

Nondeductible contributions

An individual who cannot (or does not) make contributions to a deductible IRA or a Roth IRA (¶ 3225) can still make nondeductible contributions to an IRA (see ¶ 3206). Because nondeductible IRA contributions are made using income which has already been taxed, the portion of the IRA distributions consisting of nondeductible contributions will not be taxed again when received by the individual. Thus, if an individual makes any nondeductible IRA contributions, each distribution from the IRA will consist of a nontaxable portion (return of nontaxable contributions) and a taxable portion (return of deductible contributions, if any, and account earnings).[6]

The following formula is used to determine the nontaxable portion of the individual's distribution for a taxable year:

$$\frac{\text{Total nondeductible contributions}}{\substack{\text{Year-end total IRA accountable} \\ \text{balances (plus distributions for the year)}}} \times \substack{\text{Total distributions for the} \\ \text{year}}$$

$$= \text{Nontaxable distributions for the year}$$

Example: Arnold King makes a $2,000 IRA contribution in 2010, $1,500 of which is deductible. No prior IRA contributions were made by Arnold. In 2011, Arnold makes a $2,000 IRA contribution to another IRA account, none of which is deductible. In 2012, Arnold makes no IRA contributions and $1,000 is withdrawn from the IRA to which he contributed in 2010. On December 31, 2012, the aggregate account balance in both IRAs is $4,000. The nontaxable portion of the $1,000 distribution taken in 2012 is figured as follows:

$$\frac{\text{Total nondeductible contributions}}{\substack{\text{Total account balance in the IRA as of} \\ \text{12/31/12 (incl. distribution in 2012)}}} \quad \frac{(\$2,500)}{(\$5,000)} \times \$1,000 = \$500$$

Thus, $500 of the $1,000 distribution in 2012 will not be included in King's taxable income. The remaining $500 will be taxable.

Assignments and involuntary distributions

Funds invested in IRAs are generally not intended to be alienated or assigned, but rather are intended to accumulate for the benefit of the IRA participant upon retirement. However, in certain circumstances, an assignment or involuntary distribution of IRA funds is permitted, with varying tax consequences. For example, the assignment of an ownership interest in a rollover distribution from a plan will constitute constructive receipt of the assigned amount and will be taxable in the year assigned.[7]

Bankruptcy. A qualified retirement plan must provide that the benefits under the plan cannot be assigned or alienated (see ¶ 1500). The U.S. Supreme Court has held that this provision protects employees in bankruptcy from claims against their interests in qualified plans.[8] Similar protections have now been accorded to IRAs, including SIMPLE IRAs and SEPs, under the Bankruptcy Abuse Prevention and Consumer Protection Act of 2005.[9] The creditor protections accorded to IRAs, however, are generally subject to a statutory limit of $1 million, not including amounts attributable to rollovers. The $1 million limit does not apply to SIMPLE IRAs and SEPs. The Bankruptcy Act is generally effective on October 17, 2005, but only with respect to bankruptcy cases commenced on or after that date. For cases commencing on or after October 17, 2005, state bankruptcy exemption statutes will not affect IRAs. For further information, see ¶ 2560.

Distributions to charities (pre-2012)

An exclusion from gross income is provided to individuals age 70½ and older for otherwise taxable IRA distributions of up to $100,000 in "qualified charitable distributions" from either a traditional or Roth IRA.[10] Such distributions are not to be taken into account for charitable deduction purposes.[11] This rule sunsets for distributions made in tax years beginning after December 31, 2011.[12]

Distributions to HSAs

A health savings account (HSA) can receive a one-time contribution from an IRA, effective for tax years beginning after December 31, 2006.[13] The contribution must be made via a direct trustee-to-trustee transfer. Amounts distributed from an IRA that would otherwise be includible in gross income are excludible to the extent the distribution is a qualified HSA funding distribution. The distributions also are not subject to the 10% additional tax on early distributions. The amount that can be distributed from the IRA and contributed to an HSA is limited to the otherwise maximum deductible contribution amount to the HSA.

A qualified HSA funding distribution may be made from a traditional or Roth IRA, but not from an ongoing SIMPLE IRA or an ongoing SEP-IRA. For this purpose, a SEP-IRA or SIMPLE IRA is treated as ongoing if an employer contribution is made for the plan year ending with or within the IRA owner's taxable year in which the qualified HSA funding distribution would be made.[14]

☐ The HSA contribution limits are discussed in detail in the CCH U.S. MASTER EMPLOYEE BENEFITS GUIDE.

---

[1] Code Sec. 408(d)(1) and (2).

[2] Code Sec. 408(d)(4); IRS Reg. § 1.408-4(c).

[3] IRS Reg. § 1.408-11.

[4] Code Sec. 408(d)(5)(A).

[5] Code Sec. 408(d)(5)(B).

[6] Code Sec. 72(e); IRS Notice 89-25, 1989-1 CB 662, CCH PENSION PLAN GUIDE ¶ 17,102A-1; IRS Notice 87-16, 1987-1 CB 446, CCH PENSION PLAN GUIDE ¶ 17,100M; IRS Announcement 86-121, I.R.B. 1986-50, 13, CCH PENSION PLAN GUIDE ¶ 17,097L-22.

[7] IRS Letter Ruling 7944077, 8-2-79.

[8] *Patterson v. Shumate*, US Sup Ct (1992), 504 U.S. 753, aff'g CA-4 (1991), 943 F2d 362.

[9] P.L. 109-8.

[10] Code Sec. 408(d)(8)(A), as added by P.L. 109-280 (Pension Protection Act of 2006), Act Sec. 1201(a).

[11] Code Sec. 408(d)(8)(E), as added by P.L. 109-280 (Pension Protection Act of 2006), Act Sec. 1201(a).

[12] Code Sec. 408(d)(8)(F), as added by P.L. 109-280 (Pension Protection Act of 2006), Act Sec. 1201(a) and amended by P.L. 111-312 (Tax Relief, Unemployment Insurance Reauthorization, and Job Creation Act of 2010), Act Sec. 725(a).

[13] Code Sec. 408(d)(9), as added by P.L. 109-432 (Tax Relief and Health Care Act of 2006), DIVISION A, Sec. 307(a).

[14] IRS Notice 2008-51, I.R.B. 2008-25, 6-23-08, CCH PENSION PLAN GUIDE ¶ 17,139N.

¶ 3214
INDIVIDUAL RETIREMENT ARRANGEMENTS: IRA
Beneficiaries

Any number of individuals may be named as beneficiaries of an IRA. For instance, an IRA owner may name as a beneficiary a surviving spouse, children or grandchildren, the estate, a trustee, or other family or nonfamily members. An IRA owner's right to change the beneficiary continues until death. The treatment of an IRA beneficiary often varies depending on whether the beneficiary is a surviving spouse or other type of beneficiary.

Inherited IRAs

The IRS has defined which beneficiaries may be allowed to "step into the shoes" of the IRA decedent. According to the IRS, the only beneficiary of a deceased IRA holder who may elect to treat the beneficiary's entire interest in the IRA trust as the beneficiary's own account is the IRA holder's surviving spouse.[1] A spouse who makes such an election is considered to be the individual for whose benefit the trust is maintained.

Spousal election. An election is considered made by the surviving spouse if either of the following occurs:

1. any required amounts in the account have not been distributed within the appropriate time period applicable to the decedent; or

2. any additional amounts are contributed to the accounts which are subject, or deemed to be subject, to the required distribution rules.

CCH Pointer: IRS regulations clarify that this deemed election is permitted to be made only after the distribution of the required minimum amount for the account, if any, for the year of the individual's death. Further, the regulations clarify that this deemed election is permitted only if the spouse is the sole beneficiary of the account and has an unlimited right to make withdrawals from the account. This requirement is not satisfied if a trust is named as beneficiary of the IRA, even if the spouse is the sole beneficiary of the trust.[2]

Nonspousal beneficiaries. On the other hand, if an individual other than the IRA holder's spouse is the designated beneficiary, that nonspousal beneficiary may not treat the IRA as one established on that individual's own behalf. As a result, the nonspousal beneficiary may not use the IRA to receive, or be the source of, rollover contributions. Moreover, neither deductible nor nondeductible contributions may be made to the inherited IRA (a term, which under the Tax Code, refers only to IRAs acquired by a person other than the surviving spouse).[3]

In the event an IRA holder names a nonspouse as beneficiary, dies soon thereafter, and the entire balance in the IRA is distributed to the beneficiary in a lump sum, the IRS has ruled that the balance in the IRA at the decedent's death, including unrealized appreciation of account assets and accrued income, minus the aggregate amount of the decedent's nondeductible IRA contributions, is gross income to the beneficiary in the tax year of receipt. This amount is includible in the beneficiary's gross income in the tax year of receipt. The remaining portion of the distribution, which represents appreciation and income accruing between the date of death and the date of distribution, is taxable to the beneficiary under Code Secs. 72 and 408(d).[4]

☐ See ¶ 1961 for the rules relating to rollovers by nonspouse beneficiaries from eligible retirement plans to transfer IRAs.

Determination of designated beneficiary

The rules for determining the designated beneficiary are covered at ¶ 1820. Generally, the determination of a designated beneficiary does not become final until September 30 of the calendar year following the calendar year of the employee's death. If by September 30, the beneficiary validly "disclaims" entitlement to the IRA owner's account, thereby allowing other beneficiaries to receive the benefit, the disclaiming person is not taken into account in determining the designated beneficiary. The IRS has made it clear that a disclaimer can be valid even though prior to making the disclaimer the beneficiary receives the minimum required distribution from the IRA for the year of the decedent's death.[5]

Estate planning arrangement blessed by DOL

Neither a trustee's decision to take a benefit distribution from the IRA in accordance with the terms of the IRA, nor the trust's receipt of the benefit distribution as the IRA beneficiary, is a prohibited transaction under Code Sec. 4975(c), according to an EBSA advisory opinion.[6] Thus, IRA distributions to a revocable trust established for the benefit of the IRA owner's grandson and the payment of statutory commissions associated with the IRA distributions to the IRA owner's son would not constitute prohibited transactions.

---

[1] IRS Reg. § 1.408-8, A-5.

[2] *Ibid.*

[3] Code Sec. 408(d)(3)(C).

[4] Rev. Rul. 92-47, 1992-1 CB 191, CCH PENSION PLAN GUIDE ¶ 19,754.

[5] Rev. Rul. 2005-36, I.R.B. 2005-26, 6-7-05, CCH PENSION PLAN GUIDE ¶ 19,948Z-114.

[6] ERISA Opinion Letter 2009-02A, 9-28-09, CCH PENSION PLAN GUIDE ¶ 19,992I.

¶ 3216

INDIVIDUAL RETIREMENT ARRANGEMENTS: Transfers Incident to Divorce

The transfer of an interest in an IRA is treated as nontaxable if the transfer is to a spouse or former spouse pursuant to a divorce or separation instrument.[1] Thus, neither the IRA owner nor the recipient is subject to taxation. This rule applies to individual retirement annuities, as well as to individual retirement accounts.

---

[1] Code Sec. 408(d)(6); IRS Reg. § 1.408-4(g)(1).

¶ 3218
INDIVIDUAL RETIREMENT ARRANGEMENTS:
Rollovers

In order to permit greater investment flexibility, an individual is permitted to shift investment in one type of IRA to another type, by "rolling over" the amount, without tax liability.[1]

Rollover rules also apply to transfers from qualified retirement plans to IRAs. These rules are discussed in detail at ¶ 1950 and following. The discussion below deals with IRA-to-IRA rollovers.

General rules

Two general conditions must be met before amounts may be transferred from one IRA to an individual who then transfers the amount to another IRA:

1. The amount distributed by the IRA to the individual must be transferred to the new IRA no later than the sixtieth day after it was received; and

2. A tax-free rollover of the old-account-to-individual-to-new-account type can occur only once a year.

An eligible rollover distribution from an IRA may be rolled over into a qualified employer plan, 403(b) tax-sheltered annuity, or Code Sec. 457 deferred compensation plan, effective for distributions after December 31, 2001.[2] For purposes of the expanded rollover provisions, an eligible rollover distribution from an IRA is generally the amount of the distribution that is includible in gross income. A special formula applies for determining the portion of an IRA distribution that is includible in income and thus eligible for rollover to an employer plan. The distribution is attributed first to amounts other than after-tax contributions held in any of the IRAs owned by the recipient.[3]

CCH Pointer: Employees are permitted to roll over after-tax contributions to an employee plan or an IRA, effective for post-2001 distributions.[4] Rollovers of after-tax contributions must be accomplished by means of a direct trustee-to-trustee transfer and the plan must agree to separately account for the nontaxable portion.

60-day rollover period

If the amount withdrawn from an IRA is not rolled over within a 60-day period, it must be included in the individual's gross income in the year of receipt.

Waiver or extension of 60-day period. For post-2001 distributions, the IRS may grant a hardship waiver of the 60-day rule.[5]

Rollovers of less than full amount

IRA distributions are eligible for tax-free rollover treatment to the extent that the distribution is rolled over to another IRA.[6] Accordingly, if an IRA recipient makes a rollover contribution of less than the full amount received in an IRA distribution, the amount retained will be taxed in the year of receipt as ordinary income. In addition, the retained amount will be subject to the 10% premature distribution penalty (see ¶ 3222).

> **Example:** John Monroe, who is age 40, withdraws $12,000 from his IRA. He rolls over $10,000 of the withdrawal to another IRA within 60 days. He has not received a rollover distribution within the prior 12 months. The $10,000, therefore, is rolled over tax free to the second IRA. The retained $2,000 is subject to tax at ordinary income rates. Also, a premature distribution tax of $200 (10% × $2,000) is imposed.

Inherited IRAs

Tax-free rollover treatment is denied for any amount received by an individual from an "inherited IRA." An IRA is treated as inherited if the individual for whose benefit the IRA is maintained acquired it because of the death of another individual.[7]

Exception for surviving spouses. An IRA that is received by an individual who is a surviving spouse of the original IRA owner is not subject to the inherited IRA rule.[8] Thus, a surviving spouse who receives IRA assets from, and by reason of the death of, a spouse may treat the IRA proceeds as his or her own and roll them over into an IRA.

Rollovers of property

If property other than money is distributed to the individual from the old plan, the same property must be transferred to the new plan.[9] For example, if stock is received from the old IRA, the same stock must be rolled over to the new IRA. However, if the property includes life insurance, the life insurance contract cannot be rolled over into the IRA.[10]

The use of the assets of the IRA by a trustee or custodian to buy an endowment contract for the individual for whose benefit the account is established is considered a rollover entitled to tax-free treatment to the extent that the assets so used are not attributable to the purchase of life insurance.[11] The cost of the life insurance part of the endowment contract is treated as if that amount was distributed to that individual and included in his or her gross income. However, this amount is not subject to the 10% premature distribution tax.[12] A tax-free rollover does not take place, however, if an individual receives a distribution from his or her IRA and uses it to purchase an endowment contract.[13]

---

[1] Code Sec. 408(d)(3)(A).

[2] Code Sec. 408(d)(3)(A)(ii).

[3] Code Sec. 408(d)(3)(H).

[4] Code Sec. 401(a)(31).

[5] Code Sec. 402(c)(3). Guidance in applying for a waiver of the 60-day rule is supplied in Rev. Proc. 2003-16, I.R.B. 2003-4, CCH PENSION PLAN GUIDE ¶ 17,299Q-63. For pre-2002 distributions, the IRS is not generally authorized to waive or grant extensions to the 60-day period.

[6] Code Sec. 408(d)(3)(D).

[7] Code Secs. 219(d)(4) and 408(d)(3)(C).

[8] Code Sec. 408(d)(3)(C)(ii).

[9] Code Sec. 408(d)(3)(A) and (B).

[10] Rev. Rul. 81-275, 1981-2 CB 92, CCH PENSION PLAN GUIDE ¶ 19,610.

[11] Code Sec. 408(e)(5)(A); IRS Reg. § 1.408.4(f)(1).

[12] Code Sec. 408(e)(5)(B); IRS Reg. § 1.408.4(f)(2).

[13] Code Sec. 408(d)(3)(A).

¶ 3220

INDIVIDUAL RETIREMENT ARRANGEMENTS: Special IRA Reporting and Disclosure Rules

The trustee or custodian of an individual retirement account and the issuer of an individual retirement annuity are required to furnish annual information reports to the individual participant. The information report may be furnished to the participant by the trustee or issuer on a form of its own design or on Form 5498. Also, the IRA trustee or custodian or issuer of an individual retirement annuity must report to the IRS contributions it receives from each person for the calendar year and certain other information. Form 5498 is also used for this purpose.

Taxable distributions from individual retirement accounts or annuities are to be reported to the IRS on Form 1099-R for periodic and total distributions. Copies of Form 1099-R also are to be sent to individual participants. See below for reporting of required minimum distributions.

☐ General reporting and disclosure requirements are discussed beginning at ¶ 2200.

Annual returns/reports for employer-sponsored IRAs

An employer or employee association can establish an IRA trust for some or all of its employees. The administrator of an employer-or employee association- sponsored IRA trust must file an annual report for the plan as a whole. Form 5500 is used for this purpose.

Withholding tax election notices provided to recipients

The IRS requires that IRA payors withhold taxes from taxable plan benefits paid to a recipient unless the recipient directs that such withholding not be made. To this end, payors must furnish recipients of periodic or nonperiodic plan distributions a notice of their right to make, renew, or revoke an election.

Quarterly reports of withheld taxes also must be filed with the IRS. IRA trustees and issuers of insurance or annuity contracts also will be responsible for the preparation of reports for taxable plan distributions. These reports are to be made to the IRS, participants, and beneficiaries, and to such other persons as the Secretary of Treasury may prescribe. Certain information must be maintained for purposes of making the required reports.

Reporting of IRA penalty taxes

An individual who maintains an IRA and incurs a penalty tax (see ¶ 3222) must file annual return Form 5329 to report and pay the tax.

The IRA penalty taxes that must be reported on Form 5329 are excess contribution taxes, premature distribution taxes, and insufficient distribution taxes.[1] But individuals who make only deductible contributions or receive only permissible distributions are not required to file Form 5329.[2]

Minimum required distributions

IRS regulations require the trustee, custodian, or issuer of an IRA to report amounts required to distributed from the IRA to the IRA owner and, beginning in 2004, to the IRS.[3] This reporting requirement is intended to assist individuals in complying with the minimum distribution rule (see ¶ 1800 and following).

If a minimum distribution is required for a calendar year and the IRA owner is alive at the beginning of the year, the trustee that held the IRA as of December 31 of the prior year must provide a statement to the IRA owner by January 31 of the calendar year. The IRS has provided two alternative ways of satisfying this requirement.[4]

In either case, the statement must inform the IRA owner that the trustee will be reporting to the IRS that the IRA owner is required to receive a required minimum distribution for the calendar year. The statement can be provided to the IRA owner in conjunction with the statement of the fair market value of the IRA as of December 31 of the prior year that is otherwise required to be provided to the IRA owner by January 31 of a year. If a minimum distribution is required for a calendar year, the IRA trustee must make this indication on Form 5498 for the immediately preceding year (i.e., on a 2011 Form 5498 for a 2012 required minimum distribution). However, the trustee need not indicate the amount on the form.

Mergers and acquisitions

Under the generally applicable "standard procedure," the predecessor and successor employers involved in a merger or acquisition must each file the required Form 1099-R, Reporting IRA distributions, and Form 5498, Reporting contributions to a traditional IRA, SIMPLE IRA, or Roth IRA. However, the IRS has approved an alternative procedure that allows the successor business entity, under stipulated conditions, to assume the information reporting obligations of the predecessor employer for reportable transactions occurring in the acquisition year.[5]

Death of IRA owner

In the year in which an IRA owner dies, a trustee must submit at least two Forms 5498: one reporting the fair market value of the IRA with respect to the decedent (including contributions made by the decedent) and another reporting the value of the IRA for each beneficiary.[6]

---

[1] Code Sec. 6058(e).

[2] Code Secs. 6058(d) and 7701(a)(37).

[3] IRS Reg. § 1.408-8, A-10.

[4] IRS Notice 2002-27, 2002-1 CB 814, CCH PENSION PLAN GUIDE ¶ 17,123S clarified by IRS Notice 2003-3, I.R.B. 2003-2, CCH PENSION PLAN GUIDE ¶ 17,125M.

[5] Rev. Proc. 99-50, 1999-2 CB 757, CCH PENSION PLAN GUIDE ¶ 17,299P-6. The alternative procedure is generally effective for forms filed after 1999.

[6] Rev. Proc. 89-52, 1989-2 CB 632, CCH PENSION PLAN GUIDE ¶ 17,299L-68.

¶ 3222
INDIVIDUAL RETIREMENT ARRANGEMENTS: IRA
Penalties

An individual who establishes an IRA faces a number of potential penalties with regard to contributions to and distributions from the IRA.

Premature distributions

Distributions from an individual retirement account or annuity to the individual for whose benefit the account or annuity was established can be subject to a 10% penalty tax if the individual has not reached age 59½.[1] See ¶ 1918.

The 10% tax does not apply to the following types of distributions:[2]

1. distributions made due to the IRA owner's death or disability;

2. distributions that are part of a series of substantially equal periodic payments made for the IRA owner's life or the joint lives of the IRA owner and his or her beneficiary;

3. distributions for medical expenses in excess of the Code Sec. 213 limit (7.5% of adjusted gross income);

4. distributions used to pay health insurance premiums to an individual after separation from employment.

5. distributions used to pay "qualified higher education expenses" of the individual, the individual's spouse, or any child or grandchild of the individual or the individual's spouse;

6. distributions used to pay expenses incurred by qualified first-time homebuyers;

7. qualified hurricane distributions as defined in Code Sec. 1400Q (see ¶ 1920); and

8. distributions to individuals called to active duty in excess of 179 days after September 11, 2001 (referred to as "qualified reservist distributions").

"Qualified first-time homebuyer distributions" are withdrawals from an IRA of up to $10,000 during an individual's lifetime that are used within 120 days of withdrawal to buy, build, or rebuild a "first" home that is the principal residence of the individual, spouse, child, or grandchild of the individual or spouse. In order to be considered a first-time homebuyer, the individual and spouse, if married, must not have had an ownership interest in a principal residence during a two- year period ending on the date the new home is acquired.

CCH Pointer: The exception for qualified reservist distributions is contained in Code Sec. 72(t)(2)(G), which was added by the Pension Protection Act of 2006 (P.L. 109-280). A qualified reservist distribution is a distribution made from an IRA to an individual who is a reservist or national guardsman (as defined in 37 U.S.C. 101(24)), and who was ordered or called to active duty for a period in excess of 179 days or for an indefinite period, and that is made during the period beginning on the date of the order or call to duty and ending at the close of the active duty period. An individual who receives a qualified reservist distribution may repay (in one or more contributions) the amount of the distribution at any time during the two-year period after the end of the active duty period. To permit repayment, the dollar limitations that would otherwise apply to IRA contributions do not apply to repayment contributions during the applicable two-year period. However, no deduction is allowed for any contribution made under this provision. This provision applies to individuals ordered or called to active duty after September 11, 2001. The two-year period for making recontributions of qualified reservist distributions does not end before the date that is two years after August 17, 2006.

Insufficient distributions

Minimum distributions are required for individuals following the attainment of age 70½. See ¶ 1865. A 50% penalty tax will be imposed in any year in which the individual receives insufficient distributions.[3] This 50% tax is imposed on the amount by which the minimum required distributions exceed the distributions actually received by the individual.

Excess contributions

If more than the deductible amount is contributed to an IRA, the excess is subject to a cumulative 6% excise tax.[4] The tax may be avoided under certain circumstances. See ¶ 3206.

Prohibited transactions

Individuals who establish IRAs must not engage in any of the transactions prohibited by Code Sec. 4975.[5] The penalty imposed on an IRA owner who engages in a prohibited transaction with his or her IRA is disqualification of the account or annuity with unfavorable income tax consequences.

☐ See ¶ 2400 and following for a general discussion of the prohibited transaction rules. Specific prohibited transaction exemptions applicable to IRAs are also discussed at ¶ 3208.

Provision of investment advice

The Pension Protection Act of 2006 (P.L. 109-280) added a new category of prohibited transaction exemption under the Code and ERISA in connection with providing investment advice through an "eligible investment advice arrangement" to participants and beneficiaries of individual account plans that who direct the investment or their accounts under the plan.[6] The Act specifically directs the Secretary of Labor, in conjunction with the Secretary of Transportation, to gather information to determine whether investment advice provided through a computer model would be feasible for IRAs.[7] Final regulations were issued by the Labor Department, effective December 27, 2011.[8]

☐ For further discussion of the investment advice rules, see ¶ 2312.

---

[1] Code Sec. 72(t).   [2] Code Sec. 72(t)(2), (3), (7), and (8).

[3] Code Sec. 4974; IRS Reg. § 54.4974-1.

[4] Code Sec. 4973(a).

[5] Code Sec. 408(e)(2).

[6] Code Sec.4975(d)(17), as added by P.L. 109-280 (Pension Protection Act of 2006), Act Sec.

601(b)(1)(C); ERISA Sec. 408(b)(14), as added by P.L. 109-280 (Pension Protection Act of 2006), Act Sec. 601(a)(1).

[7] P.L. 109-280 (Pension Protection Act of 2006), Act Sec. 601(b)(3)(A).

[8] 76 FR 66136, October 25, 2011.

¶ 3223

INDIVIDUAL RETIREMENT ARRANGEMENTS: Withholding Rules for IRAs

Federal income tax is withheld from IRA distributions unless the recipient chooses not to have tax withheld.[1] The amount withheld from an IRA distribution varies depending on whether the distribution is a periodic distribution (such as from an annuity) or a nonperiodic distribution (such as a lump-sum).

Periodic distributions

For annuities or other periodic distributions from an IRA, the tax withheld is based on the recipient's marital status and the number of withholding allowances claimed on the Form W-4P withholding certificate.[2] If no withholding certificate has been filed, the tax withheld is determined by treating the recipient as a married individual claiming three withholding allowances.[3]

Nonperiodic distributions

In general, tax is withheld at a 10% rate on lump-sum distributions.[4]

IRA distributions outside the U.S.

IRA distributions are subject to withholding if the distributions are delivered outside the United States or its possessions. In general, taxpayers receiving such payments cannot make an election to forego withholding on their IRA distributions.[5] However, this withholding may be avoided if the IRA recipient certifies to the payor that the recipient is not (1) a U.S. citizen; (2) a resident alien of the U.S.; or (3) a tax-avoidance expatriate.

[1] Code Sec. 3405(e)(5) and (6).

[2] Code Sec. 3405(a)(1).

[3] Code Sec. 3405(a)(4).

[4] Code Sec. 3405(b).

[5] Code Sec. 3405(e)(13).

¶ 3224

INDIVIDUAL RETIREMENT ARRANGEMENTS: SIMPLE IRAs

An employer may adopt a Savings Incentive Match Plan for Employees (SIMPLE plan), structured as an IRA, if it employs no more than 100 employees who received at least $5,000 in compensation from the employer for the *preceding* year.[1] Employers who maintain a SIMPLE IRA for at least one year, but who fail to be eligible in subsequent years, may continue to maintain the plan for two years following the last year in which the employer was eligible.[2] Also, employers setting up SIMPLE plans after 2001 may be eligible for a tax credit to cover some of the costs incurred in establishing the new plan (see ¶ 101).

A SIMPLE IRA relieves smaller employers of the need to perform complex nondiscrimination testing and to comply with burdensome top-heavy plan and reporting rules.

Maintaining another qualified plan

A SIMPLE IRA may not be established if the employer (or a predecessor employer) maintains another qualified plan (i.e., qualified retirement plan, governmental plan, tax-sheltered annuity, or SEP), with respect to which contributions were made, or benefits were accrued, for service in the period beginning with the year the SIMPLE plan became effective and ending with the year for which the determination is made.[3]

However, employers may adopt a SIMPLE IRA for noncollectively bargained employees, even if the employer also maintains a qualified plan for collectively bargained employees. Collectively bargained employees may be excluded from participation in a SIMPLE IRA, but may be covered under another qualified plan of the employer. The fact the employer maintains a qualified plan in which only collectively bargained employees may participate will not prevent it from establishing a SIMPLE IRA in which only noncollectively bargained employees may participate.[4]

Mergers and acquisitions

An employer that fails to meet the 100-employee limit, the exclusive plan requirement, or the participation rules because of an acquisition, disposition, or similar transaction may continue to maintain a SIMPLE IRA as a qualified salary reduction arrangement during a transition period that begins on the date of the transaction and ends on the last day of the second calendar year following the calendar year in which the transaction occurs.[5]

In order for the grace period to apply, however, the employer must satisfy rules similar to the coverage requirements of Code Sec. 410(b)(6)(C)(i)(II), which generally stipulate that coverage under the plan may not be significantly changed during the transition period. In addition, the SIMPLE IRA may not be maintained during the transition period unless it would have met the requirements applicable to qualified salary reduction arrangements after the transaction, if the employer maintaining the arrangement had remained a separate employer.

Eligibility to participate

A SIMPLE IRA must be open to every employee who:[6]

1. received at least $5,000 in compensation from the employer during *any* two preceding years and

2. is reasonably expected to receive at least $5,000 in compensation during the year.

Self-employed individuals may also participate in a SIMPLE plan. However, certain nonresident aliens and employees who are covered under a collective bargaining agreement may be excluded from participation.[7]

Elective deferrals and matching contributions to SIMPLE IRA

Contributions to a SIMPLE IRA are limited to employee elective contributions and required employer matching contributions or nonelective contributions. Under a SIMPLE plan, an employee may make elective, pre-tax contributions (expressed as a percentage of compensation, not as a flat dollar amount) to an IRA of up to $11,500 in tax year 2012 (and 2011).[8]

Catch-up contributions. Individuals who will attain at least age 50 by the end of the tax year are permitted to make catch-up contributions to the SIMPLE IRA in which they participate. The limits on additional catch-up deferrals for SIMPLE plans are $2,500 for the 2011 and 2012 tax year.[9]

Two contribution formulas. Employers must satisfy one of two contribution formulas. Under the matching contribution formula, employers are generally required to match employee contributions on a dollar-for-dollar basis, up to 3% of an employee's compensation for the year.[10] However, an employer may also elect to match contributions for *all* eligible employees for a given year at a rate lower than 3% (but no lower than 1%) of each employee's compensation.[11] In order to apply the lower matching percentage, the employer must notify employees of the lower percentage within a reasonable time before the 60-day election period during which employees are allowed to determine whether to participate in the SIMPLE plan.[12] In addition, the lower percentage may not be elected for a year if that would cause the matching percentage to drop below 3% of employee compensation in more than two years in a five-year period ending with that year.

Under an alternative formula, an employer may make a nonelective contribution of 2% of compensation for each eligible employee who has earned at least $5,000 in compensation from the employer during the year.[13] The nonelective contribution must be made even if the eligible employee did not elect a salary reduction contribution for the year.[14] The employer is required to notify each eligible employee of the nonelective contributions within a reasonable period of time before the 60-day election period during which an employee must determine whether to participate in the SIMPLE plan. The 2% nonelective contribution is subject to the Code Sec. 401(a)(17) limit on compensation that applies to qualified plans. This limit is $250,000 in 2012 and $245,000 in 2011.[15]

Matching contributions to SIMPLE IRA that are made on behalf of self-employed persons are not treated as elective employer contributions and are not, therefore, subject to the limit on elective deferrals for SIMPLE IRA.[16]

All contributions to an employee's SIMPLE account must be nonforfeitable. Thus, employees vest immediately in contributions made by the employer.[17]

Employers may generally deduct contributions (including pre-tax employee contributions) to the SIMPLE IRA for the year in which they are made.[18] The contributions to the SIMPLE IRA are excludable from an employee's income.[19]

¶3224

CCH Pointer: Wages paid to domestic workers are treated as compensation in determining SIMPLE plan contributions, even though such amounts are not subject to income tax withholding.[20]

Automatic enrollment. A SIMPLE IRA plan may include an automatic contribution arrangement. The arrangement may provide that default salary reduction contributions are made only for employees who are first eligible under the SIMPLE IRA plan on or after the effective date of the automatic contribution arrangement and who do not make an affirmative election (including an affirmative election of zero). The arrangement may provide that the percentage of compensation at which default salary reduction contributions are made for an employee increases based on the number of years or portions of years for which default salary reduction contributions have been made for the employee. The IRS has set out the notice requirements that apply to a SIMPLE IRA plan that includes an automatic contribution arrangement.[21] In addition, the IRS has provided a sample plan amendment that a prototype sponsor of a SIMPLE IRA plan (using a designated financial institution) can use to add an automatic contribution arrangement to the plan. [22]

When amounts must be contributed

Employers must contribute an employee's elective deferrals to the employee's SIMPLE IRA no later than 30 days after the last day of the month for which contributions are made.[23]

Contributions may be made to designated trustee

Generally, an employer must allow an employee to select the financial institution for the SIMPLE IRA to which the employer will make all contributions for the employee.[24] However, an employer may bypass the financial institution selected by the employee and require that all contributions on behalf of eligible employees be made to a trustee or issuer designated by the employer.[25]

Distributions under a SIMPLE IRA

Distributions from a SIMPLE account are generally taxed like distributions from an ordinary IRA.[26] Accordingly, distributions are includible in a participant's income when withdrawn from the account.

Participants who take early withdrawals from a SIMPLE account are generally subject to the 10% early withdrawal penalty applicable to IRAs. However, employees who withdraw contributions during the two-year period beginning on the date that they first began participating in the SIMPLE plan will be assessed a 25% penalty tax.[27]

Rollovers

Participants in a SIMPLE IRA may roll over distributions from one SIMPLE account to another free of tax.[28] In addition, a participant may roll over a distribution from a SIMPLE account to an IRA without penalty if the individual has participated in the SIMPLE plan for two years. For distributions after 2001, SIMPLE IRA distributions made after the employee has participated for two years may be

¶3224

rolled over to another SIMPLE plan, a traditional IRA, a qualified plan, a 403(b) plan, or a Code Sec. 457 plan.[29]

Model forms

The IRS has provided model plan documents (Form 5305-SIMPLE and Form 5304-SIMPLE) that employers can use to adopt SIMPLE plans in conjunction with an IRA.[30] The IRS has also issued two model IRA forms that may be used by trustees and custodians to hold contributions under a SIMPLE IRA. Form 5305-S is a model trust account agreement that is filed by the participant and the trustee. Form 5305-SA is a model custodial account agreement that is filed by the participant and the custodian. These model forms may be used with Form 5305-SIMPLE.[31]

---

[1] Code Sec. 408(p)(2)(C)(i)(I).

[2] Code Sec. 408(p)(2)(C)(i)(II).

[3] Code Sec. 408(p)(2)(D).

[4] Code Sec. 408(p)(2)(D)(i); IRS Notice 98-4, I.R.B. 1998-2, January 12, 1998, Q&A B-3, CCH PENSION PLAN GUIDE ¶ 17,113R.

[5] Code Sec. 408(p)(10).

[6] Code Sec. 408(p)(4)(A).

[7] IRS Notice 98-4, 1998-1 CB 269, January 12, 1998, Q&A B-1 and C-1, CCH PENSION PLAN GUIDE ¶ 17,113R.

[8] Code Sec. 408(p)(2)(A) and Code Sec. 408(p)(2)(E); IRS News Release IR-2011-103, 10-20-11, CCH PENSION PLAN GUIDE ¶ 17,037Q.

[9] Code Sec. 414(v)(2)(b)(ii); IRS News Release IR-2011-103, 10-20-11, CCH PENSION PLAN GUIDE ¶ 17,037Q.

[10] Code Sec. 408(p)(2)(A)(iii) and 408(p)(2)(C)(ii)(I); IRS Notice 98-4, 1998-1 CB 269, January 12, 1998, Q&A D-4, CCH PENSION PLAN GUIDE ¶ 17,113R.

[11] Code Sec. 408(p)(2)(C)(ii)(II).

[12] See Code Sec. 408(p)(5)(C).

[13] Code Sec. 408(p)(2)(B).

[14] IRS Notice 98-4, 1998-1 CB 269, January 12, 1998, Q&A D-6, CCH PENSION PLAN GUIDE ¶ 17,113R.

[15] Code Sec. 408(p)(2)(B)(ii); Code Sec. 401(a)(17); IRS Notice 98-4, 1998-1 CB 269, January 12, 1998, Q&A D-6, CCH PENSION PLAN GUIDE ¶ 17,113R; IRS News Release IR-2011-103, 10-20-11, CCH PENSION PLAN GUIDE ¶ 17,037Q.

[16] Code Sec. 408(p)(8).

[17] Code Sec. 408(p)(3).

[18] Code Sec. 404(m)(2)(A).

[19] Code Sec. 219(b)(4).

[20] Code Sec. 408(p)(6)(A)(i), as amended by the Working Families Tax Relief Act of 2004 (P.L. 108-311).

[21] IRS Notice 2009-66, I.R.B. 2009-39, 9-28-09, CCH PENSION PLAN GUIDE ¶ 17,143H.

[22] IRS Notice 2009-67, I.R.B. 2009-39, 9-28-09, CCH PENSION PLAN GUIDE ¶ 17,143H-3.

[23] Code Sec. 408(p)(5)(A)(i). In order to harmonize ERISA's plan asset regulations and the Internal Revenue Code rules governing the timing of deposits for SIMPLE IRAs, ERISA Reg. § 2510.3-102(b) was amended, effective November 25, 1997, to provide that the maximum period during which salary reduction elective contributions under a SIMPLE IRA may be treated as other than plan assets is no later than the 30th calendar day following the month in which participant amounts would otherwise have been payable to the participant in cash. Note: the 7-day safe harbor during which employers maintaining plans with less than 100 participants at the beginning of the plan year may deposit participant contributions also applies to SIMPLE IRAs. The governing rules are detailed at ¶ 2948.

[24] IRS Notice 98-4, 1998-1 CB 269, January 12, 1998, Q&A E-4, CCH PENSION PLAN GUIDE ¶ 17,113R.

[25] Code Sec. 408(p)(7); IRS Notice 98-4, 1998-1 CB 269, January 12, 1998, Q&A J-1, CCH PENSION PLAN GUIDE ¶ 17,113R.

[26] Code Sec. 402(k).

[27] Code Sec. 72(t)(6).

[28] Code Sec. 408(d)(3)(G).

[29] Code Sec. 408(d)(3)(A)(ii).

[30] Form 5304-SIMPLE and Form 5305-SIMPLE are at ¶ 10,764B and ¶ 10,768A, respectively, of the CCH PENSION PLAN GUIDE.

[31] Form 5305-S and Form 5305-SA are at ¶ 10,768B and ¶ 10,768C, respectively, of the CCH PENSION PLAN GUIDE.

¶ 3225

INDIVIDUAL RETIREMENT ARRANGEMENTS: Roth IRAs

A "Roth IRA" is a distinct type of IRA vehicle under which contributions are nondeductible and the tax advantages are "backloaded." The buildup (e.g., interest and dividends) within the account may be tax free depending on how and when the taxpayer withdraws money from the account. To be treated as a Roth IRA, the account must be designated as such when it is established.[1] A Roth IRA is treated like a traditional IRA except for the special rules described below.[2]

Contribution limits

The maximum total yearly contribution that can be made by an individual to all IRAs (that is, all the deductible, nondeductible, and Roth IRAs maintained by an individual) is $5,000 for tax year 2011 and 2012, not counting rollover contributions.[3]

Unlike traditional IRAs, individuals are allowed to make contributions to a Roth IRA even after age 70½.[4]

Excess contributions. Excess contributions to a Roth IRA are subject to the 6% tax under Code Sec. 4973.[5] Excess contributions are defined as:

1. The excess (if any) of the amount contributed for the tax year to a Roth IRA (other than a rollover) over the amount allowed as a contribution to a Roth IRA and

2. The excess contribution to a Roth IRA for the preceding tax year reduced by the sum of the distributions made from the Roth IRA for the tax year and the excess of the maximum amount allowed as a contribution to a Roth IRA for the tax year over the amount contributed to the Roth IRA for the tax year.

Any contribution that is distributed, together with net income, from a Roth IRA on or before the tax return due date (plus extensions) for the tax year of the contribution is treated as not contributed.[6]

Contribution limits inapplicable to contributions of military death gratuities. An individual who receives a military death gratuity or payment under the Servicemembers' Group Life Insurance (SGLI) program may contribute an amount up to the sum of the gratuity and SGLI payments received to a Roth IRA, notwithstanding the annual contribution limit and the income phase-out of the contribution limit that otherwise apply to contributions to Roth IRAs.[7] This provision generally applies with respect to deaths from injuries occurring on or after June 17, 2008 (the date of enactment of the Heroes Earnings Assistance and Relief Tax (HEART) Act of 2008). The contribution to a Roth IRA of an amount received as a military death gratuity or SGLI payment will be considered a qualified rollover contribution if the contribution is made before the end of the one-year period beginning on the date on which the amount is received, and the amount of the contribution does not exceed the sum of the gratuity and SGLI payments received, less the amount of gratuity and SGLI payments that were contributed to a Coverdell ESA. [8] Such rollovers will be disregarded for purposes of the rule in Code Sec. 408(d)(3)(B), which generally limits the number of rollovers to one per year. [9] In the case of a subsequent distribution from a Roth IRA that is not a qualified distribution, the distribution of the amount attributable to the contribution of a military death gratuity or SGLI payment will be treated as a nontaxable investment in the contract for purposes of applying Code Sec. 72. [10]

IRS scrutiny of tax-shelters designed to avoid Roth IRA contribution limits. The IRS has identified tax-avoidance transactions that are designed to enable taxpayers to avoid the limits on contributions to Roth IRAs by shifting taxable income or otherwise making indirect contributions from the individual's business to the Roth IRA.[11] The transactions being targeted by the IRS typically involve: (1) an individual taxpayer who owns a pre-existing business (e.g., corporation or sole proprietorship); (2) a Roth IRA that is maintained by the taxpayer, and (3) a corporation (i.e., the "Roth IRA corporation") in which substantially all shares are owned or acquired by the Roth IRA. The business and the Roth IRA, both of which are controlled by the taxpayer, enter into a transaction that shifts value into the Roth IRA without fairly or accurately reflecting the value shift. Such a transaction, for example, could involve the acquisition by the Roth IRA corporation of property (e.g., accounts receivable) from the business for less than fair market value, or another arrangement that has the effect of transferring value to the Roth IRA corporation. The difference between the fair market value of the assets acquired by the Roth IRA corporation and the amount actually paid for the assets would be, in effect, a disguised contribution to the Roth IRA. By attempting to make the contribution in this manner, the taxpayer seeks to avoid the statutory limits on Roth IRA contributions. In the event such a transaction is detected, the IRS will deny or reduce the deduction to the business; require the corporation to recognize gain on the transfer, or require the taxpayer to include the payment in income (e.g., as a taxable dividend). The transactions discussed above are treated, effective December 31, 2003, as "listed transactions." Accordingly, the transactions are subject to the Code Sec. 6011 disclosure requirements, the Code Sec. 6111 tax-shelter registration rules, and the Code Sec. 6112 list maintenance requirements. Pursuant to these requirements, taxpayers must disclose their participation in the listed transaction to the IRS and firms promoting such tax-shelters must maintain a list of customers.

Income limits

Eligibility to make contributions to a Roth IRA depends on the income level of the individual. For 2012, the maximum yearly contribution that can be made to a Roth IRA is phased out for single taxpayers with adjusted gross income (AGI) between $110,000 and $125,000 and for joint filers with AGI between $173,000 and $183,000. For 2011, the maximum yearly contribution that can be made to a Roth IRA is phased out for single taxpayers with AGI between $107,000 and $122,000 and for joint filers with AGI between $169,000 and $179,000.[12]

Example: John Monroe, a single taxpayer with AGI of $200,000, is ineligible to contribute to a Roth IRA because his income exceeds the legal threshold. However, he may contribute to a nondeductible IRA.

Taxation of distributions

Qualified distributions from a Roth IRA are not included in the taxpayer's gross income and are not subject to the additional 10% early withdrawal tax.[13] To be a qualified distribution, the distribution must satisfy a five-year holding period and must meet one of four requirements (see below).

To satisfy the five-year holding period, the Roth IRA distribution may not be made before the end of the five-tax-year period beginning with the first tax year for which the individual (or the individual's spouse) made a contribution to the Roth IRA.[14]

CCH Pointer: As is the case with traditional IRAs, a contribution to a Roth IRA for a tax year can be made by the due date for filing the individual's tax return for the year (without regard to extensions). In such a case, the five-year holding period begins to run with the tax year to which the contribution relates, not the year in which the contribution is actually made.

Qualifying types of distributions. In addition to satisfying the five-year holding period, a qualified distribution must be:[15]

1. made on or after the date on which individual attains age 59½;
2. made to a beneficiary (or the individual's estate) on or after the individual's death;
3. attributable to the individual being disabled; or
4. used to pay for "qualified first-time homebuyer expenses" (see ¶ 3222).

Example: Sandra Smith establishes a Roth IRA at age 40 and contributes $2,000 per year to the account for 20 years. The account is now worth $100,000, consisting of $40,000 in contributions plus $60,000 in accumulated earnings. Smith may make withdrawals from her Roth IRA tax-free because she has held the funds for the requisite five years and is over age 59½. (This example assumes that Smith met the income limits for contributing to the account.)

Nonqualified distributions. Distributions that do not meet the 5-year holding period or are not made for one of the specified purposes are referred to as "nonqualified distributions." There is an ordering rule for purposes of determining what portion of a nonqualified distribution is includible in income. Under this rule, distributions are treated as made from contributions first. Thus, no portion of a distribution is treated as attributable to earnings, or includible in gross income, until the total of *all* distributions from the Roth IRA exceeds the amount of contributions.[16]

Note that a distribution may be nonqualified, meaning that the earnings are included in gross income, but may escape the 10% early withdrawal penalty. This

¶3225

can occur if the distribution is covered under one of the general exemptions to the early withdrawal penalty under Code Sec. 72(t) (see ¶ 3222). Thus, for example, a Roth IRA holder who makes a withdrawal from a Roth IRA to pay qualified higher education expenses prior to age 59½ would owe income taxes on any earnings withdrawn (because the distribution is nonqualified) but would not owe the 10% early withdrawal tax.[17]

Minimum distribution rules

The pre-death required beginning distribution rules of Code Sec. 401(a)(9)(A) (see ¶ 1805) that apply to qualified plans and traditional IRAs do not apply to Roth IRAs. This means that Roth IRAs are not subject to minimum required distribution rules during the account holder's lifetime. Thus, unlike with traditional IRAs, the holders of a Roth IRA need not take a distribution by April 1 of the calendar year following the year in which they attain age 70½. Also, the incidental death benefit rules of Code Sec. 401(a) (see ¶ 324) and do not apply to Roth IRAs.[18]

Rollovers and conversions

In addition to receiving ordinary contributions, Roth IRAs may be funded by means of a rollover or conversion. Part or all of the assets of one Roth IRA can be rolled over or converted tax free to another Roth IRA. In addition, part or all of the assets in a traditional IRA can be rolled over or converted to an Roth IRA.

The rollover contribution must meet the general IRA rollover rules of Code Sec. 408(d)(3), such as the 60-day limit.[19] However, rollovers from traditional IRAs to Roth IRAs are disregarded for purposes of the general one-rollover-per-year rule.

Where amounts in a traditional IRA are rolled over or converted to a Roth IRA, the taxpayer must include in gross income any amount that would have been includible if the distribution had not been part of a qualified rollover contribution. However, the 10% early withdrawal tax does not apply.[20]

Income limits for Roth IRA conversions repealed after 2009. Prior to 2010, in order to be eligible for a Roth IRA conversion, a taxpayer's adjusted gross income for the tax year could not exceed $100,000. The income limits on conversions of traditional IRAs to Roth IRAs were eliminated, effective for tax years beginning after December 31, 2009.[21] Thus, beginning in 2010, taxpayers may make such conversions without regard to their AGI.

Special rules for conversions occurring in 2010. For conversions occurring in 2010, such amounts are included in a taxpayer's gross income in equal installments in 2011 and 2012, unless the taxpayer elects otherwise.[22] Accordingly, unless a taxpayer elects otherwise, none of the amount includible in gross income as a result of a conversion occurring in 2010 is included in income in 2010, half of the income resulting from the conversion is includible in gross income in 2011, and the other half is includible in income in 2012.

However, income inclusion is accelerated if converted amounts are distributed before 2012.[23] In that case, the amount included in income in the year of the distribution is increased by the amount distributed, and the amount included in income in 2012 (or 2011 and 2012 in the case of a distribution in 2010) is the lesser of: (1) half of the amount includible in income as a result of the conversion; and (2) the remaining portion of such amount not already included in income.

Conversions from eligible retirement plans. Beginning January 1, 2008, distributions from tax-qualified retirement plans, tax-sheltered annuities and Code Sec. 457 plans can be rolled over directly into a Roth IRA, subject to the restrictions that currently apply to rollovers from a traditional IRA into a Roth IRA (see ¶ 1970A).

Rollovers from Roth 401(k) plans. An eligible rollover distribution from a Roth 401(k) plan (¶ 2941) can be rolled over to a Roth IRA. However, amounts distributed from a Roth IRA may be rolled over or transferred only to another Roth IRA and may not be rolled over to a Roth 401(k) plan.[24]

> **CCH Pointer:** A qualified rollover contribution to a Roth IRA from another Roth IRA or a designated Roth account (a Roth 401(k) or Roth 403(b) plan) is not subject to the gross income inclusion, adjusted gross income limit, and filing status requirements that apply to rollovers from non-Roth eligible plans.[25] The IRS has clarified that if an eligible rollover distribution from an eligible employer plan is rolled over to a Roth IRA and the distribution is not made from a designated Roth account, then the amount that would be includible in gross income were it not part of a qualified rollover contribution is included in the distributee's gross income for the year of the distribution. On the other hand, if an eligible rollover distribution made from a designated Roth account is rolled over to a Roth IRA, the amount rolled over is not includible in the distributee's gross income, whether or not the distribution is a qualified distribution from the designated Roth account. [26]

Roth IRA rollovers of airline bankruptcy payments

A qualified airline employee may transfer any portion of an airline payment amount to a Roth IRA within 180 days of receipt (or, if later, within 180 days of enactment of the Worker, Retiree, and Employer Recovery Act of 2008 (December 23, 2008). [27] Such a transfer is treated as a qualified rollover contribution to the Roth IRA. An airline payment amount is any payment of money or other property payable by a commercial passenger airline carrier to a qualified airline employee under the approval of an order of a federal bankruptcy court in a case filed after September 11, 2001, and before January 1, 2007, and in respect of the qualified airline employee's interest in a bankruptcy claim against the carrier, any note of the carrier (or amount paid in lieu of a note being issued), or any other fixed obligation of the carrier to pay a lump sum amount. A qualified airline employee is an employee or former employee of a commercial passenger airline carrier who was a participant in a defined benefit plan maintained by the carrier which is a qualified plan under Code Sec. 401(a) and was terminated or became subject to the benefit accrual and other restrictions applicable to airline plans that elected alternative funding schedules under the Pension Protection Act of 2006.

¶3225

Computing adjusted gross income

For purposes of the rollover and conversion rules, the applicable adjusted gross income (AGI) is the AGI for the year of the distribution for which the conversion relates. AGI is determined before any amount is included in income as a result of the rollover or conversion.[28]

Minimum required distributions. Generally, uniform minimum required distribution rules apply to tax-qualified plans and traditional IRAs. These rules require that participants must begin taking minimum distributions no later than the "required beginning date" (see ¶ 1805 and ¶ 3210). Prior to 2005, minimum required distributions were included in AGI for purposes of calculating the $100,000 threshold.[29]

Beginning with the 2005 tax year, however, minimum required distributions are excluded from AGI solely for the purposes of determining eligibility to convert a traditional IRA to a Roth IRA.[30]

However, it should be noted that the required minimum distributions are not eligible for conversion to a Roth IRA and are included in gross income.

Taxation of distributions involving rollovers or conversions

Two special rules govern the taxation of distributions of amounts attributable to a rollover or conversion from a traditional IRA to a Roth IRA. One provision accelerates the inclusion in income of any amounts converted in 1998 and withdrawn before the end of the four-year spread period. The second provision applies the 10% early withdrawal tax to amounts converted within the five-year period beginning with the year of the conversion.

Application of early withdrawal tax. If converted amounts are withdrawn within the five-year period beginning with the year of the conversion, then, only to the extent attributable to amounts that were includible in income due to the conversion, the amount withdrawn will be subject to the 10% early withdrawal tax.[31]

Application of ordering rules

The law provides "ordering rules" to determine which amounts are withdrawn for tax purposes where a Roth IRA contains both conversion and contributory amounts, or conversion amounts from different years.[32] Under these rules, traditional Roth IRA contributions will be deemed to be withdrawn first, then converted amounts (starting with the amounts first converted). Withdrawals of converted amounts will be treated as coming first from converted amounts that were includible in income. Earnings will continue to be treated as withdrawn after contributions. All Roth IRAs, whether or not maintained in separate accounts, are treated as a single Roth IRA.

Valuation of IRA annuities involved in Roth conversions

When a traditional IRA annuity is converted to a Roth IRA, the amount includible in income upon conversion is the fair market value of the annuity contract on the date the annuity contract is converted.[33] IRS final regulations use a

¶3225

modified form of the gift tax regulations to determine the fair market value of an annuity contract.[34] If there are comparable annuity contracts being sold, the fair market value of the contract is determined as the price of the comparable contract. If no comparable contract is available to make a comparison, the fair market value is established through an approximation based on the interpolated terminal reserve at the date of the conversion, plus the proportionate part of the gross premium paid before the date of the conversion which covers the period extending beyond that date. The final regulations also provide authority for the IRS Commissioner to issue additional guidance regarding the fair market value of an IRA annuity, including formulas to be used for determining fair market value.

Recharacterizations and reconversions

Generally, if an individual makes a contribution to an IRA for a tax year and then transfers the contribution (or a portion of the contribution) to another IRA in a trustee-to-trustee transfer, the individual can elect to treat the contribution as having been made to the transferee IRA and not the transferor IRA.[35] This transfer must be made on or before the federal income tax due date (including extensions) for the tax year for which the original contribution was made. The transfer must include allocable net income on the contribution and no deduction is permitted for the contribution to the transferor IRA. The IRS refers to these transfers as "recharacterized contributions." A taxpayer can make a recharacterization of an IRA contribution for any reason. However, tax-free rollovers, SIMPLE IRA contributions, and SEP-IRA contributions may not be recharacterized.[36]

Calculation of "attributable net income." The net income attributable to a recharacterized contribution is calculated under a method prescribed in IRS regulations.[37] Under this method, the calculation of the amount of net income attributable to a contribution is based on actual earnings and losses of the IRA during the time it held the contribution.

Effect of recharacterization. A contribution made to the first (transferor) IRA that is being recharacterized as a contribution to the second (transferee) IRA is treated as having been originally contributed to the second IRA on the same date and (in the case of a regular contribution) for the same tax year that the contribution was made to the first IRA.[38]

Reconversions. An individual is permitted to "reconvert" an amount that has been transferred from a Roth IRA to a traditional IRA by means of a recharacterization after having been earlier converted from a traditional IRA to a Roth IRA.

An IRA owner who converts an amount from a traditional IRA to a Roth IRA during any tax year and then transfers that amount back to a traditional IRA by means of a recharacterization may not reconvert that amount from the traditional IRA to a Roth IRA before the beginning of the tax year following the tax year in which the amount was converted to a Roth IRA or, if later, the end of the 30-day period beginning on the day on which the IRA owner transfers the amount from the Roth IRA back to a traditional IRA by means of a recharacterization (regardless of whether the recharacterization occurs during the tax year in which the amount was converted to a Roth IRA or the following tax year).[39]

¶3225

Example 1: On March 1, 2011, Joe converts an amount from his traditional IRA to a Roth IRA. On July 1, 2011, Joe transfers the funds back to a traditional IRA by means of a recharacterization. Joe must wait until January 1, 2012, to convert back to the Roth IRA.

Example 2: Assume the same facts as in Example (1), except that Joe completed the recharacterization on December 20, 2011. In this situation, Joe would have to wait until January 20, 2012, to reconvert.

Reporting requirements

As with traditional IRAs, Roth IRA trustees and issuers are required to report to the IRS annual contributions made by participants and the tax year to which the contributions relate. Form 5498 is used to report contributions for the year. This form is also used to report the fair market value of the account to the participant. Roth IRA trustees and issuers are required to report distributions on Form 1099-R and transmittal Form 1096. There are, however, special reporting requirements that are unique to Roth IRAs, particularly relating to conversion and recharacterized contributions and distributions of converted amounts. The IRS has provided special guidance on these special Roth IRA reporting rules.[40]

☐ General IRA reporting requirements are discussed at ¶ 3220.

Model forms

The IRS has issued model forms for use by financial institutions that offer Roth IRAs to their customers. Form 5305-R (Roth Individual Retirement Trust Account) is for use by trustees. Form 5305-RA (Roth Individual Retirement Custodial Account) is for use by custodians. Form 5305-RB (Roth Individual Retirement Annuity Endorsement) is for use by annuity issuers.[41]

The IRS has also issued procedures for applying to the IRS for an opinion letter for a Roth IRA. An application for approval of a prototype Roth IRA must be submitted using Form 5306 (Application for Approval of Prototype or Employer Sponsored Individual Retirement Account) with the words "Roth IRA" written in the upper margin of the form, and accompanied by the appropriate user fee.[42]

Sponsors of prototype Roth IRAs who wish to accept rollover contributions from designated Roth contribution programs established as part of a 401(k) plan or 403(b) plan (¶ 2941) must amend their documentation to reflect that the prototype Roth IRA permits these rollover contributions.[43]

[1] Code Sec. 408A(b).

[2] Code Sec. 408A(a).

[3] Code Sec. 408A(c)(2) and (c)(6)(B).

[4] Code Sec. 408A(c)(4).

[5] Code Sec. 4973(f).

[6] IRS Reg. § 1.408A-3, Q&A-7.

[7] Code Sec. 408A(e)(2), as amended by P.L. 110-245 (Heroes Earnings Assistance and Relief Tax Act of 2008), Act Sec. 109. See also IRS Notice 2010-15, Sec. VI, I.R.B. 2010-6, CCH PENSION PLAN GUIDE ¶ 17,144L.

[8] Code Sec. 408A(e)(2)(A), as amended by P.L. 110-245 (Heroes Earnings Assistance and Relief Tax Act of 2008), Act Sec. 109.

[9] Code Sec. 408A(e)(2)(B), as amended by P.L. 110-245 (Heroes Earnings Assistance and Relief Tax Act of 2008), Act Sec. 109.

[10] Code Sec. 408A(e)(2)(C), as amended by P.L. 110-245 (Heroes Earnings Assistance and Relief Tax Act of 2008), Act Sec. 109. See also Joint Committee on Taxation (J.C.T. Rep. No. JCX-44-08).

[11]IRS Notice 2004-8, I.R.B. 2004-4, 1-26-04, CCH Pension Plan Guide ¶ 17,127Z.

[12] Code Sec. 408A(c)(3)(A) and (C). Under Code Sec. 408A(c)(3)(C), enacted by P.L. 109-280 (Pension Protection Act of 2006), the income limits for Roth IRA contributions are indexed for inflation beginning in the 2007 tax year. The indexed amount will be rounded to the nearest multiple of $1,000. The 2012 inflation adjustments are contained in IRS News Release IR-2011-103, 10-20-11, CCH Pension Plan Guide ¶ 17,037Q. The 2011 inflation adjustments are contained in IRS News Release IR-2010-108, 10-28-10, CCH Pension Plan Guide ¶ 17,037O.

[13] Code Sec.408A(d)(1).

[14] Code Sec. 408A(d)(2)(B).

[15] Code Sec. 408A(d)(2)(A).

[16] Code Sec. 408A(d)(4)(B)(i).

[17] IRS Notice 97-60, 1997-2 CB 310, 11-17-97, CCH Pension Plan Guide ¶ 17,113F.

[18] Code Sec. 408A(c)(5).

[19] Code Sec. 408A(e).

[20] Code Sec. 408A(d)(3)(A)(i) and (ii). If a rollover from a traditional IRA to a Roth IRA was made before January 1, 1999, the individual was allowed to use a "four year spread"—that is, the individual could have recognized income "ratably" over a four-tax-year period beginning with the tax year in which the payment or distribution was made. The decision to use the four-year spread was elective. See Code Sec. 408A(d)(3)(A)(iii).

[21]P.L. 109-222 (Tax Increase Prevention and Reconciliation Act of 2005), Act Sec. 512(a), repealing Code Sec. 408A(c)(3)(B), effective for taxable years beginning after December 31, 2009.

[22] Code Sec. 408A(d)(3)(A)(iii), as amended by P.L. 109-222 (Tax Increase Prevention and Reconciliation Act of 2005), Act Sec. 512(b)(1).

[23] Code Sec. 408A(d)(3)(E)(i), as amended by P.L. 109-222 (Tax Increase Prevention and Reconciliation Act of 2005), Act Sec. 512(b)(2).

[24] IRS Reg. § 1.408A-10.

[25] Code Sec. 408A(c)(3)(B) and Code Sec. 408A(d)(3)(B) as amended by P.L. 110-458 (Worker, Retiree, and Employer Recovery Act of 2008), Act Sec. 108(a).

[26]IRS Notice 2009-75, I.R.B. 2009-38, 9-28-09, CCH Pension Plan Guide ¶ 17,143L.

[27] P.L. 110-458 (Worker, Retiree, and Employer Recovery Act of 2008), Act Sec. 125.

[28] Code Sec. 408A(c)(3)(B)(i).

[29] Code Sec. 408A(c)(3)(C)(i) prior to amendment by P.L. 105-206 (IRS Restructuring and Reform Act of 1998).

[30] Code Sec. 408A(c)(3)(B)(i).

[31] Code Sec. 408A(d)(3)(F).

[32] Code Sec. 408A(d)(4)(B).

[33] IRS Reg. § 1.408A-4, A-14(a).

[34] IRS Reg. § 1.408A-4, A-14(b).

[35] Code Sec. 408A(d)(6)(A); Code Sec. 408A(d)(6)(B); Code Sec. 408A(d)(7).

[36] IRS Reg. § 1.408A-5.

[37] IRS Reg. § 1.408-11.

[38] IRS Reg. § 1.408A-5.

[39] IRS Reg. § 1.408A-5, Q&A-9.

[40] IRS Notice 98-49, 1998-2 CB 365, 9-21-98, CCH Pension Plan Guide ¶ 17,114Z; IRS Announcement 98-113, I.R.B. 1998-51, 12-21-98, CCH Pension Plan Guide ¶ 17,097P-92.

[41]Form 5305-R, Form 5305-RA, and Form 5305-RB are reproduced at ¶ 10,766J, ¶ 10,766K, and ¶ 10,766L, respectively, of the CCH Pension Plan Guide.

[42] Rev. Proc. 98-59, 1998-2 CB 365, 12-14-98, CCH Pension Plan Guide ¶ 17,299O-57.

[43] IRS Announcement 2007-55, I.R.B. 2007-23, 6-4-07, CCH Pension Plan Guide ¶ 17,097T-8.

¶ 3226

SIMPLIFIED EMPLOYEE PENSIONS: SEPs Defined

A simplified employee pension (SEP) is basically an IRA that is allowed to receive an increased rate of contributions from the IRA holder's employer.[1] *Any* employer, whether it is a corporation, a partnership, or even a one-person sole-proprietorship with no other employees, may establish a SEP.[2] Because the employer is not required to establish a trust, as with other retirement plans, it is relieved of several of the fiduciary and administrative responsibilities associated with those plans.

Characteristics of a SEP

In order for an IRA to qualify as a SEP, certain requirements must be met:

1. The employer must contribute to the IRA of every employee who is at least 21 years old, has worked during the year for which the contribution is made and for at least three of the previous five years, and has received at least $550 in compensation (for 2011 and 2012) for the year in which the contribution is made.[3] Employees covered by a collective bargaining agreement under which retirement benefits were negotiated and nonresident aliens who received no income from sources within the United States may be excluded from coverage.[4]

2. Employer contributions must be made under a written formula which specifies the manner in which they are computed and the requirements an employee must satisfy to share in an allocation. Under the SEP rules, contributions by the employer are limited to 25% of the employee's compensation or $50,000 in 2012 ($49,000 for 2011), whichever is less.[5] SEP contributions need not be made every year.

3. Employer contributions must not discriminate in favor of highly compensated employees and must bear a uniform relationship to total compensation or earned income that does not exceed $250,000 for 2012 ($245,000 for 2011).[6] In addition, if the plan becomes "top-heavy," (see ¶ 3232), certain minimum contributions have to be made.[7]

4. The employer may not restrict the employee's ability to withdraw funds from an IRA that receives SEP contributions.[8]

☐ SEP requirements are more fully discussed at ¶ 3230.

---

[1] Code Sec. 402(h).

[2] Code Sec. 408(k).

[3] Code Sec. 408(k)(2) and (k)(8); IRS Prop. Reg. § 1.408-7(d)(2); IRS News Release IR-2011-103, 10-20-11, CCH Pension Plan Guide ¶ 17,037Q.

[4] Code Sec. 408(k)(2).

[5] Code Sec. 408(k)(5); Code Sec. 408(j); IRS Prop. Reg. §§ 1.408-7(e)(2) and 1.408-7(f); IRS

News Release IR-2011-103, 10-20-11, CCH Pension Plan Guide ¶ 17,037Q.

[6] Code Secs. 408(k)(3)(A) and (C). This figure is adjusted for inflation. IRS News Release IR-2011-103, 10-20-11, CCH Pension Plan Guide ¶ 17,037Q.

[7] Code Sec. 416(c)(2).

[8] Code Sec. 408(k)(4).

¶ 3228

SIMPLIFIED EMPLOYEE PENSIONS: Establishing a SEP

In order to establish a SEP, an employer must execute a written document by the due date of its business's income tax return for the year that it is contributing and taking a deduction for contributions to the SEP. The written document must include the following information:[1]

1. the employer's name;

2. a specific formula for the allocation of contributions;

3. provisions on participation, vesting, and nondiscrimination; and

4. the signature of a responsible official.

A favorable determination letter from the Internal Revenue Service for IRAs, including IRAs which are part of a SEP, is not required to obtain the benefits of a SEP. However, the IRS has developed a one-page tax form, 5305-SEP, that meets all the requirements of a simplified employee pension plan and does not require any special document preparation.

The requirements for an employer to be able to utilize Form 5305-SEP are:

1. The employer must not maintain any other retirement plan and must not have maintained a defined benefit plan at any time in the past (see ¶ 103 for the definition of a defined benefit plan).

2. Each eligible employee must have established an IRA.

3. The employer must not utilize leased employees.

4. The plan may not integrate contributions with Social Security taxes.

Form 5305-SEP should not be filed with the IRS. However, the employer should retain a signed, dated copy with its business records.

☐ Form 5305-SEP is at CCH PENSION PLAN GUIDE ¶ 10,767.

Prototype SEPs

The IRS has also set forth procedures by which prototype SEPs can obtain opinion letters and determination letters[2] and has established a schedule of fees for requesting such rulings from the IRS.[3] Form 5306-A may be used to obtain a favorable opinion letter stating that a SEP agreement, which will be used by more than one employer, is acceptable in form. One copy of all documents that make up the SEP agreement must be filed with the Form 5306-A. If the filing is for an amendment of the SEP, a copy of the amendment and an explanation of its effect on the SEP agreement must be attached. The IRS will not issue an opinion letter on a document submitted with Form 5306-A that is a combination of a prototype SEP and a prototype individual retirement account or annuity. As of April 1, 2002, the IRS began accepting applications for opinion letters on prototype SEPs that incorporate changes under P.L. 107-16 (Economic Growth and Tax Relief Reconciliation Act of 2001).[4] Protoype SEPs must have been amended and an application for an opinion letter on the amended documents must have been submitted no later than December 31, 2002.

☐ Form 5306-A is at CCH PENSION PLAN GUIDE ¶ 10,769A.

---

[1] Code Sec. 408(k)(5); IRS Prop. Reg. §§ 1.408-7(e)(2) and 1.408-7(f).

[2] Rev. Proc. 87-50, 1987-2 CB 647, CCH PENSION PLAN GUIDE ¶ 17,299L-40.

[3] Rev. Proc. 2012-8, I.R.B. 2012-1, CCH PENSION PLAN GUIDE ¶ 17,299T-88.

[4] See Rev. Proc. 2002-10, 2002-1 CB 401, 1-28-02, CCH PENSION PLAN GUIDE ¶ 17,299P-97 and Announcement 2002-49, I.R.B. 2002-19, CCH PENSION PLAN GUIDE ¶ 17,097R-95.

¶ 3230
SIMPLIFIED EMPLOYEE PENSIONS: Requirements for a SEP

An employer must make a SEP contribution for each employee who has reached the age of 21, has worked for the employer in at least three of the preceding five years, and received at least $550 in compensation (for 2011 and 2012) from that employer for the year that the contribution is made.[1]

> **Example:** Jones Hardware maintains a SEP. Rob Douglas worked for Jones while in college in 2008, 2009, and 2010, never working more than 35 days in a particular year. In August 2011, Rob turns 21. In September, Rob begins working for Jones on a full-time basis, earning $10,000. Jones Hardware must make a SEP contribution for Rob in 2011 because he has met the minimum age requirement, has worked for Jones in three of the five years preceding 2011, and has meet the minimum compensation requirement for 2011.

Employer contributions must not discriminate in favor of highly compensated employees.[2] A SEP will be considered discriminatory unless its employer contributions bear a uniform relationship to compensation. The total amount of annual compensation that may be taken into consideration when making a SEP contribution is $250,000 for 2012 ($245,000 for 2011).[3] Interestingly, the IRS has stated that a rate of contribution that actually *decreases* as compensation *increases* is considered uniform.[4]

> **Example 1:** Jones Hardware Store installs a SEP to which it wants to contribute for each active employee. The company would like to contribute to the SEP 10% of the total compensation of each employee who has completed up to five years of service and 12% of the total compensation of each employee who has completed *more* than five years of service. Its SEP *will* be considered discriminatory because employer contributions *do not bear a uniform relationship to each employee's compensation.*

> **Example 2:** U-Do-It-Rite Hardware Store installs a SEP under which it will contribute 15% of an employee's first $15,000 in compensation and 10% of all compensation *above* $15,000. The company's SEP will *not* be considered discriminatory merely because the rate of contribution *decreases* as compensation *increases.*

The employee's right to employer contributions in a SEP is *always* 100% vested. In other words, the employee has the full right to withdraw the contributions in his account at all times.[5] This is a significant difference from other types of qualified plans, which generally allow more gradual forms of vesting. SEP benefits are also portable. Employees may take the benefits with them in the form of an IRA when they terminate employment.

---

[1] Code Sec. 408(k)(2); IRS News Release IR-2011-103, 10-20-11, CCH PENSION PLAN GUIDE ¶ 17,037Q.

[2] Code Sec. 408(k)(3).

[3] Code Sec. 408(k)(3)(C); IRS News Release IR-2011-103, 10-20-11, CCH PENSION PLAN GUIDE ¶ 17,037Q.

[4] IRS Prop. Reg. § 1.408-8(c)(1).

[5] Code Sec. 408(k)(4).

¶ 3232

SIMPLIFIED EMPLOYEE PENSIONS: Contributions and Deductions

The amounts contributed to a SEP by an employer on behalf of an employee are *not* taxable as income in the year they are contributed.[1]

Example: Mike Douglas earns $20,000 in compensation from his employer. His employer contributes $3,000 to his IRA which qualifies as a SEP. The $3,000 contributed by Mike's employer to his SEP is not taxable as income in the year that it is contributed.

An employer may deduct contributions to a SEP just as it may deduct contributions to any other type of tax-qualified retirement plan.[2] However, the following special deduction rules apply to SEPs:[3]

1. Where a SEP is maintained on a calendar year (called the "plan year"), contributions are deductible for the taxable year with which *or within which* the calendar year ends. Contributions are deductible for that tax year if they are made by the due date of the employer's tax return, plus any extensions of the due date of the tax return to which the employer is entitled.

2. Where a SEP is maintained on a taxable year basis (i.e., the plan year of the SEP and the tax year of the employer are the same) contributions are deductible for the taxable year if the contributions are made by the due date of the employer's tax return, plus extensions.

3. The deduction cannot exceed 25% of the compensation paid to the employees for the calendar year ending with or within the tax year. However, any excess may be carried over and deducted in succeeding years, up to the 25% limit for those years.[4]

Employers are allowed to take Social Security into account in calculating SEP contributions.[5] This process is known as "integration" and is discussed in detail in at ¶ 1200 and following.

Nondiscrimination rules

Employer contributions must not discriminate in favor of any officer, shareholder, or "highly compensated employee" as defined in the Internal Revenue Code.[6] However, employees who are covered by a collective bargaining agreement and who are nonresident aliens may be excluded from consideration if they would also be excluded under rules that apply to other qualified pension plans. For 2012, employer contributions will be considered discriminatory unless they bear a uniform relationship to the first $250,000 ($245,000 for 2011) of the total compensation of each employee who has a SEP-IRA.[7]

Top-heavy rules

Qualified plans that are classified as "top-heavy" must meet additional nondiscrimination requirements, including faster vesting, minimum contributions or benefits for plan participants who are non-key employees, and limitations on the amount of a participant's compensation which may be taken into account.[8] For purposes of the top-heavy plan rules, a SEP is treated as a defined contribution plan.[9] Defined contribution plans are top-heavy if, as of a certain date (called the "determination date"), the sum of the account balances of participants who are "key employees" for that plan year exceeds 60% of the sum of the account balances of all employees under the plan.[10] The plan is also considered top-heavy when it is in a top-heavy group of plans of commonly controlled or affiliated employers.[11]

A special rule for testing the 60% limit applies to SEPs. Under this rule, an employer may use the aggregate of employer contributions made for SEP participants instead of the sum of their account balances.[12]

The determination date for valuing SEP account balances is the last day of the preceding plan year.[13] In the case of the first plan year of a plan's existence, the last day of that year is the determination date.

If a SEP is determined to be top-heavy, an employer must make a minimum contribution of 3% of compensation for each participant who is not a key employee.[14]

☐ Top-heavy plans are discussed at ¶ 900 and following.

---

[1] Code Sec. 402(h).

[2] Code Sec. 404(g)(1).

[3] Code Sec. 404(h)(1).

[4] Code Sec. 404(h)(1)(C).

[5] Code Sec. 408(k)(3)(D).

[6] Code Sec. 408(k)(3).

[7] Code Sec. 408(k)(3)(C); IRS News Release IR-2011-103, 10-20-11, CCH PENSION PLAN GUIDE ¶ 17,037Q.

[8] Code Sec. 416.

[9] Code Sec. 416(i)(6).

[10] Code Sec. 416(g)(1).

[11] Code Sec. 416(g)(2).

[12] Code Sec. 416(i)(6).

[13] Code Sec. 416(g)(4)(C).

[14] Code Sec. 416(c)(2).

¶ 3234

SIMPLIFIED EMPLOYEE PENSIONS: Distribution Rules

The rules governing distributions from SEP accounts are identical to those governing IRAs (because a SEP's funding mechanism *is* an IRA).[1] Thus, a discussion of these rules may be found at ¶ 3210.

---

[1] Code Sec. 408(k)(1).

¶ 3236

SIMPLIFIED EMPLOYEE PENSIONS: Salary Reduction SEPs (SARSEPs)

Under a salary reduction SEP (SARSEP), employees can choose to have the employer make contributions to their SEP-IRAs instead of paying them the equivalent amount as salaries.[1]

The elective deferral limit applicable to SARSEPs is $17,000 for 2012 ($16,500 for 2011). The limit is subject to cost-of-living increases in $500 increments.[2]

SARSEPs repealed in 1997

Because of the enactment of SIMPLE plans (see ¶ 170 and ¶ 3224), SARSEPs may not be established after December 31, 1996.[3] Employers, however, may continue to make contributions, under pre-1997 rules, to SARSEPs established before January 1, 1997. In addition, employees hired after December 31, 1996, may continue to participate in SARSEPs that were established before 1997.

CCH Pointer: In light of the repeal of SARSEPs in 1997, the rules below only apply to SARSEPs already established by December 31, 1996.

Elective deferrals

If the employee elects to have contributions made on his or her behalf to a SEP (that is, an "elective deferral"), the contribution is not treated as having been distributed or made available to the employee.[4] In addition, the elective deferral is not treated as an employee contribution merely because the SEP provides the employee with such an election. Therefore, one advantage to the employee in electing to have amounts contributed to the SEP is that the employee is not required to include the elective deferral in gross income.

The rules permitting salary reduction SEPs do not apply to SEPs maintained by a state or local government or a political subdivision of a state or local government.[5]

Participation

An employer must allow SARSEP contributions by each employee who has reached the age of 21, has worked for the employer in at least three of the preceding five years, and received at least $550 in compensation for 2012 (and 2011) from that employer for the year that the contribution is made.[6]

The election to have amounts contributed to a SARSEP is available only if:[7]

1. at least 50% of the employees who are eligible to participate elect to have amounts contributed to the SEP; and

2. the employer did not have more than 25 eligible employees at any time during the preceding tax year.

Nondiscrimination requirement

The salary reduction arrangement is also subject to a nondiscrimination test similar to the test imposed on a 401(k) plan.[8] This is known as the Actual Deferral Percentage (ADP) test (see ¶ 2951). Under the ADP test for a SARSEP, the annual amount deferred as a percentage of compensation for each highly compensated employee may not exceed 125% of the average deferral percentage of all other eligible employees.

Vesting

The employee's right to employer contributions in a SARSEP is *always* 100% vested.[9] In other words, the employee has the full right to the contributions in his account *at all times*. This is a significant difference from other types of qualified plans, which generally allow more gradual forms of vesting. Although the employee retains an absolute right to his employer's SARSEP contributions at all times, there are substantial *tax* penalties for early withdrawal of contributions (see ¶ 3222).

Taxability of contributions to participants

The amount contributed by the employer and the amount electively deferred by the participant to a SARSEP is not taxable as income and is not includible on Form W-2 as taxable wages in the year contributed.[10] However, elective deferral amounts *are* subject to FICA and FUTA taxes.[11]

---

[1] Code Sec. 408(k)(6).

[2] Code Secs. 402(g)(1), (g)(4), and 402(h)(2). IRS News Release IR-2011-103, 10-20-11, CCH PENSION PLAN GUIDE ¶ 17,037Q.

[3] Code Sec. 408(k)(6)(H).

[4] Code Sec. 408(k)(6)(A).

[5] Code Sec. 408(k)(6)(E).

[6] Code Sec. 408(k)(2); Code Sec. 408(k)(8); IRS News Release IR-2011-103, 10-20-11, CCH PENSION PLAN GUIDE ¶ 17,037Q.

[7] Code Sec. 408(k)(6)(A)(ii) and (B).

[8] Code Sec. 408(k)(6)(A)(iii).

[9] Code Sec. 408(k)(4).

[10] Code Sec. 402(h).

[11] Code Secs. 3121(a)(5)(C) and 3306(b)(5)(C).

¶ 3238

SIMPLIFIED EMPLOYEE PENSIONS: SEP Reporting and Disclosure Rules

An employer is permitted to establish a simplified employee pension plan by using an IRS model Form 5305-SEP plan or by using a non-model plan (a SEP created other than by the use of a Form 5305-SEP). The IRS requires an employer who adopts a Form 5305-SEP to furnish each participant with information about the SEP and the SEP agreement.[1] This requirement will be satisfied by furnishing the participant with a copy of the completed Form 5305-SEP contribution agreement, the questions and answers that are printed on the Form 5305-SEP, and a statement each year showing any contribution made to the participant's individual retirement account or annuity. The employer should retain the original Form 5305-SEP agreement.

Form 5498 (Individual Retirement Arrangement Information) must be submitted to the IRS by the trustee or issuer of an IRA to which SEP contributions are made.[2] Form 5498 is submitted to the IRS along with transmittal Form 1096. Form 1096 transmitting Form 5498 is to be filed on or before May 31 following the calendar year for which Form 5498 is required. Form 5498 may also be used to provide annual report required information to SEP participants and beneficiaries.

Distributions made during the calendar year from IRAs are to be reported on Form 1099-R. Payments representing a total distribution closing the account or annuity are also to be reported on Form 1099-R. Form 1099-R must be filed with the IRS with transmittal Form 1096 by February 28 of the year following the calendar year during which payments were made.

☐ See ¶ 3220 for a discussion of IRA reporting and disclosure rules.

ERISA reporting and disclosure requirements

A SEP is subject to the ERISA reporting and disclosure requirements (annual reports, summary annual reports, disclosures to participants, etc.).[3] However, a plan administrator (ordinarily, the employer) of a model SEP may be *exempted* from the ERISA reporting and disclosure requirements.[4] To qualify for this exemption, when an employee becomes eligible to participate in a model SEP, the administrator must furnish the employee with a copy of the complete and unmodified two-page IRS Form 5305-SEP used to establish the SEP.

The Department of Labor has also issued an alternative method of compliance for most employers who adopt a non-model SEP.[5] Under this alternative method, administrators of non-model SEPs must provide eligible employees with the following specific information items:

1. the requirements for employee participation in the SEP,

2. the formula under which employer contributions to the SEP will be allocated among participants' IRAs,

3. the name or title of the individual who is designated by the employer to provide additional information to participants concerning the SEP and employer contributions to it, and

4. if the employer selects or substantially influences employees to choose the IRAs into which employer contributions will be made, the terms of those IRAs.

Administrators of non-model SEPs must also provide certain general information about SEPs and individual retirement accounts, such as:

1. what a SEP is and how it operates,

2. statutory provisions prohibiting discrimination in favor of highly paid employees,

3. a participant's right to receive contributions under a SEP and the allowable sources of contributions to a SEP-IRA,

4. the statutory limit on contributions to SEP-IRAs,

5. consequences of excess contributions to a SEP-IRA and how to avoid them,

¶3238

6. how a participant must treat contributions to a SEP-IRA for tax purposes,

7. statutory provisions concerning withdrawal of funds from a SEP-IRA and the consequences of premature withdrawal,

8. a participant's rights regarding contributions made under a SEP to his or her IRA, and

9. a participant's ability to roll over or transfer funds from a SEP-IRA to another IRA, SEP-IRA, or retirement bond, and how such a rollover or transfer may be effected without causing adverse tax consequences.

[1] IRS Announcement 80-58, I.R.B. 1980-19.

[2] IRS Prop. Reg. § 1.408-5; IRS Announcement 85-7, I.R.B. 1985-4, 42.

[3] ERISA Secs. 104 and 110.

[4] ERISA Reg. § 2520.104-48.

[5] ERISA Reg. § 2520.104-49.

¶ 3240

SIMPLIFIED EMPLOYEE PENSIONS: Tax Penalties

Premature and insufficient SEP distributions are subject to tax penalties. Since the rules governing distributions from SEP accounts are identical to those governing IRAs (because a SEP's funding mechanism is an IRA), a discussion of these rules may be found under the discussion of IRAs at ¶ 3222.

Excess contributions to SARSEP

To the extent that the amount deferred to a SARSEP exceeds the dollar and percent limitation it is treated like an excess contribution under a 401(k) plan (see ¶ 2984). [1] Deferrals in excess of those allowed under the discrimination test (see ¶ 3236) are included in the employee's income. In addition, the excess contribution may also be subject to a 10% excise tax on the employer.

The employer is required to notify a participant by March 15 if the participant has made any excess SARSEP contributions for the preceding calendar year. The employer must notify the participant by providing him with a required form (which is included in the instructions to Form 5305A-SEP). Any distribution or transfer made *before* the employer has determined that excess contributions have been made will be subject *both* to ordinary income tax and to the premature distribution penalty tax, regardless of whether the penalty tax would otherwise not apply.[2] If the employer fails to notify a participant by December 31 of the calendar year following the year of an excess SEP contribution, the SEP may no longer be considered tax-qualified.

[1] Code Sec. 408(k)(6)(C)(i).

[2] Code Sec. 408(d)(7).

¶ 3242

KEOGH PLANS: Parity with Corporate Plans

Plans for the self-employed are commonly referred to as Keogh plans and were first introduced in 1963. The Tax Equity and Fiscal Responsibility Act of 1982

(TEFRA) generally eliminated distinctions in the tax law between qualified plans of corporations and those of Keogh plans.[1] These provisions were effective beginning in 1984.

However, even after TEFRA, there still remain special requirements, definitions, and other provisions that apply only to Keogh plans. Accordingly, the general qualification requirements for Keogh plans are discussed at ¶ 300 and following. The special requirements which still exist for Keogh plans are covered in detail at ¶ 3244—¶ 3260 below.

[1] P.L. 97-248.

¶ 3244

KEOGH PLANS: Self-Employed Person Defined

A self-employed person is anyone (1) who has net earnings from self- employment to the extent that those net earnings constitute "earned income" or compensation for personal services actually rendered, and (2) who is subject to the self-employment tax under Social Security.[1]

IRS regulations also include within the definition of self-employed, certain categories of persons who are not (or are not necessarily) subject to self-employment tax.[2]

A self-employed person also includes a person who would or could be subject to self-employment tax *except* for the fact that his business had no net profits for the taxable year. But any person who is a regular or "common law" employee is not self-employed with respect to income received from that employment, even though that income constitutes net earnings from self-employment.[3]

For any person to be considered self-employed, the individual must be in business for himself or herself. Sole proprietors and partners are self-employed.[4]

[1] Code Secs. 401(c) and 401(c)(2).   [3] IRS Reg. § 1.401-10(b).
[2] See IRS Reg. § 1.401-10(a)-(d).   [4] IRS Publication 560, p. 5.

¶ 3246

KEOGH PLANS: Owner-Employee Defined

Self-employed individuals can be divided into two groups—those who are "owner-employees" and those who are not. This distinction is important for an understanding of the Keogh plan rules.

An "owner-employee" is a self-employed person who owns the entire interest in an unincorporated trade or business (e.g., a sole proprietor) or, in the case of a partnership, a partner who owns either (1) more than 10% of the capital interest or (2) more than 10% of the profits interest of the partnership.[1] For instance, a person who owns only 2% of the profits interest but 11% of the capital interest of a partnership is an owner-employee.

The partnership agreement will ordinarily determine a partner's interest in the profits and the capital of the partnership. If there is no provision concerning the sharing of profits, the profits interest of the partners will be ascertained on the same basis as their distributive shares of partnership taxable income, excluding any guaranteed payments which may be due any of the partners. If the partnership agreement is silent concerning the capital interests of the partners, the capital interests will be determined on the basis of the partner's interest in the partnership assets which would be distributable to the partner upon his withdrawal from the partnership or upon its liquidation, whichever is greater.[2]

Employer defined

A qualified plan must be the plan "of an employer." Prior to enactment of the "Self-Employed Individuals Tax Retirement Act of 1962," the term "employer" was never defined. A general definition is still lacking, but the term has been defined to the following extent: a sole proprietor (an individual who owns the entire interest in an unincorporated trade or business) is considered to be his own employer and a partnership is considered to be the employer of each partner.[3]

This definition has important practical consequences. Since a qualified plan must be a plan "of an employer," a partner could not establish a retirement plan for himself—only the partnership may establish a plan.[4] Thus, a partner without the controlling interest in his partnership would have to secure agreement from the other partners (at least enough of them to constitute a voting majority) before a plan could be established from which the partner would benefit.

Common law employee

An employee is someone who owns no part of the business and works for a self-employed person. The regulations refer to this type of employee as a "common-law employee." [5] The fact that a common-law employee is required to pay self-employment tax does not give the employee the right to set up a retirement plan. Thus, a U. S. citizen who was employed by a foreign government was denied the right to set up a retirement plan as a self-employed person even though his compensation was subject to the self-employment tax.[6]

---

[1] Code Sec. 401(c)(3).

[2] IRS Reg. § 1.401-10(b)(3).

[3] Code Sec. 401(c)(4); IRS Reg. § 1.401-10(e)(1).

[4] Rev. Rul. 67-3, 1967-1 CB 94, CCH Pension Plan Guide ¶ 18,541.

[5] IRS Reg. § 1.401-10(b)(3); IRS Publication 560.

[6] Rev. Rul. 73-384, 1973-2 CB 141, CCH Pension Plan Guide ¶ 19,263.

¶ 3248

KEOGH PLANS: Earned Income Defined

Keogh plan contributions on behalf of self-employed individuals (including owner-employees) are geared to "earned income." Earned income is defined as gross income from a trade or business (which includes professional fees and other compensation for personal services) less deductions[1] (see below). Basing contributions and deductions on earned income usually requires that a separate account be established for each self-employed person covered by the plan.[2] Generally, the limitations on contributions and deductions for Keogh plans are the same as those for corporate plans (see ¶ 500 and following).

The main concern of the law is that the personal efforts of the self-employed person be involved in the production of earned income.[3] The fact that capital also plays a significant role in producing the income of a self-employed person's business is not considered significant.

Earned income is figured after reductions

When figuring the deduction for employer contributions made on behalf of a self-employed person, the following are *subtracted* from net earnings:[4]

1. the deduction allowed the self-employed person for one-half of the self- employment tax; and

2. the deduction for contributions on behalf of the self-employed person to the plan.

Figuring deductions based on earned income

In the case of a plan under which employer contributions are expressed as a percentage of the compensation of each participant (such as in a "money purchase pension plan" or a "SEP"), the requirement that net earnings be *reduced* by the deduction for contributions is satisfied if the plan's stated rate of contribution is reduced, for each self-employed participant, to a rate determined by the following formula: divide the stated rate by the integer 1 plus that stated rate (expressed as a decimal). For example, if the plan calls for an employer contribution on behalf of each participant equal to 10% of that participant's compensation, the rate for a self-employed participant is reduced to 9.0909%— that is, 10% divided by 1.10.

Table of percentage equivalents

The following table shows (in Column II) the percentage of earned income (*unreduced* for the contribution made on behalf of a self-employed participant) that will produce the dollar equivalent of a given percentage (Column I) of earned income (*reduced* for the contribution made on behalf of a self-employed participant). For plans covering common-law employees, Column I represents the percentage of current compensation to be contributed on behalf of such employees. Column II represents the percentage of unreduced earned income that is the equivalent of the Column I percentage of current compensation. The equivalency rate for self-employed persons in Column II is computed by dividing the rate of contributions shown in Column I by 1 plus that rate of contributions. Thus, if the contribution rate for common-law employees was 10%, the equivalency rate for a self-employed individual would be 10% divided by 1.10 or 9.0909%.

(I) Percentage of Reduced Earned Income	(II) Percentage of Unreduced Earned Income
1	.9901
2	1.9608

(I) Percentage of Reduced Earned Income	(II) Percentage of Unreduced Earned Income
3	2.9126
4	3.8462
5	4.7619
6	5.6604
7	6.5421
8	7.4074
9	8.2569
10	9.0909
11	9.9099
12	10.7143
13	11.5044
14	12.2807
15	13.0435
16	13.7931
17	14.5299
18	15.2542
19	15.9664
20	16.6667
21	17.3554
22	18.0328
23	18.6992
24	19.3548
25	20.0000

The deduction for annual employer contributions to a SEP or profit-sharing plan cannot exceed 25% of the common-law employee participants' compensation, or 20% of the owner's net earnings (before computing the deduction for contributions on behalf of the owner) from the business that has the plan.

Incorporating the self-employment tax deduction

The IRS has provided guidance as to the impact of the second required reduction—that for 50% of self-employment tax. Step-by-step guidance for computing this reduction can be found at ¶ 8995 of the CCH PENSION PLAN GUIDE.

Contributions on behalf of owner-employees

For purposes of contributions made on behalf of owner-employees, earned income is limited to amounts derived from the trade or business with respect to which the plan is established. In other words, if an owner-employee is engaged in more than one business, but only one business has a plan, contributions to that plan on behalf of an owner-employee can be based only on the earned income from the business which established the plan.

1 Code Sec. 401(c)(2).

2 Rev. Rul. 69-628, 1969-2 CB 97, CCH Pension Plan Guide ¶ 18,782.

3 IRS Reg. § 1.401-10(b)(3).

4 IRS Publication 560.

¶ 3250
KEOGH PLANS: Aggregation of Plans

Prior to 1997, if an individual was an owner-employee of more than one business and if he controlled at least one of these businesses, he could participate in the plans of the noncontrolled businesses only if the other businesses he controlled had qualified plans.[1] If the owner-employee controlled more than one business, each must have had a plan if he was to participate in any one, and the plans of the controlled businesses were required to be aggregated.

The aggregation rule has been repealed, effective for years beginning in 1997.[2]

1 Code Secs. 401(d)(1) and (2), prior to repeal by P.L. 104-188 (Small Business Job Protection Act); IRS Reg. § 1.401-12(l)1-3.

2 Code Sec. 401(d).

¶ 3252
KEOGH PLANS: Contributions, Benefits, and Deductions

The limits on contributions to and benefits from a Keogh plan are the same as for qualified plans generally. The rules are discussed at ¶ 515 for defined benefit plans and ¶ 525 for defined contribution plans.

Deductions for contributions to Keogh plans are subject to the limitations stated in Code Sec. 404 that apply to all qualified plans. These rules are explained in detail at ¶ 600 and following.

Time for making contributions

Both "cash-basis" and "accrual basis" taxpayers may make contributions to a Keogh plan after the close of the taxable year if they are based on that taxable year and are made on or before the due date, including extensions, for filing the income tax return for that taxable year.[1]

Example: Mark Hogan, a sole proprietor and calendar-year cash basis taxpayer, maintains a Keogh plan. Hogan can make his contribution for 2011 at any time up through April 17, 2012 (plus extensions), and take the allowable deduction on his 2011 income tax return.

A Keogh plan must be in existence by the end of the taxable year in order for contributions made to it by the due date of the tax return to be deductible for that taxable year.

1 Code Sec. 404(a)(8).

¶ 3254

KEOGH PLANS: Special Prohibited Transaction Rules

An owner-employee is subject to the same prohibited transaction rules that apply to others who have dealings with a plan (see ¶ 2400 and following). However, certain exemptions for transactions that do not involve an owner-employee are not available for transactions between an owner-employee and his plan. These are transactions in which a plan:[1]

1. lends any part of the income or the corpus (principal) of the plan to the owner-employee,

2. pays any compensation to the owner-employee for services rendered to the plan, or

3. acquires any property from an owner-employee or sells any property to an owner-employee. These rules also apply to a member of an owner-employee's family and to a corporation in which the owner-employee owns 50% or more of the combined voting power of all classes of stock entitled to vote or 50% or more of the value of all classes of stock.

Loans to owner-employees and 50% shareholders may qualify for an exemption from the prohibited transaction rules if they meet certain criteria (see ¶ 2436 and ¶ 2448).[2]

Offering of financial services

Banks may offer financial services to Keogh plan customers only if the following conditions are met:[3]

1. Keogh accounts must be treated in the same manner as other accounts maintained by the financial institution.

2. The provision of services may not result in a return on the Keogh investment that is lower than the return on comparable investments generally offered by the financial institution to all customers.

3. The services must be generally available to other customers of the financial institution.

Offerings of cash or property

The IRS has stated that it will not raise issues concerning the tax effects resulting from possible prohibited transactions that may arise from certain cash or property offered by financial institutions to Keogh plan customers.[4]

However, the U.S. Supreme Court has ruled that the contribution of unencumbered property by an employer to satisfy its minimum funding obligation to a defined benefit plan is a "sale or exchange" that would constitute a prohibited transaction.[5]

---

[1] Code Sec. 4975.

[2] Prohibited Transaction Class Exemption 92-5, 2-11-92, CCH PENSION PLAN GUIDE ¶ 16,636.

[3] IRS Announcement 90-1, I.R.B. 1990-2, CCH Pension Plan Guide ¶ 17,097L-77.

[4] Prohibited Transaction Class Exemption 93-33, 5-28-93, CCH Pension Plan Guide ¶ 16,640.

[5] *Commissioner v. Keystone Consolidated Industries, Inc.*, US Sup Ct (1993), 113 SCt 2006.

¶ 3256

KEOGH PLANS: Distributions

The rules on distributions from a Keogh plan are the same as for qualified plans generally. The rules are discussed at ¶ 1800 and following.

¶ 3258

KEOGH PLANS: Reporting and Disclosure

The reporting and disclosure requirements for Keogh plans are the same as for qualified plans generally. The rules are discussed at ¶ 2200 and following.

¶ 3260

KEOGH PLANS: Funding Rules

An employee retirement plan that covers a self-employed person (whether or not the person is an owner-employee) is, in general, subject to the same funding requirements that apply to other qualified plans (see ¶ 1400 and following).

Funding methods for owner-employee plans

There are few differences between the methods which a plan benefiting owner-employees may choose for funding and the choices open to any other plan. The major methods of funding are:

1. funding through a trust;

2. direct purchase of annuity or other insurance contracts from an insurance company;

3. funding through a special custodial account,[1] under which the funds are deposited with a third party but with less formality than in the case of a trust; and

4. funding through the purchase of special U.S. government retirement bonds (issued before May 1, 1982).

---

[1] Code Sec. 401(f).

¶ 3262

For More Information

☐ For more information on IRAs, SEPs, and Keogh plans, see ¶ 8500-9065 of the CCH Pension Plan Guide.

Nonqualified Plans and Stock Arrangements

¶ 3300

General Rules

In addition to direct compensation, fringe benefits, and retirement benefits under qualified plans, a key means by which companies attract and retain top executive employees is nonqualified deferred compensation. By providing executive compensation through a nonqualified plan employers can effectively furnish benefits beyond the benefits typically available to non-management personnel.

Nonqualified deferred compensation plans, by definition, do not meet the qualification requirements under Code Sec. 401 and, therefore, do not afford the tax advantages available under qualified plans. Benefits under a nonqualified plan are also not guaranteed and, thus, offer employees less security than benefits provided pursuant to a qualified plan.

Nonetheless, nonqualified plans are a key element in executive compensation packages. Note that as of 2005, election, distribution, and funding restrictions have applied to nonqualified plans (see ¶ 3302).

Tax treatment of executive compensation. Distributions from nonqualified deferred compensation plans are taxed to an employee if they are distributed or made available to the employee. The employer receives a corresponding deduction in the same year. Even though a nonqualified plan is structured to defer the recognition of gain until some future date, the doctrine of constructive receipt or the economic benefit rule may force immediate taxation. In addition, compensation deferred under nonqualified deferred compensation plans that do not satisfy the applicable election, distribution, and funding restrictions under Code Sec. 409A, is subject to tax and interest assessments in the year of deferral, to the extent not subject to a substantial risk of forfeiture and not previously included in gross income (see ¶ 3302).

¶ 3302
Post-2004 Requirements for Nonqualified Plans

Generally effective beginning in 2005, nonqualified deferred compensation plans are subject to election, distribution, and funding restrictions under Code Sec. 409A.[1] Individuals who defer compensation under plans that fail to comply with the new rules will be subject to current taxation on all deferrals and to enhanced penalties unless the amounts are subject to a substantial risk of forfeiture.

Nonqualified plans affected by post-2004 rules

Nonqualified plans subject to the election, distribution, and funding restrictions (and the attendant tax consequences) include all nonqualified deferred compensation plans other than: (1) qualified employer plans (including SEPs and SIMPLE plans), (2) bona fide vacation leave, sick leave, compensatory time, disability pay, or death benefit plans.[2] In addition, note that the Code Sec. 409A rules are not limited to arrangements between an employer and employees, but also apply to one person arrangements. However, deferred compensation provided to independent contractors who perform non-management (and significant) services for two or more unrelated service recipients is excluded from coverage under Code Sec. 409A.[3]

Deferral of compensation

A nonqualified plan is subject to the restrictions of Code Sec. 409A only if it provides for the deferral of compensation. A plan provides for the deferral of compensation if the service provider has a legally binding right (i.e., compensation may not be unilaterally reduced or eliminated after services have been performed) during a tax year to compensation that is payable to (or on behalf of) the service provider in a later year.[4]

Short-term deferrals: 2 1/2 month rule. A deferral of compensation does not occur if the payment under the plan is actually or constructively received within 2 1/2 months from the later of the end of the service provider's or the service recipient's first tax year in which the amount is not subject to a substantial risk of forfeiture.[5] An exception is provided for certain delayed payments that are not made within the 2 1/2 month period because of unforeseen events that make payment administratively impracticable or threaten the solvency of the employer, as long as the payment is made as soon as is reasonably practicable.

Stock options and stock appreciation rights. Stock options and stock appreciation rights will not be treated as a deferral of compensation subject to Code Sec. 409A if issued with an exercise price that is not less than the fair market value (FMV) of the underlying stock on the date the right is granted, and the stock right does not contain an additional deferral feature.[6]

Plan aggregation. All amounts deferred under an account balance plan are treated as deferred under a single plan; all amounts deferred under a nonaccount balance plan are treated as deferred under a single plan; and all amounts deferred under any other type of plan (e.g., equity based compensation) are treated as deferred under a single plan. In addition, all amounts deferred under certain separation pay arrangements are treated as a single plan.[7]

Separation pay plans. Certain "separation pay plans" do not provide for the deferral of compensation for purposes of Code Sec. 409A.[8] This includes separation pay provided upon an involuntary separation from service or pursuant to a window program.

Election restrictions applicable to nonqualified plans after 2004

The election restrictions govern both a participant's election to defer compensation and the election of the form of a distribution.

Initial election must be made before the close of preceding year. Initial elections to defer compensation for services performed during a year must generally be made no later than the close of the preceding tax year.[9] Thus, a plan may not authorize a participant to make deferral elections during the year in which services are provided.

Two exceptions apply. First, newly eligible employees are allowed to make the election within 30 days after becoming eligible to participate in the plan. Second, a participant may make an election to defer "performance-based" compensation (that is based on services performed over no less than a 12-month period) no later than 6 months before the end of the service period.[10]

Performance-based compensation. Compensation is "performance-based" for this purpose if the receipt of the compensation is contingent upon the satisfaction of preestablished or individual performance criteria relating to a performance period of at least 12 months.[11]

Subsequent election to change time and form of payments. Plan participants must generally specify the time and form of distributions at the time of the initial election. However, participants are allowed to make a subsequent election to delay a payment or change the form of payment.[12] The election may not take effect, however, under specified plan terms, for at least 12 months after the date on which the election is made. In addition, the payment for which the additional deferral election is made (other than payments related to death, disability, or the occurrence of an unforeseeable emergency) must be deferred for no less than five years from the date the payment would otherwise have been made.[13] Finally, for a payment at a specified time or pursuant to a fixed schedule, the rescheduled election may not be made less than 12 months before the originally scheduled date of payment.

Domestic relations orders. The limits on changing deferral elections do not apply to subsequent elections made in connection with payments intended for someone other than the service provider and made in connection with a domestic relations order.[14]

Distribution restrictions

In order to qualify for favorable tax treatment under Code Sec. 409A, deferred compensation plans must limit the instances in which distributions may be made to the occurrence of the following "permissible payment" events:

- separation from service;
- disability;
- death;
- a specified time or pursuant to a fixed schedule (specified under the plan at the date of deferral);
- change in control of the corporation; or
- unforeseeable emergency.[15]

Additional restrictions on distributions to key employees upon separation from service. Distributions are generally authorized upon a participant's separation from service. However, distributions may not be made to key employees (see ¶ 925) of a publicly traded corporation immediately upon their separation from service. A key employee may not take a distribution from a nonqualified deferred compensation plan until at least 6 months after the date of separation from service or death.[16]

> **CCH Pointer:** The employer aggregation rules continue to apply. Accordingly, a participant's separation from service from an entity within a controlled group would not be a permissible distribution event if the employee continued to perform services for another entity within the group.[17]

Distributions made at a specified time. Distributions may be made at a specified time (pursuant to a fixed schedule) provided in the plan. The amount payable must be specified under the plan at the time the compensation is deferred. Accordingly, amounts payable upon the occurrence of an event (e.g., the entrance to college of an individual's child) rather than at a specified time (e.g., attainment by participant of age 65) would be subject to tax.[18]

Some flexibility is permitted: payments need not be made on the exact date specified in the plan. Payments may be made by the end of the calendar year in which a specified fixed payment date (or due date of a payment under a fixed schedule) occurs, or, if later, the 15th day of the third month following such fixed date or due date.[19]

Change in ownership or effective control. Distributions are authorized upon a change in ownership or effective control, or in the ownership of a substantial portion of the assets of the corporation.[20] Note that a change in effective control of the corporation occurs only on either of the following dates: (1) the date any one person acquires ownership of stock of the corporation possessing 30 percent or more of the total voting power of the stock of the corporation or (2) the date a majority of members of the corporation's board of directors is replaced during any 12-month period by directors whose election is not endorsed by a majority of the members of the board before the date of the election.

¶3302

Unforeseeable emergency. An unforeseeable emergency is defined as a "severe financial hardship" to the participant resulting from an illness or accident of the participant, the participant's spouse, dependent or other beneficiary.[21]

Distribution limited to amount needed to relieve hardship. The distribution made in response to an unforeseeable emergency may not exceed the amount necessary to satisfy the resultant hardship presented by the emergency, plus the amount needed to pay taxes reasonably anticipated to result from the distribution.[22] In addition, a distribution would not be authorized to the extent the hardship could be relieved through reimbursement or compensation by insurance or otherwise, or by liquidation of the participant's assets (if the liquidation of the participant's assets would not result in a severe financial hardship).

CCH Pointer: Imminent foreclosure on the participant's primary residence or funeral expenses for a spouse, dependent or beneficiary may constitute unforeseeable emergencies. Generally speaking, the purchase of a home and payment of college tuition will not.[23] Similarly, the need to repair significant water damage to the taxpayer's principal residence, or to pay the funeral expenses for an adult child are unforeseeable emergencies, but a need to pay accumulated credit card debt is not.[24]

Accelerated benefit payments prohibited. A deferred compensation plan may not permit the acceleration of the time or schedule of any payment under the plan. Code Sec. 409A(a)(3) authorizes the Treasury Secretary to provide exceptions to this general rule.[25] Generally, for plans that permit multiple alternative events, the anti-acceleration rules will apply to the addition or deletion of a permissible payment event.[26]

Exceptions to general rule prohibiting accelerations. Situations in which a deferred compensation plan may provide for the acceleration of a payment, or may provide the employer or service recipient with the discretion to accelerate payment, include the following:[27]

- **Domestic relations order.** Payments may be accelerated in order to comply with a domestic relations order.
- **Cashout rules.** Cashout provisions will not violate the anti-acceleration rules.
- **Payment of employment taxes.** Accelerated payments may be permitted in order to pay FICA or Railroad Retirement Act taxes on compensation deferred under a plan.
- **Plan termination and liquidation.** A plan may provide for an accelerated payment if the payment is made pursuant to a termination and liquidation of the plan under certain scenarios.

Tax rules

Individuals who defer compensation under plans that fail to comply with the post-2004 rules discussed above will be subject to current taxation on all deferrals and to enhanced penalties. Specifically, compensation deferred under nonqualified deferred compensation plans that do not satisfy the requirements will be subject to tax (and interest and penalty assessments) in the year of deferral, to the extent not subject to a substantial risk of forfeiture and not previously included in gross income. The provision imposing current year taxation on deferred amounts applies to "all" compensation deferred under the plan by the participant for the year and "all preceding" tax years.[28]

> **CCH POINTER:** *Calculating income and taxes resulting from Code Sec. 409A compliance failures.* The IRS has issued proposed regulations on the calculation of amounts includible in income under Code Sec.409A(a), and the calculation of the additional taxes applicable to such income in the event of a plan compliance failure. The regulations are proposed to be generally applicable for taxable years beginning on or after the issuance of final regulations.[29]

> *Interest and penalty assessments.* The tax resulting from noncompliance with the restrictions of Code Sec. 409A will be further increased by interest and penalty taxes.[30]

Interest will be assessed at the underpayment rate plus 1 percentage point on the underpayment that would have occurred had the deferred compensation been included in the participant's gross income for the tax year in which it was first deferred, or, if later, the first tax year in which the deferred compensation is not subject to a substantial risk of forfeiture.[31]

The participant will also be subject to a 20% penalty tax imposed on the amount of compensation required to be included in income.[32]

> *Taxable transfer of property triggered by changes in employer's financial health.* Assets set aside for the payment of nonqualified deferred compensation are subject to tax if the amounts are available to satisfy the claims of general creditors and the participant has a vested right to the amounts set aside. However, assets set aside (directly or indirectly) in a trust (or other arrangement) for the purpose of paying nonqualified deferred compensation shall be treated as property transferred in connection with the performance of services under Code Sec. 83, whether or not assets are available to satisfy the claims of general creditors: (1) at the time set aside, if such assets (or trust or other arrangement) are located outside of the United States, or, (2) at the time transferred, if the assets (or trust or other arrangement) are subsequently transferred outside of the United States.[33]

A taxable transfer of property under Code Sec. 83 will also occur with respect to compensation deferred under a nonqualified plan that provides that, upon a change in the employer's financial health, assets will be restricted to the payment of nonqualified deferred compensation (e.g., transferred to a rabbi trust (see ¶ 3345) or other trust).[34] Under such a provision, participants would be subject to current year taxation on amounts deferred under the plan, as transferred property under Code Sec. 83.

> *Restriction on funding of nonqualified plans by employers maintaining underfunded qualified plans.* Generally, assets set aside for the payment of deferred compensation to a "covered employee" (e.g., chief executive officer, four highest paid officers, and insiders) by an employer maintaining an at-risk plan during a "restricted period" are subject to tax under Code Sec. 83 as property

transferred in connection with the performance of services. The assets are also subject to penalty tax and interest assessments under Code Sec. 409A.[35]

If, during a restricted period in which a defined benefit plan of an employer is in at-risk status (as defined under the funding rules, see discussion beginning at ¶ 1400), assets are set aside or reserved (directly or indirectly) in a trust or other arrangement, or transferred to such a trust or other arrangement, for the purpose of paying deferred compensation of an applicable covered employee under a nonqualified deferred compensation plan of the plan sponsor (or a member of a controlled group which includes the plan sponsor), the assets will be treated, under Code Sec. 83, as transferred in connection with the performance of services, whether or not the assets are available to satisfy the claims of general creditors.[36] However, the restriction will not apply to assets that are set aside *before* the restricted period during which the defined benefit plan is in at-risk status.[37] Interest and penalties may apply.[38]

Reporting requirements

The IRS has issued guidance regarding reporting and wage withholding requirements with respect to deferrals of compensation and amounts includible in gross income under Code Sec. 409A.[39]

Transition rules for implementing Code Sec. 409A requirements

The modifications to the nonqualified deferred compensation rules implemented by the American Jobs Creation Act of 2004 generally apply to amounts deferred in tax years beginning after 2004.[40] However, the IRS issued a series of guidance providing transition relief for implementing the governing requirements prior to January 1, 2009.[41]

Plan correction under Code Sec. 409A

Operational failures. Effective for taxable years beginning on or after January 1, 2009, the IRS has issued transition relief and guidance on the correction of certain failures of nonqualified deferred compensation plans to comply with the operational requirements of Code Sec. 409A(a).[42]

The guidance provides procedures under which taxpayers can obtain relief from the full application of the income inclusion and additional tax provisions of Code Sec. 409A. Procedures provided include:

- Methods for correcting certain operational failures during the same tax year of the service provider in which the failure occurred;

- Methods for correcting certain operational failures during the subsequent tax year, if the affected service provider is not an "insider" (generally, a 10% or more owner of the employer's stock);

- Relief for certain operational failures under Code Sec. 409A during a service provider's year that involve only limited amounts; and

- Relief for certain operational failures regardless of whether the failure involves only limited amounts.

Document failures. Taxpayers may voluntarily correct many types of failures to comply with the document requirements applicable to nonqualified plans under Code Sec. 409A.[43] Certain document failures may be corrected without current income inclusion or additional taxes under Code Sec. 409A, as long as the corrected plan provision does not affect the operation of the plan within one year following the date of correction. Plans eligible for relief include a nonqualified plan linked to a qualified plan or to another nonqualified plan if the linkage does not affect the time and form of payments under the plans.[44]

---

[1] Code Sec. 409A, as added by P.L. 108-357 (American Jobs Creation Act of 2004), Act Sec. 885(a); Reg. § 1.409A-1—Reg. § 1.409A-6.

[2] Code Sec. 409A(d).

[3] Reg. § 1.409A-1(f).

[4] Reg. § 1.409A-1(b)(1).

[5] Reg. § 1.409A-1(b)(4).

[6] Reg. § 1.409A-1(b)(5). For stock rights issued after the effective date of the final regulations, the IRS has declined to apply the valuation rules applicable to incentive stock options for purposes of the exclusion from Code Sec. 409A. See Preamble to T.D. 9321 (72 FR 19234, 4-17-07) at CCH PENSION PLAN GUIDE ¶ 24,508O. However, for stock rights issued prior to January 1, 2008, transition rules continue to apply. Thus, for stock rights issued before January 1, 2005, the determination of fair market value (FMV) will be made in accordance with the rules governing incentive stock options, pursuant to which the exercise price of the stock right is deemed to be FMV if a good faith attempt was made to set the exercise price at no less than the FMV of the underlying stock at the time of the grant. However, with respect to stock rights issued on or after January 1, 2005, but before January 1, 2008, the determination of FMV, in accordance with IRS Notice 2005-1, may be made using any reasonable valuation method. See IRS Notice 2006-4, I.R.B. 2006-3, 1-16-06 at CCH PENSION PLAN GUIDE ¶ 17,132U, IRS Notice 2005-1, I.R.B. 2005-1, 1-10-05 at CCH PENSION PLAN GUIDE ¶ 17,130K, and Preamble to T.D. 9321, Section XII. Section XII of the Preamble to T.D. 9321 also offers guidance as to the treatment of stock rights created before January 1, 2008 that remain outstanding on or after January 1, 2008.

[7] Reg. § 1.409A-1(c)(2).

[8] Reg. § 1.409A-1(b)(9)

[9] Code Sec. 409A(a)(4); Reg. § 1.409A-2(a)(3).

[10] Code Sec. 409A(a)(4)(B)(ii) and (iii).

[11] Reg. § 1.409A-1(e)(1).

[12] Code Sec. 409A(a)(4)(C).

[13] Code Sec. 409A(a)(4)(C)(ii).

[14] Reg. § 1.409A-2(b)(4).

[15] Code Sec. 409A(a)(2).

[16] Code Sec. 409A(a)(2)(B)(i).

[17] Code Sec. 409A(d)(6).

[18] Code Sec. 409A(a)(2)(A)(iv).

[19] Reg. § 1.409A-3(d).

[20] Reg. § 1.409A-3(i)(5). A change in ownership or control for this purpose does not occur if the Treasury Department or a designee acquires common stock or other equity interests in a financial institution or other entity pursuant to the Emergency Economic Stabilization Act of 2008. See IRS Notice 2009-49, I.R.B. 2009-25, 6/22/2009, at CCH PENSION PLAN GUIDE ¶ 17,142W.

[21] Code Sec. 409A(a)(2)(B)(ii)(I).

[22] Code Sec. 409A(a)(2)(B)(ii)(II).

[23] Reg. § 1.409A-3(i)(3).

[24] Rev. Rul. 2010-27, I.R.B. 2010-45, 11-8-2010, CCH PENSION PLAN GUIDE ¶ 19,948Z-286.

[25] Code Sec. 409A(a)(3); Reg. § 1.409A-3(j)(1).

[26] Reg. § 1.409A-3(j)(2). Note, however, that death, disability or unforeseen emergency may be added as alternative payment events without triggering the anti-acceleration rules.

[27] Reg. § 1.409A-3(j)(4). Note that as part of the Troubled Asset Relief Program as established by the Emergency Economic Stabilization Act of 2008, a Special Master was required to approve any compensation payments to certain employees of a TARP recipient. If compliance with a Special Master Advisory Opinion would require a delay or acceleration of nonqualified deferred compensation payments, the compliance will not trigger adverse tax consequences under Code Sec. 409A. See IRS Notice 2009-92, I.R.B. 2009-52, 12/28/2009, at CCH PENSION PLAN GUIDE ¶ 17,143X.

[28] Code Sec. 409A(a)(1)(A). See also Rev. Rul. 2007-48, I.R.B. 2007-30, 7-23-07 at CCH PENSION PLAN GUIDE ¶ 19,948Z-197, which details the federal tax consequences of contributions to a nonqualified employees' trust established on behalf of highly compensated employees.

[29] Prop. Reg. § 1.409A-4 (12-8-2008, 73 FR 74380).

[30] Code Sec. 409A(a)(1)(B)(i). Under a compliance resolution program announced in 2007, employers could opt to pay the penalty and interest taxes under Code Sec. 409A that would otherwise have been assessed against rank-and-file employees who exercised discounted or "backdated" stock options in 2006. Employers were required to inform the IRS of their intent to participate in the program by February 17, 2007, and to pay applicable taxes by June 30, 2007. See IRS Announcement 2007-18, I.R.B. 2007-9, 2-26-07 at CCH Pension Plan Guide ¶ 17,097T-1.

[31] Code Sec. 409A(a)(1)(B)(ii).

[32] Code Sec. 409A(a)(1)(B)(i)(II).

[33] Code Sec.409A(b). Special rules may apply to offshore hedge or private equity funds. See Code Sec. 457A(a), as added by P.L. 110-343 (Emergency Economic Stabilization Act of 2008), Division C, Act Sec. 801(a). For more on the coordination of Code Sec. 457A with Code Sec. 409A, see IRS Notice 2009-8, I.R.B. 2009-4, 1/26/2009, at CCH Pension Plan Guide ¶ 17,141X.

[34] Code Sec. 409A(b)(2).

[35] Code Sec. 409A(b)(3), as added by P.L. 109-280 (Pension Protection Act of 2006), Act Sec. 116(a), effective for transfers or other reservations of assets occurring after August 17, 2006.

[36] Code Sec. 409A(b)(3)(A)(i), as added by P.L. 109-280 (Pension Protection Act of 2006), Act Sec. 116(a).

[37] Code Sec. 409A(b)(3)(A).

[38] Code Sec.409A(b)(5).

[39] IRS Notice 2008-115, I.R.B. 2008-52, 12-29-2008 at CCH Pension Plan Guide ¶ 17,141L, as modified by Notice 2010-6, I.R.B. 2010-3, 1-19-2010, at CCH Pension Plan Guide ¶ 17,144H. The IRS does not anticipate issuing future guidance on this subject until finalization of proposed regulations under Code Sec. 409A that address the calculation of the amount includible in income and the calculation of additional taxes (see CCH Pension Plan Guide ¶ 20,262S).

[40] P.L. 108-357 (American Jobs Creation Act of 2004), Act Sec. 885(d)(1).

[41] See IRS Notice 2007-86, I.R.B. 2007-46, 11-13-07, at CCH Pension Plan Guide ¶ 17,137H; IRS Notice 2007-78, I.R.B. 2007-41, 10-9-07 at CCH Pension Plan Guide ¶ 17,137; IRS Notice 2006-79, I.R.B. 2006-43, 10-23-06 at CCH Pension Plan Guide ¶ 17,134Q; and IRS Notice 2005-1, I.R.B. 2005-2 at CCH Pension Plan Guide ¶ 17,132M. Note that the IRS has announced a limited expansion of the areas collateral to Code Sec. 409A arrangements in which determination letters may be issued. See Rev. Proc. 2008-61, I.R.B. 2008-42, 10-20-2008, at CCH Pension Plan Guide ¶ 17,299S-75.

[42] IRS Notice 2008-113, I.R.B. 2008-51, 12-22-08, at CCH Pension Plan Guide ¶ 17,141J, as modified by IRS Notice 2010-80, I.R.B. 2010-51, 12-20-2010, at ¶ 17,146B. Information and reporting requirements apply.

[43] Notice 2010-6, I.R.B. 2010-3, 1-19-2010, at CCH Pension Plan Guide ¶ 17,144H. The notice is generally applicable for tax years beginning on or after January 1, 2009.

[44] IRS Notice 2010-80, I.R.B. 2010-51, 12-20-2010, CCH Pension Plan Guide ¶ 17,146B, modifying IRS Notice 2010-6, I.R.B. 2010-3, 1-19-2010, at CCH Pension Plan Guide ¶ 17,144H.

¶ 3305

Insurance Methods for Funding Executive Compensation

Life insurance is an effective means by which employers may fund executive compensation. The most common types of insurance arrangements are highlighted below.

Key-employee insurance

Key-employee insurance allows an employer to insure the life of a key employee in order to protect the business from monetary loss that may be caused by the employee's death. Generally, an employer has an "insurable interest" in any person actively associated with the company who would continue to provide a financial benefit to the company during their lifetime.

An employer may not deduct premiums paid for key-employee life insurance where the employer is directly or indirectly a beneficiary under the policy. Similarly, interest on loans incurred to purchase insurance generally may not be deducted by the employer. However, note that a limited exception applies to deductions for interest on debt incurred for life insurance policies (or annuity or endowment contracts) owned by a company on key persons. Such interest is deductible to the extent that the aggregate amount of debt with respect to the policies and contracts do not exceed $50,000 per individual.[1]

☐ See CCH PENSION PLAN GUIDE ¶ 9625 for more information on key persons and the cap on interest deductions.

Employees who retain incidents of ownership in the policy, such as the right to change premiums, are subject to tax on the premiums paid by the employer.[2] Amounts received under a life insurance contract following the death of an insured employee prior to retirement are not taxable to the employer or to the estate of the insured.[3] However, the surviving spouse may be required to include payments from the company in income.

If the employee lives until retirement, the policy may be cashed in to provide the deferred compensation benefits. On surrender, the employer is taxed only on the amount of the policy in excess of the premiums and other consideration paid for the policy.[4]

Group-term life insurance

Group-term life insurance allows an employee to exclude from income the first $50,000 of insurance. However, key employees are subject to tax on the cost of insurance provided under a discriminatory plan.[5]

Split-dollar plan

Under a split-dollar plan, the employer pays the part of the annual premium equal to the increase in cash value of the policy during the policy year. The balance is paid by the executive. The employer is the beneficiary of the cash value of the policy. The executive's named beneficiary is entitled to the remaining proceeds. The nondiscrimination rules do not apply to split-dollar arrangements and such insurance may be provided to officers and key employees exclusively.

Employees under split-dollar arrangements are generally taxed on the net premium cost of the current insurance (i.e., the value of the insurance protection) reduced by the amount of the premium that they pay.[6] The IRS has provided two mutually exclusive regimes for taxing split-dollar life insurance arrangements: an economic benefit regime and a loan regime. Ownership of the life insurance contract determines which regime applies. If the executive is the owner, the employer's premium payments are treated as loans to the executive. If the employer is the owner, the employer's premium payments are treated as providing taxable economic benefits to the executive. Such benefits include the executive's interest in the policy cash value and current life insurance protection.[7]

¶3305

Generally, split-dollar life insurance arrangements that provide for deferred comepnsation as defined under Reg. § 1.409A-1(b) are subject to the requirements of Code Sec. 409A.[8]

Reverse split-dollar plan

Under a reverse split-dollar life insurance arrangement, the employer and the employee split the premium payments and, upon the employee's death, the employee's beneficiary receives the amount of the employee's premium payments, plus interest. The employer receives the balance of the insurance proceeds.

An employee may not deduct premiums paid for reverse split-dollar insurance. The employee is not taxed on the cost of current life insurance protection because the employee does not receive the actual amount of insurance coverage.

□ See the CCH PENSION PLAN GUIDE at ¶ 9610-9645 for more information on insurance arrangements for executives.

Reporting requirements

Policyholders of certain employer-owned life insurance contracts are required to report certain information to the IRS on an annual basis.[9]

---

[1] Code Sec. 264(a)(1) and 264(d)(1).

[2] IRS Reg. § 1.61-2(d)(2).

[3] Code Sec. 101(a)(1).

[4] Code Sec. 72(e).

[5] Code Sec. 79(d)(1).

[6] IRS Reg. § 1.61-2(d)(2)(ii)(A).

[7] IRS Reg. § 1.61-22 (68 FR 54336, September 17, 2003). In 2006, Code Sec.101(j) was added by Sec. 863(a) of P.L. 109-280 (Pension Protection Act of 2006) to limit the extent to which death benefits from an employer-provided life insurance contract could be excluded from a policyholder's gross income. These limits apply to contracts issued, or materially modified, after August 17, 2006. Guidance issued in 2008 clarified that if the parties to a split-dollar life insurance arrangement modify the terms of the arrangement but do not modify the terms of the life insurance contract underlying the arrangement, the modification will not be treated as a material change in the life insurance contract for purposes of Code Sec.101(j), even if the modification is treated as a material modification of the split-dollar arrangement for purposes of Prop. Reg. § 1.61-22(j). See IRS Notice 2008-42, I.R.B. 2008-17, 4-28-2008, at CCH PENSION PLAN GUIDE ¶ 17,139G. For information on the definition of an employer-owned life insurance contract, the notice and consent requirements under Code Sec. 104(j)(4) and the information reporting requirements under Code Sec. 6039I, see IRS Notice 2009-48, I.R.B. 2009-24, 6/15/2009, at CCH PENSION PLAN GUIDE ¶ 17,142V.

[8] See IRS Notice 2007-34, I.R.B. 2007-17, 4-23-07 at CCH PENSION PLAN GUIDE ¶ 17,136I for more on the application of Code Sec. 409A to split-dollar life insurance arrangements.

[9] Code Sec.6039I, as added by P.L. 109-280 (Pension Protection Act of 2006), Act Sec. 863(b); Prop. Reg. § 1.6039-1 (11-6-2008, T.D. 9431, 73 FR 65981), preamble at CCH PENSION PLAN GUIDE ¶ 24,509A.

¶ 3310
Statutory Stock Options

Statutory stock option plans are those option arrangements that meet various requirements set forth in the Internal Revenue Code and IRS regulations.

General rules

An employee does not recognize ordinary income when a statutory stock option is granted or exercised. Compensation income is deferred until the sale or other disposition of the stock acquired pursuant to the exercise of a statutory stock option. Accordingly, upon the disposition of the option stock, the employee must recognize income on the difference between the disposition proceeds and the option price.[1] However, the IRS will not treat the disposition of stock acquired by an employee pursuant to the exercise of an option as subject to income tax withholding.[2] In addition, federal income tax need not be withheld on a disqualifying disposition, or when compensation is recognized in connection with an employee stock purchase plan discount (i.e., option price between 85% to 100% of the value of stock).[3]

FICA and FUTA tax. Remuneration received on account of the transfer of stock pursuant to the exercise of an incentive stock option or under an employee stock purchase plan, or any disposition of such stock, is excluded from FICA and FUTA tax. However, note that such remuneration will not be taken into account in determining Social Security benefits.[4]

Employee relationship. The individual receiving the statutory stock option must be an employee of the granting corporation or of its parent or subsidiary and must continue such employment for at least three months before the option is exercised.[5]

Deductions for grantor corporations. The grant or exercise of a stock option does not generate a business deduction for the grantor corporation.[6] The corporation may take a deduction when the executive disposes of the stock prior to expiration of the applicable holding period. Different holding requirements apply, depending on whether the stock option is a qualified stock option, an incentive stock option, an employee stock purchase plan, or restricted stock option.

Reporting requirements of stock option plans. Corporations must comply with several information reporting requirements in connection with stock option plans. Corporations must generally furnish statements for each calendar year to anyone for whom they transfer stock pursuant to the exercise of an incentive stock option. Corporations must also file an information statement with the IRS following a stock transfer. [7]

From an executive's standpoint, one of the practical problems of stock option plans, whether statutory or nonstatutory, is that the grantee often has to make large capital outlays when exercising the options (i.e., when purchasing the stock). The key question is how to remedy that capitalization drawback without having to dip into cash reserves, sell other assets, or borrow from the employer or a third party.

Options issued in connection with employee stock purchase plans

Employee stock purchase plans are designed to allow employees to purchase stock of their employer at a discount and to receive favorable tax treatment upon a qualified disposition of the option stock.

The terms of an employee stock purchase plan must comply with requirements specified in IRS Reg. § 1.423-2(c), that define the option price, the option period, and the rights of employees under the plan.[8]

¶3310

☐ See the CCH PENSION PLAN GUIDE at ¶ 9700-9710 for more detailed information on statutory stock option plans.

[1] Code Sec. 421(a).

[2] IRS Notice 2002-47, 2002-8, I.R.B. 97 at CCH PENSION PLAN GUIDE ¶ 17,124I.

[3] Code Sec. 421(b), as amended by P.L. 108-357 (American Jobs Creation Act of 2004), Act Sec. 251(b); Code Sec. 423(c), as amended by P.L. 108-357 (American Jobs Creation Act of 2004), Act Sec. 251(c).

[4] Soc. Sec. Act Sec. 209(a)(19), as added by P.L. 108-357 (American Jobs Creation Act of 2004), Act Sec. 251(a).

[5] IRS Reg. § 1.421-7(h).

[6] Code Sec. 421(a)(2); IRS Reg. § 1.421-8.

[7] Code Sec. 6039(a), as amended by P.L. 109-432 (Tax Relief and Health Care Act of 2006); § 1.6039-1 (as amended by T.D. 9472, 11/24/2009, 74 FR 61270). Note, however, this requirement was waived for stock transfers that occurred during 2007—2009.

[8] IRS Reg. § 1.423-2(c) Note that for the first time since 1988 the IRS has amended its regulations under Code Sec. 423. These amended regulations apply to any statutory option granted on or after January 1, 2010. See IRS Reg. § 1.423-1 and IRS Reg. § 1.423-2 (11/17/2009, 74 FR 59074).

¶ 3315

Incentive Stock Option Plans

Incentive stock options (ISOs) are a form of statutory stock option under which tax consequences apply not when the stock option is granted or exercised, but only when the stock received under the option is sold. Gain received from the subsequent sale is taxed as capital gain, but the employer generally may not claim a related business deduction unless there is a "premature" disposal and the executive must recognize ordinary gain.[1]

Unlike qualified and restricted statutory stock options (¶ 3310), ISOs need not be exercised by any particular date to receive tax deferred treatment, although they are likewise subject to a holding period requirement.

Another key advantage of an ISO is that it can be granted to a "class" of employees, such as executives. As a result, an ISO plan may discriminate, unlike ESOPs and other qualified plans. On the other hand, ISO grantees generally cannot own (at the time the option is offered) stock possessing more than 10% of the total combined voting power of all classes of company stock.

General requirements for granting ISOs

An incentive stock option (ISO) is defined in the Code as an option granted to an individual, for any reason connected with his employment, to purchase stock of the corporation.[2] It must meet the following requirements:

1. *Written plan*—the option must be granted pursuant to a written plan that details particular information about the number of shares and the employees that may receive them.[3]

2. *Stockholder approval*—the plan must be approved by the corporation's stockholders within 12 months before or after it is adopted.[4] In addition, the approval must comply with the corporate charter and applicable state laws or, in the absence of state regulation, with additional procedural rules.

3. ***Time for granting and order of exercising options***—an option must be granted within 10 years after the ISO plan is adopted or within 10 years after the plan is approved by the shareholders, whichever is earlier.[5]

ISOs granted *after* December 31, 1986, may be exercised in any order.[6] An ISO granted *before* 1987 cannot be exercised while an ISO that was granted earlier is outstanding.[7] An option granted prior to 1987 is treated as outstanding until it is exercised in full under its initial terms or expires after a given time.[8]

4. ***10% stock ownership rule***—an individual who receives a stock option grant cannot (at the time the option is offered) own stock that totals more than 10% of the total combined voting power of all classes of stock of the employer-corporation, its parent, or subsidiary corporations.[9] However, this rule does not apply if the option price is at least 110% of the fair market value of the stock covered by the option and the option has a five-year expiration date.[10]

5. ***$100,000 limit***—stock options are not considered to be ISOs to the extent that the aggregate fair market value (determined at the time the option is granted) of stock for options that meet the ISO requirements and that are first exercisable during any calendar year exceeds $100,000.[11]

6. ***Options granted before 1987***—in the case of options granted *before* 1987, the terms of the plan had to limit the amount of aggregate fair market value of the stock (determined at the time of the grant of the option) for which any individual could be granted ISOs in any calendar year to no more than $100,000 *plus* any carryover amount.[12] The carryover amount from any year was one-half of the amount by which $100,000 exceeded the value of the stock for which incentive stock options were granted in a prior year.

7. ***Option price***—the option price offered the grantee by the corporation may not be less than the fair market value of the stock at the time the option is granted.[13]

8. ***Fair market value***—in order to ensure that the fair market value requirements cannot be avoided, the fair market value of stock must be determined without regard to any restriction other than a restriction which, by its terms, will never lapse for options granted after March 20, 1984. However, a September 20, 1984 date is substituted for March 20, 1984, with respect to options issued after March 20, 1984, pursuant to a plan adopted or corporate action taken by the board of directors of the grantor corporation before May 15, 1984.[14]

9. ***Alternative minimum tax***—if an individual purchases stock under an ISO at less than the stock's fair market value at the

time of purchase, the difference is a tax preference item for minimum tax purposes.

Holding period

In order for a stock option to be considered an ISO and to receive special tax treatment, an employee must not sell or dispose of stock received under an option within two years after the option is granted. The employee must also hold the shares of stock for at least one year after they have been transferred to him or her.[15]

Tax treatment on disposition of ISO stock

Taxable compensation does not result when an incentive stock option is granted or exercised.[16] Compensation income is generally deferred until the sale or other disposition of the stock acquired pursuant to the exercise of the statutory stock option. When the option stock is disposed of, however, any gain recognized is generally subject to capital gains treatment and the employer-corporation receives no business deduction.[17]

Failure to meet holding period requirements. If all of the requirements necessary for ISO treatment are met, *except* the holding period requirements, tax is imposed on the sale of the stock and the gain is treated as ordinary income. Ordinary income tax treatment is limited, however, to the excess of the amount realized on the sale or exchange over the adjusted basis of the stock.[18] In this instance, the employer granting the option receives a corresponding business expense deduction.[19]

FICA and FUTA taxes. The IRS will not treat the disposition of stock acquired by an employee pursuant to the exercise of the option as subject to income tax withholding or FICA and FUTA tax (see ¶ 3310).[20]

Impact of Code Sec. 409A. The grant of an incentive stock option as described in Code Sec. 422 does not constitute a deferral of compensation under Code Sec. 409A.[21]

Special rule for losses within two years

A special rule applies to executives who dispose of stock *before* the prescribed two-year holding period when the amount realized on the sale is less than the value of the stock at the time the option was exercised. In this case, the amount that is included in the gross income of the executive and that is also deductible from the income of the employer corporation as compensation attributable to the exercise of the option cannot exceed the excess (if any) of the amount realized on the sale over the adjusted basis of the stock.[22]

Using statutory options to purchase ISOs

If stock acquired under a statutory option is used to acquire other stock offered under an ISO, certain rules must be followed when the stock is acquired and sold. If stock acquired under a statutory option is used to acquire other stock offered under an ISO, the result will be ordinary income. However, the acquired ISO would still qualify for favorable tax treatment.[23]

Modification, extension, or renewal

If the terms of any incentive stock option or stock purchase plan option are modified, extended, or renewed, certain rules apply with respect to transfers of the stock made on the exercise of the option after this alteration. Generally, a modification, extension, or renewal is considered the granting of a new option.[24]

---

[1] Code Sec. 422; IRS Reg. § 1.422-5.

[2] Code Sec. 422(b).

[3] Code Sec. 422(b)(1).

[4] Code Sec. 422(b)(1).

[5] Code Sec. 422(b)(3)-(4).

[6] P.L. 99-514 (Tax Reform Act of 1986), Act Sec. 321(a).

[7] Code Sec. 422(b)(7).

[8] Code Sec. 422A(c)(7), prior to repeal by P.L. 99-514 (Tax Reform Act of 1986), Act Sec. 321(b)(1)(A)-(B); P.L. 97-34 (Economic Recovery Tax Act of 1981), Senate Committee Report on Act Sec. 251.

[9] Code Sec. 422(b)(6).

[10] Code Sec. 422(c)(6).

[11] Code Sec. 422(d), applicable to options granted after 1986.

[12] Code Sec. 422(b)(8), prior to repeal by P.L. 99-514 (Tax Reform Act of 1986), Act Sec. 321(a).

[13] Code Sec. 422(b)(4) and (c)(1).

[14] Code Sec. 422(c)(8).

[15] Code Sec. 422(a)(1).

[16] Code Secs. 421(a) and 422(a).

[17] Code Sec. 421(a)(2).

[18] Code Sec. 422(c)(2)(A).

[19] Code Sec. 421(b).

[20] Code Sec. 421(b), as amended by P.L. 108-357 (American Jobs Creation Act of 2004), Act Sec. 251(b); Code Sec. 3121(a)(22), as added by P.L. 108-357 (American Jobs Creation Act of 2004), Act Sec. 251(a)(1); Code Sec. 3306(b)(19), as added by P.L. 108-357 (American Jobs Creation Act of 2004), Act Sec. 251(a)(3).

[21] Reg. § 1.409A-1(b)(5)(ii).

[22] Code Sec. 422(c)(2).

[23] Code Sec. 424(c).

[24] Code Sec. 424(h)(1); IRS Reg. § 1.421-4(b); IRS Reg. § 1.425-1(e).

¶ 3320

Nonstatutory Stock Options

"Nonstatutory stock options" are those options that do not qualify for favorable tax treatment because they fail to satisfy one or more of the necessary qualifying criteria.

Tax treatment of nonstatutory stock options

Generally, an employee is considered to receive compensation at the time a nonstatutory option is exercised. However, the tax treatment of an option depends on whether the option has a "readily ascertainable" fair market value when granted to the employee.

Nonetheless, nonstatutory stock options do offer some advantages as a device for compensating executives and key employees. For example, the employer is entitled to a deduction for the amount that the employee is required to include in income upon exercising the option.[1]

Another advantage of nonstatutory stock options arises because an employee can select the year in which the employee will receive the income. The employee can exercise the option in the year in which his or her tax liability will be smallest with regard to the amount includible as compensation on account of exercising the option. As a result, the nonstatutory stock option, rather than an annuity, might prove to be the more effective way to provide retirement compensation. If an annuity is purchased for an employee, there is the possibility that the entire value may be taxed to the employee as compensation in the year in which the annuity is purchased.

Generally, an employee who acquires stock under a *statutory* option arrangement is taxed only when he or she disposes of the stock, and the employer may not take a corresponding business expense deduction.

In contrast, if an option is acquired under a *nonstatutory* program, the executive may be taxed:

1. when the option is granted;
2. when the employee exercises the option;
3. when the employee sells or otherwise disposes of the option; or
4. when restrictions on disposition of the option-acquired stock lapse.[2]

The income that the employee must recognize is considered compensation and thus is taxed at ordinary income rates, and the employer may take a corresponding business expense deduction at that time.

Impact of Code Sec. 409A. Nonstatutory stock options that do not provide for the deferral of compensation are not subject to the requirements of Code Sec. 409A (see ¶ 3302). An option to purchase service recipient stock (i.e., the employer's stock) does not provide for a deferral of compensation if (1) the exercise price may never be less than the fair market value of the stock on the date the option is granted; (2) the exercise of the option is subject to Code Sec. 83 and (3) the option contains no feature for the deferral of compensation (other than delayed recognition of income until exercise).[3]

Readily ascertainable value

If the option has a readily ascertainable fair market value at the time it is granted in connection with the performance of services, the employee who performed the services realizes compensation or ordinary gain:

1. when the employee's rights in the option are transferable; or
2. when the right in the option is not subject to a substantial risk of forfeiture.[4]

Value not readily ascertainable

If the option does *not* have an ascertainable fair market value at the time it is granted, taxation occurs when the option is exercised or otherwise disposed of, even though the fair market value may have been ascertainable before then.

☐ See CCH PENSION PLAN GUIDE ¶ 9740—9750 for more information on nonstatutory stock options.

---

[1] The IRS has provided guidance on the circumstances under which employers involved in a merger or acquisition may deduct an employee's compensation resulting from the exercise or dis-

position of nonstatutory stock options. See Rev. Rul. 2003-98, I.R.B. 2003-34, August 25, 2003.

[2] Code Sec. 83. See also Rev. Rul. 2005-48, at CCH PENSION PLAN GUIDE ¶ 19,948Z-119 (employee who exercised a nonstatutory stock option

more than six months after the date the option was granted was required to recognize income under Code Sec. 83 at the time of the exercise of the option, even though the ability to sell the stock obtained thereby remained legally and contractually restricted after the exercise date by an indemnity agreement and an insider trading compliance program).

[3] Reg. § 1.409A-1(b)(5)(A). However, see IRS Letter Ruling 200728042, 5-31-07 at CCH PENSION

PLAN GUIDE ¶ 17,427Q (compensatory nonstatutory stock options granted by an employer to two non-key employees were both subject to Code Sec. 409A as a nonqualified deferred compensation plan. Whether the exercise of an option was subject to tax under Code Sec. 409A was determined by whether the option was set to terminate 10 years after the date of the grant or 90 days after the employee terminated employment).

[4] IRS Reg. § 1.83-7(a).

¶ 3325
Other Stock Arrangements

In addition to stock options, there are a number of other types of executive compensation that are stock-related. Such stock arrangements include stock appreciation rights ("SARs"), SARs in tandem with options, and restricted stock.

Stock appreciation rights (SARs)

From an executive's standpoint, one of the problems with stock options and other stock purchase plans as compensation is that the executive must make a capital outlay or commitment to acquire the shares. The commitment may be softened by favorable credit terms, but it remains a commitment for a capital investment that may or may not be of long-term benefit to the executive. The executive, for example, could suffer a loss on the stock acquired. Stock appreciation rights (SARs) are designed to give the executive a stake in the company's growth without such a capital outlay or commitment.

SARs provide an executive with a cash bonus measured by appreciation in the value of company stock from the time the rights are granted over a set or determinable period of time.

Example: XYZ Corp. provides an SAR to John Smith, one of its executives. The period specified in the SAR is five years. At the time the SAR is granted, XYZ Corp. stock has a fair market value of $20. At the end of the specified five-year period, XYZ Corp. has a value of $40. Smith will be entitled to a payment of $20 (the amount that XYZ Corp. stock has increased over the five- year period).

In addition to rights in the appreciation, which may not be realized for some time, the executive may be awarded further payments equal to the amount of dividends paid on the stock. These payments are also to be treated as earned income.

Payments made under an SAR are includible in the employee's gross income when paid. The employer may take a corresponding business deduction.[1]

SARs in tandem with options

One simple method of providing flexibility of financing for the executive is to issue stock appreciation rights (SARs) in tandem with various kinds of stock options. Under these types of arrangements, the executive may choose to exercise only the options, only the SARs, or some combination of the two, depending on the executive's wishes and specific cash flow situation. Usually, under these types of plans, there is a fixed number of SARs/options which may be exercised, so that the exercise of SARs will reduce the number of shares which may be acquired through the options.

SARs in tandem with nonqualified stock options. The tax treatment of SARs in tandem with nonqualified stock options is relatively simple in the sense that they are taxed the same. That is, with the exception of corporate insiders, the executive recognizes taxable income on the date of exercise in the amount of the spread between the market price of the stock (as of the exercise date) and the exercise price of the nonqualified stock option or SAR.[2] Therefore, regardless of the combination of options and SARs exercised, the taxable income is the same.

In this financing scenario, the exercise of the SAR cancels the executive's right to purchase stock by exercising his or her option. Similarly, exercise of the option cancels the related SAR.[3]

SARs in tandem with incentive stock options. The tax treatment of SARs in tandem with incentive stock options (ISOs) is equally simple, because each is taxed individually, as if the other were not attached. The executive recognizes income on the exercise date only to the extent the SAR is exercised.[4] SARs issued in tandem with ISOs should also expire no later than the expiration of the underlying ISO and meet certain other requirements. See CCH PENSION PLAN GUIDE ¶ 9765 for more details.

Impact of Code Sec. 409A. SARs that do not provide for the deferral of compensation are not subject to the requirements of Code Sec. 409A (see ¶ 3302). An option to purchase service recipient stock (i.e., the employer's stock) does not provide for a deferral of compensation if (1) the exercise price may never be less than the fair market value of the stock on the date the option is granted; (2) the exercise of the option is subject to Code Sec. 83 and (3) the option contains no feature for the deferral of compensation (other than delayed recognition of income until exercise).[3]

Restricted stock. The IRS has provided guidance on the tax consequences under Code Sec. 83 when restrictions are imposed on substantially vested stock, causing that stock to become substantially nonvested. The IRS ruled that if the imposition of restrictions on substantially vested stock causes that stock to become substantially nonvested, but there was no exchange of stock, the substantially nonvested stock is not subject to Code Sec. 83. However, if substantially vested stock is exchanged for substantially nonvested stock, the nonvested stock is subject to Code Sec. 83.[6]

☐ Additional stock arrangements, including: phantom stock, stock swaps, stock pyramiding, performance shares, junior stock, and stock repurchase agreements are discussed at CCH PENSION PLAN GUIDE ¶ ¶ 9770—¶ 9790.

☐ See the CCH PENSION PLAN GUIDE at ¶ 9685 for a discussion of reporting requirements of stock option plans.

☐ See ¶ 10,185 and following of the CCH PENSION PLAN GUIDE for more information on SEC reporting requirements.

¹ Code Secs. 61, 83 and 161.

² Rev. Rul. 80-300, 1980-2 CB 165, CCH PENSION PLAN GUIDE ¶ 19,544.

³ Rev. Rul. 82-121, 1982-1 CB 79, CCH PENSION PLAN GUIDE ¶ 19,620.

³Reg. § 1.409A-1(b)(5)(A).

⁴ Code Sec. 422.

⁶Rev. Rul. 2007-49, I.R.B. 2007-31, 7-30-07 at CCH PENSION PLAN GUIDE ¶ 19,948Z-198.

¶ 3330
Golden Parachutes

Golden parachutes are executive compensation arrangements under which a corporation agrees to pay amounts, often in excess of the executive's usual compensation, in the event that the corporation undergoes a change in ownership or control.[1] Golden parachutes are often used by employers as a defensive measure to prevent hostile takeovers under the assumption that the guarantee of additional financial benefits to executives will increase the cost of the acquisition and, thereby, discourage prospective purchasers.

Golden parachute arrangements, however, have also been used as an inducement to company officers to approve of an acquisition that may be contrary to the best interests of shareholders. Because of the potential for abuse implicit in such arrangements, "excess" parachute payments that exceed three times an executive's compensation are subject to tax penalties that are borne by the executive and the employer. The executive receiving the excess payment is subject to a nondeductible 20% excise tax on the excess payment. The corporation will be denied a deduction for the entire parachute payment, and not just the amount of the excess payment.[2]

Legally enforceable agreement not required

Golden parachute payments that are contingent on a change in ownership or control need not be made pursuant to a legally enforceable agreement or contract. Payments may be treated as parachute payments if made pursuant to either a "formal or informal understanding." [3]

Parachute payment

A parachute payment is any payment (other than exempt payments discussed below) in the nature of compensation to (or for the benefit of) a "disqualified individual" (e.g., shareholders, officers, or highly compensated individuals, including corporate directors) that is contingent on a change in ownership or effective control of a corporation or in the ownership of a substantial portion of its assets. In addition, the aggregate present value of payments in the "nature of compensation" must equal or exceed three times the individual's base compensation amount.[4]

Securities violation parachute payments. Payments that are not contingent on a change in control may still be treated as parachute payments. Payments in the nature of compensation that are made to or for the benefit of a disqualified individual, pursuant to an agreement that violates generally enforced securities laws or regulations are subject to regulation as "securities violation parachute payments".[5]

Form of parachute payment. A parachute payment can come in the form of cash (including the value of the right to receive cash) or property, including the spread on the exercise of a stock option, pension proceeds, insurance or annuity proceeds, and payments made pursuant to a covenant not to compete.[6]

Excess parachute payments

Amounts equal to the excess of any parachute payment made over the portion of the base compensation amount allocated to the payment are "excess parachute payments".[7] Excess parachute payments may not be deducted by the employer (payor). The disqualified individual is also subject to a nondeductible excise tax (in addition to applicable state and federal income taxes and Social Security taxes) of 20% of the amount of the excess parachute payment.[8] The excise tax is withheld by the employer as the payor.

Reasonable compensation reduces excess payment. The amount of an excess parachute payment (other than a securities violation parachute payment) may be reduced by clear and convincing evidence that the payment was "reasonable compensation" for services rendered by the disqualified individual before the change in ownership or control.[9]

Value of stock options. The IRS has provided a safe harbor method for valuing compensatory stock options.[10]

Exempt parachute payments

The following payments are exempt from treatment as parachute payments and, thus, may be deducted by the employer and do not subject the recipient to the 20% excise tax:[11]

1. payments with respect to a small domestic business corporation;

2. payments (a) with respect to a corporation in which immediately before the change in ownership or control, no stock is readily tradable on an established securities market or otherwise and (b) which have been approved by more than 75% of the corporation's shareholders[12];

3. payments to or from a qualified plan, including a tax-sheltered annuity, SEP, or SIMPLE plan;

4. payments made by a tax-exempt organization undergoing a change in ownership or control;

5. payments of reasonable compensation for services to be rendered on or after the change in ownership or control (including payments made pursuant to a covenant not to compete).

☐ The rules governing golden parachute arrangements are detailed in the CCH PENSION PLAN GUIDE at ¶ 9798—¶ 9835.

---

[1] A change in ownership of corporation occurs when any one person (or more than one person acting as a group) acquires ownership of stock of a corporation that together with stock held by the person (or group) is more than 50% of the total fair market value of voting power of the stock of the corporation (IRS Reg. § 1.280G-1, Q&A 27(a)). The IRS has further ruled that, in determining whether a change in ownership or control has occurred, unvested shares of restricted stock for which a Code Sec. 83(b) election is made, are treated as outstanding stock (Rev. Rul. 2005-39, I.R.B. 2005-27, 7-5-05, at CCH PENSION PLAN GUIDE ¶ 19,948Z-116).

[2] Code Secs. 280G and 4999(a). Note: the golden parachute rules were expanded in 2008 to apply in the event of a severance from employment by a covered executive of an employer that participated in the Treasury Department's "troubled assets relief program" (TARP). See Code Sec.280G(e), added by P.L. 110-343 (Emergency Economic Stabilization Act of 2008), Division A, Act Sec. 302(b). "Covered executives" include the chief executive officer, the chief financial officer, and the three other highest compensated officers. See also Notice 2008-94, I.R.B. 2008-44, 11-3-2008, at CCH PENSION PLAN GUIDE ¶ 17,140U and interim final Treasury regulations (74 FR 28393, 6/15/2009).

[3] General Explanation of the Tax Reform Act of 1984 (P.L. 98-369), as proposed by the Staff of the Joint Committee on Taxation.

[4] Code Sec. 280G(b)(2); IRS Reg. § 280G-1, Q&A-(2)(a) and 15(a).

[5] Code Sec. 280G(b)(2)(B); IRS Reg. § 1.280G-1, Q&A-2(c) and Q&A-37(a).

[6] Reg. § 1.280G-1, Q&A-11(a).

[7] Code Sec.280G(a); IRS Reg. § 1.280G-1, Q&A-3.

[8] Code Sec. 4999; IRS Reg. § 1.280G-1, Q&A-1.

[9] Code Sec. 280G(b)(4); IRS Reg. § 280G-1, Q&A-3 and Q&A-39(a).

[10] Rev. Proc. 2003-68, I.R.B. 2003-34, 8-25-2003, CCH PENSION PLAN GUIDE ¶ 17,299Q-83, modifying Rev. Proc. 2002-45, I.R.B. 2002-27, CCH PENSION PLAN GUIDE ¶ 17,299Q-22.

[11] Code Sec. 280G(b)(5) and (6); IRS Reg. 1.280G-1, Q&A-5(a)-9 and 1.280G-1, Q&A-40(b).

[12] See Rev. Rul. 2004-87, I.R.B. 2004-32, 8-9-04, at CCH PENSION PLAN GUIDE ¶ 19,948Z-85, in which the IRS ruled that a debtor corporation's stock was not readily tradable where it was de-listed from the New York Stock Exchange and no trading in the corporation's stock took place on any other market, including any over-the-counter market. The IRS further noted that securities of a corporation in bankruptcy that continue to be traded on an over-the-counter market following de-listing will not be considered readily tradable, as the trading of the stock would be impaired.

¶ 3335
Silver, Tin, and Pension Parachutes

Whereas golden parachutes are primarily used to shelter top executives in the event of a hostile takeover, "silver," "tin," and "pension" parachutes are used to provide similar benefits to a more broadly based group of employees in the event of a change in ownership or corporate control.

Silver and pension parachutes

Silver parachutes provide benefits to a broad base of employees in the event of a hostile takeover, while pension parachutes increase retirement payments to employees participating in an employer's defined benefit pension plan.

Pension parachutes become activated only after a change of corporate control, resulting in the automatic termination of the company's retirement plan. The excess assets are then used to provide additional benefits for all active and retired participants.

Tin parachutes

Tin parachutes are essentially severance payments for rank-and-file employees in the event of a hostile takeover that costs employees their jobs. Many see these plans as an even better takeover defense than golden parachutes because greater numbers can add up to a larger total package, even if individual payments are less.

Rules and tax consequences

The same rules and tax consequences applicable to golden parachute payments apply to silver, tin, and pension parachutes.[1] However, because the tin, silver, and pension parachute payments are made to rank-and-file employees, these payments are not subject to the 20% excise tax on excess parachute payments (see ¶ 3330).

---

[1] Code Secs. 280G and 4999; IRS Reg. § 1.280G-1.

¶ 3340

Employer Loans

In order to prevent perceived tax avoidance schemes, the tax law imputes interest to below-market loans and provides that the imputed interest is treated as income or deductions to the parties involved.[1] The imputed interest rules similarly apply to loans involving foregone interest. These loans are treated as if a realistic rate of interest had been used by both parties.

The imputed interest rules apply to:

1. gift loans;
2. loans between a corporation and a shareholder;
3. compensation-related loans between an employer and an employee (or between an independent contractor and a person for whom the independent contractor provides services); or
4. loans that are motivated by a tax-avoidance purpose.

Types of loans

Employer loans often involve business executives. Demand loans, term loans, and gift loans are the basic types of loans that may be made to the executive. A "demand loan" is any loan that is payable in full on the demand of the lender.[2] Nontransferable loans with beneficial interest arrangements that are conditioned on an individual's future performance of substantial services are also demand loans (for purposes other than determining the statutory rate of interest). Loans with indefinite maturities may also be treated as demand loans.

A demand loan that is not a gift loan is considered to be a below-market loan if interest on the loan is payable at a rate less than the applicable federal rate (AFR). When an employer lends an employee money through a demand loan, the employee realizes income equal to the imputed interest on the loan. The employer realizes the imputed interest as income but may claim a deduction for the imputed compensation paid.

Below-market loans. All loans that are not demand loans are considered "term loans." [3] A term loan is a below-market loan if the amount loaned exceeds the present value of all payments due under the loan. Present value for this and all purposes is determined by discounting the loan at the AFR.

In general, the imputed interest on below-market loans is treated as income. Also, deductions are allowed according to their economic substance. For all below-market loans, the amount treated as loaned is the amount received by the borrower.

Any below-market loan is a "gift loan" if the foregoing of interest on the loan is in the nature of a gift.[4]

☐ See CCH PENSION PLAN GUIDE ¶ 9845-9860 for more information on below-market employer loans.

---

[1] Code Sec. 7872. The imputed interest rules are generally applicable to term loans made after June 6, 1984, and demand loans outstanding after that date.

[2] Code Sec. 7872(f)(5).

[3] Code Sec. 7872(f)(6).

[4] Code Sec. 7872(f)(3).

¶ 3345
Nonqualified Deferred Pay Arrangements

Ordinarily, the purpose of entering into deferred pay arrangements with executives and key employees is to postpone payment of a part of their compensation to taxable years in which their compensation is lower than would otherwise be the case. Provision is made for payment of additional compensation over a period of future years. It is another financial incentive to spur greater performance or strengthen company loyalty.

Different types of nonqualified deferred pay arrangements

Nonqualified deferred pay arrangements may come in the form of an individual contract. For instance, a contract may provide for installment payments of a fixed amount over a period of years, payments only after retirement, purchase of annuity or endowment policies for the executive, and so on. Alternatively, these deferred pay arrangements may be established under a plan. Various types of nonqualified deferred pay arrangements are discussed below.

Note that nearly all nonqualified deferred compensation plans, including those discussed below, may be subject to the election, distribution, funding, and other restrictions implemented under Code Sec. 409A (see ¶ 3302).[1] Individuals who defer compensation under plans that fail to comply with the rules are subject to current taxation on all deferrals and to enhanced penalties.

Rabbi trusts. A "rabbi trust" is a nonqualified deferred compensation arrangement in which amounts are transferred to an *irrevocable* trust to be held for the benefit of the executive employees. The arrangement is called a rabbi trust because a rabbi received the first favorable letter ruling.[2]

The IRS has issued "model" rabbi trust provisions. Among the provisions of the model rabbi trust are requirements that: the trust assets be subject to the claims of the employer's general creditors, the trust be an unfunded arrangement, the trust not change the status of the plan as an unfunded plan maintained to provide excess benefits for a select group of management or highly compensated employees, plan participants have no preferred claim on, or beneficial interest in, the assets of the trust, and benefits not be assigned or alienated.[3]

Taxable transfer of property triggered by change in employer's financial condition. The IRS will generally not issue a favorable ruling to a rabbi trust that contains an "insolvency trigger" which provides for payments, in the event an employer experiences financial difficulties, that are made to an employee prior to the time creditors are notified of the insolvency. Employers may have used insolvency triggers in nonqualified plans to shield assets from creditors. However, a taxable transfer of property will be deemed to occur under Code 83 where a nonqualified deferred compensation plan provides that, upon a change in the employer's financial health, assets will be restricted to the payment of nonqualified deferred compensation.[4] Amounts are treated as restricted even if the assets are available to satisfy the claims of general creditors. Accordingly, the restriction would apply where a plan authorizes the transfer of assets to a rabbi trust following a change in the employer's financial condition.[5] For example, if a plan provides that, upon a change in the employer's financial condition, the trust will become funded to the extent of all deferrals, all amounts deferred under the plan would be taxable under Code Sec. 83 as transferred property.

Offshore rabbi trusts subject to current taxation. Employers may not use foreign offshore rabbi trusts to shield plan assets from creditors. Assets set aside (directly or indirectly) in a foreign offshore rabbi trust in order to fund nonqualified deferred compensation are treated as property transferred in connection with the performance of services and, thus, currently taxable under Code Sec. 83.[6] The assets are subject to tax regardless of whether or not the amounts were subject to the claims of general creditors. Specifically, the assets are subject to tax (and an additional interest assessment on the underpayment): (1) at the time set aside, if the assets (or such trust or other arrangement) were located outside of the United States, or (2) at the time of any subsequent transfer of the assets outside of the United States. In addition, any increase in the value of or earnings on assets set aside in the foreign rabbi trust would be treated as an additional transfer of property.

Exception for deferred compensation for services performed in foreign jurisdiction. The rules effectively prevent a foreign offshore rabbi trust from realizing the tax benefits available under a domestic rabbi trust. However, an exception is provided for assets located in a foreign jurisdiction if substantially all of the services to which the nonqualified deferred compensation relates are performed in the foreign jurisdiction.[7]

Secular trusts. Secular trusts are a funded type of nonqualified deferred compensation arrangement used to compensate executive employees.

A major distinction between a secular trust and a rabbi trust is that, while creditors can claim assets held in a rabbi trust after a bankruptcy, money held in secular trust funds cannot be reached by creditors. As a result, unlike a rabbi trust, an employer's contributions to a secular trust and the trust's earnings are generally taxable income to the executive-employee.[8] Under a secular trust, however, an executive may benefit from contributions to help pay the increased tax liability.

In addition, the employer is allowed a current tax deduction for its contributions, or when the contributions become vested.[9] Subsequent distributions (from already taxed contributions) made to executives are tax-free.

Excess benefit plans. Excess benefit plans are nonqualified deferred compensation plans that are established by an employer solely to provide certain employees benefits that are in excess of the limitations on contributions and benefits to qualified plans imposed by the Internal Revenue Code.[10]

Generally, excess benefit plans make up benefits lost by the executive because of the maximum limits on benefits and contributions applicable to qualified retirement plans. However, the related supplemental executive retirement plans (SERPs) are often used for broader purposes, such as increasing benefits for shorter service employees, recognizing bonus payments in the retirement plan formula, or making early retirement more attractive.

An excess benefit plan that is *unfunded* is exempt from all of the labor (Title I) and termination insurance (Title IV) provisions of ERISA.[11] By contrast, if a plan is *funded,* it is subject to the reporting and disclosure provisions, the administrative provisions, and the fiduciary standards of Title I.[12] However, the Secretary of Labor has the authority to exempt a funded excess benefit plan from the trust requirement.[13] A funded excess benefit is exempt from all other requirements of Title I and is also exempt from the plan termination insurance requirements of Title IV.[14]

Top-hat plans. A top-hat plan is *unfunded* and maintained by an employer primarily for the purpose of providing deferred compensation for a select group of management or highly compensated employees.

Top-hat plans are generally not subject to ERISA, but will satisfy the Act's reporting and disclosure requirements by filing a statement with the Secretary of Labor that includes a declaration that the employer maintains the plan or plans primarily for the purpose of providing deferred compensation for a select group of management or highly compensated employees and by providing plan documents, if any, to the Secretary upon request.[15] Note that a plan covering a controlled group of corporations can file a single registration statement that satisfies the alternative method of compliance. [16]

Deferred bonuses. From the tax standpoint, an executive is typically ahead if income can be spread to lower income years until retirement. In addition, money paid after retirement, of course, is usually taxed at a much lower rate.

Bonus deferral plans are subject to the Code Sec.409A rules.[17] However, the rules do not apply to annual bonuses (or other annual compensation) that is paid within 2½ months after the end of the tax year in which the services for which payment has been provided have been performed.[18]

---

[1] Code Sec. 409A, as added by P.L. 108-357 (American Jobs Creation Act of 2004), Act Sec. 885(a).

[2] IRS Letter Ruling 8113107, 12-31-80.

[3] Rev. Proc. 92-64, 1992-2 CB 422, CCH PENSION PLAN GUIDE ¶ 17,299M-28. See also IRS Notice

2000-56, I.R.B. 2000-43, 10-23-2000, CCH PENSION PLAN GUIDE ¶ 17,199G.

[4] Code Sec. 409A(b)(2), generally effective beginning in 2005.

[5]Conference Committee Report to P.L. 108-357 (American Jobs Creation Act of 2004).

[6] Code Sec. 409A(b)(1), effective after 2004.

[7] *Ibid.*

[8] Code Secs. 83 and 402(b).

[9] Code Sec. 404(a)(5).

[10] Code Sec. 415; ERISA Sec. 3(36).

[11] ERISA Secs. 4(b)(5) and 4021(b)(8).

[12] ERISA Secs. 101-111, 401-414, and 501-514.

[13] ERISA Sec. 403(b)(4).

[14] ERISA Secs. 201(7), 301(a)(9), and 4021(b)(8).

[15] ERISA Reg. § 2520.104-23(b).

[16] EBSA Advisory Opinion 2008-08A, 12/19/2008, at CCH PENSION PLAN GUIDE ¶ 19,992G.

[17] Code Sec. 409A(d).

[18]Reg. § 1.409A-1(b)(4).

¶ 3350

For More Information

☐ For more information on nonqualified plans, stock arrangements, and other forms of executive compensation, see the CCH PENSION PLAN GUIDE, ¶ 9502-9895.

Topical Index

References are to paragraph (¶) numbers.

CRO

TEN